Eastern Europe

Estonia
p178

Russia
p360

Latvia p232

Lithuania
p248

Belarus
p60

Poland
p308

Ukraine p448

Czech Republic
p144

Slovakia
p410

Moldova
p264

Slovenia
p430

Hungary
p198

Romania
p338

Croatia
p116

Serbia
p392

Bosnia &
Hercegovina
p74

Montenegro
p276

Kosovo p222

Bulgaria p92

North
Macedonia
p290

Albania
p42

Mark ...ch, Steve Fallon,
Anita ... Ragozin, Brana
Vla... e, Kevin Raub

Contents

POČITELJ (P87), BOSNIA & HERCEGOVINA

LUKASZ MILENAV/SHUTTERSTOCK ©

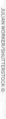

TIRASPOL (P273), MOLDOVA

JULIAN WORKER/SHUTTERSTOCK ©

BLUE PLANET STUDIO/SHUTTERSTOCK ©

Contents

STARI GRAD, HVAR ISLAND
(P134), CROATIA

ON THE ROAD

SPECTRAL-DESIGN/SHUTTERSTOCK ©

ČESKÝ KRUMLOV (P164),
CZECH REPUBLIC

Contents

TATRA MOUNTAINS (P420), SLOVAKIA

Welcome to Eastern Europe

From soaring mountains to golden sands, Eastern Europe reveals a tapestry of quaint and contemporary cultures – always with enough rough edges to keep you intrigued.

Cultural Explosion

Eastern Europe is a warehouse of culture, whether your preference is fine art or folk singing. Cities such as Prague, St Petersburg and Budapest are effortlessly elegant, housing remarkable art collections in palatial surrounds. Some locations are akin to open-air museums, like Kraków's Main Market Square, Moscow's vast Red Square and art-nouveau-rich Rīga. For every age-old powerhouse of classical music and opera, you'll also discover a plucky up-and-comer, building a reputation for avant-garde nightlife (Belgrade) or gritty galleries (Cluj-Napoca).

Spectacular Scenery

Sandy beaches, windswept plains, rugged mountain ranges – Eastern Europe has it all. Glide down the Danube River, bob across North Macedonia's Lake Ohrid, or splash around in Hungary's Lake Balaton. Gulp down fresh air in Albania's Accursed Mountains, Transylvania's criss-crossing ranges, or the High Tatras, which rumble along the Poland–Slovakia border. Test the white water in Slovenia's Triglav National Park, or explore canyons and caverns in Montenegro or Bosnia and Hercegovina.

Historic Overload

History lives on in Eastern Europe. Gaze at St Basil's Cathedral on Moscow's Red Square, a legacy of Ivan the Terrible's brutal reign; cross the bridge where Archduke Ferdinand was assassinated in Sarajevo in 1914; feel the echo of the Romanian Revolution in Bucharest or more recent tragic events on Kyiv's Maydan Nezalezhnosti. Stroll further back in time through the remains of Diocletian's Palace in Split, Croatia; or through Sofia and Plovdiv in Bulgaria, where ancient ruins continue to be unearthed beneath modern buildings and metro systems.

Folklore & Festivals

A living heritage of folklore sets Eastern Europe apart. This is the heartland of Orthodox Christianity: the religion's rites permeate cultural life, particularly in Russia and Ukraine. Roman Catholic, Muslim and Jewish communities add their own influences, while whiffs of pagan tradition can be felt in the Baltics. Baltica International Folklore Festival, Slovakia's Východná and Bulgaria's Rose Festival are captivating events, full of insight into age-old Europe. Traditional woodcarvers still hunch over benches in Slovakia, while glass icons continue to be painted in Romania.

Why I Love Eastern Europe

By Mark Baker, Writer

In the decades following the collapse of communism in 1989, intrepid travellers have discovered that real adventure in Europe lies not to the West, but rather the East. Western-leaning cities like Budapest, Kraków and my adopted hometown of Prague allow visitors to dip a toe in the old Eastern Bloc, while places further east, like Moldova, Belarus and Russia, offer heaps of unvarnished modern history. But banish forever those dated black-and-white, Cold War images from your mind: today's Eastern Europe brims with colour, culture and natural beauty. These days, this 'other' Europe might just be the continent's better half.

For more about our writers, see p512

Above: St Basil's Cathedral (p366), Moscow, Russia

Eastern Europe

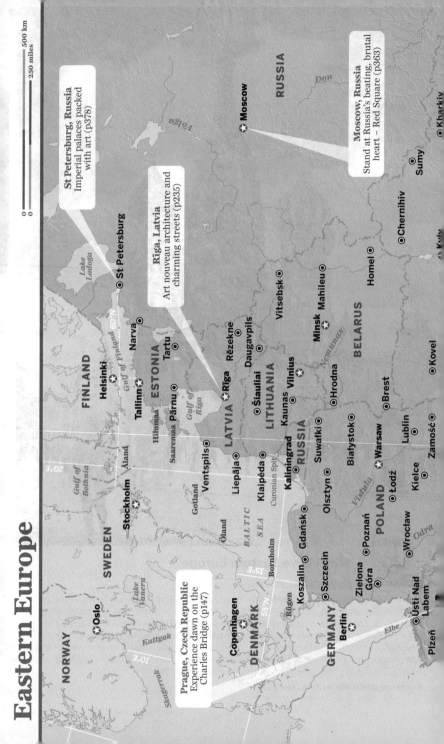

0 ——— 500 km
0 ——— 250 miles

St Petersburg, Russia Imperial palaces packed with art (p378)

Rīga, Latvia Art nouveau architecture and charming streets (p235)

Moscow, Russia Stand at Russia's beating, brutal heart – Red Square (p363)

Prague, Czech Republic Experience dawn on the Charles Bridge (p147)

NORWAY
Oslo

SWEDEN
Stockholm

FINLAND
Helsinki
Narva
St Petersburg
Lake Ladoga
Volga

Tallinn
ESTONIA
Tartu

Hiiumaa
Pärnu
Saaremaa
Gulf of Riga

LATVIA
Rīga
Rēzekne
Daugavpils

Vitsebsk

RUSSIA
Moscow
Don

Ventspils
Liepāja
Gulf of Bothnia

Gotland
Öland
Åland

BALTIC SEA

Bornholm

Rügen

Copenhagen
DENMARK

GERMANY
Berlin

Klaipėda
Curonian Spit
Kaliningrad
RUSSIA

Šiauliai
LITHUANIA
Kaunas
Vilnius
Hrodna

Nemunas

Minsk
Mahilueu

BELARUS

Homel

Chernihiv

Sumy

Kharkiv

Kovel

Koszalin
Szczecin
Gdańsk
Poznań

Zielona Góra
Wrocław

Suwałki
Olsztyn
Białystok

POLAND
Łódź
Warsaw

Lublin
Zamość

Brest

Kovel

Kiev

Odra

Vistula

Kielce

Plzeň
Ústí Nad Labem

Elbe

Eastern Europe Top Sights

Kraków, Poland
Radiating history from its medieval core (p316)

High Tatras, Slovakia
Spectacular hikes in marvellous mountains (p421)

Transylvania, Romania
Dracula-worthy castles and stunning scenery (p346)

Budapest, Hungary
Mineral baths and nonstop nightlife (p200)

Belgrade, Serbia
The 'White City' is red hot (p395)

Ohrid, North Macedonia
Magnificent monastery overlooking a holy lake (p301)

Lake Balaton, Hungary
Swim and sunbathe in Hungary's haven (p212)

Island-Hopping, Adriatic
Secret coves and sandy beaches (p134)

Mostar, Bosnia & Hercegovina
Historic bridge and rejuvenated Ottoman quarter (p82)

Accursed Mountains, Albania
Hiking trails and stunning Lake Koman (p56)

Bay of Kotor, Montenegro
Historic towns hemmed in by limestone cliffs (p279)

BLACK SEA

Sea of Azov

CRIMEA

Sea of Marmara

TURKEY

Ankara

UKRAINE

Luhansk
Donetsk
Zaporizhzhya
Dnipro
Kirovohrad
Kherson
Odesa
Simferopol
Yalta

Lviv
Uzhhorod
Chernivtsi
Chişinău
Iaşi
MOLDOVA

Zakopane
Košice
Suceava

SLOVAKIA
Bratislava
Trenčín

AUSTRIA
Vienna

Olomouc
Brno
Český Krumlov

CARPATHIAN MOUNTAINS

Bistriţa
Cluj-Napoca
Sibiu
Braşov
TRANSYLVANIA
Timişoara
ROMANIA
Craiova
Bucharest
Constanţa
Tulcea
Danube Delta
Varna
Burgas

HUNGARY
Debrecen
Szeged
Győr
Pécs
Budapest

Montana
Niš
STARA PLANINA
Sofia
Plovdiv
Kârdzhali
BULGARIA
Veliko Târnovo
Rodopi Mountains

SLOVENIA
Ljubljana
Zagreb
Rijeka
Pula
Trieste

CROATIA
Novi Sad
Belgrade
SERBIA
Banja Luka
Sarajevo
BOSNIA & HERCEGOVINA
Mostar
Split
Brač
Hvar
Zadar
Dubrovnik

Dinaric Alps

Podgorica
Kotor
MONTENEGRO
Shkodra
Skopje
NORTH MACEDONIA
Pristina
KOSOVO
Ohrid

ALBANIA
Tirana
Berat
Korça

GREECE
Corfu
Lesvos
AEGEAN SEA

ITALY
Rome
San Marino
Sicily

ADRIATIC SEA
IONIAN SEA
TYRRHENIAN SEA

Lake Balaton
Danube
Sava
Drava

Dnipro
Dniester
Don
Prut

45°N
40°N
35°N
30°E

Eastern Europe's
Top 25

Budapest, Hungary

1 Straddling the romantic Danube River, with the Buda Hills to the west and the start of the Great Plain to the east, Budapest (p200) is one of Europe's most beautiful cities. Its famous thermal baths huff steam, the stately architecture is second to none, while museums and churches brim with treasures. Its active cultural life unfolds to a backdrop of verdant parks and pleasure boats gliding up and down the Danube Bend. Meanwhile, a diverse social scene, with coffee houses, intimate wine spots and rambunctious 'ruin bars', throbs until dawn. Fisherman's Bastion, Matthias Church (p201)

Island-Hopping on the Adriatic, Croatia

2 Board a boat and zoom past some of Croatia's 1244 islands, strung like jewels along the Adriatic coast. Drop anchor for golden shores, glide past rocky coves, and look out for a beach of your own (only 50 islands are inhabited) on islands such as Hvar (p134). Travelling by sea is the most thrilling way to experience the Adriatic, whether it's a short jaunt from Dubrovnik or overnight rides along the length of the coast. If you have cash to splash, take it up a couple of notches and charter a sailboat to island-hop in style. Hvar Town (p134)

KAYO/SHUTTERSTOCK ©

DALIU/SHUTTERSTOCK ©

Prague, Czech Republic

3 The Czech capital (p147) is a near-perfectly preserved museum of European architecture through the ages. From the Old Town Square, across the Charles Bridge and up to Prague Castle, it's almost as if a 14th-century metropolis has been transported in time and plunked down in the heart of modern Europe. After you've meandered the alleyways, neck sore from craning to spy the statues and gargoyles, retire to a local pub for some Czech beer – the country's pride and joy.

Bay of Kotor, Montenegro

4 There's a sense of secrecy and mystery to the Bay of Kotor (p279). Grey mountains rise steeply from steely-blue waters, protectively hugging the inner bay. Here, ancient stone settlements cling to the shoreline, with the old alleyways of Kotor (pictured) concealed in its innermost reaches behind hefty stone walls. It's a majestic, timeless view: a fusion of fjord-like cliffs dropping to cobalt water, and the warm-hued stone of medieval streets and Venetian palaces. And life here is exuberantly Mediterranean, lived full of passion on these time-worn streets.

Walking Dubrovnik's Old City Walls, Croatia

5 History is unfurled from the battlements of Dubrovnik's spectacular city walls (p137). No visit is complete without a leisurely stroll along these ramparts, the finest in the world and Dubrovnik's main claim to fame. Built between the 9th and 16th centuries, the walls are still remarkably intact. Vistas over terracotta rooftops and the Adriatic Sea are sublime, especially at sunset. The views may even look a little familiar, thanks to Dubrovnik's starring role in the fantasy TV series *Game of Thrones*.

Castles & Mountains of Transylvania, Romania

6 Fiends from both fiction and history enjoy eternal repose in this Romanian region (p346). Castles nested high in the Carpathian Mountains inspired Irish writer Bram Stoker to set his *Dracula* novel in Transylvania. The region was also the reputed birthplace of the historical Dracula, otherwise known as Vlad the Impaler. Monumental Bran Castle is suitably vampiric, but our favourite haunt is Râşnov Fortress (pictured; p348). If (unlike the count) you don't shrink from sunlight, Transylvania is ideal for hiking, biking and skiing.

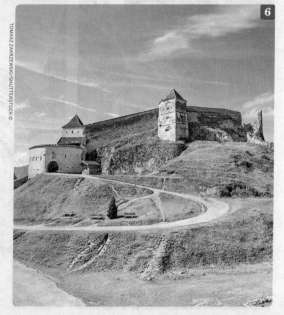

TOMASZ ZAKRZEWSKI/SHUTTERSTOCK ©

Moscow's Red Square, Russia

7 With the gravitational pull of a black hole, Red Square (p363) sucks in every visitor to Russia's capital, leaving them slack-jawed with wonder. Standing on the rectangular cobblestoned expanse – surrounded by the candy-coloured swirls of the cupolas atop St Basil's Cathedral (pictured; p366), the red-star-tipped towers of the Kremlin, Lenin's squat granite mausoleum, the handsome red-brick facade of the State History Museum, and GUM, a grand emporium of consumption – you are literally at the centre of Russia's modern history.

Art Nouveau Architecture, Rīga, Latvia

8 In between cobblestones and Gothic spires, Latvia's capital, Rīga (p235), dazzles visitors with art nouveau architecture. More than 750 buildings (the most of any city in Europe) boast this style – a menagerie of mythical beasts, screaming masks, twisting flora, goddesses and goblins, often set to vibrant colours and layer-cake roofs. Rīga's compelling jigsaw puzzle of buildings propels you between elaborate mansions, weathered apartments, and steaming coffee houses tucked behind pastel-painted facades.

KSENIA VOROBEVA/SHUTTERSTOCK ©

Hiking the High Tatras, Slovakia

9 The rocky, alpine peaks of the High Tatras (p421) are the highest in the Carpathians, with 25 peaks soaring over 2500m. But hiking this impressive little range doesn't necessarily demand Olympian effort. From Starý Smokovec you can ride a funicular to Hrebienok, the starting point for numerous mid-elevation trails among thick forest and yawning valleys. Stop at a log-cabin hikers' hut, drink in a cold beer along with the views, and you can still trundle down to another of the Tatras' dinky resort towns in time for dinner.

Kraków, Poland

10 As popular as it is, Poland's former royal capital (p316) never disappoints. An aura of history radiates from the sloping stone buttresses of medieval buildings in the Old Town. The enormous main square is enlivened by flower sellers, a bustling market hall, and the clippety-clop of horses and carriages, which ferry enraptured tourists beneath the spires. Throw in the extremes of a castle complex with remarkable art and subterranean chambers, plus the low-key chic of revived Jewish quarter Kazimierz, and it's a city you'll want to seriously get to know. Cloth Hall (p317)

Lake Ohrid, North Macedonia

11 Whether you come to sublime, hilly Ohrid (p300) for its sturdy medieval castle, to wander the stone laneways of its Old Town or to gaze at Plaošnik, its restored multidome basilica, every visitor pauses at the Church of Sveti Jovan at Kaneo (pictured), set high on a bluff overlooking Lake Ohrid and its popular beaches. It's the prime spot for absorbing the town's beautiful architecture, idling sunbathers and distant fishing skiffs – all framed by the rippling green of Mt Galičica to the southeast and the endless expanse of lake.

State Hermitage Museum, St Petersburg, Russia

12 Standing proudly at the end of Nevsky Prospekt, Russia's most famous palace houses its most famous museum (p379). Little can prepare you for the scale of the exhibits, nor for their quality. Within lies an almost unrivalled history of Western art, including a staggering number of Rembrandts, Rubens, Picassos and Matisses. If so much finery overloads your senses, content yourself with wandering through the private apartments of the Romanovs, for whom the Winter Palace was home until 1917.

GÜNTER KIRSCH/ALAMY STOCK PHOTO ©

MARISHA_SL/SHUTTERSTOCK ©

Belgrade, Serbia

13 Belgrade (p395) is a fascinating living museum of its turbulent past; its measured rise from former Yugoslavian ashes is today its catalyst for cool. By day, a gritty melange of communist-era blocks and art nouveau architecture corrals an ever-evolving cocktail of old-world culture and cutting-edge cosmopolitanism. By night, Belgrade throbs to the beat of its infamous *splavovi* (river-barge nightclubs), born of the city's contagious live-for-the-moment ethos and sociable Serbian spirit. A capital in transition, the 'White City' now teeters between comfortably unhurried and overzealously progressive.

Lake Balaton, Hungary

14 Hungary's 'sea' (and central Europe's largest freshwater lake) is where the populace comes in summertime to sun, swim and try stand-up paddleboarding. The quieter side of Lake Balaton (p212) mixes sizzling beaches and oodles of fun on the water with historic waterside towns such as Keszthely and Balatonfüred. Tihany, a protected peninsula jutting 4km into the lake, is home to a stunning abbey church, and Hévíz (pictured; p214) boasts a thermal length where you can bathe even when it's snowing.

Hiking in the Accursed Mountains, Albania

15 Albania's natural landscape is its greatest drawcard. It's best experienced in the country's north, where the Accursed Mountains (p56) offer superb hiking and traditional mountain villages that still look like they're part of the 19th century. The most popular hike is the gorgeous and moderately challenging day trek from Valbona to Theth (pictured). For long-distance trekkers, the Peaks of the Balkans Trail winds through not only Albania but the mountains of Kosovo and Montenegro.

ARTBA_NWH/SHUTTERSTOCK ©

Tallinn, Estonia

16 The Estonian capital (p181) is rightly famous for its Old Town, a maze of intertwining alleys, picturesque courtyards and red-rooftop views from medieval turrets. But be sure to step outside its time-worn walls and experience the other treasures of Tallinn. No visit is complete without sampling the city's stylish restaurants, its buzzing Scandinavian-influenced design community, and its ever-growing number of galleries, including the award-winning modern-art repository Kumu. Contemporary architecture and venerable domed churches form an enthralling contrast in this city perched by the Baltic Sea.

Cycling the Curonian Spit, Lithuania

17 Allegedly created by the giantess Neringa, the fragile sliver of land forming the Curonian Spit (p261) juts out into the Baltic Sea. Its celestial origins infuse it with otherworldly ambience, heightened by folkloric wood carvings and the giant sand dunes that earned it the nickname 'Lithuania's Sahara'. The best way to explore is by bicycle, riding through dense pine forest from one cheerful village to the next, stopping to sample freshly smoked fish, or – if you're lucky – to glimpse elusive wildlife: elk, deer and wild boar.

Black Sea Beaches, Bulgaria

18 Bulgaria has almost 400km of sparkling Black Sea coastline, dotted with resorts and a fair few hidden beaches. Sunning yourself along the so-called Bulgarian Riviera (p109) is easy on the wallet and there is a stretch of sand to suit every taste. Party-hard playgrounds like Sunny Beach attract international tourists keen on water sports and wild nightlife, cosmopolitan Varna offers long, white-sand beaches and pleasant parks, while the heritage-rich harbours of Nesebâr and Sozopol dish up culture by the spadeful.

Mostar, Bosnia & Hercegovina

19 If the 1993 bombardment of the iconic 16th-century stone bridge in Mostar (p82) underlined the heartbreaking pointlessness of Yugoslavia's brutal civil war, its reconstruction has proved symbolic of a peaceful post-conflict era. The charming Ottoman quarter has been convincingly restored and is once again an atmospheric patchwork of stone mosques, souvenir stalls and street cafes. Meanwhile, rows of bombed-out buildings hint at out how far there is to go until full reconciliation is achieved in this still-divided town.

Mt Triglav & Vršič Pass, Slovenia

20 For such a small country, Slovenia's got it all: quaint towns, epic lakes, great wines, a Venetian-inspired seashore and, most of all, mountains. The highest, Mt Triglav (pictured; p441), stands at 2864m, particularly tall in local lore. Indeed, the saying goes that you're not really Slovene until you've climbed to the top of this triple-peaked mountain. If time is an issue and you're driving, head for the Vršič Pass (p442): the highest road in Slovenia, it ducks and dives across the Julian Alps in one hair-raising, spine-tingling hour.

Wine Tasting, Moldova

21 Only dedicated oenophiles are aware of Eastern Europe's greatest wine secret: little-touristed Moldova has the ideal soil and climate for growing grapes, and offers some of the region's best wines. Whites include chardonnay, riesling and the local Fetească Albă, while cabernet sauvignon, merlot and Fetească Neagră are all popular for reds. The most renowned wineries are Cricova (p270) and Mileştii Mici (p270; pictured), with underground storage cellars that stretch for hundreds of kilometres. Tour them by car or linger for an in-depth tasting session.

Český Krumlov, Czech Republic

22 Showcasing a magnificent Old Town, Český Krumlov (p164) is the most popular day trip from Prague. But a rushed few hours navigating the town's meandering lanes and audacious clifftop castle (pictured) sells short the ČK experience. Stay at least one night to lose yourself in the Old Town's shapeshifting after-dark shadows and get cosy in riverside restaurants and pubs. The following morning, get active with rafting on the Vltava River, exploring surrounding meadows by horse or mountain bike, or touring neighbouring towns.

Prizren, Kosovo

23 Kosovo's most charming town is Prizren (p229), nestled in the valley of the Bistrica River and dominated by minarets and church towers. Despite the dark legacy of war, Prizren today is a progressive and upbeat sort of place, with one of Eastern Europe's best documentary film festivals, Dokufest, bringing a splash of international sophistication every summer. The rest of the year you can explore the town's rich heritage in the form of its hilltop fortress, grand mosques and ancient churches.

Lviv, Ukraine

24 Elegant and idyllic, Lviv (p457) is an island of sophistication in a post-Soviet sea. Ukraine's great hope for tourism is this moody city of arabica-scented coffee houses, verdant old parks, trundling trams and Austro-Hungarian manners. Tourists are beginning to wise up to Lviv, though it remains a haven, untouched by the crowds of Prague or Kraków. Melodiously accented Ukrainian provides the soundtrack while incense billows through medieval churches that miraculously avoided their dates with Soviet dynamite. Lviv coffee house

Minsk, Belarus

25 Minsk (p63) is no typical Eastern European capital. Almost totally destroyed in WWII, the ancient city underwent a Stalinist rebirth in the 1950s and is now a masterpiece of socialist architecture. Minsk is a riveting starting point to explore the Soviet time capsule that is modern Belarus. While its initial appearance is severe and austere, a few days in Minsk allows you to feel the city's pulse: lofty lookouts gazing across a bizarre and compelling urban skyline, green spaces galore, and the lively street scene of the Old Town.

Need to Know

For more information, see Survival Guide (p463)

Currency
Euro (€) in Estonia, Kosovo, Latvia, Lithuania, Montenegro, Slovakia and Slovenia, local currency elsewhere.

Languages
Apart from national languages, Russian, German and English are also widely understood.

Visas
Generally not required for most Eastern European countries for stays of up to 90 days, but a few countries do require visas.

Money
ATMS are common, cards are accepted in major towns. Always carry some cash though.

Mobile Phones
Be wary of roaming charges. If you're coming from outside Europe it's usually worth buying a local SIM card to swap into your (unlocked) phone.

Time
GMT/UTC plus one, two or three hours, depending on country.

When to Go

Warm to hot summers, mild winters
Warm to hot summers, cold winters
Mild summers, cold winters
Cold climate

- Moscow GO May–Oct
- Rīga GO May–Sep
- Warsaw GO May–Sep
- Kyiv GO Apr–Oct
- Prague GO Apr–Oct
- Bucharest GO May–Sep
- Dubrovnik GO Year-round

High Season
(Jul–Aug)

➡ Expect high temperatures and long evenings.

➡ Hotels prices rise by up to 30% and you'll need to reserve in advance.

➡ Big draws such as Prague, Budapest and Kraków will be crowded, as will beaches and hiking trails.

Shoulder
(May–Jun, Sep–Oct)

➡ Crowds and prices drop off but weather remains pleasant.

➡ Spring, music and wine festivals unfold.

➡ Overall the best time to travel in Eastern Europe.

Low Season
(Nov–Apr)

➡ Hotel prices drop to their lowest, except in ski zones.

➡ Days are short and weather is cold – in some places brutally so.

➡ Summer resorts are like ghost towns, while winter-sports areas fill to the brim.

Useful Websites

Lonely Planet (www.lonely planet.com/europe) Destination information, hotel bookings, traveller forum and more.

Deutsche Bahn (www.bahn.de) The best online train timetable for the region.

Like a Local (www.likealocal guide.com) Free online guides to cities across the region, written by locals.

Atlas Obscura (www.atlas obscura.com) Crowd-sourced travel guide to offbeat attractions around the world; plenty on Eastern Europe.

VisitEurope (www.visiteurope. com) Info and inspiration for travel in 36 European countries.

Spotted by Locals (www.spot tedbylocals.com) Insider tips for cities across Europe.

What to Take

→ Flip-flops (thongs) for overnight trains, hostel bathrooms and beaches

→ Hiking boots for treks and cobbled streets

→ Earplugs and eyeshades for hostels and overnight trains

→ European plug adaptors

→ Unlocked mobile phone to use local SIM cards

→ Spork or cutlery for hikes, markets and train picnics

Exchange Rates

	EURO	RUSSIAN ROUBLE
AUD $1	€0.63	₽47
CAD $1	€0.66	₽50
JPY ¥100	€0.79	₽60
NZD $1	€0.61	₽45
GBP £1	€1.14	₽86
USD $1	€0.88	₽66

For current exchange rates, see www.xe.com.

Daily Costs

Budget: Less than €40

→ Hostel bed: €10–25

→ Admission to museums: €1–15

→ Canteen meals: €3–6

→ Beer: €1.50–4

Midrange: €40–150

→ Midrange hotel room: €40

→ Main meal in a decent restaurant: from €10

→ Inner-city taxi trip: €10–15

→ Half-day activity like horse riding or rafting: €30–50

Top End: More than €150

→ Top-end hotel room: from €100

→ Swanky, big-city restaurant meal: from €20

→ Hire cars per day: around €30

→ Private hiking or tour guide per day: €75–150

Accommodation

Hotels From Soviet-era behemoths to palatial five-stars.

Guesthouses and Pensions Small, family-run, and generally good value.

Hostels From barebones to hipster chic.

Homestays and Farmstays Find out how locals live.

Campgrounds Cheap, though quality is variable. Wild camping is usually forbidden.

Mountain Huts Mattresses on floors or private rooms in no-frills lodges. Book in advance where possible.

Arriving in Eastern Europe

Václav Havel Airport Prague (p158) Public bus no. 119 costs 32Kč and runs from 5am to 11pm, every 10 minutes, connecting to a metro to the centre. The journey takes 30 minutes. Taxis cost from 500Kč to 700Kč.

Domodedovo and **Sheremetyevo airports** (p390; Moscow) Accessible by train (one way R420 to/from the centre). Alternatively, order an official airport taxi in the terminal (R2000 to R2500 one way).

Ferenc Liszt International Airport (p209; Budapest) The 100E coach (900Ft) departs for the centre every half hour between 5am and 12.30am. Taxis cost from 6000Ft.

Getting Around

Train Connects nearly all major cities, but not all countries have straightforward train links to neighbours.

Bus Covers almost all of Eastern Europe; particularly useful for reaching remote areas.

Car Drive on the right. Main roads are generally good. Many car-rental companies limit which countries their vehicles can go to.

Ferry International sea services connect Baltic countries with Russia, while Danube ferries travel between Hungary and Slovakia, as well as between Romania and Bulgaria.

Plane International flights connect most capitals to neighbouring countries and Western European hubs.

Bicycle Cycling infrastructure varies by country. Where bike-hire schemes exist, it's a great way to explore.

For much more on **getting around**, see p475

If You Like...

Old Towns

Kraków, Poland Arguably Eastern Europe's finest old town; the incredible Rynek Główny shouldn't be missed. (p316)

Prague, Czech Republic Fall instantly in love with the incredibly preserved Staré Město's spiky spires and narrow lanes. (p147)

Dubrovnik, Croatia Prowl the city's fantastical defensive walls before strolling marble-paved Stradun down below. (p136)

Vilnius, Lithuania One of Europe's largest old towns offers cobbled streets, artists' workshops and countless church steeples. (p250)

Tallinn, Estonia As fairy-tale as they come, conical watchtowers guard the historic heart of Estonia's capital. (p181)

Plovdiv, Bulgaria A visual feast of cobbled lanes, Bulgarian Revival–era mansions, boutique galleries and quirky bars. (p103)

Ohrid, North Macedonia Picturesque churches and ancient ruins perched above one of Europe's deepest and oldest lakes. (p301)

Berat, Albania White Ottoman houses on a rugged mountainside in this 'town of a thousand windows'. (p49)

Castles & Palaces

Bran Castle, Romania This Transylvanian beauty looks straight out of a horror movie. (p348)

Bojnice Castle, Slovakia As if from a storybook, this fortress has soaring towers and beautifully landscaped grounds. (p419)

Malbork Castle, Poland Live out medieval fantasies at this whopping brick castle, founded by 13th-century Teutonic knights. (p332)

Catherine Palace, Russia Marvel at this glittering baroque palace, restored to tsarist splendour after destruction in WWII. (p386)

Karlštejn Castle, Czech Republic An apparition of fairy-tale Gothic, this Bohemian beauty near Prague makes a great day trip. (p159)

Ljubljana Castle, Slovenia Amazing views from the watchtower and gourmet food in one of the city's top restaurants. (p433)

Mir Castle, Belarus A stocky castle painstakingly restored to 16th-century splendour, from gilded interiors to manicured grounds. (p68)

Coasts & Beaches

Hvar Island, Croatia This sun-dappled and herb-scented Adriatic isle is a jumping-off point for the Pakleni Islands. (p134)

Curonian Spit, Lithuania World Heritage sand dunes slide into bracing Baltic waters along this enchanting sliver of land. (p261)

Black Sea Coast, Bulgaria The best beaches on the Black Sea, from Varna's big resorts to less hectic Sozopol. (p109)

Jūrmala, Latvia Dip into the spa scene at Soviet-era sanatoriums along the Baltic Riviera. (p242)

Baltic Coast, Poland Family holidaymakers spill across the golden sands in Pomerania. (p330)

Historical Sites

Diocletian's Palace, Croatia Imposing Roman ruin in the beating heart of Split, encompassing 220 ancient buildings. (p130)

Rila Monastery, Bulgaria Heavenly monastery, dating back more than 1000 years and an enduring stronghold of Bulgarian culture. (p101)

Kremlin, Russia The seat of power to medieval tsars and modern presidents alike, packed with incredible sights. (p363)

Butrint, Albania Ruins of an ancient Greek fortified city in a tranquil national-park location. (p54)

Lepenski Vir, Serbia This Mesolithic-era settlement is famous for its stone idols with fishlike faces. (p407)

Museum on Water – Bay of Bones, North Macedonia A prehistoric pile dwellers' settlement on Lake Ohrid, excavated by an underwater team. (p300)

Mountains & Hiking

Slovenský Raj National Park, Slovakia Waterfalls, gorges and thick forests decorate Slovakia's outstanding national park. (p425)

Bulgaria's mountains Don't miss the trails around stunning Rila Monastery or the beautiful Rodopi Mountains. (p101)

Carpathian Mountains, Poland Use Zakopane as a base for long walks, including to emerald-green Lake Morskie Oko. (p324)

Mt Triglav, Slovenia Slovenia's highest mountain is the centrepiece of its biggest nature reserve and a terrific two-day climb. (p441)

Via Dinarica, Montenegro The Montenegrin part of this 'mega-trail' connects Durmitor National Park with Bosnia and Hercegovina's Sutjeska National Park. (p286)

Accursed Mountains, Albania Snow-capped peaks and traditional mountain villages in one of Europe's most remote corners. (p56)

Food & Drink

Hungarian cuisine Savour the national dish, goulash, with gulps of blood-red wine in this gastronomically inclined country. (p198)

Istrian delights, Croatia Truffles, wild asparagus and fresh seafood

Top: Malbork Castle (p332), Poland

Bottom: *Gulyás* (goulash), Hungary

are on the menu; there's also superb local wine. (p124)

Slow food, North Macedonia Homespun cooking, from paprika-tinged sausages to foraged mushrooms, is putting North Macedonia on the menu. (p290)

Nordic cuisine, Estonia Dip into cutting-edge Nordic cuisine at Ö and seasonal game at Rataskaevu 16. (p187)

Wine tasting, Moldova Sip a lesser-known vintage in plucky little Moldova, producer of world-class wines. (p264)

Fast food, Bosnia & Hercegovina There's no better place for *burek* (savoury pastries) or *ćevapi* (skinless sausages) than Sarajevo. (p77)

Art Collections

State Hermitage Museum, St Petersburg, Russia One of the world's greatest art collections, stuffed full of treasures from mummies to Picassos. (p379)

Danubiana Meulensteen Art Museum, Slovakia Sculptures as special as the windblown setting at this inspiring out-of-town gallery on the Danube. (p420)

State Tretyakov Gallery, Moscow, Russia This fabulous repository of Russian culture covers it all, from religious icons to contemporary sculpture. (p366)

Mucha Museum, Prague, Czech Republic Be seduced by sensuous art-nouveau posters, paintings and decorative panels of Alfonse Mucha. (p153)

Art Museum Rīga Bourse, Rīga, Latvia The old stock exchange is a worthy showcase for the city's art treasures. (p235)

Kumu, Tallinn, Estonia An ark of copper and glass housing a

lavish collection of Estonian art. (p185)

Fabrica de Pensule, Cluj-Napoca, Romania The grungy, avant-garde 'Paintbrush Factory' is a workspace for up-and-coming artists. (p353)

Museum of Contemporary Art, Belgrade, Serbia The premier collection of art from the former Yugoslavia. (p395)

Folk & Traditional Culture

Budapest's spa culture, Hungary Czech spa spots and Russia's *bani* (saunas) are good, but Budapest's baths are best. (p200)

Salaši, Serbia Traditional *salaši* (farmsteads) dot the Vojvodina province, offering cosy lodgings, slow-food feasts and rural hospitality. (p402)

Valley of the Roses, Bulgaria Petal-processing methods have barely changed in Bulgaria's flowered valleys, producing rose liqueurs, soaps and oils. (p105)

Hill of Crosses, Lithuania Thousands of crosses are amassed at this site north of Šiauliai, including folk-art masterpieces. (p260)

Outdoor Activities

Water sports, Bovec, Slovenia An unrivalled location for high-adrenaline water sports, offering everything from canyoning to hydrospeeding. (p442)

Technical-assist hikes, Slovenský Raj, Slovakia Scramble up ladders and balance on walkways in thrilling Slovenský Raj. (p425)

Rafting the Tara Canyon, Montenegro Hit the rapids of

the Tara River, hidden within Europe's deepest canyon. (p286)

Skiing, Bulgaria The Rila and Rodopi mountain ranges are speckled with ski resorts like Bansko and Borovets. (p101)

Swimming and paddleboading, Lake Balaton, Hungary From sunbathing to stand-up paddleboarding, all activity levels are possible at this scenic lake. (p212)

Belavezhskaya Pushcha National Park, Belarus Cycle or hike around Europe's oldest wildlife refuge, home to 300-odd European bison. (p71)

Spectacular Scenery

Train from Belgrade to Bar Eastern Europe's most impressive train journey through the spectacular canyons of Montenegro. (p289)

Lake Koman Ferry, Albania Witness the majesty of Albania's remote, mountainous north on this stunning ferry ride. (p56)

Triglav National Park, Slovenia A three-headed mountain presides over a swathe of turquoise river gorges and placid meadows. (p441)

Danube Delta, Romania Wild, reedy wetlands teeming with birds where the Danube flows into the Black Sea. (p351)

Hortobágy National Park, Hungary Windswept grasslands speckled with long-horned cattle and occasional *csikósok* (cowboys). (p217)

Nightlife

Belgrade, Serbia One of the most exciting, vibrant – not to mention affordable – places to party until daybreak. (p395)

Pekka Vapaavuori–designed Kumu (p185), Tallinn, Estonia

Budapest, Hungary Pop-up clubs in abandoned buildings have put Budapest's nightlife on a par with Berlin. (p200)

Moscow, Russia Evolving into an essential stop on the club-ber's world map, with bars and clubs aplenty. (p363)

Cluj-Napoca, Romania Cluj's historic backstreets house perhaps the friendliest bunch of student party animals in Europe. (p352)

Plovdiv, Bulgaria Hipster haunts and cocktail bars spill into the cobbled lanes of Kapana artistic quarter. (p103)

Budva, Montenegro Scores of beachside bars and clubs have earned Budva the nickname 'the Montenegrin Miami'. (p282)

Contemporary Architecture

Kumu, Tallinn, Estonia A world-class concrete-and-glass building that holds an excellent art collection. (p185)

Bratislava, Slovakia Its zany skyline includes a seemingly upside-down radio building and a UFO-topped bridge. (p413)

Garage Museum of Contemporary Art, Moscow, Russia In Moscow's revitalised Gorky Park, this museum occupies a 1960s pavilion redesigned by Rem Koolhaas. (p367)

Skopje, North Macedonia Several modernist masterpieces survive in Skopje, including the train station built by Kenzo Tange. (p292)

Month by Month

January

January is an enchanting time to experience countryside blanketed with snow and Old Towns dusted with frost. Most towns are relatively tourist-free and hotel prices are at rock-bottom, though ski resorts are lively.

🎭 Küstendorf Film & Music Festival, Serbia

Created and curated by Serbian director Emir Kusturica, this international indie fest (www.kustendorf-filmandmusicfestival.org) in the town of Drvengrad, near Zlatibor in Serbia, eschews traditional red-carpet glitz for oddball inclusions vying for the 'Golden Egg' prize.

February

Still cold, but with longer days, February is when colourful carnivals are held across the region, while skiers and snowboarders enjoy more sunshine. Low hotel prices and the off-season feel continue.

🎭 Golden Grapes Festival, Bulgaria

Melnik and other Bulgarian winemaking towns have their vines blessed by a priest before lavishly toasting the patron saint of wine. It's celebrated on the first and/or 14th day of the month. (p102)

🎭 Rijeka Carnival, Croatia

A kaleidoscope of costume and colour unfolds in Rijeka, host to Croatia's dazzling pre-Lent celebrations (www.rijecki-karneval.hr). Other events kick off in Zadar, Split and Dubrovnik too.

🎭 Kurentovanje, Slovenia

A procession of hairy masks, bell-ringing and the occasional wry slap form the dramatic rites of spring in Ptuj for Kurentovanje (www.kurentovanje.net), Slovenia's most distinctive Mardi Gras festival.

March

Spring arrives in southern regions, northerly countries remain in winter's slushy grip, and skiers continue to make merry in the mountains. Days can be bright and sunny, though hiking trails are perilous with melting snow.

☆ Vitranc Cup, Slovenia

Slovenia's major downhill skiing event (www.pokal-vitranc.com), held annually in early March in Kranjska Gora, will elicit gasps from both dedicated snowheads and casual observers.

🎭 Maslenitsa (Pancake Week), Russia

There is no such thing as too many pancakes at this Shrovetide festival. Maslenitsa celebrates the end of winter and encourages pre-Lenten pancake guzzling. Folk dancing and pancake stalls can be enjoyed across Russia.

🎭 Drowning of Marzanna, Poland

Head to Poland in March for the rite of the Drowning of Marzanna, a surviving pagan ritual in which an effigy of the goddess of winter is immersed in water at the advent of spring.

⭐ Ski-Jumping World Cup, Slovenia

Held on the third weekend in March, this international competition (www.planica.si) in Planica is the place to marvel at world-record-making ski jumps.

🎊 Easter Festival of Sacred Music, Czech Republic

Choral and orchestral concerts (www.mhf-brno.cz) take place in the oldest churches in Brno, including the beautiful Cathedral of Sts Peter & Paul, during the two weeks following Palm Sunday.

April

Spring kicks off in April, though the winter-sports season sometimes lingers and lofty mountain passes may still be treacherous. Days are getting warmer and sunnier, and, outside the Easter holidays, hotel prices remain low.

⭐ Budapest Spring Festival, Hungary

One of Europe's top classical music events is this two-week festival in mid-April. Concerts are held in a number of beautiful venues including several stunning churches, the Hungarian State Opera House and the National Theatre. (p205)

⭐ Moscow International Film Festival, Russia

Russia's premier film festival (www.moscowfilm festival.ru) runs toward the end of the month and includes retrospective and documentary film programs as well as the usual awards.

⭐ Music Biennale Zagreb, Croatia

Held during odd-numbered years since the 1960s, Croatia's lauded live-music highlight (www.mbz.hr) features modern-day classical concerts across a multitude of venues.

May

An excellent time to visit Eastern Europe, May is sunny and warm and full of things to do, but never too hot. Big destinations feel busy, though hiking areas and villages remain quiet.

📅 International Labour Day, Russia

Bigger than Christmas back in communist times, International Labour Day (1 May) may have dropped in status since the fall of the Berlin Wall, but it's still a national holiday in Russia and several other former Soviet republics. You'll find fireworks, concerts and even military parades.

🎊 Czech Beer Festival, Czech Republic

Beer lovers won't want to miss the Czech Beer Festival (www.ceskypivni festival.cz), where lots of food, music and – most importantly – more than 150 beers from around the country are on offer in Prague from mid- to late May.

⭐ Prague Spring & Fringe, Czech Republic

Three-week international music festival Prague Spring is the most prestigious event in the Czech capital's cultural calendar, with concerts held in an array of venues. Meanwhile, the Prague Fringe Festival (www.praguefringe.com) hosts a more irreverent line-up of theatre, comedy and music. (p154)

June

Shoulder season is well under way – it's already summer in southeastern Europe and the sun barely sets in the Baltic as the solstice approaches. One of the best times to travel, if not the cheapest.

🎊 Mikser Festival, Serbia

Creative thinking is at the heart of Belgrade's Mikser Festival (www.festival.mikser.rs), which hosts thought-provoking art exhibitions, cultural forums and cutting-edge design around the edgy Savamala district.

🎊 Rose Festival, Bulgaria

Join Bulgaria's celebration of its most fragrant export as the Valley of the Roses bursts into bloom. Kazanlâk's main square holds the main event on the first weekend in June, but smaller villages have their own rituals, from folk dancing to sipping rose liqueur. (p108)

★ White Nights, Russia

The barely setting sun across the Baltic encourages locals to party through the night. The best place to join the fun is in the imperial Russian capital, St Petersburg, where classical concerts, an international music festival (www.wnfestival.ru) and other summer events keep spirits high.

St John's Eve & St John's Day, Baltic Countries

The Baltic region's biggest annual night out is a celebration of midsummer on 23 and 24 June. It's best experienced out in the country, where huge bonfires flare for all-night revellers who sing, dance and leap over fires.

★ Jewish Culture Festival, Poland

Kraków rediscovers its Jewish heritage during a packed week of music, art exhibitions and lectures (www.jewishfestival.pl) in late June/early July. Poland's festival is the biggest and most exciting Jewish festival in the region.

July

The middle of summer sees Eastern Europe packed with both people and things to do. Temperatures and prices soar by the end of July, but hotel room rates remain reasonable early in the month.

★ Východná, Slovakia

Slovakia's top folk festival (www.festivalvychodna.

sk) is held over the first weekend of July each year in the tiny Tatras Mountain village of Východná. More than 1400 performers converge here to celebrate traditional music, dance, arts and crafts.

★ Ohrid Summer Festival, North Macedonia

The month-long Ohrid Summer Festival comprises a wealth of performances from classical, opera and rock acts to theatre and literature, all celebrating North Macedonian culture. (p303)

☆ Karlovy Vary International Film Festival, Czech Republic

Held in one of the most beautiful spa towns in the Czech Republic, the region's own Cannes (www.kviff. com) is a far smaller affair than its French cousin, but it still shows hundreds of movies in its packed program.

Ivan Kupala (Kupalle), Ukraine & Belarus

Fern wreaths, leaping over bonfires and late-night dancing are the mystical hallmarks of this suggestive fertility festival, held on the night of 6 or 7 July to purify participants in time for midsummer.

★ Festival of Medieval Arts & Crafts, Romania

During July the beautiful Romanian city of Sighişoara hosts open-air concerts, parades and ceremonies, all glorifying medieval Transylvania and

taking the town back to its fascinating 12th-century origins.

☆ EXIT Festival, Serbia

Eastern Europe's most talked-about music festival takes place each July within the walls of the Petrovaradin Citadel in Serbia's second city, Novi Sad. Book early for tickets as big international headlining acts attract music lovers from all over the continent. (p403)

★ Slavyansky Bazaar, Belarus

Held in the old Russian city of Vitsebsk (in modern Belarus), this festival is one of the biggest cultural events in the former Soviet Union, featuring theatrical performances, music concerts and exhibits from all over the Slavic world. (p69)

☆ Pohoda Festival, Slovakia

Slovakia's largest music and arts festival (www.pohodafestival.sk), held in Trenčín, represents all genres of music, from rock to orchestral, over multiple stages.

☆ Ultra Europe, Croatia

Now one of the largest electronic music festivals in the world, Ultra Europe (www.ultraeurope.com) lights up the city of Split before continuing the action in Bol, Hvar and Vis.

☆ Belgrade Summer Festival, Serbia

BELEF (www.belef.rs), a dynamic sampling of innovative music, dance, theatre and visual-arts displays, takes over the Serbian capital for a month from mid-July.

☆ Baltica International Folklore Festival, Baltic Countries

This rotating festival (www.cioff.org) of traditional Baltic folk music and dance will be hosted in Estonia in 2019 and Lithuania in 2020.

☆ International Music Festival, Czech Republic

Thousands of music lovers congregate in Český Krumlov for classical concerts, as well as jazz, rock and folk music, at this impressive month-long festival (www.festivalkrumlov.cz), which runs from mid-July to mid-August.

☆ Dubrovnik Summer Festival, Croatia

From mid-July to late August, Croatia's most prestigious summer festival (www.dubrovnik-festival.hr) presents a program of theatre, opera, concerts and dance on open-air stages throughout the city.

August

It's easy enough to escape crowds and expense, even at summer's height. There's a huge amount to see and do in August, and the weather – from the Baltic coast to the Adriatic – is sizzlingly hot.

☆ Kaliningrad City Jazz, Russia

Kaliningrad's jazz fest (www.jazzfestival.ru) at-tracts performers from across Europe. It's held over three days around the city, with nightclub jams, big concerts and even free open-air sessions.

☆ Untold, Romania

Untold is Romania's largest music festival (www.untold.com). It's held in Cluj-Napoca near the start of the month and has been scooping up awards since it began in 2015.

☆ Sziget Festival, Hungary

A week-long music festival held all over Budapest, Sziget features bands from around the world representing a dizzying array of genres, from hypnotic trance to the blackest heavy metal. (p205)

☆ Nišville International Jazz Festival, Serbia

The sprawling Niš Fortress hosts this jazz festival each August with acts from around the world on the program. (p406)

☆ Guča Festival, Serbia

Much more than old brass, Guča's trumpet festival (www.gucafestival.rs) is one of the most exciting and bizarre events in Eastern Europe. Thousands of revellers descend on the small Serbian town of Guča to damage their eardrums, livers and sanity over four cacophonous days.

☆ Sarajevo Film Festival, Bosnia & Hercegovina

This globally acclaimed festival (www.sff.ba) that grew out of the ruins of the '90s civil war screens commercial and art-house movies side by side in the Bosnian capital.

September

Summer crowds have dropped off and prices are no longer sky high, but great weather lingers across the region. September is a fantastic month to head to Eastern Europe, particular for hiking and outdoor activities.

☆ Coffee Festival, Ukraine

Eastern European coffee culture thrives in Lviv, even more so during the annual coffee festival (www.coffeefest.lviv.ua). Taste coffees from all over the world and channel the buzz into bike rides, film screenings and other events.

☆ Apollonia Arts Festival, Bulgaria

Seaside Sozopol hosts a vast festival (www.apollonia.bg) of music, drama and dance for the first week of September.

☆ Cow's Ball, Slovenia

This Slovenian mid-September weekend of folk dancing, music, eating and drinking in Bohinj marks the return of the cows from their high pastures to the valleys in typically ebullient Balkan style.

☆ Dvořák Autumn, Czech Republic

This classical-music festival honours the work of the Czech Republic's best-known composer, Antonín Dvořák. The event is held over three weeks in the spa town of Karlovy Vary (www.kso.cz).

October

October remains mild in the south but gets chilly in the north. Prices stay low and crowds lessen with each passing day. Some hiking and biking trails are off limits. Summer resorts may start hibernating.

⭐ Wine Festival, Moldova

Winemakers, wine tasting, wine buying and wine-enriched folkloric performances in and around Chişinău draw buyers and more casual oenophiles to this wine festival. (p267)

November

Eastern Europe's in-between days: after hikers shuffle home and before snow brings winter-sports fans. Days are short, weather is cold, but you'll have most of Eastern Europe's attractions to yourself and accommodation is cheap.

⭐ Tirana International Film Festival, Albania

From the end of October through the first week of November Tirana holds a short- and feature-film festival (www.tiranafilmfest.com), the only one of its kind in tiny Albania. It's a great way to take stock of Eastern European film-making.

⭐ Jazz Festival, Bosnia & Hercegovina

Held in Sarajevo in early November, this festival (www.jazzfest.ba) showcases the sultry sounds of local and international jazz musicians.

📅 Martinje, Croatia

Martinje (St Martin's Day) is celebrated in all the wine-producing regions across Croatia on 11 November. There are wine celebrations and lots of feasting and sampling of new wines.

December

Christmas decorations brighten dark streets and, despite the cold across much of the region, as long as you avoid Christmas and New Year's Eve, prices remain surprisingly low. Ski season starts towards the month's end.

🛍 Christmas Markets

Throughout December Eastern Europe heaves with German-style Christmas markets. You'll find these in many cities in the region, though we recommend Bratislava for its charm and beautiful setting.

📅 Christmas

Most countries celebrate on Christmas Eve (24 December) with an evening meal and midnight Mass. However, in Russia, Ukraine, Belarus, Moldova, Serbia, Montenegro and North Macedonia, Christmas falls in January.

📅 New Year's Eve

Even back when communist officials frowned on Christmas, New Year's Eve remained a big holiday in Eastern Europe. Join the party wherever you are and see in the new year with locals.

Itineraries

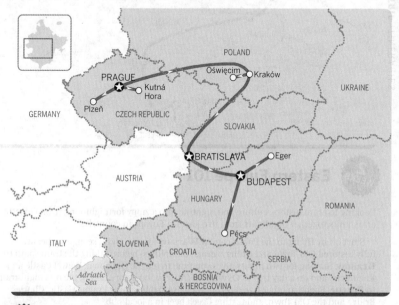

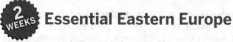 **Essential Eastern Europe**

Combine highlights of the Czech Republic, Poland, Slovakia and Hungary for an introduction to Eastern Europe's charms.

Start in **Prague**, spending two days absorbing the Old Town. Day-trip to **Kutná Hora**, to peep at its eerie ossuary and medieval silver history, and take a beer pilgrimage to **Plzeň**.

On day five head by train into Poland to reach **Kraków**, with its gob-smacking Main Square. Over three days, ramble Wawel Castle and off-beat Kazimierz, and take a trip to harrowing **Oświęcim** (Auschwitz).

On day eight head to Slovakia, passing through the High Tatras before reaching **Bratislava**, with its Danube views. Spend the evening in wine bars and beer halls; the next morning, take a half-day excursion to crumbling Devín Castle.

On day 10 take a boat down the Danube to **Budapest**. Spend a couple days simmering in outdoor baths, exploring coffee houses and ruin bars, and admiring the architecture. From here bolt to the baroque **Eger** and finish with a day trip to **Pécs**, full of relics from the Turkish occupation.

2 WEEKS Eastern Europe 101

Looking to cram history, culture and nightlife into a zippy fortnight-long trip? This itinerary knits together highlights from five Eastern European countries.

Start off by flying to the Polish capital **Warsaw** for one night, seeing the beautifully restored Old Town and eating pierogi (dumplings) before taking the train south to **Kraków**. Staying for two nights gives you time to see the Old Town, Wawel Castle and Kazimierz, and do a day trip to **Oświęcim** (Auschwitz) before taking the overnight train to **Prague**. Spend another two days on intensive sightseeing – Prague Castle, Charles Bridge and the Old Town, and tasting Czech beer in a local pub.

At the end of day five, take another overnight train to **Budapest** for two nights in Hungary. Soak in the glorious Gellért Baths, take a cruise on the Danube, see the magnificent Parliament building and wander Castle Hill before yet another overnight train (at the end of day seven) to Romania's underrated capital, **Bucharest**. With a one-night stay you can cover the main sights, including the Palace of Parliament, wander the historic centre and pick up the city's energy in its bars and clubs.

On day nine, continue by bus or train to **Plovdiv** in Bulgaria, equally rich in Roman ruins, creaky Bulgarian Revival–era mansions, inventive galleries and bars. Stay two nights here, allowing time to amble through the Old Town, pose in the Roman Amphitheatre, and take a half-day trip to vertiginous Asen's Fortress. On day 11, take the train to **Sofia** for two nights exploring the glamour of the Bulgarian capital, in particular the golden-domed Aleksander Nevski Cathedral and the Ancient Serdica Complex.

On your last day, take a day trip from Sofia through the Rila Mountains to the country's spiritual nucleus. Thousand-year-old **Rila Monastery** is Bulgaria's holiest site, in a mountain setting as spine-tingling as its apocalyptic frescoes. From here, fly out of Sofia or continue to bigger regional air hubs, such as Athens or İstanbul, to get a flight home.

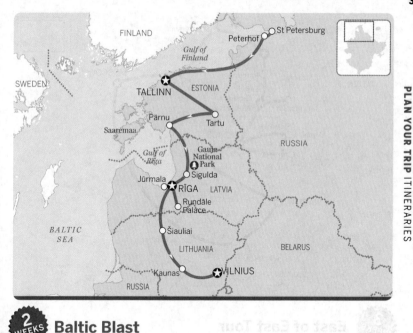

Baltic Blast

2 WEEKS

This trip weaves through four very different countries: skirting the Baltic coast, plunging through thick forests, and taking in treasured art. In the space of a fortnight you'll see rolling countryside and discover three capitals – Tallinn, Rīga and Vilnius – along with timeless St Petersburg and quirky Baltic towns.

Set aside three nights for heart-stoppingly beautiful **St Petersburg** to see the Hermitage, Nevsky Prospekt's mansions, and the amazing Church on the Spilled Blood. Head out of town to the reconstructed palaces and manicured gardens of **Peterhof**, which belonged to Peter the Great.

Take a bus or train to the Estonian capital **Tallinn** for two days. Wander the chocolate-box streets and stone towers of the 14th- and 15th-century Old Town before heading to the university town of **Tartu**, packed with interesting museums, parks and handsome wooden buildings. Duck west to the Baltic coast to find the inviting Estonian beach resort of **Pärnu**. Rest here for a day to indulge in the pleasures of summer holiday-making: mud baths, Bacchanalian nightlife and golden-sand beaches.

At the beginning of week two, continue into Latvia, stopping off in cheerful **Sigulda**. Spend a day walking in the tranquil landscapes and dense forests of **Gauja National Park**. On day 10, continue on to **Rīga**, Latvia's delightful capital, where you can soak up fantastic art-nouveau architecture, plus bleak history and a contrastingly friendly Old Town, over two days. On one of the days, take an excursion to the opulent **Rundāle Palace** to see how the aristocrats lived. On day 12, day-trip to the beaches of **Jūrmala**.

Lithuania is next, and it greets you with the astounding Hill of Crosses in **Šiauliai**, an icon of Lithuanian identity. Spirited university town **Kaunas** is Lithuania's second city, boasting a leafy old centre and bookish cafes, as well as being just a short distance away from the chilling history of war and deportation at Ninth Fort. Finally, end your journey in beautiful **Vilnius**, the country's crowning glory.

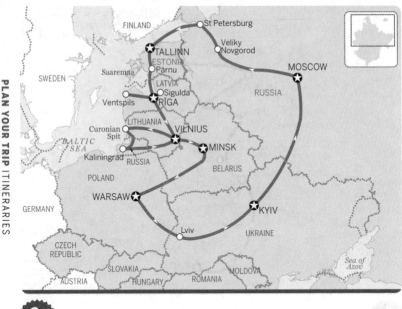

East of East Tour

3 WEEKS

Pull back the old Iron Curtain to discover the history and beauty of these one-time Soviet satellites of regional heavyweight Russia.

Begin with two days in dynamic **Warsaw**, with its revamped Old Town, museums and royal parks. From here take a train to **Lviv**, Ukraine's most beautiful city, and spend a day enjoying Old Town churches and enchanting Lychakiv Cemetery. After Lviv, continue by train to imposing **Kyiv**, where sacred relics repose beneath gilded domes.

After a couple of days enjoying the sights in the Ukrainian capital, and perhaps a guided tour of Chornobyl's exclusion zone, take the sleeper train to the megalopolis **Moscow**, a place of striking extremes, dazzling wealth and gridlocked traffic. Drink in the history of the Kremlin, see Lenin's Mausoleum, St Basil's Cathedral and Red Square, and sample the nightlife and fashion.

Once you've had your fill, leave Moscow and visit picturesque **Veliky Novgorod** en route to the beautiful baroque and neoclassical architecture of **St Petersburg**. You could easily spend three days here, although there are abundant sights around as well, such as the tsarist palace Tsarskoe Selo.

When you're ready to head off, grab a train to Estonia's magical capital, **Tallinn**, where you can soak up the medieval Old Town. Head south and relax on the golden-sand beaches of **Pärnu** before continuing to the Latvian capital **Rīga**, and its fine collection of art-nouveau architecture. Squeeze in trips to the caves and medieval castles of **Sigulda**, and the breathtaking coastline around **Ventspils**.

Cross into Lithuania, where a night or two in **Vilnius** will reveal the Baltic's most underrated capital. From Vilnius travel to the huge sand dunes of the amazing **Curonian Spit**. If you've arranged a double-entry visa for Russia, cross over into the melting-pot exclave of **Kaliningrad**. Alternatively, if you've sorted a Belarus visa, take the train to this isolated republic with its pleasant capital **Minsk** before re-entering Poland and heading back to Warsaw.

Top: Kotor's Old Town (p279), Montenegro

Bottom: Cathedral of St Sophia in Veliky Novgorod, Russia

MARINA ZEZELINA2/SHUTTERSTOCK ©

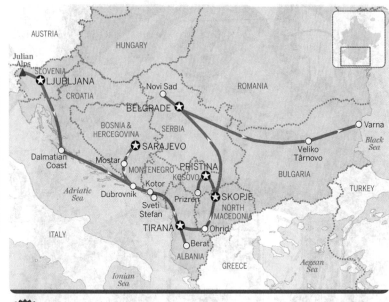

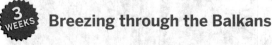

3 WEEKS

Breezing through the Balkans

Taking its name from the Balkan Mountains, this is a fascinating region of Eastern Europe lapped by different seas, with enigmatic fortresses and intriguing towns.

Begin in Slovenia, where the capital **Ljubljana** is a delight with a castle, beautiful buildings and bridges. Indulge in superb scenery and adrenaline-rush sports in the **Julian Alps** before heading south to Croatia and to the beaches along the **Dalmatian Coast**. Stop in **Dubrovnik** to explore the Old Town and the surrounding islands.

Detour into Bosnia and Herzegovina – first visit **Mostar** to see the legendary bridge and the multi-ethnic community that has enjoyed rejuvenation since the Balkan Wars, then spend a night or two in bustling **Sarajevo**. Head south to the coast and east into Montenegro: visit the historic walled city of **Kotor**, see the impressive coastline and mountains, and enjoy the beaches around the fortified island village of **Sveti Stefan** before pressing south into Albania.

After exploring **Tirana**, a mountain-shrouded, ramshackle capital, make an excursion to the Unesco-listed town of **Berat**, before taking a bus into little-explored North Macedonia, ending in sublime **Ohrid**. Spend at least two days here, enjoying the ancient churches and swimming in the eponymous lake. Make your way to **Skopje**, North Macedonia's capital, where an abundance of gleaming, modern Italianate structures are redefining the city for the 21st century. Take the train to **Pristina**, Kosovo's cosmopolitan capital, from where it's an easy hop to **Prizren**, a mosque-filled old town.

To reach Serbia's capital **Belgrade**, you'll need to backtrack to Skopje and board the international train. Don't miss the city's ancient Kalemegdan Citadel and the hip restaurant and clubbing scenes. Take a detour to laid-back **Novi Sad** with its neoclassical buildings, outdoor cafes and Danube views.

A cross-border bus or train will take you into Bulgaria. Head east to **Veliko Târnovo**, the ancient capital with a dramatic, river-wrapped setting. From here it's an easy bus to **Varna** by the Black Sea, complete with beaches, Roman ruins and open-air clubs.

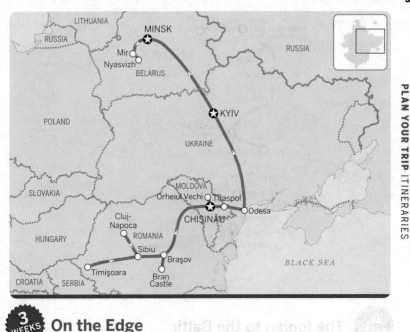

3 WEEKS — On the Edge

Covering the easternmost edge of the region (before Russia), this itinerary balances pretty towns and fortresses with time-trapped Belarus and border anomaly Transdniestr.

Start in one of Romania's underrated westerly cities: either lively **Timişoara**, with its history of anti-Ceauşescu revolt, or edgy **Cluj-Napoca**, harbouring avant-garde nightlife and coffee spots. On day three, head east to elegant **Sibiu**, before pressing on to **Braşov** on day four. Allow three days to traipse Braşov's forested hills, meander medieval laneways and day-trip to bear country or dramatic **Bran Castle**.

Start week two by entering lost-in-time Moldova. Spend a day or two exploring gritty but green capital **Chişinău**; excellent local wine is plentiful and cheap. Allow a day to visit the stunning cave monastery at **Orheiul Vechi**, and another to time-travel into Transdniestr, a country that doesn't officially exist. Little appears to have changed in the 'capital' **Tiraspol** since the Soviet era.

Entering Ukraine on day 11, make a beeline for **Odesa**, which is only two hours by train or bus from Tiraspol, to enjoy the seaside setting of Ukraine's Black Sea resort. Next, head north and devote around four days to the country's dynamic capital, **Kyiv**. An ancient seat of Slavic and Orthodox culture, it's a modern metropolis that played a starring role in the 2014 Maidan Revolution. Don't miss the Pecherska Lavra complex and St Sophia's Cathedral, as well as ousted ex-president Viktor Yanukovych's opulent mansion Mezhyhirya.

The final stop takes you to Belarus, Europe's so-called 'last dictatorship'. To avoid having to arrange a Belarus visa, fly from Kyiv to monolithic **Minsk**, a city dominated by Stalinist avenues and Soviet memorials. Minsk is generating buzz for its scintillating nightlife, centred around the up-and-coming arts quarter vul Katrychnitskaya. End your journey with a trip to the provinces. Check out the castle in **Mir**, then experience provincial life in **Nyasvizh** with its ancient churches and 16th-century castle.

4 WEEKS The Ionian to the Baltic

This eight-country odyssey extends from the Ionian to Baltic Seas, darting between sea-facing fortresses, mountainous vistas and undiscovered towns.

Arrive in Albania by ferry at the port of **Saranda**, and head to the ruins in **Butrint**. Continue through Albania to Unesco-listed **Gjirokastra**, whose stone-and-slate Old Town is Albania's loveliest. Press on to the capital **Tirana** for a couple of days of colourful cityscapes and inventive museums, before journeying on to Montenegro.

Move first to **Budva** with its atmospheric Old Town and beaches and then discover ancient, walled **Kotor**. Head north to the cliff-face-hugging **Ostrog Monastery** and on to **Durmitor National Park** for hiking, rafting and canyoning.

From Montenegro's capital Podgorica, catch an overnight train to vibrant Serbian capital **Belgrade**. Stroll the citadels and drink by the Danube, then continue north to convivial, Austro-Hungarian-influenced **Novi Sad** and explore the **Fruška Gora** monasteries and vineyards. Cross into Hungary at culture-crammed **Szeged** and head for **Lake Balaton**. Keep surging north into Slovakia, aiming for plucky **Bratislava**, to spend a few days hopping between cafes and castles. Venture onward to chilly gorges and cascades in high-octane **Slovenský Raj National Park**.

Crossing the Tatra Mountains into Poland, travel to cultural hive **Wrocław**, spending a few days admiring street art and edgy galleries before dropping in on pastel-coloured **Poznań**. From here, head for the Baltic coast: **Gdańsk** is a thriving port where WWII broke out. From here, make day trips to beaches and to **Malbork**, famed for Europe's biggest Gothic castle.

Next up is the Russian exclave of **Kaliningrad**, which combines elements of Prussia, the USSR and modern Russia. Return to the coast to travel through Kaliningrad's **Kurshskaya Kosa National Park** and cross into the Lithuanian section of birch-forested Curonian Spit, aiming for **Klaipėda**, Lithuania's main port. End your trip in many-steepled **Vilnius**.

On the Road

Estonia p178

Russia p360

Latvia p232

Lithuania p248

Belarus p60

Poland p308

Ukraine p448

Czech Republic p144

Slovakia p410

Moldova p264

Hungary p198

Slovenia p430

Romania p338

Croatia p116

Serbia p392

Bosnia & Hercegovina p74

Montenegro p276

Bulgaria p92

Kosovo p222

Albania p42

North Macedonia p290

Albania

POP 2.93 MILLION

Best Places to Eat

➡ Onufri (p51)

➡ Pasta e Vino (p55)

➡ Met Kodra (p46)

➡ Otium (p48)

➡ Mrizi i Zanave (p48)

Best Places to Stay

➡ Stone City Hostel (p52)

➡ Rose Garden Hotel (p55)

➡ Trip'n'Hostel (p46)

➡ Hotel Mangalemi (p51)

➡ Hotel Rilindja (p57)

➡ B&B Tirana Smile (p46)

Why Go?

Closed to outsiders for much of the 20th century, Albania has long been Mediterranean Europe's enigma. Until fairly recently its rumpled mountains, fortress towns and sparkling beaches were merely a rumour on most travel maps. But, with the end of a particularly brutal strain of communism in 1991, Albania tentatively swung open its gates. The first curious tourists to arrive discovered a land where ancient codes of conduct still held sway and where the wind whistled through the shattered remnants of half-forgotten ancient Greek and Roman sites. A quarter of a century after throwing off the shackles of communism, Albania's stunning mountain scenery, crumbling castles, boisterous capital and dreamy beaches rivalling any in the Mediterranean continue to enchant. But hurry here because as word gets out about what Albania is hiding, the still-tiny trickle of tourists threatens to become a flood.

When to Go
Tirana

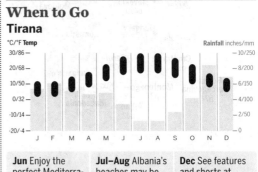

Jun Enjoy the perfect Mediterranean climate and deserted beaches.

Jul–Aug Albania's beaches may be packed, but this is a great time to explore the mountains.

Dec See features and shorts at the Tirana Film Festival, while the intrepid can snowshoe to Theth.

Entering the Country

Albania has good connections in all directions: daily buses go to Kosovo, Montenegro, North Macedonia and Greece. There are no international train routes to/from Albania. The southern seaport of Saranda is a short boat trip from Greece's Corfu, while in summer ferries also connect Himara and Vlora to Corfu. Durrës has regular ferries to Italy.

ITINERARIES

One Week

Spend a day in busy Tirana (p45), checking out the various excellent museums as well as the Blloku bars and cafes. On day two, make the three-hour trip to the Ottoman-era town of Berat (p49). Overnight there before continuing down the coast for a couple of days on the beach in Himara (p54) or Ksamil (p53). Make sure you leave time for Butrint (p54) before spending your last night in charming Gjirokastra (p51) and returning to Tirana.

Two Weeks

Follow the first week itinerary and then head north into Albania's incredible Accursed Mountains (p56). Start in Italian-flavoured Shkodra (p54), from where you can get transport to Koman (p56) for the stunning morning ferry ride to Fierzë. Continue the same day to the charming mountain village of Valbona (p56) for the night, before trekking to Theth (p57) and spending your last couple of nights in the beautiful Theth National Park before heading back to Tirana.

Essential Food & Drink

Byrek Pastry with cheese or meat.

Fergesë Baked peppers, egg and cheese, and occasionally meat.

Midhje Wild or farmed mussels, often served fried.

Paçë koke Sheep's head soup, usually served for breakfast.

Qofta Flat or cylindrical minced-meat rissoles.

Sufllaqë Doner kebab.

Tavë Meat baked with cheese and egg.

Konjak Local brandy.

Raki Popular spirit made from grapes.

Raki mani Spirit made from mulberries.

AT A GLANCE

Area 28,748 sq km

Capital Tirana

Country Code ☏ 355

Currency Lek (plural lekë); the euro (€) is widely accepted.

Emergency Ambulance ☏127; Fire ☏128; Police ☏129

Language Albanian

Time Central European Time (GMT/UTC plus one hour)

Visas Nearly all visitors can travel visa-free to Albania for a period of up to 90 days

ALBANIA

Sleeping Price Ranges

The following price categories are based on the cost of a double room in high season.

€ less than €40

€€ €40–80

€€€ more than €80

Eating Price Ranges

The following price categories are based on the cost of a main course.

€ less than 500 lekë

€€ 500–1200 lekë

€€€ more than 1200 lekë

Albania Highlights

1 Accursed Mountains (p56) Doing the wonderful day trek between the isolated mountain villages of Valbona and Theth and experiencing some of Albania's best scenery.

2 Berat (p49) Exploring this Unesco World Heritage–listed museum town, known as the 'city of a thousand windows'.

3 Albanian Riviera (p52) Catching some sun at just one of the many gorgeous beaches on the Albanian Riviera.

4 Tirana (p45) Feasting your eyes on the wild colour schemes and experiencing Blloku cafe culture in the plucky Albanian capital.

5 Gjirokastra (p51) Taking a trip to this traditional Albanian mountain town, with its spectacular Ottoman-era mansions and impressive hilltop fortress.

6 Butrint (p54) Searching for the ghosts of Ancient Greece and Rome among the forest-dappled ruins of one of Europe's finest archaeological sites.

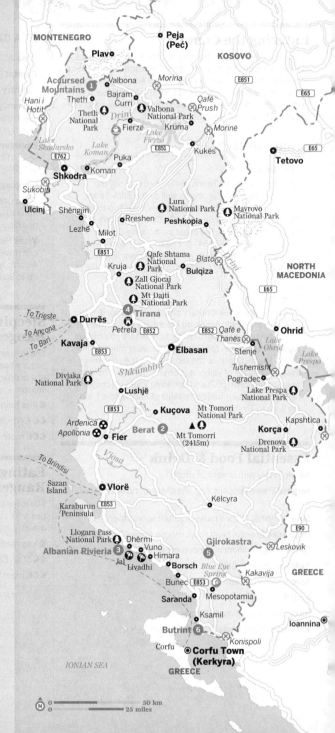

TIRANA

📍 04 / POP 557,000

Lively, colourful Tirana is where this tiny nation's hopes and dreams coalesce into a vibrant whirl of traffic, brash consumerism and unfettered fun. Having undergone a transformation of extraordinary proportions since awaking from its communist slumber in the early 1990s, Tirana's centre is now unrecognisable from those grey days, with buildings painted in primary colours, and public squares and pedestrianised streets that are a pleasure to wander.

Trendy Blloku buzzes with the well-heeled hanging out in bars and cafes, while the city's grand boulevards are lined with fascinating relics of its Ottoman, Italian and communist past – from delicate minarets to loud socialist murals. Add to this some excellent museums and you have a compelling list of reasons to visit.

◎ Sights

The centre of Tirana is Sheshi Skënderbej (Skanderbeg Sq), a large traffic island with an equestrian statue of the eponymous Albanian national hero at its centre. Most of the city's sights are within walking distance of the square.

★ Bunk'Art   MUSEUM

(📞 067 207 2905; www.bunkart.al; Rr Fadil Deliu; 500 lekë; ⊙ 9am-4pm Wed-Sun) This fantastic conversion – from a massive Cold War bunker on the outskirts of Tirana into a history and contemporary art museum – is Albania's most exciting new sight and easily a Tirana highlight. With almost 3000 sq metres of space underground spread over several floors, the bunker was built for Albania's political elite in the 1970s and remained a secret for much of its existence. Now it hosts exhibits that combine the modern history of Albania with pieces of contemporary art.

★ National History Museum   MUSEUM

(Muzeu Historik Kombëtar; www.mhk.gov.al; Sheshi Skënderbej; 200 lekë; ⊙ 9am-7pm) The largest museum in Albania holds many of the country's archaeological treasures and a replica of Skanderbeg's massive sword (how he held it, rode his horse and fought at the same time is a mystery). The lighting might be poor but fortunately the excellent collection is almost entirely signed in English and takes you chronologically from ancient Illyria to the postcommunist era. The collection

of statues, mosaics and columns from Greek and Roman times is breathtaking.

National Gallery of Arts   GALLERY

(Galeria Kombëtare e Arteve; 📞 04 223 3975; www.galeriakombetare.gov.al/en/home/index.shtml; Blvd Dëshmorët e Kombit; adult/student 200/60 lekë; ⊙ 9am-7pm) Tracing the relatively brief history of Albanian painting from the early 19th century to the present day, this beautiful space also has temporary exhibitions. The interesting collection includes 19th-century paintings depicting scenes from daily Albanian life and others with a far more political dimension including some truly fabulous examples of Albanian socialist realism.

The ground-floor part of the gallery is given over to temporary exhibitions of a far more modern and challenging kind.

Bunk'Art 2   MUSEUM

(📞 067 207 2905; www.bunkart.al; Rr Sermedin Toptani; 500 lekë; ⊙ 9am-9pm) The little cousin to the main Bunk'Art (p45), this museum, which is within a communist-era bunker and underground tunnel system below the Ministry of Internal Affairs, focuses on the role of the police and security services in Albania through the turbulent 20th century. While this might not sound especially interesting, the whole thing has been very well put together and makes for a fascinating journey behind police lines.

House of Leaves   MUSEUM

(📞 04 222 2612; www.muzeugjethi.gov.al; Rr Ibrahim Rugova; 700 lekë; ⊙ 9am-7pm May–mid-Oct, 10am-5pm Tue-Sat, 9am-2pm Sun mid-Oct–Apr) This grand old 1930s building started life as Albania's first maternity hospital, but within a few years the focus turned from creating new life to ending lives as the hospital was converted to an interrogation and surveillance centre (read: torture house). It remained as such until the fall of the communist regime. Today, the House of Leaves is a museum dedicated to surveillance and interrogation in Albania.

Mt Dajti National Park   NATIONAL PARK

Just 25km east of Tirana is Mt Dajti National Park. It is the most accessible mountain in the country, and many locals go there to escape the city rush and have a spit-roast lamb lunch. A sky-high, Austrian-made cable car, **Dajti Express** (📞 067 208 4471; www.dajtiekspres.com; Rr Dibrës; one-way/return 500/800 lekë; ⊙ 9am-10pm Jul-Aug, to 9pm May-Jun & Sep-Oct, to 7pm Nov-Apr), takes 15 minutes to make the scenic trip (almost) to the top (1611m).

National Archaeological Museum   MUSEUM
(Muzeu Arkeologjik Nacional; Sheshi Nënë Tereza;
300 lekë; ⊙10am-2.30pm Mon-Fri) The collection here is comprehensive and impressive
in parts, but there's only minimal labelling
in Albanian and none at all in English (nor
are tours in English offered), so you may
find yourself a little at a loss unless this is
your field. A total renovation is on the cards,
but as one staff member pointed out to us,
they've been waiting for that since 1985 – so
don't hold your breath.

⟁ Tours

Tirana Free Tour   TOURS
(⊡069 631 5858; www.tiranafreetour.com) This
enterprising tour agency has made its name
by offering a free daily tour of Tirana that
leaves at 10am year-round. In July, August
and September a second tour is offered at
3pm. Tours meet outside the Opera House
on Sheshi Skënderbej (look on the website
for a photo indicating the exact meeting
spot).

⨭ Sleeping

★Trip'n'Hostel   HOSTEL €
(⊡068 304 8905; www.tripnhostel.com; Rr Musa
Maci 1; dm/d from €10/30; ⊚) Tirana's coolest hostel is on a small side street, housed
in a design-conscious self-contained house
with a leafy garden out the back, a bar lined
with old records, a kitchen and a cellar-like
chill-out lounge downstairs. Dorms have
handmade fixtures, curtains between beds
for privacy and private lockable drawers,
while there's also a roof terrace strewn with
hammocks.

Tirana Backpacker Hostel   HOSTEL €
(⊡068 313 3451, 068 468 2353; www.tiranahostel.
com; Rr Bogdani 3; dm from €8, d €27; ❄@⊚) Albania's first-ever hostel continues to go from
strength to strength. Housed in a charmingly decorated house, which has something of
the air of the hazy hippy backpacker days
of the 1970s to it, this super-friendly place
has a funky design and an excellent location.
There's always a big crew of globally wandering backpackers staying.

★B&B Tirana Smile   HOTEL €€
(⊡068 406 1507, 068 406 1561; www.bbtirana
smile.com; Rr Bogdani; d incl breakfast €42; ❄⊚)
The owners could not have picked a better
name for this inspirational hotel. The eight
rooms are bright, modern, colourful and
all have light summery touches. Each has

a big workspace and good beds (though
bathrooms are small). The best part is the
communal lounge with sofas, books and a
large table where a breakfast of homemade
products is served.

Green House   BOUTIQUE HOTEL €€
(⊡069 205 7599; www.greenhouse.al; Rr Jul Varibo-
ba 6; d incl breakfast €60; P❄⊚) You've got a
fantastic location at this 10-room hotel with
downlit, stylish rooms that might be some
of the city's coolest. Some have balconies, all
have low-slung beds, shag-pile carpets, minibars and sleek furnishings. Downstairs is a
large terrace restaurant where guests take
breakfast each morning, and the whole place
looks up at one of Tirana's more quirkily decorated buildings.

✕ Eating

Most of Tirana's best eating is in and around
Blloku, a square of some 10 blocks of shops,
restaurants, cafes and hotels situated west
of Blvd Dëshmorët e Kombit, but there are
other options elsewhere. Particularly good
kebabs can be found on Rr e Kavajës. The
area known as the new market (Pazari i ri),
where Rr Luigj Gurakuqi runs into Sheshi
Avni Rustemi, has a growing number of
good traditional restaurants.

★Met Kodra   ALBANIAN €
(Sheshi Avni Rustemi; qofte 100 lekë; ⊙6am-
9.30pm Sun-Thu, to midnight Fri & Sat) One of
the great classics of Tirana dining. This tiny
place which consists of nothing but a small
smoky grill, does one thing and one thing
only – qoftas (rissoles) – and the same lady
and her family have been making them to
exactly the same recipe since 1957.

King House   ALBANIAN €
(⊡067 223 3335; www.king-house.net; Rr Ibrahim
Rugova 12; mains 300-800 lekë; ⊙8am-11pm)
Enough Albanian traditional artefacts to
shame an ethnographic museum bedeck the
walls of this charming Blloku place. There's
an excellent selection of traditional Albanian
cooking – try the delicious Korça meatballs –
as well as Italian pasta and pizza, and prices
are low. There's a good terrace dining area if
the interior is a little too much for you.

Era   ALBANIAN, ITALIAN €€
(⊡04 224 3845; www.era.al; Rr Ismail Qemali;
mains 400-900 lekë; ⊙11am-midnight; ⊘) This
local institution serves traditional Albanian
and Italian fare in the heart of Blloku. The
inventive menu includes oven-baked veal

Tirana

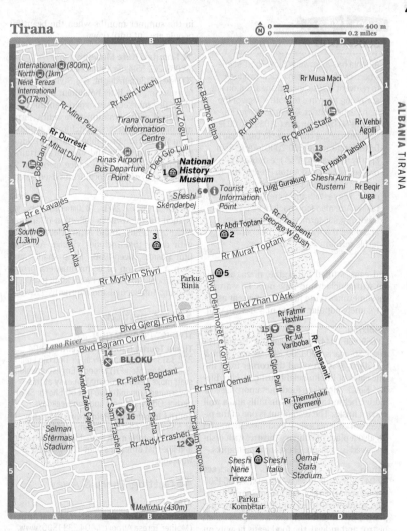

ALBANIA TIRANA

SLOW FOOD

Albania has a growing 'Slow Food' scene where chefs use organic local produce to reinvent classic local dishes. Set on a sprawling farm in a remote village of the lush Lezhë District, 65km north of Tirana, the **Mrizi i Zanave** (☑069 210 8032; www.mrizizanave.com/mrizi; Rr Lezhë-Vau i Dejës, Fishtë; mains 600-2000 lekë; ☺from 8pm by reservation; ☎♋♒) restaurant is owned by Altin and Anton Prenga, the pioneers of Albania's slow-food movement. The restaurant is credited with taking Albanian food back to basics: fresh, organic farm-to-table produce and meat that celebrates the country's fertile terrain.

and eggs, stuffed aubergine, pizza, and pilau with chicken and pine nuts. Be warned: it's sometimes quite hard to get a seat as it's fearsomely popular, so you may have to wait.

Mullixhiu　　　　　　　　ALBANIAN €€
(☑069 666 0444; www.mullixhiu.al; Lazgush Poradeci St; mains 800-1200 lekë; ☺noon-4pm & 6-10.30pm; ♒♋) Around the corner from the chic cafes of Blloku neighbourhood, chef Bledar Kola's Albanian food metamorphosis is hidden behind a row of grain mills and a wall of corn husks. The restaurant is one of the pioneers of Albania's slow-food movement and it's also a place of culinary theatre, with dishes served in treasure chests or atop teapots.

Otium　　　　　　　　　　FRENCH €€€
(☑04 222 3570; Rr Brigada e VIII; mains 1000-1500 lekë; ☺noon-11pm Mon-Sat, to 6pm Sun) With its lace window curtains and tubs of flowering plants, this might look like a simple French bistrot and indeed, the food leans heavily on Gallic cuisine. But a meal here reveals a refined operation as attentive waiters talk you through the daily menu of artfully executed seasonal dishes, typically including seafood options and some fabulous starters.

🍷 Drinking & Nightlife

Tirana runs on caffeine during the day then switches over to alcohol after nightfall. Popular places to get both are concentrated in the Blloku neighbourhood, and indeed several streets are almost nothing but bars and cafes, and become jam-packed at night. Nightlife in Tirana goes late, particularly in the summer months when the beautiful people are out until dawn.

★**Komiteti Kafe Muzeum**　　　　BAR
(☑069 262 5514; Rr Fatmir Haxhiu; raki around 200 lekë; ☺8am-midnight; ♒) Styled as a cafe-museum, this little bohemian place looks like a flea market. Every spare centimetre is crammed with communist-era relics, farming implements (those pitchforks hanging from the bar are probably a warning), Japanese fans, old clocks and so on. It's certainly a memorable spot for a coffee or one of 25 varieties of *raki*, the local fruit-based spirit.

Radio　　　　　　　　　　　BAR
(Rr Ismail Qemali 29/1; ☺10am-midnight; ♒) Named for the owner's collection of antique Albanian radios, Radio is an eclectic dream with decor that includes vintage Albanian film posters, deep-1950s lamp shades and even a collection of communist-era propaganda books to read over a cocktail. It attracts a young, intellectual and alternative crowd.

ℹ Information

TOURIST INFORMATION

Tirana Tourist Information Centre (☑04 222 3313; www.tirana.gov.al; Rr Ded Gjo Luli; ☺8am-4pm Mon-Fri) Friendly English-speaking staff make getting information easy at this government-run initiative just off Sheshi Skënderbej. Oddly, it's only open on weekdays.

Tourist Information Point (www.tirana.gov.al; Sheshi Skënderbej; ☺8am-4pm Mon-Fri) A sub-office of the main tourist information office and like that office, it's unhelpfully closed at weekends.

ℹ Getting There & Away

AIR

The modern **Nënë Tereza International Airport** (Mother Teresa Airport; ☑04 238 1800; www.tirana-airport.com; Rinas) is at Rinas, 17km northwest of Tirana. The Rinas Express airport bus operates an on-the-hour (6am to 6pm) service, with **departures** from the corner of Rr Mine Peza and Rr e Durrësit (a few blocks from the National History Museum) for 250 lekë one way. The going taxi rate is 2000 to 2500 lekë. The airport is about 20 minutes' drive away, but plan for possible traffic jams and give yourself plenty of time to get there if you're catching a flight.

BUS

There is no one official bus station in Tirana. Instead, there are numerous bus stations around the city from which buses to specific destinations leave.

International services depart from the aptly named **International Bus Station** (off Rr Durresit) just off Rr Durresit. There are multiple services to Skopje (€13 to €20, eight hours) and Ohrid (€17.50, four hours) in North Macedonia, to Pristina (via Prizren) in Kosovo (€10, four hours), and services to Budva, Kotor and Podgorica in Montenegro (€20 to €25, four hours). At present there is no direct bus to Ulcinj from Tirana, and your best bet is to change buses in Shkodra. Other international destinations include Istanbul, Dubrovnik, Sofia, Thessaloniki and Athens. It's best to double-check all international services locally, as routes and timings change with great frequency.

Furgons (shared minibuses) to Bajram Curri (1000 lekë, 5½ hours, hourly 5am to 2pm), the jumping-off point for Valbona or the far side of Lake Koman, leave from **North Station** on Rr Dritan Hoxha, a short distance from the Zogu i Zi roundabout. Note that this service passes through Kosovo. Services to Shkodra (300 lekë, two hours, hourly until 5pm) also leave from here.

Departures to the south leave from – yes, you guessed it – **South Station** (Rr Muhedin Llagani) on Rr Muhedin Llagani. These include services to Berat (400 lekë, 2½ to three hours, every 30 minutes until 6pm), Himara (1000 lekë, five hours, 1pm and 6pm), Saranda (1300 lekë, seven hours, roughly hourly 5am to midday) and Gjirokastra (1000 lekë, five to six hours, regular departures until midday, also at 2.30pm and 6.30pm). Services to Himara and Saranda will drop you off at any of the coastal villages along the way.

❶ Getting Around

There's now a good network of city buses running around Tirana costing 40 lekë per journey (payable to the conductor), although most of the sights can be covered easily on foot.

TAXI

Taxi stands dot the city, and taxis charge from 300 to 400 lekë for a ride within Tirana, and from 500 to 600 lekë at night and to destinations outside the city centre. Reach an agreement on the fare with the driver before setting off; while drivers are supposed to use meters, they almost never do. **Speed Taxi** (☑ 04 222 2555; www.speedtaxi.al), with 24-hour service, is reliable.

CENTRAL ALBANIA

Berat

☑ 032 / POP 35,000

Berat weaves its own very special magic, and is easily a highlight of visiting Albania. Its most striking feature is the collection of white Ottoman houses climbing up the hill to its castle, earning it the title of 'town of a thousand windows' and helping it join Gjirokastra on the list of Unesco World Heritage sites in 2008. Its rugged mountain setting is particularly evocative when the clouds swirl around the tops of the minarets, or break up to show the icy peak of Mt Tomorri. Despite now being a big centre for tourism in Albania, Berat has managed to retain its easy-going charm and friendly atmosphere.

◉ Sights

★ Kalaja   FORTRESS

(100 lekë; ⊙ 24hr, ticket booth 9am-6pm) Hidden behind the crumbling walls of the fortress that crowns the hill above Berat is the whitewashed, village-like neighbourhood of Kala; if you walk around the quiet cobbled streets of this ancient neighbourhood for long enough you'll invariably stumble into someone's courtyard thinking it's a church or ruin (no one seems to mind, though).

★ Onufri Museum   GALLERY

(Kalaja; 200 lekë; ⊙ 9am-6pm May–mid-Oct, to 4pm Tue-Sat, to 2pm Sun mid-Oct–Apr) The Onufri Museum is situated in the Kala quarter's biggest church, the **Church of the Dormition of St Mary** (Kisha Fjetja e Shën Mërisë). The church itself dates from 1797 and was built on the foundations of an earlier 10th-century chapel. Today Onufri's spectacular 16th-century religious paintings are displayed along with the church's beautifully gilded 19th-century iconostasis. Don't miss the chapel behind the iconostasis, or

---

WORTH A TRIP

APOLLONIA

The evocative ruins of the ancient Illyirian city of **Apollonia** (Pojan; 400 lekë; ⊙ 8am-6pm Apr-Oct, to 5pm Nov-Mar) sit on a windswept hilltop some 12km west of the city of Fier. While a large part of the ruins remains buried under the ground, what has been excavated within the 4km of city walls is pure poetry. The highlights include the theatre and the elegant pillars of the restored facade of the city's 2nd-century-AD administrative centre.

Few foreigners visit, but Apollonia is popular with locals for afternoon picnics.

Berat

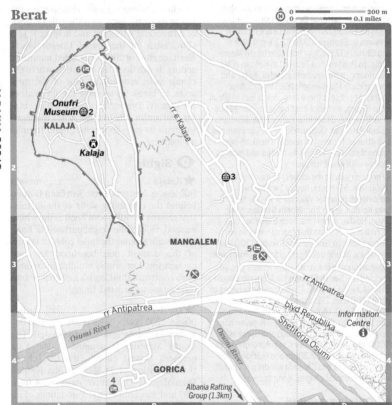

N 0 ——————— 200 m
   0 ——————— 0.1 miles

Berat

⊙ Top Sights
1 Kalaja	A2
2 Onufri Museum	A1

⊙ Sights
3 Ethnographic Museum	C2

🛏 Sleeping
4 Berat Backpackers	B4
5 Hotel Mangalemi	C3
6 Hotel Restaurant Klea	A1

🍴 Eating
7 Lili Homemade Food	B3
8 Mangalemi Restaurant	C3
9 Onufri	A1

its painted cupola, whose frescoes are now faded almost to invisibility.

Ethnographic Museum　　　MUSEUM
(🖉 032 232 224; www.muzeumet-berat.al; 200 lekë; ⊙ 9am-7.30pm May-Sep, to 4pm Mon-Sat & to 2pm Sun Oct-Apr) Just off the steep hillside that leads up to Berat's castle is this excellent museum, which is housed in a beautiful 18th-century Ottoman house that's as much of an attraction as the exhibits within. The ground floor has displays of traditional clothes and the tools used by silversmiths and weavers, while the upper storey has kitchens, bedrooms and guest rooms decked out in traditional style.

🏃 Activities

Albania Rafting Group　　　RAFTING
(🖉 067 200 6623; www.albrafting.com; Hotel Castle Park, Rr Berat–Përmet) 🍃 This pioneering group runs rafting tours for all levels to some stunning gorges around Berat and

Përmet. Everyone from children to pensioners is welcome. Rafting starts at €50 per person and hiking tours start from €20 per person per day.

Sleeping

★ Berat Backpackers
HOSTEL €

(☑ 069 785 4219; www.beratbackpackers.com; 295 Gorica; tents/dm/r without bathroom €7/10/25; ☉ Apr–Oct; @ 🛜) This transformed traditional house in the Gorica quarter houses one of Albania's friendliest hostels. The vine-clad establishment contains a basement bar and restaurant, an alfresco drinking area and a relaxed atmosphere that money can't buy. There are two airy dorms with original ceilings, and four gorgeous, excellent-value double rooms with antique furnishings. Shaded camping area and cheap laundry also available.

Hotel Restaurant Klea
GUESTHOUSE €

(☑ 032 234 970; Rr Shën Triadha, Kala; tw/d/tr incl breakfast €31/33/35) From the castle gates, go straight ahead and you'll find this gorgeous hilltop hideaway, run by a friendly English-speaking family. There are just five compact wood-panelled rooms, each with its own clean and modern bathroom. The downstairs restaurant adjoins a wonderful garden and has a daily changing specials menu featuring tasty Albanian fare (200 lekë to 450 lekë).

★ Hotel Mangalemi
HISTORIC HOTEL €

(☑ 068 232 3238; www.mangalemihotel.com; Rr Mihail Komneno; s/d/tr from €25/35/50; P ✳ @ 🛜) A true highlight of Berat is this gorgeous place inside two sprawling Ottoman houses where all the rooms are beautifully furnished in traditional Berati style and balconies (superior rooms only) give memorable views. Its terrace **restaurant** (mains 300-800 lekë; ☉ noon-11pm; 🛜) is the best place to eat in town with great Albanian food with bonus views of Mt Tomorri.

✕ Eating

★ Onufri
ALBANIAN €

(Rr Shën Triadha, Kalaja; mains 200-300 lekë, mixed plates from 1500 lekë; ☉ noon-4pm) In the pretty village-like cobbled streets of the kalaja (castle; p49), Onufri is the closest you'll get to a homestyle Albanian feast without actually gatecrashing a family lunch. Expect to be brought a heaving plate of stuffed peppers, *byrek* (stuffed savoury pastries), *qofta* (rissoles), stuffed aubergines and grilled chicken. Finish up with a slice of homemade honey cake and you've got a meal to remember.

Lili Homemade Food
ALBANIAN €€

(☑ 069 234 9362; Mangalem; mains 500-700 lekë; ☉ noon-3pm & 6.30-10pm) This charming family home deep in the Mangalem Quarter below the castle is the setting for one of Berat's best restaurants. Lili speaks English and will invite you to take a table in his backyard where you can order a meal of traditional Berati cooking. We heartily recommend the *gjize ferges*, a delicious mash of tomato, garlic and cheese.

❶ Information

TOURIST INFORMATION

Information Centre (Rr Antipatrea; ☉ 9am-noon & 2-6pm Mon-Fri) This tourist information centre can be found on Berat's main square, and has lots of local information and English-speaking staff.

❶ Getting There & Away

Berat now has a bus terminal, around 3km from the town centre on the main road to Tirana. Bus services run to Tirana (400 lekë, three hours, half-hourly until 3pm). There are also buses to Vlora (300 lekë, two hours, hourly until 2pm), Durrës (300 lekë, two hours, six per day) and Saranda (1600 lekë, six hours, two daily at 8am and 2pm), one of which goes via Gjirokastra (1000 lekë, four hours, 8am). To get to the bus station from the centre, ask locals to put you on a bus to 'Terminali Autobusave'.

Gjirokastra

☑ 084 / POP 43,000

Defined by its castle, roads paved with chunky limestone and shale, imposing slate-roofed houses and views out to the Drina Valley, Gjirokastra is a magical hillside town described beautifully by Albania's most famous author, Ismail Kadare (b 1936), in *Chronicle in Stone*. There has been a settlement here for 2500 years, though these days it's the 600 'monumental' Ottoman-era houses in town that attract visitors.

◎ Sights

★ Gjirokastra Castle
CASTLE

(200 lekë; ☉ 9am-6pm mid-Apr–mid-Oct, 8am-4pm mid-Oct–mid-Apr) Gjirokastra's eerie hilltop castle is one of the biggest in the Balkans. There's been a fortress here since the 12th century, although much of what can be seen today dates to the early 19th century.

The castle remains somewhat infamous due to its use as a prison under the communists. Inside there's a collection of armoury, two good museums, plenty of crumbling ruins to scramble around and superb views over the valley.

Cold War Tunnel
TUNNEL

(Sheshi Çerçiz Topulli; 200 lekë; ⊙8am-4pm Mon-Fri, 10am-2pm Sat, 9am-3pm Sun) Gjirokastra's most interesting sight in no way relates to its traditional architecture, but instead to its far more modern kind: this is a giant bunker built deep under the castle for use by the local authorities during the full-scale invasion that communist leader Enver Hoxha was so paranoid about. Built in secret during the 1960s, it has 80 rooms and its existence remained unknown to locals until the 1990s. Personal guided tours run from the tourist information booth on the main square all day.

🛏 Sleeping & Eating

★ Stone City Hostel
HOSTEL €

(☑069 348 4271; www.stonecityhostel.com; Rr Alqi Kond; dm/d without bathroom incl breakfast €11/27; ⊙Apr-Oct; ❄🖥🛜) This hostel is a fantastic conversion of an Old Town house, created and run by Dutchman Walter. The attention to detail and respect for traditional craftsmanship is extremely heartening, with beautiful carved wooden panels in all the rooms. Choose between the dorm rooms with custom-made bunks or a double room, all of which share spotless communal facilities.

Gjirokastra Hotel
HISTORIC HOTEL €

(☑068 409 9669, 084 265 982; hhotelgjirokastra@ yahoo.com; Rr Sheazi Çomo; tw/d incl breakfast €35/40; ❄🛜) Combining modern facilities with traditional touches, this lovely family-run hotel inside a 300-year-old house has rooms that boast huge balconies and gorgeously carved wooden ceilings. If you can afford the extra then the suite (which sleeps four), with its long Ottoman-style sofa, original wooden doors and ceiling, and magnificent stone walls, is like sleeping inside a museum.

Odaja Restaurant
ALBANIAN €

(☑069 580 8687; Rr Gjin Bue Shpata; mains 250-600 lekë; ⊙10am-11pm) Cooking up a storm since 1937, Odaja is a small and cute 1st-floor restaurant serving good, honest home-cooked Albanian mountain dishes. Tuck into the oh-so-succulent meatballs with cheese, devour some stuffed peppers and relish the superb moussaka and you'll quickly come to understand just how good Albanian food can be.

ℹ Information

TOURIST INFORMATION

Information Centre (☑084 269 044; www. gjirokastra.org; Sheshi Çerçiz Topulli; ⊙9am-5pm Mar-Nov, to 3pm Dec-Feb) In a kiosk on the main square at the entrance to the Old Town, the staff here are suitably clued up on things to do and places to stay in and around the town. Tickets for the Cold War Tunnel (p52) are also on sale here. In low season it might be briefly closed when staff are conducting a tour.

ℹ Getting There & Away

Buses stop at the ad hoc bus station just after the Eida petrol station on the new town's main road. Services include Tirana (1000 lekë, seven hours, every one to two hours until 5pm), Saranda (300 lekë, one hour, hourly) and Berat (1000 lekë, four hours, 9.15am). A taxi between the Old Town and the bus station is 300 lekë.

THE ALBANIAN RIVIERA & THE EAST

The Albanian Riviera was a revelation a decade or so ago, when backpackers discovered the last virgin stretch of the Mediterranean coast in Europe, flocking here in droves, setting up ad hoc campsites and exploring scores of little-known beaches. Since then, things have become significantly less pristine, with overdevelopment blighting many of the once-charming coastal villages. But worry not: while some beaches may be well and truly swarming in summer, with a little persistence you can still find spots to kick back and enjoy the empty beaches the region was once so famous for.

ℹ Getting There & Away

The best way to explore this part of Albania is with your own wheels. Buses do connect the towns along the coast, but they're irregular and sometimes full – give yourself plenty of time and be patient when things don't go to plan.

From Tirana, buses to Saranda (1300 lekë, five hours) leave at 6am, 9am and midday and take the coastal road via the riviera villages. From Saranda, a daily bus travels up the riviera to Vlora (1300 lekë, three hours, 7am) and can drop you anywhere along the way, while there are also Vlora buses (900 lekë; also three hours) at 7.30am and 1pm that go via the coast. An 11.30am bus from Saranda heads to Himara (500 lekë, two hours) via the coast.

Saranda

📞 0852 / POP 38,000

Saranda is the unofficial capital of the Albanian Riviera, and come the summer months it seems like half of Tirana relocates here to enjoy the busy beach and busier nightlife along its crowd-filled seaside promenade. What was once a sleepy fishing village is now a thriving city, and while Saranda has lost much of its quaintness in the past two decades, it has retained much of its charisma. The town's beaches are nothing special, but Saranda is a great base for exploring the beaches of the riviera if you have your own transport.

🛏 Sleeping & Eating

SR Backpackers   HOSTEL €

(📞 069 434 5426; www.backpackerssr.hostel. com; Rr Mitat Hoxha 10; dm from €11; @ 🛜) Your host at Saranda's most central hostel is the gregarious, English-speaking Tomi and he does much to give this place its party atmosphere. The 14 beds here are spread over three dorms, each with its own balcony, but sharing one bathroom and a communal kitchen. In Tomi's own words, 'It's not really suitable for couples after privacy'. You've been warned!

Hairy Lemon   HOSTEL €

(📞 069 889 9196; cnr Mitat Hoxha & E Arberit, 8th fl; dm incl breakfast from €9; 🛜) With a prime 8th-floor location, a clean beach at its base and a friendly, helpful atmosphere, this Irish-run backpacker hostel is a good place to chill. There's an open-plan kitchen and lounge, and two cramped and often quite hot dorm rooms, although the fans and sea breezes help temper things a bit. The unlimited breakfast pancakes are always a hit.

Follow the port road for around 10 minutes and continue when it becomes dirt; it's the orange-and-yellow apartment block on your right.

★ Mare Nostrum   INTERNATIONAL €€

(📞 0852 24 342; Rr Jonianët; mains 700-1200 lekë; ⊙ 8am-2pm & 6.30pm-midnight Apr-Oct) This sleek restaurant immediately feels different to the others along the seafront: here there's elegant decor that wouldn't look out of place in a major European capital, the buzz of a smart, in-the-know crowd and an imagina-

tive menu that combines the seafood and fish you'll find everywhere else with dishes such as Indonesian chicken curry and burgers.

❶ Information

ZIT Information Centre (📞 0852 24 124; Rr Skënderbeu; ⊙ 8am-midnight May-Sep, to 4pm Mar-Apr & Oct-Nov, 9am-5pm Dec-Feb) Saranda's tiny but excellent ZIT information centre provides information about transport and local sights and is staffed by friendly and helpful English-speaking staff. It's in a UFO-shaped building right on the waterfront.

❶ Getting There & Away

BUS

The ZIT Information Centre has up-to-date bus timetables. Most buses leave just uphill from the ruins on Rr Vangjel Pando, right in the centre of town. Buses to Tirana (1300 lekë, eight hours) go inland via Gjirokastra (300 lekë, two hours) and leave regularly between 5am and 10.30am. There are later buses at 2pm and 10pm. The 7am Tirana bus takes the coastal route (1300 lekë, eight hours). There is also one bus a day to Himara at 11.30am (500 lekë, two hours), which can stop at any point along the way to let you off at riviera villages.

Ksamil

📞 0852 / POP 3000

Delightful Ksamil, 17km south of Saranda, sits on a narrow arm of land between a sparkling lagoon famed for its mussels and a cobalt-coloured sea. The entire area surrounding the small town is a protected zone and the dusty tracks and pathways leading over olive-studded hills and along ancient water canals are a joy to explore. The coastline around Ksamil is also unusually attractive. Blessed with three small, dreamy islands (sadly, one of which is being quarried for construction material) within swimming distance of shore and dozens of pretty cove beaches, Ksamil is the kind of place where you can happily while away many sun-drenched days. However, do try and avoid high season when the place is overrun with other Nirvana seekers. Late September is idyllic.

Ksamil is an ideal base for the stunning ruins of nearby Butrint (p54).

🛏 Sleeping & Eating

Hotel Joni   HOTEL €€

(📞 069 543 1378, 069 209 1554; Sheshi Miqesia; d incl breakfast from €70; ❄ 🛜) This popular hotel in the middle of Ksamil is not on the

BUTRINT

Early in the morning, before the tourist crowds arrive and when the rocks are still tinged in the yellow dawn light, you might just imagine that the ancient walls of **Butrint** (www. butrint.al; Butrint National Park; adult 700 lekë, children under 8yrs free, family ticket per person 300 lekë; ⊗8am-sunset, museum 8am-4pm) are whispering secrets to you of long-past lives. Easily the most romantic and beautiful – not to mention the largest – of Albania's ancient sites, Butrint, 18km south of Saranda, is worth travelling a long way to see.

Although the site was inhabited long before, Greeks from Corfu settled on the hill in Butrint (Buthrotum) in the 6th century BC. Within a century Butrint had become a fortified trading city with an acropolis. The lower town began to develop in the 3rd century BC, and many large stone buildings had already been built by the time the Romans took over in 167 BC. Butrint's prosperity continued throughout the Roman period, and the Byzantines made it an ecclesiastical centre. The city then went into a long decline and was abandoned until 1927, when Italian archaeologists arrived.

Buses from Saranda (100 lekë, 20 minutes, hourly from 8.30am to 5.30pm) leave from outside the ZIT Information Centre (p53), returning from Butrint hourly on the hour.

beach, but its smart brick-and-timber-lined rooms are some of the best value around. It's within easy walking distance of several good places to swim, not to mention dozens of good eating and drinking spots.

Mussel House
SEAFOOD €€
(Km 10, Rr Sarande-Butrint; mains 500-1000 lekë; ⊗noon-midnight) With a winning view out over the vast Butrint lagoon and fronting the famed mussel beds, this laid-back, beach-shack-like restaurant a kilometre or so back along the road to Saranda dishes up mussels in any style you might care to think of. It also serves excellent grilled fish and other seafood.

❶ Getting There & Away

Any bus running between Saranda and Butrint will drop you off in Ksamil. The cost is 100 lekë.

Himara

☑0393 / POP 5700
The busy resort of Himara is the biggest town on the riviera north of Saranda. Despite this, the beaches here – book-ended by forested cliffs – are fairly attractive and the whole place has a more well-kept feel than some quieter beaches elsewhere on the coast. For those with their own wheels, there are heaps of other attractive beaches within a short drive.

▐ Sleeping & Eating

The seafront promenade along the main town beach is lined with restaurants, all of which sell a fairly similar, but decent, range of seafood and Italian dishes.

Himara Downtown Hostel
HOSTEL €
(☑067 201 7574; https://himaradowntownhostel. business.site; dm/d €10/30) This small hostel has helpful staff and just three dorms each with six beds, plus there's one double room for couples who want some privacy. The hostel walls are covered in squiggly bright wall art. When full it can feel a bit claustrophobic. It's just one block back from the town's main beach and is in the thick of the action.

Kamping Himare
CAMPGROUND €
(☑068 529 8940; www.himaracamping.com; Potami Beach; camping per person/car/electricity 700/420/240 lekë; ⊗May-Oct; ☜) Set up a tent under the olive trees at this chilled-out camping ground across the main road from the beach. Facilities are basic but nice touches include midnight movies in an open-air cinema and a lamp-lit bar-restaurant that serves as a natural social centre for guests. It's on the second (southern) beach in Himara if you're coming from Tirana.

❶ Getting There & Away

There are four buses a day (most in the morning) to Tirana (1000 lekë, five to six hours) and five a day to Saranda with the last one leaving at 1pm (500 lekë, two hours).

Shkodra

☑022 / POP 135,000
Shkodra, the traditional centre of the Gheg cultural region, is one of the oldest cities in Europe and arguably the most attractive urban centre in Albania. The ancient Rozafa Fortress has stunning views over Lake

Shkodra, while the pastel-painted buildings in the Old Town have a distinct Italian ambience. Many travellers rush through here while travelling between Tirana and Montenegro, or en route to the Lake Koman Ferry and the villages of Theth and Valbona, but it's worth spending a night or two to soak up this pleasant and welcoming place and to check out the interesting museums before moving on to the mountains, the coast or the capital.

◉ Sights

★ Rozafa Fortress   CASTLE
(200 lekë; ⊙ 9am-8pm Apr-Oct, to 4pm Nov-Mar) With spectacular views over the city and Lake Shkodra, the Rozafa Fortress is the most impressive sight in town. Founded by the Illyrians in antiquity and rebuilt much later by the Venetians and then the Turks, the fortress takes its name from a woman who was allegedly walled into the ramparts as an offering to the gods so that the construction would stand.

★ Marubi National
Photography Museum   GALLERY
(Muzeu Kombëtari i Fotografise Marubi; ☑ 022 400 500; Rr Kolë Idromeno 32; adult/student 700/200 lekë; ⊙ 9am-7pm Apr-Oct, to 5pm Nov-Mar) The Marubi Museum is a one-of-a-kind Albanian photographic museum. The core of the collection is the impressive work of the Marubi 'dynasty', Albania's first and foremost family of photographers. The collection includes the first-ever photograph taken in Albania, by Pjetër Marubi in 1858, as well as fascinating portraits, street scenes and early photojournalism, all giving a fascinating glimpse into old Albania and the rise and fall of communism.

Site of Witness &
Memory Museum   MUSEUM
(Vendi i Dëshmisë dhe Kujtesës; Blvd Skënderbeu; 150 lekë; ⊙ 9am-2.30pm Mon-Fri, 9.30am-12.30pm Sat) During the communist period this building, which started life as a Franciscan seminary, was officially used as the Shkodra headquarters of the Ministry of Internal Affairs. What that actually means is that it was an interrogation centre and prison for political detainees. Over the years, thousands of people spent time here – some never to re-emerge. The museum does a reasonable job of illustrating the horrors that took place here although much of the signage is in Albanian.

🛏 Sleeping

Wanderers Hostel   HOSTEL €
(☑ 069 212 1062; www.thewanderershostel.com; Rr Gjuhadol; dm/d incl breakfast €8/25; ❄ 🛜) Very popular with a young Anglophone crowd, this central and convivial hostel is a great place to hang out by the garden bar and make fast travel buddies. Dorms are frills-free and the bathrooms basic, but everyone seems to be having too much of a good time to care. Bikes are available for hire.

Mi Casa Es Tu Casa   HOSTEL €
(☑ 069 381 2054; www.micasaestucasa.it; Blvd Skenderbeu 22; dm €10-13, d €35, apt €40, campsites per person with/without own tent €5/7; @ 🛜) Shkodra's original hostel is a gorgeous arty space, and with a peaceful garden and open-air bar (selling local craft beers) you'd hardly guess that you were almost right in the heart of the city. There are attractive communal spaces littered with musical instruments and artwork and a bunch of friendly dogs. Dorms have between six and 10 beds.

★ Rose Garden Hotel   BOUTIQUE HOTEL €
(☑ 022 245 296, 069 311 7127; www.rosegarden hotel.al; Rr Justin Godard 18; d incl breakfast from €36; ❄ 🛜) A wonderfully restored old townhouse, the Rose Garden is all clean modern lines dusted with touches of old-fashioned class. Rooms are exceptionally inviting and include filigree door frames. The real highlight of a stay, though, is the hidden courtyard garden (which extends its botanical knowledge to more than just roses); sitting here with a good book is just perfect.

🍴 Eating

★ Pasta e Vino   ITALIAN €€
(☑ 069 724 3751; www.facebook.com/pastaevino shkoder; Rr Gjergj Fishta; mains 400-600 lekë; ⊙ noon-11pm) Casually dressed waiters with tattoos, dried tree branches dressed with herbs, and artworks made from wine corks all help to make this one of the more visually memorable places to eat in Shkodra. But what about the food? Well, it's classic Italian, it's authentic and it's very well prepared and presented. What's not to like?!

Restaurant Elita   ALBANIAN €€
(☑ 069 206 2193; Rr Gjergj Fishta; mains 600-800 lekë; ⊙ 8am-4pm & 6.30-11pm) Respected and smart restaurant with an emphasis on imaginative recreations of classic Albanian and Italian dishes. The slow-cooked pork served

in an inverted wine glass is just one such example. Very good value considering the quality of the food. Earlier in the evening it seems to be mainly other foreigners eating here, so for a more Albanian clientele, come later.

ℹ Information

Tourist Information (Rr Teuta; ⊘ 9am-7pm Mon-Sat) The small tourist information office has a few token leaflets to hand out but not much else of use. As it's a new office, there was no telephone number available at the time of research.

ℹ Getting There & Away

BUS

There is no bus station in Shkodra, but most services leave from around Sheshi Demokracia in the centre of town. There are hourly *furgons* (minibuses; 400 lekë) and buses (300 lekë) to Tirana (two hours, 6am to 5pm), which depart from outside Radio Shkodra near Hotel Rozafa. There are also several daily buses to Kotor, Ulcinj and Podgorica in Montenegro (€5 to €8, two to three hours) from outside the Ebu Bekr Mosque.

To get up into the mountains, catch the 6.30am bus to Lake Koman (600 lekë, two hours) in time for the wonderful Lake Koman Ferry to Fierzë. Several *furgons* also depart daily for Theth between 6am and 7am (1200 lekë, four hours). In both cases hotels can call ahead to get the *furgon* to pick you up on its way out of town.

THE ACCURSED MOUNTAINS & THE NORTH

Names don't come much more evocative than the 'Accursed Mountains' (Bjeshkët e Namuna; also known as the Albanian Alps), but the dramatic peaks of northern Albania truly live up to the wonder in their name. Offering some of the country's most impressive scenery, and easily its finest hiking, the mountains spread over the borders of Albania, Kosovo and Montenegro, and in Albania they reach a respectable height of 2694m. But as we all know, size isn't everything and what these mountains lack in Himalayan greatness, they more than make up for with lyrical beauty. There are deep green valleys, thick forests where wolves prowl, icy-grey rock pinnacles and quaint stone villages where old traditions hold strong. Indeed, this is where shepherds still take their flocks to high summer pastures and blood feuds continue to hold sway, and it feels as if you're far, far away from 21st-century Europe.

Valbona

📒 0213 / POP 200

Valbona has a gorgeous setting on a wide plain surrounded by towering mountain peaks, and its summer tourism industry is increasingly well organised. The village itself consists virtually only of guesthouses and

---

WORTH A TRIP

THE LAKE KOMAN FERRY

One of Albania's undisputed highlights is the superb three-hour **ferry ride** (www.komanilakeferry.com/en/ferry-lines-in-the-komani-lake) across vast Lake Koman, connecting the towns of Koman and Fierzë.

The best way to experience the journey is to make a three-day, two-night loop beginning and ending in Shkodra, and taking in Koman, Fierzë, Valbona and Theth. Every hotel in Shkodra and Valbona organises packages for the route for 2000 lekë. This includes a 6.30am *furgon* (shared minibus) pick-up from your hotel in Shkodra which will get you to the ferry departure point at Koman by 8.30am. There are normally two ferries daily and both leave from Koman at 9am. One of the two, the Berisha, carries up to ten cars, which cost 700 lekë per square metre of space they occupy. There's also a big car ferry that leaves at 1pm, but it only runs when demand is high enough – call ahead to make a reservation.

On arrival in Fierzë, the boats are met by furgons that will take you to either Bajram Curri or to Valbon. Hikers will want to head straight for Valbona, where you can stay for a night or two before doing the stunning day hike to Theth. After the hike you can stay for another night or two in glorious Theth before taking a furgon back to Shkodra (not included in the standard packages). It's also possible to do the whole thing independently, though you won't save any money or time by doing so.

DON'T MISS

HIKING

Most people come here to do the popular hike between Valbona and Theth, which takes between five and seven hours depending on your fitness and where in either village you start or end. It's not a particularly hard walk and it is attempted by many first-time mountain walkers. Even so, it's quite long and steep and can get very hot, and if you don't have much mountain walking experience you should allow extra time.

You can walk it either way, though the majority of people seem to go from Valbona to Theth as this allows for a neat circle going from Shkodra via the Lake Koman ferry. The trail begins a couple of kilometres beyond Valbona, and many people get a lift to the trailhead; it's a tiring and monotonous walk over a dry – and often very hot – stone riverbed otherwise. On the whole the trail itself is decently marked with red and white way markings and there are a number of tea houses where you can get refreshments (and even a bed). Eventually you will arrive at the Valbona Pass (1800m) for memorable views over an ocean of jagged mountains.

camping grounds, nearly all of which have their own restaurants attached. Most travellers just spend a night here before trekking to Theth, which is a shame as there are a wealth of other excellent hikes to do in the area.

🛏 Sleeping

★ Hotel Rilindja GUESTHOUSE €
(☑ 067 301 4637; www.journeytovalbona.com; Quku i Valbonës; tent/dm/d incl breakfast €4/12/35; ☏) Pioneering tourism in Valbona since 2005, the Albanian-American–run Rilindja is a fairy-tale wooden house in the forest 3km downhill from Valbona village centre. It's hugely popular with travellers, who love the comfortable accommodation, easy attitude and excellent food. The simple rooms in the atmospheric farmhouse share a bathroom, except for one with private facilities.

Jezerca GUESTHOUSE €
(☑ 067 309 3202; r from €30; ☏) Named after one of the soaring mountain peaks nearby, this guesthouse on Valbona's main (well, only) street has freestanding pine huts in a pleasant field, which sleep two, three or five people. The best huts have attached bathrooms and little terraces with hanging flower baskets. There's a small restaurant which tries hard to use only locally sourced products.

❶ Getting There & Away

Valbona can be reached from Shkodra via the Lake Koman Ferry and a connecting *furgon* (minibus) from Fierzë (400 lekë, one hour). Alternatively it can be reached by *furgon* from Bajram Curri (200 lekë, 45 minutes). In general most people just organise the entire trip as one package from Shkodra (2000 lekë).

Theth

☑ 022 / POP 400

This unique mountain village easily has the most dramatic setting in Albania. Just the journey here is quite incredible, whether you approach over the mountains on foot from Valbona or by vehicle over the high passes from Shkodra. Both a sprawling village along the valley floor amid an amphitheatre of slate-grey mountains and a national park containing stunning landscapes and excellent hiking routes, Theth is now well on its way to being Albania's next big thing. An improved – though still incomplete – asphalt road from Shkodra has made access to this once virtually unknown village far easier in recent years, bringing with it the familiar problem of overdevelopment. Come quickly while Theth retains its incomparable romance and unique charm.

◉ Sights

Blue Eye NATURAL POOL
A superb half-day hike from Theth is to the Blue Eye, a natural pool of turquoise waters fed by a small waterfall, up in the mountains to the southwest of Theth. The walk will take you through forests and steeply up into the mountains and in summer it can get very hot, so you'll probably be keen for a swim when you get to the pool. But, be warned: the water is glacier cold. Are you brave enough?

🛏 Sleeping

Vila Pisha GUESTHOUSE €€
(☑ 069 325 6415, 068 278 5057; r per person incl breakfast €34; ☏) Next to the church, right in the centre of the village, this place has been

totally rebuilt from the ground upwards. It is one of the best guesthouses in the village, with friendly, English-speaking owners, smart en-suite rooms with radiators for those cold mountain nights, large beds and wooden floors.

Vila Zorgji GUESTHOUSE €
(☑ 068 231 9610, 068 361 7309; pellumbkola@ gmail.com; r per person incl full board €35; ☺ Apr-Oct; 🖥) Zorgji is a gorgeous stone farmhouse with big, bright en-suite rooms and a dining room full of drying corn and old farming implements. The garden is equally attractive and is lined with grape vines and tomato plants. It's a little to the north of the village centre and up on the hillside near the turquoise-painted school.

❶ Getting There & Away

A daily *furgon* (1200 lekë, two hours) leaves from Shkodra at 7am and will pick you up from your hotel if your hotel owner calls ahead for you. The return trip leaves between 1pm and 2pm, arriving late afternoon in Shkodra. During the summer months it's also easy to arrange a shared *furgon* (around €50) transfer to Shkodra with other hikers from Valbona.

SURVIVAL GUIDE

❶ Directory A–Z

ACCESSIBLE TRAVEL

High footpaths and unannounced potholes make life difficult for mobility-impaired travellers. Tirana's top hotels do cater to people with disabilities, and some smaller hotels are making an effort to be more accessible. The roads and castle entrances in Gjirokastra, Shkodra, Berat and Kruja are cobblestone, although taxis can get reasonably close.

ACCOMMODATION

Hotels and guesthouses, including an expanding number of boutique and heritage properties, are easily found throughout Albania as tourism continues to grow. You will rarely have trouble finding a room for the night, though seaside towns are often booked out in late July and August.

Homestays abound in Theth and Valbona, while the number of camping grounds is increasing; you'll find them at Himara, Livadhi, Dhërmi and Drymades. Most have hot showers and on-site restaurants.

LGBT+ TRAVELLERS

Extensive antidiscrimination legislation became law in 2010, but did not extend to legalising same-sex marriage. Gay and lesbian life in Albania is alive and well but is not yet organised into clubs or organisations. The alternative music and party scene in Tirana is queer-friendly, but most contacts are made on the internet. As with elsewhere in the Balkans, discretion is generally the way to go for LGBT+ travellers.

MONEY

ATMs are widely available in most towns. Acceptance of credit cards is normally confined to upper-end hotels, restaurants and shops, although every year their usage becomes more widespread.

OPENING HOURS

Banks 9am to 3.30pm Monday to Friday
Cafes & Bars 8am to midnight
Offices 8am to 5pm Monday to Friday
Restaurants 8am to midnight
Shops 8am to 7pm; siesta time can be any time between noon and 4pm

PUBLIC HOLIDAYS

New Year's Day 1 January
Summer Day 16 March
Nevruz 23 March
Catholic Easter March or April
Orthodox Easter March or April
May Day 1 May
Mother Teresa Day 19 October
Independence Day 28 November
Liberation Day 29 November
Christmas Day 25 December

TELEPHONE

Albania's country phone code is 355. Mobile coverage is excellent, though it's limited in very remote areas (though most places have some form of connection including Theth).

TOURIST INFORMATION

The country's main tourist board website is www.albaniantourist.com.

WOMEN TRAVELLERS

Albania is a safe country for women travellers, but outside Tirana it is mainly men who go out and sit in bars and cafes in the evenings. You may tire of being asked why you're travelling alone, but you'll rarely feel the target of more than curiosity.

❶ Getting There & Away

ENTERING THE COUNTRY

All citizens of European and North American countries may enter Albania visa-free for up to 90 days. This is also true for Australians, New Zealanders, Japanese and South Korean citizens. Citizens of most other countries must apply for a visa.

AIR

Nënë Tereza International Airport (p48) is a modern, well-run terminal 17km northwest of Tirana. There are no domestic flights within Albania. Airlines flying to and from Tirana include **Adria Airways** (www.adria.si), **Alitalia** (www.alitalia.com), **Austrian Airlines** (www.austrian.com), **Lufthansa** (www.lufthansa.com), **Olympic Air** (www.olympicair.com), **Pegasus Airlines** (www.flypgs.com) and **Turkish Airlines** (www.turkishairlines.com).

LAND
Border Crossings

There are no passenger trains into Albania, so your border-crossing options are buses, *furgons* (minibuses), taxis or walking to a border and picking up transport on the other side.

Montenegro The main crossings link Shkodra to Ulcinj (via Muriqan, Albania, and Sukobin, Montenegro) and to Podgorica (via Hani i Hotit).

Kosovo The closest border crossing to the Lake Koman Ferry terminal is Morina, and further south is Qafë Prush. Near Kukës, use Morinë for the highway to Tirana.

North Macedonia Use Blato to get to Debar, and Qafë e Thanës or Tushemisht, each to one side of Pogradec, for accessing Ohrid.

Greece The main border crossing to and from Greece is Kakavija on the road from Athens to Tirana. It's about half an hour from Gjirokastra and 250km southeast of Tirana, and can take up to three hours to pass through in summer. Kapshtica (near Korça) to Krystallopigi also gets long lines in summer. Konispoli (near Butrint in Albania's south) and Leskovik (between Gjirokastra and Korça) are both far less busy.

Bus

From Tirana, regular buses head to Pristina, Kosovo; to Skopje in North Macedonia; to Ulcinj in Montenegro; and to Athens and Thessaloniki in Greece. *Furgons* (minibuses) and buses leave Shkodra for Montenegro, and buses head to Kosovo from Durrës. Buses travel to Greece from Albanian towns on the southern coast as well as from Tirana.

Car & Motorcycle

Travellers heading south from Croatia can pass through Montenegro to Shkodra (via Ulcinj), and loop through Albania before heading into North Macedonia via Pogradec or into Kosovo via the Lake Koman Ferry or the excellent Albania–Kosovo highway.

To enter Albania with you own vehicle you'll need a Green Card (proof of third-party insurance; issued by your insurer); check that your insurance covers Albania.

Taxi

Heading to North Macedonia, taxis from Pogradec will drop you off just before the border at Tushemisht/Sveti Naum. Alternatively, it's an easy 4km walk to the border from Pogradec. It's possible to organise a taxi (or, more usually, a person with a car) from where the Lake Koman Ferry stops in Fierzë to Gjakova in Kosovo. Taxis commonly charge €50 from Shkodra to Ulcinj in Montenegro.

SEA

Two or three boats per day ply the route between Saranda and Corfu, in Greece, and there are plenty of ferry companies making the journey to Italy from Vlora and Durrës. There are additional ferries from Vlora and Himara to Corfu in the summer.

ⓘ Getting Around

BUS

Bus and *furgon* (privately run minibuses) are the main forms of public transport in Albania. Fares are low, and you either pay the conductor on board or when you hop off, which can be anywhere along the route.

Municipal buses operate in Tirana, Durrës, Shkodra, Berat, Korça and Vlora, and trips usually cost 40 lekë.

CAR & MOTORCYCLE

Despite severe neglect under the communists, nowadays the road infrastructure is improving; there's an excellent highway from Tirana to Kosovo, and the coastal route from the Montenegro border to Butrint, near Saranda, is in good condition.

Tourists are driving cars, motorbikes and mobile homes into the country in greater numbers, and, apart from heavy traffic and bad drivers, it's generally hassle free. One issue is the huge number of traffic cops running speed traps. If they stop you for speeding, you'll have to pay a 'fine' in cash (around €20).

Off the main routes a 4WD isn't a bad idea. Driving at night is particularly hazardous; following another car on the road is a good idea as there are rarely any road markings or street lighting. A valid foreign driving licence is all that's required to drive a car in Albania.

Belarus

POP 9.55 MILLION

Best Places to Eat

➡ Bistro de Luxe (p66)

➡ Jules Verne (p69)

➡ Kukhmystr (p66)

➡ Provence (p72)

➡ Enzo (p66)

Best Places to Stay

➡ Hotel Manastyrski (p65)

➡ Hermitage Hotel (p69)

➡ Willing Hotel (p66)

➡ Kamyanyuki Hotel Complex (p71)

Why Go?

Long regarded by travellers as little more than a curiosity, Belarus has suddenly emerged as one of Europe's 'it' destinations. Fuelling that rise are relaxed visa requirements, a sneaky-good art and cafe scene, and hospitable locals. While political dissent remains muted, the country seems to be having fun again.

The capital has a pulsing nightlife, excellent museums and an impressive ensemble of Stalin-era architecture. Minsk has also become a hub for global summits and sporting events such as the 2019 European Games. Elsewhere, the western cities of Brest and Hrodna are Europeanised nooks, while around the Belarusian heartland you'll turn up ancient castles and national parks where rare *zubr* (European bison) roam.

When to Go
Minsk

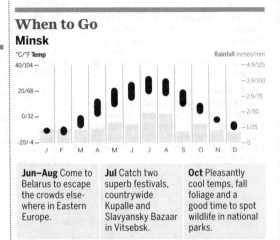

Jun–Aug Come to Belarus to escape the crowds elsewhere in Eastern Europe.

Jul Catch two superb festivals, countrywide Kupalle and Slavyansky Bazaar in Vitsebsk.

Oct Pleasantly cool temps, fall foliage and a good time to spot wildlife in national parks.

Entering the Country

You must arrive and depart by air in Minsk to take advantage of the 30-day visa-free regime. You'll generally need a visa if you arrive overland – visa-free zones (p71) in Brest and Hrodna are the exceptions.

ITINERARIES

Five Days

Five days gives you enough time to explore Minsk (p63) and get a taste of rural Belarus. Spend day one exploring the capital's Soviet past. Walk along massive pr Nezalezhnastsi (p63), take in the the Great Patriotic War Museum (p63), and pop in for a vodka at Tsentralny (p66). Day two is for culture. Check out an art museum, pop into a gallery on vul Kastrychnitskaya (p63), and go bar-hopping in the lively Old Town. Next, explore castle towns Mir (p68) and Nyasvizh (p68), with a potential overnight in either. Spend your last day cycling around Minsk's outskirts, or do another day trip.

Ten Days

After a few days in and around Minsk, hop a train or drive to the appealing western city of Brest (p68), which mixes European cafe culture with a slew of Soviet historical attractions. On day seven, head north along the Polish border to Belavezhskaya Pushcha National Park (p71), where lovely cycling trails and rare European bison await. Next, keep driving north to pleasant Hrodna (p71) with its preserved pre-WWII architecture. Alternatively, take a night train from Brest (or drive) east to Chagall's hometown, Vitsebsk (p69), before heading back to Minsk.

Essential Food & Drink

Belavezhskaya A bitter herbal alcoholic drink.

Draniki Potato pancakes, usually served with sour cream (*smetana*).

Khaladnik A local variation on cold *borshch*, a soup made from beetroot and garnished with sour cream, chopped-up hard-boiled eggs and potatoes.

Kindziuk A pig-stomach sausage filled with minced pork, herbs and spices.

Kletsky Dumplings stuffed with mushrooms, cheese or potato.

Kolduni Potato dumplings stuffed with meat.

Kvas A mildly alcoholic drink made from black or rye bread and commonly sold on the streets.

Machanka Pork stew served over pancakes.

AT A GLANCE

Area 207,600 sq km

Capital Minsk

Country Code ☏ 375

Currency Belarusian rouble (BYN)

Emergency Ambulance ☏ 03, Fire ☏ 01, Police ☏ 02

Language Belarusian, Russian

Time Eastern European time (GMT/UTC plus three hours)

Visas Not required for stays of 30 days or less for citizens of 74 countries, but must fly in/out of Minsk.

BELARUS

Sleeping Price Ranges

The following price ranges refer to a double room with bathroom during high season.

€ less than US$40

€€ US$40–100

€€€ more than US$100

Eating Price Ranges

The following price ranges refer to a main course.

€ less than BYN10

€€ BYN10–20

€€€ more than BYN20

Useful Websites

Belarus Feed (www.belarusfeed.com)

Belarus Tourism (www.belarus.by/en)

Minsk Tourism (http://minsktourism.by/en)

Belarus Highlights

1 Minsk (p63) Taking in the architecture, the rowdy nightlife and the burgeoning arts scene of Belarus' capital.

2 Brest (p68) Strolling through the streets of this cosmopolitan city and gaping at its epic WWII memorials.

3 Mir Castle (p68) Training your lens on this fairy-tale

16th-century castle – and its equally famous reflection.

4 Nyasvizh (p68) Exploring this tranquil provincial town's parks and impeccably restored castle.

5 Belavezhskaya Pushcha National Park (p71) Cycling around Europe's oldest

wildlife refuge in search of rare European bison.

6 Hrodna (p71) Checking out its ruined Old Castle, museums and pre-WWII architecture.

7 Vitsebsk (p69) Discovering the childhood home of painter Marc Chagall and excellent art museums.

MINSK

MIHCK

♪17 / POP 2.01 MILLION

Minsk will almost certainly surprise you. The capital of Belarus is, contrary to its dreary reputation, a progressive, modern and clean place. Fashionable cafes, impressive restaurants and crowded nightclubs vie for your attention, while sushi bars and art galleries have taken up residence in a city centre once totally remodelled to the tastes of Stalin. Despite the strong police presence and obedient citizenry, Minsk is a thoroughly pleasant place that's easy to become fond of.

◎ Sights

If you're short on time, have a wander around the attractive Old Town, or Verkhni Horad (Upper City). This was once the city's thriving Jewish quarter, and while most of it was destroyed in the war, a smattering of pre-war buildings along vul Internatsyanalnaya and a rebuilt **ratusha** (Town Hall; pl Svabody) on **pl Svabody** emit a whiff of history.

Many of the most bombastic buildings from the Soviet and Lukashenko eras lie well outside the centre. The most jaw-dropping specimens are northeast of the centre along pr Nezalezhnastsi and out toward **Minsk Arena** (♪17 3634 598; http://minskarena.

by; pr Peramozhtsaŭ) on pr Peramozhtsaŭ (take the #1 bus from pl Svabody). A good way to see a bunch of these is to take a **City Tour** (♪17 3996 969; http://citytour.by; pl Privakzalnaya; adult/child BYN30/15; ⊙tours 11am, 1.30pm, 4pm & 6.30pm) bus tour.

★**Museum of the Great Patriotic War**   MUSEUM
(♪17 2030 792; www.warmuseum.by; pr Peramozhtsaŭ 8; adult/student BYN9/7, audioguide BYN4, guided tours BYN35; ⊙10am-6pm Tue-Sun) Housed in a garish new building, Minsk's best museum houses an excellent display detailing Belarus' suffering and heroism during the Nazi occupation. With English explanations throughout, atmospheric dioramas and a range of real tanks, airplanes and artillery from WWII, it's one of the capital's few must-see attractions.

★**Vul Kastrychnitskaya**   STREET
Vul Kastrychnitskaya – still known by its Soviet name, ulitsa Oktyabrskaya – has blossomed into Minsk's unofficial arts district. Brazilian street artists have spray-painted brilliant murals on the giant facades of the street's apartment blocks, warehouses and factories, many of which now house event spaces, galleries and hipster cafes. President

BELARUS MINSK

MINSK'S MAIN DRAG

Inconspicuous **pr Nezalezhnastsi** (Independence Ave) is a good way to take Minsk's pulse while also taking in a few sights. It runs the length of the modern city, from stubbornly austere and expansive **pl Nezalezhnastsi** (Independence Sq) to the pinnacle of Lukashenko-approved hubris, the rhombicuboctahedron-shaped **National Library of Belarus** (♪17 2932 966; www.nlb.by; pr Nezalezhnastsi 116; library BYN1.50, viewing platform BYN3.50; ⊙library 10am-8pm, closed Sun & last Mon of the month; viewing platform noon-11pm; Ⓜ Uschod). The avenue is the world's premier embodiment of the post-WWII Stalinist Empire style, marked by expansive squares, utopian parks and palatial architectural gems like the **Central Post Office** (pr Nezalezhnastsi 10).

At pl Nezalezhnastsi you can't miss the imposing Belarusian Government Building, fronted by a Lenin Statue. It is one of several fine examples of pre-WWII constructivist architecture in Minsk. Heading northeast you'll pass the post office, the ominous **KGB headquarters** (pr Nezalezhnastsi 17) and daunting **Kastrychnitskaya pl** (Oktyabrskaya Pl) before crossing the Svislach River, straddled by the city's two main parks.

Just across the bridge is the **former residence of Lee Harvey Oswald** (vul Kamyunistychnaya 4). The alleged assassin of former US president John F Kennedy lived here for a couple of years in his early 20s. He arrived in Minsk in January 1960 after leaving the US Marines and defecting to the USSR. Once here, he truly went native: he got a job in a radio factory, married a Minsk woman, had a child – and even changed his name to Alek. But soon he returned to the United States and...you know the rest. His apartment is thought to be at the far left (northwest) side of the building on the 3rd floor.

Just 100m northeast of here, **pl Peramohi** (Victory Sq) is marked by a giant Victory Obelisk and its eternal flame, which is directly beneath the obelisk underground. From here you can hop on the Metro to go out to the National Library 5km away.

Minsk

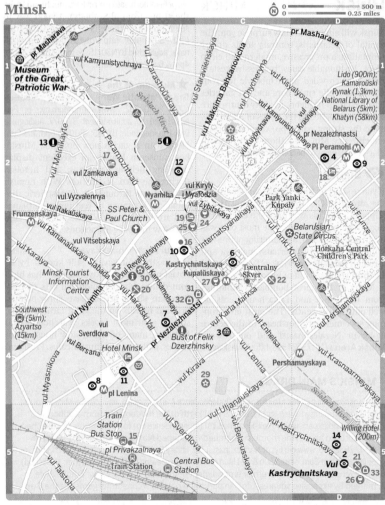

Lukashenko has allowed creative expression to flourish here with the expectation that it not spread to other parts of the capital, which remain sanitised and generally free of street art.

The district exudes a refreshing counter-culture spirit and is one of the few places where you'll hear locals speaking Belarusian and/or talking about politics. While you're out here drop into the Ў Gallery of Contemporary Art (http://ygallery.by; vul Kastrychnitskaya 19; gallery BYN4; ⊙noon-8pm), which has two cavernous post-industrial exhibition spaces and a delightful cafe that morphs into a wine bar by night. It is named after

a letter unique to the Belarusian language called 'u nieskladovaye', a symbol of sorts of the Belarusian national identity.

Belarusian State Art Museum   MUSEUM
(⌂17 3277 163; vul Lenina 20; adult/student BYN8/4, audioguide BYN3, excursion BYN20; ⊙11am-7pm Wed-Mon) This excellent museum in one of Minsk's iconic buildings (built in 1939) includes definitive works by Soviet social realists and Russian masters, including Valentin Volkov's social realist *Minsk on July 3, 1944* (1944–5), depicting the Red Army's arrival in the ruined city. Several works by Yudel Pen, Chagall's teacher, are here, includ-

Minsk

ing his 1914 portrait of Chagall, and Chagall exhibitions often rotate through here.

Trinity Hill HISTORIC SITE
(Traetskae Pradmestse) Trinity Hill is a pleasant – if tiny – recreation of Minsk's pre-war buildings on a pretty bend of the river just a little north of the centre. It has a few little cafes, restaurants and shops, and a walking bridge leads over to the **Island of Courage & Sorrow** (Island of Tears), an evocative Afghan war memorial known locally as the Island of Tears.

Kamaroŭski Rynak MARKET
(Komarovskiy Market; vul Very Kharuzhay; ⊙9am-7pm; Ⓜ Ploshcha Jakuba Kolasa) Market buffs should not miss Minsk's air-hangar-like main market, one of Minsk's collectivist masterpieces. It's a colourful smorgasbord of seasonal (and unseasonal) fruits and vegetables, breads and all manner of meat.

Tours

Minsk Guide TOURS
(☑29 3846 689; www.minsktours.by) Andrei is a professional guide who speaks excellent English and leads tours around the country. He specialises in Jewish heritage tours but is well versed on all things Belarus. He also has a lovely, log-cabin-like farmstay southwest of Minsk out towards Mir.

Free Walking Tour Minsk WALKING
(☑44 5398 306; http://freewalkingtour.by) In addition to the two-hour free walking tour, which kicks off daily at 11am in front of the ratusha on pl Svabody, this group leads Soviet tours, Jewish tours and more.

Sleeping

Hostel Tower 31/18 HOSTEL €
(☑33 6250 305; pr Nezalezhnastsi 31; dm/r BYN20/55; @⊛) JFK assassin Lee Harvey Oswald lived under the same roof (in a different apartment) in the 1960s. If that doesn't interest you, then the welcoming vibe, clean dorms and pleasant kitchen/hangout area at this quiet hostel will. It's five storeys up (no lift), in apartment 18; the door access code is 18C.

★**Hotel Manastyrski** HISTORIC HOTEL €€
(☑17 3290 300; http://monastyrski.by/en; vul Kiryly i Myafodzia 6; s/d incl breakfast from US$65/$75; ⊛⊛) Housed in the converted remains of a Benedictine Monastery in the heart of Minsk's bustling Old Town, this 48-room gem cannot be beaten for location or atmosphere. Rooms are smart and comfortably furnished with dark-wood fittings, while the impressive corridors are decorated with frescoes (found during the renovation) and wrought-iron chandeliers.

Booking directly on the website nets a 10% discount.

Willing Hotel BOUTIQUE HOTEL €€
(☑17 3369 000; vul Lenina 50; r US$70-100, ste US$150; ❋@☎; Ⓜ Praletarskaya) This new hotel announces its presence with a giant mural facing artsy vul Kastrychnitskaya. The creativity continues inside, where a circular atrium awaits and colourful carpeting with a squiggly motif covers all floor space. The suitably snazzy rooms feature contemporary art and bathtubs, and the deluxe rooms have kitchenettes with bar seating. The in-house Simple Cafe is wonderful.

DoubleTree by Hilton HOTEL €€€
(☑17 3098 000; www.doubletree.com; pr Peramozhtsaŭ 9; s/d incl breakfast from US$160/170; ❋@☎) A short walk from the Old Town, this 21-storey high-rise is the capital's best all-around hotel. The ship-shape, well-appointed rooms are what you'd expect from a four-star hotel. It's the extras that make it stand out: the excellent gym, the ground-level coffee shop and adjacent patio bar, the bike-rental service, and the sumptuous breakfast complete with a unique 'honey bar'.

✖ Eating

Lido CAFETERIA €
(pr Nezalezhnastsi 49/1; mains BYN3-7; ⊘8am-11pm Mon-Fri, from 11am Sat & Sun; ☎🍴; Ⓜ Ploshcha Jakuba Kolasa) This large, upscale *stolovaya* (cafeteria) with Latvian roots has a huge array of food on display, so it's easy for non-Russian speakers: just point at what you want. Classic Russian soups and salads, grilled trout and cheesy meat dishes are highlights.

Another branch is on **vul Nyamiha** (vul Nyamiha 5; dishes BYN3-7; ⊘10am-10pm; ☎).

★Enzo BISTRO €€
(☑29 1770 088; vul Kastrychnitskaya 23; mains BYN10-20, steaks BYN30-60; ⊘11am-midnight Sun-Thu, to 3am Fri & Sat; ❋☎) A hip and happening bistro worthy of the hip and happening street that it's on, Enzo is justifiably popular, mainly for its burgers and succulent steaks served on bread boards, but also for its towering salads and inventive desserts. Outside is prime people-watching, while inside classic-rock and alternative music videos are projected onto a brick wall behind the bar.

★Kukhmystr BELARUSIAN €€
(☑17 3274 848; vul Karla Marksa 40; mains BYN15-30; ⊘noon-11pm, closed last Sat of month; ❋☎) A stone's throw from the president's office, this charming Belarusian place boasts wooden beams, a tiled fireplace, wrought-iron light fittings and antique knick-knacks. Staff are equally pleasant, and the menu is among the most authentically Belarusian in town.

★Bistro de Luxe BISTRO €€€
(☑44 7891 111; vul Haradski Val 10; mains BYN15-45; ⊘8am-midnight Mon-Fri, from 11am Sat & Sun; ❋☎) Housed in a gorgeous space with chandeliers, sleek brasserie-style furnishings, a chessboard floor and luxury toilets, Bistro de Luxe has charm and atmosphere in spades. The food is excellent – it leans towards French – and service is impeccable. Breakfast is served until noon. Reservations recommended, especially if you want to sit outside.

🍸 Drinking & Nightlife

★Hooligan BAR
(vul Kastrychnitskaya 16; ⊘5pm-midnight, from 8am Sat & Sun, to 4am Fri & Sat; ☎) The haphazard look is very much by design at this brick-walled hipster hangout on vul Kastrychnitskaya. Belly up to the recycled-wood bar, play table football under exposed pipes or kick back in old leather couches. It offers 'twisted and classic' cocktails (BYN10 to BYN12), beer, and a few single malts and other high-end spirits.

Bessonitsa COCKTAIL BAR
(Insomnia; vul Hertsena 1; ⊘noon-late) *The* place in the Old Town for professional cocktails (try the bourbon sour or a gimlet) and late-night eats. It has Minsk's longest bar, a lively interior and a bustling patio tailor-made for people-watching.

Tsentralny BAR
(pr Nezalezhnastsi 23; ⊘8am-11pm) It's known as a place where you can drown your sorrows with BYN1.80 vodka shots – and therein lies its beauty. While models and hipsters crash the Old Town, real people with real problems hit the ground floor of this department store on Minsk's main drag. Order from the cashier and take a window seat.

Beercap Barshop CRAFT BEER
(vul Hertsena 10; ⊘5-11pm, to 1am Fri & Sat; ☎) This is a generously stocked craft-beer place at the very centre of the Old Town action. Choose from about a dozen draught beers inside, with about half a dozen additional varieties on tap outside. Tunes roar and the whole place gets jumping at weekends.

☆ Entertainment

TNT
LIVE MUSIC

(☏ 29 6555 555; www.tntrock.by; vul Revalyut-siynaya 9a; cover Fri & Sat BYN10; ⊙ noon-2am Sun-Thu, to 4am Fri & Sat) An early pioneer of Minsk's rock-music renaissance, this multi-room venue in the centre of town draws top local and regional talent and is a good bet for those who want to rock out midweek. The cocktails are strong, and on some nights it gets several bands.

Bolshoi Theatre
of Belarus
PERFORMING ARTS

(☏ 17 2895 493; http://bolshoibelarus.by; pl Parizh-skoy Kamunni 1; tickets BYN5-120; ⊙ performances 7pm, closed Jul & Aug) In an iconic pre-WWII collectivist building, the national opera has an excellent reputation and stages a range of classical ballets and operas.

🛍 Shopping

Kirmash
CLOTHING

(www.kirmash.by; pr Nezalezhnastsi 19; ⊙ 10am-9pm Mon-Fri, to 6pm Sat & Sun) This is *the* place buy embroidered shirts and dresses, table-cloths and other national-flavoured textiles. Much of the clothing blends traditional and modern motifs, with several contemporary designers represented.

Vialiki Dziakuj
GIFTS & SOUVENIRS

(vul Kastrychnitskaya 23; ⊙ noon-10pm) Per-sonable, Belarusian-speaking Valentin is a printer and brander by trade, and it shows in his wonderful collection of original mugs and T-shirts. You'll also find cool wallets, handbags, pins and other knick-knacks, plus bottled craft beer that can be enjoyed in the courtyard outside.

ℹ Information

MEDICAL SERVICES

24-Hour Pharmacy (vul Karla Marksa 20; ⊙ 24hr) Well stocked.
Apteka #4 (vul Kirava 3; ⊙ 24hr) A 24-hour pharmacy.
Ecomedservice (☏ 160, 17 2077 474; www.ems.by; vul Talstoha 4; ⊙ 8am-9pm; 🔊) Relia-ble, Western-style clinic. Bring a translator.

TOURIST INFORMATION

Minsk Tourist Information Centre (☏ 17 2033 995; www.minsktourism.by/en; vul Revaly-utsiynaya 13-119; ⊙ 8.45am-1pm & 2-6pm Mon-Fri) The main tourist office is central but well hidden in the courtyard behind vul Revalyutsiynaya 13.

BelarusTourService (☏ 33 3332 666; www.visa.by; vul Rozy Lyuksemburg 89) An excellent source for visa support, hotel bookings and transfers, plus tours.

ℹ Getting There & Away

AIR

Minsk National Airport (☏ 17 2791 300; www.airport.by) All flights in and out of Belarus are through this airport about 40km east of the centre. There are no domestic flights in Belarus.

BUS

The vast majority of intercity domestic and international services leave from the **Central Bus Station** (Tsentralny Aŭtavakzal; ☏ 114; vul Babruyskaya 6).

TRAIN

The busy and modern **Minsk train station** (☏ 105, 17 2257 000; pl Privakzalnaya; ⊙ 24hr) is pretty easy to deal with. You can buy tickets here, or opposite the station at the less crowded **International Train Ticket Office** (vul Kirava 2; ⊙ 8am-noon & 1-5pm). Downstairs is a well-signed **left luggage office** (per 24hr BYN1.25-1.50; ⊙ 24hr).

ℹ Getting Around

TO/FROM THE AIRPORT

Minsk National Airport Handy Bus A300Э goes to/from the Central Bus Station (platform 2), passing by the train station (BYN4.40, 55 minutes). It runs roughly hourly around the clock. Head left when you exit the terminal and look for the dedicated **bus stop** (Minsk National Airport).

The 35-minute taxi ride into town costs a flat BYN30 provided you book it at one of several dedicated taxi booths in the arrivals area.

BICYCLE

Renting a bicycle is an ideal way to explore Minsk and its vast boulevards. Riding on the sidewalk is encouraged – indeed many sidewalks have designated bike lanes – and a beautiful 26km two-way bike route cuts right through the centre of Minsk. **City Bike** (vul Kastrychnitskaya 16; per day BYN15-20; ⊙ 7am-10pm) and **Speedy Go** (☏ 29 1445 030; http://speedygo.by; pr Nezalezhnastsi 37a; bicycles per day BYN15; ⊙ 10am-10pm) rent bikes.

CAR

Rental cars are widely available and work great for day trips out of town. **Avis** (☏ 17 2099 489; www.avis.by; Hotel Minsk, pr Nezalezhnastsi 11) and **Europcar** (☏ 29 1336 553; www.europcar.by; Hotel Minsk, pr Nezalezhnastsi 11; ⊙ 9am-6pm) both have outlets at Hotel Minsk and at the air-port; for a cheaper local option try **AvtoGurman**

(☑ 29 6887 070; http://auto-rent.by; vul Chycheryna 4; per day from €25).

PUBLIC TRANSPORT

Minsk's metro isn't hugely useful to travellers unless you're exploring the vast suburbs. It's open daily from dawn until just after midnight. One ride costs 65 kopeks.

Buses, trams and trolleybuses cost 60 kopeks per ride, and you can buy tickets on board. The most useful services for travellers are bus 1 and bus 69, which depart from the **train station bus stop** (vul Kirava), pass by pl Svabody in the Old Town, then continue along pr Peramozhtsaŭ.

TAXI

Ordering a taxi via a ride-hailing app or by phone is the way forward. Trips within the centre cost just BYN3 to BYN5 – much cheaper and less hassle than negotiating with street taxis. Yandex Taxi and NextApp are apps that work well in Minsk (Uber also works, via Yandex). Otherwise dial 152 or 7788 for a taxi (find a translator, though, in case the operators don't speak English).

AROUND MINSK

Worthwhile trips from the capital include **Dudutki** (☑ 29 6025 250; www.dudutki.by; adult/child BYN10/6; audioguide BYN3; ⊙10am-5pm Tue-Wed, to 6pm Thu-Sun), an open-air folk museum 40km south of Minsk (take bus 323 from Minsk's Central Bus Station; p67); and **Khatyn** (☑1774 55 787; www.khatyn.by; photo exhibit BYN1; ⊙complex 24hr, photo exhibit 10.30am-4pm Tue-Sun) **FREE**, a sobering memorial to a village wiped out by the Nazis 60km north of Minsk (accessible only by private transport). The latter can be combined with the **Stalin Line Museum** (http://stalin-line.by; Rt 28, Lashany; adult/student BYN14/7; ⊙10am-6pm), 25km northwest of Minsk in Lashany – a must for military buffs with all manner of Soviet war paraphernalia on display in an open field.

Nyasvizh   Нясвіж

This green and attractive town 120km southwest of Minsk is home to the splendid **Nyasvizh Castle** (☑1770 20 602; www.niasvizh.by/en; adult/student BYN16/8, audioguide BYN3, excursion BYN39; ⊙10am-7pm May-Sep, to 6pm Oct-Apr, closed last Wed of month). It was erected by the Radziwill family in 1583 but was rebuilt and restored often over the centuries and encompasses many styles. With more than 30 fully refurbished state rooms, a very impressive inner courtyard and clear-ly labelled displays, you can easily spend a couple of hours looking around. Access to the castle is via a causeway leading away from the parking lot, with lovely lakes on either side.

From Minsk's Central Bus Station, there are five daily buses to and from Nyasvizh (BYN8, two hours). The last trip back to Minsk is around 6pm. There's a 2.30pm bus to Hrodna (BYN16, six hours) via Mir (BYN2, 45 minutes).

Mir   Мір

The charming small town of Mir, 85km southwest of Minsk, is dominated by the impossibly romantic 16th-century **Mir Castle** (☑1596 28 270; www.mirzamak.by; adult/student BYN14/7, audioguide BYN3; ⊙museum 10am-6pm, 9am-7pm Fri-Sun Jun-Aug; courtyard 24hr), reflected magnificently in an adjoining pond. A recent renovation has the place looking simply lovely, with gorgeous grounds and impressively restored interiors that have been converted into a museum with beautifully done displays on the life and times of the Radziwills. Definitely splash out for the audioguide, which offers fascinating descriptions of more than 120 items.

From Minsk's Central Bus Station, buses to Mir's small **bus station** (pl 17 Sentyabrya), on the town square, depart roughly hourly (BYN7, 1½ hours). The last trip back to Minsk is around 4.15pm; buy a return ticket when you arrive to avoid getting stuck. There's also a daily bus to Nyasvizh around 5pm (BYN2, 45 minutes) and a daily bus to Hrodna around 3pm (BYN14, five hours).

BREST   БРЕСТ

☑162 / POP 300,000

This prosperous and cosmopolitan border town looks far more to the neighbouring EU than to Minsk. Brest and the city of Hrodna to the north can now be visited visa-free for 10 days if you are arriving overland from Poland, provided you secure the proper paperwork.

⊙ Sights

Most sights are in and around Brest Fortress (p70), which flanks the Bug and Mukhavets rivers just a whisper from the Polish border. It's about a 4km walk from central **vul Savetskaya**, a pleasant walking street lined with bars and restaurants.

VITSEBSK

The historic city of Vitsebsk (known universally outside Belarus by its Russian name, Vitebsk) lies a short distance from the Russian border and almost 300km from Minsk. It was an important centre of Jewish culture when it was one of the major cities of the 'Pale of Settlement', where Jews were allowed to live in the Russian Empire. The city was immortalised in the early work of Marc Chagall, the city's most famous son.

Today Vitsebsk is an agreeable regional centre with pedestrianised vul Suvorova at its heart, along with several fine churches and museums, including two dedicated to Chagall. First and foremost among these is the **Marc Chagall Art Center** (www.chagall. vitebsk.by; vul Putna 2; adult/student BYN2.50/1.50, tours in Russian BYN9; ⊙11am-7pm Tue-Sun Apr-Sep, Wed-Sun Oct-Mar), which has about 300 of Chagall's graphic works, less than one-quarter of which is on display at any given time. Across the town's river is the **Marc Chagall House Museum** (☑212 663 468; vul Pokrovskaya 11; adult/student BYN2.50/1.50; ⊙11am-7pm Tue-Sun Apr-Sep, Wed-Sun Oct-Mar), where the artist lived as a child from 1897 to 1910 – a period beautifully evoked in his autobiography, *My Life*.

The dining and drinking scene in Vitsebsk is concentrated in the Old Town on vul Talstoha near the base of pedestrianised vul Suvorova – just follow the music. It's worth trying to time your visit for **Slavyansky Bazaar** (Slavic Bazaar; www.festival.vitebsk.by; ⊙mid-Jul), a popular festival that takes place over 10 days in July and brings in dozens of singers and performers from Slavic countries for a week-long series of concerts.

One or two daily express trains (BYN8, 3¾ hours) and a handful of slower trains (from BYN8.60, four to nine hours) head to Minsk. The **train station** (vul Kasmanaŭtaŭ) is just over the main bridge on the west side of the Dvina River.

★**Museum of Railway Technology** MUSEUM

(pr Masherava 2; adult/student BYN2.50/2; ⊙10am-6pm Tue-Sun) The outdoor Museum of Railway Technology has a superb collection of locomotives and carriages dating from 1903 (eg the Moscow–Brest Express, with shower rooms and a very comfy main bedroom) to 1988 (far more proletarian Soviet passenger carriages).

St Nicholas Brotherly Church CHURCH

(cnr vul Savetskaya & vul Mitskevicha) With its gold cupolas and yellow-and-blue facades shining gaily in the sunshine, this finely detailed 200-year-old Orthodox church is one of several lovely churches in Brest.

⎣⁼⁼ Sleeping

★**Dream Hostel** HOSTEL €

(☑33 3610 315, 162 531 499; www.dreamhostel.by; Apt 5, vul Mayakoŭskaha 17/1; dm BYN20; ❋ 🛜) Brest's finest hostel is in an apartment building right in the middle of town. It's modern and bright, with self-contained bunks, a large TV room, a beautifully equipped kitchen and a laundry. Spot two adjacent archways on vul Mayakoŭskaha; go through the right archway and follow the footpath around to the right. The entry code is 5K; it's otherwise unsigned.

Hotel Bug HOTEL €€

(☑162 278 800; www.hotelbug.by; vul Lenina 2; s/d from BYN64/90; 🛜) An unfortunate name, but this 1950s hotel near the train station is great value. The functional rooms have hot water, desks, and working wi-fi. The vintage Soviet foyer, with utopian murals and white-marble statues of Lenin and others, is definitely a highlight. The staff do not speak English but are friendly.

Hermitage Hotel HOTEL €€€

(☑162 276 000; www.hermitagehotel.by; vul Chkalova 7; s/d incl breakfast from BYN215/260; 🅿❂❋🛜) This 55-room hotel is heads above the local competition and is priced accordingly. Housed in a sensitively designed modern building, it has more than a little old-world style, with spacious, grand and well-appointed rooms, as well as impressive public areas and a top-notch restaurant.

✖ Eating & Drinking

★**Jules Verne** INTERNATIONAL €€

(vul Hoholya 29; mains BYN10-25; ⊙5pm-1am Mon-Fri, from noon Sat & Sun; 🛜🍽) Decked out like a traditional gentlemen's club and with a travel theme, this dark, atmospheric joint manages to be refined without being stuffy. It serves up cracking dishes, from mouthwatering Indian curries and French

BREST FORTRESS

The city's main sight is the **Brest Fortress** (Brestskaya krepost; www.brest-fortress.by; pr Masherava) **FREE**, a moving WWII memorial where Soviet troops held out far longer than expected against the Nazi onslaught in the early days of Operation Barbarossa.

The fortress was built between 1833 and 1842, but by WWII it was being used mainly as a barracks. The two regiments bunking here when German troops launched a surprise attack in 1941 defended the fort for an astounding month and became venerated as national legends thanks to Stalin's propaganda machine.

Enter the Brest Fortress complex through a tunnel in the shape of a huge socialist star, then walk straight ahead several hundred metres to the fortress's most iconic site: **Courage**, a chiselled soldier's head projecting from a massive rock, flanked by a sky-scraping memorial obelisk.

There are several museums in and around the sprawling grounds, the most interesting of which are a pair museums that commemorate the siege and related events in WWII: the comprehensive **Defence of Brest Fortress Museum** (adult/student BYN5/2.50, audioguide BYN3; ⊘9am-6pm, closed Mon & last Tue of month) inside the fortresses' northern bastion; and the newer, more visual **Museum of War, Territory of Peace** (adult/student BYN5/2.50, audioguide BYN3; ⊘10am-7pm, closed Tue & last Wed of month) in the southern bastion.

specialities to sumptuous desserts and the best coffee in town. Don't miss it.

Fania Braverman's House
EASTERN EUROPEAN €€

(vul Savetskaya 53; mains BYN10-25; ❋☏) Who was Fania Braverman? We have no idea. But we know there is possibly no more pleasant place in Brest to spend an evening people-watching. Top-quality acoustic musicians play out on the terrace most evenings in the warm months. Order from the meat-heavy menu or just have a drink.

★ Korova
COCKTAIL BAR

(vul Savetskaya 73; ⊘noon-2am Sun-Thu, to 5am Fri & Sat) Just an average grill and bar along vul Savetskaya by day, Korova morphs at night into a superb lounge-club, with slick bartenders serving expertly made cocktails and craft beer, while an all-types, somewhat older crowd gets their groove on to talented DJs and live bands at weekends.

Paragraph Cafe
CAFE

(vul Savetskaya 30; ⊘8am-11pm Mon-Fri, from 10am Sat & Sun) This little space on Brest's main drag caters to writers and artists with strong coffee and a paint-splattered interior. Besides coffee it also has smoothies, shakes, lemonade and a few light bites, such as muesli for breakfast.

Coyote Club
LIVE MUSIC

(vul Dzyarzhynskaha 14; BYN10 after 11pm Fri & Sat; ⊘4pm-midnight Sun-Thu, to 3am Fri & Sat) Bartenders dancing on the bar and loud live music are the calling cards of this raucous bar. Terrific fun any night of the week, it really gets going on weekends, when the best bands play and shots flow.

🛍 Shopping

Knyaz Vitaŭt
CLOTHING

(vul Savetskaya 55; ⊘10am-9pm) Absolutely original clothing including wonderful T-shirts and embroidered traditional shirts and dresses. Also has handbags, leather goods and even socks and playing cards with national motifs.

ℹ Information

MEDICAL SERVICES

Vita Fari (vul Hoholya 32; ⊘24hr) Pharmacy open 24 hours.

City Emergency Hospital (☏103; vul Lenina 15)

TRAVEL AGENCIES

Contact travel agencies in advance to arrange paperwork for visa-free entry. They charge €10 to €15.

Brest City Tour (☏333 444 223; www.brestcitytour.by; vul Zubachova 25/1) This useful agency at Brest Fortress has English-speaking guides for BYN40 per hour and leads two-hour city tours in a brightly painted van (BYN10 to BYN12 per person, minimum five people).

ℹ Getting There & Away

From the **train station** (☏105), express business-class trains serve Minsk (from BYN12, 3¼ hours, three to four daily), while slower *pasazhirsky* (passenger) trains trundle to Minsk (from BYN7, 4½ hours to nine hours, frequent), Homel (from BYN 13, 9½ hours, two daily) and Vitsebsk (from BYN15, nine to 17 hours, three daily).

From the **bus station** (📋114; vul Mitskevicha), there are *marshrutky* (fixed-route minivans) to Hrodna (BYN13 to BYN17, 3½ to four hours, six daily), plus a slower bus or two.

Daily train 127 serves Warsaw (BYN35 to BYN55, two hours). Other trains to Warsaw are possible but are less regular and cost triple or quadruple. Ecolines (www.ecolines.net) buses to Warsaw (€18, 3½ hours, three daily), which originate in Minsk, are another option.

You'll need a proper Belarusian visa for international bus travel to Ukrainian destinations such as Lviv (BYN23, 7½ hours, two daily).

❶ Getting Around

For a taxi, try the 7220 ride-sharing app, or call 7220 or 5656.

Bike N' Roll (📋29 5051 286; vul Hoholya 32; bicycles per day BYN15; ⏱10am-7pm Mon-Fri, to 5pm Sat & Sun) Nice selection of mountain and city bikes available for hourly or daily rental.

Koleso (📋162 566 699; https://prokatkoles.by/en; pr Masherava 22) The best place to rent cars in town, with a good website and prices starting at €20 per day.

AROUND BREST

Belavezhskaya Pushcha National Park
Белавежская Пушча

Unesco World Heritage Site **Belavezhskaya Pushcha National Park** (📋1631 56 398; www.npbp.by; cost varies per activity; ⏱ticket office 9am-6pm) is the oldest wildlife refuge in Europe and the pride of Belarus. At least 55 mammal species call this park home, but the area is most celebrated for its 300 or so European bison, the continent's largest land mammal. You have a chance to spot these beasts in the wild on a tour of the park, although you have to be a bit lucky.

At the National Park headquarters in Kamyanyuki, 55km north of Brest, you can arrange to tour the park by bus tour (adult/child BYN10/6, three hours, 11am and 2pm, in Russian only) or by bicycle (BYN9 to BYN15), which can be hired at the park entrance. There are several sealed bike trails to choose from; the 27km 'big journey' and the

16km 'animal crossing' offer the best chance of spotting wildlife.

You can spend the night at one of several comfortable hotels in the **Kamyanyuki Hotel Complex** (📋1631 56 200; https://npbp.by/eng; s/d incl breakfast from BYN74/148; ❄🛜♨) near the park entrance. To get to the park from Brest, take a bus or *marshrutka* from the bus station (BYN5, 1¼ hours, seven daily).

HRODNA ГРОДНА

📋152 / POP 320,000

Hrodna is a laid-back, friendly city with plenty of intact pre-WW2 architecture and a host of good bars and cafes. You can visit the city overland from Poland or Lithuania without a visa – just play by the rules and do not wander outside the fairly limited confines of Hrodna district (*rayon*).

⊙ Sights

Hrodna's two main sights are right next to each other on the banks of the Neman River. While mostly in ruins, the **Old Castle** (vul Zamkavaya 20; grounds free, museum adult/student BYN6.20/4.90; ⏱10am-6pm Tue-Sun) does have one restored wing that houses the Hrodna History and Archaeology Museum, a comprehensive walk through the history of the Hrodna region. The rococo **New Castle** (vul Zamkavaya 20; admission BYN7, or per exhibit BYN3, audioguide BYN3; ⏱10am-6pm Tue-Sun), built in the 18th century by Polish-Lithuanian rulers to replace the Old Castle, is an eclectic art museum that features attractive 19th-centu-

❶ VISA-FREE TRAVEL TO BREST & HRODNA

You can travel to Brest and Hrodna visa-free for up to 10 days provided you have the proper paperwork (€8 to €15) secured in advance through a travel agency like Nemnovo Tour (p72) in Hrodna. The regimes for Brest and Hrodna are separate – you cannot travel between the two, and there are strict limits on which borders you can cross and where you can travel once over the border (ask your supporting travel agency). The law requires you to purchase a minimum of two travel services in advance from your supporting travel agency, but these can be as minor as a taxi reservation or museum entry.

BELARUS BELAVEZHSKAYA PUSHCHA NATIONAL PARK

ry oils and the brilliant *Man with a Shovel*, thought to be by Russian avant-garde master Kazimir Malevich.

🛏 Sleeping

★Hostel Sarmatiya HOSTEL €

(📞152 723 027; www.hostelgrodno.by; vul Karla Marksa 11; dm BYN25) This mid-sized hostel is a real find, with a perfect central location, an airy and attractive common room, and the best dorm beds in town complete with personal lights and charging stations. Features include lockers, laundry, six-bed female dorm, small kitchen, and bike rental (BYN3 per hour).

🍴 Eating & Drinking

★Nesterka VEGAN €

(vul Davyda Haradzenskaha; dishes BYN4-8; ⊙2pm-midnight, to 2am Fri & Sat; 🖋) 🌱 Hrodna's alternative kids head here for falafel sandwiches, craft beer and poetry slams – you get the idea. The dirt-cheap food satisfies the impoverished artists among the crowd. DJs or live bands occasionally play inside or in a separate space downstairs.

Nasha Kava COFFEE

(vul Zamkavaya 11; ⊙9am-11pm Mon-Thu, to 1am Fri & Sat; 🛜) The cool crowd gravitates to this cosy and contemporary coffee shop with huge mirrors, pendant lighting, lovely wood tables, a small patio out front and great specialty coffee. There are sweets to nibble on plus mulled wine and hot grog.

Faradey COCKTAIL BAR

(vul Satsiyalistychnaya 32; ⊙6pm-4am Sun-Thu, to 6am Fri & Sat) Marked by an eccentric design and strong cocktails, this self-described 'emotion lab' is the best all-around bar in town. You'll see plenty of good-looking faces here on weekends when the DJs fire it up and it morphs into an intimate club.

ℹ Information

Nemnovo Tour (📞152 742 943; www.nemno votour.by; vul Elizy Azheshka 38; ⊙9am-6pm Mon-Fri; 🛜) This super-friendly agency near the train station arranges visa-free travel to both Hrodna and Brest, and has useful hardcopy and online maps highlighting Hrodna's main attractions.

ℹ Getting There & Away

Trains to Minsk (from BYN10, 4¾ to eight hours, six daily) leave from the **train station** (vul Budzyonnaha 37). *Marshrutky* (fixed-route mini-

vans) from Hrodna's **central bus station** (📞152 752 292; vul Chyrvonarmeyskaya 7) do the trip faster (BYN7, three hours, hourly).

For Brest, you're best off with a *marshrutka* (BYN13 to BYN17, 3½ to four hours, six daily). There is an 11.35am bus to Nyasvizh (BR16, six hours) via Mir (BR14, five hours).

For Białystok in Poland via the Bruzgi–Kuźnica border (4½ hours) there are frequent minibuses (BYN15) and a daily Ecolines (www.ecolines. net) bus (€15, 1.40pm); the latter continues to Warsaw (€20, 7½ hours). There's also a daily late-afternoon train to Kraków (BYN52, seven hours) via Białystok (BYN18, two hours) and Warsaw (BYN38, 3½ hours).

About four buses per day serve Druskinikai in Lithuania via the Pryvalki border (BYN10, three hours).

ℹ Getting Around

Buses 14 and 3 link the train station and central pl Savetskaya, with the latter also passing by the bus station. To hail a taxi, download the 'Taxi 7220' app.

SURVIVAL GUIDE

ℹ Directory A–Z

INTERNET ACCESS

Wi-fi is ubiquitous at restaurants and hotels and is almost always free. Local SIM cards with data (4G) are easy to purchase. Data is cheap and fast and coverage is excellent, including on major highways.

LEGAL MATTERS

Police take quality-of-life infractions such as jaywalking or public alcohol consumption seriously. Should you be cited, police will issue a ticket for about BYN25 that you can pay in most banks.

MONEY

ATMs are the best way to obtain Belarusian roubles (BYN). Credit cards are widely used for payment in Minsk and other cities, but are unlikely to be accepted in rural areas.

OPENING HOURS

Banks 9am to 5pm Monday to Friday

Office hours 9am to 6pm Monday to Friday

Restaurants and bars 10am or noon to 10pm or midnight

Shops 9am or 10am to 9pm Monday to Saturday, to 6pm Sunday (if at all)

PUBLIC HOLIDAYS

New Year's Day 1 January

Orthodox Christmas 7 January

International Women's Day 8 March

Constitution Day 15 March

Catholic & Orthodox Easter March/April

Unity of Peoples of Russia and Belarus Day 2 April

International Labour Day (May Day) 1 May

Victory Day 9 May

Independence Day 3 July

Dzyady (Day of the Dead) 2 November

Catholic Christmas 25 December

TELEPHONE

There are four mobile-phone companies that can sell you a SIM-card package with oodles of data for next to nothing. Bring your passport, a Belarusian address and your unlocked phone. To place a call or send a text from a local mobile phone, dial either +375 or 80, plus the nine-digit number.

VISAS

Citizens of 74 countries can enter Belarus visa-free for up to 30 days as long as they arrive and depart from Minsk National Airport (p67). If arriving or departing by land, everybody needs a visa – unless going to either Brest or Hrodna, the two special visa-free zones. If arriving visa-free, you must purchase a Belarusian health insurance policy upon landing in Minsk to cover the length of your stay (about €1 per day). Your home policy may work if you can prove to authorities that it covers Belarus.

Registration

If you are staying in Belarus for more than five working days, you must register with the local authorities. Most hotels do this automatically, and it's included in the room price. If you are staying with an individual or with a hostel that does not handle registration, you or your host will have to register your visa at the main **AGIM** (Citizenship & Migration Department; ☑ 17 284 5923, 17 284 5960; vul Very Kharuzhay 3; ☉ 8am-5pm Tue & Fri, 11am-8pm Wed, 8am-1pm Thu & Sat; Ⓜ Ploshcha Jakuba Kolasa) office in Minsk, or at any regional AGIM office. The cost is BYN24. Do not lose your white registration slips – border officers may demand to see these when you leave the country.

❶ Getting There & Away

Minsk is the main hub for all domestic travel and is also surprisingly well connected by both air

---

❶ WARNING: TRANSITING THROUGH RUSSIA

Via Air Flying via Moscow when departing or arriving in Minsk will require a Russian transit visa; you will not be allowed to board your flight without one.

Via Land It is illegal for foreigners to enter or leave Belarus overland via Russia – even if you have valid Russian and Belarusian visas.

---

and land to Eastern and Western Europe, as well as, of course, most former Soviet countries.

AIR

All international flights to Belarus fly in and out of Minsk National Airport (p67). Belarus' national airline, **Belavia** (☑ 17 2202 555; www.belavia. by; vul Nyamiha 14, Minsk; ☉ 9am-8pm Mon-Sat, to 6pm Sun), has lots of flights to Moscow and former Soviet states, and it also serves a few Western European cities.

LAND

Car & Motorcycle

➡ You can drive your own car or motorcycle into Belarus via legal border crossings (see http://gpk.gov.by/en/maps for the list). Make sure your vehicle insurance and other documents are in order.

➡ Foreign-registered cars (not motorcycles) are subject to stiff tolls on major Belarusian highways. Study up on the system and pre-purchase your electronic payment device at http://beltoll.by/index.php/en.

❶ Getting Around

Trains are extremely cheap and plenty comfortable; buses are cheap but less comfortable. For train schedules and prices, see www.rw.by.

Air There are no domestic flights within Belarus.

Bus A bit cheaper than trains, but can be slower. Zippy *marshrutky* (public minivans), on the other hand, are less comfortable but generally faster than buses or trains.

Car Hiring a car is recommended for exploring around Minsk, with car-hire widely available.

Train Efficient and usually on time. Try the business-class express trains for quick hops between cities.

Bosnia & Hercegovina

POP 3.51 MILLION

Best Places to Eat

➡ Tima-Irma (p85)

➡ Avlija (p80)

➡ Rajska Vrata (p81)

➡ Željo (p80)

➡ Park Prinčeva (p80)

Best Places to Stay

➡ Isa-begov Hamam Hotel (p80)

➡ Pansion Čardak (p85)

➡ Halvat Guest House (p80)

➡ Hotel Aziza (p80)

➡ Hostel Polako (p88)

Why Go?

Craggily beautiful Bosnia and Hercegovina is most intriguing for its East-meets-West atmosphere born of blended Ottoman and Austro-Hungarian histories filtered through a Southern Slavic lens. Many still associate the country with the heartbreaking civil war of the 1990s, and the scars from that time are all too visible. But today's visitors are likely to remember the country for its deep, unassuming human warmth, its beautiful mountains, numerous medieval castle ruins, raftable rivers, impressive waterfalls and bargain-value skiing.

Major drawcards include the reincarnated historical centres of Sarajevo and Mostar, counterpointing splendid Turkish-era stone architecture with quirky bars, inviting street-terrace cafes, traditional barbecue restaurants and vibrant arts scenes. There's plenty of interest to discover in the largely rural hinterland too, all at prices that make the country one of Europe's best-value destinations.

When to Go
Sarajevo

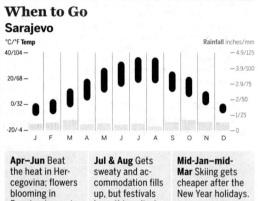

Apr–Jun Beat the heat in Hercegovina; flowers blooming in Bosnia; rivers at peak flows.

Jul & Aug Gets sweaty and accommodation fills up, but festivals keep things lively.

Mid-Jan–mid-Mar Skiing gets cheaper after the New Year holidays.

Entering the Country

Bosnia has four main international airports, although only Sarajevo has an extensive range of flights. Depending on where in the country you're heading to, it's often worth comparing prices on flights to Dubrovnik, Split or Zagreb in Croatia, then connecting to Bosnia by land. Belgrade (Serbia) and Podgorica (Montenegro) are also options.

Bosnia has multiple border crossings with Croatia, Serbia and Montenegro.

ITINERARIES

Four Days

Devote your first two days to exploring Sarajevo (p77). On day three, stop to admire the rebuilt Ottoman bridge in Konjic (p83) on your way to the even more famous rebuilt Ottoman bridge in Mostar (p82). The next day, stop in Blagaj (p86), the Kravica Waterfall (p86) and Počitelj (p87) en route to Trebinje (p87).

Seven Days

Spend your first day soaking up the sights of the Una River Valley (p88) and your second exploring the lakes, waterfall and historical old centre of Jajce (p89). The next day, take a leisurely trip to Sarajevo then continue with the four-day itinerary above.

Essential Food & Drink

Bosanska Kava Traditional Bosnian coffee, made and served in a *džezva* (small long-handled brass pot).

Burek Bosnian *burek* are cylindrical or spiral lengths of filo pastry usually filled with minced meat. *Sirnica* is filled with cheese, *krompiruša* with potato and *zeljanica* with spinach. Collectively these pies are called *pita*.

Ćevapi (Ćevapčići) Minced meat formed into cylindrical pellets and served in fresh bread with melting *kajmak*.

Hurmašice Syrup-soaked sponge fingers.

Kajmak Thick semi-soured cream.

Lokum Turkish delight.

Pljeskavica Patty-shaped *ćevapi*.

Rakija Grappa or fruit brandy.

Sarma Steamed dolma-parcels of rice and minced meat wrapped in cabbage or other green leaves.

Tufahija Whole stewed apple with walnut filling.

AT A GLANCE

Area 51,129 sq km

Capital Sarajevo

Country Code ☑387

Currency Convertible mark (KM, BAM)

Emergency Ambulance ☑124, Fire ☑123, Police ☑122

Languages Bosnian, Serbian and Croatian (all variants of the same language)

Money ATMs accepting Visa and MasterCard are ubiquitous

Time Central European Time (GMT/UTC plus one hour)

Visas Not required for most visitors (see www.mvp.gov.ba)

Sleeping Price Ranges

The following price ranges refer to a double room with bathroom during high season.

€ less than 80KM

€€ 80KM–190KM

€€€ more than 190KM

Eating Price Ranges

The following price ranges refer to a main course.

€ less than 10KM

€€ 10KM–20KM

€€€ more than 20KM

Bosnia & Hercegovina Highlights

1 **Sarajevo** (p77) Padding around Baščaršija's fascinating Turkic-era alleyways and downing heart-stopping Bosnian coffee and the nation's best *burek* and *ćevapi*.

2 **Mostar** (p82) Gawping as young men throw themselves off the magnificently rebuilt stone bridge at the centre of the city's old Ottoman quarter.

3 **Jajce** (p89) Watching the waterfall tumble photogenically past castle-crowned Old Town.

4 **Trebinje** (p87) Enjoying this fetching regional centre's low-key pace, with its walled riverside Old Town and leafy squares and parks.

5 **Kravica Waterfall** (p86) Cooling off in the turquoise waters beneath the fantastical falls.

6 **Počitelj** (p87) Soaking up the atmosphere of a tiny, picture-perfect Ottoman hillside town.

SARAJEVO

📞 033 / POP 395.000

Ringed by mountains, Sarajevo is a singular city with a enticing East-meets-West vibe all of its own. It was once renowned as a religious melting pot, earning it the epithet 'the Jerusalem of Europe'. Within a few blocks you can still find large Catholic and Orthodox cathedrals, Ashkenazi and Sephardic synagogues, and numerous mosques. However, the Jewish population was decimated during WWII and Sarajevo is now a divided city, with most of the Orthodox Christians living in Istočno Sarajevo (East Sarajevo) on the Republika Srpska side.

During the 20th century, two violent events thrust Sarajevo into the world's consciousness: the assassination which sparked WWI, and the brutal almost-four-year siege of the city in the 1990s. The scars of the longest siege in modern European history are still painfully visible, yet Sarajevo is once again a wonderful place to visit – for its intriguing architectural medley, vibrant street life and irrepressible spirit.

◎ Sights

◉ Baščaršija

Centred on what foreigners call Pigeon Square, Baščaršija (pronounced barsh-*char*-shi-ya) is the very heart of old Sarajevo. The name is derived from the Turkish for 'main market' and it's still lined with stalls, a lively (if tourist-centric) coppersmiths' alley, grand Ottoman mosques, *caravanserai* (inn) restaurants and lots of inviting little cafes. The east-west lane, Sarači, broadens out into the wide pedestrian boulevard Ferhadija, where Austro-Hungarian–era buildings take over. Some particularly grand examples line the waterfront.

⭐ **Sarajevo City Hall**   ARCHITECTURE

(Gradska vijećnica Sarajeva; Obala Kulina bana bb, Baščaršija; adult/child 10/5KM; ⊙9am-6pm) A storybook neo-Moorish striped facade makes the triangular Vijećnica (1896) Sarajevo's most beautiful Austro-Hungarian–era building. Seriously damaged during the 1990s siege, it finally reopened in 2014 after laborious reconstruction. Its colourfully restored interior and stained-glass ceiling are superb. Your ticket also allows you to peruse the excellent *Sarajevo 1914–2014* exhibition in the octagonal basement. This gives well-explained potted histories of the city's various 20th-century periods, insights into fashion and music subcultures, and revelations about Franz Ferdinand's love life.

⭐ **Galerija 11/07/95**   MUSEUM

(📞 033-953 170; www.galerija110795.ba; 3rd fl, Trg Fra Grge Martića 2, Baščaršija; admission/audioguide/tour 12/3/4KM; ⊙9am-10pm, guided tours 10.15am & 7.15pm) This gallery uses stirring photography, video footage and audio testimonies of survivors and family members to create a powerful memorial to the 8372 victims of the Srebrenica massacre, one of the most infamous events of the Bosnian civil war. You'll need well over an hour to make the most of a visit, and it's worth paying the extra for the audioguide to get more insight.

Museum of Crimes Against Humanity & Genocide 1992–1995   MUSEUM

(Muzej zločina protiv čovječnosti i genocida; 📞 062 467 764; Muvekita 11, Baščaršija; adult/child 10/8KM; ⊙9am-10pm Apr-Oct, to 6pm Nov-Mar) Nothing is sugar-coated in this confronting museum covering the many atrocities that took place throughout Bosnia during the 1990s war. Video footage combined with photographs, artefacts and personal testimonies illustrates the horror and brutality of the times. We wouldn't recommend bringing younger children.

Gazi Husrev-beg Mosque   MOSQUE

(Gazi Husrev-begova džamija; 📞 033-573 151; www.begovadzamija.ba; Sarači 18, Baščaršija; mosque 3KM, incl museum 5KM; ⊙9am-noon, 2.30-4pm & 5.30-7pm May-Sep, 9am-11am Oct-Apr) Bosnia's second Ottoman governor, Gazi Husrev-beg, funded a series of splendid 16th-century buildings of which this 1531 mosque, with its 45m minaret, is the greatest. The domed interior is beautifully proportioned and even if you can't look inside, it's worth walking through the courtyard with its lovely fountain, chestnut trees and the *turbe* (tomb) of its founder.

◉ Other Areas

⭐ **Sarajevo Cable Car**   CABLE CAR

(Sarajevska žičara; 📞 033-292 800; www.zicara.ba; off Franjevačka, Babića bašča; single/return 15/20KM; ⊙10am-8pm) Reopened in 2018 after being destroyed during the war, Sarajevo's cable car once again shuttles people on a nine-minute ride, climbing 500m to a viewpoint 1164m up on Mt Trebević. From here

Central Sarajevo

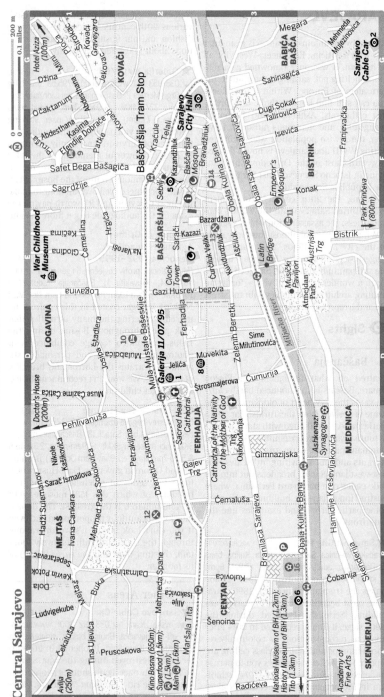

200 m
0.1 miles

G

Hotel Aziza (100m)
Šoroke
Ploča
Kovači
Graveyard
Jekovac
Džina
KOVAČI
Megara
BABIĆA BAŠČA
Mehmeda Mujezinovića
Sarajevo Cable Car 2
Očaktanum
Abdesthana
Kasima Efendije Dobrače
Patke
Kovač
Bečar
Baščaršija Tram Stop
Sarajevo City Hall 3
Šahinagića
Dugi Sokak
Talirovića
Isevića
BISTRIK
Safet Bega Bašagiča
Sagrdžije
Kračule
Telali
Kazandžiluk
Baščaršija Mosque
Bravadžiluk
14
Obala Kulina Bana
Emperor's Mosque
Franjevačka
Sebilj 5
8
Konak
Obala Isa-bega Isakovića
Park Prinčeva (800m)
War Childhood Museum 4
Kečina
Glodina
Čemerlina
Hrgića
Na Varoši
BAŠČARŠIJA
Saráči
Kazazi
Bazardžani
Kazandžiluk 13
Ašćiluk
Curčiluk Veliki
Kundurdžiluk
Latin Bridge
11
Bistrik
Austrijski Trg
LOGAVINA
Logavina
Josipa Štadlera
Mulabdića
10
Galerija 11/07/95 1
Jelića
Muše Čazime Čatića
Mula Mustafe Bašeskije
Clock Tower
Gazi Husrev- begova
Ferhadija
Muvekita
Zelenih Beretki
7
Sime Milutinovića
Čumurija
Miljacka River
Musički Pavilion
Atmejdan Park
Pehlivanuša
Petrakijina
Dženetića čikma
Sacred Heart Cathedral
FERHADIJA
Strosmajerova
8
Gajev Trg
Cathedral of the Nativity of the Mother of God
Trg Oslobođenja
Gimnazijska
MJEDENICA
Ashkenazi Synagogue
Doctor's House (200m)
MEJTAŠ
Hadži Sulejman
Nikole Kašiković
Sarač Ismailova
Ivana Cankara
Mehmeda Paše Sokolovića
Dalmatinska
Čemaluša
Branilaca Sarajeva
Obala Kulina Bana
16
Hamidije Kreševljakovića
Čobanija
Skenderija
Kevrin Potok
Šepetarevac
Buka
12
15
Kulovića
CENTAR
P
B
Kino Bosna (650m);
Superfood (1.5km);
(1.5km);
Main (1.6km)
Dola
Čekaluša
Ludvigekube
Tina Ujevića
Pruscakova
Alije Isaković
Maršala Tita
Mehmeda Spahe
Šenoina
National Museum of BiH (1.2km);
History Museum of BiH (1.3km);
Tito (1.3km)
Radićeva
6
SKENDERIJA
Academy of Fine Arts

Avlija (250m)

1   2   3   4

A   B   C   D   E   F   G

Central Sarajevo

it's a short walk to the wreck of the Olympic bobsled track, seemingly held together by layers of graffiti.

★ **War Childhood Museum** MUSEUM
(Muzej ratnog djetinjstva; ☑ 033-535 558; www.warchildhood.org; Logavina 32, Logavina; adult/child 10/5KM; ☉11am-7pm) This affecting museum had its genesis in a 2013 book edited by Jasminko Halilović, in which he asked a simple question of survivors of the Sarajevo siege: 'What was a war childhood for you?' Of the hundreds of replies received, 50 short written testimonies are presented here, each illustrated by personal effects donated by the writer, such as diaries, drawings, toys and ballet slippers. It's a lighter, less gore-filled approach to the conflict than you'll find elsewhere, but equally devastating.

National Museum of BiH MUSEUM
(Zemaljski muzej BiH; www.zemaljskimuzej.ba; Zmaja od Bosne 3, Marijin dvor; adult/child 6/3KM; ☉10am-7pm Tue-Fri, to 2pm Sat & Sun) Bosnia's biggest and best-endowed museum of ancient and natural history is housed in an impressive, purpose-built quadrangle of neoclassical 1913 buildings. It's best known for housing the priceless Sarajevo Haggadah

illuminated manuscript, but there's much more to see. Along with the Haggadah, the main building houses extraordinary Greek pottery and Roman mosaics. Behind this, the central courtyard has a pretty little botanical garden and an exceptional collection of medieval *stećci* (stone funerary monuments).

History Museum of BiH MUSEUM
(☑ 033-226 098; www.muzej.ba; Zmaja od Bosne 5, Novo Sarajevo; adult/child 5/2KM; ☉9am-7pm) Somewhat misleadingly named, this small yet engrossing museum occupies a striking, still partly war-damaged 1960s socialist-modernist building originally dubbed the Museum of the Revolution. It regularly hosts high-profile international exhibitions but the main attraction is the permanent *Surrounded Sarajevo* display, which charts local people's life-and-death battles for survival between 1992 and 1995. Alongside some heartbreaking photographs are personal effects such as self-made lamps, examples of food aid, stacks of Monopoly-style 1990s dinars and a makeshift siege-time 'home'.

Also interesting is the collection of 1996–2011 before-and-after Sarajevo images in the hallway. Directly behind the building, the tongue-in-cheek Tito (Zmaja od Bosne 5, Novo Sarajevo; ☉7am-11pm) bar is a museum in its own right.

Tunnel of Hope MUSEUM
(Tunel Spasa; ☑ 033-778 672; www.tunelspasa.ba; Tuneli 1, Ilidža; adult/child 10/5KM; ☉9am-4pm) During the 1992–95 siege, when Sarajevo was surrounded by Bosnian Serb forces, the only link to the outside world was an 800m-long, 1m-wide, 1.6m-high tunnel between two houses on opposite sides of the airport runway. Walking through a 25m section is the moving culmination of a visit to the shell-pounded house which hid the western tunnel entrance. The story of the siege and the tunnel's construction is told via video, information boards and an audioguide accessible via free wi-fi.

🛏 Sleeping

Doctor's House HOSTEL €
(☑ 061 222 914; www.thedoctorshousehostel.com; Pehlivanuša 67, Bjelave; dm/d from 24/70KM; 🖥) The Doctor's House is a healthy choice, if only for the workout you'll get walking up the hill from the centre of town. It's a nice neighbourhood; the French ambassador lives next door. The dorms all have privacy

curtains, reading lights, power points and lockers, and there are also a couple of tidy private rooms.

★ Halvat Guest House GUESTHOUSE €€

(☎033-237 715; www.halvat.com.ba; Kasima Efendije Dobrače 13, Kovači; s/d/tr 80/113/132KM; P❄️📶) The six rooms at this friendly, family-run guesthouse are clean and spacious, and surprisingly quiet for such a central location. Breakfast is available at an additional charge – but with Baščaršija (p77) just down the road, you might choose to skip it. Only the narrowest of vehicles and drivers should brave the secure garage (charged separately).

Hotel VIP HOTEL €€

(☎033-535 533; www.hotelvip.info; Jaroslava Černija 3, Baščaršija; s/d 138/177KM; P❄️📶) Tucked away on a quiet lane in the centre of town, this smart modern block only has a dozen rooms but the ambience, professional service, valet parking and well-provisioned breakfast buffet might have you think you're staying somewhere far ritzier. The bathrooms are excellent, and some rooms have balconies.

★ Isa-begov Hamam Hotel HERITAGE HOTEL €€€

(☎033-570 050; www.isabegovhotel.com; Bistrik 1, Bistrik; s/d from €80/100; ❄️) After many years of restoration this ornate 19th-century *hammam* (Turkish bath), founded in 1462, reopened with a hotel attached in 2015. The 15 rooms are designed to evoke the spirit of the age, with lashings of handcrafted dark-wood furniture, ornately carved bedsteads and tube-glass chandeliers. Guests get free use of the *hammam,* which is also open to the general public.

Hotel Aziza HOTEL €€€

(☎033-257 940; www.hotelaziza.ba; Saburina 2, Vratnik; r/ste 196/235KM; P❄️📶) Not just an extremely comfortable and friendly family-run hotel, this place invites you to enter into the love story of its owners, Mehmed and Aziza Poričanin. The 17 spacious, light-filled rooms are numbered according to significant years in the couple's life, such as the births of children and grandchildren. A daily sauna is included in the rates.

Eating

★ Željo BALKAN €

(☎033-447 000; Kundurdžiluk 19 & 20, Baščaršija; mains 3.5-7KM; ☺8am-10pm; 📶) Locals are willing to brave the tourist throngs at Željo as it's quite possibly the best place for *ćevapi* (spicy beef or pork meatballs) in Sarajevo. There are two branches diagonally across from each other. Both have street seating; neither serves alcohol.

★ Avlija EUROPEAN €€

(☎033-444 483; www.avlija.ba; Sumbula Avde 2, Višnjik; mains 7-15KM; ☺8am-11pm Mon-Sat; 📶) Locals and a few in-the-know expats cosy up at painted wooden benches in this colourful, buzzing covered yard, dangling with trailing pot plants, strings of peppers and the odd birdcage. Local specialities are served, along with pasta, risotto and schnitzel. Wash them down with inexpensive local draught beers and wines.

Superfood INTERNATIONAL €€

(www.facebook.com/SuperfoodStrEatArt; Husrefa Redžića 14, Ciglane; mains 5-27KM; ☺11am-11pm Tue-Sat, noon-8pm Sun; 📶) Tucked away among a set of much-graffitied apartment blocks, this hip cafe/restaurant wouldn't be out of place on the back streets of Auckland or Melbourne. It's a great place for brunch or a lunchtime sandwich, and they're particularly proud of their gourmet hamburgers here. Most of the ingredients are local, organic and free range.

Cakum Pakum EUROPEAN €€

(☎061 955 310; Kaptol 10, Centar; mains 7-26KM; ☺11am-11pm) A collection of antique suitcases, fringed lamps, gingham curtains and bright tartan tablecloths set the scene at this hip, wee restaurant with only half a dozen small tables. The food is simple but delicious – think savoury pancakes, salads, a large range of pasta and a small selection of grills.

Park Prinčeva BALKAN €€€

(☎061 222 708; www.parkprinceva.ba; Iza Hrida 7, Hrid; mains 14-30KM; ☺9am-11pm; P❄️) Gaze out over a superb city panorama from this hillside perch, like Bono and Bill Clinton before you. From the open-sided terrace, the City Hall (p77) is beautifully framed between rooftops, mosques and twinkling lights. Charming waiters in bow ties and red waistcoats deliver traditional dishes such as dumplings with cheese, veal *ispod sača* (roasted under a metal dome) and skewers.

⬤ Drinking & Entertainment

★ Zlatna Ribica BAR

(☎033-836 348; Kaptol 5, Centar; ☺8am-late) Sedate and outwardly grand, the tiny and

OLYMPIC SKIING

Bjelašnica

The modest ski resort of **Bjelašnica** (www.bjelasnica.org; Babin Do bb; ski pass day/night 35/25KM, lift from 10KM in summer; ☒8am-4pm & 6.30-9pm ski season, 10am-5pm May-Oct), around 25km south of Sarajevo, hosted the men's alpine events during the 1984 Winter Olympics. There's usually enough snow to ski from around Christmas, and New Year is the busiest time, though February is more reliable for good piste conditions. Floodlit night skiing is offered and the main lift also operates May to October, allowing walkers easy access to high-altitude paths. In summer, there are magical mountain villages to explore.

Jahorina

Of Sarajevo's two Olympic skiing resorts, multi-piste **Jahorina** (☒057-270 020; www. oc-jahorina.com; Olimpijska bb, Jahorina; ski pass per day 44-50KM, night 30-38KM, day & night 61-73KM; ☒Nov-Mar) (26km southeast of the city, on the Republika Srpska side) has the widest range of hotels, each within 300m of one of seven main ski lifts. There are still lots of bombed-out buildings to be seen, but reconstruction is continuing apace. The ski season usually starts in mid-November and continues through to late March. The resort is at its busiest during the New Year holidays.

Beside the longest slope, **Rajska Vrata** (☒057-272 020; www.jahorina-rajskavrata. com; Olimpijska 41, Jahorina; mains 8-20KM; ☒9am-10pm Dec-Mar, to 5pm Apr-Nov; ⓟ🖤) is a charming ski-in alpine chalet restaurant that sets diners beside a central fire with a giant metallic chimney or on the piste-side terrace. Upstairs, six Goldilocks-esque pine-walled guest bedrooms have handmade beds fashioned from gnarled old branches.

eccentric 'Golden Fish' adds understated humour to a cosy treasure trove of antiques and kitsch, reflected in big art nouveau mirrors. Drink menus are hidden in old books that dangle by phone cords and the toilet is an experience in itself. Music swerves unpredictably between jazz, Parisian crooners, opera, reggae and the Muppets.

Art Kuća Sevdaha   CAFE
(Halači 5, Baščaršija; ☒10am-6pm Tue-Sun; 🖤) Sit in the intimate fountain courtyard of an Ottoman-era building sipping Bosnian coffee, juniper or rose sherbet, or herb-tea infusions while nibbling local sweets. The experience is accompanied by the lilting wails of *sevdah* (traditional Bosnian music) – usually recorded, but sometimes live. Within the building is a museum celebrating great 20th-century *sevdah* performers (5KM) along with a store selling CDs.

Kino Bosna   ARTS CENTRE
(Kinoteka BiH; www.facebook.com/kinobosna; Alipašina 19, Koševo; ☒hours vary) This historical cinema overflows on Mondays during smoky singalongs to the house band playing Bosnian *sevdah* songs. Yugo-nostalgics pack in for New Wave nights and other themed parties. The building, originally industrial,

was adapted into a workers' club, then a theatre from the 1940s. It houses the national film archive.

National Theatre Sarajevo   PERFORMING ARTS
(Narodno pozorište Sarajevo; ☒033-221 682; www. nps.ba; Obala Kulina bana 9, Centar) Classically adorned with fiddly gilt mouldings, this proscenium-arch theatre hosts a ballet, opera, play or classical concert most nights from mid-September to mid-June. The grand, column-fronted, Renaissance-style building dates from 1921, adapted from its 1899 original form.

ℹ️ Information

Sarajevo University Clinical Centre (Klinički centar univerziteta u Sarajevu; ☒033-445 522, 033-297 000; www.kcus.ba; Bolnička 25) Within the vast Koševo Hospital complex there's an English-speaking VIP outpatient clinic for people with foreign health insurance. The hospital also offers emergency care, including an emergency paediatrics department.

Tourist Information Centre (Turistički informativni centar; ☒033-580 999; www. sarajevo-tourism.com; Sarači 58, Baščaršija; ☒9am-9pm May-Oct, to 5pm Nov-Apr) Helpful official information centre. Beware of commercial imitations.

ℹ Getting There & Away

AIR

The centrally located **Sarajevo International Airport** (SJJ; www.sarajevo-airport.ba; Kurta Schorka 36; ☺5am-11pm) is about 10km southwest of Baščaršija (p80).

BUS

➜ Sarajevo's main **bus station** (☑033-213 100; Put života 8, Novo Sarajevo; ☺24hr) has daily services to all neighbouring countries and to as far afield as Amsterdam and Istanbul. There are good links to Bosnian destinations including Mostar (20KM, 2½ hours, 10 daily) and Bihać (42KM, 6½ hours, four daily).

➜ Further services to Republika Srpska (RS) and Serbia leave from the **Istočno Sarajevo Bus Station** (☑057-317 377; www.centrotrans-ad.com; Srpskih vladara 2, Lukavica; ☺6am-11.15pm), although this isn't convenient for most travellers.

TRAIN

Trains departing Sarajevo's **railway station** (Željeznička stanica; ☑033-655 330; www.zfbh.ba; Trg žrtava genocida u Srebrenici, Novo Sarajevo; ☺ticket office 6.30am-8pm), adjacent to the bus station (p82), head to destinations including Konjic (7.90KM, one hour, three daily), Mostar (18KM, two hours, two daily) and Bihać (37KM, 6¼ hours, daily).

ℹ Getting Around

TO/FROM THE AIRPORT

➜ On the meter, airport-bound taxis charge around 7KM from Ilidža or 16KM from Baščaršija, plus 2KM per bag for luggage in some cabs. However, at the terminal it's not always easy to find a taxi prepared to use the meter.

➜ A Centrotrans bus marked Aerodrom-Baščaršija (5KM, pay on-board) departs from outside the terminal and takes around 30 minutes to central Sarajevo. However, departures are (at most) once an hour. Buses follow the main tram route, heading east along the river via Obala Kulina bana and then looping back to the airport along Mula Mustafe Bašeskije, stopping on demand at all the main stops along the way.

PUBLIC TRANSPORT

Sarajevo has an extensive network of trams, buses, trolleybuses and minibuses, all operated by **GRAS** (☑033-293 333; www.gras.ba). Except for the airport bus (p82), all single-ride tickets cost 1.60KM if pre-purchased from kiosks, or 1.80KM if bought from the driver; they must be stamped once aboard. Two-ride (3KM), five-ride (7.10KM) and day tickets (*dnevna karta*, 5.30KM)

are also available, but these are sold at official GRAS kiosks, which are few and far between.

HERCEGOVINA

Hercegovina ('hair-tse-go-*vi*-na') is the sun-scorched southern part of the country, shadowing Croatia's Dalmatian coast. It takes its name from 15th-century duke (*herceg* in the local lingo) Stjepan Vukčić Kosača, under whose rule it became a semi-independent duchy of the Kingdom of Bosnia.

Its arid Mediterranean landscape has a distinctive beauty punctuated by barren mountain ridges and photogenic river valleys. Famed for its fine wines and sun-packed fruits, Hercegovina is sparsely populated but has some intriguing historical towns and even has one little toehold on the Adriatic coast.

These days Western Hercegovina is dominated by Bosnian Croats while Eastern Hercegovina is part of the Republika Srpska. Bosniak Muslims maintain an uneasy position between the two, especially in the divided but fascinating city of Mostar. Not counting the Catholic pilgrims who flood Međugorje, Mostar is far and away Hercegovina's biggest tourist drawcard. Trebinje is lesser known but has an appealing old core.

Mostar

☑036 / POP 105,800

Mostar is the largest city in Hercegovina, with a small but thoroughly enchanting old town centre. At dusk, the lights of numerous millhouse restaurants twinkle across gushing streams, narrow **Kujundžiluk** bustles joyously with trinket sellers and, in between, the Balkans' most celebrated bridge forms a majestic stone arc between medieval towers.

Stay into the evening to see it without the summer hordes of day trippers. Stay even longer to enjoy memorable attractions in the surrounding area and to ponder the city's darker side – beyond the cobbled lanes of the attractively restored Ottoman quarter are whole blocks of bombed-out buildings, a poignant legacy of the 1990s conflict.

Between November and April most tourist facilities go into hibernation, while summer here is scorchingly hot. Spring and autumn are ideal times to visit.

KONJIC

Resting alongside the icy green Neretva River, the small town of Konjic was battered in both WWII and the 1990s war, but has revived its compact historical core centred on a beautiful six-span **Old Stone Bridge** (Stara kamena ćuprija; Konjic). Originally built in 1682, it was dynamited at the end of WWII by retreating Nazi forces but accurately reconstructed in 2009 on its original footings.

The area is also home to **D-O ARK** (Tito's Bunker; ☑036-734 811; www.titosbunker.ba; per person 20KM; ⊙ tours 10am, noon & 2pm), one of the most extraordinary remnants of the Cold War, designed to keep Yugoslav president Tito and his high command safe from a 25-megaton blast. Built in secret between 1953 and 1979, this extensive subterranean command centre is reputed to have cost the equivalent of US$4 billion. It's located 4km southeast of Konjic; follow the signs.

There's also good hiking in the surrounding mountains and rafting downstream on the Neretva. **RaftKor** (☑061 474 507; www.raft-kor.com; Varda 40/1; per person €35) is a reliable outfit that starts its tours with a visit to Boračko Lake. Rafting and canyoning trips can also be booked through **Visit Konjic** (☑061 072 027; www.visitkonjic.com; Donje polje bb; ⊙8am-8pm).

Numerous buses, including all Sarajevo–Mostar services, pass through Konjic. Three trains a day head north to Sarajevo (7.90KM, one hour) and south to Mostar (11KM, 50 minutes).

⊙ Sights

★ Stari Most
BRIDGE

The world-famous Stari Most (meaning simply 'Old Bridge') is Mostar's indisputable visual focus. Its pale stone magnificently reflects the golden glow of sunset or the tasteful night-time floodlighting. The bridge's swooping arch was originally built between 1557 and 1566 on the orders of Suleiman the Magnificent. The current structure is a very convincing 21st-century rebuild following the bridge's 1990s bombardment during the civil war. Numerous well-positioned cafes and restaurants tempt you to sit and savour the splendidly restored scene.

Partisan Memorial Cemetery
MEMORIAL

(Partizansko spomen-groblje; Kralja Petra Krešimira IV bb) Although sadly neglected and badly vandalised, fans of 20th-century socialist architecture should seek out this magnificent memorial complex, designed by leading Yugoslav-era architect Bogdan Bogdanović and completed in 1965. Paths wind up past a broken bridge, a no-longer-functioning water feature and cosmological symbols to an almost Gaudi-esque upper section made of curved and fluted concrete, which contains the graves of 810 Mostar Partisans who died fighting fascism during WWII.

Kajtaz House
MUSEUM

(Kajtazova kuća; ☑061 339 897; www.facebook. com/KajtazsHouse; Gaše Ilića 21; adult/child 4KM/ free; ⊙9am-6pm Apr-Oct) Hidden behind tall walls, Mostar's most interesting old house was once the harem (women's) section of a larger homestead built for a 16th-century Turkish judge. Full of original artefacts, it still belongs to descendants of the original family but is now under Unesco protection. A visit includes a very extensive personal tour.

Hamam Museum
MUSEUM

(☑036-580 200; www.facebook.com/thehamam museum; Rade Bitange bb; adult/child 4/3KM; ⊙10am-6pm) This late 16th-century bathhouse has been attractively restored with whitewashed interiors, bilingual panels explaining *hammam* (Turkish bath) culture and glass cabinets displaying associated traditional accoutrements. A wordless five-minute video gives a slickly sensual evocation of an imagined latter-day bathhouse experience.

War Photo Exhibition
GALLERY

(Stari Most; admission 6KM; ⊙9am-9pm Jul-Sep, 10am-6pm Mar-Jun & Oct) This collection of around 50 powerful wartime photos by New Zealand photojournalist Wade Goddard is displayed in the western tower guarding Stari Most, above the Bridge Divers' Club.

Bridge Divers' Club
ADVENTURE SPORTS

(☑061 388 552; Stari Most; training/membership €10/25; ⊙10am-dusk) In summer, young men leap from the parapet of Stari Most in a

Mostar

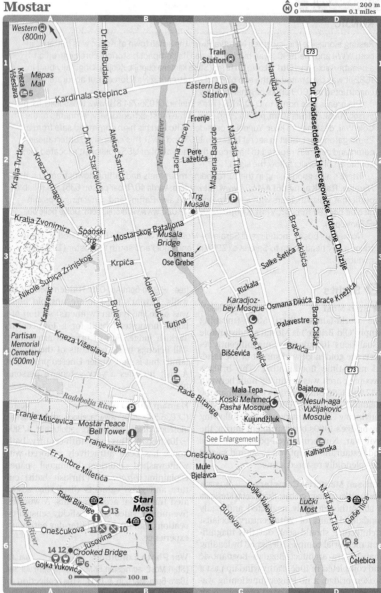

tradition dating back centuries, plummeting more than 20m into the freezing cold Neretva. It's a hilarious spectacle, involving much stretching, preening and posing in speedos and cajoling the crowd for donations. Divers won't leap until 50KM has been collected (in winter it's double).

If you want to experience one of Bosnia's ultimate adrenaline rushes for yourself, you'll first need to pay for training dives from a much lower perch at the riverside downstream. If you prove capable you can then join the club and test your mettle with the real thing. You'll get a certificate to prove

Mostar

your achievement. Don't underestimate the dangers – diving badly can prove fatal. But if you love it, your life membership means you can subsequently dive as often as you like.

🛏 Sleeping

Taso's House HOSTEL €
(📞061 523 149; www.guesthousetaso.com; Maršala Tita 187; dm/r from €8/20; ❄🖧) There's nothing flash about this cramped little hostel, but backpackers love it for its chilled-out vibe and the friendliness of the family who runs it. There's only one private twin room and three dorms, one of which is in an annex nearby.

★Pansion Čardak GUESTHOUSE €€
(📞036-578 249; www.pansion-cardak.com; Jusovina 3; r from €60; P❄🖧) This old stone house on a central lane has been thoroughly modernised and now offers seven spacious en-suite rooms with feature walls emblazoned with forest scenes. There's also a small guest kitchen.

Villa Fortuna HOTEL €€
(📞036-580 625; www.villafortuna.ba; Rade Bitange 34; s/d 68/95KM; P❄🖧) Set back from a street leading to the old bridge, this

eight-room family-run hotel offers welcome drinks in a sweet little private courtyard area at the rear. Fresh if compact rooms lead off a hallway decorated with a museum-like collection of local tools and metalwork.

Shangri La GUESTHOUSE €€
(📞061 169 362; www.shangrila.com.ba; Kalhanska 10; r €53-69; P❄🖧) Behind an imposing 1887 facade, eight individually themed rooms are presented to hotel standards, and there's a fine roof terrace with comfy parasol-shaded seating, dwarf citrus trees and panoramic city views. The English-speaking hosts are faultlessly welcoming without being intrusive. Breakfast costs €6 extra. The location is wonderfully peaceful, just three minutes' walk from Stari Most (p83) up a narrow lane.

Hotel Mepas HOTEL €€€
(📞036-382 000; www.mepas-hotel.ba; Kneza Višeslava bb; s/d from 167/203KM; P❄🖧▨) Mostar's first five-star hotel inhabits a corner of the large Mepas Mall complex. The bright, glitzy reception is on the ground floor, but rooms, pool and spa centre are all on the 8th and 9th floors.

🍴 Eating

★Tima-Irma BALKAN €
(📞066 905 070; www.cevabdzinica-tima.com; Onešćukova bb; mains 5-11KM; ⊙8am-11pm; 🖧) Despite the constant queues at this insanely popular little grill joint, the staff maintain an impressive equanimity while delivering groaning platters of ćevapi (skinless sausage), pljeskavica (burger meat) and shish kebabs. Unusually for this kind of eatery, most dishes are served with salad. Sandwiches and burgers are also on offer.

Šadrvan BALKAN €€
(📞061 891 189; www.facebook.com/SadrvanMostar; Jusovina 11; mains 3.60-20KM; ⊙9am-midnight; 🖧) On a vine- and tree-shaded corner where the pedestrian lane from Stari Most (p83) divides, this tourist favourite has tables set around a trickling fountain made of old Turkish-style metalwork. Obliging, costumed waiters can help explain a menu that covers many bases and takes a stab at some vegetarian options.

🍸 Drinking & Nightlife

Black Dog Pub PUB
(www.facebook.com/Blackdogpubmostar; Jusovina 5; ⊙4pm-midnight) This Black Dog really starts to howl on summer nights, when

BOSNIA & HERCEGOVINA MOSTAR

musicians set up on the cobbles facing the Crooked Bridge and everyone lounges around on cushions. Inside, the historical millhouse is decked out with flags and car number plates. Grab a seat on the riverside terrace and sip on some local craft beer.

Ima i Može Craft Beer Garden　　CRAFT BEER
(☑061 799 398; www.facebook.com/oldbridz; Južni logor bb; ☺9am-11pm) You're liable to hear old-school punk or Bowie blasting out of this open-sided wooden pavilion above the Radobolja River, given the predilections of the owner-manager, who's also behind the OldbridZ Brewery. Take a tasting flight of their excellent range, then start sampling the guest craft brews from elsewhere in Bosnia, Croatia and Serbia, accompanied by Mexican food or Bosnian cheese.

Café de Alma　　CAFE
(☑063 315 572; www.facebook.com/cafedealma; Rade Bitange bb; ☺9.30am-6pm Apr-Dec) Step back to Ottoman times at this excellent coffee roastery, with a shady front terrace and cool interior. The only things served are homemade juices and Bosnian-style coffee, and on your first visit you'll be taken through the whole traditional coffee-drinking ritual. Enquire about Alma's Tales personalised city tours (€30).

❶ Information

Grad Mostar (www.turizam.mostar.ba)
Tourist Info Centre (☑036-580 275; www.hercegovina.ba; Rade Bitange 5; ☺9am-noon May-Oct)
Visit Mostar (www.visitmostar.org)

❶ Getting There & Away

AIR
Mostar Airport (OMO; ☑036-352 770; www.mostar-airport.ba) is 7km south of town off the

Čapljina road. The only year-round flights are to Zagreb on Croatia Airlines, with additional airlines running seasonal services.

BUS
Mostar has two bus stations, only 1.5km apart – one for each half of its ethnic divide. The main one is the **eastern bus station** (Autobusni stanica; ☑036-552 025; Trg Ivana Krndelja), located right beside the train station (p86); it's more convenient for travellers than the **western bus station** (Autobusni kolodvor; ☑036-348 680; Vukovarska bb; ☺5.30am-10pm). Domestic destinations include Trebinje (21KM, 3½ hours, four daily), Sarajevo (20KM, 2½ hours, 10 daily) and Jajce (26KM, 4¼ hours, three daily); most services stop at both stations.

TRAIN
Trains from Mostar's **railway station** (Željeznička stanica; ☑036-550 608; www.zfbh.ba; Trg Ivana Krndelja 1), adjacent to the eastern bus station (p86), depart every morning and evening for Konjic (11KM, 50 minutes) and Sarajevo (18KM, two hours).

❶ Getting Around

Local bus services, which extend as far as peripheral towns such as Blagaj, are operated by **Mostar Bus** (☑036-552 250; www.mostarbus.ba).

Blagaj

☑036 / POPULATION 2530
An easy day trip from Mostar, pretty Blagaj hugs the turquoise Buna River as it gushes out of a cave past a historical tekke (Sufi dervish spiritual house), several enticing restaurants and Ottoman-era homesteads.

Blagaj Tekke　　ISLAMIC SITE
(Blagajska tekija; ☑061 371 005; www.tekijablagaj.ba/en; Blagaj bb; admission 5KM; ☺8am-10pm May-Oct, to 6pm Nov-Apr) Forming Blagaj's signature attraction, the centrepiece of this

---

DON'T MISS

KRAVICA WATERFALL

There's a slightly unreal Disney-esque quality to this outstanding waterfall (Slap Kravica; www.kravica.ba; adult/child 10/5KM; ☺7am-10pm Jun-Sep, to 6pm Oct-Apr, to 8pm May), where the Trebižat River plummets in a broad 25m-high arc into an emerald pool. In spring, this gorgeous mini-Niagara pounds itself into a dramatic, steamy fury. In summer it's a more gentle cascade, but the basin offers an idyllic respite from the sweltering heat for hundreds of locals and tourists.

The falls are a 15-minute walk from a car park that's 4km down a dead-end road that is well signposted from the M6 (Čapljina–Ljubuški Rd). There's no public transport, but many Mostar group tours combine a stop at the falls with visits to Blagaj and Počitelj.

POČITELJ

The stepped medieval fortress village of Počitelj is one of the most picture-perfect architectural ensembles in the country. Cupped in a steep rocky amphitheatre, it's a warren of steps climbing between ramshackle stone-roofed houses and pomegranate bushes.

The village was badly damaged by Bosnian Croat forces in 1993, including the beautiful **Hajji Alija Mosque** (Hadži Alijina džamija; adult/child 3KM/free; ⊙9am-6pm Apr-Oct), which was deliberately targeted. This 1563 structure has now been restored, although photos displayed within show how much of the decorative paintwork has been lost.

Nearby is a 16m Ottoman **clock tower**, while further up the hill is a partly ruined fortress, capped by the octagonal **Gavrakapetan Tower**. You can climb up the tower or save your energy for even better panoramas from the uppermost rampart bastions.

Počitelj is 28km south of Mostar. Buses from Mostar to Čapljina or Metković (Croatia) take this route.

complex of traditional stone-roofed buildings is a very pretty half-timbered dervish house with wobbly rug-covered floors, carved doorways, curious niches and a bathroom with star-shaped coloured glass set into the ceiling. The dervishes follow a mystical strand of Islam in which the peaceful contemplation of nature plays a part, hence the *tekke*'s idyllic positioning above the cave mouth from which the Buna River's surreally blue-green waters flow forth.

🛏 Sleeping & Eating

Hotel Blagaj HOTEL €€
(☎036-573 805; www.hotel-blagaj.com; Blagaj bb; s/d/apt €34/49/70; ⊙reception 7am-midnight; P❄🖃) Built in 2015, this professional 27-room hotel contrasts white and lavender-wash walls with sepia scenes of old Mostar. It's just beyond the main town car park en route to Blagaj Tekke.

Restoran Vrelo INTERNATIONAL €€
(☎036-572 556; www.restoranvrelo.com; Blagaj bb; mains 9-30KM; ⊙10am-10.30pm; 🖃) Across the river from the tekke, this restaurant serves reliably good food on terraces overlooking a horseshoe of rapids. Local trout is served in a variety of styles, including *'probaj ova'* (literally 'try this') which comes in lemon sauce with pumpkin seeds. There are also schnitzels, steaks, seafood or meat platters, and delicious squid stuffed with three cheeses.

ℹ Information

The small **tourist information booth** (⊙8am-8pm May-Sep) is in the main car park, 650m short of the tekke.

ℹ Getting There & Away

City bus routes 10 and 11 from Mostar run to Blagaj (2.10KM, 30 minutes), with a total of 10 services on weekdays (fewer on weekends).

Trebinje

📞 059 / POP 31,500

By far the prettiest city in Republika Srpska, Trebinje has a compact centre with a tiny walled Old Town flanked by a leafy market square. The Trebišnjica River is slow and shallow as it passes through, its banks lined with swimming spots and replicas of waterwheels, which were once used for irrigation. Mountains provide a sun-baked backdrop, while hills topped with Orthodox churches punctuate the suburbs.

It's barely 30km from Dubrovnik, but in tourist terms it's a world away – not to mention vastly cheaper. Some canny travellers base themselves here and 'commute'.

Trebinje's always been a Serb-majority town but more so since the war, with the proportion rising from 70% to 94%.

◉ Sights

Hercegovačka Gračanica CHURCH
(Херцеговачка Грачаница; Miloša Šarabe bb) Offering phenomenal views, this hilltop complex comprises a bell tower, gallery, cafe-bar and bishop's palace, but most notably the compact but eye-catching Presvete Bogorodice (Annunciation) Church. The latter's design is based very symbolically on the 1321 Gračanica monastery in Kosovo, a historically significant building that's considered sacred by many Serbs. The Trebinje version

was erected in 2000 to rehouse the bones of local poet-hero Jovan Dučić.

Arslanagić Bridge
BRIDGE

(Perovića Most, Перовића мост) This unique double-backed structure was built in 1574 under the direction of Grand Vizier Mehmed Pasha Sokolović, who was also behind the Višegrad bridge (Most Mehmed-paše Sokolovića; P), though this one was named for the toll collector. It was originally 10km further upstream from its present location but in 1965 it disappeared beneath the rising waters of the Gorica reservoir. Rescued stone by stone, it took six years to be finally reassembled.

🛏 Sleeping

★ Hostel Polako
HOSTEL €

(066 380 722; www.hostelpolakotrebinje.com; Vožda Karađorđa 7; dm/r from €11/28; Jan-Nov; 🛜) Run by a friendly American/Polish couple, this much-loved hostel offers dorms and two private doubles; bathrooms are shared. It's a ten-minute walk from both the bus station and the Old Town. Rates include pancakes for breakfast.

Hotel Platani
HOTEL €€

(059-274 050; www.hotel-platani-trebinje.com; Riste i Bete Vukanović 1; s/d/apt 72/105/164KM; P ✳ 🛜) Taking pride of place on Trebinje's pretty, central square (Трг слободе), this landmark hotel evokes the elegance of the Austro-Hungarian era. Downstairs is one of Trebinje's best restaurants (mains 10KM to 34KM), while upstairs are spacious, well-presented rooms. One huge corner room is after named *Matrix* actress Monica Bellucci who stayed here while filming locally. There's also an annex across the square.

Sesto Senso
HOTEL €€

(059-261 160; www.facebook.com/sestosenso trebinje; Obala Mića Ljubibratića 3; s/d from €42/52; P ✳ 🛜) Wrapped up in an attractive white-stone-and-glass package, this modern four-storey block is big on 21st-century style. The cheapest rooms only have tiny, high windows; it's worth paying extra for a balcony and river view. Downstairs on the terrace is one of Trebinje's best international restaurants (7am to 11pm; mains 8KM to 29KM), serving everything from local grills to chicken curries.

ℹ Information

The extremely helpful **tourist office** (059-273 410; www.gotrebinje.com; Jovan Dučića bb;

8am-4pm Mon-Fri, 9am-2pm Sat) is next to the Catholic cathedral, across the park from the Old Town's western gate.

ℹ Getting There & Away

Trebinje's **bus station** (Autobuska stanica; 059-220 466; Vojvode Stepe Stepanovića bb) is 600m southwest of the Old Town. Destinations include Mostar (21KM, 3½ hours, four daily), Konjic (26KM, two daily), Istočno Sarajevo (27KM, 4¾ hours, three daily) and Dubrovnik (8KM, one hour, one or two daily).

WESTERN BOSNIA

Travelling through this region of green wooded hills, river canyons, rocky crags and mildly interesting historical towns you'll find yourself constantly passing in and out of Bosniak-Croat Federation territory and the Republika Srpska. You'll always know when you're in the latter by the red-blue-and-white Serbian flags which sprout in profusion whenever you enter it. Prominent towns include the old Ottoman administrative capital Travnik, the gorgeous hilltop settlement of Jajce, and Republika Srpska's quasi capital Banja Luka. In the west, the Una River gushes flamboyantly over a series of waterfalls before joining the Sava on its rush to the Danube and, ultimately, the Black Sea.

Una River Valley

The adorable Una River goes through widely varying moods. In the lush green gorges to the northeast, some sections are as calm as mirrored opal, while others gush over widely fanned rafting rapids. The river broadens and gurgles over a series of shallow falls as it passes through the unassuming town of Bihać (population 39,700). Occasionally it leaps over impressive falls, notably at Štrbački Buk (p89), which forms the centrepiece of the 198-sq-km **Una National Park** (www.nationalpark-una.ba).

⊙ Sights & Activities

Rafting is a draw here; in addition, there's kayaking, fly-fishing (day's licence 40KM; two-fish maximum) and 'speed river diving', a sport invented here involving scuba diving in fast-flowing waters. Each activity centre has its own campsite and provides transfers from Bihać.

JAJCE & THE VRBAS RIVER

Jajce is a historical gem, with a highly evocative walled Old Town and **fortress** (Tvrđava u Jajcu; adult/child 2/1KM; ☉8am-8pm May-Oct, to 4pm Nov-Apr) clinging to a steep rocky knoll with rivers on two sides. The Pliva River tumbles into the Vrbas River by way of an impressive urban **waterfall** (Vodopad) right at the very foot of the town walls. Immediately to the west, the Pliva is dammed to form two pretty **lakes** (Plivsko Jezero) which are popular with swimmers, strollers, bikers and boaters.

Further up the Vrbas towards Banja Luka, **Kanjon Rafting Centre** (☑066 714 169; www.raftingnavrbasu.com; Karanovac bb; ☉9am-8pm Apr-Oct) is a reliable extreme-sports outfit specialising in rafting (35-70KM) but also offering guided hiking and canyoning trips (40KM, six person minimum). Rafting requires at least four people but joining with others is sometimes possible in summer; phone to enquire.

Jajce's centrally located bus station has services to Bihać (25KM, 3½ hours, five daily), Sarajevo (27KM, 3½ hours, five daily) and Mostar (26KM, 4¼ hours, three daily).

Ostrožac Fortress   FORTRESS

(☑061 236 641; www.ostrozac.com; Ostrožac; admission 2KM; ☉9am-dusk) Ostrožac is one of Bosnia's most photogenic castles, a spooky Gothic place high above the Una Valley, up 3km of hairpins towards Cazin. There's plenty to explore from various epochs, ramparts to walk, towers to climb and a manor house on the verge of collapse that all add to the thrill (and danger) of poking about. Off-season you might have to call the caretaker to get in, but it's only officially closed if it's snowing.

Štrbački Buk   WATERFALL

(Una National Park Entry Gate 3; adult/child 6/4KM; ☉dawn-dusk) A strong contender for the title of the nation's most impressive waterfall, Štrbački Buk is a seriously dramatic 40m-wide cascade, pounding 23.5m down three travertine sections, including over a superbly photogenic 18m drop-off, overlooked by a network of viewing platforms. The easiest access is 8km along a graded but potholed unpaved road from Orašac on the Kulen Vakuf road. There are swimming spots to stop at along the way.

Milančev Buk   WATERFALL

(Una National Park Entry Gate 5, Martin Brod; adult/child 2/1.50KM; ☉dawn-dusk) Collectively, this group of cascades tumbles down a vertical height of more than 50m, with a wide arc of rivulets pouring into a series of pools surrounded by lush, green foliage. The main viewpoint is a minute's walk from the ticket gate, 1.3km off the Bihać–Dravar Rd in Martin Brod village. Make sure you check out the view from the red footbridge near the car park, too.

❶ Getting There & Away

➸ Bihać's **bus station** (Autobuska stanica Bihać; ☑037-311 939; www.unatransport.ba; Put Armije Republike BiH bb) is 1km west of the centre. Destinations include Jajce (25KM, 3½ hours, five daily) and Sarajevo (42KM, 6½ hours, four daily).

➸ A daily train heads to **Bihać Railway Station** (☑037-312 282; www.zfbh.ba; Bihaćkih Branilaca 20) from Sarajevo (37KM, 6¼ hours).

SURVIVAL GUIDE

❶ Directory A–Z

ACCOMMODATION

Accommodation is remarkably fair value by European standards. There's a good supply of guesthouses, rental apartments, motels and hostels (many homestay-style), plus some boutique and character hotels. Business and five-star hotels are rarer. Ski areas have some upmarket resorts. Most hotels in Bosnia include some type of breakfast in the rates.

LGBT+ TRAVELLERS

Although Bosnia decriminalised homosexuality in 1998 (2000 in the Republika Srpska), attitudes remain very conservative and attacks have occurred at queer festivals in the past. LGBTI advocacy organisation Sarajevo Open Centre (www.soc.ba) is active in fighting sexuality-based discrimination. In Sarajevo, the highlight of the queer year is the Merlinka Film Festival (www.merlinka.com) held in January or February. Sarajevo has a weekend-only gay bar but you won't find any elsewhere.

MONEY

ATMs accepting Visa and MasterCard are ubiquitous.

OPENING HOURS

Closing times for many eateries and bars depends on custom. In tourist areas such as Mostar, hotels and restaurants may close in the off season.

Banks 8am to 6pm Monday to Friday, 8.30am to 1.30pm Saturday.

Bars and clubs Most bars are cafes by day, opening at 8am and closing at 11pm or later. Pubs and clubs open later and, at weekends, might close at 3am.

Office hours Typically 8am to 4pm Monday to Friday.

Restaurants 7am to 10.30pm or until the last customer.

Shops 8am to 6pm daily, many stay open later.

PUBLIC HOLIDAYS

Nationwide holidays:

New Year's Day 1 and 2 January

May Day 1 and 2 May

Additional holidays in the Federation:

Independence Day 1 March

Catholic Easter Sunday March or April (in majority-Croat areas)

Catholic Easter Monday March or April (in majority-Croat areas)

Ramadan Bajram June (in majority-Bosniak areas)

Kurban Bajram August or September (in majority-Bosniak areas)

All Saints Day 1 November (in majority-Croat areas)

Statehood Day 25 November

Catholic Christmas 25 December (in majority-Croat areas)

Additional holidays in the Republika Srpska:

Orthodox Christmas 7 January

Republika Day 9 January

Orthodox New Year 14 January

Orthodox Good Friday March or April

Orthodox Easter Saturday March or April

Orthodox Easter Sunday March or April

Victory Day 9 May

Dayton Agreement Day 21 November

SAFE TRAVEL

Landmines and unexploded ordnance still affect 2% of Bosnia and Hercegovina's land area. **BHMAC** (www.bhmac.org) removes more every year with the aim of full clearance by 2019. However, progress was slowed by floods in 2014 which added to the complexity of locating the last mines. For your safety, stick to asphalt/concrete surfaces or well-worn paths in affected areas, and avoid exploring war-damaged buildings.

TELEPHONE

Country code 387

International access code 00

Local directory information 1182 (Federation), 1185 (Republika Srpska), 1188 (Hrvatska pošta Mostar)

VISAS

It's wise to double-check the latest visa requirements by entering your nationality on the Ministry of Foreign Affairs website (www.mvp.gov.ba). Currently stays of less than 90 days require no visa for citizens of most European and American nations, plus Australia, New Zealand, Israel and several Arab and East Asian countries. If none of the visa-free conditions apply then check carefully at which specified embassies you are expected to apply (eg that means London or Tripoli for South Africans). Visitors without access to 150KM per day could be refused entry.

Note that you do not need a Bosnia and Hercegovina visa to transit (without stopping) through Neum between Split and Dubrovnik, as long as you have the right to reenter Croatia.

ⓘ Getting There & Away

AIR

Bosnia doesn't have a national carrier.

Sarajevo International Airport (p82) Bosnia's busiest, with flights all over Europe and the Middle East.

Banja Luka International Airport (BNX, Међународни аеродром Бања Лука; ☑ 051-535 210; www.banjaluka-airport.com; Mahovljani bb, Laktaši) Only used by Air Serbia (to Belgrade) and Ryanair (Charleroi, Memmingen and Stockholm-Skavsta).

Mostar Airport (p86) Year-round Croatia Airlines flights to Zagreb plus seasonal services.

Tuzla International Airport (www.tuzla-airport.ba) Tiny but a hub for budget airline WizzAir, with flights to Austria, Switzerland, Germany, The Netherlands and Sweden.

LAND
Bus

Direct bus connections link Bosnia to all of its neighbours and to as far afield as Sweden. In most cases, passports are collected on the bus and handed over at the border; you usually won't leave the bus unless there's an issue that needs resolving. Useful websites include www.busticket4.me, www.eurolines.com, www.getbybus.com and www.vollo.net.

Car & Motorcyle

Drivers need Green Card insurance and an EU or International Driving Permit. Transiting Neum in a Croatian hire car is usually not problematic.

Note that while most cars rented in Bosnia are covered for visits to neighbouring countries, Kosovo tends to be an exception, with insurance voided if you drive there. Since Croatia joined the EU in July 2013, many previously open minor border crossings with Bosnia and Hercegovina have been closed to international traffic, and border queues can be annoyingly long at busy times.

ⓘ Getting Around

BUS

Bus services are excellent and relatively inexpensive. There are often different companies handling each route, so prices can vary substantially. Luggage stowed in the baggage compartment under the bus costs extra (around 2KM a piece).

Bus stations pre-sell tickets. Between towns it's normally easy enough to wave down any bus en route. Advance reservations are sometimes necessary for overnight routes or at peak holiday times. The biggest companies include Auto-prevoz (www.autoprevoz.ba), Centrotrans (www.centrotrans.com) and Globtour (www.globtour.com). Useful websites offering schedules and bookings include www.busticket4.me, www.vollo.net and www.getbybus.com.

Frequency on some routes drops drastically at weekends. Some shorter routes stop on Sundays.

CAR & MOTORCYCLE

Bosnia and Hercegovina's winding roads are lightly trafficked and a delight for driving if you aren't in a hurry. Driving makes sense to reach the country's more remote areas. There are a few toll motorways in the centre of the country; collect your ticket from the machine at the set of booths where you enter, then pay at the booths where you leave the motorway.

TRAIN

Trains are slower and far less frequent than buses but generally slightly cheaper. ŽFBH (www.zfbh.ba) has an online rail timetable search. The main routes are Sarajevo–Bihać and Sarajevo–Konjic–Mostar.

BOSNIA & HERCEGOVINA SURVIVAL GUIDE

Bulgaria

POP 7.19 MILLION

Best Places to Eat

➡ Rosé (p112)

➡ Ethno (p112)

➡ Niko'las (p98)

➡ Pavaj (p104)

➡ Tam's House (p105)

Best Places to Stay

➡ Hotel Doro (p112)

➡ Canapé Connection (p97)

➡ Hostel Old Plovdiv (p103)

➡ At Renaissance Square (p103)

➡ Hotel Astra (p106)

Why Go?

Soul-stirring mountains, golden beaches and cities that hum with music and art. There's a lot to love about Bulgaria: no wonder the Greeks, Romans, Byzantines and Turks all fought to claim it as their own. Billed as the oldest nation on the continent, Bulgaria is rich with ancient treasure. The mysterious Thracians left behind dazzling hauls of gold and silver, and tombs that can be explored to this day. The Romans built cities of breathtaking scale, the bathhouses, walls and amphitheatres of which sit nonchalantly in the midst of modern cities. Centuries later, Bulgaria still beguiles with its come-hither coastline and fertile valleys laden with vines and roses. Plovdiv is the European Capital of Culture for 2019, Sofia has cool cred to rival any major metropolis, and lively Black Sea resorts teem with modern-day pleasure pilgrims.

When to Go
Sofia

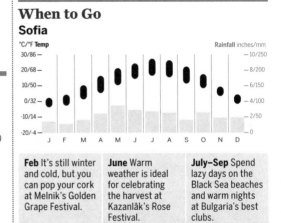

Feb It's still winter and cold, but you can pop your cork at Melnik's Golden Grape Festival.

June Warm weather is ideal for celebrating the harvest at Kazanlâk's Rose Festival.

July–Sep Spend lazy days on the Black Sea beaches and warm nights at Bulgaria's best clubs.

Entering the Country

Travel to Bulgaria does not pose any unusual problems. Sofia has air connections with many European cities, and train and long-haul bus services are frequent. At the time of research, Bulgaria was not a member of the EU's common customs and border area, the Schengen area, so even if you're entering from an EU member state (including Romania), you'll still have to show a passport or valid EU identity card. Note that border and ferry crossings can get crowded, so be sure to allow yourself plenty of time.

ITINERARIES

One Week
Take a full day to hit Sofia (p95) and its main attractions, then take the bus to Veliko Târnovo (p107) for a few days of sightseeing and hiking. For the rest of the week, head to Varna (p109) for some sea and sand, or veer south to the ancient beach towns of Nesebâr (p111) and Sozopol (p113).

Two Weeks
Spend a few extra days in Sofia (p95), adding in a day trip to Rila Monastery (p101), then catch a bus to Plovdiv (p103) to wander the cobbled lanes of the Old Town. From there, take the mountain air in majestic Veliko Târnovo (p107). Make for the coast, with a few nights in Varna (p109) and lively Sozopol (p113).

Essential Food & Drink

Fresh fruit, vegetables, dairy produce and grilled meat form the basis of Bulgarian cuisine, which has been heavily influenced by Greek and Turkish cookery. Tripe features heavily on traditional menus.

Banitsa Flaky cheese pastry, often served fresh and hot.

Beer Zagorka, Kamenitza and Shumensko are the most popular nationwide brands.

Kavarma This 'claypot meal', or meat stew, is normally made with either chicken or pork.

Kebabche Thin, grilled pork sausage, a staple of every *mehana* (tavern) in the country.

Mish-Mash Summer favourite made from tomatoes, capsicum, eggs, feta and spices.

Shishcheta Shish-kebab consisting of chicken or pork on wooden skewers with mushrooms and peppers.

Shkembe chorba Traditional stomach soup is one of the more adventurous highlights of Bulgarian cuisine.

Tarator Delicious chilled cucumber and yoghurt soup, served with garlic, dill and crushed walnuts.

Wine They've been producing wine here since Thracian times and there are some excellent varieties to try.

Sleeping Price Ranges

The following price ranges refer to a double room with bathroom in high season. Unless otherwise stated, breakfast is included in the price.

€ less than 60 lv

€€ 60–120 lv (to 200 lv in Sofia)

€€€ more than 120 lv (more than 200 lv in Sofia)

Eating Price Ranges

The following price ranges refer to a standard main course. Unless otherwise stated, service charge is included in the price.

€ less than 10 lv

€€ 10–20 lv

€€€ more than 20 lv

BULGARIA

Bulgaria Highlights

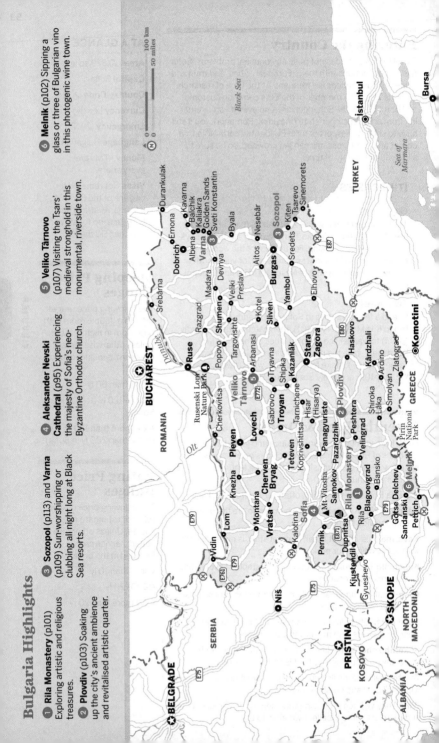

1 Rila Monastery (p101)
Exploring artistic and religious treasures.

2 Plovdiv (p103) Soaking up the city's ancient ambience and revitalised artistic quarter.

3 Sozopol (p109) Sun-worshipping or clubbing all night long at Black Sea resorts.

4 Aleksander Nevski Cathedral (p95) Experiencing the majesty of Sofia's neo-Byzantine Orthodox church.

5 Veliko Tărnovo (p107) Visiting the Tsars' medieval stronghold in this monumental, riverside town.

6 Melnik (p102) Sipping a glass or three of Bulgarian vino in this photogenic wine town.

0   50 miles
0   100 km

SOFIA СОФИЯ

📑 02 / POP 1.2 MILLION

Bulgaria's pleasingly laid-back capital is often overlooked by visitors heading to the coast or the ski resorts, but they're missing something special. Sofia is no grand metropolis, but it's a modern, youthful city, with a scattering of onion-domed churches, Ottoman mosques and stubborn Red Army monuments that lend an eclectic, exotic feel. Excavation work carried out during construction of the metro unveiled a treasure trove of Roman ruins from nearly 2000 years ago, when the city was called 'Serdica'. Away from the buildings and boulevards, vast parks and manicured gardens offer a welcome respite, and the ski slopes and hiking trails of mighty Mt Vitosha are just a short bus ride from the centre. Home to many of Bulgaria's finest museums, galleries, restaurants and clubs, Sofia may persuade you to stick around and explore further.

◎ Sights

◎ Ploshtad Aleksander Nevski

★ Aleksander Nevski Cathedral   CHURCH
(pl Aleksander Nevski; ⊘ 7am-7pm; Ⓜ Sofiyski Universitet) One of *the* symbols not just of Sofia but of Bulgaria itself, this massive, awe-inspiring church was built between 1882 and 1912 in memory of the 200,000 Russian soldiers who died fighting for Bulgaria's independence during the Russo-Turkish War (1877–78). It is named in honour of a 13th-century Russian warrior-prince.

★ Sveta Sofia Church   CHURCH
(📑 02-987 0971; ul Parizh 2; museum adult/child 6/2 lv; ⊘ church 7am-7pm Mar-Sep, to 5pm Oct-Feb, museum 9am-5pm Tue-Sun; Ⓜ Sofiyski Universitet) Sveta Sofia is one of the capital's oldest churches, and gave the city its name. A subterranean **museum** houses an ancient necropolis, with 56 tombs and the remains of four other churches. Outside are the Tomb of the Unknown Soldier and an eternal flame, and the grave of Ivan Vazov, Bulgaria's most revered writer.

Aleksander Nevski Crypt   GALLERY
(Museum of Icons; pl Aleksander Nevski; adult/child 6/3 lv; ⊘ 10am-5.30pm Tue-Sun; Ⓜ Sofiyski Universitet) Originally built as a final resting place for Bulgarian kings, this crypt now houses Bulgaria's biggest and best collection of icons, stretching back to the 5th century. Enter to the left of the eponymous church's main entrance.

◎ Sofia City Garden & Around

Archaeological Museum   MUSEUM
(📑 02-988 2406; www.naim.bg; ul Saborna 2; adult/child 10/2 lv; ⊘ 10am-6pm daily May-Oct, to 5pm Tue-Sun Nov-Apr; Ⓜ Serdika) Housed in a former mosque built in 1496, this museum displays a wealth of Thracian, Roman and medieval artefacts. Highlights include a mosaic floor from the Church of Sveta Sofia, a 4th-century BC Thracian gold burial mask, and a magnificent bronze head, thought to represent a Thracian king.

Ancient Serdica Complex   RUINS
(pl Nezavisimost; ⊘ 6am-11pm; Ⓜ Serdika) **FREE**
This remarkable, partly covered excavation site, situated just above the Serdika metro station, displays the remains of the Roman city, Serdica, that once occupied this area. The remains were unearthed from 2010 to 2012 during construction of the metro. There are fragments of eight streets, an early Christian basilica, baths and houses dating from the 4th to 6th centuries. Plenty of signage in English.

Sveti Georgi Rotunda   CHURCH
(Church of St George; 📑 02-980 9216; www.svgeorgi-rotonda.com; bul Dondukov 2; ⊘ services daily 8am, 9am & 5pm; Ⓜ Serdika) Built in the 4th century AD, this tiny red-brick church is Sofia's oldest preserved building. The murals inside were painted between the 10th and 14th centuries. It's a busy, working church, but visitors are welcome. To find the church, enter through an opening on ul Sâborna.

Sveta Petka Samardzhiiska Church   CHURCH
(bul Maria Luisa 2; ⊘ 9am-5pm; Ⓜ Serdika) This tiny church, located in the centre of the Serdika metro complex, was built during the early years of Ottoman rule (late 14th century), which explains its sunken profile and inconspicuous exterior. Inside are some 16th-century murals. It's rumoured that the Bulgarian national hero Vasil Levski is buried here.

Museum of Socialist Art   MUSEUM
(📑 02-902 1862; www.nationalgallery.bg; ul Lachezar Stanchev 7, Iztok; 6 lv; ⊘ 10am-5.30pm Tue-Sun; Ⓜ GM Dimitrov) If you wondered where all those unwanted statues of Lenin ended up, you'll find some here, along with the red star from atop Sofia's Party House. There's a gallery of paintings, with catchy titles such as *Youth Meeting at Kilifarevo Village to Send Worker-Peasant Delegation to the USSR*, and stirring old propaganda films are shown.

Sofia

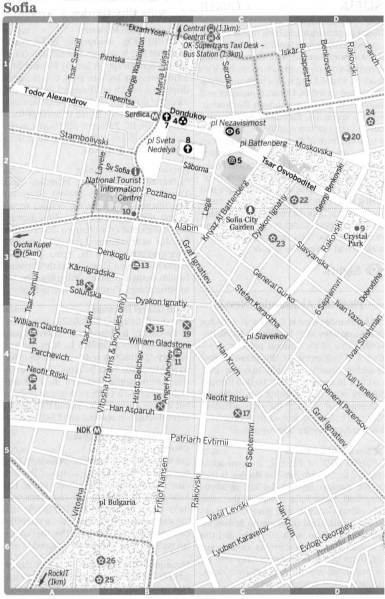

Sofia City Garden
PARK

(MSerdika) This small, central park, bounded on its northern end by ul Tsar Osvoboditel, is favoured by Sofia's chess-playing pensioners. It's home to the National Theatre (p99), and until 1999 held the mausoleum of Bulgaria's first communist ruler, Georgi Dimitrov.

Tours

Free Sofia Tour
WALKING

(☎0988920461; www.freesofiatour.com; cnr ul Alabin & bul Vitosha; ⊙10am, 11am & 6pm Apr-Oct, 11am, 2pm & 6pm Nov-Mar; MSerdika) FREE Explore Sofia's sights in the company of friendly and enthusiastic English-speaking

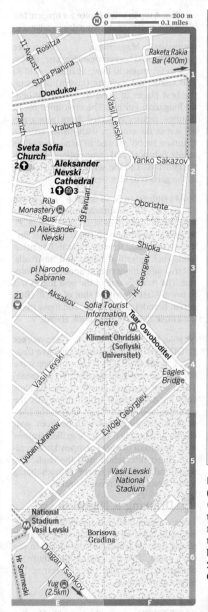

BULGARIA SOFIA

Balkan Bites   FOOD & DRINK
(📞0877613992; www.balkanbites.bg; by donation;
⏰tours 2pm; Ⓜ Sofiyski Universitet, 🚌9) This
two-hour guided walking tour focuses on
food and includes tastings and drinks at restaurants around town. The basic tour is free
but a donation is expected. Walks depart at
2pm from the statue of Stefan Stambolov in
Crystal Park.

🛏 Sleeping

★**Canapé Connection**   GUESTHOUSE €€
(📞0896893278; www.canapeconnection.com; ul
William Gladstone 12a; s/d from 60/80 lv; 🖥; 🚌1, 6,
7) Formerly a hostel, Canapé reinvented itself
as a guesthouse in 2016, retaining its same
attention to cleanliness and a refreshingly
simple, rustic design. The six rooms are divided into singles and doubles, with a larger

young locals on this two-hour guided walk.
No reservation is needed; just show up outside the Palace of Justice on the corner of
ul Alabin and bul Vitosha a few minutes
before the tour. Check the website for other themed, paid tours, including on culture,
communism and alternative Sofia.

room upstairs to accommodate families. There's a quiet garden outside to relax in.

Art Hostel
HOSTEL €€

(📞02-987 0545; www.art-hostel.com; ul Angel Kânchev 21a; dm/s/d from 22/50/64 lv; @🛜; 🖥12) This bohemian hostel stands out from the crowd with its summertime art exhibitions, live music, dance performances and more. Dorms are appropriately arty and bright; private rooms are airy and very welcoming. There's a great basement bar and a peaceful little garden at the back.

Hotel Niky
HOTEL €€

(📞02-952 3058; www.hotel-niky.com; ul Neofit Rilski 16; r/ste from 150/200 lv; P🅿😊❄🛜; Ⓜ NDK, 🖥1) The hotel's popularity has allowed the owners to hike prices in recent years, though the excellent city-centre location, comfortable rooms and gleaming bathrooms make the place still a decent value. The smart suites come with kitchenettes. Frequently full; be sure to book ahead.

Hotel Les Fleurs
BOUTIQUE HOTEL €€€

(📞02-810 0800; www.lesfleurshotel.com; bul Vitosha 21; r from 250 lv; P😊❄🛜; Ⓜ Serdika, 🖥10) You can hardly miss this very central hotel with gigantic blooms on its facade. The flowery motif is continued in the large, carefully styled rooms, and there's a very good restaurant on site. The location, right at the start of the pedestrian-only stretch of bul Vitosha, is ideal.

✖️ Eating

Made In Home
INTERNATIONAL €€

(📞0876884014; ul Angel Kânchev 30a; mains 14-23 lv; ⊙noon-9pm Sun, to 10pm Mon, to 10.30pm Tue-Thur, to 11pm Fri & Sat; 🛜🍴; Ⓜ NDK) Sofia's popular entrant into the worldwide, locally sourced, slow-food trend (the name refers to the fact that all items are made in-house). The cooking is eclectic, with dollops of Middle Eastern (eg hummus) and Turkish items, as well as ample vegetarian and vegan offerings. The playfully rustic interior feels straight out of a Winnie-the-Pooh book. Reservations essential.

Boho
INTERNATIONAL €€

(📞0896451458; www.facebook.com/boho.sofia; ul Hristo Belchev 29; mains 9-16 lv; ⊙noon-11pm; 🛜) Contemporary eclectic favorites like burgers and sweet-potato fries, hummus, pulled pork, avocado toast, and pancakes -- all reasonably priced and served in a bright, stylish locale. There's a huge garden out back for nice

weather. A top in-town choice for brunch, but it's worth reserving at least a day in advance.

Manastirska Magernitsa
BULGARIAN €€

(📞02-980 3883; www.magernitsa.com; ul Han Asparuh 67; mains 10-18 lv; ⊙11-2am; Ⓜ NDK) This traditional *mehana* (tavern) is among the best places in Sofia to sample authentic Bulgarian cuisine. The enormous menu features recipes collected from monasteries across the country, with dishes such as 'drunken rabbit' stewed in wine, as well as salads, fish, pork and game options. Portions are generous and the service attentive. Dine in the garden in nice weather.

MoMa Bulgarian Food & Wine
BULGARIAN €€

(📞0885622 20; www.moma-restaurant.com; ul Solunska 28; mains 10-24 lv; ⊙11am-10pm; 🛜🍴; Ⓜ Serdika) An update on the traditional *mehana* (taverna), serving typical Bulgarian foods such as grilled meats and meatballs, but in a more modern and understated interior. The result is one of the best nights out in town. Start off with a shot of *rakia* (Bulgarian brandy) and a salad, and move on to the ample main courses. Book ahead.

★ Niko'las
BULGARIAN €€€

(📞0876888471; www.nikolas.bg; pl Rayko Daskalov 3; mains 21-28 lv, 5-/7-course tasting menu 60/80 lv; ⊙noon-11pm Mon-Sat; 🛜; Ⓜ Serdika) The menu boasts a 'taste of the Balkans with an Asian twist', which undersells the amazing food on offer here. Expect the likes of smoked trout topped with beetroot, goat cheese and poached pear, or grilled seabass with Bulgarian caviar. The open kitchen allows direct interaction with the chefs. The wood-clad walls are warm without being folksy. Reservations recommended.

🍸 Drinking & Nightlife

There's a seemingly inexhaustible supply of watering holes all over Sofia. The cheapest places to grab a beer are the kiosks in the city's parks; if you're looking for a more sophisticated ambience, the city centre has plenty of swish bars.

One More Bar
BAR

(📞0882539592; www.facebook.com/OneMoreBar; ul Shishman 12; ⊙8.30am-2am; 🛜; Ⓜ Sofiyski Universitet) Inside a gorgeous old house, this shabby-chic hot spot wouldn't be out of place in Melbourne or Manhattan; an extensive cocktail list, a delightful summer garden and jazzy background music add to its cosmopolitan appeal.

Raketa Rakia Bar BAR

(☑02-444 6111; www.facebook.com/RaketaRaki-aBar; ul Yanko Sakazov 17; ☉11am-midnight; ☎; ☐11, Ⓜ Sofiyski Universitet) Unsurprisingly, this rakish communist-era retro bar has a huge selection of *rakia* on hand; before you start working your way down the list, line your stomach with meat-and-cream-heavy snacks and meals. Reservations essential.

DaDa Cultural Bar BAR

(☑0877062455; www.dadaculturalbar.com; ul Georgi Benkovski 10; ☉5pm-midnight Mon-Thu, to 2am Fri & Sat, to 10pm Sun; ☎; Ⓜ Serdika, ☐20, 22) A local institution, DaDa bar is far more than a place to drink. The mission here is culture, and expect to find live music, art installations, readings or happenings. The website usually has an up-to-date program. Friendly staff and a welcoming vibe.

☆ Entertainment

If you read Bulgarian, or at least can decipher some Cyrillic, the magazine *Programata* is the most comprehensive source of entertainment listings; otherwise check out its excellent English-language website, www.programata.bg.

You can search for events and book tickets online at www.eventim.bg or www.ticketpro.bg.

Live Music

Sofia Live Club LIVE MUSIC

(☑0886661045; www.sofialiveclub.com; pl Bulgaria 1; ☉8pm-7am; Ⓜ NDK) This slick venue, located in the National Palace of Culture (NDK), is the city's largest live-music club. All swished up in cabaret style, it hosts local and international jazz, alternative, world-music and rock acts.

Bulgaria Hall CLASSICAL MUSIC

(☑02-988 3195; www.sofiaphilharmonic.com; ul Aksakov 1; ☉box office 9.30am-2.30pm & 3pm-7.30pm Mon-Fri, from 11am Sat & Sun; Ⓜ Serdika) Home of the excellent Sofia Philharmonic Orchestra.

RockIT LIVE MUSIC

(☑0888666991; www.facebook.com/bar.Rock-IT; bul Petko Karavelov 5; ☉8pm-7am; ☐1, 6) If you're into rock and metal, get your horns up here. Dance parties are best on Friday and Saturday nights, while the scene is mellower during the week. In addition to metal music and beers, the kitchen pushes out decent burgers and bar food.

Performing Arts

National Palace of Culture CONCERT VENUE

(NDK; ☑02-916 6300; www.ndk.bg; pl Bulgaria; ☉ticket office 10am-8pm; ☎; Ⓜ NDK) The 'NDK' (as it's usually called) has 15 halls and is the country's largest cultural complex. It maintains a regular program of events throughout the year, including film screenings, trade shows and big-name international music acts.

National Opera House OPERA

(☑tickets 02-987 7011; www.operasofia.bg; bul Dondukov 30; ☉box office 9am-2pm & 2.30-7pm Mon-Fri, 11am-7pm Sat, 11am-4pm Sun; ☐20, 22) Opened in 1953, this monumental edifice is the venue for classical opera and ballet performances, as well as special concerts for children. Enter from ul Vrabcha.

Ivan Vazov National Theatre THEATRE

(☑02-811 9219; www.nationaltheatre.bg; ul Dyakon Ignatiy 5; ☉ticket office 9.30am-7.30pm Mon-Fri, from 11.30am Sat & Sun; Ⓜ Serdika) One of Sofia's most elegant buildings, the Viennese-style National Theatre opened in 1907 and is the city's main stage for Bulgarian drama.

❶ Information

National Tourist Information Centre (☑02-933 5826; www.tourism.government.bg; pl Sveta Nedelya 1; ☉9am-5.30pm Mon-Fri; Ⓜ Serdika) Helpful, English-speaking staff and glossy brochures for destinations around Bulgaria. The office is a little hard to find, hidden near a small side street, a few steps southwest of pl Sveta Nedelya.

Sofia Tourist Information Centre (☑02-491 8344; www.visitsofia.bg; Sofiyski Universitet metro underpass; ☉9.30am-6pm Mon-Fri; Ⓜ Sofiyski Universitet) Lots of free leaflets and maps, and helpful English-speaking staff.

Pirogov Hospital (☑emergency 02-915 4411; www.pirogov.eu; bul General Totleben 21; ☐4, 5) Sofia's main public hospital for emergencies.

❶ Getting There & Away

AIR

Sofia Airport (☑info 24hr 02-937 2211; www.sofia-airport.bg; off bul Brussels; ☎; ☐84, Ⓜ Sofia Airport), the city's and country's main air gateway, is located 10km east of the centre. The airport has two terminals (1 and 2). Most flights use the more modern Terminal 2, but a few budget carriers fly in and out of Terminal 1. Both terminals have basic services, ATMs and OK-Supertrans Taxi (p100) desks.

The only domestic flights within Bulgaria are between Sofia and the Black Sea coast. **Bulgaria Air** (☑02-402 0400; www.air.bg; ul Ivan Vazov

WORTH A TRIP

MT VITOSHA & BOYANA

The Mt Vitosha range, 23km long and 13km wide, lies just south of Sofia; it's sometimes referred to as the 'lungs of Sofia' for the refreshing breezes it deflects onto the capital. The mountain is part of the 227-sq-km **Vitosha Nature Park** (www.park-vitosha. org), the oldest of its kind in Bulgaria (created in 1934). The main activities are hiking in summer and skiing in winter (mid-December to April). All of the park's areas have good hiking; Aleko, the country's highest ski resort, is best for skiing.

On weekends chairlifts, starting around 4km from the village of **Dragalevtsi**, run all year up to Goli Vrâh (1837m); take bus 66 or 93. Another option is the six-person gondola at Simeonovo, reachable by buses 122 or 123 (also weekends only).

A trip out here could be combined with a visit to **Boyana**, home to the fabulous, Unesco-listed **Boyana Church** (☑02-959 0939; www.boyanachurch.org; ul Boyansko Ezero 3, Boyana; adult/child 10/2 lv, combined ticket with National Historical Museum 12 lv, guide 10 lv; ☺9.30am-5.30pm Apr-Oct, 9am-5pm Nov-Mar; ☒64, 107), located en route between central Sofia and the mountains. This tiny church is adorned with 90 colourful murals dating to the 13th century, considered among the most important examples of medieval Bulgarian art. A combined ticket includes entry to both the church and the **National Museum of History** (☑02-955 4280; www.historymuseum.org/en; ul Vitoshko Lale 16, Boyana; adult/child 10/1 lv, combined ticket with Boyana Church 12 lv, guided tours in English 30 lv; ☺9.30am-6pm Apr-Oct, 9am-5.30pm Nov-Mar; ☒63, 111, ☒2), 2km away. Take bus 64 or 107 to reach Boyana.

2; ☺9.30am-noon & 12.30-5.30pm Mon-Fri; Ⓜ Serdika) flies daily to Varna, with two or three daily flights running between July and September. Bulgaria Air also flies between the capital and Burgas.

BUS

Sofia's **Central Bus Station** (Tsentralna Avtogara; ☑info 090063099; www.bgrazpisanie. com; bul Maria Luisa 100; ☺24hr; ☎; Ⓜ Central Railway Station) is located beside the train station and accessed via the same metro stop. It handles services to most big towns in Bulgaria as well as international destinations. There are dozens of counters for individual private companies, as well as an information desk and an **OK-Supertrans taxi desk** (☑02-973 2121; www.oktaxi.net; Centrail Bus Station; ☺6am-10pm; Ⓜ Central Railway Station).

Departures are less frequent between November and April. Sample destinations and fares include Burgas (32 lv, eight hours, eight daily), Kazanlâk (16 lv, 3½ hours, five daily), Nesebâr (37 lv, seven hours, five daily), Plovdiv (14 lv, 2½ hours, hourly), Sozopol (32 lv, seven hours, seven daily), Varna (33 lv, eight hours, every 45 minutes) and Veliko Târnovo (22 lv, four hours, hourly).

TRAIN

Sofia's **Central Train Station** (☑info 0700 10 200, international services 02-931 0972, tickets 0884 193 758; www.bdz.bg; bul Maria Luisa 102a; ☺ticket office 7.30am-7pm; Ⓜ Central Railway Station) is the city's and country's main rail gateway. The station itself is a massive, cheerless modern structure that's been extensively renovated, but which feels empty

and lacks many basic services. It's located in an isolated part of town about 1km north of the centre, though it's the terminus of a metro line and easy to reach. It's 100m (a five-minute walk) from the Central Bus Station.

Same-day tickets are sold at counters on the ground floor, while advance tickets are sold in the gloomy basement, accessed via an unsigned flight of stairs near some snack bars. Counters are open 24 hours, but normally only a few are staffed and queues are long, so don't turn up at the last moment to purchase your ticket, and allow some extra time to work out the confusing system of platforms (indicated with Roman numerals) and tracks.

Sample destinations and fares include Burgas (26 lv, seven hours, six daily), Plovdiv (10 lv, three hours, several daily) and Varna (39 lv, eight hours, six daily).

❶ Getting Around

TO/FROM THE AIRPORT

Sofia's metro connects Terminal 2 to the centre (Serdika station) in around 30 minutes. Buy tickets in the station, which is located just outside the terminal exit. Bus 84 also shuttles between the centre and both terminals. Buy tickets (1.60 lv, plus an extra fare for large luggage) from the driver.

A taxi to the centre will cost anywhere from 12 lv to 16 lv. Prebook your taxi at the **OK-Supertrans Taxi** (☑02-973 2121; www.oktaxi.net; 0.79/0.90 lv per km day/night) counter. They will give you a slip of paper with the three-digit code of your cab. The driver will be waiting outside.

CAR & MOTORCYCLE

Sofia's public transport is excellent and traffic can be heavy, so there's no need to drive a private or rented car in Sofia. If you wish to explore further afield, however, a car might come in handy. The **Union of Bulgarian Motorists** (☑ 02-935 7935, road assistance 02-91 146; www.uab.org) provides emergency roadside service.

PUBLIC TRANSPORT

Sofia has a comprehensive public transport system based on trams, buses, trolleybuses and underground metro. Public transport generally runs from 5.30am to around 11pm every day. The **Sofia Urban Mobility Centre** (☑ info 070013233; www.sofiatraffic.bg) maintains a helpful website with fares and an updated transport map. Attractions in the centre are normally located within easy walking distance, and you're not likely to need the tram or trolley in most instances.

Sofia's shiny metro links the city centre to both Sofia Airport and the central train and bus stations. It's divided into two lines, with the lines crossing at central Serdika station. Other helpful stations include NDK, at the southern end of bul Vitosha, and Sofiyski Universitet, close to Sofia University. Tickets cost 1.60 lv, but cannot be used on other forms of public transport. Buy tickets at windows and ticket machines located in the stations.

Tickets for trams, buses and trolleybuses cost 1.60 lv each and can be purchased at kiosks near stops or from on-board ticket machines. Consider buying a day pass (4 lv) to save the hassle of buying individual tickets.

TAXI

Taxis are an affordable alternative to public transport. By law, taxis must use meters, but those that wait around the airport, luxury hotels and within 100m of pl Sveta Nedelya may try to negotiate an unmetered fare – which, of course, will be considerably more than the metered fare. All official taxis are yellow, have fares per kilometre displayed in the window, and have obvious taxi signs (in English or Bulgarian) on top. The standard fare is 0.79 lv per minute during the day, 0.90 lv per minute at night. Never accept a lift in a private, unlicensed vehicle.

SOUTHERN BULGARIA

Some of Bulgaria's most precious treasures are scattered in the towns, villages and forests of the stunning south. The must-visit medieval Rila Monastery is nestled in the deep forest but easily reached by bus; tiny Melnik is awash in ancient wine; and the cobbled streets of Plovdiv, Bulgaria's second city, are lined with timeless reminders of civilisations come and gone.

The region is a scenic and craggy one; the **Rila Mountains** (www.rilanationalpark.bg) are just south of Sofia, the **Pirin Mountains** (www.pirin-np.com) rise towards the Greek border, and the **Rodopi Mountains** loom to the east and south of Plovdiv. There's great hiking to be had, and the south is also home to three of Bulgaria's most popular ski resorts: Borovets, Bansko and Pamporovo; see www.bulgariaski.com for information.

Rila Monastery
Рилски Манастир

Rising out of a forested valley in the Rila Mountains, 120km south of Sofia, Bulgaria's most famous monastery has been a spiritual centre for more than 1000 years. Rila Monastery's fortress-like complex engulfs 8800 sq m, and within its stone walls you'll find remarkably colourful architecture and religious art. Visitors can't fail to be struck by its elegant colonnades, archways striped in black, red and white, and the bright yellow domes of its main church, beneath which dance apocalyptic frescoes. Most travellers visit Rila Monastery on a day trip, but you can stay at or near the monastery to experience its tranquillity after the tour buses leave, or explore the hiking trails that begin here.

The monastery was founded in AD 927 and, inspired by the powerful spiritual influence of hermit monk Ivan Rilski, the monastery complex was heavily restored in 1469 after raids. It became a stronghold of Bulgarian culture and language during Ottoman rule. Set in a magnificent forested valley, the monastery is famous for its mural-plastered **Church of Rozhdestvo Bogorodichno** (Church of the Nativity; Rila Monastery; ☺ 7am-8pm) dating from the 1830s. The attached **museum** (5 lv; ☺ 8.30am-4.30pm) is home to the astonishing **Rafail's Cross**, an early-19th-century double-sided crucifix, with biblical scenes painstakingly carved in miniature. The monastery compound is open from 6am to 10pm. Visitors should dress modestly.

You can stay in simple **rooms** (☑ 0896872010; www.rilamonastery.pmg-blg.com; r 30-60 lv) at the monastery or, for something slightly more upmarket, try **Gorski Kut** (☑ 0888710348, 07054-2170; www.gorski-kut.eu; d/tr/ste 55/65/80 lv; ☐ ✱), 5km west. Tour buses such as **Rila Monastery Bus** (☑ 02-

489 0885; www.rilamonasterybus.com; adult/child 60/50 lv) are a popular option for a day trip from Sofia. By public transport, one daily morning bus (11 lv, 2½ hours) goes from Sofia's Ovcha Kupel (Zapad) bus station, returning in the afternoon.

Melnik   Мелник

ℤ 07437 / POP 390

Steep sandstone pyramids form a magnificent backdrop in tiny Melnik, 20km north of the Bulgaria–Greece border. These natural rock formations, some 100m in height, resemble wizard hats and mushrooms, and they gave the village its name (the Old Slavonic word *mel* means 'sandy chalk').

But it's a 600-year-old wine culture that has made Melnik famous, and the village's wonderfully restored National Revival architecture looks all the better after a glass or two of the town's signature 'Melnik 55' red. Seeing the village only requires a day, even with an earnest ramble around its many ruins, though an overnight stop is best to soak up its peaceful charms after the tour buses leave.

The major sights here, unsurprisingly, are wineries. Melnik's wines, celebrated for more than 600 years, include the signature dark red, Shiroka Melnishka Loza; it was a favourite tipple of Winston Churchill. Shops and stands dot Melnik's cobblestone paths; better yet, learn the history and tools of Melnik's winemaking trade at the **Museum of Wine** (ℤ 0878661930; www.facebook.com/Muzeinavinoto; Melnik 91; 5 lv; ☺ 10am-7pm).

Kordopulov House   MUSEUM
(ℤ 0877576120; www.kordopulova-house.com; 3.50 lv; ☺ 9.30am-6.30pm Apr-Sep, to 4pm Oct-Mar) Bulgaria's largest Revival-era building, this whitewashed and wooden mansion beams down from a cliff face at the eastern end of Melnik's main road. Dating from 1754, the four-storey mansion was formerly the home of a prestigious wine merchant family. Its naturally cool rooms steep visitors in luxurious period flavour, from floral stained-glass windows to Oriental-style fireplaces and a sauna. It's located at the top of a hill at the far eastern end of the town.

Golden Grapes Festival   WINE
(Zlaten Grozd; ☺ 2nd weekend Feb) It's hardly Bacchanalian – this is small-town Bulgaria, after all – but this annual knees-up gathers local wine producers to showcase their wares and tempt tourists with wine tastings,

all set to a backdrop of singing competitions and other folkish entertainment. It's usually on the second weekend of February; ask at the tourist office for details.

★ **Hotel Bolyarka**   HOTEL €€
(ℤ 07437-2383; www.melnikhotels.com; Melnik 34; s/d/apt 50/60/130 lv; P ✿ @ ☎) The right blend of old-world nostalgia and modern comfort has made this one of Melnik's favourite hotels. The Bolyarka has elegant rooms, a snug lobby bar, a Finnish-style sauna and one of Melnik's best restaurants. For a touch of added charm, reserve a deluxe apartment (130 lv) with fireplace.

Hotel Melnik   HOTEL €€
(ℤ 0879131459, 07437-2272; www.hotelmelnik.com; ul Vardar 2; s/d/apt 40/60/120 lv; P ✿ ☎) This pleasant hotel is shaded by fig and cherry trees, and peeps down over Melnik's main road. White-walled rooms with simple furnishings don't quite match the old-world reception and the *mehana* (tavern) with a bird's-eye view. But it's great value and the location – up a cobbled lane, just on the right as you enter the village – is very convenient.

★ **Mehana Chavkova Kâshta**   BULGARIAN €€
(ℤ 0893505090; www.themelnikhouse.com; 8-15 lv) Sit beneath 500-year-old trees and watch Melnik meander past at this superb spot. Like many places in town, grilled meats and Bulgarian dishes are specialities (try the *satch*, a sizzling flat pan of meat and vegetables); the atmosphere and friendly service give it an extra nudge above the rest. It's 200m from the bus stop, on the left side along the main road.

ⓘ Information

Melnik Tourist Information Centre (www.sandanskicrossborder.com; Obshtina Building; ☺ 9am-5pm) Located behind the bus stop, on the *obshtina* (municipality) building's upper floor, this centre advises on accommodation and local activities, though opening times can be spotty (especially outside summer). Bus and train timetables are posted outside.

ⓘ Getting There & Away

Direct buses connect Melnik with Sofia (18 lv, 4½ hours, one daily) and Blagoevgrad (8 lv, two hours, two daily). Two daily minibuses go from Sandanski to Melnik, continuing to Rozhen, though there may be insufficient seats if local shoppers are out in force.

By train, the closest station is Damyanitsa, 12km west.

Plovdiv Пловдив

032 / POP 343,420

With an easy grace, Plovdiv mingles invigorating nightlife among millennia-old ruins. Like Rome, Plovdiv straddles seven hills; but as Europe's oldest continuously inhabited city, it's far more ancient. It is best loved for its romantic old town, packed with colourful and creaky 19th-century mansions that are now house-museums, galleries and guesthouses.

But cobblestoned lanes and National Revival–era nostalgia are only part of the story. Bulgaria's cosmopolitan second city has always been hot on the heels of Sofia, and a stint as European Capital of Culture 2019 has given Plovdiv an edge. Music and art festivals draw increasing crowds, while renovations in the Kapana creative quarter and Tsar Simeon Gardens have given the city new confidence. Once an amiable waystation between Bulgaria and Greece or Turkey, the city has flowered into a destination in its own right – and one that should be on any itinerary through central Bulgaria.

Sights

Most of Plovdiv's main sights are in and around the Old Town. Its meandering cobblestone streets, overflowing with atmospheric house museums, art galleries, antique stores, are also home to welcoming nooks for eating, drinking and people-watching.

★ **Roman Amphitheatre** HISTORIC SITE
(Ancient Theatre of Philippopolis; 032-622 209; www.oldplovdiv.com; ul Hemus; adult/student 5/2 lv; 9am-6pm) Plovdiv's magnificent 2nd-century AD amphitheatre, built during the reign of Emperor Trajan, was uncovered during a freak landslide in 1972. It once held about 7000 spectators. Now largely restored, it's one of Bulgaria's most magical venues, once again hosting large-scale special events and concerts. Visitors can admire the amphitheatre for free from several look-outs along ul Hemus, or pay admission for a scarper around.

Balabanov House MUSEUM
(032-622 209; www.oldplovdiv.com; ul K Stoilov 57; adult/child 5/2 lv; 9am-6pm Apr-Oct, to 5.30pm Nov-Mar) One of Plovdiv's most beautiful Bulgarian National Revival–era mansions, Balabanov House is an enjoyable way to experience old town nostalgia as well as contemporary art. The house was faithfully reconstructed in 19th-century style during the 1970s. The lower floor has an impressive collection of paintings by local artists, while upper rooms are decorated with antiques and elaborately carved ceilings.

Ethnographical Museum MUSEUM
(032-625 654; www.ethnograph.info; ul Dr Chomakov 2; adult/student 6/2 lv; 9am-6pm Tue-Sun May-Oct, to 5pm Nov-Apr) Even if you don't have time to step inside, it would be criminal to leave Plovdiv's old town without glancing into the courtyard of this stunning National Revival–era building. Well-manicured flower gardens surround a navy-blue mansion ornamented with golden filigree and topped with a distinctive peaked roof. There is more to admire inside, especially the upper floor's sunshine-yellow walls and carved wooden ceiling hovering above displays of regional costumes.

Sleeping

Hikers Hostel HOSTEL €
(0896764854; www.hikers-hostel.org; ul Sâborna 53; 14-/8-bed dm 18/20 lv; @) In a mellow Old Town location, Hikers has wood-floored dorms and standard hostel perks such as a laundry and a shared kitchen. Bonuses such as a garden lounge, hammocks and mega-friendly staff make it a worthy option. Staff can help organise excursions to Bachkovo Monastery (southern mountains), Buzludzha Monument (central mountains) and more. Off-site private rooms (from 50 lv) are available in the Kapana area.

★ **Hostel Old Plovdiv** HOSTEL €€
(032-260 925; www.hosteloldplovdiv.com; ul Chetvarti Yanuari 3; dm/s/d/tr/q 22/58/78/98/118 lv; P) This marvellous old building (1868) is more akin to a boutique hotel than a hostel. Remarkably restored by charismatic owner Hristo Giulev and his wife, this genial place in the middle of the Old Town is all about old-world charm. Every room features hand-picked antiques (from the decor to the beds themselves), and the courtyard is desperately romantic.

At Renaissance Square BOUTIQUE HOTEL €€€
(032-266 966; www.atrenaissancesq.com; pl Vâzhrazhdane 1; s/d from 135/155 lv; P @) Recreating National Revival–era grandeur is a labour of love at this charming little hotel, between the old town and Plovdiv's shopping streets. Its five rooms are individually decorated with handsome wood floors, billowy drapes, and floral wall and ceiling

BULGARIA PLOVDIV

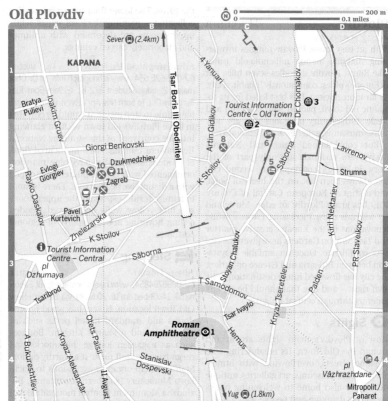

Old Plovdiv

paintings. The friendly, English-speaking owner is a font of local knowledge and extends the warmest of welcomes.

🍴 Eating & Drinking

Green Library
VEGAN €

(📞 0894796657; www.facebook.com/GoGreen.Enjoy Life; ul Pavel Kurtevich 1; mains 5-8 lv; ⊙ 9am-7pm Mon-Sat, 10am-6pm Sun; 🛜📶) You can't miss the screaming bright green facade of Kapana's 'Green Library', not a repository of books but rather of healthy foods, smoothies, sandwiches, cakes and breads. Eat in, take away, or simply enjoy a vegan chocolate-cherry cake and coffee on the pavement terrace.

★ Pavaj
BULGARIAN €€

(📞 0878111876; www.facebook.com/pavaj.plovdiv; ul Zlatarska 7; mains 10-15 lv; ⊙ noon-11pm Tue-

MYSTERIES OF THRACE

Plovdiv makes an excellent base for half-day trips to the windblown ruins and spiritual sights of Bulgarian Thrace. Magnificent **Bachkovo Monastery** (☑ 03327-2277; www.bachkovskimanastir.com; Bachkovo; monastery free, refectory 6 lv, museum 2 lv, ossuary 6 lv; ☺ 7am-8pm Jun-Sep, to 7pm Oct-May), founded in 1083, is about 30km south of Plovdiv. Its church is decorated with 1850s frescoes by renowned artist Zahari Zograf and houses a much-cherished icon of the Virgin Mary. Take any bus to Smolyan from Plovdiv's Rodopi bus station, disembark at the turn-off about 1.2km south of Bachkovo village and walk about 500m uphill.

Asen's Fortress (Assenovgrad; adult/student 4/2 lv; ☺ 9am-6pm Wed-Sun Apr-Oct, to 5pm Nov-Mar), 19km southeast of Plovdiv, squats precariously on the edge of a cliff. Over the centuries, Roman, Byzantine and Ottoman rulers admired its impenetrable position so much that they continued to build and rebuild, adding chapels and thickening its walls to a battering-ram-proof 3m. Taxis from Plovdiv will charge about 40 lv for a return trip to the fortress; better yet, negotiate for a driver to take you to both the fortress and Bachkovo Monastery.

Sun) This tiny hole-in-the-wall is one of Kapana's most happening restaurants. The formula for success follows can't-miss international trends like seasonal, farm-fresh ingredients and local favorites like sausages, meatballs and baked lamb given a lighter, more modern gloss. The wine list is superb. The space is cramped and you'll have to book in advance or turn up at odd hours.

Tam's House INTERNATIONAL €€
(☑ 0887242727; www.facebook.com/TamssHouse; ul Zagreb 4; mains 12-15 lv; ☺ 11am-11pm) One of the hit openings of 2018 was this labour of love fusing Bulgarian and South American cuisines by way of California. Expect a little of everything: steaks, burgers, tapas, and pilafs, prepared with care and given appealing, minimalist platings. Finish off with Tam's star attraction: a cheesecake 'egg' (mango cheesecake encased in white chocolate). Reserve in advance.

⭐ **Hebros Restaurant** BULGARIAN €€€
(☑ 032-625 929; www.hebros-hotel.com; ul K Stoilov 51; mains 16-28 lv; ☎) Genteel service and a tranquil setting is exactly what you would expect from the restaurant of the boutique Hebros Hotel. Classic Bulgarian flavours are gently muddled with Western European influences, creating mouth-watering morsels such as Smilyan beans with parmesan, rabbit with prunes, and grilled sea bream.

Kotka i Mishka BAR
(☑ 0878407578; www.facebook.com/Cat.and.Mouse.Craft.Beer.Bar; ul Hristo Dyukmedjiev 14; ☺ 10am-midnight) The crowd at this hole-in-the-wall craft-beer hangout spills onto the street – such is the bar's deserved popular-

ity, even against stiff competition in buzzing Kapana. The industrial-feel decorations – such as hamster cages hanging from the ceiling – are a nod to its name: 'cat and mouse'. Decent stop for afternoon tea or coffee and a perfect choice to start a late-night crawl.

Monkey House CAFE
(☑ 0889678333; www.facebook.com/monkeyhouse cafe; ul Zlatarska 3; ☺ 10am-midnight) Coffee lovers can rest easy in the stripped-bare decor of Monkey House, purveyors of Plovdiv's best flat white. The interior is ornamented with bicycles and moustachioed pillows; seats range from tree stumps and wheelbarrows to comfy chairs; and light bulbs dangle on ropes from the beamed ceiling. It's good fun, and the coffee's even better. Cocktails emerge after sundown.

ℹ️ Information

Tourist Information Centre – Central (☑ 032-620 229; www.visitplovdiv.com; ul Rayko Daskalov 1; ☺ 9am-5.30pm) Multilingual, friendly information centre near the main post office.

Tourist Information Centre – Old Town
(☑ 032-620 453; www.visitplovdiv.com; ul Sâborna 22; ☺ 9am-5.30pm) Helpful tourist information office in Plovdiv's Old Town.

ℹ️ Getting There & Away

BUS

Plovdiv has several bus stations; find more info on www.avtogara-plovdiv.info. Schedules can be found on www.bgrazpisanie.com. Most destinations of interest to travellers are served from the **Yug bus station** (South Bus Station; ☑ 032-626 937; www.bgrazpisanie.com; bul Hristo Botev 47), diagonally opposite the train station and a

15-minute walk from the centre. Both public and private buses operate from here, and there's often no way of predicting whether you'll get a big, modern bus or a cramped minibus – though the latter is likely for rural destinations. The following services typically leave from Yug: Sofia (14 lv, 2½ hours, many daily) and Varna (24-26 lv, seven hours, three daily).

Sever bus station (North Bus Station; ☑ 032-953 705; www.bgrazpisanie.com; ul Dimitar Stambolov 2; 🖵 99), 3.5km from the old town in the northern suburbs, also serves several useful destinations, including Burgas (14 lv, 2½ hours, many daily), Kazanlâk (9 lv, two hours, three daily), Nesebâr (22 lv, five hours, one daily) and Veliko Târnovo (18 lv, 4½ hours, three daily).

TRAIN

Plovdiv **train station** (www.bdz.bg; bul Hristo Botev) is well organised. Computer screens at the entrance and in the underpass leading to the platforms list recent arrivals and upcoming departures. International bus and train tickets can be booked along with domestic tickets at the **Yug bus station** and the train station. The following direct services leave from the train station: Burgas (15 lv, six hours, two daily), Sofia (10 lv, three hours, 15 daily) and Varna (18-22 lv, six hours, four daily).

CENTRAL BULGARIA

Bulgaria's mountainous centre is arguably the country's historic heart. Dramatic past events played out on both sides of the Stara Planina range: to the west is museum village Koprivshtitsa, while the lowlands town of Kazanlâk accesses Thracian tombs and the famously fragrant Valley of the Roses. The hub is magnificent Veliko Târnovo, former capital of the Bulgarian tsars, crowned with one of Europe's most spectacular citadels.

Koprivshtitsa Копривщица

☑ 07184 / POP 2500

Behind colourful house fronts and babbling streams broods Koprivshtitsa's revolutionary spirit. This museum-village immediately pleases the eye with its numerous restored National Revival–period mansions. It's a peaceful, touristy place, but Koprivshtitsa was once the heart of Bulgaria's revolution against the Ottomans. Todor Kableshkov declared an uprising against the Turks on 20 April 1876 from Kalachev Bridge (also called 'First Shot Bridge'). Today, Koprivshtitsa's few streets are dotted with historic homes interspersed with rambling, overgrown lanes, making it a romantic getaway and a good place for families.

◉ Sights

Oslekov House　　　　　　　　MUSEUM
(☑ 0878175613; www.koprivshtitza.com; ul Gerenilo-to 4; 2 lv; ⊙ 9.30am-6.30pm Apr-Oct, 9am-5pm Nov-Mar, closed Mon) With its triple-arched entrance and interior restored in shades from scarlet to sapphire blue, Oslekov House is arguably the most beautifully restored example of Bulgarian National Revival–period architecture in Koprivshtitsa. It was built between 1853 and 1856 by a rich merchant who was executed after his arrest during the 1876 April Uprising. Now a house-museum, it features informative, multilingual displays (in Bulgarian, English and French) about 19th-century Bulgaria.

Kableshkov House　　　　　　　MUSEUM
(www.koprivshtitza.com; ul Todor Kableshkov 8; adult/student 4/2 lv; ⊙ 9.30am-5.30pm Tue-Sun Apr-Oct, 9am-5pm Tue-Sun Nov-Mar) Todor Kableshkov is revered as having (probably) been the person who fired the first shot in the 1876 uprising against the Turks. After his arrest, he committed suicide rather than allowing his captors to decide his fate. This, his glorious former home (built in 1845), contains exhibits about the April Uprising.

◉ Sleeping

Hotel Astra　　　　　　　　GUESTHOUSE €€
(☑ 07184-2033; bul Hadzhi Nencho Palaveev 11; d/apt incl breakfast 80/90 lv; Ⓟ) Beautifully set in a garden at the northern end of Koprivshtitsa, the hospitable Astra has large, well-kept rooms and serves an epic homemade breakfast spread of pancakes, thick yoghurt and more. Book well in advance.

◉ Eating

Chuchura　　　　　　　　　BULGARIAN €€
(☑ 0888347770; www.mehana.eu; bul Hadzhi Nencho Palaveev 66; mains 8-15 lv; ⊙ 11am-11pm) This family-run tavern is the place to visit for authentic Bulgarian cooking. Nothing fancy, just well-done classics like pork *kavarma* (cooked in a clay pot), meatballs or roast lamb, all served in suitably rustic surrounds.

Dyado Liben　　　　　　　　BULGARIAN €€
(☑ 0887532096; bul Hadzhi Nencho Palaveev 47; mains 8-15 lv; ⊙ 11am-midnight; 🛜) Traditional fare is served at this atmospheric 1852 mansion with tables set in a warren of halls, graced with ornate painted walls and worn wood floors. Find it just across the bridge

leading from the main square, inside the facing courtyard.

ⓘ Information

Tourist Information Centre (☑ 07184-2191; www.koprivshtitza.com; pl 20 April 6; ⊙ 9.30am-5.30pm Tue, Wed & Fri-Sun Apr-Oct, to 5pm Nov-Mar) Information centre in a small building on the main square.

ⓘ Getting There & Away

Without private transport, getting to Koprivshtitsa can be inconvenient: the train station is 9km north of the village, requiring a taxi or shuttle bus (4 lv, 15 minutes), which isn't always dependably timed to meet incoming and outgoing trains. Find timetables for the shuttle bus posted at the train station or bus station.

Trains come from Sofia (6 lv to 9 lv, two hours, four daily) and Karlovo (3 lv to 4 lv, one to 1½ hours, two to four daily). Alternatively, Koprivshtitsa's **bus stop** (☑ 07184-3044; bul Palaveev 76) is central and has decent connections to Sofia (13 lv, two hours) and sporadic service to Plovdiv (12 lv, two hours).

Veliko Târnovo
Велико Търново

☑ 062 / POP 72,938

Medieval history emanates from Veliko Târnovo's fortified walls and cobbled lanes. One of Bulgaria's oldest towns, Veliko Târnovo has as its centrepiece the magnificent restored Tsarevets Fortress, citadel of the Second Bulgarian Empire. Historic Târnovo is tucked into the dramatic bends of the Yantra River, clasped by an amphitheatre of forested hills. Bulgaria's 19th-century National Revival splendour is easy to relive along historic lanes such as ul Gurko; similarly evocative is the handicraft market, Samovodska Charshiya, which retains the same atmosphere it must have had two centuries ago. The modern town has burst these tidy seams, splaying west from busy bul Bulgaria. Today's Târnovo has Bulgaria's second-largest university and is home to a multicultural expat scene.

⦿ Sights

★ **Tsarevets Fortress** FORTRESS
(☑ 0885105282; adult/student 6/2 lv, scenic elevator 2 lv; ⊙ 8am-7pm Apr-Oct, 9am-5pm Nov-Mar) The inescapable symbol of Veliko Târnovo, this reconstructed fortress dominates the skyline and is one of Bulgaria's most beloved monuments. The former seat of the medieval tsars, it hosts the remains of more than 400 houses, 18 churches, the royal palace, an execution rock and more. Watch your step: there are lots of potholes, broken steps and unfenced drops. The fortress morphs into a psychedelic spectacle with a magnificent night-time Sound & Light Show (p108).

Ulitsa General Gurko STREET
(ul General Gurko) The oldest street in Veliko Târnovo, ul Gurko is a must-stroll with arresting views towards the Yantra River and Asen Monument. Its charmingly crumbling period houses – which appear to be haphazardly piled on one another – provide a million photo opportunities and conversations that start with 'Imagine living here...'. Sturdy shoes are a must.

Sarafkina Kâshta MUSEUM
(☑ 0885105282; ul General Gurko 88; adult/student 6/2 lv; ⊙ 9am-5.30pm Tue-Sat) Built for a wealthy banker in 1861, this National Revival–style house-museum spans five storeys. Within, 19th-century earrings, bracelets and other delicate silverware are on display, alongside antique ceramics, woodcarvings and traditional costumes and jewellery.

🛏 Sleeping

Hotel Anhea HOTEL €
(☑ 062-577 713; www.anheabg.com; ul Nezavisimost 32; s/d/tr from 32/50/60 lv; ❄ 🐾 🛜) This superb budget hotel in an early-1900s building has a restful air, despite its central location. Crisp beige and cream rooms are arranged across two buildings, between which lies a peaceful courtyard and breakfast area – this secret garden is decorated with pretty iron railings and fountains, and is overseen by resident rabbit Emma.

Hostel Mostel HOSTEL €
(☑ 0897859359; www.hostelmostel.com; ul Iordan Indjeto 10; campsites/dm/s/d incl breakfast 18/20/46/60 lv; @ 🛜) The famous Sofia-based Hostel Mostel has a welcoming branch in Târnovo, with clean, modern dorm rooms and doubles with sparkling bathrooms. It's just 150m from Tsarevets Fortress – good for exploring there, but a long walk from the city centre. Service is cheerful and multilingual, and there's barbecue equipment out back.

★ **Hotel-Mehana Gurko** HISTORIC HOTEL €€
(☑ 0887858965; www.hotel-gurko.com; ul General Gurko 33; d/apt incl breakfast from 110/150 lv;

BULGARIA VELIKO TÂRNOVO

TOMBS & BLOOMS: KAZANLÂK

For centuries Kazanlâk has been the sweet-smelling centre of European rose-oil production. This nondescript town is also the gateway to the Valley of the Thracian Kings, meaning you can combine fragrant flowers with awe-inspiring tombs in a single visit.

Roses (the aromatic *Rosa damascena*, to be precise) bloom around mid-May to mid-June. Their delicate oils are used in everything from moisturising balms, liqueurs, jams and candies. Kazanlâk's **Rose Festival** (⊙1st weekend Jun) is the highlight of the season. You can explore the history of rose-oil production year-round at the **Museum of Roses** (☑0431-64 057; www.muzei-kazanlak.org; bul Osvobozhdenie 10; adult/student 6/2 lv; ⊙9am-5.30pm), or on a visit to **Enio Bonchev Rose Distillery** (☑0885640999; www.eniobonchev.com; Tarnichene; with/without rose picking 10/7 lv), 27km west of Kazanlâk (call or email in advance to fix a time).

Long before a single seed was sown, the Thracians – a fierce Indo-European tribe – ruled the roost. Archaeologists believe there are at least 1500 Thracian burial mounds and tombs in the vicinity. Most visitors to Kazanlâk head to a nearby replica of the **Thracian Tomb of Kazanlâk** (www.muzei-kazanlak.org; Tyulbe Park; adult/child 6/2 lv; ⊙9am-5pm). More (and better) tombs can be reached via tour bus or your own vehicle: between Kazanlâk and the village of Shipka you can step inside 4th-century BC **Shushmanets Tomb** (☑0431-99 031; www.muzei-kazanlak.org; adult/student 6/2 lv; ⊙9am-5pm) and the mysterious **Ostrusha Tomb** (☑0431-99 050; www.muzei-kazanlak.org; adult/student 6/2 lv; ⊙9am-5pm), whose sarcophagus was carved from a single slab of stone.

Day trips taking in both regions can be arranged at the Kazanlâk **tourist information centre** (☑0431-99 553; ul Iskra 4; ⊙8am-5pm Mon-Fri). The **Roza Hotel** (☑0431-50 005; www.hotelrozabg.com; ul Rozova Dolina 2; r 60-120 lv; P✳@🖰) in town makes a comfortable and good-value base. Buses run from Kazanlâk to Sofia (17 lv, three hours, five daily) and Plovdiv (10 lv, two hours, three daily). See www.bdz.bg/en for train schedules.

P✳@🖰) Sitting pretty on Veliko Tărnovo's oldest street, with blooms spilling over its wooden balconies and agricultural curios littering the exterior, the Gurko is one of the best places to sleep (and eat) in town. Its 21 rooms are spacious and soothing, each individually decorated and offering great views.

🍴 Eating & Drinking

Shtastliveca   BULGARIAN €€
(☑062-600 656; www.shtastliveca.com; ul Stefan Stambolov 79; mains 10-20 lv; ⊙11am-midnight; 🖰✎) Inventive dishes and amiable service have solidified the 'Lucky Man' as a favourite among locals and expats. Sauces pairing chocolate and cheese are drizzled over chicken, while strawberry and balsamic vinegar lend piquancy to meaty dishes. There is a pleasing range for vegetarians.

★Han Hadji Nikoli   INTERNATIONAL €€€
(☑062-651 291; www.hanhadjinikoli.com; ul Rakovski 19; mains 17-30 lv; ⊙10am-11pm; 🖰) Countless Veliko Tărnovo inns were ransacked under Ottoman rule, as they were popular meeting places for revolution-minded locals. Fortunately Han Hadji Nikoli survived, and today the town's finest restaurant occupies this beautifully restored 1858 building with an upstairs gallery. Well-executed dishes include Trakia chicken marinated in herbs and yoghurt, mussels sautéed in white wine, and exquisitely prepared pork neck.

Tam   BAR
(☑0889879693; www.facebook.com/TAMVELIKO TARNOVO; ul Marno Pole 2A; ⊙4pm-3am Mon-Sat) Open the nondescript door, and up the stairs you'll find the city's friendliest, most-open-minded hang-out. Tam is the place to feel the pulse of VT's arty crowd. You might stumble on art installations, movie screenings, or language nights in English, French or Spanish. Punters and staff extend a genuine welcome and drinks flow late.

☆ Entertainment

Sound & Light Show   LIVE PERFORMANCE
(☑0885080865; www.soundandlight.bg; ul N Pikolo 6; 20-25 lv) Marvel as Veliko Tărnovo's Tsarevets Fortress (p107) skyline is bathed in multicoloured light and lasers during the Sound & Light Show. This 40-minute audiovisual display uses choral music and flashes of light in homage to the rise and fall of the Second Bulgarian Empire. Check the web-

site for a current schedule and to buy tickets for paid performances.

🔒 Shopping

★**Samovodska Charshiya**   ARTS & CRAFTS
(ul Rakovski) Veliko Tărnovo's historic quarter is a true centre of craftsmanship, with genuine blacksmiths, potters and cutlers, among other artisans, still practising their trades here. Wander the cobblestone streets to discover bookshops and purveyors of antiques, jewellery and art, housed in appealing National Revival houses.

ℹ Information

Tourist Information Centre (☑ 062-622 148; www.velikoturnovo.info; ul Hristo Botev 5; ⊙9am-6pm Mon-Fri, 10am-5pm Sat & Sun) Helpful English-speaking staff offering local info and advice.

ℹ Getting There & Away

BUS

Most services arrive at and depart from the city's two main bus stations; always double-check the timetable to get the right station. **Zapad Bus Station** (West Bus Station; ☑ 062-640 908; ul Nikola Gabrovski 74), about 3km south of the tourist information centre, is the main intercity one (it's sometimes labelled simply as 'Bus Station' on timetables). Local buses 10, 12, 14, 70 and 110 go there, along ul Vasil Levski. There's also a left-luggage office. Closer to the centre is **Yug bus station** (South Bus Station; ☑ 062-620 014; ul Hristo Botev 74), 700m south of the tourist information centre.

Sample destinations and fares from Zapad include Burgas (18 lv to 25 lv, four hours, four daily), Kazanlăk (9 lv, three hours, five daily) and Plovdiv (20 lv, four hours, four daily). Destinations served from Yug include Sofia (22 lv, four hours, several daily) and Varna (21 lv, four hours, several daily).

TRAIN

Check train schedules with the tourist information centre (p109), or on www.bdz.bg, as Veliko Tărnovo's two main train stations are located 10km apart. Irregular trains link the two stations (1.50 lv, 20 minutes, seven daily).

The more walkable of the two is **Veliko Tărnovo train station** (☑ 0885397701; www.bdz.bg), 1.5km west of town. Direct connections from this station are limited, and services to cities like Plovdiv, Sofia and the coastal resorts require a change of trains in Gorna Oryakhovitsa, Stara Zagora or Dabovo. **Gorna Oryakhovitsa train station** (☑ 061-826 118; www.bdz.bg; ul Tsar Osvoboditel), 8.5km northeast of town, is along

the main line between Sofia and Varna. There are daily services to/from Sofia (18 lv, four to five hours, eight daily). Direct trains also reach Varna (13 lv, 3½ to four hours, five daily).

BLACK SEA COAST

Bulgaria's long Black Sea coastline is the country's summertime playground, attracting not just Bulgarians but tourists from across Europe and beyond. The big, purpose-built resorts here have become serious rivals to those of Spain and Greece, while independent travellers will find plenty to explore away from the parasols and jet skis. Sparsely populated sandy beaches to the far south and north, the bird-filled lakes around Burgas, and picturesque ancient towns such as Nesebăr and Sozopol are rewarding destinations. The 'maritime capital' of Varna and its seaside rival, Burgas, are two of Bulgaria's most vibrant cities. Both are famous for summer festivals and nightlife as well as their many museums and galleries.

Varna   Варна
☑052 / POP 335,170
Bulgaria's third city and maritime capital, Varna is the most interesting and cosmopolitan town on the Black Sea coast. A combination of port city, naval base and seaside resort, it's an appealing place to while away a few days, packed with history yet thoroughly modern, with an enormous park to amble round and a lengthy beach to lounge on. In the city centre you'll find Bulgaria's largest Roman baths complex and its finest archaeological museum, as well as a lively cultural and restaurant scene.

◎ Sights & Activities

★**Archaeological Museum**   MUSEUM
(☑052-681 030; www.archaeo.museumvarna.com; ul Maria Luisa 41; adult/child 10/2 lv; ⊙10am-5pm Apr-Sep, Tue-Sat Oct-Mar; ☐8, 9, 109, 409) Exhibits at this vast museum, the best of its kind in Bulgaria, include 6000-year-old bangles, necklaces and earrings said to be the oldest worked gold found in the world. You'll also find Roman surgical implements, Hellenistic tombstones and touching oddments including a marble plaque listing, in Greek, the names of the city's school graduates for AD 221. All of the exhibits are helpfully signposted in English, with excellent

explanatory text. There's a large collection of icons on the 2nd floor.

Beach
BEACH

(⊙9am-6pm) Varna has a long stretch of public beach, starting near the port and stretching north some 4km. Generally, the quality of the sand and water improve and the crowds thin as you stroll north. The easiest way to access the beach is to walk south on bul Slivnitsa to Primorski Park and follow the stairs to the beach.

Baracuda Dive Center
DIVING

(☑0898706604; www.baracudadive.com; ul General Gurko 43; half-day beginning instruction from 110 lv) Offers diving instruction for beginners and advanced divers, as well as guided diving excursions along the Black Sea coast. Rates include equipment.

🛏 Sleeping

Varna has no shortage of accommodation, although the better (or at least more central) places get very busy during the summer months.

★ Yo Ho Hostel
HOSTEL €

(☑0884729144; www.yohohostel.com; ul Ruse 23; dm/s/d from 15/38/55 lv; @ 🤶; 🚌8, 9, 109) Shiver your timbers at this cheerful, pirate-themed place, with four- and 11-bed dorm rooms, an all-female dorm and private options. Staff offer free pick-ups and can organise camping and rafting trips. The location is an easy walk to the main sights.

Hotel Odessos
HOTEL €€

(☑052-640 300; www.odessos-bg.com; bul Slivnitsa 1; s/d from 85/105 lv; 🅿 ❄ 🤶) Enjoying a great location opposite the main entrance to Primorski Park, this is an older establishment with smallish and pretty average rooms, but it's convenient for the beach. Only the pricier 'sea view' rooms have balconies.

🍴 Eating & Drinking

Varna has some of the best eating on the Black Sea coast, with everything from beachside shacks to fine dining.

Morsko Konche
PIZZA €

(☑052-600 418; www.morskokonche.bg; pl Nezavisimost, cnr ul Zamenhof; pizzas 5-10 lv; ⊙8.30am-10pm; 🤶 ☑; 🚌8, 9, 109) The 'Seahorse' is a cheap and cheerful pizza place with a big menu featuring all the standard varieties, plus some inventive creations of its own: the 'exotic' pizza comes with bananas and blueberries.

★ Stariya Chinar
BULGARIAN €€

(☑052-949 400; www.stariachinar.com; ul Preslav 11; mains 12-20 lv; ⊙8am-midnight) This is upmarket Balkan soul food at its best. Try the baked lamb, made to an old Bulgarian recipe, or the barbecued pork ribs; it also boasts some rather ornate salads. Outdoor seating is lovely in summer; park yourself in the traditional interior when the cooler weather strikes.

Mr Baba
SEAFOOD €€€

(☑0896505050; www.mrbaba.net; bul Primorski; mains 15-30 lv; ⊙8am-midnight; 🤶; 🚌20) The coast-long trend for novelty ship restaurants has come to Varna, with this handsome, wooden-hulled venture stranded at the far southern end of the beach off bul Primorski, near the port. It features a pricey but tasty menu of steak and fish dishes, including sea bass, trout and bluefish. Indoor and outdoor seating. Reserve in advance.

The Black Sheep Beer House
PUB

(☑0878623426; www.theblacksheep.bg; bul Knyaz Boris I 62; ⊙9am-2am) This centrally located pub and microbrewery is always hopping. Stop by to try out the house brew, Zlatna Varna, or nibble on some very decent pub grub like salads, burgers and grilled pork ribs. Tables can normally be had on off nights, like Mondays or Tuesdays, but book in advance over the weekend.

☆ Entertainment

Varna Opera Theatre
OPERA

(☑box office 052-665 022; www.tmpcvarna.com; pl Nezavisimost 1; ⊙ticket office 10am-1pm & 2-7pm; 🚌8, 9, 109, 409) Varna's grand opera house hosts performances by the Varna Opera and Philharmonic Orchestra all year, except July and August, when some performances are staged at the Open-Air Theatre in Primorski Park.

ⓘ Information

Tourist Information Centre (☑052-820 690; www.visit.varna.bg; pl Kiril & Metodii; ⊙9am-7pm May-Sep, 8.30am-5.30pm Mon-Fri Oct-Apr; 🚌8, 9, 109, 409) Plenty of free brochures and maps, and helpful multilingual staff. The Tourist Information Centre also operates free three-hour walking tours of the city on select days from June to September.

ⓘ Getting There & Away

AIR

Varna's international **airport** (VAR; ☑052-573 323; www.varna-airport.bg; Aksakovo; 🚌409) has scheduled and charter flights from all over Europe, as well as regular flights to and from Sofia. Bus 409 goes to the airport from the centre.

BUS

Varna's **central bus station** (Avtoexpress; ☑ information 052-757 044, tickets 052-748 349; www.autogaravn.com; bul Vladislav Varenchik 158; ☺24hr; ☐148, 409) is about 2km northwest of the city centre. Most intercity coaches depart from here. There are regular buses to Sofia (33 lv, seven hours, 10 daily), Burgas (14 lv, 21/2 hours, several daily) and other major destinations in Bulgaria: see www.bgrazpisanie.com/en for fares and schedules.

TRAIN

Facilities at Varna's **train station** (☑ 052-630 444; www.bdz.bg; pl Slaveikov; ☐8, 9, 109) include a **left luggage office** (pl Slaveikov; per day 2 lv; ☺7am-7pm) and cafe. Rail destinations from Varna include Ruse (15 lv, four hours, two daily), Sofia (30 lv, seven to eight hours, seven daily), Plovdiv (25 lv, seven hours, three daily) and Shumen (7 lv, 1½ hours, 10 daily).

Nesebâr   Несебър
☑0554 / POP 13,340

On a small rocky outcrop 37km northeast of Burgas and connected to the mainland by a narrow, artificial isthmus, pretty-as-a-postcard Nesebâr is famous for its surprisingly numerous, albeit mostly ruined, medieval churches. It has become heavily commercialised and transforms into one huge, open-air souvenir market during the high season; outside summer, it's a ghost town. Designated by Unesco as a World Heritage site, Nesebâr has its charms, but in summer these can be overpowered by the crowds and the relentless parade of tacky shops. With Sunny Beach (Slânchev Bryag) just across the bay, meanwhile, you have every conceivable water sport on hand. The 'new town' on the other side of the isthmus has the newest and biggest hotels and the main beach, but the sights are all in the old town.

⦿ Sights & Activities

Archaeological Museum   MUSEUM

(☑0554-46 019; www.ancient-nessebar.com; ul Mesembria 2; adult/child 6/3 lv; ☺9am-7pm Jun & Sep, to 8pm Jul & Aug, to 5pm Oct-May) Explore the rich history of Nesebâr – formerly Mesembria – at this fine museum. Greek and Roman pottery, statues and tombstones, as well as Thracian gold jewellery and ancient anchors, are displayed here. There's also a collection of icons from Nesebâr's numerous churches.

Sveti Stefan Church   CHURCH

(☑0554-46 019; www.ancient-nessebar.com; ul Ribarska; adult/child 6/3 lv; ☺9am-7pm Mon-Fri, 10.30am-2pm & 2.30-7pm Sat & Sun May-Sep, 9am-5pm Mon-Fri, from 10am Sat & Sun Oct-Apr) Built in the 11th century and reconstructed 500 years later, this is the best-preserved church in town. If you only visit one, this is the church to choose. Its beautiful 16th- to 18th-century murals cover virtually the entire interior. Come early, as it's popular with tour groups.

Aqua Paradise   WATER PARK

(☑0885208055; www.aquaparadise-bg.com; Hwy E87, Ravda; adult/child 42/21 lv, after 3pm 30/15 lv; ☺10am-6.30pm Jun-Sep; ⊞) Organised watery fun is on hand at Aqua Paradise, a huge water park just off the main highway on the western outskirts of Nesebâr, with a variety of pools, slides and chutes. A free minibus, running every 15 minutes, makes pick-ups at signed stops around Nesebâr and Sunny Beach.

🛏 Sleeping & Eating

★ Boutique
Hotel St Stefan   BOUTIQUE HOTEL €€

(☑0554-43 603; www.hotelsaintstefan.com; ul Ribarska 11; r/ste 95/160 lv; ᴾ❋ᴪ) One of the nicest hotels in Nesebâr, the St Stefan offers rooms with views out over the harbour and Black Sea. There's a small sauna on the premises as well as a terrace for drinks and light meals. Rooms feature original artwork by Bulgarian artists. Breakfast costs 8 lv. Book well in advance for summer dates.

★ Gloria Mar   BULGARIAN €€€

(☑0893550055; www.gloriamar-bg.com; ul Kraybrezhna 9; mains 12-30 lv; ☺11am-11pm) For our money, this is the best dining option in touristy Nesebâr. Fresh seafood, wood-fired pizzas and grilled meats are on offer, as well as harder-to-find risottos and paellas. There's an extensive wine list and dining on three levels, including a rooftop terrace. It's on the southern side of old Nesebâr, facing the marina and passenger ferry terminal.

ⓘ Getting There & Away

Nesebâr is well connected to coastal destinations by public transport, and the town's **bus station** (☑0554-42 721; www.bgrazpisanie.com; ul Andzhelo Ronkali) is on the small square just outside the city walls. The stop before this on the mainland is for the new town. Buses run in season every few minutes to Sunny Beach (1 lv, 10 minutes). Longer-haul destinations include Burgas (7 lv, one hour, hourly), Varna (14 lv, two hours, four daily) and Sofia (37 lv, seven hours, three daily). In season, high-speed **Fast Ferry** (☑0885808001; www.fastferry.bg; Passenger Ferry Port; ☺8.30am-8.30pm Jun-Sep) hydrofoils and catamarans run daily from Nesebâr's passenger ferry port (on the southern side of Nesebâr) to Sozopol.

Burgas   Бургас

☑056 / POP 202,766

For most visitors, the port city of Burgas (sometimes written as 'Bourgas') is no more than a transit point for the more appealing resorts and historic towns further up and down the coast. If you do decide to stop over, you'll find a lively, well-kept city with a neat, pedestrianised centre, a long, uncrowded beach, a gorgeous seafront **Maritime Park**, and some interesting museums. A clutch of reasonably priced hotels, as well as some of the best restaurants in this part of the country, makes it a practical base for exploring the southern coast, too.

◎ Sights

St Anastasia Island   ISLAND

(☑0882004124; www.anastasia-island.com; return boat trip adult/child 12/10 lv; ☺departures 10.30am & 1.30pm May-Oct) This small volcanic island makes for a fun day of exploring. The island, which has served as a religious retreat, a prison and pirate bait (according to legend, a golden treasure is buried in its sands), is today dominated by a lighthouse and a monastery, where visitors can sample various healing herb potions. At least two (and usually more) ships leave daily from May to October from the **passenger ferry terminal** (☑information 882004124; Magazia 1, Southeast of ul Knyaz Al Battenberg 1) south of the bus and train stations.

🛏 Sleeping

Old House Hostel   HOSTEL €

(☑056-841 558; www.burgashostel.com; ul Sofroniy 3; dm/d 18/41 lv; ✴🛜) This charming hostel makes itself right at home in a lovely 1895 house. Dorms are airy and bright (and bunk-free!), while doubles have access to a sweet little courtyard. The location is central and about 400m from the beach.

Hotel Doro   HOTEL €€

(☑056-820 808; www.hoteldoro.com; ul Sredna Gora 28; s/d 70/80 lv; ℗➔✴🛜) The location is better than it looks at first glance: ignore the slightly depressed neighbourhood setting by keeping in mind that the central restaurants

and Maritime Park are both just a short walk away. Once inside the hotel, things brighten considerably. Enjoy spotlessly clean rooms (some with balconies) and what might very well be Bulgaria's best breakfast buffet.

✗ Eating

★ Rosé   INTERNATIONAL €€

(☑0885855099; www.facebook.com/roseburgas; bul Aleko Bogoridi 19; mains 8-20 lv; ☺11am-11pm; 🛜) Choose from a wide menu of grilled meats and fish, including a superlative lamb-shank offering, or fresh pasta at this superb restaurant in the city centre. Finish off with a cake or homemade ice cream. There's a small terrace for nice weather; otherwise, eat in the main dining room, which is just formal enough for a special night out.

Ethno   SEAFOOD €€

(☑0887877966; www.facebook.com/EthnoRestaurant; ul Aleksandrovska 49; mains 7-20 lv; ☺11am-11pm; 🛜) This downtown restaurant does splendid things with seafood: the Black Sea mussels alone are worth a trip to Burgas. With inviting blue-and-white surrounds that recall the city's Greek heritage, superb (English-speaking) service and a summery vibe, Ethno is classy without being uptight.

HashtagSTUDIO   CAFE

(☑0883376370; www.facebook.com/HashtagStudioBurgas; ul Aboba 1; ☺7am-11pm) As hip as it gets in Burgas: artisanal coffees, craft beers, a stylish interior of exposed concrete walls and hanging lightbulbs, attentive service, and an all-round cool vibe. Check the Facebook page for occasional parties and live events.

ℹ Getting There & Away

AIR

Bulgaria Air (www.air.bg) links **Burgas Airport** (BOJ; ☑information 056-870 248; www.burgas-airport.bg; Hwy E87, Sarafovo; 🛜; 🚌15), 10km northeast of town, with Sofia daily (April to October). **Wizz Air** (www.wizzair.com) connects Burgas with London Luton. Other carriers service cities throughout Europe and select destinations in the Middle East, including Tel Aviv and Beirut. The airport is linked to the centre via public bus 15.

BUS

Outside the train station at the southern end of ul Aleksandrovska, **Yug bus station** (☑0884981220; www.bgrazpisanie.com; pl Tsaritsa Yoanna) is where most travellers will arrive or leave. There are regular buses to coastal destinations. Departures are less frequent outside summer. A **left-luggage office** (☺ 6am-10pm) is located inside the station. There are regular buses to coastal destinations, including Nesebâr (5 lv, 40 minutes, half-hourly), Varna (12 lv, two hours, half-hourly) and Sozopol (5 lv, 40 minutes, every 45 minutes). Several daily buses also go to and from Sofia (30 lv, seven to eight hours) and Plovdiv (20 lv, four hours). Departures are less frequent outside summer.

The Burgas Bus website (www.burgasbus.info) is in Bulgarian only, but has a handy timetable for both major bus stations (on the upper left side of the opening page).

TRAIN

The historic and well-maintained **train station** (🚆 information 056-845 022; www.bdz.bg; ul Ivan Vazov; ☺ information office 6am-10pm) was built in 1902. There are clearly marked ticket windows for buying both domestic and international tickets. There's also an ATM and a cafe. Trains run to Plovdiv (16 lv, five to six hours, five daily) and Sofia (22 lv, seven to eight hours, five daily).

Sozopol   Созопол

🚆 0550 / POP 5700

Ancient Sozopol, with its charming old town of meandering cobbled streets and pretty wooden houses, huddled together on a narrow peninsula, is one of the coast's highlights. With two superb beaches, a genial atmosphere, plentiful accommodation and good transport links, it has long been a popular seaside resort and makes an excellent base for exploring the area. Although not quite as crowded as Nesebâr, it is becoming ever more popular with international visitors. There's a lively cultural scene, too, with plenty of free concerts and other events in summer.

The new town, known as 'Harmanite', lies south of the tiny bus station. The best beach is in this part of town, but otherwise, it's mainly modern hotels and residential areas.

◎ Sights

Sozopol has two great beaches: **Harmanite Beach** has all the good-time gear (waterslide, paddle boats, beach bar), while to the north, the smaller **Town Beach** packs in the serious sun-worshippers.

Archaeological Museum   MUSEUM

(🚆 0550-22 226; ul Han Krum 2; adult/child 7/2 lv; ☺ 8.30am-6pm Jun-Sep, 8.30am-noon & 1.30pm-5.30pm Mon-Fri Oct-May) Housed in a drab concrete box near the port, this museum has a small but fascinating collection of local finds from its Apollonian glory days and beyond.

In addition to a wealth of Hellenic treasures, the museum occasionally exhibits the skeleton of a local 'vampire', found with a stake driven through its chest.

Sveti Ivan   ISLAND

The largest Bulgarian island in the Black Sea (0.7 sq km), Sveti Ivan lies 3km north of Sozopol's old town. The island's history stretches back to Thracian and Roman times, and includes a monastery from the 4th century AD. Sveti Ivan made international headlines in 2010 with the purported discovery of the remains of St John the Baptist. There are no scheduled excursions to the island, but private trips (from around 60 lv) can be arranged along the **Fishing Harbour** (ul Kraybrezhna).

★☆ Festivals & Events

Apollonia Arts Festival   ART, MUSIC

(www.apollonia.bg; ☺ late Aug–mid-Sep) This is the highlight of Sozopol's cultural calendar, with concerts, theatrical performances, art exhibitions, film screenings and more held across town.

🛏 Sleeping & Eating

★ Just a Hostel   HOSTEL €

(🚆 0550-22 175; ul Apolonia 20; dm 20 lv; 🛜) This clean, cosy, centrally located hostel sits in the centre of the Old Town, a few minutes' walk from the beach. Dorm-bed accommodation with shared bath and shower. The price includes traditional breakfast (pancakes) and coffee.

Art Hotel   HOTEL €€

(🚆 0550-24 081, 0878650160; www.arthotel-sbh.com; ul Kiril & Metodii 72; d/studios 85/105 lv; ❄🛜) This peaceful old house, belonging to the Union of Bulgarian Artists, is within a walled courtyard towards the tip of the peninsula, away from the crowds. It has a small selection of bright, comfortable rooms with balconies, most with sea views; breakfast is served on the terraces overlooking the sea.

Panorama Sv. Ivan   SEAFOOD €€

(🚆 0888260820; ul Morski Skali 21; mains 10-22 lv; ☺ 10am-11pm) This lively place has an open terrace with a fantastic view towards Sveti Ivan island. Fresh, locally caught fish is the mainstay of the menu. It's one of the best of many seafood spots on this street.

ℹ Getting There & Away

The small public **bus station** (🚆 0550-23 460; www.bgrazpisanie.com; ul Han Krum) is just

BULGARIA SOZOPOL

south of the old town walls. Buses leave for Burgas (6 lv, 40 minutes) about every 30 minutes between 6am and 9pm in summer, and about once an hour in the low season. Public buses leave two to three times a day for Sofia (30 lv, seven hours). **Fast Ferry** (☑ 0889182914, booking 0885808001; www.fastferry.bg) operates from a kiosk at the harbour and runs three daily high-speed catamarans or hydrofoils to Nesebâr (one way/return from 27/54 lv, 40 minutes) from June to September.

SURVIVAL GUIDE

❶ Directory A–Z

ACCESSIBLE TRAVEL

Bulgaria is not an easy destination for travellers with disabilities. Uneven and broken footpaths pose challenges, and ramps and toilets designed for disabled people are few and far between, other than in a handful of top-end hotels in Sofia and other big cities. Public transport is not generally geared toward the needs of travellers with disabilities. One organisation worth contacting is the Center for Independent Living (www.cil.bg) in Sofia.

ACCOMMODATION

Accommodation is most expensive in Sofia and other big cities, notably Plovdiv and Varna. Elsewhere, prices are relatively cheap by Western European standards. Demand and prices are highest in coastal resorts between July and August, and in the skiing resorts between December and February. Outside the holiday seasons, these hotels often close down, or operate on a reduced basis.

Guesthouses Usually small, family-run places and great value, with cosy rooms and home-cooked breakfasts.

Hizhas The mountain huts in Bulgaria's hiking terrain are convenient, though basic, places to sleep.

Hotels Bulgaria has a good range of hotels from budget to luxury.

INTERNET ACCESS

Most hotels and hostels offer free internet access to guests, and wi-fi hotspots can be found in many restaurants, cafes and other businesses. With the increasing availability of wi-fi, internet cafes have become something of a rarity in Bulgaria.

LGBT+ TRAVELLERS

Homosexuality is legal in Bulgaria, but gay culture remains discreet. Same-sex relationships have no legal recognition. Attitudes are changing, and there are several gay clubs and bars in Sofia and small scenes in Varna and Plovdiv. There is an annual Gay Pride march in Sofia (www.sofiapride.org). For more information see www.gay.bg.

MONEY

ATMs are widely available. Credit cards are accepted in most hotels and restaurants; smaller guesthouses or rural businesses may only accept cash.

Currency

The local currency is the lev (plural: leva), comprised of 100 stotinki. It is almost always abbreviated as lv (лв). The lev is a stable currency and linked to the euro at a rate of around 2 leva per 1 euro. For major purchases, such as organised tours, airfares, car rental and midrange and top-end hotels, prices are sometimes quoted in euros, although payment is carried out in leva.

Money Changers

Foreign-exchange offices can be found in all large towns, and rates are always displayed prominently. They are no longer allowed to charge commission, but that doesn't always stop them trying; always check the final amount that you will be offered before handing over your cash. Avoid exchange offices at train stations, airports or in tourist resorts, as rates are often poor.

OPENING HOURS

Standard opening hours are as follows:

Banks 9am to 4pm Monday to Friday

Bars 11am to midnight

Government offices 9am to 5pm Monday to Friday

Post offices 8.30am to 5pm Monday to Friday

Restaurants 11am to 11pm

Shops 9am to 6pm

PUBLIC HOLIDAYS

New Year's Day 1 January

Liberation Day 3 March

Orthodox Easter March/April/May

May Day 1 May

St George's Day/Bulgarian Army Day 6 May

Cyrillic Alphabet/Culture and Literacy Day 24 May

Unification Day 6 September

Bulgarian Independence Day 22 September

Christmas 25 and 26 December

TELEPHONE

➔ To call Bulgaria from abroad, dial the international access code (which varies from country to country), add 359 (the country code for Bulgaria), the area code (minus the first zero) and then the number.

➔ To make an international call from Bulgaria, dial 00 followed by the code of the country you are calling, then the local area code, minus the initial 0.

→ To make domestic calls within Bulgaria, dial the area code, which will be between 2 and 5 digits long, followed by the number you wish to call. If you are making a domestic call from your mobile phone, you will also have to insert the country code (+359) first, unless you are using a Bulgarian SIM card.

→ To call a Bulgarian mobile phone from within Bulgaria, dial the full number, including the initial 0.

Mobile Phones

Visitors from elsewhere in Europe will be able to use their mobile phones in Bulgaria. Local SIM cards are easy to buy in mobile phone stores (bring your passport) and can be used in most phones.

TOURIST INFORMATION

Bigger cities, and smaller towns popular with tourists, have dedicated tourist information centres, which provide free maps, leaflets and brochures. National parks often have information centres offering advice.

ⓘ Getting There & Away

Most international visitors enter and leave Bulgaria via Sofia Airport (p99), and there are frequent flights to the capital from other European cities. Bulgaria is also easily accessible by road and rail from neighbouring countries, and its railway is part of the InterRail system and so can be included in a longer European rail journey. Long-distance coaches reach Bulgarian cities from Turkey, Greece, Romania, Serbia and North Macedonia. There are regular ferry crossings that carry both vehicles and foot passengers across the Danube from Romania.

If you prefer something more structured, several companies offer organised tours and package holidays to Bulgaria.

Flights, cars and tours can be booked online at www.lonelyplanet.com/bookings.

AIR

Bulgaria has good air links with numerous European cities, as well as some cities in the Middle East. There are currently no direct flights to Bulgaria from further afield, so visitors from, for example, North America or Australia will need to pick up a connecting flight elsewhere in Europe.

LAND
Bus

Buses travel to Bulgarian cities from destinations all over Europe, most arriving at Sofia, with some direct to Plovdiv. You will either get off the bus at the border and walk through customs to present your passport, or be visited on the bus by officials. Long delays can be expected. A good timetable for international connections can be found at www.bgrazpisanie.com.

Car & Motorcycle

In order to drive on Bulgarian roads, you will need to display a vignette (15/30 lv for one week/month) sold at all border crossings into Bulgaria, petrol stations and post offices. Rental cars hired within Bulgaria should already have a vignette. Petrol stations and car-repair shops are common around border crossing areas and along main roads.

Train

Trains run to/from destinations in Romania, Serbia and Turkey, though at present, no trains travel directly between Bulgaria and North Macedonia. Bulgarian international train services are operated by Bulgarian State Railways (BDZ; www.bdz.bg).

ⓘ Getting Around

AIR

The only scheduled domestic flights within Bulgaria are between Sofia and Varna and Sofia and Burgas. Both routes are operated by Bulgaria Air (www.air.bg).

BUS

Buses link all cities and major towns and connect villages with the nearest transport hub. Several private companies operate frequent modern, comfortable buses between larger towns, while older, often cramped minibuses run on routes between smaller towns. Buses provide the most comfortable and quickest mode of public transport in Bulgaria, though the type of bus you get can be a lottery.

Though it isn't exhaustive, many bus and train schedules can be accessed at www.bgrazpisanie.com.

CAR & MOTORCYCLE

The best way to travel around Bulgaria – especially when visiting remote villages, monasteries and national parks – is to hire a car or motorbike. The Union of Bulgarian Motorists (p101) is the main national organisation for motorists, though little information is available in English.

TRAIN

The Bulgarian State Railways (БДЖ; www.bdz.bg) links most towns and cities, although some are on a spur track and only connected to a major railway line by infrequent services. Most trains tend to be antiquated, shabby and not especially comfortable, and journey times are usually longer than for buses. On the plus side, the scenery is likely to be more rewarding.

Croatia

POP 4.3 MILLION

Best Places to Eat

➡ Pelegrini (p128)

➡ Restaurant 360° (p140)

➡ Konoba Marjan (p132)

➡ Bistro Apetit (p121)

Best Places to Stay

➡ Art Hotel Kalelarga (p127)

➡ Meneghetti (p125)

➡ Studio Kairos (p121)

➡ Karmen Apartments (p139)

➡ Korta (p132)

Why Go?

If your Mediterranean fantasies feature balmy days by sapphire waters in the shade of ancient walled towns, Croatia is the place to turn them into reality.

The extraordinary Adriatic coastline, speckled with 1244 islands and strewn with historic towns, is Croatia's main attraction. The standout is Dubrovnik, its remarkable Old Town ringed by mighty defensive walls. Split showcases Diocletian's Palace, one of the world's most impressive Roman monuments, where bars, restaurants and shops thrive amid the ancient walls. In the heart-shaped peninsula of Istria, Rovinj is a charm-packed fishing port with narrow cobbled streets.

Away from the coast, Zagreb, Croatia's lovely capital, has a booming cafe culture and art scene, while Plitvice Lakes National Park offers a verdant maze of turquoise lakes and cascading waterfalls.

When to Go
Zagreb

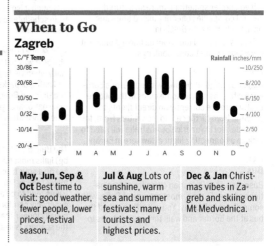

May, Jun, Sep & Oct Best time to visit: good weather, fewer people, lower prices, festival season.

Jul & Aug Lots of sunshine, warm sea and summer festivals; many tourists and highest prices.

Dec & Jan Christmas vibes in Zagreb and skiing on Mt Medvednica.

Entering the Country

Getting to Croatia is becoming easier year-on-year, with both budget and full-service airlines flying to various airports in summer. On top of this, buses, trains and ferries also shepherd holidaymakers into the country. Flights, cars and tours can be booked online at lonelyplanet.com/bookings.

ITINERARIES

Three Days

Base yourself in Dubrovnik (p136) and explore the compact old town; start early and take a walk along the city walls (p137) before it gets too hot. Catch the cable car up Srđ (p137) and explore the surrounding beaches. Once you've seen the sights and had a swim, consider boat trips to Cavtat (p141) and Lokrum (p140).

One Week

Base yourself in Croatia's exuberant second city Split (p129) for two days of sightseeing and nightlife, including a trip to the nearby postcard-perfect walled town of Trogir (p128). Spend the next few days island hopping by fast catamaran to Hvar Town (p134), the vibrant capital of the island of the same name, and photogenic walled Korčula Town (p136). Continue by catamaran to Dubrovnik (p136) and follow the itinerary above.

Essential Food & Drink

Croatian food echoes the varied cultures that have influenced the country over its history. There's a sharp divide between the Italian-style cuisine along the coast and the flavours of Hungary, Austria and Turkey in the continental parts. From grilled sea bass smothered in olive oil in Dalmatia to robust, paprika-heavy meat stews in Slavonia, each region proudly touts its own speciality, but regardless of the region you'll find tasty food made from fresh, seasonal ingredients. Here are a few essential food and drink items to look out for while in Croatia:

Beer Two popular brands of Croatian *pivo* (beer) are Zagreb's Ožujsko and Karlovačko from Karlovac.

Brodet/Brodetto/Brudet/Brujet Slightly spicy seafood stew served with polenta.

Paški sir Pungent sheep's cheese from the island of Pag, soaked in olive oil.

Pašticada Beef stewed in wine, prunes and spices and served with gnocchi.

Rakija Strong Croatian grappa comes in different flavours, from plum to honey.

Ražnjići Small chunks of pork grilled on a skewer.

AT A GLANCE

Area 56,538 sq km

Capital Zagreb

Country Code ☑ 385

Currency Kuna (KN)

Emergency Ambulance ☑ 94, Police ☑ 92

Language Croatian

Time Central European Time (GMT/UTC plus one hour)

Visas Not required for most nationalities for stays of up to 90 days.

Sleeping Price Ranges

The following price ranges refer to a double room with a bathroom in July and August.

€ less than 450KN

€€ 450KN–900KN

€€€ more than 900KN

Eating Price Ranges

The following price ranges refer to a main course.

€ less than 70KN

€€ 70KN–120KN

€€€ more than 120KN

Resources

Chasing the Donkey (www.chasingthedonkey.com)

Croatian Tourism (www.croatia.hr)

CROATIA

Croatia Highlights

1 **Dubrovnik** (p136)
Circling the historic city's mighty walls and then catching the cable car up Mt Srđ for breathtaking views from above.

2 **Plitvice Lakes National Park**
(p125) Marvelling at the otherworldly turquoise lakes and dramatic waterfalls of Croatia's top natural attraction.

3 **Hvar Town** (p134)
Capping off endless beach days with sunset cocktails and back-lane boogie sessions.

4 **Split** (p129)
Discovering the city's ancient heart in Diocletian's Palace, a quarter that buzzes day and night.

5 **Zagreb** (p120)
Exploring the quirky museums and cafes of Croatia's cute little capital.

6 **Rovinj** (p124)
Roam the steep cobbled streets and piazzas of Istria's showpiece coastal town.

7 **Zadar** (p126)
Exploring Roman ruins, intriguing museums, local eateries and hip bars within the marbled streets of the old town.

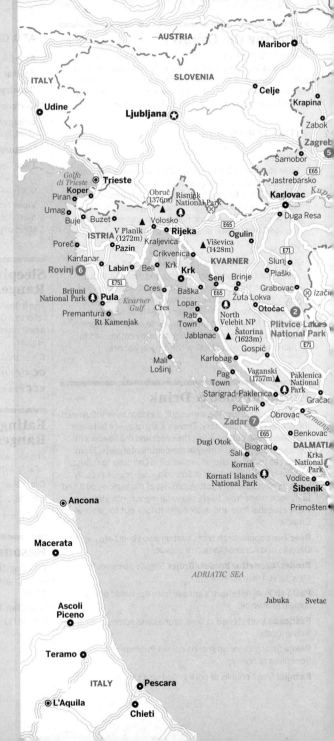

ZAGREB

📓 01 / POP 803,700

Zagreb is made for strolling. Wander through the Upper Town's red-roof and cobblestone glory, peppered with church spires. Crane your neck to see the domes and ornate upper-floor frippery of the Lower Town's mash-up of secessionist, neobaroque and art deco buildings. Search out the grittier pockets of town where ugly-bland concrete walls have been transformed into colourful murals by local street artists. This city rewards those on foot.

Afterwards, do as the locals do and head to a cafe. The cafe culture here is just one facet of this city's vibrant street life, egged on by a year-round swag of events that bring music, pop-up markets and food stalls to the plazas and parks. Even when there's nothing on, the centre thrums with youthful energy, so it's no surprise that Croatia's capital is now bringing in the city-break crowd. Zagreb is the little city that could.

⊙ Sights

As the oldest part of Zagreb, the Upper Town (Gornji Grad), which includes the neighbourhoods of Gradec and Kaptol, has landmark buildings and churches from the earlier centuries of Zagreb's history. The Lower Town (Donji Grad), which runs between the Upper Town and the train station, has the city's most interesting art museums and fine examples of 19th- and 20th-century architecture.

★ **Mirogoj** CEMETERY

(Aleja Hermanna Bollea 27; ⊙ 6am-8pm Apr-Oct, 7.30am-6pm Nov-Mar) A 10-minute ride north of the city centre (or a 30-minute walk through leafy streets) takes you to one of the most beautiful cemeteries in Europe, sited at the base of Mt Medvednica. It was designed in 1876 by Austrian-born architect Herman Bollé, who created numerous buildings around Zagreb. The majestic arcade, topped by a string of cupolas, looks like a fortress from the outside, but feels calm and graceful on the inside.

Museum of Broken Relationships MUSEUM

(www.brokenships.com; Ćirilometodska 2; adult/student 40/30KN; ⊙ 9am-10.30pm Jun-Sep, to 9pm Oct-May) From romances that withered to broken family connections, this wonderfully quirky museum explores the mementos left over after a relationship ends. Displayed amid a string of all-white rooms are donations from around the globe, each with a story attached. Exhibits range from the hilarious (the toaster someone nicked so their ex could never make toast again) to the heartbreaking (the suicide note from somebody's mother). In turns funny, poignant and moving, it's a perfect summing-up of the human condition.

Croatian Museum of Naïve Art MUSEUM

(Hrvatski Muzej Naivne Umjetnosti; ☑ 01-48 51 911; www.hmnu.hr; Ćirilometodska 3; adult/concession 25/15KN; ⊙ 10am-6pm Mon-Sat, to 1pm Sun) A feast for fans of Croatia's naive art (a form that was highly fashionable locally and worldwide during the 1960s and '70s and has declined somewhat since), this small museum displays 80 artworks (a smidgen of the museum's total 1900 holdings) that illustrate the full range of colourful, and often dreamlike, styles within the genre. The discipline's most important artists, such as Generalić, Mraz, Rabuzin and Smajić, are all displayed here.

Dolac Market MARKET

(off Trg Bana Jelačića; ⊙ open-air market 6.30am-3pm Mon-Sat, to 1pm Sun, covered market 7am-2pm Mon-Fri, to 3pm Sat, to 1pm Sun) Right in the heart of the city, Zagreb's bustling fruit and vegetable market has been trader-central since the 1930s when the city authorities set up a market space on the 'border' between the Upper and Lower Towns. Sellers from all over Croatia descend here daily to hawk fresh produce.

Katarinin Trg VIEWPOINT

(Katarinin trg) One of the best views in town – across red-tile roofs towards the cathedral – is from this square behind the **Jesuit Church of St Catherine** (Crkva Svete Katarine; Katarinin trg bb; ⊙ Mass 6pm Mon-Fri, 11am Sun). It's the perfect spot to begin or end an Upper Town wander. The square is also home to Zagreb's most famous street art; the **Whale**, gracing the facade of the abandoned Galerija Gradec building, is a 3D work by French artist Etien.

Cathedral of the Assumption of the Blessed Virgin Mary CHURCH

(Katedrala Marijina Uznešenja; Kaptol 31; ⊙ 10am-5pm Mon-Sat, 1-5pm Sun) This cathedral's twin spires – seemingly permanently under repair – soar over the city. Formerly known as St Stephen's, the cathedral's original Gothic structure has been transformed many times over, but the sacristy still contains a cycle of frescos dating from the 13th century. An earthquake in 1880 badly damaged the building and reconstruction in a neo-Gothic style began around the turn of the 20th century.

CROATIA ZAGREB

Archaeological Museum
MUSEUM

(Arheološki Muzej; 📞 01-48 73 101; www.amz.hr; Trg Nikole Šubića Zrinskog 19; adult/child/family 30/15/50KN; ⊙ 10am-6pm Tue, Wed, Fri & Sat, to 8pm Thu, to 1pm Sun) Spread over three floors, the artefacts housed here stretch from the prehistoric era to the medieval age. The 2nd floor holds the most interesting – and well-curated – exhibits. Here, displays of intricate Roman minor arts, such as decorative combs and oil lamps, and metal curse tablets are given as much prominence as the more usual show-stopping marble statuary. An exhibit devoted to Croatia's early-medieval Bijelo Brdo culture displays a wealth of grave finds unearthed in the 1920s.

Zrinjevac
SQUARE

(Trg Nikole Šubića Zrinskog) Officially called Trg Nikole Šubića Zrinskog but lovingly known as Zrinjevac, this verdant square is a major hang-out during sunny weekends and hosts pop-up cafe stalls during the summer months. It's also a venue for many festivals and events, most centred on the ornate music pavilion that dates from 1891.

🛏 Sleeping

Swanky Mint Hostel
HOSTEL €

(📞 01-40 04 248; www.swanky-hostel.com/mint; Ilica 50; dm 170-200KN; s/d 400/600KN; ✳@🌐⊠) This backpacker vortex, converted from a 19th-century textile-dye factory, has a very happening bar at its heart. Dorms are small but thoughtfully kitted out with lockers, privacy curtains and reading lamps, while private rooms are bright and large. The hostel's popularity, however, lies in its supersocial, friendly vibe, with welcome shots of *rakija* (grappa), organised pub crawls and an on-site travel agency.

Studio Kairos
B&B €

(📞 01-46 40 690; Vlaška 92; s/d/tr/q from €36/50/65/70; ✳🌐) This adorable B&B in a street-level apartment has four well-appointed rooms decked out by theme – Writers, Crafts, Music and Granny's. The cosy common space, where a delicious breakfast is served, and the enthusiastic hosts, who are a fount of knowledge on all things Zagreb, add to this place's intimate and homely appeal. Bikes are also available for rent.

★ Hotel Jägerhorn
HISTORIC HOTEL €€€

(📞 01-48 33 877; www.hotel-jagerhorn.hr; Ilica 14; s/d/ste 950/1050/1500KN; P✳@🌐) The oldest hotel in Zagreb (around since 1827) is a peaceful oasis, brimming with character.

The 18 rooms are elegantly outfitted, with soft neutral decor offset by blue accents, king-sized beds, kettles, and swish, contemporary bathrooms. Top-floor rooms have views over leafy Gradec. Staff are charming and the downstairs terrace cafe is the perfect hang-out after your sightseeing is done.

🍴 Eating

Heritage
CROATIAN €

(Petrinjska 14; mains 18-39KN; ⊙ 11am-8pm Mon-Sat; ✳) Tapas dishes, Croatian-style. This teensy place, with just one counter and a few bar stools, serves cheese and meat platters using all locally sourced ingredients. Try the flatbreads with prosciutto from Zagora, black-truffle spread and cheese from Ika, or the *kulen* (spicy paprika-flavoured sausage) with grilled peppers and cream cheese. Service is warm and friendly.

★ Mali Bar
TAPAS €€

(📞 01-55 31 014; www.facebook.com/MaliBarZagreb; Vlaška 63; dishes 45-150KN; ⊙ 12.30pm-midnight Mon-Sat; 🅿) This earthy-toned spot by star chef Ana Ugarković is all about small plates, with influences cherry-picked from across the Mediterranean, the Middle East and Asia. Dig into *labneh* (strained yoghurt cheese) balls on a bed of chard and roasted beetroot, smoked tuna dressed in saffron and Chinese pork dumplings all in the same sitting.

★ Bistro Apetit
EUROPEAN €€€

(📞 01-46 77 335; www.bistroapetit.com; Jurjevska 65a; mains 132-202KN; ⊙ 10am-midnight Tue-Sun; ✳) High up on villa-lined Jurjevska steet, this restaurant run by chef Marin Rendić, who previously worked at Copenhagen's Noma, serves up Zagreb's suavest contemporary dishes. Start with tuna tartare with pear and sesame seeds then move on to beef cheeks on bean spread, laced by carrot and pistachio. Opt for a degustation menu (five/seven courses 420/620KN) for flavour-packed feasting.

Zinfandel's
INTERNATIONAL €€€

(📞 01-45 66 644; www.zinfandels.hr; Mihanovićeva 1; mains 165-230KN; ⊙ 6am-11pm Mon-Sat, 6.30am-11pm Sun; ✳🅿) One of the top tables in town, Zinfandel's is headed by chef Ana Grgić, whose menu of creative flair is served in the grand dining room of the **Esplanade Zagreb Hotel** (📞 01-45 66 666; www.esplanade.hr; r from €130; P⊖✳@🌐). Don't miss the confit pigeon with beetroot and cherries with a rhubarb sauce. After dinner move onto the Oleander Terrace for a drink and prime people-watching across Starčevićev Trg.

CROATIA ZAGREB

Zagreb

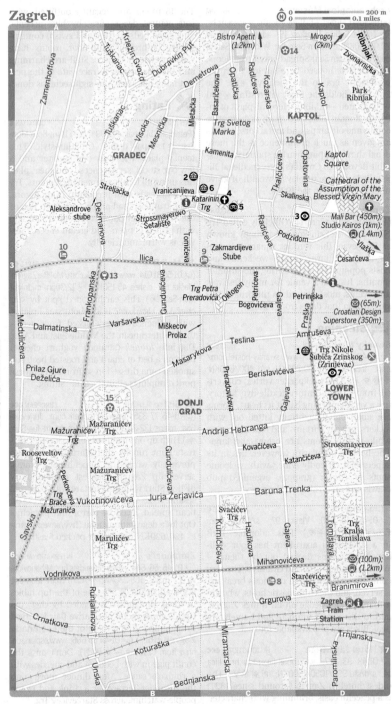

Zagreb

🍷 Drinking & Entertainment

In the Upper Town, Tkalčićeva is throbbing with bars and cafes. With half a dozen bars and sidewalk cafes between Trg Petra Preradovića (known locally as Cvjetni trg) and Bogovićeva in the Lower Town, the scene on summer nights resembles a vast outdoor party. Things wind down by midnight, though, and get quieter from mid-July through late August.

Pupitres WINE BAR
(☎ 098 16 58 073; http://pupitres.hr; Frankopanska 1; ⊙ 9am-11pm Mon-Thu, to 1am Fri & Sat; 🔊) When a wine bar is run by a top sommelier, you know you're in good hands. Jelene Šimić Valentić's casual-chic place is the best spot in town to get acquainted with Croatia's plethora of wines. Service is charming and genuinely helpful and the wine list is (unsurprisingly) a roll-call of the country's best cellars.

Craft Room CRAFT BEER
(www.facebook.com/craftroombeer; Opatovina 35; ⊙ 10am-2am; 🔊) In the city centre, this is the number-one stop for anyone interested in Croatia's craft-beer scene. Plenty of local beers are on tap and there's a huge menu of bottled international brands.

Booze & Blues LIVE MUSIC
(www.booze-and-blues.com; Tkalčićeva 84; ⊙ 8am-midnight Sun-Tue, to 2am Wed-Sat; 🔊) It does what it says on the tin. Perched at the top of the buzzy Tkalča strip, this haven of jazz, blues and soul rhythms stands out with its weekend live-music line-up. The interior is designed in the tradition of American blues and jazz clubs, with music-history memorabilia, and Heineken on tap flowing from a functioning saxophone.

ℹ Information

Emergency Health Clinic (☎ 01-63 02 911; Heinzelova 87; ⊙ 24hr)

KBC Rebro Hospital (☎ 8am-4pm 01-23 88 029; www.kbc-zagreb.hr; Kišpatićeva 12; ⊙ 24hr) Good public hospital with an emergency department. It's the teaching hospital of the University of Zagreb.

Main Tourist Office (☎ information 0800 53 53, office 01-48 14 051; www.infozagreb.hr; Trg Bana Jelačića 11; ⊙ 8.30am-8pm Mon-Fri, 9am-6pm Sat, 10am-4pm Sun) Distributes free city maps and leaflets. Has branches throughout the city.

ℹ Getting There & Away

AIR

Located 17km southeast of the city, **Zagreb Airport** (☎ 01-45 62 170; www.zagreb-airport. hr; Rudolfa Fizira 21, Velika Gorica), with its supermodern terminal opened in 2018, is Croatia's major airport, offering a range of international and domestic services.

BUS

The **Zagreb bus station** (☎ 060 313 333; www. akz.hr; Avenija M Držića 4) is located 1km east of the train station. If you need to store bags, there's a *garderoba* (per hour 5KN). Major destinations include Zadar (from 89KN, 4½ hours, 30 daily), Split (from 120KN, five to 8½ hours, 32 daily) and Dubrovnik (from 188KN, 10 hours, 12 daily).

TRAIN

The **train station** (www.hzpp.hr; Trg Kralja Tomislava 12) is in the southern part of the city centre. The station has a *garderoba* (locker per 24 hours 15KN) if you need to store bags. Destinations include Split (208KN, seven hours, three daily).

ℹ Getting Around

TO/FROM THE AIRPORT

The **Croatia Airlines bus** (www.plesoprijevoz. hr) runs from the airport to Zagreb bus station every half-hour or hour (depending on flight schedules) from 7am to 10.30pm (30KN, 40 minutes). Returning to the airport, bus services run from 4am to 8.30pm.

Bus line 290 (8KN, 1¼ hour) runs between Kvaternik Trg, just east of the city centre, and the airport every 35 minutes between 4.20am and midnight.

Taxis cost between 150KN and 200KN from the airport to the city centre.

PUBLIC TRANSPORT

Zagreb's public transport (www.zet.hr) is based on an efficient network of trams and buses. Tram maps are posted at most stations, making the system easy to navigate. Buy single-use tickets at newspaper kiosks or from the driver for 4KN (for 30 minutes) or 10KN (90 minutes). You can use the same ticket when transferring trams or buses but only in one direction. Night tram single-use tickets are 15KN. Make sure you validate your ticket when you get on the tram or bus by getting it time-stamped in the yellow ticket-validation box at the front of the vehicle – the other boxes only work for multi-use transport cards.

ISTRIA

📱 052

Continental Croatia meets the Adriatic in Istria (Istra to Croats), the heart-shaped, 3600-sq-km peninsula in the country's northwest. The bucolic interior of rolling hills and fertile plains attracts food- and culture-focused visitors to Istria's hilltop villages, rural hotels and farmhouse restaurants, while the indented coastline is enormously popular with the sun-and-sea set. Though vast hotel complexes line much of the coast and the rocky beaches are not Croatia's best, facilities are wide-ranging, the sea is clean and secluded spots are still plentiful.

Istria's madly popular coast gets flooded with central European tourists in summer, but you can still feel alone and undisturbed in the peninsula's interior, even in mid-August. Add acclaimed gastronomy (starring fresh seafood, prime white truffles, wild asparagus, top-rated olive oils and award-winning wines), sprinkle it with historical charm and you have a little slice of heaven.

Rovinj

POP 14,300

Rovinj (Rovigno in Italian) is coastal Istria's star attraction. While it can get overrun with tourists in summer and there aren't a lot of actual sights, it remains an intensely charming place. The old town is contained within an egg-shaped peninsula, webbed with steep cobbled streets and small squares, and punctuated by a tall church tower rising from the highest point. Originally an island, it was only connected to the mainland in 1763 when the narrow channel separating it was filled.

The main residential part of Rovinj spreads back from the old town and up the low hills that surround it, while resort-style hotels hug the coast to the north and south. When the crowds get too much, the 14 islands of the Rovinj archipelago make for a pleasant afternoon away.

☉ Sights

★ **St Euphemia's Church**　　　　　　CHURCH
(Crkva Sv Eufemije; Trg Sv Eufemije bb; tower 20KN; ☉ 10am-6pm Jun-Sep, to 4pm May, to 2pm Apr) **FREE** Built from 1725 to 1736, this imposing structure – the largest baroque church in Istria – dominates Rovinj from its hilltop location in the middle of the old town. Its 61m-high bell tower is older than the present church; construction commenced in 1654 and lasted 26 years. It's modelled on the campanile of St Mark's in Venice, and is topped by a 4m copper statue of St Euphemia, who shows the direction of the wind by turning on a spindle.

Rovinj City Museum　　　　　　　MUSEUM
(Muzej grada Rovinj; 📱 052-816 720; www.muzej-rovinj.hr; Trg Maršala Tita 11; adult/child Jun-Aug 65/40KN, Sep-May 15/10KN; ☉ 10am-10pm Jun-Aug, to 1pm Tue-Sat Sep-May) Housed in a 17th-century baroque palace, this museum displays temporary exhibitions on the ground floor, 20th-century and contemporary art on the 1st floor, and 16th- to 19th-century works on the top floor. Croatian artists are well represented, along with Venetian luminaries such as Jacopo Bassano.

🛏 Sleeping

Roundabout Hostel　　　　　　　HOSTEL €
(📱 052-817 387; www.roundabouthostel.com; Trg na križu 6; dm 140-187KN; 🅿 ❄ 🛜) This simple budget option has bunks with individual reading lights, lockers and a small shared kitchen. It's located on the big roundabout as you come into Rovinj, about a kilometre from the old town.

Villa Dobravac　　　　　　　　　HOTEL €€
(📱 052-813 006; www.villa-dobravac.com; Karmelo 1; r €100-128; 🅿 ❄ 🛜) As well as making wine and olive oil, the Dobravac family rents a set of 10 spacious, modern rooms in this lovely old peach-coloured villa in the residential

part of Rovinj. Most have a terrace and a sea view.

★ Casa Alice
HOTEL €€€

(☑ 052-821 104; www.casaalice.com; Paola Deperisa 1; r €200-220; P ❋ ☎ ⚐) Escape the masses in this lovely 10-room hotel in Rovinj's suburban fringes, a 20-minute walk from the centre but only five minutes from the sea. If walking sounds too hard you can always laze around the blue-tiled pool and help yourself to coffee and cake. Some of the rooms have terraces and most have a spa bath.

✖ Eating & Drinking

Pizzeria Da Sergio
PIZZA €

(☑ 052-816 949; www.facebook.com/DaSergioRv; Grisia 11; pizzas 35-82KN; ⊙ 11am-3pm & 6-11pm; ☎ ⚐) It's worth waiting in line to get a table at this old-fashioned, two-floor pizzeria. It dishes out Rovinj's best thin-crust pizza, with a huge range of toppings to choose from. It also serves decent house wine.

Monte
ISTRIAN €€€

(☑ 052-830 203; www.monte.hr; Montalbano 75; 3-/4-/6-course menu 619/719/849KN; ⊙ 6.30-11pm May-Sep; ⚐) The first restaurant in Croatia to be awarded a Michelin star, Monte offers a choice of three differently themed six-course Modern Istrian menus (one focused on local ingredients, one exclusively vegetarian and the last emphasising modern techniques). Or you can build your own three- or four-course meal, mixing and matching from all three.

Mediterraneo
COCKTAIL BAR

(www.facebook.com/mediterraneo.rovinj; Sv Križa 24; ⊙ 9am-2am Apr-Sep; ☎) Clinging to the old-town sea cliffs, this gorgeous little bar feels like a secret. It's not, of course – Rovinj's fashionable set are already here, holding court on the pastel-coloured stools right by the water. It's a very relaxed Adriatic scene, with friendly waitstaff and good cocktails, too.

❶ Information

Medical Centre (☑ 052-840 702; Istarska bb; ⊙ 24hr)

Tourist Office (☑ 052-811 566; www.rovinj-tourism.com; Pina Budicina 12; ⊙ 8am-10pm Jul & Aug, to 8pm mid-May–Jun & Sep)

❶ Getting There & Away

The **bus station** (☑ 060 333 111; Trg na Iokvi 6) is just to the southeast of the old town, with services to/from Zagreb (150KN, 4½ hours, 10 daily).

WORTH A TRIP

RURAL LUXURY

The focus is firmly on quality at **Meneghetti** (☑ 052-528 800; www.meneghetti.hr; Stancija Meneghetti 1; r from €279, mains 190-290KN; ⊙ Apr-Dec; P ❋ ☎ ⚐) – whether that be the estate's top-notch wine and olive oil, the architecture of the guest blocks, which sympathetically embrace the historic house at its core, or the exquisite modern Istrian cuisine served at the **restaurant**. Plus there's a private beach, accessed by a 25-minute walk through the vineyard. Sheer bliss.

PLITVICE LAKES NATIONAL PARK

☑ 053

By far Croatia's top natural attraction and the absolute highlight of Croatia's Adriatic hinterland, this glorious expanse of forested hills and turquoise lakes is exquisitely scenic – so much so that in 1979 Unesco proclaimed it a World Heritage Site. The name is slightly misleading though, as it's not so much the lakes that are the attraction here but the hundreds of waterfalls that link them. It's as though Croatia decided to gather all its waterfalls in one place and charge admission to view them.

The extraordinary natural beauty of the **park** (☑ 053-751 015; www.np-plitvicka-jezera.hr; adult/child Jul & Aug 250/110KN, Apr-Jun, Sep & Oct 150/80KN, Nov-Mar 55/35KN; ⊙ 7am-8pm) merits a full day's exploration, but you can still experience a lot on a half-day trip from Zadar or Zagreb. You must be able to walk a fair distance to get the most out of the place.

🛏 Sleeping & Eating

★ House Župan
GUESTHOUSE €

(☑ 047-784 057; www.sobe-zupan.com; Rakovica 35, Rakovica; s/d 250/370KN; P ❋ ☎) With an exceptionally welcoming hostess and clean, contemporary and reasonably priced rooms, this is a superb choice. There's even a guest kitchen and plenty of other diversions when you want to relax after a hike. It's set back from the highway in the small town of Rakovica, 11km north of Plitvice Lakes National Park.

Lička Kuća
CROATIAN €€

(☑ 053-751 024; Rastovača; mains 70-195KN; ⊙ 11am-10pm Mar-Nov) Built in 1972 and fully rebuilt in traditional stone-walled style in 2015 after burning to the ground three years earlier, Lička Kuća is touristy and extremely busy in high season, but the food is excellent. Specialities include slow-cooked lamb, dry-cured local prosciutto, and mountain trout, making it one of the best places for traditional dishes in the Northern Dalmatian interior.

ℹ️ Information

Both of the park's two main entrances have parking (7/70KN per hour/day) and an information office stocking brochures and maps. The main park **office** (☑ 053-751 014; www. np-plitvicka-jezera.hr; Josipa Jovića 19, Plitvička Jezera) is in Plitvička Jezera.

ℹ️ Getting There & Away

Buses stop at both park entrances; there's a small ticket office at the stop near Entrance 2. Destinations include Šibenik (118KN, four hours, three daily), Split (174KN, 4½ hours, six daily), Zadar (95KN, 2½ hours, seven daily) and Zagreb (89KN, two hours, frequent).

DALMATIA

Serving the classic cocktail of historic towns, jewel-like waters, rugged limestone mountains, sun-kissed islands, gorgeous climate and Mediterranean cuisine, Dalmatia is a holidaymaker's dream.

Hot spots include the buzzing Mediterranean-flavoured cities of Zadar and Split, and gorgeous little Hvar Town, where the cashed meet the trashed on the Adriatic's most glamorous party island. Yet one location understandably eclipses any discussion of Dalmatia: the remarkable old town of Dubrovnik. Ringed by mighty defensive walls that dip their feet in the cerulean sea, the city encapsulates the very essence of a medieval fantasy.

If it's relaxation you're after, there are seductive sandy beaches and pebbly coves scattered about islands near and far. Yachties can still sail between unpopulated islands without a shred of development, lost in dreams of the Mediterranean of old, while hikers can wander lonely trails in the mountainous hinterland, where bears and wolves still dwell.

Zadar

☑ 023 / POP 75,437

Boasting a historic old town of Roman ruins, medieval churches, cosmopolitan cafes and quality museums set on a small peninsula, Zadar is an intriguing city. It's not too crowded and its two unique attractions – the sound-and-light spectacle of the Sea Organ and the Sun Salutation – need to be seen and heard to be believed.

While it's not a picture-postcard kind of place from every angle, the mix of ancient relics, Habsburg elegance and its coastal setting all offset the unsightly tower blocks climbing up the hilly hinterland. It's no Dubrovnik, but it's not a museum town either – this is a living, vibrant city, enjoyed by residents and visitors alike.

Zadar is also a key transport hub, with superb ferry connections to the surrounding islands.

◉ Sights

★**Sea Organ**   MONUMENT
(Morske orgulje; Istarska Obala) FREE Zadar's incredible *Sea Organ,* designed by local architect Nikola Bašić, is unique. Set within the perforated stone stairs that descend into the sea is a system of pipes and whistles that exudes wistful sighs when the movement of the sea pushes air through it. The effect is hypnotic, the mellifluous tones increasing in volume when a boat or ferry passes by. You can swim from the steps off the promenade while listening to the sounds.

★**Sun Salutation**   MONUMENT
(Pozdrav Suncu; Istarska Obala) Another wacky and wonderful creation by Nikola Bašić, this 22m-wide circle set into the pavement is filled with 300 multilayered glass plates that collect the sun's energy during the day. Together with the wave energy that makes the *Sea Organ's* sound, it produces a trippy light show from sunset to sunrise that's meant to simulate the solar system. It also collects enough energy to power the entire harbour-front lighting system.

Roman Forum   RUINS
(Zeleni trg) One of the most intriguing things about Zadar is the way Roman ruins seem to sprout randomly from the city's streets. Nowhere is this more evident than at the site of the ancient Forum, constructed between the 1st century BC and the 3rd century AD. As in Roman times, it's the centre of civic and religious life, with St Donatus' Church dominating one side of it.

St Donatus' Church   CHURCH
(Crkva Sv Donata; Šimuna Kožičića Benje bb; 20KN; ⊙9am-9pm May-Sep, to 4pm Oct-Apr) Dating from the beginning of the 9th century, this unusual circular Byzantine-style church was

named after the bishop who commissioned it. As one of only a handful of buildings from the early Croatian kingdom to have survived the Mongol invasion of the 13th century, it's a particularly important cultural relic. The simple and unadorned interior includes two complete Roman columns, recycled from the Forum. Also from the Forum are the paving slabs that were revealed after the original floor was removed.

St Anastasia's Cathedral CATHEDRAL
(Katedrala Sv Stošije; Trg Sv Stošije; ⊙ 6.30-7pm Mon-Fri, 8-9am Sat, 8-9am & 6-7pm Sun) FREE Built in the 12th and 13th centuries, Zadar's cathedral has a richly decorated facade and an impressive three-nave interior with the remains of frescoes in the side apses. The cathedral was badly bombed during WWII and has since been reconstructed. On the altar in the left apse is a marble sarcophagus containing the relics of St Anastasia, while the choir contains lavishly carved stalls. A glass vestibule allows you to peer inside when the cathedral's closed, which is often.

Archaeological Museum MUSEUM
(Arheološki Muzej; ☑ 023-250 516; www.amzd.hr; Trg Opatice Čike 1; adult/child 30/15KN; ⊙ 9am-9pm Jun & Sep, to 10pm Jul & Aug, to 3pm Apr, May & Oct, 9am-2pm Mon-Fri, to 1pm Sat Nov-Mar) A wealth of prehistoric, ancient and medieval relics, mainly from Zadar and its surrounds, awaits at this fascinating museum. Highlights include a 2.5m-high marble statue of Augustus from the 1st century AD, and a model of the Forum as it once looked.

🛌 Sleeping

Windward Hostel HOSTEL €
(☑ 091 62 19 197; www.facebook.com/windward. hostel.zadar; Gazića 12; dm/d 112/450KN; ❄ 🛜) Just 1.5km from the old town, this 20-bed, yachting-themed hostel is run by a passionate sailor. Rooms are immaculate, with big lockers, electric window blinds and private reading lights. There's a supermarket and bakery nearby, and staff can organise sailing tours and lessons.

Boutique Hostel Forum HOSTEL €€
(☑ 023-253 031; www.hostelforumzadar.com; Široka 20; dm/d/ste from 155/665/725KN) Wonderfully colourful dorm rooms and stylish, white-and-black doubles and suites, some with top skyline and partial water views, make this easily the best hostel and midrange hotel in the old centre. The location couldn't be better and the rooms are terrific for the price.

★**Art Hotel Kalelarga** HOTEL €€€
(☑ 023-233 000; www.arthotel-kalelarga.com; Majke Margarite 3; s/d incl breakfast 1515/1810KN; ❄ 🛜) Built and designed under strict conservation rules due to its old-town location, this 10-room boutique hotel is an understated and luxurious beauty. Exposed stonework and mushroom hues imbue the spacious rooms with plenty of style and character. The gourmet breakfast is served in the hotel's own stylish cafe, **Gourmet Kalelarga** (www.arthotel-kalelarga.com/gourmet; Široka 23; breakfast 28-60KN, mains 59-155KN; ⊙ 7am-10pm).

🍴 Eating

★**Kaštel** MEDITERRANEAN €€
(☑ 023-494 950; www.hotel-bastion.hr; Bedemi Zadarskih Pobuna 13; mains 70-190KN; ⊙ 7am-11pm) Hotel Bastion's fine-dining restaurant offers contemporary takes on classic Croatian cuisine (octopus stew, stuffed squid, Pag cheese). France and Italy also make their presence felt, particularly in the delectable dessert list. Opt for the white-linen experience inside or dine on the battlements overlooking the harbour for a memorable evening.

Pet Bunara DALMATIAN €€
(☑ 023-224 010; www.petbunara.com; Stratico 1; mains 65-160KN; ⊙ noon-11pm) With exposed stone walls inside and a pretty terrace lined with olive trees, this is an atmospheric place to tuck into Dalmatian soups and stews, homemade pasta and local faves such as octopus and turkey. Save room for a traditional Zadar fig cake or cherry torte.

Corte Vino & More INTERNATIONAL €€€
(☑ 023-335 357; www.facebook.com/cortevinomore; Braće Bersa 2; mains 80-180KN; ⊙ noon-2.30pm & 7-10.30pm) One of the classiest dining experiences in Zadar, Corte Vino & More in the Al Mayer Heritage Hotel has a gorgeous setting, wonderfully attentive service and high-quality food that changes with the seasons, taking Croatian traditional dishes and riffing in subtle, new and creative directions. Fabulous wine list and knowledgeable waiters, too.

🍷 Drinking & Nightlife

★**La Bodega** WINE BAR
(☑ 099 46 29 440; www.labodega.hr/zadar; Široka 3; ⊙ 7am-1am Sun-Thu, to 1.30am Fri & Sat) With slick, eccentric, semi-industrial decor, a bar with a line of hams and garlic hanging above, Portuguese-style tiles and a welcoming, open-to-the-street approach, this is one of Zadar's hippest bars. There's a good range of

CROATIA ZADAR

ŠIBENIK

The coastal city of Šibenik has a magnificent medieval heart, gleaming white against the placid waters of the bay, something that may not be immediately apparent as you drive through the somewhat-shabby outskirts. The stone labyrinth of steep backstreets and alleys is a joy to explore.

It's well worth a detour here to see **St James' Cathedral** (Katedrala Svetog Jakova; Trg Republike Hrvatske; adult/child 20KN/free; ⏱ 9.30am-6.30pm), the crowning architectural glory of the Dalmatian coast and a World Heritage Site. It was constructed entirely of stone quarried from the islands of Brač, Korčula, Rab and Krk, and is reputed to be the world's largest church built completely of stone without brick or wooden supports. The structure is also unique in that the interior shape corresponds exactly to the exterior.

Other lures include **Pelegrini** (☎ 022-213 701; www.pelegrini.hr; Jurja Dalmatinca 1; mains 79-185KN, 3-/4-/5-course set menu 440/570/700KN; ⏱ noon-midnight), one of Croatia's top restaurants, and the character-filled **Medulić Palace Rooms & Apartments** (☎ 095 53 01 868; www.medulicpalace.com; Ivana Pribislavića 4; r 310-630KN, apt 365-815KN; ✳ 🔊).

Šibenik's **bus station** (☎ 060 368 368; Draga 14) has services to Dubrovnik (148KN, 6½ hours, at least two daily), Split (48KN, 1½ hours, 12 daily), Zadar (43KN, 1½ hours, at least hourly) and Zagreb (from 132KN, five to seven hours, at least hourly).

Croatian wines by the glass and an extraordinary selection by the bottle – best enjoyed with a variety of Pag cheese and prosciutto.

Podroom
CLUB

(☎ 099 74 98 451; www.podroom.club; Marka Marulića bb; ⏱ midnight-6am Fri, 1-6.30am Sat) One of Zadar's biggest clubs, Podroom draws a regular cast of Croatian and international DJs, especially in summer. It's within staggering distance of the old town and really only kicks off around 2am. Live acts also take to the stage to get things going. Admission prices vary depending on who's on the bill.

ℹ Information

Tourist Office (☎ 023-316 166; www.zadar.travel; Jurja Barakovića 5; ⏱ 8am-11pm May-Jul & Sep, to midnight Aug, 8am-8pm Mon-Fri, 9am-2pm Sat & Sun Oct-Apr; 🔊) Publishes a good colour map and rents audioguides (40KN) for a self-guided tour around the town.

Zadar General Hospital (Opća Bolnica Zadar; ☎ 023-505 505; www.bolnica-zadar.hr; Bože Peričića 5)

ℹ Getting There & Away

AIR

Recently upgraded **Zadar Airport** (☎ 023-205 800; www.zadar-airport.hr) is 12km east of the town centre. Croatia Airlines flies to Zadar from Zagreb.

BUS

The **bus station** (☎ 060 305 305; www.liburnija-zadar.hr; Ante Starčevića 1) is about 1km southeast of the old town. Domestic destinations include Dubrovnik (182KN, eight hours, up to six daily), Šibenik (43KN, 1½ hours, at least hourly), Split (86KN, three hours, hourly) and Zagreb (110KN, 3½ hours, hourly).

ℹ Getting Around

TO/FROM THE AIRPORT

Timed around all Croatia Airlines flights, buses (25KN one way) depart from outside the main terminal, and from the old town (Liburnska Obala) and the bus station one hour prior to flights.

A taxi will cost around 150KN to the old town and 180KN to Borik.

BUS & BIKE

Liburnija (www.liburnija-zadar.hr) runs buses on 10 routes, which all loop through the bus station. Tickets cost 10KN on board – or 16KN for two from a *tisak* (news-stand). Buses 5 and 8 (usually marked 'Puntamika') head to/from Borik regularly.

Calimero (☎ 023-311 010; www.rent-a-bike-zadar.com; Zasjedanja Zavnoh 1; per hour/day from 40/120KN; ⏱ 8am-8pm Mon-Fri, to 1pm Sat) is Zadar's best place to rent a bicycle. It's an easy walk from the old town.

Trogir

☎ 021 / POP 13,200

Gorgeous Trogir (called Trau by the Venetians) is set within medieval walls on a tiny island, linked by bridges to both the mainland and to the far larger Čiovo Island. On summer nights everyone gravitates to the wide seaside promenade lined with bars, cafes and yachts, leaving the knotted, mazelike marble streets gleaming mysteriously under old-fashioned streetlights.

The old town has retained many intact and beautiful buildings from its age of glory between the 13th and 15th centuries. In 1997 its profuse collection of Romanesque and Renaissance buildings earned it World Heritage status.

While it's easily reached on a day trip from Split, Trogir also makes a good alternative base to the big city and a relaxing place to spend a few days.

◎ Sights

★ St Lawrence's Cathedral CATHEDRAL
(Katedrala svetog Lovre; ☑ 021-881 426; Trg Ivana Pavla II; 25KN; ☺ 8am-8pm Mon-Sat, noon-6pm Sun Jun-Aug, to 6pm Sep-May) Trogir's show-stopping attraction is its three-naved Venetian cathedral, one of the finest architectural works in Croatia, built between the 13th and 15th centuries. Master Radovan carved the grand Romanesque portal in 1240, flanked by a nude Adam and Eve standing on the backs of lions. At the end of the portico is another fine piece of sculpture: the 1464 cherub-filled baptistery sculpted by Andrija Aleši.

Sacred Art Museum MUSEUM
(Muzej sakralne umjetnosti; ☑ 021-881 426; Trg Ivana Pavla II 6; 10KN; ☺ 8am-8pm Mon-Sat, 11.30am-7pm Sun Jun-Sep) Highlights of this small museum include illuminated manuscripts; a large painting of St Jerome and St John the Baptist by Bellini; an almost-life-size, brightly painted *Crucifix with Triumphant Christ;* and the darkly lit fragments of a 13th-century icon that once adorned the cathedral's altar.

⌂ Sleeping & Eating

Hostel Marina Trogir HOSTEL €
(☑ 021-883 075; www.hostelmarina-trogir.com; Cumbrijana 16; dm 175KN; ☺ May-Oct; ﹡ ﹅) Run by an expat German couple, this excellent hostel has only four dorms, each sleeping seven or eight people. The custom-built wooden bunks have suitcase-sized lockers underneath, reading lights and privacy curtains for the lower bunk (but not the top one). Plus there's a communal kitchen and separate men's and women's bathrooms.

Villa Moretti HISTORIC HOTEL €€
(☑ 021-885 326; www.villamoretti.com; Lučica 1; r €90-120; P ﹡ ﹅) Owned by the same family since 1792, this 17th-century palazzo has five spacious, antique-filled rooms accessed by a grand marble and wrought-iron stairway.

Two rooms open onto a large rear terrace, but all have million-dollar views over the old town. The bathrooms are large but a tad dated.

Konoba Trs DALMATIAN €€€
(☑ 021-796 956; www.konoba-trs.com; Matije Gupca 14; mains 105-230KN; ☺ 11am-midnight Mon-Sat, 5pm-midnight Sun) As traditional-looking as they come, this rustic little tavern has wooden benches and old stone walls inside, and an inviting courtyard shaded by grapevines. Yet the menu adds clever, contemporary twists to Dalmatian classics, featuring the likes of panko-crumbed octopus tentacles, and the signature dis:, nutmeg-spiced lamb *paštica-da* (stew), served with savoury pancakes.

❶ Information

Tourist Office (☑ 021-885 628; www.tztrogir. hr; Trg Ivana Pavla II 1; ☺ 8am-8pm May-Sep, 9am-5pm Mon-Fri Oct-Apr) Inside the town hall; distributes town maps.

❶ Getting There & Away

BOAT
Bura Line (☑ 095 83 74 320; www.buraline. com; Obala kralja Zvonimira bb; adult/child 35/18KN) has a small boat heading to and from Split that runs four to six times a day from May to September.

BUS
Intercity buses stop at the **bus station** (☑ 021-882 947; Kneza Tripimira bb) on the mainland near the bridge to Trogir. Destinations include Zagreb (148KN, 6½ hours, 10 daily), Zadar (73KN, 2½ hours, 11 daily), Split (20KN, 30 minutes, frequent) and Dubrovnik (137KN, 5½ hours, five daily). Split city bus 37 (17KN) takes the slower coastal road through Kaštela every 20 minutes, also stopping at the airport.

❶ Getting Around

In summer, small passenger **boats** depart from Obala Bana Berislavića, right in front of Hotel Concordia, heading to the beaches of Okrug Gornji (25KN) and Medena (20KN). The journey takes about 45 minutes.

Split
☑ 021 / POP 178,000
Croatia's second-largest city, Split (Spalato in Italian) is a great place to see Dalmatian life as it's really lived. Always buzzing, this exuberant city has just the right balance between tradition and modernity. Step inside

Central Split

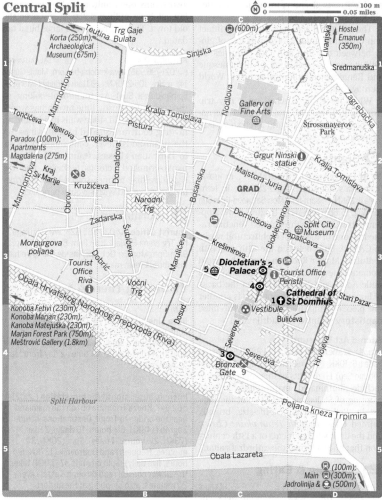

Diocletian's Palace (a Unesco World Heritage Site and one of the world's most impressive Roman monuments) and you'll see dozens of bars, restaurants and shops thriving amid the atmospheric old walls where Split has been humming along for thousands of years.

To top it off, Split has a unique setting. Its dramatic coastal mountains act as the perfect backdrop to the turquoise waters of the Adriatic and help divert attention from the dozens of shabby high-rise apartment blocks that fill its suburbs. It's this thoroughly lived-in aspect of Split that means it will never be a fantasy land like Dubrovnik, but perhaps it's all the better for that.

◉ Sights

The ever-frenetic waterfront promenade – officially called Obala hrvatskog narodnog preporoda (Croatian National Revival Waterfront) but more commonly known as the Riva – is your best central reference point in Split. East of here, past the wharf, are the buzzy beaches of Bačvice, Firule, Zenta and Trstenik bays. The wooded Marjan Hill dominates the western tip of the city and has even better beaches at its base.

★ Diocletian's Palace   HISTORIC SITE
Taking up a prime harbourside position, this extraordinary complex is one of the most

Central Split

imposing ancient Roman structures in existence today, and it's where you'll spend most of your time while in Split. Don't expect a palace, though, nor a museum – this is the city's living heart, its labyrinthine streets packed with people, bars, shops and restaurants. Built as a military fortress, imperial residence and fortified town, the palace measures 215m from north to south and 180m east to west.

➡ **Cathedral of St Domnius**

(Katedrala sv Duje; Peristil bb; cathedral/belfry 35/20KN; ☺8am-8pm Jun-Sep, 7am-noon & 5-7pm May & Oct, 7am-noon Nov-Feb, 8am-5pm Mar & Apr) Split's octagonal cathedral is one of the best-preserved ancient Roman buildings still standing. It was built as a mausoleum for Diocletian, the last famous persecutor of the Christians, who was interred here in AD 311. In the 5th century the Christians got the last laugh, destroying the emperor's sarcophagus and converting his tomb into a church dedicated to one of his victims. Note that a ticket for the cathedral includes admission to its crypt, treasury and baptistery (Temple of Jupiter).

➡ **Temple of Jupiter**

(Jupiterov hram; 10KN, free with cathedral ticket; ☺8am-7pm Mon-Sat, 12.30-6.30pm Sun May-Oct, to 5pm Nov-Apr) Although it's now the cathedral's baptistery, this wonderfully intact building was originally an ancient Roman temple dedicated to the king of the gods. It still has its original barrel-vaulted ceiling and decorative frieze, although a striking bronze statue of St John the Baptist by Ivan Meštrović now fills the spot where Jupiter once stood. The font is

made from 13th-century carved stones recycled from the cathedral's rood screen.

➡ **Split City Museum**

(Muzej grada Splita; ☑021-360 171; www.mgst.net; Papalićeva 1; adult/child 22/12KN; ☺8.30am-9pm Apr-Sep, 9am-5pm Tue-Sat, to 2pm Sun Oct-Mar) Built by Juraj Dalmatinac in the 15th century for one of the many noblemen who lived within the old town, the Large Papalić Palace is considered a fine example of late-Gothic style, with an elaborately carved entrance gate that proclaimed the importance of its original inhabitants. The interior has been thoroughly restored to house this museum, which has interesting displays on Diocletian's Palace and on the development of the city.

➡ **Diocletian's Palace Substructure**

(Supstrukcije Dioklecijanove palače; www.mgst. net; Obala hrvatskog narodnog preporoda bb; adult/child 42/22KN; ☺8.30am-9pm Apr-Sep, to 5pm Sun Oct, 9am-5pm Mon-Sat, to 2pm Sun Nov-Apr) The Bronze Gate of Diocletian's Palace once opened straight from the water into the palace basements, enabling goods to be unloaded and stored here. Now this former tradesman's entrance is the main way into the palace from the Riva. While the central part of the substructure is now a major thoroughfare lined with souvenir stalls, entry to the chambers on either side is ticketed.

Archaeological Museum   MUSEUM

(Arheološki muzej; ☑021-329 340; www.armus. hr; Zrinsko-Frankopanska 25; adult/child 20/10KN; ☺9am-2pm & 4-8pm Mon-Sat Jun-Sep, closed Sat afternoon & Sun Oct-May) A treasure trove of classical sculpture and mosaics is displayed at this excellent museum, a short walk north of the town centre. Most of the vast collection originated from the ancient Roman settlements of Split and neighbouring **Salona** (☑021-213 358; Don Frane Bulića bb, Solin; adult/child 30/15KN; ☺9am-7pm Mon-Sat, to 2pm Sun) (Solin), and there's also some Greek pottery from the island of Vis. There are displays of jewellery and coins, and a room filled with artefacts dating from the Palaeolithic to the Iron Age.

Meštrović Gallery   GALLERY

(Galerija Meštrović; ☑021-340 800; www.mestro vic.hr; Šetalište Ivana Meštrovića 46; adult/child 40/20KN; ☺9am-7pm Tue-Sun May-Sep, to 4pm Tue-Sun Oct-Apr) At this stellar art museum you'll see a comprehensive, well-arranged collection of works by Ivan Meštrović, Croatia's premier modern sculptor, who built the grand mansion as a personal residence

CROATIA SPLIT

in the 1930s. Although Meštrović intended to retire here, he emigrated to the USA soon after WWII. Admission includes entry to the nearby **Kaštilac** (Šetalište Ivana Meštrovića 39; ⊙ 9am-7pm Tue-Sun May-Sep), a fortress housing other Meštrović works.

Marjan Forest Park   PARK

(Park-šuma Marjan; www.marjan-parksuma.hr) Looming up to 178m over Split's western fringes, this nature reserve occupies a big space in Split's psyche. The views over the city and surrounding islands are extraordinary, and the shady paths provide a welcome reprieve from both the heat and the summertime tourist throngs. Trails pass through fragrant pine forests to scenic lookouts, a 16th-century Jewish cemetery, medieval chapels and cave dwellings once inhabited by Christian hermits. Climbers take to the cliffs near the end of the peninsula.

For an afternoon away from the city buzz, consider taking a long walk through the park and descending to **Kašjuni beach** (Šetalište Ivana Meštrovića bb) to cool off before catching the bus back.

🛌 Sleeping

Hostel Emanuel   HOSTEL €

(☑ 021-786 533; hostelemanuel@gmail.com; Tolstojeva 20; dm 222KN; ❄@🛜) This hip little hostel in a suburban apartment block has colourful contemporary interiors and a relaxed vibe. In the two dorms (one sleeping five, the other 10), each bunk has a large locker, curtains, a reading light and a power outlet.

★**Korta**   APARTMENT €€

(☑ 021-571 226; www.kortasplit.com; Plinarska 31; apt from €94; ❄🛜) Set around a courtyard in the historic Veli Varoš neighbourhood, these simple but elegant apartments have stone-tiled bathrooms and white walls hung with huge TVs and photos of rustic Croatian scenes. Many have balconies.

Apartments Magdalena   APARTMENT €€

(☑ 098 423 087; www.magdalena-apartments.com; Milićeva 18; apt 465-611KN; ❄🛜) You may never want to leave Magdalena's top-floor apartment once you see the old-town view from the dormer window. The three apartments are comfortable and fully furnished, and the hospitality offered by the off-site owners is exceptional: beer and juice in the fridge, a back-up toothbrush in the cupboard and even a mobile phone with credit on it.

★**Heritage Hotel Antique Split**   HERITAGE HOTEL €€€

(☑ 021-785 208; www.antique-split.com; Poljana Grgura Ninskog 1; r from €267; ❄🛜) Palace living at its most palatial, this boutique complex has eight chic rooms with stone walls and impressive bathrooms. In some you'll wake up to incredible views over the cathedral.

Villa Split   B&B €€€

(☑ 091 40 34 403; www.villasplitluxury.com; Bajamontijeva 5; r from €215; P❄🛜) Built into the Roman-built wall of Diocletian's Palace, this wonderful boutique B&B has only three rooms, the best of which is the slightly larger one in the attic. If you're happy to swap the ancient for the merely medieval, there are six larger rooms in a 10th-century building on the main square.

🍴 Eating

Kruščić   BAKERY €

(☑ 099 26 12 345; www.facebook.com/Kruscic. Split; Obrov 6; items 6-15KN; ⊙ 8am-2pm) Spit's best bakery serves delicious bread, pastries and pizza slices. The focus is more savoury than sweet, although you'll find sweet things, too.

Konoba Fetivi   DALMATIAN, SEAFOOD €€

(☑ 021-355 152; www.facebook.com/KonobaFetivi; Tomića stine 4; mains 70-95KN; ⊙ noon-11pm Tue-Sun) Informal and family-run, with a TV screening sports in the corner, Fetivi feels more like a tavern than most that bear the *konoba* name. However, that doesn't detract from the food, which is first rate. Seafood is the focus here. The cuttlefish stew with polenta is highly recommended, but the whole fish is wonderfully fresh, too.

Konoba Matejuška   DALMATIAN, SEAFOOD €€

(☑ 021-814 099; www.konobamatejuska.hr; Tomića Stine 3; mains 75-140KN; ⊙ noon-11pm Apr-Oct, to 9pm Wed-Mon Nov-Mar) This cosy, rustic tavern, in an alleyway minutes from the seafront, specialises in well-prepared seafood – as epitomised in its perfectly cooked fish platter for two. The grilled squid is also excellent, served with the archetypal Dalmatian side dish, *blitva* (Swiss chard with slightly mushy potato, drenched in olive oil). Book ahead.

★**Konoba Marjan**   DALMATIAN, SEAFOOD €€€

(☑ 098 93 46 848; www.facebook.com/konobamarjan; Senjska 1; mains 84-160KN; ⊙ noon-11pm Mon-Sat; 🛜) Offering great-quality Dalmatian fare, this friendly little Veli Varoš tavern features daily specials such as cuttlefish *brujet*

KLIS FORTRESS

Controlling the valley leading into Split, this imposing **fortress** (Tvrđava Klis; ☑ 021-240 578; www.tvrdavaklis.com; Klis bb; adult/child 40/15KN; ⊙9.30am-4pm) spreads along a limestone bluff, reaching 385m at its highest point. Its long and narrow form (304m by 53m) derives from constant extensions over the course of millennia. Inside, you can clamber all over the fortifications and visit the small museum, which has displays of swords and costumes and detailed information on the castle's brutal past.

Game of Thrones fans will recognise the fortress as Meereen, where Daenerys Targaryen had all those nasty slave-masters crucified in season four.

Klis is located 12km northeast of the city centre, and can be reached by city bus 22 (13KN) from Trg Gaje Bulata or Split's local bus station.

(a flavour-packed seafood stew – highly recommended), *gregada* (fish stew with potato) and prawn pasta. The wine list is excellent, showcasing some local boutique wineries, and there are a few seats outside on the street leading up to Marjan Hill.

Zoi   MEDITERRANEAN €€€
(☑ 021-637 491; www.zoi.hr; Obala hrvatskog narodnog preporoda 23; mains 120-180KN; ⊙6.30pm-midnight) Accessed by a discreet door on the waterfront promenade, this upstairs restaurant serves sophisticated modern Mediterranean dishes that look as divine as they taste. The decor is simultaneously elegant and extremely hip, with the exposed walls of Diocletian's Palace offset with bright bursts of magenta. Head up to the roof terrace for one of Split's most memorable dining spaces.

🍷 Drinking & Nightlife

⭐**Marcvs Marvlvs Spalatensis**   WINE BAR
(www.facebook.com/marvlvs; Papalićeva 4; ⊙11am-midnight Jun-Aug, to 11pm Mon-Sat Sep-May; 🛜) Fittingly, the 15th-century Gothic home of the 'Dante of Croatia', Marko Marulić, now houses this wonderful little 'library jazz bar' made up of small rooms crammed with books and frequented by ageless bohemians, tortured poets and wistful academics. Cheese, chess, cards and cigars are all on offer, and there's often live music.

⭐**Paradox**   WINE BAR
(☑ 021-787 778; www.paradox.hr; Bana Josipa Jelačića 3; ⊙8am-midnight; 🛜) This stylish wine and cheese bar has a fantastic rooftop terrace, a massive selection of Croatian wines (more than 120, including 40 by the glass) and an array of local cheeses to go with them. The clued-up staff members really know their stuff, and there's live music most weekends.

❶ Information

KBC Split (Klinički bolnički centar Split; ☑ 021-556 111; www.kbsplit.hr; Spinčićeva 1)

Tourist Office Riva (☑ 021-360 066; www.visit split.com; Obala hrvatskog narodnog preporoda 9; ⊙8am-9pm Jun-Sep, 8am-8pm Mon-Sat, to 5pm Sun Apr, May & Oct, 9am-4pm Mon-Fri, to 2pm Sat Nov-Mar) Stocks the free 72-hour Split Card, which offers free or discounted access to attractions, car rental, restaurants, shops and theatres. You're eligible for the card if you're staying in Split more than four nights from April to September, or staying in designated hotels for more than two nights at other times.

❶ Getting There & Away

The bus, train and ferry terminals are clustered on the eastern side of the harbour, a short walk from the old town.

AIR

Split Airport (SPU, Zračna luka Split; ☑ 021-203 555; www.split-airport.hr; Dr Franje Tuđmana 1270, Kaštel Štafilić) is in Kaštela, 24km northwest of central Split. In summer, dozens of airlines fly here from all over Europe but only Croatia Airlines, Eurowings and Trade Air fly year-round.

BOAT

Split's ferry harbour is extremely busy and can be hard to negotiate, so you're best to arrive early. Most domestic ferries depart from Gat Sv Petra, the first of the three major piers, which has **ticket booths** for both Jadrolinija and Kapetan Luka. The giant international ferries depart from Gat Sv Duje, the second of the piers, where there's a large **ferry terminal** with ticketing offices for the major lines. In July and August, and at weekends, it's often necessary to appear hours before departure for a car ferry, and put your car in the line for boarding. There is rarely a problem or a long wait obtaining a space in the low season.

Jadrolinija (☑ 021-338 333; www.jadrolinija. hr; Gat Sv Duje bb) operates most of the ferries between Split and the islands. Car ferry services include Stari Grad on Hvar (per person/car 47/310KN, two hours, up to seven daily) and Vela Luka on Korčula (60/470KN, 2¾ hours, two daily). Summertime catamaran destinations include Dubrovnik (210KN, six hours, daily), Hvar Town (55KN to 110KN, one to two hours, up to eight daily) and Korčula Town (160KN, 3¾ hours, daily).

Kapetan Luka (Krilo; ☑ 021-645 476; www. krilo.hr) has daily high-speed catamaran services to Hvar (90KN, one hour) and Korčula (130KN, 2½ hours). From May to mid-October, they also head to Dubrovnik (210KN, 4¼ hours)

BUS

Most intercity buses arrive at the **main bus station** (Autobusni Kolodvor Split; ☑ 060 327 777; www.ak-split.hr; Obala kneza Domagoja bb) beside the harbour. In summer it's best to purchase bus tickets with seat reservations in advance. If you need to store bags, there's a **garderoba** (left-luggage office; Obala kneza Domagoja 12; 1st hour 5KN, additional hours 1.50KN; ⊙ 6am-10pm May-Sep) nearby. Domestic destinations include Zagreb (157KN, five hours, at least hourly), Zadar (90KN, three hours, at least hourly) and Dubrovnik (127KN, 4½ hours, at least 11 daily).

TRAIN

Trains head to **Split Train Station** (Željeznica stanica Split; ☑ 021-338 525; www.hzpp.hr; Obala kneza Domagoja 9; ⊙ 6am-10pm) from Zagreb (194KN, 6½ hours, four daily). The station has lockers (15KN per day) that will fit suitcases, but you can't leave bags overnight. There's another **garderoba** (☑ 098 446 780; Obala kneza Domagoja 5; per day 15KN; ⊙ 6am-10pm Jul & Aug, 7.30am-9pm Sep-Jun) nearby, out on the street.

❶ Getting Around

TO/FROM THE AIRPORT

Airport Shuttle Bus (☑ 021-203 119; www. plesoprijevoz.hr; 1 way 30KN) Makes the 30-minute journey between the airport and Split's main bus station (platform 1) at least 14 times a day.

City buses 37 & 38 The regular Split–Trogir bus stops near the airport every 20 minutes. The journey takes 50 minutes from the local bus station on Domovinskog Rata, making it a slower option than the shuttle but also cheaper (17KN from Split, 13KN from Trogir).

Taxi A cab to central Split costs between 250KN and 300KN.

BUS

Promet Split (☑ 021-407 888; www.promet-split.hr) operates local buses on an extensive network throughout Split (per journey 11KN) and as far afield as Klis (13KN) and Trogir (17KN). You can buy tickets on the bus, but if you buy from

the **local bus station** or from a kiosk, a two-journey (ie return, known as a 'duplo') central-zone ticket costs only 17KN. Buses run about every 15 minutes from 5.30am to 11.30pm.

Hvar Island

☑ 021 / POP 11,080

Long, lean Hvar is vaguely shaped like the profile of a holidaymaker reclining on a sunlounger, which is altogether appropriate for the sunniest spot in the country (2724 sunny hours each year) and its most luxurious beach destination.

Hvar Town offers swanky hotels, elegant restaurants and a general sense that, if you care about seeing and being seen, this is the place to be. Rubbing shoulders with the posh yachties are hundreds of young partygoers, dancing on tables at the town's legendary beach bars. The northern coastal towns of Stari Grad and Jelsa are far more subdued.

Hvar's interior hides abandoned ancient hamlets, craggy peaks, vineyards and the lavender fields that the island is famous for. This region is worth exploring on a day trip, as is the island's southern coast, which has some of Hvar's most beautiful and isolated coves.

Hvar Town

POP 4260

The island's hub and busiest destination, Hvar Town is estimated to draw around 20,000 people a day in the high season. It's amazing that they can all fit in the small bay town, where 13th-century walls surround beautifully ornamented Gothic palaces and traffic-free marble streets, but fit they do.

Visitors wander along the main square, explore the sights on the winding stone streets, swim at the numerous beaches or pop off to the Pakleni Islands to get into their birthday suits – but most of all they come to party. Hvar's reputation as Croatia's premier party town is well deserved.

There are several good restaurants, bars and hotels here, but thanks to the island's appeal to well-heeled guests, the prices can be seriously inflated. Don't be put off if you're on a more limited budget, though, as private accommodation and multiple hostels cater to a younger, more diverse crowd.

⊙ Sights

Trg Sv Stjepana   SQUARE
(St Stephen's Sq) Stretching from the harbour to the cathedral, this impressive rectangular

square was formed by filling in an inlet that once reached out from the bay. At 4500 sq metres, it's one of the largest old squares in Dalmatia. Hvar Town's walled core, established in the 13th century, covers the slopes to the north. The town didn't spread south until the 15th century.

Fortica   FORTRESS

(Tvrđava Španjola; ☑ 021-742 608; Biskupa Jurja Dubokovica bb; adult/child 40/20KN; ☺ 8am-9pm Apr-Oct) Looming high above the town and lit with a golden glow at night, this medieval castle occupies the site of an ancient Illyrian settlement dating from before 500 BC. The views looking down over Hvar and the Pakleni Islands are magnificent, and well worth the trudge up through the old-town streets. Once you clear the town walls it's a gently sloping meander up the tree-shaded hillside to the fortress – or you can drive to the very top (100KN in a taxi).

🏃 Activities

Most of the swimming spots on the promenade heading west from the centre are tiny, rocky bays, some of which have been augmented with concrete sunbathing platforms. If you don't mind a hike, there are larger pebbly beaches in the opposite direction. A 30-minute walk will bring you to the largest of them, **Pokonji Dol**. From here, a further 25 minutes via a scenic but rocky path will bring you to secluded **Mekićevica**.

Otherwise, grab a taxi boat to the Pakleni Islands or to one of the beaches further east along the coast such as **Milna** or **Zaraće**. **Dubovica** is particularly recommended; if you have your own wheels you can park on the highway, not far from where it turns inland towards the tunnel, and reach it via a rough stony path.

🛏 Sleeping

Kapa   HOSTEL €

(☑ 091 92 41 068; karmentomasovic@gmail.com; Martina Vučetića 11; dm/r from €28/60; ☺ May-Oct; P ✱ 🠒) The advantages of Kapa's south-end-of-town location are the spacious surrounds and the brilliant sunset views. It's run by a young brother-and-sister team, operating out of a large family house. Dorms sleep four to six people, and there are private doubles with their own bathrooms.

Apartments Ana Dujmović   APARTMENT €€

(☑ 098 838 434; www.visit-hvar.com/apartments-ana-dujmovic; Biskupa Jurja Dubokovića 36; apt from €65; P ✱ 🠒) This brace of comfortable holiday apartments is set behind an olive grove, only a 10-minute walk from the centre of town and, crucially, five minutes from the beach and the Hula-Hula bar. Call ahead and the delightful owner will pick you up from the town centre.

Apartments Komazin   APARTMENT €€

(☑ 091 60 19 712; www.croatia-hvar-apartments.com; Nikice Kolumbića 2; r/apt from €80/110; ✱ 🠒) With six bright apartments and two private rooms sharing a kitchen, bougainvillea-draped Komazin is an attractive option near the top of the private-apartment heap. What the apartments may lack in style they more than compensate for in size. And the host couldn't be more welcoming.

🍴 Eating & Drinking

Dalmatino   DALMATIAN €€€

(☑ 091 52 93 121; www.dalmatino-hvar.com; Sv Marak 1; mains 80-265KN; ☺ 11am-midnight Mon-Sat Apr-Nov; 🠒) Calling itself a 'steak and fish house', this place is always popular – due, in part, to the handsome waiters and the free-flowing *rakija* (grappa). Thankfully, the food is also excellent; try the *gregada* (fish fillet served on potatoes with a thick, broth-like sauce).

Hula-Hula Hvar   BAR

(☑ 095 91 11 871; www.hulahulahvar.com; Šetalište Antuna Tomislava Petrića 10; ☺ 9am-11pm Apr-Oct) *The* spot to catch the sunset to the sound of techno and house music, Hula-Hula is known for its après-beach party (4pm to 9pm), where all of young, trendy Hvar seems to descend for sundowner cocktails. Dancing on tables is pretty much compulsory.

Kiva Bar   BAR

(☑ 091 51 22 343; www.facebook.com/kivabar.hvar; Obala Fabrika 10; ☺ 9pm-2am Apr-Dec) A happening place in an alleyway just off the waterfront, Kiva is packed to the rafters most nights, with patrons spilling out and filling up the lane. DJs spin a popular mix of old-school dance, pop and hip-hop classics to an up-for-it crowd.

ℹ Information

Emergency Clinic (Dom Zdravlja; ☑ 021-717 099; Biskupa Jurja Dubokovića 3) About 400m west of the town centre.

Tourist Office (☑ 021-741 059; www.tzhvar.hr; Trg Sv Stjepana 42; ☺ 8am-10pm Jul & Aug, 8am-8pm Mon-Sat, 8am-1pm & 4-8pm Sun Jun & Sep, 8am-2pm Mon-Fri, to noon Sat Oct-May) In the Arsenal building, right on Trg Sv Stjepana.

KORČULA ISLAND

Rich in vineyards, olive groves and small villages, the island of Korčula is the sixth-largest Adriatic island, stretching nearly 47km in length. Quiet coves and small sandy beaches dot the steep southern coast while the northern shore is flatter and more pebbly. Tradition is alive and kicking on Korčula, with age-old religious ceremonies, folk music and dances still being performed to the delight of an ever-growing influx of tourists. Arguably the best of all Croatian whites is produced from the indigenous grape *pošip*, particularly from the areas around the villages of **Čara** and **Smokvica**. The *grk* grape, cultivated around Lumbarda, also produces quality dry white wine.

Korčula Town is a stunner. Ringed by imposing defences, this coastal citadel is dripping with history, with marble streets rich in Renaissance and Gothic architecture. Its fascinating fishbone layout was cleverly designed for the comfort and safety of its inhabitants: western streets were built straight in order to open the city to the refreshing summer *maestral* (strong, steady westerly wind), while the eastern streets were curved to minimise the force of the winter *bura* (cold northeasterly wind). The town cradles a harbour, overlooked by round defensive towers and a compact cluster of red-roofed houses. There are rustling palms all around and several beaches an easy walk away.

Dominating the little square at Korčula Town's heart is the magnificent 15th-century **St Mark's Cathedral** (Katedrala svetog Marka; Trg Sv Marka; church 10KN; bell tower adult/child 20/15KN; ☉ 9am-9pm Jul & Aug, hours vary Sep-Jun), built from Korčula limestone in a Gothic-Renaissance style by Italian and local artisans. The sculptural detail of the facade is intriguing, particularly the naked squatting figures of Adam and Eve on the door pillars, and the two-tailed mermaid and elephant on the triangular gable cornice at the very top.

Some of Korčula's best eating experiences can be found at local taverns in its small villages. If you've got your own transport, it's well worth seeking out **Konoba Mate** (☑ 020-717 109; www.konobamate.hr; Pupnat 28; mains 60-118KN; ☉ 11am-2pm & 7pm-midnight Mon-Sat, 7pm-midnight Sun May-Sep; ☎) in the sleepy farming village of **Pupnat**. The turnoff to the island's best beach, **Pupnatska Luka**, is nearby.

The island has three major ferry ports: Korčula Town's West Harbour, Dominče (3km east of Korčula Town) and Vela Luka. **Jadrolinija** (☑ 020-715 410; www.jadrolinija.hr; Plokata 19 travnja 1921 br 19) has car ferries between Orebić and Domince (passenger/car 16/76KN, 15 minutes), departing roughly every hour. From June to September, a daily catamaran heads from West Harbour to Dubrovnik (130KN, two hours), Hvar (120KN, 1½ hours) and Split (160KN, 3¾ hours). **Kapetan Luka** (☑ 021-645 476; www.krilo.hr) sails daily catamarans to Hvar (110KN, 1¼ hours) and Split (130KN, 2½ hours), adding Dubrovnik (130KN, 1¾ hours) from May to mid-October. In July and August, G&V Line (p142) has four catamarans per week to West Harbour from Dubrovnik (90KN, 2½ hours).

Tourist Office Information Point (☑ 021-718 109; Trg Marka Miličića 9; ☉ 8am-9pm Mon-Sat, 9am-1pm Sun Jun-Sep) In the bus station; a summertime annexe of the main tourist office.

ℹ Getting There & Away

Jadrolinija (☑ 021-741 132; www.jadrolinija.hr; Obala Riva bb) operates the following high-speed catamarans:

➡ Daily from Split (55KN, one hour).

➡ From May to September, up to five times a day between Hvar Town and Split (110KN, one hour).

➡ From June to September, daily from Split (110KN, two hours), Korčula (120KN, 1½ hours) and Dubrovnik (210KN, 3½ hours).

Kapetan Luka (p134) tickets can be purchased from **Pelegrini Tours** (☑ 021-742 743; www.

pelegrini-hvar.hr; Obala Riva 20) for the daily catamaran to Split (90KN, one hour) and Korčula (110KN, 1¼ hours). From May to mid-October, it also heads to Dubrovnik (210KN, three hours).

Hvar Town's **bus station** (Trg Marka Miličića 9) is east of the main square. Buses head to/from the Stari Grad car-ferry port (27KN, 20 minutes, six daily).

In summer taxi boats line Hvar's harbour, offering rides to the Pakleni Islands and isolated beaches further along the coast.

Dubrovnik

☑ 020 / POP 28,500

Regardless of whether you are visiting Dubrovnik for the first time or the hundredth, the sense of awe never fails to descend when you set eyes on the beauty of the old town. Indeed it's hard to imagine anyone becoming jaded by the city's limestone streets, baroque buildings and the endless shimmer of the Adriatic, or failing to be inspired by a walk along the ancient city walls that protected the capital of a sophisticated republic for centuries.

Although the shelling of Dubrovnik in 1991 horrified the world, the city has bounced back with vigour to enchant visitors again. Marvel at the interplay of light on the old stone buildings; trace the peaks and troughs of Dubrovnik's past in museums replete with art and artefacts; take the cable car up to Mt Srđ; exhaust yourself climbing up and down narrow lanes – then plunge into the azure sea.

◉ Sights

★ City Walls & Forts   FORT
(Gradske zidine; ☏ 020-638 800; www.wallsof dubrovnik.com; adult/child 150/50KN; ⊙ 8am-6.30pm Apr-Oct, 9am-3pm Nov-Mar) No visit to Dubrovnik would be complete without a walk around the spectacular city walls, the finest in the world and the city's main claim to fame. From the top, the view over the old town and the shimmering Adriatic is sublime. You can get a good handle on the extent of the shelling damage in the 1990s by gazing over the rooftops: those sporting bright new terracotta suffered damage and had to be replaced.

Srđ   VIEWPOINT
(Srđ bb) From the top of this 412m-high hill, Dubrovnik's old town looks even more surreal than usual – like a scale model of itself or an illustration on a page. The views take in all of Dubrovnik and Lokrum, with the Elafiti Islands filling the horizon. It's this extraordinary vantage point that made Srđ a key battleground during the 1990s war. That story is told in **Dubrovnik During the Homeland War** (Dubrovnik u Domovinskom ratu; ☏ 020-324 856; adult/child 30/15KN; ⊙ 8am-10pm; Ⓟ), an exhibition housed in Fort Imperial at the summit.

The easiest and quickest way to get to the top is by **cable car** (Žičara; ☏ 020-414 355; www.dubrovnikcablecar.com; Petra Krešimira IV bb, Ploče; adult/child return 140/60KN, one way 85/40KN; ⊙ 9am-midnight Jun-Aug, to 10pm Sep, to 8pm Apr, May & Oct, to 4pm Nov-Mar), or you can drive (follow the signs to Bosanka), walk via the **Way of the Cross** (Križni put; Jadranska cesta, Srđ), or catch bus 17 from the Pile stop to Bosanka and then walk the final 1.5km.

War Photo Limited   GALLERY
(☏ 020-322 166; www.warphotoltd.com; Antuninska 6; adult/child 50/40KN; ⊙ 10am-10pm May-Sep, to 4pm Wed-Mon Apr & Oct) An immensely powerful experience, this gallery features compelling exhibitions curated by New Zealand photojournalist Wade Goddard, who worked in the Balkans in the 1990s. Its intention is to expose the everyday, horrific and unjust realities of war. There's a permanent exhibition on the upper floor devoted to the wars in Yugoslavia; the changing exhibitions cover a multitude of conflicts.

Rector's Palace   PALACE
(Knežev dvor; ☏ 020-321 497; www.dumus.hr; Pred Dvorom 3; adult/child 80/25KN, incl in multimuseum pass adult/child 120/25KN; ⊙ 9am-6pm Apr-Oct, to 4pm Nov-Mar) Built in the late 15th century for the elected rector who governed Dubrovnik, this Gothic-Renaissance palace contains the rector's office and private chambers, public halls, administrative offices and a dungeon. During his one-month term the rector was unable to leave the building without the permission of the senate. Today the palace has been turned into the **Cultural History Museum**, with artfully restored rooms, portraits, coats of arms and coins, evoking the glorious history of Ragusa.

Cathedral of the Assumption   CATHEDRAL
(Katedrala Marijina Uznesenja; Držićeva poljana; treasury 20KN; ⊙ 8am-5pm Mon-Sat, 11am-5pm Sun Easter-Oct, 9am-noon & 4-5pm Mon-Sat Nov-Easter) Built on the site of a 7th-century basilica, Dubrovnik's original cathedral was enlarged in the 12th century, supposedly funded by a gift from England's King Richard I, the

CROATIA DUBROVNIK

ⓘ MUSEUMS OF DUBROVNIK PASS

Perhaps a cunning plan to get you through the doors of some of the town's more marginal museums, a multi-museum pass (adult/child 120/25KN) allows access to nine of Dubrovnik's institutions. The only must-see among them though is the Rector's Palace, which is also the only one ticketed separately. If you're interested in visiting the excellent **Museum of Modern Art** (Umjetnička galerija; ☏ 020-426 590; www. ugdubrovnik.hr; Frana Supila 23, Ploče; ⊙ 9am-8pm Tue-Sun), then it's worth buying the pass. The other museums could easily be skipped.

Dubrovnik

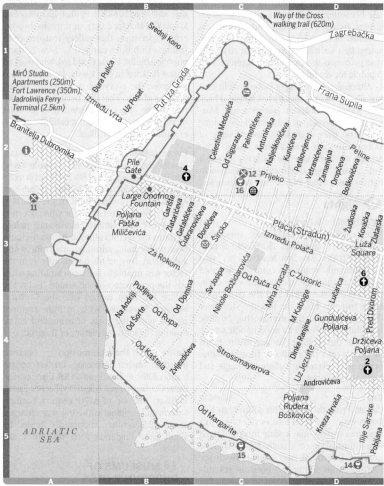

CROATIA DUBROVNIK

Lionheart, who was saved from a shipwreck on the nearby island of Lokrum. Soon after the first cathedral was destroyed in the 1667 earthquake, work began on this, its baroque replacement, which was finished in 1713.

St Blaise's Church
CHURCH

(Crkva Sv Vlahe; Luža Sq; ☺8am-noon & 4-5pm Mon-Sat, 7am-1pm Sun) Dedicated to the city's patron saint, this exceptionally beautiful church was built in 1715 in the ornate baroque style. The interior is notable for its marble altars and a 15th-century silver gilt statue of St Blaise (within the high altar), who is holding a scale model of pre-earthquake Dubrovnik.

Note also the stained-glass windows designed by local artist Ivo Dulčić in 1971.

Dominican Monastery & Museum
CHRISTIAN MONASTERY

(Dominikanski samostan i muzej; ☑020-321 423; www.dominicanmuseum.hr; Sv Dominika 4; adult/child 30/20KN; ☺9am-5pm) This imposing structure is an architectural highlight, built in a transitional Gothic-Renaissance style and containing an impressive art collection. Constructed around the same time as the city walls in the 14th century, the stark exterior resembles a fortress more than a religious complex. The interior contains a

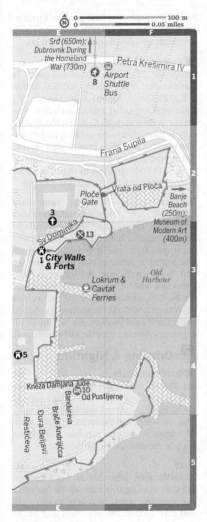

CROATIA DUBROVNIK

Fort Lawrence FORTRESS

(Tvrđava Lovrjenac; www.citywallsdubrovnik.hr; Pile; 50KN, free with city walls ticket; ⊙ 8am-6.30pm Apr-Oct, 9am-3pm Nov-Mar) St Blaise gazes down from the walls of this large free-standing fortress, constructed atop a 37m-high promontory adjacent to the old town. Built to guard the city's western approach from invasion by land or sea, its walls range from 4m to 12m thick. There's not a lot inside, but the battlements offer wonderful views over the old town and its large courtyard is often used as a venue for summer theatre and concerts.

🛏 Sleeping

Hostel Angelina HOSTEL **€**

(📞 091 89 39 089; www.hostelangelinaoldtown dubrovnik.com; Plovani skalini 17a; dm from €49; ❄ 🛜) Hidden away in a quiet nook of the old town, this cute little hostel offers bunk rooms, a small guest kitchen and a bougainvillea-shaded terrace with memorable views over the rooftops. Plus you'll get a great glute workout every time you walk up the lane. It also has private rooms in three old-town annexes (from €110).

★ **Karmen Apartments** APARTMENT **€€**

(📞 020-323 433; www.karmendu.com; Bandureva 1; apt from €95; ❄ 🛜) These four inviting

---

graceful 15th-century **cloister** constructed by local artisans after the designs of the Florentine architect Maso di Bartolomeo.

Franciscan Monastery & Museum CHRISTIAN MONASTERY

(Franjevački samostan i muzej; 📞 020-321 410; Placa 2; 30KN; ⊙ 9am-6pm Apr-Oct, to 2pm Nov-Mar) Within this monastery's solid stone walls are a gorgeous mid-14th-century **cloister**, a historic **pharmacy** and a small **museum** with a collection of relics and liturgical objects, including chalices, paintings and gold jewellery, and pharmacy items such as laboratory gear and medical books.

LOKRUM

Lush **Lokrum** (📱020-311 738; www.lokrum.hr; adult/child incl boat 150/25KN; ☺Apr-Nov) is a beautiful, forested island full of holm oaks, black ash, pines and olive trees, only a 10-minute ferry ride from Dubrovnik's Old Harbour. It's a popular swimming spot, although the beaches are rocky. Boats leave roughly hourly in summer (half-hourly in July and August). The public boat ticket price includes the entrance fee, but if you arrive with another boat, you're required to pay 120KN at the information centre on the island.

apartments enjoy a great location a stone's throw from Ploče harbour. All have plenty of character with art, splashes of colour, tasteful furnishings and books to browse. Apartment 2 has a little balcony while apartment 1 enjoys sublime port views. Book well ahead.

★Miró Studio Apartments
APARTMENT €€€

(📱099 42 42 442; www.mirostudioapartmentsdubrovnik.com; Sv Đurđa 16, Pile; apt €145-200; ❄🖧🎤) Located in a quiet residential nook only metres from the sea, hidden between the old-town walls and Fort Lawrence, this schmick complex is an absolute gem. The decor marries ancient stone walls and whitewashed ceiling beams with design features such as uplighting, contemporary bathrooms and sliding glass partitions.

✕ Eating

Shizuku
JAPANESE €€

(📱020-311 493; www.facebook.com/ShizukuDubrovnik; Kneza Domagoja 1f, Batala; mains 70-85KN; ☺5pm-midnight Tue-Sun; 🎤) Attentive local wait staff usher you to your table in the clean-lined, modern dining room of this popular restaurant, tucked away in a residential area between Gruž Harbour and Lapad Bay. The Japanese owners will be in the kitchen, preparing authentic sushi, sashimi, udon, crispy *karaage* chicken and gyoza dumplings. Wash it all down with Japanese beer or sake.

Nishta
VEGAN €€

(📱020-322 088; www.nishtarestaurant.com; Prijeko bb; mains 98-108KN; ☺11.30am-11.30pm Mon-Sat; 🖧) The popularity of this tiny old-town restaurant is testament not just to the paucity of options for vegetarians and vegans in Croatia, but also to the imaginative and beautifully presented food produced within. Each day of the week has its own menu with a separate set of cooked and raw options.

★Restaurant 360°
INTERNATIONAL €€€

(📱020-322 222; www.360dubrovnik.com; Sv Dominika bb; 2/3/5 courses 520/620/860KN; ☺6.30-10.30pm Tue-Sun Apr-Sep; 🎤) Dubrovnik's glitziest restaurant offers fine dining at its best, with flavoursome, beautifully presented, creative cuisine, an impressive wine list and slick, professional service. The setting is unrivalled – on top of the city walls with tables positioned so you can peer through the battlements over the harbour.

Nautika
EUROPEAN €€€

(📱020-442 526; www.nautikarestaurants.com; Brsalje 3, Pile; mains 290-360KN; ☺6pm-midnight Apr-Oct) Nautika bills itself as 'Dubrovnik's finest restaurant' and it comes pretty close. The setting is sublime, overlooking the sea and the city walls, and the service is faultless: black-bow-tie formal but friendly. As for the food, it's sophisticated if not particularly adventurous, with classic techniques applied to the finest local produce. For maximum silver-service drama, order the salt-crusted fish.

🍷 Drinking & Nightlife

★Bard Mala Buža
BAR

(Iza Mira 14; ☺9am-3am May-Oct) The more upmarket and slick of two cliff bars pressed up against the seaward side of the city walls. This one is lower on the rocks and has a shaded terrace where you can lose a day quite happily, mesmerised by the Adriatic vistas.

Buža
BAR

(off Od Margarite; ☺8am-2am Jun-Aug, to midnight Sep-May) Finding this ramshackle bar-on-a-cliff feels like a real discovery as you duck and dive around the city walls and finally see the entrance tunnel. However, Buža's no secret – it gets insanely busy, especially around sunset. Wait for a space on one of the concrete platforms, grab a cool drink in a plastic cup and enjoy the vibe and views.

Cave Bar More
BAR

(www.hotel-more.hr; Šetalište Nika i Meda Pucića bb, Babin Kuk; ☺10am-midnight Jun-Aug, to 10pm Sep-May) This little beach bar serves coffee, snacks and cocktails to bathers reclining by the dazzlingly clear waters of Lapad Bay, but that's not the half of it – the main bar is set in an actual cave. Cool off beneath the stalactites in the side chamber, where a glass floor exposes a water-filled cavern.

D'vino WINE BAR
(☑020-321 130; www.dvino.net; Palmotićeva 4a; ☺9am-midnight Mar-Nov; 🛜) If you're interested in sampling top-notch Croatian wine, this convivial bar is the place to go. As well as a large and varied wine list, it offers tasting flights presented by cool and knowledgeable staff (three wines from 55KN) plus savoury breakfasts, snacks and platters. Sit outside for the authentic old-town-alley ambience, but check out the whimsical wall inscriptions inside.

ℹ Information

Dubrovnik's tourist board has offices in **Pile** (☑020-312 011; www.tzdubrovnik.hr; Brsalje 5; ☺8am-8pm), **Gruž** (☑020-417 983; Obala Pape Ivana Pavla II 1; ☺8am-8pm Jun-Oct, 8am-3pm Mon-Fri, to 1pm Sat Nov-Mar, 8am-8pm Mon-Fri, to 2pm Sat & Sun Apr & May) and **Lapad** (☑020-437 460; Dvori Lapad, Masarykov put 2; ☺8am-8pm Jul & Aug, 8am-noon & 5-8pm Mon-Fri, 9am-2pm Sat Apr-Jun, Sep & Oct) that dispense maps, information and advice.

Dubrovnik General Hospital (Opća bolnica Dubrovnik; ☑020-431 777, emergency 194; www.bolnica-du.hr; Dr Roka Mišetića 2, Lapad) Public hospital with a 24-hour emergency department.

Marin Med Clinic (☑020-400 500; www.marin-med.com; Dr Ante Starčevića 45, Montovjerna; ☺8am-8pm Mon-Fri, to 1pm Sat) Large private health centre with English-speaking doctors.

Travel Corner (Avansa Travel; ☑020-492 313; www.dubrovnik-travelcorner.com; Obala Stjepana Radića 40, Gruž; internet per hr 25KN, left luggage per 2hr/day 10/40KN) This handy one-stop shop has a left-luggage service and internet terminals, dispenses tourist information, books excursions and sells Kapetan Luka ferry tickets.

ℹ Getting There & Away

AIR

Dubrovnik Airport (DBV, Zračna luka Dubrovnik; ☑020-773 100; www.airport-dubrovnik.hr; Čilipi) is in Čilipi, 19km southeast of Dubrovnik. Croatia Airlines, British Airways,

---

WORTH A TRIP

CAVTAT

Set on a petite peninsula embraced by two harbours, the ancient town of Cavtat (pronounced *tsav*-tat) has a pretty waterfront promenade peppered with restaurants, pebbly beaches and an interesting assortment of artsy attractions. These include the glorious **Račić Family Mausoleum** (Mauzolej obitelji Račić; www.migk.hr; Groblje sv Roka, Kvaternikova bb; 20KN; ☺10am-5pm Mon-Sat Apr-Oct), created in the 1920s by preeminent Croatian sculptor Ivan Meštrović. Cavtat's most revered artist is painter Vlaho Bukovac (1855–1922), whose work can be seen in **St Nicholas' Church** (Crkva svetog Nikole; Obala Ante Starčevića bb; ☺hours vary), the **Our-Lady-of-the-Snow Monastery** (Samostan Gospe od snijega; ☑020-678 064; www.franjevacki-samostan-cavtat.com; Šetalište Rat 2; ☺7am-9pm), the **Baltazar Bogišić Collection** (Obala Ante Starčevića 18; adult/child 25/10KN; ☺9.30am-1.30pm Mon-Sat Apr-Oct, 9am-1pm Mon-Fri Nov-Mar) and displayed in his childhood home, **Bukovac House** (Kuća Bukovac; ☑020-478 646; www.kuca-bukovac.hr; Bukovčeva 5; 30KN; ☺9am-6pm Mon-Sat, to 2pm Sun Apr-Oct, 10am-6pm Tue-Sat, 9am-1pm Sun Nov-Mar).

Not just the best restaurant on Cavtat's seafront strip, **Bugenvila** (☑020-479 949; www.bugenvila.eu; Obala Ante Starčevića 9; mains 90-275KN; ☺noon-4pm & 6.30-10pm; 🛜☑) is one of the culinary trendsetters of the Dalmatian coast. Local ingredients are showcased in adventurous dishes served with artistic flourishes. Visit at lunchtime to take advantage of the three-course special menu (180KN).

Without Cavtat there would be no Dubrovnik, as it was refugees from Epidaurum (the Roman incarnation of Cavtat) who established the city in 614. The walls of its famous offshoot are visible in the distance and the two are well connected by both boat and bus, making Cavtat either an easy day-trip destination from Dubrovnik or a quieter (not to mention cheaper) alternative base.

During the tourist season at least three different operators offer boats to Cavtat from Dubrovnik's Old Harbour (one-way/return 100/60KN, 45 minutes), with departures at least every half hour. In winter this reduces to three to five a day, weather dependent. Bus 10 runs roughly half-hourly to Cavtat (25KN, 30 minutes) from Dubrovnik.

Iberica, Trade Air, Turkish Airlines and Vueling fly to Dubrovnik year-round. In summer they're joined by dozens of other airlines.

BOAT

The **ferry terminal** (Obala Pape Ivana Pavla II 1, Gruž) is in Gruž, 3km northwest of the old town. Ferries for **Lokrum and Cavtat** depart from the Old Harbour.

➔ **Jadrolinija** (☑ 020-418 000; www.jadrolinija. hr; Obala Stjepana Radića 40, Gruž) has daily ferries to the Elafiti Islands. From June to September, there's also a daily catamaran to Korčula (130KN, two hours), Hvar (210KN, 3½ hours) and Split (210KN, six hours).

➔ **G&V Line** (☑ 020-313 119; www.gv-line.hr; Obala Ivana Pavla II 1, Gruž) has a catamaran to Korčula (90KN, 2½ hours) four times a week in July and August.

➔ **Kapetan Luka** (Krilo; ☑ 021-645 476; www. krilo.hr) has a daily fast boat from May to mid-October to/from Korčula (130KN, 1¾ hours), Hvar (210KN, three hours) and Split (210KN, 4¼ hours).

BUS

Buses from **Dubrovnik Bus Station** (Autobusni kolodvor; ☑ 060 305 070; www.libertasdub rovnik.hr; Obala Pape Ivana Pavla II 44a, Gruž; ⊙ 4.30am-10pm; ☎) can be crowded, so purchase tickets online or book in advance in summer. Domestic destinations include Split (127KN, 4½ hours, 11 daily), Zadar (182KN, eight hours, five daily) and Zagreb (259KN, 11¾ hours, 10 daily).

🛈 Getting Around

TO/FROM THE AIRPORT

Atlas runs the **airport shuttle bus** (☑ 020-642 286; www.atlas-croatia.com; one-way/return 40/70KN), timed around flight schedules. Buses to Dubrovnik stop at the Pile Gate and the bus station; buses to the airport pick up from the bus station and from the bus stop near the cable car.

City buses 11, 27 and 38 also stop at the airport but are less frequent and take longer (28KN, seven daily, no Sunday service).

Allow up to 280KN for a taxi to Dubrovnik. Dubrovnik Transfer Services (www. dubrovnik-transfer-services.com) offers a set-price taxi transfer service to the city (€30) and Cavtat (€16), and to as far away as Zagreb, Sara-jevo, Podgorica and Tirana.

BUS

Dubrovnik has a superb bus service. The fare is 15KN if you buy from the driver and 12KN if you buy a ticket at a *tisak* (news-stand). Timetables are available at www.libertasdubrovnik.hr.

SURVIVAL GUIDE

🛈 Directory A–Z

ACCOMMODATION

Croatia is extremely popular in summer and good places book out well in advance in July and August. It's also very busy in June and September.

Hotels These range from massive beach resorts to boutique establishments.

Apartments Privately owned holiday units are a staple of the local accommodation scene; they're especially good for families.

Guesthouses Usually family-run establish-ments where spare rooms are rented at a bargain price – sometimes with their own bathrooms, sometimes not.

Hostels Mainly in the bigger cities and more popular beach destinations, with dorms and sometimes private rooms too.

Campgrounds Tent and caravan sites, often fairly basic.

MONEY

ATMs are widely available. Credit cards are ac-cepted in most hotels and restaurants. Smaller restaurants, shops and private-accommodation owners only take cash.

OPENING HOURS

Opening hours vary throughout the year. We've provided high-season opening hours; hours gen-erally decrease in the shoulder and low seasons.

Banks 8am or 9am to 8pm weekdays and 7am to 1pm or 8am to 2pm Saturday.

Cafes and bars 8am or 9am to midnight.

Offices 8am to 4pm or 8.30am to 4.30pm weekdays.

Post offices 7am to 8pm weekdays and 7am to 1pm Saturday; longer hours in coastal towns in summer.

Restaurants Noon to 11pm or midnight; often closed Sundays outside peak season.

Shops 8am to 8pm weekdays, to 2pm or 3pm Saturday; some take a break from 2pm to 5pm. Shopping malls have longer hours.

PUBLIC HOLIDAYS

Croats take their holidays very seriously. Shops and museums are shut and boat services are reduced. On religious holidays, the churches are full; it can be a good time to check out the art-work in a church that is usually closed.

New Year's Day 1 January

Epiphany 6 January

Easter Sunday & Monday March/April

Labour Day 1 May

Corpus Christi 60 days after Easter
Day of Antifascist Resistance 22 June
Statehood Day 25 June
Homeland Thanksgiving Day 5 August
Feast of the Assumption 15 August
Independence Day 8 October
All Saints' Day 1 November
Christmas 25 & 26 December

TELEPHONE

➤ To call Croatia from abroad, dial your international access code, then 385 (the country code for Croatia), then the area code (without the initial 0) and the local number.

➤ To call from region to region within Croatia, start with the full area code (drop it when dialling within the same code).

ⓘ Getting There & Away

ENTERING THE COUNTRY/REGION

With an economy that depends heavily on tourism, Croatia has wisely kept red tape to a minimum for foreign visitors.

Passport

Your passport must be valid for at least another three months after the planned departure from Croatia, as well as issued within the previous 10 years.

Citizens of EU countries can enter Croatia with only their ID card.

Croatian authorities require all foreigners to register with the local police when they arrive in a new area of the country, but this is a routine matter normally handled by the hotel, hostel, campground or agency securing your private accommodation. If you're staying elsewhere (eg with relatives or friends), your host should take care of it for you.

AIR

There are direct flights to Croatia from a variety of European and Middle Eastern cities year-round, with dozens of seasonal routes and charters added in summer. **Croatia Airlines** (OU; ☏ 01-66 76 555; www.croatiaairlines.hr) is the national carrier; it's part of the Star Alliance. Croatia has an astonishing eight airports welcoming international flights, although some of them are highly seasonal. The main ones are Dubrovnik Airport (p141), Split Airport (p133), Zadar Airport (p128) and Zagreb Airport (p123).

LAND

Croatia has border crossings with Slovenia, Hungary, Serbia, Bosnia and Hercegovina, and Montenegro.

Bus

Direct bus connections link Croatia to all of its neighbours and to as far afield as Norway. In most cases, passports are collected on the bus and handed over at the border; you usually won't leave the bus unless there's an issue that needs resolving. Useful websites include www.eurolines.com, www.buscroatia.com, www.getbybus.com and www.vollo.net.

Train

Zagreb is Croatia's main train hub. In most cases, passports are checked on the train.

SEA

Regular ferries connect Croatia with Italy; Split is the main year-round hub.

Jadrolinija (www.jadrolinija.hr) Overnight services between Split and Ancona year-round, between Zadar and Ancona from June to September, and between Dubrovnik and Bari from April to November.

SNAV (www.snav.com) Overnight services on the Split–Ancona route from April to October.

Venezia Lines (www.venezialines.com) Ferries ply the Venice–Rovinj route from May to September.

ⓘ Getting Around

AIR

Croatia Airlines flies from Zagreb to Dubrovnik, Split and Zadar. **Trade Air** (TDR; ☏ 091 62 65 111; www.trade-air.com) flies between Split and Dubrovnik.

BOAT

Numerous ferries connect the main coastal centres and their surrounding islands year-round, with services extended in the tourist season. Split is the main hub.

BUS

Bus services are excellent and relatively inexpensive. There are often a number of different companies handling each route, so prices can vary substantially. Luggage stowed in the baggage compartment under the bus costs extra (around 10KN a piece). Note that buses between Split and Dubrovnik pass through Bosnian territory so you'll need to keep your passport handy.

TRAIN

Croatia's train network is limited and trains are less frequent than buses. For information about schedules, prices and services, contact **HŽPP** (☏ 01-37 82 583; www.hzpp.hr).

Czech Republic

POP 10.6 MILLION

Best Places to Eat

➡ Field (p156)

➡ Krčma v Šatlavské (p166)

➡ Entree (p172)

➡ Levitate Restaurant (p155)

➡ Buffalo Burger Bar (p161)

Best Places to Stay

➡ Hostel Mitte (p169)

➡ Dominican Hotel (p155)

➡ Long Story Short (p172)

➡ Hotel Myší Díra (p166)

➡ Hotel Romance Puškin (p167)

Why Go?

Since the fall of communism in 1989 and the opening up of Central and Eastern Europe, Prague has evolved into one of Europe's most popular travel destinations. The city offers an intact medieval core that transports you back – especially when strolling the hidden streets of the Old Town – some 600 years. The 14th-century Charles Bridge, traversing two historic neighbourhoods across a slow-moving river, is one of the continent's most beautiful sights.

Prague is not just about history. It's a vital urban centre with a rich array of cultural offerings. Outside the capital, in the provinces of Bohemia and Moravia, castles and palaces abound – including the audacious hilltop chateau at Český Krumlov – which illuminate the stories of powerful dynasties whose influence was felt throughout Europe. Olomouc, the historic capital of Moravia to the east, boasts much of the beauty of Prague without the crowds.

When to Go
Prague

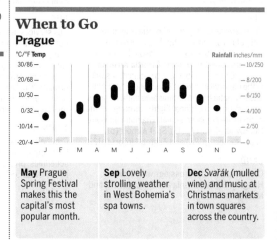

May Prague Spring Festival makes this the capital's most popular month.

Sep Lovely strolling weather in West Bohemia's spa towns.

Dec Svařák (mulled wine) and music at Christmas markets in town squares across the country.

Entering the Country

The Czech Republic lies at the centre of Europe and has good rail and road connections to surrounding countries. Prague's international airport is a major air hub for Central Europe.

Flights, cars and tours can be booked online at lonely planet.com/bookings.

ITINERARIES

One Week

Experience the exciting combination of a tumultuous past and energetic present in Prague (p147). Top experiences include the grandeur of Prague Castle (p147), Josefov's Prague Jewish Museum (p149), and getting lost amid the bewildering labyrinth of the Old Town. Take an essential day trip to Karlštejn (p159), and then head south to Český Krumlov (p164) for a few days of riverside R&R.

Two Weeks

Begin in Prague (p147) before heading west for the spa scene at Karlovy Vary (p167). Balance the virtue and vice ledger with a few Bohemian brews in Plzeň (p160) before heading south for relaxation and rigour around Český Krumlov (p164). Head east to the Renaissance grandeur of Telč (p168) and the cosmopolitan galleries and museums of Brno (p168). From Moravia's largest city, it's just a skip to stately Olomouc (p171).

Essential Food & Drink

Beer Modern pils (light, amber-coloured lager) was invented in the city of Plzeň in the 19th century, giving Czechs bragging rights to having the best beer (*pivo*) in the world.

Becherovka A shot of this sweetish herbal liqueur from Karlovy Vary is a popular way to start (or end) a big meal.

Braised beef Look out for *svíčková na smetaně* on menus. This is a satisfying slice of roast beef, served in a cream sauce, with a side of bread dumplings and a dollop of cranberry sauce.

Carp This lowly fish (*kapr* in Czech) is given pride of place every Christmas at the centre of the family meal. *Kapr na kmíní* is fried or baked carp with caraway seeds.

Dumplings Every culture has its favourite starchy side dish; for Czechs it's *knedliky* – big bread dumplings that are perfect for mopping up gravy.

Roast pork Move over beef, pork (*vepřové maso*) is king here. The classic Bohemian dish, seen on menus around the country, is *vepřo-knedlo-zelo*, local slang for roast pork, bread dumplings and sauerkraut.

AT A GLANCE

Area 78,866 sq km

Capital Prague

Country Code 420

Currency Crown (Kč)

Emergency 112

Language Czech

Time Central European Time (GMT/UTC plus one hour)

Visas Schengen rules apply; visas not required for most nationalities for stays of up to 90 days

Sleeping Price Ranges

The following price ranges refer to the cost of a standard double room per night in high season.

€ less than 1600Kč

€€ 1600–3700Kč

€€€ more than 3700Kč

Eating Price Ranges

The following price ranges refer to the price of a main course at dinner.

€ less than 200Kč

€€ 200–500Kč

€€€ more than 500Kč

Resources

CzechTourism (www.czechtourism.com)

Lonely Planet (www.lonelyplanet.com/czech-republic)

Prague City Tourism (www.prague.eu)

Czech Republic Highlights

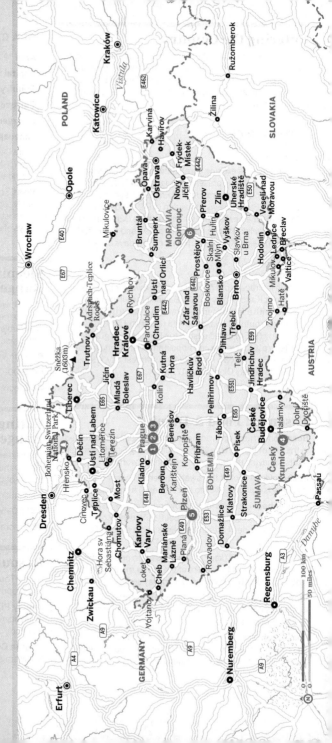

1 Charles Bridge (p152) Strolling across in the early morning or late evening when the crowds thin out.

2 U Kroka (p156) Enjoying an evening in an old-school Czech pub.

3 Astronomical Clock (p149) Joining the appreciative throngs at the top of the hour.

4 Český Krumlov (p164) Walking the streets of one of the prettiest towns in Central Europe.

5 Pilsner Urquell Brewery (p160) Touring this brewery in Plzeň to see where it all started.

6 Olomouc (p171) Ambling through this stately town, the most amazing place you've never heard of.

PRAGUE

POP 1.3 MILLION

It's the perfect irony of Prague: you're lured here by the past, but compelled to linger by the present and the future. Fill your days with its illustrious artistic and architectural heritage – from Gothic and Renaissance to art nouveau and cubist. If Prague's seasonal legions of tourists wear you down, that's OK. Just drink a glass of the country's legendary lager, relax and rest reassured that quiet moments still exist: a private dawn on Charles Bridge, the glorious cityscape of Staré Město or getting lost in the intimate lanes of Malá Strana.

◉ Sights

As seen on the map, the Vltava River winds through the middle of Prague like a giant question mark, with the city centre straddling its lower half. There is little method in Prague's haphazard sprawl – it's a city that has grown organically from its medieval roots, snagging villages and swallowing suburbs as it spread out into the wooded hills of Central Bohemia.

The oldest parts of the city cluster tightly just south of the river bend – **Hradčany**, the medieval castle district, and **Malá Strana** (Little Quarter) on the western bank; **Stáre Město** (Old Town), **Nové Město** (New Town) and the ancient citadel of **Vyšehrad** on the eastern bank.

◉ Hradčany

⭐**Prague Castle** CASTLE
(Pražský hrad; Map p148; ☎224 372 423; www.hrad.cz; Hradčanské náměstí 1; adult/concession from 250/125Kč; ⊙grounds 6am-10pm, gardens 10am-6pm Apr-Oct, historic buildings 9am-5pm Apr-Oct, to 4pm Nov-Mar; Ⓜ Malostranská, 🚋22, 23) Prague's most popular attraction. Looming above the Vltava's left bank, its serried ranks of spires, towers and palaces dominate the city centre like a fairy-tale fortress. Within its walls lies a varied and fascinating collection of historic buildings, museums and galleries that are home to some of the Czech Republic's greatest artistic and cultural treasures. Note that visitors must pass through a security check before entering the grounds, so bring your passport or EU identification card.

⭐**St Vitus Cathedral** CHURCH
(Katedrála sv Víta; Map p148; ☎257 531 622; www.katedralasvatehovita.cz; Prague Castle; ⊙9am-5pm, from noon Sun, to 4pm Nov-Mar; 🚋22, 23) Built over a time span of almost 600 years, St Vitus is one of the most richly endowed cathedrals in central Europe. It is pivotal to the religious and cultural life of the Czech Republic, housing treasures that range from the 14th-century mosaic of the Last Judgement and the tombs of St Wenceslas and Charles IV, to the baroque silver tomb of St John of Nepomuk, the ornate Chapel of St Wenceslas and art nouveau stained glass by Alfons Mucha.

Old Royal Palace PALACE
(Starý královský palác; Map p148; Prague Castle; ⊙9am-5pm, to 4pm Nov-Mar; 🚋22, 23) The Old Royal Palace is one of the oldest parts of Prague Castle, dating from 1135. It was originally used only by Czech princesses, but from the 13th to the 16th centuries it was the king's own palace. At its heart is the grand Vladislav Hall and the Bohemian Chancellery, scene of the famous Defenestration of Prague in 1618.

Golden Lane STREET
(Zlatá ulička; Map p148; Prague Castle; ⊙9am-5pm, to 4pm Nov-Mar; 🚋22, 23) This picturesque alley runs along the northern wall of the castle. Its tiny, colourful cottages were built in the 16th century for the sharpshooters of the castle guard, but were later used by goldsmiths. In the 19th and early 20th centuries they were occupied by artists, including the writer Franz Kafka (who stayed at his sister's house at No 22 from 1916 to 1917).

Story of Prague Castle MUSEUM
(Map p148; www.hrad.cz; Prague Castle; adult/child 140/70Kč; ⊙9am-5pm, to 4pm Nov-Mar; 🚋22, 23) Housed in the Gothic vaults beneath the Old Royal Palace, this huge and impressive collection of artefacts ranks alongside the Lobkowicz Palace as one of the most interesting exhibits in the castle. It traces 1000 years of the castle's history, from the building of the first wooden palisade to the present day, illustrated by models of the site at various stages in its development.

Lobkowicz Palace MUSEUM
(Lobkovický palác; Map p148; ☎233 312 925; www.lobkowicz.com; Jiřská 3; adult/concession 295/220Kč; ⊙10am-6pm; 🚋22, 23) This 16th-century palace houses a private museum known as the Princely Collections, which includes priceless paintings, furniture and musical memorabilia. Your tour includes an audio guide dictated by owner

Prague Castle

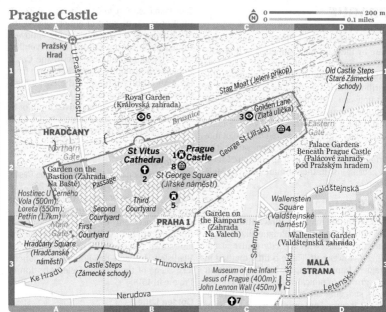

Prague Castle

◎ Top Sights

◎ Sights

William Lobkowicz and his family – this personal connection really brings the displays to life, and makes the palace one of the castle's most interesting attractions.

Strahov Library HISTORIC BUILDING
(Strahovská knihovna; ☏ 233 107 718; www.strahovskyklaster.cz; Strahovské nádvoří 1; adult/child 120/60Kč; ⊙ 9am-noon & 1-5pm; ⛟ 22, 23) Strahov Library is the largest monastic library in the country, with two magnificent baroque halls dating from the 17th and 18th centuries. You can peek through the doors but, sadly, you can't go into the halls themselves – it was found that fluctuations in humidity caused by visitors' breath was endangering the frescoes. There's also a display of historical curiosities.

Loreta CHURCH
(☏ 220 516 740; www.loreta.cz; Loretánské náměstí 7; adult/child 150/80Kč, photography permit 100Kč; ⊙ 9am-5pm Apr-Oct, 9.30am-4pm Nov-Mar; ⛟ 22, 23) The Loreta is a baroque place of pilgrimage founded by Benigna Kateřina Lobkowicz in 1626, designed as a replica of the supposed Santa Casa (Sacred House; the home of the Virgin Mary) in the Holy Land. Legend says that the original Santa Casa was carried by angels to the Italian town of Loreto as the Turks were advancing on Nazareth.

Royal Garden GARDENS
(Královská zahrada; Map p148; ⊙ 10am-6pm Apr-Oct; ⛟ 22, 23) **FREE** A gate on the northern side of Prague Castle leads to the **Powder Bridge** (Prašný most; 1540), which spans the Stag Moat and leads to the Royal Garden, which started life as a Renaissance garden built by Ferdinand I in 1534. It is graced by several gorgeous Renaissance structures.

◎ Staré Město

★ **Old Town Square** SQUARE
(Staroměstské náměstí; Map p150; Ⓜ Staroměstská) **FREE** One of Europe's biggest and most beautiful urban spaces, Old Town Square (Staroměstské náměstí, or Staromák for short) has been Prague's principal public square since the 10th century, and was its

main marketplace until the beginning of the 20th century.

Astronomical Clock
HISTORIC SITE

(Map p150; Staroměstské náměstí; ⊘ chimes on the hour 9am-9pm; Ⓜ Staroměstská) Every hour, on the hour, crowds gather beneath the Old Town Hall Tower (p149) to watch the Astronomical Clock in action. Despite a slightly underwhelming performance that takes only 45 seconds, the clock is one of Europe's best-known tourist attractions, and a 'must-see' for visitors to Prague. After all, it's historic, photogenic and – if you take time to study it – rich in intriguing symbolism.

Old Town Hall
HISTORIC BUILDING

(Staroměstská radnice; Map p150; ☎ 236 002 629; www.staromestskaradnicepraha.cz; Staroměstské náměstí 1; adult/child 250/150Kč; ⊘ 11am-6pm Mon, 9am-6pm Tue-Sun; Ⓜ Staroměstská) Prague's Old Town Hall, founded in 1338, is a hotchpotch of medieval buildings acquired piecemeal over the centuries, presided over by a tall Gothic tower with a splendid Astronomical Clock. As well as housing the Old Town's main tourist information office, the town hall has several historic attractions, and hosts art exhibitions on the ground floor and the 2nd floor.

Old Town Hall Tower
TOWER

(Věž radnice; Map p150; ☎ 236 002 629; www.staromestskaradnicepraha.cz; Staroměstské náměstí 1; adult/child 250/150Kč; ⊘ 11am-10pm Mon, 9am-10pm Tue-Sun; Ⓜ Staroměstská) The Old Town Hall's best feature is the view across the Old Town Square from its 60m-tall clock tower. It's well worth the climb up the modern, beautifully designed steel spiral staircase; there's also a lift.

Church of Our Lady Before Týn
CHURCH

(Kostel Panny Marie před Týnem; Map p150; ☎ 222 318 186; www.tyn.cz; Staroměstské náměstí; suggested donation 50Kč; ⊘ 10am-1pm & 3-5pm, to noon Sun Mar-Dec; Ⓜ Staroměstská) Its distinctive twin Gothic spires make the Týn Church an unmistakable Old Town landmark. Like something out of a 15th-century – and probably slightly cruel – fairy tale, they loom over Old Town Square, decorated with a golden image of the Virgin Mary made in the 1620s from the melted-down Hussite chalice that previously adorned the church.

Church of St James
CHURCH

(Kostel sv Jakuba; Map p150; ☎ 224 828 814; http://praha.minorite.cz; Malá Štupartská 6; ⊘ 9.30am-noon & 2-4pm Tue-Sat, 2-4pm Sun; Ⓜ Náměstí Republiky) FREE The great Gothic mass of the Church of St James began in the 14th century as a Minorite monastery church, and was given a beautiful baroque facelift in the early 18th century. But in the midst of the gilt and stucco is a grisly memento: on the inside of the western wall (look up to the right as you enter) hangs a shrivelled human arm.

DON'T MISS

PRAGUE'S JEWISH MUSEUM

The **Prague Jewish Museum** (Židovské muzeum Praha; Map p150; ☎ 222 749 211; www.jewishmuseum.cz; Reservation Centre, Maiselova 15; combined-entry ticket adult/child 350/250Kč; ⊘ 9am-6pm Sun-Fri, to 4.30pm Nov-Mar; Ⓜ Staroměstská) – a collection of four synagogues (the **Maisel**, **Pinkas**, **Spanish** and **Klaus**), the former **Ceremonial Hall** and the **Old Jewish Cemetery** – is one of the city's treasures. The monuments are clustered together in **Josefov** (Jewish Quarter), a small corner of the Old Town that was home to Prague's Jews for some 800 years before an urban renewal project at the start of the 20th century and the Nazi occupation during WWII brought this all to an end.

The monuments cannot be visited separately but require a combined-entry ticket that is good for all of the sights and available at ticket windows throughout Josefov. A fifth synagogue, the **Old-New Synagogue** (Staronová synagóga; Map p150; ☎ 222 749 211; www.jewishmuseum.cz; Červená 2; adult/child 220/150Kč; ⊘ 9am-6pm Sun-Fri, to 4.30pm Nov-Mar; 🖾 17), is still used for religious services, and requires a separate ticket or additional fee.

The museum was first established in 1906 to preserve objects from synagogues that were demolished during the slum clearance at the turn of the 20th century. The collection grew richer as a result of one of the most grotesquely ironic acts of WWII. During the Nazi occupation, the Germans took over management of the museum in order to create a 'museum of an extinct race'. To that end, they brought in objects from destroyed Jewish communities throughout Bohemia and Moravia.

Central Prague

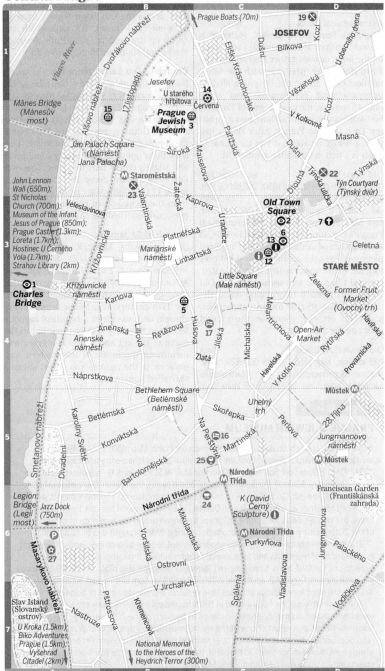

Prague Boats (70m)

JOSEFOV

19

Dušní

Bilkova

Kozí

U obecního dvora

Eliščky Krásnohorské

Vězeňská

Kozí

V Kolkovně

Josefov

U starého
hřbitova

14
Červená

Masná

**Prague
Jewish
Museum** 3

Pařížská

Dušní

Týnská

Maiselova

Široká

Dlouhá

22

Týnská ulička

Týn Courtyard
(Týnský dvůr)

Staroměstská M

23

Valentinská

Žatecká

Kaprova

U radnice

**Old Town
Square**

2

7

Mánes Bridge
(Mánesův
most)

15

Aľšovo nábřeží

17.listopadu

Dvořákovo nábřeží

Jan Palach Square
(Náměstí
Jana Palacha)

John Lennon
Wall (650m);
St Nicholas
Church (700m);
Museum of the Infant
Jesus of Prague (850m);
Prague Castle (1.3km);
Loreta (1.7km);
Hostinec U Černého
Vola (1.7km);
Strahov Library (2km)

Veleslavínova

Platnéřská

Mariánské
náměstí

Linhartská

6

13

12

Celetná

STARÉ MĚSTO

Žalezná

Křížovnické
náměstí

Karlova

Little Square
(Malé náměstí)

Former Fruit
Market
(Ovocný trh)

Melantrichova

Křížovnická

1

**Charles
Bridge**

Anenská

Liliová

Řetězová

Husova

5

17

Jilská

Michalská

Zlatá

Havelská

Rytířská

Havlíčká

Provaznická

Anenské
náměstí

Náprstkova

Bethlehem Square
(Betlémské
náměstí)

Skořepka

V Kotcích

Open-Air
Market

Můstek M

Betlémská

Karoliny Světlé

Konviktská

Na Perštýně

Martinská

Uhelný
trh

Perlová

28.října

Jungmannovo
náměstí

16

Smetanovo nábřeží

Divadelní

Bartolomějská

25

**Národní
Třída** M

Můstek M

Legion
Bridge
(Legii
most)

Jazz Dock
(750m)

Národní třída

24

K (David
Černý
Sculpture)

Národní Třída M

Purkyňova

Franciscan Garden
(Františkánská
zahrada)

Masarykovo nábřeží

27

Vorsilská

Mikulandská

Ostrovní

V Jirchářich

Spálená

Vladislavova

Jungmannova

Palackého

Vodičkova

Slav Island
(Slovanský
ostrov)

U Kroka (1.5km);
Biko Adventures
Prague (1.5km);
Vyšehrad
Citadel (2km)

Nastruze

Pstrossova

Křemencova

National Memorial
to the Heroes of the
Heydrich Terror (300m)

Vltava River

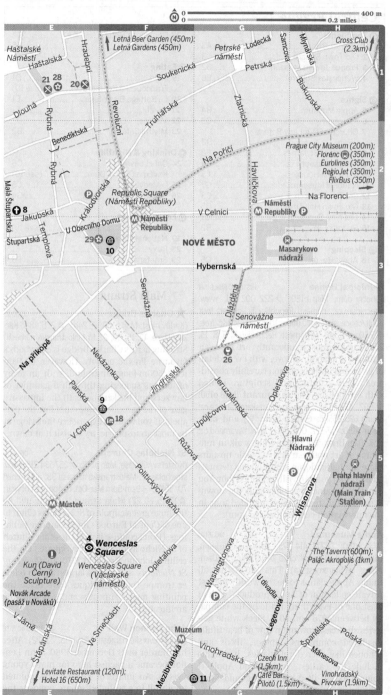

0 ———— 400 m
0 ———— 0.2 miles

Haštalské Náměstí

Haštalská

Hradební

Letná Beer Garden (450m);
Letná Gardens (450m)

Petrské náměstí

Lodecká

Samcova

Mlynářská

Cross Club
(2.3km)

Soukenická

Petrská

Biskupská

1

21 28 ⊗ 20 ⊗

Dlouhá

Rybná

Benediktská

Revoluční

Truhlářská

Zlatnická

Na Poříčí

Prague City Museum (200m);
Florenc Ⓜ (350m);
Eurolines (350m);
RegioJet (350m);
FlixBus (350m)

2

Rybná

Malá Štupartská

Jakubská

Štupartská

Templová

✚ 8

Ⓟ

Králodvorská

U Obecního Domu

Republic Square
(Náměstí Republiky)

Ⓜ Náměstí Republiky

V Celnici

Havlíčkova

Náměstí
Republiky Ⓜ Ⓟ

Na Florenci

29 ⊛ 🏛
10

NOVÉ MĚSTO

Masarykovo
nádraží

3

Hybernská

Senovážná

Dlážděná

Senovážné
náměstí

Na příkopě

Nekázanka

Jindřišská

Jeruzalémská

26

4

Panská

9 🏛

V Cípu

18

Růžová

Upújčovny

Opletalova

Hlavní
Nádraží Ⓜ

Praha hlavní
nádraží
(Main Train
Station)

5

Ⓜ Můstek

Politických Vězňů

Ⓟ

Wilsonova

4 ◎ Wenceslas
Square

Ⓘ
Kuň (David
Černý
Sculpture)

Novák Arcade
(pasáž u Nováků)

V Jámě

Štěpánská

Wenceslas Square
(Václavské
náměstí)

Opletalova

Washingtonova

U divadla

Legerova

The Tavern (600m);
Palác Akropolis (1km)

6

Ve Smečkách

Muzeum
Ⓜ

Mezibranská

Vinohradská

Czech Inn
(1.5km);
Café Bar
Pilotů (1.5km)

Španělská

Polská

Mánesova

7

Levitate Restaurant (120m);
Hotel 16 (650m)

🏛 11

Vinohradský
Pivovar (1.9km)

E | F | G | H

Central Prague

Municipal House HISTORIC BUILDING

(Obecní dům; Map p150; ☑ 222 002 101; www.
obecnidum.cz; náměstí Republiky 5; guided tour
adult/concession/child under 10yr 290/240Kč/free;
⊙ 7.30am-11pm; Ⓜ Náměstí Republiky, Ⓖ 6, 8, 15,
26) Prague's most exuberantly art nouveau
building is a labour of love, with every detail
of its design and decoration carefully considered, every painting and sculpture loaded
with symbolism. The **restaurant** (Map p150;
☑ 602 433 524; www.francouzskarestaurace.cz;
mains 695-855Kč; ⊙ noon-11pm; 🍴) and **cafe**
(Map p150; ☑ 222 002 763; www.kavarnaod.cz;
⊙ 7.30am-11pm; 🍴) here are like walk-in museums of art nouveau design, while upstairs
there are half a dozen sumptuously decorated halls that you can visit by guided tour. You
can look around the lobby and the downstairs bar for free, or book a guided tour in
the information centre (10am to 8pm).

Apple Museum MUSEUM

(Map p150; ☑ 774 414 775; www.applemuseum.
com; Husova 21; adult/child 240/110Kč; ⊙ 10am-
10pm; Ⓜ Staroměstská) This shrine to all
things Apple claims to be the world's biggest
private collection of Apple products, with at
least one of everything made by the company between 1976 and 2012. Sleek white galleries showcase row upon row of beautifully
displayed computers, laptops, iPods and
iPhones like sacred reliquaries; highlights
include the earliest Apple I and Apple II
computers, an iPod 'family tree' and Steve
Jobs' business cards.

◎ Malá Strana

★ **Charles Bridge** BRIDGE

(Karlův most; Map p150; ⊙ 24hr; 🚋 2, 17, 18 to Karlovy lázně, 12, 15, 20, 22 to Malostranské náměstí)
Strolling across Charles Bridge is everybody's
favourite Prague activity. However, by 9am
it's a 500m-long fairground, with an army
of tourists squeezing through a gauntlet of
hawkers and buskers beneath the impassive
gaze of the baroque statues that line the par-
apets. If you want to experience the bridge at
its most atmospheric, try to visit it at dawn.

St Nicholas Church CHURCH

(Kostel sv Mikuláše; Map p148; ☑ 257 534 215; www.
stnicholas.cz; Malostranské náměstí 38; adult/child
70/50Kč; ⊙ 9am-5pm Mar-Oct, to 4pm rest of year;
🚋 12, 15, 20, 22) Malá Strana is dominated by
the huge green cupola of St Nicholas Church,
one of Central Europe's finest baroque buildings. (Don't confuse it with the other Church
of St Nicholas on Old Town Square.) On the
ceiling, Johann Kracker's 1770 *Apotheosis of
St Nicholas* is Europe's largest fresco (clever trompe l'oeil techniques have made the
painting merge almost seamlessly with the
architecture).

John Lennon Wall HISTORIC SITE

(Velkopřevorské náměstí; 🚋 12, 15, 20, 22) After
his murder on 8 December 1980, John Lennon became a pacifist hero for many young
Czechs. An image of Lennon was painted
on a wall in a secluded square opposite the

French embassy (there is a niche on the wall that looks like a tombstone), along with political graffiti and occasionally Beatles lyrics.

Museum of the Infant
Jesus of Prague
CHURCH

(Muzeum Pražského Jezulátka; ☑257 533 646; www.pragjesu.cz; Karmelitská 9; ☺8.30am-7pm, to 8pm Sun; ☒12, 15, 20, 22) FREE The Church of Our Lady Victorious (kostel Panny Marie Vítězné), built in 1613, has on its central altar a 47cm-tall waxwork figure of the baby Jesus, brought from Spain in 1628 and known as the Infant Jesus of Prague (Pražské Jezulátko). At the back of the church is a museum (open from 9.30am to 5.30pm, from 1pm Sunday), displaying a selection of the frocks used to dress the Infant.

Petřín
GARDENS

(☺24h; ☒Nebozízek, Petřín) This 318m-high hill is one of Prague's largest green spaces. It's great for quiet, tree-shaded walks and fine views over the 'City of a Hundred Spires'. Most of the attractions atop the hill, including a lookout tower and mirror maze, were built in the late 19th to early 20th century, lending the place an old-fashioned, fun-fair atmosphere.

☉ Nové Město

★Wenceslas Square
SQUARE

(Václavské náměstí; Map p150; ☒Můstek, Muzeum) More a broad boulevard than a typical city square, Wenceslas Square has witnessed a great deal of Czech history – a giant Mass was held here during the revolutionary upheavals of 1848; in 1918 the creation of the new Czechoslovak Republic was celebrated here; and it was here in 1989 where many anticommunist protests took place. Originally a medieval horse market, the square was named after Bohemia's patron saint during the nationalist revival of the mid-19th century.

National Museum
MUSEUM

(Národní muzeum; Map p150; ☑224 497 111; www.nm.cz; Václavské náměstí 68; adult/child 250/170Kč; ☺10am-6pm; ☒Muzeum) Looming above Wenceslas Square is the neo-Renaissance bulk of the National Museum, designed in the 1880s by Josef Schulz as an architectural symbol of the Czech National Revival. Its magnificent interior is a shrine to the cultural, intellectual and scientific history of the Czech Republic. The museum's main building reopened in 2018 after several years of renovation work.

Mucha Museum
GALLERY

(Muchovo muzeum; Map p150; ☑224 216 415; www.mucha.cz; Panská 7; adult/child 240/160Kč; ☺10am-6pm; ☒3, 5, 6, 9, 14, 24) This fascinating (and busy) museum features the sensuous art nouveau posters, paintings and decorative panels of Alfons Mucha (1860–1939), as well as many sketches, photographs and other memorabilia. The exhibits include countless artworks showing Mucha's trademark Slavic maidens with flowing hair and piercing blue eyes, bearing symbolic garlands and linden boughs.

National Memorial to the
Heroes of the Heydrich Terror
MUSEUM

(Národní památník hrdinů Heydrichiády; ☑224 916 100; www.vhu.cz/muzea/ostatni-expozice/ krypta; Resslova 9a; ☺9am-5pm Tue-Sun; ☒Karlovo Náměstí) FREE The Church of Sts Cyril & Methodius houses a moving memorial to the seven Czech paratroopers who were involved in the assassination of Reichsprotektor Reinhard Heydrich in 1942, with an exhibit and video about Nazi persecution of the Czechs. The church appeared in the 2016 movie based on the assassination, *Anthropoid*.

Prague City Museum
MUSEUM

(Muzeum hlavního města Prahy; ☑221 709 674; www.muzeumprahy.cz; Na Poříčí 52; adult/child 150/60Kč; ☺9am-6pm Tue-Sun; ☒Florenc) This excellent museum, opened in 1898, is devoted to the history of Prague from prehistoric times to the 20th century (labels are in English as well as Czech). Among the many intriguing exhibits are an astonishing scale model of Prague, and the Astronomical Clock's original 1866 calendar wheel with Josef Mánes' beautiful painted panels representing the months – that's January at the top, toasting his toes by the fire, and August near the bottom, sickle in hand, harvesting the corn.

Kun (David Černý Sculpture)
PUBLIC ART

(Horse; Map p150; Lucerna Palace, Vodičkova 36; ☒3, 5, 6, 9, 14, 24) David Černý's wryly amusing counterpart to the equestrian statue of St Wenceslas in Wenceslas Square hangs in the middle of the Lucerna Palace shopping arcade. Here, St Wenceslas sits astride a horse that is decidedly dead; Černý never comments on the meaning of his works, but it's safe to assume that this Wenceslas (Václav in Czech) is a reference to Václav Klaus, president of the Czech Republic from 2003 to 2013.

K (David Černý Sculpture) PUBLIC ART

(Statue of Kafka; Map p150; Quadrio, Spálená 22; Ⓜ Národní Třída) FREE Located in the courtyard of the Quadrio shopping centre above Národní třída metro station, David Černý's giant rotating bust of Franz Kafka is formed from some 39 tonnes of mirrored stainless steel. It's a mesmerising show as Kafka's face rhythmically dissolves and re-emerges, possibly playing on notions of the author's ever-changing personality and sense of self-doubt.

⊙ Holešovice

Letná Gardens PARK

(Letenské sady; ⊘ 24hr; 👪; 🚊 1, 8, 12, 25, 26 to Letenské náměstí) Lovely Letná Gardens occupies a bluff over the Vltava River, north of the Old Town, and has postcard-perfect views out over the city, river and bridges. It's ideal for walking, jogging and beer-drinking at a popular **beer garden** (⊅ 233 378 200; www.letenskyzamecek.cz; Letenské sady 341; ⊘ 11am-11pm May-Sep; 🚊 1) at the eastern end of the park. From the Old Town, find the entrance up a steep staircase at the northern end of Pařížská ulice (across the bridge). Alternatively, take the tram to Letenské náměstí and walk south for about 10 minutes.

⊙ Smíchov & Vyšehrad

★ Vyšehrad Citadel FORTRESS

(⊅ 261 225 304; www.praha-vysehrad.cz; ⊘ 24hr; Ⓜ Vyšehrad) FREE The Vyšehrad Citadel refers to the complex of buildings and structures atop Vyšehrad Hill that have played an important role in Czech history for over 1000 years – as a royal residence, religious centre and military fortress. While most of the surviving structures date from the 18th century, the citadel is still viewed as the city's spiritual home. The sights are spread out over a wide area, with commanding views out over the Vltava and surrounding city.

⚑ Tours

★ Biko Adventures Prague CYCLING

(⊅ 733 750 990; www.bikoadventures.com; Vratislavova 3, Vyšehrad; bike hire per day 490Kč, tours per person from 1300Kč; ⊘ 9am-6pm Apr-Oct; 🚊 2, 3, 7, 17, 21) Italian owner Fillippo Mari loves to cycle, ski and hike and has created this small outfit dedicated to outdoor pursuits of all kinds. From April to October Biko rents bikes as well as offering day-long guided cycling trips for riders of all levels. Rental bikes include standard mountain bikes and high-end hardtails from Giant.

Prague Boats CRUISE

(Evropská Vodní Doprava; ⊅ 724 202 505; www.prague-boats.cz; Čechův most, Pier 5; adult/child from 300/200Kč; ⊘ 9am-10pm; 🚊 17) Offers a one-hour cruise to Charles Bridge and back, with views of the castle (half-hourly from 10am April to October, and hourly 11am to 7pm November to March); and a two-hour cruise to Vyšehrad and back (at 3pm year-round, plus 4.30pm April to October).

✺ Festivals & Events

Prague Spring MUSIC

(Pražské jaro; ⊅ box office 227 059 234, program 257 310 414; www.festival.cz; ⊘ May) Prague Spring is the Czech Republic's biggest annual cultural event and one of Europe's most important festivals of classical music. Concerts are held in theatres, churches and historic buildings across the city. Tickets go on sale from mid-December the preceding year. Buy tickets online or at the festival box office at the Rudolfinum (p157).

Prague Fringe Festival ART

(www.praguefringe.com; ⊘ late May/early Jun) A wild week of happenings, theatre pieces, concerts and comedy shows. Much of it is in English. Buy tickets online or at venue box offices before shows.

⌂ Sleeping

Gone are the days when Prague was a cheap destination. The Czech capital now ranks alongside most Western European cities when it comes to the quality, range and price of hotels. Accommodation ranges from cosy, romantic hotels set in historic townhouses to the new generation of modish design hotels and hostels. Book as far in advance as possible (especially during festival season in May, and at Easter and Christmas/New Year).

Czech Inn HOSTEL, HOTEL €

(⊅ 210 011 100; www.czech-inn.com; Francouzská 76, Vršovice; dm 280-500Kč, s/d 1400/1800Kč, apt from 2600Kč; 🅿 ⊝ @ 🛜; 🚊 4, 22) The Czech Inn calls itself a hostel, but a boutique label wouldn't be out of place. Everything seems sculpted by an industrial designer, from the iron beds to the brushed-steel flooring and minimalist square sinks. It offers a variety of accommodation, from standard hostel dorm rooms to good-value doubles (with or without private bathroom) and apartments.

Ahoy! Hostel HOSTEL €

(Map p150; ✎773 004 003; www.ahoyhostel.com; Na Perštýně 10; dm/r from 460/1800Kč; @奈; Ⓜ Národní Třída, 🚊2, 9, 18, 22) No big signs or branding here, just an inconspicuous card by the blue door at No 10. But inside is a very pleasant, welcoming and peaceful hostel (definitely not for the party crowd), with eager-to-please staff, some self-consciously 'arty' decoration, clean and comfortable six- or eight-bed dorms, and a couple of private twin rooms. Ideal location too.

Hotel 16 HOTEL €€

(✎224 920 636; www.hotel16.cz; Kateřinská 16; s/d from 2400/3500Kč; ➡✳@奈; 🚊4, 6, 10, 16, 22) Hotel 16 is a friendly, family-run little place with just 14 rooms, tucked away in a very quiet corner of town where you're more likely to hear birdsong than traffic. The rooms vary in size and are simply but smartly furnished; the best, at the back, have views onto the peaceful terraced garden. Staff are superb, and can't do enough to help.

NYX Hotel BOUTIQUE HOTEL €€

(Map p150; ✎226 222 800; www.leonardo-hotels.com/nyx-prague; Panská 9; r from 2800Kč; @奈; 🚊3, 5, 6, 9, 14, 24) NYX is a centrally located boutique for travellers looking for bold contemporary style and high-end amenities who are willing to splash out for it. Many of the rooms are quite spacious – the 'Heaven Suite' is a whopping 80 sq metres – and can be excellent value if sleeping four. The location, just near to Wenceslas Square, is convenient for sights and transport.

★**Dominican Hotel** HOTEL €€€

(Map p150; ✎224 248 555; www.dominicanhotel.cz; Jilská 7; r from 4900Kč; ✳@奈; Ⓜ Můstek) From the complimentary glass of wine when you arrive to the comfy king-size beds, the Dominican certainly knows how to make you feel pampered. Housed in the former monastery of St Giles, the hotel is bursting with character and is full of delightful period details including old stone fireplaces, beautiful painted timber ceilings and fragments of frescoes.

✖ Eating

In the last decade the number, quality and variety of Prague's restaurants has expanded beyond all recognition. You can now enjoy a wide range of international cuisine, from Afghan to Argentinian, Korean to Vietnamese, and even expect service with a smile in the majority of eating places. However, don't let this kaleidoscope of cuisines blind you to the pleasures of good old-fashioned Czech grub.

Mistral Café BISTRO €

(Map p150; ✎222 317 737; www.mistralcafe.cz; Valentinská 11; mains 150-260Kč; ◷8am-11pm, from 9am Sat & Sun; 奈◨; Ⓜ Staroměstská) Is this the coolest bistro in the Old Town? Pale stone, bleached birchwood and potted shrubs make for a clean, crisp, modern look, and the clientele of local students and office workers clearly appreciate the competitively priced, well-prepared food. Fish and chips in crumpled brown paper with lemon and black-pepper mayo – yum!

Lokál CZECH €

(Map p150; ✎734 283 874; www.lokal-dlouha.ambi.cz; Dlouhá 33; mains 155-265Kč; ◷11am-1am, to midnight Sun; 奈; 🚊6, 8, 15, 26) Who'd have thought it possible? A classic Czech beer hall (albeit with slick modern styling); excellent *tankové pivo* (tanked Pilsner Urquell); a daily-changing menu of traditional Bohemian dishes; and smiling, efficient, friendly service! Top restaurant chain Ambiente has turned its hand to Czech cuisine, and the result has been so successful that the place is always busy.

The Tavern BURGERS €

(www.thetavern.cz; Chopinova 26, Vinohrady; burgers 190-230Kč; ◷11.30am-10pm; 奈; Ⓜ Jiřího z Poděbrad, 🚊11, 13) This cosy sit-down burger joint is the dream of a husband-and-wife team of American expats who wanted to create the perfect burger using organic products and free-range, grass-fed beef. Great pulled-pork sandwiches, fries and bourbon-based cocktails too. Reservations are taken via the website.

★**Levitate Restaurant** GASTRONOMY €€

(✎724 516 996; www.levitaterestaurant.cz; Štěpánská 611/14; mains 250-590Kč; ◷noon-3pm Thu-Sun, 6pm-midnight Tue-Sun; ✳; 🚊Štěpánská) One of Prague's hidden treats, this gastronomy restaurant combines Asian traditions with Nordic flavours, using local ingredients. You simply can't come here 'just to eat'. A calm oasis near the bustling heart of Prague, this restaurant is aiming for the stars. Make sure to reserve your table.

Maitrea VEGETARIAN €€

(Map p150; ✎221 711 631; www.restaurace-maitrea.cz; Týnská ulička 6; weekday lunch 145Kč, mains 200-250Kč; ◷11.30am-11.30pm, from noon Sat & Sun; ✳◨; Ⓜ Staroměstská) Maitrea (a Buddhist term meaning 'the future Buddha') is a beautifully designed space full of flowing curves and organic shapes, from the sensuous polished-oak furniture and fittings to the blossom-like lampshades. The menu is inventive and wholly vegetarian, with dishes such as Tex-Mex quesadillas, spicy goulash with wholemeal dumplings, and spaghetti with spinach, crispy shredded tofu and rosemary pesto.

U Kroka
CZECH €€

(📞775 905 022; www.ukroka.cz; Vratislavova 12, Vyšehrad; mains 170-295Kč; ⊙11am-11pm; 📶; 🚊2, 3, 7, 17, 21) Cap a visit to historic Vyšehrad Citadel with a hearty meal at this traditional pub that delivers not just excellent beer but very good food as well. Classic dishes like goulash, boiled beef, rabbit and duck confit are served in a festive setting. Daily lunch specials (around 140Kč) are available from 11am to 3pm. Reservations (advisable) are only possible after 3pm.

La Bottega Bistroteka
ITALIAN €€

(Map p150; 📞222 311 372; www.bistroteka.cz; Dlouhá 39; mains 265-465Kč; ⊙9am-10.30pm, to 9pm Sun; 📶; 🚊6, 8, 15, 26) You'll find smart and snappy service at this stylish deli-cum-bistro, where the menu makes the most of all that delicious Italian produce artfully arranged on the counter; the beef-cheek cannelloni with parmesan sauce and fava beans, for example, is just exquisite. It's best to book, but you can often get a walk-in table at lunchtime.

Field
CZECH €€€

(Map p150; 📞222 316 999; www.fieldrestaurant.cz; U Milosrdných 12; mains 590-620Kč, 6-course tasting menu 2800Kč; ⊙11am-2.30pm & 6-10.30pm Mon-Fri, noon-3pm & 6-10pm Sat & Sun; 📶; 🚊17) 🍃 This Michelin-starred restaurant is unfussy and fun. The decor is an amusing art-meets-agriculture blend of farmyard implements and minimalist chic, while the chef creates painterly presentations from the finest of local produce along with freshly foraged herbs and edible flowers. You'll have to book at least a couple of weeks in advance to have a chance of a table.

🍷 Drinking & Nightlife

Bars in Prague go in and out of fashion with alarming speed, and trend spotters are forever flocking to the latest 'in' place only to desert it as soon as it becomes mainstream. The best areas to go looking for good drinking dens include Vinohrady, Žižkov, Karlín, Holešovice, the area south of Národní třída

in Nové Město and the lanes around Old Town Square in Staré Město.

★ Vinograf
WINE BAR

(Map p150; 📞214 214 681; www.vinograf.cz; Senovážné náměstí 23; ⊙11.30am-midnight, from 5pm Sat & Sun; 📶; 🚊3, 5, 6, 9, 14, 24) With knowledgeable staff, a relaxed atmosphere and an off-the-beaten-track feel, this appealingly modern wine bar is a great place to discover Moravian wines. There's good finger food, mostly cheese and charcuterie, to accompany your wine, with food and wine menus (in Czech and English) on big blackboards behind the bar. Very busy at weekends, when it's worth booking a table.

Cross Club
CLUB

(📞775 541 430; www.crossclub.cz; Plynární 23; live shows 100-200Kč; ⊙6pm-5am Sun-Thu, to 7am Fri & Sat; 📶; Ⓜ Nádraží Holešovice) An industrial club in every sense of the word: the setting in an industrial zone; the thumping music (both DJs and live acts); and the interior, an absolute must-see jumble of gadgets, shafts, cranks and pipes, many of which move and pulsate with light to the music. The program includes occasional live music, theatre performances and art happenings.

Café Bar Pilotů
COCKTAIL BAR

(📞739 765 694; www.facebook.com/cafebarpilotu; Dónská 19, Vršovice; drinks 160-180Kč; ⊙7pm-1am Mon-Thu, to 2am Fri & Sat; 📶; 🚊4, 13, 22) This old-fashioned cocktail bar, with a big wooden serving bar and walls of books behind, features inventive cocktails based on favourite locales around the neighbourhood. There are plenty of tables or you can hang out on the street until 10pm. Friendly and professional service.

Vinohradský Pivovar
PUB

(📞222 760 080; www.vinohradskypivovar.cz; Korunní 106, Vinohrady; ⊙11am-midnight; 📶; 🚊10, 16) This popular and highly recommended neighbourhood pub and restaurant offers its own home-brewed lagers as well as a well-regarded IPA. There's seating on two levels and a large events room at the back for concerts and happenings. The restaurant features classic Czech pub dishes at reasonable prices (180Kč to 230Kč). Book in advance for an evening meal.

Cafe Louvre
CAFE

(Map p150; 📞724 054 055; www.cafelouvre.cz; 1st fl, Národní třída 22; ⊙8am-11.30pm, from 9am Sat & Sun; 🚊2, 9, 18, 22) The French-style Cafe Louvre is arguably the most amenable of

Prague's grand cafes, as popular today as it was in the early 1900s when it was frequented by the likes of Franz Kafka and Albert Einstein. The atmosphere is wonderfully olde worlde, and it serves good Czech food as well as coffee. Check out the billiard hall and the ground-floor art gallery.

Hostinec U Černého Vola   PUB
(☑ 220 513 481; Loretánské náměstí 1; ☺ 10am-10pm; 🍴 22, 23) Many religious people make a pilgrimage to the Loreta, but just across the road, the 'Black Ox' is a shrine that pulls in pilgrims of a different kind. This surprisingly inexpensive beer hall is visited by real-ale aficionados for its authentic atmosphere and lip-smackingly delicious draught beer, Velkopopovický Kozel (31Kč for 0.5L), brewed in a small town southeast of Prague.

U Medvídků   BEER HALL
(At the Little Bear; Map p150; ☑ 224 211 916; www. umedvidku.cz; Na Perštýně 7; ☺ 11.30am-11pm; 🌐; Ⓜ Národní Třída, 🍴 2, 9, 18, 22) The most micro of Prague's microbreweries, with a capacity of only 250L, U Medvídků started producing its own beer in 2005, though its trad-style beer hall has been around for many years. There's also Budvar on tap (45Kč for 0.5L). The in-house restaurant serves very good Czech food. Reservations recommended.

⭐ Entertainment

Across the spectrum, from ballet to blues, jazz to rock and theatre to film, there's a bewildering range of entertainment on offer in this eclectic city. Prague is now as much a European centre for jazz, rock and hip-hop as it is for classical music. The biggest draw, however, is still the Prague Spring festival of classical music and opera.

Performing Arts

Smetana Hall   CLASSICAL MUSIC
(Smetanova síň; Map p150; ☑ 770 621 580; www. obecnidum.cz; Municipal House, náměstí Republiky 5; tickets 600-1300Kč; ☺ box office 10am-8pm; Ⓜ Náměstí Republiky) The Smetana Hall, centrepiece of the stunning Municipal House (p152), is the city's largest concert hall, seating 1200 beneath an art nouveau glass dome. The stage is framed by sculptures representing the Vyšehrad legend (to the right) and Slavonic dances (to the left). It's the home venue of the Prague Symphony Orchestra (Symfonický orchestr hlavního města Prahy; www.fok.cz), and stages performances of folk dance and music.

Dvořák Hall   CONCERT VENUE
(Dvořákova síň; Map p150; ☑ 227 059 227; www. ceskafilharmonie.cz; náměstí Jana Palacha 1, Rudolfinum; tickets 200-1400Kč; ☺ box office 10am-6pm Mon-Fri, to 3pm Jul & Aug; Ⓜ Staroměstská) The Dvořák Hall in the neo-Renaissance Rudolfinum (Map p150) is home to the world-renowned Czech Philharmonic Orchestra (Česká filharmonie). Sit back and be impressed by some of the best classical musicians in Prague.

National Theatre   OPERA, BALLET
(Národní divadlo; Map p150; ☑ 224 901 448; www. narodni-divadlo.cz; Národní třída 2; tickets 100-1290Kč; ☺ box office 9am-6pm, from 10am Sat & Sun; 🍴 2, 9, 18, 22) The much-loved National Theatre provides a stage for traditional opera, drama and ballet by the likes of Smetana, Shakespeare and Tchaikovsky, sharing the program alongside more modern works by composers and playwrights such as Philip Glass and John Osborne. The box offices are in the Nový síň building next door, in the Kolowrat Palace (opposite the Estates Theatre) and at the State Opera.

Live Music

⭐ Palác Akropolis   LIVE MUSIC
(☑ 296 330 913; www.palacakropolis.cz; Kubelíkova 27, Žižkov; ticket prices vary; ☺ 7pm-5am; 🌐; 🍴 5, 9, 15, 26) The Akropolis is a Prague institution, a labyrinthine, sticky-floored shrine to alternative music and drama. Its various performance spaces host a smorgasbord of musical and cultural events, from DJs and string quartets to Macedonian Roma bands, local rock gods and visiting talent – Marianne Faithfull, the Flaming Lips and the Strokes have all played here.

Jazz Dock   JAZZ
(☑ 774 058 838; www.jazzdock.cz; Janáčkovo nábřeží 2, Smíchov; tickets 170-400Kč; ☺ 3pm-4am Mon-Thu, from 1pm Fri-Sun Apr-Sep, 5pm-4am Mon-Thu, from 3pm Fri-Sun Oct-Mar; 🌐; Ⓜ Anděl, 🍴 9, 12, 15, 20) Most of Prague's jazz clubs are cellar affairs, but this riverside club is a definite step up, with clean, modern decor and a decidedly romantic view out over the Vltava. It draws some of the best local talent and occasional international acts. Go early or book to get a good table. Shows normally begin at 7pm and 10pm.

Roxy   LIVE MUSIC
(Map p150; ☑ 608 060 745; www.roxy.cz; Dlouhá 33; tickets 100-700Kč; ☺ 7pm-5am; 🍴 6, 8, 15, 26) Set in the ramshackle shell of an art deco

CZECH REPUBLIC PRAGUE

cinema, the legendary Roxy has nurtured the more independent end of Prague's club spectrum for more than two decades. This is the place to see the Czech Republic's top DJs. On the 1st floor is NoD, an 'experimental space' that stages drama, dance, cinema and live music.

ⓘ Information

The easiest and cheapest way to obtain Czech currency is through a bank ATM, drawn on your home credit or debit card. For exchanging cash, the big banks are preferable to private exchange booths (*směnárna*) and normally charge a lower commission (around 2% with a 50Kč minimum fee).

Na Homolce Hospital (☑ 257 271 111; www.homolka.cz; 5th fl, Foreign Pavilion, Roentgenova 2, Motol; 🚌 167, 168 to Nemocnice Na Homolce) Widely considered to be the best hospital in Prague, equipped and staffed to Western standards.

Prague City Tourism (Prague Welcome; Map p150; ☑ 221 714 714; www.prague.eu; Staroměstské náměstí 1, Old Town Hall; ⏰ 9am-7pm, to 6pm Jan & Feb; Ⓜ Staroměstská) The busiest of the Prague City Tourism branches occupies the ground floor of the Old Town Hall.

Globe Bookstore & Café (☑ 224 934 203; www.globebookstore.cz; Pštrossova 6, Nové Město; per min 1Kč; ⏰ 10am-midnight Mon-Thu, 9.30am-1am Fri-Sun; 🛜; Ⓜ Karlovo Náměstí) Offers a bank of computers for customer use; handy for visitors arriving without a laptop or web-enabled smartphone.

ⓘ Getting There & Away

AIR

Václav Havel Airport Prague (Prague Ruzyně International Airport; ☑ 220 111 888; www.prg. aero; K letišti 6, Ruzyně; 🛜; 🚌 100, 119), 17km west of the city centre, is the main international gateway to the Czech Republic and hub for the national carrier Czech Airlines, which operates direct flights to Prague from many European cities. There are also direct flights from North America (from April to October) as well as to select cities in the Middle East and Asia.

The airport has two terminals: Terminal 1 for flights to/from non–Schengen Zone countries (including the UK, Ireland and countries outside Europe); Terminal 2 for flights to/from Schengen Zone countries (most EU nations plus Switzerland, Iceland and Norway).

The arrivals halls in both terminals have exchange counters, ATMs, accommodation agencies, public-transport information desks (in Terminal 2 and in the connecting corridor to Terminal 1), tourist information offices, taxi services and 24-hour left-luggage counters (Terminal 2 only; per piece per day 120Kč). Car-hire agencies are in the 'Parking C' multistorey car park opposite Terminal 1.

BUS

Several bus companies offer long-distance coach services connecting Prague to cities around Europe. Nearly all international buses (and most domestic services) use the renovated and user-friendly **Florenc bus station** (ÚAN Praha Florenc; ☑ 900 144 444; www.florenc.cz; Pod výtopnou 13/10, Karlín; ⏰ 5am-midnight; 🛜; Ⓜ Florenc).

Important international bus operators with extensive networks and ticket offices at Florenc bus station include the following:

Flixbus (https://global.flixbus.com; Křižíkova 2b, ÚAN Florenc; ⏰ 7am-8pm)

RegioJet (Student Agency; ☑ 222 222 221; www.regiojet.cz; Křižíkova 2b, ÚAN Praha Florenc; ⏰ 5am-11.30pm)

Eurolines (☑ 731 222 111; www.elines.cz; Křižíkova 2b, ÚAN Praha Florenc; ⏰ 7am-6.30pm, to 4pm Sat; 🛜; Ⓜ Florenc)

CAR & MOTORCYCLE

Prague lies at the nexus of several European four-lane highways and is a relatively easy drive from major regional cities, including Munich (four hours), Berlin (four hours), Nuremberg (three hours), Vienna (four hours) and Budapest (five hours).

TRAIN

Prague is well integrated into European rail networks. Train travel makes the most sense if travelling to/from Berlin and Dresden to the north or Vienna, Kraków, Bratislava and Budapest to the east and south. Most domestic and all international trains arrive at **Praha hlavní nádraží** (Prague Main Train Station; ☑ information 221 111 122; www.cd.cz; Wilsonova 8, Nové Město; ⏰ 3.30am-12.30am; Ⓜ Hlavní nádraží), Prague's main station.

Most services are operated by the Czech state rail operator, České dráhy (p175), though two private rail companies, **Leo Express** (www.le.cz; Wilsonova 8, Praha hlavní nádraží; ⏰ ticket office 7.10am-8.10pm; Ⓜ Hlavní Nádraží) and **RegioJet** (Student Agency; www.regiojet.cz; Wilsonova 8, Praha Hlavní Nádraží; ⏰ 8am-8pm; Ⓜ Hlavní nádraží), compete with České dráhy on some popular lines, including travel to/from the Moravian cities Olomouc and Ostrava and points east. These companies can sometimes be cheaper and faster. Leo Express trains are identified as 'LEO' on timetables; RegioJet trains are 'RJ'.

ⓘ Getting Around

TO/FROM THE AIRPORT

The cheapest way to get into Prague from the airport is by public transport. Bus 119 stops outside both arrivals terminals every 10 minutes from 4am to midnight, taking passengers to metro stop Nádraží Veleslavín (metro line A), from where you can catch a continuing metro into the centre. The entire journey (bus plus metro) requires one full-price public-transport ticket (32Kč) plus a half-fare (16Kč) ticket for every suitcase larger than 25cm x 45cm x 70cm. Buy tickets from Prague Public Transport Authority (p159) desks (located in each arrivals hall).

For connecting directly to Praha hlavní nádraží (the main train station), the **Airport Express bus** (AE; ☑ 296 191 817; www.dpp.cz; ticket 60Kč, luggage free; ☺ 5.30am-10.30pm) stops outside both arrivals terminals and runs every half-hour. The trip takes 35 minutes. Buy tickets from the driver.

Official airport taxis line up outside the arrivals area of both terminals and can take you into the centre for 500Kč to 700Kč, depending on the destination. The drive takes about 30 minutes.

PUBLIC TRANSPORT

Prague's excellent public-transport system combines tram, metro and bus services. It's operated by the **Prague Public Transport Authority** (DPP; ☑ 296 191 817; www.dpp.cz; ☺ 7am-9pm), which has information desks in both terminals of Prague's Václav Havel Airport and in several metro stations, including the Můstek, Anděl, Hradčanská and Nádraží Veleslavín stations. The metro operates from 5am to midnight.

Tickets valid on all metros, trams and buses are sold from machines at metro stations, as well as at DPP information offices and many newsstands and kiosks. Tickets can be purchased individually or as discounted day passes valid for one or three days. A full-price individual ticket costs 32/16Kč per adult/senior aged 65 to 70, and is valid for 90 minutes of unlimited travel. For shorter journeys, buy short-term tickets that are valid for 30 minutes of unlimited travel.

TAXI

Taxis are frequent and relatively inexpensive. The official rate for licensed cabs is 40Kč flagfall plus 28Kč per kilometre and 6Kč per minute while waiting. On this basis, any trip within the city centre – say, from Wenceslas Sq to Malá Strana – should cost no more than 200Kč. The following taxi companies offer 24-hour service and English-speaking operators:

AAA Radio Taxi (☑ 14014, 222 333 222; www.aaataxi.cz)

City Taxi (☑ 257 257 257; www.citytaxi.cz)

ProfiTaxi (☑ 14015; www.profitaxi.cz)

Liftago (www.liftago.com) is a locally owned ride-share service, similar to Uber, where you download an app to your phone for ordering and paying for rides.

AROUND PRAGUE

Karlštejn

Rising above the village of Karlštejn, 30km southwest of Prague, medieval **Karlštejn Castle** (Hrad Karlštejn; ☑ tour bookings 311 681 617; www.hradkarlstejn.cz; adult/child from 260/190Kč; ☺ 9am-6.30pm Jul & Aug, 9.30am-5.30pm Tue-Sun May, Jun & Sep, shorter hours rest of year) is in such good shape it wouldn't look out of place at Disneyworld. The crowds come in theme-park proportions as well, but the peaceful surrounding countryside offers views of Karlštejn's stunning exterior that rival anything you'll see on the inside.

The castle was born of a grand pedigree, originally conceived by Emperor Charles IV in the 14th century as a bastion for hiding the crown jewels. Run by an appointed burgrave, the castle was surrounded by a network of landowning knight-vassals, who came to the castle's aid whenever enemies moved against it. Karlštejn again sheltered the Bohemian and the Holy Roman Empire crown jewels during the Hussite Wars of the 15th century, but fell into disrepair as its defences became outmoded. Considerable restoration work in the late-19th century returned the castle to its former glory.

Entry is by guided tour only (three main tours available), and best booked in advance by phone or email.

Tour 1 (50 minutes) passes through the Knight's Hall, still daubed with the coats-of-arms and names of the knight-vassals, Charles IV's Bedchamber, the Audience Hall and the Jewel House, which includes treasures from the Chapel of the Holy Cross and a replica of the St Wenceslas Crown.

Tour 2 (100 minutes, May to October only) takes in the Marian Tower, with the Church of the Virgin Mary and the Chapel of St Catherine, then moves to the Great Tower for the castle's star attraction, the exquisite Chapel of the Holy Cross, its walls and vaulted ceiling adorned with thousands of polished semiprecious stones set in gilt stucco in the form of crosses, and with religious and heraldic paintings.

Tour 3 (40 minutes, May to October only) visits the upper levels of the Great Tower, which provide stunning views over the surrounding countryside.

From Prague, there are frequent train departures daily from Prague's main station.

The journey takes 45 minutes and costs 56Kč each way.

Kutná Hora

In the 14th century, Kutná Hora, 60km southeast of Prague, rivalled the capital in importance because of the rich deposits of silver ore below the ground. The ore ran out in 1726, leaving the medieval townscape largely unaltered. Now with several fascinating and unusual historical attractions, the Unesco World Heritage–listed town is a popular day trip from Prague.

Interestingly, most visitors come not for the silver splendour but rather to see an eerie monastery, dating from the 19th century, with an interior crafted solely from human bones. Indeed, the remarkable **Sedlec Ossuary** (Kostnice; ☑ information centre 326 551 049; www.ossuary.eu; Zámecká 127; adult/concession 90/60Kč; ☺ 8am-6pm Mon-Sat, 9am-6pm Sun Apr-Sep, shorter hours rest of year), or 'bone church', features the remains of no fewer than 40,000 people who died over the years from wars and pestilence.

Closer to the centre of Kutná Hora is the town's greatest monument: the Gothic **Cathedral of St Barbara** (Chrám sv Barbora; ☑ 327 515 796; www.khfarnost.cz; Barborská; adult/concession 120/50Kč; ☺ 9am-6pm Apr-Oct, shorter hours rest of year). Rivalling Prague's St Vitus in size and magnificence, its soaring nave culminates in elegant, six-petalled ribbed vaulting, and the ambulatory chapels preserve original 15th-century frescoes. Other leading attractions include the **Hrádek** (České muzeum stříbra; ☑ 327 512 159; www.cms-kh.cz; Barborská 28; adult/concession from 70/40Kč; ☺ 10am-6pm Tue-Sun Jul & Aug, from 9am May, Jun & Sep, shorter hours rest of year) from the 15th century, which now houses the Czech Silver Museum.

Both buses and trains make the trip to Kutná Hora from Prague, though the train is usually a better bet. Direct trains depart from Prague's main train station to Kutná Hora hlavní nádraží every two hours (220Kč return, 55 minutes). It's a 10-minute walk from here to Sedlec Ossuary, and a further 2.5km (30 minutes) to the Old Town. Buses (136Kč return, 1¾ hours) depart from Prague's Háje bus station on the far southern end of the city. On weekdays, buses run hourly, with reduced services on weekdays.

BOHEMIA

Beyond the serried apartment blocks of Prague's outer suburbs, the city gives way to the surprisingly green hinterland of Bohemia, a land of rolling hills, rich farmland and thick forests dotted with castles, chateaux and picturesque towns. Rural and rustic, yet mostly within two to three hours' drive of the capital, the Czech Republic's western province has for centuries provided an escape for city-dwellers.

It's a region of surprising variety. Český Krumlov, with its riverside setting and Renaissance castle, is in a class by itself, but lesser-known towns in the south and west exude an unexpected charm. Big cities like Plzeň offer great museums and restaurants, while the famed 19th-century spa towns of western Bohemia retain an old-world lustre.

Plzeň

POP 164,180

Plzeň (Pilsen in German) is famed among beer-heads worldwide as the mother lode of all lagers, the fountain of eternal froth. Pilsner lager was invented here in 1842. It's the home of Pilsner Urquell *(Plzeňský prazdroj)*, the world's first and arguably best lager beer – 'Urquell' (in German; *prazdroj* in Czech) means 'original source' – and beer drinkers from around the world flock to worship at the Pilsner Urquell brewery.

The second-biggest city in Bohemia after Prague, Plzeň's other attractions include a pretty town square and historic underground tunnels, while the Techmania Science Centre joins the zoo and puppet museum to make this a kid-friendly destination. The city is close enough to Prague to see the sights in a long day trip, but you'll enjoy the outing much more if you plan to spend the night.

◎ Sights

★ **Pilsner Urquell Brewery** BREWERY
(Prazdroj; ☑ 377 062 888; www.prazdrojvisit.cz; U Prazdroje 7; guided tour adult/child 250/150Kč; ☺ 8.30am-6pm, to 5pm Oct-Mar) Plzeň's most popular attraction is the tour of the Pilsner Urquell Brewery, in operation since 1842 and arguably home to the world's best beer. Entry is by guided tour only, with at least four tours daily in English (10.45am, 1pm, 2.45pm and 4.30pm). Tour highlights include a trip to the old cellars (dress warmly)

and a glass of unpasteurised nectar at the end. The brewery is located about 300m east of the centre (about 10 minutes on foot).

Underground Plzeň
TUNNEL

(Plzeňské historické podzemí; ☑377 235 574; www.plzenskepodzemi.cz; Veleslavínova 6; adult/child 120/80Kč; ⊙10am-7pm Apr-Sep, to 5pm Oct-Dec & Feb-Mar) This extraordinary 60-minute guided tour explores the passageways below the old city. The earliest were probably dug in the 14th century, perhaps for beer production or defence; the latest date from the 19th century. Of an estimated 11km that have been excavated, some 500m of the tunnels are open to the public. Bring extra clothing – it's a chilly 10°C underground. Tours are given in English at 2.20pm daily from April to October; English-language audio guides are available at other times.

Brewery Museum
MUSEUM

(☑377 224 955; www.prazdrojvisit.cz; Veleslavínova 6; adult/child 90/60Kč; ⊙10am-6pm, to 5pm Oct-Mar) The Brewery Museum offers an insight into how beer was made (and drunk) in the days before Pilsner Urquell was founded. Highlights include a mock-up of a 19th-century pub, a huge wooden beer tankard from Siberia and a collection of beer mats. All have English captions and there's a good printed English text available.

Techmania Science Centre
MUSEUM

(☑737 247 585; www.techmania.cz; U Planetária 1; 190Kč; ⊙10am-6pm; ⊡⛟; ☒15, 17) Kids will have a ball at this high-tech, interactive science centre where they can play with infrared cameras, magnets and many other instructive and fun exhibits. There's a 3D planetarium (included with admission fee) and a few full-sized historic trams and trains manufactured at the Škoda engineering works. Take the trolleybus; it's a 2km hike southwest from the city centre.

🛏 Sleeping

The city has a decent range of pensions, budget and midrange hotels, many aimed at business and student visitors. The City Information Centre (p164) can find and book accommodation for a small fee.

Hotel Roudna
HOTEL €€

(☑377 259 926; www.hotelroudna.cz; Na Roudné 13; s/d 1400/1700Kč; ⊡@🛜) Perhaps the city's best-value lodging, across the river to the north of the old town, the Roudna's exterior isn't much to look at, but inside the rooms are well proportioned with high-end amenities such as flat-screen TVs, minibars and desks. Breakfasts are fresh and ample, and reception is friendly. Note there's no lift.

Hotel Rous
BOUTIQUE HOTEL €€

(☑377 320 260; www.hotelrous.cz; Zbrojnická 7; s/d from 1800/2400Kč; ⊡@🛜) This 600-year-old building combines the historic character of the original stone walls with modern furnishings. Bathrooms are art deco cool in black and white. Breakfast is taken in a garden cafe concealed amid remnants of Plzeň's defensive walls. Downstairs, the Caffe Emily serves very good coffee.

🍴 Eating & Drinking

Plzeň is a good place to try traditional Czech pub grub, washed down with excellent local Pilsner Urquell beer.

Everest Restaurant
INDIAN €

(☑774 048 597; www.indickaplzen.cz; Lochotínská 11; mains 140-180Kč; ⊙11am-10pm Mon-Thu, to 11pm Fri & Sat; 🛜☑) The region's best Indian restaurant offers a spicy alternative to pork and dumplings. All of the standard chicken and lamb dishes, plus many vegetarian options, cooked to a high standard. The location, on a busy road outside the centre, and plain appearance are not encouraging, but push through the doors to find a comfy, crowded restaurant inside. Reservations recommended.

Na Parkánu
CZECH €

(☑377 324 485; www.naparkanu.com; Veleslavínova 4; mains 169-299Kč; ⊙11am-11pm, to 1am Fri & Sat, to 10pm Sun; 🛜) Don't overlook this pleasant pub-restaurant, attached to the Brewery Museum. It may look a bit touristy, but the traditional Czech food is top-rate, and the beer, naturally, could hardly be better. Try to snag a spot in the summer garden. Don't leave without trying the *nefiltrované pivo* (unfiltered beer). Reservations are an absolute must.

⭐ Buffalo Burger Bar
AMERICAN €€

(☑733 124 514; www.facebook.com/barBuffaloBurger; Dominikánská 3; mains 165-385Kč; ⊙11am-11pm, to 1am Fri & Sat; 🛜) Tuck into some of the best burgers in the Czech Republic at this American-style diner, with cool timber decor the colour of a well-done steak. Everything is freshly made, from the hand-cooked tortilla chips, zingy salsa and guacamole, to the perfect French fries, coleslaw and the juicy burgers themselves.

MAZIARZE/SHUTTERSTOCK ©

1. The Great Synagogue (p203), Budapest, Hungary **2.** POLIN Museum of the History of Polish Jews (p311; designed by Rainer Mahlamäki), Warsaw, Poland **3.** Auschwitz-Birkenau Memorial & Museum (p321), Poland **4.** Subotica's Synagogue (p403), Serbia

PIOTRBB/SHUTTERSTOCK ©

Jewish Heritage

Jews were part of the cultural fabric of Eastern Europe for a millennium up to the Holocaust during World War II and formed a vital part of the culture of nearly every country in the region. While almost eliminated by the atrocities of World War II, Jewish culture lives on in pockets of varying sizes across Eastern Europe.

Surviving Synagogues

Traces of Jewish life are seen all around the region in the form of old synagogues. Some are abandoned and falling into disrepair. Others have been lavishly restored and may even still serve a local Jewish congregation. Budapest's Great Synagogue (p203) is the world's largest synagogue outside of New York City and includes a museum and Holocaust memorial. Serbia's Synagogue (p403), in Subotica, is a 1902 art-nouveau masterwork that's been recently restored.

Museums of Memory

Museums tell the the story of the region's Jewish communities, both in good times and bad. The Museum of the History of Polish Jews (p311), in Warsaw, is a high-tech marvel with a permanent exhibition tracing a millennium of Jewish history. Prague's Josefov (p149) is something different, a collection of restored synagogues and a historic cemetery.

Horrors of the Holocaust

The Nazi-led genocide against the Jewish people during World War II touched countries all around Eastern Europe. The Auschwitz-Birkenau Memorial & Museum (p321), in Oświęcim, Poland, is the best known of several horrific Nazi-run death camps; it's a bleak but important testament to the Holocaust.

Promoting Tolerance

The seeds of mutual understanding and tolerance can be seen all around Eastern Europe these days. The Tolerance Centre (p251) in Vilnius recalls the city's vital Jewish heritage. In the Bosnian capital, Sarajevo (p77), the country's melting-pot history is reflected in synagogues sharing neighbourhoods with churches and mosques.

Aberdeen Angus Steakhouse STEAK €€

(☑725 555 631; www.angussteakhouse.cz; Pražská 23; mains 215-600Kč; ⊙11am-11pm, to midnight Fri & Sat; 🖥) One of the best steakhouses in the Czech Republic. The meats hail from a nearby farm, where the livestock is raised organically. There are several cuts and sizes on offer; lunch options include a tantalising cheeseburger. The downstairs dining room is cosy; there's also a creek-side terrace. Book in advance.

★Měšťanská Beseda PUB

(☑reservations 378 035 415; http://web.mestanska-beseda.cz; Kopeckého sady 13; ⊙9am-10pm, from 11am Sat & Sun; 🖥) Cool heritage cafe, pub, expansive exhibition space and occasional art-house cinema – the elegant art nouveau Měšťanská Beseda is hands-down Plzeň's most versatile venue. The beautifully restored 19th-century pub is perfect for a leisurely beer or coffee. Check out who's performing at the attached theatre.

ⓘ Information

City Information Centre (Informační centrum města Plzně; ☑378 035 330; www.pilsen.eu/tourist; náměstí Republiky 41; ⊙9am-7pm, to 6pm Oct-Mar; 🖥) Plzeň's well-stocked tourist information office is a first port of call for visitors. Staff here can advise on sleeping and eating options, and there are free city maps and a stock of brochures on what to see and do.

ⓘ Getting There & Away

BUS

Plzeň's **bus station** (Centrální autobusové nádraží, CAN; ☑377 237 237; www.csadplzen.cz; Husova 60; 🚌11, 28), marked on maps and street signs as 'CAN', is 1km west of the centre. The city is well-connected by bus to regional towns and cities. **RegioJet** (Student Agency; ☑377 333 222; www.regiojet.cz; náměstí Republiky 9; ⊙9am-6pm Mon-Fri) runs half-hourly buses during the day between Plzeň and Prague (99Kč, one hour). Note most Plzeň-bound buses depart Prague from Zličín station, the last stop on metro line B (yellow).

TRAIN

Plzeň's **train station** (Plzeň hlavní nádraží; www.cd.cz; Nádražní 102) is 1km east of the historic centre. Train connections are frequent between Plzeň and Prague's main train station (120Kč, 1½ hours). There's also regular direct train service to České Budějovice (179Kč, 2 hours) and Mariánské Lázně (114Kč, 1 hour), among other regional cities.

Český Krumlov

POP 13,141

Český Krumlov, in Bohemia's deep south, is one of the most picturesque towns in Europe. It's a little like Prague in miniature – a Unesco World Heritage Site with a stunning castle above the Vltava River, an old town square, Renaissance and baroque architecture, and hordes of tourists milling through the streets – but all on a smaller scale; you can walk from one side of town to the other in 20 minutes. There are plenty of lively bars and riverside picnic spots – in summer it's a popular hangout for backpackers. It can be a magical place in winter, though, when the crowds are gone and the castle is blanketed in snow.

Český Krumlov is best approached as an overnight destination; it's too far for a comfortable day trip from Prague. Consider staying at least two nights, and spend one of the days hiking or biking in the surrounding woods and fields.

⊙ Sights

★Český Krumlov State Castle CASTLE

(☑380 704 721; www.zamek-ceskykrumlov.eu; Zámek 59; adult/concession from 240/170Kč; ⊙9am-5pm Tue-Sun Jun-Aug, to 4pm Apr, May, Sep & Oct) Český Krumlov's striking Renaissance castle, occupying a promontory high above the town, began life in the 13th century. It acquired its present appearance in the 16th to 18th centuries under the stewardship of the noble Rožmberk and Schwarzenberg families. The interiors are accessible by guided tour only, though you can stroll the grounds on your own. Book tours at castle ticket windows, over the website or through the Infocentrum (p166).

Castle Museum & Tower MUSEUM, TOWER

(☑380 704 721; www.zamek-ceskykrumlov.eu; Zámek 59; museum adult/child 100/70Kč, tower 100/70Kč; ⊙9am-5pm Jun-Aug, to 4pm Apr, May, Sep & Oct, to 3pm Tue-Sun Nov-Mar) Located within the castle complex, this small museum and adjoining tower is an ideal option if you don't have the time or energy for a full castle tour. Through a series of rooms, the museum traces the castle's history from its origins to the present day. Climb the tower for the perfect photo ops of the town below.

Museum Fotoateliér Seidel MUSEUM

(☑736 503 871; www.seidel.cz; Linecká 272; adult/child 100/40Kč; ⊙9am-noon & 1-6pm May-Sep, 9am-noon & 1-5pm Tue-Sun Oct-Apr) This photography museum presents a moving retrospective of

Český Krumlov

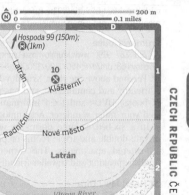

Český Krumlov

◎ Top Sights
1 Český Krumlov State Castle B1

◎ Sights
2 Castle Museum & Tower B1
3 Egon Schiele Art Centrum................. A3
4 Museum Fotoateliér Seidel B4

⬤ Sleeping
5 Hotel Myší Díra D3
6 Krumlov House D4
7 U Malého Vítka B2

⊗ Eating
8 Hospoda Na Louži B3
9 Krčma v Šatlavské B3
10 Nonna Gina C1

the work of local photographers Josef Seidel and his son František. Especially poignant are the images recording early-20th-century life in nearby villages. In the high season you should be able to join an English-language tour; if not, let the pictures tell the story.

Egon Schiele Art Centrum MUSEUM
(☑ 380 704 011; www.schieleartcentrum.cz; Široká 71; adult/child under 6yr 180Kč/free; ⊘ 10am-6pm) This excellent private gallery houses a small retrospective of the controversial Viennese painter Egon Schiele (1890–1918), who lived in Krumlov in 1911 and raised the ire of the townsfolk by hiring young girls as nude models. For this and other sins he was eventually driven out. The centre also houses interesting temporary exhibitions.

🛏 Sleeping

There are thousands of beds in Český Krumlov, but accommodation is still tight in summer. Winter rates drop by up to 30%. Ac-

commodation can be noisy in the Old Town, and parking expensive. Consider alternative accommodation a short walk out of town. For budget accommodation, expect to pay from 500Kč per person for a private room, often with breakfast included. The Infocentrum can recommend mid-range furnished apartments.

Krumlov House · HOSTEL €

(☎728 287 919; www.krumlovhostel.com; Rooseveltova 68; dm/d/tr 450/1100/1300Kč; ☻@🛜) 🚲 Perched above the river, Krumlov House is friendly and comfortable, and has plenty of books, DVDs and local information to feed your inner wanderer. Accommodation is in a six-bed en-suite dorms as well as private double and triple rooms or private, self-catered apartments. The owners are English-speaking and traveller-friendly.

★Hotel Myší Díra · HOTEL €€

(☎380 712 853; www.hotelmysidira.com; Rooseveltova 28; d/tr 2500/3100Kč; P🛜) This place has a superb location overlooking the river, and bright, spacious rooms with lots of pale wood and quirky handmade furniture; room No 12, with a huge corner bath and naughty decorations on the bed, is a favourite.

U Malého Vítka · HOTEL €€

(☎380 711 925; www.vitekhotel.cz; Radniční 27; s/d 1700/2040Kč; P☻🛜) There is a lot of charm to this small hotel in the heart of the Old Town. The simple room furnishings are of high-quality, hand-crafted wood, and each room is named after a traditional Czech fairy-tale character.

✖ Eating

Although there are dozens of places to eat in town, the large number of visitors means that booking ahead for dinner is recommended from April to October and on weekends year-round.

Nonna Gina · ITALIAN €

(☎380 717 187; www.facebook.com/pages/Pizzeria-Nonna-Gina/228366473858301; Klášterini 52; mains 130-200Kč; ⊙11am-11pm) Authentic Italian flavours from the Massaro family feature at this long-established pizzeria, where the quality of food and service knocks the socks off more expensive restaurants. Superb antipasti, great pizza and Italian wines at surprisingly low prices make for a memorable meal. Grab an outdoor table and pretend you're in Naples, or retreat to the snug and intimate upstairs dining room.

Hospoda 99 · BURGERS €

(☎380 713 813; www.hostel99.cz/hospoda-99; Věžní 99; mains 120-300Kč; ⊙10am-11pm, to 10pm Oct-May; 🛜) This pub with a big summer terrace is far enough away from the busy centre (though

only 150m walk north) to feel like something of an oasis. The menu is big on burgers, but throws in nicely prepared steaks and Mexican dishes to have something for everyone. Reserve ahead in summer for dinner.

★Krčma v Šatlavské · CZECH €€

(☎380 713 344; www.satlava.cz; Horní 157; mains 180-355Kč; ⊙11am-midnight) This medieval barbecue cellar is hugely popular with visitors and your tablemates are much more likely to be from Austria or China than from the town itself, but the grilled meats served up with gusto in a funky labyrinth illuminated by candles are excellent and perfectly in character with Český Krumlov. Advance booking is essential.

Hospoda Na Louži · CZECH €€

(☎380 711 280; www.nalouzi.cz; Kájovská 66; mains 140-280Kč) Nothing's changed in this wood-panelled *pivo* (beer) parlour for almost a century. Locals and tourists pack Na Louži for huge plates of Czech staples such as chicken schnitzels or roast pork and dumplings, as well as dark (and light) beer from the local Eggenberg brewery. Get the fruit dumplings for dessert if you see them on the menu.

❶ Information

Infocentrum (☎380 704 622; www.ckrumlov. info; náměstí Svornosti 2; ⊙9am-7pm Jun-Aug, to 5pm rest of year; closed lunch Sat & Sun) One of the country's best tourist offices. It's a good source for transport and accommodation info, maps, internet access (per five minutes 5Kč) and audio guides (per hour 100Kč). You can purchase bus tickets and the **Český Krumlov Card** (www.ckrumlov.cz/card; adult/ child 300/150Kč) here. A guide for visitors with disabilities is available.

❶ Getting There & Away

BUS

RegioJet (Student Agency; ☎841 101 101; www. regiojet.cz; Nemocniční 586) coaches (170Kč, three hours, hourly) leave from Prague's Na Knížecí bus station at Anděl metro station (Line B). Book in advance for weekends or in July and August. Český Krumlov **bus station** (Autobusové nádraží; Nemocniční 586) is about a 10-minute walk east of the historic centre.

TRAIN

The train from Prague (210Kč, 3½ hours, four to six daily) requires a change in České Budějovice. There's regular train service between České Budějovice and Český Krumlov (40Kč, 45 minutes). It is quicker and cheaper to take the bus. Český Krumlov **train station** (Vlakové nádraží; www.cd.cz;

Třída Míru 1) is located 2km north of the historic centre. A **taxi** (☑ 380 712 712; www.green-taxi.cz) from the station costs around 100Kč.

Karlovy Vary

POP 51,800

Karlovy Vary (Carlsbad), or simply 'Vary' to Czechs, has stepped up its game in recent years, thanks largely to a property boom spurred by wealthy Russian investors. Indeed, the first thing you'll notice is the high number of Russian visitors, all following in the footsteps of Tsar Peter the Great, who stayed here for treatments in the early 18th century. Day trippers come to admire the grand 19th-century spa architecture and to stroll the impressive colonnades, sipping on the supposedly health-restoring sulphurous waters from spouted ceramic drinking cups.

Despite its exalted spa reputation, Karlovy Vary is not entirely welcoming to walk-ins looking for high-end treatments such as exotic massages and peelings; these services are available but should be booked in advance.

⊙ Sights & Activities

★ Mill Colonnade
SPRING

(Mlýnská kolonáda; www.karlovyvary.cz/en/colonnades-and-springs; ⊙ 24hr) FREE The most impressive piece of architecture in Karlovy Vary is the neo-Renaissance Mill Colonnade (built 1871–81), with five different springs, rooftop statues depicting the months of the year, and a little bandstand. The Petra Restaurant, opposite, is the spot (but not the original building) where Peter the Great allegedly stayed in 1711.

Hot Spring Colonnade
SPRING

(Vřídelní kolonáda; www.karlovyvary.cz/en/colonnades-and-springs; ⊙ 9am-5pm, from 10am Sat & Sun) FREE The Hot Spring Colonnade is in an incongruous concrete-and-glass functionalist structure built in 1975 and once dedicated to Soviet cosmonaut Yuri Gagarin. It houses the most impressive of the town's geysers, Pramen Vřídlo, which spurts some 12m into the air; people lounge about inhaling the vapours or sampling the waters from a line of taps in the main hall.

Market Colonnade
SPRING

(Tržní kolonáda; www.karlovyvary.cz/en/colonnades-and-springs; Lázeňská; ⊙ 24hr) FREE The only one of the town's colonnades to be crafted from wood, this beautiful neoclassical structure dates from the 1880s and was the work

of the fabled Viennese architectural firm of Fellner & Helmer. The bronze panel above the Charles IV Spring (pramen Karla IV) depicts the discovery of the hot springs by Emperor Charles in the 14th century.

Park Colonnade
SPRING

(Sadová kolonáda; www.karlovyvary.cz/en/colonnades-and-springs; ⊙ 24hr) FREE Also known as the Garden Colonnade, this elegant wrought-iron structure dates from 1880 and is the first of the main colonnades that you reach as you enter the spa zone from the north. It was designed by the Viennese architectural firm of Fellner & Helmer, the same company that designed the Market Colonnade.

Castle Spa
SPA

(Zámecké Lázně; ☑ 353 225 502; www.castle-spa.com; Zámecký vrch 1; 30min massage from 676Kč; ⊙ 7.30am-7.30pm) Most Karlovy Vary accommodation offers some kind of spa treatment for a fee, but if you're just a casual visitor or day tripper, consider this modernised spa centre complete with a subterranean thermal pool. Visit the website for a full menu of treatments and massages.

★✦ Festivals & Events

Karlovy Vary International Film Festival
FILM

(www.kviff.com; ⊙ early Jul) This film festival always features the year's top films as well as attracting plenty of (B-list) stars. It's rather behind the pace of the likes of Cannes, Venice and Berlin but is well worth the trip.

🛏 Sleeping & Eating

Accommodation prices in Karlovy Vary have risen in recent years to be similar to those in Prague, especially in July during the annual Karlovy Vary International Film Festival. Indeed, if you're planning a July arrival, make sure to book well in advance. Infocentrum (p168) can help with hostel, pension and hotel bookings.

★ Hotel Romance Puškin
HOTEL €€

(☑ 353 222 646; www.hotelromance.cz; Tržiště 37; s/d 2800/3800Kč; ❂ 🐾 🛜) In a great location just across from the Hot Spring Colonnade (p167), the Puškin has renovated rooms with fully updated baths and very comfortable beds. These are just some of the charms at one of the nicest mid-range hotels in the spa area. The breakfast is a treat; the usual sausage and eggs is supplemented by inventive salads and smoked fish.

UNESCO HERITAGE ARCHITECTURE IN TELČ

The Unesco-protected town of Telč, perched on the border between Bohemia and Moravia, possesses one of the country's prettiest and best-preserved historic town squares. The main attraction is the beauty of the square, **náměstí Zachariáše z Hradce**, itself, which is lined with Renaissance burghers' houses. Most of the structures were built in the 16th century after a fire levelled the town in 1530. Famous houses include No 15, which shows the characteristic Renaissance sgraffito. The house at No 48 was given a baroque facade in the 18th century. **Telč Chateau** (Zámek; ☑567 243 943; www.zamek-telc.cz; náměstí Zachariáše z Hradce 1; adult/concession from 100/80Kč; ☉10am-4pm Tue-Sun May-Sep, to 3pm Apr & Oct), another Renaissance masterpiece, guards the northern end of the square.

If you decide to spend the night, the **Hotel Celerin** (☑567 243 477; www.hotelcelerin.cz; náměstí Zachariáše z Hradce 43; s/d 1300/1850Kč; ☯❋⌘) offers 12 comfortable rooms, with decor ranging from cosy wood to white-wedding chintz (take a look first).

There are a handful of daily buses that run from Prague's Florenc bus station (168Kč, 3 hours), though many connections require a change in Jihlava. The situation is similarly poor for bus travel to/from Brno (106Kč, two hours). Check the online timetable at http://jizdnirady.idnes.cz for times.

Bagel Lounge BAGELS €
(☑720 022 123; www.bagellounge.cz; TG Masaryka 45; sandwiches 99-140Kč; ☉8am-8pm; ⌘)
Ideal spot for a quick breakfast, a lunch of soup and bagel sandwich, or simply a coffee or cold drink. The terrace is great for people-watching, and the 1950s diner–inspired retro interior is fun. The 'Bacon-Bagel' sandwich (99Kč) makes for a filling breakfast.

Tusculum CZECH €€
(☑739 541 008; www.tusculumkv.cz; Sadová 31; mains 180-400Kč; ☉11am-10pm; ⌘☑) One of the better dinner options. Tusculum features organic, locally sourced ingredients on a small menu of traditional favourites like duck and pork, spiced up with surprise starters like Thai soup and hummus. There are lots of vegetarian options on the menu, and (big plus) allergy and food-sensitivity information is clearly marked on the menu. Attractive terrace for alfresco dining.

ℹ Information

Infocentrum Spa (Infocentrum Lázeňská; ☑355 321 176; www.karlovyvary.cz; Lázeňská 14; ☉8am-6pm; ⌘) The main tourist information office within the main spa area. Can provide maps and advice on accommodation, events, transport info and spa treatments.

Infocentrum TG Masaryka (Infocentrum TGM; ☑355 321 171; www.karlovyvary.cz; TG Masaryka 53; ☉8am-6pm Mon-Fri, 9am-1pm & 1.30-5pm Sat & Sun) This branch of the main tourist information office is within easy walk of the bus and train stations.

ℹ Getting There & Away

BUS
Buses from Prague (150Kč, 2¼ hours, hourly) arrive at Karlovy Vary's terminal **bus station** (Autobusové Nádraží Terminal; ☑353 504 518; Západní 2a; ☑3, 6, 18, 23). Both Flixbus (www.flixbus.cz) and **RegioJet** (☑841 101 101; www.regiojet.cz; Západní 2a; ☉7am-7pm Mon-Fri, 8.30am-6.30pm Sat & Sun; ☑3, 6, 18, 23) operate regular service to and from Karlovy Vary. Check www.vlak-bus.cz for timetables.

TRAIN
Trains from Prague (330Kč, 3¼ hours, every two hours) take a circuitous route that is much slower and more expensive than the bus. Unless you have nothing else to do, it's not recommended.

MORAVIA

The Czech Republic's eastern province, Moravia, is yin to Bohemia's yang. If Bohemians love beer, Moravians love wine. If Bohemia is about towns and cities, Moravia is all rolling hills and pretty landscapes. The Moravian capital, Brno, has the museums, but the northern city of Olomouc has the captivating architecture.

Brno
POP 377,440
Moravia's capital city just keeps getting better and better. The thousands of university students here have always ensured a lively club

and entertainment scene, but a wave of next-gen cafes, restaurants and cocktail bars in the past few years has put the city on the map and even invited positive comparisons with Prague. The churches and museums are great too. If you add in some daring modern architecture from the early 20th century, such as the Unesco-protected Vila Tugendhat, there's plenty to reward more than a transit stop.

Sights

★Vila Tugendhat ARCHITECTURE
(Villa Tugendhat; ☎515 511 015; www.tugendhat.eu; Černopolni 45; adult/concession from 300/180Kč; ⏲10am-6pm Tue-Sun Mar-Dec, 9am-5pm Wed-Sun Jan & Feb; 🚊3, 5, 9) Brno had a reputation in the 1920s as a centre for modern architecture in the Bauhaus style. Arguably the finest example is this family villa, designed by modern master Mies van der Rohe for Greta and Fritz Tugendhat in 1930. The house was the inspiration for British author Simon Mawer in his 2009 bestseller *The Glass Room*. Entry is by guided tour booked in advance by phone or email. Two tours are available: basic (one hour) and extended (1½ hours).

Labyrinth under the Cabbage Market TUNNELS
(Brněnské podzemí; ☎542 212 892; www.ticbrno.cz; Zelný trh 21; adult/concession 160/80Kč; ⏲9am-6pm Tue-Sun; 🚊4, 8, 9) In recent years, the city has opened several sections of extensive underground tunnels to the general public. This tour takes around 40 minutes to explore several cellars situated 6m to 8m below the Cabbage Market, which has served as a food market for centuries. The cellars were built for two purposes: to store goods and to hide in during wars.

Old Town Hall HISTORIC BUILDING
(Stará radnice; ☎542 427 150; www.ticbrno.cz; Radnická 8; tower adult/concession 70/40Kč; ⏲10am-10pm May-Aug, to 6pm Sep & Oct, 10am-6pm Fri-Sun Nov; 🚊4, 8, 9) No visit to Brno would be complete without a peek inside the city's medieval Old Town Hall, parts of which date back to the 13th century. The tourist office (p171) is here, plus oddities including a crocodile hanging from the ceiling (known affectionately as the Brno 'dragon') and a wooden wagon wheel with a unique story. You can also climb the tower.

Capuchin Monastery CEMETERY
(Kapucínský klášter; ☎511 145 796; www.kapucini.cz; Kapucínské náměstí; adult/concession 70/35Kč; ⏲9am-noon & 1-6pm Mon-Sat, 11am-5pm Sun, reduced hours Nov-Mar; 🚊4, 8, 9) One of the city's leading attractions is this ghoulish cellar crypt that holds the mummified remains of several city noblemen from the 18th century. Apparently, the dry, well-ventilated crypt has the natural ability to turn dead bodies into mummies. Up to 150 cadavers were deposited here prior to 1784, the desiccated corpses including monks, abbots and local notables.

Špilberk Castle CASTLE
(Hrad Špilberk; ☎542 123 677; www.spilberk.cz; Špilberk 210/1; adult/concession 280/170Kč; ⏲10am-6pm Apr-Sep, 9am-5pm Tue-Sun Oct-Mar) Brno's spooky hilltop castle is considered the city's most important landmark. Its history stretches back to the 13th century, when it was home to Moravian margraves and later a fortress. Under the Habsburgs in the 18th and 19th centuries, it served as a prison. Today it's home to the Brno City Museum, with several temporary and permanent exhibitions.

Sleeping

Brno is a popular venue for international trade fairs, and hotels routinely jack up rates by 40% or more during large events (in February, April, August, September and October especially). Check www.bvv.cz for event dates and try to plan your visit for an off week. Always book ahead if possible.

★Hostel Mitte HOSTEL €
(☎734 622 340; www.hostelmitte.com; Panská 22; incl breakfast dm 455Kč, s/d 900/1400Kč; 🚭@📶; 🚊4, 8, 9) Set in the heart of the Old Town, this clean and stylish hostel smells and looks brand new. The rooms are named after famous Moravians (eg Milan Kundera) or famous events (Austerlitz) and decorated accordingly. There are six-bed dorms and private singles, doubles and quads. Cute cafe on the ground floor.

Hotel Europa HOTEL €
(☎515 143 100; www.hotel-europa-brno.cz; třída kpt Jaroše 27; s/d 1250/1400Kč; P🚭📶; 🚊3, 5) Set in a quiet neighbourhood a 10-minute walk from the city centre, this self-proclaimed 'art' hotel (presumably for the futuristic lobby furniture) offers clean and tastefully furnished modern rooms in a historic 19th-century building. Rooms come in 'standard' and more expensive 'superior', with the chief difference being size. There is free parking out the front and in the courtyard.

Hostel Fléda
HOSTEL €

(✆731 651 005; www.hostelfleda.com; Štefánikova 24; dm/d from 270/800Kč; ☺🛜; 🖳1, 6) One of Brno's best music clubs offers funky and colourful rooms, and a cafe and good bar reinforce the social vibe. It's a quick tram ride from the centre to the Hrnčirská stop.

Barceló Brno Palace
LUXURY HOTEL €€€

(✆532 156 777; www.barcelo.com; Šilingrovo nám 2; r from 3600Kč; 🅿☺❄@🛜; 🖳4, 6, 12) Five-star heritage luxury comes to Brno at the Barceló Brno Palace. The lobby blends glorious 19th-century architecture with thoroughly modern touches, and the spacious rooms are both contemporary and romantic. The location on the edge of Brno's Old Town is excellent.

🍴 Eating

As the second-biggest city in the Czech Republic, Brno also has some of the country's best restaurants – at prices to match. For travellers on a budget, there are plenty of cafes and pubs where you can grab cheaper – but still very good – grub.

Spolek
CZECH €

(✆774 814 230; www.spolek.net; Orli 22; mains 90–180Kč; ☺9am-10pm, from 10am Sat & Sun; 🛜📶♿; 🖳2, 4, 11) You'll get friendly, unpretentious service at this coolly 'bohemian' (yes, we're in Moravia) haven with interesting salads and soups, and a concise but diverse wine list. Photojournalism on the walls is complemented by a funky mezzanine bookshop. It has excellent coffee too.

Bistro Franz
CZECH €

(✆720 113 502; www.bistrofranz.cz; Veveří 14; mains 165–195Kč; ☺8am-3.30pm Mon, to 9pm Tue-Fri, 9am-8.30pm Sat & Sun; 🛜📶; 🖳6, 12) Colourfully retro Bistro Franz is one of a new generation of restaurants that focuses on locally sourced, organic ingredients. The philosophy extends to the relatively simple menu of soups, baked chicken drumsticks, curried lentils and other student-friendly food. The wine is carefully chosen and the coffee is sustainably grown. Excellent choice for morning coffee and breakfast.

★ Pavillon
INTERNATIONAL €€

(✆541 213 497; www.restaurant-pavillon.cz; Jezuitská 6; mains 300–550Kč; ☺11am-11pm Mon-Sat, noon-10pm Sun; 📶📋; 🖳1) High-end dining in an elegant, airy space that recalls the city's heritage in functionalist architecture. The menu changes with the season, but usually features one vegetarian entrée as well as mains with locally sourced ingredients, such as wild boar or lamb raised in the Vysočina highlands. Daily lunch specials (295Kč) including soup, main and dessert, are good value.

🍷 Drinking & Nightlife

Whether your beverage of choice is coffee, beer or cocktails, Brno has you covered. Thousands of students mean dozens of watering holes, and the cafes are every bit as cool as Prague's, while the cocktail bars are even better. Central Dvořákova street, particularly the area behind the Church of St James, is a popular area for clubs and bars.

★ Cafe Podnebi
CAFE

(✆542 211 372; www.podnebi.cz; Údolní 5; ☺8am-midnight, from 9am Sat & Sun; 🛜♿; 🖳4) This homey, student-oriented cafe is famous citywide for its excellent hot chocolate, but it also serves very good espresso drinks. There are plenty of baked goods and sweets to snack on. In summer the garden terrace is a hidden oasis, and there's a small play area for kids.

Super Panda Circus
COCKTAIL BAR

(✆734 878 603; www.superpandacircus.cz; Šilingrovo náměstí 3, enter from Husova; ☺6pm-2am Mon-Sat; 🛜; 🖳4, 6, 12) From the moment the doorman ushers you through an unmarked door into this bar, you feel you've entered a secret world like out of the movie *Eyes Wide Shut*. The dark interior, lit only in crazy colours emanating from the bar, and inventive drinks add to the allure. Hope for an empty table since it's not possible to book.

Bar, Který Neexistuje
COCKTAIL BAR

(✆734 878 602; www.barkteryneexistuje.cz; Dvořákova 1; ☺5pm-2am, to 3am Wed & Thu, to 4am Fri & Sat; 🛜; 🖳4, 8, 9) 'The bar that doesn't exist' boasts a long, beautiful bar backed by every bottle of booze imaginable. It anchors a row of popular, student-oriented bars along trendy Dvořákova. For a bar that 'doesn't exist', it gets quite crowded, so it's best to book ahead.

SKØG Urban Hub
CAFE

(✆607 098 557; www.skog.cz; Dominikánské nám 5; ☺8am-1am, to 2am Fri, 10am-2am Sat, noon-10pm Sun; 🛜) Exposed brick walls, unadorned light bulbs hanging from the ceiling, loads of effortless attitude and, naturally, some of the best coffee and cakes in the centre of town. SKØG Urban Hub also moonlights as a gallery and performance space, and has pretty good salads and hummus as well.

☆ Entertainment

Fléda   LIVE MUSIC
(☑533 433 559; www.fleda.cz; Štefánikova 24; tickets 200-500Kč; ☺7pm-2am; ☒1, 6) Brno's best up-and-coming bands, occasional touring performers and DJs all rock the stage at Brno's top music club. Buy tickets at the venue. Shows start around 9pm. Take the tram to the Hrnčirská stop.

**Brno Philharmonic
Orchestra**   CLASSICAL MUSIC
(Besední dům; ☑539 092 811; www.filharmonie-brno.cz; Komenského náměstí 8; tickets 300-450Kč; ☺box office 9am-2pm Mon & Wed, 1-6pm Tue, Thu & Fri, plus 45 mins before performances; ☒5, 6, 12, 13) The Brno Philharmonic is the city's leading orchestra for classical music. It conducts some 40 concerts each year, plus tours around the Czech Republic and Europe. It's particularly strong on Moravian-born, early-20th-century composer Leoš Janáček. Most performances are held at Besední dům concert house. Buy tickets at the box office, located around the corner from the main entrance on Besední.

ℹ Information

Tourist Information Centre (TIC Brno; ☑542 427 150; www.gotobrno.cz; Radnická 8, Old Town Hall; ☺8.30am-6pm, from 9am Sat & Sun) Brno's main tourist office is located within the Old Town Hall complex. The office has loads of great information on the city in English, including events calendars and walking maps. Lots of material on the city's rich architectural heritage is also available, as well as self-guided tours. There's a free computer to check email.

Information Centre for South Moravia (Informační centrum – Jižní Morava; ☑542 211 123; www.ccrjm.cz; Radnická 2; ☺9am-noon & 12.45-5pm Mon-Fri) Just next to the main city tourist information centre, this office focuses on South Moravia, outside of the city. It's a good place to stock up on ideas and information if your travels will take you to Olomouc, Mikulov, Znojmo, Valtice-Lednice and other attractions in the region.

ℹ Getting There & Away

BUS
Hourly buses connect Brno to Prague as well as cities and towns throughout the region. Buses use one of two stations, so be sure to look at the ticket or booking closely to be sure of the station you need. Most services use Brno's central bus station, **Zvonařka** (ÚAN Zvonařka; ☑543 217 733; www.vlak-bus.cz; Zvonařka; ☺information 6am-8pm, to 4pm Sat & Sun), which is located

behind the main train station. Access is through a tunnel that begins below the train station and runs through a shopping centre.

Several popular services, however, including handy Prague-bound services with **RegioJet** (Student Agency; ☑539 000 860; www.regiojet.cz; náměstí Svobody 17; ☺9am-6pm Mon-Fri) as well as Flixbus (https://global.flixbus.com) and some others, arrive at and depart from the small **Grand Hotel Bus Stop** in front of the main train station.

There are regular coach services throughout the day to Prague (210Kč, 2½ hours), Bratislava (180Kč, two hours), Olomouc (96Kč, one hour) and Vienna (200Kč, two hours).

TRAIN
Brno's hulking **train station** (Brno hlavní nádraží; www.cd.cz; Nádraží 1) is a major domestic and international train hub, with regular services to Prague, as well as Vienna, Bratislava and Budapest. There are domestic and international ticket offices, train information, a left-luggage office and lockers, as well as several places to stock up on train provisions.

Express trains to Brno depart Prague's Hlavní nádraží (main train station; 219Kč, three hours) every couple of hours during the day. Brno is a handy junction for onward train travel to Vienna (220Kč, two hours) and Bratislava (210Kč, 1½ hours).

Olomouc

POP 100,160
Olomouc is a sleeper. Practically unknown outside the Czech Republic and underappreciated at home, the city is surprisingly majestic. The main square is among the country's nicest, surrounded by historic buildings and blessed with a Unesco-protected trinity column. The evocative central streets are dotted with beautiful churches, testament to the city's long history as a bastion of the Catholic church. Explore the foundations of ancient Olomouc Castle at the must-see Archdiocesan Museum, then head for one of the city's many pubs or microbreweries, fuelled by the thousands of students who attend university here. Don't forget to try the cheese, *Olomoucký sýr* or *tvarůžky*, reputedly the smelliest in the Czech Republic.

◉ Sights

Holy Trinity Column   MONUMENT
(Sloup Nejsvětější Trojice; Horní náměstí) The town's pride and joy is this 35m-high baroque sculpture that dominates Horní náměstí and is a popular meeting spot for

local residents. The trinity column was built between 1716 and 1754 and is allegedly the biggest single baroque sculpture in Central Europe. In 2000 the column was added to Unesco's World Heritage Site list.

Archdiocesan Museum
MUSEUM

(Arcidiecézni muzeum; ☑ 585 514 111; www.olmuart. cz; Václavské náměstí 3; adult/concession 70/35Kč; ☺ 10am-6pm Tue-Sun; ☖ 2, 3, 4, 6) The impressive holdings of the Archdiocesan Museum trace the history of Olomouc back 1000 years. The thoughtful layout, with helpful English signage, takes you through the original Romanesque foundations of Olomouc Castle, and highlights the cultural and artistic development of the city during the Gothic and baroque periods. Don't miss the magnificent Troyer Coach, definitely the stretch limo of the 18th century. Entry is free on Sundays.

St Moritz Cathedral
CHURCH

(Chrám sv Mořice; ☑ 585 223 179; www.moric-olomouc.cz; Opletalova 10; ☺ tower 9am-5pm, from noon Sun; ☖ 2, 3, 4, 6) **FREE** This vast Gothic cathedral is Olomouc's original parish church, built between 1412 and 1540. The western tower is a remnant of its 13th-century predecessor. The cathedral's amazing sense of peace is shattered every September with an International Organ Festival; the cathedral's organ is Moravia's mightiest. The tower (more than 200 steps) provides the best view in town.

Civil Defence Shelter
HISTORIC SITE

(Kryt Civilní Obrany; www.tourism.olomouc.eu; Bezručovy sady; 30Kč; ☺ tours 10am, 1pm & 4pm Sat mid-Jun–Sep) Olomouc is all about centuries-old history, but this more-recent relic of the Cold War is also worth exploring on a guided tour. The shelter was built between 1953 and 1956 and was designed to keep a lucky few protected from the ravages of a chemical or nuclear strike. Book tours at the Olomouc Information Centre (p173), which is also where they start.

🛏 Sleeping

The old centre has plenty of reasonably priced pensions, guesthouses and a couple of very good hostels.

Long Story Short
HOSTEL €

(☑ 606 090 469; www.longstoryshort.cz; Koželužská 31; dm 340-400, r 1100-2000Kč; ☻ 🛜) Clean, sleek, modern hostel has won international design awards for its creative fusion of old and new. Sleeping is in six- to 10-bed dorms, and private single and double rooms.

Facilities include an in-house bar, co-working space and garden terrace. Breakfast costs an additional 130Kč; laundry costs 200Kč.

Poets' Corner Hostel
HOSTEL €

(☑ 777 570 730; www.poetscornerhostel.com; 4th fl, Sokolská 1; dm 300-400, s/d 750/850Kč; ☻ 🛜; ☖ 2, 3, 4, 6) The couple who mind this friendly and exceptionally well-run hostel are a wealth of local information. There are eight-bed dorms, as well as private singles and doubles. Bicycles can be hired for 100Kč per day. In summer there's sometimes a two-night minimum stay, but Olomouc is worth it, and there's plenty of day-trip information on offer.

★ Penzión Na Hradě
PENSION €€

(☑ 585 203 231; www.penzionnahrade.cz; Michalská 4; s/d 1490/1890Kč; ☻ ❄ 🛜) In terms of price:quality ratio, this may be Olomouc's best deal, and worth the minor splurge if you can swing it. The location, tucked away in the shadow of St Michael's Church, is ideally central and the sleek, cool rooms have a professional design touch. There's also a small garden terrace for relaxing out the back. Book ahead in summer.

🍴 Eating & Drinking

With its large population of students, Olomouc's food options tend towards the simple and affordable. Most restaurants offer a good lunch deal of soup and main course for not much more than 100Kč. Nearly every restaurant will offer some version of the local cheese (*Olomoucký sýr* or *tvarůžky*), a stringy, fragrant dairy product that makes for either a filling starter or an accompaniment to beer.

Entree Restaurant
CZECH €€

(☑ 585 312 440; www.entree-restaurant.cz; Ostravská 1; mains 285-445Kč, 5-course tasting menu from 950Kč; ☺ 11am-2pm & 5pm-midnight; ❄ 🛜 🍴) The highest-rated restaurant in Olomouc and among the top 10 in the country, Entree emphasises locally sourced ingredients and natural materials. Award-winning Czech chef Přemek Forejt deconstructs and rearranges traditional Czech dishes in ways that make them unrecognisable yet memorable. The out-of-centre location is a 15-minute walk east of the train station or a short taxi ride. Reserve online.

Svatováclavský Pivovar
CZECH €€

(☑ 585 207 517; www.svatovaclavsky-pivovar.cz; Mariánská 4; mains 180-290Kč; ☺ 10am-11pm Mon & Tue, to midnight Wed-Fri, 11am-midnight Sat, 11am-

10pm Sun; 🛜; 🍴 2, 3, 4, 6) This warm and inviting pub makes its own beer and serves plateloads of Czech specialities such as duck confit and beer-infused *guláš* (goulash). Stop by for lunch mid-week for an excellent-value soup and main course for around 150Kč. Speciality beers include unpasteurised wheat and cherry-flavoured varieties.

★ Cafe 87
CAFE

(📞 724 211 009; Denisova 47; coffee 40Kč; ⏰ 7am-8pm, from 8am Sat & Sun; 🛜; 🍴 2, 3, 4, 6) Locals come in droves to this funky cafe beside the Olomouc Museum of Modern Art for coffee and its famous chocolate pie (50Kč). Some people still apparently prefer the dark chocolate to the white chocolate. When will they learn? It's a top spot for breakfast and toasted sandwiches too. Seating is over two floors and there's a rooftop terrace.

The Black Stuff
PUB

(📞 774 697 909; www.blackstuff.cz; 1 máje 19; ⏰ 5pm-2am, to 3am Sat, to midnight Sun; 🛜; 🍴 2, 3, 4, 6) Cosy, old-fashioned Irish bar with several beers on tap and a large and growing collection of single malts and other choice tipples. Attracts a mixed crowd of students, locals and visitors.

☆ Entertainment

Jazz Tibet Club
LIVE MUSIC

(📞 777 746 887; https://jazztibet.cz/en; Sokolská 48; tickets 100-300Kč; ⏰ 11am-midnight Mon-Sat; 🛜) Blues, jazz and world music, including occasional international acts, feature at this popular spot, which also incorporates a good restaurant and wine bar. See the website for the program during your visit. Buy tickets at the venue on the day of the show or in advance at the Olomouc Information Centre.

Moravian Philharmonic Olomouc
CLASSICAL MUSIC

(Moravská Filharmonie Olomouc; 📞 585 206 514; www.mfo.cz; Horní náměstí 23; tickets 90-270Kč) The local orchestra presents regular concerts and hosts Olomouc's International Organ Festival. Buy tickets one week in advance at the Olomouc Information Centre or at the venue one hour before the performance starts.

ℹ Information

Olomouc Information Centre (Olomoucká Informační Služba; 📞 585 513 385; www.tourism.olomouc.eu; Horní náměstí; ⏰ 9am-7pm) Located in the historic town hall and very helpful when it comes to securing maps, brochures and tickets for events around town. It also offers one-hour sightseeing tours of the city centre (70Kč) several times daily from mid-June to September.

ℹ Getting There & Away

BUS

Olomouc is connected by around 15 buses daily to/from Brno (96Kč, 1¼ hours). Regional bus services are excellent. The best way of getting to Prague, however, is by train. The **bus station** (Autobusové nádraží Olomouc; 📞 585 313 848; www.vlak-bus.cz; Sladkovského 142/37; 🍴 1, 2, 3, 4, 5, 6, 7) is located just behind the train station, about 2km east of the centre.

TRAIN

Olomouc is on a main international rail line, with regular services from both Prague (250Kč, two to three hours) and Brno (110Kč, 1½ hours). From Prague, you can take normal trains or faster, high-end private trains run by **RegioJet** (Student Agency; 📞 539 000 931; www.regiojet.cz; Jeremenkova 23; ⏰ 5.15am-8.30pm, from 6.15am Sat & Sun; 🍴 1, 2, 3, 4, 5, 6, 7) or **LEO Express** (📞 220 311 700; www.le.cz; Jeremenkova 23, Main Train Station; ⏰ 8am-7.50pm; 🍴 1, 2, 3, 4, 5, 6, 7). Buy tickets online or at ticket counters in either train station. Olomouc's **train station** (Olomouc hlavní nádraží; www.cd.cz; Jeremenkova; 🍴 1, 2, 3, 4, 5, 6, 7) is around 2km east of the centre and accessible via several tram lines.

SURVIVAL GUIDE

ℹ Directory A–Z

ACCOMMODATION

Accommodation in the Czech Republic runs the gamut from summer campsites to family pensions to hotels at all price levels. Places that pull in international tourists – Prague, Karlovy Vary and Český Krumlov – are the most expensive and beds can be hard to find during peak periods, but there's rarely any problem finding a place to stay in smaller towns.

LEGAL MATTERS

Foreigners in the Czech Republic are subject to the laws of the host country. Most visitors aren't likely to have any issues. Handy things to know:
➡ The legal blood-alcohol level for drivers is zero.
➡ Cannabis occupies a grey area; it's been decriminalised but is not technically legal. Police will rarely hassle someone for smoking a joint, but always exercise discretion and do not smoke indoors. Buying and selling drugs of any kind, including cannabis, is illegal.

LGBT+ TRAVELLERS

The Czech Republic is a relatively tolerant destination for gay and lesbian travellers. Homosexuality is legal, and since 2006, same-sex couples have been able to form registered partnerships.

Prague has a lively gay scene and is home to Eastern Europe's biggest gay pride march (www.praguepride.cz), normally held in August. Attitudes are less accepting outside the capital, but even here homosexual couples are not likely to suffer overt discrimination.

Useful websites include Prague Saints (www.praguesaints.cz) and Travel Gay Europe (www.travelgayeurope.com).

MONEY

ATMs are widely available. Credit and debit cards are accepted in most hotels and restaurants.

OPENING HOURS

Most places adhere roughly to the following hours.

Banks 9am to 4pm Monday to Friday; some 9am to 1pm Saturday

Bars 11am to 1am Tuesday to Saturday; shorter hours Sunday and Monday

Museums 9am to 6pm Tuesday to Sunday; some close or have shorter hours October to April

Restaurants 11am to 11pm; kitchens close 10pm

Shops 9am to 6pm Monday to Friday, some 9am to 1pm Saturday; tourist shops and malls have longer hours and are normally open daily.

PUBLIC HOLIDAYS

Banks, offices, department stores and some shops are closed on public holidays. Restaurants, museums and tourist attractions tend to stay open, though many may close on the first working day after a holiday.

New Year's Day 1 January

Easter Monday March/April

Labour Day 1 May

Liberation Day 8 May

Sts Cyril & Methodius Day 5 July

Jan Hus Day 6 July

Czech Statehood Day 28 September

Republic Day 28 October

Struggle for Freedom & Democracy Day 17 November

Christmas Eve (Generous Day) 24 December

Christmas Day 25 December

St Stephen's Day 26 December

TELEPHONE

Most Czech telephone numbers, both landline and mobile (cell), have nine digits. There are no city or area codes. To call any Czech number, simply dial the unique nine-digit number.

➺ To call abroad from the Czech Republic, dial the international access code (00), then the country code, then the area code (minus any initial zero) and the number.

➺ To dial the Czech Republic from abroad, dial your country's international access code, then 420 (the Czech Republic country code) and then the unique nine-digit local number.

TOURIST INFORMATION

Czech Tourism (www.czechtourism.com) maintains a wonderful website, with a trove of useful information. There's a large English-language section on festivals and events, accommodation and tips on what to see and do all around the country. **Prague City Tourism** (www.prague.eu) and **GoToBrno** (www.gotobrno.cz) are also useful.

Nearly all cities have decent tourist offices. If you turn up in a city that doesn't have a tourist office, you're pretty much on your own. Local bookshops or newsagents can sometimes sell a local map.

❶ Getting There & Away

AIR

Prague's Václav Havel Airport (p158) is one of Central Europe's busiest airports, and daily flights connect the Czech capital with major cities throughout Europe, the UK, the Middle East and Asia. From April to October, direct flights link Prague to a handful of cities in North America.

LAND

The country is integrated into the European road and rail network. Trains and buses to neighbouring countries are frequent, and road travel poses no unusual problems.

Bus

Several bus companies offer long-distance coach services connecting cities in the Czech Republic to cities around Europe. For travel to and from Prague, nearly all international buses (and most domestic services) use the city's renovated and user-friendly Florenc bus station (p158).

Important international bus operators with extensive networks and ticket offices at the Florenc bus station include Flixbus (p158), RegioJet (p158) and Eurolines (p158).

The Florenc bus station website has a good timetable of buses, both foreign and domestic, arriving in and departing from the capital.

Car & Motorcycle

The Czech Republic has generally good roads, with some limited stretches of four-lane highway.

➺ All drivers, if stopped by the police, must be prepared to show the vehicle's registration, proof of insurance (a 'green' card) and a valid driving licence.

➔ In lieu of paying highway tolls, all motorists are required to display a special prepaid sticker (dálniční známka) on car windscreens. Buy these at large petrol stations near the border or immediately after crossing the border. A sticker valid for 10 days costs 310Kč, for 30 days 440Kč, and for a year 1500Kč.

Train

The Czech national railway, České dráhy (ČD; www.cd.cz) forms part of the European rail grid, and there are decent connections to neighbouring countries. Frequent international trains connect German cities like Berlin and Dresden with Prague. From here, fast trains head southeast to Brno, with excellent onward service to points in Austria, Slovakia and Hungary. The German Rail (www.bahn.de) website has a handy international train timetable.

In addition to ČD, two private railways operate in the Czech Republic and service international destinations.

➔ RegioJet (p158) Train service to select destinations in the Czech Republic, with onward service to Slovakia. Identified as 'RJ' on timetables.

➔ LEO Express (p158) Train service to select destinations in the Czech Republic, with onward coach service to destinations in Poland, Slovakia and Ukraine. Identified as 'LEO' on timetables.

ⓘ Getting Around

AIR

Czech Airlines (www.csa.cz) runs a handful of flights weekly from Prague to the eastern city of Ostrava, but the country is small enough that air travel is usually impractical. There are no flights between Prague and Brno.

BICYCLE

Cycling is a popular weekend activity in nice weather, though its full potential has yet to be realised. Southern Moravia, especially along a marked wine trail that runs between vineyards, is ideal for cycling.

➔ A handful of large cities, including Prague, do have dedicated cycling lanes, but these are often half-hearted efforts and leave cyclists at the mercy of often-aggressive drivers.

➔ It's possible to hire or buy bicycles in many major towns, though not all. Rates average from 400Kč to 600Kč per day.

➔ A helpful website for getting started and planning a cyclist route in the Czech Republic is Cyclists Welcome (Cyklisté vítáni; www.cykliste vitani.cz).

BUS

Long-haul and regional bus services are an important part of the transport system in the Czech Republic. Buses are often faster, cheaper and more convenient than trains, and are especially handy for accessing areas where train services are poor, such as Karlovy Vary and Český Krumlov.

➔ Bus stations are usually (but not always) located near train stations to allow for easy transfer between the two. In Prague, the Florenc bus station (p158) is the main departure and arrival point, though some buses arrive at and depart from smaller stations along outlying metro lines.

➔ Check the online timetable at IDOS (http://jizdnirady.idnes.cz) to make sure you have the right station.

➔ RegioJet (p158) and Flixbus (p158) are popular private carriers with extensive national networks to key destinations, including Prague, Brno, Karlovy Vary, Plzeň and Český Krumlov. Buy tickets online or at station ticket windows.

CAR & MOTORCYCLE

Driving has compelling advantages. With your own wheels, you're free to explore off-the-beaten-track destinations and small towns. That said, driving in the Czech Republic is not ideal, and if you have the chance to use alternatives like the train and bus, these can be more relaxing options.

➔ Roads, including the most important highways, are in the midst of a long-term rebuilding process, and delays and detours are more the norm than the exception.

➔ Most highways are two lanes, and can be choked with cars and trucks. When calculating arrival times, figure on covering about 60km to 70km per hour.

TRAIN

The Czech rail network is operated by **České dráhy** (ČD, Czech Rail; ☑ national hotline 221 111 122; www.cd.cz). Train travel is generally comfortable, reasonably priced and efficient. Trains are particularly useful for covering relatively long distances between major cities, such as between Prague and Brno, or Prague and Olomouc.

Two smaller private operators, RegioJet (p158) and LEO Express (p158), operate daily high-speed trains from Prague to the Moravian cities of Olomouc and Ostrava, with the possibility to connect to onward coach services to Slovakia and Poland. Timetable information for all trains is available online at IDOS (http://jizdnirady.idnes.cz).

1. Lenin statue in Grūtas Park (p258), Lithuania 2. Buzludzha, designed by Georgi Soilov, Bulgaria 3. Museum of Yugoslavia (p395; designed by Mihailo Janković), Belgrade, Serbia 4. Bunk'Art 2 (p45), Tirana, Albania

MARIANNA IANOVSKA/SHUTTERSTOCK ©

Relics of Communism

Eastern Europe is still strongly associated in the Western consciousness with communism and the Cold War. The Soviet Union lasted for around 70 years, to 1991. Communism in Central Europe was shorter, about four decades, but equally impactful.

Where Communism Lives On

Communism is gone but some places apparently never got the memo. At Lenin's Mausoleum (p363) in Moscow, a waxy Lenin still lays in state much as he did for years during Soviet times. Transdniestr (p273), formally part of Moldova, is a living relic of Soviet history. The capital of Belarus, Minsk (p63), was rebuilt in the 1950s in Stalinist style after WWII destruction and has barely changed since.

Making Light of Dark Times

Eastern Europe, generally, is known for harbouring a dark sense of humour, and communist-era 'theme parks' provide a way of processing the past through laughter. At Budapest's Memento Park (p201), once-imposing statues of Lenin look forlorn in a haphazard graveyard. Grūtas Park (aka 'Stalin Land'; p258), in Lithuania, is an assemblage of Soviet-era statuary standing jarringly in a leafy park.

Museums to the Madness

Many cities across Eastern Europe have excellent museums dedicated to life under communism. The Museum of Yugoslavia (p395), in Belgrade, is an especially fascinating look at life in Yugoslavia; Tito, himself, is entombed here. The Bunk'Art (p45), in the Albanian capital Tirana, is a creative conversion of a massive Cold War bunker into a history and art museum.

Memorable Monuments

Communists went crazy for monuments back in the day. The mother of all monuments might be Bulgaria's **Buzludzha**, a crumbling dome near Shipka, in the middle of nowhere.

Estonia

POP 1.3 MILLION

Best Places to Eat

➡ Mr Jakob (p190)

➡ Manna La Roosa (p187)

➡ Ö (p187)

➡ Rataskaevu 16 (p187)

➡ Retro (p195)

Best Places to Stay

➡ Pädaste Manor (p194)

➡ Antonius Hotel (p192)

➡ Georg Ots Spa Hotel (p195)

➡ Hektor Design Hostel (p191)

➡ Tabinoya (p186)

Why Go?

Estonia doesn't have to struggle to find a point of difference; it's completely unique. It shares a similar geography and history with Latvia and Lithuania, but culturally it's distinct. Its closest ethnic and linguistic buddy is Finland, though 50 years of Soviet rule in Estonia have separated the two. For the last 300 years Estonia has been linked to Russia, but the two states have as much in common as a barn swallow and a bear (their respective national symbols).

With a newfound confidence, singular Estonia has crept from under the Soviet blanket and leapt into the arms of Europe. The love affair is mutual. Europe has fallen head over heels for the charms of Tallinn and its Unesco-protected Old Town. Put simply, Tallinn is now one of the continent's most captivating cities. And in overcrowded Europe, Estonia's sparsely populated countryside and extensive swathes of forest provide spiritual sustenance for nature-lovers.

When to Go
Tallinn

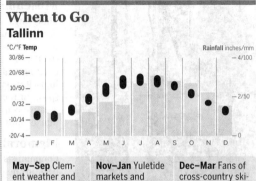

May–Sep Clement weather and summer festivals make this the best time to visit.

Nov–Jan Yuletide markets and the raising of a Christmas tree on Tallinn's main square.

Dec–Mar Fans of cross-country skiing should make for Otepää, the unofficial winter capital.

Entering the Country

Seventeen European airlines have scheduled services to Tallinn year-round, with additional routes and airlines added in summer. There are reliable bus services between Estonia and the other Baltic states.

Estonia is easily accessed by boat from major port cities around the Baltic Sea. Ferries run from Tallinn to Helsinki, St Petersburg, Mariehamn and Stockholm.

There are no border checks when driving between Estonia and Latvia thanks to the Schengen agreement.

Trains between Estonia and Latvia route through Valga, but services aren't linked. Estonian trains operated by Elron (www.elron.ee) head to Elva, Tartu and Tallinn from Valga. There is direct service to Tallinn from St Petersburg and Moscow.

ITINERARIES

Three Days

Base yourself in Tallinn (p181) and spend your first day exploring Old Town. The following day, venture to the other side of the tracks to Telliskivi Creative City (p184) before heading out of town to the wonderful Estonian Open-Air Museum (p184). On your last day, hire a car or take a day tour to Lahemaa National Park (p189).

One Week

Spend your first three days in Tallinn (p181), then allow a full day to explore Lahemaa (p189) before bedding down within the national park. The following day, continue on to Tartu (p191) for a night or two and then finish up in Pärnu (p192).

Essential Food & Drink

Estonian gastronomy mixes Nordic, Russian and German influences, and prizes local and seasonal produce.

Desserts On the sweet side, you'll find delicious chocolates, marzipan and cakes.

Favourite drinks *Õlu* (beer) is the favourite alcoholic drink. Popular brands include Saku and A Le Coq, and aficionados should seek out the product of the local microbreweries such as Tallinn's Põhjala. Other tipples include vodka (Viru Valge and Saremaa are the best-known local brands) and Vana Tallinn, a syrupy sweet liqueur, also available in a cream version.

Other favourites Black bread, sauerkraut, black pudding, smoked meat and fish, creamy salted butter and sour cream, which is served with almost everything.

Pork and potatoes The traditional stodgy standbys, prepared a hundred different ways.

Seasonal Summer menus feature berries in sweet and savoury dishes; forest mushrooms are the craze in autumn.

AT A GLANCE

Area 45,339 sq km

Capital Tallinn

Country Code ☏ 372

Currency euro (€)

Emergency Police ☏ 110; ambulance & fire ☏ 112

Language Estonian

Time Eastern European Time (GMT/UTC plus two hours)

Visas Not required for citizens of the EU, USA, Canada, Japan, New Zealand and Australia.

ESTONIA

Sleeping Price Ranges

The following price ranges refer to a double room in high (but not necessarily peak) season.

€ less than €35

€€ €35–100

€€€ more than €100

Eating Price Ranges

The following Estonian price ranges refer to a standard main course.

€ less than €10

€€ €10–15

€€€ more than €15

Estonia Highlights

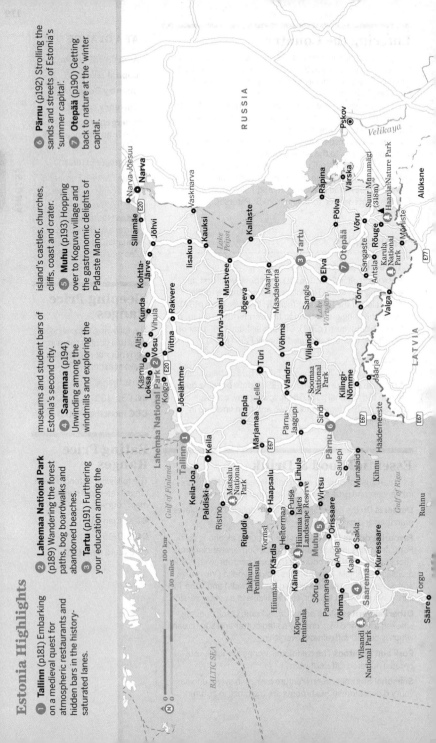

1 Tallinn (p181) Embarking on a medieval quest for atmospheric restaurants and hidden bars in the history-saturated lanes.

2 Lahemaa National Park (p189) Wandering the forest paths, bog boardwalks and abandoned beaches.

3 Tartu (p191) Furthering your education among the

museums and student bars of Estonia's second city.

4 Saaremaa (p194) Unwinding among the windmills and exploring the

island's castles, churches, cliffs, coast and crater.

5 Muhu (p193) Hopping over to Koguva village and the gastronomic delights of Pädaste Manor.

6 Pärnu (p192) Strolling the sands and streets of Estonia's 'summer capital'.

7 Otepää (p190) Getting back to nature at the 'winter capital'.

TALLINN

POP 426,540

No longer the plaything of greater powers – Danish, Swedish, Polish, German and Soviet – Tallinn is now a proud European capital with an allure all of its own. It's lively yet peaceful, absurdly photogenic and bursting with wonderful sights – ancient churches, medieval streetscapes and noble merchants' houses. Throw in delightful food and vibrant modern culture and it's no wonder Tallinn seems in danger of being loved to death, especially after a few cruise ships dock. But it's one of those blessed places that seems to cope with all the attention.

Despite the boom of 21st-century development, Tallinn safeguards the fairy-tale charms of its Unesco-listed Old Town – one of Europe's most complete walled cities. Some examples of exuberant post-Soviet development aside, the city clearly realises it's better to be classy than brassy. Hence the blossoming of first-rate restaurants, atmospheric hotels and a well-oiled tourist machine that makes visiting a breeze.

◉ Sights

◉ Old Town

Tallinn's medieval Old Town (Vanalinn) is without doubt the country's most fascinating locality. It's divided into Toompea (the upper town) and the lower town, which is still surrounded by much of its 2.5km defensive wall.

Toompea

Lording it over the Lower Town is the ancient hilltop citadel of Toompea. In German times this was the preserve of the feudal nobility, literally looking down on the traders and lesser beings below. It's now almost completely given over to government buildings, churches, embassies and shops selling amber knick-knacks and fridge magnets.

Alexander Nevsky Orthodox Cathedral   CATHEDRAL

(⌨644 3484; http://tallinnanevskikatedraal.eu; Lossi plats 10; ☉8am-7pm, to 4pm winter) The positioning of this magnificent, onion-domed Russian Orthodox cathedral (completed in 1900) at the heart of the country's main administrative hub was no accident: the church was one of many built in the last part of the 19th century as part of a general wave of Russification in the empire's Baltic provinces. Orthodox believers come here

in droves, alongside tourists ogling the interior's striking icons and frescoes. Quiet, respectful, demurely dressed visitors are welcome, but cameras aren't.

St Mary's Lutheran Cathedral   CHURCH

(Tallinna Püha Neitsi Maarja Piiskoplik toomkirik; ⌨644 4140; www.toomkirik.ee; Toom-Kooli 6; church/tower €2/5; ☉9am-5pm May & Sep, to 6pm Jun-Aug, shorter hrs/days rest of year) Tallinn's cathedral (now Lutheran, originally Catholic) had been initially built by the Danes by at least 1233, although the exterior dates mainly from the 15th century, with the tower completed in 1779. This impressive building was a burial ground for the rich and titled, and the whitewashed walls are decorated with the elaborate coats of arms of Estonia's noble families. Fit view-seekers can climb the tower.

Lower Town

Picking your way along the lower town's narrow, cobbled streets is like strolling into the 15th century – not least due to the tendency of local businesses to dress their staff up in medieval garb. The most interesting street is Pikk (Long St), which starts at the Great Coast Gate and includes Tallinn's historic guild buildings.

Tallinn Town Hall   HISTORIC BUILDING

(Tallinna raekoda; ⌨645 7900; www.raekoda.tallinn.ee; Raekoja plats; adult/student €5/3; ☉10am-4pm Mon-Sat Jul & Aug, shorter hrs rest of year; ♿) Completed in 1404, this is the only surviving Gothic town hall in northern Europe. Inside, you can visit the Trade Hall (whose visitor book drips with royal signatures), the Council Chamber (featuring Estonia's oldest woodcarvings, dating from 1374), the vaulted Citizens' Hall, a yellow-and-black-tiled councillor's office and a small kitchen. The steeply sloped attic has displays on the building and its restoration. Details such as brightly painted columns and intricately carved wooden friezes give some sense of the original splendour.

★Town Hall Square   SQUARE

(Raekoja plats) In Tallinn all roads lead to Raekoja plats, the city's pulsing heart since markets began setting up here in the 11th century. One side is dominated by the Gothic town hall (p181), while the rest is ringed by pretty pastel-coloured buildings dating from the 15th to 17th centuries. Whether bathed in sunlight or sprinkled with snow, it's always a photogenic spot.

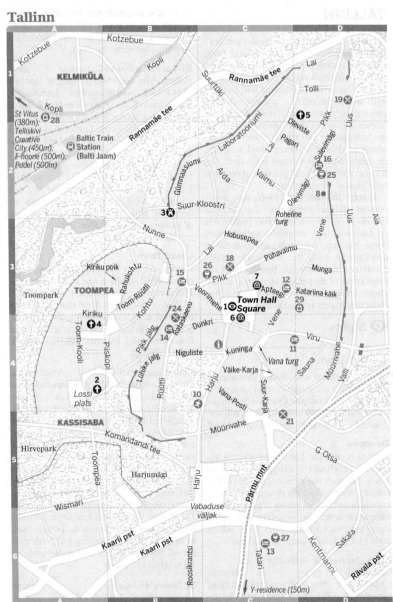

ESTONIA TALLINN

Town Council Pharmacy   HISTORIC BUILDING
(Raeapteek; ☎ 631 4860; www.raeapteek.ee; Raekoja plats 11; ◷10am-6pm Mon-Sat) Nobody's too sure on the exact date it opened but by 1422 this pharmacy was already on to its third owner, making it the oldest continually operating pharmacy in Europe. In 1583 Johann Burchardt took the helm, and a descendant with the same name ran the shop right up until 1913 – 10 generations in all! Inside there are painted beams and a small historical display, or you can just drop in to stock up on painkillers and prophylactics.

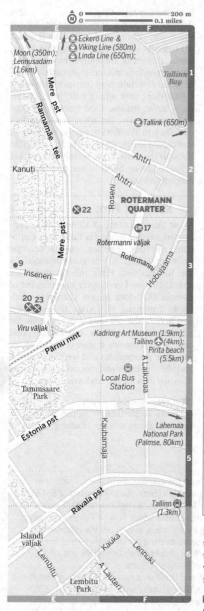

Tallinn

reaches a still-respectable 124m and you can take a tight, confined, 258-step staircase up the tower (adult/child €3/1) for wonderful views of Toompea and over the lower town's rooftops.

Lower Town Wall　　　　　　FORTRESS
(Linnamüür; ☎644 9867; Väike-Kloostri 1; adult/child €2/1; ☉11am-7pm Jun-Aug, shorter hrs/days rest of year) The most photogenic stretch of Tallinn's remaining walls connects nine towers lining the western edge of Old Town. Visitors can explore the barren nooks and crannies of three of them (there are modest displays on weaponry and castle-craft

St Olaf's Church　　　　　　CHURCH
(Oleviste kirik; ☎641 2241; www.oleviste.ee; Lai 50; ☉10am-6pm Apr-Jun & Sep-Oct, to 8pm Jul & Aug) From 1549 to 1625, when its 159m steeple was struck by lightning and burnt down, this (now Baptist) church was one of the tallest buildings in the world. The current spire

inside) with cameras at the ready for the red-rooftop views. The gardens outside the wall are pretty and relaxing.

👁 Kalamaja

Immediately northwest of the Old Town, this enclave of tumbledown wooden houses and crumbling factories swiftly transitioned into one of Tallinn's most interesting neighbourhoods thanks to local hipsters opening cafes and bars in abandoned warehouses and rickety storefronts. The intimidating hulk of Patarei Prison had seemed to cast a malevolent shadow over this part of town, so its transformation over the last several years has been nothing short of extraordinary.

★ Lennusadam   MUSEUM

(Seaplane Harbour; ☑ 620 0550; www.meremuuseum.ee; Vesilennuki 6; adult/child €14/7; ⊙ 10am-7pm daily May-Sep, to 6pm Tue-Sun Oct-Apr; P) Surrounded on two sides by island-dotted waters, Estonia has a rich maritime history, explored in this fascinating museum filled with interactive displays. When the building, with its triple-domed hangar, was completed in 1917, its reinforced-concrete shell frame construction was unique in the world. Resembling a classic Bond-villain lair, the vast space was completely restored and opened to the public in 2012. Highlights include exploring the cramped corridors of a 1930s naval submarine, and the ice-breaker and minehunter ships moored outside.

Telliskivi Creative City   AREA

(Telliskivi Loomelinnak; www.telliskivi.eu; Telliskivi 60a; ⊙ shops 10am-6pm Mon-Sat, 11am-5pm Sun; 🚶) Once literally on the wrong side of the tracks, this set of abandoned factory buildings is now Tallinn's most alternative shopping and entertainment precinct, with cafes, a bike shop, bars selling craft beer, graffiti walls, artist studios, food trucks and pop-up concept stores. But it's not only hipsters who flock to Telliskivi to peruse the fashion and design stores, drink espressos and riffle through the stalls at the weekly flea market – you're just as likely to see families rummaging and sipping.

👁 Kadriorg Park

About 2km east of the Old Town, this beautiful park's ample acreage is Tallinn's favourite patch of green. Together with the baroque Kadriorg Palace, it was commissioned by the Russian tsar Peter the Great for his wife Catherine I soon after his conquest of Estonia (Kadriorg means Catherine's Valley in Estonian). Nowadays the oak, lilac and horse chestnut trees provide shade for strollers and picnickers, the formal pond and gardens provide a genteel backdrop for romantic promenades and wedding photos, and the children's playground is a favourite off-leash area for the city's youngsters.

★ Kadriorg Art Museum   MUSEUM

(Kardrioru kunstimuuseum; ☑ 606 6400; www.kadriorumuuseum.ekm.ee; Kadriorg Palace, A

ESTONIAN OPEN-AIR MUSEUM

If tourists won't go to the countryside, let's bring the countryside to them. That's the modus operandi of this excellent sprawling complex (Eesti vabaõhumuuseum; ☑ 654 9101; www.evm.ee; Vabaõhumuuseumi tee 12, Rocca Al Mare; adult/child high season €10/7, low season €8/6; ⊙ 10am-8pm 23 Apr–28 Sep, to 5pm 29 Sep–22 Apr), where historic Estonian buildings have been plucked and transplanted among the tall trees. In summer the time-warping effect is highlighted by staff in period costume performing traditional activities among the wooden farmhouses and windmills. There's a chapel dating from 1699 and an old wooden tavern, Kolu Kõrts, serving traditional Estonian cuisine.

Activities such as weaving, blacksmithing, and traditional cooking are put on, kids love the horse-and-carriage rides (adult/child €9/6) and bikes can be hired (per hour €3). If you find yourself in Tallinn on Midsummer's Eve (23 June), come here to witness the traditional celebrations, bonfire and all.

To get here from the centre, take Paldiski mnt. When the road nears the water, veer right onto Vabaõhumuuseumi tee. Bus 21, which departs from the railway station (p189) at least hourly, stops right out front. Combined family tickets are available that include Tallinn Zoo (Tallinna loomaaed; ☑ 694 3300; www.tallinnzoo.ee; Paldiski mnt 145, Veskimetsa; adult/child €8/5; ⊙ 9am-8pm May-Aug, to 7pm Mar, Apr, Sep & Oct, to 5pm Nov-Feb), which is a 20-minute walk away.

Weizenbergi 37; adult/child €6.50/4.50; ⊙10am-6pm Tue & Thu-Sun, to 8pm Wed May-Sep, 10am-8pm Wed, to 5pm Thu-Sun Oct-Apr) Kadriorg Palace, a baroque beauty built by Peter the Great between 1718 and 1736, houses a branch of the Estonian Art Museum devoted to Dutch, German and Italian paintings from the 16th to the 18th centuries, and Russian works from the 18th to early 20th centuries (check out the decorative porcelain with communist imagery upstairs). The pink building is exactly as frilly and fabulous as a palace ought to be, and there's a handsome French-style formal garden at the rear.

★**Kumu**   GALLERY

(☑602 6000; www.kumu.ekm.ee; A Weizenbergi 34; adult/student €8/6; ⊙10am-6pm Wed & Fri-Sun, to 8pm Thu year-round, plus 10am-6pm Tue Apr-Sep) This futuristic, Finnish-designed, seven-storey building is a spectacular structure of limestone, glass and copper that's nicely integrated into the landscape. Kumu (the name is short for *kunstimuuseum,* or art museum) contains the country's largest repository of Estonian art as well as constantly changing contemporary exhibits. There's everything from venerable painted altarpieces to the work of contemporary Estonian artists such as Adamson-Eric.

◉ **Pirita**

Pirita's main claim to fame is that it was the base for the sailing events of the 1980 Moscow Olympics; international regattas are still held here. It's also home to Tallinn's largest and most popular beach.

Tallinn TV Tower   VIEWPOINT

(Tallinna teletorn; ☑686 3005; www.teletorn.ee; Kloostrimetsa tee 58a; adult/child €13/7; ⊙10am-6pm) Opened in time for the 1980 Olympics, this futuristic 314m tower offers brilliant views from its 22nd floor (175m). Press a button and frosted glass discs set in the floor suddenly clear, giving a view straight down. Once you're done gawping, check out the interactive displays in the space-age pods. Daredevils can try the exterior, 175m-high 'edge walk' (€30, 10am to 6pm).

🏃 **Activities**

Harju Ice Rink   ICE SKATING

(Harju tänava uisuplats; ☑56246739; www.uisuplats.ee; Harju; per hr adult/child €7/5; ⊙10am-10pm Dec-Mar; ⍟) Wrap up warmly to join the locals at Old Town's outdoor ice rink –

very popular in the winter months. You'll have earned a *hõõgvein* (mulled or 'glowing' wine) in the warm indoor cafe by the end of your skating session. Skate rental costs €3.

Sage Traveling   TOUR

(www.sagetraveling.com) This worldwide outfit bills itself as a European travel expert for disabled travellers. Its three-hour 'Essential Tallinn Accessible Walking Tour' thoughtfully traces a step-free route without missing out on the major sights.

☞ **Tours**

Tallinn Traveller Tours   TOURS

(☑58374800; www.traveller.ee) This outfit runs entertaining tours, including a two-hour Old Town walk departing from outside the tourist office (p188) (private groups of one to 15 people from €80), or there's a larger free tour (which also starts at the tourist office – you should tip the engaging guides). There are also ghost tours (€15), bike tours (from €19), pub crawls (€20) and day trips as far afield as Rīga (€55).

City Bike   CYCLING

(☑5111819; www.citybike.ee; Vene 33; ⊙10am-7pm, to 6pm Oct-Apr) This friendly den of cycle-monkeys offers 'Welcome to Tallinn' tours (€19, two hours) from 11am year-round that include Kadriorg and Pirita. 'Other Side' tours take in Kalamaja and Stroomi Beach (from €19, 2½ hours), while 'Countryside Cycling & Old Town Walking' tours head as far as the Open-Air Museum (€47, four hours). It also hires out bikes from €7/15 per hour/day.

Epic Bar Crawl   TOURS

(☑56243088; www.freetour.com; €15; ⊙10pm Thu-Sat) Billing itself as 'the most fun and disorderly pub crawl in Tallinn' (although somehow also the best organised), this five-hour tour includes a welcome beer or cider, a shot in each of three bars and entry to a nightclub. Epic Bar Crawl also offers particularly ignominious packages designed for stags. The meeting point is Red Emperor bar on Aia 10.

🛏 **Sleeping**

🛏 **Old Town**

★**Welcome Hostel**   HOSTEL €€

(☑650 4100; www.welcomehostel.ee; Rotermanni 12; dm/d from €15/47; ⍟) Plush beds, exposed brick walls, high ceilings and mid-century modern furnishings put this Rotermann

Quarter hostel at the top of the heap for cheaper picks in Tallinn. The 26 rooms sleep between two and 11 people and each floor has a fully-stocked kitchen. Snacks and drinks are available for purchase, and there are plenty of food options nearby.

Tabinoya HOSTEL €€

(☑ 632 0062; www.tabinoya.com; Nunne 1; dm/d from €17/50; @ 🛜) The Baltic's first Japanese-run hostel occupies the two top floors of a charming old building, with dorms (the four-person one is for females only) and a communal lounge at the top, and spacious private rooms, a kitchen and a sauna below. Bathroom facilities are shared. The vibe's a bit more comfortable and quiet than most of Tallinn's hostels. Book ahead.

Tallinn Backpackers HOSTEL €€

(☑ 644 0298; www.tallinnbackpackers.com; Olevimägi 11; dm/r from €10/72; @ 🛜) In an ideal Old Town location, this place has a global feel and a roll-call of traveller-happy features: a convivial common room, free wi-fi and lockers, cheap dinners, a games room with tabletop football, and a kitchen and laundry. There's also a regular roster of pub crawls and day trips to nearby attractions.

Old House Apartments APARTMENT €€€

(☑ 641 1464; www.oldhouseapartments.ee; Rataskaevu 16; apt from €109; 🅿 🛜) The name 'Old House' does poor justice to this wonderfully refurbished 14th-century merchant's house. It's been split into beautifully furnished apartments (including a spacious two-bedroom unit with traces of a medieval painted ceiling), and there are a further 20-odd units scattered around Old Town. All are in similar buildings, but the quality and facilities vary.

★ Hotel Cru HOTEL €€€

(☑ 611 7600; www.cruhotel.eu; Viru 8; s/d/ste €170/285/585; 🛜) Behind the pretty powder-blue facade of this boutique hotel you'll find 15 richly furnished rooms scattered along a rabbit warren of corridors. All make sensitive use of original 14th-century features such as timber beams and limestone walls, but the cheapest are a little snug. The attached restaurant prides itself as one of Tallinn's best.

🛏 City Centre

Monk's Bunk HOSTEL €

(☑ 636 3924; www.themonksbunk.com; Tatari 1; dm/r from €15/50; @ 🛜) The only monk we can imagine fitting in here, at Tallinn's

self-described 'Number One Party Hostel', is Friar Tuck. There are organised activities every night, including legendary pub crawls aimed at maximum intoxication (Wednesday to Sunday nights, €15, with shots at each bar). The facilities are good, with high ceilings, free lockers and underfloor heating in the bathrooms.

Y-residence APARTMENT €€

(☑ 5021477; www.facebook.com/YResidence; Pärnu mnt 32; apt from €65; 🛜) The 'Y' stands for 'yoga', which seems a strange name for a collection of clean-lined new apartments in several locations around Tallinn, until you realise the operators also run yoga, tai chi and meditation sessions. You can expect friendly staff, a basic kitchenette and, joy of joys, a washing machine!

Hotel Telegraaf HOTEL €€€

(☑ 600 0600; www.telegraafhotel.com; Vene 9; r €225-255; 🅿 ❄ 🛜 ⬚) This upmarket hotel in a converted 19th-century former telegraph station delivers style in spades. It boasts a spa, a pretty courtyard, an acclaimed restaurant, swanky modern-art decor, and smart, efficient service. 'Superior' rooms, in the older part of the building, have more historical detail but we prefer the marginally cheaper 'executive' rooms for their bigger proportions and sharp decor.

🍴 Eating

🍽 Old Town

Vegan Restoran V VEGAN €

(☑ 626 9087; www.veganrestoran.ee; Rataskaevu 12; mains €8-13; ☻ noon-11pm Sun-Thu, to 11.30pm Fri-Sat; 🖋) Visiting vegans are spoiled for choice in this wonderful restaurant. In summer everyone wants one of the four tables on the street, but the atmospheric interior is just as appealing. The food is excellent – expect the likes of quinoa and turnip cutlet with roasted garlic purée and spicy oven-baked seitan tacos.

Clayhills Gastropub PUB FOOD €€

(☑ 641 9312; www.clayhills.ee; Pikk 13; mains €10-20; ☻ 10am-midnight Sun-Wed, to 2am Thu-Sat; 🛜) With live bands, comfy couches, a stone-walled upstairs room and sunny summer terrace, Clayhills is a very pleasant place to take a break from a day's wandering of Old Town. It serves up quality grub too: try the miso/sesame-glazed duck breast, the wild mushroom risotto or the ribeye with chimichurri.

Rataskaevu 16 ESTONIAN €€

(☑ 642 4025; www.rataskaevu16.ee; Rataskaevu 16; mains €9-20; ⊙ noon-11pm Sun-Thu, to midnight Fri & Sat; ☞) If you've ever had a hankering for braised elk roast, this warm, stone-walled place, named simply for its Old Town address, can sate it. Although it's hardly traditional, plenty of Estonian faves fill the menu – fried Baltic herring, grilled pork tenderloin and Estonian cheeses among them. Finish, if you can, with a serve of the legendary warm chocolate cake.

Must Puudel CAFE €€

(☑ 5056258; www.facebook.com/mustpuudel; Müürivahe 20; mains €7-16; ⊙ 9am-11pm Sun-Tue, to 2am Wed-Sat; ☎) With eclectic retro furniture matched by an equally wide-roaming soundtrack, courtyard seating, excellent coffee, long opening hours and select nights of live music and DJs, the 'Black Poodle' must be Old Town's hippest cafe. It's also charming, welcoming and capable of slinging seriously good cocktails and casual meals.

★Manna La Roosa GASTRONOMY €€€

(☑ 620 0249; www.mannalaroosa.com; Vana-Viru 15; mains €15-23; ⊙ noon-11pm Sun-Tue, to 1am Wed-Thu, to 3am Fri-Sat) This restaurant-bar is truly a multi-sensory adventure. Housed in an old apothecary, the interior is a curated kaleidoscope of wacky sculptures, nonsensical paintings and plush furnishings, all sourced from around the world by revered Estonian designer Soho Fond. It's a lot to take in – thankfully the top-notch gastronomy, deliciously inventive cocktails and super-cool staff make it easy to linger.

★Tchaikovsky RUSSIAN, FRENCH €€€

(☑ 600 0600; www.telegraafhotel.com; Vene 9; mains €20-30; ⊙ 6-11pm; ☎) Located in a glassed-in pavilion within the Hotel Telegraaf (p186), Tchaikovsky offers a dazzling tableau of blinged-up chandeliers, gilt frames and greenery. Service is formal and faultless (as is the carefully contemporised menu of Franco-Russian classics) and the experience is capped by live chamber music. The €25 three-course weekday lunch is excellent value and there's terrace seating in summer.

★Tai Boh ASIAN €€€

(☑ 629 9218; www.taiboh.com; Vana-Viru 15; mains €11-24; ⊙ 5-11pm Mon-Thu, 5pm-1am Fri-Sat, 2-11pm Sun) Located above Manna La Roosa (p187), this superb pan-Asian eatery feels like a Brutalist-meets-Baroque fever dream. It's

hard to pick a focal point among the opulent kitsch...until your eye catches the chandelier adorned with mannequin arms and dove feathers. Images of historical icons span the ceiling – diners savour quality sashimi, curry or satay under the watchful eye of Barack Obama in the Dalai Lama's garb.

★Leib ESTONIAN €€€

(☑ 611 9026; www.leibresto.ee; Uus 31; mains €15-24; ⊙ noon-11pm Mon-Sat) *Leib* (Estonian black bread) is a thing of great beauty and quiet national pride, and you'll find a peerless rendition here: dense, moist, almost fruity in its Christmas-cake complexity. Thick-sliced and served with salt-flaked butter, it's the ideal accompaniment to the delightful new-Nordic ('new Estonian'?) food at this garden restaurant in the Old Town headquarters of Tallinn's Scottish club (really!).

✖ City Centre

★Ö NEW NORDIC €€€

(☑ 661 6150; www.restoran-o.ee; Mere pst 6e; degustation menus €59-76; ⊙ 6-11pm Mon-Sat, closed Jul) Award-winning Ö (pronounced 'er' and named for Estonia's biggest island, Saaremaa) has carved a unique space in Tallinn's culinary world, delivering inventive degustation menus showcasing seasonal Estonian produce. There's a distinct 'New Nordic' influence at play, deploying unusual ingredients such as fermented birch sap and spruce shoots, and the understated dining room nicely complements the theatrical but always delicious cuisine.

✖ Kalamaja

F-hoone PUB FOOD €

(☑ 53226855; www.fhoone.ee; Telliskivi 60a; mains €5-11; ⊙ kitchen 9am-11pm Mon-Sat, to 9pm Sun; ☎☞) The trailblazing watering hole of the uberhip Telliskivi complex (p184), the industrial-chic 'Building F' offers a quality menu of pasta, burgers, soups, salads and desserts in an always-lively atmosphere. Wash down your food with a craft beer from the extensive selection and remember to book a table on buzzing weekend evenings.

★Moon RUSSIAN €€€

(☑ 631 4575; www.restoranmoon.ee; Võrgu 3; mains €15-19; ⊙ noon-11pm Mon-Sat, 1-9pm Sun, closed some of Jul) Quietly but consistently the best restaurant in increasingly hip Kalamaja, Moon ('poppy') is a Tallinn gem, combining Russian and broader European influences to delicious effect. The staff are delightfully friendly and switched-on, the decor is cheerily whimsical, and dishes such as *piroshki* (little stuffed pies) and reputation-transforming chicken Kiev showcase a kitchen as dedicated to pleasure as to technical excellence.

✕ Pirita

★ NOA INTERNATIONAL €€€

(☑5080589; www.noaresto.ee; Ranna tee 3; mains €14-28; ⊙noon-11pm Mon-Thu, to midnight Fri & Sat, to 10pm Sun; 🖍) It's worth the trek out to the far side of Pirita to reach this top-notch waterside restaurant, which consistently backs up its elevated reputation. Housed in a stylish low-slung pavilion with superb views over Tallinn Bay to Old Town, it plays knowledgeably with Asian influences while keeping a focus on the best Estonian and European ingredients and techniques.

🍷 Drinking & Nightlife

★ No Ku Klubi BAR

(☑631 3929; Pikk 5; ⊙noon-1am Mon-Thu, to 3am Fri, 2pm-3am Sat, 6pm-1am Sun) A nondescript red-and-blue door, a key-code to enter, a clubbable atmosphere of regulars lounging in mismatched armchairs – could this be Tallinn's ultimate 'secret' bar? Once the surreptitious haunt of artists in Soviet times, it's now free for all to enter – just ask one of the smokers outside for the code. Occasional evenings of low-key music and film are arranged.

★ Levist Väljas BAR

(☑504 6048; www.facebook.com/levistvaljas; Olevimägi 12; ⊙5pm-3am Sun-Thu, to 6am Fri & Sat) Inside this much-loved Tallinn cellar bar (usually the last pit stop of the night) you'll find broken furniture, cheap booze and a refreshingly motley crew of friendly punks, grunge kids and anyone else who strays from the well-trodden tourist path. The discreet entrance is down a flight of stairs.

St Vitus CRAFT BEER

(☑655 5354; www.vitus.ee; Telliskivi 61b; beers from €3.50, mains €7-11; ⊙noon-9pm Sun-Mon, to 11pm Tue-Thu, to 2am Fri-Sat) Friendly staff, tasty food and ultra-slick Scandi design are all an added bonus to the fantastic craft beers at this hip Telliskivi pub. You'll find a vast selection of Estonian brews, plus several from around Europe and a handful from the US and Asia. Cider- and wine-lovers are looked after, too, with enough selection to appease a range of tastes.

Pudel BAR

(☑58664496; www.pudel.ee; Telliskivi 60a; ⊙4pm-midnight Sun, Tue & Wed, 4pm-2am Thu & Fri, noon-2am Sat) Laid-back and intimate, this friendly spot in the Telliskivi Creative City (p184) complex offers plenty of craft beers on tap, plus great booze-soaking snacks to go with them.

X-Baar GAY & LESBIAN

(☑641 9478; www.facebook.com/xbaar; Tatari 1; ⊙4pm-1am Sun-Thu, to 4am Fri & Sat) Tucked behind a sex shop and a hostel, this stalwart of Tallinn's tiny gay scene hosts a mixed and welcoming crowd.

🛍 Shopping

★ Masters' Courtyard ARTS & CRAFTS

(Meistrite Hoov; www.hoov.ee; Vene 6; ⊙10am-6pm) Archetypal of Tallinn's amber-suspended medieval beauty, this cobbled 13th-century courtyard offers rich pickings – a cosy chocolaterie/cafe, a guesthouse and artisans' stores and workshops selling quality ceramics, glass, jewellery, knitwear, woodwork and candles.

Balti Jaama Turg MARKET

(Baltic Station Market; https://astri.ee/bjt; Kopli 1; ⊙9am-7pm Mon-Sat, to 5pm Sun) The gentrification of the train station precinct is manifest in this sleek market complex, where niche food vendors trade from tidy huts on the former site of a famed but slightly seedy outdoor market. There's also a supermarket, meat, dairy and seafood halls, green grocers, fashion retailers, a gym and underground parking.

ℹ Information

Tallinn Tourist Information Centre (☑645 7777; www.visittallinn.ee; Niguliste 2; ⊙9am-7pm Mon-Sat, to 6pm Sun Jun-Aug, shorter hrs rest of year) Has a full range of brochures, maps, event schedules and other info for Tallinn and for Estonia generally.

ℹ Getting There & Away

BUS

Regional and international buses depart from Tallinn's **Central Bus Station** (Tallinna bussijaam; ☑12550; www.bussijaam.ee; Lastekodu 46; ⊙ticket office 7am-9pm Mon-Sat, 8am-8pm Sun), about 2km southeast of Old Town and linked by two tram lines and eight buses. Services depart from here for Latvia, Lithuania, Poland and other European destinations.

The national bus network is extensive, linking Tallinn to pretty much everywhere you might care to go. All services are summarised on the extremely handy Tpilet site (www.tpilet.ee). The following are some of the main routes:

Tartu (€7 to €14, 2½ hours, at least every half-hour)

Pärnu (€6.50 to €11, two hours, at least hourly)

Kuressaare (€15 to €17, four hours, 11 daily)

TRAIN

The **Baltic Train Station** (Balti Jaam; Toompuiestee 35) is on the northwestern edge of Old Town; despite the name, it has no direct services to other Baltic states. **GoRail** (www.gorail.ee) runs a daily service stopping in Narva (€8.10, 2½ hours) en route to St Petersburg and Moscow.

Domestic routes are operated by **Elron** (www.elron.ee) and include the following destinations:

Narva (€11.50, 2¾ hours, three daily)

Tartu (€10.60, two to 2½ hours, eight daily)

Pärnu (€7.90, 2¼ hours, three daily)

ⓘ Getting Around

Tallinn has an excellent network of buses, trams and trolleybuses running from around 6am to 11pm or midnight. The major **local bus station** is beneath the Viru Keskus shopping centre, although some buses terminate their routes on the surrounding streets. All local public transport timetables are online at www.tallinn.ee.

Public transport is free for Tallinn residents, children under seven and adults with children under three. Others need to pay, either buying a paper ticket from the driver (€2 for a single journey, exact change required) or by using the e-ticketing system. Buy a Ühiskaart (a smart card, requiring a €2 deposit that can't be recouped within six months of validation) at an R-Kiosk, post office or the Tallinn City Government customer service desk, add credit, then validate the card at the start of each journey using the orange card-readers. E-ticket fares are €1.10/3/6 for an hour/day/five days.

The Tallinn Card (www.tallinncard.ee) includes free public transport on all services for the duration of its validity.

NORTHERN ESTONIA

Lahemaa National Park

Estonia's largest *rahvuspark* (national park), the 'Land of Bays' is 725 sq km of rural landscape and the perfect retreat from the nearby capital. A microcosm of Estonia's natural charms, the park takes in a stretch of deeply indented coast with several peninsulas and bays, plus 475 sq km of pine-fresh hinterland encompassing forest, lakes, rivers and peat bogs, and areas of historical and cultural interest.

There is an extensive network of forest trails for walkers, cyclists and even neo-knights on horseback. In winter, the park is transformed into a magical wonderland of snowy shores, frozen seas and sparkling black trees.

Loksa, the main town within the park, has a popular sandy beach but is otherwise rather down-at-heel. Võsu, the next largest settlement, is much nicer, with its long sandy beach and summertime bars. It fills up with young revellers in peak season, despite being just a somewhat overgrown village.

Palmse Manor   HISTORIC BUILDING

(☑ 55599977; www.palmse.ee; adult/child €9/7; ☉ 10am-6pm) Fully restored Palmse Manor is the showpiece of Lahemaa National Park, housing the visitor centre in its former stables. The pretty manor house (1720, rebuilt in the 1780s) is now a museum containing period furniture and clothing. Other estate buildings have also been restored and put to new use: the distillery is a hotel, the steward's residence is a guesthouse, the lakeside bathhouse is a summertime restaurant and the farm labourers' quarters became a tavern.

★**Merekalda**   APARTMENT **€€**

(☑ 323 8451; www.merekalda.ee; Neeme tee 2, Käsmu; r €49, apt €69-99; ☉ May-Sep; 🅿🛜) At the entrance to Käsmu, this peaceful retreat is set around a lovely large garden right on the bay. Ideally you'll plump for an apartment with a sea view and terrace, but you'll need to book ahead. Boat and bike hire are available.

Altja Kõrts   ESTONIAN **€€**

(☑ 324 0070; www.palmse.ee; Altja; mains €10-16; ☉ noon-8pm Apr-Sep) Set in a thatched, wooden building with a large terrace, this uber-rustic place is run by the same folks behind Palmse Manor. Operating in spring and summer, it serves delicious plates of traditional fare (baked pork with sauerkraut, for instance) at candlelit wooden tables. It's extremely atmospheric and a lot of fun.

ⓘ Information

Lahemaa National Park Visitor Centre

(☑ 329 5555; www.loodusegakoos.ee; ☉ 9am-5pm daily mid-May–mid-Sep, 9am-5pm Mon-Fri mid-Sep–mid-May) This excellent centre stocks the essential map of Lahemaa (€1.90), as well as information on hiking trails, accommodation and guiding services. It's worth starting your park visit with the free 17-minute film titled *Lahemaa – Nature and Man*.

❶ Getting There & Away

If you have your own wheels, Lahemaa National Park is an easy 45-minute drive from Tallinn or Rakvere. Note that most roads within the park are narrow and unmarked. There is next to nothing in terms of street lighting, so plan accordingly if arriving later in the day.

Direct buses can get you from Rakvere to Palmse, Altja, Võsu and Käsmu – but you'll still have to hike a considerable amount to get deep into nature.

❶ Getting Around

Lahemaa is best explored by car or bicycle as there are only limited bus connections within the park. The main bus routes through the park include Rakvere to Sagadi (€1.55 to €2.55, 45 minutes, one to four daily), Palmse (€1.75 to €2, 50 minutes, one daily), Altja (€1.90 to €2.25, one hour, most days), Võsu (€1.95 to €2.30, one hour, six daily) and Käsmu (€2.20 to €2.55, one hour, four daily).

SOUTHERN ESTONIA

Otepää

POP 1900

The small hilltop town of Otepää, 44km south of Tartu, is the centre of a picturesque area of forests, lakes and rivers. The district is beloved by Estonians for its natural beauty and its many possibilities for hiking, biking and swimming in summer, and cross-country skiing in winter. It's often referred to as Estonia's winter capital, and winter weekends here are busy and loads of fun. Some have even dubbed the area (tongue firmly in cheek) the 'Estonian Alps' – a reference not to its peaks but to its excellent ski trails. The 63km Tartu Ski Marathon kicks off here every February but even in summer you'll see professional athletes and enthusiasts hurtling around on roller skis.

The main part of Otepää is centred on the intersection of the Tartu, Võru and Valga highways, where you'll find the main square, shops and some patchy residential streets.

◎ Sights

Pühajärv　　　　　　　　　　　　LAKE
According to legend, 3.5km-long, 8.5m-deep Pühajärv (Holy Lake) was formed from the tears of the mothers who lost their sons in a battle of the *Kalevipoeg* epic. Its five islands are said to be their burial mounds. Pagan associations linger, with major midsummer festivities held here every year. The popular sandy **beach** (Ranna tee) on the northeastern shore has waterslides, a swimming pontoon, a cafe and lifeguards in summer.

🛏 Sleeping

Murakas　　　　　　　　　　HOTEL €€
(📞 731 1410; www.murakas.ee; Valga mnt 23a; s/d €50/60; 🅿 🤶) With only 10 bedrooms, Murakas is more like a large, friendly guesthouse than a hotel. Stripey carpets, blonde wood and balconies give the rooms a fresh feel and there's a similarly breezy breakfast room downstairs (breakfast €7 per person).

GMP Clubhotel　　　　　　APARTMENT €€€
(📞 799 7000; www.clubhotel.ee; Tennisevälja 1; apt from €105; 🅿 🤶) This super-slick lakeside block is decked out with kitchenettes, funky furniture, comfy beds and oversized photos. The icing on the cake is the luxurious pair of single-sex saunas on the top level, open in the evenings for those who fancy a sunset sweat.

🍴 Eating

Pühajärve Restaurant　　MODERN EUROPEAN €€
(📞 799 7000; www.clubhotel.ee; Tennisevälja 1; mains €13-27; ⏱ noon-10pm) From the 1960s to 1980s this was Otepää's most famous restaurant, but when the Soviet Union went down the gurgler it followed in its wake. The opening of the attached Clubhotel gave Pühajärve a new lease of life and it now offers a tasty menu on a terrace above its namesake.

★**Mr Jakob**　　　　　MODERN ESTONIAN €€€
(📞 53753307; www.otepaagolf.ee; Mäha küla; mains €14-18; ⏱ noon-9pm daily, closed Mon-Thu Nov-Mar; 🤶) Otepää's best restaurant is hidden away at the golf club, 4km west of Pühajärv. The menu is as contemporary and playful as the decor, taking Estonian classics such as pork ribs and marinated herring fillets and producing something quite extraordinary. Add to that charming service and blissful views over the course and surrounding fields.

❶ Information

Otepää Tourist Information Centre (📞 766 1200; www.otepaa.eu; Tartu mnt 1; ⏱ 10am-5pm Mon-Fri, to 3pm Sat & Sun mid-May–mid-Sep, 10am-5pm Mon-Fri, to 2pm Sat rest of year) Well-informed staff distribute maps and brochures, and make recommendations for activities, guide services and lodging in the area.

ℹ Getting There & Away

The **bus station** (Tartu mnt 1) is next to the tourist office. Destinations include Tallinn (€13, 3½ hours, daily), Narva (€12, 4¼ hours, twice weekly), Tartu (€4.20, one hour, 10 daily), Sangaste (€1.70, 30 minutes, six daily) and Valga (€3.30, one hour, four daily).

Tartu

POP 98,000

Tartu lays claim to being Estonia's spiritual capital, with locals talking about a special Tartu *vaim* (spirit), created by the time-stands-still feel of its wooden houses and stately buildings, and the beauty of its parks and riverfront. Tartu was the cradle of Estonia's 19th-century national revival, and escaped Soviet town planning to a greater degree than Tallinn. Its handsome centre is lined with classically designed 18th-century buildings, many of which have been put to innovative uses.

Small and provincial, with the tranquil Emajõgi River flowing through it, Tartu is Estonia's premier university town; students comprise nearly a seventh of the population. This injects a boisterous vitality into the leafy, historic setting and grants it a vibrant nightlife for a city of its size. On long summer nights, those students who haven't abandoned the city for the beach can be found on the hill behind the Town Hall, flirting and drinking.

◉ Sights

★ **Estonian Print & Paper Museum**   MUSEUM
(Eesti Trüki- ja Paberimuuseum; ☑ 56828117; www. trykimuuseum.ee; Kastani 48f; adult/child €5/2; ⊙ noon-6pm Wed-Sun) A treat for word nerds, design hounds and print junkies alike, this interactive museum focuses on the history of printing and paper-making. Machinery from across the ages is on permanent display, and there's a gallery with rotating exhibitions plus a small selection of handmade notebooks for sale. Tickets include an hour-long tour in English by the lovely museum director, Lemmit, complete with demonstrations and the opportunity to make your own paper or prints on one of the antique presses.

University of Tartu Museum   MUSEUM
(Tartu Ülikool muuseum; ☑ 737 5674; www.muuse um.ut.ee; Lossi 25; adult/child €5/4; ⊙ 10am-6pm Tue-Sun May-Sep, 11am-5pm Wed-Sun Oct-Apr) Atop Toomemägi are the ruins of a Gothic cathedral, originally built by German knights in the 13th century. It was substantially rebuilt in the 15th century, despoiled during the Reformation in 1525, used as a barn, and partly rebuilt between 1804 and 1809 to house the university library, and is now a museum. Inside there are a range of interesting exhibits chronicling student life.

★ **Estonian National Museum**   MUSEUM
(Eesti rahva muuseum; ☑ 736 3051; www.erm.ee; Muuseumi tee 2; adult/child €14/10; ⊙ 10am-6pm Tue & Thu-Sun, 10am-8pm Wed) This immense, low-slung, architectural showcase is a striking sight and had both Estonian patriots and architecture-lovers purring when it opened in late 2016. The permanent exhibition covers national prehistory and history in some detail. Fittingly, for a museum built over a former Soviet airstrip, the Russian occupation is given in-depth treatment, while the 'Echo of the Urals' exhibition gives an overview of the various peoples that speak tongues in the Estonian language family. There's also a restaurant and cafe.

Town Hall Square   SQUARE
(Raekoja plats) Tartu's main square is lined with grand buildings and echoes with the chink of glasses and plates in summer. The centrepiece is the Town Hall itself, fronted by a statue of students kissing under a spouting umbrella. On the south side of the square, look out for the communist hammer-and-sickle relief that still remains on the facade of No 5.

Aparaaditehas   AREA
(☑ 56674704; www.aparaaditehas.ee; Kastani 42) Aparaaditehas (the Widget Factory) is an old 14,000-sq-metre industrial complex that once functioned as a factory for refrigeration equipment and secret submarine parts during the Soviet era. It underwent development in 2014 and has since been resurrected as Tartu's hippest dining, drinking, shopping and cultural hub, akin to the extremely popular Telliskivi Creative City in Tallinn.

🛏 Sleeping

★ **Hektor Design Hostel**   HOSTEL €
(☑ 740 5100; www.hektorhostels.com; Riia mnt 26; dm/s/d from €15/31/35) Set in a warehouse

built in the 1950s, this clever hostel is a far cry from the dross of typical backpacker digs. Modern, functional design and super-cosy beds are just the start – there's also a gym, a yoga room and sauna, plus a movie projector and laundry room. Private rooms have fridges and microwaves, some with their own bathrooms.

Villa Margaretha BOUTIQUE HOTEL €€
(☑731 1820; www.margaretha.ee; Tähe 11/13; s €55-85, d €65-95, ste €175; P 🛜) Like something out of a fairy tale, this wooden art-nouveau house has a sweet little turret and romantic rooms decked out with sleigh beds and art-fully draped fabrics. The cheaper rooms in the modern extension at the rear are bland in comparison. It's a little away from the action but still within walking distance of Old Town.

Tampere Maja GUESTHOUSE €€
(☑738 6300; www.tamperemaja.ee; Jaani 4; s/d/tr/q from €54/84/110/132; P ✳@🛜) With strong links to the Finnish city of Tampere (Tartu's sister city), this cosy guesthouse fea-tures seven warm, light-filled guest rooms in a range of sizes. Breakfast is included and each room has access to cooking facilities. And it wouldn't be Finnish if it didn't offer an authentic sauna (one to four people €15; open to nonguests).

Antonius Hotel HOTEL €€€
(☑737 0377; www.hotelantonius.ee; Ülikooli 15; s/d/ste from €95/120/220; ✳🛜) Sitting plumb opposite the main university building, this first-rate 18-room boutique hotel is loaded with antiques and period features. Breakfast is served in the 18th-century vaulted cellar, which in the evening morphs into a top-notch restaurant.

🍴 Eating

Aparaat INTERNATIONAL €
(☑730 3090; www.aparaadiresto.ee; Kastani 42; mains €5-14; ⊙noon-11pm Mon-Thu, to 1am Fri-Sat, to 6pm Sun) Set in the courtyard of Aparaa-ditehas (p191), Tartu's hipster outpost, Aparaat serves simple and well-executed international fare. Dishes aren't nearly as creative as the artsy types that frequent the place, but diners should hold out until the end for the excellent blue-cheese cheese-cake. There's a play area for kids, plus regu-lar concerts and other events.

Meat Market STEAK €€€
(☑653 3455; www.meatmarket.ee; Küütri 3; mains €9-19; ⊙noon-11pm Mon-Thu, to 1am Fri & Sat, to

10pm Sun) The name says it all, with dish-es ranging from standards like sirloin with truffle butter or black-garlic lamb chops, to bull testicles or wild goose with duck heart sauce. The veggie accompaniments (think buckthorn-potato purée and mushroom pâté) are excellent too. It's open late for cocktails.

ℹ️ Information

Tartu Tourist Information Centre (☑744 2111; www.visittartu.com; Town Hall, Raekoja plats; ⊙9am-6pm Mon, 9am-5pm tue-Fri, 10am-2pm Sat mid-Sep–mid-May, shorter hours rest of year) Stocks local maps and bro-chures, books accommodation and tour guides, and has free internet access.

ℹ️ Getting There & Away

Tartu's beautifully restored wooden **train sta-tion** (☑673 7400; www.elron.ee; Vaksali 6), built in 1877, is 1.5km southwest of the Old Town at the end of Kuperjanovi street. Six express (two-hour) and four regular (2½-hour) services head to Tallinn daily (both €12), and there are also three trains a day to Sangaste (€4.20, one hour) and Valga (€4.90, 70 minutes).

ℹ️ Getting Around

Tartu is easily explored on foot but there is also a local bus service. You can buy a single-use ticket from any kiosk (€0.83) or from the bus driver (€1.50); be sure to validate the ticket once on board or risk a fine. Kiosks also sell day passes (€2.50).

WESTERN ESTONIA & THE ISLANDS

Pärnu

POP 52,000
Local families, hormone-sozzled youths and German, Swedish and Finnish holidaymakers join together in a collective prayer for sunny weather while strolling the beaches, sprawl-ing parks and picturesque historic centre of Pärnu (*pair*-nu), Estonia's premier seaside re-sort. In these parts, the name Pärnu is synon-ymous with fun in the sun; one hyperbolic lo-cal described it to us as 'Estonia's Miami', but it's usually called by its slightly more prosaic moniker, the nation's 'summer capital'.

In truth, most of Pärnu is quite docile, with leafy streets and expansive parks inter-mingling with turn-of-the-20th-century vil-las that reflect the town's fashionable, more decorous past. Older visitors from Finland and the former Soviet Union still visit, seeking rest, rejuvenation and Pärnu's vaunted mud treatments.

◉ Sights

★ Pärnu Beach
BEACH

Pärnu's long, wide, sandy beach – sprinkled with volleyball courts, cafes and changing cubicles – is easily the city's main draw. A curving path stretches along the sand, lined with fountains, park benches and an excellent playground. Early-20th-century buildings are strung along Ranna pst, the avenue that runs parallel to the beach. Across the road, the formal gardens of **Rannapark** are ideal for a summertime picnic.

★ Museum of New Art
GALLERY

(Uue kunstimuuseum; ☑443 0772; www.mona. ee; Esplanaadi 10; adult/child €4/2; ⊙9am-9pm Jun-Aug, 9am-7pm Sep-May) Pärnu's former Communist Party headquarters now houses one of Estonia's edgiest galleries. As part of its commitment to pushing the cultural envelope, it stages an international nude art exhibition every summer. The gallery also hosts the annual **Pärnu Film Festival**, founded by film-maker Mark Soosaar.

⌚ Sleeping

Inge Villa
GUESTHOUSE €€

(☑443 8510; www.ingevilla.fi; Kaarli 20; s/d/ ste €56/70/82; ❀🛜) Describing itself as a 'Swedish-Estonian villa hotel', low-key and lovely Inge Villa occupies a prime patch of real estate near the beach. Its 11 rooms are simply decorated in muted tones with Nordic minimalism to the fore. The garden, lounge and sauna seal the deal.

Villa Ammende
HOTEL €€€

(☑447 3888; www.ammende.ee; Mere pst 7; s/d/ ste €225/275/475; 🅿❀🛜) Luxury abounds in this refurbished 1904 art-nouveau mansion, which lords it over handsomely manicured grounds. The gorgeous exterior – looking like a Paris metro stop writ large – is matched by an elegant lobby and individually antique-furnished rooms. Rooms in the gardener's house are more affordable but lack a little of the wow factor. It's a lot cheaper outside of July.

✕ Eating

★ Piccadilly
CAFE €

(☑442 0085; www.kohvila.com; Pühavaimu 15; dishes €4-12; ⊙9am-7pm Mon-Thu, 11am-11pm Fri-Sat, 11am-3pm Sun; ⏣) Piccadilly offers a downtempo haven for wine-lovers and vegetarians and an extensive range of hot beverages. Savoury options include delicious salads, sandwiches and omelettes, but really it's all about the sweeties, including moreish cheesecake and handmade chocolates.

★ Lime Lounge
INTERNATIONAL €€€

(☑449 2190; www.limelounge.ee; Hommiku 17; mains €10-22; ⊙noon-10pm Mon-Thu, to midnight Fri & Sat; 🛜🍴) Bright and zesty Lime Lounge feels more like a cocktail bar than a restaurant, although the food really is excellent. Classics from around the globe are represented on the menu, from Russia (borscht) to France (duck breast), Italy (delicious pasta) and all the way to Thailand (*tom kha gai* soup).

ℹ Information

Pärnu Tourist Information Centre (☑447 3000; www.visitparnu.com; Uus 4; ⊙9am-6pm mid-May–mid-Sep, 9am-5pm Mon-Fri, 10am-2pm Sat & Sun mid-Sep–mid-May) A very helpful centre stocking maps and brochures, booking accommodation and rental cars (for a small fee), and providing a left-luggage service (per day €2). There's a small gallery attached as well as a toilet and showers.

ℹ Getting There & Away

Three daily trains run between Tallinn and Pärnu (€7.90, 2¼ hours), but this isn't a great option given that **Pärnu station** (Liivi tee) is an inconvenient 5km east of the town centre in a spot that's difficult to find and to access, on a major road. There's no station office; buy tickets on the train. Note, if you're coming from Tallinn, make sure you get in the right carriages, as part of the train unhooks at Lelle and continues on a different track to Viljandi.

ℹ Getting Around

There are local buses but given that all the sights are within walking distance of each other, you probably won't need to bother with them. Tickets for local journeys are €0.64 if pre-purchased or €1 from the driver.

Muhu

POP 1560

Connected to Saaremaa by a 2.5km causeway, the island of Muhu has the undeserved reputation as the 'doormat' for the bigger island – lots of people passing through on their way from the ferry, but few stopping. In fact, Estonia's third-biggest island offers

ESTONIA MUHU

plenty of excuses to hang around, including one of the country's best restaurants and some excellent accommodation options.

◎ Sights

Muhu Museum   MUSEUM
(☑ 454 8872; www.muhumuuseum.ee; Koguva; adult/concession €4/3; ◎ 9am-6pm mid-May–mid-Sep, 10am-5pm Tue-Sat rest of year) Koguva, 6km off the main road on the western tip of Muhu, is an exceptionally well-preserved, old-fashioned island village, now protected as an open-air museum. One ticket allows you to wander through an old schoolhouse, a house displaying beautiful traditional textiles from the area (including painstakingly detailed folk costumes) and a farm that was the ancestral home of author Juhan Smuul (1922–71). You can poke around various farm buildings, one of which contains a collection of Singer sewing machines.

⎙ Sleeping

★ **Pädaste Manor**   HOTEL €€€
(☑ 454 8800; www.padaste.ee; Pädaste; r €254-481, ste €416-875; ◎ Mar-Oct; 🅿 🛜) If money's no object, here's where to part with it. This manicured bayside estate encompasses the restored manor house (14 rooms and a fine-dining restaurant), a stone carriage house (nine rooms and a spa centre) and a separate stone 'sea house' brasserie. The attention to detail is second-to-none, from the pop-up TVs to the antique furnishings and Muhu embroidery.

ⓘ Getting There & Away

Buses take the ferry from the mainland and continue through to Saaremaa via the causeway, stopping along the main road. Some Kuressaare–Kuivastu services also divert to Koguva and Pädaste on weekdays. Major destinations include Tallinn (€12 to €14, three hours, 15 daily), Tartu (€17, five hours, two daily), Viljandi (€15, four hours, two daily), Pärnu (€8.80, 2½ hours, two daily) and Kuressaare (€5 to €5.60, one hour, 27 daily).

Saaremaa

POP 33,950

To Estonians, Saaremaa (literally 'island land') is synonymous with space, spruce and fresh air – and bottled water, vodka and killer beer. Estonia's largest island (roughly the size of Luxembourg) is still substantially covered in forests of pine, spruce and juniper, while its

windmills, lighthouses and tiny villages seem largely unbothered by the passage of time.

Kuressaare, the capital of Saaremaa, is on the south coast (75km from the Muhu ferry terminal) and is a natural base for visitors. It's here among the upmarket hotels that you'll understand where the island got its nickname, 'Spa-remaa'. When the long days arrive, so too do the Finns and Swedes, jostling for beach and sauna space with Estonian urban-escapees.

ⓘ Getting There & Away

Most travellers reach Saaremaa by taking the ferry from Virtsu to Muhu and then driving in a personal vehicle or by bus across the 2.5km causeway connecting the islands.

ⓘ Getting Around

There are more than 400km of paved roads on Saaremaa and many more dirt roads. Hitching is not uncommon on the main routes but you'll need time on your hands; there's not much traffic on minor roads.

Local buses putter around the island, but not very frequently. The main terminus is **Kuressaare bus station** (Kuressaare Bussijaam; ☑ 453 1661; www.bussipilet.ee; Pihtla tee 2) and there's a route planner online at www.bussipilet.ee.

Kuressaare

POP 13,540

What passes for the big smoke in these parts, Kuressaare has a picturesque town centre with leafy streets and a magnificent castle rising up in its midst, surrounded by the usual scrappy sprawl of housing and light industry. The town built a reputation as a health centre as early as the 19th century, when the ameliorative properties of its coastal mud were discovered and the first spas opened. Now they're a dime a dozen, ranging from Eastern-bloc sanatoriums to sleek and stylish resorts.

Apart from the castle, the best of Kuressaare's historic buildings are grouped around the central square, Keskväljak. The tourist office is housed in the town hall (1670), a baroque building guarded by a fine pair of stone lions. Directly across the square the Vaekoja pub inhabits a former weigh-house, also from the 17th century.

◎ Sights

★ **Kuressaare Castle**   CASTLE
(www.saaremaamuuseum.ee) Majestic Kuressaare Castle stands facing the sea at the

southern end of the town, on an artificial island ringed by a moat. It's the best-preserved castle in the Baltic and the region's only medieval stone castle that has remained intact. The castle grounds are open to the public at all times but to visit the keep you'll need to buy a ticket to Saaremaa Museum (p195).

Saaremaa Museum MUSEUM
(☑455 4463; www.saaremaamuuseum.ee; adult/concession €6/3; ☺10am-7pm May-Aug, 11am-6pm Wed-Sun Sep-Apr) Occupying the keep of Kuressaare Castle, this museum is devoted to the island's nature and history. A large part of the fun is exploring the warren of chambers, halls, passages and stairways, apt to fuel anyone's *Game of Thrones* fantasies. One room near the bishop's chamber looks down to a dungeon where, according to legend, condemned prisoners were dispatched to be devoured by hungry lions (recorded growls reinforce the mental image).

🛏 Sleeping

⭐**Ekesparre** BOUTIQUE HOTEL €€€
(☑453 8778; www.ekesparre.ee; Lossi 27; r €175-215; ☺Apr-Oct; P🖥) Holding pole position on the castle grounds, this elegant 10-room hotel has been returned to its art-nouveau glory. Period wallpaper and carpet, Tiffany lamps and a smattering of orchids add to the refined, clubby atmosphere, while the 3rd-floor guests' library is a gem. As you'd expect from the price, it's a polished operator.

⭐**Georg Ots Spa Hotel** HOTEL €€€
(Gospa; ☑455 0000; www.gospa.ee; Tori 2; r €185-225, ste €295; P✳🖥⛶) Named after a renowned Estonian opera singer, Gospa has modern rooms with wildly striped carpet, enormous king-sized beds and a warm but minimalist design. Most rooms have balconies, and there's a fitness centre and excellent spa centre, including a pool and multiple saunas. Separate freestanding 'residences' are also available, and families are very well catered to. Prices vary widely.

🍴 Eating

⭐**Retro** CAFE €€
(☑5683 8400; www.kohvikretro.ee; Lossi 5; mains €9-14; ☺noon-9pm Mon-Thu, to midnight Fri & Sat; 🖥♿) The menu at this hip little cafe-bar is deceptively simple (pasta, burgers, wraps, grilled fish), but Retro takes things to the next level, making its own pasta and burger buns, and using the best fresh, local produce. Desserts are delicious, too. There's

also a great selection of Estonian craft beer, perfect for supping on the large rear terrace.

Ku Kuu MODERN EUROPEAN €€
(☑453 9749; www.kuressaarekuursaal.ee; Lossipark 1; mains €8-15; ☺11am-midnight May–mid-Sep; 🖥) Occupying the elegant Spa Hall from which it takes its name (Ku Kuu is short for Kuressaare Kuursaal), this is Saaremaa's loveliest dining room. The wood panelling and panes of coloured glass provide an atmospheric backdrop for a tasty menu of seafood and island produce, prepared with a strong French accent.

ℹ Information

Kuressaare Tourist Office (☑453 3120; www.kuressaare.ee; Tallinna 2; ☺9am-6pm Mon-Fri, 10am-4pm Sat & Sun mid-May–mid-Sep, 9am-5pm Mon-Fri rest of year) Inside the old town hall, it sells maps and guides, arranges accommodation and has information on boat trips and island tours.

SURVIVAL GUIDE

ℹ Directory A–Z

ACCOMMODATION

During July and August, the best accommodation books up quickly in Tallinn, which is especially busy on most weekends. Book a month ahead anytime from May to September.

High season in Estonia means summer. Prices drop substantially at other times. The exception is Otepää, when there's also a corresponding peak in winter.

LEGAL MATTERS

After dark, pedestrians are required to wear reflectors in order to remain visible to passing drivers. This is regularly enforced by police and violators may face a fine up to €40.

LGBT+ TRAVELLERS

Estonia is a fairly tolerant and safe home to its gay and lesbian citizens – certainly much more so than its neighbours. Unfortunately, that general acceptance hasn't translated into a wildly exciting scene (only Tallinn has gay venues).

OPENING HOURS

Opening hours vary considerably throughout the year due to the stark contrast of weather conditions during summer and winter – some places close entirely from October to March. The hours indicated here are during high summer season (June to August) when most places are open, and working hours are longest.

Banks 9am or 10am to 5pm or 6pm Monday to Friday

Restaurants noon to midnight

Cafes 8am to 4pm

Bars noon to midnight

Museums 10am to 6pm

Shops 10am to 6pm Monday to Friday, 11am to 5pm Saturday and Sunday

Shopping Centres 9am to 9pm

Supermarkets 8am to 11pm

PUBLIC HOLIDAYS

New Year's Day (Uusaasta) 1 January

Independence Day (Iseseisvuspäev; Anniversary of 1918 declaration) 24 February

Good Friday (Suur reede) March/April

Easter Sunday (Lihavõtted) March/April

Spring Day (Kevadpüha) 1 May

Pentecost (Nelipühade) Seventh Sunday after Easter (May/June)

Victory Day (Võidupüha; commemorating the anniversary of the Battle of Võnnu, 1919); 23 June

St John's Day (Jaanipäev, Midsummer's Day) 24 June

Day of Restoration of Independence (Taasiseseisvumispäev; marking the country's return to Independence in 1991); 20 August

Christmas Eve (Jõululaupäev) 24 December

Christmas Day (Jõulupüha) 25 December

Boxing Day (Teine jõulupüha) 26 December

Taken together, Victory Day and St John's Day are the excuse for a week-long midsummer break for many people.

TELEPHONE

There are no area codes in Estonia; if you're calling anywhere within the country, just dial the number as it's listed. All landline phone numbers have seven digits; mobile (cell) numbers have seven or eight digits and begin with 5. Estonia's country code is 372. To make a collect call dial 16116, followed by the desired number. To make an international call, dial 00 before the country code.

Public telephones accept chip cards, available at post offices, hotels and most kiosks. For placing calls outside Estonia, an international telephone card with a pin, available at many kiosks and supermarkets, is better value. Note that these cards can only be used from landlines, not mobile phones.

ⓘ Getting There & Away

ENTERING THE COUNTRY

Entering Estonia from other parts of the EU is usually a breeze – no border checkpoints and no customs – thanks to the Schengen Agreement.

If arriving from outside the Schengen area, old-fashioned travel document and customs checks are required. For more information, check the Estonian Foreign Ministry's website at www.vm.ee

AIR

The following airlines operate services to Tallinn year-round, with additional routes and airlines added in summer:

airBaltic (www.airbaltic.com) Multiple daily flights between Tallinn and Rīga.

Finnair (www.finnair.ee) Up to seven flights a day between Helsinki and Tallinn, and daily flights between Helsinki and Tartu.

LAND
Bus

The following bus companies all have services between Estonia and the other Baltic states:

Ecolines (www.ecolines.net) Major routes: Tallinn–Pärnu–Rīga (seven daily), six of which continue on to Vilnius; Tallinn–St Petersburg (six daily); Tartu–Valga–Rīga (two daily); Vilnius–Rīga–Tartu–Narva–St Petersburg (four daily).

Lux Express & Simple Express (www.luxexpress.eu) Major routes: Tallinn–Pärnu–Rīga (up to 13 daily), eight of which continue on to Panevėžys and Vilnius; Tallinn–Rakvere–Sillamäe–Narva–St Petersburg (four daily); Tallinn–Tartu–Võru–Moscow (daily); Rīga–Valmiera–Tartu–Sillamäe–Narva–St Petersburg (nine to 10 daily).

Eurolines (www.eurolines.lt) Two daily Tallinn–Pärnu–Rīga–Panevėžys–Vilnius–Kaunas–Warsaw buses.

Car & Motorcycle

With the Schengen agreement, there are no border checks when driving between Estonia and Latvia. There's usually no problem taking hire cars across the border but you'll need to let the rental company know at the time of hire if you intend to do so; some companies will charge an additional fee.

Train

Valga is the terminus for both the Estonian and Latvian rail systems, but the train services don't connect up. From Valga, Estonian trains operated by **Elron** (www.elron.ee) head to Elva, Tartu and Tallinn, while Latvian trains operated by **Pasažieru vilciens** (www.pv.lv) head to Valmiera, Cēsis, Sigulda and Rīga. There are also direct trains to Tallinn from St Petersburg and Moscow.

SEA

Eckerö Line (☑ 6000 4300; www.eckeroline.fi; Passenger Terminal A, Vanasadam; adult/child/car from €15/10/19; ☺ ticket office

8.30am-7pm Mon-Fri, to 3pm Sat & Sun) Twice-daily car ferry from Helsinki to Tallinn (2½ hours).

Linda Line (☑ 699 9331; www.lindaliini.ee; Patarei Sadam, Linnahall Terminal) Smaller and faster vessels operate from late March to late December.

Tallink (☑ 631 8320; www.tallink.com; Terminal D, Lootsi 13) Daily services between Tallinn and Helsinki plus an overnight ferry to Stockholm and Tallinn, via the Åland islands.

Viking Line (☑ 666 3966; www.vikingline.com; Terminal A, Vanasadam; passenger & vehicle from €42) At least four daily car ferries between Helsinki and Tallinn (2½ hours).

🛈 Getting Around

AIR

There is very little in the way of domestic flights in Estonia. Direct flights run from Tallinn to Kuressaare and Tallinn to Kärdla, operated by **Saartelennuliinid** (www.saartelennuliinid.ee) twice daily on weekdays and once on Saturdays and Sundays. Other flights from Tallinn to the rest of the country require a connection outside of Estonia.

In winter, when sea travel is impossible, **Luftverkehr Friesland-Harle** (LFH, www.len-dame.ee) operates flights between Pärnu and Kuressaare to the island of Ruhnu on Thursdays, Fridays and Sundays.

BOAT

There are ferries between mainland Estonia and its many islands, Saaremaa, Hiiumaa, Kihnu, Ruhnu and Vormsi being the most frequented by visitors. **Praamid** (www.praamid.ee) and **Kihnu Veeteed** (www.veeteed.com) are the major operators – check websites for exact routes and prices.

BUS

The national bus network is extensive, linking all the major cities to each other and the smaller towns to their regional hubs. All services are summarised on the extremely handy **T pilet** (www.tpilet.ee) site.

CAR & MOTORCYCLE

Estonian roads are generally very good and driving is easy. In rural areas, particularly on the islands, some roads are unsealed and without lines indicating lanes, but they're usually kept in good condition.

TRAIN

Train services have been steadily improving in recent years. Domestic routes are run by **Elron** (www.elron.ee) but it's also possible to travel between Tallinn and Narva on the Russian-bound services run by **GoRail** (www.gorail.ee).

The major domestic routes are Tallinn–Rakvere (five daily, with four continuing to Narva), Tallinn–Tartu (11 daily), Tallinn–Viljandi (five daily) and Tartu–Sangaste–Valga (four daily).

Hungary

POP 9.78 MILLION

Best Places to Eat

➡ Borkonyha (p207)

➡ Tiszavirág Restaurant (p217)

➡ Macok Bistro & Wine Bar (p218)

➡ Kispiac (p207)

➡ Impostor (p206)

Best Places to Stay

➡ Aria Hotel Budapest (p206)

➡ Sopronbánfalva Monastery Hotel (p211)

➡ Shantee House (p205)

➡ Hotel Senator Ház (p218)

➡ Club Hotel Füred (p212)

Why Go?

Stunning architecture, vital folk art, thermal spas and Europe's most exciting capital after dark: Hungary is just the place to kick off a European adventure. Lying virtually in the centre of the continent, this land of Franz Liszt and Béla Bartók, paprika-lashed dishes, superb wines and the romantic Danube River continues to enchant visitors. The allure of Budapest, once an imperial city, is immediate at first sight, and it also boasts the region's liveliest nightlife.

Pécs, the warm heart of the south, and Eger, wine capital of the north, also have much to offer travellers, as does the Great Plain, where cowboys ride and cattle roam. And how about lazing in an open-air thermal spa while snow patches glisten around you? That's at Hévíz, at the western edge of Lake Balaton, continental Europe's largest lake and Hungary's 'inland sea', which offers innumerable opportunities for rest and recreation.

When to Go
Budapest

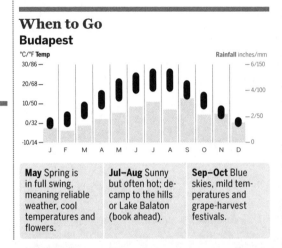

May Spring is in full swing, meaning reliable weather, cool temperatures and flowers.

Jul–Aug Sunny but often hot; decamp to the hills or Lake Balaton (book ahead).

Sep–Oct Blue skies, mild temperatures and grape-harvest festivals.

Entering the Country

Hungary is well connected with frequent air, bus and train services to its seven neighbouring countries and beyond.

ITINERARIES

One Week

Spend at least three days in Budapest (p200), checking out the sights, museums, cafes and 'ruin pubs'. On your fourth day take a day trip to a Danube Bend town such as Szentendre (p210) or Esztergom (p211). Day five can be spent getting a morning train to Pécs (p214) to see Turkish remains, museums and galleries. If you've still got the travel bug, on day six head for Eger (p217), a baroque town set in red-wine country. On your last day recuperate back in one of Budapest's wonderful thermal baths.

Two Weeks

After a week in Budapest and the Danube Bend towns, spend two days exploring the towns and grassy beaches around Lake Balaton (p212). Tihany (p215) is a rambling hillside village set on a protected peninsula, Keszthely (p213) is an old town with a great palace in addition to beaches, and Hévíz (p214) has a thermal lake. On day 10, head to the Great Plain (p215) – Szeged (p216) is a splendid university town on the Tisza River, and Kecskemét (p216) a centre of art nouveau architecture. Finish your trip in Tokaj (p218), home of Hungary's famous sweet wine.

Essential Food & Drink

Traditional Hungarian food is heavy and rich. Meat, sour cream and fat abound, and the omnipresent seasoning is paprika. Things are lightening up, though, with vegetarian, 'New Hungarian' and world cuisines increasingly available.

Gulyás (goulash) Hungary's signature dish, though here it's more like a soup than a stew and made with beef, onions and tomatoes.

Halászlé Highly recommended freshwater fish soup.

Lángos Street food; fried dough topped with cheese and/or *tejföl* (sour cream).

Palacsinta Thin crêpes eaten as a savoury main course or filled with jam, sweet cheese or chocolate sauce for dessert.

Pálinka A strong brandy distilled from all kinds of fruit but especially plums and apricots.

Paprika The omnipresent seasoning in Hungarian cooking, which comes in two varieties: strong (*erős*) and sweet (*édes*).

Pörkölt Paprika-infused stew; closer to what non-Hungarians would call goulash.

Wine Best known are the sweet dessert wine Tokaji Aszú and Egri Bikavér (Eger Bull's Blood), a full-bodied red.

AT A GLANCE

Area 93,030 sq km

Capital Budapest

Country Code ⏢36

Currency Forint (Ft)

Emergency Ambulance ⏢104, emergency assistance ⏢112, fire ⏢105, police ⏢107

Language Hungarian

Time Central European Time (GMT/UTC plus one hour)

Visas Not required for citizens of the EU, USA, Canada, Israel, Japan, Australia and New Zealand

HUNGARY

Sleeping Price Ranges

The following price ranges refer to a double room with bathroom in high season.

Budapest
€ less than 15,000Ft
€€ 15,000–33,500Ft
€€€ more than 33,500Ft

Provinces
€ less than 9000Ft
€€ 9000–16,500Ft
€€€ more than 16,500Ft

Eating Price Ranges

The following price ranges refer to a main course in the provinces and the cost of a two-course meal with a drink in Budapest.

Budapest
€ less than 3500Ft
€€ 3500–7500Ft
€€€ more than 7500Ft

Provinces
€ less than 2000Ft
€€ 2000–3500Ft
€€€ more than 3500Ft

Hungary Highlights

1 Budapest (p200) Losing yourself in the 'ruin pubs', wine bars and nightclubs of Hungary's capital.

2 Eger (p217) Understanding the sobering history of Turkish attacks, and sampling the region's famed Bull's Blood wine.

3 Pécs (p214) Absorbing the mild climate and historic architecture.

4 Lake Balaton (p212) Taking a pleasure cruise across Central Europe's largest body of fresh water.

5 Hévíz (p214) Easing your aching muscles year-round in the warm waters of this thermal lake.

6 Hortobágy National Park (p217) Watching Hungarian cowboys' shows in the Great Plain.

7 Szentendre (p210) Mill about with artists and day trippers at cute town.

BUDAPEST

📮 1 / POP 1.75 MILLION

The beauty of Hungary's capital is both natural and built. Straddling a gentle curve in the Danube, the city is flanked by the Buda Hills on the west bank and the beginnings of the Great Plain to the east. Architecturally, the city is a treasure trove of baroque, neoclassical, Eclectic and art nouveau buildings. The city is also blessed with an abundance of hot springs, and in recent years Budapest has taken on the role of the region's party town.

👁 Sights & Activities

👁 Buda

Castle Hill (Várhegy) is Buda's biggest tourist draw and a first port of call for any visit to the city. Here, you'll find most of Budapest's remaining medieval buildings, the Royal Palace and sweeping views of Pest across the river. You can walk to Castle Hill up the Király lépcső, the 'Royal Steps' that lead northwest off Clark Ádám tér, or take the **Sikló** (www.bkv.hu; I Szent György tér & Clark Ádám tér; one-way/return adult 1200/1800Ft, child 3-14yr 700/1100Ft; ☉7.30am-10pm, closed 1st & 3rd Mon of month; ☐16, 105, ☐19, 41), a funicular railway built in 1870 that ascends from Clark Ádám tér to Szent György tér near the Royal Palace.

★**Royal Palace**   PALACE
(Királyi Palota; Map p202; I Szent György tér; ☐16, 16A, 116) The former Royal Palace has been razed and rebuilt at least half a dozen times over the past seven centuries. Béla IV established a royal residence here in the mid-13th century, and subsequent kings added to the complex. The palace was levelled in the battle to drive out the Turks in 1686; the Habsburgs rebuilt it but spent very little time here. The Royal Palace now contains the **Hungarian National Gallery** (Magyar Nemzeti Galéria; Map p202; ☑1-201 9082; www.mng.hu; Bldgs A-D; adult/concession 1800/900Ft, audio guide 800Ft; ☉10am-6pm Tue-Sun), the **Castle Museum** (Vármúzeum; Map p202; ☑1-487 8800; www.btm.hu; Bldg E; adult/concession 2400/1200Ft; ☉10am-6pm Tue-Sun Mar-Oct, to 4pm Tue-Sun Nov-Feb; ☐19, 41), and the **National Széchenyi Library** (Országos Széchenyi Könyvtár, OSZK; Map p202; ☑1-224 3700; www.oszk.hu; Bldg F; ☉9am-8pm Tue-Sat, stacks to 7pm Tue-Fri, to 5pm Sat).

Matthias Church   CHURCH
(Mátyás templom; Map p202; ☑1-489 0716; www.matyas-templom.hu; I Szentháromság tér 2; adult/concession 1500/1000Ft; ☉9am-5pm Mon-Fri, 9am-noon Sat, 1-5pm Sun; ☐16, 16A, 116) Parts of Matthias Church date back 500 years, notably the carvings above the southern entrance, but essentially the church (named after King Matthias Corvinus who married Queen Beatrix here in 1474) is a neo-Gothic confection designed by the architect Frigyes Schulek in 1896.

★**Gellért Baths**   BATHHOUSE
(Gellért Gyógyfürdő; ☑06 30 849 9514, 1-466 6166; www.gellertbath.hu; XI Kelenhegyi út 4, Danubius Hotel Gellért; incl locker/cabin Mon-Fri 5600/6000Ft, Sat & Sun 5800/6200Ft; ☉6am-8pm; ☐7, 86, ☐M4 Szent Gellért tér, ☐18, 19, 47, 49) Soaking in the art nouveau Gellért Baths, open to both men and women in mixed sections (bring a swimsuit), has been likened to taking a bath

in a cathedral. The six thermal pools (one outdoors and one a swimming pool) range in temperature from 35°C to 40°C.

Memento Park   HISTORIC SITE
(☑1-424 7500; www.mementopark.hu; XXII Balatoni út & Szabadkai utca; adult/student 1500/1200Ft; ☉10am-dusk; ☐101B, 101E, 150) Home to more than 40 statues, busts and plaques of Lenin, Marx, Béla Kun and others whose likenesses have ended up on trash heaps elsewhere, Memento Park, 10km southwest of the city centre, is truly a mind-blowing place to visit. Ogle the socialist realism and try to imagine that some of these relics were erected as recently as the late 1980s.

⊙ Margaret Island

Leafy Margaret Island is neither Buda nor Pest, but its shaded walkways, gardens, thermal spa and large swimming complexes offer refuge to the denizens of both sides of the river. The largest and best series of indoor and outdoor pools in the capital is the now year-round **Palatinus Strand** (☑1-340 4500; www.palatinusstrand.hu; XIII Margit-sziget; adult/child May-Sep Mon-Fri 3100/2400Ft, Sat & Sun 3500/2600Ft, Oct-Apr Mon-Fri 2400/2000Ft, Sat & Sun 2800/2300Ft; ☉8am-8pm; ☐26), with 10 pools (two with thermal water), wave machines, water slides and kids' pools.

⊙ Pest

Andrássy út   ARCHITECTURE
(Map p204; ☐M1 Opera) Andrássy út starts a short distance northeast of Deák Ferenc tér and stretches for 2.5km, ending at **Heroes' Sq** (Hősök tere; ☐105, ☐M1 Hősök tere) and the sprawling **City Park** (Városliget; ☐20E, 30, ☐M1 Hősök tere, Széchenyi fürdő, ☐trolleybus 70, 72, 75, 79). Listed by Unesco as a World Heritage Site in 2002, it is a tree-lined parade of knock-out architecture and is best enjoyed as a long stroll from the **Hungarian State Opera House** (Magyar Állami Operaház; Map p204; ☑06 30 279 5677, 1-332 8197; www.operavisit.hu; VI Andrássy út 22; adult/concession 2490/2200Ft; ☉tours in English 2pm, 3pm & 4pm; ☐M1 Opera) out to the park.

★**Parliament**   HISTORIC BUILDING
(Országház; Map p204; ☑1-441 4904, 1-441 4415; http://latogatokozpont.parlament.hu/en; V Kossuth Lajos tér 1-3; adult/student EU citizen 2400/1200Ft, non-EU citizen 6000/3100Ft; ☉8am-6pm Apr-Oct, to 4pm Nov-Mar; ☐M2 Kossuth Lajos tér, ☐2) The Eclectic-style Parliament, designed by Imre

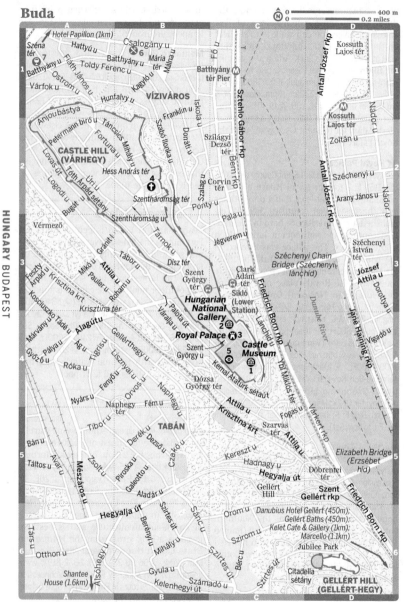

Steindl and completed in 1902, has 691 sumptuously decorated rooms. You'll get to see several of these and other features on a guided tour of the North Wing: the Golden Staircase; the Dome Hall, where the **Crown of St Stephen**, the nation's most important national icon, is on display; the **Grand Staircase** and its wonderful landing; **Loge Hall**; and **Congress Hall**, where the House of Lords of the one-time bicameral assembly sat until 1944.

Basilica of St Stephen   CATHEDRAL
(Szent István Bazilika; Map p204; ☑1-338 2151, 06 30 703 6599; www.basilica.hu; V Szent István tér;

Buda

◉ Top Sights

◉ Sights

✖ Eating

☕ Drinking & Nightlife

requested donation 200Ft; ⊙9am-7pm Mon-Sat, 7.45am-7pm Sun; Ⓜ M3 Arany János utca) **FREE** Budapest's neoclassical cathedral is the most sacred Catholic church in all of Hungary and contains its most revered relic: the mummified right hand of the church's patron, King St Stephen. It was built over half a century to 1905. Much of the interruption during construction had to do with a fiasco in 1868 when the dome collapsed during a storm, and the structure had to be demolished and then rebuilt from the ground up. The view from the **dome** (Panoráma kilátó; Map p204; ☑1-269 1849; adult/child 600/400Ft; ⊙10am-6pm Jun-Sep, to 5.30pm Apr, May & Oct, to 4.30pm Nov-Mar) is phenomenal.

House of Terror   MUSEUM

(Terror Háza; Map p204; ☑1-374 2600; www.terror haza.hu; VI Andrássy út 60; adult/concession 3000/1500Ft, audio guide 1500Ft; ⊙10am-6pm Tue-Sun; Ⓜ M1 Vörösmarty utca, ☒4, 6) The headquarters of the dreaded ÁVH secret police houses the disturbing House of Terror, focusing on the crimes and atrocities of Hungary's fascist and Stalinist regimes in a permanent exhibition called Double Occupation. The years after WWII leading up to the 1956 Uprising get the lion's share of the exhibition space (almost three-dozen spaces on three levels). The reconstructed prison cells in the basement and the Perpetrators' Gallery on the staircase, featuring photographs of turncoats, spies and torturers, are chilling.

Hungarian National Museum   MUSEUM

(Magyar Nemzeti Múzeum; Map p204; ☑1-327 7773, 1-338 2122; www.hnm.hu; VIII Múzeum körút 14-16; adult/concession/family 1600/800/3600Ft; ⊙10am-6pm Tue-Sun; Ⓜ M3/4 Kálvin tér, ☒47, 49) The Hungarian National Museum houses the nation's most important collection of historical relics in an impressive neoclassi-

cal building, purpose built in 1847. Exhibits on the 1st floor trace the history of the Carpathian Basin from earliest times to the arrival of the Magyars in the 9th century; the ongoing story of the Magyar people resumes on the 2nd floor, from the conquest of the basin to the end of communism.

★ Great Synagogue   SYNAGOGUE

(Nagy Zsinagóga; Map p204; ☑1-413 5584, 1-413 1515; www.greatsynagogue.hu/gallery_syn.html; VII Dohány utca 2; adult/concession/family incl museum 4000/3000/9000Ft; ⊙10am-7.30pm Sun-Thu, to 3.30pm Fri May-Sep, 10am-5.30pm Sun-Thu, to 3.30pm Fri Mar, Apr & Oct, 10am-3.30pm Sun-Thu, to 1.30pm Fri Nov-Feb; Ⓜ M2 Astoria, ☒47, 49) Budapest's stunning Great Synagogue is the world's largest Jewish house of worship outside New York City. Built in 1859, the synagogue has both Romantic and Moorish architectural elements. Inside, the **Hungarian Jewish Museum & Archives** (Magyar Zsidó Múzeum és Levéltár; Map p204; ☑1-413 5500; www.milev.hu) contains objects relating to both religious and everyday life. On the synagogue's north side, the **Holocaust Tree of Life Memorial** (Map p204; Raoul Wallenberg Memorial Park, opp VII Wesselényi utca 6; Ⓜ M2 Astoria, ☒47, 49) presides over the mass graves of those murdered by the Nazis.

Széchenyi Baths   BATHHOUSE

(Széchenyi Gyógyfürdő; ☑1-363 3210, 06 30 462 8236; www.szechenyibath.hu; XIV Állatkerti körút 9-11; tickets incl locker/cabin Mon-Fri 5200/5700Ft, Sat & Sun 5400/5900Ft; ⊙6am-10pm; Ⓜ M1 Széchenyi fürdő) These thermal baths are particularly popular with visitors and have helpful, English-speaking attendants. There are 15 indoor thermal pools (water temperatures up to 40°C) and three outdoor pools, including an activity pool with whirlpool. The baths are open year-round, and it's quite a sight to watch men and women playing chess on floating boards when it's snowing.

György Ráth Museum   MUSEUM

(Ráth György Múzeum; ☑1-416 9601; www.imm. hu/en/contents/262; VI Városligeti fasor 12; adult/ concession 2000/1000Ft; ⊙10am-6pm Tue-Sun; ☒trolleybus 70,78, Ⓜ M1 Bajza utca) The one-time home of the eponymous first director (1828–1905) of the Museum of Applied Arts has recently opened and is a shrine to art nouveau/Secessionist art, showing items from the museum (now under renovation). Rooms on the first floor include Ráth's fully furnished study and dining and sitting rooms; other galleries on the same floor and

Central Pest

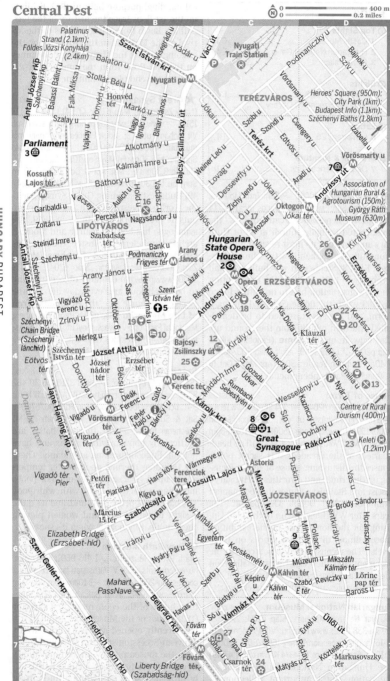

HUNGARY BUDAPEST

Central Pest

the one above walk you through the history of the style in France, Austria and Britain as well as Hungary. An absolute gem.

✪✪ Festivals & Events

Sziget Festival MUSIC
(www.szigetfestival.com; ⊙mid-Aug) One of Europe's biggest and most popular music festivals is held in mid-August on Budapest's Hajógyár (Óbuda) Island, with a plethora of Hungarian and international bands and as many as 500,000 revellers.

Budapest Spring Festival PERFORMING ARTS
(www.springfestival.hu; ⊙mid-Apr) The capital's largest and most important cultural festival, with 200 events, takes place over 18 days in mid-April at dozens of venues across the city.

⊨ Sleeping

⊨ Buda

★Shantee House HOSTEL €
(☑06 30 402 0328, 1-385 8946; www.shantee house.com; XI Takács Menyhért utca 33; beds in yurt €10-13, large/small dm from €11/14, d €32-55; ⓟ☒⊚; ⊡7, 153, ⊡19, 49) Budapest's first hostel (then known as the Back-Pack Guesthouse), the Shantee has added two floors to its colourful suburban 'villa' in south Buda. It's all good and the fun (and sleeping bodies in high season) spills out into a lovely back garden, with hammocks, a yurt and a gazebo. Two of the five doubles are en suite.

Hotel Papillon HOTEL €€
(☑1-212 4750; www.hotelpapillon.hu; II Rózsahegy utca 3/b; s/d/tr €49/69/75, apt €84-99; ⓟ☒☀☒; ⊡4, 6) This cosy hotel in Rózsadomb (Rose Hill) has a delightful back garden with a small swimming pool, and some of the 20 rooms have balconies. There are also four apartments available in the same building, one boasting a lovely roof terrace, as well as more apartments (studio to three-bedroom ones) next door. The staff are on the ball and helpful.

Danubius Hotel Gellért HOTEL €€€
(☑1-889 5500; www.danubiushotels.com/our-hotels-budapest/danubius-hotel-gellert; XI Szent Gellért tér 1; s/d/ste from €84/170/268; ⓟ☀@☒☒; Ⓜ M4 Szent Gellért tér, ⊡18, 19, 47, 49) Buda's grande dame is a 234-room four-star hotel with loads of character. Completed in 1918, the hotel contains examples of art nouveau, notably the thermal spa's entrance hall and Zsolnay ceramic fountains. Prices depend on which way your room faces and what sort of bathroom it has. Hotel guests get a 30% discount for the thermal bath.

The Gellért was the inspiration (but not the actual film location) for the hotel in Wes Anderson's *The Grand Budapest Hotel* (2014).

⊨ Pest

Brody House BOUTIQUE HOTEL €€
(Map p204; ☑06 70 774 9621, 1-550 7363; www.brody.land; VIII Bródy Sándor utca 10; r €80-120;

❄ @ 🔊 ; Ⓜ M3 Kálvin tér, 🚊 47, 49) Offering retro chic at its hippest, this one-time residence of the prime minister when parliament sat at No 8 (today's Italian Cultural Centre) has been refurbished but not altered substantially. It features antique furnishings and modern art blending seamlessly in its eight unique guestrooms and three suites dedicated to local and international artists. A minor drawback is the lack of a lift.

Wombat's
HOSTEL €€

(Map p204; 🖉 1-883 5065; http://wombats.rocks/; Király utca 20; dm €13-21, d €50-65; 🔊 ; Ⓜ M1/2/3 Deák Ferenc tér) Directly opposite the Király utca entrance to buzzing Gozsdu udvar, this slick and well-equipped hostel can accommodate a whopping 465 guests in its 120 rooms. Choose from four- to eight-bed dorms or doubles, all of which are en suite. There's a clean, cool design throughout and a large common area set in a colourful glassroofed atrium.

★ Aria Hotel Budapest
HOTEL €€€

(Map p204; 🖉 1-445 4055; www.ariahotelbudapest. com; V Hercegprímás utca 5; d/ste from €220/640; 🅿 ❄ 🔊 ; 🚊 15,115, Ⓜ M1 Bajcsy-Zsilinszky út) Our favourite new hotel in Budapest, the Aria is a music-themed affair built around an old townhouse, with Jazz, Opera, Classical and Pop Wings. Each of the 49 rooms has a balcony and bears the name of a musician or composer – they are also filled with portraits of, books about and CDs by the same. There's a fabulous wellness centre in the basement.

✗ Eating

✗ Buda

Marcello
ITALIAN €

(🖉 1-466 6231, 06 30 243 5229; www.marcelloetterem.hu/en; XI Bartók Béla út 40; mains 1600-3600Ft; ⊘ noon-10pm Sun-Wed, to 11pm Thu-Sat; 🚊 19, 47, 49) A long-time favourite with students from the nearby university since it opened almost three decades ago, this family-owned operation just down the road from XI Szent Gellért tér offers reliable Italian fare at affordable prices. The pizzas (1350Ft to 1900Ft) and the salad bar are good value, as is the lasagne (1800Ft), which is legendary in these parts.

★ Csalogány 26
INTERNATIONAL €€

(Map p202; 🖉 1-201 7892; www.csalogany26.hu; I Csalogány utca 26; mains 4500-6500Ft; ⊘ noon-3pm & 7-10pm Tue-Sat; 🚊 11, 39, 111) The decor

is spartan at this intimate restaurant, which turns out creative and superb food. Try the roasted lamb with butter squash *lecsó* (a kind of ratatouille, 5000Ft) or other meat-heavy dishes that make the most of local ingredients. An eight-course tasting menu costs 6000Ft (23,000Ft with paired wines) though there is a budget-pleasing three-course set lunch on weekdays for just 3100Ft.

Földes Józsi Konyhája
HUNGARIAN €€

(🖉 06 70 500 0222; www.foldesjozsikonyhaja.hu; II Bécsi út 31; mains 2100-4400Ft; ⊘ 11.30am-3.30pm Mon, 11.30am-4pm & 6-10pm Tue-Sun; 🚊 4, 6, 17) In a lovely old townhouse, this rustic place established by former hotel chef Joe Earthy – hey, that's what his name means! – some years back still serves excellent Hungarian homestyle dishes, including veal stew with dumplings (2750Ft) and a good range of *főzelék* (vegetables in a roux, 850Ft). Lovely garden seating in the warmer months too

✗ Pest

Pizzica
PIZZA €

(Map p204; 🖉 06 30 993 5481; www.facebook. com/pizzicapizza; VI Nagymező utca 21; pizza slices 290-490Ft; ⊘ 11am-midnight Mon-Thu, to 3am Fri & Sat; Ⓜ M1 Oktogon) If there is better pizza in Budapest, we don't know where to find it. Owned and operated by Italians Paolo and Enrico, Pizzica serves the real McCoy, with such toppings as potato and sage and mortadella. It's a tiny place but there's more seating in the small art gallery upstairs.

★ Impostor
ASIAN €€

(Map p204; 🖉 06 30 505 3632; http://impostor. hu/impostor; V Vitkovits Mihály 8; mains 2990-3690Ft; ⊘ noon-10pm Mon-Thu, to midnight Fri & Sat; Ⓜ M1/2/3 Deák Ferenc tér, 🚊 47, 49) Now in a new, more central location, elegant Impostor serves hybrid dishes that echo the owners' passion for Asia and Latin America. Though there are more elaborate main courses on offer, it's well worth trying the delectable (and quite inspired) mixed dumplings (1350Ft) and *bao* (steamed, filled rice-flour buns, 1490Ft to 1990Ft).

Barack & Szilva
HUNGARIAN €€

(Peach & Plum; Map p204; 🖉 1-798 8285, 06 30 258 0965; www.barackesszilva.hu; VII Klauzál utca 13; mains 3300-6200Ft; ⊘ 6pm-midnight Mon-Sat; 🚊 trolleybus 74, Ⓜ M2 Blaha Lujza tér) This is the kind of perfectly formed restaurant that every neighbourhood wishes it could claim. Run by a friendly husband-and-wife team, the 'Peach & Plum' serves high-quality and exceptionally well-prepared Hungarian provincial food in a bistro setting. Try the duck pâté with dried plums (2970Ft) and the red-wine beef *pörkölt* (goulash, 4200Ft). Lovely terrace in summer and live music, too.

Kispiac
HUNGARIAN €€
(Map p204; ☑1-269 4231, 06 30 430 0142; www.kispiac.eu; V Hold utca 13; mains 2450-4450Ft; ⊗noon-10pm Mon-Sat; Ⓜ M3 Arany János utca) This small retro-style restaurant – an absolute favourite – serves seriously Hungarian things like stuffed *csülök* (pig's trotter – and way better than it sounds, 2950Ft), roast *malac* (piglet, 3250Ft) and the ever-popular wild boar spare ribs (3950Ft), as well as an infinite variety of *savanyúság* (pickled vegetables). Perfectly selected wine list and a warm welcome.

★ Borkonyha
HUNGARIAN €€€
(Wine Kitchen; Map p204; ☑1-266 0835; www.borkonyha.hu; V Sas utca 3; mains 3450-7950Ft; ⊗noon-4pm & 6pm-midnight Mon-Sat; ☐15, 115, Ⓜ M1 Bajcsy-Zsilinszky út) Chef Ákos Sárközi's approach to Hungarian cuisine at this Michelin-starred restaurant is contemporary, and the menu changes every week or two. Go for the signature foie gras appetiser with apple and celeriac and a glass of sweet Tokaji Aszú wine. If *mangalica* (a special type of Hungarian pork) is on the menu, try it with a glass of dry Furmint.

🍷 Drinking & Nightlife

🍷 Buda

Kelet Cafe & Gallery
CAFE
(Kelet Kávézó és Galéria; ☑06 20 456 5507; www.facebook.com/keletkavezo; XI Bartók Béla út 29; ⊗7.30am-11pm Mon-Fri, 9am-11pm Sat & Sun;

Ⓜ M4 Móricz Zsigmond körtér, ☐18, 19, 47, 49) This super-cool cafe moonlights as a used-book exchange on the ground floor and boasts a large, bright gallery with additional seating upstairs. There are foreign newspapers to read and soups (890Ft to 1100Ft), sandwiches (from 1200Ft) and fried rice or curry (1890Ft), should you feel peckish. Try the super hot chocolate.

Oscar American Bar
BAR
(Map p202; ☑06 70 700 0222; http://oscarbudapest.hu; I Ostrom utca 14; ⊗5pm-midnight Wed, to 4am Thu-Sat; Ⓜ M2 Széll Kálmán tér) The decor is cinema-inspired (Hollywood memorabilia on the wood-panelled walls, leather director's chairs) and the beautiful crowd often act like they're on camera. Not to worry: the potent cocktails (950Ft to 2250Ft) – from daiquiris and cosmopolitans to champagne cocktails and mojitos – go down a treat. There's music most nights.

🍷 Pest

★ Neked Csak Dezső!
CRAFT BEER
(You're only Dezső!; Map p204; ☑06 20 316 0931, 06 30 177 7424; www.nekedcsak.hu; VIII Rákóczi út 29; ⊗9am-midnight Sun-Tue, to 1am Wed, to 2am Thu-Sat) This temple to craft beer, which takes its odd name from the slaughtered pig (note the wooden portrait on the wall) in the iconic Hungarian 1969 film *A Tanú* (The Witness), has 32 taps a-flowing, with such essential local IPAs and lagers as Horizont, Mad Scientist and four of their own brewed in house. Great place to start (or end) an evening.

★ Instant
CLUB
(Map p204; ☑06 70 638 5040; www.instant.co.hu; VII Akácfa utca 51; ⊗4pm-6am; ☐trolleybus 70, 74, 78, ☐4, 6) Many still love this 'ruin bar' even

---

BUDAPEST'S RUIN PUBS

Ruin pubs (*romkocsmák*) began to appear in the city from the early 2000s, when entrepreneurial freethinkers took over abandoned buildings and turned them into pop-up bars. At first very much a word-of-mouth scene, the ruin bars' popularity grew exponentially, and many have transformed from ramshackle, temporary sites full of flea-market furniture to more slick, year-round fixtures with covered areas to protect patrons from the winter elements. Start with **Anker't** (Map p204; ☑06 30 360 3389; www.facebook.com/ankertbar; VI Paulay Ede utca 33; ⊗2pm-midnight Sun-Tue, to 1am Wed, to 2am Thu, to 3am Fri & Sat; 🛜; Ⓜ M1 Opera), an achingly cool, grown-up courtyard pub surrounded by seriously ruined buildings, and move on to **Füge Udvar** (Map p204; ☑06 20 200 1000; http://legjobbkocsma.hu; VII Klauzál utca 19; ⊗4pm-4am; Ⓜ M2 Blaha Lujza tér, ☐4, 6), an enormous ruin pub with a large covered courtyard (all are on the Pest side).

in its new location as part of the **Fogas** (Map p204; ☑06 70 638 5040; www.fogashaz.hu; VII Akácfa utca 49; ☺4pm-6am; ☎; ☐trolleybus 70, 74, 78, ☐4, 6) stable and so do all our friends. It has a couple of dozen rooms to get lost in, seven bars, seven stages and two gardens with underground DJs and dance parties. It's always heaving.

DiVino Borbár   WINE BAR
(Map p204; ☑06 70 935 3980; www.divinoborbar. hu; V Szent István tér 3; ☺4pm-midnight Sun-Wed, to 2am Thu-Sat; Ⓜ M1 Bajcsy-Zsilinszky út) Central and always heaving, DiVino is Budapest's most popular wine bar, as the crowds spilling out onto the square in front of the Basilica of St Stephen in the warm weather will attest. Choose from more than 120 wines produced by some three-dozen winemakers, but be careful: those 150mL glasses (from 850Ft) go down quickly. Wine glass deposit is 500Ft.

☆ Entertainment

Handy websites for booking theatre and concert tickets include www.jegymester.hu and www.kulturinfo.hu.

★Liszt Music Academy   CLASSICAL MUSIC
(Liszt Zeneakadémia; Map p204; ☑1-462 4600, box office 1-321 0690; www.zeneakademia.hu; VI Liszt Ferenc tér 8; 1400-19,800Ft; ☺box office 10am-6pm; Ⓜ M1 Oktogon, ☐4, 6) Performances at Budapest's most important concert hall are usually booked up at least a week in advance, but more expensive (though still affordable) last-minute ones can sometimes be available. It's always worth checking.

Budapest Music Center   CONCERT VENUE
(BMC; Map p204; ☑1-216 7894; www.bmc.hu; IX Mátyás utca 8; tickets 1500-3000Ft; ☺library 9am-4.30pm Mon-Fri; Ⓜ M4 Fővám tér) Hosting a fantastic line-up of mainly Hungarian jazz and classical performances, the Budapest Music Center comprises a classy 350-capacity concert hall (tickets 1500Ft to 3000Ft), the **Opus Jazz Club** (and restaurant) with concerts at 8pm Tuesday to Saturday, a library and recording studios.

Gödör Klub   LIVE MUSIC
(Map p204; ☑06 20 201 3868; www.godorklub.hu; VI Király utca 8-10, Central Passage; ☺6pm-2am Mon-Wed, to 4am Thu-Sat; ☎; Ⓜ M1/2/3 Deák Ferenc tér) In the bowels of the Central Passage shopping centre on Király utca, Gödör has maintained its reputation for scheduling an excellent variety of indie, rock, jazz,

electronic and experimental music, as well as hosting quality club nights in its spare, industrial space. Exhibitions and movies in summer too.

🛍 Shopping

★Nagycsarnok   MARKET
(Great Market Hall; Map p204; ☑1-366 3300; www.piaconline.hu; IX Vámház körút 1-3; ☺6am-5pm Mon, to 6pm Tue-Fri, to 3pm Sat; Ⓜ M4 Fővám tér, ☐47, 49) Completed in 1897, this is Budapest's biggest market, though it has become a tourist magnet since its renovation for the millecentenary celebrations in 1996. Still, plenty of locals come here for fruit, vegetables, deli items, fish and meat. Head up to the 1st floor for Hungarian folk costumes, dolls, painted eggs, embroidered tablecloths, carved hunting knives and other souvenirs.

ℹ Information

ATMs are everywhere in Budapest, including in train and bus stations and at airport terminals. Avoid moneychangers (especially those on V Váci utca) in favour of banks if possible. Arrive about an hour before closing time to ensure the bureau de change desk is still open.

INTERNET ACCESS
Wireless (wi-fi) access is available at all hostels and hotels and very few hotels charge for the service. Many restaurants and bars and most cafes offer wi-fi, usually free to paying customers.

Electric Cafe (☑1-781 0098; www.electric cafe.hu; VII Dohány utca 37; per hr 300Ft; ☺9am-midnight; ☎; Ⓜ M2 Blaha Lujza tér) Large place with attached laundrette.

Vist@netcafe (☑06 70 585 3924; www.vistanetcafe.com; XIII Váci út 6; per hour 500Ft; ☺7am-midnight; Ⓜ M3 Nyugati pályaudvar) Another of the very few internet cafes open late.

MEDICAL SERVICES
Foreigners are entitled to first-aid and ambulance services only when they have suffered an accident; follow-up treatment and medicine must be paid for.

FirstMed Centers (☑1-224 9090; www. firstmedcenters.com; I Hattyú utca 14, 5th fl; ☺8am-8pm Mon-Fri, 9am-3pm Sat, urgent care 24hr; Ⓜ M2 Széll Kálmán tér) Modern private medical clinic with very expensive round-the-clock emergency treatment.

Király Dent (☑06 30 971 4812, 1-411 1511; https://kiralydent.hu/en; VI Király utca 14; ☺24hr Mon-Sat, 8am-9pm Sun; Ⓜ M1/2/3

Deák Ferenc tér) Reputable dental clinic with three branches in Budapest.

TOURIST INFORMATION

Budapest Info (Map p204; ☑1-576 1401; www.budapestinfo.hu; V Sütő utca 2; ☺8am-8pm; Ⓜ M1/2/3 Deák Ferenc tér, ☒47, 49) This office near Deák Ferenc tér is about the best single source of information about Budapest; stocks information about attractions, purchasable maps; can be crowded in summer.

ℹ Getting There & Away

AIR

Budapest's **Ferenc Liszt International Airport** (BUD; ☑1-296 7000; www.bud.hu/en) has two modern terminals side by side 24km southeast of the city centre.

BUS

All international buses and domestic ones to/from western Hungary and some destinations in the southeast of the country arrive at and depart from **Népliget bus station** (☑1-219 8086, international ticket office 1-219-8040; IX Üllői út 131; ☺ticket office 6am-6pm Mon-Fri, to 5pm Sat & Sun; Ⓜ M3 Népliget) in Pest. The international ticket office is upstairs. The German line FlixBus (p220) is represented here, as is the Hungarian Volánbusz (p220). There are left-luggage lockers in the basement costing 600/880Ft for a small/large backpack or suitcase for 24 hours. Népliget bus station is on the blue metro M3 (station: Népliget).

Stadion bus station (☑1-220-6227; XIV Hungária körút 48-52; ☺ticket office 6am-6pm Mon-Fri, to 4pm Sat & Sun; Ⓜ M2 Puskás Ferenc Stadion, ☒1) Generally serves cities and towns in eastern and northeastern Hungary.

Árpád-híd bus station (☑1-412 2597; XIII Árbóc utca 1; Ⓜ M3 Árpád Híd) Located on the Pest side of Árpád Bridge, this is the place to catch buses for the Danube Bend and towns to the northwest of Budapest.

CAR & MOTORCYCLE

All the international car-hire firms, including **Avis** (☑1-318 4240; www.avis.hu; V Arany János utca 26-28; ☺7am-6pm Mon-Fri, 8am-2pm Sat & Sun; Ⓜ M3 Arany János utca) and **Europcar** (☑1-505 4400; www.europcar.hu; V Erzsébet tér 7-8; ☺8am-6pm Mon & Fri, to 4.30pm Tue-Thu, to noon Sat; Ⓜ M1/2/3 Deák Ferenc tér), have offices in Budapest, and online rates, particularly if you choose the 'pay now' option, are very reasonable.

TRAIN

MÁV (p221) links up with the European rail network in all directions. Most international trains (and domestic traffic to/from the north

and northeast) arrive at **Keleti train station** (Keleti pályaudvar; ☑06 40 494 949; www.mavcsoport.hu; VIII Kerepesi út 2-6; Ⓜ M2/M4 Keleti pályaudvar).

Trains from some international destinations (eg Romania) and from the Danube Bend and Great Plain generally arrive at **Nyugati train station** (Western Train Station; ☑1-349 4949; VI Nyugati tér). Trains from some destinations in the south, eg Osijek in Croatia and Sarajevo in Bosnia, as well as some trains from Vienna, arrive at **Déli train station** (Déli pályaudvar; ☑1-349 4949; I Krisztina körút 37; Ⓜ M2 Déli pályaudvar).

All three stations are on metro lines.

ℹ Getting Around

TO/FROM THE AIRPORT

Minibuses, buses and trains to central Budapest from Ferenc Liszt International Airport run from 4.30am to 11.50pm (700Ft to 2000Ft). Taxis cost from 6000Ft to Pest and 7000Ft to Buda.

PUBLIC TRANSPORT

Public transport operates from 4.30am to between 9am and 11.50pm, depending on the line. After hours some 40 bus lines run along main roads. Tram 6 on the Big Ring Rd operates round the clock.

A single ticket for all forms of transport is 350Ft (60 minutes of uninterrupted travel on the same metro, bus, trolleybus or tram line without transferring/changing); a book of 10 tickets is 3000Ft. A 'transfer ticket' allowing unlimited stations with one change within one hour costs 530Ft. The three-day travel card (4150Ft) or the seven-day pass (4950Ft) make things easier, allowing unlimited travel inside the city limits. The fine for riding without a ticket is 8000Ft on the spot, or 16,000Ft if you pay within 30 days at the **BKK penalty office** (☑1-258 4636; www. bkk.hu; VII Akácfa utca 22; ☺9am-8pm Mon-Fri; Ⓜ M2 Blaha Lujza tér).

TAXI

Taxis in Budapest are cheap by European standards, and are – at long last – fully regulated, with uniform flagfall (700Ft) and per-kilometre charges (300Ft). Never get into a taxi that does not have a yellow licence plate and an identification badge displayed on the dashboard (as required by law), plus the logo of one of the reputable taxi firms on the outside of the side doors and a table of fares clearly visible on the right-side back door. Reputable taxi firms include **Budapest Taxi** (☑1-777 7777; www.budapesttaxi.hu), **City Taxi** (☑1-211 1111; www.citytaxi.hu), **Fő Taxi** (☑1-222 2222; www. fotaxi.hu) and **Taxi 4** (☑1-444 4444; www. taxi4.hu)

HUNGARY BUDAPEST

DANUBE BEND & WESTERN TRANSDANUBIA

The Danube Bend is a region of peaks and picturesque river towns to the north of Budapest. The name is quite literal: this is where hills on both banks force the river to turn sharply and flow southward. It is the most beautiful stretch of the Danube along its entire course, and several historical towns vie for visitors' attention. Szentendre has its roots in Serbian culture and became an important centre for art early in the 20th century. Around the bend is tiny Visegrád, Hungary's 'Camelot' in the 15th century and home to Renaissance-era palace ruins and an enchanting hilltop fortress. Esztergom, once the pope's 'eyes and ears' in Hungary, is now a sleepy town with the nation's biggest cathedral. The Danube meanders towards Western Transdanubia where you'll find Sopron, a historic city that's been around since the Roman Empire.

❶ Getting There & Away

BUS & TRAIN

Regular buses serve towns on the west bank of the Danube, but trains only go as far as Szentendre and (on a separate line) Esztergom. For Visegrád, you can take one of the regular trains from Budapest to the opposite bank of the river and then take a ferry across (sailings are linked to train arrivals).

BOAT

Regular **Mahart PassNave** (Map p204; ☑1-484 4013, 1-484 4013; www.mahartpassnave.hu; V Belgrád rakpart; ◷ 8am-5pm Mon-Fri) boats run to and from Budapest in season. From May to August, a boat departs Pest's Vigadó tér at 9am (from Batthyány tér in Buda 10 minutes later) from Tuesday to Sunday bound for Szentendre (one way/return 2310/3470Ft, 1½ hours) and Visegrád (2890/4330Ft, 3½ hours) before carrying on to Esztergom (3470/5200Ft, 5½ hours). It returns from Esztergom at 4pm, Visegrád at 5.40pm and Szentendre at 7pm, reaching Budapest at 8pm. The service is reduced to Saturday-only in April and September.

In addition, there is a boat to Szentendre (only) at 10.30am daily in July and August, from Tuesday to Sunday in May, June, September and October, and on Saturday in April. It returns from Szentendre at 5pm. A 2pm sailing to Szentendre departs Tuesday to Sunday in July and August, returning from Szentendre at 7pm

Hydrofoils travel from Budapest to Visegrád (one way/return 4300/6500Ft, one hour) and Esztergom (5300/8000Ft, 1½ hours) Tuesday to Sunday from May to September; boats leave at 10am and return at 5.30pm from Esztergom and 6pm from Visegrád.

Szentendre

☑ 26 / POP 26,450

Szentendre ('St Andrew' in Hungarian) is the southern gateway to the Danube Bend but has none of the imperial history or drama of Visegrád or Esztergom. As an art colony turned lucrative tourist centre, Szentendre strikes many travellers as a little too 'cute', and it is rammed with visitors most of the year. Still, it's an easy train trip from the capital 19km away, and the town's dozens of art museums, galleries and churches are well worth the trip. Just try to avoid visiting on weekends in summer.

The charming old centre around **Fő tér** (Main Square) (Main Square) has plentiful cafes and galleries, as well as beautiful baroque Serbian Orthodox churches. Meanwhile the **Art Mill** (Művészet Malom; ☑ 06 20 779 6657; www.muzeumicentrum.hu/en/artmill; Bogdányi utca 32; adult/6-26yr 1400/700Ft; ◷ 10am-6pm) exhibits cutting-edge art installations across three floors.

❶ Information

Tourinform (☑ 26-317 965; https://iranyszentendre.hu/en; Dumtsa Jenő utca 22; ◷ 10am-6pm), on the way to/from the train station, has lots of information about Szentendre and the Danube Bend.

❶ Getting There & Away

The easiest way to reach Szentendre from Budapest is to catch the H5 HÉV suburban train from Batthyány tér in Buda (660Ft, 40 minutes, every 10 to 20 minutes). In addition, there are efficient ferry services to Szentendre from Budapest between April and October

---

Visegrád

☑ 26 / POP 1840

Soporific, leafy Visegrád (from the Slavic words for 'high castle') has the most history of the main towns on the Danube Bend. While much of it has crumbled to dust over the centuries, reminders of its grand past can still be seen in its mighty 13th-century **Citadel** (Fellegvár; ☑ 26-398 101; https://parkerdo.hu/turizmus/latnivalok/visegradi-fellegvar; Várhegy; adult/concession 1700/850Ft; ◷ 9am-5pm mid-Mar-Apr & Oct, to 6pm May-Sep, to 4pm

Nov–mid-Mar), which offers spectacular views from high above a curve in the river, and its partially Renaissance **Royal Palace** (Mátyás Király Múzeum, Királyi Palota; ☑ 26-597 010; http://visegradmuzeum.hu/en/palota2; Fő utca 23; adult/concession 1100/550Ft; ⊙ 9am-5pm Tue-Sun Mar-Oct, 10am-4pm Tue-Sun Nov-Feb), seat of power during Visegrád's golden age in the 15th century under the reign of King Matthias Corvinus and to whom the museum there is dedicated.

ℹ Information

Visegrád Info (☑ 26-397 188; www.visitvisegrad.hu; Dunaparti út 1; ⊙ 10am-6pm daily Apr-Oct, to 4pm Tue-Sun Nov-Mar) is a good source of local information.

ℹ Getting There & Away

Visegrád buses are very frequent to/from Budapest's Újpest-Városkapu train station (745Ft, 1¼ hours, 39km). You can also reach Szentendre (465Ft, 45 minutes, 24km, hourly) and Esztergom (465Ft, 45 minutes, 25km). Regular ferry services link Visegrád with Budapest between April and September.

Esztergom

☑ 33 / POP 27,850

Esztergom's massive basilica, sitting high above the town and Danube River, is an incredible sight, rising out of what seems like nowhere in a rural stretch of country. But Esztergom's attraction goes deeper than that domed structure: the nation's first king, St Stephen, was born here in 975. It was a royal seat from the late 10th to the mid-13th centuries and has been the seat of Roman Catholicism in Hungary for more than a thousand years. In fact, **Esztergom Basilica** (Esztergomi Bazilika; ☑ 33-402 354; www.bazilika-esztergom.hu; Szent István tér 1; basilica free, crypt 300Ft, dome adult/concession 700/500Ft, treasury adult/concession 900/450Ft, combination ticket 1500/1000Ft; ⊙ 8am-6pm, crypt & treasury 9am-5pm, dome 9am-6pm) is Hungary's largest church. At the southern end of the hill is the extensive **Castle Museum** (Vármúzeum; ☑ 33-415 986; www.mnmvarmuzeuma.hu; Szent István tér 1; adult/concession 1600/800Ft; ⊙ 10am-6pm Tue-Sun Apr-Oct, to 4pm Tue-Sun Nov-Mar), housed in the former Royal Palace built during Esztergom's golden age. Below Castle Hill in the former Bishop's Palace, the **Christian Museum** (Keresztény Múzeum; ☑ 33-413 880; www.christianmuseum.hu; Mindszenty hercegprímás

tere 2; adult/concession 900/450Ft; ⊙ 10am-5pm Wed-Sun Mar-Dec) contains the finest collection of medieval religious art in Hungary. A picturesque town, packed with historic attractions, Esztergom makes a great day trip from Budapest and amply rewards those who linger longer.

ℹ Information

A private travel agency in the centre called **Cathedralis Tours** (☑ 33-520 260; Bajcsy-Zsilinszky utca 26; ⊙ 9am-5pm Mon-Fri, to noon Sat) is the only place in town for information.

ℹ Getting There & Away

Frequent buses run to/from Budapest (1120Ft, 1¼ hours), Visegrád (465Ft, 45 minutes) and Szentendre (930Ft, 1½ hours). Trains depart from Budapest's Nyugati train station (1120Ft, one hour) half-hourly. Ferries travel regularly from Budapest to Esztergom between April and September.

Sopron

☑ 99 / POP 62,450

Sopron is the most beautiful town in western Hungary. Its medieval Inner Town (Belváros) is intact and its cobbled streets are a pleasure to wander. And if that weren't enough, it's also famous for its wine, surrounded as it is by flourishing vineyards.

⊙ Sights

★ **Storno House & Collection**　MUSEUM
(Storno-ház és Gyűjtemény; ☑ 99-311 327; www.muzeum.sopron.hu; Fő tér 8; adult/concession Storno House 1000/500Ft, Boundless Story 700/350Ft; ⊙ 10am-6pm Tue-Sun) Built in 1417, Storno House has an illustrious history: King Matthias stayed here in 1482–83, and Franz Liszt played a number of concerts here in the mid-19th century. Later it was taken over by the Swiss-Italian family of Ferenc Storno, chimney sweep turned art restorer, whose re-carving of Romanesque and Gothic monuments throughout Transdanubia remains controversial. Don't miss the **Storno Collection**, the family's treasure trove. The **Boundless Story** exhibition of local history is also worth a peek.

🛏 Sleeping

★ **Sopronbánfalva Monastery Hotel**　MONASTERY €€€
(Sopronbánfalvi Kolostor Hotel; ☑ 06 70 684 9117, 99-505 895; www.banfalvakolostor.hu;

Kolostorhegy utca 1; s/d/ste €84/128/174; (P 🛜) Having worn many hats over the centuries – Carmelite convent, home for coal miners, mental hospital – this 15th-century monastery has now been sensitively restored as a beautiful 20-room hotel/retreat. The vaulted singles and light-filled doubles look out on to the forest. Upstairs there's an art gallery and a tranquil common space, the library. The **Refektórium** (📞99-505 895; www.banfalvakolostor.hu; Kolostorhegy utca 2, Sopronbánfalva Monastery Hotel; mains 3800-7600Ft; ⏰6-9pm daily, noon-3pm Sat & Sun; 🍴) restaurant serves among the best meals in Sopron.

Erhardt Pension   GUESTHOUSE €€€
(📞99-506 711; www.erhardts.hu; Balfi út 10; s/d from €68/83; P ✳ 🛜) This great central spot comprises nine compact and homey rooms decked out in soothing creams and browns, complete with super-comfy mattresses, and one of the best **restaurants** (📞99-506 711; www.erhardts.hu; Balfi út 10; mains 2990-4990Ft; ⏰11.30am-10pm Sun-Thu, to 11pm Fri & Sat; 🍴) in town. Three newer and more up-to-date rooms are in a separate building on nearby Halász utca.

🍸 Drinking

TasteVino Borbár & Vinotéka   WINE BAR
(📞06 30 519 8285; www.tastevino.hu; Várkerület 5; ⏰noon-midnight Tue-Sat) This is a vaulted bar and wine shop all in one, where you can sample the best that Sopron's wineries have to offer and also purchase your tipples of choice.

ℹ Information

Tourinform (📞99-951 975; http://turizmus.sopron.hu; Szent György utca 2; ⏰10am-6pm) in the Inner Town has information on Sopron and surrounds, including local vintners.

ℹ Getting There & Away

BUS

There are direct buses to Esztergom (3410Ft, four hours, daily), Keszthely (2520Ft, 3¼ hours, two daily) and Balatonfüred (3130Ft, four hours, two daily).

TRAIN

Direct services from the **train station** (Állomás utca), a 10-minute walk from the heart of Sopron, run to Budapest's Keleti train station (4735Ft, 2½ hours, six daily) and Vienna's Hauptbahnhof and Meidling (5000Ft, 1½ hours, three daily).

LAKE BALATON & SOUTHERN TRANSDANUBIA

Extending roughly 80km like a skinny, lop-sided paprika, at first glance Lake Balaton seems to simply be a happy, sunny expanse of opaque tourmaline-coloured water in which to play. But step beyond the beaches of Europe's biggest and shallowest body of water and you'll encounter vine-filled forested hills, historic towns and a wild peninsula jutting out 4km, nearly cutting the lake in half.

Then there's Southern Transdanubia, where whitewashed farmhouses with thatched roofs dominate a countryside that hasn't changed in centuries. Anchoring its centre is one of Hungary's most alluring cities, Pécs, where a Mediterranean feel permeates streets filled with relics of Hungary's Ottoman past and a head-spinning number of exceptional museums.

Balatonfüred

📞87 / POP 13,140

Balatonfüred is not only the oldest resort on Lake Balaton's northern shore, it's also the most fashionable. In days gone by the wealthy and famous built large villas on its tree-lined streets, and their architectural legacy can still be seen today. Yes, it's highly touristy, but it's an excellent place to base yourself on the lake, with its endless lodging and dining options, and a superb tree-lined promenade along the shore where everyone goes for their pre- or postprandial dinner strolls. The town also has the most stylish marina on the lake and is known for the thermal waters of its world-famous heart hospital.

🛏 Sleeping

Aqua Haz   PENSION €€
(Aqua House; 📞87-342 813; www.aquahaz.hu; Garay utca 2; s/d/tr 9500/11,500/15,000Ft; P 🛜) This family-run pension, in a pale-yellow three-storey house, is conveniently located between the lake and the train and bus stations. Most of the 21 rooms feature bright balconies, and free bikes are available for tooling around town. Excellent breakfast (1100Ft).

⭐ **Club Hotel Füred**   RESORT €€€
(📞06 70 458 1242, 87-482 411; www.clubhotelfured.hu; Anna sétány 1-3; r/ste from €70/185; P ✳ 🛜 🏊) This stunner of a resort hotel, right on the lake, about 1.5km from the town

centre, has 43 rooms and suites in several buildings spread over 2.5 hectares of parkland and lush gardens. There's an excellent spa centre with sauna, steam room and pool, but the real delight is the private beach at the end of the garden. Stellar service.

✖ Eating & Drinking

★ Bistro Sparhelt
BISTRO €€€

(☑87-950 406, 06 70 639 9944; http://bistro sparhelt.hu; Szent István tér 7; mains 3190-6990Ft; ⊙11.30am-10pm Wed-Sun; ☑) Head inland from the lake to the town hall for a rare gastronomic treat. Chef Balázs Elek presides over a sleek, minimalist restaurant with a succinct menu that changes monthly, its dishes dictated by whatever is market-fresh. Expect to be treated to the likes of duck liver with crab and wakame or leg of lamb with plum and sweet potatoes. Superb stuff.

Baricska Csárda
HUNGARIAN €€€

(☑87-950 738; www.baricska.hu; Baricska dűlő; mains 3100-5500Ft; ⊙noon-10pm Thu-Mon, 5-10pm Wed) If you are going to eat typical Hungarian fare, let it be here, under the trellises covered in creeping vines and among the vineyards. The setting is particularly magical in the evenings, and the dishes – paprika catfish with cottage cheese noodles, smoked duck breast with red cabbage and other Hungarian classics – are beautifully presented. There's an extensive list of Balaton wines.

Kredenc Borbisztró
WINE BAR

(☑06 20 518 9960, 87-343 229; www.kredencbor bisztro.hu; Blaha Lujza utca 7; ⊙9am-midnight) This family-run retro-style wine bar and bistro is a peaceful retreat near the lakefront. The menu is stacked with local wines, and the owner is often on hand to recommend the best tipple according to your tastes. The wine bar sells bottles of everything they serve plus an extensive selection of regional wines. Weekend DJ sets and live music.

ℹ Information

Tourinform (☑87-580 480; www.balaton fured.info.hu; Blaha Lujza utca 5; ⊙9am-7pm Mon-Fri, to 5pm Sat, 10am-4pm Sun Jun-Aug, 9am-5pm Mon-Fri, 9am-3pm Sat Sep-May) in the centre has scads of information on Balatonfüred and other towns along the lake.

ℹ Getting There & Away

BOAT

In July and August up to seven daily **Balaton Shipping Company** (Balatoni Hajózási Rt; ☑84-

310 050; www.balatonihajozas.hu; Krúdy sétány 2, Siófok) ferries link Balatonfüred with Siófok and Tihany (adult/child 1400/700Ft). From April to June and September to late October, at least four daily ferries depart for those same ports.

BUS & TRAIN

Buses reach Tihany (310Ft, 30 minutes, 14 daily) and Keszthely (1300Ft, 1½ hours, eight daily). For Budapest buses (2520, three hours) and trains (2725Ft, two hours) are much of a muchness but bus departures are more frequent (up to nine daily) against the three trains.

Keszthely

☑83 / POP 19,390

Keszthely is a town of gently crumbling grand town houses perched at the western edge of Lake Balaton. It's hands down one of the loveliest spots to stay in the area, and far removed from the tourist hot spots on the lake. You can take a dip in small, shallow beaches by day, absorb the lively yet relaxed ambience by night, and get a dose of culture by popping into the town's handful of museums and admiring its historical buildings. Whatever you do, don't miss the Festetics Palace, a lavish baroque home fit for royalty.

◎ Sights

★ Festetics Palace
PALACE

(Festetics Kastély; ☑06 30 556 7719, 83-314 194; www.helikonkastely.hu; Kastély utca 1; Palace & Coach Museum adult/6-26yr 2500/1250Ft; ⊙9am-6pm Jul & Aug, to 5pm May, Jun & Sep, to 5pm Tue-Sun Oct-Apr) The glimmering white, 100-room Festetics Palace was begun in 1745, and the two wings were extended out from the original building 150 years later. Some 18 splendid rooms in the baroque south wing are now part of the **Helikon Palace Museum**, as is the palace's greatest treasure, the **Helikon Library**, with its 90,000 volumes and splendid carved furniture.

Helikon Beach
BEACH

(Helikon Strand; adult/concession 500/350Ft; ⊙8am-7pm May–mid-Sep) Reedy Helikon Beach, north of City Beach, is good for swimming and sunbathing. It has a unique view of both the north and south shores of the lake.

🛏 Sleeping & Eating

★ Ilona Kis Kastély Panzió
PENSION €€

(Ilona Little Castle Pansion; ☑83-312 514; www. balaton-airport.com; Móra Ferenc utca 22; s/d/apt incl breakfast 9500/12,500/17,500Ft; ℗✳🛜)

WORTH A TRIP

HOT SPRINGS OF HÉVÍZ

Hévíz (population 4630), just 8km northwest of Keszthely, is the most famous of Hungary's spa towns because of the **Gyógy-tó** (Hévíz Thermal Lake; ☑83-342 830, 06 30 959 1002; www.spaheviz.hu; Dr Schulhof Vilmos sétány 1; per 3hr/4hr/day 3000/3700/5200Ft; ☺8am-7pm Jun-Aug, 9am-6pm May & Sep, to 5.30pm Apr & Oct, to 5pm Nov-Mar) – Europe's largest 'thermal lake'. A dip into this water-lily-filled lake is essential for anyone visiting the Lake Balaton region.

Fed by 80 million litres of thermal water daily, the lake is an astonishing sight. The temperature averages 33°C and never drops below 22°C in winter, allowing bathing even when there's ice on the fir trees of the surrounding Park Wood.

Buses link Hévíz with Keszthely (250Ft, 20 minutes) every half-hour.

With its pointed turrets, this delightful pension resembles a miniature castle. The five rooms might be on the compact side, but some have balconies, while the apartments are positively spacious. A generous, varied breakfast is included.

⭐ **Pura Vida Port**   MEDITERRANEAN €€€
(☑06 30 860 4629; www.facebook.com/puravida portkeszthely; Vitorlás-kikötő; mains 3690-5690Ft; ☺11am-10pm) On a breezy terrace by the marina, this new Mediterranean restaurant serves up mains such as osso bucco and confit leg of lamb but keeps holidaymakers happy with less complicated fare such as pizzas (1700Ft to 3200Ft) and burgers (2990Ft to 3490Ft). The dishes are well executed, and the staff are amiable and prompt.

ℹ️ Information

Tourinform (☑83-314 144; www.keszthely.hu; Kossuth Lajos utca 30; ☺9am-7pm mid-Jun–Aug, 9am-5pm Mon-Fri, to 1pm Sat Sep–mid-Jun) on the main street is an excellent source of information on Keszthely and the west Balaton area. Lots of brochures, plus bicycles for rent (2200Ft per day).

ℹ️ Getting There & Away

BUS

Buses link Keszthely with Hévíz (250Ft, 20 minutes, half-hourly), Budapest (3410Ft, three to

four hours, up to 12 daily) and Pécs (3130Ft, 3¼ hours, up to six daily).

TRAIN

Keszthely has train links to Balatonfüred (1490Ft, two hours, 10 daily) with a change at Tapolca, and to Budapest (3705Ft, 3¼ hours, nine daily). Budapest trains mostly arrive at Déli station, but occasionally go to Budapest Keleti.

Pécs

☑72 / POP 144,190

Blessed with a mild climate, an illustrious past and a number of fine museums and monuments, Pécs is one of the most pleasant and interesting cities to visit in Hungary. With its handful of universities, the nearby Mecsek Hills and the lively nightlife, it's second only to Budapest on many travellers' Hungarian bucket lists.

⊙ Sights

⭐ **Zsolnay**
Cultural Quarter   NOTABLE BUILDING
(Zsolnay Kulturális Negyed; ☑72-500 350; www.zskn.hu; 48hr combination ticket adult/concession/family 4990/3000/10,000Ft; ☺9am-6pm daily Apr-Oct, to 5pm Tue-Sun Nov-Mar) The sprawling Zsolnay Cultural Quarter, built on the grounds of the original Zsolnay porcelain factory, is divided into four sections (craftspeople, family and children, creative, and university) and is a lovely place to stroll around. Highlights include the **Gyugi Collection** of 700 Zsolnay pieces, the street of artisans' shops, the exhibition tracing the history of the Zsolnay factory and its founding family, and the still-functioning **Hamerli Glove Manufactury** dating from 1861.

Mosque Church   CHURCH
(Mecset templom; ☑06 30 373 8900; https://pecsi egyhazmegye.hu/en/attractions/mosque-of-pasha-gazi-kassim; Hunyadi János út 4; adult/concession 1800/900Ft; ☺9am-5pm Mon-Sat, 1-5pm Sun) The largest building extant from the time of the Turkish occupation, the former Pasha Gazi Kassim Mosque (now the Inner Town Parish Church) dominates the main square in Pécs. The Ottomans built the square-based mosque in the mid-16th century with the stones of the ruined Gothic Church of St Bertalan. The Catholics moved back in the early 18th century. The Islamic elements include windows with distinctive Turkish ogee arches, a *mihrab* (prayer niche), faded verses from the Koran and lovely geometric frescoes.

🛏 Sleeping

Nap Hostel HOSTEL €
(✆ 06 30 252 2972; www.naphostel.com; Király utca 23-25; dm 3000-3500Ft, d 9000Ft, apt 10,000Ft; @ 🛜) This welcoming hostel has three dorm rooms (each with between six and eight beds), a double with washbasin and a three-person apartment on the 1st floor of a former bank (dating from 1885). One of the six-bed dorm rooms has a corner balcony, and there's a communal kitchen. Enter through the main entrance of the hostel bar.

★ Hotel Arkadia BOUTIQUE HOTEL €€€
(✆ 72-512 550; www.hotelarkadiapecs.hu; Hunyadi János út 1; s/d/tr €53/65/90; P ❄ 🛜) This Bauhaus-style hostelry, spread across two buildings, has plenty of polished steel, exposed brick and Corbusier-style furniture in its public areas. The 32 guestrooms follow in the same vein with lots of straight lines and solid colours, but thick throws and ample doses of natural light lend them a cosy vibe. Avoid the mansard rooms at the top.

🍴 Eating & Drinking

★ Blöff Bisztró BALKAN €€
(✆ 72-497 469; Jókai tér 5; mains 1800-4500Ft; ⊗ 11am-midnight) This (mostly) Balkan bad boy has quickly acquired a solid following in town. It may be to do with its super-central location, but really the main draw is the quality of the simple, satisfying dishes – fried *papalina* (sprats) with garlic and parsley, carp crackling, *csevap* (Balkan-style grilled meat) and not-often-seen *lepények* (pies stuffed with meat or cheese) – and the friendly service.

Nappali Bar BAR
(✆ 72-585 705; www.facebook.com/nappali.bar; Király utca 23-25; ⊗ 9am-2am Sun-Thu, to 3am Fri & Sat) Nappali is one of the hippest gathering spots in town for a coffee or a glass of wine. Its outdoor seating fills up on warm, lazy evenings, and there's live music some nights. For breakfast (from 1500Ft) or lunch, head next door to sister-establishment Reggeli Bar, open from 8am to 3pm daily.

ℹ Information

Tourinform (✆ 06 30 681 7195, 72-213 315; www.iranypecs.hu; Széchenyi tér 1; ⊗ 8am-6pm Mon-Fri, 10am-6pm Sat & Sun) has both knowledgeable staff and copious information on Pécs and surrounds.

ℹ Getting There & Away

BUS
Buses connect Pécs with Budapest (3690Ft, 4¼ hours, 10 daily), Szeged (3410Ft, 3¼ hours, eight daily) and Kecskemét (3410Ft, 3¼ hours, two daily).

TRAIN
Up to nine direct trains connect Pécs with Budapest's Keleti station (4305Ft, three hours, daily). Most destinations in Southern Transdanubia are best reached by bus.

GREAT PLAIN

Like the outback for Australians or the Wild West for Americans, the Nagyalföld (Great Plain) – also known as the *puszta* – holds a romantic appeal for Hungarians. Many

---

WORTH A TRIP

HISTORIC TIHANY

While in Balatonfüred, don't miss the chance to visit Tihany (population 1480), a peninsula jutting 5km into the lake and the place with the greatest historical significance on Lake Balaton. Tihany is home to the celebrated **Benedictine Abbey Church** (Bencés Apátság Templom; ✆ 87-538 200; www.tihanyiapatsag.hu; András tér 1; adult/concession/family incl abbey museum 1200/700/3200Ft; ⊗ 9am-6pm Mon-Sat, 11.15am-6pm Sun May-Sep, 10am-5pm Mon-Sat, 11.15am-5pm Sun Apr & Oct, 10am-4pm Mon-Sat, 11.15am-4pm Sun Nov-Mar), filled with fantastic altars, pulpits and screens carved in the mid-18th century by an Austrian lay brother; all are baroque-rococo masterpieces. The church attracts a lot of tourists, but the peninsula itself has an isolated, almost wild feel. Hiking is one of Tihany's main attractions; a good map outlining the trails is available from the **Tourinform** (✆ 87-448 804; www.tihany.hu; Kossuth Lajos utca 20; ⊗ 9am-6pm Mon-Fri, 10am-6pm Sat & Sun mid-Jun–Aug, 9am-5pm Mon-Fri, 10am-4pm Sat & Sun Sep–mid-Jun) office just down from the church. Buses bound for Tihany depart from Balatonfüred's bus/train station (310Ft, 30 minutes, 15 daily). The bus stops at both ferry landings before climbing to Tihany village.

of these notions come as much from the collective imagination as they do from history, but there's no arguing the spellbinding potential of big-sky country. The Hortobágy region is where the myth of the lonely *pásztor* (shepherd), the wayside *csárda* (inn) and Gypsy violinists – kept alive in literature and art – was born. The horse and herding show at Hortobágy National Park recreates this pastoral tradition. The Great Plain is also home to cities of graceful architecture and history. Szeged is a centre of art and culture, Kecskemét is full of art nouveau gems and Debrecen is the 'Calvinist Rome'.

Szeged

🗹 62 / POP 161,120

Szeged is a bustling border town with a handful of historic sights that line the embankment along the Tisza River and a clutch of sumptuous art nouveau town palaces. Importantly, it's also a big university town, which means lots of culture, lots of partying and an active festival scene that lasts throughout the year.

◉ Sights

Reök Palace ARCHITECTURE
(Reök Palota; 🗹 62-471 411; www.reok.hu; Magyar Ede tér 2; ◎ 10am-6pm Tue-Sun) The Reök Palace

---

WORTH A TRIP

TREASURES OF KECSKEMÉT

Ringed with vineyards and orchards, the lovely city of Kecskemét (population 110,640) lies halfway between the Danube and the Tisza Rivers in the heart of the southern Great Plain. It's a green, pedestrian-friendly place with beautiful art nouveau architecture, including the masterful **Ornamental Palace** (Cifrapalota; Rákóczi út 1), the sandy-pink, stepped-roof **City Hall** (Városház; 🗹 76-513 513; Kossuth tér 1; ◎ by arrangement) and the restored **Otthon Cinema** (Széchenyi tér 4).

Tourinform (🗹 76-481 065; www.iranykecskemet.hu/en; Kossuth tér 1; ◎ 8.30am-5.30pm Mon-Fri, 9am-1pm Sat mid-May–Sep, 8am-4pm Mon-Fri Oct–mid-May) is centrally located in City Hall on the main square. Kecskemét is served by hourly buses to/from Budapest (1680Ft, 1½ hours) and Szeged (1680Ft, two hours).

---

is a mind-blowing green-and-lilac art nouveau structure, built in 1907, that looks like a decoration at the bottom of an aquarium. It's been polished up to regain its original lustre in recent years and now hosts regular photography and visual-arts exhibitions. There's also a lovely retro-style **cafe** (Reök Craft Cakeshop; 🗹 06 30 668 8059; www.facebook.com/reokcukraszda; cakes 300-750Ft; ◎ 8am-9pm) here.

Anna Baths SPA
(Anna Fürdő; 🗹 62-553 330; www.szegedsport.hu/intezmenyek/anna-furdo; Tisza Lajos körút 24; adult/child 1900/1600Ft, after 9pm 1200Ft; ◎ 6am-8pm & 9pm-midnight Mon-Fri, 6am-8pm Sat & Sun) The lovely, cream-coloured Anna Baths were built in 1896 to imitate the tilework and soaring dome of a Turkish bath. Rich architectural detail surrounds all the modern saunas and bubbly pools you'd expect. There's a fountain spouting free thermal drinking water in front of the building.

⚜ Festivals & Events

★ **Szeged Open-Air Festival** CULTURAL
(Szegedi Szabadtéri Játékok; 🗹 62-541 205; www.szegediszabadteri.hu; ◎ Jun-Aug) The Szeged Open-Air Festival held in Dóm tér from June to August is the largest cultural festival in Hungary outside of Budapest. The outdoor theatre in front of the Votive Church seats up to 6000 people. Main events include an opera, an operetta, a play, folk dancing, classical music, ballet and a rock opera.

🛏 Sleeping

Familia Vendégház GUESTHOUSE €€
(Family Guesthouse; 🗹 62-441 122; www.familia panzio.hu; Szentháromság utca 71; s/d/tr 7500/12,000/14,000Ft; P ❋ 🞀) Families and international travellers love this family-run guesthouse with contemporary, if nondescript, furnishings in a great Old Town building close to the train station. The 24 rooms have high ceilings, lots of wood and brick walls, and loads of light from tall windows. Air-conditioning costs an extra 500Ft.

Art Hotel Szeged BUSINESS HOTEL €€€
(🗹 62-592 888, 06 30 697 4681; www.arthotel szeged.hu; Somogyi utca 16; s/d/ste from €90/106/120; ❋ 🞀) Business travellers love this upbeat 71-room hotel for its ubercentral location just off Somogyi utca and its large underground garage (parking costs €11 extra). Other travellers will love the primary colours, the neon and the interesting artwork. Rooms are generously proportioned,

DEBRECEN: CULTURE & COWBOY COUNTRY

Debrecen (population 202,210) is Hungary's second-largest city, and its array of museums and thermal baths will keep you busy for a day or two. Start with the colourful **Calvinist College** (Református Kollégium; ☑ 52-614 370; www.reformatuskollegium.ttre. hu; Kálvin tér 16; adult/concession/family 900/500/2000Ft; ⊙10am-4pm Mon-Sat Mar-Oct, 10am-4pm Mon-Fri Nov-Feb), before splashing around the slides and waterfalls within **Aquaticum Debrecen Spa** (☑ 52-514 1174; www.aquaticum.hu/en; Nagyerdei Park 1; adult/ concession thermal baths 2050/1650Ft, with saunas 2900/2600Ft; ⊙7am-9pm); you can sleep here, too.

Next take a trip to **Hortobágy National Park**, 40km west, once celebrated for its sturdy *csikósok* (cowboys), inns and Gypsy bands. You can see a staged historical recreation at the **Máta Stud Farm** (Mátai Ménes; ☑ 06 70 492 7655, 52-589 368; www.hortobagy. eu/hu/matai-menes; Hortobágy-Máta; adult/child 3000/1500Ft; ⊙10am, noon & 2pm mid-Mar-Oct, plus 4pm Apr-mid-Oct).

Buses reach Debrecen from Eger (2520Ft, 2½ hours, six daily) and Szeged (3950Ft, five hours, four daily), while trains go direct from Budapest (3950Ft, 3½ hours, hourly). Six buses stop daily at Hortobágy village on runs between Debrecen (745Ft, 40 minutes) and Eger (1680Ft, 1¾ hours).

and some bathrooms have tubs. The centrepiece of the 3rd-floor fitness centre is a hot tub facing the Votive Church.

✖ Eating

Malata BURGERS €€
(☑ 06 30 190 2500; www.facebook.com/malata kezmuves; Somogyi utca 13; mains 1590-3590Ft; ⊙noon-11pm Sun-Thu, to 1am Fri & Sat; ☑) This great new hipster hang-out is part ruin garden, part pub/cafe and counts upwards of a dozen craft beers on tap. The food is mostly gourmet burgers but not exclusively so, with good choices for vegetarians. Order and pay at the bar. In winter and rain, sit in the colourful cafe, where books and frying pans dangle from the ceiling.

★ Tiszavirág Restaurant HUNGARIAN €€€
(☑ 62-554 888; http://tiszaviragszeged.hu; Hajnóczy utca 1/b; mains 3250-4900Ft; ⊙noon-3pm & 6-10pm Tue-Sat) The restaurant at the **Tiszavirág Hotel** (d/ste €110/160; ❉ �fi) serves beautifully presented international and modernised Hungarian dishes, such as guinea fowl with Jerusalem artichokes, and pigeon with couscous and beetroot. The selection of Hungarian wines by the glass is excellent and the service both warm and efficient. Simple but elegant decor, with great lighting.

❶ Information

The exceptionally helpful **Tourinform** (☑ 62-488 699; www.szegedtourism.hu; Széchenyi tér 12; ⊙9am-6pm Mon-Fri , to 1pm Sat Jun-Aug, 9am-5pm Mon-Fri, to 1pm Sat Apr, May, Sep & Oct,

9am-5pm Mon-Fri Nov-Mar) office is in swanky new premises facing leafy Széchenyi tér.

❶ Getting There & Away

BUS

Buses run to Pécs (3410Ft, 3¼ hours, eight daily) and Debrecen (3950Ft, five hours, four daily). You can also get to the Serbian cities of to Novi Sad (2520Ft, 3½ hours, once daily) and to Subotica (1300Ft, 1½ hours, three to four times daily).

TRAIN

Szeged is on the main rail line to Budapest's Nyugati train station (3705Ft, 2½ hours, hourly); many trains also stop halfway along in Kecskemét (1830Ft, one hour).

NORTHERN HUNGARY

Northern Hungary is the home of Hungary's two most famous wines – honey-sweet Tokaj and Eger's famed Bull's Blood – and a region of microclimates conducive to wine production. The chain of wooded hills in the northeast constitutes the foothills of the Carpathian Mountains, which stretch along the Hungarian border with Slovakia.

Eger

☑ 36 / POP 53,440

Filled with beautifully preserved baroque buildings, Eger is a jewellery box of a town with loads to see and do. Explore the bloody

TOKAJ WINE COUNTRY

Since the 15th century, the world-renowned sweet wines of Tokaj (population 4150) have been produced in this picturesque little town of old buildings, nesting storks and cellars. **Tourinform** (☑ 47-352 125, 06 70 388 8870; www.visittokaj.com; Serház utca 1; ⊙ 9am-6pm Mon-Fri, 10am-6pm Sat, 10am-2pm Sun Jun-Aug, 9am-4pm Mon-Fri, 10am-2pm Sat & Sun Sep-May) can help with winery tours and accommodation. Up to 16 trains a day head west for Budapest (4485Ft, 3¼ hours) through Miskolc, and south to Debrecen (1680Ft, two hours).

history of Turkish occupation and defeat at the hilltop castle; climb an original Ottoman minaret; listen to an organ performance at the colossal basilica; or relax in a renovated Turkish bath. Then spend time traipsing from cellar to cellar in the Valley of Beautiful Women, tasting the celebrated Eger Bull's Blood (Egri Bikavér) and other local wines from the cask. Flanked by northern Hungary's most inviting range of hills, the Bükk, Eger also provides nearby opportunities for hiking and other outdoor excursions.

◉ Sights

★Eger Castle FORTRESS

(Egri Vár; ☑ 36-312 744; www.egrivar.hu; Vár köz 1; castle grounds adult/child 850/425Ft, incl museum 1700/850Ft; ⊙ exhibits 10am-6pm daily Apr-Oct, to 4pm Tue-Sun Nov-Mar, castle grounds 8am-10pm Apr-Oct, to 6pm Nov-Mar) Climb up cobbled Vár köz from Tinódi Sebestyén tér to reach the castle, erected in the 13th century after the Mongol invasion. Models, drawings and artefacts such as armour and Turkish uniforms in the **Castle History Exhibition**, on the 1st floor of the former Bishop's Palace (1470), painlessly explain the castle's story. On the eastern side of the complex are foundations of the Gothic 12th-century **St John's Cathedral**. Enter the **castle casemates** (Kazamata), hewn from solid rock, via the nearby **Dark Gate**.

Lyceum Library LIBRARY

(Liceumi Könyvtar; ☑ 06 30 328 3030, 36-325 211; Eszterházy tér 1, Lyceum, Room 223; adult/child 1000/500Ft; ⊙ 9.30am-3.30pm Tue-Sun May-Sep, 9.30am-1.30pm Tue-Sun Oct, Nov, Mar &

Apr) This 160,000-volume, all-wood library on the 1st floor of the Lyceum's south wing contains hundreds of priceless manuscripts, medical codices and incunabula. The trompe l'oeil ceiling fresco painted by Bohemian artist Johann Lukas Kracker in 1778 depicts the Counter-Reformation's Council of Trent (1545–63), with a lightning bolt setting heretical manuscripts ablaze. It was Eger's – and its archbishop's – response to the Enlightenment and the Reformation.

Valley of the Beautiful Women WINE

(Szépasszony-völgy; www.ieger.com/valley-beautiful-woman.html) More than 24 wine cellars are carved into rock at the evocatively named Valley of the Beautiful Women. The choice can be daunting, so walk around first and have a look. Try ruby-red Bull's Blood or any of the whites – *leányka, olaszrizling* and *hárslevelű* – from nearby Debrő. The valley is a little more than 1km southwest across Rte 25 and off Király utca. Walk, or hop on a **Dottika** (☑ 06 30 928 8161; www.facebook.com/KisvonatEger; Kisvölgy 21; 1000Ft; ⊙ 10.30am-6.30pm Apr-Oct) mini-train.

🛏 Sleeping

Agria Retur Vendégház GUESTHOUSE €

(☑ 06 20 259 7291; www.returvendeghaz.hu; Knézich Károly utca 18; s/d/tr 4400/7800/10,800Ft; @🛜) You couldn't receive a more inviting welcome than the one you'll get at this guesthouse near the minaret. Walking up three flights of stairs, you enter a cheery, communal, fully equipped kitchen/eating area that's central to four mansard rooms. Out the back is a huge garden with tables and a barbecue at your disposal. Just read the fan mail on the wall.

★Hotel Senator Ház BOUTIQUE HOTEL €€€

(Senator House Hotel; ☑ 06 30 489 8744, 36-411 711; www.senatorhaz.hu; Dobó István tér 11; s/d €55/76; ✺@🛜) Eleven cosy rooms with traditional furnishings fill the upper floors of this delightful 18th-century inn – a home away from home – on the main square. The ground floor is shared between a quality restaurant and a reception area stuffed with antiques and curios. Expect the warmest of welcomes.

🍴 Eating & Drinking

★Macok Bistro & Wine Bar HUNGARIAN €€€

(Macok Bisztró és Borbár; ☑ 36-516 180; www.imolaudvarhaz.hu/en/the-macok-bisztro-wine-bar.html; Tinódi Sebestyén tér 4; mains 3190-5290Ft;

⊙ noon-10pm Sun-Thu, to 11pm Fri & Sat) With its inventive menu and excellent wine cellar, this stylish eatery at the foot of the castle has been named among the top dozen restaurants in Hungary, and who are we to disagree? We'll come back in particular for the duck liver *brûlée* (2590Ft) and the roasted rabbit with liver 'crisps' (3250Ft). There's a lovely dining-room courtyard with a water feature.

Biboros   CLUB
(✐ 06 70 199 2733; www.facebook.com/biboros eger; Bajcsy-Zsilinszky utca 6; ⊙ 11am-3am Mon-Fri, 1pm-3am Sat, 3pm-midnight Sun) A subdued ruin bar by day, the 'Cardinal' transforms into a raucous dance club late in the evening; the cops at the door most weekend nights are a dead giveaway. Enjoy.

ℹ Information

Meant to promote both the town and areas surrounding Eger, **Tourinform** (✐ 06 20 378 0514, 36-517 715; www.eger.hu; Bajcsy-Zsilinszky utca 9; ⊙ 8am-6pm Mon-Fri, 9am-1pm Sat & Sun Jul & Aug, 8am-5pm Mon-Fri, 9am-1pm Sat Apr-Jun, Sep & Oct, 8am-5pm Mon-Fri Nov-Mar) here is surprisingly unhelpful.

ℹ Getting There & Away

BUS

From Eger, buses serve Debrecen (2520Ft, 2½ hours, six daily), Kecskemét (3130Ft, four hours, two daily) and Szeged (3950Ft, five hours, two daily).

TRAIN

Up to seven direct trains a day head for Budapest's Keleti train station (2520Ft, two hours).

SURVIVAL GUIDE

ℹ Directory A–Z

ACCESSIBLE TRAVEL

Hungary has made great strides in recent years in making public areas and facilities more accessible to the disabled. Wheelchair ramps, toilets fitted for the disabled and inward-opening doors, though not as common as they are in Western Europe, do exist, and audible traffic signals for the blind are becoming commonplace in the cities.

For more information, contact the **Hungarian Federation of Disabled Persons' Associations** (MEOSZ; ✐ 1-388 2387; www.meosz.hu; III San Marco utca 76).

ACCOMMODATION

Hungary has a wide range of accommodation. Book a couple of months in advance for Budapest, Lake Balaton and the Danube Bend in high season.

Camping Options range from private sites with few facilities to enormous caravan campgrounds with swimming pools.

Hostels Inexpensive, prevalent in Budapest, and with lots of backpacker facilities.

Hotels Anything from socialist-era brutalist architecture to elegant five-star places, quirky boutique hotels and converted manor houses.

Pensions, inns and B&Bs Often cosy, family-run places with all the facilities of a small hotel.

Private homes and apartments Book a room or an entire place (usually) with English-speaking hosts.

Booking Services

Camping One of the best resources for finding a campsite in a particular part of the country is http://en.camping.info; another good website is www.camping.hu.

Farmhouses For information, contact the **Association of Hungarian Rural & Agrotourism** (FATOSZ; ✐ 1-352 9804; www.fatosz. eu; VII Király utca 93; ▣ trolleybus 70, 78) or the **Centre of Rural Tourism** (✐ 1-788-9932; www.falutur.hu; VII Dohány utca 86; ▣ 4, 6) in Budapest.

Hostels The Hungarian Youth Hostel Association (www.miszsz.hu) lists a number of places across the country associated with Hostelling International (HI), but not all HI-associated hostels provide discounts to HI card-holders.

Pensions, Inns & B&Bs A useful website is www.hoteltelnet.hu/en/pensions.

LEGAL MATTERS

There is a 100% ban on alcohol when driving and it is taken very seriously. Police conduct routine roadside checks with breathalysers and if you are found to have even 0.005% of alcohol in your blood, you could be fined up to 300,000Ft on the spot; police have been known to fine for less than that level of alcohol, so it's best not to drink at all. In the event of an accident, the drinking party is automatically regarded as guilty.

LGBT+ TRAVELLERS

Budapest offers a reasonable gay scene for its size but there's not much going on publicly elsewhere in Hungary.

Háttér Society (Háttér Társaság; ✐ info & counselling hotline 1-329 3380, office 1-329 2670; www.hatter.hu) Operates an information and counselling hotline from 6pm to 11pm.

Labrisz Lesbian Association (✐ 06 30 295 5415; www.labrisz.hu) Has info on Hungary's lesbian scene.

MONEY

ATMs are widely available. Credit and debit cards are accepted in most hotels and restaurants.

OPENING HOURS

With rare exceptions, opening hours (nyitva-tartás) are posted on the front doors of businesses; nyitva means 'open' and zárva 'closed'.

Banks 7.45am or 8am to 5pm Monday to Thursday, to 2pm or 4pm Friday

Bars 11am to midnight Sunday to Thursday, to 2am Friday and Saturday

Businesses 9am or 10am to 6pm Monday to Friday, to 1pm or 2pm Saturday

Clubs 4pm to 2am Sunday to Thursday, to 4am Friday and Saturday; some only open on weekends

Grocery stores and supermarkets 7am to 7pm Monday to Friday, to 3pm Saturday; some also 7am to noon Sunday

Restaurants 11am to 11pm; breakfast venues open by 8am

Shops 10am to 6pm Monday to Friday, to 1pm Saturday

PUBLIC HOLIDAYS

Hungary celebrates 10 ünnep (public holidays) each year.

New Year's Day 1 January

1848 Revolution/National Day 15 March

Easter Monday March/April

International Labour Day 1 May

Whit Monday May/June

St Stephen's/Constitution Day 20 August

1956 Remembrance Day/Republic Day 23 October

All Saints' Day 1 November

Christmas holidays 25 and 26 December

TELEPHONE

Hungary has extensive mobile (cell) phone network coverage. You can make domestic and international calls from public telephones, though these are all but obsolete with the advent of cheap mobile phone calls and WhatsApp, Skype and other VOIP services.

⚊ Getting There & Away

ENTERING THE COUNTRY/REGION

Hungary maintains 65 or so border road crossings with its neighbours. Border formalities with Austria, Slovenia and Slovakia are virtually non-existent. However, you may only enter or leave Hungary via designated border-crossing points during opening hours when travelling to/from the non-Schengen nations of Croatia, Romania, Ukraine and Serbia. In the wake of the Syrian refugee crisis, a controversial border wall now stretches along Hungary's border with Serbia and Croatia. For the latest on border formalities, check www.police.hu.

AIR

International flights land at Ferenc Liszt International Airport (p209), 24km southeast of Budapest. In general, flights to/from Schengen countries use Terminal 2A, while Terminal 2B serves non-Schengen countries.

Hungary's only other year-round commercial international airport is **Debrecen International Airport** (DEB; ☑ 06 20 467 9899; www.debrecenairport.com; Mikepércsi út), 5km south of Debrecen, with Wizz Air and Lufthansa flights to half a dozen cities, including London, Munich, Paris and Tel Aviv.

LAND

Hungary is well connected to neighbouring countries by road and rail, though most transport begins or ends its journey in Budapest.

Timetables for both domestic and international trains and buses use the 24-hour system. Be aware that Hungarian names are sometimes used for cities and towns in neighbouring countries on bus and train schedules.

Bus

Crossing the continent by bus is the cheapest option. Most international buses are run by the German company **FlixBus** (www.flixbus.hu) and link with its Hungarian associate **Volánbusz** (☑ 1-382 0888; www.volanbusz.hu). Buses depart Budapest's Népliget station to many cities across Western Europe. From the same station there are good bus connections with destinations in Croatia, Romania, the Czech Republic and Poland, among others.

Car & Motorcycle

Drivers and motorbike riders will need the vehicle's registration papers, liability insurance and an international driver's permit in addition to their domestic licence.

Hungary's motorways may only be accessed with a motorway pass (matrica), to be purchased beforehand from petrol stations and post offices (see www.autopalya.hu for more details).

Train

MÁV links up with international rail networks in all directions, and its schedule is available online. Some direct train connections from Budapest include Austria, Slovakia, Romania, Ukraine, Croatia, Serbia, Germany, Slovenia, Czech Republic, Poland, Switzerland, Italy and Bulgaria.

Seat reservations are required for international destinations and are included in the price of the ticket.

RIVER

Mahart PassNave (p210), which runs hydrofoils and other passenger boats to and from the towns of the Danube Bend, no longer offers a regularly scheduled hydrofoil service between Budapest and Vienna. It does, however, offer two-day excursions (adult/child under 12 years 53,990/43,990Ft) to the Austrian capital and back over selected weekends in June, July and August.

❶ Getting Around

AIR

There are no scheduled flights within Hungary. Hungary is small enough to get everywhere by train or bus within the span of a day.

BOAT

From April to late October Budapest-based **Mahart PassNave** (☑1-484 4010, 1-484 4013; www.mahartpassnave.hu; V Belgrád rakpart; ⊙9am-5pm Mon-Fri; ☑2) runs excursion boats on the Danube from Budapest to Szentendre, Visegrád and Esztergom, and, between May and September, hydrofoils from Budapest to Vác, Visegrád and Esztergom.

From spring to autumn, some 20 ports around Lake Balaton are well served by Balaton Shipping Company (p213) passenger ferries.

BUS

Hungary's Volánbusz (p220) network comprehensively covers the whole country.

Some larger bus stations have luggage lockers or left-luggage rooms that generally close early (around 6pm). The left-luggage offices at nearby train stations keep much longer hours.

Tickets can be purchased directly from the driver. There are sometimes queues for intercity buses, so arrive around 30 minutes before departure time. Buses are reasonably comfortable and have adequate leg room. On long journeys there are rest stops every couple of hours.

CAR & MOTORCYCLE

Driving in Hungary is useful for exploring the remotest rural corners of the country; trains and buses take care of the rest.

LOCAL TRANSPORT

Public transport is efficient and extensive in Hungarian cities, with bus and, in some case, trolleybus services. Budapest, Szeged and Debrecen also have trams, and there's an extensive metro and a suburban commuter railway in Budapest. Purchase tickets (around 300Ft to 350Ft) at news stands before travelling and validate them once aboard. Inspectors frequently check tickets.

TRAIN

MÁV (Magyar Államvasutak, Hungarian State Railways; ☑1-349 4949; www.mavcsoport.hu) operates clean, punctual and relatively comfortable (if not ultramodern) train services with free wi-fi. Budapest is the hub for main railway lines, though many secondary lines link provincial cities and towns. There are three mainline stations in Budapest, each serving largely (but not exclusively) destinations from the following regions:

Keleti (Eastern Railway) station Northern Uplands and the Northeast

Nyugati (Western Railway) station Great Plain and Danube Bend

Déli (Southern Railway) station Transdanubia and Lake Balaton

Departures and arrivals are always shown on a printed timetable: yellow is for *indul* (departures) and white for *érkezik* (arrivals); fast trains are marked in red and local trains in black. The number (or sometimes letter) next to the word *vágány* indicates the platform from which the train departs or arrives.

All train stations have left-luggage offices, some of which stay open 24 hours.

Kosovo

POP 1.92 MILLION

Best Places to Eat

➡ Tiffany (p226)

➡ Renaissance (p225)

➡ Soma Book Station (p225)

➡ Te Syla 'Al Hambra' (p230)

Best Places to Stay

➡ Hotel Prima (p225)

➡ White Tree Hostel (p225)

➡ Dukagjini Hotel (p228)

➡ Driza's House (p229)

➡ Hotel Prizreni (p229)

Why Go?

Europe's newest country, Kosovo is a fascinating land at the heart of the Balkans rewarding visitors with welcoming smiles, charming mountain towns, incredible hiking opportunities and 13th-century domed Serbian monasteries brushed in medieval art – and that's just for starters.

Kosovo declared independence from Serbia in 2008, and while it has been diplomatically recognised by 111 countries, there are still many nations that do not accept Kosovan independence, including Serbia. The country has been the recipient of massive aid from the international community, particularly the EU and NATO. Barbs of its past are impossible to miss, though: roads are dotted with memorials to those killed in 1999, while NATO forces still guard Serbian monasteries. No matter what many people who've never been to Kosovo might tell you, it's perfectly safe to travel here. Despite this, Kosovo remains one of the last truly off-the-beaten-path destinations in Europe.

When to Go
Pristina

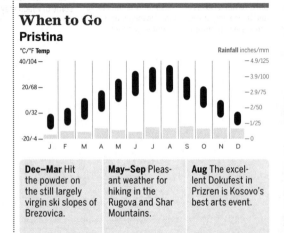

Dec–Mar Hit the powder on the still largely virgin ski slopes of Brezovica.

May–Sep Pleasant weather for hiking in the Rugova and Shar Mountains.

Aug The excellent Dokufest in Prizren is Kosovo's best arts event.

Entering the Country

Despite Kosovo's slightly ambiguous international status, it's well connected with other European countries by air and, with most neighbouring countries, by land. Whichever way you come, entering Kosovo is generally a breeze, with very welcoming and bureaucracy-free immigration and customs. One thing to be aware of, though, is that if you wish to travel between Serbia and Kosovo, you'll need to enter Kosovo from Serbia first.

ITINERARIES

Three Days

Spend a day in cool little Pristina (p224) and get to know Kosovo's charmingly chaotic capital. The next day, visit Visoki Dečani Monastery (p228), then head on to Prizren (p229) to see the old town's Ottoman sights and enjoy the view from the castle.

One Week

After a couple of days in the capital and visits to Gračanica Monastery (p229) and the Bear Sanctuary (p229), loop to lovely Prizren (p229) for a night before continuing to Peja (p228) for monasteries and markets. End with a few days of hiking and climbing in the beautiful Rugova Valley (p227).

Essential Food & Drink

Byrek Pastry with cheese or meat.

Gjuveç Baked meat and vegetables.

Fli Flaky pastry pie served with honey.

Kos Goat's-milk yoghurt.

Pershut Dried meat.

Qofta Flat or cylindrical minced-meat rissoles.

Tavë Meat baked with cheese and egg.

Vranac Red wine from the Rahovec (Orahovac) region of Kosovo.

AT A GLANCE

Area 10,887 sq km

Capital Pristina

Country Code ☑383

Currency euro (€)

Emergency Ambulance ☑94, Police ☑92

Language Albanian, Serbian

Time Central European Time (GMT/UTC plus one hour)

Visas Kosovo is visa-free for many travellers for a stay of up to 90 days.

Sleeping Price Ranges

The following price ranges are for a double room with bathroom.

€ less than €40

€€ €40–80

€€€ more than €80

Eating Price Ranges

The following price categories are for the average cost of a main course.

€ less than €5

€€ €5–10

€€€ more than €10

Resources

UN Mission in Kosovo Online (unmik.unmissions.org)

Balkan Insight (www.balkaninsight.com)

Kosovo Guide (www.kosovoguide.com)

KOSOVO

Pančićev Vrh (2017m)

Sjenica

Jarninje

Leskovac

Novi Pazar

Merdare

Gazivoda Lake

Bërnjak/Banja

Zubin Potok

Mitrovica

SERBIA

E65

Krstača (1755m)

MONTENEGRO

Bac

Berim (1731m)

Mokra Gora

Mutivodë/Medevce

Rožaje

Kulla/Rožaje

Bear Sanctuary Pristina

Novo Brdo

Pristina **3** **5**

Fortress

Mt Hajla (2403m)

Reka Allages

Peja (Peć) **4**

Gračanica Monastery

Dheu i Bardhë/ Bujanovac

Drelaj

Kuqishta & Drelaj Lakes

Mt Guni i Kuq (2522m)

Lipjan

Gjilan

Plav

Đeravica (2656m) **2**

Visoki Dečani Monastery

Mirusha Waterfalls

Gadimë Cave

Grbaja Valley

Rahovec

Muçibabë/Oraovica

Shar National Park

Preševo

Morina

Gjakova

Beli Drim

Ferizaj

Bajram Curri

Qafë Prušit

Qafë Prush

Brezovica

Blace

Kumanovo

Prizren **1**

Gllobocicë

Han i Elezit/Blace

Drini

Kruma

Vrbnica

Fierzë

Morina

Lake Fierza

Dragash

Popova Šapka

Tetovo

SKOPJE

Puka

Kukës

Brod

Titov Vrv (2748m)

ALBANIA

MACEDONIA

Drini

Gostivar

Vardar River

KOSOVO PRISTINA

0 ——— 40 km
0 ——— 20 miles

Kosovo Highlights

① **Prizren's old town** (p229) Discovering the picturesque, mosque-studded streets of Prizren's charming old quarter and getting a breathtaking view from the fortress.

② **Visoki Dečani Monastery** (p228) Taking in gorgeous frescoes, then buying monk-made wine and cheese at this serene 14th-century Serbian monastery.

③ **Pristina** (p224) Exploring Europe's youngest country through its plucky and idiosyncratic capital city and enjoying its excellent dining and nightlife.

④ **Patriarchate of Peć** (p228) Travelling back in time as you listen to haunting chanting at this medieval church.

⑤ **Bear Sanctuary** (p229) Visiting the rescued bears living in excellent conditions at this wonderful lakeside sanctuary that's just a short trip from the capital.

PRISTINA

♩ 038 / POP 211,000

Pristina is a fast-changing city that feels full of optimism and potential, even if its traffic-clogged streets and mismatched architectural styles don't make it an obviously attractive place. While the city does have a couple of worthwhile museums and galleries and serves as a base for interesting nearby sights, for most visitors Pristina is a place where the atmosphere is as much an attraction as any classic tourist sight.

◉ Sights

Central Pristina has been impressively redesigned and is focused on the Ibrahim Rugova

Sq, the centrepiece of the city at the end of the attractive, pedestrianised Blvd Nënë Tereza. On summer evenings the square comes alive with strolling families, street performers and little tots racing around on miniature cars.

★ **Emin Gjiku**
Ethnographic Museum   HISTORIC BUILDING
(Rr Iliaz Agushi; ⊙ 10am-5pm Tue-Sat, to 3pm Sun) FREE This wonderful annex of the Museum of Kosovo is located in two beautifully preserved Ottoman houses enclosed in a large walled garden. The English-speaking staff will give you a fascinating tour of both properties and point out the various unique pieces of clothing, weaponry, jewellery and household items on display in each. There's no better introduction to Kosovar culture.

It's not the easiest place to find and it's not always open during stated hours. The best bet is to ask staff at the Museum of Kosovo.

Museum of Kosovo   MUSEUM
(Sheshi Adam Jashari; ⊙ 10am-6pm Tue-Sun) FREE Pristina's main museum has recently reopened after extensive renovations. Displays begin back in the misty times of the Bronze Age. There are some wonderful statues and monuments to Dardanian gods and goddesses, plus a large stone relief depicting a Dardanian funeral procession.

National Gallery of Kosovo   GALLERY
(✉ 038 225 627; Rr Agim Ramadani 60; ⊙ 10am-6pm Mon-Fri, to 5pm Sat & Sun) FREE This excellent space approaches Kosovan art from a contemporary perspective (don't expect to see paintings from the country's history here) and is worth a look around. Exhibitions change frequently and the gallery space is normally given over to a single artist at any one time. At the time of research, the 'art' included a stable of live cows.

🛏 Sleeping

★ **White Tree Hostel**   HOSTEL €
(✉ 049 166 777; www.whitetreehostel.com; Rr Mujo Ulqinaku 15; dm €10-12, d €34; ❀ ☎) Pristina's best hostel is run by a group of well-travelled locals who took a derelict house into their care, painted the tree in the courtyard white and gradually began to attract travellers with a cool backpacker vibe. It feels more like an Albanian beach resort than a downtown Pristina bolthole.

Dorms have between four and eight beds plus there are a couple of decent double rooms with private bathrooms. There's also a fully equipped kitchen and it adjoins a very chilled, semi-open-air lounge bar (open to nonguests), which is a perfect place to meet other young travellers. With bicycles attached to the walls and giant metal sculptures, it's all very Instagramable. The crew also runs a cocktail bar/nightclub in the same building.

Han Hostel   HOSTEL €
(✉ 044 396 852; www.hostelhan.com; Rr Fehmi Agani 2/4; dm €9-10, d €25; @ ☎) Pristina's cheapest hostel is on the 4th floor of a residential building right in the heart of town. Cobbled together from two apartments that have been joined and converted, it all looks a bit grubby from the outside, but in fact this great space has a large communal kitchen, balconies and smart rooms with clean bathrooms.

★ **Hotel Prima**   BOUTIQUE HOTEL €€
(✉ 044 111 298; Lldhja e Prizrenit 24; s/d incl breakfast from €30/50; ❀ ☎) This small family-run hotel on a quiet side street gets pretty much everything right and is easily one of the best sleeps in Pristina. The understated rooms have work desks, wardrobes, and thoughtful extras such as hair-dryers. The beds are solid and comfortable and the showers are always hot. English-speaking staff are full of tips and ideas for Kosovo travel. Excellent value.

🍴 Eating & Drinking

★ **Soma Book Station**   MEDITERRANEAN €€
(✉ 038 748818; 4/a Fazli Grajqevci; mains €5-11; ⊙ 8am-1am Mon-Sat; ☎) Soma is a local institution among the young, and nearly all visitors to Pristina end up here at some point. The shady garden hums with activity at lunchtime, while the red-brick industrial-chic interior is lined with bookshelves and has a relaxed vibe. Food combines various tastes of the Mediterranean, including tuna salad, beef carpaccio, grilled fish, steaks and burgers.

There's a terrific selection of books and vinyl on sale, the central bar area is one of the best places to drink in town, and the entire place is run with passion, politeness and an attention to detail you simply won't find anywhere else in the city.

Renaissance   BALKAN €€€
(Renesansa; ✉ 044 239 377; Rr Musine Kokollari 35; set meals €15; ⊙ 6pm-midnight Mon-Sat)

KOSOVO PRISTINA

Pristina

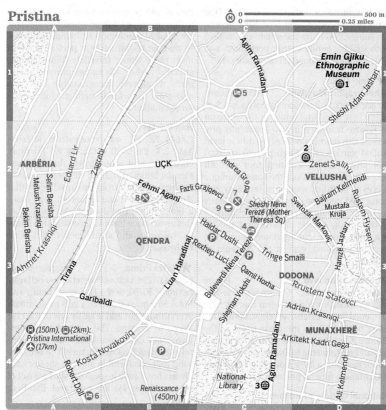

Pristina

◉ Top Sights
1 Emin Gjiku Ethnographic
   Museum..D1

◉ Sights
2 Museum of Kosovo D2
3 National Gallery of Kosovo C4

🛏 Sleeping
4 Han Hostel...C3

5 Hotel Prima...C1
6 White Tree Hostel A4

✕ Eating
7 Soma Book Station................................C2
8 Tiffany B2

◉ Drinking & Nightlife
9 Dit' e Nat'...C2

This atmospheric place might be Pristina's best-kept secret. Wooden doors open to a traditional stone-walled dining room where tables are brimming with local wine, delicious mezze and meaty main courses prepared by the family's matriarch. There's no menu and you'll just be brought a whole array of different dishes. Come with friends and prepare for a long, leisurely meal.

Vegetarians can be catered for but should call ahead. The restaurant can be rather tricky to find, as it's unsigned; taxi drivers usually know it.

Tiffany   BALKAN €€€
(☎ 038 244 040; off Rr Fehmi Agani; meals €12; ⊙ 9am-10.30pm Mon-Sat, from 6pm Sun; 🛜) The organic menu here (delivered by efficient, if somewhat terse, English-speaking staff) is simply dazzling: sit on the sun-dappled

terrace and enjoy the day's grilled special, beautifully cooked seasonal vegetables drenched in olive oil, and freshly baked bread. Understandably much prized by the foreign community, this brilliant place is unsigned and somewhat hidden behind a well-tended bush on Fehmi Agani.

Dit' e Nat' CAFE

(📞 038 742 037; www.ditenat.com/en; Rr Fazli Grajqevci 5; ⊙ 8am-midnight Mon-Sat, from noon Sun; 🛜) 'Day and night', a bookshop-cafe-bar-performance space, is a home away from home for bookish expats and locals alike. There's a great selection of books in English, strong espresso, excellent cocktails, friendly English-speaking staff and occasional live music in the evenings, including jazz. Unusually for meat-loving Kosovo, Dit' e Nat' serves a few vegetarian light lunches and snacks.

ℹ️ Getting There & Away

AIR

Pristina International Airport (📞 038 501 502 1214; www.airportpristina.com) is 18km from the centre of town. There is currently no public transport to and from the airport, so you'll have to get a taxi into the city. Taxis charge €20 for the 20-minute trip to the city centre, though many will try to ask for more – always agree on a price before you get in. Going from the city to the airport, the cost is normally €13 to €15.

BUS

The **bus station** (Stacioni i Autobusëve; 📞 038 550 011; Rr Lidja e Pejes) is 2km southwest of the centre off Blvd Bil Klinton. Taxis to the centre should cost €2, but drivers will often try to charge tourists €5 to €7.

International buses from Pristina include Belgrade (€15.50, seven hours, 11pm) and Novi Pazar (€7.50, three hours, three daily) in Serbia; Tirana, Albania (€10.50, five hours, every one to two hours); Skopje, North Macedonia (€5.50, two hours, hourly from 5.30am to 5pm); Podgorica, Montenegro (€15.50, seven hours, 7pm) and Ulcinj, Montenegro (€15.50, seven hours, 8am and 9pm).

Domestically there are buses to all corners of the country, including Prizren (€4, 75 minutes, every 20 minutes) and Peja (€4, 1½ hours, every 20 minutes).

TRAIN

Trains run from Pristina's small train station in the suburb of Fushë Kosovo to Peja (€3, two hours, twice daily at 8.01am and 4.41pm) and to Skopje in North Macedonia (€4, three hours, 7.22am daily).

ℹ️ Getting Around

Pristina has a comprehensive bus network. Tickets cost 40c and can be bought on board. With the city centre being as small as it is, few travellers ever need to make use of these buses. Taxi meters start at €1.50, and most trips around the city can be done for under €3. Try **Radio Taxi Victory** (📞 038 555 333).

OFF THE BEATEN TRACK

RUGOVA VALLEY

The **Rugova Valley** and the mountains that hem it in are Kosovo's adventure playground. The serpentine valley itself winds westward out of Peja and climbs steadily upwards towards the border of Montenegro. Narrow side-roads spin off this main route, giving access to high mountain pastures, glacial lakes and fairy-tale pine forests. Activities include caving, rafting, *via ferrata*, zip-lining, skiing and snowshoeing, but it's the hiking that really makes this a stand out tourist destination. This knot of mountains (which also extends into parts of Albania and Montenegro) is one of the most beautiful mountain ranges in eastern Europe and remains deliciously unspoiled. Slowly, though, facilities for trekkers are increasing.

The world-renowned **Peaks of the Balkans** long-distance hiking route crosses through the heart of these mountains, and throughout the area hiking trails are becoming better way-marked. If you don't have time to embark on the epic multi-day Peaks of the Balkans trail then there are lots of excellent day hikes. Two of our favourites are the half-day hike to the beautiful, forest-shrouded Kuqishta and Drelej lakes with a possible extension on to the summit of 2522m Mt Guni i Kuq (which would make for a full day hike) or the full day hike to the knife-ridge summit of Mt Hajila (2403m) with its extraordinary views down onto the plains of Montenegro. For any of these walks, it's advisable to hire an experienced guide through one of the Peja tour agencies such as Balkan Natural Adventure (p228).

WESTERN KOSOVO

Peja (Peć)

📶 039 / POP 97,000

Peja (Peć in Serbian) is Kosovo's third-largest city and one flanked by sites sacred to Orthodox Serbians. With a Turkish-style bazaar at its heart Peja would be a worthwhile stop on its own, but for most visitors the real reason to visit is to use the town as the launch pad to some wonderful mountain adventures in the spectacular nearby Rugova Valley and surrounding mountains. All of this means that Peja is fast becoming Kosovo's international tourism hub.

◉ Sights

★Patriarchate of Peć   MONASTERY
(Pećka Patrijaršija; 📶 044 150 755; with audio guide €2; ⊙ 8am-6pm) This church and nunnery complex on the outskirts of Peja are a raw slice of Serbian Orthodoxy that has existed here since the late 13th century. Outside in the landscaped grounds all is bright and colourful, but once inside the church it feels more like you're within a dark cave with magnificent faded frescoes covering the walls and ceiling. The entire complex dates from between the 1230s and the 1330s.

👉 Tours

★Balkan Natural Adventure   ADVENTURE
(📶 049 661 105; www.bnadventure.com; Mberteresha Teute) Balkan Natural Adventure is easily the stand out local adventure tour operator. In fact, it was the friendly English-speaking team here who first established many of the trekking trails in the surrounding mountains and put in the *via ferrata* and zipline. They can also organise caving, rock climbing or snowshoeing and they lead Peaks of the Balkans hiking tours.

🛏 Sleeping & Eating

Stone Bridge Guesthouse   HOTEL €
(📶 049 797 112; stonebridge.gh@gmail.com; Rr Lidhja e Pejës 6; d €25; 🛜) This new, 10-room hotel in the heart of the town offers superb value for money. The modern, white-and-grey rooms have ubercomfortable mattresses and there are small, modern bathrooms. Try to nab a back room to cut out the worst of the street noise.

★Dukagjini Hotel   HOTEL €€
(📶 038 771 177; www.hoteldukagjini.com; Sheshi i Dëshmorëve 2; d incl breakfast from €55; 🅿❄✳ 🛜🍽) The regal stone-walled Dukagjini is the smartest address in town (and a popular wedding venue). Rooms can be rather small but are grandly appointed and have supremely comfortable beds; many on the 1st floor have huge terraces overlooking the central square. There's a pool and gym and a huge restaurant with views of the river. Free parking.

★Art Design   BALKAN €
(📶 049 585 885, 044 222 254; Rr Enver Hadri 53; mains €3.50-6; ⊙ 8am-midnight) Despite sounding flash and modern, Art Design is actually an old house brimming with character and full of local arts and crafts. Choose between dining outside over a little stream or in one of the two rather chintzy dining rooms. Traditional dishes here include *sarma* (meat and rice rolled in grape leaves) and *speca dollma* (peppers filled with meat and rice).

WORTH A TRIP

VISOKI DEČANI MONASTERY

Built in the early 14th century by Serbian king Stefan Dečanski, the **Visoki Dečani Monastery** (📶 049 776 254; www.decani.org; ⊙ 10am-2.30pm & 3.30-5.30pm Mon-Sat, 10am-5.30pm Sun) FREE is in a beautiful spot beneath the mountains and surrounded by pine and chestnut trees. If you think the setting is attractive then you'll gasp in wonder as you push open the wooden doors of the church and first lay eyes on the treasures within. With its floor-to-ceiling, Biblical murals it's like stepping into an enormous medieval paintbox. There can be few more beautiful churches in Europe.

It's on the outskirts of Dečani, 15km south of Peja (Peć). Buses go to Dečani from Peja (€1, 30 minutes, frequent) on their way to Gjakova. It's a pleasant 1km walk to the monastery from the bus stop. From the roundabout in the middle of town, take the second exit if you're coming from Peja. You will need to leave your passport or ID card with the soldiers at the entrance gate if you wish to enter the complex.

GRAČANICA MONASTERY & BEAR SANCTUARY

Explore beyond Pristina by heading southeast to two of the country's best sights. Dusty fingers of sunlight pierce the darkness of **Gračanica Monastery** (€2; ⊙ 8am-6pm), completed in 1321 by Serbian King Milutin. It's an oasis in a town that is the cultural centre of Serbs in central Kosovo. Do dress respectably (that means no shorts or sleeveless tops for anyone, and head scarves for women) and you'll be very welcome to look around this historical complex and to view the gorgeous icons in the main church. The medieval-era paintings here are impressive enough but the real treat is saved for the smaller side chapel, which is an enchanted cavern of vivid, lifelike murals. Take a Gjilan-bound bus (€0.50, 15 minutes, every 30 minutes); the monastery's on your left.

Further along the road to Gjilan is the excellent **Bear Sanctuary** (☑ 045 826 072; www.facebook.com/PylliiArinjvePrishtina; Mramor; adult/child Apr-Oct €2/1, Nov-Mar €1/0.50c; ⊙ 10am-7pm Apr-Oct, to 4pm Nov-Mar), in the village of Mramor. Here you can visit a number of brown bears that were rescued from cruel captivity by the charity Four Paws. All the bears here were once kept in tiny cages as mascots for restaurants, but when the keeping of bears was outlawed in Kosovo in 2010, Four Paws stepped in to care for these wonderful animals. Sadly some of them still suffer from trauma and don't socialise well, but their excellent conditions are heartening indeed. Ask to be let off any Gjilan-bound bus by the Delfina gas station at the entrance to Mramor, then follow the road back past the lakeside, and then follow the track around to the right.

❶ Getting There & Away

BUS

The town's **bus station** (Rr Adem Jashar) is a 15-minute walk from the town centre. Frequent buses run to Pristina (€4, 1½ hours, every 20 minutes), Prizren (€3, 80 minutes to two hours, frequent) and Deçan (€1, 30 minutes, frequent). International buses link Peja with Ulcinj (€20, 10 hours, 10am and 8.30pm) and Podgorica in Montenegro (€15, seven hours, 10am).

TRAIN

Trains depart Peja for Pristina (€3, two hours, twice daily) from the town's small **train station** (Rr Emrush Miftari). To find the station, walk away from the Hotel Dukagjini down Rr Emrush Miftari for 1.4km.

SOUTHERN KOSOVO

Prizren

☑ 029 / POP 185,000

Picturesque Prizren, with its charming mosque- and church-filled old town, shines with an enthusiasm that's infectious. It's Kosovo's second city and most obvious tourist town, and is well worth a day or two's lingering exploration. Prizren is equally known for Dokufest, a documentary film festival held each August that attracts documentary makers and fans from all over the world.

◉ Sights

Prizren Fortress CASTLE

(Kalaja; ⊙ dawn-dusk) FREE It's well worth making the steep 15-minute hike up from Prizren's old town (follow the road past the Orthodox Church on the hillside; it's well signed and pretty obvious) for the superb views over the city and on into the distance. The fortress itself is a little tumble-down but restoration work is currently underway. In the evening heaps of locals come up here and a slight carnival atmosphere prevails. In the white-heat of day, it can be quite lifeless.

⌂ Sleeping

Driza's House HOSTEL €

(☑ 049 618 181; www.drizas-house.com; Remzi Ademaj 7; dm incl breakfast €9-15, tw/tr €25/42; ❋ ☎) This former family home in a courtyard just off the river embankment retains a welcoming, homey vibe and is full of local charm. It's made up of two (10- and four-bed) dorms with custom-made bunk beds, all of which include curtains, reading lights, personal electricity plugs and lockable storage cupboards, and there's a comfortable private three-bed room.

★**Hotel Prizreni** HOTEL €

(☑ 029 225 200; www.hotelprizreni.com; Rr Shën Flori 2; s/d incl breakfast from €30/34; ▣ ❋ ☎) With an unbeatable location just behind the Sinan Pasha Mosque (though some may be less pleased with the location during the dawn call to prayer), the Prizreni is a pleasant combination of traditional and modern, with 12 small but stylish and contemporary rooms, great views and enthusiastic staff. There's a good restaurant downstairs (open 8am to 11pm).

✗ Eating

★ Te Syla 'Al Hambra' KEBAB €
(☑ 049 157 400; www.tesyla.com; Shuaib Spahiu; kebabs €2-4; ⊘ 8am-11pm) Unlike most riverside places in Prizren, there's nothing pretentious about this place. It was first established in the 1960s by a street vendor who just sizzled up kebabs on the corner. From such humble beginnings grew this local classic. The kebabs are as sensational as ever, with the meat literally melting in your mouth.

❶ Getting There & Away

Prizren is well connected by bus to Pristina (€4, two hours, every 20 minutes), Peja (€3, 80 minutes to two hours, frequent), Skopje in North Macedonia (€10, three hours, two daily) and Tirana in Albania (€12, three hours, seven daily).

The **bus station** is on the right bank of the river, a short walk from the old town: follow the right-hand side of the river embankment away from the castle until you come to the traffic circle, then turn left onto Rr De Rada. The bus station will be on your left after around 200m.

SURVIVAL GUIDE

❶ Directory A–Z

ACCOMMODATION
Accommodation is booming in Kosovo, with most large towns now offering a good range of options. There are now backpacker-style hostels in all major cities and plenty of midrange and even top-end accommodation in Pristina.

LGBT+ TRAVELLERS
While legal, homosexuality remains taboo in Kosovo, and it's not a subject that many people will be comfortable broaching. That said, gay and lesbian travellers should generally have no problems, though public displays of affection are definitely inadvisable. There are no gay bars or clubs in the country, though there are a few gay-friendly bars in Pristina and Prizren. Most contact happens online.

MONEY
Kosovo's currency is the euro, despite not being part of the eurozone or the EU. ATMs are com-

mon, and established businesses accept credit cards.

OPENING HOURS
Opening hours vary, but these are the usual hours of business.
Banks 8am to 5pm Monday to Friday, until 2pm Saturday
Bars 8am to 11pm
Shops 8am to 6pm Monday to Friday, until 3pm Saturday
Restaurants 8am to midnight

PUBLIC HOLIDAYS
Note that traditional Islamic and Orthodox Christian holidays are also observed, including Ramadan.
New Year's Day 1 January
Independence Day 17 February
Kosovo Constitution Day 9 April
Labour Day 1 May
Europe Day 9 May

SAFE TRAVEL
Northern Kosovo Sporadic violence does occur in north Mitrovica and a few other flashpoints where Serbian and Kosovar communities live in close proximity.

Landmines Unexploded ordnance has been cleared from roads and paths, but you should seek KFOR advice (http://jfcnaples.nato.int/kfor) before venturing too remotely. That said, the situation is improving fast, with mine-clearance programmes all over the country.

Driving While it's perfectly legal, it's not a good idea to travel in Kosovo with Serbian plates on your car: you'll potentially leave yourself open to random attacks or vandalism from locals.

TELEPHONE
Mobile coverage is excellent throughout the country, and it's easy to obtain a SIM card with data for as little as €10; simply bring your passport to one of the offices of the three mobile phone providers. Kosovo uses the GSM phone system and American CDMA phones won't work here.

VISAS
Kosovo is visa-free for EU, Australian, Canadian, Japanese, New Zealand, South African and US passport holders for stays of up to 90 days.

❶ Getting There & Away

AIR
Pristina International Airport (p227) is 18km from the centre of Pristina. Airlines flying to Kosovo include Air Pristina, Adria, Austrian Airlines, easyJet, Norwegian, Pegasus and Turkish Airlines.

ℹ BORDER CROSSINGS

Albania There are three border crossings between Kosovo and Albania. To get to Albania's Koman Ferry, use the Qafa Morina border crossing west of Gjakova. A short distance further south is the Qafë Prush crossing, though the road continuing into Albania is bad here. The busiest border is at Vërmicë, where a modern motorway connects to Tirana.

North Macedonia Cross into Blace from Pristina and Gllobocicë from Prizren.

Montenegro The main crossing is the Kulla/Rožaje crossing on the road between Rožaje and Peja.

Serbia There are six border crossings between Kosovo and Serbia. Be aware that Kosovo's independence is not recognised by Serbia, so if you plan to continue to Serbia but entered Kosovo via Albania, North Macedonia or Montenegro, officials at the Serbian border will deem that you entered Serbia illegally and you will not be let in. You'll need to exit Kosovo to a third country and then enter Serbia from there. If you entered Kosovo from Serbia, there's no problem returning to Serbia.

LAND

Kosovo has good bus connections between Albania, Montenegro and North Macedonia, with regular services from Pristina, Peja and Prizren to Tirana (Albania), Skopje (North Macedonia) and Podgorica (Montenegro). There's also a train line from Pristina to Skopje. You can take international bus trips to and from all neighbouring capital cities; note that buses to and from Belgrade in Serbia travel via Montenegro.

ℹ Getting Around

BUS

Buses stop at distinct blue signs but can be flagged down anywhere. Bus journeys are generally cheap, but the going can be slow on Kosovo's single-lane roads.

CAR & MOTORCYCLE

Drivers should carry their licences with them whenever on the road, as police checks are not uncommon. Road conditions in Kosovo are generally good, though watch out for potholes on some poorly maintained stretches. Driving techniques in Kosovo are erratic at best. When driving, keep alert!

European Green Card vehicle insurance is not valid in Kosovo, so you'll need to purchase vehicle insurance at the border when you enter with a car; this is a hassle-free and inexpensive procedure.

It's perfectly easy to hire cars here and travel with them to neighbouring countries (with the exception of Serbia). Note that Serbian-plated cars have been attacked in Kosovo, and rental companies do not let cars hired in Kosovo travel to Serbia and vice versa.

TRAIN

The train system is something of a novelty, but services connect Pristina to Peja and to Skopje in neighbouring North Macedonia. Locals generally take buses.

Latvia

POP 1.9 MILLION

Best Places to Eat

➜ Istaba (p240)

➜ International (p240)

➜ 36.Line (p242)

➜ 3 Pavaru (p239)

➜ Fazenda Bazārs (p240)

Best Places to Stay

➜ Neiburgs (p239)

➜ Hotel Bergs (p239)

➜ Hotel MaMa (p242)

➜ Art Hotel Laine (p239)

➜ 2 Baloži (p244)

Why Go?

A tapestry of sea, lakes and woods, Latvia is best described as a vast, unspoilt parkland with just one real city – its cosmopolitan capital, Rīga. The country might be small, but the amount of personal space it provides is enormous. You can always secure a chunk of pristine nature all for yourself, be it for trekking, cycling or dreaming away on a white-sand beach amid pine-covered dunes.

Having been invaded by every regional power, Latvia has more cultural layers and a less homogenous population than its neighbours. People here fancy themselves to be the least pragmatic and the most artistic of the Baltic lot. They prove the point with myriad festivals and a merry, devil-may-care attitude – well, a subdued Nordic version of it.

When to Go
Rīga

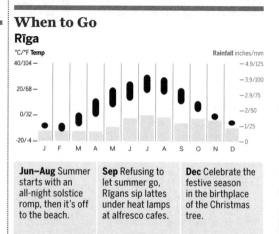

Jun–Aug Summer starts with an all-night solstice romp, then it's off to the beach.

Sep Refusing to let summer go, Rīgans sip lattes under heat lamps at alfresco cafes.

Dec Celebrate the festive season in the birthplace of the Christmas tree.

Entering the Country

Air travel to Latvia is primarily via Rīga International Airport (p241), about 13km southwest of the city centre. **Liepāja International Airport** (www.liepaja-airport.lv) serves more than 60 destinations with connections through Rīga.

Thanks to the Schengen Agreement, there are no border checks when traveling between Estonia and Lithuania by car. International bus service is operated by **Ecolines** (www.ecolines.net) and **Lux Express & Simple Express** (www.luxexpress.eu).

International trains head from Rīga to Moscow (16 hours), St Petersburg (15 hours) and Minsk (12 hours) daily. There are no direct trains to Estonia; you'll need to change at Valga.

Ferry services from Rīga, Liepāja and Ventspils connect Latvia to Swedish and German ports.

ITINERARIES

Three Days
Fill your first two days with a feast of architectural eye candy in Rīga (p235) and then take a day trip to opulent Rundāle Palace (p243).

One Week
After following the above itinerary, spend day four lazing on the beach and coveting the gracious wooden houses of Jūrmala (p242). The following morning head west to Kuldīga (p243) before continuing on to Ventspils (p244). Spend your last days exploring Sigulda (p245) and Cēsis (p246) within the leafy confines of Gauja National Park.

Essential Food & Drink

These are the pillars of Lavtian gastronomy:

Black Balzam The jet-black, 45%-proof concoction is a secret recipe of more than a dozen fairy-tale ingredients.

Mushrooms A national obsession; mushroom-picking takes the country by storm during the first showers of autumn.

Alus For such a tiny nation there's definitely no shortage of *alus* (beer) – each major town has its own brew. You can't go wrong with Užavas (Ventspils' contribution).

Kvass A beloved beverage made from fermented rye bread. It's surprisingly popular with kids!

Rye bread Apart from being tasty and arguably healthier than their wheat peers, these large brown loafs have aesthetic value too, matching nicely the dark wood of Latvia's Nordic interiors.

Berries Sold at markets all over the country, so you needn't go deep into the woods to collect a jar of them yourself.

AT A GLANCE

Area 64,589 sq km

Capital Rīga

Country Code ☑ 371

Currency euro (€)

Emergency ☑ 112

Language Latvian, Russian (unofficial)

Time Eastern European Time (GMT/UTC plus two hours)

Visas Not required for citizens of the EU, USA, Canada, Japan, New Zealand and Australia for stays of up to 90 days.

Sleeping Price Ranges

The following price ranges refer to the cost of a double room with private bathroom.

€ less than €40

€€ €40–80

€€€ more than €80

Eating Price Ranges

We've based the following Latvian price ranges on the average price of a main dish.

€ less than €7

€€ €7–14

€€€ more than €14

Resources

1188 (www.1188.lv)

Latvian Tourism Development Agency (www.latvia.travel)

Latvia Institute (www.li.lv)

LATVIA

Latvia Highlights

1 Riga (p235) Clicking your camera at the nightmarish menagerie of gargoyles, mythical beasts, goddesses and twisting vines that inhabits the city's art nouveau architecture.

2 Old Riga (p235) Losing yourself in the Unesco-protected maze of cobblestones, church spires and gingerbread trim.

3 Cēsis (p246) Launching lighting raids into Gauja National Park from the castle fortress.

4 Ventas Rumba (p244) Joining swarms of fish trying to jump over the waterfall, the widest (and possibly the shortest) in Europe.

5 Rundāle Palace (p243) Sneaking away from the capital and indulging in aristocratic decadence.

6 Jūrmala (p242) Hobnobbing with Russian jet-setters in the heart of the swanky spa scene.

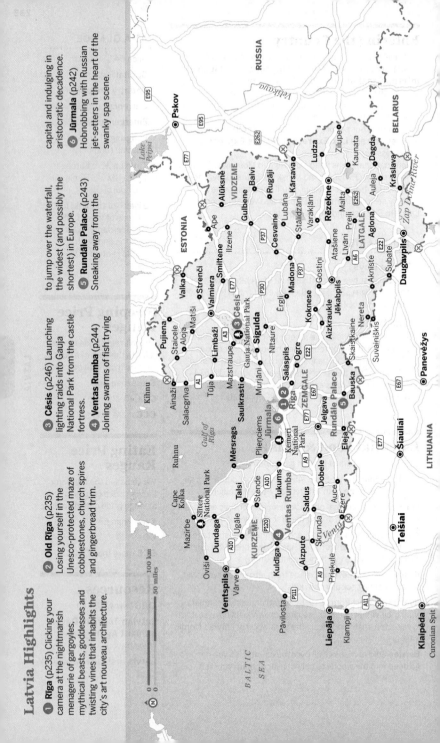

RĪGA

POP 641,400

The Gothic spires that dominate Rīga's cityscape might suggest austerity, but it is the flamboyant art nouveau that forms the flesh and the spirit of this vibrant cosmopolitan city, the largest of all three Baltic capitals. Like all northerners, it is quiet and reserved on the outside, but there is some powerful chemistry going on inside its hip bars and modern art centres, and in the kitchens of its cool experimental restaurants. Standing next to a gulf named after itself, Rīga is a short drive from jet-setting sea resort, Jūrmala, which comes with a stunning white-sand beach. But if you are craving solitude and a pristine environment, gorgeous sea dunes and blueberry-filled forests begin right outside the city boundaries.

◉ Sights

Kalnciema Kvartāls
AREA

(✆6761 4322; www.kalnciemaiela.lv; Kalnciema iela 35) A lovingly restored courtyard with several wooden buildings is the location of a very popular weekend market, where Rīgans hawk their local produce – meats, cheeses, vegetables and even spirits. But there is more to it, with live concerts, performances and art exhibitions taking place outside the market days. Even if nothing is going on, sipping coffee in one of the on-site cafes and soaking in the atmosphere of an old Rīga suburb is worthwhile. Check the website for upcoming events.

◉ Old Rīga (Vecrīga)

The curving cobbled streets of Rīga's medieval core are best explored at random. Once you're sufficiently lost amid the tangle of gabled roofs, church spires and crooked alleyways, you will begin to uncover a stunning, World Heritage–listed realm of sky-scraping cathedrals, gaping city squares and crumbling castle walls.

★ Rīga Cathedral
CHURCH

(Rīgas Doms; ✆6722 7573; www.doms.lv; Doma laukums 1; €3; ◷9am-6pm Mon-Tue & Sat, 9am-5pm Wed & Fri, 9am-5.30pm Thu, 2-5pm Sun May-Sep) Founded in 1211 as the seat of the Rīga diocese, this enormous (once Catholic, now Evangelical Lutheran) cathedral is the largest medieval church in the Baltic. The architecture is an amalgam of styles from the 13th to the 18th centuries: the eastern end, the oldest portion, has Romanesque features; the tower is 18th-century baroque; and much of the rest dates from a 15th-century Gothic rebuilding.

St Peter's Church
CHURCH

(Sv Pētera baznīca; www.peterbaznica.riga.lv; Skārņu iela 19; adult/child €9/3; ◷10am-7pm Tue-Sat, noon-7pm Sun) Forming the centrepiece of Rīga's skyline, this Gothic church is thought to be around 800 years old, making it one of the oldest medieval buildings in the Baltic. Its soaring red-brick interior is relatively unadorned, except for heraldic shields mounted on the columns. A colourful contrast is provided by the art exhibitions staged in the side aisles. At the rear of the church, a lift whisks visitors to a viewing platform 72m up the steeple.

★ Art Museum Rīga Bourse
MUSEUM

(Mākslas muzejs Rīgas Birža; ✆6732 4461; www.lnmm.lv; Doma laukums 6; adult/child €6/3; ◷10am-6pm Tue-Thu, Sat & Sun, to 8pm Fri) Rīga's lavishly restored stock exchange building is a worthy showcase for the city's art treasures. The elaborate facade features a coterie of deities that dance between the windows, while inside, gilt chandeliers sparkle from ornately moulded ceilings. The Oriental section features beautiful Chinese and Japanese ceramics and an Egyptian mummy, but the main halls are devoted to Western art, including a Monet painting and a scaled-down cast of Rodin's *The Kiss*.

Rīga History & Navigation Museum
MUSEUM

(Rīgas vēstures un kuģniecības muzejs; ✆6735 6676; www.rigamuz.lv; Palasta iela 4; adult/child €5/1; ◷10am-5pm) Founded in 1773, this is the oldest museum in the Baltic, situated in the old cathedral monastery. The permanent collection features artefacts from the Bronze Age all the way to WWII, ranging from lovely pre-Christian jewellery to preserved hands removed from medieval forgers. A highlight is the beautiful neoclassical Column Hall, built when Latvia was part of the Russian empire and filled with relics from that time.

★ Blackheads House
HISTORIC BUILDING

(Melngalvju nams; ✆6704 3678; www.melngalvju nams.lv; Rātslaukums 7; adult/child €6/3; ◷11am-6pm Tue-Sun) Built in 1344 as a veritable fraternity house for the Blackheads guild of unmarried German merchants, the original house was bombed in 1941 and flattened by

LATVIA RĪGA

Rīga

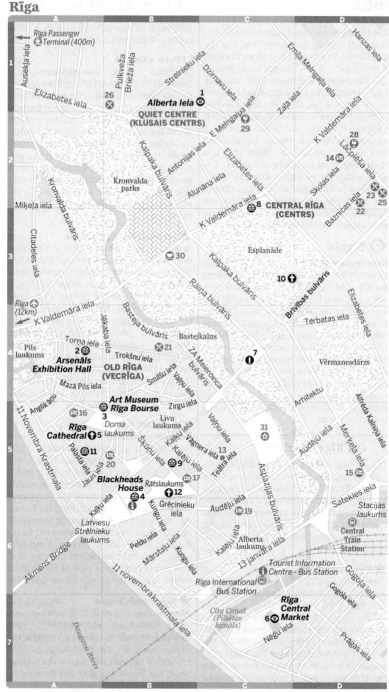

Rīga Passenger Terminal (400m)

Ausekļa iela

Elizabetes iela

Pulkveža Brieža iela

Strēlnieku iela

Dzirnavu iela

Emila Melngaiļa iela

Hanzas iela

26

Alberta iela 1

QUIET CENTRE
(KLUSAIS CENTRS)

E Melngaiļa iela

29

Zala iela

K Valdemāra iela

28

Lāčplēša iela

14

Skolas iela

23

22

25

Antonijas iela

Elizabetes iela

Kalpaka bulvāris

Kronvalda parks

Alunāna iela

K Valdemāra iela

8 CENTRAL RĪGA
(CENTRS)

Baznīcas iela

Mikeļa iela

Kronvalda bulvāris

Citadeles iela

30

Esplanāde

Kalpaka bulvāris

Rīga
(12km)

K Valdemāra iela

Jēkaba iela

Basteja bulvāris

Raiņa bulvāris

10

Brīvības bulvāris

Elizabetes iela

Tērbatas iela

Torna iela

2 Arsenāls
Exhibition Hall

Trokšņu iela

Bastejkalns

21

ZA Meierovica bulvāris

7

Vērmanesdārzs

Pils laukums

Smilšu iela

Maza Pils iela

OLD RĪGA
(VECRĪGA)

Valņu iela

Arhitektu

Angliķāņu

16

Art Museum
Rīga Bourse

Zirgu iela

Valņu iela

Alfrēda Kalniņa iela

Merkela iela

3 Doma laukums

Līvu laukums

11 Novembra Krastmala

Rīga
Cathedral 5

11

20

Šķūņu iela

Kaļķu iela

Vagnera iela

13

31

Audēju iela

15

Pils iela

Palasta iela

Jaun

Blackheads
House 4

Rātslaukums

17

Kaļēju iela

Teātra iela

9

12

Grēcinieku iela

Audēju iela

19

Aspazijas bulvāris

Satekles iela

Stacijas laukums

Kaļķu iela

Latviešu
Strēlnieku
laukums

Peldu iela

Maršala iela

Kungu iela

Kaļēju iela

Alberta laukums

Central
Train
Station

Akmens Bridge

11 novembra krastmala iela

Rīga International
Bus Station

13 Janvāra iela

Tourist Information
Centre - Bus Station

Gogoļa iela

Daugava River

City Canal
(Pilsētas
kanāls)

Rīga
Central
Market 6

Nēģu iela

Gogoļa iela

Prāgas iela

Rīga

◎ Top Sights

◎ Sights

✦ Activities, Courses & Tours

🛏 Sleeping

✦ Eating

◔ Drinking & Nightlife

✹ Entertainment

the Soviets seven years later. Somehow the original blueprints survived and an exact replica of this fantastically ornate structure was completed in 2001 for Rīga's 800th birthday.

Museum of Decorative Arts & Design MUSEUM
(Dekoratīvi lietišķās mākslas muzejs; ☎6732 4461; www.lnmm.lv; Skārņu iela 10/20; adult/child €5/2.50; ⊙11am-5pm Tue & Thu-Sun, to 7pm Wed) The former St George's Church houses a museum devoted to applied art from the art

LATVIA RĪGA

ART NOUVEAU IN RĪGA

If you ask any Rīgan where to find the city's world-famous art nouveau architecture, you will always get the same answer: 'Look up!'

Rīga has the greatest number of art nouveau buildings of any city in Europe. More than 750 buildings boast this flamboyant style of decor which is also known as *Jugendstil*, meaning 'youth style'. It was named after Munich-based magazine, *Die Jugend*, which popularised it around the turn of the 20th century.

Rīga's art nouveau district (known more formally as the 'Quiet Centre') is anchored around Alberta iela – check out 2a, 4 and 13 in particular – but you'll find fine examples throughout the city.

nouveau period to the present, including an impressive collection of furniture, woodcuts, tapestries and ceramics. The building's foundations date back to 1207 when the Livonian Brothers of the Sword erected their castle here. Since the rest of the original knights' castle was levelled by rioting citizens at the end of the same century, it is the only building that remains intact since the birth of Rīga.

★ **Arsenāls Exhibition Hall** GALLERY
(Izstāžu zāle Arsenāls; ☑ 6735 7527; www.lnmm.lv; Torņa iela 1; adult/child €3.50/2; ☺ 11am-6pm Tue, Wed & Fri, to 8pm Thu, noon-5pm Sat & Sun) Behind a row of spooky granite heads depicting Latvia's most prominent artists, the imperial arsenal, constructed in 1832 to store weapons for the Russian tsar's army, is now a prime spot for international and local art exhibitions. Also check out the massive wooden stairs at the back of the building – their simple yet funky geometry predates modern architecture.

◉ Central Rīga (Centrs)

★ **Alberta Iela** ARCHITECTURE
It's like a huge painting, which you can spend hours staring at, as your eye detects more and more intriguing details. But in fact, this must-see Rīga sight is a rather functional street with residential houses, restaurants and shops. Art nouveau, otherwise known as *Jugendstil*, is the style, and the master responsible for most of these is Mikhail Eisenstein (father of filmmaker Sergei Eisenstein). Named after the founder of Rīga, Bishop Albert von Buxthoeven, the street was the architect's gift to Rīga on its 700th anniversary.

Freedom Monument MONUMENT
(Brīvības bulvāris) Affectionately known as 'Milda', Rīga's Freedom Monument towers above the city between Old and Central Rīga. Paid for by public donations, the monument was designed by Kārlis Zāle and erected in 1935 where a statue of Russian ruler Peter the Great once stood.

Latvian National Museum of Art GALLERY
(Latvijas Nacionālā mākslas muzeja; ☑ 6732 4461; www.lnmm.lv; K Valdemāra iela 10a; adult/child €6/3; ☺ 10am-6pm Tue-Thu, to 8pm Fri, to 5pm Sat & Sun) Latvia's main gallery, sitting within the Esplanāde's leafy grounds, is an impressive building that was purpose-built in a baroque-classical style in 1905. Well-displayed paintings form a who's-who of Latvian art from the 18th to late 20th centuries. Temporary exhibitions supplement the interesting permanent collection.

Nativity of Christ Cathedral CHURCH
(Kristus Piedzimšanas katedrāle; ☑ 6721 1207; www.pravoslavie.lv; Brīvības bulvāris 23; ☺ 7am-7pm) With gilded cupolas peeking through the trees, this Byzantine-styled Orthodox cathedral (1883) adds a dazzling dash of Russian bling to the skyline. During the Soviet period the church was converted into a planetarium, but it's since been restored to its former use. Mind the dress code – definitely no shorts; women are asked to cover their heads.

◉ Moscow Suburb (Maskavas forštate)

★ **Rīga Central Market** MARKET
(Rīgas Centrāltirgus; ☑ 6722 9985; www.rct.lv; Nēģu iela 7; ☺ 7am-6pm) Haggle for your huckleberries at this vast market, housed in a series of WWI Zeppelin hangars and spilling outdoors as well. It's an essential Rīga experience, providing bountiful opportunities both for people-watching and to stock up for a picnic lunch. Although the number of traders is dwindling, the dairy and fish departments, each occupying a separate hangar, present a colourful picture of abundance

that activates ancient foraging instincts in the visitors.

🖝 Tours

Rīga Bike Tours   CYCLING
(☑ 28225773; www.rigabiketours.com; Riharda Vagnera iela 14; ☉ 10am-6pm) These folks run daily bicycle tours of Rīga that last for three hours and cost €20 (€15 with your own bike). Longer cycling tours of Latvia are also on offer. Its useful office operates under the Rīga Explorers Club brand.

E.A.T. Rīga   WALKING, CYCLING
(☑ 22469888; www.eatriga.lv; tours from €20) Foodies may be initially disappointed to discover that the name stands for 'Experience Alternative Tours' and the focus is on off-the-beaten-track themed walking tours (Old Rīga, Art Nouveau, Alternative Rīga, Retro Rīga). But don't fret – Rīga Food Tasting is an option. It also offers a cycling tour of Jūrmala.

🛏 Sleeping

🛏 Old Rīga (Vecrīga)

Cinnamon Sally   HOSTEL €
(☑ 22042280; www.cinnamonsally.com; Merķeļa iela 1; dm €11-17; @ 🛜) Convenient for the train and bus stations, Cinnamon Sally comes with perfectly clean rooms, very helpful staff and a common area cluttered with sociable characters. It might feel odd to be asked to take off your shoes at the reception, but it's all part of its relentless effort to create a homey atmosphere.

★ Naughty Squirrel   HOSTEL €€
(☑ 6722 0073; www.thenaughtysquirrel.com; Kaļķu iela 50; dm €12-16, r €45-80; ✴ @ 🛜) Slashes of bright paint and cartoon graffiti brighten up the city's capital of backpackerdom, which buzzes with travellers rattling the foosball table and chilling out in the TV room. Plush pillows and blankets in private rooms and homey wooden bunks in dorms make the place feel anything but institutional.

★ Ekes Konvents   HOTEL €€
(☑ 6735 8393; www.facebook.com/ekes.konvents; Skārņu iela 22; r €65; 🛜) Not to be confused with Konventa Sēta next door, the 600-year-old Ekes Konvents oozes wobbly medieval charm from every crooked nook and cranny. Curl up with a book in the adorable stone

alcoves on the landing of each storey. Breakfast is served down the block.

★ Dome Hotel   HOTEL €€€
(☑ 6750 9010; www.domehotel.lv; Miesnieku iela 4; r €261-432; 🛜) It's hard to imagine that this centuries-old structure was once part of a row of butcheries. Today a gorgeous wooden staircase leads guests up to a charming assortment of uniquely decorated rooms that sport eaved ceilings, wooden panelling, upholstered furniture and picture windows with city views.

★ Neiburgs   HOTEL €€€
(☑ 6711 5522; www.neiburgs.com; Jaun iela 25/27; r €194-287; ✴ 🛜) Occupying one of Old Rīga's finest art nouveau buildings, Neiburgs blends preserved details with contemporary touches to achieve its signature boutique-chic style. Try for a room on one of the higher floors – you'll be treated to a view of a colourful clutter of gabled roofs and twisting medieval spires.

🛏 Central Rīga (Centrs)

★ Art Hotel Laine   HOTEL €€
(☑ 6728 8816; www.laine.lv; Skolas iela 11; s €55, d €65-77, superior d €126; P ✴ 🛜) Embedded in an apartment block with an antiquated lift taking guests to the reception on the 3rd floor, this place brings you closer to having your own home in Rīga than most hotels can or indeed wish to do. Dark green walls and armchair velvet, art on the walls, and bathtubs and furniture from yesteryear only complement the overall homey feeling.

Hotel Bergs   HOTEL €€€
(☑ 6777 0900; www.hotelbergs.lv; Elizabetes iela 83/85; ste from €203; P ✴ 🛜) A refurbished 19th-century building embellished with a Scandi-sleek extension, Hotel Bergs embodies the term 'luxury'. The spacious suites are lavished with high-quality monochromatic furnishings and some have kitchens. There's even a 'pillow menu', allowing guests to choose from an array of different bed pillows based on material and texture.

✗ Eating

✗ Old Rīga (Vecrīga)

★ 3 Pavaru   MODERN EUROPEAN €€€
(☑ 20370537; www.3pavari.lv; Torņa iela 4; mains €18-26; ☉ noon-11pm) The stellar trio of chefs

who run this show have a jazzy approach to cooking, with improvisation at the heart of the compact and ever-changing menu. The emphasis is on experimentation (leg of lamb with anchovies, anyone?) and artful visual presentation that could have made Mark Rothko or Joan Miró gasp in admiration.

★ **Istaba** CAFE €€€
(☑ 6728 1141; www.facebook.com/galerijaISTABA; K Barona iela 31a; mains €17; ⊙ noon-11pm) Owned by local chef and TV personality Mārtiņš Sirmais, 'The Room' sits in the rafters above a gallery and occasional performance space. There's no set menu – you're subject to the cook's fancy – but expect lots of free extras (bread, dips, salad, veggies), adding up to a massive serving.

✕ Central Rīga (Centrs)

Miit CAFE €
(www.miit.lv; Lāčplēša iela 10; mains €5; ⊙ 7am-9pm Mon, to 11pm Tue-Thu, 9am-11pm Sat, 10am-6pm Sun) Rīga's hipster students head here to sip espresso and blog about Nietzsche amid comfy couches and discarded bicycle parts. The two-course lunch is a fantastic deal for penny-pinchers – expect a soup and a main course for under €5 (dishes change daily).

Big Bad Bagels BAGELS €
(☑ 24556585; www.bigbadbagels.lv; Baznīcas 8; bagels from €4.20; ⊙ 8am-8pm Mon-Fri, 10am-7pm Sat, 10am-6pm Sun) US expats aching for lox or a bacon-egg-and-cheese bagel can get a fix at this real-deal joint. Fresh bagels come with cream cheese or as a sandwich with a destination theme (Chicken in Thailand, Prosciutto in Modena – you get the point). Fresh juice, smoothies and coffee are top notch, too.

★ **Fazenda Bazārs** MODERN EUROPEAN €€
(☑ 6724 0809; www.fazenda.lv; Baznīcas iela 14; mains €11-18; ⊙ 9am-10pm Mon-Fri, from 10am Sat, from 11am Sun) Although right in the centre, this place feels like you've gone a long way and suddenly found a warm tavern in the middle of nowhere. Complete with a tiled stove, this wooden house oozes mega-tonnes of charm and the food on offer feels as homey as it gets, despite its international, fusion nature.

★ **International** INTERNATIONAL €€
(☑ 6749 1212; www.international.lv; Hospitālu iela 1; dishes €6-12; ⊙ noon-10pm Sun-Thu, to 11pm

Fri-Sat; 🛜) It's well worth a quick tram ride (take tram 11 and get off at Mēness iela) to this wonderful eatery for multiple small plates of yumminess. The name couldn't be more accurate, with a menu containing the likes of 'Tsar's fish soup', sushi, Thai curry and an exceptional Beef Wellington.

Vincents EUROPEAN €€€
(☑ 6733 2830; www.restorans.lv; Elizabetes iela 19; mains €29-39; ⊙ 6-10pm Tue-Sat) 🍃 Rīga's ritziest restaurant has served royalty and rock stars (Emperor Akihito, Prince Charles, Elton John) amid its eye-catching van Gogh-inspired decor. The head chef, Martins Ritins, is a stalwart of the Slow Food movement and crafts his ever-changing menu mainly from produce sourced directly from small-scale Latvian farmers.

🍺 Drinking & Nightlife

★ **Kaņepes Kultūras Centrs** BAR
(☑ 6734 7050; www.kanepes.lv; Skolas iela 15; ⊙ 3pm-2am or later) The crumbling building of a former musical school, which half of Rīgans over 40 seem to have attended, is now a bar with a large outdoor area filled with an artsy, studenty crowd. Wild dancing regularly erupts in the large room, where the parents of the patrons once suffered through their violin drills.

Autentika (B2) CLUB
(☑ 28348453; www.facebook.com/autentika.b2; Bruņinieku iela 2; ⊙ 11am-11pm Mon-Tue, to midnight Wed, to 1am Thu, to 5am Sat, to 10pm Sun) Set in an old brewery, this multifunctional cultural space is a local hub for all things indie. Free-spirited locals mingle over cocktails, weekend brunch, art exhibitions, emerging live bands and more. Check the Facebook page for events.

Left Door Bar COCKTAIL BAR
(☑ 26300368; www.theleftdoorbar.lv; Antonijas iela 12; ⊙ noon-midnight Mon-Thu, noon-1am Fri, 6pm-1am Sat, 6pm-midnight Sun) Rīga's grand lodge of cocktail masters masquerades as an assuming bar in the art nouveau district. Never satisfied with past achievements, the award-winning prodigies in charge are constantly experimenting with the aim to impress globetrotting connoisseurs, not your average Joe. All cocktails come in individually shaped glasses.

Leningrad CAFE
(☑ 26161335; www.leningrad.lv; K Valdemāra iela 4; ⊙ noon-3am Sun-Wed, to 7am Fri & Sat) Punk

lives on at this Soviet-themed cafe – which indeed feels like the average cafe by day, but by night, shows a grittier side with a live music scene that can linger until morning. The beer selection is good and cheap, and the staff are friendly and relaxed.

Alus darbnīca Labietis   BEER HALL
(☑ 25655958; www.labietis.lv; Aristida Briāna iela 9a-2; ☺ 1pm-1am) Its minimalist design making it feel a bit like a Gothic church, this place is on a mission to promote more obscure Latvian breweries and local craft beer. A great addition to the gradually gentrifying old factory area at the end of Miera iela.

☆ Entertainment

Latvian National Opera   OPERA, BALLET
(Latvijas Nacionālajā operā; ☑ 6707 3777; www. opera.lv; Aspazijas bulvāris 3) With a hefty international reputation as one of the finest opera companies in all of Europe, the national opera is the pride of Latvia. It's also home to the Rīga Ballet; locally born lad Mikhail Baryshnikov got his start here. Performances happen most nights of the week – check the schedule on the website for details.

ℹ Information

Tourist Information Centre (☑ 6703 7900; www.liveriga.com; Rātslaukums 6; ☺ 9am-7pm) Dispenses tourist maps and walking-tour brochures, helps with accommodation, books day trips and sells concert tickets. It also stocks the **Rīga Card** (www.liveriga.com), which offers discounts on sights and restaurants, and free rides on public transport. Satellite offices can be found in **Līvu laukums** (May to September only) and at the **bus station** (Prāgas iela 1).

ℹ Getting There & Away

AIR

Rīga International Airport (Starptautiskā Lidosta Rīga; ☑ 1817; www.riga-airport.com; Mārupe District; ☑ 22) is in the suburb of Skulte, 13km southwest of the city centre. It's the primary hub for air travel to the country – Latvia's national carrier, airBaltic (www.airbaltic.com), offers direct flights to 70 destinations within Europe.

BOAT

Rīga's **passenger ferry terminal** (☑ 6732 6200; www.portofriga.lv; Eksporta iela 3a), located about 1km downstream (north) of Akmens Bridge, offers services to Stockholm aboard Tallink (www. tallink.lv; 18 hours, three to four weekly).

It's possible to get to Jūrmala on the New Way (p242) river boat (daily, 2½ hours).

OH CHRISTMAS TREE

Rīga's Blackheads House (p235) was known for its wild parties; it was, after all, a clubhouse for unmarried merchants. On a cold Christmas Eve in 1510, the squad of bachelors, full of holiday spirit (and other spirits, so to speak), hauled a great pine tree up to their clubhouse and smothered it with flowers. At the end of the evening they burned the tree to the ground in an impressive blaze. From then on, decorating the 'Christmas tree' became an annual tradition, which eventually spread across the globe (as you probably know, the burning part never really caught on).

An octagonal commemorative plaque, inlaid in cobbled Rātslaukums, marks the spot where the original tree once stood.

BUS

Buses depart from Rīga's **international bus station** (Rīgas starptautiskā autoosta; ☑ 9000 0009; www.autoosta.lv; Prāgas iela 1), located behind the railway embankment just beyond the southeastern edge of Old Rīga. International destinations include Tallinn, Vilnius, Warsaw, Pärnu, Kaunas, St Petersburg and Moscow. Try **Ecolines** (www.ecolines.net), **Eurolines Lux Express** (www.luxexpress.eu) or **Nordeka** (www. nordeka.lv).

TRAIN

Rīga's **central train station** (Centrālā stacija; ☑ 6723 2135; www.pv.lv; Stacijas laukums 2) is convenient to Old and Central Rīga, and is housed in a Soviet-era concrete box (now built into a glass-encased shopping mall), just outside Old Town.

Found in a large hall to the right from the main entrance, cash offices 1 to 6 sell tickets to international destinations, which now include Moscow (from €153, 16 hours, daily), St Petersburg (from €92, 15 hours, daily) and Minsk (from €28, 12 hours, weekly). Domestic tickets are sold in cash offices 7 to 15. The information office (open 7am to 7pm) is located next to the latter.

ℹ Getting Around

BICYCLE

Zip around town with **Sixt Bicycle Rental** (Sixt velo noma; ☑ 6767 6780; www.sixtbicycle.lv; per 30min/day €1/10). A handful of stands are conveniently positioned around Rīga and Jūrmala; simply choose your bike, call the rental service and receive the code to unlock your wheels.

CAR

Rīga is divided into six parking zones. Municipal parking in the centre of Rīga costs between €2 and €3 per hour. If you need to drop a car in Rīga for longer, consult www.europark.lv – it runs parking lots all around the city and offers more flexibility time- and moneywise.

PUBLIC TRANSPORT

The centre of Rīga is too compact for most visitors even to consider public transport, but trams, buses or trolleybuses may come in handy if you are venturing further out. For routes and schedules, consult www.rigassatiksme.lv. Tickets cost €2; unlimited tickets are available for 24 hours (€5), three days (€10) and five days (€15). Tickets are available from Narvessen newspaper kiosks as well as vending machines on board new trams and in the underground pass by the train station.

TAXI

Taxis charge €0.60 to €0.80 per kilometre. Insist on having the meter on before you set off. Meters usually start running at around €1.50. It shouldn't cost more than €5 for a short journey (like crossing the Daugava for dinner in Ķīpsala). There are taxi ranks outside the bus and train stations, at the airport and in front of a few major hotels in Central Rīga, such as Radisson Blu Hotel Latvija.

WESTERN LATVIA

Jūrmala

POP 48,600

Jūrmala (pronounced *yoor*-muh-lah) is a 32-km string of 14 townships with Prussian-style villas, each unique in shape and decor. Even during the height of communism, Jūrmala was always a place to *'sea'* and be seen. These days, on summer weekends vehicles clog the roads when jetsetters and day-tripping Rīgans flock to the resort town for some serious fun in the sun. Jomas iela is Jūrmala's main drag, with loads of tourist-centric venues. Unlike many European resort towns, most of Jūrmala's restaurants and hotels are several blocks away from the beach, which keeps the seashore (somewhat) pristine.

🛏 Sleeping & Eating

Hotel MaMa BOUTIQUE HOTEL €€€
(✏ 6776 1271; www.hotelmama.lv; Tirgonu iela 22; r €175-360; 🖥) The bedroom doors have thick, mattress-like padding on the interior (psycho-chic?) and the suites themselves are a veritable blizzard of white drapery. A mix of silver paint and pixie dust accents the ultramodern furnishings and amenities. If heaven had a bordello, it would probably look something like this.

★ 36.Line LATVIAN €€€
(✏ 22010696; www.36line.com; Līnija 36; mains €12-52; ⊙ 1-11pm; ✏) Popular local chef Lauris Alekseyevs delivers modern twists on traditional Latvian dishes at this wonderful restaurant, occupying a slice of sand at the eastern end of Jūrmala. Enjoy the beach, then switch to casual attire for lunch or glam up for dinner. In the evening it's not uncommon to find DJs spinning beats.

ℹ Information

Tourist Office (✏ 6714 7900; www.visitjurmala. lv; Lienes iela 5; ⊙ 9am-5pm Mon-Fri, 10am-5pm Sat, 10am-3pm Sun) Located across from Majori train station, this helpful office has scores of brochures outlining walks, bike routes and attractions. Staff can assist with accommodation bookings and bike rental. A giant map outside helps orient visitors when the centre is closed.

ℹ Getting There & Away

BOAT

The river boat **New Way** (✏ 2923 7123; www.pie-kapteina.lv; return adult/child €30/15) departs from Rīga Riflemen Sq and docks in Majori, near the train station. The journey takes one hour, and only runs on weekends.

BUS

A common mode of transport between Rīga and Jūrmala; take minibuses (30 minutes) in the direction of Sloka, Jaunķemeri or Dubulti and ask the driver to let you off at Majori. These vans depart every five to 15 minutes between 6am and midnight and leave opposite Rīga's central train station. Catch the bus at Majori train station for a lift back. These regularly running minibuses can also be used to access other townships within Jūrmala's long sandy stretch. From 9am to midnight, minibuses also connect Jūrmala to Rīga International Airport.

CAR

Motorists driving into Jūrmala must pay a €2 toll per day from April to September before they cross the Lielupe river, even if you are just passing through. There is plenty of (mostly) free-of-charge parking space along Jūras iela.

TRAIN

Two to three trains per hour link the sandy shores of Jūrmala to Central Rīga. Take a suburban train bound for Sloka, Tukums or Dubulti and disembark at Majori station (€1.40 to €1.90, 20 to 50 minutes). The first train departs Rīga around 5.50am and the last train leaves Majori around 10.44pm. Jūrmala-bound trains usually depart from tracks 3 and 4, and stop six or seven times within the resort's 'city limits' if you wish to get off in another neighbourhood. Visit www.pv.lv or www.1188.lv for the most up-to-date information.

Kuldīga

POP 23,000

Home to what Latvians brand 'the widest waterfall in Europe', Kuldīga is also the place where your immersion into the epoch of chivalry won't be spoiled by day-tripping camera-clickers – the place is simply too far

RUNDĀLE PALACE

Built as a grand residence for the Duke of Courland, this magnificent **palace** (Rundāles pils; ☑ 6396 2274; www.rundale.net; whole complex/house long route/short route/short route & garden/garden €13/10/8/11/4; ⊙10am-6pm) is a monument to 18th-century aristocratic ostentatiousness, and is rural Latvia's architectural highlight. It was designed by Italian baroque genius Bartolomeo Rastrelli, who is best known for the Winter Palace in St Petersburg. About 40 of the palace's 138 rooms are open to visitors, as are the wonderful formal gardens, inspired by those at Versailles.

Ernst Johann Biron started his career as a groom and lover of Anna Ioanovna, the Russian-born Duchess of Courland. She gave him the duchy when she became Russian empress, but he stayed with her in St Petersburg, turning into the most powerful political figure of the empire. In 1736 he commissioned the Italian architect Bartholomeo Rastrelli to construct his summer residence near Bauska.

Russian authors later blamed Biron for ushering in a era of terror, but many historians believe his role in the persecution of the nobility was exaggerated. On her death bed, the empress proclaimed Biron the Regent of Russia, but two months later his rivals arrested him and sentenced him to death by quartering. The sentence was commuted to exile. The unfinished palace stood as an empty shell for another 22 years when, pardoned by Catherine II, Ernst Johann returned home. Rastrelli resumed the construction and in 1768 the palace was finished. Ernst Johann died four years later at the age of 82. A succession of Russian nobles inhabited (and altered) the palace after the the Duchy of Courland was incorporated into Russian Empire in 1795.

The castle is divided into two halves; the **East Wing** was devoted to formal occasions, while the **West Wing** was the private royal residence. The **Royal Gardens**, inspired by the gardens at Versailles, were also used for public affairs. The rooms were heated by a network of 80 porcelain stoves (only six authentic stoves remain), as the castle was mostly used during the warmer months.

The palace was badly damaged in the Franco-Russian War in 1812 and again during the Latvian War of Independence in 1919 – what you see now is the result of a painstaking restoration started by experts from Leningrad in 1972 and officially finished in 2015. Definitely spend an extra €2 and opt for the 'long route' option when buying the ticket. Unlike the short route, it includes the duke's and duchess's private chambers, which is your chance to peek into the everyday life of 18th-century aristocrats as well as to admire the opulent interior design. Even the duke's chamber pot, adorned with a delightful painting of swimming salmon, is on display.

Like any good castle, Rundāle has loads of eerie ghost tales, but the most famous spectre that haunts the palace grounds is the 'White Lady'. In the 19th century the royal doctor had a young daughter who was courted by many men, but on her 18th birthday she suddenly grew ill and died. Obsessed with her untimely demise, the doctor kept her corpse in his laboratory to study her and tried to figure out why she was ravaged by illness (or was she poisoned by a lovelorn suitor?). Unable to rest eternally, the daughter's spirit began haunting the castle and cackling wildly in the middle of the night. During Rundāle's restorations, several art historians and masons heard her wicked laughter and brought in a priest to exorcise the grounds.

From Bauska (12km away) there are hourly buses to Rundāle Castle (€0.90 to 1.75) between 6am and 7.30pm. Make sure you get off at Pilsrundāle, the villlage before Rundāle.

from Rīga. In its heyday, Kuldīga (or Goldingen, as its German founders called it) served as the capital of the Duchy of Courland (1596–1616), but it was badly damaged during the Great Northern War and was never quite able to regain its former lustre. Today, this blast from the past is a favourite spot to shoot Latvian period-piece films.

◉ Sights

Ventas Rumba
WATERFALL

In a country that is acutely short of verticals but rich on horizontals, landscape features appear to be blatantly two-dimensional – even waterfalls. Spanning 240m, Ventas Rumba is branded Europe's widest, but as it is hardly taller than a basketball player, it would risk being dismissed by vile competitors a mere rapid, were it ever to attend an international waterfall congress. That said, it does look like a cute toy Niagara, when observed from the Kuldīga castle hill.

Kuldīga Historic Museum
MUSEUM

(Kuldīgas novada muzejs; ☑ 6335 0179; www.kuldigasmuzejs.lv; Pils iela; adult/child €1.50/1; ⊙ noon-6pm Tue, 10am-6pm Wed-Sun) Founded by a local German school director, the museum is housed in what a local legend claims to be a Russian pavilion from the 1900 World Exhibition in Paris. Its 2nd floor has been redesigned as an apartment of a rich early-20th-century local family, which features an international playing-cards collection in the 'master's room'. A cluster of Duke Jakob's cannons sits on the front lawn.

⌸ Sleeping & Eating

★ 2 Baloži
GUESTHOUSE €€

(☑ 22000523; www.facebook.com/2balozi; Pasta iela 5; r from €50) Perched above the Alekšupīte stream, this old wooden house has rooms designed in the laconic Scandinavian style with lots of aged wood that creates a pleasant, nostalgic ambience. Goldingen Room restaurant, across the square, serves as the reception.

★ Pagrabiņš
INTERNATIONAL €€

(☑ 6632 0034; www.pagrabins.lv; Baznīcas iela 5; mains €5-15; ⊙ 11am-11pm Mon-Thu, to 3am Fri & Sat, noon-11pm Sun; ☑) Pagrabiņš inhabits a cellar that was once used as the town's prison. Today a combination of Latvian and Asian dishes is served under low-slung alcoves lined with honey-coloured bricks. In warmer weather, enjoy your snacks on the small verandah, which sits atop the trickling Alekšupīte stream out the back.

ⓘ Information

Tourist Information Centre (☑ 6332 2259; www.visit.kuldiga.lv; Baznīcas iela 5; ⊙ 9am-5pm)

ⓘ Getting There & Away

From the **bus station** (☑ 6332 2061; Adatu iela 9), buses run to/from Rīga (€6.40, 2½ to 3½ hours, every two hours), Liepāja (€3.85 to €4.70, 1¾ hours, seven daily), Ventspils (€3, 1¼ hours, six daily) and Alsunga (€1.60, 35 minutes, five daily).

Ventspils

POP 35,360

Fabulous amounts of oil and shipping money have turned Ventspils into one of Latvia's most beautiful and dynamic cities. The air is brisk and clean, and the well-kept buildings are done up in an assortment of cheery colours – even the towering industrial machinery is coated in bright paint. Latvia's biggest and busiest port wasn't always smiles and rainbows, though – Ventspils' strategic, ice-free location served as the naval and industrial workhorse for the original settlement of Cours in the 12th century, the Livonian Order in the 13th century, the Hanseatic League through the 16th century and finally the USSR in recent times.

Although locals coddle their Užavas beer and claim that there's not much to do, tourists will find a weekend's worth of fun in the form of brilliant beaches, interactive museums and winding Old Town streets dotted with the odd boutique and cafe.

◉ Sights

Ventspils Beach
BEACH

For Ventspils, the wide stretch of dazzlingly white sand south of the Venta River is what the Louvre is for Paris – its main treasure. During the warmer months, beach bums of every ilk – from nudists to kiteboarders – line the sands to absorb the sun's rays. Backed by a belt of dunes and a lush manicured park, the Blue Flag beach feels as pristine and well cared for as an urban beach can get.

⌸ Sleeping & Eating

Kupfernams
B&B €€

(☑ 27677107; www.hotelkupfernams.lv; Kārļa iela 5; s/d €44/65; ☎) This charming wooden house at the centre of Old Town has a set of cheery upstairs rooms with slanted ceilings, opening onto a communal lounge. Below, there's a cafe and a hair salon (which doubles as the reception).

Krogs Zītari
EASTERN EUROPEAN €€

(📞 25708337; www.facebook.com/KrogsZitari; Tirgus iela 11; mains €7-15; ⏰ 11am-midnight) Tucked in the courtyard of a pretty timber-framed German house, this beer garden serves large portions of meat- and seafood-heavy fare. Whether it is beer-braised pork shank or fried rainbow trout with almond butter, all food is designed to make a perfect match for excellent Latvian brews.

ℹ️ Information

Tourist Information Centre (📞 6362 2263; www.visitventspils.com; Dārzu iela 6; ⏰ 8am-6pm Mon-Fri, 10am-4pm Sat & Sun) In the ferry terminal.

ℹ️ Getting There & Away

Ventspils' **bus terminal** (📞 6362 9904; Kuldīgas iela 5) is served by buses to/from Rīga (€7.55, 2¾ to four hours, hourly), Kuldīga (€3, 1¼ hours, six daily) and Liepāja (€5.20, 2¼ to three hours, six daily) via Jūrkalne (€2.50, one hour) and Pāvilosta (€3.25, 1¼ hours).

Stena Line (www.stenaline.lv) operates ferry service to Nynäshamn, Sweden, up to twice daily from the Ventspils **ferry terminal** (€49, 8½ hours).

NORTHERN LATVIA

Sigulda
POP 11,300

With a name that sounds like a mythical ogress, it comes as no surprise that the gateway to the Gauja Valley is an enchanting spot with delightful surprises tucked behind every dappled tree. Locals proudly call their town the 'Switzerland of Latvia', but if you're expecting the majesty of a mountainous snow-capped realm, you'll be rather disappointed. Instead, Sigulda mixes its own brew of scenic trails, extreme sports and 800-year-old castles steeped in legends.

🔘 Sights & Activities

⭐ **Turaida Museum Reserve**
CASTLE

(Turaidas muzejrezervāts; 📞 6797 1402; www.turaida-muzejs.lv; Turaidas iela 10; adult/child summer €6/1.15, winter €3.50/0.70; ⏰ 9am-8pm) Turaida means 'God's Garden' in ancient Livonian,

and this green knoll capped with a fairy-tale castle is certainly a heavenly place. The red-brick castle with its tall cylindrical tower was built in 1214 on the site of a Liv stronghold. A museum inside the castle's 15th-century granary offers an interesting account of the Livonian state from 1319 to 1561, and additional exhibitions can be viewed in the 42m-high Donjon Tower and the castle's western and southern towers.

Bobsled Track
ADVENTURE SPORTS

(Bob trase; 📞 6797 3813; www.bobtrase.lv; Šveices iela 13; ⏰ noon-5pm Sat & Sun) Sigulda's 1200m bobsled track was built for the Soviet team. In winter you can fly down the 16-bend track at 80km/h in a five-person Vučko **soft bob** (per adult/child €10/7, from November to March). Summer speed fiends can ride a wheeled **summer bob** (per adult/child €10/7, from May to September).

🍴 Eating

⭐ **Mr Biskvīts**
CAFE, BAKERY €

(📞 6797 6611; www.mr.biskvits.lv; Ausekļa iela 9; mains €4-9; ⏰ 8am-9pm Mon-Fri, 9am-9pm Sat, 9am-7pm Sun) Mr Biskvīts' candy-striped lair is filled with delicious cakes and pastries, but it's also a good spot for a cooked breakfast, a lunchtime soup or sandwich, and an evening pasta or stir-fry. The coffee's great too.

ℹ️ Information

Sigulda Tourism Information Centre (📞 6797 1335; www.tourism.sigulda.lv; Ausekļa iela 6; ⏰ 9am-6pm; 📶) Located within the train station, this extremely helpful centre has stacks of information about activities and accommodation.

Gauja National Park Visitors Centre (📞 6130 3030; www.entergauja.com/en; Turaidas iela 2a; ⏰ 9am-7pm) Sells maps of the park, town and cycle routes nearby.

ℹ️ Getting There & Away

Buses trundle the 50-odd kilometers between Sigulda's **bus station** and Rīga (€2.75, one hour, every 30 minutes between 8am and 10.30pm).

One train per hour (between 6am and 9pm) travels the Rīga–Sigulda–Cēsis–Valmiera line. Fares from Sigulda include Rīga (€1.90, one or 1¼ hours), Līgatne (€.70, 10 minutes) and Cēsis (€2, 40 minutes).

ℹ️ Getting Around

Sigulda's attractions are quite spread out and after a long day of walking, bus 12 (€2.35) will become your new best friend. It plies the route to/from New Sigulda Castle, Turaida Castle and Krimulda Manor hourly during business hours (more on weekends).

Cēsis

POP 18,600

With its stunning medieval castle, cobbled streets, green hills and landscaped gardens, Cēsis is simply the cutest little town in Latvia. There is a lot of history here, too: it started eight centuries ago as a Livonian Order's stronghold in the land of unruly pagans and saw horrific battles right under (or inside) the castle walls. Although it's an easy day trip from Rīga, Cēsis is definitely worth a longer stay, especially since there is the whole of Gauja National Park around it to explore.

◉ Sights

★ Cēsis Castle   CASTLE

(Cēsu pils; ☑ 6412 1815; www.cesupils.lv; adult/student €6/3.50, tours from €35; ⊙ 10am-6pm) Cēsis Castle is actually two castles in one. The first is the sorrowful dark-stone towers of the old Wenden castle. Founded by Livonian knights in 1214, it was sacked by Russian tsar Ivan the Terrible in 1577, but only after its 300 defenders blew themselves up with gunpowder. The other is the more cheerful, castle-like, 18th-century manor house once inhabited by the dynasty of German counts von Sievers. It houses a museum that features original fin-de-siècle interiors.

⊨ Sleeping

Hotel Cēsis   HOTEL €€

(☑ 6412 0122; www.hotelcesis.com; Vienības laukums 1; s/d €45/60; @ 🛜) The exterior is vaguely neoclassical while the inside features rows of standard upmarket rooms. Its in-house restaurant serves top-notch Latvian and European cuisine in a formal setting or outdoors in the pristine garden.

❶ Information

Cēsis Tourism Information Centre

(☑ 28318318; www.tourism.cesis.lv; Baznīcas laukums 1; ⊙ 10am-6pm) Just outside the walls of the Cēsis Castle.

❶ Getting There & Away

Cēsis' **bus station** and train station can be found in the same location, at the roundabout

connecting Raunas iela to Raiņa iela. There are up to five trains per day between 6.35am and 9pm linking Cēsis and Rīga (€3.50, two hours). Bikes are allowed on board. Two or three buses per hour between 6.15am and 10.20pm ply the route from Cēsis to Rīga, stopping in Līgatne and Sigulda. Trains also run to Valmiera (€1.55, 30 minutes).

SURVIVAL GUIDE

❶ Directory A–Z

ACCOMMODATION

➡ We highly advise booking ahead during the high season (summer). Rates drop significantly in the colder months.

➡ Most rooms are en suite. Smoking in rooms is normally prohibited.

➡ Check out www.camping.lv for details on pitching a tent.

LGBT+ TRAVELLERS

Rīga has a few gay venues and it was the first former-Soviet city to host EuroPride in 2015. The following organisations offer resources for LGBT+ people in Latvia, as well as listings and events.

Mozaika (www.mozaika.lv) Latvia's only LGBTIQ alliance.

Latvian Gay Portal (www.gay.lv) Social networking and classifieds.

Latvia Pride (www.pride.lv) Resources, media and events

MONEY

Latvia abandoned its national currency, the lats, and switched to the euro in January 2014.

ATMs are easy to find and credit cards are widely accepted.

OPENING HOURS

Opening hours vary throughout the year. We list high-season opening hours, but remember these longer summer hours often decrease in shoulder and low seasons.

Shops 10am–7pm Monday to Friday, until 5pm on Saturdays. Some stay open on Sundays. Supermarkets are open up to 10pm, with some open 24 hours.

Restaurants Generally from 11am until 3pm for lunch and from 6pm to 11pm for dinner.

Banks 10am–2pm and 3pm-5pm Monday to Friday.

PUBLIC HOLIDAYS

The Latvia Institute website (www.li.lv) has a page devoted to special Latvian Remembrance Days under the 'About Latvia' link.

New Year's Day 1 January

Easter March/April

Labour Day 1 May

Restoration of Independence of the Republic of Latvia 4 May

Mothers' Day Second Sunday in May

Whitsunday A Sunday in May or June

Līgo Eve (Midsummer festival) 23 June

Jāņi (St John's Day and Summer Solstice) 24 June

National Day 18 November; Anniversary of the Proclamation of the Republic of Latvia, 1918

Christmas (Ziemsvētki) 25 December

Second Holiday 26 December

New Year's Eve 31 December

TELEPHONE

Latvian telephone numbers have eight digits; landlines start with '6' and mobile numbers start with '2'. To make any call within Latvia, simply dial the eight-digit number. To call a Latvian telephone number from abroad, dial the international access code, then the country code for Latvia (371) followed by the subscriber's eight-digit number.

ⓘ Getting Around

BICYCLE

Latvia's rural roads are forgivingly flat, to the delight of touring cyclists. Bikes and equipment can be hired from Rīga Bike Tours (p239), which also organises cycling holiday packages.

BUS

Buses are much more convenient than trains if you're travelling beyond the capital's clutch of suburban rail lines. Updated timetables are available at www.autoosta.lv and www.1188.lv.

TRAIN

Train travel is convenient for a limited number of destinations, most notably Jūrmala, Gauja National Park and Daugavpils. The city's network of commuter rails makes it easy for tourists to reach day-tripping destinations. Latvia's further attractions are best explored by bus.

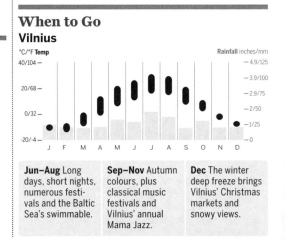

Lithuania

POP 2.82 MILLION

Best Places to Eat

➜ Saula (p254)

➜ Senoji Kibininė (p257)

➜ Balzac (p254)

➜ Tik Pas Joną (p261)

➜ Stora Antis (p260)

➜ Sweet Root (p255)

Best Places to Stay

➜ Hotel Pacai (p254)

➜ Bernardinu B&B (p254)

➜ Miško Namas (p261)

➜ Litinterp Guesthouse (p260)

➜ Domus Maria (p254)

➜ Narutis (p254)

Why Go?

Blame it on the Baltic sea breeze or the almost-endless midsummer days: Lithuania has an otherworldly quality. In the southernmost of the Baltic states, beaches are spangled with amber and woodlands are alive with demonic statues.

Medieval-style mead and traditional wood-carving never went out of style but there's also a spirited counterculture, particularly in compact capital Vilnius. Less visited are second city Kaunas and spa resort Druskininkai, where 19th-century architecture nudges against brooding Soviet buildings.

As Europe's last country to be Christianised, pagan history still soaks the land. Curonian Spit, splintering from the Baltic coast, is awash in folklore. Cyclists, hikers and beach-goers eagerly board ferries to its voluptuous dunes. Cloaking the rest of Lithuania are lakes, forests of birch and pine, and pancake-flat farmland; in Lithuania, there's ample space to breathe.

When to Go
Vilnius

Jun–Aug Long days, short nights, numerous festivals and the Baltic Sea's swimmable.	**Sep–Nov** Autumn colours, plus classical music festivals and Vilnius' annual Mama Jazz.	**Dec** The winter deep freeze brings Vilnius' Christmas markets and snowy views.

Entering the Country

With budget flights into Vilnius and Kaunas, and rail routes from other destinations in Eastern Europe, it's easy and inexpensive to reach Lithuania from within Europe. Ryanair (www.ryanair.com) operates routes to Vilnius and Kaunas from several European cities. AirBaltic (www.airbaltic.com) flies to Vilnius from Rīga several times daily and from Tallinn on most days.

ITINERARIES

Three Days
Devote two days to exploring the baroque heart of Vilnius (p250). Then day-trip to Trakai (p256) to experience its island castle and the history and cuisine of the Karaite people, stopping off at Paneriai (p256) on the way.

One Week
Start by spending four nights in Vilnius (p250), including a day trip to Trakai (p256) and the memorial at Paneriai (p256). Travel cross-country to the Hill of Crosses (p260), near Šiauliai (p259), then explore some serious nature on Curonian Spit (p261) for a couple of days. Head back east via Klaipėda (p259) and Kaunas (p257).

Essential Food & Drink

Beer and mead Švyturys, Utenos and Kalnapilis are regional beers; *midus* (mead) is a honey-tinged nobleman's drink returning to popularity.

Beer snacks No drinking session is complete without smoked pigs' ears or *kepta duona* (deep-fried garlicky bread sticks).

Beetroot delight Cold *šaltibarščiai* (beetroot soup) is a summer speciality, served with potatoes; sour cream turns it neon pink. Hot beetroot soups, with or without cream, are common year-round.

Potato creations Pop a button for *cepelinai* (potato-dough 'zeppelins' stuffed with meat, mushrooms or curd cheese), *bulviniai blynai* (potato pancakes) or *žemaičių blynai* (heart-shaped mashed potato stuffed and fried), or *vedarai* (intestines stuffed with mashed potato).

Smoked fish Curonian Spit is famous for smoked fish, particularly the superb *rūkytas ungurys* (smoked eel).

Pastries Bite into Trakai specialities *kibinai*, pasties crammed with mutton, or sate your sweet tooth with *šakotis*, sweet, spit-roasted batter.

Hunter's table Sample local game, such as beaver stew or boar sausages.

AT A GLANCE

Area 65,300 sq km

Capital Vilnius

Country code ☑ 370

Currency euro (€)

Emergency General ☑ 112, fire ☑ 01, police ☑ 02, ambulance ☑ 03

Language Lithuanian

Time Eastern European Time (GMT/UTC plus two hours)

Visas Not required for citizens of the EU, USA, Canada, Japan, New Zealand and Australia for visits up to 90 days.

LITHUANIA

Sleeping Price Ranges

The following price ranges refer to the cost of a double room with private bathroom.

€ less than €50

€€ €50–100

€€€ more than €100

Eating Price Ranges

The following price ranges are based on the cost of a typical main course.

€ less than €7

€€ €7–14

€€€ more than €14

Resources

Lonely Planet (www.lonelyplanet.com/lithuania)

Visit Vilnius (www.vilnius-tourism.lt)

Lithuania Travel (https://www.lithuania.travel/en/)

Baltic Times (www.baltictimes.com/news_lithuania)

Lithuania Highlights

1 Vilnius (p250)
Wandering the backstreets of the beautiful baroque capital, looking for that perfect bar or bistro.

2 Curonian Spit (p261)
Cycling between beaches, birch forests and sand dunes on this peaceful sliver of land in the Baltic Sea.

3 Hill of Crosses (p260)
Being awestruck at this storied pilgrimage site, a hill entirely cloaked in crucifixes.

4 Trakai (p256) Exploring Lithuania's smallest national park and its postcard-perfect island castle.

5 Kaunas (p257) Drinking in Old Town's atmosphere and WWII history in Lithuania's spirited second city.

6 Grūtas Park (p258)
Feeling spooked by a Soviet sculpture gallery at forested 'Stalin World' near Druskininkai.

VILNIUS

♪ 5 / POP 574,147

There is a dreamy quality to Vilnius (vilnyus), especially in the golden glow of a midsummer evening. Lithuania's capital has an Old Town of rare authenticity: marvellously intact, its pebbly streets are lined with weather-worn period buildings that hide cafes, boutiques and dainty guesthouses.

Vilnius doesn't hide its battle scars. Reminders of loss are everywhere: museums dedicated to the Holocaust, former ghettos, preserved KGB torture chambers and cemeteries filled with the war dead.

Though carpeted with green spaces and studded with venerable Catholic and Orthodox church spires, this is no Eastern European antique. Artists, punks and even a self-declared micro-nation, the **Republic of Užupis**, keep Vilnius cutting-edge.

◉ Sights

◉ Cathedral Square & Gediminis Hill

★ Palace of the Grand Dukes of Lithuania   MUSEUM
(Valdovų Rumai; ☑ 5-262 0007; www.valdovuru mai.lt; Katedros aikštė 4; full admission €6, per exhibition €2-3, guided tour €20-30; ☺ 10am-6pm Mon-Wed & Sun, to 8pm Thu-Sat) On a site that has been settled since at least the 4th century AD stands the latest in a procession of fortified palaces, repeatedly remodelled, destroyed and rebuilt. One of its grandest manifestations, the baroque palace built for the 17th-century grand dukes, has been faithfully rebuilt to house an atmospheric museum of art and history. Visitors with a couple of hours can opt for full admission, accessing four 'routes' through Lithuanian history; otherwise choose one or two.

Gediminas Castle & Museum   MUSEUM
(Gedimino Pilis ir Muziejus; ☑ 5-261 7453; www. lnm.lt; Gediminas Hill, Arsenalo gatvė 5; adult/child €5/2; ☺ museum 10am-9pm, castle hill 7am-9pm) With its hilltop location above the junction of the Neris and Vilnia rivers, Gediminas Castle is the last of a series of settlements and fortified buildings occupying this site since Neolithic times. This brick version, built by Grand Duke Vytautas in the early 15th century, harbours a museum about the city with successive floors elaborating on past centuries of warfare, medieval weaponry and contemporary history. For most visitors, the highlight is the 360-degree panorama of Vilnius from the roof.

Vilnius Cathedral   CATHEDRAL
(Vilniaus Arkikatedra; ☑ 5-269 7800; www.katedra. lt; Katedros aikštė 1; cathedral admission free, crypt tours adult/child €4.50/2.50; ☺ 7am-7pm, crypt tours 4pm Tue, Thu & Sat) Stately Vilnius Cathedral, divorced from its freestanding **belfry** (☑ 8-600 12080; www.bpmuziejus.lt; adult/student €4.50/2.50; ☺ 10am-7pm Mon-Sat May-Sep), is a national symbol and the city's most instantly recognisable building. Known in full as the Cathedral of St Stanislav and St Vladislav, this columned neoclassical cathedral occupies a spot originally used for the worship of Perkūnas, the Lithuanian thunder god.

Register in advance to tour the crypts, the final resting place of many prominent Lithuanians including Vytautas the Great (1350–1430).

National Museum of Lithuania   MUSEUM
(Lietuvos Nacionalinis Muziejus; ☑ 5-262 7774; www.lnm.lt; Arsenalo gatvė 1; adult/child €3/1.50; ☺ 10am-6pm Tue-Sun) This wide-ranging museum exhibits art and artefacts from Lithuanian life from Neolithic times to the present day. Early history is revealed in 2nd-millennium-BC arrowheads and 7th-century grave hauls (signage isn't always good), while the lives of well-to-do Lithuanians of recent

---

JEWISH VILNIUS

Over the centuries, Vilnius developed into a leading centre of Jewish scholarship with more than 100 synagogues, earning itself the nickname 'Jerusalem of the north'. The Jewish community was largely destroyed in WWII. The former Jewish quarter lay in the streets west of Didžioji gatvė, including present-day Žydų gatvė (Jews St) and Gaono gatvė, named after Vilnius' most famous Jewish resident, Gaon Elijahu ben Shlomo Zalman (1720–97).

One of the three main branches of the Vilna Gaon Jewish State Museum, the **Tolerance Centre** (Tolerancijos Centras; ☑ 5-212 0112; www.jmuseum.lt; Naugarduko gatvė 10/2; adult/concession €4/2; ☺ 10am-6pm Mon-Thu, to 4pm Fri & Sun) is simultaneously a museum of Jewish history and culture, and a performance space. The **Holocaust Museum** (Holokausto Ekspozicija; ☑ 5-262 0730; www.jmuseum.lt; Pamėnkalnio gatvė 12; adult/child €3/1.50; ☺ 9am-5pm Mon-Thu, 9am-4pm Fri, 10am-4pm Sun), or 'Green House', exhibits the unvarnished truth behind the destruction of Lithuania's once-vibrant Jewish community, the Litvaks. This profoundly disturbing chapter of history is essential to understanding Vilnius. Many items on display were donated by survivors and victims' families.

The **Choral Synagogue** (Choralinė Sinagoga; ☑ 5-261 2523; Pylimo gatvė 39; €1; ☺ 10am-4pm Mon-Fri, to 2pm Sun), built in 1903, is now Vilnius' sole surviving Jewish temple. The exterior is an intriguing blend of oriental and modern Romanesque styles; ring the buzzer to enter and view its vaulted interior and ornate Torah ark.

Central Vilnius

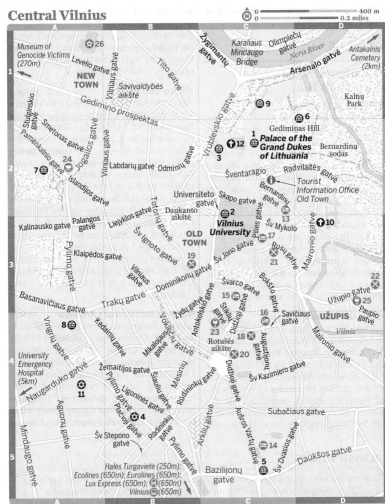

centuries are unveiled with velvet-lined sleds and elaborately painted furniture. The highlight is the colourful folk traditions room, replete with floral-decorated furnishings, linens and carved wooden crosses.

Old Town

★ Vilnius University   HISTORIC BUILDING
(Vilniaus Universitetas; ☑ 5-219 3029; www.muzie jus.vu.lt; Universiteto gatvė 3; campus adult/child €1.50/0.50, bell tower adult/child €2.50/1.50; ☉ campus 9am-6pm Mon-Sat, bell tower 10am-7pm May-Sep) Founded in 1579 during the Catholic Counter Reformation, Vilnius University

was run by Jesuits for two centuries. During the 19th century it became one of Europe's greatest centres of learning, and the university survived shutdown by Tsar Nicholas I, rebranding under Soviet rule, and closure by the Nazis. Its spectacular architectural ensemble includes a 64m bell tower, baroque church, courtyard and fresco-laden hall, all of which are open to visitors.

Gates of Dawn   HISTORIC BUILDING
(Aušros Vartai; ☑ 5-212 3513; www.ausrosvartai. lt; Aušros Vartų gatvė 12; ☉ 6am-7pm) **FREE** The southern border of Old Town is marked by the last-standing of five 16th-century portals

Central Vilnius

LITHUANIA VILNIUS

that were once built into the city walls. A suitably grand way to enter the Old Town, the focal point of the Gates of Dawn is the Chapel of Mary the Mother of Mercy, housing the 'Vilnius Madonna'. Framed in silver, this 17th-century painting of the Virgin Mary attracts pilgrims from across Europe.

St Anne's Church   CHURCH
(Šv Onos Bažnyčia; www.onosbaznycia.lt; Maironio gatvė 8-1; ☉10.30am-6.30pm Tue-Sat, 8am-7pm Sun) Flamboyant and Gothic St Anne's Church, a vision of undulating lines and red-brick arches, was built in 1500 on the site of a wooden church that burned to the ground. Today it's among Vilnius' most famous buildings; the turreted facade (marrying 33 different kinds of brick) inspires countless photo ops from the grassy plaza opposite. Within, rib vaults trace graceful lines of brick through a rosy interior. Napoleon was reportedly so charmed that he wanted to relocate the church to Paris.

MO Museum   GALLERY
(☑6-098 3764; https://mo.lt; Pylimo gatvė 17; adult/student/child under 7 €7/3.50/free; ☉10am-8pm Sat-Mon, Wed & Thu, to 10pm Fri) Opened in October 2018, this assemblage of contemporary Lithuanian art and photography is the country's first private museum. An orderly union of sharp angles, polished glass and white plaster, the ultra-modern gallery was designed by visionary Daniel Libeskind, the architect behind Berlin's Jewish Museum. Around 5000 20th-century artworks are assembled within, freshened by rotating exhibitions and occasional cultural events.

◉ New Town & Beyond

★**Museum of Genocide Victims**   MUSEUM
(Genocido Aukų Muziejus; ☑5-249 8156; www.genocid.lt/muziejus; Aukų gatvė 2a; adult/concession €4/1; ☉10am-6pm Wed-Sat, to 5pm Sun) This former headquarters of the KGB (and before them the Gestapo, Polish occupiers and Tsarist judiciary) houses a museum dedicated to thousands of Lithuanians who were murdered, imprisoned or deported by the Soviet Union from WWII until the 1960s. Back-lit photographs, wooden annexes and a disorienting layout sharpen the impact of past horrors outlined in graphic detail. Most unsettling is the descent to the prison cells and execution yard.

Antakalnis Cemetery   CEMETERY
(Antakalnio Kapinės; off Karių kapų gatvė; ☉9am-dusk) In this leafy suburb, little-visited by tourists, Antakalnis Cemetery is the final resting place of Lithuanian luminaries and locals lost to war. Brutalist, art-nouveau and modernist headstones give the cemetery, a half-hour walk east of the centre, the feel of an open-air sculpture gallery. Those killed by Soviet special forces on 13 January 1991 are memorialised by a sculpture of the Madonna.

A taxi or ride-share service from the train station costs around €6; hailing a ride back is near-impossible.

📛 Sleeping

Jimmy Jumps House
HOSTEL €

(☎5-231 3847; www.jimmyjumpshouse.com; Savičiaus gatvė 12-1; dm €9-15, d/tr with shared bathroom incl breakfast from €30/36; @🛜) Movie nights, pub crawls, free waffles...this clean, well-run, centrally located hostel is justifiably popular among backpackers. The pinewood bunks are in modest four- to 12-bed rooms, but hands-on service, lockers, a sociable lounge, games and a well-priced bar add up to money well spent.

Bernardinu B&B
GUESTHOUSE €€

(☎5-261 5134; www.bernardinuhouse.com; Bernardinų gatvė 5; d €50-60, d/tr with shared bathroom from €45/69; P🛜) Baroque flourishes and original frescoes make every room unique at this friendly, family-owned B&B, stylishly restored within an 18th-century townhouse. Old timber flooring and ceilings have been carefully preserved, and stripped patches of brick allow you to see through the patina of the years. Breakfast (€6) is brought to your door on a tray.

Domus Maria
GUESTHOUSE €€

(☎5-264 4880; www.domusmaria.lt; Aušros Vartų gatvė 12; s/d/tr/q incl breakfast from €60/83/100/113; P🛜) Austere and occasionally spooky, the guesthouse of the Vilnius archdiocese is housed in a former 17th-century monastery. Rooms are plain but ample, history almost echoes along the long corridors, and the location at the foot of Old-Town artery Aušros Vartų gatvė couldn't be better. Two rooms, 207 and 307, have views of the Gates of Dawn – book far in advance.

★Hotel Pacai
DESIGN HOTEL €€€

(☎5-277 0000; https://hotelpacai.com; Didžioji gatvė 7; d from €180; P✳@🛜) Staying at luxurious Pacai, in a restored 17th-century palace, you snooze beneath the same timber beams as past nobles...except nowadays there's modern art decking the walls, and individually styled chambers have discreet sundecks and lustrous marbled bathrooms. Murals and vaulted corridors preserve the history while a glamorous inner courtyard and top-end bar and restaurants bring Pacai bang up to date.

Narutis
HISTORIC HOTEL €€€

(☎5-212 2894; www.narutis.com; Pilies gatvė 24; d/ste incl breakfast from €144/207; P✳@🛜🏊) In a townhouse built in 1581, rooms at this classy pad have satin drapes, huge comfy beds and, in some cases, original 19th-century frescoes. The opulence continues in the brick-lined spa (the pool and Jacuzzi are free in the mornings). Breakfast steals the show: served in a vaulted Gothic cellar, it's a banquet spread of bubbly, smoked fish and dainty desserts.

🍴 Eating

Senamiesčio Krautuvė
DELI €

(☎5-231 2836; www.senamiesciokrautuve.lt; Literatų gatvė 5; ⏰10am-8pm Mon-Sat, 11am-5pm Sun) Look no further than this quiet hobbit-hole deli for the very best Lithuanian comestibles, many unique to the country. Wicker baskets brim with fruit and vegetables, cheeses and yoghurts fill the chiller cabinets, and jars of honey and jam line the shelves. Grab breads and cookies to eat on the hoof while admiring the arty tributes along Literatų gatvė.

★Saula
LITHUANIAN, EUROPEAN €€

(☎5-250 7473; www.facebook.com/saularestoranas; Didžioji gatve 26; mains €9-16; ⏰11am-10pm Mon-Thu, to 11pm Fri & Sat, noon-10pm Sun) 🍴 Lithuanian staples find elegant expression at this contemporary cellar restaurant: herring with dill foam, duck drizzled with blackcurrant and buckthorn-garnished panna cotta. Birch tables and pale stone walls impart a light, airy feel, while pagan statuettes and modern-art knick-knacks mirror the old-meets-new menu. Best of all, the produce is locally sourced and informed by the seasons.

Balzac
FRENCH €€

(☎8-614 89223; www.balzac.lt; Savičiaus gatvė 7; mains €11-17; ⏰11.30am-11pm Sun-Wed, to midnight Thu-Sat) This faithfully *français* bistro serves classic French dishes in an elegantly distressed setting: melt-in-mouth duck confit with lentils, *tournedos de boeuf* (beef tenderloin wrapped in bacon) and its signature *tarte tatin* (caramelised apple cake). The dining area is small, so book to avoid disappointment.

SHOP LIKE A LOCAL

Traditional market stalls mingle effortlessly with on-trend cafes at **Halles Market** (Halės Turgavietė; ☎5-262 5536; www.halesturgaviete.lt; Pylimo gatvė 58; ⏰7am-6pm Tue-Sat, to 3pm Sun), one of the city's oldest food markets. The glossy metal and glass construction, completed in 1906, is a delightful place to browse fruit and veg, buckets of flowers and deli fare like honeys and jams.

Meat Lovers' Pub
PUB FOOD €€

(☑8-652 51233; www.meatloverspub.lt; Šv Ignoto gatvė14; mains €7-18; ☺11.30am-midnight Mon-Fri, noon-midnight Sat, noon-8pm Sun; ☎) Order lager, wheat beer or dark ale. Nibble fried cheese and moreish smoked ribs. Find that you're thirsty again, and start the cycle anew. Meat Lovers' Pub delivers exactly what it promises: unapologetically carnivorous pub food, like German sausages, T-bone steaks and juicy burgers, in a convivial setting that somehow suits everyone from merry-making groups to solo travellers with books.

★ Sweet Root
LITHUANIAN €€€

(☑8-685 60767; www.sweetroot.lt; Užupio gatvė 22; 7-course degustation €75; ☺6-11pm Wed-Sat) Led by the seasons, Sweet Root pairs locally sourced ingredients – pike and nettles, beetroot leaves and chanterelles – and presents them exquisitely in a smart modern dining room. It's an evening-long degustation experience, elevated to greater heights if you opt for wines thoughtfully matched to each course (extra €55). Vegetarian, vegan and other diets require a few days' notice. Book ahead.

🍷 Drinking & Nightlife

Alinė Leičiai
PUB

(☑5-260 9087; www.bambalyne.lt; Stiklių gatvė 4; ☺11am-midnight; ☎) With draught mead, numerous local brews and a flower-filled beer garden, Leičiai is a cheerful place to clink glasses with locals. Mop up the damage with hearty Lithuanian fare: soup served in bread bowls, trout with hazelnuts and pork neck with cabbage.

Špunka
BAR

(☑8-652 32361; www.spunka.lt; Užupio gatvė 9; ☺3-10pm Tue-Sun, from 5pm Mon) This tiny, charismatic bar does a great line in craft ales from Lithuania and further afield. If you need sustenance to keep the drink and chat flowing, crunchy beer snacks, soups and garlic bread are close at hand.

Elska
COFFEE

(☑8-608 21028; www.facebook.com/elska.coffee; Pamėnkalnio gatvė 1; ☺7am-9pm Mon-Fri, 8am-8pm Sat & Sun; ☎) A front-runner of Vilnius' latest wave of smart coffee shops, Elska distinguishes itself with a pocket-sized library and adjoining gallery of modern art. This bookish cafe attracts a mix of grab-and-go commuters and students seeking to linger over avocado toast, chia-seed pudding and one of the best flat whites in the city.

★ Entertainment

Lithuanian National Opera & Ballet Theatre
OPERA

(Lietuvos Nacionalinis Operos ir Baleto Teatras; ☑5-262 0727; www.opera.lt; Vienuolio gatvė 1; ☺box office 10am-7pm Mon-Fri, to 6.30pm Sat, to 3pm Sun) This stunning (or gaudy, depending on your taste) Soviet-era building, with huge, cascading chandeliers and grandiose dimensions, is home to Lithuania's national ballet and opera companies. You can see world-class performers for as little as €10.

ℹ Information

Tourist Information Office Old Town (☑5-262 9660; www.vilnius-tourism.lt; cnr Pilies & Radvilaitės gatvė; ☺9am-noon & 1-6pm) The head office of Vilnius' tourist information service has free maps, transport advice and can help book accommodation.

University Emergency Hospital (☑5-236 5000; www.santa.lt; Santariškių gatvė 2; ☺24hr) This teaching hospital takes serious and emergency cases.

ℹ Getting There & Away

BUS

Vilnius' **bus station** (Autobusų Stotis; ☑1661; www.autobusustotis.lt; Sodų gatvė 22; ☺5am-10.45pm) is just south of the Old Town. Inside its ticket hall, domestic tickets are sold from 6am to 7pm, and it has a *bagažinė* (left luggage service). Buses travel to/from Druskininkai (€11, two hours, 15 daily), Kaunas (€6 to €7, 1¾ hours, regular), Klaipėda (€17 to €21, four to 5¾ hours, 15 daily) and Šiauliai (€13.70 to €18, three to 4½ hours, 12 daily). Beyond Lithuania, direct services also reach Rīga in Latvia (€15 to €23, 4¼ to 6¼ hours, eight daily) and Tallinn in Estonia (€26 to €35, 9¼ hours, four daily).

Ecolines (☑5-213 3300; www.ecolines.net; Geležinkelio gatvė 15; ☺8.30am-9.30pm) Serves large cities across Europe.

Eurolines (☑5-233 5277; www.eurolines.lt; Sodų gatvė 22; ☺6.30am-9.30pm) A reliable long-distance carrier with services to Rīga, Tallinn, Warsaw (Poland) and Lviv (Ukraine).

Lux Express (☑5-233 6666; www.luxexpress.eu; Sodų 20b-1; ☺8am-7pm Mon-Fri, 9am-7pm Sat & Sun) Luxurious coaches connecting Vilnius with Rīga, Tallinn, St Petersburg, Warsaw and Helsinki.

TRAIN

There is no direct or convenient rail link between Vilnius' **train station** (Geležinkelio Stotis; ☑5-269 3722; www.litrail.lt; Geležinkelio gatvė 16) and Rīga or Tallinn. Direct trains link Warsaw to Vilnius; browse schedules on www.intercity.pl.

There are also regular services linking Minsk and Vilnius (see www.rw.by).

ⓘ Getting Around

TO/FROM THE AIRPORT

Buses 1 and 2 (€1) run between the **Vilnius International Airport** (Tarptautinis Vilniaus Oro Uostas; ☑ 6-124 4442; www.vno.lt; Rodūnios kelias 10a; ☎; ☐ 1, 2) and town, trains (€0.70) trundle to the main station.

BICYCLE

Vilnius is becoming increasingly bike-friendly, although bike lanes are rarer outside Old Town and along the banks of the Neris. The tourist office has free cycling maps, and orange **Cyclocity** (☑ 8-800 22008; www.cyclocity.lt; ⊙ Apr-Oct) stations dot the city. A three-day ticket is €2.90 and the first half-hour is free, then charges are between €0.39 to €3.39 per 30 minutes.

PUBLIC TRANSPORT

The city is efficiently served by buses and trolleybuses from 5am to midnight; Sunday services are less frequent. Single-trip tickets cost €1 when bought from the driver. If you get a *Vilniečio kortelė* (electronic ticket) for €1.50, single journeys cost €0.65 or you can buy 24-/72-hour passes for €5/8 (www.vilniusticket.lt). Read more on www.vilniustransport.lt and www.stops.lt.

TAXI

Taxis are generally cheaper if ordered in advance by telephone (ask the hotel reception desk or restaurant to call). Reliable companies:

Ekipažas (☑ 1446; www.ekipazastaksi.lt)
Martono Taksi (☑ 240 0004)

EASTERN & SOUTHERN LITHUANIA

Paneriai

☑ 5 / POP 9000

A bleak chapter of Lithuania's wartime history is commemorated in this neighbourhood of Vilnius, 11km southwest of the centre. Paneriai is notorious as the site of 100,000 murders – the exact figure is unknown – by subunits of the Nazi secret police.

Around 70% of the people slaughtered in Paneriai were Jewish. Other victims were Lithuanian and Polish soldiers and partisan fighters, prisoners of war and priests.

A small **museum** (☑ tours 699 90 384; www.jmuseum.lt; Agrastų gatvė 15; ⊙ 9am-5pm Tue-Sun May-Sep, by appointment Oct-Apr; Ⓟ) FREE exhibits testimonies from the Burners Brigade, prisoners of war forced to dispose of bodies, and eyewitness reports detailing how massacres unfolded to the glee of commanders. Nearby, a **walking path** connects Jewish, Soviet and Polish monuments and locations associated with the killings, such as prison bunkers and pits where victims were shot.

ⓘ Getting There & Away

Daily trains (some terminating in Trakai or Kaunas) travel between Vilnius and Paneriai station (€0.60, 10 minutes, at least hourly). To reach the museum, make a right down Agrastų gatvė upon leaving the train station and it's a 1km walk southwest.

Trakai

☑ 528 / POP 4500

Rising like an apparition from the waters of Lake Galvė, a rosy brick Gothic castle is the crowning attraction of Trakai. Spread along a 2km-long peninsula only 28km from Vilnius, this attractive town is a popular day trip.

With practically the entire town gazetted as an 82-sq-km **national park** (www.seniejitrakai.lt), it's fitting that Trakai's very name derives from the Lithuanian word for a forest glade. Its castle roosts on one of 21 islands in Lake Galvė, which opens out from the northern end of the peninsula.

★ Trakai Castle   CASTLE

(Trakų Pilis; ☑ 8-528 53946; www.trakaimuziejus.lt; adult/concession €8/4; ⊙ 10am-7pm; ☛) Stepping across the wooden walkway to Trakai's Gothic castle is like tripping into a fairy tale. The castle is estimated to date from around 1400, when Grand Duke Vytautas needed stronger defences than the peninsula castle afforded. Arranged between its coral-coloured brick towers, the excellent **Trakai History Museum** conveys the flavour of past eras: chainmail, medieval weapons, 19th-century embroidery and glassware, plus talking knights, projected onto the stone walls.

North North East   KAYAKING

(☑ 8-677 93441; www.facebook.com/northnortheastkayaking; kayak rental €15, guided tour from €25; ⊙ May-Oct) Trakai's castle is even lovelier when seen from the water, and on these beginner-friendly guided kayak tours – in Lithuanian, Russian or English – the epic views are amplified by local knowledge and the odd picnic. Our pick is the sunset tour, to see the lakes dappled with golden light.

DON'T MISS

KARAITE CULTURE

Trakai is well-known for Karaite culture and cuisine, belonging to a Judaic minority group who have lived here since medieval times. Grand Duke Vytautas brought 383 Karaite families from Crimea to Trakai, initially installing them as castle guards. The **Karaite Ethnographic Museum** (Karaimų etnografinė paroda; ☑528-55 286; www.trakaimuziejus. lt; Karaimų gatvė 22; adult/child €2/1; ⊙10am-6pm Wed-Sun) displays their traditional dress and arresting photographs of Karaite people, past and present.

Draped with antiques and wood-carved finery, **Senoji Kibininė** (☑528-55 865; www.kibi-nas.lt; Karaimų gatvė 65; pasties from €1.50, mains €5.50-12; ⊙10am-10pm) is a popular place for the full Karaite culinary experience; it's worth braving the crowds for *kibinai* (pasties usually stuffed with lamb or mushrooms) served with a bowl of chicken broth. Alternatively, grab *kibinai* from the takeaway counter at **Kybynlar** (☑8-698 06320; www.kybynlar.lt; Karaimų gatvė 29; pasties from €2, mains €7-12; ⊙noon-9pm Mon, 11am-9pm Tue-Thu & Sun, 11am-10pm Fri & Sat).

ℹ Getting There & Away

Eight or nine daily trains (€1.80, 30 minutes) travel between Trakai's **train station** (☑7005 5111; www.litrail.lt; Vilniaus gatvė 5) and Vilnius. Regular buses also link the two (€2, 30 minutes).

CENTRAL LITHUANIA

Kaunas

☑37 / POP 288,363

A scrappy little sister compared to debonair Vilnius, Kaunas (kow-nas) sprawls out from its dainty Old Town and 14th-century fort. Strategically wedged at the confluence of the Nemunas and Neris Rivers, Kaunas gained a taste for the limelight during a brief spell as Lithuania's capital in the interwar period; the town owes some of its most attractive architecture to this era. You'll find uninhibited nightlife and arguably the country's best galleries, and plucky Kaunas is increasingly appealing as it prepares for a stint as European Capital of Culture for 2022.

◎ Sights

◉ Old Town

The heart of Kaunas' lovely Old Town is the city's former **Town Hall** (Kauno rotušė; Rotušės aikštė 15), built in the mid-16th century and formerly a theatre, prison and palace.

House of Perkūnas   HISTORIC BUILDING
(Perkūno namas; ☑8-641 44614; www.perkunona mas.lt; Aleksoto gatvė 6; adult/child €2/1; ⊙10am-4.30pm Mon-Fri) With ornate arches and turrets rippling from its brick facade, this late-15th-century mansion is a treasure of Kaunas' late-Gothic architecture. Built by merchants of the Hanseatic League, its interior is laid out to evoke the noble lifestyles of yesteryear: chandeliers, dining tables and a library with a small exhibition dedicated to 19th-century Romantic poet Adam Mickiewicz. The magnificent house is named for the thunder god Perkūnas, whose likeness was discovered during renovations in 1818.

**Maironis Lithuanian
Literary Museum**   MUSEUM
(Maironio Lietuvių Literatūros Muziejus; ☑37-206 842; http://maironiomuziejus.lt; Rotušės aikštė 13; adult/child €3/1; ⊙9am-5pm Tue-Sat) Even travellers unenthused by turn-of-the-20th-century literature will be enchanted by this museum dedicated to Lithuanian luminary Maironis (aka Jonas Mačiulis). The museum is inside a beautifully attired 18th-century mansion, bought and furnished by Maironis in 1909. Highlights include the rococo **Red Room** (actually baby blue) and the **Great Dining Room**, gloriously decorated with traditional heraldry rendered in bold graphic art.

**St Francis Xavier
Church & Monastery**   CHURCH
(☑37-432 098; www.kjb.lt; Rotušės aikštė 7-9; tower €1.50; ⊙4-6pm Mon-Fri, 7am-1pm & 4-6pm Sun) The southern side of Rotušės aikštė is dominated by rosy-pink late-Baroque facade of the St Francis Xavier Church, college and Jesuit monastery complex. Peek inside the twin-towered church, built between 1666 and 1720, and climb up to the viewing platform for a bird's-eye vantage point over Kaunas' Old Town.

◉ New Town

Laisvės alėja (Freedom Ave), a striking 1.7km pedestrian street, runs east from Old Town to New Town, ending at the blue-domed neo-Byzantine **St Michael the Archangel Church** (Šv Archangelo Mykolo Rektoratas; ☑ 37-226 676; Nepriklausomybės aikštė 14; ☺ 9am-2.30pm).

★ MK Čiurlionis

National Museum of Art   GALLERY
(MK Čiurlionio Valstybinis Dailės Muziejus; ☑ 37-229 475; www.ciurlionis.lt; Putvinskio gatvė 55; adult/child €4/2, audio guide €4; ☺ 11am-5pm Tue, Wed & Fri-Sun, to 7pm Thu) One Lithuania's oldest and grandest galleries, Kaunas' leading art museum (founded 1921) is the place to acquaint yourself with the dreamlike paintings of Mikalojus Konstantinas Čiurlionis (1875–1911), one of the country's greatest artists and composers. Elsewhere in the sizeable gallery are contemporary sculpture exhibitions flooded with natural light, Lithuanian folk and religious art, and 16th- to 20th-century European works.

Museum of the Ninth Fort   MUSEUM
(IX Forto Muziejus; ☑ 37-377 750; www.9fortomuziejus.lt; Žemaičių plentas 73; adult/child €3/1.50; ☺ 10am-6pm Tue-Sun Apr-Oct) Lithuania's dark 20th-century history is powerfully and poignantly told at the Museum of the Ninth Fort, 7km north of Kaunas. Begin in the main **museum**, a modern gallery space with a church-like interior, which details the country's WWII experience. With the same entrance ticket, continue uphill to the WWI-era **fort**, converted into a hard-labour prison in the early 20th century and a centre of torture, interrogation and mass killings in WWII.

Kaunas Picture Gallery   GALLERY
(Kauno Paveikslų Galerija; ☑ 37-221 789; www.ciurlionis.lt/kaunas-art-gallery; Donelaičio gatvė 16; adult/student €2/1; ☺ 11am-5pm Tue, Wed & Fri-Sun, to 7pm Thu) This underrated gem, a branch of the many-tentacled Čiurlionis museum (p258), exhibits works by 20th-century Lithuanian artists. Most explanation is in Lithuanian but the art does the talking: 1920s and '30s watercolours depict bucolic countryside and fishing villages (an enjoyable primer, if you're travelling into rural Lithuania) along with treasured artworks like a vivid triptych by 20th-century painter Adomas Galdikas.

🛏 Sleeping

Kauno Arkivyskupijos
Svečių Namai   GUESTHOUSE €
(Kaunas Archdiocese Guesthouse; ☑ 37-322 597; www.kaunas.lcn.lt/sveciunamai; Rotušės aikštė 21; s/d/tr without bathroom €26/37/42, d/tr with bathroom from €40/49; 🅿 ✳ @ 🛜) The location of this Catholic archdiocesan guesthouse couldn't be better, snuggled between venerable churches and overlooking the Old Town square. Rooms are unadorned, but they have high ceilings and big windows. There's a communal kitchen to cook breakfast (which isn't offered) and parking spaces through the main archway – unless the local parishioners get there first.

Apple Economy Hotel   HOTEL €
(☑ 37-321 404; www.applehotel.lt; Valančiaus gatvė 19; s/d from €32/36; 🅿 @ 🛜) Fourteen tiny but brightly decorated rooms are stacked into this simple but friendly hotel. There are no frills

---

WORTH A TRIP

FROM SPAS TO 'STALIN WORLD': DRUSKININKAI

Towering forests, toasty waters and a Soviet theme park...sound like your kind of trip? **Grūtas Park** (Grūto Parkas; ☑ 6-824 2320; www.grutoparkas.lt; Grūtas; adult/child €7.50/4; ☺ 9am-10pm Jun-Aug; 🅿 🚼) is a curious amusement park that educates with a gallery of socialist realist art and an information centre, packed with newspapers and USSR maps. Statues of Lenin that once dominated Lithuanian towns now sulk along tree-lined paths. Explore the surreal grounds, but it's better to skip the on-site zoo. It's 8km east of Druskininkai; take bus 2 via Viečiūnai (two to five daily).

The reputation of Druskininkai's healing mineral waters dates back centuries; test them at **Grand Spa Lietuva** (☑ 313-51 200; www.grandspa.lt; Kudirkos gatvė 43; ☺ 9am-5pm Mon-Thu, to 6pm Fri & Sat, to 4pm Sun) then kick back in **Kolonada** (☑ 662 06062; www.sventejums.lt/kolonada; Kudirkos gatvė 22; mains €6-12; ☺ 11am-11pm Sun-Thu, to 1am Fri & Sat) with a cocktail. Classic, slightly time-worn **Regina** (☑ 313-51 243; www.regina.lt; Kosciuškos gatvė 3; s/d/tr/q incl breakfast from €54/58/97/113; 🅿 🛜), with its own little spa, is a good place to stay the night.

To reach Druskininkai, there are daily direct buses from Vilnius (€11, two hours, 10 daily) and Kaunas (€9 to €11, 2¼ to 3½ hours, 12 daily).

but it's a serviceable economy option in an excellent location, tucked into a quiet courtyard on the northwestern flank of Old Town.

Daugirdas BOUTIQUE HOTEL €€
(✆ 37-301 561; www.daugirdas.lt; Daugirdo gatvė 4; s/d/ste incl breakfast €60/79/90; ❋ 🤖) This boutique hotel, wedged between central Old Town and the Nemunas, is one of the most charismatic in Kaunas. Parts of the building date to the 16th century, and the standard rooms are cosy and modern with good-quality beds and bathrooms with heated floors. For something extra special, luxuriate in a Jacuzzi in the timber-beamed Gothic Room (€175).

✖ Eating

Motiejaus Kepyklėlė BAKERY €
(📱 8-616 15599; Vilniaus gatvė 7; pastries from €1; ⊙ 7.30am-8pm Mon-Sat, 9am-7pm Sun) Perhaps the best bakery in Kaunas, Motiejaus prepares traditional Lithuanian cakes and cookies, alongside desserts and coffee with a Franco-Italian flavour. Cooked breakfasts can be hit and miss, but it's hard to go wrong with international dainties such as *canelés* (French vanilla cakes), muffins and croissants.

Senieji Rūsiai EUROPEAN €€€
(Old Cellars; 📱 37-202 806; www.seniejirusiai.lt; Vilniaus gatvė 34; mains €12-25; ⊙ 11am-midnight Mon-Thu, to 1am Fri, noon-1am Sat, noon-11pm Sun; 🤖) Named for its 17th-century subterranean vaults lined with frescoes, 'Old Cellars' is one of the most atmospheric places in Kaunas for a candlelit dinner. Choose flame-cooked beef or duck with wine-poached pears to match the medieval banquet ambience, or peruse pan-European options like steak with foie gras or salmon with cream of fennel.

🍷 Drinking & Nightlife

Kultūra Kavinė PUB, CAFE
(www.facebook.com/kauno.kultura; Donelaičio gatvė 14-16; ⊙ noon-2am Tue-Fri, 3pm-2am Sat, noon-midnight Sun & Mon; 🤖) If revolution brews in Kaunas, they'll trace it back to Kultūra Kavinė. The town's dreamers and debaters spill out from this shabby-chic pub, smoking and sipping beers on the concrete terrace. Close to the New Town's galleries and beloved by students, this artful hangout has a raw, earnest feel and open-minded clientele. The best spot in town to mingle.

2½ Ubuolio PUB
(📱 8-650 66422; www.facebook.com/2supuseobuolio; Palangos gatvė 9; ⊙ 5pm-2am) A den for locals to glug a cold one over trivia nights and

VEGETARIAN KAUNAS

Discard those stereotypes about endless dumplings, Kaunas' dining scene is diverse. **Moksha** (✆ 8-676 71649; www.facebook.com/cafemoksha; Vasario 16-osios gatvė 6; mains €6-12; ⊙ 11am-9pm Mon-Fri, noon-9pm Sat, noon-8pm Sun; 🤖) reels you in with ambient, plucked-string music, chilli-spiked aromas and personable service; try the vegan mango curry. Cosy **Radharanė** (✆ 37-320 800; www.radharane.lt/kaunas; Daukšos gatvė 28; mains €4-6; ⊙ 11am-9pm; 🤖) also has a broad menu, from soy goulash to Thai vegetable curry and curried aubergine.

sports screenings, this cider pub in a vaulted cellar gets packed out even on weeknights. Bonus: there's free popcorn.

ℹ Information

Tourist Office (✆ 8-616 50991; www.visit.kaunas.lt; Rotušės aikštė 15; ⊙ 9am-1pm & 2-6pm Mon-Fri, 10am-1pm & 2-4pm Sat, 10am-1pm & 2-3pm Sun) Inside Kaunas' Town Hall, this friendly and multilingual tourist office can book accommodation, sell maps and guides, and arrange bicycle rental and guided tours of the Old Town.

ℹ Getting There & Away

Kaunas' bus and train stations are not far from each other, about 2km south of the city centre. From the **bus station** (Autobusų Stotis; 📱 37-409 060; www.autobusubilietai.lt; Vytauto prospektas 24; ⊙ ticket office 6am-9.30pm), frequent services leave for Klaipėda (€14.50 to €16.80, 2¾ to four hours) and Vilnius (€6.40 to €7, 1¾ hours). From the **train station** (Geležinkelio Stotis; 📱 7005 5111; www.litrail.lt; MK Čiurlionio gatvė 16; ⊙ ticket office 4.10am-9.45pm) there are plenty of trains each day to Vilnius (€4.80 to €6.60, 1¼ to 1¾ hours).

There are also services to Tallinn in Estonia (two daily) and Rīga in Latvia (four daily).

WESTERN LITHUANIA

Klaipėda

📱 46 / POP 148,100

There's a distinctly German flavour to Klaipėda (klai-pey-da). Lithuania's third-largest city, formerly known as Memel, was part of

LITHUANIA KLAIPĖDA

HILL OF CROSSES

Lithuania's fabled **Hill of Crosses** (Kryžių kalnas; ☑41-370 860; Jurgaičiai; ⊙information centre 9am-6pm) is a symbol of defiance as much as a pilgrimage site. More than 100,000 crosses have been planted on this low hill, many of them strung with rosary beads that rattle softly in the breeze. The tradition began during the 1831 Uprising and reached its height in the 1960s, in defiance of anti-religious Soviet rule. At night locals crept here to lay crosses, infuriating their oppressors.

It's 12km north of Šiauliai (2km off Hwy A12) near Jurgaičiai. To reach the Hill of Crosses from Šiauliai, take a Joniškis-bound bus (€1.50, 10 minutes, up to seven daily) to the 'Domantai' stop and walk for 15 minutes, or grab a taxi (around €20).

the Prussian Kingdom until the region wrestled to autonomy in 1923. Most travellers barely glimpse Klaipėda as they rush headlong for the ferry to Curonian Spit, but it's rewarding to hang around. Buildings in compact, cobblestoned Old Town are constructed in the German *fachwerk* style (with distinctive half-timbered facades) and there's a bevy of bars in which to sip beers by the water.

⊙ Sights

Klaipėda Castle Museum MUSEUM
(Klaipėda Pilies Muziejus; ☑46-453 098; www.mlimuziejus.lt; Pilies gatvė 4; adult/child €1.74/0.87; ⊙10am-6pm Tue-Sat) Spread across four exhibition spaces around Klaipėda's castle, these warren-like galleries introduce different eras of regional history. The most atmospheric is the stone-lined medieval exhibition but the highlight is the **39/45 Museum**, a state-of-the-art space capturing the fear and disarray of wartime Klaipėda in evocative ways.

History Museum
of Lithuania Minor MUSEUM
(Mažosios Lietuvos Istorijos Muziejus; ☑46-410 524; www.mlimuziejus.lt; Didžioji Vandens gatvė 6; adult/child €1.45/0.72; ⊙10am-6pm Tue-Sat) This creaky-floored little museum traces the origins of 'Lithuania Minor' (Kleinlitauen) – as this coastal region was known during its several centuries as part of East Prussia. It exhibits Prussian maps, coins and artefacts

of the Teutonic order. Most attractive are the wooden furnishings, displays of folk art and traditional weaving machines.

🛏 Sleeping

Litinterp Guesthouse GUESTHOUSE €
(☑46-410 644; www.litinterp.com; Puodžių gatvė 17; s with/without bathroom €28/23, d €46/40; 🅿🛜) For its price range, this guesthouse in an 18th-century building is a standout star. High ceilings with wooden beams and sizeable beds ensure charm and comfort in equal supply, and it's efficiently run, with English-speaking staff. The 19 rooms vary from standard doubles to kitchen-equipped suites; there's a shared kitchen and enclosed parking, too. Breakfast costs €3.

✕ Eating

★**Stora Antis** LITHUANIAN €€€
(☑6-862 5020; www.storaantis.lt; Tiltų gatvė 6; mains €15-18; ⊙5pm-midnight Tue & Thu-Sat) Taking full advantage of a stunning 19th-century cellar, brick-lined Stora Antis elevates classic Lithuanian fare (baked duck, bean soups, pan-fried plaice) to haute-cuisine heights. A restaurant was first established here in 1856 and it's retained its charms, laden with antiques and bric-a-brac. One of the best places to eat in Klaipėda's Old Town.

★**Momo Grill** STEAK €€€
(☑8-693 12355; https://momogrill.lt; Liepų gatvė 20; mains €10-18; ⊙11am-10pm Tue-Fri, noon-10pm Sat; 🛜) This tiny, modern, minimalist steakhouse is foodie heaven and the hardest table to book in town. The small menu consists of just three cuts of beef plus grilled fish and leg of duck, and allows the chef to focus on what he does best. The austere interior of white tiles is soothing and the wine list is marvellous.

🍷 Drinking & Nightlife

Timbered portside pub **Žvejų Baras** (☑6-866 0405; www.zvejubaras.lt; Kurpių gatvė 8; ⊙5pm-midnight Sun-Wed, to 2am Thu, to 4am Fri & Sat) lives up to its name (which means 'Fisherman's Bar'). Set aglow by lead-lined lamps, this is one of Klaipėda's nicest places to catch live music or sports screenings.

If you prefer your people-watching with a side-serve of meringues, macarons or little *sablés* (French shortbreads), head to cute corner cafe **Vanilės Namai** (☑8-612 02010; www.vanilesnamai.lt; cnr Manto & Vytauto gatvė; ⊙9am-8pm Sun-Thu, to 9pm Fri & Sat; 🛜).

ℹ Information

Tourist Office (☑ 46-412 186; www.klaipe-dainfo.lt; Turgaus gatvė 7; ☺ 9am-6pm Mon-Fri) Exceptionally efficient tourist office selling maps and locally published guidebooks, and arranging accommodation, tours and more. Open weekends in summer.

ℹ Getting There & Away

BOAT

Smiltynės Perkėla (www.keltas.lt) runs car and foot passenger ferries between Klaipėda and Smiltynė on Curonian Spit.

BUS

Services to/from Klaipėda's **bus station** (Autobusų Stotis; ☑ 46-411 547; www.klap.lt; Butkų Juzės 9; ☺ ticket office 3.30am-7.30pm) reach Kaunas (€14 to €16, 2¾ to 4½ hours, 18 daily), Šiauliai (€11, three to 3½ hours, seven daily) and Vilnius (€18 to €21, four to 5½ hours, 16 daily). Most buses to/from Juodkrantė and Nida depart from Smiltynė ferry landing on Curonian Spit.

Buses also reach Kaliningrad in Russia (€11.40, 4½ hours, two daily), Rīga in Latvia (€19, five hours, one daily) and Tallinn in Estonia (€47 to €56, 13 hours, one daily via Vilnius or Kaunas). Ecolines (https://ecolines.net) sells tickets for international destinations.

Curonian Spit

POP 3371

On this bewitching tendril of land, winds caress the sand dunes, pine scents the breeze and amber washes up on beaches. Designated a national park (Kuršių Nerijos Nacionalinis Parkas) in 1991, Curonian Spit trails down the Baltic Sea from Lithuania to Russian territory Kaliningrad. Pine forests populated by deer, elk and wild boar cover about 70% of the area and only a fraction is urban. Until the first decades of the 20th century, most of the spit was German territory. Today, locals joke that the spit's sand dunes are 'Lithuania's Sahara'.

⊙ Sights

★Parnidis Dune   DUNES

(Parnidžio kopa) The 52m-high Parnidis Dune is simultaneously mighty and fragile. Past settlements around Nida have been engulfed by the moving sand dune but this is a delicate landscape of mountain pines, meadows and fine blonde sand speckled with purple searocket flowers. A 1700m-long path picks its way to a grand panorama at the height of

the dune, where you'll find a sundial with a granite obelisk (constructed in 1995).

Don't stray from the footpath, and take all rubbish with you.

Amber Gallery   GALLERY

(Gintaro Galerija; ☑ 469-52 573; www.ambergallery.lt; Pamario gatvė 20; adult/child €2.50/1.20; ☺ 10am-7pm Apr-Oct) In an old fisher's hut on the north side of town is this museum and shop devoted to amber. Staff introduce the mythic and supposed health-boosting properties of this caramel-coloured fossilised resin. Visitors can peer through magnifying glasses at insects trapped in amber and explore the amber-ornamented garden. The museum doubles as a boutique selling truly unusual jewellery studded with amber. Enquire ahead for hour-long amber-processing classes (€6).

🛏 Sleeping & Eating

★Miško Namas   GUESTHOUSE €€

(☑ 469-52 290; www.miskonamas.com; Pamario gatvė 11; d €65-85, 2-/4-person apt from €85/95; P 🛜) Overlooking a peaceful garden, this immaculately maintained guesthouse is picked out in Curonian blue-and-white and filled with elegant furnishings, ornaments and lace. Every room has a fridge and a kettle, and some have fully fledged kitchens and balconies. Guests can browse books from the small library or laze in the garden.

★Tik Pas Joną   SEAFOOD €

(☑ 8-620 82084; www.facebook.com/Rukytos ZuvysTikPasJona; Naglių gatvė 6-1; mains €3; ☺ 10am-10pm Apr-Nov, Sat & Sun only Dec-Mar) Picture the scene: you select mackerel or eel from a traditional smoking rack, lay it on a paper plate with a slice of rye bread, and eat with your hands while watching the lagoon glow orange at sunset. This is the best spot in Neringa to feast on the region's famous smoked fish – accompany it with cold beer and crunchy veggies.

Kepykla Gardumėlis   BAKERY €

(☑ 469-52 021; www.kepykla-gardumelis.lt; Pamario gatvė 3; snacks from €1.20; ☺ 8am-6pm) Curonian Spit's best place for freshly baked goods, Gardumėlis makes bread only with stone-ground organic flour. Similar perfectionism is applied to the ingredients destined for their cookies, mille-feuille pastries and poppyseed rolls. Their most unusual treat is *morkų saldainiai*, bright-orange carrot candy: chewy, zesty and with a slight vegetal note.

ⓘ Information

Curonian Spit National Park Visitors Centre
(☑ 46-402 256; www.nerija.lt; Smiltynės gatvė
11; ☺9am-noon & 1-6pm Tue-Sat Jun-Aug)
The summer-only visitors centre in Smiltynė is
packed with information about the park's ecol-
ogy and attractions, and can arrange guided
nature tours (€31 to €36, two to eight people).

Juodkrantė Tourist Information Centre
(☑469-53 490; www.visitneringa.com; L
Rėzos gatvė 8; ☺10am-8pm Mon-Sat, to 3pm
Sun) Located opposite the bus stop inside the
cultural centre.

Nida Tourist Information Centre (☑469-52
345; www.visitneringa.com; Taikos gatvė 4;
☺9am-7pm Mon-Sat, 10am-5pm Sun; ☜)

ⓘ Getting There & Away

Curonian Spit is accessible only via boat or ferry
(there are no bridges linking the spit to the mainland). From Klaipėda, two ferries run regularly:
a passenger ferry goes to Smiltynė from the **Old
Ferry Port** (Senoji perkėla; ☑46-311 117; www.
keltas.lt; Danės gatvė 1; per passenger/bicycle
€1/free) for cyclists and foot passengers (at
least hourly between 7am and 9pm). There's a
vehicle ferry from the **New Ferry Port** (Naujoji
perkėla; ☑46-311 117; www.keltas.lt; Nemuno
gatvė 8; per foot passenger/motorbike/car
€1/4.90/12.30, bicycle free) 2km south of
Klaipėda's Old Town that connects to a point on
the spit around 2km south of Smiltynė (one to
three ferries per hour between 5am and 9pm);
pay as you drive on.

You can also reach the Russian Kaliningrad
Region from here. The Russian border post is
3km south of Nida on the main road and daily
buses depart from Nida (€7.80, two hours).
Don't contemplate this without the necessary
Russian visa and paperwork.

DON'T MISS

WITCHES' HILL

A coven of wooden sculptures is gathered on a forest-clad hill in Juodkrantė,
carved by Lithuanian artists over the
years since 1979. **Witches' Hill** (Raganų
Kalnas; ☋) is an open-air sculpture
gallery where devils grimace beneath
decorative arches, while warty-nosed
witches and grinning peasants peep out
from among the pine trees. The figures
represent various characters from regional folklore, and some have an interactive quality: slide down a demon's
tongue, sit on a throne, and try to resist
taking a dozen photos.

ⓘ Getting Around

Hire bikes in Klaipėda and take them across
the lagoon via the passenger ferry for free. Alternatively, there are bike-rental places in Nida
(usually around €3/10 per hour/day). There is a
well-marked trail that runs the entire length of
the spit from Smiltynė to Nida via Juodkrantė
(about 50km).

Buses travel from the northerly ferry port
Smiltynė to Juodkrantė (€1.90, 15 to 20 minutes) down to Nida (€4, one hour), between
seven and 10 times daily.

SURVIVAL GUIDE

ⓘ Directory A-Z

ACCOMMODATION

➡ Prices rise from June to August (book ahead)
and drop outside the summer, when some
places close.

➡ Most hostels are located in large cities like
Vilnius and Kaunas; outside of these you're
better off choosing guesthouses or farmstays.

LGBT+ TRAVELLERS

Vilnius has a handful of LGBT+-specific venues,
and many more gay-friendly ones. The National
LGBT Rights Organization (www.lgl.lt) has a map
of gay venues on their website.

MONEY

➡ Cash is preferred for small purchases and at
smaller-scale guesthouses.

➡ Tip 10% to reward good service in restaurants. Say *ačiū* (thank you) to show you aren't
expecting change back.

OPENING HOURS

We have listed high-season opening hours, but
remember these longer summer hours often
decrease in shoulder and low seasons.

Banks 9am to 5pm Monday to Friday

Bars 11am to midnight Sunday to Thursday,
11am to 2am Friday and Saturday

Clubs 10pm to 3am Thursday or Friday to
Saturday

Post offices 9am to 7pm Monday to Friday,
9am to 2pm Saturday

Restaurants noon to 11pm; later on weekends

Shops 9am or 10am to 6pm or 7pm Monday to
Saturday; some open Sunday

TELEPHONE

➡ To call other cities from a landline within
Lithuania, dial 8, wait for the tone, then dial the
area code and telephone number.

➡ To make an international call from Lithuania,
dial 00 followed by the country code.

→ For travellers with unlocked phones, SIM cards are cheap (usually €1 or €2) and easy to pick up at convenience stores.

❶ Getting There & Away

AIR
The airports at Vilnius (p256) and **Kaunas** (☑ 8-612 44442; www.kaunas-airport.lt; Vilniaus gatvė, Karmėlava; ☉ 6am–midnight; 🚌 29, 29E) both have good connections within Europe. From the US and beyond, you're likely to change planes in a hub airport such as Amsterdam, Warsaw or Frankfurt.
→ **AirBaltic** (www.airbaltic.com) flies to Vilnius from Rīga several times daily and from Tallinn on most days, and also offers scheduled if sporadic service from Rīga to Palanga. These flights are more frequent in summer (May to September).
→ Many travellers arrive via low-cost carrier **Ryanair** (www.ryanair.com).

BOAT
From Klaipėda's **International Ferry Port** (☑ 46-499 799; www.portofklaipeda.lt; Perkėlos gatvė 10), **DFDS Seaways** (☑ 46-323 232; www.dfdsseaways.lt; Baltijos prospektas 40; ☉ 10am–5.30pm) runs passenger and car ferries to/from Kiel, Germany (per pedestrian/car from €28/80, daily, 20 hours) and Karlshamn, Sweden (per pedestrian/car from €39/74, 14 hours, at least daily).

BUS
Long-distance bus routes link Vilnius to neighbouring countries Poland, **Belarus and the Baltics. Browse routes on Eurolines (www.eurolines.lt) and** Lux Express (https://lux express.eu), whose coaches link Vilnius with Rīga, Tallinn, St Petersburg, Warsaw and Helsinki.

CAR & MOTORCYCLE
→ Poland and Latvia are part of the EU's common-border Schengen Agreement, so there are no border checks when driving between them and Lithuania.
→ Inform your car-rental company ahead of time if you are planning to drive across borders.
→ For neighbouring Belarus and Russian region Kaliningrad, where most visitors require a visa to enter, checks are stricter and cross-border car rental is unlikely to be possible.

TRAIN
→ Direct trains link Warsaw to Kaunas and Vilnius; browse schedules on www.intercity.pl.
→ There are regular services linking Minsk and Vilnius (see www.rw.by).

❶ TICK WARNING
Travellers planning to spend time camping, hiking or walking in forests should strongly consider a tick-borne encephalitis (TBE) vaccination. Compared to other European countries, Lithuania has a relatively high incidence of TBE, a potentially very serious illness that attacks the brain. If you find a tick attached to your body, remove it as quickly as possible using a clean pair of tweezers and wash the affected area. TBE symptoms may not appear until one or two weeks after a tick bite; seek medical attention.

→ To/from Rīga or Tallinn, buses are quicker and more direct.

❶ Getting Around

BICYCLE
→ Bike hire is offered in all major cities, and often in small villages along the coast.
→ Curonian Spit, the Baltic coast and Šiauliai's surrounds are scenic, unchallenging destinations for cyclists. Ferries to Curonian Spit allow passengers to bring their bicycle for free.
→ Some **Kautra** (www.kautra.lt) intercity buses have bike racks (no extra charge; look for the bicycle symbol next to routes when booking a ticket on www.autobusubilietai.lt).

BUS
→ Most services are summarised on the extremely handy bus tickets website Autobusų Bilietai (www.autobusubilietai.lt).

CAR & MOTORCYCLE
→ Car hire is offered in all the major cities and Lithuanian roads are generally very good.
→ To cope with snowy conditions, winter tyres are compulsory from mid-November through March; rental vehicles should have them.

LOCAL TRANSPORT
→ Lithuanian cities generally have good public transport, based on buses, trolleybuses and minibuses.

TRAIN
→ The **Lithuanian Rail** website (www.litrail.lt) has routes, times and prices in English.
→ For common train journeys like Vilnius to Kaunas or to Klaipėda, the train is often more comfortable and better value than the bus. For other routes, such as Klaipėda to Kaunas or Šiauliai to Kaunas, the opposite is true.

Moldova

POP 3.44 MILLION (INCLUDING TRANSDNIESTR)

Best Places to Eat

➡ Popasul Dacilor (p269)

➡ Gok-Oguz (p269)

➡ Kumanyok (p274)

➡ Vatra Neamului (p269)

➡ Stolovka SSSR (p274)

Best Places to Stay

➡ Art Rustic Hotel (p268)

➡ Butuceni Eco-Resort (p272)

➡ Château Purcari (p270)

➡ City Park Hotel (p268)

➡ Costel Hostel (p273)

Why Go?

The world is finally waking up to the charms of this little nation wedged between Romania and Ukraine. Moldova was famously dubbed the world's least happy place in a bestselling book in 2008, but today it's better known for its unspoiled countryside and superb wine tours. As one of Europe's least visited countries, Moldova retains a measure of roads-less-travelled charm. But that's changing quickly as budget flights from Western Europe take off.

Moldova may be entering the consciousness of the global traveller, but those seeking the remote and obscure still have their Shangri-La in the form of the breakaway republic of Transdniestr, where the Soviet Union reigns supreme. As for the unhappy thing, well that's a thing of the past. According to the most recent UN survey, today's Moldova is the world's 67th *happiest* country.

When to Go
Chişinău

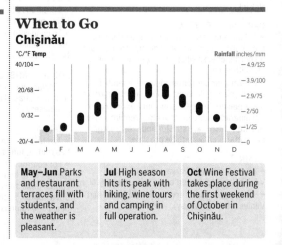

°C/°F Temp / Rainfall inches/mm

May–Jun Parks and restaurant terraces fill with students, and the weather is pleasant.

Jul High season hits its peak with hiking, wine tours and camping in full operation.

Oct Wine Festival takes place during the first weekend of October in Chişinău.

Entering the Country

Entering and leaving Moldova is usually a breeze, though you may experience queues and delays.

ITINERARIES

Three Days

Use the capital Chişinău (p266) as your base for a long-weekend getaway in Moldova. Spend day one strolling the pleasant parks of this fast-changing city, and checking out its museums and excellent restaurants. On the second day, take a day trip out to the stunning cave monastery at Orheiul Vechi (p271) and, if you don't mind a bit of driving, Tipova (p272) monastery with its incredible views of the Dniestr River and Transdniestr beyond. On day three take a day trip to one of the many vineyards (p270) around Chişinău for a tour and wine tasting.

One Week

Spend a night or two in surreal Transdniestr (p273), a bastion of Russian-ness on the fringes of Moldova. Take an overnight trip to Soroca (p272) to see the impressive fortress on the lazy Dniestr. Lastly, reserve two or three days to explore more-remote bits of the country – kayaking on the Dniestr, birdwatching on the Lower Prut River near Cahul, exploring the Soviet sites of Gagauzia (p272) or staying a couple of nights in a boutique wine chalet.

Essential Food & Drink

Muşchi de vacă/porc/miel A cutlet of beef/pork/lamb.

Piept de pui The ubiquitous chicken breast.

Mămăligă Cornmeal mush with a consistency between porridge and bread that accompanies many dishes.

Brânză Moldova's most common cheese is a slightly salty-sour sheep's milk product that often comes grated. Put it on *mămăligă*.

Sarma Cabbage-wrapped minced meat or pilau rice packages, similar to Turkish dolma or Russian *goluptsy*.

Wine Look for bottles from quality local wineries like Cricova, Chateau Vartely and Purcari, among many others.

Fresh produce Moldova is essentially one big, very rewarding farmers market.

AT A GLANCE

Area 33,851 sq km

Capital Chişinău

Country Code 🕿373

Currency Moldovan leu (plural lei)

Emergency Ambulance 🕿903, fire 🕿901, police 🕿902

Language Moldovan

Time Eastern European Time (GMT/UTC plus three hours)

Visas None for EU, USA, Canada, Japan, Australia and New Zealand, but required for South Africa and many other countries

Sleeping Price Ranges

The following price ranges refer to the cost of a double room with private bathroom.

€ less than €35

€€ €35–85

€€€ more than €85

Eating Price Ranges

The following price ranges refer to the cost of an average main-course meal.

€ less than 90 lei

€€ 90–180 lei

€€€ more than 180 lei

Resources

Moldova Holiday (www.moldovaholiday.travel)

Moldova.org (www.moldova.org/en)

Fest (www.fest.md)

Moldova Highlights

1 Chişinău (p266)
Strolling the cafe-lined streets and leafy parks of Moldova's friendly capital.

2 Cricova (p270)
Designating a driver for tours to world-famous wine cellars and boutique wineries, like this one, outside Chişinău.

3 Orheiul Vechi (p271)
Exploring this fantastic historic cave monastery, burrowed by 13th-century monks.

4 Transdniestr (p273)
Leaving Europe behind in this self-styled 'republic', a surreal, living homage to the Soviet Union.

5 Soroca (p272) Ogling Gypsy-king mansions in Moldova's Roma capital, and visiting its medieval fortress.

6 Tipova (p272) Enjoying jaw-dropping views from this mystical monastery built into a cliff high above the Dniestr.

CHIŞINĂU

♪ 22 / POP 510,000

Pretty much all roads in Moldova lead to its wine-and-food-loving capital. Chişinău is a city of parks where retirees play chess in the shade of old-growth trees, of street festivals, and of sidewalk cafes where you can have a beverage and watch the world go by. A dozen superb wineries are within a 90-minute drive,

and the super-central location puts the entire country within a day trip. Throw in a hip and happening nightlife, and Chişinău ticks off all the boxes for an effective weekend break.

◎ Sights

Parcul Catedralei PARK
(Cathedral Park; B-dul Ştefan cel Mare; 🚸) Dab in the middle of Chişinău, this park is popu-

lar with families and canoodling teenagers on benches, and makes for great strolling. The highlight is the **Nativity of Christ Metropolitan Cathedral** (Catedrala Mitropolitană Naşterea Domnului; http://en.mitropolia. md) `FREE`, dating from the 1830s, and its lovely bell tower (1836). Along B-dul Ştefan cel Mare the main entrance to the park is marked by the Holy Gates (1841), also known as Chişinău's own **Arc de Triomphe**. On the northwestern side of the park is a colourful 24-hour **Flower Market** (Str Mitropolit G Bănulescu-Bodoni; ⊙10am-10pm).

Diagonally opposite Parcul Caedralei is **Grădina Publică Ştefan cel Mare şi Sfînt** (Ştefan cel Mare Park; B-dul Ştefan cel Mare;), named after national hero Ştefan cel Mare, whose 1928 statue lords over the entrance.

National Archaeology & History Museum
MUSEUM

(Muzeul Naţional de Istorie a Moldovei; www.national museum.md/en; Str 31 August 1989, 121a; adult/student 10/5 lei, photos 15 lei, tour in English 100 lei; ⊙10am-6pm Sat-Thu Apr-Oct, to 5pm Nov-Mar) This impressive museum contains artefacts from the region of Orheiul Vechi, including Golden Horde coins and 14th-century ceramics; a rare, 2000-year-old Sarmatian fired-clay urn in the shape of a curly-coated ram; a beautiful amorpha (Greek jar) painted with anthropomorphic deities; and weapons dating from ancient times to the present. A huge late-Soviet-era diorama on the 1st floor depicts a battle near the village of Leuşeni on the Prut River during the pivotal WWII Iaşi-Chişinău Offensive.

Army Museum
MUSEUM

(Str Tighina 47; adult/child 10/3 lei, photos 10 lei; ⊙9am-5pm Tue-Sun) Occupying one end of the Centre of Culture and Military History, this once-musty museum now hosts a moving exhibit on Soviet-era repression. Stories of Red Terror, forced famines, mass deportations and gulag slave labour are told through photographs, videos, newspaper clippings and dioramas. While little is in English, the museum nevertheless gives you a good sense of the horrific scale of the crimes perpetrated by Lenin and Stalin.

National Art Museum
MUSEUM

(Muzeul Naţional de Artă al Moldovei; Str 31 August 1989, 115; adult/student 10/5 lei; ⊙10am-6pm Tue-Sun Apr-Oct, to 5pm Nov-Mar) A massive facelift was half-finished at the end of 2018, with the gorgeously restored main wing open to visitors. The focus is on contemporary Mol-

dovan art, with a room or two of European works (mainly Dutch, Flemish and Italian) plus space for rotating exhibitions. The annex at the back contains a more extensive European collection, plus folk art and icons, but it remains closed indefinitely.

National Museum of Ethnography & Natural History
MUSEUM

(Muzeul Naţional de Etnografie şi Istorie Naturală; www.muzeu.md; Str M Kogălniceanu 82; adult/student 10/5 lei, photos 15 lei; ⊙10am-6pm Tue-Sun, closed last Wed of month;) The highlight of this massive and wonderful exhibition is a life-sized reconstruction of the skeleton of a dinothere – an 8-tonne elephant-like mammal that lived during the Pliocene epoch – 5.3 million to 1.8 million years ago – discovered in the Rezine region in 1966. Sweeping dioramas depict national customs and dress, while other exhibits cover geology, botany and zoology (including bizarre deformed animals in jars).

👉 Tours

Tour companies can arrange the standard wine, monastery and Transdniestr tours in addition to more specialised offerings, such as multiday excursions out of the capital. **Best Moldova** (☑022 874 027; www.bestmoldova. md; B-dul Ştefan cel Mare 71; ⊙9am-7pm Mon-Fri, to 4pm Sat) and **Tatra-Bis** (☑022 844 304; www.tatrabis.md; Str Alexandru Bernardazzi 59/3; ⊙9am-6pm Mon-Fri, 10am-3pm Sat) are two of the better ones.

🎊 Festivals & Events

⭐ Wine Festival
WINE

(http://wineday.wineofmoldova.com; Piaţa Marii Adunări Naţionale; ⊙Oct) The nectar that makes Moldova tick is celebrated on the first weekend in October to coincide with the end of the grape harvest. A long block of B-dul Ştefan cel Mare is taken over by stalls selling wine, food and crafts as folk bands fill the air with traditional music. Tourists are encouraged to learn the national dances and don traditional clothing.

🛏 Sleeping

Ionika Hostel
HOSTEL €

(☑060 639 551; Str M Kogălniceanu 62; dm €7-9, d €19-20) The best all-around hostel in Chişinău, Ionika scores points with an excellent kitchen, flamboyant common areas, spacious dorms, individual bed lights and outlets, huge lockers, a musical massage shower and a pleasant outdoor patio.

Central Chişinău

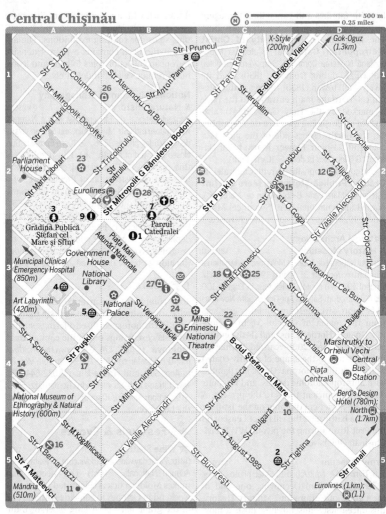

★ **City Park Hotel**　　　　　HOTEL **€€**
(☎022 249 249; www.citipark.md; Str E Doga 2; s/d
incl breakfast €70/80; P ⓢ) This fashionable
hotel on the main walking street in town
is popular, so book ahead to enjoy its bold,
bright rooms, crisp English-speaking service
and excellent breakfast in its street-side beer
restaurant. Outstanding value, especially
throwing in top-end perks like bathrobes
and contemporary art.

★ **Art Rustic Hotel**　　　　　HOTEL **€€**
(☎022 232 593; www.art-rustic.md; Str Alexandru Hajdeu 79/1; s/d incl breakfast from €35/45;
P ✳ ⓢ) This small boutique hotel, a

15-minute walk from the centre, offers excellent value. The 13 rooms are individually and
imaginatively furnished and come in two
classes: '*standart*' and cheaper '*econom*',
with the former being much bigger, and the
latter boasting balconies.

Berd's Design Hotel　　BOUTIQUE HOTEL **€€€**
(☎022 022 222; www.berdshotel.com; B-dul D
Cantemir 12; s/d incl breakfast from €125/140, ste
€290) Leviathan doors that must weigh several tonnes open to Chişinău's most design-
conscious rooms, rendered in elegant silver
tones. Quarters have plenty of space and
giant beds, plus ultra-boutique bathrooms

Central Chişinău

with square sinks and wall-mounted toilets. Minimalism rules the day – no extra fabrics here.

 Eating

The neighbourhood along Str Bucureşti and Str 31 August 1989 is a good place to browse for restaurants. Northeast of the parks, pedestrianised Str E Doga is another cafe and restaurant row.

★ **Coffee Molka** CAFE €
(Str Octavian Goga; dishes 25-50 lei; ⊘8am-10.30pm Mon-Fri, noon-10.30pm Sat & Sun; 🛜) The charismatic owner's love of coffee is on display everywhere, from Turkish coffee faithfully prepared according to an ancient style, to shelves of antique coffee grinders that make up part of the on-site coffee 'museum'. Vintage record and book collections and groovy lighting add to the ambience. Light bites are best taken on the rooftop terrace.

★ **Popasul Dacilor** MOLDOVAN €€
(☑069 150 543; Str Valea Crucii St 13; mains 50-250 lei; ⊘11am-midnight; ⊛🛜) Chişinău's most eccentric eatery is a bit like a *Game of Thrones* set, awash in furs, totem poles and gnarled wood. Out back open-air dining options take all shapes and sizes, and a two-tonne door leads to a secret stash of rare Moldovan wines. The traditional Bessarabian fare and service are superb. It's out towards the airport.

★ **Gok-Oguz** MOLDOVAN €€
(☑022 468 852; Str Calea Orheiului 19a; mains 100-175 lei; ⊘10am-11pm) It's well worth the short taxi ride north of the centre to Chişinău's only Gagauzian restaurant. Gagauzian food has Turkic, Romanian and Russian influences, and the offerings here include *carne de miel po Gheorhievski* (baked mutton with rice and vegetables), lamb *cavurma* (a spicy stew) and *ghiozlemea* (gözleme – or Turkic pastries) with ewes' milk cheese.

Vatra Neamului MOLDOVAN €€
(☑022 226 839; Str Puşkin 20b; mains 75-300 lei; ⊘11am-midnight; Ⓟ⊛🛜) This superb place boasts charming old-world decor, unfailingly genial staff and – by night – a duet strumming traditional Moldovan instruments. A long menu of imaginatively dressed-up meats – think stewed pork with *mămăligă* (boiled cornmeal), baked rabbit and grilled trout, not to mention *varenyky* (Ukrainian dumplings) and *plăcintă* (stuffed pastries) – may prompt repeat visits.

Gastrobar MEDITERRANEAN €€€
(☑068 906 545; Str A Bernardazzi 66; mains 100-250 lei; ⊘noon-11pm; ⊛🛜🍴) The food is both healthy and outstanding – what you might expect from a place with the motto 'bread, wine, life'. Warm up with a berry smoothie infused with flax seeds, then pick from light *meze* (tzatziki, hummus) or envelope-pushing mains like duck breast in orange and cranberry sauce or grilled octopus.

🍷 Drinking & Nightlife

★ Kira's Club
CLUB

(www.facebook.com/kirasclub; Str Veronica Micle 7; Fri & Sat cover 40 lei; ⊙ 11am-11pm Sun-Thu, to 5am Fri & Sat) More than a club, this intimate basement venue might better be described as a multifaceted counterculture haven. DJs are the norm, but on any given night you might encounter live music, hip-hop or poetry slams. In the warm months the party moves outside, taking over the sidewalk in front of the edgy Luceafărul theatre next door.

★ Invino enoteca
WINE BAR

(📞 022 909 944; www.invino.md; Str Mitropolit G Bănulescu Bodini 41; ⊙ 11am-9pm; 🛜) Chișinău, as you might imagine, has its share of wine bars. Invino occupies a refined, minimalist space just off the central park. It has a big blonde-wood bar, an extensive wine list with virtually all of Moldova's wineries represented, plus cheeses and other hors d'oeuvres for pairing and palate cleansing. And this being Moldova, it ain't expensive.

Bandabar
CLUB

(📞 079 500 277; Str Mihai Eminescu 55; cover 100-200 lei; ⊙ 11pm-6am Fri & Sat; 🛜) This club opened to much fanfare in late 2018 and quickly became the hottest thing in town. Sister of hipster club **Barbar** (www.facebook. com/barbarmd; Str Mihai Eminescu 45; Fri & Sat cover 150 lei; ⊙ 11am-11pm Sun-Thu, to 5am Fri & Sat), this is comparatively huge, with a giant dance hall and a smaller chill space. Draws top DJs and bands.

Smokehouse
CRAFT BEER

(B-dul Ștefan cel Mare 128; ⊙ 11am-midnight Sun-Thu, to 2am Fri & Sat; 🛜) Twinned with the adjacent Taproom 27, the motto is 'hoppiness on tap' and they deliver with a small but carefully curated list of craft beers on tap. Grab a flight of four/eight beers for 65/130 lei. It's also known for ribs, corn succotash and other barbecuestaples of the American South.

☆ Entertainment

Posters listing what's on are displayed on boards outside the city's various theatres. Culture vultures should not miss a performance at the **Maria Bieșu National Opera & Ballet Theatre** (www.nationalopera.md; B-dul Ștefan cel Mare 152; tickets 50-200 lei; ⊙ box office 11am-6pm Tue-Mon, to 2pm Sat & Sun) or the architecturally splendid **Organ Hall** (Sala cu Orgă; www.organhall.md; B-dul Ștefan cel Mare 81; ⊙ box office 11am-6pm, performances 6pm).

TOURING MOLDOVA'S WINE COUNTRY

Moldova was the Rhone Valley of the Soviet Union, and two of the largest wineries in the world are within 20km of Chișinău: **Cricova** (📞 069 077 734; www.cricovavin.md; Str Chișinăului 124, Cricova; ⊙ 10am-5pm Mon-Fri) and **Mileștii Mici** (📞 069 500 262, 022 382 777; www.milestii-mici.md; Mileștii Mici town; tours 350-1500 lei; ⊙ 8am-5pm Mon-Fri). The latter has a collection of about 1.5 million bottles – which makes it the world's largest wine collection, according to the Guinness Book of World Records. Tours of these two giants are popular; email well in advance to book a spot.

To avoid crowds, you might consider booking a more intimate wine-tasting experience at one of the several boutique wineries around Chișinău. These have the added benefit of better wine. A few of the best:

Castel Mimi (📞 062 001 893; www.castelmimi.md; Str Dacia 1, Bulboaca; tasting tours 300-780 lei; ⊙ 10am-6pm Wed-Sun, restaurant to 10pm) This legendary winery 40km southeast of Chișinău occupies a beautifully restored stone manor dating from 1893. It's a picture of modern luxury, with an interactive tasting table, an exquisite restaurant, and grove of *domiki* (small houses) and palatial rooms for rent.

Château Purcari (📞 024 230 411; www.purcari.md; Purcari; tasting tours from 300 lei) Nestled in the extreme southeast corner of Moldova, about 115km from Chișinău, Purcari's wines are arguably Moldova's finest. Tours here can last from one to several days, with luxurious lakeside **accommodation** (📞 060 121 221; https://purcari.md; Purcari; s/d from €65/75; ❄🛜) and an array of activities.

Château Vartely (📞 022 829 891; www.vartely.md; Str Eliberării 170b, Orhei/New Orhei; basic tour without tasting 150 lei) Established in 2008, it offers not just very good whites and reds, but excellent food and cosy accommodation (rooms from €83) in one of 12 pretty wooden bungalows, just 50km north of Chișinău.

Art Labyrinth ARTS CENTRE

(www.art-labyrinth.org; Str A Şciusev 98; ⊙noon-9pm; 🔊) 🍴 Difficult to categorise, this charmingly derelict multipurpose collective is of most interest as a performing-arts and concert venue, but also contains galleries, yoga and dance studios, and a vegan cafe. Events happen two or three times per week, and the place is at its best during weekend parties fuelled by DJs or live bands.

🛍 Shopping

Wine is the most obvious gift. **Carpe Diem** (www.wineshop.md; Str Columna 136, 3a; ⊙11am-11pm) is the best wine shop in town, with highly knowledgeable, English-speaking owners. **Mândria** (www.mandria.md; Str Mitropolit G Bănulescu Bodini 5; ⊙9am-6pm Mon-Fri) is highly recommended for beautiful, hand-embroidered national outfits and blankets. For all-around souvenirs, drop into **Fantezie** (☑022 222 475; B-dul Ştefan cel Mare 83; ⊙9am-7pm Mon-Fri, 10am-5pm Sat, 10am-2pm Sun) in the marvellous city hall building.

ℹ Information

Moldova Tourist Information Center (www.moldova.travel; B-dul Ştefan cel Mare 83; ⊙10am-7pm Mon-Fri, to 3pm Sat; 🔊) The enthusiastic staff can organise just about everything, from hotels to car rentals to guided excursions around Moldova.

Victoriabank (Str Puşkin 26; ⊙9am-5pm Mon-Fri, to 2pm Sat) Has ATM, Western Union and Moneygram.

ℹ Getting There & Away

AIR

Moldova's only international airport is the modern **Chişinău International Airport** (KIV; ☑022 525 111; www.airport.md; Str Aeroportului 80/3), 13km southeast of the city centre, with regular flights (p275) to many major European capitals.

BUS

Buses heading south to Bucharest and east to Transdniestr and Odesa (Ukraine) use the **Central Bus Station** (Gara Centrala; ☑022 542 185; www.autogara.md; Str Mitropolit Varlaam 58). Most but not all buses to Odesa go via Palanca and avoid Transdniestr, and only a few go to the preferred Privoz Station in Odesa.

The **North Bus Station** (Autogara Nord; ☑022 411 338; Str Caleja Moşilor) serves Soroca and points north, and has international departures to Kyiv and Moscow. The **South Bus Station** (Autogara Sud; ☑022 713 983; Şoseaua Hînceşti 143) serves Comrat and most southern destinations, and also serves Iaşi, Romania.

With offices at the **train station** (☑022 549 813; www.eurolines.md; Aleea Garii 1; ⊙9am-6pm Mon-Fri) and in the **centre** (☑022 222 827; www.eurolines.md; Str Teatrului 4/1), Eurolines has nicer buses to major cities around Europe.

TRAIN

International trains depart from the eclectic **train station** (Gara Feroviară Chişinău; ☑022 833 333; Aleea Gării). Services run to Bucharest (from 600 lei, 14 hours, 4.56pm daily), Kyiv (from 700 lei, 14 to 18 hours, two to three daily), Moscow (from 1500 lei, 29 to 32 hours, two to three daily) and Odesa (185 lei, 4 hours, 6.57am Thursday to Sunday). **Left luggage** (per day 11-15 lei; ⊙24hr) is available.

ℹ Getting Around

TO/FROM THE AIRPORT

From the airport, trolleybus 30 (2 lei) services central Chişinău's main artery, B-dul Ştefan cel Mare (35 minutes).

Cabs ordered from taxi booths at the airport cost 100 lei to 120 lei to the centre.

CAR

Hiring a car is a good way to get around. Moldova's highways are in great shape, although rural roads still present some challenges.

The major rental agencies have booths at the airport. Several local companies prominently advertise cheaper rates around town, but be careful of these guys.

PUBLIC TRANSPORT

Buses, trolleybuses and marshrutky (fixed-route minivans; 2 lei to 3 lei) criss-cross the city in dizzying fashion from about 5.30am until 10.30pm. Trolleybus 30 wings its way down Str 31 August 1989 then veers onto B-dul Ştefan cel Mare and continues all the way to the airport. Trolleybuses 1, 5 and 8 connect the train station with the centre via B-dul Ştefan cel Mare, passing within a block of the Central Bus Station. See www.fest.md/en/map for route maps.

TAXI

Taxis ordered by phone or via a ride-hailing app (try Yandex taxi or iTaxi) cost just 30 lei to 50 lei for trips around the centre. Call 14 222, 14 428, 14 008 or 14 499.

AROUND CHIŞINĂU

Orheiul Vechi

The archaeological and ecclesiastical complex at **Orheiul Vechi** (Old Orhei; Butuceni), about 50km north of Chişinău, is the country's most important historical site and a place of stark natural beauty. Occupying a remote cliff high above the Răut River, the complex is known for its **Cave Monastery** (Mănăstire în Peşteră; Orheiul Vechi; voluntary donation; ⊙ 8am-6pm) **FREE**, but also includes baths, fortifications and ruins dating back as much as 2000 years.

The complex is in the village of Butuceni, where a small bridge over the Răut takes you to the trailhead for a 15-minute hike up to the Cave Monastery, dug by Orthodox monks in the 13th century. Dress appropriately at the monastery: long skirts or pants for women, long shorts or trousers for men, and no tank tops.

The **Orheiul Vechi Exhibition Centre** (Butuceni; adult/student incl ethnographic museum 10/5 lei; ⊙ 9am-5pm Tue-Sun), located just before the bridge, contains objects recovered during archaeological digs, and also sells a handy English-language map and guide (40 lei) of the complex.

There are two fabulous sleeping options in Butuceni should you want to get a taste of village life. About 1km east of the bridge, **Eco-Resort Butuceni** (☑ 079 617 870; www. pensiuneabutuceni.md; Butuceni; s/d/tr/q incl breakfast €30/46/65/75; ✱ ☎ ✱) has 19 rooms done up in peasant style, a fabulous restaurant (mains 50–100 lei) and an indoor swimming pool. **Vila Etnica** (www.etnica.md; Butuceni; r

---

WORTH A TRIP

TIPOVA CAVE MONASTERY

This fantastic **monastery** (Tipova; 10 lei, photos 15 lei) **FREE** is built into cliffs that tower some 200m above the Dniestr River's right (west) bank, in the tiny village of Tipova some 95km northeast of Chişinău. The monastery consists of three religious chambers and monastic cells linked by precarious steps built into the rock face. The oldest of the three chambers, the **Elevation of the Holy Cross** cave church, is thought to date from the 11th century. Dress appropriately to enter any religious areas.

Arriving by private car is recommended. Otherwise, take the 10.30am *marshrutka* to Tipova (2½ hours) from Chişinău's North Bus Station. It returns to Chişinău in the late afternoon (around 3pm), so consider overnighting at lovely **Vila Serenada** (☑ 079 842 662; vent-dest@hotmail.fr; Horodişte; d incl breakfast €40; ✱) in nearby Horodişte.

€70-80; ✱ ☎) is a rambling complex with a pleasant restaurant on a babbling brook.

❶ Getting There & Away

From Chişinău, *marshrutky* to Butuceni depart from a **bus stand** (Str Metropolit Varlaam) roughly opposite the Central Bus Station entrance (26 lei, 1¼ hours, five or six daily). Placards will say 'Butuceni', 'Trebujeni' or 'Orheiul Vechi'. The last trip back is at 4.15pm (6.20pm in the summer). A taxi round trip shouldn't cost more than €40.

Soroca

The northern city of Soroca (population 22,000) occupies a prominent position on the Dniestr River and is Moldova's unofficial 'Roma capital'. The incredibly gaudy, fantastical mansions of the Roma 'kings' that line the streets up on the hill above the centre are a sight to behold.

The gloriously solid **Soroca Fortress** (Cetatea Soroca; ☑ 069 323 734; Str Petru Rareş 1; adult/student 10/5 lei, tours in English 100 lei; ⊙ 9am-1pm & 2-6pm Wed-Sun) on the banks of the Dniestr dates to the late 15th century and the reign of Moldavian Prince Ştefan cel Mare. It was built on the remains of a wooden fortress in the shape of a circle, with five bastions. Today those bastions contain medieval-themed exhibits, with a few English placards posted about that shed light on the history of the fortress.

You can get fantastic views of the Dniestr and the perfectly partitioned fields of Ukraine beyond by climbing the 660 steps (not an exact count) up to the **Candle of Gratitude** (Str Independenţei) **FREE** on the town's southern outskirts.

There are a few passable places to stay in town but really only one restaurant of note, pizzeria **Salat** (Parcu Central; mains 40-100 lei; ⊙ 9am-11pm) on the town square.

From the **bus station** (Str Independenţei) south of town, *marshrutky* head to Chişinău's North Bus Station every hour or so until 6pm (75 lei, 2½ hours). There are daily buses to Bucharest and Kyiv.

Gagauzia

The autonomous region of Gagauzia (Gagauz Yeri) lies 100km due south of Chişinău but is a world apart from the cosmopolitan capital. This Turkic-influenced Christian ethnic minority forfeited full independence for autonomy in the early 1990s, thus making

INTO THE WILD

Moldova has several playgrounds for lovers of the great outdoors. The bird-laden **Prutul de Jos (Lower Prut) Biosphere Reserve** in the country's extreme southwest corner was recognised as a Unesco site in 2018. You can base yourself near the reserve at **Costel Hostel** (☑ 069 072 674; www.costelhostel.com; Roşu Village, Cahul; per person from €15; ☎) in the village of Roşu, near Cahul. Owner Constantin is a permaculture maverick who cooks traditional meals with ingredients sourced from his bountiful garden. His relatives in Slobozia Mare, about 40km south of Roşu, lead informal rowing-boat tours on the reserve's Lake Beleu.

Other outdoorsy highlights around the country include multiday kayaking and camping expeditions on the **Dniestr River**; and the **Plaiul Fagului (Land of Beeches) Natural Scientific Reserve**, where you can bike through beech forests or climb Moldova's highest peak (430m). With a fleet of kayaks and mountain bikes, outdoor shop **X-Style** (☑ 069 107 435, 069 692 265; www.xstyle.md; B-dul Grigore Vieru 27; ☺9am-8pm) in Chişinău runs trips to these places, sometimes dipping into Romania. Ask for Natalie or Alexandru.

it subordinate to Moldova constitutionally and for defence. But politically the Gagauz generally look towards Russia for patronage, while increasingly looking towards Turkey for both cultural inspiration and economic investment.

Comrat, the capital, has a nice church, the requisite Lenin statue and the eclectic **Comrat Regional History Museum** (vul Lenina 162; 10 lei; ☺9am-4pm Tue-Sat), but its main appeal lies in being a cultural oddity. Tiraspol Hostel & Tours (p274) runs excellent tours to Gagauzia out of Chişinău or Tiraspol.

Comrat is easy to reach from Chişinău, with hourly *marshrutky* departures from the South Bus Station (45 lei, two hours).

TRANSDNIESTR

POP 469,000

The self-declared republic of Transdniestr, a narrow strip of land on the eastern bank of the Dniestr River, is a ministate that doesn't officially exist in anyone's eyes but its own.

From the Moldovan perspective, Transdniestr (also spelled Transnistria; in Russian: Prednestrove) is still officially part of its sovereign territory that was illegally grabbed in the early 1990s with Russian support. Officials in Transdniestr see it differently and proudly point to the territory having won its 'independence' in a bloody civil war in 1992. A bitter truce has ensued ever since.

These days, a trip to Transdniestr is easier than ever thanks to relaxed registration rules. Visitors will be stunned by this idiosyncratic region that still fully embraces the iconography of the Soviet period.

Tiraspol

☑ 533 / POP 130,000

The 'capital' of Transdniestr is also, officially at least, the second-largest city in Moldova. With eerily quiet streets, flower beds tended with military precision and old-school Soviet everything from street signs to parks named after communist grandees, Tiraspol will be one of the strangest places you'll ever visit.

◉ Sights & Activities

Noul Neamţ Monastery MONASTERY
(Kitskany Monastery; Kitskany Village) A stunning 70m bell tower marks this serene monastery (1861), 7km south of Tiraspol. You can climb the bell tower for a bird's-eye view of the monastery's four churches and a sweeping panorama of the countryside. You'll need to ask around for the key to be let up. Frequent *marshrutky* serve Kitskany from Tiraspol (4 roubles, 10 minutes); the stop is just over the central bridge spanning the Dniestr.

Tiraspol National History Museum MUSEUM
(ul 25 Oktober 46; 26 roubles; ☺9am-5pm Tue-Sun) No period of Transdniestran history is ignored at this relatively interesting museum, starting with photos of late-19th-century Tiraspol, moving to the Soviet period and the Great Patriotic War, to the civil war of 1992.

Kvint Factory FACTORY
(☑ 0533 96 577; www.kvint.md; ul Lenina 38; ☺store 9am-1pm & 2-10pm) Since 1897 Kvint has been making some of Moldova's finest brandies. Book private tasting tours in English two days in advance (US$10 to US$70

per person, five-person minimum). Wine tastings are also available (US$8 to US$17, three-person minimum), or join one-hour standard tours of the factory (in Russian), which take place Monday to Friday at 3pm (45 roubles per person, no tastings).

👉 Tours

Tiraspol Hostel & Tours   TOURS
(☑ 068 571 472; www.moldovahostels.com) Run by Tim, an American, this operator runs truly creative tours to less explored corners of Transdniestr or multiday combo tours taking in Gagauzia and/or Odesa as well. The focus is on Soviet sights and experiences, often with a heavy local element (eg, a homestay and traditional meal in an isolated village).

Transnistria Tour   TOURS
(☑ 069 427 502, 077 741 678; www.transnistria-tour. com) This highly recommended company offers a full range of tours and travel services to foreign visitors. Company head and guide Andrey Smolenskiy speaks German and Swedish in addition to English and Russian.

🛏 Sleeping

Like Home Hostel   HOSTEL €
(☑ 0777 66 188; http://htno.ru; Sadovyi pereulok 9b; dm €10; ❄ 🛜) The best hostel in town, and not just because it's the only one with signage (making it viable for walk-ins). It's homey and friendly with a real common area, two spacious eight-bed dorm rooms with air-con,

and some of the best food in town served in the Vkusnii Dom cafe at the back.

City Club   HOTEL €€€
(☑ 0533 59 000; www.cityclub.md; ul Gorkogo 18; r without/with breakfast from €50/60; 🅿 ❄ 🛜) One of the better deals in the region, City Club features lovely staff and well-appointed, spacious rooms. There are classy inside-and-out dining choices and a sauna, but the highlight is the truly impressive gym – even nongym-rats will be tempted to work out.

🍴 Eating & Drinking

⭐ Kumanyok   UKRAINIAN €
(☑ 0533 72 034; ul Sverdlova 37; mains 50-125 roubles; ⏲ 9am-11pm; 🛜) This smart, super-friendly, traditional Ukrainian place is set in a kitsch faux-countryside home, where diners are attended to by a fleet of peasant-dressed waitresses. The menu is hearty Ukrainian fare; think *varenyky* (dumplings), *bliny* (pancakes), *golubtsi* (stuffed cabbage rolls) and, above all, authentic *borshch* (beetroot soup).

Stolovka SSSR   CAFETERIA €
(Bus Station, ul Sovetskaya 1, 2nd fl, Bendery; dishes 8-18 roubles; ⏲ 9am-4pm; ❄ 🛜) In this retro-Soviet *stolovaya* (cafeteria) above the bus station, you can dine amid USSR-vintage paraphernalia on egalitarian fare like *solyanka* (pickled vegetables and potato soup), *olivye* (potato) salad and *kotleta* (minced meat cutlet). No English menu, just point and pick from the buffet.

Vintage   CLUB
(www.clubvintage.ru; ul Klary Tsetkin 14/2; from 7pm Fri & Sat 100 roubles; ⏲ 24hr) The hottest club in Tiraspol, often pulling top DJs from Moscow and elsewhere. Serious fun.

ℹ Information

MONEY
The Transdniestran rouble is the only way to pay for stuff in the breakaway republic, as credit cards are not accepted. You can exchange dollars, euros, Russian roubles or Moldovan lei for roubles at exchange kiosks and banks.

TOURIST INFORMATION
Tourist Information Centre (☑ 0533 53 559; tourism@ngo.ardt.com; ul Sovetskaya 135; ⏲ 9.30am-6.30pm Mon-Sat) This helpful new office covers all of Transdniestr and is a good place to stop if you're planning to hit less-visited parts of the republic. They have the only decent map of Tiraspol, sell souvenirs and can help find guides.

ⓘ CROSSING INTO TRANSDNIESTR

All visitors to Transdniestr are required to show a valid passport at the 'border' (if arriving by train this happens at the train station). The formalities are fairly straightforward and take about five minutes.

Your passport will be scanned and used to generate a slip of paper called a 'migration card'. You must keep the paper with your passport at all times and surrender it when leaving (so don't lose it!). Migration cards allow for stays of up to 45 days. If you plan to stay overnight you must provide the border officials with an address for each day of your stay.

Be sure to ask for a Moldovan entry stamp if you enter Transdniestr from Ukraine and plan on continuing to Moldova proper. If you fail to secure one, you must register your presence at the **Bureau for Migration and Asylum** (B-dul Ştefan cel Mare 124; ⊙ 9am–4pm Mon-Fri) in Chişinău within three business days of arriving in Moldova proper.

The above rules are subject to change, especially if tensions with Moldova increase.

ⓘ Getting There & Away

From the bus station, *marshrutky* go to Chişinău (40 roubles, 1¾ hours, every 20 minutes) and Odesa in Ukraine (60 roubles, 2½ hours to three hours, six daily).

The Odesa–Chişinău train passes through Tiraspol, but it only runs from Friday to Sunday (plus Thursdays in summer). The departure to Odesa is at 8.06am (170 roubles, three hours), while to Chişinău the departure is at 9.21pm (110 roubles, one hour). There's an additional train to Chişinău on odd days (5.58pm).

The bus station and train station share a parking lot about 1.5km north of the centre. Trolley-bus 1 takes you into the centre via ul Lenina and ul 25 Oktober (3 roubles).

SURVIVAL GUIDE

ⓘ Directory A–Z

MONEY

ATMs widely available, particularly in Chişinău and other cities. Credit cards usually accepted in urban centres, less so in rural areas. Transdniestr has its own currency.

OPENING HOURS

Banks 9am–3pm Monday to Friday
Businesses 8am–7pm Monday to Friday, to 4pm Saturday
Museums 9am–5pm Tuesday to Sunday
Restaurants 10am–11pm
Shops 9am or 10am–6pm or 7pm Monday to Saturday

PUBLIC HOLIDAYS

New Year's Day 1 January
Orthodox Christmas 7–8 January
International Women's Day 8 March
Orthodox Easter Sunday & Monday April/May
Labour Day 1 May
Victory (1945) Day 9 May
Independence Day 27 August
National Language Day 31 August
Western Christmas 25 December

TELEPHONE

It's straightforward to buy a local prepaid SIM card with one of the two main mobile-phone providers, Moldcell and Orange, and use it in any unlocked handset. To place a call or send a text from a local mobile phone, dial +373 or 0, plus the two-digit prefix and the six-digit number.

VISAS

None for European countries, USA, Canada, Japan, Australia and New Zealand, but required for South Africa and many other countries.

ⓘ Getting There & Away

AIR

Moldova's only international airport is in Chişinău (p271). The national carrier, **Air Moldova** (☑ 022 830 830; www.airmoldova.md; B-dul Negruzzi 10, Chişinău; ⊙ 8am-8pm), and local budget carrier **Fly One** (☑ 022 100 003; www.flyone.aero) serve several European cities.

LAND

Motorists must purchase a highway sticker (vignette) to drive on Moldovan roads. Buy these online (http://vinieta.gov.md) or at border crossings. Rates per seven/15/30 days are €4/8/16.

ⓘ Getting Around

Moldova has a comprehensive network of buses running to most towns and villages. *Marshrutky*, or fixed-route minivans (also known by their Romanian name, maxitaxis), follow the same routes as the buses and are quicker. Car hire makes sense as Moldova's roads are good these days and you can reach just about any part of the country on a day trip out of Chişinău.

Montenegro

☏ 382 / POP 676,900

Best Places to Eat

➡ Belveder (p284)

➡ Hotel Soa (p288)

➡ Restaurant Conte (p279)

➡ Antigona (p283)

➡ One (p281)

Best Places to Stay

➡ La Vecchia Casa (p285)

➡ Palazzo Drusko (p282)

➡ Palazzo Radomiri (p282)

➡ Old Town Hostel (p281)

➡ Hostel Pirate (p283)

Why Go?

Imagine a place with sapphire beaches as spectacular as Croatia's, rugged peaks as dramatic as Switzerland's, canyons nearly as deep as Colorado's, palazzi as elegant as Venice's and towns as old as Greece's. Now wrap it up in a Mediterranean climate and squish it into an area two-thirds the size of Wales, and you start to get a picture of Montenegro (Црна Гора).

More-adventurous travellers can easily sidestep the peak-season hordes on the coast by heading to the rugged mountains of the north. This is, after all, a country where wolves and bears still lurk in forgotten corners.

Montenegro, Crna Gora, Black Mountain: the name itself conjures up romance and drama. There are plenty of both on offer as you explore this perfumed land, bathed in the scent of wild herbs, conifers and Mediterranean blossoms. Yes, it really is as magical as it sounds.

When to Go
Podgorica

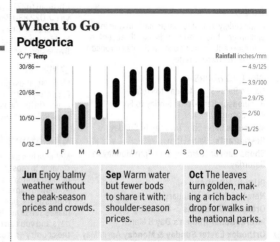

Jun Enjoy balmy weather without the peak-season prices and crowds.

Sep Warm water but fewer bods to share it with; shoulder-season prices.

Oct The leaves turn golden, making a rich backdrop for walks in the national parks.

Entering the Country

Whether you choose to fly, train, ferry, bus or drive, it's not difficult to get to Montenegro these days. New routes – including those served by low-cost carriers – are continually being added to the busy timetable at the country's two airports. It's also possible to make your way from neighbouring countries, especially Croatia. Dubrovnik's airport is very close to the border and the beautiful city makes an impressive starting point to a Montenegro holiday. Flights, cars and tours can be booked online at lonelyplanet.com/bookings.

ITINERARIES

Five Days

Basing yourself in the atmospheric walled town of Kotor (p279), spend an afternoon in palazzi-packed Perast (p279) and a whole day in buzzy Budva (p282). Allow another day to explore mountainous Lovćen National Park (p283) and the old royal capital, Cetinje (p283).

One Week

For your final two days, head north to the mountains of Durmitor National Park (p285), making sure to stop at the historic Ostrog Monastery (p285) on the way. Spend your time hiking, rafting (in season) and canyoning.

Essential Food & Drink

Loosen your belt; you're in for a treat. By default, most Montenegrin food is local, fresh and organic, and hence very seasonal. The food on the coast is virtually indistinguishable from Dalmatian cuisine: lots of grilled seafood, garlic, olive oil and Italian dishes. Inland it's much more meaty and Serbian-influenced. The village of Njeguši in the Montenegrin heartland is famous for its *pršut* (prosciutto, air-dried ham) and *sir* (cheese). Anything with Njeguški in its name is going to be a true Montenegrin dish and stuffed with these goodies.

Here are some local favourites:

Riblja čorba Fish soup, a staple of the coast.

Crni rižoto Black risotto, coloured and flavoured with squid ink.

Lignje na žaru Grilled squid, sometimes stuffed (*punjene*) with cheese and smoke-dried ham.

Jagnjetina ispod sača Lamb cooked (often with potatoes) under a metal lid covered with hot coals.

Rakija Domestic brandy, made from nearly anything. The local favourite is grape-based *loza*.

Vranac & Krstač The most famous indigenous red and white wine varietals (respectively).

AT A GLANCE

Area 13,812 sq km

Capital Podgorica

Country Code 382

Currency euro (€)

Emergency Ambulance 124, Fire 123, Police 122

Language Montenegrin

Time Central European time (GMT/UTC plus one hour)

Visas None for citizens of EU, Canada, USA, Australia, New Zealand and many other countries.

MONTENEGRO

Sleeping Price Ranges

The following price ranges are based on a standard double with bathroom in high season.

€ less than €45

€€ €45–100

€€€ more than €100

Eating Price Ranges

The following ranges refer to the average price of a main course.

€ less than €5

€€ €5–15

€€€ more than €15

Resources

Montenegrin National Tourist Organisation (www.montenegro.travel)

Montenegro Highlights

1 Kotor (p279) Randomly roaming the atmospheric streets until you're a little lost.

2 Lovćen National Park (p283) Driving the vertiginous route from Kotor to the Njegoš Mausoleum.

3 Perast (p279) Admiring the baroque palaces and churches.

4 Ostrog Monastery (p285) Seeking out the spiritual at this impressive cliff-clinging monastery.

5 Tara Canyon (p285) Floating through paradise, rafting between the plunging walls of this canyon.

6 Cetinje (p283) Diving into Montenegro's history, art

and culture in the old royal capital.

7 Ulcinj (p282) Beaching by day and soaking up the Eastern-tinged vibe on the streets after dark.

8 Durmitor National Park (p285) Admiring the mountain vistas reflected in glacial lakes during walks.

COASTAL MONTENEGRO

There's less than 100km as the crow flies from the fjord-like Bay of Kotor in the north to the long sandy beaches abutting Albania, yet Montenegro's coast can still claim some of the most dramatic scenery on the entire Mediterranean.

Perast   Пераст

☑ 032 / POP 270

Looking like a chunk of Venice that has floated down the Adriatic and anchored itself onto the Bay of Kotor, Perast hums with melancholy memories of the days when it was rich and powerful. Despite having only one main street, this tiny town boasts 16 churches and 17 formerly grand palazzi. While some are just enigmatic ruins sprouting bougainvillea and wild fig, others are caught up in the whirlwind of renovation that has hit the town.

The town slopes down from the highway to a narrow waterfront road (Obala Marka Martinovića) that runs along its length. At its heart is **St Nicholas' Church** (Crkva Sv Nikole; Obala Marka Martinovića bb; treasury €1; ⊙8am-6pm), set on a small square lined with date palms and the bronze busts of famous citizens.

Perast's most famous landmarks aren't on land at all: two peculiarly picturesque islands with equally peculiar histories.

⊙ Sights

★ **Gospa od Škrpjela**   ISLAND
(Our-Lady-of-the-Rock Island; ⊙church 9am-7pm Jul & Aug, to 5pm Apr-Jun & Sep-Nov, to 3pm Dec-Mar) This picturesque island was artificially created (on 22 July 1452, to be precise) around a rock where an image of the Madonna was found; every year on that same day, the locals row over with stones to continue the task. In summer, boats line up on the Perast waterfront to ferry people there and back (€5 return); off season, you may need to ask around.

The magnificent **church** at its centre was erected in 1630 and has sumptuous Venetian paintings, hundreds of silver votive tablets and a small museum (€1.50). The most unusual – and famous – exhibit is an embroidered icon of the Madonna and Child partly made with the hair of its maker.

⫝̸ Sleeping & Eating

GudCo Apartments   APARTMENT €€
(☑ 032-373 589; gudco@t-com.me; Perast 152; apt from €75; ❄ ☎) There are only two spacious, stone-walled apartments available here, positioned directly above the extremely welcoming owners' house. Wake up to extraordinary bay views in your spacious Perast pad, then play with the kittens on the rear terrace while you catch up on your laundry (units have washing machines and dishwashers).

Konoba Školji   MONTENEGRIN, SEAFOOD €€
(☑ 069-419 745; www.skolji.com; Obala Marka Martinovića bb; mains €8-24; ⊙10am-midnight; ☎) This appealing traditional restaurant is all about the thrill of the grill: fresh seafood and falling-off-the-bone meats are barbecued to perfection in full view of salivating diners. Thankfully they're not shy with the portion sizes; the delightful/maddening smell of the cooking and the sea air will have you ravenous by the time your meal arrives. The pasta is good too.

★ **Restaurant Conte**   SEAFOOD €€€
(☑ 032-373 722; www.hotelconte.me; Obala Marka Martinovića bb; mains €10-25; ⊙8am-midnight; ☎) If you don't fall in love here – with Perast, with your dining partner, with a random waiter – consider your heart stone; with its island views, table-top flowers and super-fresh oysters, this place is ridiculously romantic. You'll be presented with platters of whole fish to select from; the chosen one will return, cooked and silver-served, to your table.

❶ Getting There & Away

➡ Paid parking is available on either approach to town (per day €2) but, in summer, it's in hot demand.

➡ Car access into the town itself is restricted.

➡ There's no bus station but buses to and from Kotor (€1.50, 25 minutes) stop at least every 30 minutes on the main road at the top of town.

➡ Water taxis zoom around the bay during summer and call into all ports, including Perast.

➡ Regular taxis from Kotor to Perast cost around €15.

Kotor   Котор

☑ 032 / POP 13,000

Wedged between brooding mountains and a moody corner of the bay, achingly atmospheric Kotor is perfectly at one with its setting. Hemmed in by staunch walls snaking improbably up the surrounding slopes, the town is a medieval maze of museums, churches, cafe-strewn squares, and Venetian

Kotor

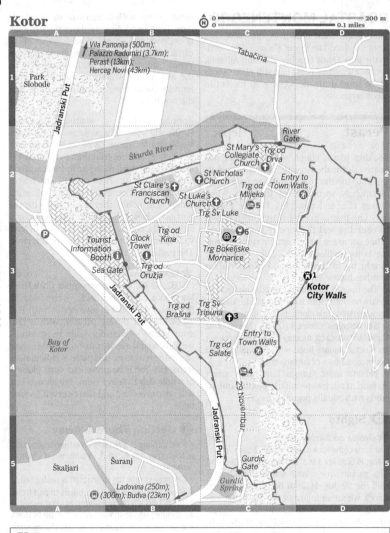

MONTENEGRO KOTOR

Kotor

palaces and pillories. It's a dramatic and delightful place where the past coexists with the present; its cobblestones ring with the sound of children racing to school in centuries-old buildings, lines of laundry flutter from wrought-iron balconies, and hundreds of cats – the descendants of seafaring felines – loll in marble laneways. Come nightfall, Kotor's spectacularly lit-up walls glow as serenely as a halo. Behind the bulwarks, the

> **WORTH A TRIP**
>
> ### TIVAT ТИВАТ
>
> With its bobbing super yachts, a posh promenade and rows of swanky apartment blocks, visitors to Tivat could be forgiven for wondering if they're in Monaco or Montenegro. The erstwhile-mediocre seaside town has undergone a major makeover – courtesy of the multimillion-dollar redevelopment of its old naval base into a first-class marina – and while it bears no resemblance to anywhere else in the country, Tivat is now attracting the uberwealthy (and less-loaded rubberneckers) in droves.
>
> Single-handedly responsible for Tivat's transformation is **Porto Montenegro** (www.portomontenegro.com), a surreal 24-hectare town-within-a-town occupying the former Arsenal shipyard and naval base. Primped, preening and planned right down to the last polished pebble, the almost impossibly glamorous marina complex includes upmarket apartment buildings; a 'lifestyle village' of fancy boutiques, bars, restaurants and leisure facilities; a **maritime museum** (Zbirka pomorskog nasljeđa; ☑ 067-637 781; Porto Montenegro; museum/submarine €3/2; ⊙ 9am-4pm Mon-Fri, 1-5pm Sat); a resort-style hotel; and berths for 450 yachts (with a total of 850 berths planned by completion). The best restaurant is brasserie-style **One** (☑ 067-486 045; www.facebook.com/jettyone; mains €10-22; ⊙ 8.30am-midnight), with views over the megayachts moored in the marina.
>
> Tivat has a reputation as being one of the sunniest spots in the Bay of Kotor. While it will never rival Kotor for charm, it makes a pleasant stop on a trip around the bay.

streets buzz with bars, live music – from soul to serenades – and castle-top clubbing.

Budva's got the beaches, and nearby Dubrovnik's got the bling, but for romance, ambience and living history, this Old Town outflanks them all.

◉ Sights

★ Kotor City Walls   FORTRESS
(Bedemi grada Kotora; €8; ⊙ 24hr, fees apply 8am-8pm May-Sep) Kotor's fortifications started to head up St John's Hill in the 9th century and by the 14th century a protective loop was completed, which was added to right up until the 19th century. The energetic can make a 1200m ascent up the fortifications via 1350 steps to a height of 260m above sea level; the views from St John's Fortress, at the top, are glorious. There are entry points near the River Gate and behind Trg od Salate.

St Tryphon's Cathedral   CHURCH
(Katedrale Sv Tripuna; Trg Sv Tripuna; church & museum €2.50; ⊙ 9am-8pm Apr-Oct, to 5pm Nov, Dec & Mar, to 1pm Jan & Feb) Kotor's most impressive building, this Catholic cathedral was consecrated in 1166 but reconstructed after several earthquakes. When the entire frontage was destroyed in 1667, the baroque bell towers were added; the left one remains unfinished. The cathedral's gently hued interior is a masterpiece of Romanesque architecture with slender Corinthian columns alternating with pillars of pink stone, thrusting upwards to support a series of vaulted roofs. Look for

the remains of Byzantine-style frescoes in the arches.

Maritime Museum of Montenegro   MUSEUM
(Pomorski muzej Crne Gore; ☑ 032-304 720; www.museummaritimum.com; Trg Bokeljske Mornarice; adult/child €4/1; ⊙ 9am-8pm Mon-Sat, 10am-4pm Sun Jul & Aug, 8am-6pm Mon-Sat, 9am-1pm Sun May, Jun & Sep, 9am-5pm Mon-Fri, to noon Sat & Sun Oct-Apr) Kotor's proud history as a naval power is celebrated in three storeys of displays housed in a wonderful early-18th-century palace. An audio guide helps explain the collection of photographs, paintings, uniforms, exquisitely decorated weapons and models of ships.

🛏 Sleeping

Old Town Hostel   HOSTEL €€
(☑ 032-325 317; www.hostel-kotor.me; 29 Novembar bb; dm from €14, r €75, without bathroom €60; ✴ 🛜 🛏) If the ghosts of the Bisanti family had any concerns when their 13th-century palazzo was converted into a hostel, they must be overjoyed now. Sympathetic renovations have brought the place to life, and the ancient stone walls echo with the cheerful chatter of happy travellers. A second building, directly across the road, has modern rooms and a small pool.

Vila Panonija   HOTEL €€
(☑ 032-334 893; www.vilapanonija.com; Dobrota bb; r €80-110; 🅿 ✴ 🛜) Set back from the waterfront in Dobrota, this old stone house

has been converted into a small hotel – or is it a large guesthouse? The stained glass in the breakfast room is a little 'belle époque' but the bedrooms, with their midnight-blue feature walls, are much more modern. Some have balconies; all have en-suite bathrooms.

★ **Palazzo Drusko** BOUTIQUE HOTEL €€€
(☎ 067-333 172; www.palazzodrusko.me; near Trg od Mlijeka; s/d from €69/139; ❋ ☎) Loaded with character and filled with antiques, this venerable 600-year-old palazzo is a memorable place to stay, right in the heart of the Old Town. Thoughtful extras include water jugs loaded with lemon and mint, a guest kitchen, 3D TVs and old-fashioned radios rigged to play Montenegrin music.

Palazzo Radomiri HOTEL €€€
(☎ 032-333 176; www.palazzoradomiri.com; Dobrota 220; s/d/ste from €160/180/250; ☺ Apr-Oct; ⓟ ❋ ☎ ☒) This honey-coloured early-18th-century palazzo on the Dobrota waterfront, 4km north of Kotor's Old Town, has been transformed into a first-rate boutique hotel. Some rooms are bigger and grander than others, but all 10 have sea views and luxurious furnishings. Guests can avail themselves of a small workout area, sauna, pool, private jetty, bar and restaurant.

WORTH A TRIP

BUDVA БУДВА

Budva is the poster child of Montenegrin tourism. Easily the country's most-visited destination, it attracts hordes of holidaymakers intent on exploring its atmospheric Stari Grad (Old Town), sunning themselves on the bonny beaches of the Budva Riviera and partying until dawn; with scores of buzzy bars and clanging clubs, it's not nicknamed 'the Montenegrin Miami' for nothing.

Though Budva has been settled since the 5th century BC, you'll be hard-pressed finding much – outside of the Old Town – that isn't shiny and relatively new. Development has run rampant here, and not all of it appears to be particularly well thought out. In the height of the season, Budva's sands are blanketed with package holidaymakers from Russia and Ukraine, while the nouveau riche park their multimillion-dollar yachts in the town's guarded marina. That said, Budva has a hectic charm all of its own.

✖ Eating & Drinking

Ladovina MONTENEGRIN, DALMATIAN €€
(☎ 063-422 472; www.ladovina.me; Njegoševa 209; mains €9-20; ☺ 8am-1am) Tucked away in the Škaljari neighbourhood, south of the Old Town, this relaxed cafe-restaurant has tables beneath an open-sided pagoda under a canopy of trees. The menu includes veal, lamb and octopus claypots, and a mix of seafood and meat grills. There's a terrific selection of wine by the glass and craft beer. Save room for the Kotor cream pie.

★ **Letrika** COCKTAIL BAR
(www.facebook.com/artbarletrika; near Trg Bokeljske Mornarice; ☺ 8am-1am) By day, Letrika is a quiet place for a sneaky drink, with a steampunk aesthetic and side-alley location. On summer nights DJs set up outside and the lane gets jammed with hip young things dancing and sipping cocktails.

ⓘ Information

Kotor Health Centre (Dom zdravlja Kotor; ☎ 032-334 533; www.dzkotor.me; Jadranski Put bb) Kotor's main clinic.

Tourist Information Booth (☎ 032-325 951; www.tokotor.me; Jadranski Put; ☺ 8am-8pm Apr-Oct, to 6pm Nov-Mar) Stocks free maps and brochures, and can help with contacts for private accommodation.

ⓘ Getting There & Away

The **bus station** (☎ 032-325 809; www.autobuskastanicakotor.me; Škaljari bb; ☺ 6am-8pm) is to the south of town, just off the road leading to the tunnel. Buses to Tivat (€1.50, 20 minutes), Budva (€4, 40 minutes) and Cetinje (€5, 1½ hours) are at least hourly.

A taxi to Tivat airport should cost around €10.

Ulcinj Улцињ

☎ 030 / POP 10,700

For a taste of Albania without actually crossing the border, head down to buzzy, beautiful Ulcinj. The population is 61% Albanian (68% Muslim), and in summertime it swells with Kosovar holidaymakers for the simple reason that it's a lot nicer than the Albanian seaside towns. The elegant minarets of numerous mosques give Ulcinj (Ulqin in Albanian) a distinctly Eastern feel, as does the lively music echoing out of the kebab stands around Mala Plaža (Small Beach). Ulcinj's ramshackle Old Town looms above the heaving beach and is a fantastic spot for people-watching without being surrounded by people.

⭐**Hostel Pirate** HOSTEL €
(☑068-212 552; www.hostel-pirate.com; Nikole Djakonovića bb; dm/r with shared bathroom from €12/30; [P][❄][📶]) Just because it's Ulcinj's only hostel doesn't mean this jolly Pirate rests on its laurels. This is an immaculate, friendly, comfortable and flat-out-wonderful place that installs fierce love and loyalty in its guests. The hostel organises bike rentals, kayaking and boat trips. It also turns on free barbecue dinners fuelled by shots of equally gratis *rakija*.

⭐**Antigona** SEAFOOD €€€
(☑069-154 117; Stari Grad bb; mains €8-27; ⊙10am-midnight) Antigona's clifftop terrace offers perhaps the most romantic aspect of any eatery in Ulcinj, and handsome waiters in bow ties only add to the impression. The seafood is excellent too – but be sure to check the price and weight of the fish in advance if you wish to avoid any nasty surprises come bill time. It also rents rooms.

ⓘ Information

Tourism Information Centre (☑030-412 333; www.ulcinj.travel; Gjergj Kastrioti Skënderbeu bb; ⊙7am-10pm Jun-Aug, 8am-3pm Mon-Fri Sep-May)

ⓘ Getting There & Away

The **bus station** (☑030-413 225; www.bussta tionulcinj.com; Vëllazërit Frashëri bb; ⊙5am-10pm) is on the northeastern edge of town. Services head to Kotor (€9, 2½ hours, daily) and Budva (€7, two hours, nine daily).

INLAND MONTENEGRO

To truly get to know Montenegro, a visit to the country's mountainous core is a must. Its beating heart is Mt Lovćen, a symbol of national identity.

Lovćen National Park

Directly behind Kotor is **Mt Lovćen** (Ловћен; 1749m), the black mountain that gave Crna Gora (Montenegro) its name; *crna/negro* means 'black', and *gora/monte* means 'mountain' in Montenegrin and Italian respectively. This locale occupies a special place in the hearts of all Montenegrins. For most of its history it represented the entire nation – a rocky island of Slavic resistance in an Ottoman sea. A striking shrine to Montenegro's most famous son, Petar II Petrović Njegoš,

peers down from its heights, with views stretching as far as Albania and Croatia.

The park's main hub is **Ivanova Korita**, near its centre, where there are a few eateries and accommodation providers and, in winter, a beginners' ski slope. **Njeguši**, on the park's northern edge, is famous for being the home village of the Petrović dynasty and for making the country's best *pršut* (smoke-dried ham) and *sir* (cheese). Roadside stalls sell both, along with honey.

⭐**Njegoš Mausoleum** MAUSOLEUM
(Njegošev mauzolej; adult/child €3/1.50; ⊙9am-6pm) Lovćen's star attraction, this magnificent mausoleum (built 1970 to 1974) sits at the top of its second-highest peak, Jezerski Vrh (1657m). Take the 461 steps up to the entry where two granite giantesses guard the tomb of Montenegro's greatest hero. Inside, under a golden mosaic canopy, a 28-tonne Petar II Petrović Njegoš rests in the wings of an eagle, carved from a single block of black granite.

Konoba kod Radonjića MONTENEGRIN €€
(☑041-239 820; Njeguši bb; mains €6-13; ⊙8am-7pm; 📶) With stone walls and meat hanging from the ceiling, this atmospheric family-run tavern serves up delicious roast lamb as well as the local specialities, *pršut* and *sir*. Enjoy dining with olives on a Njeguški plate (€9.50) or in sandwiches (€2.50).

ⓘ Information

National Park Visitor Centre (☑067-344 678; www.nparkovi.me; Ivanova Korita bb; ⊙9am-5pm) As well as providing information on the national park, this centre also rents bikes (per hour/day €2/10), offers accommodation in four-bed bungalows (€30) and takes camping bookings (from €3).

ⓘ Getting There & Away

If you're driving, the park can be approached from either Kotor (20km) or Cetinje (7km); pay the entry fee (€2) at the booths on each approach. Tour buses are the only buses that head into the park. Be aware that this is a *very* twisty-turny and narrow road; the large tour buses that hog it in summer don't make the driving experience any easier. Don't be distracted by the beyond-spectacular views.

Cetinje Цетиње

☑041 / POP 13,900

Rising from a green vale surrounded by rough grey mountains, Cetinje is an odd mix of erstwhile capital and overgrown village,

MONTENEGRO LOVĆEN NATIONAL PARK

WORTH A TRIP

DELVE DEEP & DINE HIGH

Lipa Cave (Lipska pećina; ☑ 067-003 040; www.lipa-cave.me; adult/child €11/7; ⊗ tours 10am, 11.30am, 1pm, 2.30pm and 4pm May-Oct) Cetinje may indeed be littered with old-time reminders of its days as Montenegro's capital city, but just 4km away lies an attraction that makes the town look positively modern. Millions of years old, Lipa Cave is one of the country's largest caves – and the only one open for organised visits – with 2.5km of illuminated passages and halls filled with stalactites, stalagmites and freaky natural pillars. Tours take 60 minutes, including a road-train ride and short walk to the entrance.

Belveder (☑ 067-567 217; mains €6-10; ⊗ 10am-11pm; 🐾) Occupying a scenic eyrie, well signposted on the way to Lipa Cave, this wonderful roadside restaurant serves traditional fare including freshwater fish, grilled squid, and lamb and veal slow-roasted *ispod sača* (under a domed metal lid topped with charcoal), accompanied by the smokiest paprika-laced potatoes you could hope for. The views from the wooden-roofed terrace gaze towards Lake Skadar.

where single-storey cottages and stately mansions share the same street. Several of those mansions – dating from the days when European ambassadors rubbed shoulders with Montenegrin princesses – have become museums or schools for art and music.

The city was founded in 1482 by Ivan Crnojević, the ruler of the Zeta state, after abandoning his previous capital near Lake Skadar, Žabljak Crnojevića, to the Ottomans. A large statue of him stands near the main square. Cetinje was the capital of Montenegro until the country was subsumed into the first Yugoslavia in 1918. After WWII, when Montenegro became a republic within federal Yugoslavia, it passed the baton – somewhat reluctantly – to Titograd (now Podgorica). Today it's billed as the 'royal capital', and is home to the country's most impressive collection of museums.

◉ Sights

Cetinje's collection of four museums (History, King Nikola, Njegoš Biljarda and Ethnographic) and two galleries (Montenegrin Art and its offshoot, Miodrag Dado Đurić) is known collectively as the **National Museum of Montenegro** (www.mnmuseum.org). A joint ticket (adult/child €10/5) will get you into all of them or you can buy individual tickets.

Some of the grandest buildings in town are former international embassies from Cetinje's days as Montenegro's capital.

History Museum   MUSEUM
(Istorijski muzej; ☑ 041-230 310; www.mnmuseum. org; Novice Cerovića 7; adult/child €3/1.50; ⊗ 9am-5pm Apr-Oct, to 4pm Mon-Sat Nov-Mar) Housed in the imposing former parliament building (1910), this fascinating museum follows a timeline from the Stone Age onwards. His-

torical relics include the tunic that Prince Danilo was wearing when he was assassinated, and Prince Nikola's bullet-riddled standard from the battle of Vučji Do. It's also the most even-handed museum in the entire region in its coverage of the break-up of Yugoslavia, honestly examining Montenegrin involvement in the bombardment of Dubrovnik and war crimes in Bosnia.

Montenegrin Art Gallery   GALLERY
(Crnogorska galerija umjetnosti; www.mnmuseum. org; Novice Cerovića 7; adult/child €4/2; ⊗ 9am-5pm Apr-Oct, to 4pm Mon-Sat Nov-Mar) All of Montenegro's great artists are represented here, with the most famous (Milunović, Lubarda, Đurić etc) having their own separate spaces. There's a small collection of icons, the most important being the precious 9th-century *Our Lady of Philermos*, traditionally believed to have been painted by St Luke himself. It's spectacularly presented in its own blue-lit 'chapel', but the Madonna's darkened face is only just visible behind its spectacular golden casing mounted with diamonds, rubies and sapphires.

Miodrag Dado Đurić Gallery   GALLERY
(Galerija; Balšića Pazar; ⊗ 10am-2pm & 5-9pm Tue-Sun) **FREE** This edgy establishment is an offshoot of the Montenegrin Art Gallery, and is dedicated to one of Montenegro's most important artists, who died in 2010. Housed in a striking five-storey concrete and glass building, it promotes and displays 20th-century and contemporary Montenegrin art.

King Nikola Museum   PALACE
(Muzej kralja Nikole; www.mnmuseum.org; Dvorski Trg; adult/child €5/2.50; ⊗ 9am-5pm Apr-Oct, to 4pm Mon-Sat Nov-Mar) Entry to this maroon-

and-white palace (1871), home to the last sovereign of Montenegro, is by guided tour (you may need to wait for a group to form). Although looted during WWII, more than enough plush furnishings, stern portraits and taxidermal animals remain to capture the spirit of the court.

🛏 Sleeping & Eating

⭐ La Vecchia Casa   GUESTHOUSE €

(☑ 067-629 660; www.lavecchiacasa.com; Vojvode Batrica 6; s/d/apt €20/34/38; 🅿 ❋ 🛜) With its gorgeous rear garden and pervading sense of tranquillity, this period house captures the essence of old Cetinje. The clean, antique-strewn rooms retain a sense of the home's history, and there's a guest kitchen (stocked with do-it-yourself breakfast supplies) and a laundry.

Kole   MONTENEGRIN €€

(☑ 069-606 660; www.restaurantkole.me; Bul Crnogorskih junaka 12; mains €4-16; ⏱7am-midnight) They serve omelettes and pasta at this popular restaurant, but it's worth delving into artery-clogging local specialities such as *Njeguški ražanj* (smoky spit-roasted meat stuffed with prosciutto and cheese) or *popeci na cetinjski način* ('Cetinje-style' veal schnitzel, similarly stuffed, rolled into logs, breaded and deep-fried). Serves are massive; try one between two, with a side salad.

ℹ Information

Accident & Emergency Clinic (Hitna pomoć; ☑ 041-233 002; Vuka Mićunovića 2)

Tourist Information (☑ 041-230 250; www.cetinje.travel; Novice Cerovića bb; ⏱8am-6pm Mar-Oct, to 4pm Nov-Feb) Helpful office which also rents bikes (per half-/full day €2/3). Short sightseeing tours start from here, taking to Cetinje's streets in golf buggies (30/45 minutes €2/3).

ℹ Getting There & Away

➠ Cetinje is just off the main Budva–Podgorica highway and can also be reached by a glorious back road from Kotor via Lovćen National Park.

➠ The **bus station** (☑ 041-241 744; Trg Golootočkih Žrtava; ⏱6am-10pm) has regular services from Tivat (€5, 1¼ hours), Budva (€4, 40 minutes) and Kotor (€5, 1½ hours).

Durmitor National Park

The impossibly rugged and dramatic Durmitor (Дурмитор) is one of Montenegro's – and Mother Nature's – showpieces. Carved out by glaciers and underground streams, Durmitor stuns with dizzying canyons, glittering glacial lakes and nearly 50 limestone peaks soaring to over 2000m; the highest, **Bobotov Kuk**, hits 2523m. From December to March, Durmitor is a major ski resort, while in summer it's popular for hiking, rafting and other active pursuits.

The national park covers the Durmitor mountain range and a narrow branch heading east along the Tara River towards Mojkovac. West of the park, the mighty Tara marks the border with Bosnia and joins the Piva River near Šćepan Polje.

Durmitor is home to 163 bird species, about 50 types of mammals and purportedly the greatest variety of butterflies in Europe. It's very unlikely you'll spot bears and wolves, which is either a good or bad thing depending on your perspective.

👁 Sights

⭐ Black Lake   LAKE

(Crno jezero) Eighteen glittering glacial lakes known as *gorske oči* (mountain eyes) dot the Durmitor range. The spectacular Black Lake, a pleasant 3km walk from Žabljak, is the largest of them and the most visited part of the national park. The rounded mass of Međed (the Bear; 2287m) rears up behind it, casting an inky shadow into the pine-walled waters. An easy 3.6km walking track circles the lake.

⭐ Tara Canyon   CANYON

Slicing through the mountains at the northern edge of the national park, the Tara River forms a canyon that is 1300m deep at its

---

DON'T MISS

OSTROG MONASTERY

Resting improbably – miraculously? – in a cliff face 900m above the Zeta valley, the gleaming white **Ostrog Monastery** (Manastir Ostrog; www.manastirostrog.com) is the most important site in Montenegro for Orthodox Christians, attracting up to a million visitors annually. Even with its numerous pilgrims, tourists and souvenir stands, it's a strangely affecting place. A **guesthouse** (☑ 068-080 133; office@mostrog.me; dm €5) near the Lower Monastery offers tidy single-sex dorm rooms, while in summer sleeping mats are provided for free to pilgrims in front of the Upper Monastery.

peak (the Grand Canyon plummets a mere 200m deeper). The best views are from the water, and rafting (p286) along the river is one of the country's most popular tourist activities. If you'd rather admire the canyon from afar, head to the top of **Mt Ćurevac** (1625m) – although even this view is restricted by the canyon walls.

Tara Bridge
BRIDGE

(Đurđevića Tara) The elegant spans of the 150m-high Tara Bridge were completed just as WWII was starting. At the time it was the largest concrete arched vehicular bridge in Europe. Its 365m length is carried on five sweeping arches, the largest of which is 116m wide.

Dobrilovina Monastery
CHRISTIAN MONASTERY

Near the eastern boundary of the national park, 28km from Mojkovac, this monastery has an idyllic setting in lush fields hemmed in by the mountains and the Tara River. If you knock at the accommodation wing, a black-robed nun will unlock the church, but only if she's satisfied that you're appropriately attired. The frescoes that remain inside the church, dedicated to St George (Sv Đorđe), are faded but very beautiful.

Stećci Sites
CEMETERY

These mysterious carved stone tomb monuments – dating from between the 12th and 16th centuries – can be found across northern Montenegro and neighbouring Bosnia. There are two extremely significant *stećci* sites in Durmitor National Park (both were added to Unesco's World Heritage list in 2016): the Bare Žugića necropolis, with 300 *stećci*, and Grčko groblje (Greek graveyard) with 49. Many of the stones at both sites are intricately decorated.

🏃 Activities

Hiking

Durmitor is one of the best-marked mountain ranges in Europe, with 25 marked trails making up a total of 150km. Some suggest it's a little *too* well labelled, encouraging novices to wander around seriously high-altitude paths that are prone to fog and summer thunderstorms. Ask the staff at the National Park Visitors Centre (p288) about tracks that suit your level of experience and fitness.

One rewarding route is the hike to the two **Škrčka Lakes** (Škrčka jezera), in the centre of a tectonic valley, where you can enjoy magnificent scenery and stay overnight in a mountain hut (June to September only). Another popular hike is from the Black Lake to the **ice cave** *(ledina pećina)* – home in cooler months to stalactite- and stalagmite-like shapes made of ice – on Obla Glava. It's a six- to seven-hour return hike.

If you're considering an assault on **Bobotov Kuk** or a serious winter expedition, you're best to arrange a local guide.

In any case, check the weather forecast before you set out, stick to the tracks, and prepare for rain and sudden drops in temperature. A compass could be a lifesaver. *Durmitor and the Tara Canyon* by Branislav Cerović (€12 from the visitors centre) is a great resource for mountaineers and serious hikers. The **Mountaineering Association of Montenegro** (www.pscg.me) has contacts and info on the peaks and paths of Durmitor.

Via Dinarica Hiking Trail
HIKING

(www.viadinarica.com) The Montenegrin part of this 1930km 'megatrail' – which traverses Slovenia, Croatia, Bosnia, Montenegro and Albania – connects Durmitor with Bosnia's Sutjeska National Park. See the website for details, or contact **Black Mountain** (☑067-076 676; www.montenegroholiday.com) 📞 to organise hiking tours.

Rafting

A rafting expedition along the Tara is the best way to revel in glorious river scenery that's impossible to catch from land. Trips are suitable for everyone from the white-water novice to experienced foam-hounds. Though it's not the world's most white-knuckled ride, there are a few rapids; if you're after speed, visit in April and May, when the last of the melting snow revs up the flow. Various operators run trips between April and October.

The 82km section that is raftable starts from Splavište, south of the Tara Bridge, and ends at Šćepan Polje on the Bosnian border. The classic two-day trip heads through the deepest part of the canyon on the first day, stopping overnight at Radovan Luka. **Summit Travel Agency** (☑068-535 535; www.summit.co.me; Njegoševa 12, Žabljak; half-/1-/2-day rafting trips €45/110/200) offers a range of rafting trips on this route, with transfers from Žabljak.

Most of the day tours from the coast traverse only the last 18km from Brstanovica – this is outside the national park and hence avoids hefty fees. You'll miss out on the canyon's depths, but it's still a beautiful stretch, including most of the rapids. The buses follow a spectacular road along the Piva River, giving you a double dose of canyon action.

It's important to use a reputable operator; in 2010 two people died in one day on a trip with inexperienced guides. At a minimum make sure you're given a helmet and life jacket – wear them and do them up. Some noteworthy operators are **Camp Grab** (☑ 069-101 002; www.tara-grab.com; half-day incl lunch €44, 3-day all-inclusive rafting trips from €200), **Tara Tour** (☑ 069-086 106; www.taratour.com; Šćepan Polje bb) and **Waterfall Rafting Centre** (☑ 069-310 848; www.raftingmontenegro.com). Many of the rafting groups also offer other activities, including horse riding, canyoning and jeep safaris. If you've got your own wheels you can save a few bucks and avoid a lengthy coach tour by heading directly to Šćepan Polje and hooking up with the rafting tours there.

Skiing

With 120 days of snow cover, Durmitor offers the most reliable – and cheapest – skiing in Montenegro.

Savin Kuk Ski Centar (☑ 052-363 036; www.tcdurmitor.me; ski passes day/week €12/60) and **Javorovača Ski Centar** (☑ 067-800 971; www.javorovaca.me; adult/child day passes €8/5, week passes €48/30) both rent out equipment and offer lessons. See www.skiresortmontenegro.com (in Montenegrin) for more information on all of Montenegro's ski centres.

Free-riding snowboarders and skiers should check out www.riders.me for off-piste adventure ideas.

Adventure Sports

Red Rock Zipline   ADVENTURE SPORTS
(☑ 069-440 290; www.redrockzipline.com; Đurđevića Tara; adult €10; ☉ 10am-8pm Apr-Oct) Feel the wind in your hair (and the collywobbles in your stomach) with a 50km per hour flight across the Tara Canyon. The 350m-long zipline is strung alongside the magnificent Tara Bridge with a starting point 170m above the river. It's scary as hell, but fret not: it's run by an extremely professional outfit. Look for the red flags.

Crno Jezero

Avanturistički Park   ADVENTURE SPORTS
(☑ 069-214 110; www.avanturistickipark.me; Black Lake; adult/child €9/8; ☉ 10am-7pm Jul & Aug, 10am-6pm Sat & Sun Jun & Sep) Want to take flight? Two ziplines have been set up by the shores of Black Lake, offering criminal amounts of fun. The shorter one zips across the forest from a height of 14m, while the longer one will hurtle you for 350m clear across the lake. There are also obstacle courses and plenty of activities set up for kids, including a zipline with toboggan.

Nevidio Canyon   CANYONING
Just south of the national park, near Šavnik, is the remarkable 2.7km-long Nevidio Canyon. Cut by the Komarnica River, at points it is only metres wide, hence the name (*nevidio* means 'invisible'). It's extremely beautiful but equally dangerous. Canyoning expeditions generally take about three to four hours and participants should be able to swim and have a high level of fitness.

July and August are the safest months to explore, and then only in the company of professional guides. **Montenegro Canyoning** (☑ 069-565 311; www.montenegro-canyoning.com; trips without/with lunch per person €90/100) is a highly recommended group that focuses solely on expeditions to Nevidio. Otherwise, **Anitra/Grab** (www.tara-grab.com) organises expeditions out of Nikšić (price on application), and Summit Travel Agency and **Durmitor Adventure** (☑ 069-629 516; www.durmitoradventure.com) do so out of Žabljak (€100 per person including lunch, minimum two people).

🛏 Sleeping & Eating

★**Hikers Den**   HOSTEL €
(☑ 067-854 433; www.hostelzabljak.com; Božidara Žugića bb, Žabljak; dm/r from €13/35; ☉ Apr-Oct; ☏) Split between three neighbouring houses, this laid-back and sociable place is by far the best hostel in the north. If you're keen on rafting, canyoning or a jeep safari, the charming English-speaking hosts will happily make the arrangements. They also offer a four-hour 'Durmitor in a day' minivan tour (€20).

★**Eko-Oaza Tear of Europe**   CAMPGROUND €
(Eko-Oaza suza Evrope; ☑ 069-444 590; www.ekooaza.me; Gornja Dobrilovina; campsites per 1/2/3 people €7.50/11/15, campervans €13-15, cabins €50, without bathroom €20; ☉ Apr-Oct; ☏) Consisting of a handful of comfortable wooden cottages with bathrooms (each sleeping five people), small cabins without bathrooms, well-equipped apartments and a fine stretch of lawn above the river, this magical, family-run 'eco oasis' offers a genuine experience of Montenegrin hospitality. Home-cooked meals are provided on request, and rafting,

kayaking, canyoning and jeep safaris can be arranged. Truly memorable.

Hotel Soa HOTEL €€€
(☑ 052-360 110; www.hotelsoa.com; Njegoševa bb, Žabljak; s/ste/apt from €67/105/124; P 🗬) The rooms at this snazzy, modern hotel are kitted out with monsoon shower heads, robes and slippers. There's also a playground, bikes for hire and one of the country's best restaurants (mains €5 to €17); try the lamb baked in cream, served with *ajvar* (roasted-red-capsicum dip).

O'ro MONTENEGRIN €€
(Njegoševa bb, Žabljak; mains €8-11; ⊙ 7am-1am; 🗬) The focus is firmly on local specialities at this appealing wood-and-glass restaurant. In summer, grab a seat on the large terrace and tuck into a *Durmitorska večera* (Durmitor dinner) platter featuring air-dried beef, sausages, local cheese, *ajvar* and crispy roast potatoes. They also serve lamb, veal, trout and *kačamak* (polenta, cheese and potato porridge).

❶ Orientation

All roads (and ski runs and bumpy trails) lead to **Žabljak**, regional capital and – at 1450m – one of the highest towns in the Balkans. Quaintly ramshackle – though slowly smartening up – it's the gateway to Durmitor's mountain adventures. You'll find restaurants, hotels and a supermarket gathered around the car park that masquerades as Žabljak's main square.

❶ Information

The road to the Black Lake is blocked off just past the National Park Visitors Centre and an entry fee is charged (per person per one/three/seven days €3/6/12). Drivers will need to park outside the gates (€2) and walk the remaining 500m to the lake. Keep hold of your ticket, in case you bump into a ranger.

National Park Visitors Centre (☑ 052-360 228; www.nparkovi.me; Njegoševa bb, Žabljak; ⊙ 7am-5pm Mon-Fri, 10am-5pm Sat & Sun Jan & Jun–mid-Sep, 7am-3pm Mon-Fri mid-Sep–Dec & Feb-May) On the road to the Black Lake, this centre includes a wonderful micromuseum focusing on the park's flora and fauna. The knowledgeable staff answer queries and sell local craft, maps, hiking guides and fishing permits (€20). They also rent bikes (per hour/day €3/8), assist with accommodation and can organise local guides (€15 to €100, depending on the trail).

Žabljak Tourist Office (☑ 052-361 802; www.tozabljak.com; Trg Durmitorskih ratnika, Žabljak; ⊙ 7am-10pm mid-Jun–Sep, 8am-8pm

Oct–mid-Jun) Operates in a wooden hut in Žabljak's main square/car park.

The website **www.durmitor.rs** has heaps of information on activities and accommodation in the region, plus the latest news and events listings.

❶ Getting There & Away

All of the approaches to Durmitor are spectacular. The most reliable road to Žabljak follows the Tara River west from Mojkovac. In summer this 70km drive takes about 90 minutes. If you're coming from Podgorica, the quickest way is through Nikšić and Šavnik. The main highway north from Nikšić follows the dramatic Piva Canyon to Šćepan Polje. There's a wonderful back road through the mountains leaving the highway near Plužine, but it's impassable as soon as the snows fall.

The bus station is at the southern edge of Žabljak, on the Šavnik road. Buses head to Podgorica (€8, 2½ hours, eight daily), Belgrade (€21, nine hours, daily) and, in summer, to the Bay of Kotor.

SURVIVAL GUIDE

❶ Directory A–Z

ACCOMMODATION

Montenegro offers a great variety of accommodation. Booking ahead in the summer – especially on the coast – is essential.

Hotels Range from slick seaside offerings to off-the-beaten-track Yugoslav-style digs. Prices range accordingly.

Hostels Popping up in popular destinations but thin on the ground elsewhere.

Campgrounds Usually offer million-dollar views for penny-pinching prices. Facilities vary wildly.

Private accommodation Almost every town and village has private rooms *(sobe)* and/or apartments *(apartmani)* for rent.

Eco villages Wooden cabins in the countryside.

MONEY

ATMs widely available. Credit cards are accepted in larger hotels but aren't widely accepted elsewhere.

OPENING HOURS

Montenegrins have a flexible approach to opening times. Even if hours are posted on the door of an establishment, don't be surprised if they're not heeded. Many tourist-orientated businesses close between November and March.

Banks 8am to 5pm Monday to Friday, 8am to noon Saturday.

Post offices 7am to 8pm Monday to Friday, sometimes Saturday. In smaller towns they may close midafternoon, or close at noon and reopen at 5pm.

Restaurants, cafes & bars 8am to midnight. If the joint is jumping, cafe-bars may stay open until 2am or 3am.

Shops 9am to 8pm. Sometimes they'll close for a few hours in the late afternoon.

PUBLIC HOLIDAYS

New Year's Day 1 and 2 January
Orthodox Christmas 6, 7 and 8 January
Orthodox Good Friday & Easter Monday date varies, usually April/May
Labour Day 1 and 2 May
Independence Day 21 and 22 May
Statehood Day 13 and 14 July

TELEPHONE

➡ The international access prefix is 00, or + from a mobile phone.

➡ The country code is 382.

➡ Press the *i* button on public phones for dialling commands in English.

➡ Mobile numbers start with 06.

➡ The prefix 80 indicates a toll-free number.

➡ You can make phone calls at most larger post offices. Phone boxes are otherwise few and far between.

ⓘ Getting There & Away

ENTERING THE COUNTRY

Entering Montenegro doesn't pose any particular bureaucratic challenges. In fact, the country's dead keen to shuffle tourists in. Unfortunately, Croatia seems less happy to let them go, if the long waits at their side of the Adriatic highway checkpoint are any indication; if you need to be somewhere at a certain time, it pays to allow an hour. The main crossing from Serbia at Dobrakovo can also be slow at peak times.

AIR

➡ **Montenegro Airlines** (www.montenegroair lines.com) is the national carrier, running a small fleet of 116-seater planes.

➡ Montenegro's largest and most modern airport is immediately south of the capital, **Podgorica** (TGD; ☑ 020-444 244; www.monte negroairports.com).

➡ The second international airport, at **Tivat** (TIV; ☑ 032-670 930; www.montenegroair

ports.com; Jadranski Put bb), is well positioned for holidaymakers heading to the Bay of Kotor or Budva.

➡ Montenegro's de facto third airport is actually in neighbouring Croatia. Dubrovnik Airport (p141) is only 17km from the border and the closest airport to Herceg Novi.

LAND

Montenegro may be a wee slip of a thing but it borders five other states: Croatia, Bosnia and Hercegovina (BiH), Serbia, Kosovo and Albania. You can easily enter Montenegro by land from any of its neighbours.

Bus

There's a well-developed bus network linking Montenegro with the major cities of the former Yugoslavia and onward to Western Europe and Turkey. At the border, guards will often enter the bus and collect passports, checking the photos as they go. Once they're happy with them they return them to the bus conductor, who will return them as the driver speeds off.

Useful websites include www.busticket4.me, www.eurolines.com, www.getbybus.com and www.vollo.net.

Train

Montenegro's main train line starts at Bar and heads north through Podgorica and into Serbia. At least two trains head between Bar and Belgrade daily (€21, 11¾ hours). You'll find timetables on the website of **Montenegro Railways** (www.zcg-prevoz.me).

SEA

Montenegro Lines (www.montenegrolines. com) has boats from Bar to Bari (Italy), at least weekly from May to November (deck ticket €44 to €48, cabin €63 to €210, 11 hours); and from Bar to Ancona (Italy), at least weekly from July to August (deck €60, cabin €80 to €230, 16 hours). Cars cost €56 to €90.

ⓘ Getting Around

Bus Buses link all major towns and are affordable, reliable and reasonably comfortable. Up-to-date timetable information and online booking can be found on www.busticket4.me.

Car While you can get to many places by bus, hiring a car will give you freedom to explore some of Montenegro's scenic back roads. Some of these are extremely narrow and cling to the sides of canyons, so they may not suit the inexperienced or faint-hearted.

North Macedonia

✔ 389 / POP 2.08 MILLION

Best Places to Eat

➡ Letna Bavča Kaneo (p304)

➡ Hotel Tutto Restaurant (p299)

➡ Vila Raskrsnica (p306)

➡ Nadžak (p296)

➡ Kebapčilnica Destan (p296)

Best Places to Stay

➡ Vila Raskrsnica (p306)

➡ Villa Dihovo (p306)

➡ Sunny Lake Hostel (p303)

➡ Villa Jovan (p303)

➡ Urban Hostel & Apartments (p295)

Why Go?

Part Balkan, part Mediterranean and rich in Greek, Roman and Ottoman heritage, North Macedonia has a fascinating past and a complex national identity.

Glittering Lake Ohrid and its historic town have etched out a place for North Macedonia on the tourist map, but there is a wealth of natural beauty in this small country.

Dramatic mountains have blissfully quiet walking trails, lakes and riding opportunities. The national parks of Mavrovo, Galičica and Pelister are cultivating some excellent cultural and culinary tourism initiatives; if you want to get off the beaten track in Europe – this is the place.

Skopje's centre has suffered from a building spree of grotesque faux-neoclassical monuments, buildings and fountains, funded by the previous government. Luckily, its Ottoman old town and buzzing modern areas are untouched, and remain charming and authentic.

When to Go
Skopje

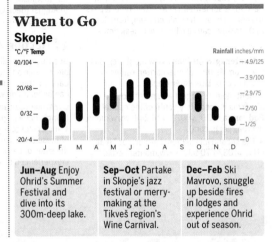

Jun–Aug Enjoy Ohrid's Summer Festival and dive into its 300m-deep lake.	Sep–Oct Partake in Skopje's jazz festival or merry-making at the Tikveš region's Wine Carnival.	Dec–Feb Ski Mavrovo, snuggle up beside fires in lodges and experience Ohrid out of season.

Entering the Country

Skopje and Ohrid are well connected to other Balkan tourist hubs as well as some international destinations further afield. Air connections have increased thanks to the growing number of budget airlines flying here. Buses are generally more frequent and cover a broader range of destinations than trains (they're also just as fast).

Some travellers have reported being denied entry to Serbia from North Macedonia if they have a stamp from Kosovo in their passport.

ITINERARIES

One Week

Spend a couple of days in Skopje (p292) amid the mind-boggling faux neoclassical architecture and in the Čaršija (p293) with its historic mosques, churches, museums and Ottoman castle. Visit the nearby Canyon Matka (p297) for kayaking and swimming in the cool waters.

Next head to North Macedonia's most charming and historic town, Ohrid (p301), for swimming in the spectacular lake. Stay in a village guesthouse on the edge of Pelister National Park (p305), with hiking and home cooking. Cross Lake Prespa for the pelican-inhabited, ruin-strewn island of Golem Grad (p301).

Two Weeks

Linger in Pelister National Park (p305) in order to stop in Bitola (p306), loved for its buzz, elegance and ancient Heraclea Lyncestis (p306) ruins.

Next visit Mavrovo National Park (p298) and stay in historic Janče (p299) and Galičnik (p299) villages for superb cuisine and horse riding. Visit the impressive Sveti Jovan Bigorski Monastery (p298).

Make a pit stop in the Tikveš Wine Region (p304) for tastings and a tour.

Essential Food & Drink

Ajvar Sweet red-capsicum dip; accompanies meats and cheeses.

Lukanci Homemade chorizo-like pork sausages, laced with paprika.

Pita A pie made of a coil of flaky pastry stuffed with local cheese and spinach or leek.

Rakija Grape-based fruit brandy.

Šopska salata Tomatoes, onions and cucumbers topped with grated *sirenje* (white cheese).

Tavče gravče Baked beans cooked with spices, onions and herbs, and served in earthenware.

Vranec & Temjanika North Macedonia's favourite red/white wine varietals.

AT A GLANCE

Area 25,713 sq km

Capital Skopje

Country Code ☑ 389

Currency North Macedonian denar (MKD)

Emergency Ambulance ☑ 194, Police ☑ 192

Language Macedonian, Albanian

Time Eastern European Time (GMT/UTC plus two hours)

Visas None for EU, US, Australian, Canadian or New Zealand citizens for stays of up to three months.

Sleeping Price Ranges

The following price ranges are based on a standard double with bathroom.

€ less than 3000MKD/€50

€€ 3000MKD/€50–5000MKD/€80

€€€ more than 5000MKD/€80

Eating Price Ranges

The following ranges refer to the average price of a main course.

€ less than 200MKD

€€ 200MKD–350MKD

€€€ more than 350MKD

Resources

Balkan Insight (www.balkaninsight.com)

Exploring Macedonia (www.exploringmacedonia.com)

North Macedonia Highlights

1 Ohrid's Old Town
(p301) Exploring Ohrid's distinctive historic quarter, right to the end of the boardwalk and pebble beach, and up to the clifftop Church of Sveti Jovan at Kaneo.

2 Skopje (p292) Diving into the historic Čaršija (Old Ottoman Bazaar) of North Macedonia's friendly capital, seeking out its modernist architecture and marvelling

at the supersized riverside monuments.

3 Pelister National Park
(p305) Eating your fill at food-focused village tourism initiatives in this underrated national park, then walking it off the next day.

4 Golem Grad (p301) Chasing ghosts, pelicans and tortoises around this eerie Lake Prespa island, fecund with overgrown ruins.

5 Popova Kula (p304) Sipping your way through North Macedonia's premier wine region, Tikveš, using this wonderful winery hotel as your base.

6 Sveti Jovan Bigorski Monastery (p298) Taking tea with monks at this majestic complex teetering in the hills of Mavrovo National Park.

SKOPJE   СКОПЈE

♪ 02 / POP 506.930

Skopje has plenty of charm. Its Ottoman- and Byzantine-era sights are focused around the city's delightful Čaršija, bordered by the 15th-century Kameni Most (Stone Bridge)

and Tvrdina Kale Fortress – Skopje's guardian since the 5th century. Don't miss the excellent eating and drinking scene in Debar Maalo, a lovely tree-lined neighbourhood.

For most of its existence, Skopje has been a modest Balkan city known for its rich local life, but the last decade has seen its centre transformed into a bizarre set design for an ancient civilisation. Towering warrior statues, gleaming, enormous neoclassical buildings, marble-clad museums, hypnotic megafountains...and plenty of lions.

This is the result of a controversial, nationalistic project called 'Skopje 2014' implemented by ex–Prime Minister Nikola Gruevski. Some of the buildings along the riverbank are already suffering flooding and have unsteady foundations.

◉ Sights

★ Čaršija
AREA

(Old Ottoman Bazaar) Čaršija is Skopje's hillside Ottoman old town, evoking the city's past with its winding lanes filled with teahouses, mosques, craftspeople's shops, and even good nightlife. It also boasts Skopje's best historic structures and a handful of museums, and is the first place any visitor should head. Čaršija runs from the Stone Bridge to the **Bit Pazar** (⊙8am-3pm), a big vegetable and household goods market. Expect to get pleasantly lost in its maze of narrow streets.

★ National Gallery of Macedonia
GALLERY

(Daut Paša Amam; www.nationalgallery.mk; Kruševska 1a; adult/student & child 50/20MKD; ⊙10am-6pm Tue-Sun Oct-Mar, to 9pm Apr-Sep) The Daut Paša Amam (1473) were once the largest Turkish baths outside of İstanbul and they make a magical setting for the permanent collection of Skopje's national art gallery, just by the entrance to the Čaršija. The seven restored rooms house mainly modern art and sculpture from North Macedonia, brought to life by the sun piercing through the small star-shaped holes in the domed ceilings. Two other National Gallery sites – **Čifte Amam** (Bitpazarska; adult/student & child 50/20MKD; ⊙10am-6pm Tue-Sun Oct-Mar, to 9pm Apr-Sep) and **Mala Stanica** (www.nationalgallery.mk; Jordan Mijalkov 18; adult/student & child 50/20MKD; ⊙8am-6pm Tue-Sun Oct-Mar, to 9pm Apr-Sep) – house rotating, temporary exhibitions.

★ Tvrdina Kale Fortress
FORTRESS

(Samoilova; ⊙7am-7pm) FREE Dominating the skyline of Skopje, this *Game of Thrones*–worthy, 6th-century AD Byzantine (and later, Ottoman) fortress is an easy walk up from the Čaršija and its ramparts offer great views over the city and river. Inside the ruins, two mini museums were being built at the time of writing to house various archaeological finds from Neolithic to Ottoman times. This will be a welcome addition to the site, as there are no information boards at the fortress at present.

Archaeological Museum of Macedonia
MUSEUM

(www.amm.org.mk; bul Goce Delčev; adult/student & child 300/150MKD; ⊙10am-6pm Tue-Sun) This supersized pile of Italianate-styled marble has been a giant receptacle for Skopje's recent splurge on government-led monuments to boost national pride. Inside, there are three floors displaying the cream of Macedonian archaeological excavations beneath the dazzle of hundreds of lights. Highlights include Byzantine treasures; sophisticated 3D reconstructions of early Macedonian faces from skulls; a pint-sized replica of an early Christian basilica showing the life phases of mosaic conservation; and a Phoenician royal necropolis.

Ploštad Makedonija
SQUARE

(Macedonia Sq) This gigantic square is the centrepiece of Skopje's audacious nation-building-through-architecture project and it has massive statues dedicated to national heroes, as well as an incongruous Triumphal Arch in the southeast corner. The towering, central warrior on a horse – Alexander the Great – is bedecked by fountains that are illuminated at night. Home to a number of cafes and hotels, it's a popular stomping ground for locals as well as tourists, particularly when the sun goes down.

Museum of Contemporary Art
MUSEUM

(NIMoCA; ☑02 311 7734; https://msu.mk; Samoilova 17; 300MKD, free 1st Fri of month; ⊙9am-5pm Tue-Sat, to 1pm Sun) Housed in a stunning modernist building with floor-to-ceiling windows and perched atop a hill with wonderful city views, this museum was built in the aftermath of Skopje's devastating 1963 earthquake. Artists and collections around the world donated works to form a collection that includes Picasso, Léger, Hockney, Meret Oppenheim and Bridget Riley. Unfortunately, its collection isn't always on display – you may come here and find its exhibitions extraordinary or mundane, depending on what's been put on display.

Sveti Spas Church
CHURCH

(Church of the Holy Saviour; Makarije Frčkoski 8; adult/student 120/50MKD; ⊙9am-5pm Tue-Fri, to 3pm Sat & Sun) Partially submerged 2m underground (the Ottomans banned churches from being taller than mosques), this church dates from the 14th century and is the most historically important in Skopje. Its sunken design means it doesn't look like a church, so you might not

Skopje

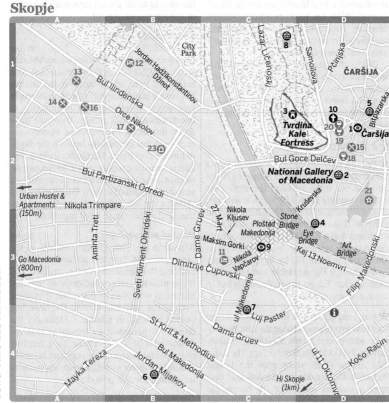

Skopje

◎ Top Sights

◎ Sights

✪ Activities, Courses & Tours

⌂ Sleeping

✖ Eating

◆ Drinking & Nightlife

✿ Entertainment

⌂ Shopping

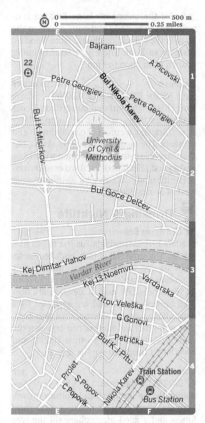

notice it at first: it's opposite the Old Town Brewery – look for the pretty bell tower that watches over it, built into its outer courtyard wall. Inside the church an elaborate carved iconostasis shines out of the dark.

🏃 Activities

Bicycle Tours & Guides Macedonia CYCLING
(📞 078 982 981; www.bicycle.mk; per day from 800MKD) Skopje's long riverside walkway is a magnet for cyclists, especially at dusk when joggers, strollers, kids playing football and anglers all come out too. Rent bikes by the day from this outfit; it'll even drop the bike (including helmet, lights and high-vis vest) at your hotel. Guided Skopje day tours and North Macedonia–wide adventures are also offered.

👉 Tours

Skopje Walks WALKING
(www.skopjewalks.com; ul Makedonija; donations welcome; ⊙10am) **FREE** These excellent free tours run for three hours and cover every important corner of Skopje's inner city. Highly recommended for insights into the city, its history and residents from local guides who are passionate about Skopje. Tours meet outside the **Memorial House of Mother Teresa** (ul Makedonija 9) – look out for the blue ID badge – at 10am daily.

Go Macedonia TOURS
(📞 02 306 4647; www.gomacedonia.com; ul Ankarska 29a) This company focuses on sustainable tourism, and can arrange hiking, cycling, caving and winery tours across the country. It also runs a Galičnik Wedding (p299) trip each year, including transport, guided activities, local accommodation and a monastery tour at Sveti Jovan Bigorski (p298).

🎊 Festivals & Events

Skopje Jazz Festival MUSIC
(📞 02 313 1090; www.skopjejazzfest.com.mk; ⊙Oct) The festival features artists from across the globe, always including a world-renowned player or group (Chick Corea, McCoy Tyner, Herbie Hancock and Tito Puente are some past headliners).

🛏 Sleeping

⭐**Urban Hostel & Apartments** HOSTEL €
(📞 02 614 2785; www.urbanhostel.com.mk; Adolf Ciborovski 22; dm/s/d €10/24/35, apt €35-70; ❄🞮) In a converted residential house with a sociable front garden for summer lounging, Urban is an excellent budget option on the outskirts of the leafy Debar Maalo neighbourhood, a 15-minute walk west of central Skopje. Decor is eclectic, with a fireplace for cosy winter nights and even a piano. The hostel's modern apartments, on the same road, are great value.

Lounge Hostel HOSTEL €
(📞 076 547 165; www.loungehostel.mk; 1st fl, Naum Naumovski Borče 80; dm €9-10, s/d €25/30; ❄🞮🞮) A lovely large common area, orthopaedic mattresses and bright, breezy balconies attached to every room are some of the highlights of this sociable, retro-styled hostel with a view over City Park. Staff are a little less clued-up here than at some other hostels, but will bend over backwards to help make guests' lives easier.

Hi Skopje HOSTEL €
(📞 02 609 1242; www.hihostelskopje.com; Crniche 15; dm/d from €9/20) In a leafy, affluent suburb in the cool shade of Mt Vodno, this hostel's greatest assets are its garden and

sprawling layout, which makes it feel more spacious than many others in town. It's a 15-minute walk to Ploštad Makedonija from here (and a 120MKD taxi ride from the bus and train stations), but the trade-off is a relaxing atmosphere.

★**Hotel Solun** HOTEL €€€
(☑02 323 2512, 071 238 599; www.hotelsolun.com; Nikola Vapčarov 10; s/d from €83/103; 🅿 @ 🛜 🌊) Accessed through an alley just off the main square, this is a stylish, beautifully designed place, with modern and elegantly decorated rooms, and an excellent art collection on the walls. A spa and an indoor pool beckon downstairs. Hotel Solun sits in a different stratosphere to most of North Macedonia's faded 'high-end' hotels.

✖ Eating

★**Nadžak** MACEDONIAN €
(☑02 312 8113; Orce Nikolov 105; mains from 100MKD; ⊙8am-midnight; 🛜) It doesn't look like much, but the food at Nadžak is excellent, cheap and always fresh. All sorts of Macedonian specialities are on the menu, from *skara* (grilled meat) to liver to peppers and *tavče gravče* (oven-baked beans in tomato sauce). Everything tastes great – order several dishes and share. Seating is inside and on a covered terrace, in the heart of Debar Maalo.

★**Kebapčilnica Destan** KEBAB €
(ul 104 6; mains 180MKD; ⊙8am-11pm) Skopje's best beef kebabs, accompanied by seasoned grilled bread, peppers and a little raw onion, are served at this classic Čaršija place. The terrace is often full. Ten stubby kebabs constitute a serious meat feast (180MKD), or you can ask for a half portion (120MKD). Pair the kebabs with *ajvar* (red-pepper dip) and a cabbage salad.

Barik MACEDONIAN €
(☑070 360 601; Mihail Cokov 8; mains from 100MKD; ⊙8am-midnight) An excellent little taverna in Debar Maalo, with a great range of Macedonian specialities – try the veal liver with onion with some red wine or the baked cheese. Tables are scattered across the pavement and the whole place has a Mediterranean feel. It's very popular with the locals.

Sushico ASIAN €€
(☑02 321 7874; www.sushico.com.mk; Aminta Treti 29; mains from 350MKD; ⊙11am-11.30pm; 🛜 🅿) If you fancy a change of palate, this international chain serves a good range of pan-Asian specialities in an elegant setting (that

includes the obligatory large Buddha statues). Try the avocado and quinoa rolls or the staple crispy duck, or choose from noodles, sushi or sashimi. There is a Sunday buffet brunch from noon to 4pm.

Kaj Pero MACEDONIAN €€
(Orce Nikolov 109; mains 120-800MKD; ⊙9am-1am) This neighbourhood favourite in Debar Maalo has tables spilling out onto a leafy street, drawing a crowd of casual diners and drinkers. The menu is focused on *skara*, but there are also some inventive nongrill dishes and a good selection of local wines and *rakija* (fruit brandy). It's about a 10-minute walk west of central Skopje.

🍷 Drinking & Nightlife

★**Old Town Brewery** CRAFT BEER
(Gradište 1; ⊙9am-midnight Sun-Thu, to 1am Fri & Sat; 🛜) The siren call of tasty craft beer sings to locals and tourists alike at Skopje's only microbrewery, which is justifiably popular for its Weiss beer, IPA, golden ale and dark beer – all brewed on-site and accompanied by a dependable menu of international pub grub. The sunny terrace, sandwiched between the walls of Tvrdina Kale Fortress (p293) and Sveti Spas Church, crowns its appeal.

Menada BAR
(☑070 256 171; Kazandžiska 2; ⊙8am-1am) Popular with the local art and culture crowd, Menada often has live music – jazz, rock, folk – and a good atmosphere till the wee hours. The wood-panelled bar and terrace can get quite busy, so grab a table while you can. There are palatable snacks. It's right at the entry into the Čaršija.

Vinoteka Temov WINE BAR
(Gradište 1a; ⊙9am-midnight) Skopje's best wine bar, in a restored wooden building near Sveti Spas Church, is refined and atmospheric. Knowledgeable staff offer a vast wine list starring the cream of North Macedonia's vineyards, though if you want to taste any of the better wines you'll need to buy a bottle as the glass selection is limited (as it is everywhere in North Macedonia, unfortunately).

☆ Entertainment

Macedonian National Opera and Ballet OPERA
(☑02 311 8451; http://mob.mk; Goce Delčev 4; tickets 400MKD) Set inside the most beautiful modernist building – designed by the Slovene architects Biro 71, completed in 1981 –

MT VODNO

Framing Skopje to the south, Vodno's towering mass – pinpointed by the 66m Millennium Cross – is an enduring symbol of the city. A popular (shaded) hiking trail cuts a swathe up its wooded slopes and there's also a gondola that climbs the mountainside from halfway up, where a couple of restaurants cater to day trippers. To get here, take the 'Millennium Cross' special bus (35MKD, 12 daily) from the bus station to the gondola. A taxi to the gondola costs about 200MKD, and the gondola round trip is 100MKD.

Up in the gods around the western side of Vodno, the village of Gorno Nerezi is home to Sveti Pantelejmon Monastery (1164), one of North Macedonia's most significant churches. Its Byzantine frescoes, such as the Lamentation of Christ, depict a pathos and realism predating the Renaissance by two centuries. It's 5km from Skopje city centre and it takes about 20 minutes to get here by taxi (350MKD, using the meter) because of the steep, windy road. The views from the monastery's terrace are sublime. Admission is 120MKD.

this is where one can see classic opera and ballet pieces. Check the website for seasonal performances.

Shopping

★ Monozero   ARTS & CRAFTS
(☑ 070 255 093; http://mono-zero.com; Kliment Ohridski 30; ⊕ 10.30am-6.30pm Mon-Fri, 10am-4pm Sat) A brilliant local carpentry enterprise, Monozero makes everything out of solid wood sourced from responsibly harvested forests. Each object is hand made using traditional craft techniques. You can pick up cheeseboards, chopping boards and candleholders, each smooth and beautiful and perfect for remembering North Macedonia, sustainably.

❶ Information

Skopje's **tourist information centre** (Filip Makedonski; ⊕ 8.30am-4.30pm Mon-Fri) has maps and a range of countrywide promotional literature. Note that the advertised opening hours are not kept.

❶ Getting There & Away

Skopje International Airport (☑ 02 314 8333; www.airports.com.mk; 1043, Petrovec) is located 21km east of the city centre.

Vardar Express (☑ 02 311 8263; www.vardar express.com) shuttle bus runs between the airport and the city; check the website for its timetable. Taxis to and from the airport cost 1200MKD.

Skopje's **bus station** (☑ 02 246 6313; www. sas.com.mk; bul Nikola Karev), with ATM, exchange office and English-language information office, adjoins the train station. Bus schedules are only available online in Macedonian (your hotel/hostel staff should be more than happy to translate for you, though).

❶ Getting Around

➡ Buses congregate under the bus/train station; for Matka you need bus number 60 (70MKD) and for Vodno take the special 'Millennium Cross' bus (35MKD).

➡ Skopje's taxis aren't bad value, with the first kilometre costing just 40MKD, and 25MKD for subsequent kilometres.

➡ Drivers rarely speak English, but they do use their meters (if they don't, just ask/point).

AROUND SKOPJE

Canyon Matka

Ah, Matka. Early Christians, ascetics and revolutionaries picked a sublime spot when they retreated into the hills here from Ottoman advances: the setting is truly reverential. Matka means 'womb' in Macedonian and the site has a traditional link with the Virgin Mary.

Churches, chapels and monasteries have long been guarded by these forested mountains, though most have now been left to rack and ruin. Many of the modern-day villages in this area are majority Macedonian Albanian Muslim, though the population is sparse.

Canyon Matka is a popular day trip from Skopje and crowded at weekends; if you want peace and quiet, come early or stay overnight.

◎ Sights & Activities

★ Sveta Bogorodica
Monastery   MONASTERY
(Lake Matka; ⊕ 8am-8pm) FREE Framed by mountains and with a serene, peaceful atmosphere, Sveta Bogorodica is a really special spot. Still home to nuns, this working

monastery has 18th-century wooden-bal-ustraded living quarters. The beautiful 14th-century chapel has frescoes from the 1500s. A church has stood on this spot since the 6th century, evident from the crosses on the left-hand side of the entrance.

Bogorodica is clearly signposted from the road that leads to the Canyon Matka car park (buses drop passengers off here); walk up the short, steep hill directly above.

Church of Sveti Andrej CHURCH
(Lake Matka; ⊙10am-4pm) FREE The most eas-ily accessible of Canyon Matka's 14th-century churches and also one of the finest, the pe-tite Church of St Andrew (1389) is practical-ly attached to the Canyon Matka Hotel and backed by the towering massif of the canyon walls. Inside, well-preserved painted frescoes depict apostles, holy warriors and archan-gels. Opening hours can be a bit erratic.

Cave Vrelo CAVE
(Matka boat kiosk; 400MKD; ⊙9am-7pm) A team of scuba divers from Italy and Belgium have explored Matka's underwater caverns to a depth of 212m and still not found the bot-tom, making these caves among the deepest in Europe. Cave Vrelo is open to the public – you can enter the inky depths of the bat-in-habited cave by boat or hired kayak.

Canyon Matka Kayaking KAYAKING
(single/double kayak per 30min 150/250MKD; ⊙9am-7pm) Kayaking through Matka's pre-cipitous canyon is divine. This is a light paddle, where you can enjoy the rock forma-tions and gorgeous sunlight – kayaks are the only watercraft allowed on the lake beside the licensed boat plying the route to Cave Vrelo. You can kayak to the cave and back; count on around two hours in total.

Sleeping & Eating

Canyon Matka Hotel LODGE €€
(☑02 205 2655; www.canyonmatka.mk; Lake Mat-ka; d €39-60) The premium lakefront setting by the canyon walls makes this hotel a fine place for a night's rest, but it's more rough around the edges than might be expected and feels like an adjunct to its successful res-taurant. The 2nd-floor rooms have charm-ing wooden beams but are slightly smaller than those on the 1st floor.

Restaurant Canyon Matka MACEDONIAN €€
(☑02 205 2655; www.canyonmatka.mk/restaurant; Lake Matka; mains from 600MKD; ⊙8am-midnight) With a prime location just above the water,

this is fine dining with a focus on the Mac-edonian and the Mediterranean. Order the grilled trout and salad with any of the good local wines and enjoy the beautiful views. Bring mosquito repellent for evenings.

Getting There & Away

From Skopje, catch bus 60 from Bul Partizanski Odredi or from the bus/train station (return 70MKD, 40 minutes, nine daily).

It is not possible to get to the main section of the lake, where the Canyon Matka Hotel and boat kiosk are, by car or bus. Taxis (450MKD) and the bus from Skopje will drop you about a 10- to 15-minute walk from there, at the public car park and a couple of riverside restaurants.

If you have your own wheels, the closest public car park to the lake is just before the pedestri-an-only walkway, but it's a small car park up a steep hill and fills up quickly in summer and on weekends. Both car parks are free.

WESTERN NORTH MACEDONIA

Mavrovo National Park
Маврово Национален Парк

The gorges, pine forests, karst fields and waterfalls of Mavrovo National Park offer a breath of fresh, rarefied air for visitors travelling between Skopje and Ohrid. Beau-tiful vistas abound, and the park is home to North Macedonia's highest peak, Mt Korab (2764m). Locally the park is best known for its ski resort (the country's biggest) near Mavrovo town, but by international stand-ards the skiing is fairly average. In summer-time, the park is glorious.

Driving in the park is extremely scenic, but a word of caution: car GPS doesn't work well here and signposting is poor.

Sights & Activities

★Sveti Jovan
Bigorski Monastery MONASTERY
(⊙services 5.30am, 4pm & 6pm) FREE This revered 1020 Byzantine monastery is locat-ed, fittingly, up in the gods along a track of switchbacks off the Debar road, close to Janče village. Legend attests an icon of Sveti Jovan Bigorski (St John the Baptist) miraculously appeared here, inspiring the monastery's foundation; since then the monastery has been rebuilt often – apparently, the icon has

occasionally reappeared too. The complex went into demise during communist rule but has been painstakingly reconstructed and today is as impressive as ever, with some excellent views over Mavrovo's mountains.

Jance   VILLAGE

Just a blip on the map, the small village of Jance is one of the few places in Mavrovo (besides the ski resort) where it's possible to get decent accommodation. It's a picturesque spot that scales the hillside; the views from up here are awesome, even if the village itself feels like a forgotten corner of the country. Its cluster of stone houses includes some fascinating examples of decaying rural architecture with *bondruk* wooden frames, packed earthen walls and creaking wooden porches.

Galicnik   VILLAGE

Up a winding, tree-lined road ending in a rocky moonscape 17km southwest of Mavrovo, almost depopulated Galicnik features traditional houses along the mountainside. It's also famed for its traditional cheesemaking. The village is placid except during the Galicnik Wedding Festival. A wonderful food and accommodation option is available with one of the few local families that live here year-round, and you can hike in the surrounding area, including to Jance.

Horse Club Bistra Galicnik   HORSE RIDING

(☑ 077 648 679; www.horseriding.com.mk) You can go on daily rides (2½ hours to 5½ hours) through Mavrovo's mountain valleys, departing from the village of Galicnik and dropping by traditional villages. The daily treks have cheese-tasting stops. Multiday excursions involve camping, cheese tasting and going up to the Medenica peak.

✺ Festivals & Events

★ Galicnik Wedding Festival   CULTURAL

(www.galichnik.mk; ⊙ 12–13 Jul) The small Mavrovo village of Galicnik is a placid rural outpost that bursts into life each July with a traditional wedding festival, when one or two lucky couples have their wedding here. It's a big two-day party that you can join, along with 3000 happy Macedonians. Everyone eats, drinks, and enjoys traditional folk dancing and music.

⊨ Sleeping & Eating

Baba i Dede   GUESTHOUSE €

(☑ 070 370 843, 077 854 256; Galicnik; r per person €20; ⓟ ⓢ) Baba i Dede means Grandpa and

Grandma – and indeed it's a pair of Galicnik ancients (more or less the only two people who live in the village year-round) who welcome you at this charming guesthouse with a restaurant. The four rooms are spacious and homely, and the traditional food is delicious, prepared by the ever-smiling Baba.

Sveti Jovan Bigorski Monastery   HOSTEL €

(☑ Father Serges 070 304 316, Father Silvan 078 383 771; www.bigorski.org; Mavrovo National Park; dm €15-20; ❇ ⓢ) For a unique experience, you can bed down in one of North Macedonia's most famous monasteries for the night. Rooms are clustered in one wing of the religious complex and decorated, naturally, with traditional monastic furniture. Although the sleeping arrangements are effectively dorms, it's a far cry from the hard wooden bunks you might associate with the monks' pared-back lifestyle.

Hotel Tutto   HOTEL €€

(☑ 042 470 999; www.tutto.com.mk; Jance; s/d/t €30/50/60, apt €40-50; ⓟ ❇ ⓢ) Welcome to one of North Macedonia's most enterprising community projects – an eco-hotel with a restaurant to die for. The setting in Jance is peaceful and lovely, and there are hiking trails at the hotel's front door. The 1st-floor rooms are exceedingly comfy: ask for one at the front to appreciate the view from your balcony.

★ Hotel Tutto Restaurant   MACEDONIAN €€

(☑ 042 470 999; www.tutto.com.mk; Jance; mains from 400MKD; ⊙ 8am-midnight) The owner of Tutto is a founding member of North Macedonia's Slow Food organisation, and his enthusiasm for local produce is infused in the restaurant kitchen. Macedonian specialities such as slow-roast lamb and *pita* (coiled filo pastry pies stuffed with spinach and cheese) are a must, and there are always fresh mushrooms on the menu, picked from the surrounding forest.

❶ Information

Go Macedonia (p295), in Skopje, arranges Galicnik wedding festival trips including transport, guided activities, local accommodation and a monastery tour at Sveti Jovan Bigorski. Book ahead.

❶ Getting There & Away

➜ Without your own wheels, it's difficult to reach the various places of interest in the national park independently, or to do any hiking.

➜ For Sveti Jovan Bigorski Monastery, buses transiting Debar for Ohrid or Struga will be able to drop you off.

Lake Ohrid

♪ 046

Lake Ohrid, in its vastness and mystery, is a monumentally seductive attraction. Mirror-like and dazzling on sunny days, it's a truly beautiful place – especially in and around the ancient town of Ohrid.

At 300m deep, 34km long and three million years old, shared by North Macedonia (two-thirds) and Albania (one-third), Lake Ohrid is among Europe's deepest and oldest. The Macedonian portion is inscribed on the Unesco World Heritage list for its cultural heritage and unique nature – it's considered the most biodiverse lake of its size in the world.

◉ Sights

★ Sveti Naum Monastery   MONASTERY

(100MKD, parking 50MKD; ⊗7am-8pm Jun-Aug, closes at sunset rest of year) Sveti Naum, 29km south of Ohrid, is an imposing sight on a bluff near the Albanian border and a popular day trip from Ohrid. Naum was a contemporary of St Kliment, and their monastery an educational centre. The iconostasis inside the church dates to 1711 and the frescoes to the 19th century; it's well worth paying the fee to enter. Sandy beaches hem the monastery in on two sides and are some of the best places to swim around Lake Ohrid.

Vevčani   VILLAGE

Keeping one sleepy eye on Lake Ohrid from its mountain perch, Vevčani dates to the 9th century and is a quiet rural settlement beloved by locals for its traditional restaurants and **natural springs** (adult/child 20/10MKD; ⊗9am-5pm). The old brick streets flaunt distinctive 19th-century rural architecture and the village is watched over by the Church of St Nicholas. Vevčani lies 14km north of Struga, at the northerly edge of the lake. Buses from Struga run hourly (50MKD); a taxi should cost around 400MKD.

Museum on Water – Bay of Bones   MUSEUM

(♪078 909 806; adult/student & child 100/30MKD; ⊗9am-7pm Jul-Aug, to 4pm Sep-Jun, closed Mon Oct-Apr) In prehistoric times Lake Ohrid was home to a settlement of pile dwellers who lived literally on top of the water, on a platform supported by up to 10,000 wooden piles anchored to the lake bed. The remains of the settlement were discovered at this spot and were gradually excavated by an underwater team between 1997 and 2005; the museum is an elaborate reconstruction of the settlement

as archaeologists think it would have looked between 1200 and 600 BC.

✦ Activities

Springs of St Naum   BOATING

(Sveti Naum Monastery; per boat 600MKD) Inside the Sveti Naum Monastery, colourful covered motorboats sit waiting to whisk visitors over the lake to see the Springs of St Naum. The water here is fed by Lake Prespa and is astoundingly clear – at some points it is 3.5m deep and still you can see the bottom.

⊨ Sleeping

Robinson Sunset House   HOSTEL €

(♪075 727 252; Lagadin; dm/d/apt €12/30/45; ❄🕏) Sweeping lake views, free surfboards (for paddling) and a sprawling garden with lots of relaxing nooks and crannies make this ramshackle hostel a winner if you don't fancy the bustle of Ohrid itself. It sits on a hill above the village of Lagadin, a short bus ride south of Ohrid town. Rooms are spacious and charming, if quite basic.

Hotel Sveti Naum   HOTEL €

(♪046 283 080; www.hotel-stnaum.com.mk; Sveti Naum; s/d/ste from 1890/2500/4990MKD; 🕏) Inside the grounds of the Sveti Naum Monastery, some of this hotel's rooms and suites have lovely lake views. Designed in line with traditional building principles, the rooms feature monastic-style furniture and are quite spacious, if a little dated. It's also right by one of Lake Ohrid's best beaches. For the price, it's a steal.

✗ Eating & Drinking

Restaurant Ostrovo   MACEDONIAN €€

(Sveti Naum Monastery; mains 120-850MKD; ⊗8am-9pm) Of all the restaurants at Sveti Naum, this one has the prettiest setting by the water. Cross the little bridge and there's a seemingly endless garden for dining as well as a unique feature: moored pontoons that you can eat on. Staff speak very little English but are friendly and helpful. Fish features heavily on the menu and breakfast here is good.

Kutmičevica   MACEDONIAN €€

(♪046 798 399; www.kutmicevica.com.mk; Vevčani; mains 250-900MKD; ⊗9am-midnight) This restaurant, which reverberates with the chatter of locals, is a great find: the views from its dining room are immense, right out over the village. It spills onto a terrace on sunny days. The traditional wood-beamed setting matches the menu, where you'll see some Macedo-

GALIČICA NATIONAL PARK

The rippling, rock-crested massif of Galičica separates Lakes Ohrid and Prespa, and is home to Magaro Peak (2254m), a handful of mountain villages and 1100 species of plant, 12 of which can be found only here. **Lake Prespa** is home to the island of **Golem Grad**. The whole area is protected as a 228-sq-km national park, stretching down to Sveti Naum.

Adrift on Lake Prespa, Golem Grad was once the king's summer playground but is now home to wild tortoises, cormorants and pelicans, and perhaps a few ghosts. A settlement endured here from the 4th century BC to the 6th century AD and during medieval times there was a monastery complex. The ruins, birdlife and otherworldly beauty make it well worth exploring. Vila Raskrsnica (p306) or Dzani Dimovski (070 678 123), who owns the cafe at Dupeni Beach, organise trips.

Prespa is separated from its sister lake, Ohrid, by Galičica National Park and a road crosses the ridge of the park, linking the two. Prespa's mirrorlike surface stretches for 176.8 sq km and it is the highest tectonic lake in the Balkans (853m) – the borders of North Macedonia, Albania and Greece converge in its centre. **Dupeni Beach**, near the Greek border on its eastern side, is a (sandy!) spot for swimming.

nian specialities you won't find in Ohrid, and some inventive takes on classic foods.

Orevche Beach Bar   BAR
(Orevche; ⏰10am-8pm; 🛜) A twisted cliffside path sloping steeply downwards into the unknown makes Orevche feel like a secret hideaway, and really it is because hardly anybody knows it's here. The Lake Ohrid water is clear and it would be easy to lose a few hours lounging on the rustic beach bar's day beds and swimming, particularly at sunset.

ℹ Information

Once you leave Ohrid town, ATMs are surprisingly hard to find. There's a reliable one in the foyer of Hotel Bellevue, a giant waterfront high-rise just south of Ohrid town.

ℹ Getting There & Away

The major regional bus hub is Ohrid town, and the northerly lake town of Struga also has some bus connections to other Macedonian towns.

ℹ Getting Around

Bus Frequent buses ply the Ohrid–Sveti Naum route (€1) in summer, stopping off at various points along the lake road, including the village of Lagadin and the Bay of Bones (p300).

Boat Transfers from Ohrid to Sveti Naum (€10 return) run every day in summer.

Ohrid   Охрид
☑ 046 / POP 55,750

Sublime Ohrid is North Macedonia's most seductive destination. It sits on the edge of serene Lake Ohrid, with an atmospheric old

quarter that cascades down steep streets, dotted with beautiful churches and topped by the bones of a medieval castle. Traditional restaurants and lakeside cafes liven up the cobblestone streets. Outside of July and August, the tourist circus subsides and the town becomes more lived in.

Ohrid is small enough to hop from historic monuments into a deck chair and dip your toes in the water – a lovely little town beach and boardwalk make the most of the town's natural charms. A holiday atmosphere prevails all summer, when it's a good idea to book accommodation in advance. Ohrid's busiest time is from mid-July to mid-August.

◉ Sights

★**Ohrid Boardwalk & City Beach**   BEACH
Skimming the surface of the water along Ohrid's shore, snaking towards Kaneo fishing village and the town's most famous church, this over-water boardwalk takes you to a beautiful outcrop of rocky beaches and a handful of restaurants and bars. On a hot day the area is thronged by bathers, drinkers and diners. The cool waters are translucent and inviting, the cliff-backed setting is sublime, and strolling this stretch of coast up to the Church of Sveti Jovan at Kaneo is an Ohrid must.

★**Church of Sveti Jovan at Kaneo**   CHURCH
(Kaneo; 100MKD; ⏰9am-6pm) This stunning 13th-century church is set on a cliff over the lake, about a 15-minute walk west of Ohrid's port area, and is possibly North Macedonia's most photographed structure. Peer down into the azure waters and you'll see why medieval monks found spiritual inspiration

Ohrid

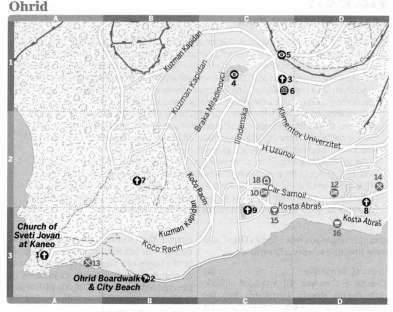

Church of Sveti Jovan at Kaneo

Ohrid Boardwalk & City Beach

here. The small church has original frescoes behind the altar.

Plaošnik
CHURCH
(adult/student & child 100/30MKD; ⊙8am-7pm) Saluting the lake from Ohrid's hilltop, Plaošnik is home to the multidomed medieval Church of Sveti Kliment i Pantelejmon, the foundations of a 5th-century basilica and a garden of intricate early Christian flora-and-fauna mosaics. The central church was restored in 2002; though it lacks the ancient wall frescoes of many other Macedonian churches, it is unusual in having glass floor segments revealing the original foundations and framed relics from the medieval church, which dated to the 9th century.

Sveta Bogorodica Bolnička & Sveti Nikola Bolnički
CHURCH
(off Car Samoil; admission to each church 50MKD; ⊙9am-1pm) *Bolnica* means 'hospital' in Macedonian; during plagues visitors faced 40-day quarantines inside the walled confines of these petite churches, which are thought to date to the 14th century. Sandwiched between Car Samoil and Kosta Abraš in the heart of the Old Town, the churches have somewhat irregular opening hours, but don't miss going in if they are open. Both are small and low-lying, but have intricate interiors heaving under elaborate icons.

Church of Sveta Bogorodica Perivlepta
CHURCH
(Klimentov Univerzitet; 100MKD; ⊙9am-4pm) Just inside the **Gorna Porta** (Upper Gate; Ilindenska), this 13th-century Byzantine church, whose name translates as 'Our Lady the Most Glorious', has vivid biblical frescoes (newly restored in 2017) painted by masters Michael and Eutychius, and superb lake and Old Town views from its terrace. There's also an **icon gallery** (☑046 251 935; 100MKD; ⊙10am-2pm & 6-9pm Tue-Sun) highlighting the founders' artistic achievements.

Sveta Sofija Cathedral
CHURCH
(Car Samoil; adult/student & child 100/30MKD; ⊙9am-7pm) Ohrid's grandest church, 11th-century Sveta Sofija is supported by columns and decorated with elaborate, if very faded, Byzantine frescoes, though they are still well preserved and very vivid in the apse. Its superb acoustics mean it's often used for concerts. To one side of the church there's a peaceful, manicured garden providing a small oasis of green in the heart of the Old Town.

☞ Tours

★ Free Pass Ohrid
TOURS
(☑070 488 231; www.freepassohrid.mk; Kosta Abraš 74) Run by twin sisters and offering a whole array of tailored tours – from hiking

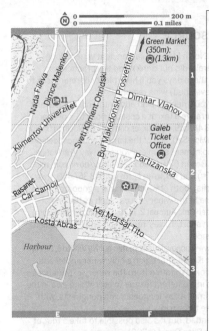

Map scale: 0 — 200 m / 0 — 0.1 miles

Green Market (350m); (1.3km)

Galeb Ticket Office

Harbour

NORTH MACEDONIA OHRID

in Galičica National Park, to wine touring around Tikveš, and boat trips and paragliding around Lake Ohrid, among others – this is local enterprise and alternative tourism at its best. They also have stacks of cultural and adventure tours from their Ohrid base.

✪ Festivals & Events

★ **Ohrid Summer Festival**   PERFORMING ARTS
(☑ 046 262 304; http://ohridskoleto.com.mk; Kej Maršal Tito; ⊗ box office 9am-10pm Jul & Aug) This is Ohrid's most celebrated festival and one of the biggest cultural events in North Macedonia. It hits town in late July and features classical and opera concerts, theatre and dance staged at venues all over the city, including the **Classical Amphitheatre** (Braka Miladinovci; ⊗ 24hr) **FREE**. Buy tickets from the box office kiosk on Kej Maršal Tito, next to the Jazz & Blues cafe-bar.

⌂ Sleeping

★ **Villa Jovan**   HISTORIC HOTEL €
(☑ 076 236 606; vila.jovan@gmail.com; Car Samoil 44; s/d/ste €27/59/98; ❄ 중) By far the most charming place to stay in Ohrid, this 1856 mansion offers nine rooms in the heart of the Old Town. There are old-world furnishings, creaky floors and wooden beams, and a cosy atmosphere. The two top-floor rooms

have quirky sunken baths sitting behind a glass wall, looking out onto the tiny sun-trap terraces.

Sunny Lake Hostel   HOSTEL €
(☑ 075 629 571; www.sunnylakehostel.mk; 11 Oktombri 15; dm €10-12, d €24; ❄ 중) This excellent hostel is a bustling hub for backpackers. Though it could be more spacious, nobody cares because they have such a good time here. The common areas are a highlight: a snug upstairs terrace with lake views and a garden down below for beer drinking. Facilities include a laundry, free breakfast, a kitchen, lockers and bike hire (€5 per day).

★ **Jovanovic Guest House**   GUESTHOUSE €€
(☑ 070 589 218; jovanovic.guesthouse@hotmail.com; Boro Šain 5; apt €40-65; ❄ 중) This property has two studio apartments, both of which sleep four, set in the heart of the Old Town. Each is well equipped and comes with a shady balcony. The apartment on the

DON'T MISS

TASTING TIKVEŠ WINES AT THE SOURCE

Five hundred years of Ottoman rule buried North Macedonia's ancient winemaking culture (the Ottomans, being Muslim, generally did not drink), and the practice was confined to monasteries for centuries. But these days you'll hear plenty of references to Tikveš – the country's most lauded (and developed) wine region.

None of the wineries accept walk-ins, so you'll need to plan appointments to taste and tour by calling ahead (if you're not driving, arrange a taxi at a cost of about €25 per car for five or so hours). **Tikveš Winery** (☏ 043 447 519; www.tikves.com.mk; 29 Noemvri 5; wine tasting per person from 300MKD; ⊘ 10am-6pm Mon-Sat), one of the largest and most celebrated, can be virtually impossible to get an appointment at unless you plan way in advance.

Most vineyards – with the exceptions of **Bovin** (☏ 043 365 322; http://bovin.com.mk/; Industriska, 1440 Negotino; ⊘ 8am-4pm Mon-Fri) and **Popova Kula** (☏ 043 367 400; www. popovakula.com.mk; bul Na Vinoto 1, Demir Kapija), both of which are well signposted – are extremely difficult to find on your own. Some of the winery 'tours', such as the one at **Stobi Winery** (☏ 078 221 427; www.stobiwinery.mk; Autopat 2, 1420 Gradsko; ⊘ 9am-6pm) **FREE**, are really not worth bothering with. In short, Tikveš' reputation and Macedonian enthusiasm somewhat oversell the experience.

Happily, **Popova Kula** (☏ 043 367 400; www.popovakula.com.mk; bul Na Vinoto 1, Demir Kapija; s €35-45, d €50-110; P❋☎) in Demir Kapija, the region's only winery hotel and restaurant, is worth the effort. The owner took inspiration from the winery experiences of California and what he's achieved here is in a different league to everything else in the region. Tours of the property are held four times a day for guests and nonguests, with fascinating insight into the history of the site thrown in.

A stay at Popova Kula is highly recommended, but it's also possible to take a tour of the region from Ohrid (a long day) with Free Pass Ohrid (p302).

North Macedonia's key unique grape varietal is *vranac* (a full-bodied red), while Popova Kula in particular prizes a little-known grape called *stanushina*.

1st floor is slightly bigger, but the top-floor apartment's balcony is more private and has one of the best views in town, right over the lake and Sveta Sofija Cathedral.

✖ Eating

Green Market MARKET €
(off Goce Delčev; ⊘ 7am-9pm Mon-Sat, to 2pm Sun, closes 7pm Mon-Sat in winter) Ohrid's main outdoor fruit and vegetable market is great for self-caterers and sells everything from local produce to electronics and kids' toys. Enter directly behind the fountain on Goce Delčev, near the Činar tree. Monday is the market's biggest day.

★ **Letna Bavča Kaneo** SEAFOOD €€
(☏ 070 776 837; Kočo Racin 43; mains 220-500MKD; ⊘ 8am-midnight; ☎) Of the three terrace restaurants by the water at Kaneo, this one is the best – the atmosphere is right, the food is fantastic and the service professional. The traditional menu has had a facelift; truffle oil accompanies the potatoes, trout is both fresh and smoked, courgettes are stuffed with aromatic herbs and rice. There are good local wines.

Restaurant Antiko MACEDONIAN €€
(Car Samoil 30; mains 200-800MKD; ⊘ 11am-11pm) In an old Ohrid mansion in the middle of the Old Town, the famous Antiko has great traditional ambience and is a good place to try classic Macedonian dishes such as *tavče gravče* (beans and peppers baked in the oven with spices), and top-quality Macedonian wines.

🍷 Drinking & Nightlife

★ **Jazz Inn** BAR
(Kosta Abraš 74; ⊘ 9pm-1am) This unassuming little jazz-themed bar sways to a different rhythm than the strip of bars down on Ohrid's lakefront, with an alternative vibe, a distinct soundtrack and arty clientele. Tucked down a cobbled backstreet away from the touristy hubbub, the low-lit interior has a speakeasy feel, though revellers can be found spilling out onto the road by midnight on weekends and throughout summer.

Liquid CAFE
(Kosta Abraš 17; ⊘ 8am-1am; ☎) Ohrid's most stylish lakefront bar is a relaxed chill-out place by day, serving coffee and drinks (no

food). At night it morphs into the town's most lively bar with a beautiful crowd and pumping music. Its patio jutting into the lake has the best views and ambience on this strip. During the day this place is kid-friendly too.

🔒 Shopping

⭐ **Atelier Marta Pejoska** JEWELLERY
(☑ 070 691 251; whatisfiligree.tumblr.com/; Car Samoil 52; ⊙ noon-6.30pm) Ohrid-born Marta trained as an architect and decided to dedicate herself to the traditional Macedonian craft of filigree – silver thread weaving that has the appearance of silver lace (pieces from €25). Marta is a charming host and works to order as well as displaying and selling her existing designs. She often has exhibitions in her small shop.

ℹ️ Information

Ohrid does not have an official tourist office (despite the fact that many city maps suggest it does); www.visitohrid.org is the municipal website.

ℹ️ Getting There & Away

Ohrid's **St Paul the Apostle Airport** (☑ 046 252 820; www.airports.com.mk) is 10km north of the town.

There is no public transport to and from the airport. Taxis cost 500MKD one way (don't bother haggling because it's a set fare) and are easy to pick up without prebooking.

Ohrid's **bus station** (cnr 7 Noemvri & Klanoec) is 1.5km northeast of the town centre. Tickets can either be bought at the station itself or from the **Galeb** (☑ 046 251 882; www.galeb.mk; Partizanska; ⊙ 9am-5pm) bus company ticket office just outside Ohrid Old Town. A taxi to Ohrid's bus station from the port area on the edge of the Old Town is a set fare of 150MKD.

CENTRAL NORTH MACEDONIA

Pelister National Park
Пелистер Национален Парк

North Macedonia's oldest national park, created in 1948, Pelister covers 171 sq km of the country's third-highest mountain range, the quartz-filled Baba massif. Eight peaks top 2000m, crowned by Mt Pelister (2601m). Two glacial lakes, known as 'Pelister's Eyes', sit at the top. Summiting both Mt Pelister

and the lakes is one of the park's biggest hiking attractions.

Pelister has excellent village guesthouses nearby and is just 30 minutes away by car from historic Bitola. With its fresh alpine air and good day hikes, the park is an underrated Macedonian stopover.

◉ Sights

Dihovo VILLAGE
Propping up the base of Pelister, just 5km from Bitola, the 830m-high mountainside hamlet of Dihovo is a charming spot, surrounded by thick pine forests and rushing mountain streams. The village's proximity to the main access road into the Pelister National Park makes it a popular base for walkers, and locals have shown impressive initiative in developing their traditional community into a pioneering village tourism destination.

Brajčino VILLAGE
Cradled by the foothills on the western edge of Pelister, little Brajčino's lungs are fit to bursting with fresh mountain air, making it a thoroughly idyllic place to pitch up. Rushing water resounds around the village, cherry trees blossom in spring and migrating swallows stop by; traditional rural architecture adds further charm. There are five churches and a monastery hidden in the leafy environs circling this well-kept village and a two-to-three-hour, well-marked trail takes in all of them.

🏃 Activities

⭐ **Bee Garden BN** FOOD
(☑ 097 526 9535; www.pcelarnikbn.com; Dihovo; ⊙ by appointment) A fantastic opportunity to learn about bee-keeping and taste local honey, pollen and royal jelly. The friendly apiarist will demonstrate the workings of the hives, and you can buy some of the delicious products – perfect for gifts back home. The bee-keeper's family also do excellent traditional home cooking, which can be booked by phoning in advance.

Mt Pelister & Lakes WALKING
Pelister's signature hike is the full-day ascent to the national park's highest peak (2601m) and nearby mountain lakes – Big Lake and Small Lake – that puncture the mountain top like a pair of deep blue eyes, hence their nickname, 'Pelister's Eyes'. There are numerous starting points for the hike but none are reliably marked so it's advisable to take a guide.

🛏 Sleeping

★ Vila Raskrsnica
BOUTIQUE HOTEL €

(☎ 075 796 796; vila.raskrsnica@gmail.com; Brajčino; r per person €25; ᴘ ❋ ⬢) It's worth detouring from the tourist trail just to stay at this utterly lovely village hotel, which offers four rooms in a chalet-style house and lip-smacking country food. Rooms are comfortable and elegant, with exposed stone walls and wooden floors, but it's the expansive mountain-backed garden, rustic picnic tables and a peeping view of Lake Prespa that make Raskrsnica so special.

Villa Dihovo
GUESTHOUSE €€

(☎ 047 293 040, 070 544 743; www.villadihovo. com; Dihovo; room rates at your discretion; ⬢) A remarkable guesthouse, Villa Dihovo comprises three traditionally decorated rooms in a historic house that's home to former professional footballer Petar Cvetkovski and family. There's a big, private flowering lawn and cosy living room with an open fireplace for winter. The only fixed prices are for the homemade wine, beer and *rakija* (fruit brandy); all else, room price included, is your choice.

ⓘ Information

Pelister National Park Information Centre
(☎ 047 237 010; www.park-pelister.com; Nizhepole; ⊙ 9am-3pm Tue-Sun) sells a detailed map of the park and its trails (120MKD). The centre is accessible from the Dihovo road shortly after you enter the park.

ⓘ Getting There & Away

There is one main road into Pelister, which enters from the eastern side coming from Bitola and skirts very close to the village of Dihovo. If you enter the park in your own car, you'll be stopped at a checkpoint and charged 50MKD.

Public transport does not service the park. A taxi from Bitola or Dihovo costs 360MKD one way.

Bitola
Битола

☎ 047 / POP 95,390

Buttressing Pelister National Park, elevated Bitola (660m) has a sophistication inherited from its Ottoman days when it was known as the 'City of Consuls'. Macedonians wax lyrical about its elegant buildings, nationally important ruins and cafe culture – yet as far as tourists are concerned it's still a little off the beaten track.

Join the locals in sipping a coffee and people-watching along pedestrianised Širok Sokak (ul Maršal Tito), the main promenade and heart of the city, and explore the wonderful Stara Čaršija (Old Ottoman Bazaar).

★ Heraclea Lyncestis
ARCHAEOLOGICAL SITE

(adult/child 100MKD/20MKD; ⊙ daylight-8pm) Located 1km south of central Bitola, Heraclea Lyncestis is among North Macedonia's best archaeological sites, though the neglected state of the on-site museum might make you think otherwise. See the Roman baths, portico and amphitheatre, and the striking early Christian basilica and episcopal palace ruins, with beautiful, well-preserved floor mosaics – they're unique in depicting endemic trees and animals. There's a small shady cafe in the grounds and the setting is bucolic.

★ Hotel Teatar
BOUTIQUE HOTEL €

(☎ 047 610 188; Stiv Naumov 35; s/d/t from €24/40/55; ᴘ ❋ ⬢) Sensitively designed in the image of a traditional Macedonian (Ottoman) house, Hotel Teatar is without doubt one of the loveliest hotels in the country. Rooms are spacious, simple and stylish, with large comfortable beds. The common areas display ethnographic costumes, and there's a secluded central courtyard with tables for drinks and breakfast.

Via Apartments
APARTMENT €

(☎ 075 552 343; www.via.mk; off ul Elpida Karamandi 4; s/d/tr/q €13/24/31/40; ❋ ⬢) Set back from the road, hidden away down a dingy alley, Via's lovely front garden/patio is a surprising oasis. Inside the well-designed, modern apartments share a kitchen, laundry and lounge. The location is excellent: just off Širok Sokak.

Vino Bar Bure
MEDITERRANEAN €

(☎ 047 227 744; Širok Sokak 37; mains from 90MKD; ⊙ 8am-midnight; ⬢) Positioned at the end of Širok Sokak, overlooking the street and the square, this restaurant specialises in Macedonian and Turkish cuisine, and good local wines. It has a modern terrace with a bustling atmosphere and a cosy interior. Order a *pide* – a flatbread with toppings of meat and/or cheese – or a *lahmacun* (Turkish pizza) and watch the world go by.

★ Porta Jazz
BAR

(Kiril i Metodij; ⊙ 8am-1am, to midnight Sep-May; ⬢) There's a notably bohemian vibe at this popular place that's packed every night in summer, and when live jazz and blues bands play during the rest of the year (September to May). It's located near the Church of Sveti Dimitrij, one block back from Širok Sokak.

Jagoda
BAR

(☎ 047 203 030; Širok Sokak 154; ⊘ 7am-midnight; 🛜) Right at the end of Širok Sokak, this is a great place for coffee, beer and DJ parties – the red-and-white chequered tablecloths, the good music and the airy terrace opposite the little park mean you can spend quite a few hours hanging out here. It's where the local art crowd goes. It serves meze, too.

ℹ Information

Bitola Tourist Office has no walk-in office. There is a decent website – http://bitola.info/ – with information about the town.

ℹ Getting There & Away

The **bus** and **train stations** (ul Nikola Tesla) are adjacent, 1km south of the centre.

SURVIVAL GUIDE

ℹ Directory A–Z

LGBT+ TRAVELLERS

Macedonians are religious conservatives and the country's LGBT scene is very small. The Rainbow Europe Index continues to rank the country's gay rights among the worst in the region.

MONEY

North Macedonia's national currency is the denar (MKD), but many tourist-related prices (such as transport and hotel costs) are quoted in euros – you may even find that the business owner doesn't immediately know the denar price if you ask for it. Hence Lonely Planet lists prices as they are quoted rather than in denars only.

Macedonian exchange offices *(menuvačnici)* work commission-free. ATMs are widespread. Credit cards can be used in larger cities (especially in restaurants), but don't rely on them outside Skopje.

OPENING HOURS

Banks 7am to 5pm Monday to Friday
Cafes 8am to midnight
Museums Many close on Mondays
Shops 9am to 6pm

PUBLIC HOLIDAYS

New Year's Day 1 January
Orthodox Christmas 7 January
Orthodox Easter Week March/April/May
Labour Day 1 May
Sts Cyril and Methodius Day 24 May
Ilinden Day 2 August
Independence Day 8 September

Revolution Day 11 October
St Clement of Ohrid Day 8 December

ℹ Getting There & Away

AIR

Budget airlines have improved Skopje's modest number of air connections, and it's now connected pretty well to major European cities. Wizz Air still flies Skopje–London, but has stopped its Ohrid–London flights, and the Skopje–Barcelona connection was stopped in autumn 2018.

See the Airports of Macedonia website (www. airports.com.mk) for information about flying in and out of North Macedonia, including timetables, carriers and weather conditions.

LAND
Bus

International routes generally arrive at and depart from Skopje or Ohrid. Pristina, Tirana, Sofia, Belgrade and Thessaloniki are the most common connections.

Car & Motorcycle

Bringing your own vehicle into North Macedonia is hassle free, though you do need a Green Card (proof of third-party insurance, issued by your insurer) endorsed for North Macedonia. You also need to bring the vehicle registration/ownership documents.

Train

➡ The Macedonian Railway network is limited and trains are less frequent than buses.

➡ Trains connect Skopje to Pristina, Belgrade and Thessaloniki (though the last is via a train-and-bus combo because of the fraught relationship with Greece).

➡ Timetables and fares are viewable online (http://mktransport.mk/en).

ℹ Getting Around

BUS

➡ Skopje serves most domestic destinations.

➡ Larger buses are new and air-conditioned; kombis (minibuses) are usually not.

➡ During summer, prebook for Ohrid.

➡ Sunday is often the busiest day for intercity bus travel among locals, so book ahead.

CAR & MOTORCYCLE

There are occasional police checkpoints; make sure you have the correct documentation. Call 196 for roadside assistance.

TRAIN

Domestic trains are reliable but slow. From Skopje, one train line runs to Negotino and another to Bitola via Veles and Prilep. A smaller line runs Skopje–Kičevo. Ohrid does not have a train station.

Poland

POP 38.5 MILLION

Best Places to Eat

➡ Warszawa Wschodnia (p314)

➡ Krako Slow Wines (p320)

➡ Kardamon (p323)

➡ Szeroka 9 (p335)

➡ Tawerna Mestwin (p333)

Best Places to Stay

➡ Dream Hostel (p313)

➡ Aparthotel Vanilla (p319)

➡ Mamas & Papas Hostel (p332)

➡ Puro Poznań Stare Miasto (p329)

➡ Hotel Spichrz (p334)

Why Go?

If they were handing out prizes for 'most eventful past', Poland would score a gold medal. The nation has spent centuries at the pointy end of history, grappling with war and invasion. Nothing, however, has succeeded in suppressing Poles' strong sense of nationhood and cultural identity. As a result, bustling centres like Warsaw and Kraków exude a sophisticated energy that's a heady mix of old and new.

Away from the cities, Poland is surprisingly diverse, from its northern beaches to the long chain of mountains on its southern border. In between, towns and cities are dotted with ruined castles, picturesque market squares and historic churches.

Although prices have steadily risen in the postcommunist era, Poland is still good value. As the Poles continue to reconcile their distinctive national identity with their location at the heart of Europe, it's a fascinating time to pay a visit.

When to Go
Warsaw

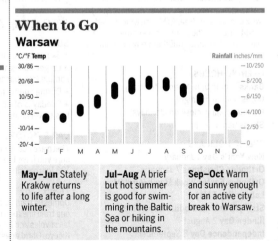

May–Jun Stately Kraków returns to life after a long winter.

Jul–Aug A brief but hot summer is good for swimming in the Baltic Sea or hiking in the mountains.

Sep–Oct Warm and sunny enough for an active city break to Warsaw.

Entering the Country

As a member of the EU, Poland has open borders (and plenty of rail and road crossings) on its western and southern frontiers with Germany, the Czech Republic and Slovakia. Crossings with EU-member Lithuania, on the northeastern end of the country, are also open.

It's a different story crossing into Ukraine, Belarus and Russia's Kaliningrad enclave, which form part of the EU's external border and may require visas and advance planning.

The following is a list of 24-hour border crossings into Poland's non-EU neighbours.

Belarusian border (south to north): Terespol, Kuźnica

Russian (Kaliningrad) border (east to west): Bezledy–Bagrationowsk, Gronowo

Ukrainian border (south to north): Medyka, Hrebenne–Rawa Ruska, Dorohusk

ITINERARIES

One Week

Spend a day exploring Warsaw (p310), with a stroll around the Old Town and a stop at the Museum of the History of Polish Jews. Next day, head to historic Kraków (p316) for three days, visiting the beautiful Old Town, Wawel Castle and former Jewish district of Kazimierz. Take a day trip to Auschwitz-Birkenau (p321), the former Nazi German extermination camp. Afterwards, head to Zakopane (p324) for a day in the mountains.

Two Weeks

Follow the above itinerary, then travel to Wrocław (p326) for two days, taking in its historic Cathedral Island. Head north to Gothic Toruń (p334) for a day, then onward to Gdańsk (p330) for two days, exploring the attractive Old Town, the superb Museum of WWII and the magnificent castle at Malbork (p332).

Essential Food & Drink

Barszcz Famous beetroot soup comes in two varieties: red (made from beetroot) and white (with wheat flour and sausage).

Bigos Thick stew with sauerkraut and meat.

Pierogi Flour dumplings, usually stuffed with cheese, mushrooms or meat.

Szarlotka Apple cake with cream; a Polish classic.

Wódka Vodka: try it plain, or ask for *myśliwska* (flavoured with juniper berries).

Żurek Hearty, sour rye soup includes sausage and hard-boiled egg.

AT A GLANCE

Area 312,696 sq km

Capital Warsaw

Country Code ☑48

Currency Polish złoty (zł)

Emergency Ambulance ☑999, fire ☑998, police ☑997; from mobile phones ☑112

Language Polish

Time GMT/UTC+1

Visas Generally not required for stays of up to 90 days

Sleeping Price Ranges

Prices listed are for an average double room in high season, with private bathroom and including breakfast.

€ less than 150zł

€€ 150zł–400zł

€€€ more than 400zł

Eating Price Ranges

The following price ranges refer to the cost of an average main-course item.

€ less than 20zł

€€ 20zł–40zł

€€€ more than 40zł

POLAND

Poland Highlights

1 Kraków (p316)
Experiencing the beauty and history of the Old Town.

2 Wrocław (p326)
Enjoying the city's student-fuelled party vibe.

3 Auschwitz-Birkenau (p321) Remembering the victims of the Holocaust.

4 Museum of WWII (p330) Discovering Poland's wartime history in Gdańsk's superb modern museum.

5 Zakopane (p324)
Skiing or hiking the Tatra Mountains from this alpine resort.

6 Warsaw Rising Museum (p311) Being dazzled by one of Warsaw's best museums.

WARSAW

POP 1.76 MILLION

Once you've travelled around Poland, you realise this: Warsaw is different. Rather than being centred on an old market square, the capital is spread across a broad area with diverse architecture: restored Gothic, communist concrete, modern glass and steel.

This jumble is a sign of the city's tumultuous past. Warsaw has suffered the worst history could throw at it, including near destruction at the end of WWII – and survived. As a result, it's a fascinating collection of neighbourhoods and landmarks. Excellent museums interpret its complex story, from the joys of Chopin's music to the tragedy of the Jewish ghetto.

It's not all about the past, however. Warsaw's restaurant and entertainment scene is the best in Poland. You can dine well and affordably here on cuisines from around the world, and take your choice of lively bars and clubs. This gritty city knows how to have fun.

⊙ Sights

★ Royal Castle
MUSEUM

(Zamek Królewski; ☑ 22 355 5170; www.zamek-krolewski.pl; Plac Zamkowy 4, Stare Miasto; adult/concession 30/20zł, free Wed; ⊙ 10am-6pm Tue-Thu & Sat, to 8pm Fri, 11am-6pm Sun, closes 4pm Oct-Apr; ⓜ Stare Miasto) This massive brick edifice, a copy of the original blown up by the Germans in WWII, began life as a wooden stronghold of the dukes of Mazovia in the 14th century. Its heyday came in the mid-17th century, when it became one of Europe's most splendid royal residences. It then served the Russian tsars and, in 1918, after Poland regained independence, became the residence of the president. Today it is filled with period furniture and works of art.

★ Old Town Square
SQUARE

(Rynek Starego Miasta, Stare Miasto; ⓜ Stare Miasto) At the centre of the partially walled Old Town (Stare Miasto), the Old Town Square is, for those with an eye for historic buildings, the loveliest square in Warsaw. It's lined with tall houses exhibiting a fine blend of Renaissance, baroque, Gothic and neoclassical elements; aside from the facades at Nos 34 and 36, all were rebuilt after being reduced to rubble by the Germans at the close of WWII.

Church of the Holy Cross
CHURCH

(Kościół św Krzyża; ☑ 22 826 8910; www.swkrzyz.pl; ul Krakowskie Przedmieście 3, Śródmieście Północne; ⊙ 10-11am & 1-4pm Mon-Sat, 2-4pm Sun; ⓜ Nowy Świat-Uniwersytet) FREE Of Warsaw's many impressive churches, this is the one most visitors want to see. Not so much to admire the fine baroque altarpieces that miraculously survived the Warsaw Rising reprisals, but to glimpse a small urn by the second pillar on the left side of the nave. This urn, adorned with an epitaph to Frédéric Chopin, contains what remains of the composer's heart. It was brought here from Paris after the his death.

★ Palace of Culture & Science
HISTORIC BUILDING

(PKiN, Pałac Kultury i Nauki; ☑ 22 656 7600; www.pkin.pl; Plac Defilad 1, Śródmieście Północne; observation deck adult/concession 20/15zł; ⊙ observation deck 10am-8pm; ⓜ Centrum) Love it or hate it, every visitor to Warsaw should visit the iconic, socialist-realist PKiN (as its full Polish name is abbreviated). This 'gift of friendship' from the Soviet Union was built in the early 1950s, and at 231m high remains the tallest building in Poland. It's home to a huge congress hall, theatres, a multiscreen cinema and museums. Take the high-speed lift to the 30th-floor (115m) observation terrace *(taras widokowy)* to take it all in.

★ Warsaw Rising Museum
MUSEUM

(Muzeum Powstania Warszawskiego; www.1944.pl; ul Grzybowska 79, Czyste; adult/concession 25/20zł, Sun free; ⊙ 8am-6pm Mon, Wed & Fri, to 8pm Thu, 10am-6pm Sat & Sun; ⓜ Rondo Daszyńskiego, ⓜ Muzeum Powstania Warszawskiego) One of Warsaw's best, this museum traces the history of the city's heroic but doomed uprising against the German occupation in 1944 via three levels of interactive displays, photographs, film archives and personal accounts. The volume of material is overwhelming, but the museum does an excellent job of instilling a sense of the desperation residents felt in deciding to oppose the occupation by force, and of illustrating the dark consequences, including the Germans' destruction of the city in the aftermath.

★ POLIN Museum of the History of Polish Jews
MUSEUM

(☑ 22 471 0301; www.polin.pl; ul Anielewicza 6, Muranów; main exhibition adult/concession 25/15zł, temporary exhibits adult/concession 12/8zł, Thu free; ⊙ 10am-6pm Mon, Thu & Fri, to 8pm Wed, Sat & Sun; ⓜ Ratusz Arsenał, ⓜ Muranów, Anielewicza) This exceptional museum's permanent exhibition opened in late 2014. Impressive multimedia exhibits document 1000 years of Jewish history in Poland, from accounts of the earliest Jewish traders in the region through waves of mass migration, progress and pogroms, all the way to WWII and the destruction of Europe's largest Jewish community. It's worth booking online, and you can hire an audio guide (10zł) to get the most out of the many rooms of displays, interactive maps, photos and videos.

★ Fryderyk Chopin Museum
MUSEUM

(☑ 22 441 6251; www.chopin.museum; ul Okólnik 1, Śródmieście Północne; adult/concession 22/13zł, Wed free; ⊙ 11am-8pm Tue-Sun; ⓜ Nowy Świat-Uniwersytet) A high-tech, multimedia museum within the baroque Ostrogski Palace, showcasing the work of the country's most famous composer. You're encouraged to take your time through four floors of displays, including stopping by the listening booths in the basement where you can browse Chopin's oeuvre to your heart's content. Limited visitation is allowed each hour; your best bet is to book your visit in advance by phone or email. Entrance at ul Tamka 43.

Central Warsaw

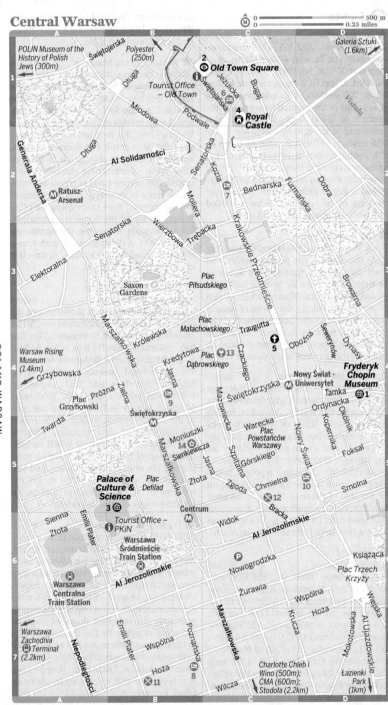

0 — 500 m
0 — 0.25 miles

POLIN Museum of the
History of Polish
Jews (300m)

Świętojerska

Polyester
(250m)

Galeria Sztuki
(1.6km)

Długa

Miodowa

2 Old Town Square

Tourist Office
– Old Town

Jezuicka

6 Świętojańska

Bugaj

Vistula

4 Royal
Castle

Podwale

Długa

Senatorska

Al Solidarności

Kozia

Bednarska

Furmańska

Dobra

M Ratusz-
Arsenał

Generała Andersa

Senatorska

Wierzbowa

Trębacka

Mołiera

Krakowskie Przedmieście

Browarna

Elektoralna

Saxon
Gardens

Plac
Piłsudskiego

Marszałkowska

Królewska

Plac
Małachowskiego

Traugutta

Obozna

Sewerynów

Dynasy

Warsaw Rising
Museum
(1.4km)

Grzybowska

Zielna

Kredytowa

Plac
Dąbrowskiego

13

Czackiego

5

Nowy Świat -
Uniwersytet M

Tamka

**Fryderyk
Chopin
Museum**

1

Plac
Próżna
Grzybowski

Jasna

9

Świętokrzyska

Mazowiecka

Świętokrzyska

Ordynacka

Okólnik

Kopernika

Foksal

Twarda

Świętokrzyska M

Moniuszki
14
Sienkiewicza

Warecka

Plac
Powstańców
Warszawy

Jasna

Szpitalna

Górskiego

Nowy Świat

**Palace of
Culture &
Science**

Plac
Defilad

Złota

Zgoda

10

Smolna

3

Tourist Office –
PKiN

Centrum M

Widok

Chmielna

12

Bracka

Al Jerozolimskie

Sienna

Złota

Emilii Plater

Warszawa
Śródmieście
Train Station

Al Jerozolimskie

Nowogrodzka

P

Żurawia

Książęca

Plac Trzech
Krzyży

Warszawa
Centralna
Train Station

Wspólna

Hoża

Wiejska

Warszawa
Zachodnia
Terminal
(2.2km)

Niepodległości

Emilii Plater

Wspólna

Poznańska

Hoża

8

11

Wilcza

Marszałkowska

Krucza

Charlotte Chleb i
Wino (500m);
ĆMA (600m);
Stodoła (2.2km)

Mokotowska

Al Ujazdowskie

Łazienki
Park
(1km)

Central Warsaw

◉ Top Sights
1 Fryderyk Chopin Museum D4
2 Old Town Square C1
3 Palace of Culture & Science B5
4 Royal Castle C1

◉ Sights
5 Church of the Holy Cross C4

🛏 Sleeping
6 Castle Inn C1
7 Dream Hostel C2
8 H15 .... B7
9 Oki Doki City Hostel B4
10 Royal Route Residence D5

✴ Eating
11 Flambéeria B7
12 Mango C5

◉ Drinking & Nightlife
13 Enklawa C4

✪ Entertainment
14 Filharmonia Narodowa B5

Łazienki Park   GARDENS
(Park Łazienkowski; ☑504 243 783; www.lazienki-krolewskie.pl; ul Agrykola 1, Ujazdów; ⊙24 hours; ☐Plac Na Rozdrożu) FREE Pronounced wah-zhen-kee, this park is a beautiful place of manicured greens, wooded glades and strutting peacocks. Once a hunting ground attached to **Ujazdów Castle** (ul Jazdów 2), Łazienki was acquired by King Stanisław August Poniatowski in 1764 and transformed into a splendid park complete with palace, amphitheatre, and various follies and other buildings.

Neon Museum   MUSEUM
(Muzeum Neonów; ☑665 711635; www.neonmuzeum.org; ul Mińska 25, Kamionek; adult/concession 12/10zł; ⊙noon-5pm Mon, Tue, Thu & Fri, noon-6pm Sat, 11am-5pm Sun; ☐Bliska) Situated within the cool Soho Factory complex of old industrial buildings housing designers and artists, this museum is devoted to the preservation of the iconic neon signs of the communist era. The collection is arrayed within a historic factory, with many large pieces fully lit. Other exhibits are dotted around the complex and are illuminated after dark. It's well worth the trek across the river. Get off the tram at the Bliska stop.

🛏 Sleeping

Warsaw has a huge range of accommodation, from backpacker hostels to luxury boutique hotels, spread widely across the city centre. However, you'll get cheaper rates at places outside the centre in exchange for a short tram or metro ride. Many business hotels offer discounted rates at weekends.

★ Dream Hostel   HOSTEL €
(☑22 419 4848; https://dream-hostels.com; Krakowskie Przedmieście 55, Śródmieście Północne; dm/d or tw from 50/193zł; ☞; ☐Plac Zamkowy) This large and lively hostel has everything going for it – comfy beds, clean bathrooms, well-equipped kitchens, a choice of dorms (some women-only) and private rooms, a friendly on-site bar and helpful staff.

Oki Doki City Hostel   HOSTEL €
(☑22 828 0122; www.okidoki.pl; Plac Dąbrowskiego 3, Śródmieście Północne; dm/d from 38/168zł; ☞; Ⓜ Świętokrzyska) Arguably Warsaw's most popular hostel and certainly one of the best, each of its bright, large rooms is individually named and decorated. Accommodation is in three- to eight-bed dorms, with a special three-bed dorm for women only. The owners are well travelled and know the needs of backpackers, providing a kitchen and a laundry service. Breakfast available (15zł).

Castle Inn   HOTEL €€
(☑22 425 0100; http://castleinn.pl; ul Świętojańska 2, Stare Miasto; s/d from 356/376zł; ❄☞; ☐Stare Miasto) This 'art hotel' is housed in a 17th-century townhouse, one of the few that was not totally destroyed during WWII. All rooms overlook either Castle Sq or St John's Cathedral, and come in a range of quirky designs, such as 'Viktor', named for a reclusive street artist, complete with tasteful graffiti and a gorgeous castle view. Note: there are lots of steep stairs, and no lift.

Royal Route Residence   APARTMENT €€
(☑22 887 9800; www.royalrouteresidencewarsaw.com; ul Nowy Świat 29/3, Śródmieście Północne; 2-person apt from 430zł; P☞🖥; ☐Foksal) Wonderfully central accommodation in an attractive historic building, offering well-equipped apartments that sleep from two to seven people. Furnishings are bright and modern, and mod cons include microwave, espresso machine and washing machine. Go through the passageway into the courtyard; reception is tucked in the corner on the right.

★ H15   BOUTIQUE HOTEL €€€
(☑22 553 8700; www.h15boutiqueapartments.com; ul Poznanska 15, Śródmieście Południowe; r/apt from 540/1250zł; P❄☞; ☐Hoża) Set in a gorgeous late-19th-century apartment block that once housed the Soviet Union's embassy,

this is one of Warsaw's most luxurious hotels. Modern art and designer furniture vie for your attention with elements of retained communist-era decor. Rooms are quirky and individual, and the location is bang in the middle of the city's trendiest district.

✕ Eating

The largest concentration of eateries is on and around Krakowskie Przedmieście and Nowy Świat, and south of al Jerozolimskie. The Old Town generally houses expensive tourist traps, but there are a few quality spots.

Mango   VEGAN €
(☑ 535 533 629; www.mangovegan.pl; ul Bracka 20, Śródmieście Północne; mains 19-45zł; ⊙ 11am-10pm; 🖋 ; Ⓜ Centrum) Mango is a stylish all-vegan eatery with a simple contemporary interior and pleasant outdoor terrace. Excellent menu items range from quinoa burgers to veggie kebabs. The 'Mango Plate' *(talerz mango)* of hummus, mango, falafel, eggplant, olives, sweet peppers and harissa paste served with pita bread is top value at 25zł.

Charlotte Chleb i Wino   FRENCH €
(☑ 662 204 555; www.bistrocharlotte.pl; Plac Zbawiciela, Śródmieście Południowe; mains 10-19zł; ⊙ 7am-midnight Mon-Thu, to 1am Fri, 8am-1am Sat, 8am-10pm Sun; 🖋 ; 🚌 Plac Zbawiciela) This French-Polish bakery and bistro dishes up tantalising croissants and pastries at the break of dawn, then transitions to big salads and crusty sandwiches through the lunch and dinner hours, and finally to wine on the terrace in the evening. Great value for money.

★ ĆMA   POLISH €€
(☑ 22 221 8176; www.mateuszgessler.com.pl; Unit 31, Hala Koszyki, ul Koszykowa 63, Śródmieście Południowe; mains 25-68zł; ⊙ 24hr; 🖋 ; 🚌 Plac Konstytucji) 🖋 Star chef Mateusz Gessler established this informal, brasserie-style eatery in the hipster heartland of the Hala Koszyki (a converted market hall filled with artisan shops and eateries). The menu brings a deft modern touch to the most traditional of Polish dishes, from head cheese (pig's-head brawn) to goose stomachs (stewed in gravy).

Flambéeria   FRENCH €€
(☑ 730 267 772; www.facebook.com/flambeeria; ul Hoża 61, Śródmieście Południowe; mains 19-28zł; ⊙ 10am-9pm Mon, to 10pm Tue-Thu, to 11pm Fri, noon-11pm Sat, noon-9pm Sun; 🚌 Koszykowa) Slick modern restaurant with a cool interior that's fitted with artistically cracked tiles and bare light bulbs, serving traditional *tartes flambées* (savoury tarts from the French region of Alsace) with a range of fillings. Enter from ul Emilii Plater.

★ Warszawa Wschodnia   MODERN EUROPEAN €€€
(☑ 22 870 2918; www.mateuszgessler.com.pl; Soho Factory, ul Mińska 25, Kamionek; mains 58-78zł; tasting menu 150zł; ⊙ 24hr; 🖋 ; 🚌 Bliska) 🖋 Fabulous restaurant in a huge industrial building, taking its name from the neon sign salvaged from the nearby train station of the same name. Serves a modern interpretation of Polish cuisine with French influences. The bar-kitchen area to the right of the entrance is open 24 hours.

🍸 Drinking & Nightlife

Bars are concentrated around the Old Town, ul Nowy Świat and south of Al Jerozolimskie. For clubbing check out ul Mazowiecka in the city centre, and ul Ząbkowska in Praga.

★ Galeria Sztuki   CAFE
(☑ 22 619 8109; http://.caffee.stanowski.pl; ul Ząbkowska 13, Stara Praga; ⊙ 9am-11pm Mon-Thu, to midnight Fri, from 10am Sat, to 10pm Sun; 🖋 ; Ⓜ Dworzec Wileński) If you're staying on the east side of the river, this cosy spot – part cafe-bar, part antique shop – is a great place to escape to. It serves some of the best coffee in town, has a good choice of wines by the glass and does breakfasts (mostly egg-based) until noon.

Polyester   BAR
(☑ 733 464 600; ul Freta 49/51, Nove Miasto; ⊙ noon-12.30am Sun-Thu, to 1.30am Fri-Sat; 🖋 ; 🚌 Plac Krasińskich) Smooth establishment with retro furnishings and a laid-back vibe. Serves good cocktails, as well as a full range of coffee drinks and light food.

Enklawa   CLUB
(☑ 22 827 3151; www.enklawa.com; ul Mazowiecka 12, Śródmieście Północne; ⊙ 10pm-3am Tue, to 4am Wed-Sat; Ⓜ Świętokrzyska) Blue and purple light illuminates this space with comfy plush seating, mirrored ceilings, two bars and plenty of room to dance. Check out the extensive drinks menu, hit the dance floor or observe the action from a stool on the upper balcony. Wednesday night is 'old school' night, with music from the '70s to the '90s. Smart dress code.

☆ Entertainment

Filharmonia Narodowa   CLASSICAL MUSIC
(National Philharmonic; ☑ 22 551 7130; www.filharmonia.pl; ul Jasna 5, Śródmieście Północne; tickets

ŁÓDŹ

Łódź (pronounced *woodge*) is a red-brick city that grew fabulously wealthy in the 19th century on the back of its massive textile industry. Today it's famous for its architecture (both historic and modern), its colourful street art, its Jewish heritage and its many fine museums and art galleries. It is also the centre of Poland's film industry.

The city's abundant **street art** grew out of the Urban Forms Festival in 2009; today more than 100 murals and installations add colour and life to the city's rapidly rejuvenating centre. The **tourist office** (Centrum Informacji Turystycznej; ☑ 42 208 8181; www.lodz. travel; ul Piotrkowska 28; ⊙ 9am-7pm Mon-Fri, 10am-6pm Sat, to-4pm Sun, shorter hours Oct-Apr; ☎; ☐ Zachodnia-Więckowskiego) will point you to the best-known examples, and many are documented on the Urban Forms (www.urbanforms.org) website.

Łódź is an easy day trip from Warsaw, with a fast and frequent rail service (31zł, 90 minutes, at least hourly).

from 60zł; ⊙ box office 10am-2pm & 3-7pm Mon-Sat; Ⓜ Świętokrzyska) Home of the world-famous National Philharmonic Orchestra and Choir of Poland, founded in 1901, this venue has a concert hall (enter from ul Sienkiewicza 10) and a chamber-music hall (enter from ul Moniuszki 5), both of which stage regular concerts. There are box offices at both entrances.

Stodoła   LIVE MUSIC

(☑ 22 825 6031; www.stodola.pl; ul Batorego 10, Śródmieście Południowe; ⊙ box office 9am-9pm Mon-Fri, to 2pm Sat; Ⓜ Pole Mokotowskie) Opened in 1956, and originally a cafeteria and social club for builders working on the Palace of Culture & Science (p311), this venue is one of Warsaw's biggest and longest-running live-music stages. A great place to catch touring bands.

❶ Information

Tourist Office – PKiN (www.warsawtour.pl; Plac Defilad 1, Śródmieście Północne; ⊙ 8am-7pm May-Sep, to 6pm Oct-Apr; ☎; Ⓜ Centrum; ☐ Warszawa Śródmieście) The Palace of Culture & Science branch of Warsaw's official tourist information organisation is a central resource for maps and advice. The staff can also help with accommodation. There's no phone number, so visit in person. The entrance is on ul Emilii Plater.

Tourist Office – Old Town (www.warsawtour. pl; Rynek Starego Miasta 19/21, Stare Miasto; ⊙ 9am-8pm May-Sep, to 6pm Oct-Apr; ☎; ☐ Stare Miasto) Hands out free maps and booklets, and dispenses information on what to see and do during your stay. There's no phone, so visit in person or contact by email.

❶ Getting There & Away

AIR

Warsaw Chopin Airport (Lotnisko Chopina Warszawa; ☑ 22 650 4220; www.lotnisko-

chopina.pl; ul Żwirki i Wigury 1, Włochy; ☐ Warszawa Lotnisko Chopina) Warsaw's main airport lies in the suburb of Okęcie, 10km south of the city centre; it handles most domestic and international flights.

Warsaw Modlin Airport (Modlin Lotnisko; ☑ 22 315 1880; www.modlinairport.pl; ul Generała Wiktora Thommée 1a, Nowy Dwór Mazowiecki; ☐ Modlin) Smaller airport 35km north of Warsaw used by budget carriers, including Ryanair for flights to and from the UK.

Buy tickets for public transport from the tourist office or from one of several newsagents.

BUS

Warszawa Zachodnia bus terminal (Dworzec Autobusowy Warszawa Zachodnia; ☑ 703 403 403; www.dawz.pl; al Jerozolimskie 144, Czyste; ⊙ information & tickets 5.30am-10pm), west of the city centre, handles the majority of international and domestic routes from the capital, run by various operators.

FlixBus (https://global.flixbus.com) operates buses to cities across Poland and beyond from **Młociny bus station** (Dworzec Autobusowy Młociny; ul Kasprowicza 145, Bielany; Ⓜ Młociny) north of the city centre, and **Wilanowska bus station** (Dworzec Autobusowy Wilanowska; ul Puławska 145, Wilanowska; Ⓜ Wilanowska) south of the centre, as well as from Warszawa Zachodnia. Each station is next to the Metro station of the same name. Book on its website for the lowest fares.

TRAIN

Warsaw has several train stations, but the one most travellers use is **Warszawa Centralna** (Warsaw Central; www.pkp.pl; al Jerozolimskie 54, Śródmieście Północne; ⊙ 24hr; ☐ Warszawa Centralna), with connections to every major Polish city and many other places in between; check the online timetable in English at http:// rozklad-pkp.pl for times and fares.

POLAND WARSAW

You can buy tickets from ticket machines (instructions available in English), or one of the many ticket counters in both the main hall and the shopping concourse. It's best to write down your destination and travel dates/times to show the ticket seller, as not all ticket agents speak English.

❶ Getting Around

TO/FROM THE AIRPORT

Train is the easiest way of getting from **Warsaw Chopin Airport** to the city. Regular services run to Warszawa Centralna station every 30 minutes between 5am and 10.30pm (4.40zł, 20 minutes). Bus 175 (4.40zł, every 15 minutes, 5am to 11pm) runs to the city, passing along ul Jerozolimskie and ul Nowy Świat before terminating at Plac Piłsudskiego, within walking distance of the Old Town.

A shuttle bus transfers passengers from **Warsaw Modlin Airport** to nearby Modlin station, where you can catch a train to Warszawa Centralna (19zł, one hour, at least hourly). **Modlin Bus** (☑ 703 403 993; www.modlinbus.com) services run from Modlin airport and the Palace of Culture & Science in central Warsaw (35zł, one hour, hourly). Buy tickets from the driver; lower fares available online.

PUBLIC TRANSPORT

Warsaw's integrated public transport system is operated by **ZTM** (Zarząd Transportu Miejskiego, Urban Transport Authority; ☑ 19 115; www.ztm.waw.pl) and consists of tram, bus and metro lines, all using the same ticketing system.

Buy tickets at news stands – look for a sign saying 'Sprzedaży Biletów ZTM' – and ticket machines (*automat biletów*; instructions available in English) at metro stations and major tram and bus stops (coins, banknotes and credit cards). There are also machines on newer trams and buses (exact fare in coins only, or credit card).

For most trips, a *jednorazowy bilet* (single-journey ticket, 3.40zł) is sufficient. It is valid for 20 minutes, including transfers between bus, tram and metro. For longer journeys, consider a 40- or 90-minute ticket (4.40zł and 7zł respectively). These tickets also allow unlimited transfers.

KRAKÓW

POP 767,350

Many Polish cities are centred on an attractive Old Town, but none compare to Kraków (pronounced krak-oof) for effortless beauty. As it was the royal capital of Poland until 1596 and miraculously escaped destruction in WWII, Kraków is packed with appealing historic buildings and streetscapes. One of the most important sights is Wawel Castle, from where the ancient Polish kingdom was once ruled.

South of the castle lies the former Jewish quarter of Kazimierz. Its silent synagogues are a reminder of the tragedy of WWII. These days, the quarter has been injected with new life and is home to some of the city's best bars and clubs.

◉ Sights

◉ Wawel Hill

South of Old Town, this prominent hilltop is crowned with the former Royal Castle and cathedral – both enduring symbols of Poland.

★ **Wawel Royal Castle** CASTLE
(Zamek Królewski na Wawelu; ☑ Wawel Visitor Centre 12 422 5155; www.wawel.krakow.pl; grounds free, attractions priced separately; ⊘ grounds 6am-dusk; 🚊 6, 8, 10, 13, 18) As the political and cultural heart of Poland through the 16th century, Wawel Castle is a potent symbol of national identity. It's now a museum containing five separate sections: Crown Treasury & Armoury, State Rooms, Royal Private Apartments, Lost Wawel and the Exhibition of Oriental Art. Each requires a separate ticket. Of the five, the State Rooms and Royal Private Apartments are the most impressive, but to be honest, the best part is just wandering around the castle grounds.

The Renaissance palace you see today dates from the 16th century. An original, smaller residence was built in the early 11th century by King Bolesław I Chrobry. Kazimierz III Wielki (Casimir III the Great) turned it into a formidable Gothic castle, but when it burned down in 1499, Zygmunt I Stary (Sigismund I the Old; 1506–48) commissioned a new residence. Within 30 years, the current Italian-inspired palace was in place. Despite further extensions and alterations, the three-storey structure, complete with a courtyard arcaded on three sides, has been preserved to this day.

Repeatedly sacked and vandalised by the Swedish and Prussian armies, the castle was occupied in the 19th century by the Austrians, who intended to make Wawel a barracks, while moving the royal tombs elsewhere. They never got that far, but they did turn the royal kitchen and coach house into a military hospital and raze two churches. They also built a new ring of massive brick walls, largely ruining the original Gothic fortifications.

After Kraków was incorporated into re-established Poland after WWI, restoration work began and continued until the outbreak of WWII. The work was resumed after the war and has been able to recover a good deal of the castle's earlier external form and interior decoration.

Wawel Cathedral CHURCH

(☎12 429 9515; www.katedra-wawelska.pl; cathedral free, combined entry for crypts, bell tower & museum adult/concession 12/7zł; ⏲9am-5pm Mon-Sat, from 12.30pm Sun Apr-Oct, to 4pm Nov-Mar; 🚋6, 8, 10, 13, 18) Wawel Cathedral has witnessed many coronations, funerals and burials of Poland's monarchs and nobles over the centuries. The present-day cathedral is basically a Gothic structure, but chapels in different styles were built around it later. The showpiece chapel is the **Sigismund Chapel** (Kaplica Zygmuntowska) on the southern wall. It's often referred to as the most beautiful Renaissance chapel north of the Alps, recognisable from the outside by its gilded dome. An audio guide (7zł) helps to put it all in context.

Old Town

The vast Rynek Główny (main square) is the focus of the Old Town, and is Europe's largest medieval town square (200m by 200m).

★**Rynek Underground** MUSEUM

(☎12 426 5060; www.podziemiarynku.com; Rynek Główny 1; adult/concession 21/18zł, Tue free; ⏲10am-8pm Wed-Mon, to 4pm Tue, longer hours Apr-Oct; 🚋1, 6, 8, 13, 18) This fascinating attraction beneath the market square consists of an underground route through medieval market stalls and other long-forgotten chambers. The 'Middle Ages meets 21st century' experience is enhanced by holograms and audiovisual wizardry. Buy tickets at an office on the western side of the Cloth Hall (Sukiennice 21), where an electronic board shows tour times and tickets available. The entrance to the tunnels is on the northeastern end of the Cloth Hall.

St Mary's Basilica CHURCH

(Basilica of the Assumption of Our Lady; ☎12 422 0521; www.mariacki.com; Plac Mariacki 5, Rynek Główny; adult/concession church 10/5zł, tower 15/10zł; ⏲11.30am-6pm Mon-Sat, from 2pm Sun; 🚋1, 6, 8, 13, 18) This striking brick church, best known simply as St Mary's, is dominated by two towers of different heights. The first church here was built in the 1220s and following its destruction during a Tatar raid, construction of the basilica began. Tour the exquisite interior, with its remarkable carved wooden altarpiece, and in summer climb the tower for excellent views. Don't miss the hourly *hejnał* (bugle call) from the taller tower.

Cloth Hall HISTORIC BUILDING

(Sukiennice; Rynek Główny 1/3; 🚋1, 6, 8, 13, 18) FREE Dominating the middle of Rynek Główny, this building was once the centre of Kraków's medieval clothing trade. Created in the early 14th century when a roof was put over two rows of stalls, it was extended into a 108m-long Gothic structure, then rebuilt in Renaissance style after a 1555 fire; the arcades were a late-19th-century addition. The ground floor is now a busy trading centre for crafts and souvenirs; the upper

WORTH A TRIP

A UNESCO-PROTECTED SALT MINE

Some 14km southeast of Kraków, the **Wieliczka** (☎12 278 7302; www.kopalnia.pl; ul Daniłowicza 10; adult/concession 94/74zł; ⏲7.30am-7.30pm Apr-Oct, 8am-5pm Nov-Mar; 📶👪) (vyeh-leech-kah) salt mine has been welcoming tourists since 1722 and today is one of Poland's most popular attractions. It's a subterranean labyrinth of tunnels and chambers – about 300km distributed over nine levels, the deepest being 327m underground – of which a small part is open to the public via two-hour guided tours.

The salt-hewn formations include chapels with altarpieces and figures, while others are adorned with statues and monuments – and there are even underground lakes. The climax of the tour is the vast chamber (54m by 18m, and 12m high) housing the ornamented **Chapel of St Kinga** (Kaplica Św Kingi). Every single element here, from chandeliers to altarpieces, is made of salt.

English-language tours depart every half-hour from 8.30am to 6pm. During the rest of the year there are between six and eight daily tours in English.

Minibuses to Wieliczka (3zł) depart Kraków frequently between 6am and 8pm from stands along ul Pawia, across from the Galeria Krakowska mall.

Kraków – Old Town & Wawel

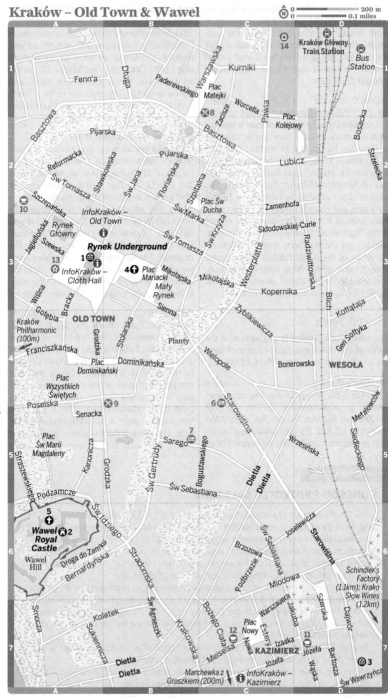

N
0 ——————————— 200 m
0 ——————————— 0.1 miles

Kraków Główny Train Station
14

Bus Station

Kurniki

Warszawska

Fenn'a

Długa

Paderewskiego

Plac Matejki

Worcella

Zacisze

Prawia

Plac Kolejowy

8

Basztowa

Pijarska

Reformacka

Sławkowska

Pijarska

Basztowa

Lubicz

Bosacka

Strzelecka

Św Tomasza

Św Jana

Florjańska

Szpitalna

Plac Św Ducha

Zamenhofa

Szczepańska

InfoKraków – Old Town

Św Marka

Św Krzyża

Skłodowskiej-Curie

10

Rynek Główny

Szewska

Jagiellońska

Św Tomasza

Westerplatte

Radziwiłłowska

Rynek Underground

13   1

InfoKraków – Cloth Hall

4   Plac Mariacki

Mały Rynek

Mikołajska

Mikołajska

Kopernika

Blich

Kołłątaja

Wiślna

Bracka

Gołębia

OLD TOWN

Grodzka

Stolarska

Sienna

Zyblikiewicza

Gen Sołtyka

Kraków Philharmonic (100m)

Franciszkańska

Planty

Wielopole

Bonerowska

WESOŁA

Metalowców

Plac Dominikański

Dominikańska

Plac Wszystkich Świętych

Poselska

Senacka

9

Starowiślna

6

Wrzesińska

Siedleckiego

Straszewskiego

Plac Św Marii Magdaleny

Kanonicza

Grodzka

Św Gertrudy

Sarego

7

Bogusławskiego

Dietla

Dietla

Podzamcze

Św Idziego

Św Sebastiana

Józefa

5

Wawel Royal Castle   2

Wawel Hill

Droga do Zamku

Bernardyńska

Stradomska

Św Agnieszki

Brzozowa

Św Sebastiana

Joselewicza

Starowiślna

Schindler's Factory (1.1km); Krako Słow Wines (1.2km)

Smocza

Koletek

Sukiennicza

Krakowska

Bożego Ciała

Meiselsa

Podbrzezie

Miodowa

Warszauera

Estery

Jakuba

Szeroka

Dajwor

Dietla

Dietla

Marchewka z Groszkiem (200m)

12

Plac Nowy

Nowa

InfoKraków – Kazimierz

Izaaka

KAZIMIERZ

Józefa

11

Bartosza

Wąska

Św Wawrzyńca

3

POLAND KRAKÓW

Kraków – Old Town & Wawel

floor houses the **Gallery of 19th-Century Polish Painting** (☑12 433 5400; www.mnk.pl; adult/concession 20/15zł, Sun free; ⊙9am-5pm Tue-Fri, 10am-6pm Sat, to 4pm Sun).

◎ Kazimierz & Podgórze

Founded by King Kazimierz III Wielki in 1335, Kazimierz was originally an independent town that later became a Jewish district. During WWII, the Germans relocated Jews south across the Vistula River to a walled ghetto in Podgórze. They were exterminated in the nearby Płaszów Concentration Camp, as portrayed in the Steven Spielberg film *Schindler's List*. In addition to the attractions below, many synagogues are still standing and can be visited individually.

★Schindler's Factory   MUSEUM
(Fabryka Schindlera; ☑12 257 1017; www.muzeum krakowa.pl; ul Lipowa 4; adult/concession 24/18zł, Mon free; ⊙10am-4pm Mon, 9am-8pm Tue-Sun; ⊞3, 19, 24) This impressive interactive museum covers the German occupation of Kraków in WWII. It's housed in the former enamel factory of Oskar Schindler, the German industrialist who famously saved the lives of members of his Jewish labour force during the Holocaust. Well-organised, innovative exhibits tell the moving story of the city from 1939 to 1945. Take a tram to Plac Bohaterów Getta, then follow the signs east under the railway line to the museum.

Galicia Jewish Museum   MUSEUM
(☑12 421 6842; www.galiciajewishmuseum.org; ul Dajwór 18; adult/concession 16/11zł; ⊙10am-6pm; ⊞3, 19, 24) This museum both commemorates Jewish victims of the Holocaust and celebrates the Jewish culture and history of the former Austro-Hungarian region of Gali-

cia. It features an impressive photographic exhibition depicting modern-day remnants of southeastern Poland's once-thriving Jewish community, called 'Traces of Memory', along with video testimony of survivors and regular temporary exhibits. The museum also leads guided tours of the Jewish sites of Kazimierz; call or email for details.

⊨ Sleeping

As Poland's premier tourist destination, Kraków has plenty of accommodation options. However, advance booking is recommended for anywhere central.

★Mundo Hostel   HOSTEL €
(☑12 422 6113; www.mundohostel.eu; ul Sarego 10; dm 60-65zł, d 170-190zł; ⊛⊜; ⊞1, 6, 8, 10, 13, 18) Attractive, well-maintained hostel in a quiet courtyard location neatly placed between the Old Town and Kazimierz. Each room is decorated for a different country; for example, the Tibet room is decked out with colourful prayer flags. Barbecues take place in summer. There's a bright, fully equipped kitchen for do-it-yourself meals.

★Aparthotel Vanilla   APARTMENT €€
(☑12 354 0150; www.aparthotelvanilla.pl; ul Bobrzyńskiego 33; apt from 250zł; P⊛⊜; ⊞11, 17, 18, 52) This place is a great choice for motorists, easily accessible from the A4 motorway, offering secure parking, and with a tram stop across the street (20 minutes to the centre). Standard rooms are superb value, effectively mini apartments with kitchenette and balcony; a buffet breakfast is served in the ground-floor restaurant.

Hamilton Suites   APARTMENT €€
(☑12 346 4670; www.krakow-apartments.biz; apt 300-600zł; ⊜) Provides high-quality

apartment rentals suited to longer stays (at least three days) and corporate rentals. The apartments are scattered around the Old Town as well as further afield in Podgórze. Most feature bright, modern design, and longer stays come with cleaning services. Check the website for an overview of the apartments.

★ Hotel Pugetów   HISTORIC HOTEL €€€

(☑ 12 432 4950; www.donimirski.com/hotel-puge tow; ul Starowiślna 15a; s/d 500/700zł; P ❄ 🗇; 🚌 1, 3, 17, 19, 22, 24, 52) This charming historic hotel stands proudly next to the 19th-century neo-Renaissance palace of the same name. It offers just seven rooms with distinctive names (Conrad, Bonaparte) and identities. Think embroidered bathrobes, black-marble baths and a fabulous breakfast room in the basement.

✕ Eating

Glonojad   VEGETARIAN €

(☑ 12 346 1677; www.glonojad.com; Plac Matejki 2; mains 15-22zł; ⊗ 8am-10pm Mon-Fri, from 9am Sat & Sun; 🗇 ☑ 🖷; 🚌 2, 4, 14, 18, 20, 24, 44) This appealing and popular self-service cafeteria has a great view onto Plac Matejki, just north of the Barbican. The diverse menu has a variety of tempting vegetarian dishes including samosas, curries, potato pancakes, falafel, veggie lasagne and soups. The breakfast menu is served till noon, so there's no need to jump out of that hotel bed too early.

★ Krako Slow Wines   INTERNATIONAL €€

(☑ 669 225 222; www.krakoslowwines.pl; ul Lipowa 6f; mains 22-40zł; ⊗ 10am-10pm Sun-Thu, to midnight Fri & Sat; 🗇 ☑ 🖷 🗷; 🚌 3, 19, 24) It's hard to accurately characterise this little wine bar and restaurant, which serves the best-value lunches within 100m of Schindler's Factory (p319). The emphasis is on the wine, but it also serves excellent beer, coffee, salads, snacks and hummus sandwiches, and its Caucasian barbecue (Tuesday to Saturday) turns out mouth-watering Georgian- and Armenian-style shashlik and kebab.

Marchewka z Groszkiem   POLISH €€

(☑ 12 430 0795; www.marchewkazgroszkiem.pl; ul Mostowa 2; mains 15-35zł; ⊗ 9am-10pm; 🗇 ☑ 🖷; 🚌 6, 8, 10, 13) Traditional Polish cooking, with hints of influence from neighbouring countries such as Ukraine, Hungary and Lithuania. Excellent potato pancakes and a delicious boiled beef with horseradish sauce are highlights of the menu. There are a few

sidewalk tables to admire the parade of people down one of Kazimierz's up-and-coming streets.

★ Miód Malina   POLISH €€€

(☑ 12 430 0411; www.miodmalina.pl; ul Grodzka 40; mains 40-80zł; ⊗ noon-11pm; 🗇 ☑ 🖷; 🚌 1, 6, 8, 13, 18) The charmingly named 'Honey Raspberry' serves Polish dishes in colourful surrounds. Grab a window seat and order the wild mushrooms in cream, and any of the duck or veal dishes. There's a variety of beef steaks on the menu as well. The grilled sheep's-cheese appetiser, served with cranberry jelly, is a regional speciality. Reservations essential.

🍷 Drinking & Nightlife

The Rynek Główny is literally ringed on all sides by bars and cafes, where outdoor tables offer great people-watching spots. Kazimierz also has a lively bar scene, centred on Plac Nowy.

★ Bunkier Cafe   CAFE

(☑ 12 431 0585; www.bunkiercafe.pl; Plac Szczepański 3a; ⊗ 9am-1am; 🗇; 🚌 2, 4, 14, 18, 20, 24, 44) The 'Bunker' is a wonderful cafe with an enormous glassed-in terrace tacked on to the Bunkier Sztuki (Art Bunker), a cutting-edge gallery northwest of the Rynek. The garden space is heated in winter and always has a buzz. There is excellent coffee, nonfiltered beers and homemade lemonades, plus light bites such as burgers and salads. Enter from the Planty.

Cheder   CAFE

(☑ 515 732 226; www.cheder.pl; ul Józefa 36; ⊗ 10am-10pm; 🚌 3, 19, 24) Unlike most of the other Jewish-themed places in Kazimierz, this one aims to entertain *and* educate. Named after a traditional Hebrew school, the cafe offers access to a decent library in Polish and English, regular readings and films, real Israeli coffee, brewed in a traditional Turkish copper pot with cinnamon and cardamom, and snacks such as homemade hummus.

Mleczarnia   CAFE

(☑ 12 421 8532; www.mle.pl; ul Meiselsa 20; ⊗ 10am-1am; 🗇; 🚌 6, 8, 10, 13) Wins the prize for best beer garden – located across the street from the cafe. Shady trees and blooming roses make this place tops for a sunny-afternoon drink. If it's raining, the cafe itself is warm and cosy, with crowded bookshelves and portrait-covered walls. Interesting beverages available include mead and cocoa with cherry vodka. Self-service.

AUSCHWITZ-BIRKENAU MEMORIAL & MUSEUM

Many visitors combine a stay in Kraków with a trip to the **Auschwitz-Birkenau Memorial & Museum** (Auschwitz-Birkenau Miejsce Pamięci i Muzeum; ☑ guides 33 844 8100; www. auschwitz.org; ul Stanisławy Leszczyńskiej; ⊙ 7.30am-7pm Jun-Aug, to 6pm Apr-May & Sep, to 5pm Mar & Oct, to 4pm Feb, to 3pm Jan & Nov, to 2pm Dec) **FREE**, a name synonymous with the horror of the Holocaust. More than a million Jews, and many thousands of Poles and Roma, were murdered here by German occupiers during WWII.

Both sections of the camp – **Auschwitz I** and the much larger outlying **Birkenau (Auschwitz II)** – have been preserved and are open to visitors free of charge. It's essential to visit both to appreciate the extent and the inhumanity of the place. From April to October it's compulsory to join a tour if you arrive between 10am and 3pm, otherwise you can explore at your own pace.

The tour begins at the main camp, Auschwitz I, which began life as a Polish military barracks but was co-opted by the Germans in 1940 as an extermination camp. Here is the infamous gate, displaying the grimly cynical message: 'Arbeit Macht Frei' (Work Makes You Free). Some 13 of 30 surviving prison blocks house museum exhibitions.

From here, the tour moves to Birkenau (Auschwitz II), 2km to the west, where most of the killing took place. Massive and purpose-built for efficiency, the camp had more than 300 prison barracks. Here you'll find the remnants of gas chambers and crematoria.

Auschwitz-Birkenau is a workable day trip from Kraków. There are hourly buses to Oświęcim (10zł, one hour), departing from the bus station in Kraków. There are also numerous minibuses to Oświęcim from the minibus stands off ul Pawia, next to Galeria Krakowska.

☆ Entertainment

★ Harris Piano Jazz Bar   JAZZ
(☑ 12 421 5741; www.harris.krakow.pl; Rynek Główny 28; tickets 20-80zł; ⊙ 11am-2am; ☐ 1, 6, 8, 13, 18) This lively jazz haunt is housed in an atmospheric, intimate cellar space right on the Rynek Główny. Harris hosts jazz and blues bands most nights from around 9.30pm, but try to arrive an hour earlier to get a seat (or book in advance by phone). Wednesday nights see weekly jam sessions (admission free).

Kraków Philharmonic   CLASSICAL MUSIC
(Filharmonia im Karola Szymanowskiego w Krakowie; ☑ 12 619 8733; www.filharmonia.krakow.pl; ul Zwierzyniecka 1; ⊙ box office 10am-2pm & 3-7pm Tue-Fri; ☐ 1, 2, 6) Home to one of Poland's best orchestras. Tickets cost 30zł to 40zł.

ℹ Information

The official tourist information office, **Info-Kraków** (www.infokrakow.pl), maintains branches around town. Expect cheerful service, loads of free maps and promotional materials, help in sorting out accommodation and transport, and a computer on hand (in some branches) for free, short-term web-surfing.

ℹ Getting There & Away

AIR
Kraków's **John Paul II International Airport** (KRK; ☑ 801 055 000, 12 295 5800; www.

krakowairport.pl; ul Kapitana Mieczysława Medweckiego 1, Balice; ☎) is located in the town of Balice, about 15km west of the centre. The airport has car-hire desks, bank ATMs, a tourist information office and currency exchanges.

LOT (www.lot.com) flies to Warsaw, and Ryanair has direct flights to Gdańsk. There are also direct flights from Kraków to many cities in the UK and Europe.

BUS
Kraków's **bus station** (☑ 703 403 340; www. mda.malopolska.pl; ul Bosacka 18; ⊙ information desk 9am-5pm; ☎ ; ☐ 2, 3, 4, 5, 10, 14, 17, 19, 20, 44, 50, 52) is next to the main train station northeast of the Old Town. Access the station through the train station and follow the signs. The station has ticket and information counters, storage lockers and vending machines.

Nearly all intercity coaches, both international and domestic, arrive at or depart from this station. Handy bus services include **FlixBus** (https://global.flixbus.com), **Leo Express** (www. leoexpress.com) and **Majer Bus** (www.majerbus. pl). Consult the websites for destinations, departure times and prices.

TRAIN
The modern **Kraków Main Station** (Kraków Główny; ☑ 22 391 9757; www.pkp.pl; ul Pawia 5a; ⊙ information desk 7am-9pm; ☎ ; ☐ 2, 3, 4, 5, 10, 14, 17, 19, 20, 44, 50, 52) is on the northeastern edge of the Old Town, entered via the **Galeria Krakowska** (☑ 12 428 9902; www. galeriakrakowska.pl; ul Pawia 5; ⊙ 9am-10pm

Mon-Sat, 10am-9pm Sun; 🚇 2, 3, 4, 10, 14, 20, 44, 52) shopping centre. Mostly underground, the station is beautifully laid out, with information booths and ticket offices on several levels. Find the left-luggage office (6zł/day) and storage lockers (per day big/small locker 12/8zł) below platform 5. There are plenty of bank ATMs, restaurants and shops.

ℹ️ Getting Around

The city's extensive network of trams is operated by the **Kraków Public Transport Authority** (Miejskie Przedsiębiorstwo Komunikacyjne/ MPK; 📞 12 19150; www.mpk.krakow.pl) abbreviated as MPK. The system runs daily from about 5am to 11pm.

Rides require a valid ticket that can be bought from automated ticketing machines *(automat biletów)* onboard or at important stops. Some machines only take coins, while others also take bills and credit cards, though using coins remains the quickest way to buy a ticket. You can also buy tickets from some news kiosks.

Tickets are valid for various time periods, from 20 minutes (2.80zł) and 40 minutes (3.80zł) to 24/48/72 hours (15/24/36zł). Remember to validate your ticket in stamping machines when you first board; spot checks are frequent.

The network is logically laid out and tram numbers and routes are prominently displayed at stops. The only issue is that the routes and numbers change frequently as lines are upgraded and repaired. InfoKraków tourist offices can supply a transport map, though that may too be out of date.

MAŁOPOLSKA

Małopolska (literally 'Lesser Poland') covers southeastern Poland from the former royal capital of Kraków to the eastern Lublin Uplands. The name does not refer to size or relative importance, but rather that Lesser Poland was mentioned in atlases more recently than Wielkopolska ('Greater Poland'). It's a colourful region filled with remnants of traditional life and historic cities.

Lublin

POP 339,850

Lublin is the largest city in southeastern Poland, with a thriving cultural and academic scene. That said, it's not a looker. Lublin was ravaged during WWII and the forced industrialisation of the communist period added insult to injury. Nevertheless, the city's historic core, the Rynek, is slowly being gentrified,

and trendy clubs and restaurants are giving new lustre to the Old Town's impressive stock of Renaissance and baroque town houses.

Lublin is of special interest to travellers seeking Poland's Jewish past. For centuries the city was a leading centre of Jewish scholarship, giving rise to Lublin's nickname the 'Jewish Oxford'. That heritage came to a brutal end in WWII, but here and there you can still find traces.

👁 Sights & Activities

Majdanek HISTORIC SITE
(Państwowe Muzeum na Majdanku; 📞 81 710 2833; www.majdanek.eu; Droga Męczenników Majdanka 67; parking 5zł; ⏰ 9am-6pm Apr-Oct, to 4pm Nov-Mar, exhibition closed Mon; 🅿) **FREE** Majdanek extermination camp, where tens of thousands of people, mainly Jews, were murdered by the Germans during WWII, lies on the outskirts of Lublin – guard towers and barbed-wire fences interrupting the suburban sprawl are disquieting. Allow half a day for the 5km walk around the camp; if pushed for time, visit the historical exhibition in building 62, the photographic display in building 45, and the skin-crawlingly chilling gas chambers. Majdanek is 4km southeast of the Kraków Gate; take bus 23.

Lublin Castle MUSEUM
(www.muzeumlubelskie.pl; ul Zamkowa 9; adult/concession 30/23zł; ⏰10am-6pm Tue-Sun May-Sep, 9am-5pm Oct-Apr) Lublin's royal castle dates from the 12th and 13th centuries, though it's been rebuilt many times since; the oldest surviving part is the impressive Romanesque **round tower** that dominates the courtyard; it was here in 1569 that Poland's union with Lithuania was signed. The castle is home to **Lublin Museum** and the 14th-century Gothic **Chapel of the Holy Trinity**, which contains Poland's finest examples of medieval frescoes; the ticket gives access to both and also to the tower.

Kraków Gate MUSEUM
(Brama Krakowska; www.muzeumlubelskie.pl; Plac Łokietka 3; adult/concession 5.50/4.50zł; ⏰10am-6pm Tue-Sun Jun-Aug, to 4pm Sep-May) The only significant remnant of the fortified walls that once surrounded the Old Town is the 14th-century Gothic Kraków Gate, built during the reign of Kazimierz III Wielki following the Mongol attack in 1341. It received its octagonal Renaissance superstructure in the 16th century, and its baroque crown in 1782. These days it's home to the **Historical Muse-**

um of Lublin and its small collection of documents and photographs of the town's history.

Cathedral of St John the Baptist CHURCH
(www.archikatedra.kuria.lublin.pl; Plac Katedralny; church free, treasury & crypt adult/child 4/2zł; ⊗ treasury & crypt 10am-4pm Tue-Sat) This former Jesuit church dates from the 16th century and is the largest in Lublin; you can visit any time services are not taking place. The impressive interior is adorned with baroque trompe l'oeil frescoes by Moravian artist Józef Meyer. The **treasury** *(skarbiec)* houses precious gold and silverware, a 14th-century bronze baptismal font and more Meyer frescoes. The vaulted roof of the so-called **acoustic vestry** *(zakrystia akustyczna)* reflects whispers from one corner across to the other.

Underground Route WALKING
(☑ tour bookings 81 534 6570; www.teatrnn.pl/pod ziemia; Rynek 1; adult/concession 12/10zł; ⊗ 10am-4pm Tue-Fri, noon-5pm Sat & Sun) This 280m trail winds its way through interconnected cellars beneath the Old Town, with historical exhibitions along the way. Entry is from the southwest side of the neoclassical Old Town Hall in the centre of Market Sq (Rynek) at approximately two-hourly intervals; check with the tourist office for exact times.

🛏 Sleeping

Folk Hostel HOSTEL €
(☑ 887 223 887; www.folkhostel.pl; ul Krakowskie Przedmieście 23; dm/tr 45/159zł; P 🛜) This charming hostel ticks all the boxes, with friendly English-speaking staff, brightly decorated rooms and a superbly central location. Although it overlooks the main street, the entrance is around the back, via a gate on Zielona. Limited on-site parking.

Vanilla Hotel HOTEL €€
(☑ 81 536 6720; www.vanilla-hotel.pl; ul Krakowskie Przedmieście 12; s 265-335zł, d 315-405zł; P @ 🛜) The name must be tongue-in-cheek – this sleekly gorgeous hotel on the main pedestrian plaza is anything but plain vanilla. The rooms are filled with inspired, even bold, styling: vibrant colours, big headboards, and retro lamps and furniture. There's lots of attention to detail here, which continues in the chic restaurant and coffee bar. Lower rates on weekends.

Rezydencja Waksman HOTEL €€
(☑ 81 532 5454; www.waksman.pl; ul Grodzka 19; s/d 210/230zł, apt from 290zł; P @ 🛜) Hotel Waksman deserves a blue ribbon for many reasons, not least of which is the atmospheric Old Town location. Each standard room (named 'yellow', 'blue', 'green' or 'red' for its decor) has individual character. The two apartments on top are special; they offer ample space for lounging or working, and views over the Old Town and castle.

🍴 Eating & Drinking

Mandragora JEWISH €€
(☑ 81 536 2020; www.mandragora.lublin.pl; Rynek 9; mains 25-55zł; ⊗ 8.30am-10pm Sun-Thu, to midnight Fri & Sat; 🛜) There's good kitsch and there's bad kitsch, and at Mandragora, it's all good. Sure it's going for the *Fiddler on the Roof* effect with the lace tablecloths, knickknacks and photos of old Lublin, but in the romantic Rynek setting it works wonderfully. The food is heartily Jewish, from roast duck with *tzimmes* (stewed carrots and dried fruit) to salt beef.

★ Kardamon INTERNATIONAL €€€
(☑ 81 448 0257; www.kardamon.eu; ul Krakowskie Przedmieście 41; mains 32-72zł; ⊗ noon-11pm Mon-Sat, to 10pm Sun; 🛜) By many accounts, Lublin's best restaurant is this lush cellar on the main street. The menu is a mix of international staples such as grilled pork tenderloin, along with Polish favourites such as *żurek* (sour rye soup), roast duck served with beetroot and some regional specialities.

Szklarnia CAFE
(Centrum Kultury w Lublinie; www.facebook.com/pg/szklarniakawiarnia; ul Peowiaków 12; ⊗ 9am-1am Sun-Thu, to 2am Fri & Sat; 🛜) This sleek cafe-bar in the Lublin Cultural Centre has great coffee as well as a daily selection of cakes. There's live entertainment some nights, and a nice garden terrace at the back in warm weather (the name means 'glasshouse').

Czarna Owca PUB
(www.czarnaowcagastropub.pl; ul Narutowicza 9; ⊗ 1-11pm Sun-Thu, to 2am Fri-Sat) The 'Black Sheep' is a legendary Lublin watering hole, going strong into the small hours at weekends. In addition to Żywiec and Paulaner on draught and a selection of bottled Polish craft beers, it has a menu of gourmet burgers, pub grub and snacks to munch on.

ℹ Information

Tourist Information Centre (LOITiK; ☑ 81 532 4412; www.lublintravel.pl; ul Jezuicka 1/3; ⊗ 9am-7pm Apr-Oct, to 5pm Nov-Mar) Extremely helpful English-speaking staff. There

ZAMOŚĆ: POLAND'S RENAISSANCE HEART

While most Polish cities' attractions centre on their medieval heart, Zamość (zah-moshch) is pure 16th-century Renaissance. It was founded in 1580 by nobleman Jan Zamoyski and designed by an Italian architect. The splendid architecture of Zamość's Old Town escaped serious destruction in WWII and was added to Unesco's World Heritage List in 1992.

The **Rynek Wielki** (Great Market Square) is the heart of Zamość's attractive Old Town. This impressive Italianate Renaissance square (exactly 100m by 100m) is dominated by a lofty, pink town hall and surrounded by colourful, arcaded burghers' houses. The **Museum of Zamość** (Muzeum Zamojskie; www.muzeum-zamojskie.pl; ul Ormiańska 30; adult/concession 12/6zł; ☉9am-4pm Tue-Sun) is based in two of the loveliest buildings on the square and houses interesting exhibits, including paintings, folk costumes and a scale model of the 16th-century town.

The city's **synagogue** (www.zamosc.fodz.pl; ul Pereca 14; by donation; ☉10am-6pm Tue-Sun Mar-Oct, to 2pm Nov-Feb) was built around 1620 and served as the Jewish community's main house of worship until WWII, when it was shuttered by the Germans. The highlight of the exhibition is a gripping computer presentation on the history of the town's Jewish community, including its roots in Sephardic Judaism.

Zamość is an easy day trip from Lublin by bus (15zł, two hours, every half-hour). The helpful **tourist office** (☑84 639 2292; www.travel.zamosc.pl; Rynek Wielki 13; ☉8am-5pm Mon-Fri, from 9am Sat & Sun year-round, longer hours May-Sep; ☏) in the town hall has maps, brochures and souvenirs.

are souvenirs for sale and lots of brochures, including handy maps of the most popular walking tours in Lublin. There's also a computer for internet access.

ⓘ Getting There & Away

BUS

FlixBus (https://global.flixbus.com) services connect the **bus station** (ul Hutnicza 1, cross at Tysiąclecia) with major cities throughout Poland, including Warsaw (from 15zł, three hours, six daily) and Kraków (47zł, 5½ hours, four daily).

Private minibuses run from the **minibus station** (ul Nadstawna) north of the bus terminal to various destinations, including Zamość (15zł, two hours, hourly) and Kazimierz Dolny (8zł, one hour, every 30 minutes).

TRAIN

The train station is 2km south of the Old Town. There are direct trains to Warsaw (from 31zł, three hours, five daily); Kraków and Zamość are more easily reached by bus.

CARPATHIAN MOUNTAINS

The Carpathians (Karpaty) stretch from Poland's southern border with Slovakia into Ukraine, and their wooded hills and snowy mountains are a magnet for hikers, skiers and cyclists. The most popular destination here is the resort of Zakopane.

Zakopane

POP 27,270

Zakopane, 100km south of Kraków, is Poland's main alpine resort, situated at the foot of the Tatra Mountains. It's a popular jumping-off spot for trekking and mountain hikes, as well as skiing. The busy high street, ul Krupówki, is a jumble of souvenir shops, bars and restaurants, but away from the centre, the pace slows down. This was an artists' colony in the early 20th century, and the graceful timbered villas from those days – built in what's known as the 'Zakopane style' – are still scattered around town.

◎ Sights & Activities

Morskie Oko   LAKE
(national park per person 5zł) The most popular outing near Zakopane is to this emerald-green mountain lake, about 20km southeast of the town. Minibuses regularly depart from ul Kościuszki, across from the main bus station, for Polana Palenica (10zł, 45 minutes), from where a 9km-long road continues uphill to the lake. Cars, bikes and buses are not allowed, so you'll have to walk (about two hours each way) or take a horse-drawn carriage (50zł). Travel agencies organise day trips.

Kasprowy Wierch Cable Car · CABLE CAR
(☑18 201 5356; www.pkl.pl; Kuźnice; adult/concession return 63/53zł; ☉7.30am-4pm Jan-Mar, to 6pm Apr-Jun & Sep-Oct, 7am-9pm Jul & Aug, 9am-4pm Nov-Dec) The cable-car trip from Kuźnice (2km south of Zakopane) to the Mt Kasprowy Wierch summit (1985m) is a classic tourist experience. At the end of the ascent (20 minutes, climbing 936m), you can get off and stand with one foot in Poland and the other in Slovakia. The view from the top is spectacular (clouds permitting). The cable car normally closes for two weeks in May, and won't operate if the snow or wind conditions are dangerous.

Old Church & Cemetery · CHURCH
(Stary Kościół i Cmentarz na Pęksowym Brzyzku; ul Kościeliska 4; cemetery 2zł; ☉8am-5pm) This small wooden church and atmospheric cemetery date from the mid-19th century. The Old Church has charming carved wooden decorations and pews, and the Stations of the Cross painted on glass on the windows. The adjoining cemetery is one of the country's most beautiful, with a number of amazing wood-carved headstones, some resembling giant chess pieces. The noted Polish painter and creator of the Zakopane style, Stanisław Witkiewicz, is buried here beneath a modest wooden grave marker.

🛏 Sleeping

Private rooms provide some of the best-value accommodation in town (around 50zł per person). Check at the tourist office for details or look for signs reading '*pokoje*', '*noclegi*' or '*zimmer frei*'.

Target Hostel · HOSTEL €
(☑18 207 4596, 730 955 730; www.targethostel.pl; ul Sienkiewicza 3b; dm/tw from 39/150zł; @🛜) This private, well-run hostel is within easy walking distance of the bus station; the entrance is downstairs from the street, beneath a clinic. Accommodation is in six- to 10-bed dorms, with classic pale-wood panelling and wooden floors. There's a common room and communal kitchen, and the staff are friendly and helpful.

Czarny Potok · HOTEL €€
(☑18 202 2760; www.czarnypotok.pl; ul Tetmajera 20; s/d from 219/259zł; P🅿🛜) The 'Black Stream', set beside a pretty brook amid lovely gardens, is a 44-room pension-like hotel on a quiet backstreet just south of the pedestrian mall. Bedrooms have alpine-style pine-

wood cladding, and there's a great fitness centre with a pool and two saunas.

Hotel Sabała · HOTEL €€€
(☑18 201 5092; www.sabala.zakopane.pl; ul Krupówki 11; s/d from 380/420zł; ☜🛜🏊) Built in 1894 but thoroughly up to date, this striking timber hotel has a superb location overlooking the picturesque pedestrian thoroughfare. The hotel offers cosy, attic-style rooms, and there's a sauna, solarium and swimming pool. The restaurant here serves both local specialities and international favourites.

🍴 Eating & Drinking

Karczma Zapiecek · POLISH €€
(☑18 201 5699; www.karczmazapiecek.pl; ul Krupówki 43; mains 25-40zł; ☉10am-11pm) One of the better choices among a group of similar highlander-style restaurants along ul Krupówki, with great food, an old stove and a terrace. Traditional dishes on offer include local *oscypek grillowany* (grilled smoked cheese) served with bacon or cranberries, Slovakian *hałuski bryndzowe* (potato dumplings with sheep's cheese) and *pstrąg z pieca* (baked trout).

Pstrąg Górski · SEAFOOD €€
(☑512 351 746; www.zakopane-restauracje.pl; ul Krupówki 6a; mains 22-45zł; ☉10am-10pm; 🛜) This alpine-style restaurant (the 'Mountain Trout') done up in timber-rich decor and overlooking a narrow stream, serves some of the freshest trout, salmon and sea fish in town. Trout is priced at 6zł and up per 100g (whole fish), bringing the price of a standard fish dinner to around 35zł, not including sides.

La Mano · COFFEE
(www.facebook.com/lamanozakopane; ul Władysława Orkana 1f; ☉9am-6pm Mon & Wed-Sat, 10am-4pm Sun; 🛜) This cool and stylish cafe serves the best coffee in town, a passion reflected in the range of coffee-making equipment on sale, alongside a neat line in locally produced honey fruit juices and compotes. Sit out front overlooking the street, or head through the back for a view of the mountains.

ℹ Information

Tourist Office (Centrum Informacji Turystycznej; ☑18 201 2211; www.zakopane.pl; ul Kościuszki 7; ☉9am-5pm Mar-Aug, Mon-Fri Sep-Feb) Small but helpful municipal tourist office just south of the bus station on the walk towards the centre. It has free city maps and sells more-detailed hiking maps.

POLAND ZAKOPANE

Tatra National Park Information Point (Punkt Informacji Turystycznej; ☎ 18 20 23 300; www. tpn.pl; ul Chałubińskiego 42; ⊙ 7am-3pm) Located in a small building near the Rondo Jana Pawła II on the southern outskirts of the city. It's a good place for maps, guides and local weather and hiking information.

❶ Getting There & Around

Bus is far and away the best transport option for reaching Zakopane. The **bus station** (PKS; ☎ 300 300 143; ul Kościuszki 23) is about 400m northeast of the centre along ul Kościuszki. Most buses and minibuses depart from here or the small minibus station across the street.

Szwagropol (☎ 12 271 3550; www. szwagropol.pl) operates bus services to Kraków (20zł, two hours, twice hourly).

Dozens of privately owned minibuses depart regularly (when full) from the bus station to hiking trailheads, including Kuznice (5zł, 15 minutes, for the Kasprowy Wierch cable car) and Morskie Oko (8zł, 30 minutes).

SILESIA

Silesia (Śląsk in Polish; pronounced shlonsk), in the far southwest of the country, is a traditional industrial and mining region with a fascinating mix of landscapes.

Wrocław

POP 638,590

Everyone loves Wrocław (*vrots*-wahf) and it's easy to see why. Wrocław's location on the Odra River, with its 12 islands, 130 bridges and riverside parks, is idyllic, and the beautifully preserved Cathedral Island is a treat for lovers of Gothic architecture.

Though in some ways it's a more manageable version of Kraków, with all the cultural attributes and entertainment of that popular destination, the capital of Lower Silesia also has an appealing character all its own. Having absorbed Bohemian, Austrian and Prussian influences, the city has a unique architectural and cultural make-up, symbolised by its magnificent market square (Rynek).

But Wrocław is not just a pretty face. It is Poland's fourth-largest city and the major industrial, commercial and educational centre for the region. At the same time it's a lively cultural centre, with several theatres, major festivals, rampant nightlife and a large student community.

◎ Sights & Activities

The hub of city life is the magnificent Old Town square, the **Rynek**. Northeast of the Old Town lies historic Cathedral Island (Ostrów Tumski) – the birthplace of Wrocław.

★ **Old Town Hall** HISTORIC BUILDING
(Stary Ratusz; Rynek) This grand edifice took almost 200 years (1327–1504) to complete. The right-hand part of the eastern facade, with its austere early-Gothic features, is the oldest, while the delicate carving in the section to the left shows early-Renaissance style; the astronomical clock in the centre, made of larch wood, was built in 1580. The southern facade, dating from the early 16th century, is the most elaborate, with a pair of ornate bay windows and carved stone figures.

Wrocław Dwarves PUBLIC ART
(Wrocławskie Krasnale; www.krasnale.pl) See if you can spot the tiny bronze statue of a dwarf resting on the ground, just to the west of the **Hansel & Gretel houses** (Jaś i Małgosia; ul Odrzańska 39/40). A few metres away you'll spot firefighter dwarves, rushing to put out a blaze. These figures are part of a collection of over 300 scattered through the city. Though whimsical, they're also a reference to the symbol of the Orange Alternative, a communist-era dissident group that used ridicule as a weapon.

★ **Panorama of Racławice** MUSEUM
(Panorama Racławicka; www.panoramaraclawicka.pl; ul Purkyniego 11; adult/concession 30/23zł; ⊙ 8am-7.30pm Apr-Oct, shorter hours & closed Mon Nov-Mar; ⓟ) Wrocław's pride and joy is this giant painting of the battle for Polish independence fought at Racławice on 4 April 1794, between the Polish army led by Tadeusz Kościuszko and Russian troops under General Alexander Tormasov. The Poles won but it was all for naught: months later the nationwide insurrection was crushed by the tsarist army. The canvas measures 15m by 114m, and is wrapped around the internal walls of a rotunda.

National Museum MUSEUM
(Muzeum Narodowe; www.mnwr.pl; Plac Powstańców Warszawy 5; adult/concession 20/15zł, Sat free; ⊙ 10am-5pm Tue-Fri, 10.30am-6pm Sat & Sun, shorter hours Oct-Mar) A treasure trove of fine art. Medieval sculpture is displayed on the ground floor; exhibits include the Romanesque tympanum from the portal of the **Church of St Mary Magdalene** (ul Łaciarska; tower adult/concession 4/3zł; ⊙ tower 10am-6pm Apr-Oct), depicting the Assumption of the

Virgin Mary, and 14th-century sarcophagi from the **Church of SS Vincent & James** (Kościół Św Wincentego i Św Jakuba; Plac Biskupa Nankiera 15a). There are also collections of Silesian paintings, ceramics, silverware and furnishings from the 16th to 19th centuries.

Cathedral of St John the Baptist   CHURCH
(Archikatedra Św Jana Chrzciciela; www.katedra.archi diecezja.wroc.pl; Plac Katedralny 18; tower & chapels adult/concession 10/8zł; ⊙ 10am-5pm Mon-Sat, from 2pm Sun) The centrepiece of Cathedral Island, this three-aisled Gothic basilica was built between 1244 and 1590. Seriously damaged during WWII, it was rebuilt in its original Gothic form. Entry to the church is free, but you need to buy a ticket to visit three beautiful baroque chapels, and to ascend to the viewpoint atop the 91m-high tower (there's a lift).

Gondola Bay   CANOEING
(Zatoka Gondol; www.visitwroclaw.eu/en/event/ gondola-bay; promenada Staromiejska; kayak per hour 15zł; ⊙ Apr-Sep) You can get a different perspective of the city by viewing it from the water. Rent a kayak, rowing boat (per hour 25zł) or motorboat (per hour 80zł) and take a tour around Ostrow Tumski.

🛏 Sleeping

Hostel Mleczarnia   HOSTEL €
(✆ 71 787 7570; www.mleczarniahostel.pl; ul Włodkowica 5; dm 40-50zł, tw 220zł; 🛜) Set in a quiet courtyard not far from the Rynek (go through the passage left of Restaurant Sarah), this hostel has bags of charm, having been decorated in a deliberately old-fashioned style with antique furniture. There's a women-only dorm available, along with a kitchen and free laundry facilities. In the courtyard is the excellent **Mleczarnia** (www.mle.pl; ⊙ 8am-4am; 🛜) cafe-bar.

Hotel Patio   HOTEL €€
(✆ 71 375 0400; www.hotelpatio.pl; ul Kiełbaśnicza 24; s/d from 250/270zł; 🅿 ❄ 🛜) The Patio offers pleasant lodgings a short hop from the main square, within two buildings linked by a covered, sunlit courtyard. Rooms are clean and light, though the cheaper ones can be on the small side, and there's a spectacular breakfast spread.

Hotel Monopol   HOTEL €€€
(✆ 71 772 3777; www.monopolwroclaw.hotel.com. pl; ul Modrzejewskiej 2; r from 700zł; ❄ 🛜 🏊) In its heyday the elegant Monopol hosted such luminaries as Pablo Picasso and Marlene Dietrich (along with more notorious names such as Adolf Hitler). Along with stylishly modernised bedrooms there's a choice of upmarket restaurants, bars, a cafe, a spa and boutiques, so you won't be short of pampering options.

🍴 Eating

★ Panczo   TEX-MEX €€
(✆ 884 009 737; www.facebook.com/panczobus; ul Świętego Antoniego 35/1a; mains 15-26zł; ⊙ noon-11pm Sun-Thu, to midnight Fri & Sat; 🛜) Part of a Polish trend that has seen street-food businesses opening up in permanent premises, Panczo serves up huge portions of lip-smacking tacos, enchiladas and – the house speciality – burritos. The food is fresh, zingy and authentic, as are the margaritas. Order food at the bar (ask for an English menu if there are none on the tables).

Vega Bar Wegański   VEGAN €€
(✆ 713 443 934; www.facebook.com/vega.bar.we ganski.wroclaw; Rynek 1/2; mains 15-30zł; ⊙ 8am-8pm Mon-Thu, to 9pm Fri & Sat, 9am-8pm Sun; 🥗) This buzzing vegan restaurant in the centre of the Rynek, with a cafe upstairs, serves everything from breakfasts of oatmeal and millet with vegan milk and seasonal fruits (till noon), to hot, filling lunch dishes such as tempeh burgers, Thai curries, pizzas and meat-free pierogi (Polish dumplings). There's a good choice of gluten-free options too, and even vegan ice cream.

★ Restauracja Jadka   POLISH €€€
(✆ 71 343 6461; www.jadka.pl; ul Rzeźnicza 24/25; mains 57-83zł; ⊙ 5-11pm Mon-Sat, to 10pm Sun) One of Wrocław's top fine-dining options, presenting impeccable modern versions of Polish classics such as ox tongue served with beetroot and chard, and halibut with tarragon and fried groats, with silver-service table settings (candles, crystal, linen) in delightful Gothic surroundings. Bookings are recommended, especially at weekends.

🍷 Drinking & Entertainment

Vinyl Cafe   BAR
(✆ 508 260 288; www.facebook.com/vinylcafe. wroclaw; ul Kotlarska 35/36; ⊙ 10am-midnight Mon-Thu, to 1am Fri-Sat, to 11pm Sun; 🛜) Hitting the retro button hard, this cool cafe-bar is a jumble of mismatched furniture, old framed photos and stacks of vinyl records. It's a great place to grab a drink, both day and night.

Bezsenność   CLUB
(www.facebook.com/klubbezsennosc; ul Ruska 51; ⊙ 7pm-3am Tue & Wed, to 5am Thu-Sat) With

its alternative/rock/dance line-up and distressed decor, 'Insomnia' attracts a high-end clientele and is one of the most popular clubs in town. It's located in the Pasaż Niepolda, home to a group of bars, clubs and restaurants, just off ul Ruska.

Filharmonia CLASSICAL MUSIC
(Philharmonic Hall; ☑ tickets 71 715 9700; www.nfm.wroclaw.pl; ul Piłsudskiego 19) The city's main concert hall stages performances of orchestral music, chamber music, jazz and popular artists.

❶ Information

Tourist Office (☑ 71 344 3111; www.wroclaw-info.pl; Rynek 14; ☺ 9am-7pm)

❶ Getting There & Away

BUS
The **bus station** (Dworzec Centralny PKS; ☑ 703 400 444; ul Sucha 1/11) is 1.3km south of the Rynek, at the east end of the Wroclavia shopping mall, across the street from the main train station. Destination include Berlin (69zł, 4½ hours, four daily), Kraków (from 21zł, 3½ hours, hourly), Prague (69zł, 4½ hours, four daily) and Warsaw (29zł, 4½ hours to 5½ hours, hourly).

TRAIN
Trains depart from the impressive mock castle that is Wrocław Główny station, 1.2km south of the Rynek. Destination include Kraków (45zł, 3½ hours, hourly), Poznań (38zł, 2½ hours, hourly) and Warsaw (59zł, 3½ to six hours, 10 daily).

WIELKOPOLSKA

Wielkopolska (Greater Poland) is the region where Poland came to life in the Middle Ages. As a result of this ancient eminence, its cities and towns are full of historic and cultural attractions. The battles of WWII later caused widespread destruction in the area, though Poznań has resumed its prominent economic role.

Poznań
POP 554,700

Stroll into Poznań's Old Town square on any evening and you'll receive an instant introduction to the characteristic energy of Wielkopolska's capital. The city centre is buzzing at any time of the day, and positively jumping by night, full of people heading to its many restaurants, pubs and clubs. The combination of international business travellers attending its numerous trade fairs and the city's huge student population has created a distinctive vibe quite independent of tourism.

In addition to its energetic personality, Poznań offers many historical attractions – this is, after all, the 1000-year-old birthplace of the Polish nation – and its plentiful transport links make it a great base from which to explore the quieter surrounding countryside.

⊙ Sights

The main sights are split between the Old Town and the island of Ostrów Tumski, east of the main square and across the Warta River – the place where Poznań was founded, and with it the Polish state.

Town Hall HISTORIC BUILDING
(Ratusz; Stary Rynek 1; ⧆ Plac Wielkopolski, Wrocławska) Poznań's Renaissance town hall, topped with a 61m-high tower, instantly attracts attention. Its graceful form replaced a 13th-century Gothic structure, which burned down in the early 16th century. Every day at noon two metal goats appear through a pair of small doors above the clock and butt their horns together 12 times, in deference to an old legend. These days, the town hall is home to the city's Historical Museum.

Historical Museum of Poznań MUSEUM
(Muzeum Historii Miasta Poznania; ☑ 61 856 8000 www.mnp.art.pl; Stary Rynek 1; adult/concession 7/5zł, Sat free; ☺ 11am-5pm Tue-Thu, noon-9pm Fri, 11am-6pm Sat & Sun; ⧆ Plac Wielkopolski, Wrocławska) This museum (in the town hall) displays an interesting and well-presented exhibition on Poznań's history, though the building's original interiors are worth the entry price on their own. The richly ornamented Renaissance Hall on the 1st floor is a real gem, with its original stucco work and paintings from 1555. The 2nd floor contains artefacts from the Prussian/German period, documents illustrating city life in the 1920s and '30s, and a collection of interesting memorabilia from the past two centuries.

★ **Porta Posnania**
Interactive Heritage Centre MUSEUM
(Brama Poznania ICHOT; ☑ 61 647 7634 www.bramapoznania.pl; ul Gdańska 2; adult/concession 18/12zł incl audio guide; ☺ 9am-6pm Tue-Fri, 10am-7pm Sat & Sun; ⧆ Katedra) This cutting-edge multimedia museum provides an easily digested introduction to the birth of the Polish nation, telling the tale of Ostrów Tumski's (Cathedral Island) eventful history via in-

teractive displays, maps, movies and models. It's located opposite the island's eastern shore and is linked to the cathedral area by footbridge. The exhibitions are multilingual, but the audio guide helps bring everything together.

To reach the museum from the city centre, take tram 8 eastward to the Rondo Śródka stop.

★ Poznań Cathedral
CHURCH

(Katedra Poznańska; www.katedra.archpoznan.pl; ul Ostrów Tumski 17; church free, crypt adult/concession 3.50/2.50zł; ⊙ 9am-5pm Mon-Sat mid-Mar–mid-Nov, 9.30am-4pm mid-Nov–mid-Mar; ⛴ Katedra) Ostrów Tumski is dominated by this monumental double-towered cathedral. Basically Gothic with additions from later periods, notably the baroque upper towers, the cathedral was damaged in 1945 and took 11 years to rebuild. Early Polish kings were buried in the **crypt** – apart from fragments of their tombs, you can see the relics of the original church dating from 968, and of the Romanesque building from the second half of the 11th century.

🛏 Sleeping

Tey Hostel
HOSTEL €

(⌨ 61 639 3497; www.tey-hostel.pl; ul Świętosławska 12; dm 25-40zł, s 58-150zł, d 70-200zł; ⛴; ⛴ Wrocławska) Centrally located hostel offering comfortable accommodation with modern furniture and smart, contemporary decor in pastel shades. There's a spacious kitchen and lounge, and all beds have reading lamps and lockers. The cheaper private rooms have shared bathrooms.

Hotel Stare Miasto
HOTEL €€

(⌨ 61 663 6242; www.hotelstaremiasto.pl; ul Rybaki 36; s/d from 275/340zł; 🅿 ❄ ⛴; ⛴ Wrocławska) Stylish value-for-money hotel with a tastefully chandeliered foyer and spacious breakfast room. Rooms can be small but are clean and bright with lovely starched white sheets. Some upper rooms have skylights in place of windows.

★ Puro Poznań Stare Miasto
BOUTIQUE HOTEL €€€

(⌨ 61 333 1000; www.purohotel.pl/en/poznan; St-awna 12; r from 250zł; 🅿 ❄ ⛴; ⛴ Plac Wielkopolski) The homegrown Puro hotel chain's Poznań outpost ticks all the boxes – central location, underground car park, designer decor, comfortable lobby with free coffee machine, fast reliable wi-fi, helpful staff,

sharply styled bedrooms flooded with light and a buffet breakfast that has you coming back for more. What's not to like?

🍴 Eating

★ Cybina 13
POLISH €€

(⌨ 61 663 6334; www.cybina13.pl; Cybińska 13/2; mains 29-49zł; ⊙ noon-10pm; ⛴ ⛴; ⛴ Katedra, Rondo Śródka) 🌿 Set in the cute little enclave of Śródka, close to the Poznań Gate, this bright, modern restaurant is popular with locals, whether for a romantic dinner in the sharply styled dining room or a weekend lunch at the outdoor tables. The tempting menu puts a modern spin on traditional Polish dishes, and is accompanied by home-baked flavoured breads.

Wiejskie Jadło
POLISH €€

(⌨ 61 853 6600; www.wiejskie-jadlo.pl; Stary Rynek 77; mains 22-55zł; ⊙ noon-11pm; ⛴ Marcinskowskiego) This compact Polish restaurant, hidden a short distance back from the Rynek, serves what it says on the sign – *wiejskie jadło* (countryside food). It offers a range of filling dishes including several kinds of pierogi (dumplings), *żurek* (sour rye soup) served in a hollow loaf, roast pork knuckle and beef with beetroot, all dished up in a rustic farmhouse setting.

🍷 Drinking & Nightlife

Chmielnik
BAR

(⌨ 790 333 946; www.facebook.com/chmielnik pub; ul Żydowska 27; ⊙ 4pm-midnight Mon-Wed, 4pm-1am Thu, 4pm-2am Fri, 2pm-2am Sat, 1-11pm Sun; ⛴; ⛴ Plac Wielkopolski) This is the ideal place to sample the output of the booming Polish craft-beer scene, with over 150 brews in stock. Lounge and sip in the pleasant wood-lined interior or in the garden terrace out the back – yes, those are hops and grapevines growing amid the greenery.

Stragan
CAFE

(⌨ 789 233 965; www.facebook.com/stragankawiarnia; ul Ratajczaka 31; ⊙ 8am-9pm Mon-Fri, 9am-8pm Sat & Sun; ⛴; ⛴ Gwarna) Cool, contemporary cafe in which even the most bearded hipster would feel at home. Coffee ranges from Chemex brews to flat whites, complemented by excellent cakes and light meals. Also serves breakfast (to noon) and bagels (all day); order at the counter.

Van Diesel Music Club
CLUB

(⌨ 515 065 459; www.vandiesel.pl; Stary Rynek 88; ⊙ 9pm-5am Fri & Sat; ⛴ Plac Wielkopolski,

Wrocławska) Happening venue on the main square, with DJs varying their offerings between pop, house, R&B, soul and dance. Given the variety, you're sure to find a night that will get you on the dance floor.

☆ Entertainment

Centrum Kultury Zamek CONCERT VENUE
(Castle Cultural Centre; ☑61 646 5260; www.ckzamek.pl; ul Św Marcin 80/82; ☎; ☒Gwarna, Zamek) Within the grand neo-Romanesque **Kaiserhaus** (ul Św Marcin 80/82), built from 1904 to 1910 for German emperor Wilhelm II, this active cultural hub hosts cinema, art and music events.

❶ Information

The Poznań City Card (one day, 49zł) is available at all city information centres. It provides free entry to major museums, sizeable discounts at restaurants and recreational activities, and unlimited public transport use.

Tourist Office (Informacja Turystyczna Stary Rynek; ☑61 852 6156; www.poznan.travel; Stary Rynek 59/60; ◷9.30am-6pm Mon-Sat, 9.30am-5pm Sun; ☒Plac Wielkopolski, Wrocławska) Located conveniently on the main square.

Tourist Office – Train Station (Informacja Turystyczna Dworzec Główny PKP; ☑61 633 1016; www.poznan.travel; ul Dworcowa 2; ◷9am-5pm; ☒Poznań Główny, Most Dworcowy) At Poznań Główny train station.

❶ Getting There & Away

BUS

The **bus station** (Dworzec autobusowy w Poznaniu; ☑703 303 330; www.pks.poznan.pl; ul Stanisława Matyi 2; ☒Poznań Główny, Most Dworcowy) is at the north end of the Avenida shopping mall, downstairs from the main train station. Destinations include:

Berlin from 49zł, three to four hours, six daily

Gdańsk 25zł, five hours, three daily

Prague 69zł, eight hours, twice daily

Warsaw 35zł, four to five hours, seven daily

Wrocław 15zł, 3½ hours, twice daily

TRAIN

Poznań Główny train station is 15km southwest of the old town square, entered via Level 1 of the Avenida shopping mall.

Gdańsk 56zł, 3½ hours, eight daily

Kraków 66zł, five to six hours, eight daily

Toruń 35zł, 1½ hours, 12 daily

Warsaw from 55zł, four hours, 12 daily

Wrocław 38zł, 2½ hours, hourly

POMERANIA

Pomerania (Pomorze in Polish) is an attractive region with diverse drawcards, from beautiful beaches to architecturally pleasing cities. The historic port city of Gdańsk is situated at the region's eastern extreme, while the attractive Gothic city of Toruń lies inland.

Gdańsk

POP 474,000

Like a ministate all to itself, Gdańsk has a unique feel that sets it apart from other cities in Poland. Centuries of maritime ebb and flow as a major Baltic port; streets of distinctively un-Polish architecture influenced by a united nations of wealthy merchants who shaped the city's past; the to-ing and fro-ing of Danzig/Gdańsk between Teutonic Prussia and Slavic Poland; and the destruction wrought by WWII have all bequeathed a special atmosphere that makes Gdańsk an increasingly popular destination.

Visitors throng in ever greater numbers to wander historical thoroughfares lined with grand, elegantly proportioned buildings, and to enjoy a treasure trove of characterful bars and cafes, seafood restaurants, amber shops and intriguing museums, not to mention pleasure-boat cruises along the river and a wealth of maritime history to soak up in between brews at dockside beer gardens.

◉ Sights

Most of Gdańsk's sights are situated in the Main Town (Główne Miasto), centred on the busy **Długi Targ** (Long Market), but two modern attractions – the Museum of WWII and the European Solidarity Centre – lie a short distance to the north of this compact central area.

★ Museum of WWII MUSEUM
(Muzeum II Wojny Światowej; www.muzeum1939.pl; pl Władysława Bartoszewskiego 1; adult/concession 23/16zł; ◷10am-7pm Tue-Fri, to 8pm Sat & Sun) Opened in 2016, this striking piece of modern architecture is a bold addition to the northern end of Gdańsk's waterfront. It has rapidly become one of the city's must-visit attractions, tracing the fate of Poland during the world's greatest conflict, from amazing footage of the German battleship *Schleswig-Holstein* firing on Westerplatte on 1 September 1939, to harrowing accounts of the

Gdańsk

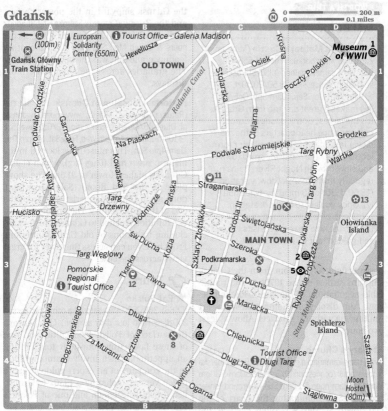

Gdańsk

◎ Top Sights
1 Museum of WWII...................................D1

◎ Sights
Historical Museum of Gdańsk........(see 4)
2 National Maritime Museum..................D3
3 St Mary's Church.................................C3
4 Town Hall...C4
5 Żuraw..D3

🛏 Sleeping
6 Gotyk House..C3
7 Hotel Podewils....................................D3

✖ Eating
8 Bar Neptun..B4
9 Restauracja Pod Łososiem..................C3
10 Tawerna Mestwin..............................C2

🍷 Drinking & Nightlife
11 Cafe Lamus..C2
12 Józef K..B3

✪ Entertainment
13 Baltic Philharmonic Hall.....................D2

horrors of Nazi extermination camps. An absolute minimum of three hours is needed to do it justice.

European Solidarity Centre MUSEUM
(Europejskie Centrum Solidarności; ☎58 772 4112; www.ecs.gda.pl; Plac Solidarności 1; building free, exhibition adult/concession 20/15zł; ⊙10am-6pm Mon-Fri, to 7pm Sat & Sun May-Sep, shorter hours Oct-Apr) Opened in 2014, and housed in a love-it-or-hate-it example of 21st-century architecture (its rusty steel plates designed to evoke ships under construction), this exhibition has quickly become one of Gdańsk's unmissables. Audio guides clamped to ears, visitors wander through seven halls examining Poland's

MALBORK

Magnificent **Malbork Castle** (Muzeum Zamkowe w Malborku; ☑ tickets 556 470 978; www.zamek.malbork.pl; ul Starościńska 1; adult/concession 29.50/20.50zł; ☺9am-7pm May-Sep, 10am-3pm Oct-Apr; ℗) makes a great day trip from Gdańsk. It's the largest Gothic castle in Europe and was once headquarters of the medieval Teutonic Knights, its sinister form looming over the relatively small town and slow-moving Nogat River. Trains run regularly from Gdańsk Głowny station (13.60zł, 30 to 50 minutes, twice hourly). Once you get to Malbork station, turn right, cross the highway and follow ul Kościuszki to the castle. Visits are by self-guided tour with audio guide.

postwar fight for freedom, from the Gdańsk shipyard strikes of the 1970s to the round-table negotiations of the late 1980s and beyond, the displays blending state-of-the-art multimedia with real artefacts. Allow at least two hours.

St Mary's Church
CHURCH

(www.bazylikamariacka.gdansk.pl; ul Podkramarska 5; tower adult/concession 10/5zł; ☺8.30am-5.30pm Mon-Sat, 11am-noon & 1-5pm Sun year-round, longer hours May-Sep) Dominating the heart of the Old Town, St Mary's is often cited as the largest brick church in the world, its massive 78m-high tower dominating the Gdańsk cityscape. Begun in 1343, the building reached its present proportions in 1502. The high altar has a Gothic polyptych from the 1510s, with the Coronation of the Virgin depicted in its central panel. Don't miss the 15th-century astronomical clock in the northern transept, and the church tower (a climb of 405 steps).

National Maritime Museum
MUSEUM

(Narodowe Muzeum Morskie w Gdańsku; ☑ Maritime Cultural Centre 58 329 8700, information 58 301 8611; www.nmm.pl; ul Ołowianka 9-13; combined ticket for all sites adult/concession 23/13zł; ☺10am-4pm Tue-Fri, to 6pm Sat & Sun) This is a sprawling exhibition covering Gdańsk's role as a Baltic seaport through the centuries. The headquarters, the multimillion-euro Maritime Cultural Centre, has a permanent interactive exhibition 'People-Ships-Ports'. Other exhibitions (which can be visited individually with separate tickets) include the MS *Sołdek*, the first vessel to be built at

the Gdańsk shipyard in the postwar years, and the **Żuraw** (Crane; ul Szeroka 67/68; adult/concession 8/5zł; ☺10am-6pm Jul & Aug, shorter hours & closed Mon Sep-Jun), a 15th-century loading crane that was the biggest in its day. The granaries across the river house more displays.

Historical Museum of Gdańsk
MUSEUM

(Ratusza Głównego Miasta; www.muzeumgdansk. pl; Długa 46/47; adult/concession 12/6zł, tower 5zł; ☺10am-1pm Tue, to 4pm Wed, Fri & Sat, to 6pm Thu, 11am-4pm Sun) This museum is located in the historic **town hall** (Długi Targ), which claims Gdańsk's highest tower at 81.5m. The showpiece is the Red Room (Sala Czerwona), done up in Dutch Mannerist style from the end of the 16th century. The 2nd floor houses exhibitions related to Gdańsk's history, including imitations of old Gdańsk interiors. From here you can access the tower for great views across the city.

👉 Tours

⭐ Eat Polska
FOOD

(☑661 368 758; www.eatpolska.com; per person 290zł; ☺Food Tour daily at noon) Get beneath the surface of Polish food culture on one of these fascinating four-hour tours (bring an appetite!), which involve sampling food in the company of an expert guide at half a dozen venues, including a 1950s food market, a fish delicatessen and one of Poland's top restaurants. Vodka and beer tours are also available.

🛏 Sleeping

⭐ Mamas & Papas Hostel
HOSTEL €

(☑792 578 933; www.facebook.com/hostelmamas papas; ul Nowiny 19; dm/tw from 50/130zł; ℗@◈) This family-run hostel set in a suburban home offers the best welcome in the Tri-City. It's a cosy affair with just 28 beds, a common room and kitchen, but it's the owners – experienced travellers who know what makes a good hostel experience – who make it special. The only drawback is the location, a 10-minute bus ride south of the centre.

Moon Hostel
HOSTEL €

(☑58 691 6700; www.moonhostel.pl; ul Długie Ogrody 6a; s/d/q from 99/119/159zł; ℗@◈✿) This colourfully decorated hostel has a superb location, a pleasant two-minute walk across the river from the Long Market. Accommodation is in bright, IKEA-furnished two- to six-bed rooms, with spotless shared or private bathrooms. Breakfast is available, but not really worth the price; there are several good breakfast cafes nearby.

Gotyk House HOTEL €€
(Kamienica Gotyk; ☑58 301 8567; www.gotyk
house.eu; ul Mariacka 1; r 339zł; P 🕏) Wonderfully located near St Mary's Church (p332), this neat, Gothic-themed guesthouse is squeezed into Gdańsk's oldest building. The seven compact rooms have Gothic touches such as pointy-arched doorways and hefty drapery, though most are thoroughly modern creations and bathrooms are definitely of the third millennium. Breakfast is served in your room. Four floors, no lift.

★**Hotel Podewils** HOTEL €€€
(☑58 300 9560; www.podewils.pl; ul Szafarnia 2; s/d from 355/455zł; P 🕸🕏) The view from the Podewils across the river to the Main Town can't be beaten, though the owners probably wish they could take its cheery baroque facade and move it away from the concrete riverside developments sprouting next door. Guestrooms are a vintage confection of elegant period furniture, classic prints and distinctive wallpaper.

🍴 Eating

Bar Neptun CAFETERIA €
(☑058 301 4988; www.barneptun.pl; ul Długa 33/34; mains 6-20zł; ☺7.30am-7pm Mon-Fri, 10am-6pm Sat & Sun, 1hr later Jun-Sep; 🕏) It's surprising where some of Poland's communist-era milk bars have survived – this one is right on the main tourist drag. However, Neptun is a cut above your run-of-the-mill bar mleczny, with potted plants and decorative tiling. Popular with foreigners on a budget, it even has an English menu of Polish favourites such as naleśniki (crepes) and gołąbki (cabbage rolls).

★**Tawerna Mestwin** POLISH €€
(☑58 301 7882; www.tawernamestwin.com; ul Straganiarska 20/23; mains 22-38zł; ☺11am-10pm Tue-Sun; 🕏🕮) 🍴 The speciality here is Kashubian regional cooking from the northwest of Poland, and dishes such as potato pancakes, stuffed cabbage rolls, fish soup and fried herring are as close to home cooking as you'll get in a restaurant. The interior is done out like a traditional farm cottage and the exposed beams and dark-green walls make for a cosy atmosphere.

Restauracja Pod Łososiem POLISH €€€
(☑58 301 7652; www.podlososiem.com.pl; ul Szeroka 52/54; mains 60-110zł; ☺noon-11pm) Founded in 1598 and famous for its fish dishes, this is one of Gdańsk's most highly regarded restaurants. Red leather seats, brass chandeliers and a gathering of gas lamps fill out the rather sober interior, illuminated by the speciality drink – Goldwasser. This gooey, sweet liqueur with flakes of gold was produced in its cellars from the 16th century until WWII.

🍷 Drinking & Nightlife

★**Józef K** BAR
(☑527 161 510; www.facebook.com/jozefk; ul Piwna 1/2; ☺10am-2am Sun-Thu, to 4am Fri & Sat; 🕏) Is it a bar or a junk shop? You decide as you relax with a cocktail or a glass of excellent Polish perry on one of the battered sofas, illuminated by an old theatre spotlight. Downstairs is an open area where the party kicks off at weekends; upstairs is more intimate with lots of soft seating and well-stocked bookcases.

Cafe Lamus BAR
(☑531 998 832; www.facebook.com/cafelamus; Lawendowa 8, enter from Straganiarska; ☺noon-1am) This fun retro-style bar has a random scattering of 1970s sofas and armchairs (and deckchairs outside), big-print wallpaper from the same period, and a menu of Polish craft beers, cider and coffee. There's also a spillover bar for the Saturday-night crowd.

☆ Entertainment

Baltic Philharmonic Hall CLASSICAL MUSIC
(☑58 320 6262; www.filharmonia.gda.pl; ul Ołowianka 1; ☺box office 9.30am-4pm Tue, 10.30am-6pm Wed-Fri) The regular host of chamber-music concerts; also organises many of the major music festivals throughout the year.

ℹ Information

Tourist Office – Długi Targ (☑58 301 4355; www.visitgdansk.com; Długi Targ 28/29; ☺9am-7pm May-Aug, to 5pm Sep-Apr)

Tourist Office – Galeria Madison (www. visitgdansk.com; Galeria Madison, ul Rajska 10; ☺9am-7pm Mon-Sat, from 10am Sun) Near the train station.

Tourist Office – Airport (☑58 348 1368; www.visitgdansk.com; ul Słowackiego 210, Gdańsk Lech Wałęsa Airport; ☺24hr)

Pomorskie Regional Tourist Office (☑58 732 7041; www.pomorskie.travel; Brama Wyżynna, Wały Jagiellońskie 2a; ☺9am-6pm year-round, to 8pm Mon-Fri Jun-Sep) Housed in the Upland Gate, this friendly regional tourist office has info on Gdańsk and the surrounding area.

POLAND GDAŃSK

ℹ Getting There & Away

AIR

Gdańsk Lech Wałęsa airport (☑ 801 066 808, 52 567 3531; www.airport.gdansk.pl; ul Słowackiego 210) is 14km west of the city centre. There are direct flights to Warsaw with LOT, and to Kraków and Wrocław with Ryanair.

International flights to many European and UK cities are operated by budget airlines Ryanair and Wizz Air.

BUS

Gdańsk's **bus terminal** (PKS Gdańsk; ul 3 Maja 12) is right behind the central train station, linked by an underground passageway.

There are plenty of connections from Gdańsk to Western European cities plus services east to Kaliningrad (40zł, 3½ hours, four daily).

TRAIN

The grand main train station, **Gdańsk Główny**, is on the western edge of the Old Town. Destinations include Malbork (13.50zł, 40 minutes, two or three an hour), Poznań (56zł, 3½ hours, eight daily), Toruń (47zł, 2½ hours, nine daily) and Warsaw (77zł, three to four hours, hourly).

Toruń

POP 202,560

Toruń escaped major damage in WWII and is famous for its well-preserved Gothic architecture, along with the quality of its famous gingerbread. The city is also renowned as the birthplace of Nicolaus Copernicus (Mikołaj Kopernik in Polish), who revolutionised the field of astronomy in 1543 by asserting the earth travelled around the sun. He's a figure you will not be able to escape – you can even buy gingerbread men in his likeness.

◎ Sights

The usual starting point on Toruń's Gothic trail is the **Old Town Market Square** (Rynek Staromiejski), lined with finely restored houses. At the southeast corner, look for the picturesque **Statue of Copernicus**.

Old Town Hall   MUSEUM

(Ratusz Staromiejski; www.muzeum.torun.pl; Rynek Staromiejski 1; adult/concession 15/10zł, tower 15/10zł, combined ticket 25/18zł; ⊙ 10am-6pm Tue-Sun May-Sep, to 4pm Oct-Apr) The Old Town Hall dates from the 14th century and hasn't changed much since, though some Renaissance additions lent an ornamental touch to the sober Gothic structure. Today it houses Gothic art (painting and stained glass), a display of local 17th- and 18th-century crafts and a gallery of Polish paintings from 1800 to the present, including a couple of Witkacys and Matejkos. Climb the tower for a fine panoramic view of Toruń's Gothic townscape.

Cathedral of SS John the Baptist & John the Evangelist   CHURCH

(www.katedra.diecezja.torun.pl; ul Żeglarska 16; tower 9zł; ⊙ 9am-5.30pm Mon-Sat, from 2pm Sun, tower closed Nov-Mar) Toruń's mammoth Gothic cathedral was begun around 1260 but only completed at the end of the 15th century. Its massive tower houses Poland's second-largest historic bell, the Tuba Dei (God's Trumpet). On the southern side of the tower, facing the Vistula, is a large 15th-century clock; its original face and single hand are still in working order. Check out the dent above the VIII – it's from a cannonball that struck the clock during the Swedish siege of 1703.

Toruń Gingerbread Museum   MUSEUM

(Muzeum Toruńskiego Piernika; www.muzeum. torun.pl; ul Strumykowa 4; adult/concession 12/9zł; ⊙ 10am-6pm Tue-Sun May-Sep, to 4pm Oct-Apr) Not to be confused with the commercial **Gingerbread Museum** (Muzeum Piernika; ☑ 56 663 6617; www.muzeumpiernika.pl; ul Rabiańska 9; adult/concession 17/12zł; ⊙ 10am-6pm, tours every hour, on the hour) across town, this branch of the Toruń Regional Museum is housed in a former gingerbread factory and looks at the 600-year-long history of the city's favourite sweet. You also get the chance to make your own gingerbread using dough prepared to the original recipe.

⌘ Sleeping

Toruń Główny Hostel   HOSTEL €

(☑ 606 564 600; www.hosteltg.com; Toruń Główny train station; dm/d 39/70zł; ☞) This hostel is housed in the old post-office building right on the platform at Toruń's main train station, with attractive wall paintings of the Old Town. The six- and eight-bed dorms are spacious with suitcase-size lockers and reading lamps; free breakfast is served in the basement kitchen. Downsides include train noise (surprise!), and only one shower per floor.

★ Hotel Spichrz   HOTEL €€

(☑ 56 657 1140; www.spichrz.pl; ul Mostowa 1; s/d from 250/310zł; ❄☞) Wonderfully situated within a historic waterfront granary, this hotel's 19 rooms are laden with personality, featuring massive exposed beams above characterful timber furniture and contemporary

WORTH A TRIP

GREAT MASURIAN LAKES

The northeastern corner of Poland features a beautiful postglacial landscape dominated by thousands of lakes. About 200km of canals connect these bodies of water, making the area a prime destination for canoeists, as well as those who love to hike, fish and mountain bike.

The towns of **Giżycko** and **Mikołajki** make good bases. Both the **Giżycko tourist office** (☑ 87 428 5265; www.gizycko.turystyka.pl; ul Wyzwolenia 2; ⊙ 9am-6pm Mon-Fri, 10am-4pm Sat & Sun Jun-Aug, shorter hours Sep-May; ☜) and the **Mikołajki tourist office** (☑ 87 421 6850; www.mikolajki.eu; Plac Wolności 7; ⊙ 10am-6pm Mon-Sat, to 5pm Sun Jun-Aug, to 6pm Mon-Sat May & Sep) supply useful maps for sailing and hiking, provide excursion boat schedules and assist in finding accommodation.

Nature aside, there are some interesting fragments of history in this region. A grim reminder of the past is the **Wolf's Lair** (Wilczy Szaniec; ☑ 89 741 0031; www.wilczyszaniec. olsztyn.lasy.gov.pl; Gierłoż; adult/concession 15/10zł, parking 5zł; ⊙ 8am-8pm Apr-Sep, to 4pm Oct-Mar; ℗). Located at **Gierłoż**, 8km east of Kętrzyn, this ruined complex was Hitler's wartime headquarters for his invasion of the Soviet Union. In 1944 a group of high-ranking German officers tried to assassinate Hitler here. These dramatic events were reprised in the 2008 Tom Cruise movie *Valkyrie*.

bathrooms. The location by the river is within walking distance of the sights but away from the crowds. The hotel's Karczma Spichrz restaurant serves traditional Polish cuisine.

Hotel Petite Fleur HOTEL €€
(☑ 56 621 5100; www.petitefleur.pl; ul Piekary 25; s/d from 210/270zł; ✺☜) One of the better midrange options in town, this place is full of historic character with an antique lobby, and understated rooms with timber beam ceilings and elegant prints, though the singles can be small and dark, and there's no lift. The French brick-cellar restaurant is one of Toruń's better dining options and the buffet breakfast is a delight.

✕ Eating & Drinking

Oberża POLISH €
(☑ 56 622 0022; www.facebook.com/oberzatorun; ul Rabiańska 9; mains 8-17zł; ⊙ 11am-10pm Mon-Thu, to midnight Fri & Sat, to 9pm Sun; ☜) This self-service cafeteria stacks 'em high and sells 'em cheap for a hungry crowd of locals and tourists. Find your very own thatched minicottage or intimate hideout amid stained-glass windows, cartwheels, bridles and other rustic knick-knacks and enjoy 11 types of pierogi (dumplings), soups, salads and classic Polish mains from a menu tuned to low-cost belly-packing.

★ Szeroka 9 INTERNATIONAL €€€
(☑ 56 622 8424; www.szeroka9.pl; ul Szeroka 9; mains 35-50zł; ⊙ noon-11pm Mon-Fri, from 10am Sat & Sun) ✐ Arguably Toruń's top restaurant,

this place offers a changing menu of seasonal gourmet fare ranging from pickled trout with horseradish to pig cheeks with creamed potato and marinated beetroot; the dessert to plump for is local gingerbread in plum sauce. The decor is contemporary urban and the staff are friendly and knowledgeable. Reservations recommended for dinner.

Jan Olbracht MICROBREWERY
(www.browar-olbracht.pl; ul Szczytna 15; ⊙ 10am-11pm Sun-Thu, to midnight Fri & Sat) Take a seat in a barrel-shaped indoor booth or at the street-side terrace to sample some of this microbrewery's unusual beers. These include pils, wheat beer, a special ale and, this being Toruń, gingerbread beer, all brewed in the gleaming copper vats at the street end of the bar.

☆ Entertainment

Dwór Artusa CLASSICAL MUSIC
(☑ 56 655 4929; www.artus.torun.pl; Rynek Staromiejski 6; ⊙ box office noon-6pm Mon-Fri) The Artus Court, an impressive late-19th-century mansion overlooking the main square, houses a major cultural centre and has an auditorium hosting musical events, including concerts and recitals.

❶ Information

Tourist Office (☑ 56 621 0930; www.it.torun. pl; Rynek Staromiejski 25; ⊙ 9am-6pm Mon-Fri, from 10am Sat & Sun; ☜) Free wi-fi access, heaps of info and professional staff who know their city.

POLAND TORUŃ

ⓘ Getting There & Away

BUS

Toruń bus station (Dworzec Autobusowy Toruń; ul Dąbrowskiego 8-24) is close to the northern edge of the Old Town and handles services to Gdańsk (from 20zł, 2½ hours, hourly) and Warsaw (from 28zł, three to four hours, at least hourly).

TRAIN

Toruń has two stations: **Toruń Główny** is about 2km south of the Old Town, on the opposite side of the Vistula, while the more convenient **Toruń Miasto** is on the Old Town's eastern edge. Not all services stop at both stations.

There are direct trains to Gdańsk (47zł, 2½ hours, four daily), Kraków (62zł, 5¼ hours, one daily) and Warsaw (from 50zł, 2¾ hours, hourly).

SURVIVAL GUIDE

ⓘ Directory A–Z

ACCOMMODATION

Poland has a wide choice of accommodation to suit all budgets. Advanced booking is recommended for popular destinations such as Kraków, Zakopane and Gdańsk.

Hotels Hotels account for the majority of accommodation in Poland, encompassing a variety of old and new places, ranging from basic to ultraplush.

Pensions *Pensjonaty* (pensions) are small, privately run guesthouses that provide breakfast and occasionally half or full board. They are generally clean, comfortable and good value.

Hostels Polish hostels include both the newer breed of privately owned hostels and the older, publicly run or municipal hostels. There are also simple, rustic mountain lodges.

LGBT+ TRAVELLERS

Homosexuality is legal in Poland but not openly tolerated. Polish society is conservative and for the most part remains hostile towards the LGBT+ community.

The Polish gay and lesbian scene is fairly discreet; Warsaw and Kraków are the best places to find bars, clubs and gay-friendly accommodation, and Sopot is noted as gay-friendly compared to the rest of Poland. The best sources of information for Poland's scene are the Warsaw and Kraków city guides on www.queerintheworld.com, and www.queer.pl (in Polish only).

MONEY

➡ The Polish currency is the *złoty*, abbreviated to zł and pronounced *zwo*-ti. It is divided into 100 *groszy*, which are abbreviated to gr.

➡ Banknotes come in denominations of 10zł, 20zł, 50zł, 100zł and 200zł, and coins in 1gr, 2gr, 5gr, 10gr, 20gr and 50gr, and 1zł, 2zł and 5zł.

➡ Keep some small-denomination notes and coins for shops, cafes and restaurants – getting change for the 100zł and 200zł notes that ATMs often spit out can be a problem.

➡ ATMs are ubiquitous in cities and towns, and even the smallest hamlet is likely to have at least one. The majority accept Visa and MasterCard.

➡ Beware of the widespread Euronet ATMs, which give a much poorer rate of exchange than bank ATMs.

➡ The best exchange rates are obtained by changing money at banks, or by taking cash out of bank ATMs.

Tipping

When to tip Customary in restaurants and at service establishments such as hairdressers; optional everywhere else.

Restaurants At smaller establishments and for smaller tabs, round the bill to the nearest 5zł or 10zł increment. Otherwise, 10% is standard.

Taxis No need to tip, though you may want to round up the fare to reward good service.

OPENING HOURS

Most places adhere to the following hours. Shopping centres generally have longer hours and are open from 9am to 8pm at weekends. Museums are usually closed on Mondays, and have shorter hours outside high season.

Banks 9am–4pm Monday to Friday, to 1pm Saturday (varies)

Offices 9am–5pm Monday to Friday, to 1pm Saturday (varies)

Post Offices 8am–7pm Monday to Friday, to 1pm Saturday (cities)

Restaurants 11am–10pm daily

Shops 8am–6pm Monday to Friday, 10am–2pm Saturday

PUBLIC HOLIDAYS

New Year's Day 1 January

Epiphany 6 January

Easter Sunday March or April

Easter Monday March or April

State Holiday 1 May

Constitution Day 3 May

Pentecost Sunday Seventh Sunday after Easter

Corpus Christi Ninth Thursday after Easter

Assumption Day 15 August

All Saints' Day 1 November

Independence Day 11 November

Christmas 25 and 26 December

TELEPHONE

➡ All telephone numbers, landline and mobile, have nine digits. Landlines are written 12 345 6789, with the first two numbers corresponding to the area code (there is no zero). Mobile-phone numbers are written 123 456 789.

➡ Poland uses the GSM 900/1800 system, the same as Europe, Australia and New Zealand. It's not compatible with most cell phones from North America or Japan (though many mobiles have multiband GSM 1900/900 phones that will work in Poland).

❶ Getting There & Away

Flights, cars and tours can be booked online at lonelyplanet.com/bookings.

AIR

➡ Most international flights to Poland arrive at Warsaw Chopin Airport (p315). Other international airports include Kraków, Gdańsk, Poznań and Wrocław.

➡ Poland's national airline is **LOT** (www.lot. com), offering regular flights to Poland from throughout Europe, and also to/from New York, Chicago, Toronto, Tel Aviv and Beijing, among others.

➡ Several budget carriers, including **Ryanair** (www.ryanair.com) and **Wizz Air** (www.wizzair. com), link European cities to Polish destinations.

LAND

Bus

➡ International buses head in all directions, including eastward to the Baltic States and Russia. From Zakopane, it's easy to hop into Slovakia via bus or minibus.

➡ Several companies operate long-haul coach services, including **Eurolines** (www.eurolines. pl), **Ecolines** (www.ecolines.net) and **FlixBus** (https://global.flixbus.com).

Car & Motorcycle

➡ The minimum legal driving age is 18.

➡ The maximum blood-alcohol limit is 0.02%.

➡ All drivers are required to carry their passport (with a valid visa if necessary), driving licence, vehicle registration document and proof of third-party insurance (called a Green Card).

Train

There are direct rail services from Warsaw to several surrounding capitals, including Berlin, Prague, Minsk and Moscow. Kraków also has useful international rail connections.

SEA

Ferry services operated by **Unity Line** (☑ 91 880 2909; www.unityline.pl) and **TT-Line** (www. ttline.com) connect Poland's Baltic coast ports of Gdańsk, Gdynia and Świnoujście to destinations in Scandinavia.

❶ Getting Around

AIR

LOT (www.lot.com) flies between Warsaw and Gdańsk, Katowice, Kraków, Poznań and Wrocław.

BUS

➡ Poland has a comprehensive bus network (far greater than the rail network) covering nearly every town and village accessible by road.

➡ Buy tickets at bus terminals or directly from the driver.

➡ **FlixBus** (https://global.flixbus.com) is the main nationwide coach operator between major cities and towns using modern coaches with free wi-fi.

CAR & MOTORCYCLE

➡ Major international car-rental companies are represented in larger cities and airports.

➡ Car-hire agencies require a passport, valid driving licence and credit card. You need to be at least 21 or 23 years of age (depending on the company).

TRAIN

➡ Poland's train network is extensive and reasonably priced.

➡ **PKP InterCity** (IC; ☑ from Poland 703 200 200, from abroad +48 22 391 97 57; www. intercity.pl) runs all of Poland's express trains, including ExpressInterCity Premium (EIP), ExpressInterCity (EIC), InterCity (IC), EuroCity (EC) and TLK trains.

➡ A second main operator, **PolRegio** (www. polregio.pl), takes care of most other trains, including relatively fast InterRegio trains and slower Regio trains.

➡ Buy tickets at ticket machines, station ticket windows or at special PKP passenger-service centres, located in major stations.

Romania

POP 19.7 MILLION

Best Places to Eat

➡ Lacrimi şi Sfinţi (p344)

➡ Roata (p353)

➡ Homemade (p356)

➡ Caru' cu Bere (p344)

➡ Bistro de l'Arte (p348)

Best Places to Stay

➡ Casa Georgius Krauss (p349)

➡ Casa del Sole (p356)

➡ Little Bucharest Old Town Hostel (p343)

➡ Bella Muzica (p347)

➡ Lol & Lola (p353)

Why Go?

Beautiful and beguiling, Romania's rural landscape remains relatively untouched by the country's urban evolution. It's a land of aesthetically stirring hand-ploughed fields, sheep-instigated traffic jams and lots of homemade plum brandy. Most visitors focus their attention on Transylvania, with its legacy of fortified Saxon towns like Braşov and Sighişoara, plus tons of eye-catching natural beauty. Across the Carpathians, the Unesco-listed painted monasteries dot Bucovina. The Danube Delta has more than 300 species of birds, including many rare varieties, and is an ideal spot for birdwatching. Energetic cities like Timişoara, Sibiu, Cluj-Napoca and, especially, Bucharest offer culture – both high- and lowbrow – and showcase Romania as a rapidly evolving European country.

When to Go
Bucharest

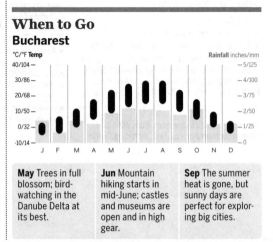

May Trees in full blossom; birdwatching in the Danube Delta at its best.

Jun Mountain hiking starts in mid-June; castles and museums are open and in high gear.

Sep The summer heat is gone, but sunny days are perfect for exploring big cities.

Entering the Country

Travel to Romania does not pose any unusual problems. Bucharest has air connections with many European capitals and large cities, and train and long-haul bus services are frequent. At the time of research, Romania was not a member of the EU's common customs and border area, the Schengen area, so even if you're entering from an EU member state (including Bulgaria or Hungary), you'll still have to show a passport or valid EU identity card. Border crossings can get crowded, particularly during weekends, so prepare for delays.

ITINERARIES

One Week
Spend a day ambling around the capital (p340), then take a train to Braşov (p346) – Transylvania's main event – for castles, activities and beer at street-side cafes. Spend a day in the medieval citadel of Sighişoara (p349), then catch a train back to Bucharest or on to Budapest.

Two Weeks
Arrive in Bucharest by plane or Timişoara by train, then head into Transylvania (p346), devoting a day or two each to Braşov (p346), Sighişoara (p349) and Sibiu (p350). Tour the southern painted monasteries in Bucovina (p354), then continue on to Bucharest (p340).

Essential Food & Drink

Romanian food borrows heavily from its neighbours, including Turkey, Hungary and the Balkans, and is centred on pork and other meats. Farm-fresh, organic fruits and vegetables are in abundance, lending flavour and colour to a long list of soups and salads. Condiments typically include sour cream, garlic sauce and grated sheep's cheese.

Ciorbă de burtă Garlicky tripe soup that's inexplicably a local favourite.

Ciorbă de perişoare A spicy soup with meatballs and vegetables.

Covrigi Oven-baked pretzels served warm from windows around town.

Mămăligă Cornmeal mush, sometimes topped with sour cream or cheese.

Papanaşi Arguably the county's most popular dessert and made of fried dough, stuffed with sweetened curd cheese and covered with jam and heavy cream.

Sarmale Spiced meat wrapped in cabbage or grape leaves.

Tochitură A hearty stew that's usually comprised of pan-fried pork, sometimes mixed with other meats, in a spicy tomato or wine sauce.

Ţuică Fiery plum brandy sold in water bottles at roadside rest stops.

AT A GLANCE

Area 238,391 sq km

Capital Bucharest

Country Code ☑40

Currency Romanian lei

Emergency ☑112

Language Romanian

Visas Not required for citizens of the EU, Australia, USA, Canada or New Zealand

Sleeping Price Ranges

The following price ranges refer to a double room with a bathroom, including breakfast (Bucharest prices tend to be higher).

€ less than 150 lei

€€ 150–300 lei

€€€ more than 300 lei

Eating Price Ranges

The following price ranges refer to an average main course.

€ less than 20 lei

€€ 20–40 lei

€€€ more than 40 lei

Resources

Autogari.ro (www.auto gari.ro)

Lonely Planet (www.lonely planet.com/romania)

Romania Ministry of Tourism (www.romania.travel)

Romania Highlights

1 Braşov (p346) Basing yourself here to ascend castles and mountains (and castles on top of mountains).

2 Bucovina (p354) Following the Unesco World Heritage line of painted monasteries.

3 Sibiu (p350) Soaking in this beautifully restored Saxon town.

4 Sighişoara (p349) Exploring this medieval citadel and birthplace of Dracula.

5 Danube Delta (p351) Rowing through the tributaries and the riot of nature.

6 Bucharest (p340) Enjoying the museums and cacophonous nightlife of the capital.

BUCHAREST

021, 031 / POP 1.86 MILLION

Romania's capital sometimes gets a bad rap, but in fact it's dynamic, energetic and lots of fun. Many travellers give the city just a night or two before heading off to Transylvania, but that's not enough time. Allow at least a few days to take in the very good museums, stroll the parks and hang out at trendy cafes and drinking gardens. While much of the centre is modern and the buildings are in various stages of disrepair, you'll find splendid 17th- and 18th-century Orthodox churches and graceful belle époque villas tucked away in quiet corners. Communism changed the face of the city forever, and nowhere is this more evident than at the gargantuan Palace of Parliament, the grandest (and arguably crassest) tribute to dictatorial megalomania you'll ever see.

◉ Sights

◉ South of the Centre

★ Palace of Parliament HISTORIC BUILDING
(Palatul Parlamentului, Casa Poporului; ☑tour bookings 0733-558 102; www.cic.cdep.ro; B-dul Naţiunile Unite; adult/student complete tours 45/23 lei, standard tours 40/20 lei; ⊙9am-5pm Mar-Oct, 10am-4pm Nov-Feb; Ⓜ Izvor) The Palace of Parliament is the world's second-largest administrative building (after the Pentagon) and former dictator Nicolae Ceauşescu's most infamous creation. Started in 1984 (and still unfinished), the 330,000-sq-metre building has more than 3000 rooms. Entry is by guided tour only (book ahead). Entry to the palace is from B-dul Naţiunile Unite on the building's northern side (to find it, face the front of the palace from B-dul Unirii and walk around the building to the right). Bring your passport.

Great Synagogue SYNAGOGUE
(☑0734-708 970; Str Adamache 11; ⊙10am-4pm Mon-Thu, to 1pm Fri & Sun; Ⓜ Piaţa Unirii) FREE This important synagogue dates from the mid-19th century and was established by migrating Polish Jews; entry is free, but a donation (10 lei) is expected. It's hard to find, hidden on three sides by public housing blocks, but worth the effort to see the meticulously restored interior and to take in the main exhibition on Jewish life and the Holocaust in Romania.

◉ Historic Centre & Piaţa Revoluţiei

Bucharest's Historic Centre (Centrul Istoric), sometimes referred to as the 'Old Town', lies south of Piaţa Revoluţiei. It was the seat of power in the 15th century but today is filled with clubs and bars. Piaţa Revoluţiei saw the heaviest fighting in the overthrow of communism in 1989. Those days are commemorated by the Rebirth Memorial (Memorialul Renaşterii; Calea Victoriei, Piaţa Revoluţiei; ⊙24hr; Ⓜ Universitate) in the centre of the square.

Stavropoleos Church CHURCH
(☑021-313 4747; www.stavropoleos.ro; Str Stavropoleos 4; ⊙8.30am-6pm; Ⓜ Piaţa Unirii) The tiny and lovely Stavropoleos Church, which dates from 1724, perches a bit oddly a block over from some of Bucharest's craziest Old Town carousing. It's one church, though, that will make a lasting impression, with its courtyard filled with tombstones, an ornate wooden interior and carved wooden doors.

★ Romanian Athenaeum HISTORIC BUILDING
(Ateneul Român; ☑box office 021-315 6875; www.fge.org.ro; Str Benjamin Franklin 1-3; tickets 20-70 lei; ⊙box office noon-7pm Tue-Fri, from 4pm Sat, 10-11am Sun; Ⓜ Universitate, Piaţa Romană) The exquisite Athenaeum is the majestic heart of Romania's classical-music tradition. Scenes from Romanian history are featured on the interior fresco inside the Big Hall on the 1st floor; the dome is 41m high. A huge appeal dubbed 'Give a Penny for the Athenaeum' saved it from disaster after funds dried up in the late 19th century. Today it's home to the George Enescu Philharmonic Orchestra and normally only open during concerts, but you can often take a peek inside.

National Art Museum MUSEUM
(Muzeul Naţional de Artă; ☑information 021-313 3030; www.mnar.arts.ro; Calea Victoriei 49-53; adult/child 25/10 lei; ⊙11am-7pm Wed-Sun; Ⓜ Universitate) Housed in the 19th-century Royal Palace, this massive, multipart museum – all signed in English – houses two permanent galleries: one for National Art and the other for European Masters. The national gallery is particularly strong on ancient and medieval art, while the European gallery includes some 12,000 pieces and is laid out by nationality.

◉ North of the Centre

Luxurious villas and parks line grand Şos Kiseleff, which begins at Piaţa Victoriei. The major landmark is the Triumphal Arch (Arcul de Triumf; Piaţa Arcul de Triumf; ⊙closed to the public; Ⓜ Aviatorilor), which stands halfway up Şos Kiseleff.

★ Former Ceauşescu Residence MUSEUM
(Primăverii Palace; ☑021-318 0989; www.casaceausescu.ro; B-dul Primăverii 50; guided tours in English adult/child 50/40 lei; ⊙10am-5pm Tue-Sun; ☐131, 282, 301, 331, 330, 335, Ⓜ Aviatorilor) This restored villa is the former main residence of Nicolae and Elena Ceauşescu, who lived here for around two decades up until the end in 1989. Everything has been returned to its former lustre, including the couple's bedroom and the private apartments of the three Ceauşescu children. Highlights include a cinema in the basement, Elena's opulent private chamber, and the back garden and swimming pool. Reserve a tour in advance by phone or on the website.

Central Bucharest

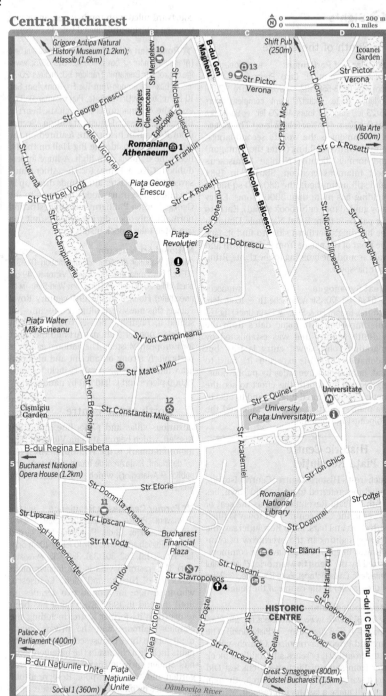

N 0 — 200 m
0 — 0.1 miles

Grigore Antipa Natural History Museum (1.2km); Atlassib (1.6km)

Shift Pub (250m)

Icoanei Garden

Str Pictor Verona

B-dul Gen Magheru

Str Georges Clemenceau

Str Mendeleev

10

13

9 Str Pictor Verona

Str Dionisie Lupu

Str Nicolae Golescu

Str Episcopiei

Str George Enescu

Calea Victoriei

Str Luterană

Romanian Athenaeum 1

Str Franklin

Str C A Rosetti

Vila Arte (500m)

Str Pitar Moş

B-dul Nicolae Bălcescu

Piaţa George Enescu

Str Ştirbei Vodă

Str C A Rosetti

Str Boteanu

Str Nicolae Filipescu

Str Tudor Arghezi

Str Ion Câmpineanu

2

Piaţa Revoluţiei

Str D I Dobrescu

3

Piaţa Walter Mărăcineanu

Str Ion Câmpineanu

Str Matei Millo

Str Ion Brezoianu

12

Str Constantin Mille

Str E Quinet

Universitate

University (Piaţa Universităţii)

Cişmigiu Garden

B-dul Regina Elisabeta

Str Academiei

Str Ion Ghica

Bucharest National Opera House (1.2km)

Str Domniţa Anastasia

Str Eforie

Romanian National Library

Str Colţei

11

Str Lipscani

Str Lipscani

Str Doamnei

Str M Vodă

Bucharest Financial Plaza

6

Str Blănari

Spl Independenţei

Str Ilfov

7

Str Stavropoleos

Str Lipscani

5

4

Str Hanul cu Tei

Palace of Parliament (400m)

Calea Victoriei

Str Poştei

HISTORIC CENTRE

Str Smârdan

Str Şelari

Str Covaci

Str Gabroveni

8

B-dul I C Brătianu

B-dul Naţiunile Unite

Piaţa Naţiunile Unite

Str Franceză

Great Synagogue (800m); Podstel Bucharest (1.5km)

Social 1 (360m)

Dâmboviţa River

Central Bucharest

Grigore Antipa Natural History Museum
MUSEUM

(Muzeul de Istorie Naturală Grigore Antipa; ☎021-312 8826; www.antipa.ro; Şos Kiseleff 1; adult/student 20/5 lei; ⊙10am-8pm Tue-Sun Apr-Oct, to 6pm Tue-Fri, to 7pm Sat & Sun Nov-Mar; 🚼; Ⓜ Piaţa Victoriei) One of the few attractions in Bucharest aimed squarely at kids, this natural-history museum, showing off Romania's plant and animal life, has been thoroughly renovated. It features lots of modern bells and whistles, such as video displays, games and interactive exhibits. Much of it has English signage.

National Village Museum
MUSEUM

(Muzeul Naţional al Satului; ☎021-317 9103; www.muzeul-satului.ro; Şos Kiseleff 28-30; adult/child 15/4 lei; ⊙9am-7pm Tue-Sun, to 5pm Mon; 🚼; Ⓜ Piaţa Victoriei) On the shores of Herăstrău Lake, this museum is a terrific open-air collection of several dozen homesteads, churches, mills and windmills relocated from rural Romania. Built in 1936 by royal decree, it is one of Europe's oldest open-air museums and a good choice for kids to boot.

🛏 Sleeping

Hotels in Bucharest are typically aimed at business people, and prices are higher than in the rest of the country; booking in advance may help secure a discount. Room rates can drop by as much as half in mid-summer (July and August), which is widely considered low season. The situation with hostels continues to improve and Bucharest now has some of the best cheap lodgings in the country.

★ Little Bucharest Old Town Hostel
HOSTEL €

(☎0786-055 287; www.littlebucharest.ro; Str Smârdan 15; dm 35-60 lei; r 145 lei; ⊛@🛜; Ⓜ Piaţa Unirii) Bucharest's most central hostel, in the middle of the lively historic centre, is superclean, white-walled and well run. Accommodation is over two floors, with dorms ranging from six to 12 beds. Private doubles are also available. The staff are travel friendly and youth-oriented and can advise on sightseeing and fun. Book over the website or by email.

Podstel Bucharest
HOSTEL €

(☎021-336 2127; www.podstel.com; Str Olimpului 13a; dm 50-65 lei, d 150 lei; @🛜; Ⓜ Piaţa Unirii) Arguably the nicest and most chill of Bucharest's hostels is a 10-minute walk southwest of Piaţa Unirii. The location is quiet and mainly residential, and there's a beautiful garden set up like a Moroccan tearoom out back. Sleeping is in six-bed mixed dorms, with one good-value private double. Friendly and welcoming staff.

Vila Arte
BOUTIQUE HOTEL €€

(☎021-210 1035; www.vilaarte.ro; Str Vasile Lascăr 78; s/d 250/300 lei; ⊛⊞@🛜; Ⓜ Piaţa Romană, 🚌5, 21) A renovated villa transformed into an excellent-value boutique hotel stuffed with original art that pushes the envelope on design and colour at this price point. The services are top drawer and the helpful reception makes every guest feel special. The 'Ottoman' room is done in an updated Turkish style, with deep-red spreads and fabrics, and oriental carpets.

Rembrandt Hotel
HOTEL €€€

(☎021-313 9315; www.rembrandt.ro; Str Smârdan 11; s/d tourist 300/400 lei, standard 500/600 lei, business from 700 lei; ⊛⊞@🛜; Ⓜ Universitate) Prices have gone through the roof here in the past couple of years, though the hotel's personal touch and stylish rooms, with big, comfy beds and parquet floors, still justify a short-stay splurge. The location, in the historic centre just opposite the landmark National Bank, is within easy reach of some of the best cafes and bars.

✕ Eating

Caru' cu Bere
ROMANIAN €€

(📞 0726-282 373; www.carucubere.ro; Str Stavropoleos 3-5; mains 25-50 lei; ⊙ 8am-midnight Sun-Thu, to 2am Fri & Sat; 🐼; Ⓜ Piaţa Unirii) Despite a decidedly touristy-leaning atmosphere, with peasant-girl hostesses and sporadic traditional song-and-dance numbers, Bucharest's oldest beerhouse continues to draw in a strong local crowd. The colourful belle-époque interior and stained-glass windows dazzle, as does the classic Romanian food. Dinner reservations are essential.

Shift Pub
INTERNATIONAL €€

(📞 021-211 2272; www.shiftpub.ro; Str General Eremia Grigorescu 17; mains 25-40 lei; ⊙ noon-11pm Sun-Thu, to 1am Fri & Sat; 🐼; Ⓜ Piaţa Romană) Great choice for salads and burgers as well as numerous beef and pork dishes, often sporting novel Asian, Middle Eastern or Mexican taste touches. Try to arrive slightly before meal times to grab a coveted table in the tree-covered garden.

Social 1
INTERNATIONAL €€

(📞 0733-222 200; www.social1.ro; B-dul Unirii 1; mains 27-50 lei; ⊙ 10am-midnight Tue-Sun, from noon Mon; 🐼🖉) Pair a visit to the Palace of Parliament with breakfast or lunch at this cheerful spot, conveniently situated just in front of Ceauşescu's behemoth. There's something for everyone on the menu: grills, burgers, ribs, fish and pasta. The quality is high, the prices are moderate and the service attentive. Sit outside in nice weather. Book in advance to be safe.

★ Lacrimi şi Sfinţi
ROMANIAN €€€

(📞 0725-558 286; www.lacrimisisfinti.com; Str Şepcari 16; mains 30-60 lei; ⊙ 12.30pm-1am Tue-Sun, from 6.30pm Mon; 🐼; Ⓜ Piaţa Unirii) A true destination restaurant in the historic centre, Lacrimi şi Sfinţi takes modern trends such as farm-to-table freshness and organic sourcing and marries them to old-school Romanian recipes. The philosophy extends to the simple, peasant-inspired interior, where the woodworking and decorative elements come from old farmhouses. The result is food that feels authentic and satisfying. Book in advance.

🍺 Drinking & Nightlife

Bucharest excels at places to drink, whether you prefer coffee, wine, beer or cocktails. The city has an exploding artisanal coffee scene, and also some very good pubs and clubs – many of them to be found in the historic centre. In summer, look out for terraces and gardens, usually in a secluded spot under a canopy of trees.

★ Grădina Verona
CAFE

(📞 0732-003 060; www.facebook.com/gradina verona; Str Pictor Verona 13-15; ⊙ 10am-midnight May-Sep; 🐼; Ⓜ Piaţa Romană) A garden oasis hidden behind the Cărtureşti bookshop, serving standard-issue but excellent espresso drinks and some of the most inspired iced-tea and lemonade infusions you're likely to find in Romania, such as peony flower, mango and lime (it's not bad).

M60
CAFE

(📞 031-410 0010; www.facebook.com/m60cafeam zei; Str Mendeleev 2; ⊙ 8am-midnight Mon-Fri, from 10am Sat & Sun; 🐼; Ⓜ Piaţa Romană) M60 is a category-buster, transforming through the day from one of the city's preeminent morning coffee houses to a handy lunch spot (healthy salads and vegetarian options) and then morphing into a meet-up and drinks bar in the evening. It's been a hit since opening day, as city residents warmed to its clean, minimalist Scandinavian design and living-room feel.

Origo
CAFE

(📞 0757-086 689; www.origocoffee.ro; Str Lipscani 9; ⊙ 7am-1am Sun, Tue & Wed, to 3am Thu-Sat; 🐼; Ⓜ Piaţa Unirii) Some of the best coffee in town and *the* best place to hang out in the morning, grab a table and gab with friends. Lots of special coffee roasts and an unlimited number of ways to imbibe. There are a dozen pavement tables for relaxing on a sunny day.

☆ Entertainment

Bucharest has a lively night scene of concerts, theatre, rock and jazz. Check the weekly guide *Şapte Seri* (www.sapteseri.ro) for entertainment listings. Another good source for what's on is the website www.iconcert.ro. To buy tickets online, visit the websites of the leading ticketing agencies: www.myticket. ro and www.eventim.ro.

Control
LIVE MUSIC

(📞 0733-927 861; www.control-club.ro; Str Constantin Mille 4; ⊙ 1pm-late; 🐼; Ⓜ Universitate) This is a favourite among club-goers who like alternative, turbo-folk, indie and garage sounds. Hosts both live acts and DJs, depending on the night.

Bucharest National Opera House
OPERA

(Opera Naţională Bucureşti; 📞 box office 0743-278 335; www.operanb.ro; B-dul Mihail Kogălniceanu

70-72; tickets 20-80 lei; ⊘box office 10am-1pm & 2-7pm; ⓂEroilor) The city's premier venue for classical opera and ballet. Buy tickets online or at the venue box office.

Shopping

Cărtureşti Verona   BOOKS
(☑0728-828 916; www.carturesti.ro; Str Pictor Verona 13-15, cnr B-dul Nicolae Bălcescu; ⊘10am-10pm; ⓂPiaţa Romană) This bookshop, music store, tearoom and funky backyard garden is a must-visit. Amazing collection of design, art and architecture books, as well as carefully selected CDs and DVDs, including many classic Romanian films with English subtitles. Also sells Lonely Planet guidebooks.

Information

You'll find hundreds of bank branches and ATMs in the centre. Banks usually have currency-exchange offices, but bring your passport as you'll have to show it to change money.

Bucharest Tourist Information Center (☑021-305 5500, ext 1003; http://seebucharest.ro; Piaţa Universităţii; ⊘10am-5pm Mon-Fri, to 2pm Sat & Sun; ⓂUniversitate) This small, poorly stocked tourist office in the underpass by the Universitate metro station is rarely open but seems to be the best the city can offer. While there's not much information on hand, the English-speaking staff can field basic questions.

Central Post Office (☑021-315 9030; www.posta-romana.ro; Str Matei Millo 12; ⊘8am-7.30pm Mon-Fri, 9am-1pm Sat; ⓂUniversitate)

Emergency Clinic Hospital (Floreasca Hospital; ☑021-599 2300; www.urgentafloreasca.ro; Calea Floreasca 8; ⊘24hr; ⓂŞtefan cel Mare) The first port of call in any serious emergency. Arguably the city's, and country's, best emergency hospital.

Getting There & Away

AIR
All international and domestic flights use **Henri Coandă International Airport** (OTP; Otopeni; ☑021-204 1000; www.bucharestairports.ro; Şos Bucureşti-Ploieşti; ▣783), often referred to in conversation by its previous name, 'Otopeni'. Henri Coandă is 17km north of Bucharest on the main road to Braşov. Arrivals and departures use separate terminals (arrivals is to the north). The airport is a modern facility, with restaurants, newsagents, currency-exchange offices and ATMs. There are 24-hour information desks at both terminals.

The airport is the hub for the national carrier **Tarom** (☑call centre 021-204 6464, office 021-316 0220; www.tarom.ro; Spl Independenţei 17,

city centre; ⊘9am-5pm Mon-Fri; ⓂPiaţa Unirii). Tarom has a comprehensive network of internal flights to major Romanian cities as well as to capitals and big cities around Europe and the Middle East. At the time of writing, there were no direct flights from Bucharest to North America or Southeast Asia.

BUS
Several coach companies dominate the market for travel from Bucharest to cities around Romania.

The best bet for finding a connection is to consult the websites www.autogari.ro and www.cditransport.ro. Both keep up-to-date timetables and are fairly easy to manage, though www.cditransport.ro is only in Romanian. Be sure to follow up with a phone call just to make sure a particular bus is running on a particular day. Another option is to ask your hotel to help with arrangements or book through a travel agency.

Bucharest has several bus stations and they don't seem to follow any discernible logic for which station should serve which destination. Even residents have a hard time making sense of it. When purchasing a bus ticket, always ask where the bus leaves from.

CAR & MOTORCYCLE
Traffic in Bucharest is heavy and you won't want to drive around for very long. If you're travelling by car and just want to visit Bucharest for the day, it's more sensible to park at a metro station on the outskirts and take the metro into the city.

TRAIN
Gara de Nord (☑reservations 021-9521; www.cfrcalatori.ro; Piaţa Gara de Nord 1; ⓂGara de Nord) is the central station for most national and all international trains. The station is accessible by metro from the centre of the city. Buy tickets at station ticket windows. A seat reservation is compulsory if you are travelling with an InterRail or Eurail pass. Check the latest train schedules on either www.cfr.ro or the German site www.bahn.de (when searching timetables, use German spellings for cities, ie 'Bukarest Nord' for Bucharest Gara de Nord).

Following are sample fares and destination times from Bucharest to major Romanian cities on faster IC (Inter-City) trains: Braşov (48 lei, three hours, 15 daily), Cluj-Napoca (90 lei, 7½ hours, five daily), Sibiu (70 lei, six hours, two daily), Sighişoara (70 lei, five hours, two daily) and Timişoara (112 lei, 9 to 10 hours, two daily).

Getting Around

TO/FROM THE AIRPORT
Bus

To get to Henri Coandă International Airport from the centre, take express bus 783, which leaves every 15 minutes between 6am and 11pm (every half-hour at weekends) from Piaţas Unirii and Victoriei and points in between. The Piaţa Unirii stop is on the south side.

Taxi

To hail a taxi at the airport, go to a series of touch screens located in the arrivals hall, where various taxi companies and their rates are listed. Choose any company offering rates from 1.69 to 1.89 lei per kilometre (there's little difference in quality). A reputable taxi to the centre should cost no more than 50 lei.

PUBLIC TRANSPORT

Bucharest's public transport system of the metro, buses, trams and trolleybuses is operated by the transport authority **RATB** (Regia Autonomă de Transport Bucureşti; ☑ 021-9391; www.ratb. ro). The system runs daily from about 4.30am to approximately 11.30pm.

To use buses, trams or trolleybuses, you must first purchase an 'Activ' or 'Multiplu' magnetic card (3.70 lei) from any STB street kiosk, which you then load with credit that is discharged as you enter the transport vehicles. Trips cost 1.30 lei each.

Metro stations are identified by a large letter 'M'. To use the metro, buy a magnetic-strip ticket available at ticketing machines or cashiers inside station entrances (have small bills handy). Tickets valid for two journeys cost 5 lei.

TRANSYLVANIA

After a century of being name-checked in literature and cinema, the word 'Transylvania' enjoys worldwide recognition. The mere mention conjures a vivid landscape of mountains, castles, spooky moonlight and at least one well-known count with a wicked overbite. Unexplained puncture wounds notwithstanding, Transylvania is all those things and more. A melange of architecture and chic sidewalk cafes punctuate the towns of Braşov, Sighişoara and Sibiu, while the vibrant student town Cluj-Napoca has some vigorous nightlife.

Braşov

☑ 0268 / POP 276.090

Gothic spires, medieval gateways, Soviet blocks and a huge Hollywood-style sign: Braşov's skyline is instantly compelling. A number of medieval watchtowers still glower over the town. Between them sparkle baroque buildings and churches, while easy-going cafes line main square Piaţa Sfat-

ului. Visible from here is forested Mt Tâmpa, sporting 'Braşov' in huge white letters.

⊙ Sights

In addition to the sights below, explore the **Old Town Fortifications** that line the centre on the eastern and western flanks. Many have been restored.

Black Church CHURCH
(Biserica Neagră; ☑ 0268-511 824; www.honterus gemeinde.ro; Curtea Johannes Honterus 2; adult/student/child 10/6/3 lei; ⊙ 10am-7pm Tue-Sat, from noon Sun Apr-Oct, 10am-4pm Tue-Sat, from noon Sun Nov-Mar) Romania's largest Gothic church rises triumphantly over Braşov's old town. Built between 1385 and 1477, this German Lutheran church was named for its charred appearance after the town's Great Fire in 1689. Restoration of the church took a century. Today it stands 65m high at its bell tower's tallest point. Organ recitals are held in the church three times a week during July and August, usually at 6pm Tuesday, Thursday and Saturday.

St Nicholas' Cathedral CHURCH
(Biserica Sfântul Nicolae; Piaţa Unirii 1; ⊙ 7am-6pm) FREE With forested hills rising behind its prickly Gothic spires, St Nicholas' Cathedral is one of Braşov's most spectacular views. First built in wood in 1392, it was replaced by a Gothic stone church in 1495 and later embellished in Byzantine style. It was once enclosed by military walls; today the site has a small cemetery. Inside are murals of Romania's last king and queen, covered by plaster to protect them from communist leaders and uncovered in 2004.

Mt Tâmpa MOUNTAIN
(Muntele Tâmpa) Rising 940m high and visible around Braşov, Mt Tâmpa is adorned with its very own Hollywood-style sign. Hard as it is to imagine, it was the site of a mass-impaling of 40 noblemen by Vlad Ţepeş. Banish such ghoulish images from your head as you take the **cable car** (Telecabina; ☑ 0268-478 657; Aleea Tiberiu Brediceanu; one way/return adult 10/18 lei, child 6/10 lei; ⊙ 9.30am-5pm Tue-Sun, noon-6pm Mon), or hike (about an hour), to reach a small viewing platform offering stunning views over the city. There's a cafe at the top.

🛏 Sleeping

Rolling Stone Hostel HOSTEL €
(☑ 0268-513 965; www.rollingstone.ro; Str Piatra Mare 2a; dm/r from 46/170 lei; P @ ☎) Powered

Braşov

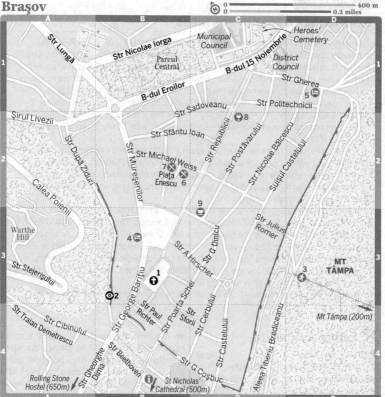

by enthusiastic staff, Rolling Stone has clean dorm rooms that sleep between six and 10. Most rooms have high ceilings and convenient touches like lockers and reading lamps for each bed. Private doubles are comfy, or sleep in the wood-beamed attic for a stowaway vibe. Maps and excellent local advice are supplied the moment you step through the door.

★ **Bella Muzica**   HOTEL **€€**

(☏ 0268-477 956; www.bellamuzica.ro; Piaţa Sfatului 19; s/d/apt from 250/290/560 lei; ❄ 🕸) A regal feel permeates Bella Muzica, housed within a 400-year-old building, thanks to its tastefully restored wooden beams, exposed brick, high ceilings and occasional antiques. The main square location of this refined hotel is hard to top.

Casa Reims   B&B **€€**

(☏ 0368-467 325; www.casareims.ro; Str Castelului 85; s/d from 210/260 lei; 🅿 ❄ 🕸) Pastels and acid tones mingle beautifully with bare

Braşov

◎ Sights

1 Black Church	B3
2 Old Town Fortifications	B3

◈ Activities, Courses & Tours

3 Mt Tâmpa Cable Car	D3

⬛ Sleeping

4 Bella Muzica	B3
5 Casa Reims	D1

⊗ Eating

6 Bistro de l'Arte	B2
7 Pilvax	B2

⊜ Drinking & Nightlife

8 Festival 39	C2
9 Tipografia	C3

brick and wooden beams at this boutique B&B. Personalised service from the friendly owners adds to the VIP feel, and most rooms have views of Mt Tâmpa.

WORTH A TRIP

BRAN CASTLE & RÂŞNOV FORTRESS

Rising above the town on a rocky promontory, **Bran Castle** (☑0268-237 700; www.bran-castle.com; Str General Traian Moşoiu 24; adult/student/child 40/25/10 lei; ⊙9am-6pm Tue-Sun, from noon Mon Apr-Sep, to 4pm Oct-Mar) holds visitors in thrall. Illuminated by the light of a pale moon, the vampire's lair glares down from its rocky bluff. An entire industry has sprouted around describing the pile as 'Dracula's Castle', and at first glance the claims look legit. Regrettably, though, Bran Castle's blood-drinking credentials don't withstand scrutiny. It's unlikely Vlad Ţepeş – either 'the Impaler' or 'protector of Wallachia' – ever passed through. Nor did the castle inspire Bram Stoker in writing his iconic Gothic novel *Dracula*.

These seem minor quibbles when you gaze up at the turreted fortress, guarded from the east by the Bucegi Mountains and from the west by Piatra Craiului massif. Meanwhile, the castle's museum pays greater homage to Romanian royals than immortal counts. Ignoring this, a gauntlet of souvenir sellers hawk fang-adorned mugs and Vlad-the-Impaler compact mirrors (really).

Commonly paired with Bran Castle on day trips from Braşov, nearby **Râşnov Fortress** (Cetatea Râşnov; ☑0268-230 115; www.rasnov-turism.ro; Strada Cetăţii; adult/child 12/6 lei; ⊙9am-6pm) might just be the more enchanting of the two. The medieval citadel, built by Teutonic Knights to guard against Tatar and Turkish invasion, roosts on a hilltop 19km southwest of Braşov by road. Visitors are free to stroll between sturdy watchtowers, browse medieval-themed souvenir and craft stalls, and admire views of rolling hills from the fortress' highest point. Walk from the village or take the lift.

Bran is a 45-minute bus ride from Braşov, with a stop in Râşnov, and makes an easy day trip.

🍴 Eating & Drinking

⭐ Bistro de l'Arte   BISTRO €€
(☑0720-535 566; www.bistrodelarte.ro; Piaţa Enescu 11; mains 32-40 lei; ⊙9am-midnight Mon-Sat, from noon Sun; 🛜🖉) Tucked down a charming side street, this bohemian joint can be spotted by the bike racks shaped like penny-farthings. There's an almost Parisian feel in Bistro de l'Arte's arty decor and Champagne breakfasts (59 lei), though its menu picks the best from France, Italy and beyond: bruschetta, fondue, German-style cream cake and a suitably hip cocktail list.

Pilvax   HUNGARIAN €€
(☑0268-475 829; www.pilvax.ro; Str Michael Weiss 16; mains 25-60 lei; ⊙8am-10pm Tue-Sun, from 1pm Mon; 🛜🖉) Centrally located Pilvax offers an upscale fusion of Transylvanian and Hungarian food – think stuffed peppers or braised spare ribs with polenta – in a bright, modern setting. The wine list is among the best in the area and there's a big terrace out front for when it's too warm to sit inside. Reserve in advance for dinner or on weekends.

Tipografia   TEAHOUSE
(☑0722-373 090; www.tipo-grafia.ro; Str Postăvarului 1; ⊙8am-1am Mon-Fri, from 9am Sat & Sun; 🛜) Tipografia calls itself a teahouse, but it's an excellent all-rounder. It makes a mean cup of coffee too, and by sunset the place morphs into one of the city's best beer joints and cocktail bars. The crowd is local and chill, and weekend nights have been known to go on far longer than closing hour.

Festival 39   BAR
(☑0743-339 909; www.festival39.com; Str Republicii 62; ⊙7am-midnight; 🛜) Jazz flows from this vintage-feel watering hole and restaurant, an art deco dream of stained glass, high ceilings, wrought-iron finery, candelabra and leather banquettes. As good for clanking together beer glasses as for cradling a hot chocolate over your travel journal.

ℹ️ Information

You'll find numerous ATMs and banks on and around Str Republicii and B-dul Eroilor.

Tourist Information Centre (☑0268-327 298; www.brasovtourism.eu; Str Prundului 1; ⊙9am-5pm Mon-Thu, 10am-3pm Fri, 11am-2pm Sat & Sun) Cordial staff offer maps and local advice.

ℹ️ Getting There & Away

BUS

Maxitaxis and microbuses are the best way to reach places near Braşov, including Bran and

Râşnov. The most accessible station is **Bus Station 1** (Autogari 1; ☑ 0268-427 267; www.autogari.ro; B-dul Gării 1), next to the train station. From 6am to 7.30pm maxitaxis leave every half-hour for Bucharest (from 40 lei, 2½ to 3½ hours). About 10 daily buses or maxitaxis leave for Sibiu (30 lei, 2½ hours). At least three go daily to Sighişoara (35 lei, two hours). Less frequent buses reach Cluj-Napoca (90 lei, four to five hours, four daily). For other destinations, check www.autogari.ro.

TRAIN

The **train station** (Gara Braşov; ☑ 0268-410 233; www.cfrcalatori.ro; B-dul Gării 5) is 2km northeast of the town centre. Left-luggage service is available at the station. Sample routes and fares: Bucharest (48 lei, three hours, 15 daily), Cluj-Napoca (75 lei, seven hours, six daily), Sibiu (45 lei, four hours, four daily) and Sighişoara (40 lei, three hours, six daily).

Sighişoara

☑ 0265 / POP 28,100

So resplendent are Sighişoara's pastel-coloured buildings, stony lanes and medieval towers, you'll rub your eyes in disbelief. Fortified walls encircle Sighişoara's lustrous merchant houses, now harbouring cafes, hotels and craft shops. Lurking behind the gingerbread roofs and turrets of the Unesco-protected old town is the history of Vlad Ţepeş, the bloodthirsty, 15th-century Wallachian prince. He was allegedly born here, in a house that is visitable to this day. Ţepeş is best remembered as Vlad the Impaler, or Dracula, fuelling a local industry of vampire-themed souvenirs. Allow time to lose yourself along Sighişoara's alleys, hike to its hilltop church and sip coffee at cafes half a millennium old.

⊙ Sights

Citadel   FORTRESS

Sighişoara's delightful medieval buildings are enclosed within its citadel, a Unesco-listed complex of protective walls and watchtowers. Walking in the citadel is today a tranquil, fairy-tale-like experience, but these towers were once packed with weapons and emergency supplies, guarding Sighişoara from Turkish attacks (note the upper windows from which arrows could be fired).

Clock Tower   MUSEUM

(Turnul cu Ceas; Piaţa Muzeului 1; adult/child 15/4 lei; ⊙ 9am-6.30pm Tue-Fri, 10am-5.30pm Sat & Sun mid-May–mid-Sep, to 3.30pm mid-Sep–mid-May)

The multicoloured-tiled roof of Sighişoara's Clock Tower glitters like the scales of a dragon. The tower was built in the 14th century and expanded 200 years later. It remains the prettiest sight in town, offering a magnificent panorama from the top. The views are as good a reason to visit as the museum inside, a patchy collection of Roman vessels, scythes and tombstones, and a scale model of the fortified town (English-language explanation is variable).

Casa Vlad Dracul   HISTORIC BUILDING

(☑ 0744-518 108; www.facebook.com/restaurant-casa-vlad-dracul-229836943748789; Str Cositorarilor 5; 5 lei; ⊙ noon-8pm) Vlad Ţepeş (aka Dracula) was reputedly born in this house in 1431 and lived here until the age of four. It's now a decent restaurant, but for a small admission the staff will show you Vlad's old room (and give you a little scare). Bubble-burster: the building is indeed centuries old, but has been completely rebuilt since Vlad's days.

🛏 Sleeping

Burg Hostel   HOSTEL €

(☑ 0265-778 489; www.burghostel.ro; Str Bastionului 4-6; dm 45 lei, s/d 90/120 lei, without bathroom 85/110 lei; ☎ ▩) A great budget choice without compromising on charm, Burg Hostel has spacious dorms (with handy touches like plug sockets close to beds). Common areas have chandeliers made from old cartwheels, plus ceramic lamps, vaulted ceilings and other rustic touches. Staff are friendly and there's a relaxing courtyard cafe. Breakfast isn't normally included, but you can buy meals from the cafe.

Pensiunea Legenda   GUESTHOUSE €€

(☑ 0748-694 368; www.legenda.ro; Str Bastionului 8; r 160 lei; ☎) The owners of this historic guesthouse whisper that Vlad Ţepeş once wooed a beautiful young woman within these walls, a myth that will either charm or chill you. All five rooms at this well-run guesthouse have snug beds and occasional vampiric twists such as black chandeliers and dungeon-like doors. Breakfast not included.

★Casa Georgius Krauss   BOUTIQUE HOTEL €€€

(☑ 0365-730 840; www.casakrauss.com; Str Bastionului 11; r 330-400 lei; P ▩ ☎) This dazzling boutique hotel is hived out of an old burgher's house at the northern end of the citadel.

The restoration left period details like wood-beamed ceilings, while adding tasteful modern bathrooms and plush-linened beds. The Krauss Room, number 2, has original paintings, including a medieval coat of arms, plus a four-poster bed.

✕ Eating

Central Park   INTERNATIONAL €€
(☑ 0365-730 006; www.hotelcentralpark.ro; Central Park Hotel, Piața Hermann Oberth 25; mains 30-45 lei; ⊙ 11am-11pm; 🅿 🛜) Even if you're not staying at the **hotel** (s/d 340/370 lei; 🅿 ❈ @ 🛜), plan a meal here. Sighișoara is short on good restaurants and this is one of the best. The food is a mix of Romanian and international dishes, including very good steaks, and the wine list offers the best domestic labels. Dress up for the lavish dining room or relax on the terrace.

Casa Vlad Dracul   ROMANIAN €€
(☑ 0265-771 596; www.facebook.com/restaurant-casa-vlad-dracul-229836943748789; Str Cositorarilor 5; mains 25-35 lei; ⊙ noon-8pm; 🚼) The link between Dracula and tomato soups, or medallions with potato and chicken roulade, we'll never quite understand. But the house where Vlad was born could have been dealt a worse blow than this atmospheric, wood-panelled restaurant. The menu of Romanian, Saxon and grilled specials is dotted with Dracula references. Embellish it a little and your kids will love it.

🛍 Shopping

★ Arts & Crafts   ARTS & CRAFTS
(☑ 0745-853 109; www.thespoonman.ro; Str Cositorarilor 5; ⊙ 10.30am-6.30pm) Inside Casa Vlad Dracul (p349), this wondrous handicraft shop is the brainchild of self-styled 'Spoonman' Mark Tudose, who employs traditional woodcarving methods to fashion Transylvanian spoons (each with a local legend behind it), as well as painted-glass icons, clay statues, painted eggs and much more. It's a beautiful place to browse, and your best bet for finding a culturally meaningful souvenir.

ℹ Information

There are numerous ATMs and banks lining Sighișoara's main street, Str 1 Decembrie 1918.
Tourist Information Centre (Centrul Național de Informare și Promovare Turistică; ☑ 0365-882 937; www.sighisoara.org.ro; Str Turnului 1; ⊙ 9am-5pm; 🛜) Cordial, multilingual information service just behind the Clock Tower (p349) as you're approaching from town. Has free maps and transport information.

ℹ Getting There & Away

BUS

Close to the train station, the **main bus station** (Autogara Cambus; ☑ 0265-771 260; www.autogari.ro; Str Libertății 53) sends buses of various sizes and colours to Brașov (from 26 lei, 2½ hours, five daily) and Sibiu (from 40 lei, 2½ hours, two daily). Note that some buses use stops other than the main bus station. Be sure to check with www.autogari.ro.

TRAIN

Direct trains connect Sighișoara's **train station** (☑ 0265-771 886; www.cfrcalatori.ro; Str Libertății 51) with Brașov (40 lei, 2½ to 3½ hours, six daily), Bucharest (70 lei, five to 5½ hours, two daily, more via Brașov), Cluj-Napoca (40 to 60 lei, 4½ to six hours, four daily, more via Teius) and Sibiu (13 lei, 2½ to three hours, two daily, more via Mediaș).

Sibiu

📞 0269 / POP 147,250

Sibiu is awash in aristocratic elegance. Noble Saxon history emanates from every art nouveau facade and gold-embossed church, all parked elegantly around graceful squares. Renowned composers Strauss, Brahms and Liszt all played here during the 19th century, and Sibiu has stayed at the forefront of Romania's cultural scene. Houses with distinctive eyelid-shaped windows (imagine a benign Amityville Horror House) watch a cast of artists and buskers bustling below them. Cafes and bars inhabit brick-walled cellars and luminously decorated attics.

◉ Sights

★ St Mary's Evangelical Church   CHURCH
(Catedrala Evanghelică Sfânta Maria; Piața Huet; adult/child 5/2 lei, with tower 8/3 lei; ⊙ 9am-8pm Mon-Sat, from 11.30am Sun) Sibiu's Gothic centrepiece rises more than 73m over the old town. Inside, marvel at ghoulish stone skeletons, 17th-century tombs and the largest organ in Romania, all framed by a magnificent arched ceiling. Built in stages from the mid-1300s to 1520, the church was planted atop the site of an older 12th-century sanctuary. At the time of research, the main chambers were closed for long-term renovation but it was still possible to visit the front room and tower.

DANUBE DELTA

After passing through several countries and absorbing countless lesser waterways, the Danube River empties into the Black Sea in eastern Romania, just south of the Ukrainian border.

The Danube Delta (Delta Dunării), included on Unesco's World Heritage list, is one of Romania's leading attractions. At the port of **Tulcea** (pronounced tool-cha), the river splits into three separate channels – the Chilia, Sulina and Sfântu Gheorghe arms – creating a constantly evolving 4187-sq-km wetland of marshes, floating reed islets and sandbars. The region provides sanctuary for 300 species of bird and 160 species of fish. Reed marshes cover 1563 sq km, constituting one of the largest single expanses of reed beds in the world.

The delta is a haven for wildlife lovers, birdwatchers, anglers and anyone wanting to get away from it all. There are beautiful, secluded beaches at both **Sulina** and **Sfântu Gheorghe**, and the fish and seafood, particularly the fish soup, are the best in Romania. Tulcea is the largest city in the delta and the main entry point for accessing the region. It's got good bus and minibus connections to the rest of the country, and is home to the main passenger ferries. There is no rail service in the delta and few paved roads, meaning the primary mode of transport is ferry boat. Regularly scheduled ferries, both traditional 'slow' ferries and faster (and more expensive) hydrofoils, leave from Tulcea's main port on select days throughout the week and access major points in the delta.

The helpful staff at the **Tourism Information Centre** (☑ 0240-519 130; www.cnipt-tulcea.ro; Str Gării 26; ☺ 8am-4pm Mon-Fri) in Tulcea can help piece together a journey depending on your time and budget.

Brukenthal Palace
GALLERY

(European Art Gallery; ☑ 0269-217 691; www.brukenthalmuseum.ro; Piața Mare 5; adult/student 20/5 lei; ☺ 9am-5pm Wed-Sun) Brukenthal Palace is worth visiting as much for its resplendent period furnishings as for the European art within. Duck beneath the Music Room's chandeliers to admire colourful friezes and 18th-century musical instruments, before sidling among chambers exhibiting 17th-century portraits amid satin chaise longues and cases packed with antique jewellery. Sumptuously curated.

History Museum
MUSEUM

(Casa Altemberger; www.brukenthalmuseum.ro/istorie; Str Mitropoliei 2; adult/child 20/5 lei; ☺ 9am-5pm Wed-Sun) This impressive museum begins with re-enactments of cave dwellers squatting in the gloom and dioramas of Dacian life. Out of these shadowy corridors, the museum opens out to illuminating exhibitions about Saxon guilds and local handicrafts (most impressive is the 19th-century glassware from Porumbacu de Sus). There's plenty of homage to Saxon efficiency: you could expect a fine for improperly crafting a copper cake tin.

ASTRA National Museum Complex
MUSEUM

(Muzeul Civilizației Populare Tradiționale ASTRA; ☑ 0269-202 447; www.muzeulastra.ro; Str Pădurea Dumbrava 16-20; adult/child 17/3.50 lei; ☺ 8am-8pm May-Sep, 9am-5pm Oct-Apr) Five kilometres from central Sibiu, this is Europe's largest open-air ethnographic museum, where churches, mills and traditional homes number among 400 folk-architecture monuments on-site. In summer, ASTRA hosts numerous fairs, dance workshops and musical performances, so it's worthwhile checking the website for events. There's also a nice gift shop and restaurant with creekside bench seats.

🛏 Sleeping

B13
HOSTEL €

(☑ 0269-701 742; www.b13hostel.ro; Str Nicolea Bălcescu 13; dm 50-75 lei; ❀@☎) Almost too chic to be dubbed a hostel, B13 offers comfy bunks in six- to 20-bed dorms (one is women-only). The best rooms face the street: they have more light and better views. There are lockers and a friendly chill-out room, and a handy American-style burger bar downstairs.

Council
BOUTIQUE HOTEL €€

(☑ 0369-452 524; www.thecouncil.ro; Piața Mică 31; s/d/apt from €50/55/109; ❀☎) Tapping into Sibiu's medieval lifeblood, this opulent hotel occupies a 14th-century hall in the heart of the old town. Individually designed rooms are equipped with desks, security safes and plenty of contemporary polish, but there are aristocratic touches such as crimson throws, bare wooden rafters and Turkish-style rugs.

Am Ring HOTEL **€€**
(☑0269-206 499; www.amringhotel.ro; Piaţa Mare 14; s/d/ste 250/290/390 lei; ❉☎) Centrally located and decorated in a smorgasbord of styles, this is arguably Sibiu's most lavish place to sleep. From the vaulted brick dining room to bedrooms styled with original wooden beams, throne-like chairs and baroque touches such as gold candelabra, Am Ring exudes old-world elegance.

✖ Eating & Drinking

★**Crama Sibiul Vechi** ROMANIAN **€€**
(☑0269-210 461; www.sibiulvechi.ro; Str Papiullarian 3; mains 25-35 lei; ☉11am-10pm) Hidden in an old wine cellar, this is the most evocative restaurant in Sibiu. Explore Romanian fare such as cheese croquettes, minced meatballs and peasant's stew with polenta. Show up early or reserve ahead; it's very popular.

Kulinarium ROMANIAN, EUROPEAN **€€**
(☑0721-506 070; www.kulinarium.ro; Piaţa Mică 12; mains 30-40 lei; ☉noon-midnight; ☎) Fresh, well-presented Italy- and France-leaning cuisine using seasonal ingredients graces plates at Kulinarium. The restaurant has an intimate, casual feel, with roughly painted stone walls and dangling modern lampshades. Choose from smoky Austrian sausages, spinach soup with quail eggs, rare-beef salad, trout with wild rice or well-executed pasta dishes.

Nod Pub BAR
(☑0745-047 070; www.facebook.com/nod.pub; Piaţa Mică 27; ☉9am-midnight Mon-Fri, from 10am Sat & Sun; ☎) Superb coffee and authentic cocktails (try the mojito) make this a special spot, night or day. There's an organic feel to the wood-accented interior, but you're better off at an outdoor table, watching people mill around grand Piaţa Mică.

Music Pub BAR
(☑0369-448 326; www.facebook.com/musicpub sibiu; Piaţa Mică 23; ☉8am-3am Mon-Fri, from 11am Sat & Sun; ☎) Skip down the graffitied corridor and rub your eyes in astonishment as a cellar bar and airy veranda open up. One of the merriest spots in town, Music Pub sparkles with straw lamps and little candles, while '90s dance and rock plays on.

There's table service, it's friendly and there's occasional live music.

❶ Information

ATMs are located all over the centre.

Tourist Information Centre (☑0269-208 913; www.turism.sibiu.ro; Str Samuel Brukenthal 2, Piaţa Mare; ☉9am-8pm Mon-Fri, 10am-6pm Sat & Sun May-Sep, 9am-5pm Mon-Fri, to 1pm Sat & Sun Oct-Apr) Based at the town hall; staff can offer free maps and plenty of local transport advice.

❶ Getting There & Away

BUS

Sibiu has two useful bus stations: the **Transmixt station** (Autogara Transmixt; ☑0269-217 757; www.autogari.ro; Piaţa 1 Decembrie 1918 no 6) is next to the train station; **bus station Q7** (Autogara Q7; ☑0269-232 826; Str Şcoala de Înot) is southwest of the centre. Both serve many of the same destinations, so it's important to verify which station your bus is using. Ask locally or look on www.autogari.ro.

Services run to Braşov (30 lei, 2½ to three hours, 12 daily), Bucharest (60 lei, 4½ hours, 10 daily), Cluj-Napoca (35 lei, 3½ to 4½ hours, 15 daily), Timişoara (60 to 80 lei, six hours, seven daily) and Târgu Mureş (30 lei, 2½ to 3½ hours, six daily).

TRAIN

Sibiu's **train station** (Gara Sibiu; ☑0269-211 139; www.cfrcalatori.ro; Piaţa 1 Decembrie 1918, 6) has direct trains to Braşov (44 lei, three hours, four daily), Bucharest (70 lei, six to eight hours, two daily, more via Braşov), Sighişoara (13 lei, three hours, one daily, more via Copşa Mică or Mediaş) and Timişoara (61 lei, 6½ hours, one daily, more via Arad). Mostly indirect services reach Cluj-Napoca (66 lei, five hours, 12 daily); change at Copşa Mică or Vinţu de Jos.

Cluj-Napoca

☑0264 / POP 324,500

Bohemian cafes, music festivals and vigorous nightlife are the soul of Cluj-Napoca, Romania's second-largest city. With increasing flight links to European cities, Cluj is welcoming more and more travellers, who usually shoot off to more-popular towns in southern Transylvania. But once arrived, first-time visitors inevitably lament their failure to allow enough time in Cluj. Don't make the same mistake. Start with the architecture, ranging from Romania's second-largest Gothic church to baroque buildings and medieval towers. Dip into galleries and gardens.

And allow at least one lazy morning to recover from Cluj's fiery nightlife.

◎ Sights

★ St Michael's Church
CHURCH

(Biserica Sfantul Mihail; ✆ 0264-592 089; Piața Unirii; ⊙ 8am-6pm) FREE The showpiece of Piața Unirii is 14th- and 15th-century St Michael's, the second-biggest Gothic church in Romania, after Brașov's Black Church (p346). Its neo-Gothic clock tower (1859) stands 80m high, while original Gothic features – such as the 1444 front portal – can still be admired. Inside, soaring rib vaults lift the gaze towards fading frescoes.

At the time of research, the church was temporarily closed for renovation.

Parcul Etnografic Romulus Vuia
MUSEUM, PARK

(✆ 0264-586 776; www.muzeul-etnografic.ro; Aleea Muzeului Etnografic; adult/child 6/3 lei; ⊙ 10am-6pm Wed-Sun Apr-Sep, 9am-4pm Oct-Mar) Traditional architecture from around Romania has been faithfully reassembled at this open-air museum, 5km northwest of central Cluj. Most impressive is the Cizer Church; get the attention of a caretaker to allow you inside to view frescoes covering its wooden interior.

Pharmacy History Collection
MUSEUM

(Piața Unirii 28; adult/child 6/3 lei; ⊙ 10am-4pm Mon-Wed & Fri, noon-6pm Thu) Cluj-Napoca's oldest pharmacy building holds an intriguing collection of medical miscellany. 'Crab eyes', skulls and powdered mummy are just a few of the cures on display in these antique-filled rooms. The prettiest is the Officina, a polished room with dark filigree swirling around its walls. You'll also learn that the 18th-century recipe for a love potion sounds suspiciously like mulled wine…

At the time of research, the museum was temporarily closed for renovation but was expected to reopen in 2020.

Fabrica de Pensule
ARTS CENTRE

(Paintbrush Factory; ✆ 0727-169 569; www.fabrica depensule.ro; Str Henri Barbusse 59-61; ⊙ tours 3-7pm Tue-Sat; 🚋 1, 6, 7, 24, 24B, 25, 30, 36B) FREE More of a living, breathing creative space than a gallery, Fabrica de Pensule teems with just-made artwork by local and foreign creators who use this former paintbrush factory as a studio. Visits are by free guided tour, and depending on how you like your art, you'll either adore visiting this artistic community in a postindustrial setting or be bemused by the work-in-progress art within boxy gallery spaces. It's 3km northeast of the centre. Walk or take the bus.

🛏 Sleeping

Youthink Hostel
HOSTEL €

(✆ 0743-014 630; www.youthinkhostel.com; Str Republicii 74; dm/d €15/35; 🅿 🐾 ⊙) 🦮 A labour-of-love restoration project has transformed a 1920 building into something between a hostel and an ecotourism retreat. Original wood beams, fireplace and hardwood floors retain the early-20th-century splendour, while the seven- and eight-bed dorms are clean and modern. Aptly for such a cheery and eco-conscious hostel, you'll be greeted by friendly dogs and a cat.

★ Lol & Lola
BOUTIQUE HOTEL €€

(✆ 0264-450 498; www.loletlolahotel.ro; Str Neagră 9; s/d €67/79; 🅿 ❄ ⊙) This enjoyably zany hotel has a rainbow of individually styled rooms to choose from, with themes ranging from Hollywood, ballet, and a rock 'n' roll room with vinyl and guitars. It's ultramodern with friendly service. The hotel is a little tricky to find, situated on a small street just east of central Str Victor Babeș.

Hotel Confort
HOTEL €€

(✆ 0264-598 410; www.hotelconfort.ro; Calea Turzii 48; s/d/ste 220/240/270 lei; 🅿 ❄ ⊙) Huge rooms with wooden floors and fuzzy rugs are accented with flower arrangements and arty prints at this chic hotel. Four rooms have balconies, and most have big windows and billowy drapes. It's a car-friendly location, a 15-minute walk outside central Cluj. Parking is free but limited; ask ahead. Breakfast is an extra 30 lei.

✗ Eating & Drinking

★ Roata
ROMANIAN €€

(✆ 0264-592 022; www.facebook.com/restaurant roatacluj; Str Alexandru Ciurea 6; mains 25-40 lei; ⊙ noon-11pm; 🍴) Transylvanian cuisine just like Granny made it, in an untouristed part of Cluj. Settle in beneath the vine-covered trellis outdoors and agonise between roasted pork ribs and pike with capers. Or go all out with a 'Transylvanian platter' for two (52 lei), with homemade sausages, meatballs, sheep's cheese, aubergine stew and spare elastic for when your pants snap (we wish).

Bujole
ROMANIAN €€

(www.bujole.com; Piața Unirii 15; mains 35-70 lei; ⊙ 8am-11pm Mon-Fri, from 9am Sat, from 10am

WORTH A TRIP

PAINTED MONASTERIES OF BUCOVINA

Bucovina's painted monasteries are among the most distinctive in all Christendom. They're cherished not only for their beauty and quality of artisanship, but also for their endurance over the centuries and cultural significance. The half-dozen or so monasteries, scattered over a large swathe of Bucovina, date mainly from the 15th and 16th centuries, a time when Orthodox Moldavia was battling for its life with forces of the expanding Ottoman Empire.

The monasteries are hailed mainly for their colourful external frescoes, many of which have survived the region's cruel winters relatively intact. The external wall paintings served as both expressions of faith and as an effective method of conveying important biblical stories to a parish of mostly illiterate soldiers and peasants. But don't pass up the rich interiors, where every nook and cranny is filled with religious and cultural symbolism.

Arbore Monastery (Mănăstirea Arbore; ☑ 0740-154 213; Hwy DN2K 732, Arbore; adult/student 5/2 lei, photography 10 lei; ☉ 8am-7pm May-Sep, to 4pm Oct-Apr), the smallest of the main monasteries, receives a fraction of the visitors the others receive. The smaller scale allows you to study the paintings up close, to appreciate the skills and techniques. The monastery dates from 1503.

Humor Monastery (Mănăstirea Humorului; ☑ 0230-572 837; Gura Humorului; adult/student 5/2 lei, photography 10 lei; ☉ 8am-7pm May-Sep, to 4pm Oct-Apr), built in 1530 near the town of Gura Humorului, boasts arguably the most impressive interior frescoes.

Voroneț Monastery (Mănăstirea Voroneț; ☑ 0230-235 323; Str Voroneț 166, Voroneț; adult/child 5/2 lei, photography 10 lei; ☉ dawn-dusk), also not far from Gura Humorului, is the only one to have a specific colour associated with it. 'Voroneț Blue', a vibrant cerulean colour created from lapis lazuli, is prominent in its frescoes. The monastery was built in just three months and three weeks by Ştefan cel Mare following a 1488 victory over the Turks.

Built in 1532, **Moldovița Monastery** (Mânăstirea Moldovița; Vatra Moldoviței; adult/student 5/2 lei, photography 10 lei; ☉ 8am-7pm May-Sep, to 4pm Oct-Apr), 35km northwest of the Voroneț Monastery, occupies a fortified quadrangular enclosure with tower, gates and flowery lawns. The central painted church has been partly restored, and features impressive frescoes from 1537.

The main gateway to the monasteries is **Suceava**, reachable by direct train from both Bucharest and Cluj-Napoca.

Sun; 🛜) The excellent French-inspired Romanian cooking, with a few welcome atypical starters such as hummus, make this a must-visit. The convenient Piața Unirii location doesn't hurt. French influences include a very good foie gras and duck confit. If too many hotel breakfast buffets have you pining for something different, the breakfast menu includes the city's best eggs Benedict (25 lei).

Roots
CAFE

(B-dul Eroilor 4; ☉ 7.30am-11.30pm Mon-Fri, from 9am Sat, to 5pm Sun; 🛜) Competition for Cluj's best brew is stiff, but Roots' silky coffee is the front runner. Staff are as friendly as the flat whites are smooth. Find it just next door to the Tourist Information Office.

Euphoria Biergarten
BEER GARDEN

(☑ 0745-393 333; www.euphoria.ro; Str Cardinal Iuliu Hossu 25; ☉ 8am-2pm; 🛜) The perfect, quiet spot for evening beers (and good food too).

Find a table out front by a small river or in the big garden out back and order from a wide range of national and craft beers. The food menu is fairly ambitious for a beer garden – mains (25 lei to 40 lei) include burgers, ribs and grilled meats.

Joben Bistro
CAFE

(www.jobenbistro.ro; Str Avram Iancu 29; ☉ 8am-2am Mon-Thu, from noon Fri-Sun; 🛜) This steampunk cafe will lubricate the gears of any traveller with a penchant for Victoriana. Aside from the fantasy decor, with skull designs, taxidermied deer heads and copper pipes on bare brick walls, it's a laid-back place to nurse a lavender-infused lemonade or perhaps the potent 'Drunky Hot Chocolate'.

ⓘ Information

There are banks and ATMs scattered around the centre.

Tourist Information Office (☎0264-452 244; www.visitcluj.ro; B-dul Eroilor 6; ⊗8.30am-8pm Mon-Fri, 10am-6pm Sat & Sun; ☎) Superfriendly office with free maps, thoughtful trekking advice and tons of info on transport links, accommodation, events and more.

ⓘ Getting There & Away

BUS

Domestic and international bus services depart mostly from **Bus Station Beta** (Autogara Beta; ☎0264-455 249; www.autogarabeta-cluj.ro; Str Giordano Bruno 1-3; ⊗6am-10.45pm). The bus station is 350m northwest of the train station (take the overpass). Check www.autogari.ro for current routes and departure/arrival stations.

Popular routes and fares include: Braşov (65 lei, five hours, six daily), Bucharest (60 to 90 lei, nine hours, six daily) and Sibiu (30 to 40 lei, 3¼ to four hours, almost hourly).

TRAIN

Trains from Cluj-Napoca's **train station** (www.cfrcalatori.ro; Str Căii Ferate) reach the following destinations: Braşov (75 lei, seven hours, six daily), Bucharest (90 lei, 10 hours, five daily), Sighişoara (60 lei, 4½ hours, four daily) and Sibiu (50 lei, five hours, one daily).

The **Agenţia de Voiaj CFR** (☎0264-432 001; Piaţa Mihai Viteazu 20; ⊗8.30am-8pm Mon-Fri) sells domestic and international train tickets in advance.

BANAT

Western Romania, with its geographic and cultural ties to neighbouring Hungary and Serbia, and its historical links to the Austro-Hungarian Empire, enjoys an ethnic diversity that much of the rest of the country lacks. Timişoara, the regional hub, has a nationwide reputation as a beautiful and lively metropolis, and for a series of 'firsts'. It was the world's first city to adopt electric street lights (in 1884) and, more importantly, the first city to rise up against dictator Nicolae Ceauşescu in 1989.

Timişoara
☎0256 / POP 315,050

Romania's third-largest city (after Bucharest and Cluj-Napoca) is also one of the country's most attractive urban areas, built around a series of beautifully restored public squares and lavish parks and gardens. The city's charms have been recognised by the EU, which named Timişoara as the Eu-

ropean Capital of Culture for 2021. Locally, Timişoara is known as 'Primul Oraş Liber' (The First Free City), for it was here that anti-Ceauşescu protests first exceeded the Securitate's capacity for violent suppression in 1989, eventually sending Ceauşescu and his wife to their deaths.

◉ Sights

★Museum of the 1989 Revolution
MUSEUM

(☎0256-294 936; www.memorialulrevolutiei.ro; Strada Popa Şapcă 3-5; adult/child 10/5 lei; ⊗8am-4pm Mon-Fri, 10am-2pm Sat) This is an ideal venue to brush up on the December 1989 anticommunist revolution that began here in Timişoara. Displays include documentation, posters and photography from those fateful days, capped by a graphic 20-minute video (not suitable for young children) with English subtitles. Enter from Str Oituz 2.

Synagogue in the Fortress
SYNAGOGUE

(Sinagoga din Cetate; Str Mărăşeşti 6) Built in 1865 by Viennese architect Ignatz Schuhmann, the synagogue acts as an important keynote in Jewish history – Jews in the Austro-Hungarian Empire were emancipated in 1864, when permission was given to build the synagogue. It was closed at the time of research for renovation, but the fine exterior is worth taking in.

Reformed Church
CHURCH

(Biserica Reformată; Str Timotei Cipariu 1) The 1989 revolution began at the Reformed Church, where Father László Tőkés spoke out against Ceauşescu. You can sometimes peek in at the church, and it is usually open during times of worship.

Timişoara Art Museum
MUSEUM

(Muzeul de Artă Timişoara; ☎0256-491 592; www.muzeuldeartatm.ro; Piaţa Unirii 1; adult 10 lei, child free; ⊗10am-6pm Tue-Sun) This museum displays a representative sample of paintings and visual arts over the centuries as well as regular, high-quality temporary exhibitions. It's housed in the baroque **Old Prefecture Palace** (built 1754), which is worth a look inside for the graceful interiors alone.

🛏 Sleeping

Hostel Costel
HOSTEL €

(☎0356-262 487; www.hostel-costel.ro; Str Petru Sfetca 1; dm 50-65 lei, d 135 lei; @☎) This charming 1920s art-nouveau villa is the city's best-run hostel. The vibe is relaxed and congenial. There are three dorm rooms with six to 10 beds and one private double, plus ample chill rooms, a kitchen and a big garden with hammocks for relaxing.

★**Casa del Sole** BOUTIQUE HOTEL €€
(☎0356-457 771; www.casadelsole.ro; Str Romulus 12; s/d 260/370 lei; P❄📶🏊) An unexpectedly attractive boutique hotel, located in a green residential district about 1km south of the centre. The hotel occupies an old villa, and the stylish, period-piece rooms are located in three buildings within the same complex. The back garden is lovely and has a restaurant and terrace for drinks. The pool is large and clean.

Vila La Residenza HOTEL €€€
(☎0256-401 080; www.laresidenza.ro; Str Independenţei 14; s/d/ste from 380/430/550 lei; P❄@📶🏊) This charming converted villa recalls an English manor, with a cosy reading room and library off the lobby and an enormous, well-tended garden in the back with swimming pool. Its 15 rooms are comfort-driven in a similarly understated way. A first choice for visiting celebrities and *the* place to stay if price is no object.

Eating & Drinking

★**Homemade** INTERNATIONAL €€
(☎0730-832 299; www.facebook.com/pg/homemadetimisoara; Str Gheorghe Doja 40; mains 25-40 lei; ⊙noon-11pm; 📶) Push your way through the unmarked doorway into what looks like someone's living room, with dark-green walls and antique rugs on parquet floors. Homemade feels like a well-kept secret. The eclectic menu runs from very well-done burgers and fries to more intricate creations built around beef and pork. Plenty of vegetarian options on the menu as well. Reserve for evenings.

Casa Bunicii ROMANIAN €€
(☎0356-100 870; www.casa-bunicii.ro; Str Virgil Onitiu 3; mains 25-60 lei; ⊙noon-midnight) The name translates to 'Granny's House' and indeed this casual, family-friendly restaurant specialises in home cooking and regional specialities from Banat, with an emphasis on dishes based on *spätzle* (egg noodles). The duck soup with dumplings (12 lei) and grilled chicken breast served in sour cherry sauce (25 lei) both come recommended. Folksy surrounds.

La Căpiţe BEER GARDEN
(☎0371-397 706; www.facebook.com/lacapitetm; B-dul Pârvan Vasile 13; ⊙10am-1am Mar-Oct; 📶) Shaggy riverside beer garden and alternative hang-out strategically located across the street from the university, ensuring lively crowds on warm summer evenings. Some nights have live music or DJs. The name translates as 'haystack', and bales of hay strewn everywhere make for comfy places to sit and chill.

Scârţ Loc Lejer CAFE
(☎0751-892 340; www.facebook.com/scartlocle jer; Str Laszlo Szekely 1; ⊙10am-11pm Mon-Fri, from 11am Sat, from 2pm Sun; 📶) An old villa that's been retro-fitted into a funky coffee house called something like the 'Creaky Door', with old prints on the walls and chill tunes on the turntable. There are several cosy rooms in which to read and relax, but our favourite is the garden out back, with shady nooks and even hammocks to stretch out on.

Entertainment

National Theatre & Opera House THEATRE, OPERA
(Teatrul Naţional şi Opera Română; ☎tickets 0256-201 117; www.tntimisoara.com; Str Mărăşeşti 2) The National Theatre & Opera House features both dramatic works and classical opera, and is highly regarded. Buy tickets (from around 50 lei) at the **box office** (☎0256-201 117; www.ort.ro; Str Mărăşeşti 2; ⊙11am-7pm Tue-Sun) or via email, but note that most of the dramatic works will be in Romanian.

Information

Timişoara Tourist Information Centre
(Info Centru Turistic; ☎0256-437 973; www.timisoara-info.ro; Str Alba Iulia 2; ⊙9am-7pm Mon-Fri, 10am-4pm Sat May-Sep, 9am-6pm Mon-Fri, 10am-3pm Sat Oct-Apr) This great tourist office can assist with accommodation and trains, and provide maps and Banat regional info.

Getting There & Away

BUS

Timişoara lacks a centralised bus station for its extensive domestic and international services. Buses and minibuses are privately operated and depart from different points around the city, depending on the company and destination. Many long-haul coach services use the **Normandia Bus Station** (Autogara Normandia; ☎0253-238 121; www.autogari.ro; Calea Stan Vidrighin 12), about 2km southeast of the centre. Another popular bus station, closer to the Northern Train station, is **Autotim** (Autogara Autotim; ☎0256-493 471; Splaiul Tudor Vladimirescu 30). Consult its website (www.autogari.ro) for departure points.

Sample fares include Bucharest (90 lei), Cluj-Napoca (60 lei) and Sibiu (75 lei). The main international operators include **Atlassib** (☏ 0757-112 370; www.atlassib.ro; Calea Stan Vidrighin 12; ☉ 9am-6pm Mon-Fri, 10am-2pm Sat), **Eurolines** (☏ 0256-288 132; www.eurolines.ro; Calea Stan Vidrighin 12; ☉ 9am-6pm Mon-Fri, 11am-3pm Sat) and **Flixbus** (www.flixbus.ro).

Belgrade-based **Gea Tours** (☏ 0316-300 257; www.geatours.rs) offers a daily minibus service between Timişoara and Belgrade (one way/return €15/30); book over the website.

TRAIN

Trains depart from the **Northern Train Station** (Gara Timişoara-Nord; ☏ 0256-493 806; www.cfrcalatori.ro; Str Gării 2; ☐ 1, 8), though it's actually 'west' of the centre. Daily express trains include services to Bucharest (112 lei, nine hours, two daily) and Cluj-Napoca (80 lei, six hours, one daily).

Agenţia de Voiaj CFR (☏ 0256-491 889, international trains 0256-294 131; www.cfr.ro; Piaţa Victoriei 7; ☉ 10am-6pm Mon-Fri) sells domestic and international train tickets and seat reservations.

SURVIVAL GUIDE

ℹ Directory A–Z

ACCESSIBLE TRAVEL

➡ Romania is not well equipped for people with disabilities, even though there has been some improvement over recent years. Wheelchair ramps are available only at some upmarket hotels and restaurants, and public transport is a challenge for anyone with mobility problems.

➡ **Romania Motivation Foundation** (www.motivation.ro) is a local organisation with offices around the country to assist people in wheelchairs and with mobility issues. It has a good website in English for people confined to wheelchairs.

➡ Download Lonely Planet's free Accessible Travel guide from http://lptravel.to/Accessible Travel.

ACCOMMODATION

Romania has a wide choice of accommodation options to suit most budgets, including hotels, pensions, hostels and camping grounds. Book summer accommodation in popular Transylvanian destinations such as Braşov and Sibiu well in advance.

Hostels Big cities like Bucharest and Cluj have modern-style hostels and are open to all age groups.

Hotels Hotels range from modest family-run affairs to boutiques and high-priced corporate chains – with a commensurate range of prices.

Pensions *(pensiunes)* Small, locally owned inns that offer excellent value and are occasionally borderline luxurious.

LEGAL MATTERS

Romanian police take a dim view towards illegal drug use of any kind, including cannabis, as well as obvious displays of public drunkenness.

LGBT+ TRAVELLERS

Public attitudes towards homosexuality remain generally negative. In spite of this, Romania has made some legal progress towards decriminalising homosexual acts and adopting antidiscrimination laws.

➡ There is no legal provision for same-sex partnerships.

➡ Bucharest remains the most tolerant city in the country, though here, too, open displays of affection between same-sex couples are rare.

➡ The Bucharest-based **Accept Association** (www.acceptromania.ro) is an NGO that defends and promotes the rights of gays and lesbians at a national level. Each year in June the group helps to organise the six-day festival **Bucharest Pride** (www.bucharestpride.ro; ☉ Jun), with films, parties, conferences and a parade.

MONEY

ATMs are widely available. Credit cards are widely accepted in hotels and restaurants.

Currency

The Romanian currency is the leu (plural: lei), listed in some banks and currency-exchange offices as RON. One leu is divided into 100 bani.

Money Changers

The best place to exchange money is at a bank. You'll pay a small commission, but get a decent rate. You can also change money at a private exchange booth *(casa de schimb)* but be wary of commission charges and always ask how many lei you will receive before handing over your bills.

You will need to show a passport to change money, so always have it handy. Never change money on the street with strangers; it's always a rip-off.

OPENING HOURS

Shopping centres and malls generally have longer hours and are open from 9am to 8pm Saturday to Sunday. Museums are usually closed on Monday, and have shorter hours outside high season.

Banks 9am to 5pm Monday to Friday, to 1pm Saturday (varies)

Museums 10am to 5pm Tuesday to Friday, to 4pm Saturday and Sunday

ⓘ TIPPING

Restaurants 10% of the bill to reward good service.

Taxis Round the fare up to reward special service.

Hotels Tip cleaning staff 3 to 5 lei per night or 20 lei per week to reward good service.

Personal services Tip hairdressers 10%.

Offices 8am to 5pm Monday to Friday

Post Offices 8am to 7pm Monday to Friday, to 1pm Saturday (cities)

Restaurants 9am to 11pm Monday to Friday, 10am to 11pm Saturday and Sunday

Shops 9am to 6pm Monday to Friday, to 2pm Saturday

PUBLIC HOLIDAYS

If you'll be travelling during public holidays it's wise to book ahead, as some hotels in popular destinations may be full.

New Year 1 and 2 January

Orthodox Easter Monday April/May

Labour Day 1 May

Pentecost May/June, 50 days after Easter Sunday

Assumption of Mary 15 August

Feast of St Andrew 30 November

Romanian National Day 1 December

Christmas 25 and 26 December

SAFE TRAVEL

Watch out for jacked-up prices for tourists in Bucharest restaurants, taxis that charge extortionate fares (call for a taxi from companies recommended by your hotel) and a lifted wallet if you're not careful in public squares or jam-packed buses. Stray dogs are an occasional annoyance but rarely pose a danger. Avoid the temptation to pet them. The best strategy is to stay out of their way and they'll stay out of yours.

TELEPHONE
Domestic & International Calls

Romania has a modern telephone network of landlines and mobile (cell) phones. It's possible to receive and make direct international calls from anywhere in the country. Romania's country code is 40.

➡ All Romanian landline numbers have 10 digits, consisting of a zero, plus a city code and the number.

➡ The formula differs slightly depending on whether the number is in Bucharest or outside Bucharest. Bucharest numbers take the form: 0 + two-digit city code (21 or 31) + seven-digit number. Outside Bucharest, numbers take the form: 0 + three-digit city code + six-digit number.

➡ Mobile-phone numbers can be identified by a three-digit prefix starting with 7. All mobile numbers have 10 digits: 0 + three-digit prefix (7xx) + six-digit number.

Mobile Phones

Local SIM cards can be used in European, Australian and some American phones. Other phones must be set to roaming.

TOURIST INFORMATION

➡ The **Romanian Ministry of Tourism** (www.romania.travel) maintains a wonderful website with a trove of useful information. There's a large English-language section on festivals and events, accommodation and tips on what to see and do all around the country. Nearly all big cities have decent tourist offices. Tourist information can still be tough to track down in rural areas.

ⓘ Getting There & Away

ENTERING THE COUNTRY
Passport

All international visitors to Romania are required to have a valid passport (EU members need only a valid EU ID card). The expiration date of the passport should exceed your travel dates by at least three months, though some airlines will not allow passengers to board unless the passport is valid for at least six months.

AIR

Romania has good air connections to Europe and the Middle East. At the time of research there were no direct flights to Romania from North America or Southeast Asia.

BUS

Long-haul bus services remain a popular way of travelling from Romania to Western Europe as well as to parts of southeastern Europe and Turkey. Bus travel is comparable in price to train travel, but can be faster and require fewer connections.

CAR & MOTORCYCLE

Romania has decent road and car-ferry connections to neighbouring countries, and entering the country by car or motorcycle will present no unexpected difficulties. At all border crossings, drivers should be prepared to show the vehicle's registration, proof of insurance (a green card) and a valid driver's licence. All visiting foreigners, including EU nationals, are required to show a valid passport (or EU identity card).

TRAIN

Romania is integrated into the European rail grid, and there are decent connections to Western Europe and neighbouring countries. Nearly all of these arrive at and depart from Bucharest's main station, Gara de Nord (p345). Budapest is the main rail gateway in and out of Romania from Western Europe. There are two daily direct trains between Budapest and Bucharest, with regular onward connections from Budapest to Prague, Munich and Vienna.

❶ Getting Around

AIR

Given the distances and poor state of the roads, flying between cities is a feasible option if time is a primary concern. The Romanian national carrier **Tarom** (www.tarom.ro) operates a comprehensive network of domestic routes and has ticket offices around the country. The airline flies regularly between Bucharest and Cluj-Napoca, Sibiu and Timişoara. The budget carrier **Blue Air** (www.blueairweb.com) also has a comprehensive network of domestic destinations that overlap with Tarom.

BUS

A mix of buses, minibuses and 'maxitaxis' form the backbone of the Romanian national transport system. Unfortunately, bus routes change frequently; often these changes are communicated between people by word of mouth. Towns and cities will sometimes have a half-dozen different bus stations (autogara) and maxitaxi stops, depending on which company is operating a particular route and the destination in question. The helpful website **Autogari.ro** (www.autogari.ro) is an up-to-date national timetable that is relatively easy to use and lists routes, times, fares and departure points.

CAR & MOTORCYCLE

Driving in Romania is not ideal, and if you have the chance to use alternatives like the train and bus, this can be a more relaxing option. Roads are generally crowded and in poor condition. The country has only a few stretches of motorway (autostrada), meaning most of your travel will be along two-lane highways. Western-style petrol stations are plentiful, but be sure to fill up before heading on long trips through the mountains or in remote areas. A litre of unleaded 95 octane cost about 5.50 lei at the time of research.

TRAIN

Romania's passenger rail network has been cut back considerably in recent years, though trains remain a reliable – if slow – way of moving between large cities.

➜ The national rail system is run by **Căile Ferate Române** (CFR, www.cfrcalatori.ro); the website has a handy online timetable (mersul trenurilor).

➜ Buy tickets at train-station windows, specialised Agenţia de Voiaj CFR ticket offices, private travel agencies or online at www.cfrcalatori.ro.

➜ Sosire means 'arrivals' and plecare, 'departures'. On posted timetables, the number of the platform from which the train departs is listed under linia.

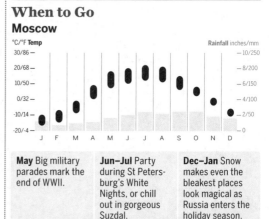

Russia

POP 144.5 MILLION

Best Places to Eat

➡ Gran Cafe Dr Zhivago (p372)

➡ White Rabbit (p372)

➡ Lavka-Lavka (p372)

➡ Cococo (p386)

➡ Banshiki (p386)

➡ Russkaya Chaynaya (p377)

Best Places to Stay

➡ Brick Design Hotel (p371)

➡ Moss Boutique Hotel (p371)

➡ Godzillas Hostel (p371)

➡ Soul Kitchen Hostel (p385)

➡ Rossi Hotel (p385)

➡ Surikov Guest House (p376)

Why Go?

Europe's ultimate eastern frontier might be shrouded in ancient enigma and modern political intrigue, but it sizzles with creative energy and offers an entirely different perspective than its neighbours.

Could there be a more iconic image of Eastern Europe than the awe-inspiring architectural ensemble of Moscow's Red Square? Fresh from a thorough revamp, Russia's brash and wealthy capital is a must on any trip to the region. St Petersburg is another stunner. The former imperial capital is still Russia's most beautiful and alluring city, with its grand Italianate mansions, wending canals and opening bridges on the enormous Neva River. East of Moscow, there is entirely different scenery – that of millennia-old little towns packed with onion-domed churches and fortress-like monasteries.

When to Go
Moscow

°C/°F Temp   Rainfall inches/mm

May Big military parades mark the end of WWII.

Jun–Jul Party during St Petersburg's White Nights, or chill out in gorgeous Suzdal.

Dec–Jan Snow makes even the bleakest places look magical as Russia enters the holiday season.

Entering the Country

There are many routes into and out of Russia. Most people fly into Moscow or St Petersburg. Using the main railway route via Belarus is now tricky due to visa squabbles between the two countries. Consider detouring via Finland, Latvia or Estonia.

ITINERARIES

One Week

Start your week in splendid St Petersburg (p378). Wander up Nevsky pr (p378), see Dvortsovaya pl and spend a half-day at the Hermitage (p379). Explore Peter & Paul Fortress (p384) and the wonderful Russian Museum (p378) the next day.

On day three, take an early-morning train to Moscow (p363). Touring the Kremlin (p363) and Red Square (p363) will take up one day, viewing the spectacular collections at the Tretyakov (p366) and Pushkin (p367) art museums another. On day five stretch your legs in the revamped Gorky Park (p367), taking in more art at New Tretyakov (p367) and Garage Museum (p367).

Take an afternoon train to Vladimir (p375) and continue to Suzdal (p376). Spend a day exploring this rural paradise before heading back to Vladimir in the morning on day seven. Check out its ancient monuments before visiting the Church of the Intercession on the Nerl (p375) just outside town. Catch a train back to Moscow in the evening.

Two Weeks

With two extra days in Moscow (p363), sweat it out in the luxurious Sanduny Baths (p372) or do a metro tour, then take a day trip to Sergiev Posad (p377). In St Petersburg (p378), spend more time in the Hermitage (p379) and other museums, and tack on an excursion to Peterhof (p386) or Tsarskoe Selo (p386).

Essential Food & Drink

Soups For example, the lemony, meat *solyanka* or the hearty fish *ukha*.

Bliny (pancakes) Served with *ikra* (caviar) or *tvorog* (cottage cheese).

Salads A wide variety usually slathered in mayonnaise, including the chopped potato Olivier.

Pelmeni (dumplings) Stuffed with meat and eaten with sour cream and vinegar.

Central Asian dishes Try *plov* (Uzbek pilaf), shashlyk (kebab) or *lagman* (noodles).

Vodka The quintessential Russian tipple.

Kvas A refreshing, beer-like nonalcoholic drink, or the red berry juice mix *mors*.

AT A GLANCE

Area 17,098,242 sq km

Capital Moscow

Country Code 7

Currency Rouble (R)

Emergency Stationary/mobile phone: Ambulance 03/103, Fire 01/101, Police 02/102

Language Russian

Time Moscow/St Petersburg (GMT/UTC plus three hours)

Visas Required by all – apply at least a month in advance of your trip

Sleeping Price Ranges

The following price ranges refer to a double room with bathroom during high season.

€ less than R1500 (less than R3000 in Moscow and St Petersburg)

€€ R1500–4000 (R3000–15,000 in Moscow and St Petersburg)

€€€ more than R4000 (more than R15,000 in Moscow and St Petersburg)

Eating Price Ranges

The following price ranges refer to a main course.

€ less than R300 (less than R500 in Moscow and St Petersburg)

€€ R300–800 (R500–1000 in Moscow and St Petersburg)

€€€ more than R800 (more than R1000 in Moscow and St Petersburg)

Russia Highlights

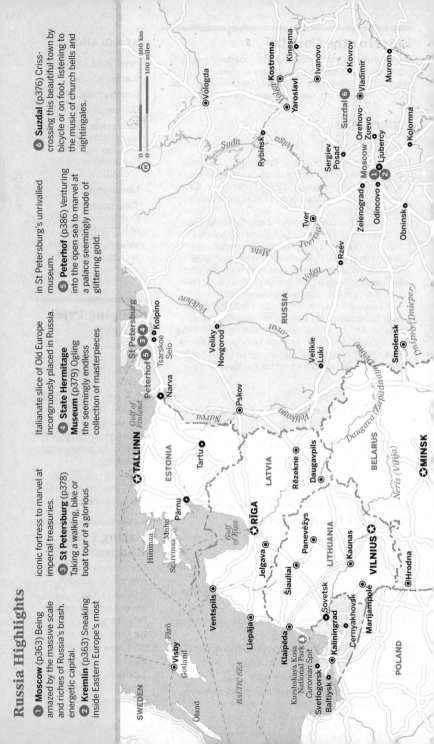

1 Moscow (p363) Being amazed by the massive scale and riches of Russia's brash, energetic capital.

2 Kremlin (p363) Sneaking inside Eastern Europe's most iconic fortress to marvel at imperial treasuries.

3 St Petersburg (p378) Taking a walking, bike or boat tour of a glorious Italianate slice of Old Europe incongruously placed in Russia.

4 State Hermitage Museum (p379) Ogling the seemingly endless collection of masterpieces in St Petersburg's unrivalled museum.

5 Peterhof (p386) Venturing into the open sea to marvel at a palace seemingly made of glittering gold.

6 Suzdal (p376) Criss-crossing this beautiful town by bicycle or on foot, listening to the music of church bells and nightingales.

MOSCOW МОСКВА

📞 495, 496, 498, 499 / POP 12.5 MILLION

Huge and prone to architectural gigantism, full of energy, both positive and dark, refined and tasteless at the same time, Moscow is overwhelming in every way. After the major spruce-up it has undergone in recent years, the mind-bogglingly eclectic Russian capital may look like hipster-ridden parts of Brooklyn at one point and a thoroughly glossed-over version of North Korea at another.

The sturdy stone walls of the Kremlin, the apex of Russian political power and once the centre of the Orthodox Church, occupy the city's founding site on the northern bank of the Moscow River. Remains of the Soviet state, such as Lenin's Tomb, are nearby in Red Square and elsewhere in the city, which radiates from the Kremlin in a series of ring roads.

⊙ Sights

⊙ Kremlin & Red Square

★ Moscow Kremlin   MUSEUM
(Кремль; 📞 495-695 4146; www.kreml.ru; R700; ⊙ 9.30am-6pm 15 May-30 Sep, ticket office 9am-5pm Fri-Wed; 10am-5pm 1 Oct-14 May, ticket office 9.30am-4.30pm Fri-Wed; Ⓜ Aleksandrovsky Sad) The apex of Russian political power and once the centre of the Orthodox Church, the Kremlin is the kernel of not only Moscow, but of the whole country. From here, autocratic tsars, communist dictators and modern-day presidents have done their best – and worst – for Russia.

Covering Borovitsky Hill on the Moscow River's north bank, it's enclosed by high walls 2.25km long (Red Square's outside the east wall). The best views of the complex are from Sofiyskaya nab across the river.

Much of what you see, both the red-brick walls and magnificent churches encircled by them, was designed by Italian architects invited to Moscow at the end of the 15th century by tsar Ivan III, or rather by his wife - Sophia Palaiologina. A niece of the last Byzantine emperor, she was raised as a fugitive in Rome and saw Moscow as heir to Constantinople and by extension - to Rome itself.

Before entering the Kremlin, deposit bags (free) at the **left-luggage office** (⊙ 9-11am, 11.30am-3.30pm & 4-6.30pm Fri-Wed), beneath the Kutafya Tower near the main **ticket office** (Кассы музеев Кремля; ⊙ 9am-5pm Fri-Wed May-Sep, 9.30am-4.30pm Fri-Wed Oct-Apr;

Ⓜ Aleksandrovsky Sad) in Alexander Garden. The entrance ticket covers admission to all five church-museums and the **Patriarch's Palace** (Патриарший дворец). It does not include the Armoury, the **Diamond Fund Exhibition** (Алмазный фонд России; 📞 495-629 2036; www.gokhran.ru; R500; ⊙ 10am-1pm & 2-5pm Fri-Wed) or the **Ivan the Great Bell Tower** (Колокольня Ивана Великого; R250; ⊙ 10am-5pm Apr-Oct), which are priced separately.

During warm months (April to October), many people try to visit the Kremlin around noon in order to watch the change of guards at Sobornaya Sq in the centre of the fortress. The ceremony involves a few dozen horses and men in historical attire performing sophisticated square-bashing choreography.

Photography is not permitted inside the Armoury or any of the buildings on Sobornaya pl (Cathedral Sq).

★ Armoury   MUSEUM
(Оружейная палата; www.kreml.ru; adult/child R1000/free; ⊙ tours 10am, noon, 2.30pm & 4.30pm Fri-Wed; Ⓜ Aleksandrovsky Sad) The Armoury dates to 1511, when it was founded under Vasily III to manufacture and store weapons, imperial arms and regalia for the royal court. Later it also produced jewellery, icon frames and embroidery. To this day, the Armoury contains plenty of treasures for ogling, and remains a highlight of any visit to the Kremlin. If possible, buy your time-specific ticket to the Armoury when you buy your ticket to the Kremlin.

★ Red Square   HISTORIC SITE
(Красная площадь; Krasnaya pl; Ⓜ Ploshchad Revolyutsii) Immediately outside the Kremlin's northeastern wall is the celebrated Red Square, the 400m-by-150m area of cobblestones that is at the very heart of Moscow. Commanding the square from the southern end is St Basil's Cathedral (p366). This panorama never fails to send the heart aflutter, especially at night.

★ Lenin's Mausoleum   MEMORIAL
(Мавзолей Ленина; www.lenin.ru; Krasnaya pl; ⊙ 10am-1pm Tue-Thu & Sat; Ⓜ Ploshchad Revolyutsii) 🆓 Although Vladimir Ilych requested that he be buried beside his mum in St Petersburg, he still lies in state at the foot of the Kremlin wall, receiving visitors who come to pay their respects. Line up at the western corner of the square (near the entrance to Alexander Garden) to see the

The Kremlin

A DAY AT THE KREMLIN

Only at the Kremlin can you see 800 years of Russian history and artistry in one day. Enter the ancient fortress through the Trinity Gate Tower and walk past the impressive Arsenal, ringed with cannons. Past the Patriarch's Palace, you'll find yourself surrounded by white-washed walls and golden domes. Your first stop is ❶ **Assumption Cathedral** with the solemn fresco over the doorway. As the most important church in prerevolutionary Russia, this 15th-century beauty was the burial site of the patriarchs. The ❷ **Ivan the Great Bell Tower** now contains a nifty multimedia exhibit on the architectural history of the Kremlin. The view from the top is worth the price of admission. The tower is flanked by the massive ❸ **Tsar Cannon & Bell**.

In the southeast corner, ❹ **Archangel Cathedral** has an elaborate interior, where three centuries of tsars and tsarinas are laid to rest. Your final stop on Sobornaya pl is ❺ **Annunciation Cathedral**, rich with frescoes and iconography.

Walk along the Great Kremlin Palace and enter the ❻ **Armoury** at the time designated on your ticket. After gawking at the goods, exit the Kremlin through Borovitsky Gate and stroll through the Alexander Garden to the ❼ **Tomb of the Unknown Soldier**.

Assumption Cathedral
Once your eyes adjust to the colourful frescoes, the gilded fixtures and the iconography, try to locate *Saviour with the Angry Eye*, a 14th-century icon that is one of the oldest in the Kremlin.

Arsenal

BOROVITSKY TOWER

Use the entrance at Borovitsky Tower if you intend to skip the churches and visit only the Armoury or Diamond Fund.

Borovitsky Tower

Trinity Gate Tower

Alexander Garden

⑥

Great Kremlin Palace

TOP TIPS

➡ **Online Purchase** Full-price tickets to the Kremlin churches and the Armoury can be purchased in advance on the Kremlin website.

➡ **Lunch** There are no eating options. Plan to eat before you arrive or stash a snack.

Armoury
Take advantage of the free audio guide to direct you to the most intriguing treasures of the Armoury, which is chock-full of precious metalworks and jewellery, armour and weapons, gowns and crowns, carriages and sledges.

Tomb of the Unknown Soldier

Visit the Tomb of the Unknown Soldier honouring the heroes of the Great Patriotic War. Come at the top of the hour to see the solemn synchronicity of the changing of the guard.

ANDREW KOTURANOV/SHUTTERSTOCK ©

Patriarch's Palace

Ivan the Great Bell Tower

Check out the artistic electronic renderings of the Kremlin's history, then climb 137 steps to the belfry's upper gallery, where you will be rewarded with super, sweeping vistas of Sobornaya pl and beyond.

Moscow River

Tsar Cannon & Bell

Peer down the barrel of the monstrous Tsar Cannon and pose for a picture beside the oversized Tsar Bell, both of which are too big to serve their intended purpose.

Sobornaya pl

Annunciation Cathedral

Admire the artistic mastery of Russia's greatest icon painters – Theophanes the Greek and Andrei Rublyov – who are responsible for many of the icons in the deesis and festival rows of the iconostasis.

Archangel Cathedral

See the final resting place of princes and emperors who ruled Russia for more than 300 years, including the visionary Ivan the Great, the tortured Ivan the Terrible and the tragic Tsarevitch Dmitry.

EKATERINA BYKOVA/SHUTTERSTOCK ©

embalmed leader, who has been here since 1924. Note that photography is not allowed and stern guards ensure that all visitors remain respectful and silent.

⭐ **St Basil's Cathedral**   CHURCH
(Покровский собор, Храм Василия Блаженного; ☑ 495-698 3304; www.shm.ru; adult/concession R1000/150; ⊙ 11am-5pm Nov-Apr, to 6pm May-Oct, from 10am Jun-Aug; Ⓜ Ploshchad Revolyutsii) At the southern end of Red Square stands the icon of Russia: St Basil's Cathedral. This crazy confusion of colours, patterns and shapes is the culmination of a style that is unique to Russian architecture. In 1552 Ivan the Terrible captured the Tatar stronghold of Kazan on the Feast of Intercession. He commissioned this landmark church, officially the Intercession Cathedral, to commemorate the victory. Created from 1555 to 1561, this masterpiece would become the ultimate symbol of Russia.

State History Museum   MUSEUM
(Государственный исторический музей; www.shm.ru; Krasnaya pl 1; adult/concession R700/100, audio guide R300; ⊙ ticket office 10am-5pm Mon, Wed, Thu & Sun, to 8pm Fri & Sat Sep-May, 10am-8pm daily Jun-Aug; Ⓜ Okhotny Ryad) At the northern end of Red Square, the State History Museum has an enormous collection covering Russian history from the time of the Stone Age. The building, dating from the late 19th century and designed in the Russian revivalist style, is itself an attraction – each room is in the style of a different period or region, some with highly decorated walls echoing old Russian churches.

⊙ **South of the Moscow River**

⭐ **State Tretyakov Gallery Main Branch**   GALLERY
(Государственная Третьяковская Галерея; www.tretyakovgallery.ru; Lavrushinsky per 10; adult/concession R700/150; ⊙ 10am-6pm Tue, Wed & Sun, to 9pm Thu-Sat, last tickets 1hr before closing; Ⓜ Tretyakovskaya) The exotic boyar (high-ranking noble) castle on a little lane in Zamoskvorechie contains the main branch of the State Tretyakov Gallery, housing the world's best collection of Russian icons and an outstanding collection of other prerevolutionary Russian art. Show up early to beat the queues. The neighbouring **Engineer's Building** is reserved for special exhibits.

SOBORNAYA PLOSHCHAD

On the northern side of Sobornaya pl, with five golden helmet domes and four semicircular gables facing the square, is the **Assumption Cathedral** (Успенский собор), built between 1475 and 1479. As the focal church of prerevolutionary Russia, it's the burial place of most heads of the Russian Orthodox Church from the 1320s to 1700. The iconostasis dates from 1652, but its lowest level contains some older icons, including the Virgin of Vladimir (Vladimirskaya Bogomater), an early-15th-century Rublyov-school copy of Russia's most revered image, the Vladimir Icon of the Mother of God (Ikona Vladimirskoy Bogomateri).

The delicate little single-domed church beside the west door of the Assumption Cathedral is the **Church of the Deposition of the Robe** (Церковь Ризоположения), built between 1484 and 1486 by masons from Pskov.

With its two golden domes rising above the eastern side of Sobornaya pl, the 16th-century Ivan the Great Bell Tower (p363) is the Kremlin's tallest structure. Beside the bell tower stands the **Tsar Bell** (Царь-колокол), a 202-tonne monster that cracked before it ever rang. North of the bell tower is the mammoth **Tsar Cannon** (Царь-пушка), cast in 1586 but never shot.

The 1508 **Archangel Cathedral** (Архангельский собор), at the square's southeastern corner, was for centuries the coronation, wedding and burial church of tsars. The tombs of all of Russia's rulers from the 1320s to the 1690s are here bar one (Boris Godunov, who was buried at Sergiev Posad).

Finally, the **Annunciation Cathedral** (Благовещенский собор), at the southwest corner of Sobornaya pl and dating from 1489, contains the celebrated icons of master painter Theophanes the Greek. He probably painted the six icons at the right-hand end of the diesis row, the biggest of the six tiers of the iconostasis. Archangel Michael (the third icon from the left on the diesis row) and the adjacent St Peter are ascribed to Russian master Andrei Rublyov.

MOSCOW'S WHITE-HOT ART SCENE

Revamped old industrial buildings and other spaces in Moscow are where you'll find gems of Russia's super-creative contemporary art scene. Apart from the following recommended spots, also see www.artguide.ru.

Garage Museum of Contemporary Art (☑495-645 0520; www.garagemca.org; ul Krymsky val 9/32; adult/student R300/150; ⏱11am-10pm; Ⓜ Oktyabrskaya) Having moved into a permanent Gorky Park location, a Soviet-era building renovated by the visionary Dutch architect Rem Koolhaas, Garage hosts exciting exhibitions by top artists.

Vinzavod (Винзавод; www.winzavod.ru; 4-y Syromyatnichesky per 1; Ⓜ Chkalovskaya) **FREE** A former wine factory has morphed into this postindustrial complex of prestigious galleries, shops, a cinema and trendy cafe. Nearby, another converted industrial space, the **Artplay** (☑495-620 0882; www.artplay.ru; ul Nizhny Syromyatnichesky per 10; ⏱noon-8pm Tue-Sun; Ⓜ Chkalovskaya) **FREE**, is home to firms specialising in urban planning and architectural design, as well as furniture showrooms and antique stores.

Red October (Завод Красный Октябрь; Bersenevskaya nab; Ⓜ Kropotkinskaya) **FREE** The red-brick buildings of this former chocolate factory now host the **Lumiere Brothers Photography Centre** (www.lumiere.ru; Bolotnaya nab 3, bldg 1; R250-400; ⏱noon-9pm Tue-Fri, to 10pm Sat & Sun) plus other galleries, cool bars and restaurants. In an adjacent building the **Strelka Institute for Media, Architecture and Design** is worth checking out for its events, bookshop and bar. Also, look out for **GES-2**, a new large contemporary art space that was due to open in an old power station in the fall of 2019.

★ **Gorky Park** PARK

(Парк Горького; ⏱24hr; ♿; Ⓜ Oktyabrskaya) **FREE** Moscow's main city escape isn't your conventional expanse of nature preserved inside an urban jungle. It's not a fun fair either, though it used to be one. Its official name says it all – Maxim Gorky's Central Park of Culture and Leisure. That's exactly what it provides: culture and leisure in all shapes and forms. Designed in the 1920s by avant-garde architect Konstantin Melnikov as a piece of communist utopia, these days it showcases the enlightened transformation Moscow has recently undergone.

Art Muzeon & Krymskaya Naberezhnaya
PUBLIC ART

(Ⓜ Park Kultury) **FREE** Moscow's answer to London's South Bank, Krymskaya Nab (Crimea Embankment) features wave-shaped street architecture with Scandinavian-style wooden elements, beautiful flower beds and a moody fountain, which ejects water randomly from many holes in the ground to the excitement of children and adults alike. It has merged with the Art Muzeon park and its motley collection of Soviet stone idols (Stalin, Sverdlov and a selection of Lenins and Brezhnevs) that were ripped from their pedestals in the post-1991 wave of anti-Soviet feeling.

New Tretyakov Gallery GALLERY

(Новая Третьяковская галерея; www.tretyakovgallery.ru; ul Krymsky val 10; adult/child R500/250; ⏱10am-6pm Tue, Wed & Sun, to 9pm Thu-Sat, last tickets 1hr before closing; Ⓜ Park Kultury) Moscow's premier venue for 20th-century Russian art, this branch of the Tretyakov Gallery has much more than the typical socialist-realist images of muscle-bound men wielding scythes and busty women milking cows (although there's that, too). The exhibits showcase avant-garde artists such as Malevich, Kandinsky, Chagall, Goncharova and Popova, as well as nonconformist artists of the 1960s and 1970s who refused to accept the official style.

◉ West of the Kremlin

★ **Pushkin Museum of Fine Arts** MUSEUM

(Музей изобразительных искусств им Пушкина; ☑495-697 9578; www.arts-museum.ru; ul Volkhonka 12; single/combined galleries R400/600; ⏱11am-7pm Tue, Wed, Sat & Sun, to 9pm Thu & Fri; Ⓜ Kropotkinskaya) This is Moscow's premier foreign-art museum, split over three branches and showing off a broad selection of European works, including masterpieces from ancient civilisations, the Italian Renaissance and the Dutch Golden Age. To see the incredible collection of Impressionist

Central Moscow

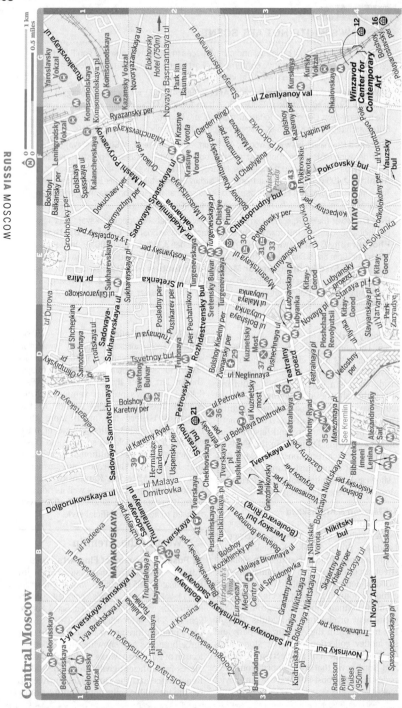

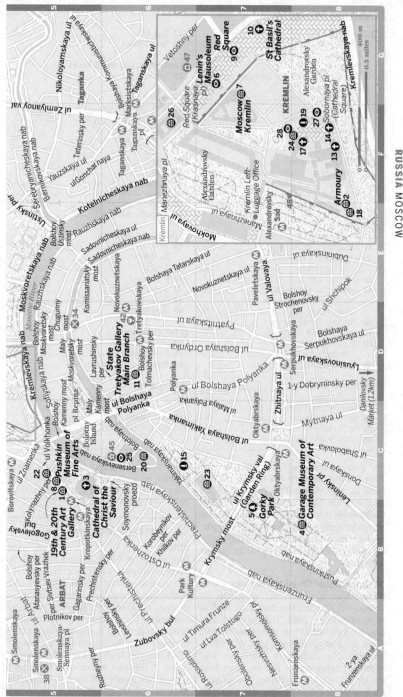

Red Square

Lenin's Mausoleum 6

Moscow Kremlin 7

47

26

KREMLIN

9

10

St Basil's Cathedral

Alexandrovsky Garden

Sobornaya pl (Cathedral Square)

19 27

28

24 17

13 14

Armoury 2

18

48

Kremlin Left-Luggage Office

Alexandrovsky Sad

Alexandrovsky Garden

Manezhnaya ul

Kremlin Manezhnaya pl

Mokhovaya ul

Vetoshny per

Red Square (Krasnaya pl)

0 400 m
0 0.2 miles

Smolenskaya

Smolenskaya-Sennaya pl

38

ARBAT

Gogolevsky bul

Bolshoy Afanasyevsky per

ul Arbat

Plotnikov per

Zubovsky bul

Park Kultury

ul Timura Frunze

ul Lva Tolstogo

Prechistenka

Prechistensky per

Gagarinsky per

ul Znamenka

Borovitskaya

19th & 20th Century Art Gallery 1

22 8

Pushkin Museum of Fine Arts

Cathedral of Christ the Saviour 3

Soymonovsky proezd

Kropotkinskaya

ul Volkhonka

pl Repina

Maly Kamenny most

Bolshoy Kamenny most

Bersenevskaya nab

45 25

20

Bolotny Island

Bolotnaya nab

Kadashevskaya nab

15

23

Gorky Park 5

Garage Museum of Contemporary Art 4

Krymsky val (Garden Ring)

Oktyabrskaya

Krymsky most

Pushkinskaya nab

Frunzenskaya nab

Frunzenskaya

2-ya Frunzenskaya ul

Komsomolsky pr

Nesvizhsky per

Obolensky per

ul Rossolimo

Khamovnichesky val

Moscow River

Moskvoretskaya nab

Sofiyskaya nab

Kremlevskaya nab

Bolshoy Moskvoretsky most

Maly Moskvoretsky most

Bolotnaya ul

ul Bolshaya Polyanka

ul Bolshaya Yakimanka

ul Malaya Polyanka

ul Bolshaya Ordynka

Polyanka

Lavrushinsky per

State Tretyakov Gallery Main Branch 11

42 34

Bolshoy Tolmachevsky per

Tretyakovskaya

Novokuznetskaya

Komissariatsky most

Chugunny most

Bolshaya Tatarskaya ul

Novokuznetskaya ul

Pyatnitskaya ul

Paveletskaya

ul Valovaya

Serpukhovskaya

Bolshaya Serpukhovskaya ul

Bolshoy Strochenovsky per

ul Shchipok

Dublinskaya ul

Oktyabrskaya

Mytnaya ul

ul Shabolovka

Donskaya ul

Leninsky pr

Lyusinovskaya ul

Zhitnaya ul

1-y Dobryninsky per

Danilovsky Market (12km)

Taganka

Nikoloyamskaya ul

ul Zemlyanoy val

Taganskaya ul

Taganskaya

Marksistskaya

Taganskaya pl

Bolshaya Kommunisticheskaya ul

Goncharnaya ul

Teterinsky per

Serebryanicheskaya nab

Bernikovskaya nab

Yauzskaya ul

Yauzskaya

Ustinsky per

Bolshoy Ustinsky most

Kotelnicheskaya nab

Sadovnicheskaya nab

Sadovnicheskaya ul

Rauzhskaya nab

Central Moscow

and post-Impressionist paintings, visit the **19th & 20th Century Art Gallery** (ul Volkhonka 14; adult/student R300/150; ⊙11am-7pm Tue-Sun, to 9pm Thu). The **Museum of Private Collections** (Музей личных коллекций; www.artprivatecollections.ru; ul Volkhonka 10; entry prices vary; ⊙noon-8pm Wed-Sun, to 9pm Thu) shows off complete collections donated by private individuals.

★**Cathedral of Christ the Saviour** CHURCH (Храм Христа Спасителя; www.xxc.ru; ul Volkhonka 15; ⊙1-5pm Mon, from 10am Tue-Sun; Ⓜ Kropotkinskaya) **FREE** This opulent and grandiose cathedral was completed in 1997 – just in time to celebrate Moscow's 850th birthday. The cathedral's sheer size and splendour guarantee its role as a love-it-or-hate-it landmark. Considering Stalin's plan for this site (a Palace of Soviets topped with a 100m statue of Lenin), Muscovites should at least be grateful they can admire the shiny domes of a church instead of the shiny dome of Ilyich's head.

◎ Northern Moscow

VDNKh PARK
(grounds free; Ⓜ VDNKh) Palaces for workers! There is no better place to see this Soviet slogan put into practice than at VDNKh, which stands for Exhibition of Achievements of the National Economy. The place feels like a Stalinesque theme park, with palatial pavilions, each designed in its own unique style to represent all the Soviet republics and various industries, from geology to space exploration. Fresh from a thorough, though not yet entirely completed reconstruction, the place looks more splendid than ever.

The top attraction is the reopened **Space Pavilion**, an opulent temple of retro-futurism filled with rockets and replicas of space stations, some of which you can walk through.

☞ Tours

Radisson River Cruises
BOATING

(www.radisson-cruise.ru; adult/child from R800/600; Ⓜ Kievskaya) The Radisson operates big riverboats that cart 140 people up and down the Moscow River on a 2½-hour cruise, departing from the dock in front of the hotel and from the dock in Gorky Park (p367). In summer, there are five or six daily departures from each location (check the website for times).

🛏 Sleeping

Godzillas Hostel
HOSTEL €

(☑ 495-699 4223; www.godzillashostel.com; Bolshoy Karetny per 6; dm R700-950, s/d R2200/2800; ❄ @ 🛜; Ⓜ Tsvetnoy Bulvar) Tried and true, Godzillas is Moscow's best-known hostel, with dozens of beds spread out over four floors. The rooms come in various sizes, but they are all spacious and light-filled, and painted in different colours. To cater to the many guests, there are bathroom facilities on each floor, three kitchens and a big living room with satellite TV.

Fasol Hostel
HOSTEL €

(☑ 495-240 9409; http://fasol.co; Arkhangelsky per 11/16 str 3; dm from R1000, d with shared bathroom R3500; Ⓜ Chistye Prudy) The entrance to this hostel, hidden in the courtyards amid 19th-century apartment blocks, looks unassuming. However, with over 80 beds, this popular and professionally run place is a major-league player. Dorms, sleeping six to eight, are decorated with psychedelic wall paintings; bunk beds come with body-friendly mattresses, curtains and individual lights, allowing guests to enjoy full autonomy.

Elokhovsky Hotel
HOTEL €€

(Отель Елоховский; ☑ 495-632 2100; www.elohotel.ru; ul Spartakovskaya 24; s/d R4500/5300; ❄ 🛜; Ⓜ Baumanskaya) Admittedly not very central and occupying the top floor of a shopping arcade, this hotel is nevertheless about the best value for money in Moscow. Rooms are painted in soothing colours, complemented by cityscapes of the world's major cities. The coffee machine in the lobby is available 24 hours. Baumanskaya metro and Yelokhovsky Cathedral are a stone's throw away.

★ Brick Design Hotel
BOUTIQUE HOTEL €€

(☑ 499-110 2470; www.brickhotel.ru; Myasnitskaya ul 24/7 str 3/4; r from R8000; ❄ 🛜; Ⓜ Chistye Prudy) Not only is this boutique hotel cosy, thoughtfully designed and very centrally located, it also doubles as an art gallery, with original works by Russian 20th-century conceptualist artists adorning the walls. That's in addition to a very tasteful combination of modern and antique furniture. Visitors also rave about the breakfast, which comes fresh from farms near Moscow.

Moss Boutique Hotel
BOUTIQUE HOTEL €€€

(☑ 495-114 5572; www.mosshotel.ru; per Krivokoleyny 10 str 4; r from R13,000; ❄ 🛜; Ⓜ Chistye Prudy) You get to see real moss growing in the elevator shaft of this elegant boutique hotel, with aged wood and black concrete surfaces dominating the interior. There's also a cool, relaxed ambience. Rooms – some really small, others bigger – are all equipped with superbly comfortable beds and formidable music centres that you can connect to your phone.

🍴 Eating

★ Danilovsky Market
MARKET €€

(www.danrinok.ru; Mytnaya ul 74; mains R400-600; ◷ 8am-8pm; Ⓜ Tulskaya) A showcase of the city's ongoing gentrification, this giant Soviet-era farmers market is now largely about deli food cooked and served in myriad little eateries, including such gems as a Dagestani dumpling shop and a Vietnamese pho-soup

METRO TOUR

For just R40 you can spend the day touring Moscow's magnificent metro stations. Many of the stations are marble-faced, frescoed, gilded works of art. Among our favourites are **Komsomolskaya**, a huge stuccoed hall, its ceiling covered with mosaics depicting military heroes; **Novokuznetskaya**, featuring military bas-reliefs done in sober khaki, and colourful ceiling mosaics depicting pictures of the happy life; and **Mayakovskaya**, Grand Prize winner at the 1939 World's Fair in New York. Another must-visit station is **Ploshchad Revolutsii**, filled with dozens of bronze statues of workers and soldiers.

kitchen. The market itself looks very orderly, if a tiny bit artificial, with uniformed vendors and thoughtfully designed premises.

★ Lavka-Lavka INTERNATIONAL €€

(Лавка-Лавка; ☑ 8-495-621 2036; www.restoran. lavkalavka.com; ul Petrovka 21 str 2; mains R500-1100; ⊙ noon-midnight Tue-Thu & Sun, to 1am Fri & Sat, 6pm-midnight Mon; 🛜 📶; Ⓜ Teatralnaya) 🍽 Welcome to the Russian Portlandia – all the food here is organic and hails from little farms where you can rest assured all the lambs and chickens lived a very happy life before being served to you on a plate. This is a great place to sample local food cooked in a funky improvisational style.

Moldova MOLDOVAN €€

(☑ 8-916-552 0353; www.restoran-moldova.ru; ul Rozhdestvenka 7; mains R450-600; ⊙ noon-midnight; Ⓜ Kuznetsky Most) When speakeasy meets post-Soviet political economy, it may result in something like this little gem tucked into the Moldovan embassy in Moscow's heart. Prepare for southern, Balkan-flavoured fare with *mititei* kebabs, *mamalyga* (polenta) with *brynza* soft cheese and paprika in all shapes and forms. The main highlight though is the excellent Moldovan wine.

Gran Cafe Dr Zhivago RUSSIAN €€

(Гранд Кафе Др Живаго; ☑ 499-922 0100; www. drzhivago.ru; Mokhovaya ul 15/1; mains R400-1200; ⊙ 24hr; Ⓜ Okhotny Ryad) An excellent

---

THE BANYA

Taking a traditional Russian *banya* is a must. These wet saunas are a social hub and a fantastic experience for any visitor to Russia. Leave your inhibitions at home and be prepared for a beating with birch twigs (far more pleasant than it sounds). Ask at your accommodation for the nearest public *banya*. In Moscow, try the luxurious **Sanduny Baths** (☑ 495-782 1808; www.sanduny.ru; ul Neglinnaya 14; R1800-2800; ⊙ 8am-10pm Wed-Mon, 2nd male top class 10am-midnight Tue-Fri, 8am-10pm Sat & Sun; Ⓜ Kuznetsky Most), where they have several classes just like on trains, and in St Petersburg the traditional **Mytninskiye Bani** (Мытнинские бани; www.mybanya.spb.ru; ul Mytninskaya 17-19; per hour R200-350, lux banya per hour R1000-2000; ⊙ 8am-10pm Fri-Tue; Ⓜ Ploshchad Vosstaniya).

---

breakfast choice before visiting the Kremlin, this round-the-clock place mixes Soviet nostalgia with a great deal of mischievous irony in both design and food. The chef has upgraded the menu of a standard pioneer camp's canteen to near-haute-cuisine level, with masterfully cooked porridge, pancakes, *vareniki* (boiled dumplings, like ravioli) and cottage-cheese pies.

★ Björn SCANDINAVIAN €€€

(☑ 495-953 9059; http://bjorn.rest; Pyatnitskaya ul 3; mains R700-1200; ⊙ noon-midnight; Ⓜ Novokuznetskaya) A neat cluster of fir trees on a busy street hides a Nordic gem that deserves a saga to glorify its many virtues. This is not an 'ethnic' restaurant, but a presentation of futuristic Scandinavian cuisine straight out of a science fiction movie. From salads to desserts, every dish looks deceptively simple, visually perfect and 23rd century.

White Rabbit INTERNATIONAL €€€

(☑ 495-510 5101; http://whiterabbitmoscow.ru; Smolenskaya pl 3; mains R800-1600; ⊙ noon-midnight, to 2am Thu-Sat; 🛜; Ⓜ Smolenskaya) Views from panoramic windows are breathtaking, but the real stunner here is the menu – playfully inventive, yet singularly Muscovite, marrying cutting-edge culinary thought with the lavishness of Tolstoy-era banquets. This results in such concoctions as baked-bean borscht with crucians or calf tongue in chokecherry dough. Definitely go for small snacks, especially pies. Booking is advisable.

🍷 Drinking & Nightlife

★ Ukuleleshnaya BAR

(Укулелешная; ☑ 495-642 5726; www.uku-uku. ru; ul Pokrovka 17 str 1; ⊙ noon-midnight Sun-Thu, noon-4am Fri & Sat; Ⓜ Chistye Prudy) In its new location, this is now more of a bar than a musical instrument shop, although ukuleles still adorn the walls, prompting an occasional jam session. Craft beer prevails on the drinks list, but Ukuleleshnaya also serves experimental cocktails of its own invention. Live concerts happen regularly and resident Pomeranian spitz Berseny (cute dog) presides over the resulting madness.

★ Noor / Electro BAR

(☑ 8-903-136 7686; www.noorbar.com; Tverskaya ul 23/12; ⊙ 8pm-3am Mon-Wed, to 6am Thu-Sun; Ⓜ Pushkinskaya) There is little to say about this misleadingly unassuming bar, apart from the fact that everything in it is close to perfection. It has it all – prime location, convivial atmosphere, eclectic DJ music, friendly bartenders and superb drinks. Though declared 'the best' by various magazines on several occasions, it doesn't feel like the owners care.

★**Enthusiast**   BAR

(Энтузиаст; Stoleshnikov per 7 str 5; ⊙ noon-11pm Sun-Thu, to 2am Fri & Sat; Ⓜ Teatralnaya) Scooter enthusiast, that is. But you don't have to be one in order to enjoy this superbly laid-back bar hidden at the far end of a fancifully shaped courtyard and disguised as a spareparts shop. On a warm day, grab a beer or cider, settle into a beach chair and let harmony descend on you.

32.05   CAFE

(☑8-905-703 3205; www.veranda3205.ru; ul Karetny Ryad 3; ⊙11am-3am; Ⓜ Pushkinskaya) The biggest drinking and eating establishment in Hermitage Gardens, this veranda positioned at the back of the park's main building looks a bit like a greenhouse. In summer, tables (and patrons) spill out into the park, making it one of the city's best places for outdoor drinking. With its long bar and joyful atmosphere, the place also heaves in winter.

Cafe Mart   CAFE

(Кафе Март; www.cafemart.ru; ul Petrovka 25; ⊙11am-midnight Sun-Wed, to 6am Thu-Sat, jazz concert 9pm Thu; ✦; Ⓜ Chekhovskaya) It looks like just another cellar bar, but if you walk all the way through the underground maze you'll find yourself in the huge overground 'orangerie' hall with mosaic-covered walls, warm lighting and possibly a jazz concert. When the weather is fine, Mart spills into the sculpture-filled courtyard of the adjacent **Moscow Museum of Modern Art** (Московский музей современного искусства; MMOMA; www.mmoma.ru; ul Petrovka 25; adult/student R450/250, joint ticket for 3 venues R500/300; ⊙noon-8pm Tue, Wed & Fri-Sun, 1-9pm Thu; Ⓜ Chekhovskaya).

★**Bar Strelka**   CAFE, CLUB

(www.barstrelka.com; Bersenevskaya nab 14/5, bldg 5a; ⊙9am-midnight Mon-Thu, to 3am Fri, noon-3am Sat, noon-midnight Sun; ☎; Ⓜ Kropotkinskaya) Located just below the Patriarshy most, the bar-restaurant at the **Strelka Institute** (www.strelkainstitute.ru) is the ideal starting point for an evening in the Red October (p367) complex. The rooftop terrace has unbeatable Moscow River views, but the interior is equally cool in a shabby-chic sort of way. The bar menu is excellent and there is usually somebody tinkling the ivories.

Parka   CRAFT BEER

(☑8-926-160 6313; www.facebook.com/parka craft; Pyatnitskaya ul 22 str 1; ⊙1pm-2am; Ⓜ Novokuznetskaya) 'Parka' is a *banya* (bathhouse) term, hence the sauna-like decor, and just like a proper *banya*, this is a very relaxing place. The friendly bartenders let you try any beer before you commit to buying a pint; the brews, many with crazy Runglish names, are mostly local.

☆ Entertainment

★**Bolshoi Theatre**   BALLET, OPERA

(Большой театр; ☑495-455 5555; www.bolshoi. ru; Teatralnaya pl 1; tickets R5500-12,000; ⊙closed late Jul–mid-Sep; Ⓜ Teatralnaya) An evening at the Bolshoi is still one of Moscow's most romantic and entertaining options for a night on the town. The glittering six-tier auditorium has an electric atmosphere, evoking over 240 years of premier music and dance. Both the ballet and opera companies perform a range of Russian and foreign works here.

Tchaikovsky Concert Hall   CLASSICAL MUSIC

(Концертный зал имени Чайковского; ☑495-232 0400; www.meloman.ru; Triumfalnaya pl 4/31; tickets R800-3000; ⊙concerts 7pm, closed Aug; Ⓜ Mayakovskaya) Established in 1921, the Tchaikovsky Concert Hall is the main venue for the country's best orchestras and stellar international acts. It's a huge auditorium, with seating for 1600 people. Expect to hear the Russian classics, such as Stravinsky, Rachmaninov and Shostakovich, as well as other European favourites. Look out for children's concerts, jazz ensembles and other special performances.

🛍 Shopping

GUM   MALL

(ГУМ; www.gum.ru; Krasnaya pl 3; ⊙10am-10pm; Ⓜ Ploshchad Revolyutsii) Behind its elaborate 240m-long facade on the northeastern side of Red Square, GUM is a bright, bustling shopping mall with hundreds of fancy stores and restaurants. With a skylight roof and three-level arcades, the spectacular interior was a revolutionary design when it was built in the 1890s, replacing the Upper Trading Rows that previously occupied this site.

Flakon   SHOPPING CENTRE

(www.flacon.ru; ul Bolshaya Novodmitrovskaya 36; Ⓜ Dmitrovskaya) Flakon is arguably the most visually attractive of all the redeveloped industrial areas around town, looking a bit like the far end of London's Portobello Rd, especially on weekends. Once a glassware plant, it is now home to dozens of funky shops and other businesses. Shopping for designer clothes and unusual souvenirs is the main reason for coming here.

Izmaylovsky Market   MARKET
(www.kremlin-izmailovo.com; Izmaylovskoye sh 73; ⊙10am-8pm; Ⓜ Partizanskaya) Never mind the kitschy faux 'tsar's palace' it surrounds, this is the ultimate place to shop for *matryoshka* dolls, military uniforms, icons, Soviet badges and some real antiques. Huge and diverse, it is almost a theme park, including shops, cafes and a couple of not terribly exciting museums.

ⓘ Information

Free wireless access is ubiquitous.

36.6 A chain of 24-hour pharmacies with many branches all around the city.

European Medical Centre (☑ 495-933 6655; www.emcmos.ru; Spirodonevsky per 5; ⊙24hr; Ⓜ Mayakovskaya) Offers 24-hour emergency

service, consultations and a full range of medical specialists.

Main Post Office (Myasnitskaya ul 26; ⊙24hr; Ⓜ Chistye Prudy)

Moscow Times (https://themoscowtimes.com) Country's main English-language publication.

ⓘ Getting There & Around

ARRIVING IN MOSCOW

Airports The three main airports are accessible by the convenient **Aeroexpress Train** (☑ 8-800 700 3377; www.aeroexpress.ru; one way R420; ⊙6am-midnight), which takes 35 to 45 minutes from the city centre. If you wish to take a taxi, book an official airport taxi through the dispatcher counter (R2000 to R2500). If you can order a taxi by phone or with a mobile-phone app it will be about 50% cheaper.

Train Stations Rail riders will arrive at one of the central train stations. All of the train stations are located in the city centre, with easy access to the metro. Alternatively, most taxi companies offer a fixed rate of R400 to R600 for a train-station transfer.

PUBLIC TRANSPORT

The rapidly expanding and super-efficient **Moscow metro** (www.mosmetro.ru; per ride R55) network is by far the most convenient way of getting around the city. But with the introduction of dedicated bus lanes and fleet upgrade, buses, trolleybuses and trams are becoming increasingly relevant.

Moscow has a unified ticketing system. Available from ticket booths and machines at metro stations and some bus stops, tickets are magnetic cards that you must tap on the reader at the turnstiles before entering a metro station or on the bus. Most convenient for short-term visitors is the red Ediny (Единый) ticket, which is good for all kinds of transport and available at metro stations. A single trip costs R55. A three-day unlimited pass goes for R438.

Metro stations are marked outside by 'M' signs. Many bus stops are now equipped with screens showing waiting time.

TAXI

Taxis are affordable, but you can't really flag them down in the street – not the metered ones anyway. These days, most people use mobile phone apps (such as Uber, Gett and Yandex Taxi) to order a cab. You can also order an official taxi by phone or book it online, or ask a Russian-speaker to do this for you. **Taxi Tsel** (☑ 495-204 2244; www.taxicel.ru) is a reliable company, but operators don't speak English. **Lingo Taxi** (www.lingotaxi.com) promises English-speaking drivers and usually delivers.

GOLDEN RING
ЗОЛОТОЕ КОЛЬЦО

The Golden Ring is textbook Russia: onion-shaped domes, kremlins and gingerbread cottages with cherry orchards. It is a string of the country's oldest towns that formed the core of eastern Kiyvan Rus. Too engrossed in fratricide, they failed to register the rise of Moscow, which elbowed them out of active politics. Largely untouched by Soviet industrialisation, places like Suzdal now attract flocks of Russian tourists in search of the lost idyll. The complete circular route, described in the Lonely Planet guide to Russia, requires about a week to be completed. But several gems can be seen on one- or two-day trips from Moscow.

Vladimir   Владимир

[phone] 4922 / POP 347,000

Founded at the dawn of the 12th century on a bluff over the Klyazma River, Vladimir became the cradle of Russian history when Prince Andrei Bogolyubsky moved his capital there from Kyiv in 1169. Thus began Vladimir's Golden Age, when many of the beautifully carved white-stone buildings for which the area is renowned were built by Bogolyubsky and his brother, Prince Vsevolod the Big Nest. After a Mongol invasion devastated the town in 1238, power shifted some 200km west to a minor settlement called Moscow. Though Vladimir eventually rebounded from the ruins, it would never regain its former glory.

Today this bustling city is the administrative centre of Vladimir Oblast. Although not as charmingly bucolic as nearby Suzdal, Vladimir's easy access from Moscow, its cluster of centrally located Unesco-listed sights and its stunning river-valley panoramas make it an ideal starting point for a Golden Ring tour.

★ Assumption Cathedral   CHURCH

(Успенский собор; [phone] 4922-325 201; www.vladmuseum.ru; Sobornaya pl; adult/student R150/75; ⏱visitors 1-4.45pm Tue-Sun) Set dramatically high above the Klyazma River, this simple but majestic piece of pre-Mongol architecture is the legacy of Prince Andrei Bogolyubsky, the man who began shifting power from Kyiv to northeastern Rus (which eventually evolved into Muscovy). A white-stone version of Kyiv's brick Byzantine churches, the cathedral was constructed from 1158 to 1160,

WORTH A TRIP

CHURCH OF THE INTERCESSION ON THE NERL

Tourists and pilgrims all flock to Bogolyubovo, just 12km northeast of Vladimir, for this perfect little jewel of a 12th-century church standing amid a flower-covered floodplain. The **Church of the Intercession on the Nerl** (Церковь Покрова на Нерли; Bogolyubovo; ⏱10am-6pm Tue-Sun) FREE is the golden standard of Russian architecture. Apart from ideal proportions, its beauty lies in a brilliantly chosen waterside location (floods aside) and the sparing use of delicate carving.

To reach it, get bus 152 (R25) from the Golden Gate or Sobornaya pl in Vladimir and get off by the blue-domed Bogolyubsky Monastery. Walk past the monastery to Vokzalnaya ul, the first street on the right, and follow it down to the train station. Cross the pedestrian bridge over the railroad tracks and follow the stone path for 1km across the meadow.

though it was rebuilt and expanded after a fire in 1185. It was added to Unesco's World Heritage List in 1992.

Cathedral of St Dmitry   CHURCH

(Дмитриевский собор; www.vladmuseum.ru; Bolshaya Moskovskaya ul 60; adult/student R150/75; ⏱10am-6pm Mon-Thu, to 8pm Fri-Sun May-Sep, reduced hours Oct-Apr) Built between 1193 and 1197, this exquisite, Unesco-listed white-stone cathedral represents the epitome of Russian stone carving. The attraction here is the cathedral's exterior walls, which are covered in an amazing profusion of images. At their top centre, the north, south and west walls all show King David bewitching the birds and beasts with music.

Voznesenskaya Sloboda   HOTEL €€€

(Вознесенская слобода; [phone] 8-800 302 5494; www.vsloboda.ru; ul Voznesenskaya 14b; d from R4900; [P][air][wifi]) Perched on a bluff with tremendous views of the valley, this hotel has one of the most scenic locations in the area. Outside is a quiet neighbourhood of old wooden cottages and villas dominated by the elegant Ascension Church, whose bells chime idyllically throughout the day. The new building's interior is tastefully designed to resemble art nouveau style c 1900.

Ginger Cat　　　　　INTERNATIONAL **€€**

(Пшеничный кот; ☎4922-472 109; https://pshenichniy-kot.ru; ul Bolshaya Moskovskaya 19; mains R340-590; ⏰11am-11pm, from 10am Sat & Sun; 🐾) This cheerfully coloured modern place is designed to keep children busy in two playrooms while adults relax with a decent meal and a glass of wine. Children or not, this is where you'll find competently cooked international fare, such as steaks and caesar *salat*. The extensive dessert menu is a treat for any sweet tooth, young or old.

★**Four Brewers Pub**　　　CRAFT BEER

(Паб Четыре Пивовара; www.4brewers.ru; Bolshaya Moskovskaya ul 12; ⏰2pm-midnight Sun-Thu, to 2am Fri & Sat) This pocket-sized pub offers 20 brews on tap and dozens more in bottles – porter, IPA, stout, ale, you name it – all from the brewers' own vats or other Russian microbreweries, with such unforgettable names as 'Banana Kraken', 'Santa Muerte', 'Roksana and the Endless Universe' and (our personal favourite) 'Black Jesus, White Pepper'. Bartenders happily offer recommendations and free tastes.

ⓘ Getting There & Away

Vladimir is on the main trans-Siberian line between Moscow and Nizhny Novgorod and on a major highway leading to Kazan. There are nine services a day from Moscow's Kursk Station (Kursky vokzal), with modern Strizh and slightly less comfortable Lastochka trains (R600 to R1600, 1¾ hours).

Suzdal　　　　Суздаль

☎49231 / POP 9750

The sparkling diamond in the Golden Ring is undoubtedly Suzdal – if you have time for only one of these towns, this is the one to see. With rolling green fields carpeted with dandelions, a gentle river curling lazily through a historic town centre, sunlight bouncing off golden church domes and the sound of horse clops and church bells carrying softly through the air, you may feel like you've stumbled into a storybook Russia.

Suzdal served as a royal capital when Moscow was still a cluster of cowsheds, and was a major monastic centre and an important commercial hub for many years as well. But in 1864, local merchants failed to get the Trans-Siberian Railway built through here (it went to Vladimir instead). Suzdal was thus bypassed both by trains and 20th-century progress, preserving its idyllic character for future visitors.

⊙ Sights

★**Kremlin**　　　　　　FORTRESS

(Кремль; ☎49231-21 624; www.vladmuseum.ru; ul Kremlyovskaya; joint ticket adult/student R350/200; ⏰exhibitions 9am-6pm Sun-Thu, to 9pm Fri & Sat, grounds to 9pm) The grandfather of the Moscow Kremlin, this citadel was the 12th-century base of Prince Yury Dolgoruky, who ruled the vast northeastern part of Kyivan Rus (and, among other things, founded a small outpost that would eventually become the Russian capital). The 1.4km-long earthen ramparts of Suzdal's kremlin enclose a few streets of houses and a handful of churches, as well as the main cathedral group on ul Kremlyovskaya.

★**Saviour Monastery of St Euthymius**　　　MONASTERY

(Спасо-Евфимиев монастырь; ☎49231-20 746; www.vladmuseum.ru; ul Lenina; adult/student R400/200; ⏰10am-7pm Sun-Thu, to 9pm Fri & Sat) Founded in the 14th century to protect the town's northern entrance, Suzdal's biggest monastery grew mighty in the 16th and 17th centuries after Vasily III, Ivan the Terrible and the noble Pozharsky family funded impressive new stone buildings and made large land and property acquisitions. It was girded with its great brick walls and towers in the 17th century.

🛏 Sleeping

★**Surikov Guest House**　　GUESTHOUSE **€€**

(Гостевой дом Суриковых; ☎8-915-752 4950, 8-961-257 9598; ul Krasnoarmeyskaya 53; d incl breakfast R2500; 🅿🐾) This 11-room boutique guesthouse is positioned at a particularly picturesque bend of the Kamenka River across from the walls of the Saviour Monastery of St Euthymius (p376). It has modestly sized but comfortable rooms equipped with rustic-style furniture (some made by the owner himself) and a Russian restaurant (for guests only) on the 1st floor. Visitors rave about this place.

Pushkarskaya Sloboda　　RESORT **€€€**

(Пушкарская слобода; ☎8-800 350 5303; www.pushkarka.ru; ul Lenina 45; d from R4300; 🅿❄🐾🏊) This attractive riverside holiday village has everything you might want for a Russian idyll, including accommodation options in traditionally styled log cabins (from

R7900). It has three restaurants (including a rustic country tavern and a formal dining room) and a spa centre with pool. The staff can also arrange all sorts of tours and classes around Suzdal.

✖ Eating & Drinking

★ Russkaya Chaynaya   RUSSIAN €
(Русская чайная; www.tea-suzdal.ru; ul Kremlyovskaya 10g; mains R250-620; ⊙10am-9pm) It's hidden behind a kitsch crafts market, but this place is a gem. Russian standards – bliny, *shchi* (cabbage soup), mushroom dishes and pickles – are prominently represented, but it's all the unusual (and rather experimental) items on the menu that make Russkaya Chaynaya so special. Cabbage stewed in apple juice with raisins and thyme, anyone?

★ Gostiny Dvor   RUSSIAN €€
(Гостиный дворъ; ☑ 49231-021 190; www.suzdal-dvor.ru; Trading Arcades, Torgovaya pl; mains R450-550; ⊙10am-10pm Mon-Thu, 9am-11pm Fri-Sun; 🛜🐕) There are so many things to like about this place: eclectic decor of rustic antiques and warm wood; outside terrace tables offering river views; hearty Russian dishes (chicken, pike, *pelmeni* dumplings) prepared with modern flair; and friendly, attentive service, to start. Finish up with a tasting set of house-made *medovukha* (honey ale) while the kids amuse themselves in the playroom.

Graf Suvorov &
Mead-Tasting Hall   BEER HALL
(Граф Суворов и зал дегустаций; ☑ 49231-20 803, 8-905-734 5404; Trading Arcades, Torgovaya pl; tasting menu R300-500; ⊙10am-6pm Mon-Fri, to 8pm Sat & Sun) Sit beneath vaulted ceilings and contemplate kitsch murals of Russian military hero Count Suvorov's exploits in the Alps as you make your way through a tasting set (10 samples) of the few dozen varieties of locally produced *medovukha*. Flavours also include berry and herb infusions. Located on the back (river) side of the Trading Arcades.

❶ Getting There & Away

There is no bus service to Suzdal from Moscow; you'll need to take a train to Vladimir and then switch to a Suzdal-bound bus there. Buses run very regularly throughout the day to and from Vladimir (R110, 45 minutes). The bus station is 2km east of the centre on Vasilievskaya ul. Some long-distance buses pass the central square on the way.

Sergiev Posad
Сергиев Посад

☑ 496 / POP 109,000

Blue-and-gold cupolas offset by snow-white walls – this colour scheme lies at the heart of the Russian perception of divinity and Sergiev Posad's monastery is a textbook example. It doesn't get any holier than this in Russia, for the place was founded in 1340 by the country's most revered saint, St Sergius of Radonezh. Since the 14th century, pilgrims have been journeying here to pay homage to him.

Although the Bolsheviks closed the monastery, it was reopened following WWII as a museum, residence of the patriarch and a working monastery. The patriarch and the church's administrative centre moved to the Danilovsky Monastery in Moscow in 1988, but the Trinity Monastery of St Sergius remains one of the most important spiritual sites in Russia.

★ Trinity Monastery
of St Sergius   MONASTERY
(Свято-Троицкая Сергиева Лавра; ☑ info 496-544 5334, tours 496-540 5721; www.stsl.ru; ⊙5am-9pm) FREE In 1340 St Sergius of Radonezh founded this *lavra* (senior monastery), which soon became the spiritual centre of Russian Orthodoxy. St Sergius was credited with providing mystic support to Prince Dmitry Donskoy in his improbable victory over the Tatars in the Battle of Kulikovo in 1380. Soon after his death at the age of 78, Sergius was named Russia's patron saint.

Old Hotel Lavra   HOTEL €€
(Старая гостиница Лавры; ☑ 496-549 9000; www.lavrahotel.ru; pr Krasnoy Armii 133; s/d from R3000/3400; 🛜) Built in 1822 as pilgrim accommodation, this massive monastery hotel has been revived in its original capacity, with nothing to distract its supposedly puritan guests from prayer and contemplation – not even TV. But despite their blandness, rooms are modern and very clean. There's a vast restaurant on the premises. Unsurprisingly, alcohol is strictly banned throughout the complex. Breakfast is R200.

★ Gostevaya Izba   RUSSIAN €€
(Гостевая Изба; ☑ 496-541 4343; www.sergiev-kanon.ru; Aptekarsky per 2; meals R350-850; ⊙10am-11pm; 🐕) Right by the monastery walls, this wonderful restaurant recreates classic dishes metropolitans of the past

RUSSIA SERGIEV POSAD

might have eaten outside fasting periods, such as apple-roasted duck breast with lingonberry sauce. Portions are ample and the food delicious. Try some *kvas* (fermented rye bread water), fireweed tea or Siberian malt lemonade straight from the monastery's own brewery.

ⓘ Getting There & Away

Considering the horrendous traffic jams on the road approaches to Moscow, train is a much better way of getting to Sergiev Posad from the capital. The fastest option is the express commuter train that departs from Moscow's Yaroslavsky vokzal (R230, one hour); there are four daily during the week, three on weekends. Cheaper but slower *elektrichki* (suburban trains; R176, 1½ hours) depart a few times per hour throughout the day.

ST PETERSBURG
САНКТ ПЕТЕРБУРГ

☑ 812 / POP 5,281,580

Affectionately known as Piter to locals, St Petersburg is a visual delight. The Neva River and surrounding canals reflect unbroken facades of handsome 18th- and 19th-century buildings that house a spellbinding collection of cultural storehouses, culminating in the incomparable Hermitage. Home to many of Russia's greatest creative talents (Pushkin, Dostoevsky, Tchaikovsky), Piter still inspires a contemporary generation of Russians, making it a liberal, hedonistic and exciting place to visit.

The city covers many islands, some real, some created through the construction of canals. The central street is Nevsky pr, which extends some 4km from the Alexander Nevsky Monastery to the Hermitage.

◉ Sights

◎ Historic Heart

Palace Square SQUARE
(Дворцовая площадь; Dvortsovaya pl; Ⓜ Admiralteyskaya) This vast expanse is simply one of the most striking squares in the world, still redolent of imperial grandeur almost a century after the end of the Romanov dynasty. For the most amazing first impression, walk from Nevsky pr, up Bolshaya Morskaya ul and under the **triumphal arch**.

★ Russian Museum MUSEUM
(Русский музей; ☑ 812-595 4248; www.rusmuseum.ru; Inzhenernaya ul 4; adult/student R500/250; ☉ 10am-8pm Mon, 10am-6pm Wed & Fri-Sun, 1-9pm Thu; Ⓜ Nevsky Prospekt) Focusing solely on Russian art, from ancient church icons to 20th-century paintings, the Russian Museum's collection is magnificent and can easily be viewed in half a day or less. The collection includes works by Karl Bryullov, Alexander Ivanov, Nicholas Ghe, Ilya Repin, Natalya Goncharova, Kazimir Malevich and

---

RUSSIA'S MOST FAMOUS STREET

Walking **Nevsky Prospekt** is an essential St Petersburg experience. Highlights along it include the Kazan Cathedral (p384), with its curved arms reaching out towards the avenue.

Opposite is the **Singer Building** (Nevsky pr 28; Ⓜ Nevsky Prospekt), a Style Moderne (art deco) beauty restored to all its splendour when it was the headquarters of the sewing-machine company; inside is the bookshop **Dom Knigi** (☑ 812-448 2355; www.spbdk.ru; Nevsky pr 28; ☉ 9am-1am; ☎; Ⓜ Nevsky Prospekt) and **Café Singer** (Кафе Зингеръ; ☑ 812-571 8223; www.singercafe.ru; Nevsky pr 28; mains R400-500; ☉ 9am-11pm; ☎; Ⓜ Nevsky Prospekt), serving good food and drinks with a great view over the street.

Further along are the covered arcades of Rastrelli's historic **Bolshoy Gostiny Dvor** (Большой Гостиный Двор; ☑ 812-630 5408; http://bgd.ru; Nevsky pr 35; ☉ 10am-10pm; Ⓜ Gostiny Dvor) department store, while on the corner of Sadovaya ul is the Style Moderne classic **Kupetz Eliseevs** (☑ 812-456 6666; www.kupetzeliseevs.ru; Nevsky pr 56; ☉ 10am-11pm; ☎; Ⓜ Gostiny Dvor) reincarnated as a luxury grocery and cafe.

An enormous **statue of Catherine the Great** (pl Ostrovskogo) stands at the centre of **Ploshchad Ostrovskogo** (Площадь Островского; Ⓜ Gostiny Dvor), commonly referred to as the Catherine Gardens; at the southern end of the gardens is **Alexandrinsky Theatre** (☑ 812-710 4103; www.alexandrinsky.ru; pl Ostrovskogo 2; tickets R900-6000; Ⓜ Gostiny Dvor), where Chekhov's The Seagull premiered (to tepid reviews) in 1896.

STATE HERMITAGE MUSEUM

Mainly set in the magnificent Winter Palace and adjoining buildings, the **Hermitage** (Государственный Эрмитаж; www.hermitagemuseum.org; Dvortsovaya pl 2; combined ticket R700; ☺10.30am-6pm Tue, Thu, Sat & Sun, to 9pm Wed & Fri; Ⓜ Admiralteyskaya) fully lives up to its sterling reputation. You can be absorbed by its treasures for days and still come out wanting more.

The enormous collection (over three million items, only a fraction of which are on display in around 360 rooms) almost amounts to a comprehensive history of Western European art. Viewing it demands a little planning, so choose the areas you'd like to concentrate on before you arrive. The museum consists of five connected buildings. From west to east:

Winter Palace Designed by Bartolomeo Rastrelli, its opulent state rooms, Great Church, Pavilion Hall and Treasure Rooms shouldn't be missed.

Small Hermitage and Old Hermitage Both were built for Catherine the Great, partly to house the art collection started by Peter the Great, which she significantly expanded. Here you'll find works by Rembrandt, Da Vinci and Caravaggio.

New Hermitage Built for Nicholas II, to hold the still-growing art collection. The Old and New Hermitages are sometimes grouped together and labelled the Large Hermitage.

General Staff Building Designed by Carlo Rossi in the 1820s, this building, located across the square from the Winter Palace, contains an amazing collection of Impressionist and post-Impressionist works.

State Hermitage Theatre Built in the 1780s by Giacomo Quarenghi. Concerts and ballets are still performed here.

Kuzma Petrov-Vodkin, among many others, and the masterpieces keep on coming as you tour the beautiful Carlo Rossi–designed Mikhailovsky Palace and its attached wings.

Entry is either from Arts Sq or via the connected **Benois Wing** (nab kanala Griboyedova; adult/student R450/200; ☺10am-8pm Mon, 10am-6pm Wed & Fri-Sun, 1-9pm Thu) on nab kanala Griboyedova. There's also an entrance from the lovely **Mikhailovsky Garden** (Михайловский сад; https://igardens.ru; ☺10am-10pm May-Sep, to 8pm Oct-Mar, closed Apr) FREE behind the palace. Permanent and temporary exhibitions by the Russian Museum are also held at the **Marble Palace** (Мраморный дворец; Millionnaya ul 5; adult/student R300/170; ☺10am-6pm Mon, Wed & Fri-Sun, 1-9pm Thu; Ⓜ Nevsky Prospekt), the **Mikhailovsky Castle** (Михайловский замок; Sadovaya ul 2; adult/student R250/130; ☺10am-6pm Mon, Wed & Fri-Sun, 1-9pm Thu; Ⓜ Gostiny Dvor) and the **Stroganov Palace** (Строгановский дворец; Nevsky pr 17; adult/student R250/130; ☺10am-6pm Wed & Fri-Mon, 1-9pm Thu; Ⓜ Nevsky Prospekt). Combined tickets, available at each palace, cover entrance either to your choice of two the same day (adult/student R600/270) or to all four within a three-day period (R850/400).

⭐**Church of the Saviour on the Spilled Blood** CHURCH
(Храм Спаса на Крови; ☎812-315 1636; http://eng.cathedral.ru/spasa_na_krovi; Konyushennaya pl; adult/student R350/200; ☺10.30am-6pm Thu-Tue; Ⓜ Nevsky Prospekt) This five-domed dazzler is St Petersburg's most elaborate church, with a classic Russian Orthodox exterior and an interior decorated with some 7000 sq metres of mosaics. Officially called the Church of the Resurrection of Christ, its far more striking colloquial name references the assassination attempt on Tsar Alexander II here in 1881.

⭐**St Isaac's Cathedral** MUSEUM
(Исаакиевский собор; ☎812-315 9732; www.cathedral.ru; Isaakievskaya pl; cathedral adult/student R250/150, colonnade R150; ☺cathedral 10.30am-10.30pm Thu-Tue May-Sep, to 6pm Oct-Apr, colonnade 10.30am-10.30pm May-Oct, to 6pm Nov-Apr; Ⓜ Admiralteyskaya) The golden dome of St Isaac's Cathedral dominates the St Petersburg skyline. Its obscenely lavish interior is open as a museum, although services are held in the cathedral throughout the year. Many people bypass the museum to climb the 262 steps to the *kolonnada* (colonnade) around the drum of the dome, providing superb city views.

The Hermitage

A HALF-DAY TOUR

Successfully navigating the State Hermitage Museum, with its four vast interconnecting buildings and around 360 rooms, is an art form in itself. Our half-day tour of the highlights can be done in four hours, or easily extended to a full day.

Once past ticket control start by ascending the grand ❶ **Jordan Staircase** to Neva Enfilade and Great Enfilade for the impressive staterooms, including the former throne room St George's Hall and the 1812 War Gallery (Room 197), and the Romanovs' private apartments. Admire the newly restored ❷ **Great Church** then make your way back to the Neva side of the building via the Western Gallery (Room 262) to find the splendid ❸ **Pavilion Hall** with its view onto the Hanging Garden and the gilded Peacock Clock, always a crowd pleaser.

Make your way along the series of smaller galleries in the Large Hermitage hung with Italian Renaissance art, including masterpieces by ❹ **Da Vinci** and ❺ **Caravaggio**. The Loggia of Raphael (Room 227) is also impressive. Linger a while in the galleries containing Spanish art before taking in the Dutch collection, the highlight of which is the hoard of ❻ **Rembrandt** canvases in Room 254.

Descend the Council Staircase (Room 206), noting the giant malachite vase, to the ground floor where the fantastic Egyptian collection awaits in Room 100 as well as the galleries of Greek and Roman Antiquities. If you have extra time, it's well worth booking tours to see the special exhibition in the ❼ **Gold Rooms** of the Treasure Gallery.

GERMAN S/SHUTTERSTOCK ©

Jordan Staircase
Originally designed by Rastrelli, in the 18th century this incredible white marble construction was known as the Ambassadorial Staircase because it was the way into the palace for official receptions.

The Gold Rooms
One of two sections of the Treasure Gallery, here you can see dazzling pieces of gold jewellery and ornamentation created by Scythian, Greek and ancient Oriental craftsmen.

IMAGE SOURCE/GETTY IMAGES ©

Great Church
This stunningly ornate church was the Romanovs' private place of worship and the venue for the marriage of the last tsar, Nicholas II, to Alexandra Feodorovna in 1895.

Rembrandt

A moving portrait of contrition and forgiveness, *Return of the Prodigal Son* (Room 254) depicts the biblical scene of a wayward son returning to his father.

Da Vinci

Along with the *Benois Madonna*, also here, *Madonna and Child (Madonna Litta;* Room 214) is one of just a handful of paintings known to be the work of Leonardo da Vinci.

St George's Hall

Hermitage Theatre

Pavilion Hall

Apart from the Peacock Clock, the Pavilion Hall also contains beautifully detailed mosaic tables made by Italian and Russian craftsmen in the mid-19th century.

Caravaggio

The Lute Player (Room 237) is the Hermitage's only Caravaggio, and a work that the master of light and shade described as the best piece he'd ever painted.

Central St Petersburg

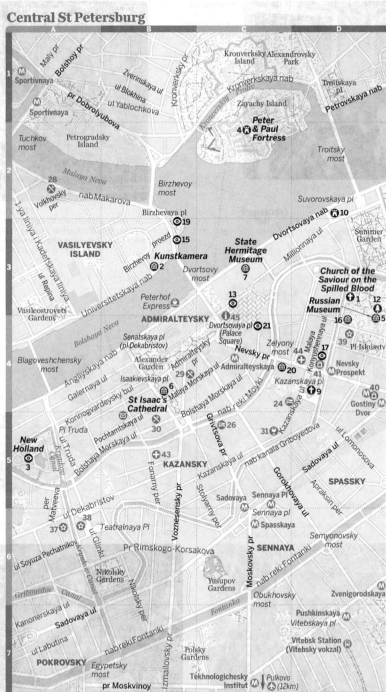

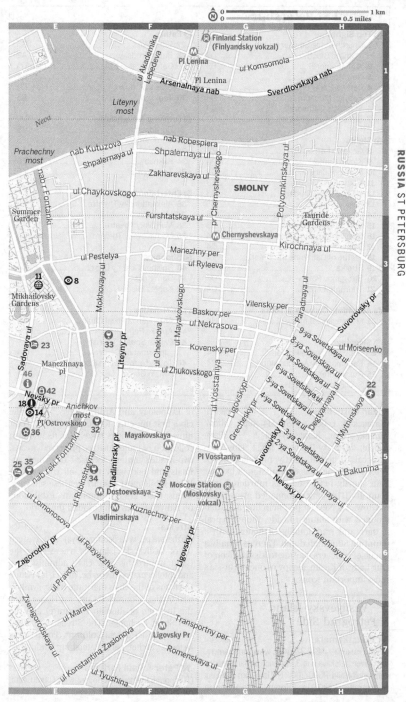

Central St Petersburg

Kazan Cathedral   CHURCH
(Казанский собор; ☎ 812-314 4663; http://
kazansky-spb.ru; Kazanskaya pl 2; ⊙ 8.30am-
7.30pm; Ⓜ Nevsky Prospekt) FREE This neoclassical cathedral, partly modelled on St
Peter's in Rome, was commissioned by Tsar
Paul shortly before he was murdered in a
coup. Its 111m-long colonnaded arms reach
out towards Nevsky pr, encircling a garden
studded with statues. Inside, the cathedral
is dark and traditionally Orthodox, with a
daunting 80m-high dome. There is usually a
queue of believers waiting to kiss the icon of
Our Lady of Kazan, a copy of one of Russia's
most important icons.

◉ Vasilyevsky Island & Petrograd Side

★ **Kunstkamera**   MUSEUM
(Кунсткамера; ☎ 812-328 1412; www.kunstkamera.
ru; Universitetskaya nab 3, entrance on Tamozhenny
per; adult/child R300/100; ⊙ 11am-7pm Tue-Sun;
Ⓜ Admiralteyskaya) Also known as the Museum
of Ethnology and Anthropology, this is the
city's first museum, founded in 1714 by Peter
himself. It is famous largely for its ghoulish
collection of monstrosities, preserved 'freaks',
two-headed mutant foetuses, deformed animals and odd body parts, all collected by
Peter. While most rush to see these sad specimens, there are also interesting exhibitions
on native peoples from around the world.

Strelka   LANDMARK
(Birzhevaya pl; Ⓜ Vasileostrovskaya) This eastern
tip of Vasilyevsky Island is where Peter the
Great wanted his new city's administrative
and intellectual centre to be. In fact, it became
the focus of the city's maritime trade, symbolised by the colonnaded Customs House (now
the Institute of Russian Literature) and the
Old Stock Exchange. The Strelka is flanked
by the pair of **Rostral Columns** (Ростральная
колонна), archetypal St Petersburg landmarks.

★ **Peter & Paul Fortress**   FORTRESS
(Петропавловская крепость; www.spbmuseum.
ru; grounds free, SS Peter & Paul Cathedral adult/

child R450/250, combined ticket for 5 exhibitions R600/350; ⊙grounds 9.30am-8pm, cathedral & bastion 10am-7pm Mon, Thu & Fri, 10am-5.45pm Sat, 11am-7pm Sun; Ⓜ Gorkovskaya) Housing a cathedral where the Romanovs are buried, a former prison and various exhibitions, this large defensive fortress on Zayachy Island is the kernel from which St Petersburg grew into the city it is today. History buffs will love it and everyone will swoon at the panoramic views from atop the fortress walls, at the foot of which lies a sandy riverside beach, a prime spot for sunbathing.

⊙ Beyond the Historic Heart

★ New Holland   ISLAND
(Новая Голландия; www.newhollandsp.ru; nab Admiralteyskogo kanala; ⊙9am-10pm Mon-Thu, to 11pm Fri-Sun; Ⓜ Sadovaya) This triangular island was closed for the most part of the last three centuries, and has opened to the public in dazzling fashion. There's plenty going on here, with hundreds of events happening throughout the year. There are summertime concerts, art exhibitions, yoga classes and film screenings, plus restaurants, cafes and shops. You can also come to enjoy a bit of quiet on the grass – or on one of the pontoons floating in the pond.

Golitsyn Loft   CULTURAL CENTRE
(nab reky Fontanki 20; Ⓜ Gostiny Dvor) The new epicentre of creativity on the Fontanka River is this mazelike complex of shops, bars, cafes, beauty salons, tattoo parlours, galleries and even a hostel with capsule-style bunks. Enter via the archway into a large courtyard, which is spread with outdoor eating and drinking spots in the summer, then head up any of the stairwells into the five buildings for some urban exploration. On weekends the centre stages one-off events, such as craft markets, concerts and film screenings.

🛏 Sleeping

Baby Lemonade Hostel   HOSTEL €
(☎812-570 7943; http://babylemonade.epoque hostels.com; Inzhenernaya ul 7; dm/d with shared bathroom from R600/2500, d from R4000; @ 🛜; Ⓜ Gostiny Dvor) The owner of Baby Lemonade is crazy about the 1960s and it shows in the pop-art, psychedelic design of this friendly, fun hostel with two pleasant, large dorms and a great kitchen and living room. However, it's worth splashing out for the boutique-hotel-worthy private rooms that are in a separate flat with great rooftop views.

★ Soul Kitchen Hostel   HOSTEL €
(☎8-965-816 3470; www.soulkitchenhostel.com; nab reki Moyki 62/2, apt 9, Sennaya; dm R780-2200, d R3200-7500; @🛜; Ⓜ Admiralteyskaya) Soul Kitchen blends boho hipness and boutique-hotel comfort, scoring perfect 10s in many key categories: private rooms (chic), dorm beds (double-width with privacy curtains), common areas and kitchen (all beautifully designed). The lounge is a fine place to hang out, with a record player, a big-screen projector (for movie nights) and an artful design.

★ Rachmaninov
Antique Hotel   BOUTIQUE HOTEL €€
(☎812-571 9778; www.hotelrachmaninov.com; Kazanskaya ul 5; s/d from R6600/7500; @🛜; Ⓜ Nevsky Prospekt) The long-established Rachmaninov still feels like a secret place for those in the know. Perfectly located and run by friendly staff, it's pleasantly old world, with hardwood floors and attractive Russian furnishings, particularly in the breakfast salon, which has a grand piano.

Rossi Hotel   BOUTIQUE HOTEL €€€
(☎812-635 6333; www.rossihotels.com; nab reki Fontanki 55; s/d/ste from R8700/9600/18,000; ❄@🛜; Ⓜ Gostiny Dvor) Occupying a beautifully restored building on one of St Petersburg's prettiest squares, the Rossi's 65 rooms are all designed differently, but their brightness and moulded ceilings are uniform. Antique beds, super-sleek bathrooms, exposed brick walls and lots of cool designer touches create a great blend of old and new.

🍴 Eating

★ Buter Brodsky   EUROPEAN €€
(Бутер Бродский; ☎8-911-922 2606; https://vk.com/buterbrodskybar; nab Makarova 16; mains R260-780; ⊙noon-midnight; 🛜; Ⓜ Sportivnaya) Shabby chic has never looked so good as it does at this cafe-bar dedicated to the poet Joseph Brodsky (the name is a pun on *buterbrod,* the Russian word for sandwich) a super-stylish part of Vasilyevsky Island's eating and drinking scene. The menu runs from excellent *smørrebrød* (open sandwiches; from R260) to fulsome Nordic- and Russian-themed mains.

★ Gräs x Madbaren   FUSION €€
(☎812-928 1818; http://grasmadbaren.com; Inzhenernaya ul 7; mains R420-550, tasting menu R2500; ⊙9am-11pm Sun-Thu, to 1am Fri & Sat; 🛜; Ⓜ Gostiny Dvor) Anton Abrezov is the talented

exec chef behind this Scandi-cool meets Russian locavore restaurant where you can sample dishes such as a delicious corned-beef salad with black garlic and pickled vegetables or an upmarket twist on ramen noodles with succulent roast pork.

Teplo
MODERN EUROPEAN €€

(☏ 812-407 2702; www.v-teple.ru; Bolshaya Morskaya ul 45; mains R360-940; ⊙ 9am-midnight Mon-Fri, from 11am Sat & Sun; ❄ ☎ ✎ ⏥; Ⓜ Admiralteyskaya) This much-feted, eclectic and original restaurant has got it all just right. The venue itself is a lot of fun to nose around, with multiple small rooms, nooks and crannies. Service is friendly and fast (when it's not too busy) and the peppy, inventive Italian-leaning menu has something for everyone. Reservations are usually required, so call ahead.

Banshiki
RUSSIAN €€

(Банщики; ☏ 8-921-941 1744; www.banshiki.spb.ru; Degtyarnaya ul 1; mains R500-1100; ⊙ 11am-11pm; ☎; Ⓜ Ploshchad Vosstaniya) Attached to a renovated *banya* (public baths) complex, this is currently the place to sample nostalgic Russian fare at affordable prices. Everything is made in-house, from its refreshing *kvas* (fermented rye bread water) to dried meats and eight types of smoked fish. Don't overlook cherry *vareniki* (dumplings) with sour cream, oxtail ragout or the rich borsch.

Cococo
RUSSIAN €€€

(☏ 812-418 2060; www.kokoko.spb.ru; Voznesensky pr 6; mains R650-1300; ⊙ 7-11am & 2pm-1am; ☎; Ⓜ Admiralteyskaya) Cococo has charmed locals with its inventive approach to contemporary Russian cuisine. Your food is likely to

AROUND ST PETERSBURG

Several palace estates around St Petersburg, country retreats for the tsars, are now among the most spectacular sights in Russia.

Peterhof (Петергоф; also known as Petrodvorets), 29km west of the city and built for Peter the Great, is best visited for its **Grand Cascade** (⊙ 11am-5pm Mon-Fri, to 6pm Sat & Sun May-Oct) and Water Avenue, a symphony of over 140 fountains and canals located in the **Lower Park** (Нижний парк; www.peterhofmuseum.ru; adult/student May-Oct R750/400, Nov-Apr free; ⊙ 9am-7pm). There are several additional palaces, villas and parks here, each of which charges its own hefty admission price.

Tsarskoe Selo (Царское Село), 25km south of the city in the town of Pushkin, is home to the baroque **Catherine Palace** (Екатерининский дворец; www.tzar.ru; Sadovaya ul 7; adult/student R1000/350, audio guide R150; ⊙ 10am-4.45pm Wed-Sun), expertly restored following its near destruction in WWII. From May to September individual visits to Catherine's Palace are limited to noon to 2pm and 4pm to 5pm, other times being reserved for tour groups. The town itself is a pleasant place for a stroll, with a few nice places to eat along the route from the train station to the palace. **Borscht** (Борщ; Moskovskaya ul 20; ⊙ 11am-6pm) is a quirky place that serves nothing but the famed beetroot soup and vodka. For a more conventional dining experience try **Solenya Varenya** (Соленья-Варенья; ☏ 8-812-465 2685; www.solenya-varenya.ru; Srednyaya ul 2; mains R420-880; ⊙ 10am-11pm; ☎).

Pavlovsk (Павловск) A less visited destination a short bus ride away from Pushkin, this town is home to the stunning 18th-century **Pavlovsk Great Palace** (Большой Павловский дворец; www.pavlovskmuseum.ru; ul Sadovaya 20; adult/child R600/250; ⊙ 10am-6pm, closed Tue, Fri & 1st Mon of month) ✎ and one of the finest green spaces in greater St Petersburg. To compare the tastes of its original owner to those of the current Russian leader, consider a lunch at Podvorye – reputedly one of Putin's favourite restaurants, located on the main road some 500m northeast from Pavlovsk train station.

By far the best (but also the priciest) way of reaching Peterhof is by **Peterhof Express** (www.peterhof-express.com; single/return adult R800/1500, student R600/1000; ⊙ 10am-6pm) hydrofoil, which leaves from jetties behind the Hermitage and the Admiralty from May to September. Buses and *marshrutky* (fixed-route minibuses) to Petrodvorets (R55, 30 minutes) run frequently from outside metro stations Avtovo and Leninsky Prospekt.

The easiest way to get to Tsarskoe Selo is by *marshrutka* (R35) from Moskovskaya metro station. For Pavlovsk; catch another *marshrutka* (R32) from Pavlovskoe sh near the southeast corner of Catherine Park. Infrequent suburban trains for Pushkin (R47, 30 minutes) and Pavlovsk, one stop away, leave from Vitebsk train station in St Petersburg.

arrive disguised as, say, a small bird's egg, a can of peas or a broken flowerpot – all rather gimmicky, theatrical and fun. The best way to sample what it does is with its tasting menu (R2900). Bookings are advised.

🍷 Drinking & Nightlife

★ Top Hops
CRAFT BEER

(☎ 8-966-757 0116; www.tophops.ru; nab reki Fontanki 55; ⊙ 4pm-1am Mon-Thu, 2pm-2am Fri-Sun; 🛜; Ⓜ Gostiny Dvor) One of the nicer craft-beer bars in town, this riverside space with friendly staff serves up a regularly changing menu of 20 beers on tap and scores more in bottles. The tasty Mexican snacks and food (go for nachos and chilli) go down exceptionally well while you sample your way through its range.

Borodabar
COCKTAIL BAR

(☎ 8-911-923 8940; www.facebook.com/Borod abar; Kazanskaya ul 11; ⊙ 5pm-2am Sun-Thu, to 6am Fri & Sat; 🛜; Ⓜ Nevsky Prospekt) *Boroda* means beard in Russian, and sure enough you'll see plenty of facial hair and tattoos in this hipster cocktail hang-out. Never mind, as the mixologists really know their stuff – we can particularly recommend their smoked Old Fashioned, which is infused with tobacco smoke, and their colourful (and potent) range of shots.

★ Commode
BAR

(www.commode.club; 2nd fl, ul Rubinshteyna 1; per hour R180; ⊙ 4pm-2am Sun-Thu, to 6am Fri & Sat) Stopping in for drinks at Commode feels more like hanging out in an upper-class friend's stylish apartment. After getting buzzed up, you can hang out in various high-ceilinged rooms, catch a small concert or poetry slam, browse books in the quasi-library room, play a round of table football, or chat with the easy-going crowd that's fallen for the place.

Hat
BAR

(ul Belinskogo 9; ⊙ 7pm-5am; Ⓜ Gostiny Dvor) The wonderfully retro-feeling Hat is a serious spot for jazz and whisky lovers, who come for the nightly live music and the cool-cat crowd that make this wonderfully designed bar feel like it's been transported out of 1950s Greenwich Village. A very welcome change of gear for St Petersburg's drinking options, but it can be extremely packed at weekends.

Kakhabar
WINE BAR

(☎ 812-965 0524; https://kakhabar.ru; ul Rubin-shteyna 24; ⊙ noon-11am, to 1am Fri & Sat) This is our ideal post-Soviet bar, specialising in Georgian wine accompanied by tapas-sized versions of succulent Georgian fare, including *khachapuri* (Georgian cheese bread) and *khinkali* (dumplings). Get a bottle of *saperavi* or *mukuzani* red if you need an introduction to Georgia's endemic wines and move on to the potent *chacha* (grappa equivalent) when things get lively.

☆ Entertainment

★ Mariinsky Theatre
BALLET, OPERA

(Мариинский театр; ☎ 812-326 4141; www.mariinsky.ru; Teatralnaya pl 1; tickets R1200-6500; Ⓜ Sadovaya) St Petersburg's most spectacular venue for ballet and opera, the Mariinsky Theatre is an attraction in its own right. Tickets can be bought online or in person; book in advance during the summer months. The magnificent interior is the epitome of imperial grandeur, and any evening here will be an impressive experience.

Known as the Kirov Ballet during the Soviet era, the Mariinsky has an illustrious history, with troupe members including such ballet greats as Nijinsky, Nureyev, Pavlova and Baryshnikov. In recent years the company has been invigorated by the current artistic and general director, Valery Gergiev, who has worked hard to make the company solvent while overseeing the construction of the impressive and much-needed second theatre, the **Mariinsky II** (Мариинский II; ul Dekabristov 34; tickets R350-6000; ⊙ ticket office 11am-7pm; Ⓜ Sadovaya), across the Kryukov Canal from the company's green-and-white wedding cake of a building. It is pretty certain that the Mariinsky Theatre will close at some point in 2019 for a full (and, again, much-needed) renovation.

★ Mikhailovsky Theatre
PERFORMING ARTS

(Михайловский театр; ☎ 812-595 4305; www.mikhailovsky.ru; pl Iskusstv 1; tickets R500-5000; Ⓜ Nevsky Prospekt) This illustrious stage delivers the Russian ballet or operatic experience, complete with multitiered theatre, frescoed ceiling and elaborate productions. Pl Iskusstv (Arts Sq) is a lovely setting for this respected venue, which is home to the State Academic Opera & Ballet Company.

ℹ Information

Free wi-fi access is common across the city.
American Medical Clinic (☎ 812-740 2090; www.amclinic.ru; nab reki Moyki 78; ⊙ 24hr; Ⓜ Admiralteyskaya) One of the city's largest private clinics.

Apteka Petrofarm (☑ 812-571 3767; Nevsky pr 22-24; ⊙ 24hr) An excellent, all-night pharmacy.

Main Post Office (Pochtamtskaya ul 9; Ⓜ Admiralteyskaya) Worth visiting for its elegant Style Moderne interior.

St Petersburg Times Published every Tuesday and Friday, when it has an indispensable listings and arts review section.

Tourist Information Bureau (☑ 812-242 3909, 812-303 0555; http://eng.ispb.info; Sadovaya ul 14/52; ⊙ 10am-7pm Mon-Sat; Ⓜ Gostiny Dvor) There are also branches outside the **Hermitage** (☑ 8-931-326 5744; Dvortsovaya pl; ⊙ 10am-7pm; Ⓜ Admiralteyskaya) and **Pulkovo airport** (⊙ 9am-8pm).

ⓘ Getting There & Around

ARRIVING IN ST PETERSBURG

Pulkovo Airport From St Petersburg's superb airport, an official taxi to the centre should cost between R800 and R1000; if you book one via an app it's likely to be R700. Alternatively, take bus 39 (35 minutes) or 39A (20 minutes) to Moskovskaya metro station for R35, then take the metro from Moskovskaya (Line 2) all over the city for R45.

Train Stations Main train stations are located in the city centre and connected to metro stations.

PUBLIC TRANSPORT

The metro is usually the quickest way around the city. *Zhetony* (tokens) and credit-loaded cards can be bought from booths in the stations (R45). Multiride cards are also available (R355 for 10 trips, R680 for 20 trips). Buses, trolleybuses and *marshrutky* fixed route minibuses (fare R40) often get you closer to the sights and are especially handy to cover long distances along main avenues like Nevsky pr.

TAXI

Taxi apps, such as Gett and Yandex Taxi, are all the rage in St Petersburg and they've brought down the prices of taxis in general, while improving the service a great deal. Aside from the apps, the best way to get a taxi is to order it by phone. **Taxi 6000000** (☑ 812-600 0000; http://6-000-000.ru) has English-speaking operators.

SURVIVAL GUIDE

ⓘ Directory A–Z

ACCESSIBLE TRAVEL

Travellers with disabilities are not well catered for in Russia. Many footpaths are in poor condition and potentially hazardous, and there is a lack of access ramps and lifts for wheelchairs. However, attitudes are enlightened and things are slowly changing.

ACCOMMODATION

For major cities and resorts it's a good idea to book a night or two in advance (especially during the busy summer season in St Petersburg). Elsewhere you can usually just turn up and find a room.

Hotels Range from contemporary and professionally run to moodily idiosyncratic DIY enterprises and an occasional Soviet-era dinosaur.

Hostels Moscow and St Petersburg have rich pickings but you'll now also find many good ones in other major cities and towns. At the time of research, laws were being passed that outlaw hostels that occupy premises in apartment blocks. Many will likely close or relocate as a result of this.

B&Bs & homestays Not so common but worth searching out for a true experience of Russian hospitality.

INTERNET ACCESS

Installing a pay-as-you-go Russian SIM card with unlimited traffic on your smartphone is the easiest way to ensure constant access. These are available at airports and most shopping malls.

Wi-fi is common across Russia and usually access is free (or available for the cost of a cup of coffee). You may have to ask for a password (*parol*) to get online. Most of the time these days you also input your mobile phone number. Sometimes this will need to be a Russian number (ie one starting with +7); if you don't have one, ask a local if you can use their number.

If you don't have your own wi-fi-enabled device, it's probably easiest to get online in the business centres of hotels or at hostels that have a computer terminal.

LEGAL MATTERS

Avoid contact with the myriad types of police. It's not uncommon for them to bolster their incomes by extracting 'fines' from the unaware; you always have the right to insist to be taken to a police station (though we don't recommend this; if possible try to resolve the problem on the spot) or that the 'fine' be paid the legal way, through Sberbank. If you need police assistance (ie you've been the victim of a robbery or an assault), go to a station with a local for both language and moral support. Be persistent and patient.

If you are arrested, the police are obliged to inform your embassy or consulate immediately and allow you to communicate with it without delay. You can't count on the rules being followed, so be polite and respectful towards officials and hopefully things will go far more smoothly for you. In Russian, the phrase 'I'd like to call my embassy' is '*Pozhaluysta, ya khotel by pozvonit v posolstvo moyey strany*'.

LGBT+ TRAVELLERS

➜ Russia is a conservative country and being gay is generally frowned upon. LGBT people face stigma, harassment and violence in their everyday lives.

➜ Homosexuality isn't illegal, but promoting it (and other LGBT lifestyles) is. What constitutes promotion is at the discretion of the authorities.

➜ There are active and relatively open gay and lesbian scenes in both Moscow and St Petersburg. Elsewhere, the gay scene tends to be underground.

➜ Visit http://english.gay.ru for information, good links and a resource for putting you in touch with personal guides for Moscow and St Petersburg.

➜ Coming Out (www.comingoutspb.com) is the site of a St Petersburg–based support organisation.

MONEY

The Russian currency is the rouble, written as 'рубль' and abbreviated as 'руб' or 'p'. Roubles are divided into 100 almost worthless *kopeyki* (kopecks). Coins come in amounts of R1, R2, R5 and R10 roubles, with banknotes in values of R10, R50, R100, R200, R500, R1000, R2000 and R5000.

ATMs that accept all major credit and debit cards are everywhere, and most restaurants, shops and hotels in major cities gladly accept plastic. Visa and MasterCard are the most widespread card types, while American Express can be problematic in some hotels and shops. You can exchange dollars and euros (and some other currencies) at most banks; when they're closed, try the exchange counters at top-end hotels. You may need your passport. Note that crumpled or old banknotes are often refused.

OPENING HOURS

Banks 9am to 6pm Monday to Friday, some open 9am to 5pm Saturday

Bars and Clubs noon to midnight Sunday to Thursday, to 6am Friday and Saturday

Cafes 9am to 10pm

Post Offices 8am to 8pm or 9pm Monday to Friday, shorter hours Saturday and Sunday

Restaurants noon to midnight

Shops 10am to 8pm

Supermarkets and Food stores 9am to 11pm or 24 hours

PUBLIC HOLIDAYS

In addition to the following official days, many businesses (but not restaurants, shops and museums) close for a week of bank holidays between 1 January and at least 8 January. Bank

holidays are typically declared to merge national holidays with the nearest weekend.

New Year's Day 1 January

Russian Orthodox Christmas Day 7 January

Defender of the Fatherland Day 23 February

International Women's Day 8 March

International Labour Day/Spring Festival 1 May

Victory Day 9 May

Russian Independence Day 12 June

Unity Day 4 November

SAFE TRAVEL

Despite the strain in relations with the West, Russia is generally a safe country in which to travel.

➜ Don't leave any valuables or bags inside your car. Valuables lying around hotel rooms also tempt providence.

➜ It's generally safe to leave your belongings unguarded when using the toilets on trains, but you'd be wise to get to know your fellow passengers first.

➜ Pickpockets and purse-snatchers operate in big cities and major towns. Keep your valuables close.

➜ Avoid drinking with dodgy strangers and discussing international politics when drunk.

TELEPHONE

Local calls from homes and most hotels are free. To make a long-distance call or to call a mobile from most phones, first dial 8, wait for a second dial tone, then dial the area code and phone number. To make an international call dial 8, wait for a second dial tone, then dial 10, then the country code etc. Some phones are for local calls only and won't give you that second dial tone.

To place an international call from a mobile phone, dial + and then the country code.

TIME

There are 11 time zones in Russia; the standard time is calculated from Moscow, which is GMT/UTC plus three hours year-round. In 2011, Russia abandoned the summer time switch, so the gap with European neighbours increases by an hour in winter.

TOILETS

➜ Pay toilets are identified by the words платный туалет (*platny tualet*). In any toilet, Ж (*zhensky*) stands for women's and M (*muzhskoy*) stands for men's.

➜ Public toilets are rare and can be dingy and uninviting. Toilets in major hotels, cafes or shopping centres are preferable.

➜ In all public toilets, the babushka you pay your R20 to can also provide miserly rations of toilet paper; it's always a good idea to carry your own.

TOURIST INFORMATION

Official tourist offices are rare in Russia.

You're mainly dependent on hotel receptionists and administrators, service bureaus and travel firms for information. The latter two exist primarily to sell accommodation, excursions and transport – if you don't look like you want to book something, staff may or may not answer questions.

VISAS

Nationals of all Western countries require a visa, but most Latin American, as well as some East Asian countries, Israel and South Africa have visa-free arrangements with Russia. Arranging a visa is generally straightforward but is likely to be time-consuming, bureaucratic and – depending on how quickly you need the visa – costly. Start the application process at least a month before your trip. Following the World Cup success in 2018, the government pondered relaxing visa requirements – look out for media announcements.

ⓘ Getting There & Away

ENTERING THE COUNTRY

➡ Searches beyond the perfunctory are quite rare, but clearing customs when you leave Russia by a land border can be lengthy.

➡ Visitors are allowed to bring in and take out up to US$10,000 (or its equivalent) in currency, and goods up to the value of €10,000, weighing less than 50kg, without making a customs declaration.

➡ Fill in a customs declaration form if you're bringing into Russia major equipment, antiques, artworks or musical instruments (including a guitar) that you plan to take out with you – get it stamped in the red channel of customs to avoid any problems leaving with the same goods.

➡ If you plan to export anything vaguely 'arty' – instruments, coins, jewellery, antiques, antiquarian manuscripts and books (older than 50 years) or art (also older than 50 years) – it should first be assessed by the **Ministry of Culture** (Коллегия экспертизы; ☑ 499-391 4212; ul Akademika Korolyova 21, bldg 1, office 505, 5th fl; ⊙11am-5pm Mon-Fri; ⓜVDNKh); it is very difficult to export anything over 100 years old. Bring your item (or a photograph, if the item is large) and your receipt. If export is allowed, you'll be issued a receipt for tax paid, which you show to customs officers on your way out of the country.

AIR

Moscow's **Sheremetyevo** (Шереметьево; ☑ 495-578 6565; www.svo.aero), **Domodedovo** (Домодедово; ☑ 495-933 6666; www.domodedovo.ru) and **Vnukovo** (Внуково; ☑ 495-937 5555; www.vnukovo.ru) and St Petersburg's **Pulkovo International Airport** (LED; ☑ 812-337 3822; www.pulkovoairport.ru; Pulkovskoye sh) host the bulk of Russia's international flights.

Plenty of other cities have direct international connections, including Arkhangelsk, Irkutsk, Kaliningrad, Kazan, Khabarovsk, Krasnodar, Mineralnye Vody, Murmansk, Nalchik, Nizhny Novgorod, Novosibirsk, Perm, Yekaterinburg and Yuzhno-Sakhalinsk.

LAND

Russia borders 14 countries. Popular land approaches include trains and buses from Central European and Baltic countries or on either the trans-Manchurian or trans-Mongolian train routes from China and Mongolia.

Border Crossings

Russia shares borders with Azerbaijan, Belarus, China, Estonia, Finland, Georgia, Kazakhstan, Latvia, Lithuania, Mongolia, North Korea, Norway, Poland and Ukraine. Before planning a journey into or out of Russia from any of these countries, check the visa situation for your nationality.

On trains, border crossings are a straightforward but drawn-out affair, with a steady stream of customs and ticket personnel scrutinising your passport and visa. If you're arriving by car or motorcycle, you'll need to show your vehicle registration and insurance papers, and your driving licence, passport and visa. These formalities are usually minimal for Western European citizens. On the Russian side, most cars are subjected to cursory inspection, with only a small percentage getting a thorough check.

SEA

Ferry routes connect St Petersburg to Helsinki (Finland), Stockholm (Sweden) and Tallinn (Estonia).

ⓘ Getting Around

AIR

Major Russian airlines, including **Aeroflot** (☑ 495-223 5555, toll free in Russia 8-800 444 5555; www.aeroflot.com), **Rossiya** (☑ 8-495 139 7777, 8-800 444 5555; www.rossiya-airlines.com), **S7 Airlines** (☑ 495-783-0707, 8-800 700-0707; www.s7.ru), **Ural Airlines** (www.uralairlines.com), **UTAir** (www.utair.ru) and budget carrier **Pobeda** (www.pobeda.aero), have online booking, with the usual discounts for advance purchases. Otherwise, it's no problem buying a ticket at ubiquitous *aviakassa* (ticket offices), which may be able to tell you about flights that you can't easily find out about online overseas. Online agencies specialising in Russian air tickets with English interfaces include **Anywayanyday** (☑ 8-800 775 7753; www.any

wayanyday.com), **Pososhok.ru** (☑ 8-800 333 8118; www.pososhok.ru), **One Two Trip!** (www.onetwotrip.ru) and **TicketsRU** (www.tickets.ru).

Whenever you book airline tickets in Russia you'll need to show your passport and visa. Tickets can also be purchased at the airport right up to the departure of the flight and sometimes even if the city centre office says that the plane is full. Return fares are usually double the one-way fares.

It's a good idea to check in online as early as possible and sign up for notifications about delays and cancellations. Most airlines have handy telephone apps, which you can use for both booking and online check-in.

Airlines may bump you if you don't check in at least an hour before departure and can be very strict about charging for checked bags that are overweight, which generally means anything over 20kg. Pobeda is notoriously strict (as well as unpredictable and arbitrary) about baggage allowances and carry-on luggage.

Have your passport and ticket handy throughout the various security and ticket checks that can occur, right up until you find a seat. Some flights have assigned seats, others don't. On the latter, seating is a free-for-all.

Many internal flights in Moscow use either Domodedovo or Vnukovo airports; if you're connecting to Moscow's Sheremetyevo international airport, allow a few hours to cross town (at least three hours if you need to go by taxi, rather than train and metro).

Big city airports are gradually being revamped and modernised, but in small towns airports offer facilities similar to the average bus shelter.

BUS & MARSHRUTKY

Long-distance buses tend to complement rather than compete with the rail network. They generally serve areas with no railway or routes on which trains are slow, infrequent or overloaded.

Most cities have an intercity bus station (автовокзал, *avtovokzal*). Tickets are sold at the station or on the bus. Fares are normally listed on the timetable and posted on a wall. As often as not you'll get a ticket with a seat assignment, either printed or scribbled on a till receipt. If you have luggage that needs to be stored in the bus baggage compartment, you may have to pay an extra fare, typically around 10% of the bus fare. Some bus stations may also apply a small fee for security measures.

Marshrutky (a Russian diminutive form of *marshrutnoye taksi*, meaning a fixed-route taxi) are minibuses that are often quicker than larger buses and rarely cost much more. Where roads are good and villages frequent, *marshrutky* can be twice as fast as buses and are well worth paying extra for.

CAR & MOTORCYCLE

Driving in Russia is not for the faint-hearted, but if you've a sense of humour, patience and a decent vehicle, it's an adventurous way to go. Both road quality and driving culture have improved a great deal in the last decade, so driving has become much more pleasant than before. There are also reliable car-hire companies.

The sheer number of vehicles and constant road improvements make traffic jams a largely unavoidable obstacle in the vicinities of Moscow, St Petersburg and other large cities. Russia's most popular navigation app, Yandex, monitors traffic jams in real time and sends you on the fastest route.

TRAIN

Russian Railways (РЖД, RZD; ☑ 8-800 775 0000; www.rzd.ru) trains are generally comfortable and, depending on the class of travel, relatively inexpensive for the distances covered. The network is highly centralised, with Moscow, which has nine large train stations, as the main transfer hub. Given large distances, a vast majority of carriages are equipped with sleeping berths, while only newer and shorter-distance trains have seats.

A handful of high-speed services aside, trains are rarely speedy, but have a remarkable record for punctuality – if you're a minute late for your train, the chances are you'll be left standing on the platform. The fact that RZD managers have a large portion of their pay determined by the timeliness of their trains not only inspires promptness, but also results in the creation of generous schedules. You'll notice this when you find your train stationary for hours in the middle of nowhere only to suddenly start up and roll into the next station right on time.

Serbia

POP 7.11 MILLION

Best Places to Eat

➡ Iris New Balkan Cuisine (p399)

➡ Šaran (p399)

➡ Bela Reka (p400)

➡ Ambar (p400)

➡ Stambolijski (p407)

Best Places to Stay

➡ Mama Shelter (p399)

➡ Savamala Bed & Breakfast (p398)

➡ Yugodom (p398)

➡ Varad Inn (p403)

➡ ArtLoft Hotel (p406)

Why Go?

Diverse, welcoming and a hell of a lot of fun – everything you never heard about Serbia is true. Best of all, this land-locked country in the heart of the Balkans is still delightfully off the tourist trail. While the feisty Serbian spirit is embodied in Belgrade's world-class nightlife and Novi Sad's epic EXIT festival, look beyond these historic metropolises and you'll discover a crucible of cultures and unsullied outdoors ripe for exploration.

The art nouveau town of Subotica revels in its Austro-Hungarian heritage, bohemian Niš echoes to the clip-clop of Roma horse carts, and minaret-studded Novi Pazar nudges the most sacred of Serbian Orthodox monasteries. Established wine regions and thermal spas cradled in rolling hills date back to Roman times. On the slopes of Kopaonik, Zlatibor and Stara Planina, ancient traditions coexist with après-ski bling, while super-scenic Tara and Đerdap national parks brim with hiking, biking, rafting and kayaking opportunities.

When to Go
Belgrade

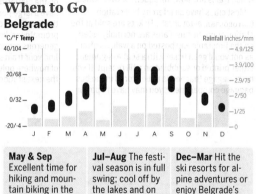

| **May & Sep** Excellent time for hiking and mountain biking in the national parks. | **Jul–Aug** The festival season is in full swing; cool off by the lakes and on the rivers. | **Dec–Mar** Hit the ski resorts for alpine adventures or enjoy Belgrade's cultural calendar. |

Entering the Country

Getting to Serbia is a cinch; it's connected to Europe by main roads, there are no seas to cross and its two airports welcome flights from across the continent and the world. All of Europe is accessible from Belgrade: Budapest, Zagreb, Sofia and Thessaloniki are a train ride away, and regular buses serve destinations including Vienna, Sarajevo and Podgorica.

ITINERARIES

Five Days

Revel in three days of cultural and culinary exploration in Belgrade (p395), allowing for at least one night of hitting the capital's legendary nightspots. Carry on north to laid-back Novi Sad (p402) on the Danube, and complete the Vojvodina tour with a day trip to Subotica (p403) to admire its art nouveau architecture.

Ten Days

Follow the above itinerary, then head to southern Serbia. Slice southwest for some hiking and a train ride in Tara National Park (p407) en route to Turkish-flavoured Novi Pazar (p403). Alternatively turn southeast for a boat trip and cycling through Đerdap National Park (p407), followed by the history and *kafana* cuisine of bohemian Niš (p406).

Essential Food & Drink

Kajmak Dairy delight akin to a salty clotted cream.

Ajvar Spread made from roasted peppers, aubergines and garlic.

Urnebes Creamy, spicy peppers-and-cheese spread.

Burek Flaky meat, cheese or vegetable pie eaten with yoghurt.

Pljeskavica Spicy hamburger, usually served with onions.

Ćevapi These skinless sausages are the national fast food.

Ražnjići Pork or veal shish kebabs.

Karađorđeva šnicla Similar to chicken Kiev, but with veal or pork and lashings of *kajmak* and tartar sauce.

Svadbarski kupus Sauerkraut and hunks of smoked pork slow-cooked in giant clay pots.

Riblja čorba Fish soup, most commonly from carp, spiced with paprika.

Gomboce Potato-dough dumplings, usually stuffed with plums.

Rakija Strong distilled spirit made from fruit – the most common variety is *šljivovica*, made from plums.

AT A GLANCE

Area 77,474 sq km

Capital Belgrade

Country Code ☑ 381

Currency Dinar (RSD)

Emergency Ambulance ☑ 194, fire ☑ 193, police ☑ 192

Language Serbian

Time Eastern European Time (GMT/UTC plus one/two hours in winter/summer)

Visas None for citizens of the EU, UK, Australia, New Zealand, Canada and the USA

Sleeping Price Ranges

The following price categories are based on the cost of a high-season double room including breakfast.

€ less than 3000RSD

€€ 3000–8000RSD

€€€ more than 8000RSD

Eating Price Ranges

The following price categories are based on the cost of a main course.

€ less than 600RSD

€€ 600–1000RSD

€€€ more than 1000RSD

Serbia Highlights

1 Belgrade (p395) Revelling in the intriguing melange of faded Yugo-nostalgia, cutting-edge Balkan cool and fascinating history.

2 Tara National Park (p407) Hiking, rafting on the Drina or riding a narrow-gauge railway around the most scenic slice of Serbia.

3 EXIT Festival (p403) Joining thousands of revellers each July for eclectic beats at Novi Sad's formidable fortress.

4 Đerdap National Park (p407) Cycling or cruising through the Danube's astounding Iron Gates gorge and millennia of history.

5 Subotica (p403) Gawking at the marvellous art nouveau architecture of this leafy town in Vojvodina province.

6 Novi Pazar (p403) Exploring the melding cultural heritages of this Turkish-flavoured town and revered Serbian Orthodox sites nearby.

BELGRADE БЕОГРАД

📃 011 / POP 1.6 MILLION

Outspoken, adventurous, proud and audacious: Belgrade ('White City') is by no means a 'pretty' capital, but its gritty exuberance makes it one of Europe's most happening cities. While it hurtles towards a brighter future, its chaotic past unfolds before your eyes: socialist blocks are squeezed between art nouveau masterpieces, and remnants of the Habsburg legacy contrast with Ottoman relics and socialist modernist monoliths. This is where the Sava and Danube Rivers kiss, an old-world culture that at once evokes time-capsuled communist-era Yugoslavia and new-world, EU-contending cradle of cool.

Grandiose coffee houses and smoky dives pepper Knez Mihailova, a lively pedestrian boulevard flanked by historical buildings all the way to the ancient Belgrade Fortress. The riverside Savamala quarter has gone from ruin to resurrection, and is the city's creative headquarters (for now). Deeper in Belgrade's bowels are museums guarding the cultural, religious and military heritage of the country.

⊙ Sights

★ **Belgrade Fortress** FORTRESS
(Beogradska tvrđava; www.beogradskatvrdjava.co.rs; ⊙24hr) FREE Some 115 battles have been fought over imposing, impressive Belgrade Fortress (aka Kalemegdan); the citadel was destroyed more than 40 times throughout the centuries. Fortifications began in Celtic times, and the Romans extended it onto the flood plains during the settlement of 'Singidunum', Belgrade's Roman name. Much of what stands today is the product of 18th-century Austro-Hungarian and Turkish reconstructions. The fort's bloody history, discernible despite today's jolly cafes and funfairs, only makes the fortress all the more fascinating.

Audio guides in six languages with a map (300RSD plus ID as deposit) are available from the souvenir shop within the Inner Stambol Gate, which is also where you must purchase tickets for the Clock Tower, Roman Well and Big Gunpowder Magazine.

★ **Museum of Yugoslavia** MUSEUM
(www.muzej-jugoslavije.org; Botićeva 6; 400RSD, incl entry to Marshal Tito's Mausoleum, 4-6pm 1st Thu of month free; ⊙10am-6pm Tue-Sun) This must-visit museum houses an invaluable collection of more than 200,000 artefacts representing the fascinating, tumultuous history of Yugoslavia. Photographs, artworks, historical documents, films, weapons, priceless treasure: it's all here. It can be a lot to take in; English-speaking guides are available if booked in advance via email, or you can join a free tour on weekends (11am in English, Serbian at noon). **Marshal Tito's Mausoleum** (Kuća Cveća, House of Flowers) is also on the museum grounds; admission is included in the ticket price.

The museum's main building, known as the May 25 Museum, is expected to reopen in 2019 after extensive renovations. Take trolleybus 40 or 41 at the south end of Parliament on Kneza Miloša; ask the driver to let you out at Kuća Cveća.

★ **Mt Avala** TOWER
(Mt Avala; tower 300RSD; ⊙tower 9am-8pm Mar-Sept, to 5pm Oct-Feb) Looming over Belgrade and topped with the tallest tower in the Balkans (204.5m), Mt Avala is a city landmark that makes for a pleasant break from the capital's bustling streets. The **broadcasting tower**, originally completed in 1965 but levelled by NATO bombs in 1999, was rebuilt in 2010 and now offers picture-perfect panoramas over Belgrade and beyond from viewing platforms and a cafe. Nearby, the **Monument to the Unknown Hero** by Ivan Meštrović honours Serbian victims of WWI.

Mt Avala is 16km from the city centre; on weekends in summer, bus 400 runs to the top of Avala from the **Voždovac** (Joakima Rakovca) stop.

★ **Museum of Contemporary Art** MUSEUM
(www.msub.org.rs; Ušće 10; 300RSD, free Wed; ⊙10am-6pm Mon, Wed & Fri-Sun, 10am-10pm Thu) One of Belgrade's top cultural sights, this recently renovated museum is a treasure trove of 20th-century art from the ex-Yugoslav cultural space. The 1960s concrete-and-glass modernist building, surrounded by a sculpture park, has great views towards the Belgrade Fortress across the Sava River.

Conceptual art features prominently, including a 1970s video called *Freeing the Memory* from the region's most famous artist (and Belgrade native), Marina Abramović. One section is dedicated to the 1920s Yugoslav avant-garde magazine *Zenit* and the Zenitism art movement associated with it.

National Museum MUSEUM
(Narodni Muzej; www.narodnimuzej.rs; Trg Republike 1a; adult/child 300/150RSD, Sun free; ⊙10am-6pm Tue, Wed, Fri & Sun, Thu & Sat noon-8pm) Lack of funding for renovations kept Serbia's National Museum mostly shuttered for 15

Central Belgrade

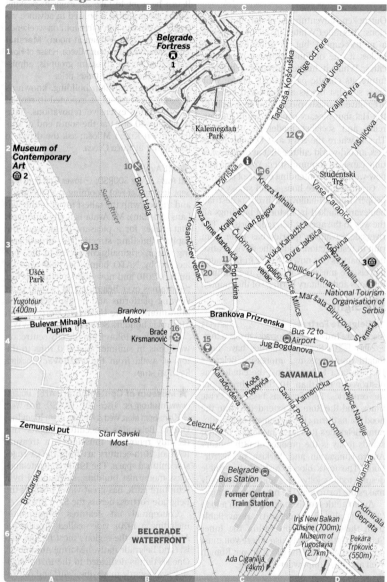

Belgrade Fortress
1

Museum of Contemporary Art
2

Kalemegdan Park

Beton Hala

Suva River

Ušće Park

Yugotour (400m)

Bulevar Mihajla Pupina

Brankov Most

Brače Krsmanović 16

Zemunski put

Stari Savski Most

Brodarska

BELGRADE WATERFRONT

Pariska

Kneza Sime Markovića

Kneza Mihaila

Kralja Petra

Čubrina

Ivan Begova

Pop Lukina

Kosančićev venac

Vuka Karadžića

Topličin venac

Carice Milice

Đure Jakšića

Obilićev Venac

Zmaj Jovina

Kneza Mihaila

Maršala Birjuzova

Tadeuša Košćuska

Rige od Fere

Cara Uroša

Kralja Petra

Višnjićeva

Studentski Trg

Vase Čarapića

Popvina

14

12

6

3

National Tourism Organisation of Serbia

Brankova Prizrenska

Bus 72 to Airport

Jug Bogdanova

Karadorđeva

Koče Popovića

Železnička

Gavrila Principa

Gavrila Kamenička

SAVAMALA

Lomina

Kraljice Natalije

Balkanska

7

15

21

Belgrade Bus Station

Former Central Train Station

Iris New Balkan Cuisine (700m); Museum of Yugoslavia (2.7km)

Admirala Geprata

Pekara Trpković (550m)

Ada Ciganlija (4km)

10

13

11

20

years, but its much ballyhooed 2018 reopening has been a great source of national pride – it awoke from the dead on Vidovdan (28 June), the country's national day – and for good reason. Built in 1903 and reconstructed multiple times over the years, the museum's latest €12 million makeover frames some 5000 sq metres of exhibition space over three floors.

Highlights include works by Croatian Ivan Meštrović, the most celebrated sculptor of the Kingdom of Yugoslavia; archaeological treasures from Roman-era Serbia; and extensive galleries dedicated to both 18th-

Central Belgrade

◎ Top Sights
1 Belgrade Fortress	B1
2 Museum of Contemporary Art	A2

◎ Sights
3 National Museum	D3

⊜ Sleeping
4 Hostel Bongo	E5
5 Hotel Moskva	E4
6 Mama Shelter	C2
7 Savamala Bed & Breakfast	C4
8 Smokvica Bed & Breakfast	E2
9 Yugodom	F3

⊗ Eating
10 Ambar	B2
11 Mayka	C3

◎ Drinking & Nightlife
12 Bar Central	D2
13 Klub 20/44	A3
14 Krafter	D1
15 Vinoteka	C4

✿ Entertainment
16 KC Grad	B4
17 National Theatre	E3

ⓐ Shopping
18 Bajloni Market	F3
19 Belgrade Design District	E4
20 Makadam	C3
21 Zeleni Venac Market	D4

Nikola Tesla Museum MUSEUM
(www.nikolateslamuseum.org; Krunska 51; admission incl guided tour in English 500RSD; ⊙10am-8pm Tue-Sun) Meet the man on the 100RSD note at one of Belgrade's best museums, where you can release your inner nerd with some wondrously sci-fi-ish interactive elements. Tesla's ashes are kept here in a glowing, golden orb: debate has been raging for years between the museum (and its secular supporters) and the Church as to whether the remains should be moved to Sveti Sava Temple.

Sveti Sava Temple CHURCH
(www.hramsvetogsave.com; Krušedolska 2a; ⊙7am-7pm) Sveti Sava is the Balkans' biggest (and the world's second biggest) Orthodox church, a fact made entirely obvious when looking at the city skyline from a distance or standing under its dome. The church is built on the site where the Turks apparently burnt relics of St Sava. Work on the church interior (frequently interrupted by wars) continues today as the cupola is being adorned with

and 19th-century Serbian art and 20th-century Yugoslavian art. Don't miss the museum's most haunting corner, where Stevan Aleksić's *The Burning of the Remains of St Sava* (1912) sits sidesaddle to Đorđe Krstić's *The Fall of Stalać* (1903), two hyper-realistic and menacing oils on canvas.

a 1248-sq-metre mosaic, one of the world's largest on a curved surface.

Work is expected to continue through 2020 – until then, visit the astonishing gold-ceilinged crypt and its ornate chandeliers, Murano glass mosaics and vibrant frescoes.

Ada Ciganlija
BEACH

(www.adaciganlija.rs; parking 250RSD; ⊘24hr) FREE In summertime, join the hordes of sea-starved locals (up to 250,000 a day) for sun and fun at this artificial island on the Sava. Cool down with a swim, kayak or windsurf after a leap from the 55m bungee tower. Take bus 52 or 53 from Zeleni Venac.

Gardoš Tower
TOWER

(Tower of Sibinjanin Janko; www.kulanagardosu.com; Gardoš fortress; 200RSD; ⊘10am-7pm) This splendid brick tower (1896) has been renovated to house a free gallery, which hosts regular exhibitions. The views from the top, especially at sunset, are breathtaking. Somewhat confusingly, it's also known as the Millennium Tower.

From Zemun's buzzy Sinđelićeva, the tower is a five-minute walk up the cobbled street of Grobljanska.

☞ Tours

★ Yugotour
DRIVING

(☏066 801 8614; www.yugotour.com; per person 2900-8900RSD; ⊘from 11am) Yugotour is a mini road trip through the history of Yugoslavia and the life of its president Tito. Belgrade's communist years are brought to life in the icon of Yugo-nostalgia: a Yugo car!

Tours are led by young locals happy to share their own perceptions of Yugoslavia; they take in the communist-era architecture of Novi Beograd, the Museum of Yugoslavia and Marshal Tito's Mausoleum, among other locations.

★ Taste Serbia
FOOD & DRINK

(☏065 236 4866; www.tasteserbia.com; 4130-35400RSD) Take your taste buds on a holiday with these deliciously diverse tasting tours run by three local foodies. Explore Belgrade's gourmet scene, head north on a bacon-centric Vojvodinian voyage, stuff yourself in western Serbia and more; all tours are customisable, informative and fun. Pack your stretchy pants. Minimum two people and maximum of 16 people per group; advance bookings essential.

Belgrade Alternative Guide
WALKING

(☏063 743 3055; www.belgradealtguide.com; tours per person 1700-9800RSD) Run by passionate locals, these tours explore Savamala rooftop hang outs, central art galleries, street art, the history of Zemun, farmers markets, secret eateries and surrounding villages. Tours generally run between three and four hours.

🛏 Sleeping

Hostel Bongo
HOSTEL €

(☏011 268 5515; www.hostelbongo.com; Terazije 36; dm/d with shared bathroom 1800/4800RSD; ❄@⑲) Guests at the modern, brightly painted and meticulously maintained Bongo can take their pick: plunge into the tons of attractions, bars and restaurants nearby, or hide from it all in the hostel's sweet garden terrace. Fantastic staff with oodles of hostelling experience.

★ Yugodom
GUESTHOUSE €€

(☏065 984 6366; www.yugodom.com; Strahinjica Bana 80; d/ste 4200/8400RSD; ❄⑲) This evocative two-room guesthouse offers more than a comfortable bed; it's also a vessel for time travel. Billed as a 'stayover museum', Yugodom (*dom* means 'house' in Serbian) is decked out with gorgeous art and Yugoslavian mid-century modern furnishings from the Tito era (though you'll find all the mod cons and self-catering facilities you need disguised among the retro trappings).

The location is as impeccable as the surrounds; on a newly pedestrianised street smack in the middle of Dorćol and across the road from **Bajloni Market** (cnr Cetinjska & Džordža Vašingtona; ⊘6am-7pm).

★ Savamala Bed & Breakfast
B&B €€

(☏011 406 0264; www.savamalahotel.rs; Kraljevića Marka 6, Savamala; s/d/tr from 6000/7200/9000RSD; ❄⑲) This brilliant B&B is all early-1900s charm out the front, and nouveau-Savamala graffiti-murals out the back. As hip as you'd expect from its location in Belgrade's coolest quarter, the digs here are furnished with a mix of period furniture and the work of up-and-coming Belgrade designers. It's close to the city's main sights, and there are tons of happening bars and restaurants within staggering distance.

Smokvica Bed & Breakfast
B&B €€

(☏069 446 4002; www.smokvica.rs; Gospodar Jovanova 45, Dorćol; d 7700RSD; ❄⑲) Smokvica's shabby-chic cafe and accommodation empire has expanded to Dorćol, where the line-up's second B&B occupies a grand whitewashed 19th-century mansion. Spacious rooms with vaulted ceilings and hardwood floors are decked out in trademark sky blue, with supersonic showers. The designer cafe at this location is also a charming retreat just steps from the six rooms.

★ Mama Shelter
BOUTIQUE HOTEL **€€€**

(☑011 333 3000; www.mamashelter.com/en/belgrade; Kneza Mihaila 54a; d from 8300RSD; P❋@🛜) Belgrade is just the 7th city worldwide to receive one of Philippe Starck's whimsical designer Mama Shelter hotels – the city's hottest – this one sitting on prime real estate at the Belgrade Fortress end of Kneza Mihaila, on the top floor of the glitzy Rajićeva Shopping Centre.

Rooms are funky and fun, but the real coup here is the 1000-sq-metre rooftop restaurant, bar and hang-space, complete with arcade games, outdoor fire pit, stupendous views and oodles of beautiful people – one of the few places in Belgrade to get an aerial perspective with a cocktail in hand. Go at sunset!

Hotel Moskva
HISTORIC HOTEL **€€€**

(Hotel Moscow; ☑011 364 2000; www.hotel moskva.rs; Terazije 20; s/d/ste from 10,500/12,800/24,700RSD; P❋@🛜) Art-nouveau icon and proud symbol of the best of Belgrade, the majestic 123-room Moskva has been wowing guests – including Albert Einstein, Indira Gandhi and Alfred Hitchcock – since 1906. Laden with ye olde glamour, this is the place to write your memoirs at a big old desk.

✖ Eating

★ Pekara Trpković
BAKERY **€**

(www.facebook.com/pekaratrpkovic; Nemanjina 32; burek per 100g 32-55RSD; ⊙6am-8.30pm Mon-Sat, to 4pm Sun) The fact that this family business has existed for over a century in Belgrade's competitive bakery market is quite an achievement. The Serbian tradition of making pastries has reached its peak in this case. Trpković delicacies and sandwiches are extremely popular so you can often see queues, especially for breakfast and lunch break.

Sometimes there are two queues – one just for *burek* (heavenly filo pastries stuffed with veal, cheese, spinach etc).

★ Ribnjak
SERBIAN **€€**

(☑011 331 8894; Jojkićev Dunavac bb; mains 400-1000RSD, fish per kg 600-2900RSD; ⊙noon-10pm) An unremarkable houseboat moored far enough from the city centre that few people know about it (or ever see it!), this undeniably simple *restoran* (restaurant) does remarkable, extra effort-worthy things with river fish.

The speciality is rarely seen fish *mućkalica* (spicy stew) – order that as an appetiser (after the fish soup!) and follow with a perfectly griddle-seared whole zander (*grillovani smuđ*) and sides of Dalmatian-style potato and mangel (chard). No English menu. It's a 600RSD or so CarGo ride from Trg Republike.

Mayka
VEGETARIAN **€€**

(☑011 328 8401; www.facebook.com/maykabeograd/; Kosančićev venac 2; mains 785-1050RSD; ⊙11am-midnight; 🛜🌱) Among Belgrade's slim offerings for vegetarians, here's a gem right in the city centre. Mayka serves up worldly vegetarian specialities in a Serbian way. Listen to the waiter's recommendations and don't miss dishes featuring their house-made seitan or stir-fried veggies with smoked sunflower cheese. Indian and Thai curries go down a treat as well, especially on the rustic front patio.

The interior evokes a bar atmosphere and, while enjoying world-class slow food, you can come across live jazz and piano acts too.

★ Iris New Balkan Cuisine
SERBIAN **€€€**

(☑064 129 6377; www.newbalkancuisine.com/iris; Sarajevska 54; tasting menus veg/non-veg 3000-3700RSD, with wine 5600/6300RSD; ⊙12.30-10pm Wed-Sat; 🛜🌱) 🌿 Belgrade's best foodie bang for the buck is this newcomer clandestinely occupying a 1st-floor apartment south of the old train station. Courses from the tasting menu are based around a single ingredient – whatever head chef Vanja Puškar has procured from organic farmers that week – and taken to new heights without leaving behind their Serbian origins.

Memorable examples when we dined: a stunning Buša beef carpaccio with yoghurt, olive oil and fried sourdough; a perfectly crisp pork schnitzel doused in green pea and mint cream with sage-perfumed zucchini foam; and a delightful fig-stuffed chicken roulade on triple-fried potato, with salty caramel and hop-orange foam. Natural wines often accompany the eight-course menus. Welcome to the New Balkans!

★ Šaran
SEAFOOD **€€€**

(☑011 261 8235; www.saran.co.rs; Kej Oslobođenja 53, Zemun; mains 1050-2090RSD; ⊙noon-11pm Sun & Mon, to 1am Tue-Sat; 🛜) Šaran (meaning 'carp') is rightfully renowned as Zemun's best quayside fish restaurant for its exceptional fish dishes, professional service and welcoming atmosphere. Freshwater river fish dishes like Smederevo-style pike (grilled, then baked under an astonishingly flavourful smothering of tomatoes, garlic, onions and red peppers) and pricier whole saltwater options (6100RSD to 8400RSD) are absolute standouts.

Live Balkan music most nights.

Bela Reka   SERBIAN €€€
(☑ 11 655 5098; www.restoranbelareka.rs; Tošin bunar 79, Novi Beograd; mains 630-1890RSD; 🐾) One of Belgrade's best new restaurants, Bela Reka is modern and sophisticated, but fiercely dedicated to the traditional craft of Serbian cuisine, and is well worth a trek to Novi Beograd, 5.5km west of Brankov Most. Gorgeously presented, meat-leaning dishes are some of Belgrade's best: perfectly spiced, Pirot-style *uštipci* (meatballs), walnut-and-hazelnut-crusted monastery chicken and *homolje* (sausage stuffed with cheese) are outstanding.

An award-winning baker fires up traditional *somun* flatbread in a clay oven and the goat's cheese comes direct from their own farm (you can pick some up in their artisan market). But wait, dessert! Go for *ledene kocke*, a dead-simple, dead-delicious sponge cake resurrected from Yugoslavian recipe books.

Ambar   BALKAN €€€
(☑ 011 328 6637; www.ambarrestaurant.com; Karađorđeva 2-4, Beton Hala; small plates 310-1150RSD; ⊙ 10am-2am; 🐾) Upmarket, innovative small-plate takes on Balkan cuisine are the go to at this chic spot – the best of a handful of trendy options overlooking the river. Everything from *ajvar* to mixed grills has been given a contemporary spin; even the *pljeskavica* (bunless hamburger) gets the five-star treatment.

Put your meal choices in the hands of the excellent and well-versed staff and you won't be disappointed, right down to the Serbian wines. You can try everything for 2990RSD.

🍸 Drinking & Nightlife

★ Restoran Tabor   TAVERNA
(☑ 011 241 2464; www.restorantabor.com; Bulevar Kralja Aleksandra 348; ⊙ noon-2am Mon-Sat; 🐾) If you want an authentic Serbian Friday-night experience, this wildly popular (reserve several days ahead) *kafana* (tavern) in Zvezdara has it all: captivating folk music, great traditional food (don't skip the *mak pita* – baklava-like dessert made with poppy seeds), sexy lighting and a room full of good-time-seeking locals (and celebs) who will eventually be dancing on the tables!

It's 5.5km west of Knez Mihailova (a 300RSD or so CarGo ride from Savamala).

★ Klub 20/44   RIVER BARGE
(www.facebook.com/klub2044; Ušće bb; ⊙ 5pm-2am Sun, Tue & Wed, to 4am Thu, to 5am Fri & Sat; 🐾) Retro, run-down and loads of fun, this alternative *splav* (river-barge nightclub) is named for Belgrade's map co-ordinates. Open year-round, it has become an electronica reference for top European DJs – despite its shabby appearance. Swimming up from the back might be your easiest way in!

★ Bar Central   COCKTAIL BAR
(www.facebook.com/BarCentral011; Kralja Petra 59; ⊙ 9am-midnight Sun-Thu, to 1am Fri & Sat; 🐾) This is the HQ of Serbia's Association of Bartenders, a fact made evident after one sip of any of the sublime cocktails (515RSD to 1165RSD) on offer. With an interior as polished as a bottle flip-pour, this ain't the place for tacky tikis and those little umbrellas – this is serious mixology territory.

Krafter   CRAFT BEER
(www.facebook.com/kftbeerbar; Strahinjića Bana 44, Dorćol; ⊙ 9am-midnight Mon-Thu, to 1pm Fri & Sat, 10am-midnight Sun; 🐾) Hopheads seeking local salvation should settle in at this intimate, industrial-chic craft beer bar featuring 14 rotating offerings on draught (pints 295RSD to 385RSD) – always Serbian – along with a small international selection in bottles. The menu is heavily weighted towards hoppy pale and India pale ales, and the lovely English-speaking staff are passionate about their suds devotion.

Vinoteka   WINE BAR
(www.facebook.com/vinotekasavamala; Karađorđeva 57, Savamala; ⊙ 11am-midnight Sun-Thu, to 1am Fri & Sat; 🐾) If you want to take a deep dive into Serbian wine, this cosy Savamala wine bar boasts 40 domestic wines by the glass (290RSD to 450RSD) and nearly 300 ex-Yugoslavian regional wines by the bottle (it's a bottle shop by day). It's not a wild place but rather perfect for a bit of juice and a conversation in a more intimate setting.

☆ Entertainment

★ KC Grad   CULTURAL CENTRE
(www.gradbeograd.eu; Braće Krsmanović 4, Savamala; ⊙ noon-1am Mon-Thu, to 5.30am Fri & Sat, 2pm-midnight Sun; 🐾) A Savamala stalwart (it's been running since 2009), this wonderful warehouse space promotes local creativi-

ty with workshops, exhibitions, a restaurant and nightly music events.

Bitef Art Cafe   LIVE MUSIC
(www.bitefartcafe.rs; Mitropolita Petra 8; ⊙9am-4am; 🛜) There's something for everyone at this delightful hotchpotch of a cafe-club. Funk, soul and jazz get a good airing, as do rock, world and classical music. In summer, Bitef moves their stage to Belgrade Fortress.

National Theatre   THEATRE
(🗹 011 262 0946; www.narodnopozoriste.rs; Fran-cuska 3; ⊙ box office 11am-3pm & 5pm-performance time) This glorious 1869 building hosts operas, dramas and ballets during autumn, winter and spring.

🔒 Shopping

⭐ **Makadam**   ARTS & CRAFTS
(www.makadam.rs; Kosančićev venac 20; ⊙noon-8pm Tue-Sun; 🛜) Make your way to Makadam across the original Turkish cobblestones of Kosančićev venac, a lovely slice of old Belgrade. The concept store only sells hand-made products from across Serbia. Shoppers will find an impressive selection of carefully chosen items by local craftspeople and designers, with the accent on the use of natural and traditional materials.

The bistro (9am to midnight daily) serves local wines, beers and more. The sidewalk seating here – in fact along a large swath of Kosančićev venac – draws a lively, in-the-know happy hour crowd.

Belgrade
Design District   FASHION & ACCESSORIES
(Čumićevo Sokače; www.belgradedesigndistrict.blogspot.com; Čumićeva 2; ⊙noon-8pm Mon-Fri, to 5pm Sat) Once Belgrade's first mall and later abandoned, this revitalised complex is now home to more than 30 boutiques showcasing up-and-coming local fashionistas, jewellers, artists and designers. It's a fabulous place to pick up original pieces you won't find anywhere else. It's in the middle of the city hidden behind buildings; follow the marked passage from Nušićeva by Trg Terazije.

ℹ️ Information

Tourist Organisation of Belgrade Hosts tourist information centres at **Nikola Tesla Airport** (Turistički informativni centri; 🗹 011 209 7828; www.tob.rs; Aerodrom Beograd 59, Belgrade Nikola Tesla Airport; ⊙9am-9.30pm), **Knez Mihailova** (Turistički informativni centri; 🗹 011 263 5622; www.tob.rs; Knez Mihailova 56, Belgrade City Library; ⊙9am-8pm) and the

now de-commissioned **Central Train Station** (Turistički informativni centri; 🗹 011 361 2732; www.tob.rs; Central Train Station; ⊙9am-2pm Mon-Sat).

National Tourism Organisation of Serbia Operates the information centre at **Trg Republike** (Tourist information Centre; 🗹 011 328 2712; www.serbia.travel; Trg Republike 5; ⊙10am-9pm Mon-Fri, to 6pm Sun) and **Mt Avala** (🗹 011 390 8517; www.serbia.travel; Mt Avala Tower; ⊙9am-8pm Mar-Sep, to 5pm Oct-Feb). More info points are planned.

ℹ️ Getting There & Away

AIR
Belgrade Nikola Tesla Airport (🗹 011 209 4444; www.beg.aero; Aerodrom Beograd 59) is 18km from Belgrade. Air Serbia (www.airserbia.com) is Serbia's domestic carrier.

BUS
➥ Belgrade's **bus station** (Glavna Beogradska autobuska stanica; 🗹 011 263 6299; Železnička 4) is near the eastern banks of the Sava River; BAS (www.bas.rs) and Lasta (www.lasta.rs) are the two main carriers.

➥ Sample international routes include Sarajevo (2510RSD, eight hours, six daily), Ljubljana (4770RSD, 7½ hours, three daily) and Pristina (2020RSD, seven hours, five daily). For Vienna (2470RSD to 4570RSD, nine hours, three daily) and some other international destinations, tickets must be purchased at **Basturist** (🗹 011 263 8982; www.basturist.com; Železnička 4) at the eastern end of the station.

➥ Frequent domestic services include Subotica (1270RSD to 1440RSD, three hours, nine daily), Novi Sad (750RSD, one hour, every 15 minutes), Niš (1280RSD, three hours, every 30 minutes) and Novi Pazar (1470RSD, three hours, every 45 minutes).

TRAIN
➥ Most local and international trains depart from **Belgrade Centar** (Prokop Station; 🗹 011 397 5533; www.srbvoz.rs; Prokupačka), while trains for Bar (Montenegro), Sofia (Bulgaria) and Thessaloniki (Greece) leave from **Topčider Station** (🗹 011 360 2899; www.srbvoz.rs; Topčiderska, Topčider), south of the city centre. See www.serbianrailways.com for updates.

➥ Frequent trains go to Novi Sad (from 388RSD, 1½ hours, eight daily), Subotica (from 660RSD, three hours, six daily) and Niš (from 884RSD, four hours, six daily). International destinations include Bar (from 2833RSD, 11½ hours, 9.05pm), Budapest (from 1770RSD, eight hours, three daily), Sofia (from 2821RSD, 12 hours, 9.06am), Thessaloniki (from 4400RSD, 15 hours, 6.21pm) and Zagreb (from 2243RSD, seven hours, 10.20am and 9.19pm).

SERBIA BELGRADE

ℹ Getting Around

TO/FROM THE AIRPORT

Local bus 72 (Jug Bogdanova, Zeleni Venac; 89RSD to 150RSD, half-hourly, 4.50am to midnight from airport, 4am to 11.40pm from town) connects the airport with Zeleni Venac (note the stop where passengers alight *from* the airport is different from the stop going *to* the airport; the cheapest tickets must be purchased from news stands. The **A1 minibus** (Kralja Milutina, Trg Slavija) also runs between the airport and the central Trg Slavija (300RSD, 5am to 3.50am from airport, 4.20am to 3.20am from the square).

Don't get swallowed up by the airport taxi shark pit. Head to the taxi information desk (near the baggage claim area); they'll give you a taxi receipt with the name of your destination and the fare price (fixed according to six zones). A taxi from the airport to central Belgrade (Zone 2) is 1800RSD (a CarGo ride-share is about 500RSD less).

PUBLIC TRANSPORT

➤ **GSP Belgrade** (www.gsp.rs) runs the city's trams, trolleybuses and buses. Rechargeable **BusPlus** (www2.busplus.rs) smart cards can be bought (250RSD) and topped up (89RSD per ticket) at kiosks across the city; tickets are 150RSD if you buy from the driver. Fares are good for 90 minutes. Unlimited paper BusPlus passes relevant to tourists are available for one, three and five days for 250RSD, 700RSD and 1000RSD, respectively.

➤ Tram 2 connects Belgrade Fortress with Trg Slavija and the bus stations.

➤ Belgrade Centar (p401) train station is connected by **bus 36** (Prokupačka) with Trg Slavija and the bus stations, and by trolleybus 40 or 41 with the city centre.

➤ Zemun is a 45-minute walk from central Belgrade (across Brankov Most, along Nikole Tesle and the Kej Oslobođenja waterside walkway). Alternatively, take bus 15 or 84 from Zeleni Venac market.

TAXI

➤ Move away from obvious taxi traps and flag down a distinctly labelled cruising cab, or get a local to call you one. Flag fall is 170RSD; reputable cabs should charge about 65RSD per kilometre between 6am and 10pm Monday to Friday, 85RSD between 10pm and 6am, and weekends and holidays. Make absolutely sure the meter is turned on.

➤ Order a **Naxis Taxi** (☑ 011 19084; www.naxis.rs) by phone, text, Twitter or mobile app. Rates are fixed, drivers speak English and major credit cards are accepted. You can also rent a driver for a day trip out of the city. CarGo (www.appcargo.net) is a popular ride-share app.

VOJVODINA ВОЈВОДИНА

Novi Sad   Нови Сад

☑ 021 / POP 341,600

Novi Sad is a chipper town with all the spoils and none of the stress of the big smoke. Locals sprawl in pretty parks and outdoor cafes, and laneway bars pack out nightly. The looming Petrovaradin Fortress keeps a stern eye on proceedings, loosening its tie each July to host Serbia's largest music festival. You can walk to all of Novi Sad's attractions from the happening pedestrian thoroughfare, Zmaj Jovina, which stretches from the main square (Trg Slobode) to Dunavska.

Novi Sad isn't nicknamed the 'Athens of Serbia' for nothing: its history as a vibrant, creative city continues today in its established galleries, alternative music scene and a vibe that's generally more liberal than that of other Serbian cities. Novi Sad is 2019's European Youth Capital, and in 2021, it will become the first non-EU city to spend a year with the prestigious title of European Capital of Culture.

⊙ Sights

★**Petrovaradin Fortress**   FORTRESS
(Petrovaradinska Tvrdjava; Beogradska; ⊙ 24hr) Towering over the river on a 40m-high volcanic slab, this mighty citadel, considered Europe's second-biggest fortress (and one of its best preserved), is aptly nicknamed 'Gibraltar on the Danube'. Constructed using slave labour between 1692 and 1780, its dungeons have held notable prisoners including Karađorđe (leader of the first Serbian uprising against the Turks and founder of a royal dynasty) and Yugoslav president Tito.

Have a good gawk at the iconic clock tower: the size of the minute and hour hands are reversed so far-flung fisherfolk can tell the time. Within the citadel walls, a **museum** (Muzej Grada Novog Sada; www.museumns.rs; 300RSD; ⊙ 9am-5pm Tue-Sun) offers insight into the site's history; it can also arrange tours (in English; 3500RSD) of Petrovaradin's 16km of creepy, but cool, unlit underground tunnels *(katakombe)*. Petrovaradin hosts Novi Sad's wildly popular EXIT Festival each July.

★**Gallery of Matica Srpska**   MUSEUM
(www.galerijamaticesrpske.rs; Trg Galerija 1; 100RSD; ⊙ 10am-8pm Tue-Thu, to 10pm Fri, to 6pm Sat & Sun) First established in Pest (part of modern Budapest) in 1826 and moved to

WORTH A TRIP

SUBOTICA & NOVI PAZAR

Sugar-spun art nouveau marvels, a laid-back populace and a sprinkling of Serbian and Hungarian flavours make Subotica (10km from the Hungarian border) a worthy day trip or stopover. Once an important hub of the Austro-Hungarian Empire, the town attracted some of the region's most influential architects and artists; their excellently preserved handiwork is today the town's biggest drawcard. The unmissable eye candy includes the 1904 **Raichle Palace**, which now houses a modern **art gallery** (Savremena galerija Subotica; www.sgsu.org.rs; Park Ferenca Rajhla 5; adult/child 100/50RSD; ⊙8am-7pm Mon-Fri, 9am-1pm Sat); the 1910 **City Hall** (Gradska kuća; ☑024 555 128; Trg Slobode; tour with/without tower 300/150RSD; ⊙tours noon Tue-Sat), with a soaring, 76m-high tower; and the 1902 **Synagogue** (Sinagoga; www.en.josu.rs; Trg Sinagoge 2; adult/child 250RSD/free; ⊙10am-6pm Tue-Fri, to 2pm Sat & Sun) that was restored to its full glory in 2018.

Down south near the Montenegrin border, Novi Pazar is the cultural centre of the Raška (Sandžak) region, with a large Muslim population. Turkish coffee, cuisine and customs abound, yet some of the most sacred Orthodox sights are in the vicinity: this was the heartland of the Serbian medieval state. The 16th-century **Altun-Alem Mosque** (Altun-Alem džamija; 1.maja 79) is one of Serbia's oldest surviving Islamic buildings, while the small 9th-century **Church of St Peter** (Petrova crkva; ☑060 059 8401; foreigners €2; ⊙8am-3pm), 3km from town, with a fascinating, photogenic cemetery, is the oldest intact church in the country. Around 14km west of town is the 13th-century, Unesco-listed **Sopoćani Monastery** (Manastir Sopoćani; foreigners €2; ⊙8am-7pm); its frescoes are sublime examples of medieval art.

Novi Sad in 1864, this is one of Serbia's most important and long-standing cultural institutions. It's not a mere gallery but rather a national treasure, with three floors covering priceless Serbian artworks from the 18th, 19th and 20th centuries in styles ranging from Byzantine to modernist, with countless icons, portraits, landscapes and graphic art (and more) in between.

Štrand BEACH
(50RSD; ⊙8am-7pm) One of Europe's best by-the-Danube beaches, this 700m-long stretch morphs into a city of its own come summertime, with bars, stalls and all manner of recreational diversions attracting thousands of sun- and fun-seekers from across the globe. It's also the ultimate Novi Sad party venue, hosting everything from local punk gigs to EXIT raves.

It's great for kids (watch them by the water: the currents here are strong), with playgrounds, trampolines and dozens of ice-cream and fast-food stalls.

Museum of Vojvodina MUSEUM
(Muzej Vojvodine; www.muzejvojvodine.org.rs; Dunavska 35-7; 200RSD; ⊙9am-7pm Tue-Fri, 10am-6pm Sat & Sun) This worthwhile museum houses historical, archaeological and ethnological exhibits. The main building covers Vojvodinian history from Palaeolithic times to the late 19th century. Nearby, at building 37, which

also houses the **Museum of Contemporary Art Vojvodina** (☑021 526 634; www.msuv.org; Dunavska 37; ⊙10am-6pm Tue-Thu, Sat & Sun, to 8pm Fri) **FREE**, the story continues to 1945 with harrowing emphasis on WWI and WWII. The highlights include three gold-plated Roman helmets from the 4th century, excavated in Srem region not far from Novi Sad, and one of the city's first bicycles, dating from 1880.

★ Festivals & Events

EXIT Festival MUSIC
(www.exitfest.org; ⊙Jul) The Petrovaradin Fortress is stormed by thousands of revellers each July during this epic festival. The first edition, in 2000, lasted 100 days and galvanised a generation of young Serbs against the Milošević regime. The festival has since been attended by the eclectic likes of Prodigy, Gogol Bordello and Motörhead...plus about 200,000 merrymakers from around the world each year.

🛏 Sleeping

★ **Varad Inn** HOSTEL €
(☑021 431 400; www.varadinn.com; Štrosmajerova 16, Petrovaradin; dm/d/q from 1230/3960/4820RSD; ❋🐾) Sitting in the shadow of Petrovaradin Fortress, this excellent budget option is housed in a gorgeous yellow baroque-style building constructed in 1714.

Novi Sad

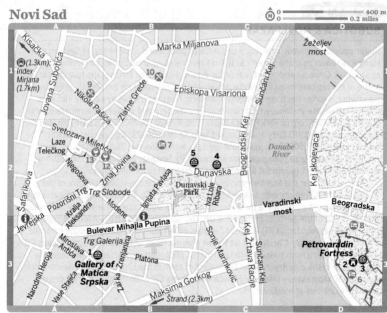

Completely renovated but making beautiful use of salvaged historical bits and bobs, the Varad Inn (get it?) has beautiful feel-at-home rooms (all with their own bathrooms, lockers and towels), a lovely cafe and garden, and communal kitchen.

★**Narator** APARTMENT €€
(☏ 060 676 7886; www.en.narator.rs; Dunavska 17 / Trg Republike 16; s/d apt from 3600/4800RSD; ❄ 🛜) The super-central designer digs at Narator do indeed tell a story; four of them, in fact, one for every themed, individually decorated apartment. With names like 'Chambermaid from Eden', 'The Bookworm' and 'Captain Honeymoon', each room's tale unfolds via a series of exquisite, original naive-style portraits scattered across the walls. All apartments are self-contained.

It's a bit tricky to find. Enter to the right of Laboratorija Medical Praxis from Dunavska and between Aldo and Jeodie's from Trg Republike.

Leopold I LUXURY HOTEL €€€
(☏ 021 488 7878; www.leopoldns.com; Petrovaradin Fortress; 1st floor r/ste incl breakfast from 16,800/24,000RSD, 2nd floor r/ste incl breakfast from 10,800/16,800RSD; 🅿 ❄ 🛜) This rock-top, 59-room hotel in the Petrovaradin complex is split into two sections, with two different names: the 1st floor, **Leopold I**, is given over to indulgent baroque-style digs while the 2nd floor, **Garni Hotel Leopold I**, comprises mod-

ern, (slightly) economical rooms. The location is unbeatable, and breakfast at the terrace restaurant is a princely way to start the day.

Eating

★ Toster Bar
BURGERS €

(www.tosterbar.rs; Zmaj Jovina 24; burgers 320-860RSD; ⊙10am-11pm Mon-Thu, to 1am Fri & Sat, 11am-11pm Sun; 🖥) There are likely better Serbian-style *pljeskavica* (hamburgers) in Novi Sad, but there certainly aren't better American-style burgers, and the beauty of wildly popular Toster is that it does both! Tucked away in a jam-packed *pasaž* (passage), it's a Croatian-owned, cash-only joint doing fat, juicy and spicy (Carolina Reaper spicy!) burgers along with a wise devotion to craft beer.

Index Mirjana
FAST FOOD €

(Braće Popović 8; sandwiches 200-290RSD; ⊙7am-11pm Sun-Thu, to midnight Fri & Sat) The consensus among Novosadjani is that this hole-in-the-wall of a sandwich shop produces the best version of the locally famous Index sandwich – an indulgent, sauce-laden spin on a ham-and-cheese sandwich – in the friendliest of manners (many folks, both Serbian and foreigners, complain about nasty customer service at many of the Novi Sad sandwich shops).

★ Fish i Zeleniš
MEDITERRANEAN €€

(Fish and Greens; ☎021 452 002; www.fishizelenis.com; Skerlićeva 2; mains 696-2900RSD; ⊙noon-11pm; 🖥🗷) This character-filled, snug little nook serves up the finest vegetarian and pescatarian meals in northern Serbia. Organic, locally sourced ingredients? Ambient? Ineffably delicious? Tick, tick, tick. Check the daily specials or spring for one of their excellently prepared Mediterranean staples, guided by the affable staff.

Project 72
SERBIAN €€

(☎021 657 2720; www.wineanddeli.rs; Kosovska 15; small plates 242-898RSD, mains 725-1692RSD; ⊙9am-11pm Mon-Thu, to 1am Fri & Sat; 🖥) 🗷 This smart bistro with lovely sidewalk seating is brought to Novi Sad by the same owners as the excellent Fish i Zeleniš, but here the concentration is on creative tapas and heartier, Mediterranean/Serbian meat dishes, which pair wonderfully with the deep wine list featuring 21 Serbian wines by the glass.

Standout dishes include oxtail with celery purée and sweet *bermet* dessert wine; wild boar with orange and red fruits; and lamb with blanched broccoli. At least 80% of the produce used is organic.

🍷 Drinking & Nightlife

Beer Store
CRAFT BEER

(www.beerstore.rs; Svetozara Miletića 17; ⊙4pm-midnight Sun-Thu, to 1am Fri & Sat; 🖥) Don't let the name confuse you, Novi Sad's top craft beer destination features 20 mostly Serbian brews on draught, along with another 180 or so in bottles. Expect several pale ales and IPAs from Novi Sad's finest, 3Bir, which go down far too easily on the outdoor patio along this atmospheric pedestrianised street.

PUBeraj
BAR

(www.facebook.com/puberajcafee; Mite Ružića; ⊙8am-11pm Mon-Thu, to 1am Fri & Sat, noon-11pm Sun; 🖥) The hippest and certainly the most local of the smattering of bars around Laze Telečkog, PUBeraj is the brainchild of local Andrija Nikitović, who figured a stylish cocktail bar sandwiched between a barbershop and salon was just what Novi Sad needed. It features at least 30 whiskeys, and hosts DJs and live music several times per week.

ℹ Information

The Tourist Organisation of the City of Novi Sad operates two tourist information centres; one at **Jevrejska** (Turistički info centri; ☎021 661 7343; www.novisad.travel; Jevrejska 10; ⊙7.30am-5pm Mon-Fri, 10am-3pm Sat) on the way to the main bus and railway stations; and on **Bulevar Mihajla Pupina** (Turistički info centri; ☎021 421 811; www.novisad.travel; Bul Mihajla Pupina 9; ⊙7.30am-5pm Mon-Fri, 10am-5pm Sat) near Petrovaradin Fortress, Belgrade Quay and the Danube.

ℹ Getting There & Away

The **bus station** (Međumesna autobuska stanica Novi Sad; ☎021 444 022; Bul Jaše Tomića 6) has regular departures to Belgrade (700RSD, one hour, every 10 to 30 minutes) and Subotica (790RSD, 1¾ hours). There are a dozen or so buses to Niš (1780RSD, 5½ hours). Two buses go daily to Budapest (3130RSD, 5¾ hours, 9.15am and 10.15pm).

Frequent trains leave the **train station** (Železnička stanica Novi Sad; ☎021 420 700; www.srbvoz.rs; Bul Jaše Tomića 4), next door to the bus station, for Belgrade (400RSD, 1¾ hours) and Subotica (490RSD, 2½ hours). At least three trains go daily to Budapest (1500RSD, 6½ hours, 9.26am, 1.17pm and 11.30pm).

ℹ Getting Around

From the Novi Sad train station, city bus 4B (65RSD) will take you to the town centre.

Crveni i Red Taxi (www.crvenitaxi.co.rs/aplik acija) is the most reliable taxi app for Novi Sad.

SOUTH SERBIA
ЈУЖНА СРБИЈА

Niš　　　　　　　　Ниш

🖉 018 / POP 183,000

Serbia's third-largest metropolis is a lively city of curious contrasts, where Roma in horse-drawn carriages trot alongside new cars, and posh cocktails are sipped in antiquated alleyways. It's a buzzy kind of place, with a high number of university students, packed-out laneway bars, a happening live-music scene, and pop-up markets and funfairs come summertime.

Niš was settled in pre-Roman times, but hit its peak during the years of the Empire. Constantine the Great (AD 280–337) was born here, as were two other Roman emperors, Constantius III and Justin I. Turkish rule lasted from 1386 until 1877, despite several Serb revolts; Ćele Kula (Tower of Skulls) and Niš Fortress are reminders of Ottoman dominion. Niš also had it rough during WWII; the Nazis built one of Serbia's most notorious concentration camps here.

◉ Sights

Mediana　　　　　　　　　RUINS
(Bul Cara Konstantina; 200RSD; ⊘9am-7pm Tue-Sun) Mediana is what remains of Constantine the Great's luxurious 4th-century Roman palace. The recently unveiled 1000 sq metres of gorgeous mosaics are the highlight here; they were hidden from public view until protective renovations were completed in 2016. Digging has revealed a palace, a forum, a church and an expansive grain-storage area. The ruins were closed until 2019 for more renovations. Mediana is on the eastern outskirts of Niš and a short walk from Ćele Kula.

Ćele Kula　　　　　　　　MONUMENT
(Tower of Skulls; Bul Zoran Đinđić; 200RSD, with Red Cross Concentration Camp & Archaeological Hall 300RSD; ⊘9am-7pm Tue-Sun) With Serbian defeat imminent at the 1809 Battle of Čegar, the Duke of Resava kamikazed towards the Turkish defences, firing at their gunpowder stores, killing himself, 4000 of his men and 10,000 Turks. The Turks triumphed regardless, and to deter future acts of rebellion, they beheaded, scalped and embedded the skulls of the dead Serbs in this tower. Only 58 of the initial 952 skulls remain. Contrary to Turkish intention, the tower serves as proud testament to Serbian resistance.

Catch bus 1 across the street from tourist information on Vožda Karađorđa (60RSD).

Red Cross Concentration Camp　　MUSEUM
(Crveni Krst; Bul 12 Februar; 200RSD, with Archaeological Hall & Ćele Kula 300RSD; ⊘9am-7pm Tue-Sun) One of the best-preserved Nazi camps in Europe, the deceptively named Red Cross (named after the adjacent train station) held about 30,000 Serbs, Roma, Jews and Partisans during the German occupation of Serbia (1941–45). Harrowing displays tell their stories, and those of the prisoners who attempted to flee in the biggest-ever breakout from a concentration camp. This was a transit camp so few were killed on the premises – they were taken to **Bubanj** (Spomen park Bubanj; Vojvode Putnika; ⊘24hr), or on to Auschwitz, Dachau etc.

The English-speaking staff are happy to provide translations and explain the exhibits in depth; and the fact that you might have it all to yourself makes it all the more distressing. The camp is a short walk north of the Niš bus station.

🎊 Festivals & Events

Nišville International Jazz Festival　　MUSIC
(www.nisville.com; Niš Fortress; from 3550RSD; ⊘Aug) This jazz festival, held at Niš Fortress, attracts big-name musos from Serbia and around the world.

🛏 Sleeping

Aurora Hostel　　　　　　HOSTEL €
(🖉063 109 5820; www.aurorahostel.rs; Dr Petra Vučinića 16; dm/r from 1120/4560RSD; ❋🤶) Set within a 19th-century former Turkish consulate, Aurora offers charm and comfort by the ladle-load. Though the building has been renovated, its wood-heavy interiors and hospitable host are redolent of a more gentle era. Rooms are spick and span – all with private bathrooms – and there's a good communal kitchen, and a lovely garden area for socialising.

★ArtLoft Hotel　　　BOUTIQUE HOTEL €€
(🖉018 305 800; www.artlofthotel.com; Oblačića Rada 8a/7; s/d/ste from 5612/6466/7320RSD; ❋🤶) Central and chic, this designer hotel takes its name literally, with original murals and paintings by local artists dominating every room. The modern feel extends to the professional staff, who take service to the next level by offering friendly assistance, advice and little touches including complimentary fruit and drinks. It's a short stroll from here to Trg Republike and Kopitareva.

GO WILD: TARA & ĐERDAP NATIONAL PARKS

If you need a breather from Serbia's urban destinations, two spectacular national parks provide fresh-air fun in droves. Contact **Wild Serbia** (☎063 273 852; www.wildserbia.com) for guided trips and outdoor adventures.

The sprawling **Đerdap National Park** (636 sq km) is home to the mighty Iron Gates gorge. Its formidable cliffs – some of which soar over 500m – dip and dive for 100km along the Danube on the border with Romania. The hulking **Golubac Fortress** (Tvrđava Golubački Grad; www.tvrdjavagolubackigrad.rs; Golubac; adult/child 600/120RSD; ⊙10am-7pm Tue-Sun Apr-Aug, to 6pm Sep, to 5pm Oct, to 4pm Nov-Mar) and the ancient settlement of **Lepenski Vir** (www.lepenski-vir.org; adult/child 400/250RSD; ⊙9am-8pm) are testimony to old-time tenacity. With marked paths and signposted viewpoints, Đerdap is an excellent hiking destination; the international EuroVelo 6 cycling path also runs through here. Boat tours through the gorge can be booked through **Serbian Adventures** (☎062 737 242; www.serbianadventures.com).

With forested slopes, dramatic ravines and jewel-like waterways, **Tara National Park** (220 sq km) is scenic Serbia at its best. Pressed up against Bosnia and Hercegovina, its main attraction is the Drina River canyon, the third-largest of its kind in the world. The emerald-green river offers ripper rafting; two lakes (Perućac and Zaovine) are ideal for calm-water kayaking. Nearby are the **Šargan Eight** (Šarganska osmica; ☎Mon-Fri 031 510 288; www.sarganskaosmica.rs; Mokra Gora; adult/child 600/300RSD; ⊙3 daily Jul & Aug, 2 daily Apr-Jun, Sep & Oct, daily Dec-Feb) heritage railway, a 2½-hour journey with disorienting twists and tunnels, and the hilltop mini village of **Drvengrad** (Küstendorf; ☎064 883 0213; www.mecavnik.info; Mećavnik hill, Mokra Gora; adult/child 250/100RSD; ⊙7am-7pm) built by filmmaker Emir Kusturica for his movie *Life is a Miracle*.

⭐ **Hotel Sole**   HOTEL €€
(☎018 524 555; www.hotelsole.rs; Kralja Stefana Prvovenčanog 11; s/d from 5782/6844RSD incl breakfast; P❄🐾🛜) Sitting pretty right in the heart of Niš, this refurbished hotel has modern, super-spacious rooms with boutique furnishings; ceiling murals are a very cool touch. Hotel Sole also dishes up one of the best breakfasts you'll find anywhere and the staff were the best we met in Serbia's cities. They'll even throw in laundry at no extra charge.

✗ Eating

Pekara Anton Plus   BAKERY €
(www.pekara-brankovic.com; Trg Pavla Stojkovića 17; burek 45-120RSD; ⊙6am-8pm Mon-Fri, to 4pm Sat, to 2pm Sun) Prepare to hurry up and wait for the Serbian breakfast of champions: *burek* (hearty filo pastries stuffed with veal, cheese and other tasty fillings). This slick *pekara* (bakery) does the best in Niš. Four versions are available – veal, cheese, spinach and pizza (ham, cheese and mushroom) – and the Nišlije can't get enough of them.

Kafana Galija   SERBIAN €€
(www.kafanagalija.com; Nikole Pasica 35; mains 260-1700RSD; ⊙10am-midnight Mon-Thu, to 2am Fri & Sat, 11am-7pm Sun; 🛜) The chefs here grill to thrill, with exceptional takes on classics, including spicy meat platters and a good *pljeskavica* (bunless burger). Rouse yourself from your food coma by sticking around for the rollicking live music and associated crowd carousals – the patio spills out onto bustling Kopitareva. Save room for the wet and wonderful baklava.

⭐ **Stambolijski**   SERBIAN €€€
(☎018 300 440; www.restoranstambolijski.rs; Nikole Pašića 36; mains 390-1950RSD; ⊙noon-10.30pm; 🛜) This upscale, standout New Balkan restaurant elegantly occupies the oldest preserved home in Niš (dating to 1878) and is easily the city's top dining destination. The accolades were quickly showered on Chef Saša Mišić for his modern takes on classics like *jagnjetina ispod sača* (lamb cooked in a clay pot), coupled with creative dishes like pork neck with beer and honey.

🍷 Drinking & Nightlife

Vespa Bar   BAR
(www.vespabar.com; Trg Republike; ⊙8am-midnight Mon-Thu, to 2am Fri & Sat, 9am-midnight Sun; 🛜) There are literally Vespas coming out of the woodwork at this happy, happening bar in the centre of town. Chat with the friendly 'bikies' over beer (local and international) or

something from the extensive cocktail list (195RSD to 420RSD). Ace people-watching.

Ministarstvo Beer Bar　　　　CRAFT BEER
(www.facebook.com/pg/ministarstvobeerbar; Vojvode Vuka 12; ⊗8.30am-midnight Mon-Thu, to 1.30am Fri, 10.30am-1.30am Sat, 5pm-midnight Sun; ⊗) Ministarstvo is one of Niš's go-to craft beer destinations, with 15 options on draught (mostly Serbian, a bit of mainstream German and Czech) and a gaggle more by the bottle. A fantastic soundtrack, lively patio and a fun, suds-swilling crowd make this a solid choice for hopheads who want to steer clear of more crowded areas such as Kopitareva.

ⓘ Information

Tourist Organisation of Niš runs several tourist information centres, including one within the **Niš Fortress** (Turistički info centri; ☑018 250 222; www.visitnis.com; Tvrđava; ⊗9am-8pm Tue-Fri, 9.30am-2.30pm Sat & Sun). Other convenient branches in the city centre include **Vožda Karađorđa** (Turistički info centri; ☑018 523 118; www.visitnis.com; Vožda Karađorđa 7; ⊗9am-8pm Mon-Fri, to 2pm Sat), **Obrenovićeva** (Turistički info centri; ☑018 520 207; www.visitnis.com; Obrenovićeva 38; ⊗9am-8pm Mon-Fri, to 2pm Sat) and **Dušanova** (Turistički info centri; ☑018 505 688; www.visitnis.com; Dušanova 30; ⊗8am-4pm Mon-Fri).

ⓘ Getting There & Away

The **bus station** (Autobuska stanica Niš; ☑018 255 177; www.nis-ekspres.rs; Bul 12 Februar) has frequent services to Belgrade (1118RSD, three hours, hourly) and one daily bus to Novi Pazar (1280RSD, four hours, 3.15pm). **Niš Ekspres** (www.nis-ekspres.rs) heads to Sofia, Bulgaria (1225RSD, five hours, 4.30am) and Skopje, North Macedonia (1234RSD, four hours, six daily).

From the **train station** (Železnička stanica Niš; ☑018 264 625; www.srbvoz.rs; Dimitrija Tucovića bb), there are four daily trains to Belgrade (from 900RSD, 4½ hours), one to Sofia (from 1100RSD, six hours, 2.16pm) and one to Skopje (from 900RSD, five hours, 11.19pm).

The **Niš Constantine The Great Airport** (☑018 458 3336; www.nis-airport.com; Vazduhoplovaca 24) is 4km from downtown Niš; destinations include Germany, Italy, Slovakia and Switzerland. **Bus 34B** (60RSD, 10 minutes) heads from the bus station to the airport, leaving from a stop just outside the station on Bul 12 Februar. From the airport, it's 34A.

A taxi to/from the airport to town is around 400RSD – be weary of solo taxis waiting for passengers and changing the tariff period from 'one' to far more expensive 'three' (reserved for long-distance trips out of town).

SURVIVAL GUIDE

ⓘ Directory A–Z

ACCOMMODATION

You'll find hotels and hostels in most Serbian towns. The **Serbian Youth Hostels Association** (Ferijalni Savez Beograd; ☑011 322 0762; www.hostels.rs; Makedonska 22/2, Belgrade) can help with hostel information and advice. Private rooms *(sobe)* and apartments *(apartmani)* offer good value and can be organised through tourist offices. 'Wild' camping is possible outside national parks; **Camping Association of Serbia** (www.camping.rs) lists official camping grounds. In rural areas, look out for *etno sela* (traditional village accommodation) or *salaši* (farmsteads). **Rural Tourism Serbia** (www.selo.co.rs) can organise village sleepovers.

Although accommodation prices are often quoted in euro, you must pay in dinar. City tax (130RSD to 155RSD per person per night) is levied on top of lodging bills.

LGBT+ TRAVELLERS

As evidenced by the furore over Belgrade's early pride parades (chronicled in the 2011 film *Parada*), life is not all rainbows for homosexuals in this conservative country. Discretion is highly advised. Check out www.gay-serbia.com and www.gej.rs for the latest news in the Serbian LGBT community, or to make local connections.

MONEY

ATMs are widespread and cards are accepted by established businesses. There's an exchange office *(menjačnica)* on every street corner. Exchange machines accept euros, US dollars and British pounds.

OPENING HOURS

Banks 9am to 5pm Monday to Friday, 9am to 1pm Saturday

Bars 8am to midnight (later on weekends)

Restaurants 8am to midnight or 1am

Shops 8am to 6pm or 7pm Monday to Friday, 8am to 3pm Saturday

PUBLIC HOLIDAYS

New Year 1 and 2 January

Orthodox Christmas 7 January

Statehood Day 15 and 16 February

Orthodox Easter April/May

Labour Day 1 and 2 May

Armistice Day 11 November

SAFE TRAVEL

Travelling around Serbia is generally safe for visitors who exercise the usual caution. The exceptions can be border areas, particularly the southeast Kosovo border where Serb–Albanian tensions remain. Check the situation before attempting to cross overland, and think thrice about driving there in Serbian-plated cars.

TELEPHONE

The country code is 381. To call abroad from Serbia, dial 00 followed by the country code. Press the *i* button on public phones for dialling commands in English. Long-distance calls can also be made from booths in post offices. A variety of local and international phonecards can be bought in post offices and news stands.

ⓘ Getting There & Away

AIR

Belgrade's Nikola Tesla Airport (p401) handles most international flights. The airport website has a full list of airlines servicing Serbia. In the south, Niš Constantine the Great Airport (p408) links Niš with countries including Germany, Italy, Slovakia and Switzerland.

Serbia's national carrier is **Air Serbia** (www.airserbia.com). It code-shares with airlines including Etihad, Aeroflot, Alitalia and KLM.

LAND
Border Crossings

Because Serbia does not acknowledge crossing points into Kosovo as international border crossings, it may not be possible to enter Serbia from Kosovo unless you first entered Kosovo from Serbia. If you wish to enter Serbia from Kosovo, consider taking a route that transits another nearby country. Check with your embassy for updates.

Bus

Bus services to Western Europe and Turkey are well developed. When crossing borders, officers will usually board the bus, take everyone's passports then return them after processing them; passengers wait in their seats.

Car & Motorcycle

Drivers need International Driving Permits. If you're in your own car, you'll need your vehicle registration and ownership documents and locally valid insurance (such as European Green Card vehicle insurance). Otherwise, border insurance costs about €150 for a car, €95 for a motorbike; www.registracija-vozila.rs has updated price lists. Check your hire-car insurance cover to be sure it covers Serbia.

Driving Serbian-plated cars into Kosovo is not a good idea, and is usually not permitted by rental agencies or insurers anyway.

Train

International rail connections leaving Serbia originate in Belgrade. Heading north, most call in at Novi Sad and Subotica. Heading southeast, they go via Niš. The scenic route to Bar on the Montenegrin coast passes through Užice in the southwest.

At border stops, officials will board the train to stamp your passport and check for relevant visas. For more information, visit the website of **Serbian Railways** (www.serbianrailways.com).

ⓘ Getting Around

BICYCLE

Bicycle paths are improving in larger cities. Mountain biking in summer is popular in regions including Tara National Park. Picturesque winding roads come with the downside of narrow shoulders.

The international **Euro Velo 6** (www.eurovelo.com) route runs through parts of Serbia including Novi Sad, Belgrade and Đerdap National Park.

BUS

Bus services are extensive, though outside major hubs, sporadic connections may leave you in the lurch for a few hours. In southern Serbia particularly, you may have to double back to larger towns.

Reservations are only worthwhile for international buses and during festivals. Tickets can be purchased from the station before departure or on board.

CAR & MOTORCYCLE

The **Automobile & Motorcycle Association of Serbia** (Auto-Moto Savez Srbije; ☏ 011 333 1100, roadside assist 1987; www.amss.org.rs; Ruzveltova 18, Belgrade; ◷ 8am-4pm Mon-Fri) provides roadside assistance and extensive information on its website. A great resource for drivers is the **Planplus** (www.planplus.rs) interactive online road atlas; *Intersistem Kartografija* publishes a useful road map of Serbia (1:550,000).

Several car-hire companies have offices at Nikola Tesla Airport in Belgrade. Small-car hire typically costs €25 to €45 per day. Check where you are not able to take the car. In Belgrade and other large towns you may have to purchase parking tickets from machines, kiosks or via SMS (in Serbian only).

Traffic police are everywhere and accidents are workaday. As of 2018, the BAC limit is 0.02%. You must drive with your headlights on, even in the daytime. An International Driving Permit is required.

TRAIN

Serbian Railways (www.serbianrailways.com) links Belgrade, Novi Sad, Subotica, Niš and Užice in the west; check the website for smaller stations between the cities.

Trains usually aren't as regular and reliable as buses, and can be murderously slow, but they're a fun way to meet locals and other travellers.

Slovakia

POP 5.45 MILLION

Best Places to Eat

➡ Sky Bar & Restaurant (p417)

➡ Vino & Tapas (p421)

➡ Modrá Hviezda (p417)

➡ Koliba Patria (p424)

➡ Pán Ryba (p427)

➡ Kupecká Bašta (p424)

Best Places to Stay

➡ Marrol's Boutique Hotel (p416)

➡ Penzión Sabato (p420)

➡ Penzión Slovakia (p427)

➡ Hostel Blues (p416)

➡ Hotel Cafe Razy (p420)

Why Go?

Right in the heart of Europe, Slovakia is a land of castles and mountains, occasionally punctuated by industrial sprawl. More than a quarter-century after Czechoslovakia's break-up, Slovakia has emerged as a self-assured, independent nation. Capital city Bratislava draws visitors to its resplendent old town but Slovakia shines brightest for lovers of the outdoors. Walking trails in the High Tatras wend through landscapes of unearthly beauty, with mirror-still glacier lakes backed by 2000m peaks.

Almost an alternate realm, Slovakia's less-visited east is speckled with quaint churches. Beyond eastern metropolis Košice, a boutique charmer of a city, the Tokaj wine region unfurls across thinly populated countryside.

Slovakia is small. For visitors, that can mean fortresses, hiking and beer-sloshing merriment – all in the space of a long weekend.

When to Go
Bratislava

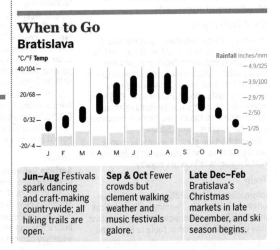

Jun–Aug Festivals spark dancing and craft-making countrywide; all hiking trails are open.	**Sep & Oct** Fewer crowds but clement walking weather and music festivals galore.	**Late Dec–Feb** Bratislava's Christmas markets in late December, and ski season begins.

Entering the Country

Bratislava and Košice are the country's main entry and exit points by air, road and rail. Poprad, with bus links to/from Zakopane in Poland and a few international flights, is in distant third place. Entering Slovakia from the EU, indeed from most of Europe, is a breeze. Lengthy customs checks make arriving from Ukraine more tedious.

Bratislava has the largest number of international flights. Well-connected Vienna International Airport is just 60km away from Bratislava, with frequent direct buses connecting the two.

Direct trains connect Bratislava to Austria, the Czech Republic, Poland, Hungary and Russia; from Košice, trains connect to the Czech Republic, Poland, Ukraine and Russia. Buses travel to Uzhhorod in Ukraine (three hours) from Košice.

ITINERARIES

Three Days

A long weekend in Bratislava (p413) is enough to experience the fine castle and old town, and take trips to forbidding Devín Castle (p419) and uplifting Danubiana Meulensteen Art Museum (p420). At nightfall, take your pick from avant-garde venues, merry beer halls and swish cocktail bars.

One Week

Spend three days experiencing Bratislava (p413), including one or two trips to castles or galleries outside the city. Press east to Poprad (p420), a base for two glorious days of hiking or skiing. Storm Spiš Castle (p424) and finish with a day or two in quirky Košice (p426).

Essential Food & Drink

Bryndzové halušky National dish of potato dumplings with sheep's cheese and diced bacon.

Guláš Known elsewhere in Central Europe as goulash, a thick shepherd's stew often rich with venison.

Kapustnica Thick sauerkraut and sausage soup, commonly with ham or mushrooms.

Lokše Potato pancakes stuffed with cabbage, mince or other fillings.

Pirohy Pillowy dumplings with a crimped edge, crammed with cheese, meat or mushrooms.

Šulance Walnut- or poppyseed-topped dumplings.

Trdelník Barbecued cone of sweet pastry sprinkled with nuts and sugar.

Vývar Chicken or beef broth often with noodles, vegetables or dumplings.

Žemlovka Bread pudding with stewed fruit, frequently pears or apples.

AT A GLANCE

Area 49,034 sq km

Capital Bratislava

Country Code ✆421

Currency euro (€)

Emergency Ambulance ✆155, fire ✆150, general emergency ✆112, police ✆158

Language Slovak

Time Central European Time (GMT/UTC plus one hour)

Visas Not required for most visitors staying less than 90 days

Sleeping Price Ranges

The following price ranges refer to a double room with bathroom.

€ less than €50

€€ €50–130

€€€ more than €130

Eating Price Ranges

The following price ranges refer to a main course.

€ less than €7

€€ €7–12

€€€ more than €12

Resources

Lonely Planet (www.lonelyplanet.com/slovakia)

Slovakia Tourist Board (http://slovakia.travel/en)

Englishman in Slovakia (www.englishmaninslovakia.co.uk)

SLOVAKIA

Slovakia Highlights

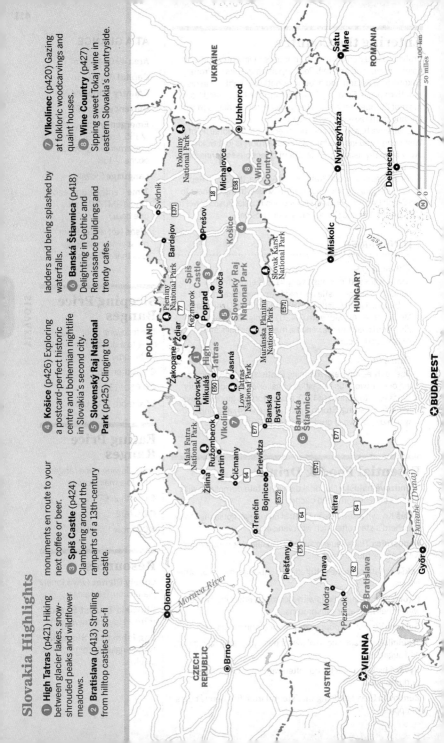

1 High Tatras (p421) Hiking between glacier lakes, snow-shrouded peaks and wildflower meadows.

2 Bratislava (p413) Strolling from hilltop castles to sci-fi monuments en route to your next coffee or beer.

3 Spiš Castle (p424) Clambering around the ramparts of a 13th-century castle.

4 Košice (p426) Exploring a postcard-perfect historic centre and bohemian nightlife in Slovakia's second city.

5 Slovenský Raj National Park (p425) Clinging to ladders and being splashed by waterfalls.

6 Banská Štiavnica (p418) Delighting in Gothic and Renaissance buildings and trendy cafes.

7 Vlkolínec (p420) Gazing at folkloric woodcarvings and quaint houses.

8 Wine Country (p427) Sipping sweet Tokaj wine in eastern Slovakia's countryside.

BRATISLAVA

📙 02 / POP 430,000

Slovakia's capital since the country's independence in 1993, Bratislava is a mosaic of illustrious history: a medieval and Gothic old town, baroque palaces commissioned by Hungarian nobles, and the crowning castle, rebuilt to Renaissance finery. Slicing through the city are stark-angled, communist-era blocks and a futurist bridge.

Recent years have added a cast of outlandish statues, boutiques and modish cafes, eagerly sought out by visiting stag party groups and day trippers from Vienna. Many arrive purely to enjoy the uproarious nightlife, from rowdy beer halls to hidden nightclubs.

Despite the march of modernism, Bratislava still has nature on its doorstep. The city banks the Danube River, only a few kilometres from the Austrian border. Rolling north are the Malé Karpaty (Small Carpathians), their lowlands draped with vineyards. Flitting between postcard-pretty, steely and gorgeously green, Bratislava never fails to intrigue.

History

First inhabited by Slavs during the 6th century, the earliest mention of Bratislava and its castle is found in AD 907. By the 12th century, Bratislava (then called Poszony in Hungarian or Pressburg in German) was a large city in greater Hungary. Many of the imposing baroque palaces you see date to the 40-year reign of Austro-Hungarian empress Maria Theresa (1740–80). From the 16th-century Turkish occupation of Budapest to the mid-1800s, the Hungarian parliament met locally and monarchs were crowned in St Martin's Cathedral.

'Bratislava' was officially born as the second city of a Czechoslovakian state after WWI. When Europe was redivided, the city was coveted by various nations – not least Austria (the population was predominantly German-speaking). US President Woodrow Wilson supported Czechoslovakian requests to have a Danube port in their newly founded country and the city was almost called Wilsonovo Mesto (Wilson City). Post-WWII, the communists razed a large part of the old town, including the synagogue, to make space for a highway.

🅾 Sights

⭐ **Bratislava Castle**   CASTLE

(Bratislavský hrad; 📙 02-2048 3110; www.bratislava-hrad.sk; grounds free, museum adult/student €8/4;

⊙ grounds 9am-1am, museum 10am-6pm Tue-Sun Apr-Oct, to 5pm Nov-Mar) Magnificently rebuilt in Renaissance style, Bratislava Castle looks as though it has been transplanted from a children's picture book. Inside is a history museum, though many chambers feel empty and underutilised. The castle's oldest original feature is the 13th-century Crown Tower; climb it for bird's-eye views. Another highlight is the late-baroque *Assumption of the Virgin Mary* (1762–3) painting by Anton Schmidt in the Music Hall. Without a ticket you can wander the manicured baroque gardens behind the castle.

Hlavné Námestie   SQUARE

The nucleus for Bratislava's history, festivals and chic cafe culture is Hlavné nám (Main Sq). There's architectural finery in almost every direction, notably the Stará Radnica (Old Town Hall), a complex of attractive 14th- and 15th-century Gothic buildings, and Palugyayov Palác, a neobaroque former palace.

⭐ **Museum of City History**   MUSEUM

(Aponiho Palace; 📙 02-5910 0847; www.muzeum. bratislava.sk; Radničná 1; adult/child €5/2.50; ⊙ 10am-5pm Tue-Fri, 11am-6pm Sat & Sun) Rove through Bratislava's past in the former town hall. First, scale the tower for a lookout over Bratislava. Then tour the exhibition rooms; loveliest of all, despite the dreary name, is the Hall of the Extended Municipal Council and the Court House, with brightly coloured ceilings, Gothic flourishes and stained glass dating to the 17th century.

Spare some time at the end for the Viticulture Museum beneath, where you can sample regional wines with a lively explanation (from €5).

Blue Church   CHURCH

(Kostol sv Alžbety; https://modrykostol.fara.sk; Bezručova 2; ⊙ 7-7.30am & 5.30-7pm Mon-Sat, 7.30am-noon & 5.30-7pm Sun) Dedicated to St Elisabeth of Hungary in 1913, the early-20th-century 'Blue Church' is a vision in sapphire and powder-blue. From its undulating arches and ceramic roof tiles to the tip of its clock tower (36.8m), it's a marvel of art nouveau design.

St Martin's Cathedral   CHURCH

(Dóm sv Martina; 📙 02-5443 1359; http://dom. fara.sk; Rudnayovo nám 1; ⊙ 9-11.30am & 1-6pm Mon-Sat, 1.30-4pm Sun May-Sep, to 4pm Mon-Sat Oct-Apr) The coronations of 19 royals have taken place within three-nave St Martin's

SLOVAKIA BRATISLAVA

Central Bratislava

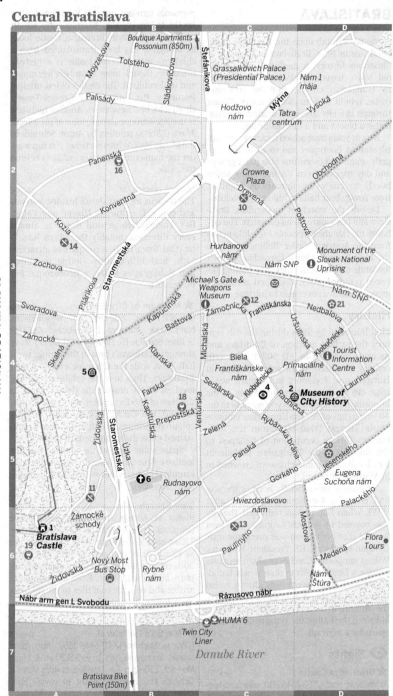

SLOVAKIA BRATISLAVA

Boutique Apartments
Possonium (850m)

Štefánikova

Grassalkovich Palace
(Presidential Palace)

Nám 1
mája

Moyzesova

Tolstého

Sládkovičova

Palisády

Hodžovo
nám

Mýtna

Vysoká

Tatra
centrum

Panenská

16

Obchodná

Konventná

Crowne
Plaza

Drevená

10

Poštová

Kozia

14

Staromestská

Piláriková

Hurbanovo
nám

Nám SNP

Monument of the
Slovak National
Uprising

Zochova

Michael's Gate &
Weapons
Museum

Nám SNP

21

Svoradova

Kapucínska

Zámočnícka

12

Františkánska

Nedbalova

Zámocká

Baštová

Uršulínska

Klobučnícka

Skalná

Klariská

Michalská

Biela

Františkánske
nám

Primaciálne
nám

Tourist
Information
Centre

5

Farská

Sedlárska

4

2

Museum of
City History

Laurinská

18

Klobučnícka

Radničná

Kapitulská

Prepoštská

Venturská

Zelená

Rybárska brána

Židovská

Staromestská

Úzka

Panská

20

Jesenského

11

Rudnayovo
nám

Gorkého

Eugena
Suchoňa nám

Palackého

6

Hviezdoslavovo
nám

Mostová

Medená

Bratislava
Castle

1

Žámocké
schody

Paulínyho

13

Flora
Tours

19

Nový Most
Bus Stop

Rybné
nám

Nám L
Štúra

Židovská

Nábr arm gen L Svobodu

Rázusovo nábr

HUMA 6

Twin City
Liner

Danube River

Bratislava Bike
Point (150m)

Central Bratislava

◎ Top Sights
1 Bratislava Castle	A6
2 Museum of City History	C4

◎ Sights
3 Blue Church	F4
4 Hlavné Námestie	C4
5 Museum of Jewish Culture	A4
6 St Martin's Cathedral	B5

🛏 Sleeping
7 Hostel Blues	F2
8 Marrol's Boutique Hotel	E6
9 Patio Hostel	F2

✖ Eating
10 Bratislavský Meštiansky Pivovar	C2
11 Modrá Hviezda	A5
12 Prašná Bašta	C3
13 Sky Bar & Restaurant	C6
14 Soupa Bistro	A3
15 Štúr	E5

◎ Drinking & Nightlife
16 Apollon Club	B2
17 Slovak Pub	E2
18 Stupavar	B4
19 Subclub	A6

◎ Entertainment
20 Historic SND	D5
21 KC Dunaj	D3

🛍 Shopping
22 Úľuv	E1

Cathedral, alluded to by the 300kg replica crown atop its spire. The interior of this 14th-century Gothic sanctuary has four chapels dedicated to saints and luminaries, a horse-back statue of St Martin, and huge rib vaults and stained-glass windows that lift the gaze.

Museum of Jewish Culture　　　MUSEUM
(Múzeum židovskej kultúry; ☎ 02-2049 0102; www.snm.sk; Židovská 17; adult/child €7/2; ⊙ 11am-5pm Sun-Fri) This enriching museum unveils the stories of Bratislava's once-thriving Jewish community through photographs and objects from daily life, with a focus on the impressive Jewish architecture lost both during and after WWII.

🏃 Activities

Bratislava Bike Point　　　CYCLING
(☎ 0907 683 112; www.bratislavabikepoint.com; Pri Suchom mlyne 84; bike rental 24hr €15, per day thereafter €13; ⊙ bike rental by arrangement, tours Apr-Oct) Book at least a day in advance to

hire a bicycle from knowledgeable Bratislava Bike Point; for an extra €3, the bike can be brought to the central Bratislava address of your choice. Bike lock and helmet are included. The website is packed with cyclist-friendly info, too. Deposit €50 per bike.

⌖ Tours

★ Authentic Slovakia   CULTURAL
(☑0908 308 234; www.authenticslovakia.com; 2/4hr tour per person from €25/39) Always with ribald humour and an eye for the dark side, Authentic Slovakia leads you into Bratislava's seamy history and wacky architecture (usually aboard a retro Škoda car). Want to see 'Bratislava's Beverly Hills', brutalist cityscapes or drink your way around Devín Castle? You're in safe hands.

Bratislava Food Tours   FOOD & DRINK
(☑0910 902 315; http://bratislavafoodtours.com; per person €45-80) Guided by the well-honed taste buds of local foodies, learn about dining etiquette and Slovak staple foods in between bites of sheep's cheese, dumplings, cookies and optional swigs of beer and liqueur. Book ahead, and definitely don't dine before the tour.

✸ Festivals & Events

Coronation Festival   CULTURAL
(www.coronation.sk; ☺late Jun; ⊞) A historically accurate recreation of a coronation ceremony, plus markets, wine and folk music, unfolds annually in the old town over the last weekend of June. A different Hungarian monarch is 'crowned' each year, and there are historical tours of Bratislava, a concert in St Martin's Cathedral (p413) and lots of costume-clad tomfoolery – dress up and get your own royal portrait.

Cultural Summer
& Castle Festival   CULTURAL
(www.visitbratislava.com; ☺Jul-Sep; ⊞) Bratislava's widest-ranging festival features classical music, folk, alternative theatre, jazz, brass bands and more, at venues across town throughout the summer. Historical buildings, town squares and even fountains transform into pop-up venues for DJs, dance parties, yoga classes and every genre of live music. Open-air theatre at Bratislava Castle (p413) is a highlight.

Bratislava Music Festival   MUSIC
(www.bhsfestival.sk; ☺Oct/Nov) One of Slovakia's most important music festivals, with

classical-music performances by international orchestras held in Slovak Philharmonic venues in late October or early November. They're presided over by visiting conductors, and include some premieres of Slovak compositions.

⌂ Sleeping

Midrange self-catering accommodation, like Apartments Bratislava (☑0918 397 924; www.apartmentsbratislava.com; studios/apt from €60/69; ☎), is a great way to stay central without paying hotel prices.

★ Hostel Blues   HOSTEL €
(☑0905 204 020; www.hostelblues.sk; Špitálska 2; dm/d from €15/54; @☎) A cracking hostel where social areas feel lovably grungy while facilities, like kitchens and bathrooms, are nicely up to date. Table football, guitars and cheap beer encourage mingling in the lounge, with its velvety sofas and blues posters. Choose from single-sex or mixed dorms, or private rooms with en-suite bathrooms (a steal for the price).

Patio Hostel   HOSTEL €
(☑02-5292 5797; www.patiohostel.com; Špitálska; dm €8-20, d/tr €70/85, tw/tr without bathroom from €59/74; ℗☎) A zesty colour scheme and on-the-ball staff make this modern backpackers a compelling choice. Accommodation options include four-bed, single-sex dorms, mixed 10-bed dorms and private rooms with or without bathrooms. A welcome drink sets the tone while lockers, free laundry service, complimentary coffee and a bar tick all the backpacker boxes.

Hotel Arcus   GUESTHOUSE €€
(☑02-5557 2522; www.hotelarcus.sk; Moskovská 5; s/d/tr incl breakfast €54/99/127; ℗☎) Family-run Arcus goes above and beyond: it's exceptionally clean with helpful reception staff and top-class breakfasts. Tucked away on a residential street, its room sizes vary but all have high ceilings and plenty of space, and there's a garden out back to relax in. Rates drop by 15% at weekends.

Marrol's Boutique Hotel   LUXURY HOTEL €€€
(☑02-5778 4600; www.hotelmarrols.sk; Tobrucká 4; d/ste incl breakfast from €138/254; ℗❄☎☎) Even travellers with aristocratic tastes will raise an approving eyebrow at the neobaroque furnishings, sophisticated restaurant and exemplary service at Marrol's. Rooms are plush, in soft shades of ivory and gold, with king-sized beds. The breakfast buffet

– sorry, banquet – is out of this world, and there's a lobby bar with fireplace.

✗ Eating

Štúr
CAFE €

(☑ 0919 399 338; www.sturcafe.sk; Štúrova 8; cakes from €3, sandwiches from €4; ⊗ 8.30am-10pm Mon-Fri, 9am-10pm Sat, 9am-9pm Sun; 🛜🅿) Wonderful coffee, gateaus in flavours ranging from carrot-almond to caramel cheesecake, and sandwiches are served in this bookish *kaviareň* (cafe) with flashes of art-nouveau style. It's named for Ľudovít Štúr, who codified the Slovak literary language.

Bratislavský Meštiansky Pivovar
SLOVAK €€

(☑ 0944 512 265; www.mestianskypivovar.sk; Drevená 8; mains €7-22; ⊗ 11am-midnight Mon-Thu & Sat, to 1am Fri, 11am-10pm Sun; 🛜) Continuing Bratislava's 600-year-old beer-making tradition, this brewery and restaurant offers home-brewed and German beers to accompany its menu of Central European stomach liners (sometimes infusing the beer into the dishes). Settle in at the vaulted hall and choose from beer and onion goulash, confit duck, beer-roasted chicken and moreish snacks from cheese plates to crackling pork.

Prašná Bašta
SLOVAK €€

(☑ 02-5443 4957; www.prasnabasta.sk; Zámočnicka 11; mains €8-21; ⊗ 11am-11pm; 🅿) Stained-glass windows cast a soft light inside Prašná Bašta, a cosy, low-ceilinged den. Similarly warm and reassuring are full-flavoured courses like chicken with camembert and walnuts, herbed trout, and veal drowned in mushroom sauce. A winning mix of atmosphere, friendly service and fine food.

★ Modrá Hviezda
SLOVAK €€€

(☑ 0948 703 070; www.modrahviezda.sk; Beblavého 14; mains €12-24; ⊗ 11am-11pm) The 'Blue Star' specialises in regally executed Slovak dishes: venison in cognac, tender lamb shank, and mangalica pork (from woolly pigs) on a silky pumpkin purée. The brick-lined cellar space, festooned with farm tools and a-twinkle with candles, feels equal parts romantic and rustic. A must-eat; reservations recommended.

★ Sky Bar & Restaurant
THAI, EUROPEAN €€€

(☑ 0948 109 400; www.skybar.sk; Hviezdoslavovo nám 7; mains €10-20; ⊗ noon-midnight Sun-Thu, to 1am Fri & Sat; 🅿) Fusion cuisine is prepared with a nod and a wink by experimental chefs at this 7th-floor restaurant. You may not be able to read your menu amid the sultry, violet lighting but no matter: everything's delicious, from salmon with Thai basil to venison with veggies. Our highlight? The 'Wild Hunter' cocktail: part beverage, part primeval diorama.

🍷 Drinking & Nightlife

Slovak Pub
PUB

(☑ 02-5292 6367; www.slovakpub.sk; Obchodná 62; ⊗ 11am-11pm Mon-Thu, to midnight Fri, noon-11pm Sat & Sun; 🛜) The name suggests a by-the-numbers tourist trap, but this rustic tavern-restaurant is a guilty pleasure among locals, too. Grab a draught beer, or perhaps a wooden paddle of *slivovica* (plum brandy), and you'll likely stay longer than planned. Before you develop beer goggles, you might learn something from the knightly regalia and portraits of Slovak heroes on show.

Stupavar
BEER HALL

(☑ 0948 343 252; www.facebook.com/stupavar beerpub; Prepoštská 4; ⊗ 3pm-midnight) A local favourite for craft beer, this vaulted drinking haunt has an excellent selection of ales and microbrews for its small size.

Subclub
CLUB

(www.subclub.sk; Nábrežie arm gen L Svobudu; ⊗ 10pm-4am Thu-Sat) Drum 'n' bass, funk, indie and hard techno vibrate the subterranean walls of this nightlife stalwart in the shadow of Bratislava Castle. The vibe depends very much on what's on, but club nights are usually so well attended, loud and lively that you'd barely notice if a meteor struck (it's a former Soviet bunker, after all).

Apollon Club
GAY & LESBIAN

(☑ 0948 900 092; http://apollon-gayclub.sk; Panenská 24; ⊗ 8pm-1am Tue & Wed, to 4am Thu-Sat) Fostering a community atmosphere, Apollon is Slovakia's oldest gay club. Rough-hewn stone walls and violet lighting create the mood, while DJs, costume parties and themed nights provide the entertainment.

☆ Entertainment

Keep an eye on **Kam do Mesta** (www.kamdomesta.sk/bratislava) for entertainment listings.

KC Dunaj
LIVE PERFORMANCE

(www.kcdunaj.sk; Nedbalova 3; ⊗ 4pm-late Mon-Sat, to midnight Sun; 🛜) An alternative cultural centre par excellence, hosting drama, live music, comedy, club nights, visual arts and more. A kicking international crowd can be found here almost nightly, particularly at the terrace bar with its rooftop view of the old town.

It's generally open until early in the morning but exact hours vary depending on the event.

Historic SND
THEATRE

(☑ box office 02-2049 4290; www.snd.sk; Gorkého, booking office cnr Jesenského & Komenského; tickets €18-40; ☺ box office 8am-7pm Mon-Fri, 9am-noon & 2-7pm Sat & Sun, plus 1hr before performances) The neo-Renaissance venue of the Slovak National Theatre, which dazzles with its silvery roof and statue-studded facade, hosts opera, ballet and modern drama within its 18th-century walls.

🛍 Shopping

Úľuv
ARTS & CRAFTS

(www.uluv.sk; Obchodná 64; ☺ noon-6pm Tue-Fri, to 2pm Sat) Woodcarving, pottery, weaving and other traditional Slovak art forms unfold expertly at this crafts cooperative. It's as much a gallery as a place to browse souvenirs, and everything is made with love.

ℹ Information

Bratislava's old town has banks and ATMs, especially along Poštova. The train and bus stations, and airport, have ATMs/exchange booths.

There is an expanding set of free wi-fi zones in the old town and beyond, including Hlavné nám, Hviezdoslavovo nám and Nám SNP.

Main Post Office (☑ 02-5443 0381; Nám SNP 35; ☺ 7am-8pm Mon-Fri, to 6pm Sat) In a beautiful building.

Police station (☑ 0961 031 705, emergency 158, emergency 112; Štúrova 15)

Tourist Information Centre (☑ 02-5441 9410; www.visitbratislava.com; Klobučnícká 2; ☺ 9am-7pm Apr-Oct, to 6pm Nov-Mar)

University Hospital (Univerzitná Nemocnica Bratislava; ☑ 02-5729 0111; www.unb.sk/nemocnica-stare-mesto; Mickiewiczova 13; 🏥 Americké nám) The closest hospital to the old town.

Poliklinika Ruzinov (☑ 02-4827 9111; www.ruzinovskapoliklinika.sk; Ružinovská 10) Hospital with emergency services and 24-hour pharmacy.

ℹ Getting There & Away

AIR

Vienna's much busier international airport is only 60km west and connected by direct buses to both Bratislava's centre and its airport.

Bratislava Airport (BTS; ☑ 02-3303 3353; www.bts.aero; Ivanská cesta) is a 12km drive northeast of central Bratislava.

BOAT

LOD (☑ 02-5293 2226; www.lod.sk; Fajnorovo nábr 2, Passenger Port; adult one way/return €24/39, child one way/return €12/19.50; ☺ mid-Apr–mid-Oct) Daily hydrofoil departures between Bratislava and Vienna in July and August (and a few per week from April to June, September to October), taking 1¾ hours there and slightly less coming back. Vessels depart from the **hydrofoil terminal** (Fajnorovo nábr 2).

Twin City Liner (☑ in Austria +43 1 904 88 80; www.twincityliner.com; Rázusovo nábr) Boats to Vienna leave daily from the **HUMA 6 terminal** (Rázusovo nábr) from late March through October. You can book through **Flora Tours** (☑ 02-5443 5803; www.floratour.sk; Kúpelná 6; ☺ 9am-5pm Mon-Fri).

BUS

To reach Bratislava, trains are usually comparably priced and more convenient than the bus.

Bratislava Bus Station (Mlynské nivy; 🚌 210) is 1km east of the old town; locals call it 'Mlynské

WORTH A TRIP

TREASURES OF BANSKÁ ŠTIAVNICA

Gold, silver and around 140 different minerals brought enormous wealth to Banská Štiavnica, in rugged central Slovakia. A considerable swathe of the town is inscribed on Unesco's World Heritage list. Much of its architectural magnificence is in and around Nám sv Trojice, the old town's 'Holy Trinity Square'. Marching around the Old Castle (Starozámocká 1; guided/self-guided tour adult €4/3, child €2/1.50; ☺ 9am-5pm daily May-Sep, 8am-4pm Wed-Sun Oct-Dec, 8am-4pm Tue-Sun Jan-Apr) is a riveting history lesson; don't miss navigating the creaking stairs of the Flamboyant Gothic clock tower. Many visitors arrive purely to see pilgrimage site Kalvária (Calvary; www.kalvaria.org; end of Pod Kalvlánou; ☺ 9am-4pm Apr-Dec, Sat & Sun only Jan-Mar; Ⓟ) FREE, the apex of baroque art in Slovakia, on a volcanic hill 2km northeast of the old town.

Divná Pani (☑ 045-679 0945; www.divnapani.sk; A Kmeťa 8; snacks from €2; ☺ 7.15am-10pm Mon-Thu, to midnight Fri, 8.30am-midnight Sat, 9am-10pm Sun) is a showy venue for cocktails and cake. Overnight, Boutique Apartments (☑ 0902 276 207; www.trotuarcafe.sk; A Kmeťa 14; apt from €39; 🕿) are comfy with a dash of steampunk chic.

Buses travel between Banská Štiavnica and Bratislava (€9.50, 3½ hours, two daily).

Nivy' (the street name). For schedules, see https://cp.hnonline.sk.

Slovak Lines (☑ 02-5542 2734; www.slovak-lines.sk; Mlynské Nivy, Bratislava bus station; ⊙ ticket sales 6.30am-6.30pm) runs services throughout the country and to Vienna (€5.50, one hour, half-hourly).

Eurolines (☑ Bratislava office 02-5556 2195; www.eurolines.sk; Mlynské Nívy, Bratislava bus station) is the contact for most international buses, including to Budapest (from €5.50, 2½ to 4½ hours, hourly), Prague (from €9.50, 4¼ hours, eight daily), Paris (from €60, 19 hours, three weekly) and more, some of which also operate under the Slovak Lines banner.

TRAIN

InterCity (IC) and EuroCity (EC) trains are quickest. To and from Bratislava's **main station** (Hlavná Stanica; www.slovakrail.sk; Franza Liszta nám), *rychlík* (R; 'fast' trains) take slightly longer, but run more frequently and cost less. *Osobný* (Ob) trains connect smaller towns. For schedules, see https://cp.hnonline.sk.

Domestic trains run to Poprad (€15 to €19.50, 3½ to 4½ hours, 12 daily, some changing in Žilina) and Košice (€19, 4¾ to six hours, 12 daily, more with changes).

International trains run to Vienna (€10.50, one hour, hourly), Prague (from €12, 4¼ hours, two direct daily) and Budapest (from €15, 2¾ hours, eight daily).

ⓘ Getting Around

TO/FROM THE AIRPORT

➜ City bus 61 links Bratislava Airport (p418) with the main train station, a 20-minute ride.

➜ Standing taxis (over)charge to town, some demanding as much as an eye-watering €25; ask the price before you get in or halve the cost by using a ride-share app like Taxify.

➜ Regular buses (€7, one hour, 14 daily) connect Vienna International Airport with Bratislava Airport (also stopping at Most SNP); find timetables on www.flixbus.com.

CAR

Abrix (☑ 0905 405 405; www.abrix.sk; Pestovateľská 1; ⊙ 8am-6pm Mon-Fri) Good-value operator offering pickup at the airport or any Bratislava address.

Buchbinder (☑ 02-4363 7821; www.buchbinder.sk; Stará Vajnorská 25; ⊙ 8am-6pm Mon-Fri, to noon Sat) Has an office at the airport.

PUBLIC TRANSPORT

The old town is small, so you won't always need to make use of Bratislava's extensive tram, bus and trolleybus network, run by Dopravný Podnik Bratislava (www.dpb.sk). Check https://imhd.sk/ba for city-wide schedules.

WORTH A TRIP

ENCHANTING CASTLE TOUR

Blushing sandstone towers and crenellated turrets make **Bojnice Castle** (☑ 046-543 0624; www.bojnicecastle.sk; Zámok a okolie 1, Bojnice; adult/child €9/3.50; ⊙ 9am-5pm May-Sep, to 3pm Oct & Apr, 10am-3pm Nov-Mar) the most visited in Slovakia. An early-20th-century reconstruction by the Pálffy family took inspiration from the castles of France's Loire Valley, lifting Bojnice to the neobaroque splendour that stands today.

Prievidza, 4km east of the castle, has buses to Bratislava (€10.50, 3¼ to 4¼ hours, three daily). Local buses connect Prievidza and Bojnice (€0.60, 10 minutes).

Tickets cost €0.70/0.90/1.20 for 15/30/60 minutes. Buy at machines next to stops and news stands, and always validate on board (or risk a legally enforceable €50 to €70 fine). Passes start at €6.90/8 for 24/72 hours.

Bus 93 Main train station to Hodžovo nám then Petržalka train station

Trolleybus 207 Hodžovo nám to Bratislava Castle

Trolleybus 210 Bratislava bus station to main train station

TAXI

Taxi companies usually charge in the realm of €0.55 per kilometre in town (or €1.20 outside the city centre) but standing taxis compulsively overcharge foreigners. An around-town trip should never cost above €10. Ride-share apps like Uber and Taxify also operate in Bratislava.

AA Euro Taxi (☑ 0903 807 022, in Slovakia 02-16 022; www.aataxieuro.sk; minimum fare €3.89) Local taxi company.

Free Taxi (☑ 02-5596 9696; www.freetaxi.sk; minimum fare €3.90) Competitive fares...but no, it's not free.

Around Bratislava

Devín Castle

Perched between Slovakia and Austria, rugged **Devín Castle** (☑ 02-6573 0105; www.muzeum.bratislava.sk; Muránská 10, Devín; adult/child €5/2.50; ⊙ 10am-6pm Mon-Fri, to 7pm Sat & Sun May-Sep, to 5pm daily Mar & Oct, to 4pm daily Nov-Feb) makes a popular day trip from Bratislava. From the ramparts there are admirable views of rivers and goat-speckled hills beyond. Inside, the museum hosts an archaeological exhibition with Neolithic grave finds and Bronze Age sculptures. In summer, kid-friendly medieval games and souvenir stalls consume the grounds. From November to March you can enter the grounds but exhibitions close. Bus 29 links Devin with Bratislava's Nový Most (stop 6); get a 30-minute ticket (€0.90).

Danubiana Meulensteen Art Museum

The windswept location of the world-class **Danubiana Meulensteen Art Museum** (📞 02-6252 8501; www.danubiana.sk; Via Danubia, Čunovo; adult/child €10/5; ⊘ 10am-6pm Tue-Sun) is as invigorating as the works on display. Inside, the gallery's floor-to-ceiling windows overlook the water, providing an organic backdrop to mostly contemporary art. It's 15km south of Bratislava with year-round bus links (bus 90, €1.20) and boat links at weekends from May to October (adult/child €16/10, including gallery entry).

TATRA MOUNTAINS

It's hard to overstate the majesty of the Tatras, whose 300-plus peaks form the central Carpathian Mountains' loftiest section. Together with the Polish national park of the same name, Slovakia's Tatra National Park is a Unesco-protected biosphere reserve.

DON'T MISS

THE VILLAGE TIME FORGOT

The squat, colourful houses of **Vlkolínec** (www.vlkolinec.sk; adult/child €2/1; ⊘ 9am-6pm Mon-Fri, to 7pm Sat & Sun) evoke medieval Europe with just a hint of Hobbiton. This tiny Unesco-listed mountain hamlet, dating to the 14th century, has 45 traditional log buildings, including an 18th-century timber bell tower, baroque Catholic chapel and cottages painted peach and powder blue. Two weekday-only buses make the 30-minute (€0.50) journey to Vlkolínec from Ružomberok train station, which is reached by train from Bratislava (€11.70 to €14, 2¾ to 3½ hours), Poprad (€4.50 to €6, one hour) and Košice (€8.70 to €11, 2¼ to 3¾ hours).

Poprad

📞 052 / POP 51.500 / ELEV 672M

Gateway to the High Tatras, Poprad is an excellent base for hiking or skiing day trips. By car or train, there are plenty of places to hike around lakes and through gorges or play in powder at winter-sports resorts. Rail links to Starý Smokovec and Štrbské Pleso are a cinch, and Slovenský Raj National Park is only a 15km drive south.

Poprad has its own attractions too, like the **Spišská Sobota** district, where well-preserved Renaissance buildings radiate charm, and the **Tatra Gallery** (Tatranská galéria; 📞 052-772 1968; www.tatragaleria.sk; cnr Hviezdoslavova & Halatova; adult/child €3/1; ⊘ 9am-6pm Mon-Fri, from 2pm Sun), housed in a former steam-power plant.

★ **Adventoura**   ADVENTURE SPORTS
(📞 0903 641 549; www.adventoura.eu) Dog sledding, trekking and adventure holidays, ski packages...this energetic outfit can arrange the works. Cultural and wildlife-spotting excursions are also expertly undertaken (with a high success rate on bear-watching trips). Day rates for private trips around the Tatras begin at around €30 per person. Book a week ahead (or a month, during peak season).

Aqua City   SWIMMING, SPA
(📞 052-785 1111; www.aquacity.sk; Športová 1397; day pass adult/student €22/19, 3hr pass adult/student €19/16; ⊘ 8am-9pm; 🚻) 🏊 With indoor and outdoor pools, saunas and slides, this heavily hyped water park is a welcome destination after skiing or hiking. Mayan-themed water slides (summer only) suit the kids, the 'Sapphire' zone has pools bathed in sultry light, and there's a swim-up bar that prepares a passable piña colada (€6). The park is also an eco-pioneer in Central Europe.

Hotel Cafe Razy   PENSION €
(📞 0911 571 568; www.hotelcaferazy.sk; Sv Egídia nám 58; s/d from €25/40; 🅿🛜) Hotel Cafe Razy's main-square location gives it reason to preen. The 16 rooms, some split-level, have individual flair: splashes of colour, tile floors and wooden beams. There's also zany clockwork on the outside of the building, which cranks into action after hours. Fortunately the 'c-razy' branding reflects the design rather than the service.

★ **Penzión Sabato**   B&B €€
(📞 052-776 9580; www.sabato.sk; Sobotské nám 6; d incl breakfast €70-110; 🅿🛜) Within this

peach-coloured mansion, dating to 1730, find eight romantic rooms with billowy drapes, wood-beamed ceilings and handsome Renaissance-era furniture. Each one is different (they're priced by size) and five have fireplaces.

★ **Vino & Tapas** INTERNATIONAL **€€€**
(✆ 0918 969 101; www.facebook.com/vinotapaspop rad; Sobotské nám 38; 4-/8-course tasting menu €25/45; ⊗ 5-11pm Tue-Sat) Truffled eggs, delicate ravioli, flower-strewn desserts... Vino & Tapas offers an exceptional dining experience in an atmospheric, brick-walled restaurant. Opt for a set menu with amuse-bouche to savour the best stuff. Phone ahead as it's rightly popular.

❶ Information

Čistiareň Boja (Dlhé Hony 1, Max Shopping Mall; laundry per 3/6kg €12/15; ⊗ 9am-8pm Mon-Sat) Overnight laundry service in the Max mall southwest of town.

City Information Centre (✆ 052-16 186; www.visitpoprad.sk; Svätého Egídia nám 86; ⊗ 8am-6pm Mon-Fri, 9am-1pm Sat, 2-5pm Sun Jul & Aug, 9am-5pm Mon-Fri, to noon Sat Sep-Jun)

❶ Getting There & Around

AIR

Poprad-Tatry International Airport (✆ 052-776 3875; www.airport-poprad.sk; Na Letisko 100), 4km west of town, has regular links to London Luton and seasonal ones to Rīga. There is no public transport to the airport. Metered **taxis** (✆ 0905 300 700, 052-776 8768; www.radiotaxi-poprad.sk) cost less than €4.

BUS

Buses serve Bratislava (€18, 5¾ hours, two daily), Košice (€4, 1¾ to 2½ hours, eight daily) and more. Between mid-June and mid-October there are buses to/from Zakopane in Poland (€5.50, two hours, two to four daily in season).

CAR

Good car-hire rates are offered by well-established **Car Rental Poprad** (✆ 0903 639 179; http://carrental-poprad.com; ⊗ by arrangement). Book ahead to pick up at Poprad's airport or train station.

TRAIN

Poprad-Tatry train station (Wolkera) is served by direct trains from Bratislava (€15 to €19.50, 3½ to 4½ hours, 12 daily, some changing in Žilina) and Košice (€5, 1¼ to two hours, almost hourly). From Poprad, direct trains travel to Starý Smokovec (€1.50, 25 minutes, hourly), from where electric trains zoom to other Tatras resorts.

High Tatras
◪ 052

The High Tatras (Vysoké Tatry), the tallest range in the Carpathian Mountains, occupy a near-mythic place in Slovak hearts. Instantly recognisable, the crooked summit of Mount Kriváň (2495m) has become a national symbol in literature and popular culture, with some Slovaks swearing it's their national duty to climb it. Twenty-five peaks reach higher than 2500m and the tallest mountains – like Gerlachovský štít (2654m) – attract the most hikers, revealing Slovakia as a nation of adventurers.

In winter, snow transforms hiking trails into small, family-friendly ski areas.

☂ Activities

Hiking routes are colour-coded and easy to follow; unmarked routes cannot be undertaken without a mountain guide.

Pick up one of the numerous detailed maps and hiking guides available at bookshops and information offices, like VKU's 1:25,000 *Vysoké Tatry*. Distances are officially given in hours rather than kilometres (and we think these estimates assume a high level of fitness).

Many hiking routes criss-cross, or form part of, the Tatranská Magistrála. This mighty trail spans 45km, though you may see it described as longer, depending on the start or end village. Best trekked between mid-June and mid-October, the challenging trail runs beneath High Tatras peaks more than 2500m high, to the edge of the Western (Západné) Tatras. The route has some demanding, technical assisted sections as well as more level rambles.

❶ Getting Around

Narrow-gauge electric trains trundle from Štrbské Pleso to Novy and Starý Smokovec, and on to Tatranská Lomnica. Tickets are priced by kilometre (€0.50 less than 2km, €1 up to 6km, etc). Maps at train stops show distances. Buy a multijourney ticket if touring resorts (one-/three-/seven-day pass €4/8/14, kids half-price).

Smokovec Resort Towns
◪ 052

The High Tatras are comfortably accessed from this string of resort towns. From west to east along Rte 537, they are Novy Smokovec, Starý Smokovec and Horný Smokovec. The region's history of holidaymaking is long: Starý Smokovec has been a mountain

ℹ️ MOUNTAIN SAFETY

Never set out into the mountains without the phone number for Slovakia's **Mountain Rescue Service** (Horská záchranná služba; ☑ 052-787 7711, emergency 18 300; www.hzs.sk), and always log your planned route and expected return time with your hostel or a friend who can raise the alarm. Download the **Mountain Rescue Service app**, which gives weather alerts and allows you to send an emergency SMS with your GPS coordinates; pre-fill the app with your information before hiking.

getaway since the late 18th century, and it retains a nostalgic air.

🏃 Activities

Hrebienok, reachable by **funicular** (Pozemná lanovka; http://hrebienok.lanovky.sk; Starý Smokovec; return adult/child Jul & Aug €11/8, Sep-Jun €9/6; ⊙ 7.30am-7pm Jul & Aug, 8.30am-6pm Sep-Jun) from Starý Smokovec, overlooks breathtaking views of the Veľká Studená Valley and has a few good hiking options, including short kid-friendly rambles. East and west from here, the red **Tatranská Magistrála Trail** transects the southern slopes of the High Tatras for 65km start to finish.

Bilíkova Chata (☑ 0949 579 777; www.bilik ovachata.sk; Hrebienok 14; s/tw without bathroom €29/46, ste from €80; 🛜), a log-lined overnight lodge and restaurant, is a short walk from the funicular railway terminus. An easy and well-signposted northbound walking trail (green) continues from Bilíkova Chata to **Studený potok waterfalls** (Vodopády Studeného potoka), taking about 20 minutes; 30 additional minutes brings you up to Zamkovského chata, a hiking lodge and restaurant. If you want to finish in Tatranská Lomnica, it's a further 3km to **Skalnaté pleso**, from where you can take a chairlift down.

Heading west from Hrebienok, you can hike along the base of Slavkovsky štít to lakeside **Sliezsky dom** hotel (red, two hours), then down a small connector trail to the yellow-marked trail back to Starý Smokovec (four hours total). Mountain climbers scale to the top of **Slavkovský štít** (2452m) via the blue trail from Starý Smokovec (eight to nine hours return).

To ascend peaks without marked trails, including the eight- or nine-hour odyssey to summit **Gerlachovský štít** (2654m), it's

mandatory to hire a certified guide; contact the **Mountain Guide Society** (☑ 0905 428 170; www.tatraguide.sk; Starý Smokovec 38; ⊙ noon-6pm daily, closed weekends Oct-May).

ℹ️ Information

Tatras Information Office (Tatranská informačná kancelária; ☑ 052-442 3440; www.tatry.sk; Starý Smokovec 23; ⊙ 8am-5.45pm Jan-Mar, to 4pm Apr-Dec) The area's largest info office, with helpful English-speaking staff and vast quantities of brochures.

ℹ️ Getting There & Away

Direct trains link Starý Smokovec and Poprad-Tatry (p421) (€1.50, 25 minutes, hourly); Poprad is on the main west–east rail line between Bratislava and Košice.

Tatranská Lomnica

☑ 052 / POP 1300 / ELEV 903M

Overlooked by fearsome Lomnický štít, the country's second-highest peak, Tatranská Lomnica is home to a spine-chillingly precipitous cable car and the region's loftiest skiing – including its steepest piste. Summer also heaves with activity, as hikers embark on view-laden trails from Skalnaté pleso, a 1751m-altitude glacier lake.

Lomnický Štít Ascent   CABLE CAR

(www.vt.sk; adult/child return Tatranská to Skalnaté pleso €22/18, return Skalnaté pleso to Lomnický štít €27/23; ⊙ 8.30am-5.30pm Jul & Aug, to 3.30pm Sep-Jun) From Tatranská Lomnica, a gondola pauses midstation at Štart; change cars for the winter-sports area, restaurant and lake at Skalnaté pleso. From there, a cable car rises another 855m to the giddy summit of Lomnický štít (2634m), a hair-raising eight-minute journey. Prices are as steep as the ascent, and timeslots sell out quickly on sunny days; try queuing as early as 7.30am.

Ski Resort Tatranská Lomnica   SKIING

(www.gopass.sk; adult one-/six-day pass €39/200; ⊙ late Nov–mid-Apr; 🚡) Nearly 12km of pistes – a mix of blue and red, with a couple of challenging black runs – make up the wondrously scenic skiing terrain above Tatranská Lomnica. Pistes top out at 2190m and there's a respectable 1300m vertical drop across the resort. Views of Slovakia's second-tallest peak, Lomnický štít, are remarkable throughout.

Zamkovského Chata   HUT €

(☑ 0905 554 471; www.zamka.sk; dm €20; ⊙ year-round) Perched at 1475m above sea level, this log chalet has been a guesthouse since the 1940s and is open year-round. Still catering to hikers, this no-frills refuge offers 23 dorm beds (crowded in summer) and a restaurant serving sausage and mustard, soups and dumplings. Breakfast (€6) and half-board (€16) are hearty and very reasonably priced.

Grandhotel Praha HOTEL €€
(☑ 044-290 1338; www.ghpraha.sk; Tatranská Lomnica 8; d/ste incl breakfast from €114/184; P 🛜 ⛷) Stepping into this art nouveau hotel (1905), the indignities of ski-lift queues and mud-spattered hikes melt away. The marble staircase and sparkling chandeliers set the tone. Its ample rooms are similarly lavish, with gilt-edged mirrors and burnished wallpaper, and breakfast is exceptional. The spa, complete with sauna and steam room, is fragrant with mountain herbs, oils and soothing salt lamps.

Slnečný Dom SLOVAK €€
(☑ 0903 406 470; www.slnecnydom.sk; Tatranská Lomnica 287; mains €8-12; ⊙ 9am-9pm Jul-Aug & Dec-Mar, reduced hours rest of year) Gaze at walls covered with antique skis while awaiting roasted trout, melt-in-your-mouth pork on lentils, or perhaps hot *encian* (soft, rinded cheese) at the 'Sunny House'. There's draft beer and central Slovak wines to wash it down.

★ **Humno Tatry** BAR, CLUB
(☑ 0911 115 603; www.humnotatry.sk; Tatranská Lomnica; ⊙ 11am-11pm Thu, noon-4am Fri & Sat, noon-11pm Sun, closed Mon-Wed) Tumble straight from the cable-car base station into this big, wood-beamed club, diner and cocktail bar. There's an outdoor deck to bask in late-afternoon sun over beers, or perhaps an apple-sage or frozen-cherry refresher. Inside, the sound of thudding hiking boots is as loud as the music. On theme nights – DJs, house, old-school pop – it's packed to the rafters.

ℹ️ Information

TIK Tatranská Lomnica (☑ 052-446 8119; www.tatry.sk; Tatranská Lomnica 98; ⊙ 8am-4pm)

ℹ️ Getting There & Away

The **train station** is off Tatranská Lomnica's main road.

Reaching Poprad-Tatry (p421) by train requires a change in Starý Smokovec or Studený Potok (€1.50, 45 minutes) but there are direct buses (€1.30, 30 minutes, hourly). Luggage storage is available at the bus station between 8.30am and 6.30pm.

Štrbské Pleso

☑ 052 / POP 3390 (REGION)

The tarn at Štrbské Pleso is one of the High Tatras' loveliest scenes – and don't visitors know it. This glacial lake (1346m) receives huge numbers of visitors around the year, thanks to lofty hiking trails and the country's longest ski season. Rent a **row boat** (☑ 0911 707 982; per 40min for 3/4 passengers €18/23; ⊙ 10am-6pm May-Sep) at the dock behind Grand Hotel Kempinski

🏃 Activities

The easiest walk is the level 2.3km trail around the lake. For a longer hike, follow the red-marked, rocky **Magistrála Trail** uphill from Hotel Patria for about 1½ hours to **Popradské pleso**, an even more idyllic lake at 1494m. You can return to the train line by following the paved road down to the Popradské pleso stop (45 minutes). The Magistrála zigzags up the mountainside from Popradské pleso and then traverses east towards **Sliezsky dom** and the Hrebienok funicular above Starý Smokovec (5½ to six hours).

The year-round **Solisko Express chairlift** (return adult/child €13/9, 8am to 3.30pm) rises to **Chata pod Soliskom** (1840m), from where it's a one-hour walk north along a red trail to the 2093m summit of **Predné Solisko**.

Higher trails close from November to mid-June; check what's open at the **tourist office** (☑ 0911 333 466; www.strbskepleso.sk; Poštová; ⊙ 8am-4pm).

🛏️ Sleeping & Eating

Chata Pod Soliskom HOSTEL €
(☑ 0917 655 446; www.chatasolisko.sk; top of Solisko Express lift; dm/d €20/80) This modern hostel with a nine-bed dorm (no bunks) and one private room is located at the top of the Solisko Express (1840m). Lodgings are ornamented in modern chalet style with sheepskin rugs, rope sculptures, black-and-white landscape photography and pinewood everywhere you look. Breakfast is €6.

Grand Hotel Kempinski HOTEL €€€
(☑ 052-326 2222; www.kempinski.com/hightatras; Kupelna 6; d/ste incl breakfast from €179/289; P ❄ @ 🛜 ⛷) Everything you'd expect from a sumptuous hotel chain, with the bonus of dreamy lake views, the Kempinski is Štrbské Pleso's best address. Elements of traditional Slovak design, like carved wooden headboards, are elegantly placed throughout the rooms, whose large windows offers views of lake or

valley. Every luxury is here, from a heated pool with chandeliers to the suave restaurant.

★ **Koliba Patria**   SLOVAK €€
(☑ 052-784 8870; http://hotelpatria.sk; eastern lakeshore, Štrbské Pleso; mains €8-18; ⊙ 11.30am-10.30pm) On a lakeshore perch, Koliba Patria's earthy decor brings nature indoors: lamps are fashioned from cowbells, and a tree appears to burst from its wooden beams and slate walls. The refined Slovak menu offers familiar dishes done exceptionally well: perfectly spiced deer goulash, zesty sauerkraut and zander fillet on a silky bed of buttery potatoes. There's an outdoor terrace, too.

ⓘ Getting There & Away

Štrbské Pleso is connected by electric railway to the Smokovec Resort Towns (€1.50, 45 minutes) and Tatranská Lomnica (€2, 1½ hours). Direct buses also travel to/from Poprad (€1.70, one hour, five daily).

EASTERN SLOVAKIA

Welcome to Slovakia's untrammelled east, home to Andy Warhol history, medieval wine cellars, mysterious churches and the best wine region you've never heard of.

Levoča

☑ 053 / POP 14,700

The medieval wealth of Levoča, a former royal town, is writ large across its Unesco-listed centre. Majstra Pavla nám, the historic main square, is an architectural treasure chest: it's lined by burgher mansions with gabled roofs, and has a dazzlingly restored town hall.

The spindles-and-spires Church of St Jacob (Chrám sv Jakuba; www.chramsvjakuba. sk; Majstra Pavla nám; adult/child €3/2; ⊙ by tour 8.30am-4pm Tue-Sat, from 11.30am Sun & Mon), built in the 14th and 15th centuries, elevates the spirits with its soaring arches and precious art. The main attraction is the Gothic altar (1517), created by medieval woodcarver extraordinaire Master Paul of Levoča.

Beaming over the town is the Church of Mariánska Hora (Bazilika Panny Márie; ☑ 053-451 2826; http://rkc.levoca.sk; ⊙ hours vary, services 2.30pm Sun summer; ℗), a Catholic pilgrimage site glowing beatifically from a hill 2km north.

Hotel U Leva   HOTEL €€
(☑ 053-450 2311; www.uleva.sk; Majstra Pavla nám 25; s/d/ste incl breakfast from €43/58/89; ℗ 🛜)

Awash in the main square's golden colour scheme, Levoča's best hotel is spread across two pyramid-roofed buildings. Rooms are painted in warming sunset shades, with rustic accents like wooden beams but modern conveniences like fridges and good TVs. There's a welcome drink on arrival, too.

★ **Kupecká Bašta**   SLOVAK, ITALIAN €€
(☑ 0908 989 626; www.kupeckabasta.sk; Kukučínová 2; mains €6-15; ⊙ 10am-10pm Mon-Thu, 11am-11pm Fri & Sat) Dine within the very walls of Levoča's old town at this outstanding Slovak restaurant. A medley of Slovak and Hungarian influences grace the menu, like chicken stroganoff and schnitzels, along with unexpected combinations: pork encrusted with almonds, or served with mozzarella and cognac sauce, and Italian dishes like prawn and lime tagliatelle. It's all good, and the service is attentive.

ⓘ Information

Everything you're likely to need, ATMs, post office and the **tourist office** (☑ 053-451 3763; http://eng.levoca.sk; Majstra Pavla nám 58; ⊙ 9am-4pm daily May-Sep, Mon-Fri only Oct-Apr) included, is on the main square.

ⓘ Getting There & Away

The **bus station** (Železničný riadok 31) is 1km by foot south of the main square. Direct services reach Košice (€5, two hours, four daily), Poprad (€1.70, 45 minutes, every one to two hours), Spišská Nová Ves (for Slovenský Raj, €0.90 to €2, 15 minutes to one hours, half-hourly) and Spišské Podhradie (for Spiš Castle, €0.90 to €2, 30 minutes, one or two hourly).

Spišské Podhradie

☑ 053 / POP 4040

Slovakia's most spectacular castle has propelled the otherwise dozy village of Spišské Podhradie to tourism stardom.

A former stomping ground of medieval watchmen and Renaissance nobles, Spiš Castle (Spišský hrad; ☑ 053-454 1336; www.facebook. com/spisskyhradsk; adult/student/child €8/6/4; ⊙ 9am-6pm May-Sep, to 4pm Apr & Oct, 10am-4pm Nov, closed Dec-Mar) looms over the village from a limestone hill. This vast, Unesco-listed fortification is one of Central Europe's biggest castle complexes. Its bulwarks and thick defensive walls date to the 12th century (at the latest), and once guarded Hungarian royals and nobles from flying arrows. Highlights of the 4-hectare site include views from the

22m-high tower, and a **museum** of medieval history within the former palace.

Home-away-from-home **Penzión Podzámok** (✆053-454 1755; www.penzionpodzamok.eu; Podzámková 28; s/d/tr from €25/30/45, without bathroom s/d €12/20; P🖥🛱) has nicely maintained rooms awash in candy colours. The view of Spiš Castle from the yard is spectacular.

By the highway, 6km west of the castle, **Spišsky Salaš** (✆053-454 1202; http://spisskysalas.sk; Levočská cesta 11; mains from €4; ⊙10am-9pm; P🖥) pulls big crowds, with its lamb goulash and *pirohy* (dumplings).

❶ Getting There & Away

BUS
Buses connect with Levoča (€0.90 to €1.20, 30 minutes, one to two per hour), Poprad (from €2.20, one hour, six daily) and Košice (€4.30, 1½ hours, two direct daily, more via Prešov or Levoča).

TRAIN
Spišské Podhradie is connected by bus to Spišské Vlachy (€0.90, 20 minutes, 10 daily), which has direct rail links west to Spišská Nová Ves (for Slovenský Raj; €1.20, 25 minutes, every two hours) and east to Košice (€2.50, one hour, every two hours).

Slovenský Raj & Around
✔053

You don't simply visit **Slovenský Raj National Park** (www.slovenskyraj.eu; Jul & Aug adult/child €1.50/0.50, Sep-Jun free). It's more accurate to say that you clamber, scramble and get thoroughly drenched in the 328-sq-km park's dynamic landscape of caves, canyons and waterfalls. Hikers in 'Slovak Paradise' climb ladders over gushing cascades, trek to ruined monasteries and shiver within an ice cave – and that's just on day one.

Among several trailhead villages, three are the best served by accommodation and food options. Most popular is Podlesok, slightly west of Hrabušice. On the east side of the park is low-key Čingov, a convenient starting point for hikes and rock climbing.

◎ Sights & Activities

Before hiking, pick up VKÚ's 1:25,000 *Slovenský Raj* hiking map (No 4) or 1:50,000 regional map (No 124). Hikes involving via ferrata ladders are open from mid-June through October. In July and August, trails can get busy to the point of queues.

One of the best-loved ascents is from Podlesok through **Suchá Belá Gorge** to Kláštorisko Chata, the site of a medieval monastery. Begin early and allow between two and four hours for this often-steep (and often-crowded) trail, along which you'll be sprayed by waterfalls as you cling to metal ladders.

Dobšinská Ice Cave   CAVE
(Dobšinská ľadová jaskyňa; ✆058-788 1470; www.ssj.sk; Dobšiná; adult/child €8/4; ⊙9am-4pm Tue-Sun by hourly tour late May-Sep, closed Oct–mid-May) More than 110,000 cubic metres of ice are packed into the gleaming walls of this Unesco-listed ice cave, near the southern edge of Slovenský Raj National Park. The atmosphere is otherworldly: icy stalagmites, resembling polished marble, bulge from the ground and chambers sparkle with dangling tendrils of frost. In places, the cave ice is 25m thick. The departure point is a half-hour walk from the car park, so arrive in good time ahead of guided tours (on the hour).

Ferrata HZS Kyseľ   CLIMBING
(per person €5; ⊙mid-Jun–mid-Oct) This one-way via-ferrata route is an exciting, hands-on way to experience Slovenský Raj's geological drama. Gear isn't included but you can hire it from operators in Podlesok or Čingov (€5 to €10); if you aren't confident, hire a guide (€50) from the national park office (p426).

⌕ Sleeping & Eating

Autocamping Podlesok   CAMPGROUND €
(✆053-429 9165; www.podlesok.sk; Podlesok; per adult/child/campsite/motorhome €4.70/3.20/3.50/4, chalets €50-150; P🖥🛱) Pitch a tent, hide out in a no-frills chalet or book a modern en-suite cottage at this well-located campground, right near Hrabušice's national park office and restaurants. Dogs are welcome (€2).

It's always a good idea to reserve in advance and it's essential to call ahead between November and March.

Reštaurácia Rumanka   SLOVAK €
(✆0907 289 262; www.podlesok.com; Podlesok; mains €4-8; ⊙11am-9pm May-Sep, to 7pm Fri-Sun only Oct-Apr) Enormously popular Rumanka serves enough varieties of *halušky* (dumplings) to satisfy ravenous hikers, as well as crispy fried *pirohy* (stuffed with mushrooms or meat), pork chops, and sheep's cheese in handy takeaway portions (from €0.95). Excellent selection of homemade desserts, too, from strudels and mascarpone cupcakes to panna cotta.

ℹ Information

Outside July and August, stop off in Spišská Nová Ves for maps and advice.

Mountain Rescue Service (☑ 052-787 7711, emergency 18 300; www.hzs.sk) For emergencies in the park. Check the website for weather conditions.

National Park Information Centre (www.npslovenskyraj.sk; Hlavná, Podlesok; ⊙ 7.30am-3pm Mon-Fri, 9.30am-4.30pm Sat & Sun Jul & Aug, closed Sep-Jun) Summer-only national park hub.

Tourist Information Centre (☑ 053-442 8292; www.spisskanovaves.eu/tic; Letná 49, Spišská Nová Ves; ⊙ 8am-6pm Mon-Fri, 9am-1pm Sat, 2-6pm Sun May-Sep, to 7pm weekdays Jul & Aug, 9am-5pm Mon-Fri Oct-Mar) Year-round information and luggage storage in town.

ℹ Getting There & Away

Consider hiring a car from Poprad or Košice, particularly during low season when connections to the park can be a chore. By public transport, you'll have to transfer at least once.

BUS

Buses (https://cp.hnonline.sk) are most frequent in July and August, and services thin out on weekends.

There are up to five daily direct buses from Poprad to Hrabušice (€1.30, 45 minutes) and Dedinky (€2.10, 1¼ hours). Alternatively, change buses in Spišský Štvrtok.

More frequent buses from Poprad reach Slovenský Raj's transport hub Spišská Nová Ves (€1.70, 45 minutes, at least hourly Monday to Friday and every one to two hours Saturday and Sunday). From Spišská Nová Ves, it's easiest to hike, cycle or arrange a transfer through your accommodation but there are infrequent daily buses to Hrabušice (for Podlesok; €1.10, 30 minutes) and Čingov (€0.60, 15 minutes).

TRAIN

Trains run from Spišská Nová Ves to Poprad (€1.55, 20 minutes, at least hourly) and Košice (€4, one to 1½ hours, every one to two hours).

Košice

☑ 055 / POP 239,000

Equal parts pretty and gritty, Košice captures attention with its old town, a jewellery box of Gothic towers, medieval bastions and baroque sculpture. Since Košice's tenure as European Capital of Culture in 2013, the cultural scene has continued to bloom: offbeat bars, Soviet city tours and vegetarian dining share the limelight with cultural draws like the showstopping Gothic cathedral.

◉ Sights

★ **Cathedral of St Elizabeth**   CHURCH
(Dóm sv Alžbety; ☑ 055-622 1555; www.dom.rimkat.sk; Hlavné nám; tower adult/child €1.50/1, crypt €1; ⊙ 1-5pm Mon, from 9am Tue-Fri, 9am-1pm Sat) This 14th-century cathedral dominates Košice's main square, its gables bristling above tall, stained-glass windows while colourful roof tiles evoke a resplendent scaled dragon. One of Europe's easternmost Gothic cathedrals, 60m-long St Elizabeth is the largest in the country. Ascend 160 stone steps up the narrow stairwell of 59.7m-tall **Sigisimund Tower** to peep out across the city.

Hlavné Nám   SQUARE
Much of Košice's finery is assembled along Hlavné nám, a long plaza with flower gardens, fountains and cafes on either side. Stroll past the central **musical fountain** (Hlavné nám) to experience its hourly chimes (and, at night, the multicoloured light show). Across from the fountain is the **State Theatre** (Štátne divadlo Košice; ☑ 055-245 2269; www.sdke.sk; Hlavné nám 58; ⊙ box office 9am-12.30pm & 1-5.30pm Mon-Fri, 9am-1pm Sat), a baroque beauty from 1899. Walking south you'll see the 1779 **Shire Hall** (Župný dom; Hlavné nám 27), crowned with a coat of arms and home to the **East Slovak Gallery** (☑ 055-681 7511; www.vsg.sk; Hlavná 27; adult/child €3/2; ⊙ 10am-6pm Tue-Sun).

Hrnčiarska   HISTORIC SITE
(Ulička Remesiel; Hrnčiarska) FREE Art studios and traditional workshops line quaint Hrnčiarska, including herbalists, blacksmiths, potters and purveyors of precious stones. Some of their crafts haven't changed in 200 years; others use timeworn techniques to create contemporary designs. A few businesses along this cobbled lane have traditional crafts demonstrations, while others house arty coffee shops.

Rodošto &
Mikluš Prison   HISTORIC BUILDING, MUSEUM
(www.vsmuzeum.sk; Hrnčiarska; bastion adult/child €3/2, prison adult/child €2/1; ⊙ 9am-5pm Tue-Sat, to 1pm Sun) This complex's motley attractions form a whirlwind tour of Košice's history. In the **bastion**, whose walls date to the 15th century, Košice is revealed as a powerhouse of medieval weapons production: you'll see cannonballs, coats of arms and well-dressed horse mannequins. Adjoining is a replica of the house in which Hungarian national hero Franz II Rákoczi was exiled in the 18th century. At the **prison**, you'll learn executioner

etiquette from a video presentation before seeing grisly restraints in the cells.

Sleeping

★ Penzión Slovakia GUESTHOUSE €€
(☑ 055-728 9820; www.penzionslovakia.sk; Orliá 6; s/d/apt incl breakfast from €64/74/95; [P][✱][🛜]) Incongruous as it sounds, the patriotic Slovak guesthouse above this Argentine steakhouse is one of Košice's most compelling places to overnight. Framing an inner courtyard, rooms feel effortless (bare brick walls, brightly coloured trimmings) but they're exceptionally well designed and each is named after a Slovak city. Hot breakfasts are cooked to order. Our only gripe? The expensive parking (€10).

Hotel Zlatý Dukat BOUTIQUE HOTEL €€
(☑ 055-727 9333; www.zlatydukat.sk; Hlavná 16; s/d/ste incl breakfast from €65/85/145; [P][✱][🛜]) Rooms at Zlatý Dukat have a classic, almost antique, style: high ceilings, areas of exposed brick and wooden beams, but modern fittings like flat-screen TVs and security boxes. There is a superb Slovak restaurant and wine cellar in the hotel's 13th-century basement.

✗ Eating

★ Republika Východu INTERNATIONAL, CAFÉ €€
(☑ 0908 704 116; www.republikavychodu.sk; Hlavná 31; mains €5-12; ◷ 8am-midnight Mon-Fri, from 10am Sat & Sun; [🛜][✎][🍴]) With its tongue-in-cheek declaration of independence from Western Slovakia, Republika Východu (Republic of the East) sets a spirited tone. The menu, too, doesn't play by any rules: breakfast on avocado toast or quinoa porridge, studded with raspberries, then hang around to lunch on steak or goat's cheese salad. Bonus: it's lined with bookshelves and there's a children's play area.

Pán Ryba SEAFOOD €€
(☑ 0905 321 441; www.facebook.com/panrybakosice; Mlynská 13; mains €9-16; ◷ 9am-10pm Mon-Fri, from 11am Sat) A revelation amid Košice's often doughy food scene, 'Mr Fish' brings inspiration from across Asia and the Mediterranean to its creative preparations of seafood. Tuna is seared beautifully, paella is generously laden with squid and mussels, and the open kitchen allows your hungry eyes a view of the proceedings.

12 Apoštolov SLOVAK, EUROPEAN €€
(☑ 0948 876 671; www.facebook.com/12apostolov Kosice; Kováčska 51; mains €6-8; ◷ 11am-11pm Mon-Wed, to midnight Thu-Sat) High-backed

pews and religious portraits seem to urge prayerful contemplation, but the chefs at 12 Apoštolov have something more decadent in mind. This venerable tavern (1910) specialises in Slovak soul food: gravy-soaked pork steak with bread dumplings, burgers, paprika-laced stews and fish with creamy risotto. There's also eight varieties of craft beer – not quite enough for each apostle.

Med Malina POLISH, SLOVAK €€
(☑ 055-622 0397; www.medmalina.sk; Hlavná 81; mains €6-14; ◷ 11am-11pm Mon-Sat, to 10pm Sun) Sour soup *żurek*, roast duck with red cabbage, and *bigos* (cabbage and mushroom stew, flavoured with sausage meat): a medley of Polish and Slovak specialities are served with cheer in a simple but homely setting. Locals scramble for the few tables here, so it's worth reserving on weekends.

🍷 Drinking & Nightlife

Enoteca Centro WINE BAR
(☑ 0905 217 329; www.facebook.com/enotecacentro; Kováčska 10; ◷ 10am-11pm Mon-Sat, 4-10pm Sun) A royal haul of Slovak wine is found in this cavernous bar, where old frescoes heighten the storied atmosphere. There's a sheltered terrace area for mild evenings – Italian-style, to suit Centro's excellent line in *aperitivi*.

Jazz Club CLUB, BAR
(www.jazzclub-ke.sk; Kováčska 39; ◷ bar 11.30am-midnight Mon-Thu, to 2am Fri & Sat, club 9pm-3am Tue-Sat) Part cafe-bar, part nightclub, Jazz Club has something to suit most revellers. An appealing mix of medieval-style arches, steampunk brass and wood decor and bright lights, the venue draws a messy young crowd to student nights and dance parties,

while a more chilled-out set lounge on its bar and terrace, or settle in for full-service meals.

ⓘ Information

City Information Centre (☑ 055-625 8888; www.visitkosice.org; Hlavná 59; ⊙ 9am-6pm Mon-Fri, to 3pm Sat & Sun)

Municipal Information Centre (Informačné centrum MiC; ☑ 0911 567 423; www.mickosice.sk; Hlavná 32; ⊙ 9.30am-6.30pm Mon-Fri, 10am-3pm Sat & Sun)

Nemocnica Košice-Šaca (☑ 055-723 4111; www.nemocnicasaca.sk; Lúčna 57, Šaca) Private hospital outside central Košice.

Police Station (☑ 158; Pribinova 6)

Post Office (☑ 055-674 1493; www.posta.sk; Poštová 20; ⊙ 7am-7pm Mon-Fri, 8am-noon Sat)

ⓘ Getting There & Away

AIR

Košice International Airport (KSC; www.airportkosice.sk; Košice-Barca) is 7km south-west of the city centre by road; bus 23 plies the route hourly.

Czech Airlines (www.csa.cz) flies to Bratislava and Prague; Austrian Airlines (www.austrian.com) to Vienna; Wizz Air (http://wizzair.com) to London Luton; LOT (www.lot.com) to Warsaw; and Turkish Airlines (www.turkishairlines.com) to Istanbul.

BUS

Direct buses reach Levoča (€5, two hours, seven daily), Poprad (€4, 1¾ to 2½ hours, eight daily) and Bratislava (€19.50 to €21, seven to 7¾ hours, two daily). There is a much bigger choice of west-bound routes if you change buses in Prešov.

Eurobus (☑ 055-680 7306; www.eurobus.sk; Staničné nám 9; ⊙ ticket office 6am-6pm Mon-Fri) has services to Uzhhorod in Ukraine (€7, four hours, six daily). Getting to Poland is easier from Poprad.

CAR

Several international car-hire companies, including Avis and Europcar, are represented at the airport. **Buchbinder** (☑ 0911 582 200, 055-683 2397; www.buchbinder.sk; Košice International Airport; ⊙ 8am-4.30pm Mon-Fri, or by arrangement) often has the most reasonable rates.

TRAIN

Direct trains from Košice **train station** (☑ general information 024-485 8188; Staničné nám, near Mestský park; ☒) run to Bratislava (€19 to €22, 4¾ to seven hours, at least every 1½ hours), Poprad in the High Tatras (€5, 1¼ to two hours, almost hourly) and Spišská Nová Ves for Slovenský Raj (€4, one hour, hourly). There are also trains over the border to Budapest (€15, four hours, one or two daily) via Miskolc.

ⓘ Getting Around

The old town is small and walkable. Transport tickets (30-/60-minute ticket €0.60/0.70, 24-hour ticket €3.20) cover buses and trams; buy them at news stands and machines, and validate as soon as you board.

SURVIVAL GUIDE

ⓘ Directory A–Z

INTERNET ACCESS

➜ Wi-fi is widely available across the country. Slovak telecommunications companies are also aiming to bring high-speed internet to lesser-populated areas in Slovakia by 2020.

➜ Most hotels and cafes have wi-fi; in rural areas most guesthouses have a connection though it may not extend beyond the reception or dining area.

LGBT+ TRAVELLERS

The Queer Slovakia (http://queerslovakia.sk) site lists events in Bratislava, Košice and beyond.

MONEY

➜ Visa and MasterCard are accepted at most hotels and restaurants in well-touristed places like Bratislava, Košice and High Tatras resorts.

➜ Guesthouses and apartments outside major cities often accept payment in cash only.

➜ Slovaks don't tip consistently, but rounding up bills to the nearest euro is common practice.

OPENING HOURS

Operating hours in villages and remote areas may be considerably shorter from October to April.

Banks 8am to 5pm Monday to Friday

Bars 11am to midnight Monday to Thursday, 11am to 2am Friday and Saturday, noon to midnight Sunday

Grocery Stores 6.30am to 6pm Monday to Friday, 7am to noon Saturday

Post Offices 8am to 6pm Monday to Friday, 8am to noon Saturday

Restaurants 11am to 10pm

PUBLIC HOLIDAYS

New Year's/Day of the Slovak Republic's Establishment 1 January

Epiphany/Three Kings Day 6 January

Good Friday and Easter Monday March/April

Labour Day 1 May

Victory over Fascism Day 8 May

Cyril and Methodius Day 5 July

SNP (National Uprising) Day 29 August

Constitution Day 1 September

Our Lady of Sorrows Day 15 September

All Saints' Day 1 November
Fight for Freedom and Democracy Day 17 November
Christmas 24 to 26 December

TELEPHONE

➡ Slovakia has very good network coverage and you only need to bring a passport to buy a local SIM card. Major providers include Orange, T-Mobile and O2.

➡ Landline numbers can have either seven or eight digits. Mobile phone numbers (10 digits) are often used for businesses; they start with 09.

➡ When dialling from abroad, you need to drop the zero from both city area codes and mobile phone numbers.

TOURIST INFORMATION

Association of Information Centres of Slovakia (www.aices.sk) Runs a wide network of city information centres.

Slovak Tourist Board (http://slovakia.travel/en) The country's over-arching tourist resource online.

ⓘ Getting There & Away

AIR

Vienna International Airport (VIE; ☑ 01-700 722 233; www.viennaairport.com; ☎) in Austria, 60km away, has the nearest big international air hub.

There are other airports in Bratislava (p418), Košice (p428) and Poprad (p421).

The main airlines operating in Slovakia are:

Austrian Airlines (www.austrian.com) Connects Košice with Vienna.

Czech Airlines (www.csa.cz) Flies from Prague to Bratislava.

LOT (www.lot.com) Flies between Warsaw and Košice.

Ryanair (www.ryanair.com) Connects Bratislava with numerous destinations across the UK and Italy, coastal Spain, Dublin, Paris and Brussels.

Wizz Air (http://wizzair.com) Connects Košice to a few UK airports, Poprad to London Luton, and Bratislava to European cities including Kyiv, London Luton, Sofia and Warsaw.

LAND

➡ Border posts between Slovakia and fellow EU Schengen member states – Czech Republic, Hungary, Poland and Austria – are almost nonexistent.

➡ It's convenient to come in by road, but drivers must buy a vignette, a toll sticker granting access to Slovak highways, at the border (https://eznamka.sk).

➡ Checks at the Ukrainian border are more strident, as you will be entering the EU (expect your vehicle to be searched). By bus or car, plan for one to two hours' wait.

➡ Direct trains operate between Bratislava and Budapest (2¾ hours), Prague (from four hours) and Vienna (from one hour). From Košice, trains travel across the border with Hungary to Budapest (four hours) via Miskolc. Čierna nad Tisou has rail links to/from Ukraine.

➡ Check www.slovakrail.sk for domestic train schedules and https://cp.hnonline.sk for domestic and international routes.

RIVER

Danube riverboats offer an alternative way to get between Bratislava and Vienna.

ⓘ Getting Around

AIR

Czech Airlines (www.csa.cz) offers the only domestic air service, between Bratislava and Košice (and you're probably better off catching the train).

BICYCLE

➡ Roads can be narrow and potholed, and in towns cobblestones and tram tracks can prove dangerous for riders.

➡ Bike rental isn't ubiquitous but it's common in mountain resorts and some national parks, and increasing in popularity in Bratislava and Košice.

➡ Charges apply for bringing bikes aboard trains and cable cars (reservations may be necessary on long-distance trains).

BUS

Read timetables carefully; different schedules apply for weekends and holidays. Find up-to-date information at https://cp.hnonline.sk.

CAR & MOTORCYCLE

Highways are in great shape, distances are short and routes are scenic: Slovakia is a good country for a road trip.

LOCAL TRANSPORT

➡ Bratislava and Košice have trams and trolleybuses, and High Tatras towns are linked by electric railway.

➡ Public transport generally operates from 5am to 10.30pm (to 11pm in Bratislava). Reduced night-bus services run in Bratislava and Košice.

➡ Buy tickets at ticket machines and news stands near the transport stop. Always validate your ticket in the machine on board or risk a fine.

TRAIN

The main Bratislava–Košice line slices west to east through the country, via Trenčín and Poprad. Search for up-to-date schedules and buy tickets through **Slovak Railways** (02-4485 8188; www.slovakrail.sk).

Slovenia

POP 2 MILLION

Best Places to Eat

➡ Castle Restaurant (p439)

➡ Monstera Bistro (p436)

➡ Pri Mari (p446)

➡ Štrud'l (p441)

➡ Ek Bistro (p435)

Best Places to Stay

➡ Jazz Hostel & Apartments (p439)

➡ Adora Hotel (p434)

➡ PachaMama (p446)

➡ Youth Hostel Proteus Postojna (p444)

➡ Vila Park (p441)

Why Go?

It's a pint-sized place, with a surface area of just over 20,000 sq km, and two million people. But 'good things come in small packages', and never was that old chestnut more appropriate than in describing Slovenia. The country has everything – from beaches, snowcapped mountains, and hills awash in grape vines to Gothic churches, baroque palaces and art-nouveau buildings. Its incredible mixture of climates brings warm Mediterranean breezes up to the foothills of the Alps, where it can snow in summer. The capital, Ljubljana, is a culturally rich city that values sustainability over unfettered growth. This sensitivity towards the environment extends to rural and lesser-developed parts of the country.

When to Go
Ljubljana

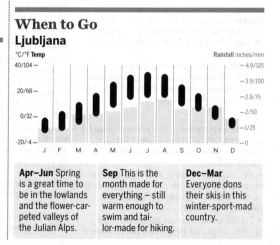

Apr–Jun Spring is a great time to be in the lowlands and the flower-carpeted valleys of the Julian Alps.

Sep This is the month made for everything – still warm enough to swim and tailor-made for hiking.

Dec–Mar Everyone dons their skis in this winter-sport-mad country.

Entering the Country

Entering Slovenia is usually a straightforward procedure. If you're arriving from an EU Schengen country, such as Austria, Italy or Hungary, you will not have to show a passport or go through customs, no matter which nationality you are. If you're coming from any non-Schengen country, ie outside of the EU but also including Croatia, full border procedures apply.

ITINERARIES

Three Days
Spend a couple of days in Ljubljana (p432), then head north to unwind in romantic Bled (p438) or Bohinj (p440) beside idyllic mountain lakes. Alternatively, head south to visit the caves at Škocjan (p444) or Postojna (p443).

One Week
A full week will allow you to see the country's top highlights. After two days in the capital (p432), head for Bled (p438) and Bohinj (p440). Depending on the season, take a bus or drive over the hair-raising Vršič Pass (p442) into the valley of the vivid-blue Soča River and take part in some adventure sports in Bovec (p442). Continue south to the caves at Škocjan (p444) and Postojna (p443), and then to the sparkling Venetian port of Piran (p445) on the Adriatic.

Essential Food & Drink

Little Slovenia boasts an incredibly diverse cuisine, with as many as two dozen different regional styles of cooking. Here are some highlights:

Gibanica Layer cake stuffed with nuts, cheese and apple.

Jota Hearty bean-and-cabbage soup.

Postrv Trout, particularly from the Soča River, is a real treat.

Potica A nut roll eaten at teatime or as a dessert.

Prekmurska gibanica A rich concoction of pastry filled with poppy seeds, walnuts, apples and cheese, and topped with cream.

Pršut Air-dried, thinly sliced ham from the Karst region.

Štruklji Scrumptious dumplings made with curd cheese and served either savoury as a main course or sweet as a dessert.

Žganci The Slovenian stodge of choice – groats made from barley or corn but usually *ajda* (buckwheat).

Žlikrofi Ravioli-like parcels filled with cheese, bacon and chives.

AT A GLANCE

Area 20,273 sq km

Capital Ljubljana

Country code ☑386

Currency euro (€)

Emergency Ambulance ☑112, Fire ☑112, Police ☑113

Language Slovene

Time Central European Time (GMT/UTC plus one hour)

Visas Not required for citizens of the EU, Australia, USA, Canada or New Zealand

Sleeping Price Ranges

The following price ranges refer to a double room with en suite toilet and bath or shower, and include tax and breakfast.

€ less than €50

€€ €50–100

€€€ more than €100

Eating Price Ranges

The following price ranges refer to a two-course, sit-down meal, including a drink, for one person. Many restaurants also offer an excellent-value set menu of two or even three courses at lunch.

€ less than €15

€€ €15–30

€€€ more than €30

Slovenia Highlights

1 Ljubljana Castle (p433) Enjoying a 'flight' on the funicular up to this spectacular hilltop castle.

2 National & University Library (p433) Considering the genius of architect Jože Plečnik at Ljubljana's historic library.

3 Lake Bled (p438) Gazing at the natural perfection of this crystal-clear green lake.

4 Škocjan Caves (p444) Gawking in awe at the 100m-high walls of this incredible cave system.

5 Mt Triglav (p441) Climbing to the top of the country's tallest mountain.

6 Piran (p445) Getting lost wandering the narrow Venetian alleyways of this seaside town.

LJUBLJANA

01 / POP 279,750 / ELEV 297M

Slovenia's capital and largest city is one of Europe's greenest and most liveable capitals. Car traffic is restricted in the centre, leaving the banks of the emerald-green Ljubljanica River free for pedestrians and cyclists. Slovenia's master of early-modern, minimalist design, Jože Plečnik, graced the capital with beautiful bridges and buildings as well as dozens of urban design elements, such as pillars, pyramids and lamp posts. Some 50,000 students support an active clubbing scene, and Ljubljana's museums and restaurants are among the best in the country.

◉ Sights

The easiest way to see Ljubljana is on foot. The oldest part of town, with the most important historical buildings and sights (including

Ljubljana Castle) lies on the right (east) bank of the Ljubljanica River. Center, which has the lion's share of the city's museums and galleries, is on the left (west) side of the river.

★Ljubljana Castle CASTLE

(Ljubljanski Grad; ☎01-306 42 93; www.ljubljanskigrad.si; Grajska Planota 1; adult/child incl funicular & castle attractions €10/7, incl Time Machine tour €12/8.40, castle attractions only €7.50/5.20; ⏲castle 9am-11pm Jun-Sep, to 9pm Apr, May & Oct, 10am-8pm Jan-Mar & Nov, to 10pm Dec) Crowning a 375m-high hill east of the Old Town, this castle is an architectural mishmash, with most of it dating from the early 16th century when it was largely rebuilt after a devastating earthquake. It's free to ramble around the castle grounds, but you'll have to pay to enter the Watchtower and the Chapel of St George, and to see the worthwhile Slovenian History Exhibition, visit the Puppet Theatre and take the Time Machine tour.

National & University Library ARCHITECTURE

(Narodna in Univerzitetna Knjižnica, NUK; ☎01-200 12 09; www.nuk.uni-lj.si; Turjaška ulica 1; ⏲8am-8pm Mon-Fri, 9am-2pm Sat) FREE This library is architect Jože Plečnik's masterpiece, completed in 1941. To appreciate this great man's philosophy, enter through the main door (note the horse-head doorknobs) on Turjaška ulica – you'll find yourself in near darkness, entombed in black marble. As you ascend the steps, you'll emerge into a colonnade suffused with light – the light of knowledge, according to the architect's plans.

Triple Bridge BRIDGE

(Tromostovje) Running south from **Prešernov trg** (Prešeren Sq) to the Old Town is the much celebrated Triple Bridge, originally called Špital (Hospital) Bridge. When it was built as a single span in 1842 it was nothing spectacular, but between 1929 and 1932 superstar architect Jože Plečnik added the two pedestrian side bridges, furnished all three with stone balustrades and lamps, and forced a name change. Stairways on each of the side bridges lead down to the poplar-lined terraces along the Ljubljanica River.

National Museum of Slovenia MUSEUM

(Narodni Muzej Slovenije; ☎01-241 44 00; www.nms.si; Prešernova cesta 20; adult/student €6/4, with National Museum of Slovenia–Metelkova or Slovenian Museum of Natural History €8.50/6, lapidarium free; ⏲10am-6pm, to 8pm Thu) Housed in a grand building from 1888 – the same building as the **Slovenian Museum of Natural History** (Prirodoslovni Muzej Slovenije; ☎01-241 09 40; www.pms-lj.si; adult/student €4/3, 1st Sun of month free; ⏲10am-6pm Fri-Wed, to 8pm Thu) – highlights include the highly embossed *Vače situla* – a Celtic pail from the 6th century BC that was unearthed in a town east of Ljubljana. There's also a Stone Age bone flute discovered near Cerkno in western Slovenia in 1995. You'll find examples of Roman jewellery found in 6th-century Slavic graves, as well as a glass-enclosed Roman lapidarium outside to the north.

City Museum of Ljubljana MUSEUM

(Mestni Muzej Ljubljana; ☎01-241 25 00; www.mgml.si; Gosposka ulica 15; adult/child €6/4; ⏲10am-6pm Tue, Wed & Fri-Sun, to 9pm Thu) The excellent city museum, established in 1935, focuses on Ljubljana's history, culture and politics via imaginative multimedia and interactive displays. The reconstructed street that once linked the eastern gates of the Roman colony of Emona (today's Ljubljana) to the Ljubljanica River and the collection of well-preserved classical artefacts in the basement treasury are worth a visit in themselves. So too are the models of buildings that the celebrated architect Jože Plečnik never got around to erecting.

Sleeping

★Hostel Vrba HOSTEL €

(☎064 133 555; www.hostelvrba.si; Gradaška ulica 10; dm €22-30, d €65-75; @📶) Definitely one of our favourite budget digs in Ljubljana, this nine-room hostel on the Gradiščica Canal is just opposite the bars and restaurants of delightful Trnovo. There are three twin doubles, dorms with four to eight beds (including a popular all-female dorm), hardwood floors and an always warm welcome. Free bikes in summer.

Celica Hostel HOSTEL €

(☎01-230 97 00; www.hostelcelica.com; Metelkova ulica 8; dm €18-26, s/d cell €58/62; @📶) This stylishly revamped former prison (1882) in Metelkova (p436) has 20 'cells', designed by different artists and architects, and complete with original bars. There are nine rooms and apartments with three to seven beds and a packed, popular 12-bed dorm. The ground floor is home to a cafe and restaurant (set lunch around €7). Bikes cost €3/6 for a half-/full day.

Hotel Galleria BOUTIQUE HOTEL €€

(☎01-421 35 60; www.hotelgalleria.eu; Gornji trg 3; s €70-110, d €90-130; ❄@📶) This attractive

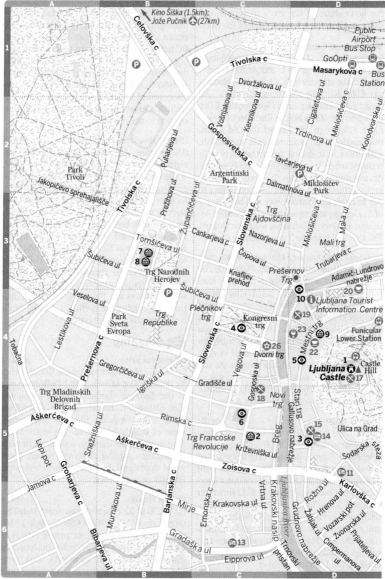

boutique hotel has been cobbled together from several Old Town town houses. There are 16 spacious rooms and a multitiered back garden. The decor is kitsch with a smirk and there are fabulous touches everywhere. Among our favourites are the enormous room 8, with views of the **Hercules**

Fountain (Levstikov trg), and room 13, with glimpses of Ljubljana Castle.

★ **Adora Hotel** HOTEL €€€
(☑ 082 057 240; www.adorahotel.si; Rožna ulica 7; s €115, d €125-155, apt €135-165; P ❋ @ 🤶) This small hotel below Gornji trg is a wel-

✕ Eating

★ **Ek Bistro**   INTERNATIONAL €
(☏ 041 937 534; www.facebook.com/ekljubljana; Petkovškovo nabrežje 65; breakfasts €8-10; ⊙ 8am-8pm Mon-Thu, to 9pm Fri & Sat, to 3pm Sun; ☎ 🖉)
Ljubljana's top spot for brunch, meaning in this case big slices of avocado toast on home-made bread, bowls of muesli and yoghurt, and eggs Benedict on fresh-baked English muffins. Wash it down with a glass of freshly squeezed something or a flat white. The fresh-cut flowers on the tables look great against the distressed brick walls.

Pop's Place   BURGERS €
(☏ 059 042 856; www.facebook.com/popsplace burgerbar; Cankarjevo nabrežje 3; burgers €8-10; ⊙ noon-midnight; ☎) Centrally located craft-beer and burger bar that's evolved into a must-visit. The burgers, with locally sourced

come addition to accommodation in the Old Town. The 10 rooms are small but fully equipped, with lovely hardwood floors and tasteful furnishings. The breakfast room looks out onto a small garden, bikes are free for guests' use, and the staff are overwhelmingly friendly and helpful.

SLOVENIA LJUBLJANA

beef and brioche-style buns, are excellent, as are the beers and cocktails. The dining area feels festive, with an open kitchen behind the bar and communal tables out front for diners to rub elbows and compare burgers. Avoid traditional meal times: Pop's gets busy.

Druga Violina SLOVENIAN €
(☑082 052 506; www.facebook.com/drugaviolina; Stari trg 21; mains €6-10; ☺8am-midnight; ☎) Just opposite the Academy of Music, the 'Second Fiddle' is an extremely pleasant and affordable place for a meal in the Old Town. There are lots of Slovenian dishes, including *ajdova kaša z jurčki* (buckwheat groats with ceps) and *obara* (a thick stew of chicken and vegetables), on the menu. It's a social enterprise designed to help those with disabilities.

Gostilna na Gradu SLOVENIAN €€
(Inn at the Castle; ☑031 301 777; www.nagradu.si; Grajska planota 1; mains €12-18; ☺10am-midnight Mon-Sat, noon-6pm Sun; ☎) Right within the Ljubljana Castle (p433) complex, Na Gradu is much too stylish to be just a *gostilna* (inn-like restaurant). The award-winning chefs use only Slovenian-sourced breads, cheeses and meats, and age-old recipes to prepare a meal to remember. If you really want to taste your way across the country, try the five-course gourmet tasting menu for €42.20.

★**Monstera Bistro** SLOVENIAN €€€
(☑040 431 123; http://monsterabistro.si; Gosposka ulica 9; 3-course lunch €19, 7-course tasting menu €55; ☺11.30am-5pm Mon-Wed, to 11pm Thu-Sat; ☎☑) ✦ The concept bistro of star TV chef Bine Volčič delivers 'best-meal-of-the-trip' quality using locally sourced, seasonal ingredients and zero-waste food-prep concepts. Most diners opt for the three-course lunch (starter, main course, dessert), though the multicourse dinners are consistently good. The light-infused dining room, with white-brick walls and light woods, feels dressy without being overly formal. Book in advance.

🍷 Drinking & Nightlife

★**Magda** CAFE
(☑01-620 26 10; https://barmagda.si; Pogačarjev trg 1; ☺7am-1am Mon-Sat, from 10am Sun; ☎) It's hard to put a finger on what makes Magda so special. Maybe it's the expertly prepared espresso (just €1 a cup purchased at the bar) or the unique 'tapas-style' breakfast menu, where you choose from local meats and cheeses, or the craft gins and local home-made brandies on offer. It's a great choice to start or end the day.

Slovenska Hiša COCKTAIL BAR
(Slovenian House; ☑083 899 811; www.slovenska hisa.si; Cankarjevo nabrežje 13; ☺8am-1am Sun-Thu, to 3am Fri & Sat; ☎) Our favourite boozer along the river is so cute it's almost twee. Choose from artisanal coffees, wines, lemonades, cocktails and spirits, featuring ingredients sourced only in Slovenia. Order one of the inventive meat and cheese plates (€4 to €7) to soak up the alcohol.

Pritličje CAFE
(Ground Floor; ☑082 058 742; www.pritlicje.si; Mestni trg 2; ☺9am-1am Sun-Wed, to 3am Thu-Sat; ☎) The ultra-inclusive 'Ground Floor' offers something for everyone: cafe, bar, live music, cultural centre and comic-book shop. Events are scheduled almost nightly and the location next to the **Town Hall** (Mestna Hiša; ☑01-306 30 00; Mestni trg 1; tours €5; ☺8am-5pm Mon-Fri) FREE, with good views across **Mestni trg** (Town Sq), couldn't be more perfect.

Metelkova Mesto CLUB
(Metelkova Town; www.metelkovamesto.org; Masarykova cesta 24) This ex-army garrison – taken over by squatters in the 1990s and converted into a free-living commune – is home to several clubs, bars and concert venues. It generally comes to life after 11pm daily in summer, and on Friday and Saturday the rest of the year. The quality of the acts varies, though there's usually a little of something for everyone.

☆ Entertainment

★**Kino Šiška** LIVE MUSIC
(☑030 310 110, box office 01-500 30 00; www. kinosiska.si; Trg Prekomorskih brigad 3; ☺box office 3-8pm Mon-Fri, pub 8am-midnight, events 8pm-2am; ☎; 🚊1, 3, 5, 8, 22, 25) This renovated old movie theatre now houses an urban cultural centre, hosting mainly indie, rock and alternative bands from around Slovenia and the rest of Europe. Buy tickets at the box office or at **Eventim** (☑090 55 77; www.eventim. si; Trg Osvobodilne Fronte 6; ☺8am-4pm) offices around town.

Slovenia Philharmonic Hall CLASSICAL MUSIC
(Slovenska Filharmonija; ☑01-241 08 00; www. filharmonija.si; Kongresni trg 10; tickets €8-16; ☺box office 11am-1pm & 3-6pm Mon-Fri) Home to the Slovenian Philharmonic, founded in 1701, this small but atmospheric venue at the southeast corner of **Kongresni trg** (Congress Sq) also stages concerts and hosts performances of the Slovenian Chamber

Choir (Slovenski Komorni Zbor). Haydn, Beethoven and Brahms were honorary Philharmonic members, and Gustav Mahler was resident conductor for a season (1881–82).

Gala Hala LIVE MUSIC
(☑ 01-431 70 63; www.galahala.com; Metelkova Mesto, Masarykova cesta 24; tickets €3-10) Metelkova (p436)'s biggest and best venue to catch live alternative, indie and rock music several nights a week. There's an open-air performance space from May to September.

ℹ️ Information

ATMs are everywhere, including several outside the Ljubljana TIC (p437). Full-service banks are all around the centre; they're the best places to exchange cash.

Ljubljana Tourist Information Centre (TIC; ☑ 01-306 12 15; www.visitljubljana.com; Adamič-Lundrovo nabrežje 2; ⊘ 8am-9pm Jun-Sep, to 7pm Oct-May) Knowledgeable and enthusiastic staff dispense information, maps and useful literature, and help with accommodation. Offers a range of interesting city and regional tours, and maintains an excellent website.

Slovenian Tourist Information Centre (STIC; ☑ 01-306 45 76; www.slovenia.info; Krekov trg 10; ⊘ 8am-9pm daily Jun-Sep, 8am-7pm Mon-Fri, 9am-5pm Sat & Sun Oct-May; 📶) Good source of information for travel to the rest of Slovenia, with internet and bicycle rental also available.

ℹ️ Getting There & Away

AIR

Jože Pučnik Airport (Aerodrom Ljubljana; ☑ 04-206 19 81; www.lju-airport.si; Zgornji Brnik 130a, Brnik), Slovenia's main international airport, is located 27km north of Ljubljana.

BUS

Buses to destinations both within Slovenia and abroad leave from the **bus station** (Avtobusna Postaja Ljubljana; ☑ 01-234 46 00; www.ap-ljubljana.si; Trg Osvobodilne Fronte 4; ⊘ 5am-10.30pm Mon-Fri, 5am-10pm Sat, 5.30am-10.30pm Sun) just next to the train station. The station website has an excellent timetable for checking departure times and prices. At the station, you'll find multilingual information phones and a touchscreen computer next to the ticket windows. You do not usually have to buy your ticket in advance; just pay as you board the bus.

Some sample one-way fares (return fares are usually double) from the capital: Bled (€7.80, 1½ hours, 57km, hourly), Bohinj (€9.80, two hours, 91km, hourly), Piran (€6, one hour, 53km, up to 24 daily).

TRAIN

Domestic and international trains arrive at and depart from central Ljubljana's **train station** (Železniška Postaja; ☑ 01-291 33 32; www.slo-zeleznice.si; Trg Osvobodilne Fronte 6; ⊘ 5am-10pm), where you'll find a separate information centre on the way to the platforms. The website has an excellent timetable with departure times and prices. Buy domestic tickets from windows No 1 to 8 and international ones from either window No 9 or the information centre.

Useful domestic destinations include Bled (€6.60, 55 minutes, 51km, up to 21 daily) and Koper (€9.60, 2½ hours, 153km, up to four services daily). Please note that these are one-way, 2nd-class domestic fares, travel times, distances and frequencies from Ljubljana. Return fares are double the price, and there's a surcharge of €1.80 on domestic InterCity (IC) and EuroCity (EC) train tickets.

ℹ️ Getting Around

TO/FROM THE AIRPORT

The cheapest way to Jože Pučnik Airport is by public bus (€4.10, 50 minutes, 27km) from **stop No 28** (€4.10 one way; ⊘ 5.20am-8.10pm) at the bus station. These run at 5.20am and hourly from 6.10am to 8.10pm Monday to Friday; at the weekend there's a bus at 6.10am and then one every two hours from 9.10am to 7.10pm. Buy tickets from the driver.

Two airport shuttle services that get consistently good reviews are **GoOpti** (☑ 01-320 45 30; www.goopti.com; Trg Osvobodilne Fronte 4; €9 one way) and **Markun Shuttle** (☑ reservations 041 792 865; www.prevozi-markun.com; €9 one way), which will transfer you from Brnik (where the airport is) to central Ljubljana in half an hour. Book by phone or online.

A taxi from the airport to Ljubljana will cost from €35 to €45.

BICYCLE

Ljubljana is a pleasure for cyclists, and there are bike lanes and special traffic lights everywhere. **Ljubljana Bike** (☑ 01-306 45 76; www.visitljubljana.si; Krekov trg 10; per 2hr/day €2/8; ⊘ 8am-7pm Mon-Fri, 9am-5pm Sat & Sun Apr, May & Oct, 8am-9pm Jun-Sep) rents two-wheelers in two-hour or full-day increments from April through October from the Slovenian Tourist Information Centre.

PUBLIC TRANSPORT

Ljubljana's city buses, many running on methane, operate every five to 15 minutes from 5am (6am on Sunday) to around 10.30pm. A flat fare of €1.20 (good for 90 minutes of unlimited travel, including transfers) is paid with a stored-value magnetic Urbana card, which can be purchased at newsstands, tourist offices and the public-transport authority's **Information Centre** (☑ 01-430 51 74; www.lpp.si/en; Slovenska cesta 56; ⊙ 6.30am-7pm Mon-Fri) for €2; credit can then be added (from €1 to €50).

THE JULIAN ALPS

This is the Slovenia of tourist posters: mountain peaks, postcard-perfect lakes and blue-green rivers. Prepare to be charmed by Lake Bled (with an island and a castle!) and surprised by Lake Bohinj (how does Bled score all that attention when down the road is Bohinj?). The lofty peak of Mt Triglav, at the centre of a national park of the same name, may dazzle you enough to prompt an ascent.

Lake Bled

☑ 04 / POP 5100 / ELEV 481M

Yes, it's every bit as lovely in real life. With its bluish-green lake, picture-postcard church on an islet, a medieval castle clinging to a rocky cliff and some of the highest peaks of the Julian Alps and the Karavanke as backdrops, Bled is Slovenia's most popular resort, drawing everyone from honeymooners lured by the over-the-top romantic setting to backpackers, who come for the hiking, biking, water-sports and canyoning possibilities.

That said, Bled can be overpriced and swarming with tourists in July and August. But as is the case with many popular destinations around the world, people come in droves – and will continue to do so – because the place is so special.

⊙ Sights

★ Lake Bled   LAKE

(Blejsko jezero) Bled's greatest attraction is its exquisite blue-green lake, measuring just 2km by 1.4km. The lake is lovely to behold from almost any vantage point, and makes a beautiful backdrop for the 6km walk along the shore. Mild thermal springs warm the water to a swimmable 22°C (72°F) from June through August. The lake is naturally the focus of the entire town: you can rent rowing boats, splash around on stand-up paddleboards (SUPs) or simply snap countless photos.

Bled Island   ISLAND

(Blejski Otok; www.blejskiotok.si; ⊙ 9am-7pm) Tiny, tear-shaped Bled Island beckons from the shore. There's the **Church of the Assumption** (Cerkev Marijinega Vnebovzetja; ☑ 04-

576 79 79; adult/child €6/1; ⊙ 9am-7pm May-Sep, to 6pm Apr & Oct, to 4pm Nov-Mar) and a small museum, the **Provost's House** (☑ 04-576 79 78; adult/child €6/1, incl with admission to Church of the Assumption; ⊙ 9am-7pm May-Sep, to 6pm Apr & Oct, to 4pm Nov-Mar), but the real thrill is the ride out by *pletna* (gondola). The *pletna* will set you down on the south side at the monumental **South Staircase** (Južno Stopnišče), built in 1655. The staircase comprises 99 steps – a local tradition is for the husband to carry his new bride up them.

Bled Castle   CASTLE

(Blejski Grad; ☑ 04-572 97 82; www.blejski-grad.si; Grajska cesta 25; adult/child €11/5; ⊙ 8am-9pm Jun-Aug, to 8pm Apr-May & Sep-Oct, to 6pm Nov-Mar) Perched atop a steep cliff more than 100m above the lake, Bled Castle is how most people imagine a medieval fortress to be, with towers, ramparts, moats and a terrace offering magnificent views. The castle houses a **museum collection** that traces the lake's history from earliest times to the development of Bled as a resort in the 19th century.

🏃 Activities

Several local outfits organise outdoor activities in and around Bled, including trekking, mountaineering, rock climbing, ski touring, cross-country skiing, mountain biking, rafting, kayaking, canyoning, horse riding, paragliding and ballooning.

★ 3glav Adventures   ADVENTURE SPORTS

(☑ 041 683 184; www.3glav.com; Ljubljanska cesta 1; ⊙ 9am-noon & 4-7pm mid-Apr–Oct) Bled's number-one adventure-sport specialist. Its most popular trip is the Emerald River Adventure (from €80), an 11-hour hiking and swimming foray into Triglav National Park and along the Soča River that covers a sightseeing loop of the region (from Bled over the Vršič Pass and down the Soča Valley, with optional rafting trip). Book by phone or via the website.

Gondola Ride   BOATING

(Pletna; ☑ 041 427 155; www.bled.si; per person return €14; ⊙ 8am-9pm Mon-Sat, to 6pm Sun Jul & Aug, 8am-7pm Mon-Sat, 11am-5pm Sun Apr-Jun, Sep & Oct, 8am-6pm Mon-Sat, to 1pm Sun Nov-Mar) Riding a piloted gondola (known as a *pletna*) out to Bled Island is the archetypal tourist experience. There is a convenient jetty just below the **TIC** and another in **Mlino** on the south shore. You get about half an hour to explore the island. In all, the trip to the island and back takes about 1¼ hours.

🛏 Sleeping & Eating

Bled has a wide range of accommodation, but book well in advance if you're travelling in July or August.

⭐ Jazz Hostel & Apartments
HOSTEL, GUESTHOUSE €€

(📱 040 634 555; www.jazzbled.com; Prešernova cesta 68; dm €35, d €80, without bathroom €60, apt d/q €90/100; P@🛜) If you don't mind being a little way (a short walk) from the action, this is a first-class budget choice. Guests rave about Jazz, mainly thanks to Jani, the superbly friendly owner who runs a sparkling, well-kitted-out complex. There are dorms (bunk-free, and with under-bed storage) and colourful en-suite rooms, plus family-sized apartments with a full kitchen. Book well in advance.

Camping Bled
CAMPGROUND €

(📱 04-575 20 00; www.sava-camping.com; Kidričeva cesta 10c; campsites from €23, glamping huts from €90; P@🛜) Bled's hugely popular, amenity-laden campground is in a rural valley at the western end of the lake, about 4km from the bus station. There's a rich array of family-friendly activities available, and a restaurant and a store on-site.

Old Parish House
GUESTHOUSE €€

(Stari Farovž; 📱 045 767 979; www.blejskiotok.si; Riklijeva cesta 22; s/d from €80/120; P🛜) In a privileged position, the Old Parish House belonging to the Parish Church of St Martin has been transformed into a simple, welcoming guesthouse, with timber beams, hardwood floors and neutral, minimalist style. Pros include car parking, lake views and waking to church bells.

Garden Village Bled
RESORT €€€

(📱 083 899 220; www.gardenvillagebled.com; Cesta Gorenjskega odreda 16; pier tent €130, tree house €320, glamping tent €370; ⏰ Apr-Oct; P@🛜🏊) Garden Village embraces and executes the eco-resort concept with aplomb, taking glamping to a whole new level and delivering lashings of wow factor. Accommodation ranges from small two-person tents (with shared bathroom) on piers over a trout-filled stream, to family-sized tree houses and large safari-style tents. Plus there are beautiful grounds, a natural swimming pool and an organic restaurant.

Slaščičarna Zima
CAFE €

(📱 04-574 16 16; www.smon.si; Grajska cesta 3; kremna rezina €3; ⏰ 7.30am-9pm) Bled's culinary speciality is the delicious *kremna rezi-*
na, also known as the *kremšnita:* a layer of vanilla custard topped with whipped cream and sandwiched between two layers of flaky pastry. While this patisserie may not be its place of birth, it remains the best place in which to try it – retro decor and all.

Gostilna Murka
SLOVENIAN €€

(📱 04-574 33 40; www.gostilna-murka.com; Riklijeva cesta 9; mains €10-20; ⏰ 10am-10pm Mon-Fri, noon-11pm Sat & Sun; 🛜) This traditional restaurant set within a large, leafy garden may at first appear a bit theme-park-ish – but this is one of the first places locals recommend and the food is authentic (lots of old-school national dishes). Offers good-value lunch specials for around €6 (but you'll have to ask the server).

Castle Restaurant
SLOVENIAN €€€

(📱 advance booking 04-620 34 44; www.jezersek.si/en/bled-castle-restaurant; Grajska cesta 61; mains €20-40, tasting menu from €50; ⏰ 10.30am-10pm; 🛜) It's hard to fault the superb location of the castle's restaurant, with a terrace and views straight from a postcard. What a relief the food is as good as it is: smoked trout, roast pork, poached fish. Note advance booking by phone is compulsory for dinner and only the multicourse tasting menu is available.

ℹ Information

Infocenter Triglavska Roža Bled (📱 04-578 02 05; www.tnp.si; Ljubljanska cesta 27; ⏰ 8am-6pm mid-Apr–mid-Oct, to 4pm mid-Oct–mid-Apr; 🛜)

Tourist Information Centre (📱 04-574 11 22; www.bled.si; Cesta Svobode 10; ⏰ 8am-9pm Mon-Sat, 9am-5pm Sun Jul & Aug, reduced hours Sep-Jun; 🛜) Open year-round: outside high season until at least 6pm Monday to Friday, to 3pm Sunday.

ℹ Getting There & Away

BUS

Bled is well connected by bus; the **bus station** (Cesta Svobode 4) is a hub of activity at the lake's northeast. **Alpetour** (📱 04-201 32 10; www.alpetour.si) runs most of the bus connections in the Julian Alps region, so check its website for schedules.

Popular services run to Lake Bohinj (€3.60, 37 minutes, 29km, up to 12 daily) and Ljubljana (€7.80, 70 to 80 minutes, 57km, up to 15 daily).

TRAIN

Bled has two train stations, though neither one is close to the town centre:

Lesce-Bled station Four kilometres east of Bled township on the road to Radovljica. It's on

SLOVENIA LAKE BLED

the rail line linking Ljubljana with Jesenice and Austria. Trains to/from Ljubljana (€5.20 to €7, 40 minutes to one hour, 51km, up to 20 daily) travel via Škofja Loka, Kranj and Radovljica. Buses connect the station with Bled.

Bled Jezero station On Kolodvorska cesta northwest of the lake. Trains to Bohinjska Bistrica (€1.85, 20 minutes, 18km, seven daily), from where you can catch a bus to Lake Bohinj, use this smaller station. You can travel on this line further south to Most na Soči and Nova Gorica.

Lake Bohinj

📌 04 / POP 5100 / ELEV 542M

Many visitors to Slovenia say they've never seen a more beautiful lake than Bled...that is, until they've seen the blue-green waters of Lake Bohinj, 26km to the southwest. Admittedly, Bohinj lacks Bled's glamour, but it's less crowded and in many ways more authentic. It's an ideal summer-holiday destination. People come primarily to chill out or to swim in the crystal-clear water, with leisurely cycling and walking trails to occupy them as well as outdoor pursuits like kayaking, hiking and horse riding.

◉ Sights

★ **Church of St John the Baptist** CHURCH
(Cerkev Sv Janeza Krstnika; 📌 04-574 60 10; Ribčev Laz 56; church & bell tower €4, church only €2.50; ⊙ 10am-4pm Jun-Aug, group bookings only May & Sep) This postcard-worthy church and bell tower, at the head of the lake and beside the stone bridge, dates back at least 700 years and is what every medieval church should be: small, surrounded by natural beauty and full of exquisite frescoes. The nave is Romanesque, but the Gothic presbytery dates from about 1440. Many walls and ceilings are covered with 15th- and 16th-century frescoes.

Savica Waterfall WATERFALL
(Slap Savica; 📌 04-574 60 10; www.bohinj.si; Ukanc; adult/child €3/1.50; ⊙ 8am-8pm Jul & Aug, 9am-7pm Apr-Jun, to 5pm Sep-Nov) The magnificent Savica Waterfall, which cuts deep into a gorge 78m below, is 4km from Ukanc and can be reached by a walking path from there in 1½ hours. By car, you can continue past Ukanc via a sealed road to a car park beside the Savica restaurant, from where it's a 25-minute walk up more than 500 steps and over rapids and streams to the falls. Wear decent shoes for the slippery path.

Vogel MOUNTAIN
(📌 04-572 97 12; www.vogel.si; cable car return adult/child €20/10; ⊙ cable car 8am-7pm) The glorious setting and spectacular panoramas make it worth a trip up Vogel – during winter, when it's a popular **ski resort** (day pass adult/child €32/16; ⊙ mid-Dec–Mar), but also in its 'green season', when walks and photo ops abound. The cable car runs every 30 minutes or so from its base near Ukanc – the base station is at 569m, the top station at 1535m.

🏃 Activities

Lake Bohinj is filled with activities of all sorts, from active pursuits like canyoning and paragliding from Vogel to more-sedate pastimes like hiking, cycling and horse riding. The TIC in Ribčev Laz maintains a list of tour operators and equipment-rental outfits, and can help arrange trips and tours.

Alpinsport ADVENTURE SPORTS
(📌 04-572 34 86; www.alpinsport.si; Ribčev Laz 53; ⊙ 10am-6pm) Rents equipment: canoes, kayaks, SUPs and bikes in summer; skis and snowboards in winter. It also operates guided rafting and canyoning trips. Its base is opposite Hotel Jezero in Ribčev Laz.

PAC Sports ADVENTURE SPORTS
(Perfect Adventure Choice; 📌 04-572 34 61; www.pac.si; Hostel Pod Voglom, Ribčev Laz 60; ⊙ 8am-10pm Jun-Sep, to 8pm Oct–May) Popular sports and adventure company, based in Hostel Pod Voglom, 2km west of Ribčev Laz; also has a summertime lakeside kiosk at Camp Zlatorog. Rents bikes, canoes, SUPs and kayaks, and operates guided canyoning, rafting and caving trips. In winter, it rents sleds and offers ice climbing and snowshoeing.

🛏 Sleeping & Eating

Camp Zlatorog CAMPGROUND €
(📌 059 923 648; www.camp-bohinj.si; Ukanc 5; per person €11-15.50; ⊙ May-Sep; 🅿🛜) This tree-filled campground can accommodate up to 750 guests and sits photogenically on the lake's southwestern corner, 5km from Ribčev Laz. Prices vary according to site location, with the most expensive (and desirable) sites right on the lake. Facilities are very good – including a restaurant, a laundry and water-sport rentals – and the tourist boat docks here. Tents can be hired.

Pension Stare PENSION €€
(📌 040 558 669; www.bohinj-hotel.com; Ukanc 128; s/d €60/90; 🅿🛜) This sweet 10-room

TRIGLAV NATIONAL PARK

Triglav National Park (Triglavski Narodni Park; commonly abbreviated as TNP), with an area of 840 sq km (over 4% of Slovenian territory), is one of the largest national reserves in Europe. It is a pristine, visually spectacular world of rocky mountains – the centre-piece of which is **Mt Triglav** (2864m), the country's highest peak – as well as river gorges, ravines, lakes, canyons, caves, rivers, waterfalls, forests and Alpine meadows.

The park has information centres in Bled (p439), Stara Fužina (p441) in Bohinj, and **Trenta** (Dom Trenta; ☑ 05-388 93 30; www.tnp.si; Trenta; ☺ 9am-7pm Jul-Aug, 10am-6pm May, Jun, Sep & Oct, 10am-2pm Mon-Fri Jan-Apr, closed Nov-Dec) on the Vršič Pass. These centres have displays on park flora and fauna, and are well worth a stop.

Good online starting points for learning about the park are www.tnp.si and www.hiking-trail.net. Several hiking maps are available from TICs. Two decent options: the laminated 1:50,000-scale *Triglavski Narodni Park* (€9.10; buy online from shop.pzs.si) from the Alpine Association of Slovenia (PZS), and Kartografija's widely available 1:50,000-scale *Triglavski Narodni Park* (€8; www.kartografija.si).

pension is on the Savica River in Ukanc, surrounded by a large, peaceful garden. If you really want to get away from it all without having to climb mountains, this is your place. Rooms are no-frills; there's a half-board option too.

★ **Vila Park**   BOUTIQUE HOTEL €€€
(☑ 04-572 3300; www.vila-park.si; Ukanc 129; d €100-120; [P] ☎) Vila Park creates a great first impression, with sunloungers set in expansive riverside grounds, and balconies overflowing with flowers. The interior is equally impressive, with eight elegant rooms plus a handsome lounge and dining area. Note: it's a kid-free zone.

★ **Štrud'l**   SLOVENIAN €
(☑ 041 541 877; www.facebook.com/gostilnica.trgovinica.strudl; Triglavska cesta 23, Bohinjska Bistrica; mains €6-12; ☺ 8am-10pm; ☎) This modern take on traditional farmhouse cooking is a must for foodies keen to sample local specialities. Overlook the incongruous location in the centre of Bohinjska Bistrica, and enjoy dishes like *ričet s klobaso* (barley porridge with sausage and beans).

Gostilna Pri Hrvatu   SLOVENIAN €€
(☑ 031 234 300; Srednja Vas 76; mains €10-18; ☺ 10am-11pm Wed-Mon) Get an eyeful of mountain views from the sweet creek-side terrace of this relaxed inn in Srednja Vas. Flavourful homemade dishes include buckwheat dumplings, polenta with porcini, local chamois in piquant sauce, and grilled trout.

ℹ Information

There are two main TICs in the Bohinj area: the office in **Ribčev Laz** (TIC; ☑ 04-574 60 10; www.

bohinj-info.com; Ribčev Laz 48; ☺ 8am-8pm Mon-Sat, to 6pm Sun Jul & Aug, 9am-5pm Mon-Sat, to 3pm Sun Nov & Dec, 8am-7pm Mon-Sat, 9am-3pm Sun Jan, Feb, May, Jun, Sep & Oct; ☎) is closer to the lake and handier for most visitors than the office in **Bohinjska Bistrica** (LD TURIZEM; ☑ 04-574 76 00; www.ld-turizem.si; Mencingerjeva ulica 10, Bohinjska Bistrica; ☺ 8am-7pm Mon-Sat, to 1pm Sun Jul & Aug, 9am-noon & 2-6pm Mon-Fri, 9am-1pm Sat, to noon Sun Sep-Jun; ☎). The **national park centre** (☑ 04-578 02 45; www.tnp.si; Stara Fužina 38; ☺ 8am-6pm Jul & Aug, 9am-5pm Apr-Jun, Sep & Oct) in Stara Fužina is worth a stop.

ℹ Getting There & Away

BUS

The easiest way to get to Lake Bohinj is by **bus** (Ribčev Laz) – services run frequently from Ljubljana, via Bled and Bohinjska Bistrica. **Alpetour** (☑ information 04-201 32 10; www.alpetour.si) is the major bus operator for the region.

Services from Lake Bohinj (departing from Ribčev Laz, near the TIC) run to Bled (€3.60, 40 minutes, 29km, up to 12 daily), Bohinjska Bistrica (€1.80, eight minutes, 7km, up to 20 daily) and Ljubljana (€9.80, two hours, 86km, up to nine daily)

TRAIN

Several trains daily make the run to Bohinjska Bistrica from Ljubljana (€7.30, two hours, six daily), though this route requires a change in Jesenice. There are also trains between Bled's small Bled Jezero station and Bohinjska Bistrica (€1.85, 20 minutes, 18km, seven daily).

From Bohinjska Bistrica, passenger trains to Nova Gorica (€5.80, 1¼ hours, 61km, up to eight daily) make use of a century-old, 6.3km tunnel under the mountains that provides the only direct option for reaching the Soča Valley.

CROSSING THE VRŠIČ PASS

A couple of kilometres from Kranjska Gora is one of the road-engineering marvels of the 20th century: a breakneck, Alpine road that connects Kranjska Gora with Bovec, 50km to the southwest. The trip involves no fewer than 50 pulse-quickening hairpin turns and dramatic vistas as you cross the **Vršič Pass** (Prelaz Vršič) at 1611m.

The road was commissioned during WWI by Germany and Austria-Hungary in their epic struggle with Italy. Much of the hard labour was done by Russian prisoners of war, and for that reason, the road from Kranjska Gora to the top of the pass is now called the Ruska cesta (Russian Road).

The road over the pass is usually open from May to October and is easiest to navigate by car, motorbike or bus (in summer, buses between Kranjska Gora and Bovec use this road). It is also possible – and increasingly popular – to cycle it.

SOČA VALLEY

The Soča Valley region (Posočje) stretches west of Triglav National Park and includes the outdoor activity centre of Bovec. Threading through it is the magically aquamarine Soča River. Most people come here for the rafting, hiking and skiing, though there are plenty of historical sights and locations, particularly relating to WWI, when millions of troops fought on the mountainous battlefront here.

Bovec

🖉 05 / POP 3150 / ELEV 456M

Soča Valley's de facto capital, Bovec offers plenty for adventure-sports enthusiasts. With the Julian Alps above, the Soča River below and Triglav National Park (p441) all around, you could spend a week here rafting, hiking, kayaking, mountain biking and, in winter, skiing, without ever doing the same thing twice. It's beautiful country and Bovec's a pleasant town in which to base yourself for these activities.

⦿ Sights

★ **Boka Waterfall**   WATERFALL
(Slap Boka) With a sheer vertical drop of 106m (and a second drop of 30m), Boka is the highest waterfall in Slovenia – and it's especially stunning in the spring, when snowmelt gives it extra oomph. It's 5.5km southwest of Bovec – you can drive or cycle to the area and park by the bridge, then walk about 15 minutes to the viewpoint.

Kanin Cable Car   CABLE CAR
(🖉 05-917 93 01; www.kanin.si; adult €10-34, child €8-28; ⊙ hours vary) This cable car whisks you up to the Bovec Kanin Ski Centre in a number of stages. It's most often used as an access for winter skiing or summer activ-

ities, but it's equally rewarding for sightseers – the views from the top station and en route are sweepingly beautiful. In summer in particular, the last departure heading up the mountain can be as early as 2pm, so it's usually best to visit in the morning.

🏃 Activities

There are dozens of adrenaline-raising companies in Bovec; some specialise in one activity (often rafting), while others offer multiday packages so you can try various activities (rafting, canyoning, kayaking, paragliding, climbing, caving, ziplining).

Nature's Ways   ADVENTURE SPORTS
(🖉 031 200 651; www.econaturesways.com; Čezsoča) Right by the river around 2km from Bovec, this company runs all the usual Bovec activities, including canyoning, rafting, kayaking, ziplining, caving and mountain biking. Reducing plastic pollution is part of its mantra.

Soca Rider   ADVENTURE SPORTS
(🖉 041 596 104; www.socarider.com; Trg Golobarskih Žrtev 40) Does all of the usual trips, but distinguishes itself by making families and beginners a key part of its offering.

🛏 Sleeping & Eating

Bovec has some excellent accommodation, across a range of budgets. In addition to hotels and hostels, the TIC has dozens of private rooms and apartments (from €20 per person) on its lists. Don't discount the many scenic options along the road to Trenta towards the Vršič Pass, especially if you have a campervan.

Adrenaline Check Eco Place   CAMPGROUND €
(🖉 041 383 662; www.adrenaline-check.com; Podklopca 4; campsite per person €15, s/d tent from €40/50, safari tent €120-150; ⊙ May-Sep; P 🛜) About 3km southwest of town, this fun, fab-

ulous campground makes camping easy: hire a tent under a lean-to shelter that comes with mattresses and linen, or a big, furnished safari-style tent. Cars are left in a car park, and you walk through to a large, picturesque clearing (so it's not for campervans).

Hotel Sanje ob Soči HOTEL €€
(📋 05-389 60 00; www.sanjeobsoci.com; Mala Vas 105a; s/d €80/110; 🅿️ 🛜) 'Dream on the Soča' is an architecturally striking hotel on the edge of town. Interiors are minimalist and colourful, and room sizes range from 'economy' on the ground floor to studios and family-sized apartments (named after the mountain you can see from the room's windows). There's friendly service, a sauna area, and a great breakfast spread (€12).

Dobra Vila BOUTIQUE HOTEL €€€
(📋 05-389 64 00; www.dobra-vila-bovec.si; Mala Vas 112; r €140-270; 🅿️ ❄️ @ 🛜) This stunning 10-room boutique hotel is housed in an erstwhile telephone-exchange building dating from 1932. Peppered with art deco flourishes, interesting artefacts and objets d'art, it has its own library and a wine cellar, and a fabulous restaurant with a winter garden and an outdoor terrace.

Gostilna Sovdat SLOVENIAN €€
(📋 05-388 60 27; www.gostilna-sovdat.si; Trg Golobarskih Žrtev 24; mains €7-22; ⏰ 10am-10pm) Sovdat isn't strong on aesthetics and its outdoor terrace isn't as pretty as others in town, but the crowd of locals attests to its popularity and value. Lots on the menu falls under €10, including plentiful pastas and bumper burgers. You can go upmarket, too, with the likes of gnocchi in a truffle sauce or roast beef with Gorgonzola.

Dobra Vila Restaurant SLOVENIAN €€€
(📋 05-389 64 00; www.dobra-vila-bovec.si; Mala Vas 112; 4-/6-course set menu €45/60) Easily the best place to eat in town is the polished restaurant at Dobra Vila – preferably in the pretty garden in summer. A carefully constructed menu of local, seasonal ingredients is served to an appreciative crowd. Setting, service and food are first-class; bookings are essential.

ℹ️ Information

Tourist Information Centre (TIC; 📋 05-302 96 47; www.bovec.si; Trg Golobarskih Žrtev 22; ⏰ 8am-8pm Jul & Aug, 9am-7pm Jun & Sep, 8.30am-12.30pm & 1.30-5pm Mon-Fri, 9am-5pm Sat & Sun May, shorter hours Oct-Apr) The TIC is open year-round. Winter hours will depend on the reopening of the local ski centre – expect long hours when the ski season is fully operating.

ℹ️ Getting There & Away

Bus routes run to Ljubljana (€14, 3¾ hours, 151km, three daily). Busline **Alpetour** (📋 04-532 04 45; www.alpetour.si) runs buses to Kranjska Gora (€7, 1¾ hours, 46km), via Trenta (€2.90, 30 minutes, 20km), for Vršič Pass.

SLOVENIAN KARST & COAST

The Karst region (*Kras* in Slovenian) of western Slovenia is a limestone plateau stretching inland from the Gulf of Trieste. Rivers, ponds and lakes can disappear and then resurface in the Karst's porous limestone through sinkholes and funnels, often resulting in underground caverns like the fabulous caves at Škocjan and Postojna. Slovenia has just 47km of coastline on the Adriatic Sea, but it certainly makes the most of it. Piran, the highlight, is full of Venetian architecture and has a lively seaside vibe.

Postojna

📋 05 / POP 9420 / ELEV 546M
The karst cave at Postojna is one of the largest in the world, and its stalagmite and stalactite formations are unequalled anywhere. Among Slovenia's most popular attractions, it's a busy spot – the amazing thing is how the large crowds at the entrance seem to get swallowed whole by the size of the cave, and the tourist activity doesn't detract from the wonder. It's a big, slick complex, and it doesn't come cheap. But it's still worth every minute you can spend in this magical underground world. The adjacent town of Postojna serves as a gateway to the caves and is otherwise a fairly attractive provincial Slovenian town.

⭐**Postojna Cave** CAVE
(Postojnska Jama; 📋 05-700 01 00; www.postojnska-jama.eu; Jamska cesta 30; adult/child €25.80/15.50, with Predjama Castle €35.70/21.40; ⏰ tours hourly 9am-6pm Jul & Aug, to 5pm May, Jun & Sep, 10am, noon & 3pm Nov-Mar, 10am-noon & 2-4pm Apr & Oct) The jaw-dropping Postojna Cave system, a series of caverns, halls and passages some 24km long and two million years old, was hollowed out by the Pivka River, which enters a subterranean tunnel near the cave's entrance.

PREDJAMA CASTLE

Predjama Castle (Predjamski Grad; ☑ 05-700 01 00; www.postojnska-jama.eu; Predjama 1; adult/child €13.80/8.30, with Postojna Cave €35.70/21.40; ☉ 9am-7pm Jul & Aug, to 6pm May, Jun & Sep, 10am-5pm Apr & Oct, to 4pm Nov-Mar), 9km from Postojna, is one of Europe's most dramatic castles. It teaches a clear lesson: if you want to build an impregnable fortification, put it in the gaping mouth of a cavern halfway up a 123m cliff. Its four storeys were built piecemeal over the years from 1202, but most of what you see today is from the 16th century. It looks simply unconquerable.

Visitors get to see 5km of the cave on 1½-hour tours; 3.2km of this is covered by a cool electric train. Postojna Cave has a constant temperature of 8°C to 10°C, with 95% humidity, so a warm jacket and decent shoes are advised.

Youth Hostel Proteus Postojna   HOSTEL €
(☑ 05-850 10 20; www.proteus.sgls.si; Tržaška cesta 36; dm/s/d €15/23/34; P @ ?) Don't be fooled by the institutional exterior – inside, this place is a riot of colour. It's surrounded by parkland and is a fun, chilled-out space, with three-bed rooms (shared bathrooms), kitchen and laundry access, and bike rental. The year-round hostel shares the building with student accommodation, so facilities are good. It's about 500m southwest of Titov trg.

★ **Lipizzaner Lodge**   GUESTHOUSE €€
(☑ 040 378 037; www.lipizzanerlodge.com; Landol 17; s/d/q from €55/80/100; P ?) In a relaxing rural setting 9km northwest of Postojna Cave, a Welsh-Finnish couple have established this very hospitable, affordable guesthouse. They offer seven well-equipped rooms (including family-sized, and a self-catering apartment); great-value, three-course evening meals on request (€20); brilliant local knowledge (check out their comprehensive website for an idea); forest walks (including to Predjama in 40 minutes); and bike rental.

Hotel Jama   HOTEL €€€
(☑ 05-700 01 00; www.postojnska-jama.eu; Jamska cesta 30; r from €129) This huge, concrete, socialist-era hotel is part of the Postojna Cave complex and has undergone a stunning renovation, reopening in 2016 with slick, contemporary rooms with striking colour schemes and lovely glass-walled bathrooms. It's worth paying extra (anywhere between €10 and €30) for a room with a view. There's also a restaurant and a bar, and the excellent buffet breakfast costs €12.

★ **Restaurant Proteus**   SLOVENIAN €€
(☑ 081 610 300; Titov trg 1; mains €12-22; ☉ 8am-10pm) The fanciest place in town: inside is modern and white, with booths fringed by curtains, while the terrace overlooking the main square is a fine vantage point. Accomplished cooking showcases fine regional produce – house specialities include venison goulash and steak with *teran* (red wine) sauce. It's hard to go past the four-course Chef's Slovenian Menu (€38) for value and local flavour.

ⓘ Information

Tourist Information Centre Galerija (☑ 040 122 318; www.visit-postojna.si; Trg Padlih Borchev 5; ☉ 9am-5pm Mon-Sat, to 3pm Sun) Well-stocked tourist office in the town centre.

Tourist Information Centre Postojna (TIC; ☑ 064 179 972; www.visit-postojna.si; Tržaška cesta 59; ☉ 8am-4pm Mon-Fri, 10am-3pm Sat) A smart new pavilion has been built in the town's west, on the road into Postojna. It's handy for those driving into town and there's adequate parking.

ⓘ Getting There & Away

BUS

Postojna's **bus station** (Titova cesta 2) is 200m southwest of Titov trg. Note some intercity buses will stop at the cave complex too (on timetables this is Postojnska jama). Destinations from Postojna include Divača (for Škocjan; €3.90, 30 minutes, seven daily), Ljubljana (€6.80, one hour, hourly) and Piran (€9.60, 1¾ hours, four daily).

TRAIN

The train station is on Kolodvorska cesta about 800m east of the square.

Postojna is on the main train line linking Ljubljana (€5.80, one hour) with Sežana and Trieste via Divača, and is an easy day trip from the capital. As many as 20 trains a day make the run from Ljubljana to Postojna and back.

Škocjan Caves

★ **Škocjan Caves**   CAVE
(Škocjanske Jame; ☑ 05-708 21 00; www.park-skocjanske-jame.si; Škocjan 2; cave tour adult/child Jul & Aug €20/10, Mar-Jun, Sep & Oct €18/9, Nov-Feb €16/7.50; ☉ tours hourly 10am-5pm Jun-Sep,

10am, noon, 1pm & 3.30pm Apr, May & Oct, 10am & 1pm Mon-Sat, 10am, 1pm & 3pm Sun Nov-Mar) Touring the huge, spectacular subterranean chambers of the 6km-long Škocjan Caves is a must. This remarkable cave system was carved out by the Reka River, which enters a gorge below the village of Škocjan and eventually flows into the Dead Lake, a sump at the end of the cave where it disappears. It surfaces again as the Timavo River at Duino in Italy, 34km northwest, before emptying into the Gulf of Trieste. Dress warmly and wear good walking shoes.

Pr' Vncki Tamara   GUESTHOUSE €€
(📋 05-763 30 73, 040 697 827; pr.vncki.tamara@gmail.com; Matavun 10; d €70; 🅿) This welcoming, relaxed spot in Matavun is just steps south of the entrance to the caves. It has four traditionally styled rooms with a total of 10 beds in a charming old farmhouse; we love the rustic old kitchen with the open fire. Bikes can be rented; meals can be arranged (and are highly praised).

Etna   ITALIAN €€
(📋 031 727 568; www.etna.si; Kolodvorska ulica 3a, Divača; mains €8-19; ⊙ 11am-11pm Tue-Sun) Etna takes the classic pizza-pasta-meat menu and gives it a creative twist, with surprisingly tasty (and beautifully presented) results. All the essentials are homemade (pasta, pizza dough from wholemeal flour); pizza choices are divided between classic or seasonal. The desserts are pretty as a picture.

❶ Getting There & Away

The Škocjan Caves are about 4.5km by road southeast of Divača. A bus connection runs from Divača's neighbouring train and bus stations to the caves a couple of times a day – the caves office recommends you call for times, as these change seasonally. Alternatively, there's a one-hour signed walking trail to the caves.

Buses between Ljubljana and the coast stop at Divača. Destinations include Ljubljana (€8.50, 1½ hours, seven daily) and Postojna (€3.90, 30 minutes, seven daily).

Train destinations from Divača include Ljubljana (€7.70, 1½ hours, up to 14 daily) and Postojna (€3.44, 35 minutes, up to 14 daily).

Piran

📋 05 / POP 3800

One of the loveliest towns anywhere along the Adriatic coast, picturesque Piran (Pirano in Italian) sits prettily at the tip of a narrow peninsula. Its Old Town – one of the best-preserved historical towns anywhere in the Mediterranean – is a gem of Venetian Gothic architecture, but it can be a mob scene at the height of summer. In quieter times, it's hard not to fall instantly in love with the atmospheric winding alleyways, the sunsets and the seafood restaurants.

⊙ Sights

★ Tartinijev Trg   SQUARE
The pastel-toned Tartinijev trg is a marble-paved square (oval, really) that was the inner harbour until it was filled in 1894. The statue of a nattily dressed gentleman in the centre is of native son, composer and violinist Giuseppe Tartini (1692–1770). East is the 1818 Church of St Peter (Cerkev Sv Petra). Across from the church is Tartini House (Tartinijeva Hiša; 📋 05-671 00 40; www.pomorskimuzej.si; Kajuhova ulica 12; adult/child €2/1; ⊙ 9am-noon & 6-9pm Jul & Aug, shorter hours Sep-Jun), the composer's birthplace. The Court House (Sodniška Palača) and the porticoed 19th-century Municipal Hall (Občinska Palača), home to the tourist information centre, dominate the western edge of the square.

Cathedral of St George   CATHEDRAL
(Župnijska Cerkev Sv Jurija; www.zupnija-piran.si; Adamičeva ulica 2) A cobbled street leads from behind the red Venetian House Tartinijev trg on to Piran's hilltop cathedral, baptistery and bell tower. The cathedral was built in baroque style in the early 17th century on the site of an earlier church from 1344.

The cathedral's doors are usually open and a metal grille allows you to see some of the richly ornate and newly restored interior, but full access is via the Parish Museum of St George (📋 05-673 34 40; adult/child €2/1; ⊙ 9am-1pm & 5-7.30pm Mon-Fri, 9am-2pm & 5-8pm Sat, from 11am Sun), which includes the church's treasury and catacombs.

Bell Tower   TOWER
(Zvonik; Adamičeva ulica; €1; ⊙ 10am-8pm summer, shorter hours rest of year) The Cathedral of St George's free-standing, 46.5m bell tower, built in 1609, was clearly modelled on the campanile of San Marco in Venice and provides a fabulous backdrop to many a town photo. Its 147 stairs can be climbed for fabulous views of the town and harbour. Next to it, the octagonal 17th-century baptistery contains altars and paintings. It is now sometimes used as an exhibition space. To the east is a 200m-long stretch of the 15th-century town wall.

SLOVENIA PIRAN

🛏 Sleeping & Eating

Piran has a number of atmospheric choices and an unusually stable accommodation offering. Prices are higher here than elsewhere along the coast, and you'd be crazy to arrive without a booking in summer. If you're looking for a private room, start at **Maona Tourist Agency** (☑05-674 03 63; www.maona. si; Cankarjevo nabrežje 7; ☉9am-8pm Mon-Sat, 10am-1pm & 5-7pm Sun) or **Turist Biro** (☑05-673 25 09; www.turistbiro-ag.si; Tomažičeva ulica 3; ☉9am-1pm & 4-7pm Mon-Sat, 10am-1pm Sun).

Max Piran   B&B €€
(☑041 692 928; www.maxpiran.com; Ulica IX Korpusa 26; d €70-88; ❉🛜) Piran's most romantic accommodation has just six handsome, compact rooms, each bearing a woman's name rather than a number, in a delightful, coral-coloured, 18th-century town house. It's just down from the Cathedral of St George, and is excellent value.

★PachaMama   GUESTHOUSE €€€
(PachaMama Pleasant Stay; ☑05-918 34 95; www.pachamama.si; Trubarjeva 8; r €80-175; ❉🛜) Built by travellers for travellers, this excellent guesthouse sits just off Tartinijev trg and offers 12 fresh rooms, decorated with timber and lots of travel photography. Cool private bathrooms and a 'secret garden' add appeal. There are also a handful of studios and family-sized apartments dotted around town, of an equally high standard.

Cantina Klet   SEAFOOD €
(Trg 1 Maja 10; mains €5-10; ☉10am-11pm) This small wine bar sits pretty under a grapevine canopy on Trg 1 Maja. You order drinks from the bar (cheap local wine from the barrel or well-priced beers), but we especially love the self-service window (labelled 'Fritolin pri Cantini') where you order from a small blackboard menu of fishy dishes, like fish fillet with polenta, fried calamari or fish tortilla.

★Pri Mari   MEDITERRANEAN €€
(☑041 616 488, 05-673 47 35; www.primari-piran. com; Dantejeva ulica 17; mains €8-24; ☉noon-4pm & 6-10pm Tue-Sun Apr-Oct, noon-4pm & 6-10pm Tue-Sat, noon-6pm Sun Nov-Mar) This stylishly rustic and welcoming restaurant run by an Italian-Slovenian couple serves the most inventive Mediterranean and Slovenian dishes in town – lots of fish – and a good selection of local wines. Space is limited, so it pays to book ahead.

ℹ Information

Tourist Information Centre (TIC; ☑05-673 44 40; www.portoroz.si; Tartinijev trg 2; ☉9am-10pm Jul & Aug, to 7pm May, to 5pm Sep-Apr & Jun) Your first stop for information on Piran and Portorož. It's in the impressive Municipal Hall.

ℹ Getting There & Away

BUS

Arriva (☑090 74 11; www.arriva.si) buses serve the coast; see the website for schedules and prices. From the **bus station** (Dantejeva ulica) south of the centre, three buses daily make the journey to Ljubljana (€13, three hours), via Divača and Postojna.

SURVIVAL GUIDE

ℹ Directory A–Z

ACCOMMODATION

Slovenia has all manner of places to bed down. You'll need to book well in advance if you're travelling during peak season (July and August on the coast and at Bled or Bohinj; spring and autumn in Ljubljana).

Hotels Runs the gamut between family-run operations to five-star boutiques.

Hostels Both indie hostels and HI-affiliated affairs are plentiful.

Pensions & Guesthouses Often family-owned and good value.

Private Rooms Single rooms or fully furnished flats. Locate via tourist information centres.

Mountain Huts Simple beds, with or without facilities, near hiking trails.

MONEY

ATMs are widely available or you can exchange money at banks. Credit and debit cards are accepted by most businesses throughout the country.

OPENING HOURS

Opening hours can vary throughout the year. We've provided high-season opening hours.

Banks 8.30am to 12.30pm and 2pm to 5pm Monday to Friday

Bars 11am to midnight Sunday to Thursday, to 1am or 2am Friday and Saturday

Restaurants 11am to 10pm

Shops 8am to 7pm Monday to Friday, to 1pm Saturday

PUBLIC HOLIDAYS

Slovenia celebrates 14 *prazniki* (holidays) each year. If any of them fall on a Sunday, the Monday becomes the holiday.

New Year's 1 and 2 January
Prešeren Day (Slovenian Culture Day) 8 February
Easter & Easter Monday March/April
Insurrection Day 27 April
Labour Day holidays 1 and 2 May
National Day 25 June
Assumption Day 15 August
Reformation Day 31 October
All Saints' Day 1 November
Christmas Day 25 December
Independence Day 26 December

TELEPHONE

Slovenia's country code is 386. Slovenia has six area codes (01 to 05 and 07). Ljubljana's area code is 01.

➞ To call a landline within Slovenia, include the area code if the number you are calling is outside the area code.

➞ To call abroad from Slovenia, dial 00 followed by the country and area codes, and then the number.

➞ To call Slovenia from abroad, dial the international access code, 386 (the country code for Slovenia), the area code (minus the initial zero) and the number.

ℹ Getting There & Away

Most travellers arrive in Slovenia by air, or by rail and road connections from neighbouring countries. Flights, cars and tours can be booked online at lonelyplanet.com/bookings.

AIR

Ljubljana's Jože Pučnik Airport (p437), 27km north of the capital, is the only air gateway for travelling to and from Slovenia. The arrivals hall has a branch of the **Slovenia Tourist Information Centre** (STIC; www.visitljubljana.si; Jože Pučnik Airport; ☺ 8am-7pm Mon-Fri, 9am-5pm Sat & Sun Oct-May, 8am-9pm Jun-Sep) and a bank of ATMs (located just outside the terminal).

The Slovenian carrier **Adria Airways** (☑ flight info 04-259 45 82, reservations 01-369 10 10; www.adria.si) serves more than 30 European destinations on regularly scheduled flights; there are useful connections to other former Yugoslav capitals. Budget carriers include **EasyJet** (www.easyjet.com) and **Wizz Air** (☑ Slovenia call centre 090 100 206; www.wizzair.com).

LAND
Bus

Several long-haul coach companies operate in Slovenia, connecting the country to destinations around Europe. This service is often cheaper and faster than trains. Buses are also useful for reaching areas where train connections from Slovenia are deficient, including to points in Italy and Bosnia & Hercegovina. Most international services arrive and depart from Ljubljana's main bus station (p437).

Train

The **Slovenian Railways** (Slovenske Železnice, SŽ; ☑ info 1999; www.slo-zeleznice.si) network links up with the European railway network via Austria (Villach, Salzburg, Graz, Vienna), Italy (Trieste), Germany (Munich, Frankfurt), Czech Republic (Prague), Croatia (Zagreb, Rijeka), Hungary (Budapest), Switzerland (Zürich) and Serbia (Belgrade). The Slovenian Railways website has full information in English on current international connections.

SEA

During summer it's possible to travel by sea between Piran and the Italian ports of Venice and Trieste.

ℹ Getting Around

BICYCLE

Cycling is a popular way to get around. Larger towns and cities have dedicated bicycle lanes and traffic lights. Bicycle-rental shops are generally concentrated in the more popular tourist areas. Expect to pay from €3/17 per hour/day.

BUS

The Slovenian bus network is extensive and you can reach every major city and town, and many smaller places, by bus. A range of companies serve the country, but prices tend to be uniform: around €4/6/10/17 for 25/50/100/200km of travel. Buy your ticket from ticket windows at the bus station *(avtobusna postaja)* or pay the driver as you board.

CAR & MOTORCYCLE

Roads in Slovenia are good. Tolls are not paid separately on motorways. Instead, cars must display a *vinjeta* (road-toll sticker) on the windscreen. The sticker costs €15/30/110 for a week/month/year for cars and €7.50/30/55 for motorbikes, and is available at petrol stations, post offices and tourist information centres. Failure to display a sticker risks a fine of up to €300. For emergency roadside assistance, call 1987 anywhere in Slovenia.

TRAIN

Domestic trains are operated by Slovenian Railways. The network is extensive and connects many major cities and towns. Trains tend to offer more space and are more comfortable than buses, and can occasionally be cheaper. Trains are useful mainly for covering long distances. The railways website has a timetable and extensive information in English.

Ukraine

POP 44.6 MILLION

Best Places to Eat

➡ Ostannya Barikada (p453)

➡ Shoti (p453)

➡ Baczewski (p458)

➡ Trapezna Idey (p458)

➡ Bernardazzi (p460)

➡ Kotelok Mussels Bar (p460)

Best Places to Stay

➡ Dream House Hostel (p452)

➡ Hotel Bontiak (p453)

➡ Villa Stanislavsky (p458)

➡ Leopolis Hotel (p458)

➡ Babushka Grand Hostel (p460)

➡ Frederic Koklen (p460)

Why Go?

Shaped like a broken heart, with the Dnipro River dividing it into two, this Slavic hinterland is a vast swathe of sage-flavoured steppe filled with sunflowers and wild poppies. Blessed with a near-ideal climate and the richest soil in Europe, it's one huge garden of a country where flowers are blossoming, fruit are ripening and farmers markets sing hymns of abundance.

If only its history were as idyllic. Just over two decades into a very troubled independence, Ukraine is dogged by a conflict with neighbouring Russia that has left Crimea and a small chunk of its eastern territory off limits to most travellers. But the country's main attractions, including eclectic and rebellious Kyiv, architecturally rich Lviv and flamboyant Odesa, are well away from the conflict zone. A long stretch of the Black Sea coast invites beach fun, while the Carpathians draw skiers in winter and cyclists in summer.

When to Go
Kyiv

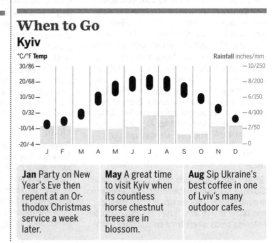

°C/°F **Temp**

Rainfall inches/mm

Jan Party on New Year's Eve then repent at an Orthodox Christmas service a week later.

May A great time to visit Kyiv when its countless horse chestnut trees are in blossom.

Aug Sip Ukraine's best coffee in one of Lviv's many outdoor cafes.

Entering the Country

The majority of visitors fly to Ukraine – generally to Kyiv. Some new direct train services to/from Poland have appeared and, as it has across Europe, international bus travel has made a big comeback.

ITINERARIES

Two Days

A couple of days are just enough to 'do' Kyiv (p452), starting at its stellar attraction, the Kyevo-Pecherska Lavra (p452) (aka the Caves Monastery). Follow this with a hike up artsy Andriyivsky uzviz (p452), before plunging into the beeswax-perfumed Byzantine interior of Unesco-listed St Sophia's Cathedral (p452).

Five Days

Having seen the sights in Kyiv, hop aboard a slow night train to Lviv (p457), Ukraine's most central European city complete with bean-scented coffee houses, Gothic and baroque churches, and quaintly rattling trams.

One Week

Take another overnight train or fly to Odesa (p459), a flamboyant port city filled with elegant Parisian architecture and boasting an outstanding culinary culture that comes close to being regarded as 'Odesa cuisine'.

Essential Food & Drink

When it comes to food, Ukraine is the land of abundance, with distinct regional variations. Here are some of the Ukrainian staples you are certain to find on restaurant menus:

Borshch The national soup made with beetroot, pork fat and herbs.

Salo Cured pig fat, cut into slices and eaten with bread.

Varenyky Pasta pockets filled with everything from mashed potato to sour cherries.

Halushky Pasta cubes served with pieces of meat or liver.

Banosh A west Ukrainian version of polenta served with cottage cheese.

AT A GLANCE

Area 603,628 sq km

Capital Kyiv

Country Code ☑ 380

Currency Hryvnya (uah)

Emergency ☑ 112

Language Ukrainian, Russian

Time East European Time (GMT/UTC plus two hours)

Visas Not required for EU, UK, US and Canadian citizens for stays of up to 90 days

Sleeping Price Ranges

The following price ranges refer to a double room in high season.

€ less than 500uah

€€ 500–1500uah

€€€ more than 1500uah

Eating Price Ranges

The following price ranges refer to a main course.

€ less than 100uah

€€ 100–200uah

€€€ more than 200uah

Ukraine Highlights

1 Kyevo-Pecherska Lavra (p452) Inspecting Kyiv's collection of mummified monks by candlelight.

2 Andriyivsky Uzviz (p452) Making an ascent of Kyiv's most atmospheric street.

3 Lviv (p457) Doing a spot of cobble-surfing in the historical centre packed with churches, museums and eccentric restaurants.

4 Lychakivsky Cemetery (p457) Exploring Lviv's final resting place of Ukraine's great and good.

KYIV КИЇВ

⌨ 044 / POP 2.9 MILLION

In the beginning there was Kyiv. Long before Ukraine and Russia existed, the city's inhabitants were already striding up and down the green hills, idling hot afternoons away on the Dnipro River and promenading along Khreshchatyk – then a stream, now the main avenue. From here, East Slavic civilisation spread all the way to Alaska.

Today, history continues to unfold. As revolution has come and gone, and as war in the east smoulders, Ukraine's capital has rebelled yet again, only this time culturally. A creative wave has swept over the city, embodied by urban art, vintage cafes and 24-hour parties. Seemingly overnight, Kyiv has become hip.

It's also cheap. You can eat at superb restaurants and drink at hidden cocktail bars for a fraction of what they would cost in the West. Kyiv's time is clearly now – or until the next revolution rolls around.

⦿ Sights

★ **St Sophia's Cathedral** CHURCH
(pl Sofiyska; grounds/cathedral/bell tower 20/80/40uah; ⊙ cathedral & museums 10am-6pm, grounds & bell tower 9am-7pm; Ⓜ Zoloti Vorota) The interior is the most astounding aspect of Kyiv's oldest standing church. Many of the mosaics and frescoes are original, dating back to 1017–31, when the cathedral was built to celebrate Prince Yaroslav's victory in protecting Kyiv from the Pechenegs (tribal raiders). While equally attractive, the building's gold domes and 76m-tall wedding-cake bell tower are 18th-century baroque additions. It's well worth climbing the bell tower for a bird's-eye view of the cathedral and 360-degree panoramas of Kyiv.

★ **Kyevo-Pecherska Lavra** MONASTERY
(Києво-Печерська лавра, Caves Monastery; ⌨ 044-406 6375; http://kplavra.kiev.ua; vul Lavrska 9; upper/lower Lavra 25uah/free; ⊙ 9am-7pm Apr-Sep, 9am-6pm Oct-Mar, caves 8.30am-4.30pm; Ⓜ Arsenalna) Tourists and Orthodox pilgrims alike flock to the Lavra, set on 28 hectares of grassy hills above the Dnipro River in Pechersk. It's easy to see why tourists come: the monastery's cluster of gold-domed churches is a feast for the eyes, the hoard of Scythian gold rivals that of the Hermitage, and the underground labyrinths lined with mummified monks are exotic and intriguing. For pilgrims, the rationale is much simpler: to them, this is the holiest ground in the country.

★ **Maidan Nezalezhnosti** SQUARE
(майдан Незалежності, Independence Sq; Ⓜ Maidan Nezalezhnosti) Be it celebration or revolution, whenever Ukrainians want to get together – and they often do – 'Maidan' is the nation's meeting point. The square saw pro-independence protests in the 1990s and the Orange Revolution in 2004. But all of that was eclipsed by the Euromaidan Revolution in 2013–14, when it was transformed into an urban guerrilla camp besieged by government forces. In peaceful times, Maidan is more about festiveness than feistiness, with weekend concerts and a popular nightly fountain show.

Yet the echo of revolution is omnipresent. Makeshift memorials on vul Instytutska serve as a sombre reminder of those slain in Euromaidan. Images of burning tyres and army tents from that fateful winter will forever linger in the Ukrainian conscience.

Andriyivsky Uzviz STREET
(Андріївський узвіз, Andrew's Descent; Ⓜ Kontraktova Pl) According to legend, a man walked up the hill here, erected a cross and prophesied, 'A great city will stand on this spot.' That man was the Apostle Andrew, hence the name of Kyiv's quaintest thoroughfare, a steep cobbled street that winds its way up from Kontraktova pl to vul Volodymyrska, with a vaguely Montparnasse feel. Along the length of 'the *uzviz*' you'll find cafes, art galleries and vendors selling all manner of souvenirs and kitsch.

🛏 Sleeping

★ **Dream House Hostel** HOSTEL €
(⌨ 044-580 2169; https://dream-hostels.com; Andriyivsky uzviz 2D; dm/s/d without bathroom from 270/855/1100uah, d with bathroom 1350uah; ❄ @ 🕾; Ⓜ Kontraktova Pl) Kyiv's most happening hostel is this gleaming 100-bed affair superbly located at the bottom of Andriyivsky uzviz. An attached **cafe-bar** (⊙ 8am-midnight; 🕾), a basement kitchen, a laundry room, key cards, bike hire, and daily events and tours make this a comfortable and engaging base from which to explore the capital. A few doubles (some with bathroom) are available in addition to dorms.

★ **Sunflower B&B Hotel** B&B €€
(⌨ 044-279 3846; www.sunflowerhotel.kiev.ua; vul Kostyolna 9/41; s/d incl breakfast 1950/2300uah;

NUKES & CROOKS

Two of the country's most visited as well as most unusual attractions can be done as day trips from Kyiv. One is **Chornobyl**, the apocalyptic site of the world's worst nuclear catastrophe, which happened in April 1986. A trip into the vast 'exclusion zone' around the troubled nuclear plant, now covered by a massive sarcophagus, is a moving journey back to the days of the Soviet Union and the most thought-provoking nine hours you'll spend in Ukraine. Radiation is low enough for the place to be proclaimed safe to visit, so many travel companies in Kyiv, such as **SoloEast Travel** (📞 044-279 3505; www.tourkiev.com; vul Prorizna 10, office 105; ⏰ 9am-6pm Mon-Fri, 10am-2pm Sat; Ⓜ Khreshchatyk), run Chornobyl tours, which typically involve bussing people from Maidan Nezalezhnosti to the site, located 110km north of Kyiv. Expect to pay US$80 to US$110 per person to join a group day tour.

Another product of Ukraine's turbulent recent history, Kyiv's newest tourist attraction is **Mezhyhirya** (📞 050 664 0080; www.mnp.org.ua; vul Ivana Franka 19, Novi Petrivtsi; adult/child 120/50uah; ⏰ 8am-9.30pm May-Sep, 8am to dark Oct-Apr; 🚌 397), the estate that once 'belonged' to ex-president Viktor Yanukovych, who was ousted in the Euromaidan Revolution of 2014 and forced to escape to Russia. A wander through the opulent grounds – totalling 137 hectares and costing hundreds of millions of dollars to create – gives visitors an idea of just how corrupt the Yanukovych regime had become. Now a national park, the estate is centred around Yanukovych's personal dacha (country house), a 620 sq-metre pinewood behemoth. Mezhyhirya is about 15km north of Kyiv. Bus 397 goes right to the park, via Vyshhorod centre, from either Petrivka (50 minutes) or Heroyiv Dnipra (35 minutes) metro stations. Departures are every hour on the hour from Petrivka.

❄ @ 🛜; Ⓜ Maidan Nezalezhnosti) Just off maidan Nezalezhnosti but well hidden from noisy traffic and crowds, this B&B (and definitely not hotel) seems to have been designed by a super-tidy granny. The airy, light-coloured rooms have a retro feel and there are extras like umbrellas and a shoe-polishing machine that you wouldn't expect. Continental breakfast is served in your room.

Hotel Bontiak — BOUTIQUE HOTEL €€€
(📞 098 538 1538; www.bontiak.com; vul Irynynska 5; incl breakfast s 2500, d 2980-3390uah; ❄ @ 🛜; Ⓜ Zoloti Vorota) Tucked in a quiet courtyard a five-minute walk from maidan Nezalezhnosti, this cosy boutique hotel is built into Kyiv's hilly landscape, which is why the reception is on the top floor. The stylishly minimalist rooms are generously sized and well equipped, and breakfast is served in your room.

🍴 Eating

⭐ Kyivska Perepichka — PIES €
(Київська перепічка; vul Bohdana Khmelnytskoho 3; perepichka 15uah; ⏰ 8.30am-9pm Mon-Sat, 10am-9pm Sun; Ⓜ Teatralna) A perpetually long queue moves with lightning speed towards a window where two women hand out pieces of fried dough enclosing a mouth-watering sausage. The place became a local institution long before the first 'hot dog' hit town. An essential Kyiv experience.

⭐ Ostannya Barikada — UKRAINIAN €€
(Last Barricade; 📞 068 907 1991; maidan Nezalezhnosti 1; mains 130-200uah; ⏰ 11am-midnight; ❄ 🛜; Ⓜ Maidan Nezalezhnosti) Hidden in a 'secret bunker' under maidan Nezalezhnosti, this is both a nationalist shrine and one of Kyiv's best restaurants. Everything – from the cheeses and *horilka* (vodka) to the craft beer and steaks – is 100% homegrown. Ukraine's three modern revolutions are eulogised everywhere. Getting in is a quest, but as poet Taras Shevchenko said, 'Fight and you'll win.'

Tintin — VIETNAMESE €€
(📞 097 828 7878; www.facebook.com/TinTin.Velo drome; vul Lypynskoho 15; mains 120-200uah; ⏰ noon-11pm; Ⓜ Zoloti Vorota) This gem enjoys a wonderfully surreal end-of-the-universe setting by the velodrome and doubles as a really cool bar. Owners seem to be positively obsessed with Vietnamese soups and curries, and super-friendly staff are trained to explain the ingredients and cooking methods. A frivolous chain of associations brings the Belgian cartoon character into the equation, but it's only for the better.

⭐ Shoti — GEORGIAN €€€
(Кафе Шоти; 📞 044-339 9399; vul Mechnykova 9; mains 160-480uah; ⏰ noon-11pm; ❄ 🛜; Ⓜ Klovska) This is modern Georgian cuisine at its finest. Try the fork-whipped egg-and-butter

Central Kyiv

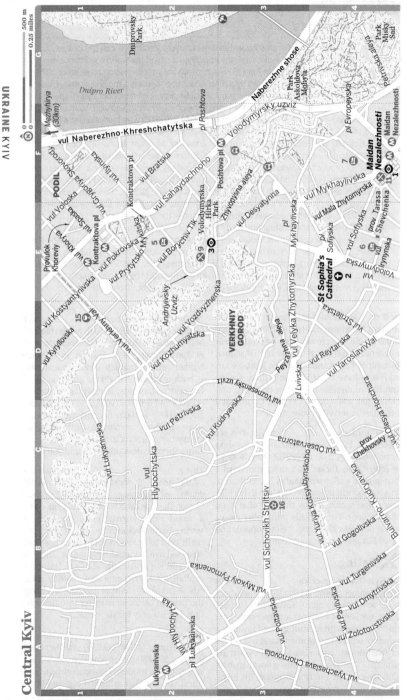

Dnipro River

Mezhyhirya (30km)

PODIL

VERKHNIY GOROD

St Sophia's Cathedral

Maidan Nezalezhnosti

vul Naberezhno-Khreshchatytska

Naberezhne shose

Dniprovsky Park

Park Misky Sad

Park Askoldova Mohyla

Petrivska aleya

pl Poshtova

Poshtova pl

Volodymyrsky uzviz

pl Evropeyska

vul Mykhaylivska

vul Mala Zhytomyrska

prov Tarasa Shevchenka

Maidan Nezalezhnosti

vul Sofiyska

vul Sahaydachnoho

vul Bratska

Kontraktova pl

vul Volodymyrska

pl Sofiyska

vul Volodymyrska

vul Trohsvyatytelska

Zhytnyorzka aleya

Zhyvopysna aleya

vul Desyatynna

pl Mykhaylivska

vul Velyka Zhytomyrska

vul Striletska

vul Volodymyrska Hirka Park

Volodymyrska

vul Borychiv Tik

vul Prytysko-Mykilska

vul Pokrovska

Kontraktova pl

vul Spaska

vul Voloska

vul Hryhoriya Skovorody

vul Illinska

Provulok Khoreviy

vul Khoryv

Andriyivsky Uzviz

vul Vozdvyzhenska

vul Kozhumyatska

Peyzazhna aleya

vul Reytarska

vul Yaroslaviv Val

vul Kostyantynivska

vul Kyrylivska

vul Verkhniy Val

vul Hlybochytska

vul Petrivska

vul Kudryavska

vul Voznesensky uzviz

pl Lvivska

vul Lvivska

vul Observatorna

prov Chekhovsky

vul Olesya Honchara

Bulvar Tarasa Shevchenka

vul Lukyanivska

vul Sichovykh Striltsiv

vul Artema Kotsyubynskoho

vul Gogolivska

vul Mykoly Pymonenka

vul Hlybochytska

vul Lukyanivska

pl Lukyanivska

vul Bulvarno-Kudryavska

vul Turgenivska

vul Dmytrivska

vul Pavlivska

vul Zolotoustivska

vul Poltavska

vul Vyacheslava Chornovola

Lukyanivska

1
2
3
5
6
7
9
11
15
16

500 m
0.25 miles

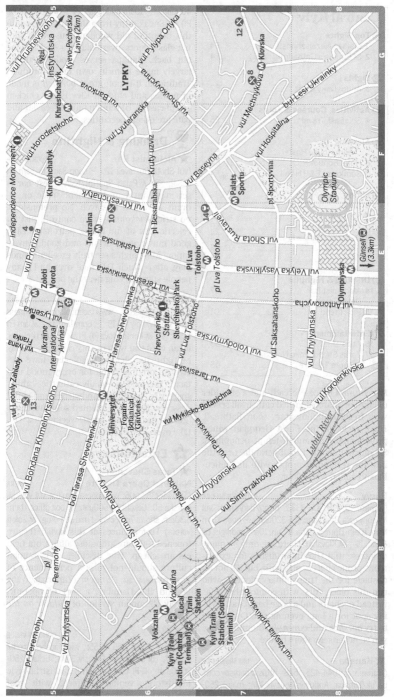

UKRAINE KYIV

Central Kyiv

khachapuri (cheese bread) and a shoulder of lamb or charcoal-grilled catfish, all served with fresh, complimentary *shoti* flatbread. Huge racks of the finest Georgian wines, professionally decanted, tempt oenophiles. Sit outside on the broad veranda, or settle into the restaurant proper with its meticulously scuffed wood floor.

Barvy UKRAINIAN €€€
(Барви; ☑ 098 306 3333; http://barvy.rest; vul Mechnykova 3; mains 125-320uah; ⊙noon-11pm Mon, 10am-11pm Tue-Thu & Sun, 10am-midnight Fri & Sat; ☎; Ⓜ Klovska) There are only so many quintessential Ukrainian dishes for experiment-prone chefs to play with, but it's not an obstacle for the true culinary pioneers who run this place. Airy, with comfortable sofas instead of chairs and a large bar, it's an inviting spot for a long evening out. Come here to try *borshch* and *varenyky* dumplings like you've never seen them before.

★**Kanapa** UKRAINIAN €€€
(Канапа; ☑ 044-425 4548; https://borysov. ua/uk/kanapa; Andriyivsky uzviz 19A; mains 250-

400uah; ⊙10am-midnight; ☎; Ⓜ Kontraktova Pl) ✦ Sneak away from the busy *uzviz* into this beautiful old wooden house with sliding-glass doors overlooking a lush ravine out back. Kanapa serves modern cuisine largely made from its own farm's produce. Traditional it is not: green *borshch* is made of nettles and chicken Kiev is not chicken but pheasant. Ukrainian mussels, caviar and pâté are other specialities.

🍷 Drinking & Nightlife

★**Alchemist Bar** COCKTAIL BAR
(vul Shota Rustaveli 12; ⊙noon-3am, to 5am Fri & Sat; ☎; Ⓜ Palats Sportu) Kyiv's best bar is set in an intimate basement space on vibrant vul Shota Rustaveli. No pretensions, no strict *feiskontrol* (face control), just an eclectic mix of fun-loving patrons chasing good music, good drinks and good conversation. Most nights see truly excellent bands play, after which DJs take over and many people start dancing near the bar.

★**Pink Freud** COCKTAIL BAR
(☑ 050 991 9818; www.facebook.com/pinkfreud kyiv; vul Nyzhniy Val 19; ⊙6pm-1am, to 2.30am Fri & Sat; ☎; Ⓜ Kontraktova Pl) Pink Freud reckons it can cure you with quality cocktails. It may be right: its talented mixologists have created an original drink for every mood and taste. The food is equally cathartic – think spare ribs, boutique sandwiches and sinful desserts. There are talented solo musicians (guitar, sax, piano) most weeknights; DJs take over at weekends.

☆ Entertainment

★**Taras Shevchenko
National Opera Theatre** OPERA
(☑ 044-235 2606; www.opera.com.ua; vul Volodymyrska 50; tickets 20-500uah; ⊙box office 11am-5.30pm, shows 7pm, closed mid-Jun–Aug; Ⓜ Zoloti Vorota) Performances at this lavish theatre (opened 1901) are grandiose affairs, but tickets are cheap. True disciples of Ukrainian culture should not miss a performance of *Zaporozhets za Dunaem* (Zaporizhzhyans Beyond the Danube), a sort of operatic, purely Ukrainian version of *Fiddler on the Roof.*

Atlas CONCERT VENUE
(Атлас; ☑ 067 155 2255; www.facebook.com/ atlas37; vul Sichovykh Striltsiv 37-41; tickets 250-2000uah; ⊡ Pl Lvivska) This industrial-style multistorey venue, complete with roof

terrace, caters to all musical tastes – from techno to heavy metal – with a sprinkling of theatre and poetry readings. The best of the best in Ukrainian and foreign music gravitate here these days.

❶ Getting Around

TO/FROM THE AIRPORT

Boryspil airport is connected to Kyiv's main station (p457) by the round-the-clock **Skybus** service (90uah, 45 minutes to one hour). There is also a new train service between the two (80uah, 35 minutes), but it is not always reliable. Zhulyany airport is served by trolleybus 9 that departs from Bessarabska pl.

PUBLIC TRANSPORT

Kyiv's crowded, but efficient metro runs between around 6am and midnight. Plastic tokens are sold at windows and dispensers at stations. Buy tickets for buses, trolleybuses, trams and *marshrutky* (fixed-route minibuses) from the driver or conductor. One ride by metro or overground transport costs 8uah.

LVIV ЛЬВІВ

📞 032 / POP 728,000

If you've spent time in other Ukrainian regions, Lviv will come as a shock. Mysterious and architecturally lovely, this Unesco-listed city is the country's least Soviet and exudes the same authentic Central European charm as pretourism Prague or Kraków once did. Its quaint cobbles, bean-perfumed coffeehouses and rattling trams are a continent away from the Soviet brutalism of the east. It's also a place where the candle of Ukrainian national identity burns brightest and where Russian is definitely a minority language.

But the secret is out, and those who foresaw that Lviv would become Ukraine's top tourist attraction are watching their prediction come true. No other city is more geared up for visitors and no other attracts so many of them. Lviv has the best range of hotels in the country, plus hostels, tour agencies, guides and English-language information abound, making this Ukraine's premier destination by a long way.

◎ Sights

★ Ploshcha Rynok SQUARE

FREE Lviv was declared a Unesco World Heritage Site in 1998, and this old market square lies at its heart. The square was progressively rebuilt after a major fire in the early 16th century destroyed the original. Around 40 townhouses hem the square's perimeter. Most of these three- and four-storey buildings have uniform dimensions, with three windows per storey overlooking the square. This was the maximum number of windows allowed tax free and those buildings with four or more belonged to the extremely wealthy.

Pl Rynok is at its best on summer evenings when crowds of people emerge to enjoy the buskers, beer and generally good-natured atmosphere.

★ Lychakivsky Cemetery CEMETERY

(Личаківський цвинтар; 📞 032-275 5415; www.lviv-lychakiv.com.ua; vul Pekarska; adult/student 25/15uah; ⊙9am-6pm Oct-Mar, to 8pm Apr-Sep; 🚍7) Don't leave town until you've seen this amazing 42-hectare cemetery, only a short ride on tram 7 from the centre. This is the Père Lachaise of Eastern Europe, with the same sort of overgrown grounds and Gothic aura as the famous Parisian necropolis (but

UKRAINE LVIV

---

❶ MOVING AROUND UKRAINE

Fast daytime trains are the preferable mode of transportation in Ukraine. These are modern, comfortable and usually have wi-fi. From Kyiv's **main train station** (Central Terminal; 📞 044-309 7005; pl Vokzalna 2; Ⓜ Vokzalna) there are three Intercity+ services daily for Lviv (360uah, five hours) and one to Odesa (370uah, 7¼ hours). There are also useful overnight services from Kyiv to Odesa (700uah, 7¾ hours) and from Odesa to Lviv (700uah, 10 hours).

Flights are also convenient, especially if you use Zhulyany airport (p462) in Kyiv, which is closer to the city and more manageable than Boryspil airport (p462). There are no direct flights between Odesa and Lviv.

Bus journeys can be arduous, so try and stick with well-established bus companies such as **Gunsel** (📞 044-525 4505; www.gunsel.com.ua; Central Bus Station), which runs useful services between Kyiv and Odesa (400uah, seven hours).

containing less-well-known people). Laid out in the late 18th century, it's packed full of western Ukraine's great and good. Pride of place goes to the grave of revered nationalist poet Ivan Franko.

Latin Cathedral CATHEDRAL
(www.lwowskabazylika.org.ua; pl Katedralna 1; ⊙8.30am-5pm Mon-Sat, 2-5.30pm Sun) With various chunks dating from between 1370 and 1480, this working cathedral is one of Lviv's most impressive churches. The exterior is most definitely Gothic, while the heavily gilded interior, one of the city's highlights, has a more baroque feel, with colourfully wreathed pillars hoisting frescoed vaulting and mysterious side chapels glowing in candlelit half-light. Services are in four languages, including English.

If you walk around the outside of the cathedral, you'll eventually come to a relief of Pope John Paul II, erected to commemorate his visit to Lviv in 2001.

🛏 Sleeping

⭐**Old City Hostel** HOSTEL €
(☑032-294 9644; www.oldcityhostel.lviv.ua; vul Beryndy 3; dm 160uah, d with/without bathroom 700/600uah; @🛜) Occupying two floors of an elegantly fading tenement just steps from pl Rynok, this expertly run hostel, with period features and views of the Shevchenko statue from the wrap-around balcony, has long established itself as the city's best. Fluff-free dorms hold four to eight beds, shower queues are unheard of, sturdy lockers keep your stuff safe and there's a well-equipped kitchen.

⭐**Villa Stanislavsky** BOUTIQUE HOTEL €€
(☑032-275 2505; www.villastanislavskyi.com. ua; vul Henerala Tarnavskoho 75; r from 850uah; 🅿❄🛜) This hilltop villa stands amid the splendid decay of what used to be a posh fin de siècle residential neighbourhood, 20 minutes on foot from the centre. The dark, polished wood of the stairs and furniture and the placid surroundings provide much-needed respite from the old town's hustle and bustle. A dedicated chess room is the cherry on the sundae.

⭐**Leopolis Hotel** HOTEL €€€
(☑032-295 9500; www.leopolishotel.com; vul Teatralna 16; s/d 2700/3050uah; ❄@🛜) One of the historical centre's finest places to catch some Zs. Every guest room in this 18th-century edifice is different, but all have a well-stocked minibar, elegant furniture and an Italian-marble bathroom with underfloor heating. Wheelchair-friendly facilities, a new spa/fitness area in the cellars and a pretty decent brasserie are extras you won't find anywhere else.

✖ Eating

⭐**Trapezna Idey** UKRAINIAN €
(Трапезна ідей; ☑032-254 6155; www.idem. org.ua; vul Valova 18A; mains 50-100uah; ⊙11am-11pm) An unmarked door behind the paper-aeroplane monument leads into the bowels of a Bernardine monastery, where this lovely local-intelligentsia fave is hiding, together with a modern art gallery called the **Museum of Ideas**. People flock here for the hearty *bohrach* (a Ukrainian version of goulash) and *banosh* (Carpathian polenta with salty cottage cheese).

Tsukor Black BREAKFAST €
(Цукор Блэк; ☑098 679 8225; http://cukor.lviv. ua/; pr Kryva Lypa 3; mains 75-150uah; ⊙8am-10pm) Come to Kryva Lypa for the best breakfasts in town. This two-storey place serves an array of wonderful toast- and waffle-based concoctions with eggs, avocado and other veggies. There is also a cool little souvenir shop on the premises, with most items featuring its trademark penguin.

⭐**Baczewski** EASTERN EUROPEAN €€
(Ресторація Бачевських; ☑032-224 4444; vul Shevska 8; mains 100-330uah; ⊙8am-midnight; ❄) Here's how you compress your Lviv cultural studies into one evening out. Start with Jewish *forschmak* (herring pate), eased down by Ukrainian *nalyvky* (digestifs) and followed by Hungarian fish soup. Proceed to Polish *pierogi* (dumplings) and finish with Viennese *Sachertorte* with Turkish coffee. An essential Lviv experience. Be sure to reserve a table for dinner at this mega-popular place.

🍷 Drinking & Nightlife

⭐**Pravda Beer Theatre** BREWERY
(www.pravda.beer; pl Rynok 32; ⊙10am-2am; 🛜) The latest addition to Lviv's drinking scene is this dramatically industrial, multistorey beer temple right on pl Rynok. The master brewer here creates several types of beer, often given imaginative and sometimes political names such Obama Hope and Summer Lviv. Live music is provided by the brewery's very own orchestra, tours run throughout the day and there's a menu of good pub food.

★**Pyana Vyshnya** BAR

(П'яна вишня; pl Rynok 11; ⊙ 10am-midnight) It's easy to find this one-drink bar – just look for the crowd of people on pl Rynok holding tiny glasses of something crimson, any time of the day. The tipple in question is the namesake, 18.5% volume, bitter-sweet cherry liqueur, sold by the crystal glass (36uah) or in bottles (200uah for 0.5L).

★**Lvivska Kopalnya Kavy** CAFE

(Львівська копальня кави; pl Rynok 10; ⊙ 8am-midnight Mon-Thu, to 2am Fri-Sun; 🛜) Lviv is Ukraine's undisputed coffee capital, and the 'Lviv Coffee Mine' is where the stratum of arabica is excavated by local colliers from deep beneath pl Rynok. You can tour the mine or just sample the heart-pumping end product inside at tables as dark as the brews, or out on the covered courtyard.

❶ Information

Tourist Information Centre (☑ 032-254 6079; www.lviv.travel; pl Rynok 1, Ratusha; ⊙ 9am-8pm May-Sep, 10am-6pm Oct-Apr) Ukraine's best tourist information centre. Branches at the **airport** (☑ 067 673 9194; www.lviv.travel; Lviv Airport; ⊙ open depending on flight schedule) and the **train station** (☑ 032-226 2005; www.lviv.travel; ticket hall, Lviv Train Station; ⊙ 9am-6pm).

❶ Getting Around

TO/FROM THE AIRPORT

To reach the city centre from the airport, take trolleybus 9 to the university (vul Universytetska, 20 minutes) or bus 48 (28 minutes) to the corner of vul Doroshenka and pr Svobody.

PUBLIC TRANSPORT

The Tourist Information Centre (p459) has comprehensive maps of the entire tram and bus network, but you are unlikely to use it as central Lviv can be easily explored on foot.

ODESA ОДЕСА

☑ 048 / POP 1 MILLION

Odesa is a city straight from literature – an energetic, decadent boom town. Its famous Potemkin Steps sweep down to the Black Sea and Ukraine's biggest commercial port. Behind them, a cosmopolitan cast of characters makes merry among neoclassical pastel buildings lining a geometric grid of leafy streets.

Immigrants from all over Europe were invited to make their fortune here when Odesa was founded in the late 18th century by Russia's Catherine the Great. These new inhabitants, particularly Jews, gave Russia's southern window on the world a singular, subversive nature.

Having weathered recent political storms, Odesa is booming again – it now substitutes for Crimea as the main domestic holiday destination. It's a golden age for local businesses, but it puts a strain on the already crowded sandy beaches.

⊙ Sights

★**Prymorsky Boulevard** STREET

(Приморський бульвар) Odesa's elegant facade, this tree-lined, clifftop promenade was designed to enchant the passengers of arriving boats with the neoclassical opulence of its architecture and civility, unexpected in these parts at the time of construction in the early 19th century. Imperial architects also transformed the cliff face into terraced gardens descending to the port, divided by the famous **Potemkin Steps** (Потьомкінські сходи) – the **Istanbul Park** lies east of the steps and the **Greek Park** west of them.

★**Vul Derybasivska** STREET

(Дерибасівська вулиця) Odesa's main commercial street, pedestrian vul Derybasivska is jam-packed with restaurants, bars and, in the summer high season, tourists. At its quieter eastern end you'll discover the **statue of José de Ribas** (vul Derybasivska), the Spanish-Neapolitan general who built Odesa's harbour and who also has a central street named after him. At the western end of the thoroughfare is the pleasant and beautifully renovated **City Garden**, surrounded by several restaurants.

History of Odesa Jews Museum MUSEUM

(Музей історії євреїв Одеси; ☑ 048-728 9743; www.migdal.org.ua/migdal/museum/; vul Nizhynska 66; recommended donation 100uah; tour 200uah; ⊙ 1-7pm Mon-Thu, 10am-4pm Sun) Less than 2% of people call themselves Jewish in today's Odesa – against 44% in the early 1920s – but the resilient and humorous Jewish spirit still permeates every aspect of local life. Hidden inside a typical run-down courtyard with clothes drying on a rope and a rusty carcass of a prehistoric car, this modest but lovingly curated exhibition consists of items donated by Odessite families, many of whom have long emigrated to America or Israel.

🛏 Sleeping

Babushka Grand Hostel
HOSTEL €

(☎063 070 5535; www.babushkagrand.com; vul Mala Arnautska 60; dm/d from 190/570uah; ❄ 🛜) While Odesa's other hostels are decidedly for the young, day-sleeping crowd, the wonderfully named Grand Babushka, occupying a palatial apartment near the train station, has a more laid-back, traveller vibe. The stuccoed interiors and crystal chandeliers are stunning, the staff fun and occasionally a real Ukrainian *babushka* arrives to cook up a feast.

Hotel Ayvazovsky
HOTEL €€

(Готель Айвазовський; ☎067 997 9711; http://aivazovskiy-hotel.org.ua; vul Bunina 19; s/d incl breakfast from 1100/1500uah; ❄❄🛜) From the Chesterfield sofas in the foyer to the spacious, European-standard bedrooms with high ceilings to the design-magazine-perfect bathrooms, this soothing, 27-room hotel in the heart of the city centre is worth every hryvnya. Continental breakfast is delivered to your room every morning, and staff can book tours and countless other services.

Frederic Koklen
BOUTIQUE HOTEL €€€

(Фредерік Коклен; ☎048-737 5553; www.koklenhotel.com; prov Nekrasova 7; d incl breakfast from 1600uah; ❄🛜) Odesa's most sumptuous boutique hotel has guests gushing about the exceptional service, the luxurious period ambience and the great location. Rooms in this renovated mansion are studies in 18th- and 19th-century imperial-era style, and the attention to detail, quality of materials and standard of maintenance are exceptional for Ukraine.

🍴 Eating

Dva Karla
MOLDOVAN €

(Bodega 2K; ☎096 524 1601; www.facebook.com/bodega2k; vul Hretska 22; mains 70-120uah; ⊙10am-11pm) This envoy from nearby Moldova occupies a super-quaint courtyard covered with a vine canopy in summer and pleasant cellar premises in winter. Come here to try *mamalyga* (a version of polenta with *brynza* goat's cheese or fried lard), paprika stuffed with rice and chopped meat, as well as juicy *mitityay* (kebabs).

Touting itself as a bodega, 2K also treats visitors to excellent Moldovan and (more experimental) Ukrainian wine. It's also a great breakfast option.

⭐ City Food Market
FOOD HALL €€

(Міський продовольчий ринок; ☎048-702 1913; www.facebook.com/odessa.cityfood.market; Rishelyevska 9A; mains 100-200uah; ⊙11am-2am; 🛜🛜) Once an itinerant tribe, congregating here and there for irregular jamborees, Odesa foodies now have a rather palatial indoors base. The two-storey building is divided between shops, each with its own kitchen dedicated to a particular product – from the Vietnamese *pho* soup and Greek pita gyros, to grilled ribs and oysters.

⭐ Bernardazzi
EUROPEAN €€€

(Бернардацці; ☎067 000 2511; www.bernardazzi.com; Odessa Philharmonic Hall, vul Bunina 15; mains 200-420uah; ⊙noon-midnight, to 2am Fri & Sat; ❄) Few Ukrainian restaurants have truly authentic settings, but the art nouveau dining room of this Italianesque palazzo (once a stock exchange, now the Philharmonic Hall) is the real deal. In addition to well-crafted Southern and Eastern European fare, there's an award-winning wine list, occasional live music and a secluded courtyard for summertime chilling.

Kotelok Mussels Bar
SEAFOOD €€€

(☎048-736 6030; http://kotelok-musselsbar.com; vul Sadova 17; mains 180-400uah; ⊙9am-11pm, to midnight Fri & Sat) This may not be obvious, but mussels are as much a part of Odesa food culture as aubergine 'caviar' (cold vegetable stew). Furnished like a bar, with a row of seats facing an open kitchen, Kotelok is all about Black Sea mussels served with a variety of dips, including the quintessentially local mixture of paprika and *brynza* goat's cheese.

🍷 Drinking & Nightlife

⭐ Shkaf
BAR

(Шкаф; ☎048-232 5017; www.shkaff.od.ua; vul Hretska 32; ⊙6pm-5am) It feels like entering a *shkaf* (wardrobe) from the outside, but what you find inside is a heaving basement bar–club, a surefire antidote to Odesa's trendy beach-club scene and pick-up bars. The inconspicuous, unmarked entrance is always surrounded by smoking/chilling-out patrons, so you won't miss it.

The Fitz
BAR

(☎068 810 2070; www.facebook.com/TheFitzCocktailBar; vul Katerynynska 6; ⊙3pm-3am) Doubling as a barbershop by day, this little bar has an edgy, decadent feel enhanced by aged walls and a magnificent chandelier that bedazzles incoming customers. Some patrons occupy barbers' work stations, complete with sinks and mirrors, which adds to the overall surreality. Mostly rum-based cocktails include all-time favourites, as well as those you've likely never tried.

❶ Getting Around

To get to the city centre from the train station (about a 20-minute walk), go to the stop near the McDonald's and take any *marshrutka* (minibus) saying 'Грецька площа' (pl Hretska, vul Bunina side), such as bus 148. From the airport, trolleybus 14 goes to the train station, while the infrequent bus 117 trundles all the way into the centre, stopping at Pl Hretska Bus Stop.

SURVIVAL GUIDE

❶ Directory A–Z

ACCOMMODATION

Book well ahead during summer in Lviv and Odesa, and across the country in early January and early May. The Carpathians are busy in summer and to a lesser extent during ski season.

Hotels (готель) From standard Western chains to unreformed Soviet dinosaurs.

Mini-hotels (мини-готель) Typically occupy one floor in an apartment block; often good value.

Hostels (хостел) Some professionally run; many are semi-amateurish affairs in converted communal apartments.

Apartments (квартира) Vary in size and quality; a good alternative to city hotels.

Homestays (приватний сектор) Room or bed in seaside towns during high season; standards usually basic.

INTERNET ACCESS

Internet is more accessible for travellers in Ukraine than it is in most Western countries.

➡ SIM-cards with fast and unlimited internet access are ubiquitous and very cheap.

➡ Free wi-fi internet access is the norm in hotels, cafes and restaurants across the country, with or without a password.

➡ Bus stations, train stations and airports often have free wi-fi.

➡ Most cities have free wi-fi hotspots.

➡ Wi-fi is available on Intercity trains and on some long-distance coaches.

➡ Upmarket hotels often have a business centre with a couple of terminals hooked up to the internet.

➡ Internet cafes are uncommon these days; many of them have devolved into dodgy gaming centres.

LEGAL MATTERS

➡ Carry your passport with you at all times; if stopped by the police, you are obliged to show it.

➡ If you are stopped by the police, ask to see their ID immediately.

➡ The police must return your documents at once.

➡ Do not get involved with drugs; penalties can be severe and the process leading up to them labyrinthine.

➡ The US embassy in Kyiv maintains a list of English-speaking lawyers.

LGBT+ TRAVELLERS

Homosexuality is legal in Ukraine, but few people are very out here and attitudes vary. Gay clubs do exist in large cities; elsewhere the gay scene is mostly underground. Ukraine lags behind most of Europe on gay rights, but pride marches do take place, heavily guarded by police and threatened by right-wing thugs.

MONEY

ATMs are widespread, even in small towns. Credit cards are accepted at most hotels and restaurants.

OPENING HOURS

Opening hours are consistent throughout the year with very few seasonal variations. Lunch breaks (1pm to 2pm or 2pm to 3pm) are an all-too-common throwback to Soviet days. Sunday closing is rare.

Banks 9am to 5pm Monday to Friday

Restaurants 11am to 11pm

Cafes 9am to 10pm

Bars and Clubs 10pm to 3am

Shops 9am to 9pm

Sights 9am to 5pm or 6pm, closed at least one day a week

PUBLIC HOLIDAYS

New Year's Day 1 January

Orthodox Christmas 7 January

International Women's Day 8 March

Orthodox Easter (Paskha) April/May

Labour Day 1–2 May

Victory Day (1945) 9 May

Constitution Day 28 June

Independence Day (1991) 24 August

Defender of Ukraine Day 14 October

SAFE TRAVEL

With Ukraine in the news for all the wrong reasons, safety is a major concern for travellers these days. But although crime is on the rise, Ukraine remains a rather safe European destination, unless you venture into the war zone, which accounts for a tiny part of the country's territory in the far east.

TELEPHONE

All numbers now start with 0, that zero being a part of the national code. If you see a number starting with 8, this is the old intercity and mobile prefix and should be left off.

VISAS

Generally, visas are not needed for stays of up to 90 days.

❶ Getting There & Away

AIR

Four international airports serve as gateways to Ukraine.

➸ **Kyiv Boryspil International Airport** (✆ 044-364 4505; www.kbp.aero) Gets the bulk of international flights and serves as the hub for the national carrier, **Ukraine International Airlines** (✆ 044-581 5050; www.flyuia.com; vul Lysenka 4; ⊗ 8am-7.30pm, to 5.30pm Sun; Ⓜ Maydan Nezalezhnosti).

➸ **Kyiv Zhulyany International Airport** (✆ 044-585 0211; www.airport.kiev.ua; vul Medova 2; 🚌 9, marshrutka 302, 368, 805) Serves domestic flights and a growing number of international flights, including flights by budget carrier Wizz Air.

➸ **Lviv Danylo Halytsky International Airport** (✆ 032 229 8112; www.lwo.aero; vul Lyubinska 168) Attracts a fair number of international flights, including Ryanair services to London.

➸ **Odesa International Airport** (www.odessa.aero) Regular flights to Istanbul and several Central/Eastern European destinations.

LAND

Providing the most useful service by far, two trains daily from Przemyśl in Poland to Lviv (two hours) and Kyiv (seven to nine hours). Considerably less convenient slow sleeper trains connect Kyiv and Lviv to Hungary and Slovakia.

Despite poor relations, trains were still running between Kyiv and Moscow (14 to 16 hours, seven daily) and destinations in Ukraine and Russia at the time of writing.

You'll find bus services to multiple European destinations at every major station in Ukraine. Check https://infobus.eu or https://busfor.ua for schedules.

❶ Getting Around

AIR

The network is very centralised, so more often than not you need to change flights in Kyiv when travelling between the southeast and the west. The number of domestic flights and carriers has fallen considerably in recent years.

BUS

Buses serve every city and small town, but they're best for short trips (three hours or less), as vehicles can often be small, old and overcrowded. However, luxury bus services run by big companies provide a good alternative to trains. Some bus stations have become quite orderly, others remain chaotic.

CAR & MOTORCYCLE

Travelling by car in Ukraine can be a rewarding if nerve-racking experience. However, road conditions are improving and drivers may even be becoming a little more disciplined.

LOCAL TRANSPORT

Ukrainian cities are navigable by trolleybus, tram, bus and (in Kyiv, Kharkiv and Dnipro) metro. Urban public-transport systems are usually overworked and overcrowded. There's no room for being shy or squeamish – learn to assert yourself quickly.

➸ A ticket (kvytok or bilyet) for one ride by bus/tram/trolleybus costs 2uah to 5uah.

➸ There are virtually no return, transfer, timed or day tickets available anywhere.

➸ It's always simplest to pay the driver or conductor.

➸ Tickets have to be punched on board (or ripped by the conductor).

➸ Unclipped or untorn tickets warrant an on-the-spot fine should you be caught.

➸ For the metros you need a plastic token (zheton), sold at the counters inside the stations. Top-up cards are now also available in Kyiv.

➸ Metros run from around 5.30am to midnight.

TRAIN

For long journeys, train is the preferred method of travel in Ukraine. The most useful and comfortable are the daytime Intercity+ trains. Many overnight trains have old, Soviet-era carriages. Services are mostly punctual.

Survival Guide

Directory A–Z

Accessible Travel

Depending on the destination, Eastern Europe is generally challenging for travellers with disabilities. While individual museums and hotels are slowly being brought up to Western European standards of accessibility, provision isn't reliable. Away from the beaten track, facilities are almost nonexistent and transport presents a challenge.

➡ In general, wheelchair-accessible rooms are available only at top-end hotels (and may be limited, so be sure to book in advance).

➡ Rental cars and taxis may be accessible, but public transport outside of places like Prague or Ljubljana rarely is.

➡ Many major museums and sites have some form of disabled access. It's best to call ahead or ask locally when it comes to castles and other ancient sites.

➡ If you have a physical disability, get in touch with your national support organisation and ask about the countries you plan to visit.

➡ Many Eastern European countries have national support organisations that can offer helpful information over their websites. Download Lonely Planet's free *Accessible Travel* guide from http://lptravel.to/AccessibleTravel.

Accommodation

Reservations

➡ Reserving online or by phone is generally a good idea in high season.

➡ Hotels and pensions often list with online booking websites.

➡ Hostels and cheap hotels fill up very quickly, especially in popular backpacker destinations such as Prague, Budapest and Kraków.

➡ Tourist offices, where they exist, may be able to make reservations on your behalf (some charge a small fee for this service). The level of English spoken, and the quality of tourist-office services, varies enormously across Eastern Europe.

Seasons

➡ High season is usually in July and August (with a winter peak season in ski areas like the Tatras, typically December to March).

➡ Rates usually drop outside the high season, sometimes by as much as 50%.

➡ In mountainous areas, some hotels close during October and November (months that typically suit neither hikers nor skiers). Accommodation in beach destinations (like the Adriatic and Black Sea coasts) may hibernate all winter.

➡ In business-oriented hotels in cities, rooms are most expensive from Monday to Friday and cheaper over the weekend.

Camping

Eastern Europe's numerous camping grounds are generally inexpensive and family-friendly places to stay. They are best suited to beach holidays or travellers with cars, as they tend to be far from city attractions (though some are accessible by public transport).

Many camping grounds in Eastern Europe rent small on-site cabins, bungalows or caravans for double or triple the regular camping fee; bungalows fill quickly in July and August. Generally, camping grounds charge per tent, plus an extra fee per person (as well as per car, per pet and other fees).

The standard of camping grounds in Eastern Europe varies from country to country. They're unreliable in Romania, crowded in Slovenia and Hungary (especially on Lake Balaton), and variable in the Czech Republic, Poland, Slovakia and Bulgaria. Some countries, including Moldova and Belarus, have very few official camping grounds, but you can usually find somewhere to pitch your tent. Croatia's coast has nudist camping grounds galore (signposted FKK, the

German acronym for naturist), which enjoy secluded locations.

➡ Camping grounds may be open from April to October, May to September, or perhaps only June to August, depending on location and demand.

➡ A few private camping grounds are open year-round.

➡ Camping in the wild is usually illegal; ask local people about the situation before you pitch your tent on a beach or an open field.

➡ In Eastern Europe you are sometimes allowed to build a campfire; ask first.

Farmhouses

Variously described as 'agro-tourism' and 'village tourism', farm lodgings and eco-minded homestays are a well-developed concept in several Eastern European countries, including Estonia, Hungary, Latvia, Lithuania, Slovenia and, increasingly, Serbia. It's like staying in a private room or pension, except that the participating farms are in picturesque rural areas and may have activities nearby such as horse riding, kayaking, skiing and cycling.

See World Wide Opportunities on Organic Farms (www.wwoof.net) for information about working on organic farms in exchange for room and board.

Guesthouses & Pensions

Small private guesthouses (or 'pensions') are common throughout Eastern Europe. Priced somewhere between hotels and private rooms, they typically have fewer than a dozen rooms and usually have a small restaurant or bar on the premises. You'll often get much more personal service at a pension than you would at a hotel, though there's a bit less privacy and it's a less polished operation (don't expect speedy wi-fi

or 24-hour reception). Call ahead to check prices and reserve – someone will usually speak some halting English, German or Russian.

Homestays, Private Rooms & Couchsurfing

Homestays can offer glimpses of local life that you might not enjoy at a hotel or hostel, though their quality and professionalism varies hugely.

➡ In many Eastern European countries, travel or tourist agencies can arrange accommodation in private rooms in local homes. In Hungary you can get a private room almost anywhere, but in other countries only the main tourist centres have them. Some rooms are like mini-apartments, with cooking facilities and private bathrooms for the sole use of guests.

➡ Prices are low but there may be a 30% to 50% surcharge if you stay fewer than three nights.

➡ People may approach you at train or bus stations in Eastern Europe offering a private room or a hostel bed. If you're interested, insist that they point to the homestay's location on a map, and negotiate a clear price. Obviously, if you are staying with strangers, don't leave your money, credit cards, passport or other essential valuables behind when you go out.

➡ Any house, cottage or farmhouse with *Zimmer Frei* (German), сниму комнату (Russian), *sobe* (Croatian) or *szoba kiadó* (Hungarian) displayed outside is advertising the availability

of private rooms; knock on the door and ask if any are available. However, in countries such as Russia or Belarus where visa registration is necessary, you may have to pay a travel agency to register your visa with a hotel.

➡ Online hospitality clubs, linking travellers with thousands of global residents who'll let you occupy their couch or spare room for free – and sometimes show you around town – include Couchsurfing (www.couchsurfing. com), Global Freeloaders (www.globalfreeloaders. com) and 5W (www. womenwelcomewomen. uk). Check the rules of each organisation.

➡ If you're staying for free with friends or strangers, make sure you bring some small gifts for your hosts – it's a deeply ingrained cultural tradition throughout the region. Flowers, chocolates or nicely packaged biscuits and cakes will work.

➡ Always let friends and family know where you're staying and carry your mobile phone with you. Solo travellers should be especially careful in homestay situations – as well as following general safety rules, if you get weird vibes from your host on arrival, back out politely rather than risk staying on.

Hostels

Hostels offer about the cheapest roof over your head in Eastern Europe and you normally don't have to be young to take advantage of them. Many hostels are part of the national Youth Hostel

---

BOOK YOUR STAY ONLINE

For more accommodation reviews by Lonely Planet authors, check out http://lonelyplanet.com/hotels/. You'll find independent reviews, as well as recommendations on the best places to stay. Best of all, you can book online.

Association (YHA), which is affiliated with the Hostelling International (HI; www. hihostels.com) umbrella organisation.

➧ Hostels vary widely in character and quality. A number of privately run hostels in Prague, Bucharest, Budapest, Moscow and St Petersburg are serious party venues, while many Hungarian hostels outside Budapest are student dormitories that open to travellers for six or seven weeks in summer only.

➧ Hostels affiliated with HI can be found in most Eastern European countries. A hostel card is seldom required, though you sometimes get a small discount if you have one.

➧ At a hostel, you get a bed for the night plus use of communal facilities; there's often a kitchen where you can prepare your own meals. You may be required to have a bed sheet or a sleeping bag, if you don't have one, you can usually hire one for a small fee.

➧ Private hostels may offer amenities like lounges, laundry facilities, libraries and game rooms.

➧ Most hostels accept reservations over a website or by phone or email, but may not be able to hold rooms during peak travel periods.

Hotels

At the bottom end of the scale, cheap hotels may be no more expensive than private rooms or guest-houses, while at the other extreme you'll find beautifully designed boutique and five-star hotels with price tags to match.

➧ Solo travellers in Eastern Europe may pay over the odds, as single rooms are often not much cheaper than doubles.

➧ Inexpensive older rooms may have a washbasin but

no bathroom, which means you'll have to go down the corridor to use the toilet and shower.

➧ Breakfast is sometimes included in the price of a room.

Rental Accommodation

In larger cities, renting an apartment is an excellent option. These are often better value than a hotel (and some are a steal for their size), and you can self-cater and be far more independent, but quality varies. Agencies operate independently and sometimes quasi-legally, so you may have no recourse if you have a disagreement. When dealing with agencies you've found online, never send money in advance unless you're sure they are genuine.

University Accommodation

Some universities rent out space in student halls in July and August. This is quite popular in the Baltic countries, the Czech Republic, Hungary, North Macedonia, Poland, Slovakia and Slovenia.

➧ Accommodation will sometimes be in single rooms (but is more commonly in doubles or triples) and will come with shared bathrooms. Basic cooking facilities may be available.

➧ Enquire at the college or university, at student-information services or at local tourist offices.

Children

Travelling with your children in Eastern Europe will be a treat and a challenge.

➧ Children will usually be adored and welcomed into cafes, restaurants and hotels.

➧ Depending on the country, children don't always blend seamlessly into evening dining and drinking scenes

(as in Western Europe, where it's not unusual for children to sit in high chairs while mum or dad sips wine).

➧ Eastern Europe offers plenty of attractions for young travellers, from kid-friendly museums to parks and zoos.

➧ Pizza and American-style food (burgers, fries) are popular in numerous countries, so fussy palates can usually be catered for. For inspiration and tips on family travel, pick up a copy of Lonely Planet's *Travel with Children* guide.

Practicalities

➧ In Eastern Europe most car-rental firms have children's safety seats for hire at a small cost, but it is essential that you book them in advance.

➧ High chairs and cots are standard in many restaurants and hotels, but numbers are limited.

➧ Find items like baby food, infant formulas, soy and cows' milk, disposable nappies and other essentials at supermarkets or drugstores/pharmacies.

➧ Discretion is advised when breastfeeding; unfortunately it remains taboo in some public places.

➧ Nappy-changing facilities aren't reliably common in public toilets (and certainly not reliably clean).

➧ Child care is considered a high-end service, but may be available at some of the swankier hotels.

Discount Cards

Camping Card International

The Camping Card International (CCI; www.camping-cardinternational.com) is an ID that can be used when checking into a camping ground. Many camping grounds offer a small discount if you sign in with one, plus it includes third-party insurance.

Hostelling International

Hostels may charge you less if you have a Hostelling International (HI; www.hihostels.com) card. Some hostels will issue one on the spot or after a few days' stay, though this might cost a bit more than getting it at home.

Rail Passes

The RailPlus card, available to buy at many international ticket outlets, entitles the holder to train-fare reductions of 25% on standard tickets for conventional international trains. It can be used on many Eastern European cross-border routes, and is sold at many international ticket offices.

If you plan to visit more than a few countries, or one or two countries in depth, you might also save money with a rail pass.

Senior Cards

Many attractions offer reduced-price admission for people over 60 or 65. EU residents, especially, are eligible for discounts in many EU countries; make sure you bring proof of age.

Senior Travel Expert (www.seniortravelexpert.com) is a useful resource with tips on senior discounts.

Student, Youth & Teacher Cards

The International Student Identity Card (ISIC; www.isic.org) is available for students, offering thousands of worldwide discounts on transport, museum entry, youth hostels and even some restaurants. Similar discounts are available with ISIC's under-30s and teacher cards. Apply for a card online or via issuing offices, which include STA Travel (www.statravel.com).

For under-26s, there's also the European Youth Card (www.euro26.org). Several countries have raised the age limit for this card to 30.

Electricity

Plugs in Eastern Europe are the standard round two-pin variety, sometimes called the europlug.

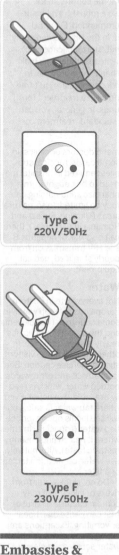

Type C
220V/50Hz

Type F
230V/50Hz

Embassies & Consulates

It's important to realise what your embassy can and cannot do to help if you get into trouble while travelling abroad. Remember that you are bound by the laws of the country you are visiting. Generally speaking, your embassy cannot help much if your emergency is of your own making. It will not post bail or otherwise act to get you out of jail.

If your documents are lost or stolen, your embassy can assist you in obtaining a new passport; this is greatly simplified if you have a photocopy or scan of your passport. Your embassy may refer you to a lawyer or a doctor, but it is highly unlikely to provide any financial assistance, no matter what your emergency.

Health

Before You Go

There are no mandatory vaccinations for entering Eastern Europe, but some are recommended. Most vaccines don't produce immunity until two weeks after they're given. Visit your doctor at least a month before departure to ensure you are up to date with routinely recommended vaccines, and in good time to make arrangements for any travel-related health needs.

The vaccinations you are most likely to need are the following:

MMR (measles, mumps and rubella)

Hepatitis A and B

Diphtheria

Tetanus

Rabies pre-exposure vaccine if you plan on spending a lot of time in remote places or in the company of animals. You will still need to seek post-exposure treatment if exposed to the virus.

Tick-borne encephalitis if hiking in wild areas is a significant part of your plans

Availability & Cost of Healthcare

In most countries, good basic healthcare is readily available and pharmacists can

EUROPEAN HEALTH INSURANCE CARD

Citizens of EU countries and Switzerland, Iceland, Norway and Liechtenstein should acquire a European Health Insurance Card (EHIC), entitling them to free or reduced-cost emergency healthcare in EU countries. Transporting you back to your home country, in the event of illness, is not covered so a robust travel-insurance policy is still strongly recommended. Every EU individual needs their own card. In the UK, you can apply online (www.ehic.org.uk/internet/startapplication.do).

The EHIC does not cover private healthcare, so make sure you are treated by a state healthcare provider. In EU countries where state-provided healthcare isn't free, you will need to pay yourself and fill in a treatment form; keep the form to claim any refunds. In general, you can claim back around 70% of the standard treatment cost.

give valuable advice and sell over-the-counter medication for minor illnesses. They can also advise when more specialised help is required and point you in the right direction.

For major hospitals with English-speaking staff, capital cities are your best bet, but large hospitals can be found in numerous towns.

By Western European or North American standards, healthcare is often cheap. It tends to be more expensive in EU member states than in non-EU member states. In most non-EU states you'll probably want to attend a private clinic for anything serious. Comprehensive health insurance is essential, as costs accumulate rapidly in private clinics. The standard of dental care is usually good, and some countries (like Slovenia, Serbia and Poland) even attract dental tourism.

The availability and standard of healthcare in Belarus isn't high; if at all possible, head overland to Poland or Lithuania. Ukraine's healthcare system is also poor by Western European standards.

Medical care is not always readily available outside major cities, but embassies, consulates and five-star hotels can usually recom-

mend doctors or clinics. In some cases, medical supplies required in hospital may need to be bought from a pharmacy and nursing care may be limited. In some rural areas (Ukraine, Russia and Romania in particular), there can be a risk of hepatitis B and HIV transmission from poorly sterilised medical equipment.

Water

Not everywhere in Eastern Europe has safe tap water. In some countries (like Slovenia and the Czech Republic) it's nearly always drinkable; in others (like Ukraine) visitors should exercise caution. Seek local advice and err towards bottled water, which is readily available, if in doubt. Even where tap water is safe, you will see locals opting for bottled water (especially in cities where it has an unpleasantly metallic taste). Alternatively, use water-purification tablets or a filter.

Do not drink water from rivers or lakes, as it may contain bacteria or viruses that can cause diarrhoea or vomiting. Exceptions are hiking areas where drinkable water sources are clearly marked. Brushing your teeth with tap water is unlikely to lead to problems, but use bottled water if you want to be very cautious.

Insurance

A travel-insurance policy to cover theft, loss and medical problems is always a good idea. The policies written by STA Travel (www.statravel.com) and other student-travel organisations are usually good value.

➡ Some insurance policies will specifically exclude 'dangerous activities', which can include scuba diving, motorcycling and even hiking. Winter-sports and car-rental cover is sometimes limited, so check the fine print.

➡ Some policies even exclude certain countries.

➡ Check that your policy covers ambulances and an emergency flight home.

➡ You may prefer a policy that pays doctors or hospitals directly rather than reimbursing your claims after the fact.

➡ Some policies ask you to call back (reverse charges) to a centre in your home country, where an immediate assessment of your problem is made.

➡ If you have to file a claim, make sure you gather and keep all documentation (like police or hospital reports). Worldwide travel insurance is available at www.lonelyplanet.com/travel-insurance. You can buy, extend and claim online at any time – even if you're already on the road.

Internet Access

With few exceptions, any decent-sized town in Eastern Europe has internet access in some shape or form. In general, the internet cafe is a thing of the past as wi-fi has become ubiquitous. Laptops and smartphones can easily connect in many cafes, bars, libraries, hotels, hostels and some public places. Some countries, like Romania and Russia, pride themselves on their wi-fi speed (and it may put your connection back home to shame). In others, like Belarus, you might find certain websites inaccessible, thanks to legislation allowing surveillance and selective blocking of the web. Connections in rural areas (especially mountainous ones) are likely to be slow.

Legal Matters

➡ Public drunkenness, or even drinking alcohol in public, is usually frowned upon and can lead to big fines.

➡ Attitudes toward drugs, including cannabis, vary across the region, though drugs remain illegal in every country in Eastern Europe. Police might turn a blind eye to a joint in the Czech Republic or Slovenia (though even here, cannabis is technically illegal), while in other countries that same behavior might get you a big fine or deportation. Harder drugs everywhere can lead to long prison sentences, particularly in countries such as Russia, Albania and Belarus.

➡ Protesting can attract severe penalties in countries like Russia and Belarus. In these same countries, journalists are advised not to advertise their profession.

➡ If arrested, most countries will honour your right to a translator and allow you to contact your embassy; do so at the first opportunity.

➡ The presumption of innocence applies across EU countries (that is, the burden of proof is on the prosecutor to prove you committed a crime). In theory, it also applies in countries such as Belarus and Russia, though there has been criticism of how this rule has been used in practice.

LGBT+ Travellers

Consensual sex between people of the same gender is legal across Eastern Europe,

but the general population isn't always open-minded.

➡ The Czech Republic, Estonia and Slovenia have the best reputations for acceptance of LGBT+ people.

➡ You are unlikely to raise eyebrows by sharing a double room with your same-sex partner in larger towns and cities, but rural areas might be a different story.

➡ In many countries, overt displays of affection between members of the same sex are likely to attract negative attention.

➡ LGBT+ travellers should be particularly cautious in Bulgaria, Belarus, Hungary, Russia and Romania.

➡ Most countries have online forums and gay advocacy groups.

➡ Many Eastern European capitals have small but active scenes, and annual pride parades, though some of these have attracted counter-demonstrations.

➡ Outside large towns, gay and lesbian life is invisible and the internet is the only realistic way to make contact with other gay people.

Maps

Paper maps might feel redundant in the age of smart phones, but they are invaluable if you go hiking or plan on taking road trips in mountainous (phone signal–free) areas.

Don't blindly follow your sat-nav: online maps aren't infallible when it comes to distinguishing gravel from paved roads, and they won't be aware of treacherously pothole-ridden routes (a particular problem in parts of Albania, Romania and Moldova). Online estimated driving times should also be taken with a pinch of salt, particularly if you're driving at night, in mountainous areas, or across borders.

Maps of Eastern European capitals and other major

towns are widely available from travel bookshops if you want a detailed map in advance. Detailed hiking maps can be bought from bookshops in capital cities, or at national park information centres (smaller local tourist offices sometimes don't offer more than city maps).

Money

Long journeys around Eastern Europe require you to flit between the kuna, złoty, forint, leu, lev, lek, and various other national currencies. The euro is used in Estonia, Latvia, Lithuania, Kosovo, Montenegro, Slovakia and Slovenia; it remains the easiest currency to change throughout the region.

Only convert as much local currency as you intend to use, and don't expect to be able to easily convert the smaller national currencies outside of the issuing country or once you are back home.

ATMs

Eastern European countries generally have plenty of ATMs in their capitals and sizeable towns. Check the specific situation in your destination before setting out from the big city – and never rely entirely on being able to find an ATM.

➡ Cash or debit cards can be used throughout Eastern Europe at ATMs linked to international networks.

➡ Before leaving home, let your bank know you'll be travelling in Eastern Europe. Transactions coming in from countries like Russia, Ukraine and Belarus, for example, can sometimes lead card-company security departments to proactively shut down your card.

➡ If you choose to rely on plastic, go for two different cards – this allows one to be used as a backup in the case of loss or if the card is rejected for some reason.

➜ A combination of cards and cash is the best approach.

Cash

➜ The two most favoured foreign currencies throughout Eastern Europe are the euro and the US dollar.

➜ Although it's not difficult to exchange other major world currencies in big cities, you are at the mercy of the exchange office and its rates.

➜ Local currency is almost always preferred, and usually the only kind accepted within a country. But some non-euro countries may accept (even prefer) payment in euros, such as Bosnia & Hercegovina and Moldova.

➜ Note that in some places banks will not change or accept damaged bank notes. This is especially true in the former Soviet Union, so bring clean and newish notes from home, whenever possible, and keep your local currency pristine.

Changing Money

➜ Banks are generally the safest and best places to exchange money, though it always pays to shop around for the best rate.

➜ Private currency exchanges can be hit or miss. In countries like Poland and Romania they are viewed as legitimate parts of the banking system, while in many other countries they are little more than rip-off booths for tourists.

➜ Bear in mind that the poorest rates are often offered in tourist areas and at places like border crossings, airports and train stations. It's usually better to use an airport or train station ATM than change money at a private exchange office.

➜ Never change money on the street or the black market. It's illegal and you'll invariably lose money.

Credit Cards

➜ Credit cards are commonly accepted. You'll usually be able to use them at upmarket restaurants, shops, hotels, car-rental firms, travel agencies and many petrol stations.

➜ Visa and MasterCard are the most widely accepted cards.

➜ It's no guarantee that small restaurants and guesthouses will take cards, even if you booked online and secured your reservation by card. Ask ahead or bring back-up cash.

➜ Bear in mind that if you use a credit card for purchases, exchange rates may have changed by the time your bill is processed, which can work out to your advantage or disadvantage.

Tipping

Tipping practices vary by country. You can't go wrong if you add 10% onto your bill at a restaurant.

Hotels Porters in upmarket hotels will appreciate a couple of euros.

Restaurants In fashionable venues, waiting staff will expect a tip; in rural locations a tip might astonish your server.

Taxi drivers Depends on the city or country but tips are generally low. Round up to the nearest unit of currency.

Travellers Cheques

It's become more difficult to find places that cash travellers cheques. In parts of Eastern Europe only a few banks handle them, and the process can be bureaucratic and costly.

Opening Hours

Opening hours vary by country; we've listed the most common hours. Saturday and Sunday are official days off, though most shops and cafes open daily. During hot summer months, some enterprises shut in the early afternoon, reopening at 3pm or 4pm and working into the evening.

Banks and offices 9am–5pm Monday to Friday (sometimes with an hour or two off for lunch); may also open Saturday morning

Museums 10am–5pm Tuesday to Sunday; shorter hours October to April

Restaurants 11am–10pm

Shops 9am or 10am–6pm or later; hours limited in winter

Photography

➜ Photographing military installations, even casually, is never a good idea. In Belarus and Russia, you may have serious explaining to do.

➜ Ask permission before taking close-up photos of people.

➜ Museums often demand that you buy permission to photograph or video their displays.

➜ Photo equipment, like digital memory, batteries and film, is widely available, though you'll have a better selection in larger towns.

➜ Lonely Planet's *Guide to Travel Photography* covers all aspects of technique and etiquette.

Post

The efficiency and cost of the national postal systems in Eastern Europe vary by country. There seem to be no set rules, but EU countries are likely to be faster, more reliable and more expensive than non-EU states.

➜ Postal service from Belarus, Moldova, Montenegro, Russia and Ukraine is slow, but mail usually reaches its destination eventually. For added assurance and speed, most of these countries offer an express service.

➜ To send a parcel from Eastern Europe you usually have to take it unwrapped to a main post office; parcels weighing more than 2kg often must be taken to a special customs post office. The post-office staff will usually wrap the parcels for you. The staff may ask to see your passport and note the number on the form; if you don't have a return address within the country, put the address of your hotel.

Public Holidays

The following list isn't exhaustive across countries in Eastern Europe, which may also have public holidays for national days, saints' days, International Women's Day and other celebrations. Dates for Orthodox Christmas and Easter are different to those of their Catholic and Protestant counterparts (though Easter sometimes falls on the same date by both calendars).

New Year's Day 1 January

Orthodox Christmas Day 7 January

Catholic Easter Country-dependent, dates vary

Orthodox Easter Country-dependent, dates vary

May Day/International Labour Day 1 May

Christmas Day 25 December

Safe Travel

Eastern Europe is as safe – or unsafe – as any other part of the developed world. Stay aware of your surroundings, and you'll probably be fine.

➡ You're most vulnerable to crime aboard transport, from crowded buses to overnight trains; keep valuables close.

➡ You're likely to encounter beggars, some may follow you. Not engaging is the simplest way to deflect interest.

➡ Taxi and currency-exchange scams are the likeliest pitfalls. Insist on taxi meters; only change money at legitimate outlets.

Corruption

➡ Low-level corruption is disappearing fast and is now rare for travellers to encounter. Do not pay bribes to people in official positions, such as police, border guards, train conductors and ticket inspectors.

➡ Be aware, however, that these systems still exist in Belarus, Moldova (and Transdniestr) and Russia. If corrupt cops want to hold you up because some obscure stamp is missing from your documentation or on some other pretext, just let them and consider the experience an integral part of your trip. Insisting on calling your embassy is always a good move; officers are likely to receive some grief if their superiors learn they are harassing tourists.

➡ If you do have to pay a fine or supplementary charge, insist on a proper receipt before turning over any money. In all of this, try to maintain your cool, as any threats from you will only make matters worse.

Landmines

Parts of Albania, Bosnia & Hercegovina, Croatia and Kosovo still have landmines in remote areas. Touristed areas and national parks have been prioritised for landmine clearance, but in some places the process is ongoing. Ask locally for the latest information, and pay careful attention to advice about hiking trails (or better yet, hire a local guide). Always stick to established roads and paths in regions where mines are still a problem.

Scams

➡ Taxi scams vary from claiming the meter is broken (so you'll have to accept an inflated, flat fee), to deliberately misquoting the currency (you assumed the price was quoted in Romanian lei? He's now claiming it's euro). Order taxis by phone or get them from taxi ranks – avoid hawkers at airports.

➡ Always watch out at bank ATMs and be careful with your credit- or debit-card PIN numbers.

➡ There have been some reports of people making duplicates of credit- or debit-card information with high-tech machines. If your card leaves your sight for longer than you think necessary, consider cancelling it.

➡ Currency-exchange scams are less prevalent than they once were. Anyone who approaches you offering suspiciously good exchange rates (an uncommon occurrence these days) is an outright thief.

GOVERNMENT TRAVEL ADVICE

The following government websites offer travel advisories and information on current areas to avoid.

Australian Department of Foreign Affairs (www.smarttraveller.gov.au)

British Foreign and Commonwealth Office (www.gov.uk/foreign-travel-advice)

Government of Canada Travel Advice and Advisories (https://travel.gc.ca/travelling/advisories)

Japan Ministry of Foreign Affairs (www.anzen.mofa.go.jp)

New Zealand Ministry of Foreign Affairs (www.safetravel.govt.nz)

US State Department (www.travel.state.gov)

Theft

Definitely a problem in Eastern Europe and the threat comes from both local thieves and fellow travellers. The most important things to guard are your passport, other documents, tickets, phone and money.

➡ Consider using a money-belt beneath your shirt or an inner zip-up pocket to keep your valuables secure and out of sight.

➡ Train-station lockers or luggage-storage counters are useful to store your luggage (though not valuables), but be suspicious of non–staff members who offer to help you operate your locker.

➡ Pickpockets are most active in dense crowds, especially in busy train stations and on public transport during peak hours.

➡ Don't leave valuables lying around in your hotel room. Carry your own padlock for hostel lockers and always use it.

➡ Parked cars containing luggage or other bags are prime targets for petty criminals; cars with foreign number plates and/or rental-agency stickers attract particular attention.

➡ In the case of theft or loss, always report the incident to the police and ask for a statement; otherwise your travel insurance company won't pay up.

Racially Motivated Violence

Some countries in Eastern Europe have thriving neo-Nazi movements, which tend to target local Roma populations and, in some cases, non-Caucasian travellers. Countries such as Poland, the Czech Republic, Slovakia and Slovenia are racially homogeneous. While stares are likely, it's unlikely that travellers will encounter any violence while in Eastern Europe.

However, Russian neo-Nazis have been known to seek out fights with nonwhite people on Hitler's birthday (20 April); St Petersburg in particular has seen an extraordinary amount of violence against ethnic minorities – and not only on this date.

Telephone

Telephone services in Eastern Europe are generally good. The mobile phone is king across the region and post office telephone centres are being phased out. Overall you can expect a good level of mobile coverage, though in remote areas you will have trouble getting a signal.

Mobile Phones

➡ Mobile phones operate on the GSM standard. If you have roaming, your phone will usually switch automatically over to a local network. This can be expensive if you use the phone a great deal (or rely on data), but is useful for ad hoc and emergency use.

➡ If you plan to spend more than a week or so in any one country, consider buying a SIM card to slip into your phone. Check with your provider at home that your handset has been unlocked.

➡ SIM cards can cost as little as €5 and can be topped up with cards available at supermarkets, kiosks, newsagents and mobile-phone dealers. With a smartphone, you can use a local SIM card for data as well.

➡ When buying a SIM card, come equipped with your passport (and in countries like Belarus and Russia, any registration paperwork).

Phone Codes

➡ To call abroad from a landline you dial the international access code for the country you are calling from (most commonly 00 in Eastern Europe, but 8-10 in Belarus and Russia).

➡ From a mobile phone simply dial + followed by the country code, the city code and the local number.

➡ To make a domestic call to another city in the same country, you generally need to dial the area code (with the initial zero) and the number; however, in some countries the area code is an integral part of the phone number and must be dialled every time – even if you're just calling next door.

Phonecards

Local telephone cards are available from post offices, telephone centres, newsstands or retail outlets. In any given country, there's a wide range of local and international phonecards available. For local calls you're usually better off with a local phonecard.

Time

➡ Eastern Europe spans three time zones: Central European Time (GMT+1), Eastern European Time (GMT+2) and Further-Eastern European Time, or 'Moscow Time' (GMT+3). At noon in New York, it's 6pm in Warsaw, 7pm in Sofia and 8pm in Moscow.

➡ All countries, except Russia, employ daylight savings. Clocks are put forward an hour at the start of daylight savings, usually on the last Sunday in March. They are set back one hour on the last Sunday in October.

Toilets

➡ The vast majority of toilets are modern, sit-down, flushing toilets.

➡ In a few countries, including Albania, Belarus, Moldova, Russia and Ukraine, you can expect to find squat toilets at transport stations and some sights (usually poorly maintained). They are rare in restaurants or hotels.

➡ You'll need to pay a small fee to use most public toilets in Eastern Europe. There may be an extra fee for toilet paper.

➡ Using hotel or restaurant facilities is nearly always free and one way to ensure you'll be using a clean bathroom.

Tourist Information

Countries that have successfully realised their potential as holiday destinations usually have a network of excellent tourist information centres (TICs). However, there are still many countries that appear to take little interest in developing their tourism offering.

➡ Countries in the latter category are Belarus, Ukraine, Romania and Moldova. Much of Russia is similarly badly organised, though there are TICs in St Petersburg.

➡ Among the best prepared are Croatia, the Czech Republic, Hungary, Poland, Slovakia and Slovenia, many of which have tourist offices abroad as well as throughout the country.

Visas

Generally not required for most Eastern European countries for stays of up to 90 days, but a few countries do require visas.

Both Russia (including Kaliningrad) and Belarus require many nationalities to obtain visas, but, under a special programme to encourage tourism, citizens of 74 countries can now enter Belarus visa-free for up to 30 days as long as they arrive at and depart from Minsk National Airport. When arriving in or departing Belarus by land, with a couple of minor exceptions, everybody needs a visa. Arranging a visa is generally straightforward but is likely to be time-consuming, bureaucratic and – depending on how quickly you need the visa – costly. Start the application process at least a month before your trip.

➡ Consulates sometimes issue visas on the spot,

although some levy a 50% to 100% surcharge for 'express service'. If there's a choice, get a visa in advance – they're often cheaper in your home country and this can save on bureaucratic procedure.

➡ If you do need to get a visa, note that it will have an expiration date and you'll be refused entry after that period has elapsed.

➡ Decide in advance if you want a tourist or transit visa; transit visas, usually valid for just 48 or 72 hours, are often cheaper and issued faster, but it's usually not possible to extend a transit visa or change it into a tourist visa.

➡ In line with the Schengen Agreement, there are no longer passport controls at the borders between most EU countries, but procedures between EU and non-EU countries (or between EU countries that are in the Schengen area and those that are not – like Romania, Bulgaria and Croatia) can still be fairly thorough.

➡ The hassles created by losing your passport and visa can be considerably reduced if you have a record of its number and issue date or, even better, photocopies of the relevant data pages. A photocopy of your birth certificate can also be useful.

Registration

Some countries, mainly those outside the EU, require visitors to register with the local authorities within 48 hours of arrival, supposedly so they know where you are staying. For more information, consult the individual country content.

➡ If you're staying at a hotel or other official accommodation, the reception desk will take care of registration for you.

➡ If you're staying with friends, relatives or in a private room, you're supposed to register with the police yourself. In some cases, this is a formality that is never

enforced, so you can skip it. In other cases (such as Russia), you can be fined if you do not go through the motions.

Women Travellers

Women travellers will generally find Eastern Europe safe and welcoming, whether you're in company or on your own. Macho attitudes prevail in some areas, so you can expect some condescension dressed as courtesy (asking about your husband, or unsolicited help parking your car).

It is not unusual for women to be propositioned by strangers on the street, which can be annoying and sometimes threatening. As a rule, the further east you go, the more exotic foreigners will seem; attention is rarely dangerous and is easily deflected with a shake of the head and a firm 'no'.

Work

EU citizens have free rein to work in many countries in the region. However, with unemployment still a problem in many areas, Eastern European countries aren't always keen on handing out jobs to foreigners.

If you're not an EU citizen, the paperwork involved in arranging a work permit can be almost impossible, especially for temporary work. That doesn't prevent enterprising travellers from topping up their funds occasionally – and they don't always have to do this illegally. If you do find a temporary job in Eastern Europe, though, the pay is likely to be low. Do it for the experience, not to earn your fortune.

➡ Teaching English is the easiest way to make some extra cash, but the market is saturated in places such as Prague and Budapest.

➡ *Work Your Way Around the World* by Susan Griffith gives good, practical advice on a wide range of issues.

Transport

GETTING THERE & AWAY

It's never been easier (or cheaper) to reach Eastern Europe, especially from major Western European cities. The region has long been easily accessible by rail and bus, with hubs like Prague particularly well-connected. There's an increasingly enormous range of routes by air, thanks to budget carriers like easyJet and Wizz Air, with budget flights (particularly from the UK) reaching airports from the Czech Republic to Ukraine.

Flights, cars and tours can be booked online at lonelyplanet.com/bookings.

Entering Eastern Europe

Most Eastern European countries can be visited visa-free by many nationals, simply with a passport with at least six months between its expiration date and your intended date of departure from the region.

Passports

All Eastern European countries require travellers to have a valid passport, preferably with at least six months between the time of departure and the passport's expiration date.

EU travellers from countries that issue national identity cards are increasingly using them to travel within the EU, although it's impossible to use them as sole travel documents outside the EU.

Air

Thanks to the budget-airline boom, there is an abundant choice of destinations in Eastern Europe to which you can fly direct. Some routes are seasonal (coming to life only in summer or for the ski season) while popular destinations – Prague, Budapest, Kraków and Moscow – are well served by year-round flights. Book up to three months in advance if possible, but low prices are often available at short notice (outside high summer).

Airports

Moscow (Russia), Prague (Czech Republic), Budapest (Hungary) and Warsaw (Poland) are the region's best-connected air hubs. They all have transatlantic flights as well as plenty of flights from Western Europe; they are also well served by budget airlines. Other smaller hubs are St Petersburg (Russia), Rīga (Latvia), Bucharest and Cluj-Napoca (Romania), Zagreb (Croatia), Kyiv (Ukraine) and Bratislava (Slovakia), all of which have daily flights to many major European cities. Most of the small hubs also have budget-airline connections, though these tend to be less frequent further east.

CLIMATE CHANGE & TRAVEL

Every form of transport that relies on carbon-based fuel generates CO_2, the main cause of human-induced climate change. Modern travel is dependent on aeroplanes, which might use less fuel per kilometre per person than most cars but travel much greater distances. The altitude at which aircraft emit gases (including CO_2) and particles also contributes to their climate change impact. Many websites offer 'carbon calculators' that allow people to estimate the carbon emissions generated by their journey and, for those who wish to do so, to offset the impact of the greenhouse gases emitted with contributions to portfolios of climate-friendly initiatives throughout the world. Lonely Planet offsets the carbon footprint of all staff and author travel.

Land

Apart from standard border queues, document checks and the occasional search, reaching Eastern Europe overland is fairly straightforward. Many travellers arrive in this way, into major rail and bus stations such as Belgrade, Budapest, Prague and Moscow. These hubs are well connected to numerous major cities in Western Europe.

Travel between EU member countries that are part of the EU's common customs Schengen area is seamless, with no border checks. Expect longer waits for travel to EU countries that are not part of the Schengen zone (Romania, Bulgaria, Croatia). Travel to non-EU countries, such as Ukraine, Belarus, Russia and Moldova, may entail even longer waits and require special entry visas.

Bus

Buses are a useful fallback if there are no trains or flights to your destination, and in many areas they may be quicker and more reliable than trains. As a means for travelling from Western Europe they are also cheap. Journeys between Schengen countries will be uninterrupted; otherwise there may be border passport checks on or off the bus.

Ecolines (www.ecolines.net/en) Runs buses between Eastern and Western Europe.

Eurolines (www.eurolines.eu) Has a vast network with member companies in many Eastern European countries and offers innumerable routes across the continent.

Flixbus (https://global.flixbus. com) Rapidly growing budget coach carrier with excellent connections from Western Europe to points around Eastern Europe.

Car & Motorcycle

Travelling by car or motorcycle into Eastern Europe gives travellers an immense amount of freedom and is generally worry-free. But keep in mind that some insurance packages, especially those covering rental cars, do not include all European countries. Be sure to ask the agency to insure the car in all the countries where you plan to travel. It's outright forbidden to take rental cars into certain countries; always double-check with your provider.

Some countries require the purchase of a *vignette*, a road-tax sticker diplayed on the windscreen, whatever the journey length on their roads. *Vignettes* can be bought, along with fuel, at almost all major road border points.

Train

There are numerous routes into the region by train. Major railway hubs are Prague (Czech Republic), Budapest (Hungary), Bucharest (Romania), Belgrade (Serbia) and Moscow (Russia). Albania has no international train services.

From Asia, the Trans-Siberian, Trans-Mongolian and Trans-Manchurian Railways connect Moscow to the Russian Far East, China, North Korea and Mongolia. Long-distance trains from Moscow reach central Asian cities such as Tashkent (Uzbekistan), Bishkek (Kyrgyzstan) and Almaty (Kazakhstan). Overnight trains also connect Belgrade, Budapest and Sofia (Bulgaria) with İstanbul (Turkey). Note that many countries are cutting back on overnight train services, and some connections may no longer be running or not available during your trip.

Depending on the countries, expect some degree of checks when crossing the border. They usually involve guards boarding a train to view travel tickets, visas (bought separately and in advance) and passports, and perform checks for stowaways in train compartments. In some places (like the Russia–China border) there may be a long wait for bogie exchange, which is needed where rail-track gauges differ between countries.

Seat 61 (www.seat61. com) is an indispensable resource to start planning long-distance train travel into Eastern Europe.

Sea

Boats from several companies connect Italy with Croatia, Slovenia, Montenegro and Albania; there are also services between Corfu (Greece) and Albania. Timetables vary greatly by season so check well ahead.

Ferries also ply the Gulf of Finland and Baltic Sea, connecting Helsinki (Finland) and Stockholm (Sweden) with Tallinn (Estonia), St Petersburg (Russia) and Rīga (Latvia). In Poland, Gdańsk and Gdynia are linked to Sweden, and Świnoujście (near Szczecin) to Denmark. Klaipėda (Lithuania) is served by ferries from Germany.

GETTING AROUND

Air

Major Eastern European cities are connected by a full schedule of regular flights within the region. Budgetairline prices are competitive with trains and sometimes with buses.

Many countries offer domestic flights, although there is rarely a need to fly internally (unless you need to cover ground quickly). Russia is the exception; flying from either Moscow or St Petersburg to Kaliningrad saves you the trouble of getting a double-entry Russian visa, which you would need if travelling to Kaliningrad overland (which crosses the border and gives your visa an exit stamp).

Bicycle

Eastern Europe is compact enough for exciting cross-border biking routes, and mountainous enough to thrill even seasoned cyclists. Easy areas to cycle include Bulgaria's Black Sea coast, flat Estonia, Hungary and parts of Poland. Cycling culture has been generally slow to catch on, though in nearly every country you'll find small but growing bike scenes. Cycling is a tough mode of transport to explore certain countries, such as Albania.

European Cyclists' Federation (www.ecf.com) Advocates bike-friendly policies and offers advice.

EuroVelo (www.eurovelo.com) Details long-distance bike routes across the continent, including many in Eastern Europe.

Hire

Except in a few of the more visited regions, it can be difficult to hire bikes. The most reliable spots are often camping grounds and resort hotels during summer months, or hostels in major cities.

Transporting a Bicycle

When flying with your own bike, it's best to take it apart and pack the pieces in a bike bag or box. Some airlines will simply tag a bike as check-in luggage, others will refuse to handle them unbagged; check ahead.

Bikes can usually be transported on trains as luggage, subject to a small supplementary fee. If it's possible, book tickets in advance. Alternatively you can look into sending your bike on to your desired destination on a cargo train.

Tours

Plenty of specialist companies offer organised cycling tours of Eastern Europe. They generally plan the itinerary, organise accommodation and transport luggage, making life a lot simpler for cyclists.

European Bike Tours (www.europe-bike-tours.eu) Short- and long-distance rides through Eastern Europe, including Russia.

Experience Plus (www.experienceplus.com) Runs tours throughout the region, including Croatian islands, the Carpathian Mountains and Slovenia's lakes.

Top Bicycle (www.topbicycle.com) This Czech company offers cycling tours of the Czech Republic, Hungary, Poland and Slovakia, as well as more extensive tours around the region.

Velo Touring (www.velo-touring.hu) Based in Budapest, this company offers tours of Hungary, as well as bike rentals for those who want to go it alone.

Boat

Eastern Europe's rivers, canals, lakes and seas provide rich opportunities for boat travel, although in almost all cases these are very much pleasure cruises rather than particularly practical ways to get around. Boat travel is usually far more expensive than the equivalent bus or train journey, but that's not necessarily the point.

Bus

Buses are a viable alternative to the rail network in many Eastern European countries (and generally a better option for getting around in countries across the Balkans, including Albania, Bulgaria, Bosnia & Hercegovina, Croatia, Kosovo, Montenegro, North Macedonia and Serbia). Buses tend to complement the rail system rather than duplicate it, though in some countries – notably Hungary, the Czech Republic and Slovakia – you'll often have a choice between the two options.

➡ Buses tend to be best for shorter hops, getting around cities and reaching remote rural villages. They are often the only option in mountainous regions.

➡ In general, buses are slightly cheaper and they may also be faster than trains. The ticketing system varies in each country, but advance reservations are rarely necessary. On long-distance buses you can often pay upon boarding, although it's safest to buy your ticket in advance at the station.

Car & Motorcycle

Travelling with your own vehicle allows you increased flexibility and the option to get off the beaten track. However, cars can be inconvenient in city centres when you have to negotiate strange one-way systems or find somewhere to park in the narrow streets of old towns. You also have to put up with often crowded and poorly maintained roads and highways.

Driving Licence & Documentation

➡ Always double-check which type of licence is required in your chosen destination before departure.

➡ An EU driving licence may be used throughout most of Eastern Europe, as may North American and Australian ones. If you want to be extra cautious – or if you have any other type of licence – you should obtain an International Driving Permit (IDP).

➡ At border crossings and police stops always be prepared to show the car's registration papers and proof of insurance.

Fuel & Spare Parts

➡ Unleaded petrol of 95 or 98 octane is widely available throughout the region and it's a bit cheaper than super (premium grade). Diesel is also usually available.

CROSSING BORDERS

The Schengen Agreement, which allows for passport-free travel within a large chunk of Europe, includes the Czech Republic, Estonia, Hungary, Latvia, Lithuania, Poland, Slovakia and Slovenia. EU member countries that are not part of the agreement – and where the usual border stops and passport checks apply – include (at the time of research) Bulgaria, Croatia and Romania. For up-to-date details see www.schengenvisainfo.com.

Russia–Belarus Border
A somewhat relaxed version of border control has been reestablished between Russia and Belarus, despite the two being part of a single customs union. You must have visas for both countries; crossing without them is a criminal offence. Don't even consider entering Belarus on a Russian visa or vice versa.

There are potentially serious implications for those transiting into Russia via Belarus on an international bus or train as you will not receive a Russian border stamp or an immigration form on entering the country. If you later plan to exit Russia via a different route this will be a problem and you could be fined.

We've not heard of any travellers running into serious difficulties but it would still be wise to make careful enquiries with visa authorities in both Belarus and Russia before you've confirmed your travel arrangements.

Russia–Ukraine Border
The two countries were essentially at war with each other at the time of writing, but it was still possible to cross in both directions by vehicle or train, with the exception of rebel-held zones in southeastern Ukraine and Russian-controlled Crimea. Crossing into the rebel-held zones or Crimea from the Russian side is a criminal offence under Ukrainian law. Ukraine has also announced that it will no longer permit foreigners to travel to Crimea from the Ukrainian side.

➡ Always fill your tank before driving into mountainous or otherwise remote areas.

➡ Spare parts are widely available from garages and dealerships around the region, although this is less the case in Belarus, Moldova and Ukraine, and of course in more rural areas.

Hire
➡ The big international companies will give you reliable service and a good standard of vehicle. Prebooked rates are generally lower than walk-in rates at rental offices.

➡ Local companies will usually offer lower prices than the multinationals, but it's best to use ones with good reputations – try asking at your hotel.

➡ Bear in mind that many companies will not allow you to take cars into certain countries. Russia, Belarus, Moldova and Kosovo all regularly feature on forbidden lists – check in advance with the car-hire company you're planning to use.

➡ Remember that even if your hire company allows the vehicle to be taken into that country, your travel-insurance policy may not cover you in that country.

Insurance
Third-party motor insurance is compulsory throughout the EU. For non-EU countries make sure you check the requirements with your insurer. For more information contact the Association of British Insurers (www.abi.org.uk).

➡ Get your insurer to issue a green card (which may cost extra), an internationally recognised proof of insurance, and check that it lists all the countries you intend to visit. Find details on www.cobx.org.

➡ If the green card doesn't list one of the countries you're visiting and your insurer cannot (or will not) add it, you will have to take out separate third-party cover at the border of the country in question (where available).

➡ The European Accident Statement is available from your insurance company and allows each party at an accident to record information for insurance purposes. The Association of British Insurers has more details. Never sign an accident statement you cannot understand – insist on a translation and sign only if it's acceptable.

➡ Taking out a European breakdown-assistance policy, such as those offered by the AA (www.theaa.com) and RAC (www.rac.co.uk), is a good investment.

➡ Non-Europeans might find it cheaper to arrange for international coverage with their own national motoring organisation before leaving home. Ask about reciprocal services offered by affiliated organisations around Europe.

Road Rules

Motoring organisations can supply members with country-by-country information on motoring regulations, or they may produce motoring guidebooks for general sale.

Standard international road signs are used in Eastern Europe. When driving in the region, keep the following rules in mind:

➡ Drive on the right-hand side of the road and overtake on the left.

➡ Seat belts are mandatory for the driver and all passengers.

➡ Motorcyclists (and passengers) must wear a helmet.

➡ Children under 12 and intoxicated passengers are not allowed to sit in the front seat in most countries.

➡ Drink-driving is a serious offence – most Eastern European countries have a 0% blood-alcohol concentration (BAC) limit.

➡ Some countries require headlights to be switched on low beam at all times; rental cars may be set up to do so automatically.

➡ Trams have priority at crossroads and when they are turning right. Don't pass a tram that's stopping to let off passengers until everyone is out and the doors have closed again, and never block a tram route.

➡ Traffic police usually administer fines on the spot; always ask for a receipt (if they refuse, it may be a scam).

➡ Almost everywhere in Europe it is compulsory to carry a red warning triangle, which you must use when parking on a highway in an emergency.

➡ A first-aid kit, fire extinguisher and reflective vest are also required in most Eastern European countries.

Road Hazards

Driving in Eastern Europe can be much more dangerous than in Western Europe. In the event of any accident, notify the police and your insurer.

➡ Theft from vehicles is a problem in many areas and foreign or rental cars make an attractive target. Never leave valuables in your car.

➡ In rural areas you may encounter horse-drawn vehicles, cyclists and domestic animals on the roads.

➡ The quality of country roads varies immensely. Don't trust your satnav over local advice or clearly marked road signs, or you may end up on a gravelled, potholed road only suited to 4WDs.

➡ Driving at night can be particularly hazardous in rural areas where roads are narrow and poorly lit.

➡ Winter tyres may be necessary in snow-clad mountainous areas or required by law during winter months; ask your rental outfit.

Hitching

Hitching is never entirely safe in any country and we don't recommend it. Travellers who hitch should understand they are taking a small but potentially serious risk.

Public transport remains relatively cheap in Eastern Europe, so hitching is more for the adventure than for the transport, except in some rural areas poorly served by public transport. In some countries, drivers will expect the equivalent of a bus fare, and a few may ask for fuel money.

If you want to give it a try, remember the following key points:

➡ Solo travellers expose themselves to the greatest risk when hitching. Hitching in pairs is safer.

➡ Don't hitch from city centres; take public transport to suburban exit routes.

➡ Make a clearly written cardboard sign indicating your intended destination, remembering to use the local name for the town or city (Praha not Prague, Warszawa not Warsaw).

➡ Don't let your luggage be put in the boot, only sit next to a door you can open, and unless you've been holding up a sign, ask drivers where they are going before you say where you're going.

Local Transport

Eastern European cities generally have good public transport.

➡ There are excellent metro networks in Moscow and St Petersburg (Russia), Warsaw (Poland), Prague (Czech Republic), Kyiv (Ukraine), Minsk (Belarus), Budapest (Hungary), Bucharest (Romania) and Sofia (Bulgaria).

➡ Throughout the region, you'll come across shared minibuses (*marshrutka* in the former Soviet Union, *furgon* in Albania) used as both inter- and intra-city transport. It's the most likely way you'll travel between mountain towns in Albania, for example.

➡ Trolleybuses are another phenomenon of Eastern Europe. Although slow, they are environmentally friendly (being powered by electricity) and can be found throughout the former Soviet Union.

➡ Trams are also popular, though they vary greatly in speed and modernity. Those in Russia and Romania are often borderline antiques, while Prague's fleet of sleek trams have electronic destination displays and automated announcements.

➤ Taxis throughout Eastern Europe are generally cheap and reliable, though the classic scams of being overcharged by sketchy drivers are common across the various countries. Avoid hailing taxis in touristy areas and train stations, and always order your taxi by telephone where possible. Ride-sharing services like Uber (www.uber.com) and Taxify (www.taxify.eu) operate in some, but not all, large cities.

Train

Trains are the most atmospheric way to make long overland journeys in Eastern Europe, though in some countries they are slower and less reliable than buses. All major cities are on the rail network and it's perfectly feasible for train travel to be your only form of intercity transport. In general, trains run efficiently.

➤ If you're travelling overnight (which is often the case when you're going between countries), the bed reservation may or may not be included in the price of your ticket, depending on the country.

➤ Each carriage is usually administered by a steward, who will look after your ticket and – crucially, if you arrive during the small hours – make sure that you get off at the correct stop.

➤ Each carriage will normally have a toilet and washbasin at either end – but the state of cleanliness will vary. Be aware that toilets may be closed while the train is at a station and for a good 30 minutes before you arrive in a big city.

➤ Overnight trains have the benefit of saving you a night's accommodation, and they are a great way to meet locals.

Train Classes

The system of train classes in Eastern Europe is similar to that in Western Europe. Short trips, or longer ones that don't involve sleeping on the train, are usually seated like a normal train – benches (on suburban trains) or aeroplane-style seats (on smarter intercity services).

There are generally three classes of sleeping accommodation on trains – each country has a different name for what are broadly 3rd, 2nd and 1st class. First-class tickets cost one-third more, or even double the price, of 2nd-class tickets.

Third class Generally consists of six berths in each compartment and is the cheapest option; not ideal if you like your privacy. In the former Soviet Union, 3rd class is called *platskartny* and does not have compartments; instead, there's just one open-plan carriage with beds everywhere. Third class is not widely available.

Second class Known as *kupe* in the former Soviet Union, 2nd class has four berths in a closed compartment; it's the option most used by travellers. If there are two of you, you will share your accommodation with two others. However, if there are three of you, you may have the compartment to yourselves.

First class SV or *myagky* in the former Soviet Union is a treat, although generally you are paying for space rather than decor. Here you'll find two berths in a compartment plus, possibly, other amenities such as TVs or meals.

Reservations

It's always advisable to buy a ticket in advance. Seat reservations are recommended (where applicable), but are only necessary if the timetable specifies that one is required. On busy routes and during the summer, always try to reserve a seat several days in advance.

➤ You can book most routes in the region from any main station in Eastern Europe.

➤ In some countries, especially when buying tickets for long-distance routes, you may be asked to show your passport.

➤ For peace of mind, you may prefer to book tickets via travel agencies before you leave home, although this will be more expensive than booking on arrival.

Resources

If you plan to travel extensively by train, the following resources are useful planning tools:

Deutsche Bahn (www.bahn.com) A useful resource for timetables (and some fares) for trains across Eastern Europe; the website is available in many languages, including English.

European Rail Timetable (www.europeanrailtimetable.co.uk) Buy complete listings of train schedules, updated monthly, that indicate where supplements apply or where reservations are necessary.

Man in Seat 61 (www.seat61.com) Tips on negotiating Eastern Europe's rail landscape by a devoted train traveller.

Voyages SNCF (https://en.oui.sncf) Provides information on fares and schedules for trains across Europe.

Safety

Trains, while generally safe, can attract petty criminals.

➤ Carry your valuables on you at all times – keep your cash, wallet and passport on you, even when visiting the bathroom.

➤ If you are sharing a compartment with others, you'll have to decide whether or not you trust them. It's always best to keep your essential documents on you.

➤ At night, make sure your door is locked from the inside. Stow your valuables in secure pockets or a money belt, or hide them in your luggage under the bed (which usually can't be accessed when someone is lying down).

➤ If you have a compartment to yourself, you can ask the steward to lock it while you go to the dining car or go for a wander outside when the train is stopped. However, be aware that most criminals strike when they can easily disembark from the train and on rare occasions stewards are complicit.

➡ In the former Soviet Union, opinions vary on open-plan 3rd-class accommodation – with so many people observing the carriage's goings-on it can be argued these are actually safer than 2nd- and 1st-class compartments.

Train Passes

Passes are available online or through most travel agents. Not all countries in Eastern Europe are covered by rail passes, but they can be worthwhile if you are concentrating your travels on a particular part of the region, and if you're planning on extensive travel by rail. Always do the maths before committing to a pass: purchasing separate advance tickets for a few journeys may be cheaper. Check out the excellent summary of available passes, and their pros and cons, at Man in Seat 61 (www.seat61.com/Railpass-and-Eurail-pass-guide.htm)

Keep in mind that all passes offer discounted 'youth' prices for travellers who are under 28 years of age on the first day of travel. Some passes allow an accompanying child to travel for free. Discounted fares are available if you are travelling in a group of two to five people (although you must always travel together).

Buy passes through Rail Europe (www.raileurope.com and www.raileurope.com. au); in Australia you can also use Rail Plus (www.railplus. com.au) or International Rail (www.internationalrail. com.au).

BALKAN FLEXIPASS

The Balkan Flexipass (www. rail.cc/en/balkan-flexi-pass) covers Bosnia & Hercegovina, Bulgaria, Greece, North Macedonia, Montenegro, Romania, Serbia and Turkey, and some ferries between Greece and Italy. It is not available to anyone who is a resident of the countries included in the pass. It's valid for 1st-class travel only.

EURAIL PASS

The famous Eurail Pass (www. eurail.com) allows the greatest flexibility for 'overseas' visitors only – if you are a resident of Europe, check out the InterRail Pass. The Eurail Global pass allows unlimited travel in up to 28 countries, including Croatia, the Czech Republic, Hungary, Romania and Slovenia. The pass is valid for a set number of consecutive days or a set number of days within a period of time.

EURAIL SELECT

Again, only non-European residents can purchase this pass, which covers travel in two to four neighbouring countries, which you choose from the 26 available. Your Eastern European options include Bulgaria, Croatia, the Czech Republic, Hungary, Montenegro, Poland, Romania, Serbia, Slovakia and Slovenia. Note that Serbia and Montenegro count as one country for Eurail pass purposes, as do Croatia and Slovenia.

INTERRAIL GLOBAL

These passes are available to European residents (proof of residency is required), including residents of Turkey. Terms and conditions vary slightly from country to country, but the InterRail pass is not valid for travel within your country of residence. For complete information, visit the InterRail website (www.interrail.eu).

InterRail Global allows unlimited travel in 30 European countries, including Bosnia & Hercegovina, Bulgaria, Croatia, the Czech Republic, Hungary, North Macedonia, Montenegro, Poland, Romania, Serbia, Slovakia and Slovenia.

INTERRAIL & EURAIL COUNTRY PASSES

If you intend to travel extensively by train within one country, you might consider buying a country pass. InterRail (www.interrail.eu) passes are cheaper, but available only to EU residents; non residents must purchase a Eurail (www.eurail.com) pass. Prices vary by country and number of days, so check out the websites for more information. You'll need to travel widely to recoup your money, but the passes may save you the time and hassle of buying individual tickets that don't require reservations.

Language

This chapter offers basic vocabulary to help you get around Eastern Europe. Read our coloured pronunciation guides as if they were English and you'll be understood. The stressed syllables are indicated with italics.

Some phrases in this chapter have both polite and informal forms (indicated by the abbreviations 'pol' and 'inf' respectively). The abbreviations 'm' and 'f' indicate masculine and feminine gender respectively.

ALBANIAN

In Albanian – also understood in Kosovo – ew is pronounced as 'ee' with rounded lips, uh as the 'a' in 'ago', dh as the 'th' in 'that', dz as the 'ds' in 'adds', and zh as the 's' in 'pleasure'. Also, ll and rr are pronounced stronger than when they are written as single letters.

Basics

Hello.	*Tungjatjeta.*	toon·dya·tye·ta
Goodbye.	*Mirupafshim.*	mee·roo·paf·sheem
Excuse me.	*Më falni.*	muh fal·nee
Sorry.	*Më vjen keq.*	muh vyen kech
Please.	*Ju lutem.*	yoo loo·tem
Thank you.	*Faleminderit.*	fa·le·meen·de·reet
Yes.	*Po.*	po
No.	*Jo.*	yo

What's your name?
Si quheni? — see choo·he·nee

My name is ...
Unë quhem ... — oo·nuh choo·hem ...

Do you speak English?
A flisni anglisht? — a flees·nee ang·leesht

I don't understand.
Unë nuk kuptoj. — oo·nuh nook koop·toy

Accommodation

campsite	*vend*	vend
	kampimi	kam·pee·mee
guesthouse	*bujtinë*	booy·tee·nuh
hotel	*hotel*	ho·tel
youth	*fjetore*	fye·to·re
hostel	*për të rinj*	puhr tuh reeny

Do you have a single/double room?
A keni një dhomë — a ke·nee nyuh dho·muh
teke/dopjo? — te·ke/dop·yo

How much is it per night/person?
Sa kushton për një — sa koosh·ton puhr nyuh
natë/njeri? — na·tuh/nye·ree

Eating & Drinking

Is there a vegetarian restaurant near here?
A ka ndonjë restorant — a ka ndo·nyuh res·to·rant
vegjetarian — ve·dye·ta·ree·an
këtu afër? — kuh·too a·fuhr

What would you recommend?
Çfarë më — chfa·ruh muh
rekomandoni? — re·ko·man·do·nee

I'd like the bill/menu, please.
Më sillni faturën/ — muh seell·nee fa·too·ruhn/
menunë, ju lutem. — me·noo·nuh yoo loo·tem

I'll have ... *Dua ...* — doo·a ...

Cheers! *Gëzuar!* — guh·zoo·ar

Emergencies

Help!	*Ndihmë!*	ndeeh·muh
Go away!	*Ik!*	eek

Call the doctor/police!
Thirrni doktorin/policinë! — theerr·nee dok·to·reen/po·lee·tsee·nuh

I'm lost.
Kam humbur rrugën. — kam *hoom*·boor *rroo*·guhn

I'm ill.
Jam i/e sëmurë. (m/f) — yam ee/e suh·*moo*·ruh

Where are the toilets?
Ku janë banjat? — koo *ya*·nuh *ba*·nyat

Shopping & Services

I'm looking for ...
Po kërkoj për ... — po kuhr·*koy* puhr ...

How much is it?
Sa kushton? — sa koosh·*ton*

That's too expensive.
Është shumë shtrenjtë. — *uhsh*·tuh *shoo*·muh *shtreny*·tuh

market	*treg*	treg
post office	*posta*	*pos*·ta
tourist office	*zyrë turistike*	*zew*·ra too·rees·*tee*·ke

Transport

boat	*anija*	a·*nee*·ya
bus	*autobusi*	a·oo·to·*boo*·see
plane	*aeroplani*	a·e·ro·*pla*·nee
train	*treni*	*tre*·nee

One ... ticket (to Shkodër), please.
Një biletë ... (për në Shkodër), ju lutem. — nyuh bee·*le*·tuh ... (puhr nuh *shko*·duhr) yoo *loo*·tem

one-way	*për vajtje*	puhr *vai*·tye
return	*kthimi*	*kthee*·mee

BULGARIAN

In Bulgarian, vowels in unstressed syllables are generally pronounced shorter and weaker than they are in stressed syllables. Note that uh is pronounced as the 'a' in 'ago' and zh as the 's' in 'pleasure'.

Basics

Hello.	Здравейте.	zdra·*vey*·te
Goodbye.	Довиждане.	do·*veezh*·da·ne
Excuse me.	Извинете.	iz·vee·*ne*·te
Sorry.	Съжалявам.	suh·zhal·*ya*·vam

NUMBERS – ALBANIAN		
1	*një*	nyuh
2	*dy*	dew
3	*tre*	tre
4	*katër*	*ka*·tuhr
5	*pesë*	*pe*·suh
6	*gjashtë*	*dyash*·tuh
7	*shtatë*	*shta*·tuh
8	*tetë*	*te*·tuh
9	*nëntë*	*nuhn*·tuh
10	*dhjetë*	*dhye*·tuh

Please.	Моля.	*mol*·ya
Thank you.	Благодаря.	bla·go·dar·*ya*
Yes.	Да.	da
No.	Не.	ne

What's your name?
Как се казвате/казваш? (pol/inf) — kak se *kaz*·va·te/*kaz*·vash

My name is ...
Казвам се ... — *kaz*·vam se ...

Do you speak English?
Говорите ли английски? — go·*vo*·ree·te lee ang·*lees*·kee

I don't understand.
Не разбирам. — ne raz·*bee*·ram

Accommodation

campsite	къмпинг	*kuhm*·peeng
guesthouse	пансион	pan·see·*on*
hotel	хотел	ho·*tel*
youth hostel	общежитие	ob·shte·*zhee*·tee·ye

Do you have a ... room?
Имате ли стая с ...? — *ee*·ma·te lee *sta*·ya s ...

single	едно легло	ed·*no* leg·*lo*
double	едно голямо легло	ed·*no* go·*lya*·mo leg·*lo*

How much is it per night/person?
Колко е на вечер/човек? — *kol*·ko e na *ve*·cher/cho·*vek*

Eating & Drinking

Do you have vegetarian food?
Имате ли вегетерианска храна? — *ee*·ma·te lee ve·ge·te·ree·*an*·ska hra·*na*

What would you recommend?

Какво ще препоръчате?		*kak·vo* shte pre·po·*ruh*·cha·te

I'd like the bill/menu, please.

Дайте ми сметката/ менюто, моля.		*dai·*te mee *smet·*ka·ta/ men·*yoo*·to *mol·*ya

I'll have ...	Ще взема …	shte *vze·*ma …
Cheers!	Наздраве!	na·*zdra·*ve

Emergencies

Help!	Помощ!	*po·*mosht
Go away!	Махайте се!	*ma·*hai·te se

Call the doctor/police!

Повикайте лекар/ полицията!		po·*vee·*kai·te le·kar/ po·*lee·*tsee·ya·ta

I'm lost.

Загубих се.		za·*goo·*beeh se

I'm ill.

Болен/Болна съм. (m/f)		*bo·*len/*bol·*na suhm

Where are the toilets?

Къде има тоалетни?		kuh·de ee·ma to·a·*let·*nee

Shopping & Services

I'm looking for ...

Търся …		*tuhr·*sya …

How much is it?

Колко струва?		*kol·*ko *stroo·*va

That's too expensive.

Скъпо е.		*skuh·*po e

bank	банка	*ban·*ka
post office	поща	*po·*shta
tourist office	бюро за туристическа информация	*byoo·*ro za too·*ree·*stee·ches·ka een·for·ma·*tsee·*ya

NUMBERS – BULGARIAN

1	един	ed·*een*
2	два	dva
3	три	tree
4	четири	che·tee·ree
5	пет	pet
6	шест	shest
7	седем	se·dem
8	осем	o·sem
9	девет	de·vet
10	десет	de·set

Transport

boat	корабът	ko·*ra·*buht
bus	автобусът	av·to·*boo·*suht
plane	самолетът	sa·mo·*le·*tuht
train	влакът	*vla·*kuht
One ... ticket (to Varna), please.	Един билет … (за Варна), моля.	e·*deen* bee·*let* … (za *var·*na), *mol·*ya
one-way	в едната посока	v ed·*na·*ta po·*so·*ka
return	за отиване и връщане	za o·*tee·*va·ne ee *vruhsh·*ta·ne

CROATIAN & SERBIAN

Croatian and Serbian are very similar and mutually intelligible. Using them, you will also be fully understood in Bosnia & Hercegovina, and Montenegro, and in parts of Kosovo.

In this section, significant differences between Croatian and Serbian are indicated with (C) and (S) respectively. Note that r is rolled and that zh is pronounced as the 's' in 'pleasure'.

Basics

Hello.	*Zdravo.*	*zdra·*vo
Goodbye.	*Zbogom.*	*zbo·*gom
Excuse me.	*Oprostite.*	o·*pro·*sti·te
Sorry.	*Žao mi je.*	*zha·*o mi ye
Please.	*Molim.*	*mo·*lim
Thank you.	*Hvala.*	*hva·*la
Yes.	*Da.*	da
No.	*Ne.*	ne

What's your name?

Kako se zovete/ zoveš? (pol/inf)		*ka·*ko se zo·ve·te/ zo·vesh

My name is ...

Zovem se ...		zo·vem se ...

Do you speak English?

Govorite/Govoriš li engleski? (pol/inf)		go·vo·ri·te/go·vo·rish li en·gle·ski

I don't understand.

Ja ne razumijem.		ya ne ra·zu·mi·yem

Accommodation

campsite	*kamp*	kamp
guesthouse	*privatni smještaj*	pri·*vat·*ni smyesh·tai
hotel	*hotel*	*ho·*tel

| youth | prenoćište | pre·no·chish·te |
| hostel | za mladež | za *mla*·dezh |

Do you have a single/double room?

| *Imate li jednokrevetnu/* | i·ma·te li yed·no·kre·vet·nu/ |
| *dvokrevetnu sobu?* | dvo·kre·vet·nu so·bu |

How much is it per night/person?

| *Koliko stoji po* | ko·li·ko sto·yi po |
| *noći/osobi?* | no·chi/o·so·bi |

Eating & Drinking

What would you recommend?

| *Što biste preporučili?* | shto bi·ste pre·po·ru·chi·li |

Do you have vegetarian food?

| *Da li imate* | da li i·ma·te |
| *vegetarijanski obrok?* | ve·ge·ta·ri·yan·ski o·brok |

I'd like the bill/menu, please.

| *Mogu li dobiti račun/* | mo·gu li do·bi·ti ra·chun/ |
| *jelovnik, molim?* | ye·lov·nik mo·lim |

| I'll have ... | Želim ... | zhe·lim ... |
| Cheers! | Živjeli! | zhi·vye·li |

Emergencies

| Help! | Upomoć! | u·po·moch |
| Go away! | Maknite se! | mak·ni·te se |

Call the ...!	Zovite ...!	zo·vi·te ...
doctor	liječnika (C)	li·yech·ni·ka
	lekara (S)	le·ka·ra
police	policiju	po·li·tsi·yu

I'm lost.

| *Izgubio/Izgubila* | iz·gu·bi·o/iz·gu·bi·la |
| *sam se.* (m/f) | sam se |

NUMBERS – CROATIAN & SERBIAN

1	jedan	ye·dan
2	dva	dva
3	tri	tri
4	četiri	che·ti·ri
5	pet	pet
6	šest	shest
7	sedam	se·dam
8	osam	o·sam
9	devet	de·vet
10	deset	de·set

I'm ill.

| *Ja sam bolestan/* | ya sam bo·le·stan/ |
| *bolesna.* (m/f) | bo·le·sna |

Where are the toilets?

| *Gdje se nalaze* | gdye se na·la·ze |
| *zahodi/toaleti?* (C/S) | za·ho·di/to·a·le·ti |

Shopping & Services

I'm looking for ...

| *Tražim ...* | tra·zhim |

How much is it?

| *Koliko stoji/* | ko·li·ko sto·yi/ |
| *košta?* (C/S) | kosh·ta |

That's too expensive.

| *To je preskupo.* | to ye pre·sku·po |

bank		
banka		ban·ka
post office	poštanski	po·shtan·skee
	ured	oo·red
tourist office	turistička	tu·ris·tich·ka
	agencija	a·gen·tsi·ya

Transport

boat	brod	brod
bus	autobus	a·u·to·bus
plane	zrakoplov (C)	zra·ko·plov
	avion (S)	a·vi·on
train	vlak/voz (C/S)	vlak/voz

One ... ticket	Jednu ... kartu	yed·nu ... kar·tu
(to Sarajevo),	(do Sarajeva),	(do sa·ra·ye·va)
please.	molim.	mo·lim
one-way	jedno-	yed·no·
	smjernu	smyer·nu
return	povratnu	po·vrat·nu

CZECH

An accent mark over a vowel in written Czech indicates it's pronounced as a long sound. Note that air is pronounced as in 'hair', aw as in 'law', oh as the 'o' in 'note', ow as in 'how', uh as the 'a' in 'ago', kh as the 'ch' in the Scottish *loch*, and zh as the 's' in 'pleasure'. Also, r is rolled in Czech and the apostrophe (') indicates a slight y sound.

Basics

Hello.	Ahoj.	uh·hoy
Goodbye.	Na shledanou.	nuh·skhle·
		duh·noh
Excuse me.	Promiňte.	pro·min'·te

Sorry.	Promiňte.	*pro*·min'·te
Please.	Prosím.	*pro*·seem
Thank you.	Děkuji.	*dye*·ku·yi
Yes.	Ano.	*uh*·no
No.	Ne.	ne

What's your name?
Jak se jmenujete/   yuhk se *yme*·nu·ye·te/
jmenuješ? (pol/inf)   *yme*·nu·yesh

My name is ...
Jmenuji se ...   *yme*·nu·yi se ...

Do you speak English?
Mluvíte anglicky?   *mlu*·vee·te *uhn*·glits·ki

I don't understand.
Nerozumím.   ne·ro·zu·meem

Accommodation

campsite	tábořiště	*ta*·bo·rzhish·tye
guesthouse	penzion	*pen*·zi·on
hotel	hotel	*ho*·tel
youth hostel	mládežnická	*mla*·dezh·nyits·ka
	ubytovna	u·bi·tov·nuh

Do you have a ... room?
Máte jednolůžkový/   *ma*·te yed·no·loozh·ko·vee
dvoulůžkový pokoj?   dvoh·loozh·ko·vee *po*·koy

How much is it per ...?	Kolik to stojí ...?	*ko*·lik to *sto*·yee ...
night	na noc	nuh nots
person	za osobu	zuh o·so·bu

Eating & Drinking

What would you recommend?
Co byste doporučil/   tso *bis*·te do·po·ru·chil/
doporučila? (m/f)   do·po·ru·chi·luh

Do you have vegetarian food?
Máte vegetariánská   *ma*·te ve·ge·tuh·ri·ans·ka
jídla?   *yeed*·luh

I'd like the bill/menu, please.
Chtěl/Chtěla bych   khtyel/*khtye*·luh bikh
účet/jídelníček,   oo·chet/yee·del·nyee·chek
prosím. (m/f)   ... *pro*·seem

| I'll have ... | Dám si ... | dam si ... |
| Cheers! | Na zdraví! | nuh *zdruh*·vee |

Emergencies

| Help! | Pomoc! | *po*·mots |
| Go away! | Běžte pryč! | *byezh*·te prich |

NUMBERS – CZECH

1	*jeden*	ye·den
2	*dva*	dvuh
3	*tři*	trzhi
4	*čtyři*	*chti*·rzhi
5	*pět*	pyet
6	*šest*	shest
7	*sedm*	se·dm
8	*osm*	o·sm
9	*devět*	de·vyet
10	*deset*	de·set

Call the doctor/police!
Zavolejte lékaře/   zuh·vo·ley·te *lair*·kuh·rzhe/
policii!   po·li·tsi·yi

I'm lost.
Zabloudil/   zuh·bloh·dyil/
Zabloudila jsem. (m/f)   zuh·bloh·dyi·luh ysem

I'm ill.
Jsem nemocný/   ysem ne·mots·nee/
nemocná. (m/f)   ne·mots·na

Where are the toilets?
Kde jsou toalety?   gde ysoh *to*·uh·le·ti

Shopping & Services

I'm looking for ...
Hledám ...   *hle*·dam ...

How much is it?
Kolik to stojí?   *ko*·lik to *sto*·yee

That's too expensive.
To je moc drahé.   to ye mots *druh*·hair

bank	banka	*buhn*·kuh
post office	pošta	*posh*·tuh
tourist office	turistická	*tu*·ris·tits·ka
	informační	in·for·muhch·nyee
	kancelář	*kuhn*·tse·larzh

Transport

bus	autobus	*ow*·to·bus
plane	letadlo	*le*·tuhd·lo
train	vlak	vluhk

One ... ticket to (Telč), please.	... jízdenku do (Telče), prosim.	... *yeez*·den·ku do (*tel*·che) *pro*·seem
one-way	Jedno-směrnou	*yed*·no-smyer·noh
return	Zpáteční	*zpa*·tech·nyee

ESTONIAN

Double vowels in written Estonian indicate they are pronounced as long sounds. Note that air is pronounced as in 'hair', aw as in 'law', ea as in 'ear', eu as the 'u' in 'nurse', ew as 'ee' with rounded lips, oh as the 'o' in 'note', ow as in 'how', uh as the 'a' in 'ago', kh as in the Scottish *loch,* and zh as the 's' in 'pleasure'.

Basics

Hello.	Tere.	te·re
Goodbye.	Nägemist.	nair·ge·mist
Excuse me.	Vabandage. (pol)	va·ban·da·ge
	Vabanda. (inf)	va·ban·da
Sorry.	Vabandust.	va·ban·dust
Please.	Palun.	pa·lun
Thank you.	Tänan.	tair·nan
Yes.	Jaa.	yaa
No.	Ei.	ay

What's your name?
Mis on teie nimi?   mis on tay·e ni·mi

My name is ...
Minu nimi on ...   mi·nu ni·mi on ...

Do you speak English?
Kas te räägite   kas te rair·git·te
inglise keelt?   ing·kli·se keylt

I don't understand.
Ma ei saa aru.   ma ay saa a·ru

Eating & Drinking

What would you recommend?
Mida te soovitate?   mi·da te saw·vit·tat·te

Do you have vegetarian food?
Kas teil on taimetoitu?   kas tayl on tai·met·toyt·tu

I'd like the bill/menu, please.
Ma sooviksin   ma saw·vik·sin
arvet/menüüd, palun.   ar·vet/me·newt pa·lun

I'll have a ...   Ma tahaksin ...   ma ta·hak·sin ...

Cheers!   Terviseks!   tair·vi·seks

Emergencies

Help!	Appi!	ap·pi
Go away!	Minge ära!	ming·ke air·ra

Call the doctor/police!
Kutsuge arst/   ku·tsu·ge arst/
politsei!   po·li·tsay

I'm lost.
Ma olen ära eksinud.   ma o·len air·ra ek·si·nud

NUMBERS – ESTONIAN

1	üks	ewks
2	kaks	kaks
3	kolm	kolm
4	neli	ne·li
5	viis	vees
6	kuus	koos
7	seitse	say·tse
8	kaheksa	ka·hek·sa
9	üheksa	ew·hek·sa
10	kümme	kewm·me

Where are the toilets?
Kus on WC?   kus on ve·se

Shopping & Services

I'm looking for ...
Ma otsin ...   ma o·tsin

How much is it?
Kui palju see maksab?   ku·i pal·yu sey mak·sab

That's too expensive.
See on liiga kallis.   sey on lee·ga kal·lis

bank	pank	pank
market	turg	turg
post office	postkontor	post·kont·tor

Transport

boat	laev	laiv
bus	buss	bus
plane	lennuk	len·nuk
train	rong	rongk

One ... ticket	Üks ... pilet	ewks ... pi·let
(to Pärnu),	(Pärnusse),	(pair·nus·se)
please.	palun.	pa·lun
one-way	ühe otsa	ew·he o·tsa
return	edasi-tagasi	e·da·si·ta·ga·si

HUNGARIAN

A symbol over a vowel in written Hungarian indicates it's pronounced as a long sound. Double consonants should be drawn out a little longer than in English. Note also that aw is pronounced as in 'law', eu as the 'u' in 'nurse', ew as 'ee' with rounded lips, and zh as the 's' in 'pleasure'. Finally, keep in mind that r is rolled in Hungarian and that the apostrophe (') indicates a slight y sound.

Basics

Hello.	Szervusz. (sg)	ser·vus
	Szervusztok. (pl)	ser·vus·tawk
Goodbye.	Viszlát.	vis·lat
Excuse me.	Elnézést kérek.	el·ney·zeysht key·rek
Sorry.	Sajnálom.	shoy·na·lawm
Please.	Kérem. (pol)	key·rem
	Kérlek. (inf)	keyr·lek
Thank you.	Köszönöm.	keu·seu·neum
Yes.	Igen.	i·gen
No.	Nem.	nem

What's your name?
Mi a neve/   mi o ne·ve/
neved? (pol/inf)   ne·ved

My name is ...
A nevem ...   o ne·vem ...

Do you speak English?
Beszél/Beszélsz   be·seyl/be·seyls
angolul? (pol/inf)   on·gaw·lul

I don't understand.
Nem értem.   nem eyr·tem

Accommodation

campsite	kemping	kem·ping
guesthouse	panzió	pon·zi·āw
hotel	szálloda	sal·law·do
youth hostel	ifjúsági szálló	if·yū·sha·gi sal·lāw

Do you have a single/double room?
Van Önnek kiadó egy   von eun·nek ki·o·dāw ed'
egyágyas/duplaágyas   ej·a·dyosh/dup·lo·a·dyosh
szobája?   saw·ba·yo

How much is it per night/person?
Mennyibe kerül egy   men'·nyi·be ke·rewl ej
éjszakára/főre?   ey·so·ka·ro/fēū·re

NUMBERS – HUNGARIAN

1	egy	ej
2	kettő	ket·tēū
3	három	ha·rawm
4	négy	neyj
5	öt	eut
6	hat	hot
7	hét	heyt
8	nyolc	nyawlts
9	kilenc	ki·lents
10	tíz	teez

Eating & Drinking

What would you recommend?
Mit ajánlana?   mit o·yan·lo·no

Do you have vegetarian food?
Vannak Önöknél   von·nok eu·neuk·neyl
vegetáriánus ételek?   ve·ge·ta·ri·a·nush ey·te·lek

I'll have ...
... kérek.   ... key·rek

Cheers! (to one person)
Egészségedre!   e·geys·shey·ged·re

Cheers! (to more than one person)
Egészségetekre!   e·geys·shey·ge·tek·re

I'd like the ...   ... szeretném.   ... se·ret·neym
| **bill** | A számlát | o sam·lat |
| **menu** | Az étlapot | oz eyt·lo·pawt |

Emergencies

| Help! | Segítség! | she·geet·sheyg |
| Go away! | Menjen innen! | men·yen in·nen |

Call the doctor!
Hívjon orvost!   heev·yawn awr·vawsht

Call the police!
Hívja a   heev·yo o
rendőrséget!   rend·ēūr·shey·get

I'm lost.
Eltévedtem.   el·tey·ved·tem

I'm ill.
Rosszul vagyok.   raws·sul vo·dyawk

Where are the toilets?
Hol a vécé?   hawl o vey·tsey

Shopping & Services

I'm looking for ...
Keresem a ...   ke·re·shem o ...

How much is it?
Mennyibe kerül?   men'·nyi·be ke·rewl

That's too expensive.
Ez túl drága.   ez tūl dra·go

market	piac	pi·ots
post office	postahivatal	pawsh·to·hi·vo·tol
tourist office	turistairoda	tu·rish·to·i·raw·do

Transport

bus	busz	bus
plane	repülőgép	re·pew·lēū·geyp
train	vonat	vaw·not

One ... ticket to (Eger), please.	Egy ... jegy (Eger)be.	ej ... yej (e·ger)·be
one-way	csak oda	chok aw·do
return	oda-vissza	aw·do·vis·so

LATVIAN

A line over a vowel in written Latvian indicates it's pronounced as a long sound. Note that air is pronounced as in 'hair', aw as in 'law', ea as in 'ear', ow as in 'how', wa as in 'water', dz as the 'ds' in 'adds', and zh as the 's' in 'pleasure'. The apostrophe (') indicates a slight y sound.

Basics

Hello.	Sveiks.	svayks
Goodbye.	Atā.	a·taa
Excuse me.	Atvainojiet.	at·vai·nwa·yeat
Sorry.	Piedodiet.	pea·dwa·deat
Please.	Lūdzu.	loo·dzu
Thank you.	Paldies.	pal·deas
Yes.	Jā.	yaa
No.	Nē.	nair

What's your name?
Kā Jūs sauc?   kaa yoos sowts

My name is ...
Mani sauc ...   ma·ni sowts ...

Do you speak English?
Vai Jūs runājat   vai yoos ru·naa·yat
angliski?   ang·li·ski

I don't understand.
Es nesaprotu.   es ne·sa·prwa·tu

Eating & Drinking

What would you recommend?
Ko Jūs iesakat?   kwa yoos ea·sa·kat

NUMBERS – LATVIAN

1	viens	veans
2	divi	di·vi
3	trīs	trees
4	četri	che·tri
5	pieci	pea·tsi
6	seši	se·shi
7	septiņi	sep·ti·nyi
8	astoņi	as·twa·nyi
9	deviņi	de·vi·nyi
10	desmit	des·mit

Do you have vegetarian food?
Vai Jums ir veģetārie   vai yums ir ve·dye·taa·rea
ēdieni?   air·dea·ni

I'd like the bill/menu, please.
Es vēlos rēķinu/   es vair·lwas rair·tyi·nu/
ēdienkarti, lūdzu.   air·dean·kar·ti loo·dzu

I'll have a ...
Man lūdzu vienu ...   man loo·dzu vea·nu ...

Cheers!
Priekā!   prea·kaa

Emergencies

| Help! | Palīgā! | pa·lee·gaa |
| Go away! | Ej prom! | ay prwam |

Call the doctor/police!
Zvani ārstam/policijai!   zva·ni aar·stam/po·li·tsi·yai

I'm lost.
Esmu apmaldījies.   es·mu ap·mal·dee·yeas

Where are the toilets?
Kur ir tualetes?   kur ir tu·a·le·tes

Shopping & Services

I'm looking for ...
Es meklēju ...   es mek·lair·yu ...

How much is it?
Cik maksā?   tsik mak·saa

That's too expensive.
Tas ir par dārgu.   tas ir par daar·gu

bank	banka	ban·ka
market	tirgus	tir·gus
post office	pasts	pasts

Transport

boat	laiva	lai·va
bus	autobus	ow·to·bus
plane	lidmašīna	lid·ma·shee·na
train	vilciens	vil·tseans

One ... ticket (to Jūrmala), please.	Vienu ... biļeti (uz Jūrmalu), lūdzu.	vea·nu ... bi·lye·ti (uz yoor·ma·lu) loo·dzu
one-way	vienvirziena	vean·vir·zea·na
return	turp-atpakaļ	turp·at·pa·kal'

LITHUANIAN

Symbols on vowels in written Lithuanian indicate they are pronounced as long sounds. Note that aw is pronounced as in 'law', ea as in 'ear', ow as in 'how', wa as in 'water', dz as the 'ds' in 'adds', and zh as the 's' in 'pleasure'.

Basics

Hello.	Sveiki.	svay·ki
Goodbye.	Viso gero.	vi·so ge·ro
Excuse me.	Atleiskite.	at·lays·ki·te
Sorry.	Atsiprašau.	at·si·pra·show
Please.	Prašau.	pra·show
Thank you.	Ačiū.	aa·choo
Yes.	Taip.	taip
No.	Ne.	ne

What's your name?
Koks jūsų vardas? · kawks yoo·soo var·das

My name is ...
Mano vardas ... ma·no var·das ...

Do you speak English?
Ar kalbate angliškai? ar kal·ba·te aang·lish·kai

I don't understand.
Aš nesuprantu. ash ne·su·pran·tu

Eating & Drinking

What would you recommend?
Ką jūs rekomenduo- kaa yoos re·ko·men·dwo·
tumėte? tu·mey·te

Do you have vegetarian food?
Ar turite vegetariško ar tu·ri·te ve·ge·taa·rish·ko
maisto? mais·to

I'd like the bill/menu, please.
Aš norėčiau ash no·rey·chyow
sąskaitos/meniu saas·kai·taws/me·nyu

I'll have a ...
Aš užsisakysiu ... ash uzh·si·sa·kee·syu ...

Cheers!
Į sveikatą! ee svay·kaa·taa

Emergencies

| Help! | Padėkit! | pa·dey·kit |
| Go away! | Eikit iš čia! | ay·kit ish chya |

Call the doctor/police!
Iškvieskit gydytoją/ ish·kveas·kit gee·dee·to·ya/
policiją! po·li·tsi·ya

I'm lost.
Aš pasiklydau. ash pa·si·klee·dow

Where are the toilets?
Kur yra tualetai? kur ee·ra tu·a·le·tai

Shopping & Services

I'm looking for ...
Aš ieškau ... ash eash·kow ...

How much is it?
Kiek kainuoja? keak kain·wo·ya

NUMBERS – LITHUANIAN

1	vienas	vea·nas
2	du	du
3	trys	trees
4	keturi	ke·tu·ri
5	penki	pen·ki
6	šeši	she·shi
7	septyni	sep·tee·ni
8	aštuoni	ash·twa·ni
9	devyni	de·vee·ni
10	dešimt	de·shimt

That's too expensive.
Per brangu. per bran·gu

bank	bankas	baan·kas
market	turgus	tur·gus
post office	paštas	paash·tas

Transport

boat	laivas	lai·vas
bus	autobusas	ow·to·bu·sas
plane	lėktuvas	leyk·tu·vas
train	traukinys	trow·ki·nees

One ... ticket Vieną vea·naa
(to Kaunas), bilietą ... bi·lye·taa ...
please. (į Kauną), (ee kow·naa)
  prašau. pra·show

one-way į vieną ee vea·naa
  pusę pu·sey

return į abi ee a·bi
  puses pu·ses

NORTH MACEDONIAN

Note that dz is pronounced as the 'ds' in 'adds', r is rolled, and zh as the 's' in 'pleasure'.

Basics

Hello.	Здраво.	zdra·vo
Goodbye.	До гледање.	do gle·da·nye
Excuse me.	Извинете.	iz·vi·ne·te
Sorry.	Простете.	pros·te·te
Please.	Молам.	mo·lam
Thank you.	Благодарам.	bla·go·da·ram
Yes.	Да.	da
No.	Не.	ne

NUMBERS – MACEDONIAN

1	еден	e·den
2	два	dva
3	три	tri
4	четири	che·ti·ri
5	пет	pet
6	шест	shest
7	седум	se·dum
8	осум	o·sum
9	девет	de·vet
10	десет	de·set

What's your name?
Како се викате/ ka·ko se vi·ka·te/
викаш? (pol/inf) vi·kash

My name is ...
Јас се викам … yas se vi·kam …

Do you speak English?
Зборувате ли zbo·ru·va·te li
англиски? an·glis·ki

I don't understand.
Јас не разбирам. yas ne raz·bi·ram

Accommodation

campsite	камп	kamp
guesthouse	приватно сместување	pri·vat·no smes·tu·va·nye
hotel	хотел	ho·tel
youth hostel	младинско преноќиште	mla·din·sko pre·no·kyish·te

Do you have a single/double room?
Дали имате da·li i·ma·te
еднокреветна/ ed·no·kre·vet·na/
двокреветна соба? dvo·kre·vet·na so·ba

How much is it per night/person?
Која е цената за ko·ya e tse·na·ta za
ноќ/еден? noky/e·den

Eating & Drinking

What would you recommend?
Што препорачувате shto pre·po·ra·chu·va·te
вие? vi·e

Do you have vegetarian food?
Дали имате da·li i·ma·te
вегетаријанска храна? ve·ge·ta·ri·yan·ska hra·na

I'd like the bill/menu, please.
Ве молам сметката/ ve mo·lam smet·ka·ta/
мени. me·ni

I'll have ...
Јас ќе земам … yas kye ze·mam …

Cheers!
На здравје! na zdrav·ye

Emergencies

Help! Помош! po·mosh
Go away! Одете си! o·de·te si

Call the doctor/police!
Викнете лекар/ vik·ne·te le·kar/
полиција! po·li·tsi·ya

I'm lost.
Се загубив. se za·gu·biv

I'm ill.
Јас сум болен/ yas sum bo·len/
болна. (m/f) bol·na

Where are the toilets?
Каде се тоалетите? ka·de se to·a·le·ti·te

Shopping & Services

I'm looking for ...
Барам … ba·ram …

How much is it?
Колку чини тоа? kol·ku chi·ni to·a

That's too expensive.
Тоа е многу скапо. to·a e mno·gu ska·po

market	пазар	pa·zar
post office	пошта	posh·ta
tourist office	туристичко биро	tu·ris·tich·ko·to bi·ro

Transport

boat	брод	brod
bus	автобус	av·to·bus
plane	авион	a·vi·on
train	воз	voz

One ... ticket (to Ohrid), please.	Еден … (за Охрид), ве молам.	e·den … (za oh·rid) ve mo·lam
one-way	билет во еден правец	bi·let vo e·den pra·vets
return	повратен билет	pov·ra·ten bi·let

POLISH

Polish vowels are generally pronounced short. Nasal vowels are pronounced as though you're trying to force the air through your nose, and are indicated with n or m following the vowel. Note that ow is pronounced as in 'how', kh as the 'ch' in the Scottish *loch*, and zh as the 's' in 'pleasure'. Also, r is rolled in Polish and the apostrophe (') indicates a slight y sound.

Basics

Hello.	*Cześć.*	cheshch
Goodbye.	*Do widzenia.*	do vee·dze·nya
Excuse me.	*Przepraszam.*	pshe·pra·sham
Sorry.	*Przepraszam.*	pshe·pra·sham
Please.	*Proszę.*	pro·she
Thank you.	*Dziękuję.*	jyen·koo·ye
Yes.	*Tak.*	tak
No.	*Nie.*	nye

What's your name?
Jak się pan/pani   yak shye pan/pa·nee
nazywa? (m/f pol)   na·zi·va
Jakie się nazywasz? (inf)   yak shye na·zi·vash

My name is ...
Nazywam się ...   na·zi·vam shye ...

Do you speak English?
Czy pan/pani mówi   chi pan/pa·nee moo·vee
po angielsku? (m/f)   po an·gyel·skoo

I don't understand.
Nie rozumiem.   nye ro·zoo·myem

Accommodation

campsite	*kamping*	kam·peeng
guesthouse	*pokoje gościnne*	po·ko·ye gosh·chee·ne
hotel	*hotel*	ho·tel
youth hostel	*schronisko młodzieżowe*	skhro·nees·ko mwo·jye·zho·ve

Do you have a ... room?   *Czy jest pokój ...?*   chi yest po·kooy ...

single   *jedno-osobowy*   yed·no·o·so·bo·vi

double   *z podwójnym łóżkiem*   z pod·vooy·nim woozh·kyem

How much is it per night/person?
Ile kosztuje   ee·le kosh·too·ye
za noc/osobę?   za nots/o·so·be

Eating & Drinking

What would you recommend?
Co by pan polecił? (m)   tso bi pan po·le·cheew
Co by pani poleciła? (f)   tso bi pa·nee po·le·chee·wa

Do you have vegetarian food?
Czy jest żywność   chi yest zhiv·noshch
wegetariańska?   ve·ge·tar·yan'·ska

I'd like the ..., please.
Proszę o rachunek/   pro·she o ra·khoo·nek/
jadłospis.   ya·dwo·spees

I'll have ...	*Proszę ...*	pro·she ...
Cheers!	*Na zdrowie!*	na zdro·vye

Emergencies

Help!	*Na pomoc!*	na po·mots
Go away!	*Odejdź!*	o·deyj

Call the doctor/police!
Zadzwoń po lekarza/   zad·zvon' po le·ka·zha/
policję!   po·lee·tsye

I'm lost.
Zgubiłem/   zgoo·bee·wem/
Zgubiłam się. (m/f)   zgoo·bee·wam shye

I'm ill.
Jestem chory/a. (m/f)   yes·tem kho·ri/a

Where are the toilets?
Gdzie są toalety?   gjye som to·a·le·ti

Shopping & Services

I'm looking for ...
Szukam ...   shoo·kam

How much is it?
Ile to kosztuje?   ee·le to kosh·too·ye

That's too expensive.
To jest za drogie.   to yest za dro·gye

market	*targ*	tark
post office	*urząd pocztowy*	oo·zhond poch·to·vi
tourist office	*biuro turystyczne*	byoo·ro too·ris·tich·ne

NUMBERS – POLISH

1	*jeden*	ye·den
2	*dwa*	dva
3	*trzy*	tshi
4	*cztery*	chte·ri
5	*pięć*	pyench
6	*sześć*	sheshch
7	*siedem*	shye·dem
8	*osiem*	o·shyem
9	*dziewięć*	jye·vyench
10	*dziesięć*	jye·shench

Transport

boat	*łódź*	wooj
bus	*autobus*	ow·to·boos
plane	*samolot*	sa·mo·lot
train	*pociąg*	po·chonk

One ... ticket (to Katowice), please.	*Proszę bilet ... (do Katowic).*	pro·she bee·let ... (do ka·to·veets)
one-way	*w jedną stronę*	v yed·nom stro·ne
return	*powrotny*	po·vro·tni

ROMANIAN

Note that ew is pronounced as 'ee' with rounded lips, oh as the 'o' in 'note', ow as in 'how', uh as the 'a' in 'ago', and zh as the 's' in 'pleasure'. The apostrophe (') indicates a very short, unstressed i (almost silent).

Basics

Hello.	*Bună ziua.*	boo·nuh zee·wa
Goodbye.	*La revedere.*	la re·ve·de·re
Excuse me.	*Scuzaţi-mă.*	skoo·za·tsee·muh
Sorry.	*Îmi pare rău.*	ewm' pa·re ruh·oo
Please.	*Vă rog.*	vuh rog
Thank you.	*Mulţumesc.*	mool·tsoo·mesk
Yes.	*Da.*	da
No.	*Nu.*	noo

What's your name?
Cum vă numiţi? koom vuh noo·meets'

My name is ...
Numele meu este ... noo·me·le me·oo yes·te ...

Do you speak English?
Vorbiţi engleza? vor·beets' en·gle·za

I don't understand.
Eu nu înţeleg. ye·oo noo ewn·tse·leg

Accommodation

campsite	*teren de camping*	te·ren de kem·peeng
guesthouse	*pensiune*	pen·syoo·ne
hotel	*hotel*	ho·tel
youth hostel	*hostel*	hos·tel

Do you have a ... room?	*Aveţi o cameră ...?*	a·vets' o ka·me·ruh ...
single	*de o persoană*	de o per·so·a·nuh
double	*dublă*	doo·bluh

How much is it per ...? *Cît costă ...?* kewt kos·tuh ...

night	*pe noapte*	pe no·ap·te
person	*de persoană*	de per·so·a·nuh

Eating & Drinking

What would you recommend?
Ce recomandaţi? che re·ko·man·dats'

Do you have vegetarian food?
Aveţi mâncare vegetariană? a·ve·tsi mewn·ka·re ve·je·ta·rya·nuh

I'll have ...	*Aş dori ...*	ash do·ree ...
Cheers!	*Noroc!*	no·rok

I'd like the ..., please.	*Vă rog, aş dori ...*	vuh rog ash do·ree ...
bill	*nota de plată*	no·ta de pla·tuh
menu	*meniul*	me·nee·ool

Emergencies

Help!	*Ajutor!*	a·zhoo·tor
Go away!	*Pleacă!*	ple·a·kuh

Call the ...!	*Chemaţi ...!*	ke·mats' ...
doctor	*un doctor*	oon dok·tor
police	*poliţia*	po·lee·tsya

I'm lost.
M-am rătăcit. mam ruh·tuh·cheet

I'm ill.
Mă simt rău. muh seemt ruh·oo

Where are the toilets?
Unde este o toaletă? oon·de yes·te o to·a·le·tuh

NUMBERS – ROMANIAN

1	*unu*	oo·noo
2	*doi*	doy
3	*trei*	trey
4	*patru*	pa·troo
5	*cinci*	cheench'
6	*şase*	sha·se
7	*şapte*	shap·te
8	*opt*	opt
9	*nouă*	no·wuh
10	*zece*	ze·che

Shopping & Services

I'm looking for ...
Caut ...   kowt ...

How much is it?
Cât costă?   kewt *koş*·tuh

That's too expensive.
E prea scump.   ye pre·a skoomp

market	piaţă	pya·tsuh
post office	poşta	posh·ta
tourist office	biroul de informaţii turistice	bee·ro·ool de een·for·ma·tsee too·rees·tee·che

Transport

boat	vapor	va·por
bus	autobuz	ow·to·booz
plane	avion	a·vyon
train	tren	tren

One ... ticket (to Cluj), please.	Un bilet ... (până la Cluj),vă rog.	oon bee·let ... (pew·nuh la kloozh) vuh rog
one-way	dus	doos
return	dus-întors	doos ewn·tors

RUSSIAN

In Russian – also widely used in Belarus – the kh is pronounced as the 'ch' in the Scottish *loch* and zh as the 's' in 'pleasure'. Also, r is rolled in Russian and the apostrophe (') indicates a slight y sound.

Basics

Hello.	Здравствуйте.	zdrast·vuyt·ye
Goodbye.	До свидания.	da svee·dan·ya
Excuse me./ Sorry.	Извините, пожалуйста.	eez·vee·neet·ye pa·zhal·sta
Please.	Пожалуйста.	pa·zhal·sta
Thank you.	Спасибо	spa·see·ba
Yes.	Да.	da
No.	Нет.	nyet

What's your name?
Как вас зовут?   kak vaz za·vut

My name is ...
Меня зовут ...   meen·ya za·vut ...

Do you speak English?
Вы говорите   vi ga·va·reet·ye
по-английски?   pa·an·glee·skee

NUMBERS – RUSSIAN

1	один	a·deen
2	два	dva
3	три	tree
4	четыре	chee·ti·ree
5	пять	pyat'
6	шесть	shest'
7	семь	syem'
8	восемь	vo·seem'
9	девять	dye·veet'
10	десять	dye·seet'

I don't understand.
Я не понимаю.   ya nye pa·nee·ma·yu

Accommodation

campsite	кемпинг	kyem·peeng
guesthouse	пансионат	pan·see·a·nat
hotel	гостиница	ga·stee·neet·sa
youth hostel	общежитие	ap·shee·zhi·tee·ye

Do you have a ... room?	У вас есть ...?	u vas yest' ...
single	одноместный номер	ad·nam·yes·ni no·meer
double	номер с двуспальней кроватью	no·meer z dvu·spaln·yey kra·vat·yu

How much is it ...?	Сколько стоит за ...?	skol'·ka sto·eet za ...
for two people	двоих	dva·eekh
per night	ночь	noch'

Eating & Drinking

What would you recommend?
Что вы   shto vi
рекомендуете?   ree·ka·meen·du·eet·ye

Do you have vegetarian food?
У вас есть   u vas yest'
вегетарианские   vi·gi·ta·ri·an·ski·ye
блюда?   blyu·da

I'd like the bill/menu, please.
Я бы хотел/хотела   ya bi khat·yel/khat·ye·la
счёт/меню. (m/f)   shot/meen·yu

I'll have ...   ..., пожалуйста. ... pa·zhal·sta

Cheers!   За здоровье!   za zda·rov·ye

Emergencies

Help!	Помогите!	pa·ma·*gee*·tye
Go away!	Идите отсюда!	ee·*deet*·ye at·*syu*·da

Call the doctor/police!
Вызовите врача/ милицию! — vi·za·veet·ye vra·*cha*/mee·*leet*·si·yu

I'm lost.
Я потерялся/ потерялась. (m/f) — ya pa·teer·*yal*·sa/ pa·teer·*ya*·las'

I'm ill.
Я болею. — ya bal·*ye*·yu

Where are the toilets?
Где здесь туалет? — gdye zdyes' tu·al·*yet*

Shopping & Services

I'd like ...
Я бы хотел/ хотела ... (m/f) — ya bi khat·*yel*/ khat·*ye*·la ...

How much is it?
Сколько стоит? — *skol'*·ka *sto*·eet

That's too expensive.
Это очень дорого. — *e*·ta o·*cheen*' *do*·ra·ga

bank	банк	bank
market	рынок	*ri*·nak
post office	почта	*poch*·ta
tourist office	туристическое бюро	tu·rees·*tee*·chee·ska·ye byu·ro

Transport

boat	параход	pa·ra·*khot*
bus	автобус	af·*to*·bus
plane	самолёт	sa·mal·*yot*
train	поезд	*po*·yeest

One ... ticket (to Novgorod), please.
Билет ... (на Новгород). — beel·*yet* ... (na *nov*·ga·rat)

one-way	в один конец	v a·*deen* kan·*yets*
return	в оба конца	v o·ba kant·*sa*

SLOVAK

An accent mark over a vowel in written Slovak indicates it's pronounced as a long sound. Note that air is pronounced as in 'hair', oh as the 'o' in 'note', ow as in 'how', uh as the 'a' in 'ago', dz as the 'ds' in 'adds', kh as the 'ch' in the Scottish *loch*, and zh as the 's' in 'pleasure'. The apostrophe (') indicates a slight y sound.

Basics

Hello.	Dobrý deň.	do·bree dyen'
Goodbye.	Do videnia.	do vi·dye·ni·yuh
Excuse me.	Prepáčte.	pre·pach·tye
Sorry.	Prepáčte.	pre·pach·tye
Please.	Prosím.	pro·seem
Thank you.	Ďakujem	dyuh·ku·yem
Yes.	Áno.	a·no
No.	Nie.	ni·ye

What's your name?
Ako sa voláte? — uh·ko suh vo·la·tye

My name is ...
Volám sa ... — vo·lam suh ...

Do you speak English?
Hovoríte po anglicky? — ho·vo·ree·tye po uhng·lits·ki

I don't understand.
Nerozumiem. — nye·ro·zu·myem

Accommodation

campsite	táborisko	ta·bo·ris·ko
guesthouse	penzión	pen·zi·awn
hotel	hotel	ho·tel
youth hostel	nocľaháreň pre mládež	nots·lyuh·ha·ren' pre mla·dyezh

Do you have a single room?
Máte jedno- posteľovú izbu? — ma·tye yed·no· pos·tye·lyo·voo iz·bu

Do you have a double room?
Máte izbu s manželskou posteľou? — ma·tye iz·bu s muhn·zhels·koh pos·tye·lyoh

How much is it per ...?
Koľko to stojí na noc/osobu? — kol'·ko to sto·yee nuh nots/o·so·bu

Eating & Drinking

What would you recommend?
Čo by ste mi odporučili? — cho bi stye mi od·po·ru·chi·li

Do you have vegetarian food?
Máte vegetariánske jedlá? — ma·tye ve·ge·tuh·ri·yan·ske yed·la

I'd like the ..., please.	Prosím si ...	pro·seem si ...
bill	účet	oo·chet
menu	jedálny lístok	ye·dal·ni lees·tok

| I'll have ... | Dám si ...! | dam si ... |
| Cheers! | Nazdravie! | nuhz·druh·vi·ye |

Emergencies

| Help! | Pomoc! | po·mots |
| Go away! | Choďte preč! | khod'·tye prech |

Call ...!	Zavolajte ...!	zuh·vo·lai·tye ...
a doctor	lekára	le·ka·ruh
the police	políciu	po·lee·tsi·yu

I'm lost.
Stratil/Stratila som sa. (m/f) — struh·tyil/struh·tyi·luh som suh

I'm ill.
Som chorý/chorá. (m/f) — som kho·ree/kho·ra

Where are the toilets?
Kde sú tu záchody? — kdye soo tu za·kho·di

Shopping & Services

I'm looking for ...
Hľadám ... — hlyuh·dam ...

How much is it?
Koľko to stojí? — kol'·ko to sto·yee

That's too expensive.
To je príliš drahé. — to ye pree·lish druh·hair

| market | trh | trh |

NUMBERS – SLOVAK

1	jeden	ye·den
2	dva	dvuh
3	tri	tri
4	štyri	shti·ri
5	päť	pet'
6	šesť	shest'
7	sedem	se·dyem
8	osem	o·sem
9	deväť	dye·vet'
10	desať	dye·suht'

| post office | pošta | posh·tuh |
| tourist office | turistická kancelária | tu·ris·tits·ka kuhn·tse·la·ri·yuh |

Transport

bus	autobus	ow·to·bus
plane	lietadlo	li·ye·tuhd·lo
train	vlak	vluhk

One ... ticket (to Poprad), please.	Jeden ... lístok (do Popradu), prosím.	ye·den ... lees·tok (do pop·ruh·du) pro·seem
one-way	jedno-smerný	yed·no-smer·nee
return	spiatočný	spyuh·toch·nee

SLOVENE

Note that uh is pronounced as the 'a' in 'ago', oh as the 'o' in 'note', ow as in 'how', zh as the 's' in 'pleasure', r is rolled, and the apostrophe (') indicates a slight y sound.

Basics

Hello.	Zdravo.	zdra·vo
Goodbye.	Na svidenje.	na svee·den·ye
Excuse me.	Dovolite.	do·vo·lee·te
Sorry.	Oprostite.	op·ros·tee·te
Please.	Prosim.	pro·seem
Thank you.	Hvala.	hva·la
Yes.	Da.	da
No.	Ne.	ne

What's your name?
Kako vam/ti je ime? (pol/inf) — ka·ko vam/tee ye ee·me

My name is ...
Ime mi je ... — ee·me mee ye ...

Do you speak English?
Ali govorite angleško? — a·lee go·vo·ree·te ang·lesh·ko

I don't understand.
Ne razumem. — ne ra·zoo·mem

Accommodation

campsite	kamp	kamp
guesthouse	gostišče	gos·teesh·che
hotel	hotel	ho·tel
youth hostel	mladinski hotel	mla·deen·skee ho·tel

LANGUAGE SLOVENE

Do you have a single/double room?
Ali imate   *a·*lee ee·*ma·*te
enoposteljno/   e·no·*pos·*tel'·no/
dvoposteljno sobo? dvo·*pos·*tel'·no so·bo

How much is it per night/person?
Koliko stane na   ko·lee·ko *sta·*ne na
noč/osebo?   noch/o·*se·*bo

Eating & Drinking

What would you recommend?
Kaj priporočate? kai pree·po·*ro·*cha·te

Do you have vegetarian food?
Ali imate   *a·*lee ee·*ma·*te
vegetarijansko hrano? ve·ge·ta·ree·*yan·*sko *hra·*no

I'll have ...	*Jaz bom ...*	yaz bom ...
Cheers!	*Na zdravje!*	na zdrav·ye
I'd like the ...,	*Želim ...,*	zhe·*leem* ...
please.	*prosim.*	pro·seem
bill	*račun*	ra·*choon*
menu	*jedilni list*	ye·*deel·*nee leest

Emergencies

Help!	*Na pomoč!*	na po·*moch*
Go away!	*Pojdite stran!*	poy·*dee·*te stran

Call the doctor/police!
Pokličite zdravnika/ pok·*lee·*chee·te zdrav·*nee·*ka
policijo!   po·lee·*tsee·*yo

I'm lost.
Izgubil/   eez·*goo·*beew/
Izgubila sem se. (m/f) eez·*goo·*bee·la sem se

I'm ill.
Bolan/Bolna sem. (m/f) bo·*lan*/*boh·*na sem

Where are the toilets?
Kje je stranišče? kye ye stra·*neesh·*che

NUMBERS – SLOVENE

1	*en*	en
2	*dva*	dva
3	*trije*	*tree·*ye
4	*štirje*	*shtee·*rye
5	*pet*	pet
6	*šest*	shest
7	*sedem*	se·dem
8	*osem*	o·sem
9	*devet*	de·vet
10	*deset*	de·set

Shopping & Services

I'm looking for ...
Iščem ...   *eesh·*chem ...

How much is this?
Koliko stane? ko·lee·ko *sta·*ne

That's too expensive.
To je predrago. to ye pre·*dra·*go

market	*tržnica*	*tuhrzh·*nee·tsa
post office	*pošta*	*posh·*taw
tourist office	*turistični urad*	too·rees·teech·nee oo·rad

Transport

boat	*ladja*	*lad·*ya
bus	*avtobus*	*av·*to·boos
plane	*letalo*	le·*ta·*lo
train	*vlak*	vlak

One ... ticket	*... vozovnico*	... vo·*zov·*nee·tso
to (Koper),	*do (Kopra),*	do (*ko·*pra)
please.	*prosim.*	pro·seem
one-way	*Enosmerno*	e·no·*smer·*no
return	*Povratno*	pov·*rat·*no

UKRAINIAN

Vowels in unstressed syllables are generally pronounced shorter and weaker than they are in stressed syllables. Note that kh is pronounced as the 'ch' in the Scottish *loch* and zh as the 's' in 'pleasure'. The apostrophe (') indicates a slight y sound.

Basics

Hello.	Добрий день.	*do·*bry den'
Goodbye.	До побачення.	do po·*ba·*chen·nya
Excuse me.	Вибачте.	*vy·*bach·te
Sorry.	Перепрошую.	pe·re·*pro·*shu·yu
Please.	Прошу.	*pro·*shu
Thank you.	Дякую.	*dya·*ku·yu
Yes.	Так.	tak
No.	Ні.	ni

What's your name?
Як вас звати? yak vas zva·ty

My name is ...
Мене звати ... me·*ne* zva·ti ...

Do you speak English?

Ви розмовляєте	vy roz·mow·*lya*·ye·te
англійською	an·*hliys'*·ko·yu
мовою?	*mo*·vo·yu

I don't understand.

| Я не розумію. | ya ne ro·zu·*mi*·yu |

Accommodation

campsite	кемпінг	*kem*·pinh
double room	номер на	*no*·mer na
	двох	dvokh
hotel	готель	ho·*tel'*
single room	номер на	*no*·mer na
	одного	o·*dno*·ho
youth hostel	молодіжний	mo·lo·*dizh*·ni
	гуртожиток	hur·*to*·zhi·tok

Do you have any rooms available?

| У вас є вільні номери? | u vas ye *vil'*·ni no·me·ri |

How much is it per night/person?

| Скільки коштує | *skil'*·ky ko·shtu·ye |
| номер за ніч/особу? | *no*·mer za nich/o·so·bu |

Eating & Drinking

What do you recommend?

| Що Ви порадите? | shcho vy po·*ra*·dy·te |

I'm a vegetarian.

| Я вегетаріанець/ | ya ve·he·ta·ri·a·nets'/ |
| вегетаріанка. (m/f) | ve·he·ta·ri·*an*·ka |

Cheers!	Будьмо!	*bud'*·mo
I'd like ...	Я візьму ...	ya viz'·*mu* ...
bill	рахунок	ra·*khu*·nok
menu	меню	me·*nyu*

Emergencies

Help!

| Допоможіть! | do·po·mo·*zhit'* |

Go away!

| Іди/Ідіть звідси! (pol/inf) | i·*di*/i·*dit'* zvid·si |

Call the doctor/police!

| Викличте лікаря/ | *vi*·klich·te *li*·ka·rya/ |
| міліцію! | mi·*li*·tsi·yu |

I'm lost.

| Я заблукав/ | ya za·blu·*kaw*/ |
| заблукала. (m/f) | za·blu·*ka*·la |

I'm ill.

| Мені погано. | me·*ni* po·*ha*·no |

NUMBERS – UKRAINIAN

1	один	o·*din*
2	два	dva
3	три	tri
4	чотири	cho·*ti*·ri
5	п'ять	pyat'
6	шість	shist'
7	сім	sim
8	вісім	*vi*·sim
9	дев'ять	de·*vyat'*
10	десять	de·*syat'*

Where's the toilet?

| Де туалети? | de tu·a·le·ti |

Shopping & Services

I'd like to buy ...

| Я б хотів/хотіла | ya b kho·*tiw*/kho·*ti*·la |
| купити ... (m/f) | ku·*pi*·ti ... |

How much is this?

| Скільки це він/вона | *skil'*·ki tse vin/vo·*na* |
| коштує? (m/f) | ko·shtu·ye? |

That's too expensive.

| Це надто дорого. | tse *nad*·to *do*·ro·ho |

ATM	банкомат	ban·ko·*mat*
market	ринок	*ri*·nok
post office	пошта	*po*·shta
tourist office	туристичне	tu·ri·*stich*·ne
	бюро	byu·*ro*

Transport

I want to go to ...

| Мені треба їхати | me·*ni* tre·ba yi·kha·ti |
| до ... | do ... |

bus	автобус	aw·*to*·bus
one-way	квиток в	kvi·*tok* v
ticket	один бік	o·*din* bik
plane	літак	li·*tak*
return	зворотний	zvo·*ro*·tni
ticket	квиток	kvi·*tok*
train	поїзд	*po*·yizd

Behind the Scenes

SEND US YOUR FEEDBACK

We love to hear from travellers – your comments keep us on our toes and help make our books better. Our well-travelled team reads every word on what you loved or loathed about this book. Although we cannot reply individually to your submissions, we always guarantee that your feedback goes straight to the appropriate authors, in time for the next edition. Each person who sends us information is thanked in the next edition – the most useful submissions are rewarded with a selection of digital PDF chapters.

Visit **lonelyplanet.com/contact** to submit your updates and suggestions or to ask for help. Our award-winning website also features inspirational travel stories, news and discussions.

Note: We may edit, reproduce and incorporate your comments in Lonely Planet products such as guidebooks, websites and digital products, so let us know if you don't want your comments reproduced or your name acknowledged. For a copy of our privacy policy visit lonelyplanet.com/privacy.

WRITER THANKS

Mark Baker

I owe a debt of gratitude to many friends and organisations on the ground in the Czech Republic, Romania and Bulgaria for helping me to update this content. An incomplete list would include Kateřina Pavlitová and the staff at Prague City Tourism. In Romania, Monica Suma, Ligia-Verkin Keşişian, Mark and Raluca Tudose. In Bulgaria, Dani Nencheva, Petia Yoncheva, Petya Lubomirova, and Tatyana Spasova. At Lonely Planet, my Destination Editors Gemma Graham and Brana Vladisavljevic.

Greg Bloom

Another big hearty bearhug to dad for tagging along for a big chunk of the research, even enduring a near flash flood in Gagauzia. Tiraspol Tim was his usual helpful self, and thanks also to the handy new tourist offices in Tiraspol and Chişinău. Thanks to Leonid in Brest for the Belevezhskaya tour. Back home, immeasurable thanks to my sanity checks, Callie and Anna. And to Windi, for holding down the fort while I was away.

Stuart Butler

The first people I must thank are my wife, Heather, and children, Jake and Grace, for their unending patience while I worked on this project and for being the best travel companions a person could want in Albania. In Kosovo huge thanks to Nol and Virtyt for their help and hiking knowledge. In Albania huge thanks to Amar in Tirana and Altin in Ksamil. Back in

LP's London office thanks to Brana for all her tips, suggestions and endless Balkan knowledge.

Peter Dragicevich

First and foremost, I'd like to say a huge hvala to Vojko, Marija, Ivan, Mario and Ivana Dragičević in Split, for the kindness and patience you've shown your distant cousin over the years. Thanks also to Hayley Wright, Slavenko Sucur, and Emma and Ben Hayward for the tips and chats. Special thanks to my destination editors, Anna Tyler and Brana Vladisavljevic, and all of the writers, editors and Lonely Planet staff who contributed to this book.

Steve Fallon

Thanks to Virág Katona, Judit Maróthy, Dávid Máté, Ildikó Nagy Moran, Bea Szirti and Adrian Zador for their very helpful suggestions. Gábor Banfalvi and Péter Lengyel showed me the correct wine roads to follow; Tony Láng and Balázs Váradi the political ones. Once again Michael Buurman opened his flat for me in Budapest; thanks to Tal Lev for hospitality. *Nagyon szépen köszönöm mindenkinek!* As always, I'd like to dedicate my share of this to partner Michael Rothschild, with love and gratitude.

Anthony Ham

Many thanks to Luca, Miriam, Lidija, Marija in Croatia, to Romana Nared, Ana Petrič and Franc Mlakar in the Lož Valley, and to Saša and Jure in Idrija, and all the staff at tourist offices across Croatia and Slovenia. At Lonely Planet, I am grateful to my editor Anna Tyler for sending me to such wonderful places, and to my fellow writers Peter, Mark and Jess for their wisdom. To my family – Marina, Jan, Carlota and Valentina: *con todo mi amor*.

Anita Isalska

My research in Slovakia and Lithuania was greatly enriched by the generous advice and local insights of Slavo Stankovic, Marek Leskovjansky, Jana Kačalová, Gintarė Kavaliūnaitė and Raimonda Patapavičienė. For cider-soaked bar research, an extra thank you to Tom Hewitson. A big *na zdravie* (and *na zdrowie*) to my parents, Barbara and Harry, for their enthusiastic participation in Bratislava bar crawls. My heartiest thanks, as ever, to Normal Matt for moral support and mountain driving.

Jessica Lee

A big thanks to the people of Croatia for being such great company. In particular, a huge thank you to the enthusiastic staff at the tourist information offices of Varaždin and Zagreb County in Croatia, and Celje, Dolenjske Toplice, Murska Sobata and Ptuj in Slovenia, for being founts of knowledge and helpful information and a big thank you to Anton, Irena, Mila, Tea, Tom, Zvonimir, Skanka and Igor, Petra, Daniel and Lea for tips and chats.

Vesna Maric

I would like to thank Maja Trajkovska, Metodi Chilimanov, Magdalena Lazarevska and Slobodan Đudurović for making my time in North Macedonia more special than I could imagine. Big thank yous go to Brana Vladisavljevic for commissioning me and always being such a great and kind editor. Thanks also to Tom Masters for his help.

MaSovaida Morgan

Deepest thanks to the wonderful souls who offered guidance, tips, recommendations, and delightfully deep conversations during this eye-opening journey. Extra special thanks to LeCiel, Didzis, Rita, Lemmit, Anna, Anet, and Davis.

Leonid Ragozin

I'd like to thank my friends Dima Zhuravlev, Dima Muzychenko and Sasha Agatov for helping out with research ideas and providing company in Moscow. Also many thanks to Anya and Yulia Semyonov for an excellent dinner at LP. On the road, thanks in Ukraine, thanks to Katya Sergatskova, Yevhen Stepanenko, Misha Friedman and Serhiy Savhcuk for joining me on daring research expeditions into the culinary temples and drinking dens of Kyiv, Odesa and Lviv.

Kevin Raub

Thanks to Brana Vladisavljevic and all my fellow partners in crime at LP. On the road, Jelena Stanković, Maja Živković, Suna Kažić, Marija Mitrović, Dejan Majić, Tijana Vujasinović, Goran Magdić, Djole Jovanović, Filip Mićić, Luka Pejović and Mihailo Subotić.

Brana Vladisavljevic

Hvala puno to James Smart and Jennifer Carey for the support, Kate Morgan for her guidebook authoring advice, co-writer Kevin Raub for excellent work on Belgrade, Novi Sad and Niš updates, Dragiša Mijačić for great tips on Stara Planina and Kragujevac, and my sister Sandra for keeping me company on the road for a few days.

Neil Wilson

A big thank you to helpful tourist office staff all over Poland, to Łukasz Śmigiel in Gdańsk, and as ever to Carol Downie. Thanks also to Gemma Graham and the rest of the Lonely Planet team.

ACKNOWLEDGEMENTS

Climate map data adapted from Peel MC, Finlayson BL & McMahon TA (2007) 'Updated World Map of the Köppen-Geiger Climate Classification', *Hydrology and Earth System Sciences*, 11, 1633–44.

Cover photograph: Windows of a Russian country house, Svetlana Sysoeva/Shutterstock ©

Illustrations p364–5, p380–1 by Javier Zarracina.

THIS BOOK

This 15th edition of Lonely Planet's *Eastern Europe* guidebook was researched and written by Mark Baker, Greg Bloom, Stuart Butler, Peter Dragicevich, Steve Fallon, Anthony Ham, Anita Isalska, Jessica Lee, Vesna Maric, MaSovaida Morgan, Leonid Ragozin, Kevin Raub, Brana Vladisavljevic and Neil Wilson. This guidebook was produced by the following:

Destination Editors Gemma Graham, Anna Tyler, Brana Vladisavljevic

Senior Product Editors Grace Dobell, Elizabeth Jones

Regional Senior Cartographers Mark Griffiths, Valentina Kremenchutskaya, Anthony Phelan

Product Editor Kathryn Rowan

Book Designer Clara Monitto

Assisting Editors Janet Austin, Sarah Bailey, Judith Bamber, Imogen Bannister, Michelle Bennett, Carolyn Boicos, Katie Connolly, Joel Cotterell, Jacqueline Danam, Samantha Forge, Emma Gibbs, Jennifer Hattam, Gabrielle Innes, Kellie Langdon, Alison Morris, Claire Naylor, Rosie Nicholson, Lauren O'Connell, Kristin Odijk, Susan Paterson, Monique Perrin, Tamara Sheward, Fionnuala Twomey, Simon Williamson

Assisting Cartographers Julie Dodkins, Rachel Imeson, Katerina Pavkova

Cover Researcher Naomi Parker

Thanks to Vesna Čelebić, Daniel Herszberg, Günther Mimm, Aristea Parissi, Rachel Rawling, Kirsten Rawlings, Tony Wheeler

Index

Map Pages **000**
Photo Pages **000**

Map Pages **000**
Photo Pages **000**

Map Legend

Sights

- 🏖 Beach
- 🐦 Bird Sanctuary
- ☸ Buddhist
- 🏰 Castle/Palace
- ✝ Christian
- 🔯 Confucian
- 🕉 Hindu
- ☪ Islamic
- Jain
- ✡ Jewish
- Monument
- 🏛 Museum/Gallery/Historic Building
- Ruin
- ⛩ Shinto
- Sikh
- ☯ Taoist
- 🍷 Winery/Vineyard
- 🦁 Zoo/Wildlife Sanctuary
- ◉ Other Sight

Activities, Courses & Tours

- Bodysurfing
- Diving
- Canoeing/Kayaking
- Course/Tour
- Sento Hot Baths/Onsen
- Skiing
- Snorkelling
- Surfing
- Swimming/Pool
- Walking
- Windsurfing
- Other Activity

Sleeping

- Sleeping
- Camping
- Hut/Shelter

Eating

- Eating

Drinking & Nightlife

- Drinking & Nightlife
- Cafe

Entertainment

- Entertainment

Shopping

- Shopping

Information

- 💲 Bank
- Embassy/Consulate
- Hospital/Medical
- @ Internet
- Police
- ✉ Post Office
- Telephone
- Toilet
- ℹ Tourist Information
- • Other Information

Geographic

- 🏖 Beach
- ⊢ Gate
- Hut/Shelter
- Lighthouse
- Lookout
- ▲ Mountain/Volcano
- Oasis
- Park
-)(Pass
- Picnic Area
- Waterfall

Population

- ★ Capital (National)
- ◉ Capital (State/Province)
- City/Large Town
- ● Town/Village

Transport

- ✈ Airport
- ⊗ Border crossing
- Bus
- ++⊕++ Cable car/Funicular
- –◉– Cycling
- –⊕– Ferry
- Ⓜ Metro station
- ⇒⊕⇐ Monorail
- Ⓟ Parking
- Petrol station
- Ⓢ S-Bahn/Subway station
- Taxi
- Ⓣ T-bane/Tunnelbana station
- +⊕– Train station/Railway
- ⇒⊕– Tram
- Ⓤ U-Bahn/Underground station
- • Other Transport

Routes

- Tollway
- Freeway
- Primary
- Secondary
- Tertiary
- Lane
- Unsealed road
- Road under construction
- Plaza/Mall
- Steps
-)–=(Tunnel
- Pedestrian overpass
- Walking Tour
- Walking Tour detour
- Path/Walking Trail

Boundaries

- International
- State/Province
- Disputed
- Regional/Suburb
- Marine Park
- Cliff
- Wall

Hydrography

- River, Creek
- Intermittent River
- Canal
- Water
- Dry/Salt/Intermittent Lake
- Reef

Areas

- Airport/Runway
- Beach/Desert
- + + Cemetery (Christian)
- × × Cemetery (Other)
- Glacier
- Mudflat
- Park/Forest
- Sight (Building)
- Sportsground
- Swamp/Mangrove

Note: Not all symbols displayed above appear on the maps in this book

Neil Wilson

Poland Neil was born in Scotland and has lived there most of his life. Based in Perthshire, he has been a full-time writer since 1988, working on more than 80 guidebooks for various publishers, including the Lonely Planet guides to Scotland, England, Ireland and Prague. An outdoors enthusiast since childhood, Neil is an active hill-walker, mountain-biker, sailor, snowboarder, fly-fisher and rock-climber, and has climbed and tramped in four continents, including ascents of Jebel Toubkal in Morocco, Mount Kinabalu in Borneo, the Old Man of Hoy in Scotland's Orkney Islands and the Northwest Face of Half Dome in California's Yosemite Valley.

Anthony Ham

Croatia, Slovenia Anthony is a freelance writer and photographer who specialises in Spain, East and Southern Africa, the Arctic and the Middle East. When he's not writing for Lonely Planet, Anthony writes about and photographs Spain, Africa and the Middle East for newspapers and magazines in Australia, the UK and the US.

Jessica Lee

Croatia, Slovenia In 2011 Jessica swapped a career as an adventure-tour leader for travel writing and since then her travels for Lonely Planet have taken her across Africa, the Middle East and Asia. She has lived in the Middle East since 2007 and tweets @jessofarabia. Jess has contributed to Lonely Planet's Egypt, Turkey, Cyprus, Morocco, Marrakesh, Middle East, Europe, Africa, Cambodia, and Vietnam guidebooks and her travel writing has appeared in *Wanderlust* magazine, the *Daily Telegraph,* the *Independent,* BBC Travel and Lonelyplanet.com.

Kevin Raub

Serbia Atlanta native Kevin Raub started his career as a music journalist in New York, working for *Men's Journal* and *Rolling Stone* magazines. He ditched the rock 'n' roll lifestyle for travel writing and has written more than 70 Lonely Planet guides, focused mainly on Brazil, Chile, Colombia, USA, India, the Caribbean and Portugal. Raub also contributes to a variety of travel magazines in both the US and UK. Along the way, the self-confessed hophead is in constant search of wildly high IBUs in local beers. Follow him on Twitter and Instagram (@RaubOnTheRoad).

Peter Dragicevich

Bosnia & Hercegovina, Croatia, Montenegro After a successful career in niche newspaper and magazine publishing, both in his native New Zealand and in Australia, Peter finally gave in to Kiwi wanderlust, giving up staff jobs to chase his diverse roots around much of Europe. Over the last decade he's written literally dozens of guidebooks for Lonely Planet on an oddly disparate collection of countries, all of which he's come to love. He once again calls Auckland, New Zealand, his home – although his current nomadic existence means he's often elsewhere.

Steve Fallon

Hungary A native of Boston, Massachusetts, Steve graduated from Georgetown University with a Bachelor of Science in modern languages. After working for several years for an American daily newspaper and earning a master's degree in journalism, his fascination with the 'new' Asia led him to Hong Kong, where he lived for over a dozen years, working for a variety of media companies and running his own travel bookshop. Steve lived in Budapest for three years before moving to London in 1994. He has written or contributed to more than 100 Lonely Planet titles. Steve is a qualified London Blue Badge Tourist Guide. Visit his website on www.steveslondon.com.

Anita Isalska

Lithuania, Slovakia Anita Isalska is a travel journalist, editor and copywriter. After several merry years as a staff writer and editor – a few of them in Lonely Planet's London office – Anita now works freelance between San Francisco, the UK and any Baltic bolthole with good wi-fi. Anita specialises in Eastern and Central Europe, Southeast Asia, France and off-beat travel. Read her stuff on www. anitaisalska.com.

Vesna Maric

North Macedonia Vesna has been a Lonely Planet author for nearly two decades, covering places as far and wide as Bolivia, Algeria, Sicily, Cyprus, Barcelona, London and Croatia, among others. Her latest work has been updating Florida, Greece and North Macedonia.

MaSovaida Morgan

Estonia, Latvia MaSovaida is a travel writer and multimedia storyteller whose wanderlust has taken her to more than 40 countries and all seven continents. Previously, she was Lonely Planet's Destination Editor for South America and Antarctica for four years and worked as an editor for newspapers and NGOs in the Middle East and United Kingdom. Follow her on Instagram @MaSovaida.

Leonid Ragozin

Russia, Ukraine Leonid Ragozin studied beach dynamics at Moscow State University, but for want of decent beaches in Russia, he switched to journalism and spent 12 years voyaging through different parts of the BBC, with a break for a four-year stint as a foreign correspondent for Newsweek Russia. Leonid is currently a freelance journalist focusing largely on the conflict between Russia and Ukraine (both his Lonely Planet destinations), which prompted him to leave Moscow and find a new home in Rīga.

Brana Vladisavljevic

Serbia Brana grew up in the former Yugoslavia and studied foreign languages and literature in Belgrade. She joined Lonely Planet's Melbourne office in 2004 and has lost count of the phrasebook and guidebook titles she edited over the years. From 2014 to 2019, she was based in the London office as the Destination Editor for Eastern and Southeastern Europe. Brana looked after destinations stretching from the Russian Far East to the Greek islands but has a soft spot for her native Western Balkans region.

OUR STORY

A beat-up old car, a few dollars in the pocket and a sense of adventure. In 1972 that's all Tony and Maureen Wheeler needed for the trip of a lifetime – across Europe and Asia overland to Australia. It took several months, and at the end – broke but inspired – they sat at their kitchen table writing and stapling together their first travel guide, *Across Asia on the Cheap.* Within a week they'd sold 1500 copies. Lonely Planet was born.

Today, Lonely Planet has offices in Franklin, London, Melbourne, Oakland, Dublin, Beijing and Delhi, with more than 600 staff and writers. We share Tony's belief that 'a great guidebook should do three things: inform, educate and amuse'.

OUR WRITERS

Mark Baker

Bulgaria, Czech Republic, Romania, Slovenia Mark is a freelance travel writer with a penchant for offbeat stories and forgotten places. He's originally from the United States, but now makes his home in the Czech capital, Prague. He writes mainly on Eastern and Central Europe for Lonely Planet as well as other leading travel publishers, but finds real satisfaction in digging up stories in places that are too remote or quirky for the guides. Prior to becoming an author, he worked as a journalist *for The Economist, Bloomberg News* and *Radio Free Europe,* among other organisations. Follow him on Instagram and Twitter (@markbakerprague), and read his blog: www.markbakerprague.com. Mark also contributed to the Plan and Survival Guide chapters.

Greg Bloom

Belarus, Moldova Greg is a freelance writer, editor, tour guide and travel planner based out of Manila and Anilao, Philippines. Greg began his writing career in the late '90s in Ukraine, working as a journalist and later editor-in-chief of the *Kyiv Post,* an English-language weekly. As a freelance travel writer, he has contributed to some 40 Lonely Planet titles, mostly in Eastern Europe and Asia. In addition to writing, he organises customised adventure tours in north Palawan and north Luzon (Philippines). Greg's travel articles have been published in the *Sydney Morning Herald,* the *South China Morning Post,* BBC.com and the Toronto *Globe and Mail,* among many other publications. Accounts of his Lonely Planet trips over the years are at www.mytripjournal.com/bloomblogs.

Stuart Butler

Albania, Kosovo Stuart has been writing for Lonely Planet for a decade and during this time he's come eye to eye with gorillas in the Congolese jungles, met a man with horns on his head who could lie in fire, huffed and puffed over snow bound Himalayan mountain passes, interviewed a king who could turn into a tree, and had his fortune told by a parrot. Oh, and he's met more than his fair share of self-proclaimed gods. When not on the road for Lonely Planet he lives on the beautiful beaches of Southwest France with his wife and two young children. He also works as a photographer and was a finalist in both the 2015 and 2016 Travel Photographer of the Year Awards. In 2015 he walked for six weeks with a Maasai friend across part of Kenya's Maasai lands in order to gather material for a book he is writing (see www.walkingwiththemaasai.com). His website is www.stuartbutlerjournalist.com.

OVER MORE
PAGE WRITERS

Published by Lonely Planet Global Limited
CRN 554153
15th edition – October 2019
ISBN 978 1 78701 370 4
© Lonely Planet 2019   Photographs © as indicated 2019
10 9 8 7 6 5 4 3 2 1
Printed in Singapore